Twentieth-Century
Literary Criticism

Twentieth-Century Literary Criticism

**Excerpts from Criticism of the
Works of Novelists, Poets, Playwrights,
Short Story Writers, and Other Creative
Writers Who Lived between 1900 and 1960,
from the First Published Critical
Appraisals to Current Sources**

**Sharon K. Hall
Editor**

**Gale Research Company
Book Tower
Detroit, Michigan 48226**

STAFF

Sharon K. Hall, *Editor*

Dennis Poupard, *Associate Editor*

Anna H. Crabtree, Thomas Ligotti, Marsha Ruth Mackenzie,
James E. Person, Jr., Lizbeth A. Purdy, *Assistant Editors*

Phyllis Carmel Mendelson, *Contributing Editor*

Carolyn Voldrich, *Production Editor*

Thomas Gunton, *Research Coordinator*
Robert J. Elster, Jr., *Research Assistant*

Linda M. Pugliese, *Manuscript Coordinator*

Bridget Broderick, Francine Melotti-Bacon, Ada Morgan,
Robyn V. Young, *Editorial Assistants*

L. Elizabeth Hardin, *Permissions Coordinator*
Dawn L. McGinty, Filomena Sgambati,
Angela J. Wilson, *Permissions Assistants*

Library of Congress Catalog Card Number 76-46132
ISBN 0-8103-0177-6

CONTENTS

PREFACE

It is impossible to overvalue the importance of literature in the intellectual, emotional, and spiritual evolution of humankind. Literature is that which both lifts us out of our everyday life and helps us to better understand it. Through the fictive life of an Emma Bovary, a Lambert Strether, a Leopold Bloom, our perceptions of the human condition are enlarged, and we are enriched.

Literary criticism is a collective term for several kinds of critical writing: criticism may be normative, descriptive, textual, interpretive, appreciative, generic. It takes many forms: the traditional essay, the aphorism, the book or play review, even the parodic poem. Perhaps the single unifying feature of literary criticism lies in its purpose: to help us to better understand what we read.

The Scope of the Book

The usefulness of Gale's *Contemporary Literary Criticism (CLC),* which excerpts criticism of current creative writing, suggests an equivalent need among literature students and teachers interested in authors of the period 1900 to 1960. The great poets, novelists, short story writers, and playwrights of this period are by far the most popular writers for study in high school and college literature courses. Moreover, since contemporary critics continue to analyze the work of this period—both in its own right and in relation to today's tastes and standards—a vast amount of relevant critical material confronts the student.

Thus, *Twentieth-Century Literary Criticism (TCLC)* will present significant passages from published criticism on authors who died between 1900 and 1960. Because of the difference in time span under consideration (*CLC* considers authors living from 1960 to the present), there will be no duplication between *CLC* and *TCLC.*

Each volume of *TCLC* will be carefully designed to present a list of authors who represent a variety of genres and nationalities. The length of an author's section is intended to be representative of the amount of critical attention he or she has received in the English language. Articles and books that have not been translated into English are excluded. An attempt has been made to identify and include excerpts from the seminal essays on each author's work. Additionally, as space permits, especially insightful essays of a more limited scope are included. Thus *TCLC* is designed to serve as an introduction for the student of twentieth-century literature to the authors of that period and to the most significant commentators on these authors. Each *TCLC* author section will represent the scope of critical response to that author's work: some early criticism will be presented to indicate initial reactions, later criticism will be selected to represent any rise or fall in an author's popularity, and current retrospective analyses will provide students with a modern view. Since a *TCLC* author section is intended to be a definitive overview, the editors will include between 40 and 50 authors in each 600-page volume (compared to approximately 150 authors in a *CLC* volume of similar size) in order to devote more attention to each author. Unlike *CLC,* no attempt will be made to update author sections in subsequent volumes, unless important new criticism warrants additional excerpts.

The Organization of the Book

An author section consists of the following elements: author heading, bio-critical introduction, principal works, excerpts of criticism (each followed by a citation), and, beginning with Volume 3, an annotated bibliography.

- The *author heading* consists of the author's full name, followed by birth and death dates. The unbracketed portion of the name denotes the form under which the author most commonly wrote. If an author wrote consistently under a pseudonym, the pseudonym will be listed in the author heading and the real name located in paren-

Preface

theses on the first line of the bio-critical introduction. Also located at the beginning of the bio-critical introduction are any name variation under which an author wrote, including transliterated forms for non-English language authors. Uncertainty as to a birth or death date is indicated by a question mark.

- The *bio-critical introduction* contains biographical and other background information about an author that will elucidate his or her creative output.

- The *list of principal works* is chronological by date of first publication and genres are identified. In those instances where the first publication was other than English language, the title and date of the first English-language edition are given in brackets. Unless otherwise indicated, dramas are dated by first publication, not first performance.

- *Criticism* is arranged chronologically in each author section to provide a perspective on any changes in critical evaluation over the years. For purposes of easier identification, the critic's name and the publication date of essay are given at the beginning of each piece of criticism.

- A complete *bibliographical citation* designed to facilitate location of the original essay or book by the interested reader accompanies each piece of criticism. An asterisk * at the end of a citation indicates the essay is on more than one author.

- The *annotated bibliography* appearing at the end of each author section suggests further reading on the author. In some cases it includes essays for which the editors could not obtain reprint rights.

Each volume of *TCLC* includes a cumulative index to critics. Under each critic's name is listed the author(s) on which the critic has written and the volume and page where the criticism may be found. *TCLC* also includes a cumulative index to authors with the volume number in which the author appears in boldface after his or her name.

Beginning with Volume 2, *TCLC* added an appendix which lists the sources from which material in the volume is reprinted. It does not, however, list every book or periodical consulted for the volume.

Acknowledgments

No work of this scope can be accomplished without the cooperation of many people. The editors especially wish to thank the copyright holders of the excerpts included in this volume, the permission managers of many book and magazine publishing companies for assisting us in locating copyright holders, and the staffs of the Detroit Public Library, University of Michigan Library, and Wayne State University Library for making their resources available to us.

Suggestions Are Welcome

If readers wish to suggest authors they would like to have covered in future volumes, or if they have other suggestions, they are cordially invited to write the editor.

AUTHORS TO APPEAR
IN FUTURE VOLUMES

Adams, Henry 1838-1918
Ady, Endre 1877-1919
Agate, James 1877-1947
Agustini, Delmira 1886-1914
Alain-Fournier (Henri Alban
  Fournier) 1886-1914
Aldrich, Thomas Bailey 1836-1907
Annensy, Innokenty Fyodorovich
  1856-1909
Anstey, Frederick 1856-1934
Arlen, Michael 1895-1956
Barbusse, Henri 1873-1935
Barea, Arturo 1897-1957
Baring, Maurice 1874-1945
Baroja, Pio 1872-1956
Barry, Philip 1896-1949
Bass, Eduard 1888-1946
Belloc, Hilaire 1870-1953
Benét, Stephen Vincent
  1898-1943
Benét, William Rose 1886-1950
Bennet, (Enoch) Arnold
  1867-1931
Benson, E(dward) F(rederic)
  1867-1940
Benson, Stella 1892-1933
Beresford, J(ohn) D(avys)
  1873-1947
Bethell, Mary Ursula 1874-1945
Betti, Ugo 1892-1953
Biely, Andrei 1880-1934
Binyon, Laurence 1869-1943
Bjørnson, Bjørnstjerne 1832-1910
Blackmore, R(ichard) D(oddridge)
  1825-1900
Blasco Ibáñez, Vicente
  1867-1928
Blok, Alexandr 1880-1921
Bojer, Johan 1872-1959
Bosman, Herman Charles
  1905-1951
Bottomley, Gordon 1874-1948
Bourne, George 1863-1927
Broch, Herman 1886-1951
Bromfield, Louis 1896-1956
Buchan, John 1870-1953
Bunin, Ivan 1870-1953
Byrne, Donn (Brian Oswald
  Donn-Byrne) 1889-1928
Cabell, James Branch 1879-1958
Cable, George Washington
  1844-1925
Caine, Hall 1853-1931
Campana, Dino 1885-1932
Campbell, (Ignatius) Roy
  1901-1957
Cannan, Gilbert 1884-1955
Capek, Karl 1890-1938
Chesnutt, Charles Waddell
  1858-1932

Churchill, Winston 1871-1947
Coppard, A(lfred) E(dgar)
  1878-1957
Corelli, Marie 1855-1924
Corvo, Baron (Frederick
  William Rolfe) 1860-1913
Crane, Stephen 1871-1900
Crawford, F. Marion 1854-1909
Croce, Benedetto 1866-1952
Cullen, Countee 1903-1946
D'Annunzio, Gabriele 1863-1938
Dario, Ruben 1867-1916
Davidson, John 1857-1909
Davies, W(illiam) H(enry)
  1871-1940
Davis, Rebecca Harding 1831-1910
Day, Clarence 1874-1935
Delafield, E.M. (Edme
  Elizabeth Monica de la
  Pasture) 1890-1943
de la Mare, Walter 1873-1956
DeMorgan, William 1839-1917
Doblin, Alfred 1878-1957
Douglas, Lloyd C(assel) 1877-1951
Douglas, (George) Norman
  1868-1952
Dowson, Ernest Christopher
  1867-1900
Doyle, Sir Arthur Conan
  1859-1930
Dreiser, Theodore 1871-1945
Drinkwater, John 1882-1937
Duun, Olav 1876-1939
Echegaray y Eizaguirre, José
  1833?-1916
Eluard, Paul 1895-1952
Esenin, Sergei Aleksandrovich
  1895-1925
Fadeyev, Alexandr 1901-1956
Feydeau, Georges 1862-1921
Field, Michael (Katharine
  Harris Bradley 1846-1914
  and Edith Emma Cooper
  1862-1913)
Field, Rachel 1894-1942
Flecker, James Elroy 1884-1915
France, Anatole (Anatole
  Thibault) 1844-1924
Freeman, John 1880-1929
Gibbon, Lewis 1901-1935
Gide, André 1869-1951
Glyn, Elinor 1864-1943
Gogarty, Oliver St. John
  1878-1957
Golding, Louis 1895-1958
Gorky, Maxim 1868-1936
Gosse, Edmund 1849-1928
Gould, Gerald 1885-1936
Grahame, Kenneth 1859-1932
Gray, John 1866-1934

Grey, Zane 1875-1939
Grove, Frederick Philip
  1871-1948
Güiraldes, Ricardo 1886-1927
Gumilyov, Nikolay 1886-1921
Gwynne, Stephen Lucius
  1864-1950
Haggard, H(enry) Rider
  1856-1925
Hale, Edward Everett 1822-1909
Hall, (Marguerite) Radclyffe
  1806-1943
Hardy, Thomas 1840-1928
Harris, Frank 1856-1931
Hašek, Jaroslav 1883-1923
Hauptmann, Gerhart 1862-1945
Hearn, Lafcadio 1850-1904
Heidenstam, Verner von
  1859-1940
Hergesheimer, Joseph 1880-1954
Hernandez, Miguel 1910-1942
Herrick, Robert 1868-1938
Hewlett, Maurice 1861-1923
Heyward, DuBose 1885-1940
Hichens, Robert 1864-1950
Hilton, James 1900-1954
Holtby, Winifred 1898-1935
Hope, Anthony 1863-1933
Housman, Laurence 1865-1959
Howard, Sidney 1891-1939
Howells, William Dean
  1837-1920
Hudson, Stephen 1868-1944
Hudson, W(illiam) H(enry)
  1841-1922
Ivanov, Vyacheslav Ivanovich
  1866-1949
Jacob, Max 1876-1944
Jacobs, W(illiam) W(ymark)
  1863-1943
James, Will 1892-1942
Jerome, Jerome K(lapka)
  1859-1927
Jimenez, Juan Ramon 1881-1958
Jones, Henry Arthur 1851-1929
Kipling, Rudyard 1865-1936
Kraus, Karl 1874-1936
Kuzmin, Mikhail Alekseyevich
  1875-1936
Lagerlöf, Selma 1858-1940
Lang, Andrew 1844-1912
Lawson, Henry 1867-1922
Lee, Vernon (Violet Paget)
  1856-1935
Leverson, Ada 1862-1933
Lewis, (Harry) Sinclair
  1885-1951
Lewisohn, Ludwig 1883-1955
Lie, Jonas 1833-1908
Lindsay, (Nicholas) Vachel
  1879-1931

London, Jack 1876-1916
Lonsdale, Frederick 1881-1954
Louys, Pierre 1870-1925
Lovecraft H(oward) P(hillips)
  1890-1937
Lowndes, Marie Belloc
  1868-1947
Lowry, Malcolm 1909-1957
Lucas, E(dward) V(errall)
  1868-1938
Lynd, Robert 1879-1949
MacArthur, Charles 1895-1956
Macaulay, Rose 1881-1958
Machen, Arthur 1863-1947
Manning, Frederic 1887-1935
Marinetti, Filippo Tommaso
  1876-1944
Marriott, Charles 1869-1957
Martin du Gard, Roger
  1881-1958
Martínez Sierra, Gregorio
  1881-1947
Mayakovsky, Vladimir
  Vladimirovich 1893-1930
Mencken, H(enry) L(ouis)
  1880-1956
Meredith, George 1828-1909
Meynell, Alice 1847-1922
Millay, Edna St. Vincent
  1892-1950
Milne, A(lan) A(lexander)
  1882-1956
Miro, Gabriel 1879-1936
Mistral, Frédéric 1830-1914
Mitchell, Margaret 1900-1949
Monro, Harold 1879-1932
Moore, George 1852-1933
Moore, Thomas Sturge
  1870-1944
Morgan, Charles 1894-1958
Morley, Christopher 1890-1957
Murray, (George) Gilbert
  1866-1957
Nervo, Armada 1870-1919
Nietzsche, Friedrich 1844-1900
Norris, Frank 1870-1902
Noyes, Alfred 1880-1958
Olbracht, Ivan (Kemil Zeman)
  1882-1952
Orczy, Baroness (Emmuska)
  1865-1947
Owen, Wilfred 1893-1918
Palamas, Kostis 1859-1943
Pinero, Arthur Wing 1855-1934
Pirandello, Luigi 1867-1936
Pontoppidan, Henrik 1857-1943
Porter, Eleanor H(odgman)
  1868-1920
Porter, Gene(va) Stratton
  1886-1924

Authors to Appear in Future Volumes

Powys, T(heodore) F(rancis) 1875-1953
Proust, Marcel 1871-1922
Quiller-Couch, Arthur 1863-1944
Rappoport, Solomon 1863-1920
Rawlings, Marjorie Kinnan 1896-1953
Reid, Forrest 1876-1947
Reymont, Ladislas (Wladyslaw Stanislaw Reymont) 1867-1925
Richardson, Henry Handel (Ethel Florence Richardson) 1870-1946
Riley, James Whitcomb 1849-1916
Rinehart, Mary Roberts 1876-1958
Roberts, Elizabeth Madox 1886-1941
Robinson, Edward Arlington 1869-1935
Rölvaag, O(le) E(dvart) 1876-1931
Rolland, Romain 1866-1944
Rostand, Edmond 1868-1918

Roussel, Raymond 1877-1933
Runyon, (Alfred) Damon 1884-1946
Sabatini, Rafael 1875-1950
Santayana, George 1863-1952
Schnitzler, Arthur 1862-1931
Schulz, Bruno 1892-1942
Scott, Duncan Campbell 1862-1947
Seeger, Alan 1888-1916
Service, Robert 1874-1958
Seton, Ernest Thompson 1860-1946
Slater, Francis Carey 1875-1958
Sologub, Fyodor 1863-1927
Squire, J(ohn) C(ollings) 1884-1958
Stephens, James 1882-1951
Stockton, Frank R. 1834-1902
Storni, Alfonsina 1892-1938
Supervielle, Jules 1884-1960
Sutro, Alfred 1863-1933
Swinburne, Algernon Charles 1837-1909

Symons, Arthur 1865-1945
Synge, John Millington 1871-1909
Tabb, John Bannister 1845-1909
Tarkington, Booth 1869-1946
Teasdale, Sara 1884-1933
Tey, Josephine (Elizabeth Mackintosh) 1897-1952
Thompson, Francis 1859-1907
Tolstoy, Count Leo (Nikolayevich) 1828-1910
Turner, W(alter) J(ames) R(edfern) 1889-1946
Twain, Mark (Samuel Langhorne Clemens) 1835-1910
Vachell, Horace Annesley 1861-1955
Valéry, Paul 1871-1945
Valle-Inclan, Ramón del 1869-1935
Van Dine, S.S. (Willard H. Wright) 1888-1939
Van Doren, Carl 1885-1950
Vazov, Ivan 1850-1921

Verne, Jules 1828-1905
Wallace, Edgar 1875-1932
Wallace, Lewis 1827-1905
Walpole, Hugh 1884-1941
Wassermann, Jakob 1873-1934
Webb, Mary 1881-1927
Webster, Jean 1876-1916
Welch, Denton 1917-1948,
Wells, Carolyn 1869-1942
Wells, H(erbert) G(eorge) 1866-1946
Werfel, Franz 1890-1945
Wister, Owen 1860-1938
Wolfe, Thomas 1900-1938
Woollcott, Alexander 1887-1943
Wren, P(ercival) C(hristopher) 1885-1941
Wylie, Francis Brett 1844-1954
Zamyatin, Yevgeniy Ivanovich 1884-1937
Zangwill, Israel 1864-1926

Readers are cordially invited to suggest additional authors to the editors.

A.E.

1867-1935

(Pseudonym of George William Russell; also wrote under pseudonym of Y.O.) Irish poet, essayist, editor, journalist, and dramatist.

A key figure in the Irish Literary Revival, A.E. contributed perhaps more by his personality than by his artistry. He was a gifted conversationalist, a popular lecturer, an acknowledged visionary—an oracle of Ireland.

A.E. had a pious upbringing and was from his youth inclined toward mysticism. It was while pursuing his interest in painting at the Dublin Metropolitan School of Art that A.E. met W. B. Yeats, his lifelong friend. Through Yeats, A.E. became involved in the Theosophical Movement, finding a channel for his mystical inclination. Together the two writers founded the Dublin Lodge of the Theosophical Society. Many of A.E.'s beliefs have their origin in this spiritual background and are the inspiration for his early poetry, *Homeward: Songs by the Way*, *The Earth Breath*, and *The Divine Vision*. A.E. was also influenced by other mystic poets. He was devoted to the work of Emerson and recognized his own image in the poetry of Blake. A.E.'s poetry, not surprisingly, has been compared to that of Blake, Emerson, and Whitman.

A.E. was central to the rise of the Irish National Theatre and is often considered one of the founders of the Abbey Theatre. His only play, *Deirdre*, a verse drama based on Irish legend, was one of the earliest productions of the modern Irish theater. Always interested in other Irish authors, A.E. hosted a weekly gathering which drew such notables as Yeats, George Moore, Padraic Colum, and James Stephens. As editor of Dublin's literary weekly, *The Irish Statesman*, he provided another forum for writers.

A.E.'s interests were more than literary; they were also political. He was involved throughout his life in Irish agrarian and political affairs and was a moving force behind the Agricultural Cooperative Movement. He edited its chief organ, *The Irish Homestead* (later *The Irish Statesman*).

In his later years, broken by the death of his wife, Violet, and saddened that the spiritual rebirth he had sought for his homeland, and often written about had not occurred, A.E. retired to England. Critical consensus is that A.E. survives not as painter, poet, or politician, but as the embodiment of the beliefs and principles of the Irish Revival.

PRINCIPAL WORKS

Homeward: Songs by the Way   (poetry)   1894
The Earth Breath, and Other Poems   (poetry)   1897
The Divine Vision, and Other Poems   (poetry)   1904
Co-operation and Nationality: A Guide for Rural Reformers from This to the Next Generation   (essays) 1912
Collected Poems   (poetry)   1913
Gods of War   (poetry)   1915
Imaginations and Reveries   (essays and drama, includes *Deirdre: A Drama*)   1915
The National Being: Some Thoughts on an Irish Polity (essays)   1916
The Candle of Vision   (essays)   1918
The Interpreters   (essay)   1922
Voices of the Stones   (poetry)   1925
Enchantment, and Other Poems   (poetry)   1930
Vale and Other Poems   (poetry)   1931
Song and Its Foundations   (essays)   1932
The Avatars: A Futurist Fantasy   (novel)   1933
The House of the Titans and Other Poems   (poetry)   1934
Selected Poems   (poetry)   1935
The Living Torch   (essays)   1937

JULIA ELLSWORTH FORD   (essay date 1905)

Among the poets whose work has added distinction to the Literary Movement in Ireland is A. E. . . . , whose volume of verse 'The Divine Vision,' recently published, has brought a new revelation of tender beauty in a glowing color of words, and has given a quickening insight into the mystic world. (p. 82)

Aside from their technical form, 'A. E.'s' poems might have been voiced in remote ages in the East, if we except those which are love poems. In these songs of personal feeling one realizes deeply the spiritual side of love. Above all they are touched with a tenderness and sadness unspeakable, but it is a noble sadness which is the dominant note of his love poetry. It renounces that it may attain to a higher fulfillment. This sad, but far from despondent note throughout 'A. E.'s' poetry, is essentially a modern phase that can as well be discerned in the painting as in the poetry of the latter part of the nineteenth century, especially among the Preraphaelites; and the twentieth century is under this same influence. (p. 83)

'A. E.' has close affinity to our master Emerson; both drew much of their inspiration from the same source, the *Upanishads*. They both found their way homeward to the strange world the seers tell of, 'the world at the back of the heavens.' While Emerson is a poet of deeper thought and broader harmony, 'A. E.' has the great gift of delicate melody. His unusual metres, often repeated, have a peculiar fitness for the thought expressed. An interesting peculiarity of his thought is his constant appeal to the power of 'Quiet' which gives us the uplifting calm that the twilight hour brings, but he has greater gifts for us in reserve; his optimism is not the outcome of mental passiveness, but the result of his philosophy of Eternal Beauty as the root of all things permanent. . . . (p. 85)

[The] heart of this great mystic, 'A. E.,' is aglow with the spirit of his time, and that the voice of Ireland's most spiritual singer is one of the greatest voices of the Irish Movement—the new Renaissance, not of learning but of feeling. (p. 86)

Julia Ellsworth Ford, "'A. E.,' The Neo-Celtic Mystic," in Poet Lore *(copyright, 1905, by Poet Lore, Inc.), Vol. XVI, No. IV, Winter, 1905, pp. 82-6.*

CORNELIUS WEYGANDT (essay date 1907)

["Reconciliation," included in "The Divine Vision,"] is a poem I do not pretend to understand in detail, but I do feel its drift. . . . Many of [Mr. Russell's] poems are like this poem in that you must content yourself with their general drift and not insist on understanding their every phrase. I suppose to the initiated mystic they are more than presentations of emotions that need not be translated into terms of thought for their desired effect.

To Mr. Russell, poetry is a high and holy thing; like Spencer he believes it the fruit of a "certain enthousiasmos and celestial inspiration:" it is his religion that Mr. Russell is celebrating in his verses, many of which are in a sense hymns to the Universal Spirit, and all of which are informed by such sincerity that you do not wonder that his followers make them their general gospel. (p. 155)

Seventeen of "A. E.'s" one hundred and sixty poems are definitely declarations of belief, but declarations so personal, so undogmatic that you would hardly write him down a didactic poet at first reading. "A New Theme" tells of his desertion of subjects "that win the easy praise," of his venturing "in the untrodden woods To carve the future ways." Here he acknowledges that the things he has to tell are "shadowy," that his breath in "the magic horn" can make but feeble murmurs. In the prologue to "The Divine Vision" he states the conditions of his inspiration: [the meditative twilight hours, when songs spring from his heart, which is "touched by the flame"]—that is the flame of his being that, "mad for the night and the deep unknown," leaps back to the "unphenomenal" world whence his spirit came and blends his spirit into one with the Universal Spirit. This same union through the soul's flame "A. E." presents in his pictures, and in his prologue to the "The Divine Vision" he writes that he wishes to give his reader

To see one elemental pain
One light of everlasting joy.

This elemental pain, as I take it, is the pain of the soul shut up in its robe of clay in this physical, phenomenal world, and so shut off from the spiritual world, the world of the unphenomenal or unknowable. The "everlasting joy" I take to be the certainty of eventual union with the Universal Spirit in the unphenomenal world, a union and a joy anticipated in the occasional temporary absorptions of the soul into the Universal Spirit in moments that Emerson experienced as "Revelation" and Plotinus as ecstasy. (p. 156)

The typical poem of "A. E." is that in which the sight of beautiful things of this phenomenal world in which we live lifts his soul to participation in the Universal Spirit. It is most often through some beauty of the sky at sunset . . . or at sunrise, when there is "fire on the altar of the hills" . . . that he becomes one with the Universal Spirit in "the rapture of the fire," that he is lost "within the Mother's being," he would say; that the soul returns to the Oversoul, Emerson would say. There are ways by which the soul homes other than these—sometimes it is "By the hand of a child I am led to the throne of the King," but it is most often by way of beauties of the sky. (p. 157)

How important the symbol is to "A. E."—as important as it is to Emerson—may be gathered from "Symbolism." . . . (p. 158)

In this poem is the proof of how intimately "A. E." could write of the sweet things of earth did he so choose. But he does not so choose, except rarely, and sometimes he leaves out the statement of beautiful material things by which he customarily bids farewell to earth in his aspiration to spiritual things, and writes only of unearthly things—as of some girl that he, an Irishman living in the Dublin of to-day, loves in the Babylon of three thousand years ago, to the annihilation of space and time. This is written in the very spirit of Emerson's declaration that "Before the revelation of the soul, Time, Space and Nature shrink away." . . . "A. E.," like Emerson, holds that the true poet is he who "gives men glimpses of the law of the Universe; shows them the circumstance as illusion; shows that Nature is only a language to express the laws, which are grand and beautiful; and lets them, by his songs, into some of the realities." Emerson yearns that "the old forgotten splendours of the Universe should glow again for us;" and "A. E." believes that we at times attain "the ancestral Self," his restless ploughman, "walking through the woodland's purple" under "the diamond night," "Deep beneath his rustic habit finds himself a King."

"A. E.'s" poems on death are little different from those in which he celebrates the soul's absorption into the Universal Spirit, since death means to him only a longer absorption into the Universal Spirit. . . . (pp. 158-59)

So sustained is the habitual altitude of Mr. Russell's thought, so preoccupied his mind with spiritual things that the human reader must feel lonely at times, must feel the regions of the poet's thought alien to him. At such times it is a positive relief to find the poet yearning for the concrete sweet things of earth. (p. 159)

It is love, love of country, love of countryside, and love of woman that he writes of when he does write of "loved earth things." "A Woman's Voice," and "Forgiveness" are poems so simple that none may misunderstand; they have the human call, so rare in "A. E.," but it is not strong human call. Of such love-songs he has written but few—poems out of the peace and not out of the passion of love; of passion other than spiritual ecstasy and rapt delight in nature there is none in his verse. Although he has been given "a ruby flaming heart," he has been given also "a pure cold spirit." Only about a fourth of his poems have the human note dominant, and even when it is so dominant, as when he writes of his country, he is very seldom content to rest with a description of the beauty of place or legend; the beautiful place must be threshold to the Other World, as "The Gates of Dreamland." . . . (pp. 159-60)

"In Connerama" and "An Irish Face," poems with earthly titles, you expect only things earthly, but in these two, he uses the picture of the concrete only as the symbol of the universal. The reason Mr. Russell must take you to the supernatural in these poems is because he sees spirits everywhere he goes in Ireland. "Never a poet," he writes, "has lain on our hillsides but gentle, stately figures, with hearts shining like the sun, move through his dreams, over radiant graves, in an enchanted world of their own," (p. 160)

When we come to consider the technique of Mr. Russell's art we find him anything but Emersonian. Mr. Russell has, in general, command of form, melody, harmony, distinction. Who reads carefully will remember many fine lines; who reads only once will be as one lost in sunfilled fog like that of "A. E.'s" own Irish mountains; but he should be patient, he should wait and look again and again, and finally he will see, even if earth be still dimmed with fogbanks, much of the heavens, free of fog, and radiant with cold white light. There are comparatively few "purple patches" in Mr. Russell's poetry, for the reason that each poem depends for its chief appeal on one mood or thought of dream immanent in it rather than on any fine phrasing. The effort to catch the meaning of the verse—seldom apparent at first glance—prevents the noting of as many purple lines as there are. Nor when noted are such lines readily memorable since they are apt to lack association with known and loved things to bring them back to the reader. And again the poems are very short, intimations, suggestions rather than expressions—and their intangible themes are often much alike, and poem becomes confused with poem in the memory. (pp. 162-63)

> *Cornelius Weygandt, "'A. E.,' the Irish Emerson," in* The Sewanee Review *(reprinted by permission of the editor; © 1907 by The University of the South), Vol. XV, No. 2, Spring, 1907, pp. 148-65.*

ERNEST A. BOYD (essay date 1915)

The very title of this exquisite little book [*Homeward: Songs by the Way*] indicates the author's attitude toward life. Home, to "A. E.," means the return of the soul to the Oversoul, the absorption of the spirit in the Universal Spirit. *Homeward* is the narrative of his spiritual adventures, the record of those ecstasies which mark the search of the soul for the Infinite. (p. 252)

Homeward was followed [by *The Earth Breath* and *The Divine Vision*.] . . . These latter volumes do not, in a sense, represent any progression; they are the utterances of a similar contemplation, and were, in essentials, contained in his

first book. . . . There is, of course, the deeper note of a more mature reflection, a certain sadness which has come with the years. The eager spirit still aspires homeward, but the goal is yet far away. In the preface to his *Collected Poems . . . ,* "A. E." confesses to the change of mood which makes his later work slightly different from the earlier. . . . This volume is . . . the complete expression of "A. E.'s" thought, no less than the final collection of his verse. So far as its content is concerned, the book is perfect. Some of the less successful poems of the earlier volumes, notably of *The Earth Breath* and *The Divine Vision*, have been omitted. It is interesting to note that only two from *Homeward* have been suppressed. This is a significant illustration of the initial perfection of his work, and of the constancy of belief it has expressed. Form has never been a preoccupation of "A. E."; his verses are sometimes marred by clumsiness and obscurity of phrase, and he openly avows his inability to remould them before giving them in their now definite arrangement. Nevertheless, *Collected Poems* is an achievement of which Irish literature may be proud. Seldom has such beauty of thought and language been accompanied by the restraint which makes this book the small but great contribution of "A. E." to contemporary poetry. (pp. 253-54)

Concerned as most of his poems are with the relation of man to Deity, of the soul to the Eternal, "A. E.'s" verse has been pronounced "inhuman" by some critics. The great themes of poetry, love and death, are not absent from his pages, but they are treated from the special standpoint of the transcendentalist. "A. E." is enamoured of beauty and mystery, he is enthralled by a sense of immortal destinies. In the love of woman he feels an emotion which goes far beyond that conveyed by the mortal senses. . . . Often one reads some exquisite evocation of the Irish countryside, only to find, after a verse or two, that the poet has peopled this landscape with the phantom figures of the heroic age, or with the flaming beings seen in mystic ecstasy. What seemed to be a simple picture becomes a glimpse behind the veil, and bog and mountain are forgotten in the splendour of the vision. Similarly in his love poems "A. E." has the faculty of projecting his emotion into regions beyond time and space. . . . Death, for him, has none of the mysterious terror which has inspired so much fine poetry. To "A. E." the immortality of man is assured, for is he not of the same divine substance as the Great Source of all being? (p. 255)

The *leitmotiv* of "A. E.'s" poetry, and the fundamental postulate of his philosophy, is the divine origin of man, the gradual falling away of the human race from its heroic destinies, and its present enslavement to materialism. It is only when he is aroused by some noble ideal, or some great memory, that man rises to a realisation of the divinity that is in him. His constant endeavour is to fan this divine spark into flame. Hence his love and admiration for the heroic figures of Celtic history and legend, when man carried latent within him all the potentialities of nature, and his faculties were not diminished by specialisation. (p. 256)

"A. E." rightly conceives it the aim and *raison d'être* of the new Anglo-Irish literature "to create a national ideal in Ireland, or rather to let that spirit incarnate fully which began among the ancient peoples, which has haunted the hearts, and whispered a dim revelation of itself, through the lips of the bards and peasant storytellers." In *The Dramatic*

Treatment of Heroic Literature are set forth the reasons which call for the re-creation of the bardic tales at the hands of the modern poets, and more particularly the use of this material in the Irish Theatre. "A. E." was afterwards to put his theories into practice by writing *Deirdre*. . . . The author has since recanted some of the views he first held as to the desirability of staging the heroic stories, perhaps as a result of his dissatisfaction with his own effort in that direction. There can, however, be no question as to the suitability of such a natural tragedy as that of *Deirdre* for the stage. [John Millington] Synge's version, incomplete as it is, shows sufficiently the power of this theme, when treated by a real dramatist. Of "A. E.'s" *Deirdre,* as of that of Yeats, it may be said that it is a work of poetic rather than dramatic merit. (p. 257)

> Ernest A. Boyd, "'A. E.'—Mystic and Economist," in The North American Review *(reprinted by permission from* The North American Review; *copyright © 1915 by the University of Northern Iowa), Vol. 202, No. 717, August, 1915, pp. 251-61.*

DARRELL FIGGIS   (essay date 1916)

[Æ] was more content to record his [discoveries] than to communicate [them]: had he as a poet been more self-aware he might by a better craft, born of brooding, have more often lit a flame in his verse, to burn intensely there and to light other brains, where it is content to tell of a fire in the poet himself altogether so much brighter than in the poetry he made. There is no poem, so sincere is this poet, and especially in his early verse, that does not tell of a vision that he does not feel that it is important we should know. He was never at heart interested in the poem only for the poem's sake; and he never in his verse took a holiday—at least in his published verse. And we feel this. We feel that there is no poem, however it fail, that does not record a spiritual discovery; but we are often baffled, because the poem, while it tells us of the discovery, is not itself the fine ritual in which the discovery is involved. The poet has his vision, we know; though visions are by no means always the starting-point for song, yet we are seldom uncertain in this case. Indeed, that is the thing that tantalizes. For the magician's sleight sometimes is lacking; and thus we hear him telling us of things, sometimes facilely and always mellifluously, but we are disappointed because he cannot make his vision ours for ever. At such times we feel that if he had brooded over his craft as he brooded over the things he wished to convey by his craft he would have made us better sharers of the things that remain his.

For the poems of these days are one continuous inspiration of theme. "Homeward, Songs by the Way" is an unbroken series. It is linked with "The Earth Breath" by the inclusion in that volume of many poems of the first song; the last of which appeared in "The Divine Vision," where the poet first begins definitely to turn to speechcraft from songcraft, and to utter in a fine pomp what he first had sung in purity, even though the song were not always uniformly magical. (pp. 30-1)

Yet a poem may be taken where the clearness of the vision is indisputable and the result one to be pondered on, where, however, the answering mood in us is not uplifted to an equal height. Such a poem is "Om." We know how it came. As the accountant sat at his desk, it and all around him were whirled away while he looked intently on the sight before his open eyes. . . . The record of the thing seen is complete, told with music and wisdom. But what have we missed? We have missed just what it brought to the poet. The ecstasy it wrought in him he has not wrought in us, for all that we know well, from the record and some alchemy in its making, that the ecstasy was there. The very chord he heard is hardly heard by us, for it is strange that the tone conveyed by the word "Om" is not the tone-dominant of the poem. (pp. 33-4)

[In "The Great Breath"] we are lifted to an equal mood; the ecstasy that was in the singer is the ecstasy that passes to us. So it is with "The Unknown God," with its higher, clearer tone, and "Refuge" from ["The Divine Vision"], with its deep mature reticence. Yet, whether we hear or do not hear his ecstasy, never was there so exact a poet as this. Many of his poems come not only from the inmost circle of spiritual insight, but also from the outer circle of psychic vision; and much that might seem, at a cursory glance, extravagant imagery, will be found to be no more than meticulous accuracy to what he has beheld. Perhaps they too much demand a knowledge of mystic signs and symbols; perhaps they unwisely, in some cases, decree for us a like psychic experience if not learning—unwisely for poetry, which should not need annotation but should address itself directly to the pure and aspiring spirit of man: that may very well be; but there are none of his poems that we may set aside as inexact. "The Robing of the King," for example, records precisely what in vision he beheld, rightly or wrongly, as the meaning of the Crucifixion, surrendering, as he does, its outward appearance to those who did not know the esoteric event that was happening. And there are many poems of this sort, that are rather less poems than texts, like the texts of the East, to be brooded upon like symbols and unravelled like mysteries. Not only, however, are the visions of the "household" so written. On the hills of Ireland, aflame once with mystic fires, this man may have beheld the great ones once again, have seen things not easy to be told, and have recorded them with the care of a man of faith. These things are not lightly to be spoken of; but to be passed from hand to hand; and Irishmen at least will read "The Child of Destiny" with attention. (pp. 35-7)

If a man has to write . . . of [the] fine intimacies [of spiritual life] the writing will be just as complex as the spiritual life is complex, and will seem obscure in exactly the same relation as his experiences and discoveries will defy expression. He will have to ambush the shy things that lurk in the thicket of his soul, and net them subtly and quickly in the tones and colours and rhythms of words rather than in their bold and limited meanings. That will not lead to clarity; clarity in such a case would be a profound lie; for precious things are precious in both meanings of the word.

It is a very delicate net of words, for instance, he has thrown round some of the intimations of the spiritual meaning of Life in his essay "The Renewal of Youth." "We came out of the Great Mother-Life for the purposes of soul," he says; and in the wonderful music of that essay he writes of the source and destiny of that experience for which we have been lent to Life. (p. 47)

That of which he writes is the same . . . as he sang of in "The Robing of the King"; and to say of it, as of the essay, that it is prose at its highest, is to give it but half its praise. It is the writing of a seër: a seër who sees the golden end with the golden uprise, and who perceives, therefore, that "every word which really inspires is spoken as if the Golden Age had never passed," for "the great teachers ignore the personal identity and speak to the eternal pilgrim." It may be true, in the opening words of this essay, that "humanity is no longer the child it was at the beginning of the world," that "its gay, wonderful childhood gave way, as cycle after cycle coiled itself into slumber, to more definite purposes, and now it is old and burdened with experiences"—experiences gathered, as his profound faith is, not merely as written in histories dealing with the outward life of nations and the race, but in renewed reincarnations of innumerable souls—but it is equally true that the life that runs now is the life that ever ran; and if we could but strike down to that depth, or if some seër could do so, or if some artist, who is the seër expressing himself in Beauty, could do so, then we would renew our youth, we would smile in the face of old Circumstance with the youngling joy that is our true heritage, and like happy children wise with understanding refashion Seeming into the ideal truth of Being. (pp. 48-9)

"The Renewal of Youth" is great prose, quite conceivably the greatest prose of its time; but it is this firstly because it is, in strict terms, a holy book. It is not concerned with dead things, with ethics and moralities, but with the fount from which these things arise, and in connection with which they are not dead but alive. (pp. 49-50)

["Deirdre" is] a pitiful tale that could be charged with so many significances—justly and truly as it came to Æ, and in pure and musical prose. It does not express Æ to us: or rather, since it is impossible for a man to write without in some degree expressing himself, it merely carries off the things that had lightly gathered on the surface of his mind. The manner of its inception precluded a deep and meditated utterance; and leaves us with the thought that if Æ had not written with that marvellous facility of his, some of his later writings might more constantly have come burthened with permanent vision rather than radiant with a wonderful casual insight. (p. 140)

> *Darrell Figgis, in his Æ (George W. Russell): A Study of a Man and a Nation, Maunsel & Co. Ltd., 1916, 159 p.*

IRWIN EDMAN   (essay date 1923)

Poetry, politics, and philosophy are by no means so dissevered in essence as they frequently are in practice, and it is a rare exhilaration to find a book which is a sincere and passionate fusion of the three. A. E. is one of the few living writers who could accomplish the feat. It is impossible offhand to think of any other literary man in this generation whose life has been at once that of a mystic philosopher and a revolutionary publicist, an intense poet and active politician. "The Interpreters" is that rare thing in philosophy, sustained and sensitive reflection upon a subject matter no less intimate and real than the author's own experience.

Not often outside the dialogues of Plato, and scarcely anywhere in recent philosophical literature, does one find ideas so completely dramatized. . . . The characters are rebels against an imagined world state whose empire and ideal are marked by world-wide uniformity. They are caught on the verge of a successful revolution and are thrown into the arsenal which they have barely failed to capture. . . . [These] doomed prisoners elect to spend their remaining

hours before execution at dawn in revealing to each other the roots of the ideals for which they have dared to die. For these are not ordinary social reformers in whose literary programs lurk no spiritual meanings, and in whose narrow perception of means gleams no heaven of deeply conceived ends. These have rebelled not against a polity but against a spirit. . . .

There are, wrapped in this exaltation, two major convictions, both dubious empirically, but both deeply true to the essential idealism of man. The first is that political creeds drive their meaning if not their origin from a spiritual insight deeper than the external facts and programs with which they are ostensibly dealing. The second is the insistence that all living thought and vital emotion derive from a universal life, that the cosmos is the source of all the varied flowers of faith that come to fulness in the human spirit. Neither of these poetic dogmas is literally true. . . . No one, perhaps, but a Celtic poet could have written a book on politics in the spirit of a Neo-Platonic mystic. . . . Perhaps no one but a man brought up on Irish folk-lore could believe so tenderly in the lyric goodness of things. In any case, it would be hard to find in contemporary literature so moving and magical an essay in "relating the politics of time to the politics of eternity." And this most Platonic symposium is written in a prose tuned to the grandeur of its theme and its intention.

> *Irwin Edman, "The Politics of Eternity," in The Nation (copyright 1923 by the Nation Associates, Inc.), Vol. CXVI, No. 3016, April 25, 1923, p. 499.*

W. B. YEATS   (essay date 1926)

A few months before I had come to Ireland [AE] had sent me some verses, which I had liked till Edwin Ellis had laughed me from my liking by proving that no line had a rhythm that agreed with any other, and that, the moment one thought he had settled upon some scheme of rhyme, he would break from it without reason. But now his verse was clear in thought and delicate in form. He wrote without premeditation or labour. It had, as it were, organized itself, and grown as nervous and living as if it had, as Dante said of his own work, paled his cheek. (p. 241)

Men watched him with awe or with bewilderment; it was known that he saw visions continually, perhaps more continually than any modern man since Swedenborg. . . . He and I often quarrelled, because I wanted him to examine and question his visions, and write them out as they occurred; and still more because I thought symbolic what he thought real like the men and women that had passed him on the road. Were they so much a part of his subconscious life that they would have vanished had he submitted them to question; were they like those voices that only speak, those strange sights that only show themselves for an instant, when the attention has been withdrawn; that phantasmagoria of which I had learnt something in London: and had his verse and his painting a like origin? And was that why . . . , after writing *Homeward; Songs by the Way,* where all is skilful and much exquisite, he would never again write a perfect book? (pp. 242-44)

[AE] had, and has, the capacity, beyond that of any man I have known, to put with entire justice not only the thoughts, but the emotions of the most opposite parties and personalities, as it were dissolving some public or private uproar into drama by Corneille or by Racine; and men who have hated each other must sometimes have been reconciled, because each heard his enemy's argument put into better words than he himself had found for his own; and this fight was in later years to give him political influence, and win him respect from Irish Nationalist and Unionist alike. It is, perhaps, because of it—joined to a too literal acceptance of those noble images of moral tradition which are so like late Graeco-Roman statues—that he has come to see all human life as a mythological system, where, though all cats are griffins, the more dangerous griffins are only found among politicians he has not spoken to, or among authors he has but glanced at; while those men and women who bring him their confessions and listen to his advice carry but the snowiest of swan's plumage. Nor has it failed to make him, as I think, a bad literary critic; demanding plays and poems where the characters must attain a stature of seven feet, and resenting as something perverse and morbid all abatement from that measure. I sometimes wonder what he would have been had he not met in early life the poetry of Emerson and Walt Whitman, writers who have begun to seem superficial precisely because they lack the Vision of Evil; and those translations of the Upanishads, which it is so much harder to study by the sinking flame of Indian tradition than by the serviceable lamp of Emerson and Walt Whitman. (pp. 245-46)

> W. B. Yeats, "The Trembling of the Veil: Ireland After Parnell" (1926), in his Autobiographies (reprinted by permission of A. P. Watt Ltd.), Macmillan & Co. Ltd., 1955, pp. 197-250.*

JOHN EGLINTON   (essay date 1935)

[When Russell's first] poems appeared, . . . the favourable reception they met with proved how widely diffused was the interest in [Theosophy's] beliefs and doctrines, some knowledge of which, one would think, was necessary for their comprehension. There is no doubt about Russell's poetic gift. . . . [Verse] is Russell's natural instrument. What is essential in his mind can only find expression poetically. The gift has remained with him all through life, and in his Collected Poems we find a progressive mastery of the lofty diction which he has elaborated for himself. The workmanship is not always fine; 'mystic', 'dreamy', 'diamond', 'starry', are tawdry substitutes for the 'inevitable' word, which is often avoided. And though there is a good deal about Beauty in the poems, beauty in his sombre twilight world is rather an object of belief than of delighted apprehension. . . . But as a poet of ideas there is no poet of his time quite like Russell. Sometimes his verses are the expression, almost crude, of the beliefs which have rooted themselves in him: the best of them are the embodiment and often perfect expression of moral intuitions; and not seldom he has been moved to utterance on public matters, as in the lines 'On behalf of some Irishmen not followers of tradition', which Ireland will carry in its memory like an arrow in the wound. The poems tell of spiritual agonies and triumphant spiritual perceptions, and often the impression one receives is of a terrible sadness, for the attitude with which this proud soul confronts the universe has not infrequently drawn upon him a response, or laid bare an irresponsiveness, which would have crushed any but the most pertinacious conviction. . . . [His] moments of illumination alternated with disconcerting avowals of doubt, and the very 'kingliness' and 'lordliness' of the beings to whose world he aspired, seemed to indicate a non-religious and

even non-philosophic dissatisfaction with his own earthly lot. Yet the consolatory power of Russell's poetry was to my knowledge more than once manifested: as when Dowden, who visited the beautiful Duchess of Leinster in her last illness, mentioned that she had found much comfort in Homeward: Songs by the Way. (pp. 48-51)

Suddenly broke out the Great War, which altered everything in this world, and not least the politics and prospects of Ireland. Russell was deeply stirred, and not, at least at first, specially as an Irishman. His horror of the slaughter was like that of Arjuna in the Bhagavad Gita, where the hero stands with Krishna in the interspace between two vast hosts drawn up for mutual destruction. . . . Russell lifted up his voice, and in a series of poems, in which his diction and sentiment reached their highest elevation, addressed the British public through the columns of The Times on the iniquity of war and of the statesmen who had brought it about. . . . [With] Russell the ethical problem was complicated by the fact that as a good Irish nationalist he would probably have reconciled himself easily enough to the collapse of the 'bubble Empire' as a thing good for the world, good for his own country, good perhaps for England itself; and this attitude, though intelligible, was hardly one to elicit any consolatory response from divine wisdom, like the agonised perplexity of Arjuna. Gods of War . . . was nevertheless, in dignity of poetic expression, one of Russell's most remarkable volumes of verse. (pp. 56-7)

> John Eglinton, "A.E. and His Story," in his Irish Literary Portraits (copyright © 1935 by Macmillan & Co. Ltd.; reprinted by permission of Macmillan, London and Basingstoke), Macmillan, 1935, pp. 39-61.

PADRAIC COLUM   (essay date 1936)

A.E.'s poetry belongs to an age remote from the modern one, and unless we have something in us which has survived from that age we will be interested only now and again in this, which is so impersonal, which makes such little innovation.

It is poetry that is close to the Vedas and Zoroastrian hymns. How little it has been influenced by the modern world with its religions, its philosophies and its social order! A. E. was aware of all of them, but they never made him dubious about the myth that gave a center to his poetry, the myth that he had evolved for himself. Men were the stayed Heaven-dwellers, the divinities who had descended into chaos to win a new empire for the spirit. "Homeward, Songs by the Way," was the title of his first volume, and it implied a return to remembrance, to the heaven that men had forgotten themselves out of. And the title-poem in his last volume, "The House of the Titans," dealt with the same myth. . . . A. E. was criticized because his verse forms were the accepted ones, because his frequent use of "immemorial," "vastness," "ancient," "dream," "beauty," made such words seem like counters rather than words with a life of their own. It has to be admitted that there is an amount of rhetoric in this poetry. But there is high distinction too: A. E. was an artist as well as a prophet. . . .

In [his] volume, "The Voices of the Stones," a poignant sense of loss makes itself felt—it is in that beautiful poem, "Promise," although there is still a faith that all losses will be restored. From this on the poet faces a lightless world:

companions have gone, age is coming on, the old simple, innocent, useful life is broken up; a cry that questions all goes up from this prophet of immortality. But A. E. would have his last utterance one of faith. And so he ends the selection that he had made just before his death with a poem [of faith] that is characteristic of his whole life. . . .

He believed in reincarnation and there was something about himself that made us suspend our disbelief in that strange doctrine. He must have existed in one of those ancient civilizations where the philosopher and the poet, the prophet and the priest, were one and the same person. (p. 23)

There are more accomplished poets and more competent philosophers left in the world. But we cannot turn to them with affection as we turned to A.E. (p. 24)

Padraic Colum, "A.E. and His Poetry," in The New Republic (© *1936 The New Republic, Inc.), Vol. 87, No. 1119, May 13, 1936, pp. 23-4.*

(essay date 1937)

The meditative twilight hour which predominated in A.E.'s poetry, with its transitory skies and delicately constellated colours, more than any other influence helped to establish in many minds the mood of the Celtic Twilight, though the poems themselves in their early matured thought owe little to that convention. The discipline of the true visionary differs from that of the imaginative artist, and the poems of A.E. do not yield their inner meaning with that sharpness of impact which we associate with vision. In their delicate impressionism, their mingling of shadow and jewel points of light, a system of worship is adumbrated, but the poems have the immediate effect of moving at a distance from the inner line of their significance. The intensity of their mystical earth-worship was expressed with an awe and reverence, a stillness of contemplation which evoked an answering mood of stillness. Even those who were but dimly conscious of the living mythus underneath, which gave the poet all the substance of his thought, could not but be aware of a self-flattering sense of spiritual expansion in themselves. . . .

But it is actually in the remote nature of his inner thought that A.E. differed so greatly from other poets who have patched up for themselves a compromise with temporal beliefs. The apparent comfort of his thought, with its expression in a modulated vowel music and tender touch, hid an implacable belief in the astounding responsibility of the human soul destined to shape and reshape itself in every circumstance of delight or terror. . . . His final belief in goodness and pity gave a tenderness to his poems and an air of mildness which did not seem incompatible with the tenets of Christianity. He was, however, a professing polytheist; and in the mythology, the intuitive symbols of older creeds, which other poets use as a state of thought, he found the actual and even visible action of spirit. . . . The poet's private devotion to [a] religion of nature, despite a multitude of world affairs, is shown by the fact that in his last narrative poem, "The House of the Titans," written in the comparative leisure of age, he attempted to re-interpret his spiritual beliefs in terms of Celtic divinity, gathering in meditation the vestigial survivals of that ancient Pantheon and reconciling it with Eastern thought. . . . (p. 765)

It is necessary to emphasize the religious nature of A.E.'s verse and clarify our own attitude, for otherwise we fail to perceive the full implications of his natural worship or account for its literary limitations. He meant what he said; and there is a direct simplicity in many of his earth hymns. . . . He employed common measures, ordinary rhymes and a modicum of rhythm and, except for an insistence on vowel patterns, which was due to a strong aural sense, he avoided technical elaboration in his own work, though it delighted him in the work of his contemporaries. Though the moods within them are many, there is no development in the ordinary sense of the word in his poems. We may note indeed a growing sparsity and clearness of outline, but there is no fundamental change. . . . Judged by the romantic canon of poetic surprise, a canon which has received many rude shocks in recent years, the religious procession of his poetry becomes self-same. But the quality which emanates from these poems seems at times a conquest of sheer spirit over matter. The compelling power of a multitudinous faith, terrible for all its tenderness and attendant calmness, is, to say the least of it, exhilarating. The visional and imaginative quality of this poetry affords us a unique experience. The sense of spiritual significance gives to it a religious power which seems beyond the analytical range of literary criticism. (pp. 765-66)

"Prose and Poetry of A.E.: 'The Candle of Vision'," in The Times Literary Supplement (© *Times Newspapers Ltd. (London) 1937; reproduced from* The Times Literary Supplement *by permission), No. 1864, October 23, 1937, pp. 765-66.*

MONK GIBBON   **(essay date 1937)**

I hesitate to dogmatise about [A. E.'s] verse. He wrote no poem in which there was not beauty of thought and sincerity of utterance but he wrote many poems in which the form seems inadequate and the imagery a little vague. Here . . . we need to beware that the fault is not sometimes our own. The mystical poets demand to be read almost a single poem at a time. Otherwise we cannot keep pace with the wheeling of systems in their metaphysical universe. The implications of his verse take us too far. Every poem really needs separate acceptance, a separate meditation; the crust of the ascetic rather than the rich and varied banquet before which appetite presently fails. As with his prose they should be read at a time when our mood is already in some measure attuned to them. Then a poem that seemed to mean little before will unlock its heart to us, speaking direct to that spiritual ear which, when it hears at all, seems to hear certainties. The journey which A.E. asks the mind to take is often a far one. It is not the surface meaning of his words which matters but their profound inner content and implication. We should be careful before we agree with the opinion of one critic that A.E. "will be remembered for his life and talk, for the personal manifestations of his gentle and radiant spirit, rather than for his poetry."

For that spirit reveals much of itself to us in the poems. His poetry is nearly always an attempt to plumb some mystery of the soul or to reveal some moment of illumination in consciousness. (pp. 53-4)

Monk Gibbon, "AE," in The Living Torch *by A.E., edited by Monk Gibbon (reprinted by permission of Macmillan, London and Basingstoke), Macmillan, 1937, pp. 3-84.*

SEAN O'FAOLAIN (essay date 1939)

There is really no progression in [Æ's] verse: it is the same note at the end and at the beginning; there is neither advance nor decline. (p. 47)

I loved him and we all loved him as a man. As for his poems, they are sweet and they are noble, but they are not Æ and they are not life. Yeats was right enough about Æ. He sought not himself but a way of life, and no man who does not find himself can find life. His best poems, like "We must pass like smoke or live within the spirit's fire," are the perfect expression of traditional wisdom as he adapts it, hardly altering it. In the volume before me, "The Living Torch," we have some of his best work, and it is almost exclusively day-by-day journalism, though journalism without peer. There he is himself as the sage who sees all things, even the most commonplace, as part of the eternal procession. But his conception of order to which all things are related is a traditional conception, not, need it be said, the less admirable and satisfying for that reason, though the less interesting for being "found" rather than "self-won."

When one places Æ and W. B. in opposition to each other it is this that finally emerges—that the poetry of Yeats is the poetry of a personality; unsure, unequal, adventurous, most satisfying when it is most personal, dismaying when it is least personal—even tiresome then, of an egregious folly; while the poetry of Æ, like the poetry of Crashaw, or Herbert, or Vaughn, is the poetry of character, satisfying when felicitous, its enemy triteness and mechanical sentiment. If I were to be wrecked with either on a desert island, or have the choice of either as a companion in death, I should not hesitate which to choose. For the desert island, I should choose Æ—and read Yeats. For the end—Yeats. Because we live as we can, but we die as we must. I should get no companionship from Yeats; he is wrapped up in his own world. . . . But, as against Æ's kindness, tolerence, journalism, sociability, and wisdom, he has what is more to the point of a crisis—pride, and passion. (pp. 56-7)

> *Sean O'Faolain, "Æ and W. B.," in* Virginia Quarterly Review *(copyright, 1939, by the* Virginia Quarterly Review, *The University of Virginia), Vol. 15, No. 1 (Winter, 1939), pp. 41-57.**

FRANK O'CONNOR (essay date 1939)

[A.E.'s] conversation, like his life, ran in patterns: well-formed phrases, ideas, quotations, and anecdotes, which he repeated over a lifetime without altering an inflection. (p. 64)

"A.E.," I once teased him, "Joyce makes you say, 'the only thing that matters about a work of art is out of how deep a life does it spring.'"

"Well, that's clever of him," A.E. exclaimed with genuine surprise, looking at me over his spectacles. "That's true, you know. I may quite well have said that." He said it at least once every day. It was one of the patterns of speech that had lasted him a lifetime. . . . (pp. 64-5)

Critics accused [A.E.] of vagueness and platitude—sometimes very bitterly—and it was hard to defend him. But for myself I feel certain that those vicious tricks of style which made him obscure a really individual perception in language where repetition killed all sense of wonder, were nothing more or less than habits of phrasing picked up heaven knows how or where in boyhood. At the first page of the first prose book of his I open, I find two clichés—"the genie in the innermost" and "an outcast from the light." The repetition of them over a hundred pages stuns the reader, yet this book, "Song and its Fountains," contains the finest criticism of Yeats ever written; it is just a few pages but full of delicate, individual perception, and it may give an idea of A.E.'s conversation when, as sometimes happened, the fog seemed to lift from his brain.

It is the same with his poems and pictures. Heaven knows from what early study of Nonconformist hymns a man so alive to the magic of poetry—and poetry simply bubbled from him—picked up those barbarous, jangling rhythms; the metrical equivalent of clichés—though there are clichés enough. (pp. 66-7)

He produced abundantly, effortlessly, and yet seemed to find no real delight in his work, because picture, essay, poem, created without the anguish of the artist, left an unsatisfied creative urge, and he can never have known the utter emptiness of the artist who exhausts himself in one supreme effort and feels there can nothing more to say. (p. 68)

[There] was too much daylight in A.E. to nourish poetry. I am reminded of that bright glare upon the crude colors of his canvases [in his home], and of the masses of shadow among the flickering candles in Yeats's [home]. These two things might almost be taken as symbolical of a contrasted objectivity and subjectivity in the two men, and when I read Synge or Lady Gregory I notice that mass of shadow which they, like Yeats, have in their work. Call it shadow, subjectivity, idealism , humbug, what you will—it is what one needs if one is to live in the garish daylight of a democracy dominated by parish priests. (p. 74)

That fable of light and shadow, of objectivity and subjectivity, is one way of expressing my idea of the old feud between Yeats and A.E., but it was a difference that expressed itself in almost every detail of their lives. (p. 75)

Why is there no development in his work? What was the "fog" in his brain? A life that was all externalization, an art that was all disguise, a philosophy that was but a prison for an abounding nature—what was the reality? Was there some sort of failure to shake off his boyhood and accept the dialectic of life? Under the platitude there was another Russell without any Nonconformist benevolence; sometimes he speaks in the poems with a harsh, clear, noble voice. . . . There should have been a Russell of middle life with a voice like that, but the dialectic breaks down, the antiself, as Yeats would say, is missing. (p. 80)

> *Frank O'Connor, "Two Friends: Yeats and A. E.," in* The Yale Review *(© 1939 by Yale University; reprinted by permission of the editors), Vol. XXIX, No. 1, September, 1939, pp. 60-88.**

HERBERT HOWARTH (essay date 1958)

In the last thirty years of his life AE was a great figure. He was not the most famous living Irishman, but he was the most famous Irishman who permanently lived in Ireland. Shaw and Joyce were abroad, Yeats was at home only for a period. It was clear that AE was not a poet of Yeats' order nor so idiosyncratic a personality, but he was better-loved as a man and perhaps better-respected as a thinker and humane arbiter. He was consulted on private and public problems, and wrote in the Press on all the issues of the day like a man who knew himself to be the national conscience. It is lucky for a nation if it has an AE to admonish it; but such work sometimes dies with the man, and the next generation cannot easily understand what made him so important to his contemporaries. By giving the greater part of his energy to arbitration and polemic he neglected his poetry and painting; he wrote poetry and painted for refreshment in scanty intervals from public life, whereas Yeats—or Eliot—made public pronouncements secondary to, and developed from, their work at their art. So his poems and paintings grew only a little; at the end of his life they still seemed much what they had been at the outset; and by the 'twenties they already had a faded air, and were loved for his sake rather than their own. Now they are largely ignored. . . . [His] mood is so different from the prevailing mood of our time that only three or four of his poems come to my mind as I go about life—and a test of a poem is whether it does this—and that if words of his come unsolicited to my help, they are more often from his polemical prose. (pp. 165-66)

AE's poems lie within a very restricted range. A limitation can also be a definition, if it is notably personal, and AE's best poems are perhaps recognisable as his own by the circumscription and the one or two personal touches within it. His vocabulary mainly depends on the romantic postulation of the vision of the heavenly courts. His imagery is of the same order, deriving partly from nineteenth-century English poetry, partly from English translations of oriental literature; it is only occasionally sharpened by the sights and sounds of the everyday world. AE once spoke of his highest delight as the "intoxication" of the Sufi, and some of his poems evidently hope to catch that divine intoxication; but only one or two kindle with it. There is nothing in the tradition of English literature to help a poet to write with the Sufi note, for the English imagination has found other routes into ecstasy; and AE was not the great technical innovator who opens a new route for future poets. He had three or four forms at his disposal: compact quatrains, such as Blake sometimes used so magnificently; compact six-line stanzas; a five-line stanza, occasionally and experimentally; couplets. Now and then he writes couplets eight trochaic feet to the line, the lines long and raking enough to dazzle, the poems short enough for the dazzle to enchant, not to overpower.

At their best the poems have a double effect: they are contained by their compact patterns, and yet we see their vision as if the compact cage were momentarily broken. When that happens AE gives the feeling that the mystical poets traditionally give, that they have riven a cleft into the frame of the universe and we look into celestial spaces. . . . But these moments, in which the poems transcend the conventions of their period and kind, and catch the timelessness which they invoke as a solvent for the wrongs of time, are few. (pp. 180-81)

Perhaps his problem as a poet was that, right to the end, he only valued the esoteric in poetry. Though as a man he had wrestled with reality effectively, he did not entirely approve of what he had done, and had a nostalgic preference for the theosophist-poet of 1894. The best of his late published poems are the natural partners of the best of his early poems, as if his life had undergone no change. Possibly his most superb verses are those on the last page of *The Candle of Vision*:

No sign is made while empires pass.
The flowers and stars are still His care,
The constellations hid in grass,
The golden miracles in air.

Life in an instant will be rent
When death is glittering, blind and wild,
The Heavenly Brooding is intent
To that last instant on Its child.

The verses have a hammered quality, which expresses the workmanship of God which they celebrate. They are written towards the end of the Great War, and the prose that precedes them shows that AE has been reflecting on the significance of that Armageddon and the terrorism and sacrifices in Ireland. "Powers that seem dreadful", he says, "things that seemed abhorrent . . . will reveal themselves as brothers and allies." But for all their excellence the stanzas do not show that AE has lived and developed for twenty-five years since he wrote the poems in *Homeward*. If they had appeared in *Homeward*, they would have seemed the best of the book, just as they seem the best of all AE, but they would not have been conspicuously maturer than the work around them nor out of place, whereas the poetic prose-sketches of early AE look almost a century apart from his mature prose. . . . Just a poem here and there assimilates the new understanding and energy that turn his prose from feminine to masculine. (pp. 182-83)

Herbert Howarth, "AE—George William Russell," in his The Irish Writers 1880-1940: Literature under Parnell's Star *(© 1958 by Herbert Howarth), Rockliff, 1958, pp. 165-211.*

RICHARD J. LOFTUS   (essay date 1964)

A.E.'s attitude toward the national political movement in Ireland, like that of Yeats, passed through various phases. (p. 99)

Occasionally A.E.'s public attitudes find expression in his verse. "On Behalf of Some Irishmen Not Followers of Tradition," for example, like Yeats' "To Ireland in the Coming Time," is a defense of an aesthetic grounded in the unorthodoxy of theosophy. In his poem A.E. exhorts the youthful poets of Ireland to reject "the sceptyred myth" of conventional belief and to dedicate themselves to "The golden heresy of truth." The Easter Rising of 1916 inspired A.E. to compose a most moving poem, "Salutation," addressed to Padraic Pearse, James Connolly, Thomas MacDonagh, Countess Markievicz, and those other rebels whom he did not know personally. . . . A.E. composed "Salutation" shortly after the abortive rebellion and had it privately printed and distributed. The poem has often been anthologized, yet A.E. omitted it from the final selection for the collected edition. Deeper and more lasting, perhaps, was his response to the death of Terence MacSwiney, the mayor of Cork, after a sixty-nine-day hunger strike in Brixton Gaol during the Black and Tan War. In a sonnet, "A Prisoner," A.E. compares MacSwiney to the "fabled Titan chained upon the hill." . . . MacSwiney's act of passive heroism demanded and won the poet's admiration; whereas his response to deeds of violence was ordinarily characterized by indignation and regret. So, in "Waste," A.E. decries the slaughter of the Irish Civil War as a "sacrifice / For words hollow as wind," . . . an allusion in general to the emptiness of political oratory and, perhaps, in particular to the fact that Eamon De Valera rejected the

Free State Treaty and thereby precipitated the year-long fratricidal struggle because he objected to the *phrasing* of the oath of allegiance to the English king.

A.E.'s attempts at public rhyming are remarkably few. He was moved by the events of World War I to compose a series of poems which have frequently been praised for their humanity but which in fact are characterized by a kind of smug exultation—unusual in A.E.—that the poet's prophecies have been borne out. Except for the war poems and the handful of Irish poems mentioned above, one will find very little in the canon of A.E.'s verse that is directly relevant to the chronicle of public affairs in Ireland. The reason for this poetic aloofness is a matter for speculation. Perhaps, for one thing, he was lacking in suitable technique; for A.E. never mastered the ballad form which Yeats employed so effectively in writing of the Parnell debacle, the Easter Rising, and the controversy surrounding Roger Casement. Again, A.E. had available for his public comments a prose outlet in the columns of *The Irish Homestead* and *The Irish Statesman,* so perhaps he felt no need to assume the role of bard. In his prose A.E. expounds endlessly on the day-to-day affairs of Ireland, but in his verse his attitudes and opinions remain fragmentary and ill-defined.

The nationalism expressed in A.E.'s verse, more so even than that of Yeats', is subjective rather than objective, romantic rather than realistic, ethereal rather than material. It proclaims an inner state of being rather than an outer actuality. . . . A.E. believed, as did Yeats, Douglas Hyde, and most of the writers of the eighteen-nineties, that the people of modern Ireland possessed the same racial and spiritual characteristics as the ancient Celts. . . . In the spirit of the times, A.E. found it a simple matter to ignore the fact that wave after wave of invaders and conquerors had made the Irish anything but a "pure race." As far as he was concerned, the spark of greatness remained. All that was needed was spiritual regeneration, and that, surely, the poet could bring about. Like Yeats, A.E. attempted to express in his verse a vision of the ideal Irish nation, a Utopian dream which he conceived in his own imagination and which he hoped would inspire his countrymen to put on once again the mantle of grandeur that belonged to the ancient Gaels. (pp. 100-02)

As a poet Yeats succeeds as very few others have done; but A.E. fails—and, considering his pretensions, fails rather badly. Except for a handful of poems scattered here and there through his canon, his work lacks vitality and, what is worse, lacks significance for modern man. Having examined his collected poems, one finds it difficult not to conclude that A.E.'s development as an artist was stunted, that in the end his aesthetic, in Yeats' words, "surrenders itself to moral and poetical commonplace," and that his verse remains soft and fleshless, a survival of nineteenth-century romanticism.

His failure may be blamed in part upon the dissipation of his talents in the practical work of agricultural reorganization and journalism. (p. 103)

Yet difference in circumstance does not begin to explain the disparity between the quality of Yeats' mature art and that of A.E.. . . . The fact of the matter would appear to be that A.E.'s genius was of a lesser sort and that he was from beginning to end Yeats' inferior creatively, if not intellectually. (p. 104)

A.E. was surely influenced by the two romantic poets from America. In Emerson the young Russell discovered a faith in the individual, in Whitman a faith in democracy; from the two together he acquired an attitude of confidence with regard to mankind. A.E., says Yeats [see excerpt above], like Emerson and Whitman (and like a great many writers of the nineteenth century), lacked "the Vision of Evil." (pp. 106-07)

What is awkward about these predispositions—for the individual, for democracy, and for moral and spiritual good—is that they are alien to the eastern religious philosophy which A.E. expounds. (p. 107)

Yeats struck closer to the essence of Hindu thought in that he recognized the conflict between Good and Evil as part of the nature of being and sought reconciliation in the intense passion generated by that conflict. For A.E., on the other hand, the struggle between Good and Evil was confined to this world; strife and evil together would be "Overthrown . . . in the unconflicting spheres" of the world to come. . . . Yeats' myth-god is an organic synthesis of the twofold nature of man; A.E.'s, like the conventional Christian conception of God, is a thing undefiled. Both Russell and Yeats attempted to create in their verse a mythology that would propagate religious "truth" among their countrymen. That neither succeeded as an apostle of theosophy among the Irish people is perfectly obvious. As a poet, however, Yeats succeeded in blending together Irish tradition and eastern occultism into a unified artistic creation of major proportions. A.E., despite his psychic disposition and power of vision (or perhaps because of them), failed to achieve the permanence of art and, considering the claims he sometimes made for his poetry, failed rather badly. More than any other Irish writer, A.E. is the poet of the Celtic Twilight. He believed—quite literally—that "Earth's faery children . . . roam the primrose-hearted eve." . . .Twilight was the magic hour, the time of day when the spiritual world was most likely to reveal itself and therefore a time especially suitable for visionary experience. (pp. 108-09)

A.E.'s obsession with the remote, the obscure, the unknown, is evident in his earliest poetry, the esoteric verse of *Homeward.* That he should have turned for the inspiration and subject matter of his art to the oldest and most obscure of the national traditions, the mythological lore of prehistoric, pagan Ireland, is not surprising. When he addressed himself to his countrymen, it was to urge them to return with him to the mysterious twilight era of Ireland's remote past. . . . (pp. 109-10)

One cannot say that A.E.'s approach to Irish legend was scholarly; he played freely with the ancient myths, turning and twisting them to his own purposes. Nevertheless, now and then his rendering of one or another old story is strangely convincing. In "The Children of Lir," for example, one of his most beautiful poems, A.E. tries to define the religious meaning hidden in what he believed to be a myth from pagan Ireland. . . . (p. 110)

In "The Children of Lir" and a few other poems A.E. treats of old Irish legends and myths with remarkable sensitivity. In much of his verse, though, he is less successful. Frequently his readings of the old saga materials lack sophistication and suffer distortion as a result of his predisposition for good and against evil, for love and against hate, for joy and against terror and fear. At times he misses the point entirely. In "Dana," for example, his speaker is the mother-goddess of pre-Christian Ireland.... Plainly A.E. has softened and sentimentalized the old goddess. True enough, Danu in Irish legend is the beneficent earth goddess, the giver of life and sustenance; but she is also the maleficent goddess of the grave and death. (pp. 111-12)

Only when as an old man he undertook to write an epic poem, *The House of Titans,* did A.E. manage to define his religious creed with much success. "AEism," as it turned out, was not particularly complex or difficult; nor, unfortunately, did it seem to justify the grandiloquence with which the poet had espoused it for some forty years.

The House of Titans is not really a poem of epic proportions; yet it represents A.E.'s only sustained effort in verse to impose an order upon the mythic vision which had obsessed him through his entire creative life. It is a national poem in that it represents a final attempt by A.E. to teach his countrymen what they must believe in and to what course of action they must devote themselves if they would maintain faith with their ancient heritage and achieve spiritual nobility in the future. *The House of Titans* is not a good poem. It has all the characteristic weaknesses of A.E.'s verse—pomposity of tone, exaggerated imagery, vagueness of language and phrasing. But it has a story, too; and in the unraveling of that story A.E.'s idea of man—his origin, his condition, his destiny—gradually emerges and becomes intelligible.

In his poem A.E. fills out the vague pattern of Celtic mythology with substantive details from Greco-Roman tradition and philosophic concepts from the East. The story begins with a reconstruction of the legendary Battle of Mag Tuired between the Tuatha Dé Danann and the race of giants, the Fomorians. In A.E.'s account the Tuatha Dé Danann are represented as spiritual beings, the overlords of the universe; the Fomorians, renamed "Titans," are children of the earth and, hence, creatures of flesh and passion.... [King] Nuada and the gods of spiritual light are victorious and become lords over the Titans. But in the ages following the conquest "evil sorcery worked on the gods" so that they forgot their divine origin and at last came to believe "the bodily form to be / Themselves. And earth had lost its first / Impenetrable strangeness and grew dear / As hearth and home." Their divine knowledge forgotten, the gods took wives from among the children of earth and at last "the being of the gods was changed / To be but lordlier titan." Only Nuada, the king, retains a vague half-memory of ancient glory and only he struggles to regain the lost knowledge of things divine; to the others he seems "a madman dreaming of lost worlds." (pp. 113-15)

In the context of the poem it becomes clear that Nuada and the corrupted gods are meant to represent the race of men who had once known the heavenly regions of immortal light but who now must endure the "dark house" of mortal existence on earth. A.E. maintained as one of his fundamental doctrines a kind of inverted theory of evolution; men were not, as Darwin would have it, improved apes, but rather degenerate gods.... [In short], the first half of *The House of Titans* is devoted to the study of man's decline from the divine to the human state.

In the second half of his poem A.E. provides a rationale for man's fall and attempts to define the means by which he may again attain to the divine state.... [A succession of unsullied gods reveal portions of divine truth to Nuada.] The "poet of heaven," for example, states that to achieve spiritual perfection man must practice "selfless" love, a love founded upon sacrifice.... True gods must suffer first, must earn their divinity. (pp. 116-17)

This, then, is the theme of *The House of Titans:* that the spirit of man must be swallowed up by the "titan" of flesh and passion; that the spirit must suffer the Titan's "brute despair and the descent to hells / Earth had not known before the spirit came"; and that somehow in the depths of the Titan's heart the spirit must discover the truth of selfless love and the "magian mind" that can transform sorrows into blessings and agonies into joys. When these things have transpired, man will progress toward union with the All-Father in the Feast of Age (i.e., eternity).... The task, then, for such enlightened ones as Nuada and A.E. is to awaken the Titans, that is, men in general and Irishmen in particular, to their noble spiritual destiny.

That *The House of Titans* is an Irish poem and that its message was intended for the edification of Irishmen is evident from the use of Celtic myth-figures as dramatis personae. For A.E., even more than for Yeats, mysticism and nationalism were joined inseparably.... Apparently he felt that the Easter Rising of 1916 was the handiwork of the ancient gods.... (pp. 117-18)

In a second long poem, "Michael," the concepts of vision and selfless sacrifice, both of which are defined in *The House of Titans,* are specifically related to the Easter rebellion.... The hero of the poem, Michael, is a boy from the rugged coast of County Donegal (where A.E. spent his summers) in the West of Ireland, an area where "fisher folk" sat and listened to old tales / Or legends of gigantic gales." Michael, a sensitive, imaginative youth, experiences a vision of "palaces of light" and "towers that faded up in the air." ...

Soon afterwards the young man leaves Donegal to find work in Dublin; and oppressed by "the city's dingy air," "the black reek of chimneys," and "the dark warehouse where he drudged," he begins to forget the wonder of his vision.

Happily, however, the youth encounters in Dublin another native of Donegal, one who still holds fast to the "spiritual heritage" of the ancient Gaels and who introduces Michael to the traditions and legendary heroes of Ireland's past.... The legends of Ireland seem to Michael "the story of the soul" and those who made those legends seem "warriors of Eternal Mind." Then on Easter Monday ... Michael goes to the barricades to give himself to Ireland's holy cause. An enemy bullet wounds him mortally; but even as death takes hold of his body, he feels "The rapture that is sacrifice" and the vision he had experienced in the mountains of Donegal returns to him—in A.E.'s words: "lofty forms of burnished air / Stood on the deck with Michael there." Michael's visionary experience and his sacrifice in the cause of nationalism both find their meaning in the sacred truth which the Druid gods brought with them when they descended to struggle against the Titans. (pp. 118-19)

Michael's curious mixture of occultism and patriotism is what A.E. desired for the Irish people. A national vision based on the idea that men can and should become gods is noble enough, certainly; but it is also a romantic vision, perhaps much too romantic for a modern world in which men seem intent on being anything but godlike. More than that, however, it is the pomposity of A.E.'s vision—the hyperbolic abstractions, the unrestrained diction—that renders it unconvincing. It seems almost incredible that he should have expected the average Irishman—a prosaic, middle-class creature at best—to comprehend and to accept his creed of nationalism; yet that is precisely what he did expect; and he was bitterly disappointed and disillusioned when his countrymen ignored his wisdom. (pp. 119-20)

One is most reluctant to term A.E. a failure. Yet, although he wrote a number of poems that have charm and grace and that no doubt will survive as anthology pieces, his total achievement as a poet is of a minor sort. More than anything else, he was lacking in art. . . . A.E.'s importance in the cultural movement was, perhaps, more as a personality than as an artist; for he served as a kind of All-Father for three generations of young Irish writers, encouraging them, helping them, printing their formative efforts. (p. 122)

Richard J. Loftus, "A.E.: The Land of Promise," in his Nationalism in Modern Anglo-Irish Poetry *(copyright © 1964 by the Regents of the University of Wisconsin), The University of Wisconsin Press, 1964, pp. 97-122.*

WILLIAM IRWIN THOMPSON   (essay date 1967)

As the protagonists of *The Interpreters* relate their life stories, one cannot help remembering Yeats's theory of the dream. The revolution takes on the quality of Yeats's dream of the centaur; the total myth is too large for a single imagination, but pieces of it, the pieces of it that are in sympathy with an individual's particular temperament, can animate an individual's imagination. And as these individuals gather, each driven by a different dream, the pieces fit together, and the total dream of the nation or culture emerges. The dream is pieced together in the gathering of the many, and the gathering of the many in Sackville Street is the beginning of the revolution. . . . Naturally, the piece of the total idea of Revolution that comes most easily to A.E.'s imagination is the mystical. A.E. can understand and keenly perceive the romanticism of [Standish James] O'Grady or the messianic nationalism of [Padraic] Pearse, but he distorts William Martin Murphy into his personal focus, and he scarcely sees Michael Collins at all. As a religious thinker there were always two subjects that A.E. never pursued intellectually: sex and evil. As a student of Eastern thought, he knew that excited violence was a sexual passion, for that is what he means when he refers to the poisoned "deeps of life" and the "sinister ecstasy," but he preferred to blot out these subjects by a meditation upon their opposites of love and goodness. Perhaps he was right; this may have been the only possible personal solution for him, but for us, who come upon history after Buchenwald and Hiroshima, it is not enough. Terror has become so much a part of our reality that we cannot accept a view of history that lacks the vision of terror. Perhaps this is why A.E. ultimately fails to hold us, fascinating though he is, and why we turn away to the tougher perceptions of other writers. There are, of course, simpler reasons, for A.E. never mastered English prose; there is always a sense of strain and stiffness, as if he were trying to round off a neat period in the manner of Dr. Johnson. A.E. could rise to a few eloquent moments, but his writing is nowhere as graceful as Yeats's *A Vision*. The speeches, though

weighted against one another with a sense of drama, do not reach the level of the drama of ideas in Shaw's *Don Juan in Hell,* and as a work of political fiction, *The Interpreters* cannot be compared in quality to either *1984* or *The Magic Mountain*. And yet, for all the work's limitations, A.E. succeeds admirable in showing how five men of conflicting philosophies can all be simultaniously right, and that is the work's singular merit. (pp. 193-95)

William Irwin Thompson, "The Mystic Image: A.E.," in his The Imagination of an Insurrection, Dublin, Easter, 1916: A Study of an Ideological Movement *(copyright © 1967 by William Irwin Thompson; reprinted by permission of Oxford University Press, Inc.), Oxford University Press, New York, 1967, pp. 167-201.*

HERBERT V. FACKLER   (essay date 1970)

[*Deirdre* is] a rather naive production. A.E. was, to begin with, no professional dramatist, and *Deirdre* was his sole dramatic creation. Criticism of the play's technical presentation and of its performance found him defenseless. (p. 2)

In its general tone, *Deirdre* is a curious blend of A.E.'s own mysticism and impressionism and the Nineteenth Century Deirdre materials of [Samuel Ferguson, Aubrey de Vere, and R. D. Joyce], . . . to name three typical examples. In various degrees the versions of the legend produced by these and other writers stress the romantic and tragic aspects of Deirdre's plight at the expense of the development of individual characters and psychological motivation. A.E.'s sentimental, romantic leanings clearly encouraged him to follow in this tradition rather than to turn to the starkness of the *Longes Mac nUsnig* or the barbarism and incidental crudeness of the *Book of Leinster*.

Of A.E.'s impressionistic mysticism more must be said. The imagery of the play is heavily freighted with "dream," "vision," and "sleep" images. In her first two speeches Deirdre refers to spring as the end of "winter's sleep" and recounts a dream vision of the Sidhe, and Naisi perishes under the delusion of the druid Cathvah's spell, only realizing at the instant of death that it has been a delusion. With the end of this delusion comes Deirdre's sudden transition to tragic self-knowledge, which more than anything else makes her a tragic figure; with her we have understood Naisi's delusion, and with her we see the unreal vision result in his death. . . . It is, I think, this tragic ending which provides us with a key to the play's central matter—the conflict between appearance and reality. In the development of this theme Lavarcam plays super-realist, seeing always the truth through her keen insight into spiritual and visionary mysteries. . . . Her function as choral figure is important to the play's development, for the other major characters choose consistently to follow their visions and suppress reality; thus she becomes a Cassandra figure, unheeded prophetess of the reality which breaks illusions. Even Lavarcam's attempt to deceive Concobar into believing that Deirdre's beauty has been lost is not a break with her character, for the high king has shown himself to be willing to suspend reality; her action, then, seems to be an attempt to take advantage of a seeming weakness in his character. That it should fail is inevitable, yet her very surrender to the power of Deirdre's attraction in the face of her role as prophetess points up dramatically the intensity of that attraction. The rejection of her utterances by Deirdre, Concobar, and Naisi transfers the play's action from contrived plot sequence controlled by Deirdre's birth prophecy to a more material sphere. Their refusal to heed Lavarcam takes on the aspect of choice, an expression of the will, and carries with it the responsibility for consequences. (pp. 2-4)

The characters themselves are the familiar figures of the Nineteenth Century treatments of the legend. Deirdre herself is an ingenue type who has marvelous beauty but little knowledge except for that which is intuitional and emotional. It is easy for her to interpret dreams as reality, for her circumscribed existence has limited her knowledge of the world. Hence she interprets the appearance of bright birds as a sign of joy for her and Naisi.... And to Lavarcam's answer that these are the Birds of Angus, bringing both love and death, she explains that the girl Deirdre has indeed died, and been replaced by a woman, and that the child-death woman-birth initiation has been administered by the force of love. At the next appearance of the Birds of Angus, however, Deirdre understands their significance and attempts to dissuade Naisi from returning to Ireland, to no avail. In the interval she has achieved some degree of mature understanding, which reinforces the pathos of her farewell to Alba.

Naisi too is a conventional figure. Afraid of nothing, loyal to his comrades of the Red Branch, able in battle, and patriotic, he is an ideal prince for Deirdre.... [He] insists upon following his vision—a vision dictated by the chivalrous notion of the veracity and goodness of kings—in insisting upon a return to Ulla. His vision, like Deirdre's, is shattered by the truth.

Nor is Concobar without illusion. In his early talk with Lavarcam he reveals his own chivalric nature through his comments on his kingdom and on his refusal to let the infant be slain.... His is a dream like that of England's Arthur, a dream of construction, of movement toward an ideal kingdom.... However, the effect of Deirdre's beauty upon him is an intrusion of reality into his dream-world which shatters his justice and ultimately makes him traitor to and destroyer of his own ideality; his justification of his acts rings false: "The death of Naisi was only the fulfiling of the law." We see the reality of both his desire and his kingship in his final, honest appraisal of his condition: "I have two divided kingdoms, and one is in my own heart." Concobar too has been defeated by reality. Ironically, however, his ideal is achieved at least partially as the death-rebirth cycle becomes again operative, for Lavarcam prophesies of the gods that "of pity for her [Deirdre] they will build up an eternal kingdom in the spirit of man." Thus A.E. includes in his drama the rationale for the play itself and for the continuing impact of Deirdre's story on the Irish imagination. (pp. 4-5)

In his use of Celtic mythology A.E. produces a symbolic parallelism to the plot of his play. We have seen how the birds function, and even a casual reading of the text impresses us with the extent to which Celtic deities and symbols appear. The "Father" of Deirdre's first speech is undoubtedly Mananaun, "the most spiritual divinity known to the Gael ... the divine imagination ... the unuttered word." Dana, the Celtic Demeter, is invoked at the beginning of Act II and entreated again at the end of the act, and it is Mananaun who is invoked by Cathvah in his spell over the mind of Naisi so that the superior deity comes to represent the illusionary power. The persistent paradox of death

as an escape into immortality is present here also, in that Mananaun's power leads directly to the deaths of the lovers and to their spiritual mythification.

Perhaps Ernest Boyd is correct in assuming that A.E.'s *Deirdre* "is a work of poetic rather than dramatic merit" [see excerpt above] but in its thematic emphasis upon the appearance-reality disparity, its impressionistic assertion that what is acted upon as real is real by virtue of that action, and its presentation of complex and often noble motives resulting in a tragic climax it is a very important version of the Deirdre myth. (pp. 5-6)

> *Herbert V. Fackler, in his introduction to* Deirdre: A Legend in Three Acts *by George W. Russell (copyright 1970 DePaul University), DePaul University, 1970, pp. 1-7.*

BIBLIOGRAPHY

Bose, Abinash Chandra. "A.E. (George William Russell)." In his *Three Mystic Poets: A Study of W. B. Yeats, A.E. and Rabindranath Tagore*, pp. 47-102. Darby, PA: Folcroft Press, 1970.*
    Examination of the mystical aspects of A.E. and his poetry.

British Broadcasting Corporation. "AE (George Russell)." In *Irish Literary Portraits: W. B. Yeats, James Joyce, George Moore, George Bernard Shaw, Oliver St. John Gogarty, F. R. Higgins, AE: W. R. Rodgers's Broadcast Conversations with Those Who Knew Them*, pp. 185-203. London: BBC, 1972.
    A collection of intimate biographical vignettes, related by Monk Gibbon, Padraic Colum, Frank O'Connor, and others.

Byrne, J. Patrick. "AE, Poet and Man." *Poet Lore* XLVII, No. 3 (Autumn 1941): 240-49.
    Essay on A.E.'s beliefs and his development as a writer.

Colum, Padraic. Foreword to *Printed Writings of George W. Russell (AE): A Bibliography with Some Notes on His Pictures and Portraits*, edited by Alan Denson, pp. 11-13. Evanston, IL: Northwestern University Press, 1961.
    An account of the preparation for and initial performance of *Deirdre*.

Eglinton, John. *A Memoir of AE: George William Russell*. London: Macmillan & Co., 1937, 290 p.
    A detailed biography of A.E.

McFate, Patricia Ann. "AE's Portraits of the Artists: A Study of *The Avatars*." *Eire-Ireland* VI, No. 4 (Winter 1971): 38-48.
    An interpretation of *The Avatars*.

Moore, George. "Ave." In *Hail and Farewell: Ave, Salve, Vale*, first annotated ed., edited by Richard Cave, pp. 128-44. Toronto: Macmillan of Canada, 1976.*
    Moore's impressions of A.E., and of other writers of the Irish Literary Revival. Incidents and thoughts of the author's daily life are also retold.

"New Books Reviewed: *The Interpreters*." *The North American Review* CCXVII, No. 810 (May 1923): 714-16.
    A review of *The Interpreters*.

O'Casey, Sean. "Dublin's Glittering Guy." In his *Inishfallen Fare Thee Well*, pp. 268-98. New York: Macmillan, 1949.
    An amusing vignette, in which three Dubliners discuss A.E.—"the old humbug."

O'Connor, Frank. "The Scholar." *The Kenyon Review* XXVII, No. 2 (Spring 1965): 336-43.*
    A series of anecdotes about A.E. and Osborn Bergin.

Russell, Diarmuid. "'Æ' (George William Russell)." *The Atlantic*

Monthly 171, No. 2 (February 1943): 51-7.
    A biographical sketch, related by A.E.'s son.

Skelton, Robin. "Division and Unity: AE and W. B. Yeats." In
The World of W. B. Yeats, rev. ed., edited by Robin Skelton and
Ann Saddlemyer, pp. 189-98. Seattle: University of Washington
Press, 1965.*
    A comparison of the attitudes and works of A.E. and Yeats.

Thornton, Weldon. "A.E.'s 'Ideal Poems: J[ame]s St[ephen]s'."
Eire-Ireland VIII, No. 3 (Autumn 1973): 26-8.
    An examination of a little-known poem that A.E. dedicated to
    James Stephens.

Leonid (Nikolaevich) Andreyev

1871-1919

(Also transliterated as Andreev, Andre'ev, or Andreyeff; also wrote under pseudonym of James Lynch) Russian novelist, short story writer, and dramatist.

Andreyev's work captures the state of mind of the Russian intellectual at the turn of the century. His writing is characterized by extreme nihilism and a preoccupation with metaphysical questions.

Like Dostoevsky, his primary influence, Andreyev often deals with pathological characters. His morbid fascination with horror, gloom, chaos, and internal conflict has led many critics to compare him to Poe, especially when discussing such works as *The Black Masks*, in which the principal character is a schizophrenic at war with himself. In addition to his examination of isolated individuals, Andreyev also displayed a concern with public issues in his powerful and influential indictments of war in *The Red Laugh* and of capital punishment in *The Seven Who Were Hanged*.

Andreyev is credited with introducing Symbolism to the Russian stage and his *He Who Gets Slapped* is considered a significant work of Russian drama. Unfortunately, many critics have concluded that he was primarily a realist who strained for symbolic effect.

Enormously popular during the first decade of this century, Andreyev's work was officially banned after the Russian Revolution, and has only recently been reinstated as a subject fit for Soviet critical interest.

PRINCIPAL WORKS

Novye razakzay (short stories) 1902
Krasnyi smelch (novella) 1904
  [*The Red Laugh: Fragments of a Discovered Manuscript*, 1905]
K zvezdam (drama) 1905
  [*To the Stars: A Drama in Four Acts* published in journal *Poet Lore*, 1907]
Gubernator (novella) 1906
Savva. Ignis sanat (drama) 1906
  [*Savva* published in *Savva. The Life of Man: Two Plays by Leonid Andreyev*, 1914]
Zhizń chelovieka (drama) 1906
  [*The Life of Man* published in *Savva. The Life of Man: Two Plays by Leonid Andreyev*, 1914]
Iuda Iskariot i drugie (novella) 1907

T'ma (novella) 1907
Chernyia maski (drama) 1908
  [*The Black Maskers* published in *Plays by Leonid Andreyeff: The Black Maskers. The Life of Man. The Sabine Women*, 1915]
Lyubov k blizhnemu (drama) 1908
  [*Love of One's Neighbor*, 1914]
Moi zapiski (novella) 1908
Razskaz o semi povieshennykh (novella) 1908
  [*The Seven Who Were Hanged*, 1909]
Tsař Golod (drama) 1908
Anatéma (drama) 1909
  [*Anathema: A Tragedy in Seven Scenes*, 1910]
Silence and Other Stories (short stories) 1910
Sobraniye sochineny (drama, novels, short stories, and essays) 1910-1916
Okean (drama) 1911
Prekrasayia sabinianki (drama) 1912
  [*The Sabine Women* published in *Plays by Leonid Andreyeff: The Black Maskers. The Life of Man. The Sabine Women*, 1915]
The Crushed Flower, and Other Stories (short stories) 1916
Ironicheskie razskazy (drama and short stories) 1916
The Little Angel, and Other Stories (short stories) 1916
Polet (short stories) 1916
Tot, kto poluchaet poshchechiny (drama) 1919
  [*He, the One Who Gets Slapped: A Play in Four Acts*, 1921]
When the King Loses His Head, and Other Stories (short stories) 1920
Abyss (novella) 1924
V tumane (short stories) 1928
Seven that Were Hanged, and Other Stories (short stories) 1958

(essay date 1908)

Andreyev has been called "the Edgar Allan Poe of Russian literature," and the characterization is suggestive. There is, indeed, in his work something weird, gruesome, haunting and vaguely reminiscent of Poe. But the comparison should not be carried too far. Poe, unhealthy as he was in certain

15

aspects of his genius, is not to be compared, in point of morbidity, with Andreyev, whose imagination at times is positively diseased; and the problems of sex, which obsess the Russian author, were not so much as touched upon by the American. Moreover, Poe was dominantly the *artist*, detached from every worldly and human interest; a dreamer weaving dreams that enchant by reason of their sheer imaginative quality. Andreyev, on the other hand, is *humanist* as well as artist; a child of the Revolution, reflecting the thwarted hopes, the confusion, and the agonies of his people. He is a grim portent, betokening disease, not health; preoccupied with the nether side of life; recalling the old saying that genius is akin to insanity. (p. 282)

[Andreyev] is incapable of treating innocence simply as innocence, and for its own sake. A darker purpose perpetually lurks in the background. . . . [In] Andreyev's stories the aspect of nature is always symbolical of an inner and spiritual event. (p. 283)

Andreyev has shown that his genius is many sided. The morbid still engages his pen. Nothing fascinates him so much as the analysis of failure and decay. But he has taken new flights, has plumbed new depths of human psychology.

At the time of the Russo-Japanese war he wrote a story called "The Red Laugh." It is a masterpiece, and depicts the gradual disintegration of a sensitive man's mind brought into intimate contact with the seamy side of militarism. No anti-militarist tract has done so much to reveal to the Russian people, and to humanity at large, the meaning of war. No reader who has scanned its pages could ever forget the impression of *horror* it conveys. (p. 284)

Andreyev is a dramatist, as well as a novelist, and has written nothing more impressive than his morality play, "The Life of Man." This deals with the five (not seven) ages of the ordinary mortal, and is regarded by Russian critics as an indictment of life and death without parallel in the world's literature. (p. 285)

It will be noted that even "The Life of Man," which seems to indicate Andreyev's philosophy more clearly than it is indicated in any other of his works, ends in crushing pessimism. Yet Andreyev himself, at least in his more hopeful moods, disclaims the title of pessimist. "His pessimism," says B. F. Botzianovsky, a Russian critic, "if pessimism it be, is of a peculiar nature." . . .

Andreyev's own words on this subject are highly significant as an aid to the interpretation of his works. "By denying everything," he says in an essay, "you arrive at a belief in the symbol. By refuting the whole of life you involuntarily become its apologist. I never believe in life so much as when I read Schopenhauer, the father of pessimism. Here is a man, I say to myself, who thought as he thought and yet lived. Hence I conclude: life is mighty, life is invincible." (p. 286)

> *"Andreyev—A New Portent in Russian Literature," in* Current Literature, *Vol. XLV, No. 3, September, 1908, pp. 282-86.*

LEO TOLSTOY (essay date 1908)

I think modern writers today are often guilty of (it's the basis of the whole Decadent movement) . . . the wish to be unusual and original, to surprise and astonish the reader. . . . [This desire] excludes simplicity. And simplicity is the necessary condition of the beautiful. What is simple and free of artificiality might be bad, but what is not simple and is artificial cannot be good. . . .

You write that the merit of your works is sincerity. I not only recognise this, but also that their purpose is a good one: the wish to contribute to the good of other people. I think you are sincere also in your modest opinion about your works. This is all the better for your part, in that the success they enjoy might have made you, on the contrary, exaggerate their importance. I have read too little by you, and that inattentively, as I generally read little fiction and take little interest in it, but from what I know and remember of your writings I would advise you to do more work on them and bring your thoughts to the last degree of clarity and precision. (p. 681)

> *Leo Tolstoy, in his letter to L. N. Andreyev in 1908, in* Tolstoy's Letters: 1880-1910, *Vol. II, edited and translated by R. F. Christian (abridged by permission of Charles Scribner's Sons; copyright © 1978 R. F. Christian), Scribner's, 1978, pp. 680-81.*

WILLIAM LYON PHELPS (essay date 1911)

[Andreev's] style, while marked by the typical yet always startling Russian simplicity, is nevertheless entirely his own, and all his tales and plays are stamped by powerful individuality. (p. 263)

Andreev's *Red Laugh* ought to be read in America as a contrast to our numerous war stories, where war is pictured as a delightful and exciting tournament. This book has not a single touch of patriotic sentiment, not a suggestion of "Hurrah for our side!" The soldiers are on the field because they were sent there, and the uninjured are too utterly tired, too tormented with lack of sleep, too hungry and thirsty to let out a single whoop. (p. 266)

In this gruesome tale of the realities of war, Andreev has given shocking physical details of torn and bleeding bodies, but true to the theme that animates all his books, he has concentrated the main interest on the Mind. Soldiers suffer in the flesh, but infinitely more in the mind. War points chiefly not to the grave, nor to the hospital, but to the madhouse. . . . Andreev is the first to show that the most common and awful form of disease among Russian soldiers is the disease of the brain. The camp becomes a vast madhouse, with the peculiar feature that the madmen are at large. (pp. 267-68)

No more terrible protest against war has ever been written than Andreev's *Red Laugh*. It shows not merely the inexpressible horror of the battlefield and the dull, weary wretchedness of the men on the march, but it follows out the farthest ramifications flowing from the central cause: the constant tragedies in the families, . . . the whole accumulation of woe.

The first two words of the book are *Madness and Horror!* and they might serve as a text for Andreev's complete works. There seems to be some taint in his mind which forces him to dwell forever on the abnormal and diseased. He is not exactly decadent, but he is decidedly pathological. Professor Brückner has said of Andreev's stories, "I do not recall a single one which would not get fearfully on a man's nerves." He has deepened the universal gloom of Russian fiction, not by descending into the slums with

Gorki, but by depicting life as seen through the strange light of a decaying mind. He has often been compared, especially among the Germans, with Edgar Allan Poe. But he is really not in the least like Poe. Poe's horrors are nearly all unreal fantasies, that vaguely haunt our minds like the shadow of a dream. Andreev is a realist, like his predecessors and contemporaries. His style is always concrete and definite, always filled with the sense of fact. There is almost something scientific in his collection of incurables.

The most cheerful thing he has written is perhaps *The Seven Who Were Hanged.* This is horrible enough to bring out a cold sweat; but it is redeemed, as the work of Dostoevski is, by a vast pity and sympathy for the condemned wretches. . . . No sentimental sympathy with murderers is shown here; he carries no flowers to the cells where each of the seven in solitude awaits his fate. Nor are the murderers in the least degree depicted as heroes—they are all different men and women, but none of them resembles the Hero-Murderer of romance. (pp. 268-70)

[The] aim of Andreev, like that of all prominent Russian novelists, is to study the secret of secrets, the human heart. (p. 270)

In [Dimitry] Merezhkovski's interesting work *Tolstoi as Man and Artist,* the author says: "We are accustomed to think that the more abstract thought is, the more cold and dispassionate it is. It is not so; or at least it is not so with us. From the heroes of Dostoevski we may see how abstract thought may be passionate, how metaphysical theories and deductions are rooted, not only in cold reason, but in the heart, emotions, and will. There are thoughts which pour oil on the fire of the passions and inflame man's flesh and blood more powerfully than the most unrestrained license. There is a logic of the passions, but there are also passions in logic. . . ." (p. 272)

Merezhkovski is talking of the heroes of Dostoevski; but his remark is applicable to the work of nearly all Russian novelists, and especially to Chekhov and Andreev. . . . Every one must have noticed how Russians are hag-ridden by an idea; but no one except Merezhkovski has observed the *passion* of abstract thought. In some characters, such as those Dostoevski has given us, it leads to deeds of wild absurdity; in Andreev, it usually leads to madness.

One of Andreev's books [*Mysl*] is indeed a whole commentary on the remark of Merezhkovski quoted above. The English title of the translation is *A Dilemma.* . . . The chief character is a physician, Kerzhentsev, who reminds one constantly of Dostoevski's Raskolnikov, but whose states of mind are even more subtly analysed. No one should read this story unless his nerves are firm, for the outcome of the tale is such as to make almost any reader for a time doubt his own sanity. It is a curious study of the border-line between reason and madness. (pp. 273-74)

The story is an excellent example of what Merezhkovski must mean by the passion of thought. . . .

Andreev is an unflinching realist, with all the Russian power of the concrete phrase. He would never say, in describing a battle, that the Russians "suffered a severe loss." He would turn a magnifying glass on each man. But, although he is a realist and above all a psychologist, he is also a poet. (p. 276)

William Lyon Phelps, "Andreev," in Essays on

Russian Novelists *(reprinted with permission of Macmillan Publishing Co., Inc.; copyright 1911 by the Macmillan Co., Inc.; renewed 1939 by William Lyon Phelps),* Macmillan, 1911 *(and reprinted by Macmillan, 1922), pp. 262-77.*

SERGE PERSKY (essay date 1913)

Andreyev is considered, to-day, as one of the most brilliant representatives of the new constellation of Russian writers, in which he takes a place immediately next to Tchekoff, whom he resembles in the melancholy tone of his work. In him, as in Tchekoff, the number of people who suffer from life, either crushed or mutilated by it, by far exceed the number of happy ones; moreover, the best of his stories are short and sketchy like those of Tchekoff. Andreyev is then, so to speak, his spiritual son. But he is a sickly son, who carries the melancholy element to its farthest limit. The grey tones of Tchekoff have, in Andreyev, become black; his rather sad humor has been transformed into tragic irony; his subtle impressionability into morbid sensibility. The two writers have had the same visions of the anomalies and the horrors of existence; but, where Tchekoff has only a disenchanted smile, Andreyev has stopped, dismayed; the sensation of horror and suffering which springs from his stories has become an obsession with him; it does not penetrate merely the souls of his heroes, but, as in Poe, it penetrates even the descriptions of nature. (p. 202)

Most of Andreyev's characters, like those of Dostoyevsky, are abnormal, madmen and neuroasthenics in whom are distinguishable marked traces of degeneration and psychic perversion. They are beings who have been fatally wounded in their life-struggle, whose minds now are completely or partially powerless. Too weak to fight against the cruel exigencies of reality, they turn their thoughts upon themselves and naturally arrive at the most desolate conclusions, and commit the most senseless acts. (p. 203)

In general, the stories of Andreyev, after passing through various catastrophes, lead the reader back to this theme,—the moral isolation of a human being, who feels that the world has become deserted, and life a game of shadows. The abyss which separates Andreyev's heroes from other men makes them weak, numb, and miserable. It seems, in fact, that there is no greater misfortune than for a man to feel himself alone in the midst of his fellow-creatures. (p. 205)

The idea that [Andreyev] mostly presents is not the power of bestial instincts, but rather the indestructible vitality of human feelings and aspirations towards a better existence, which sometimes comes to light among the most miserable and depraved people, and even among those who are in the most abject material condition.

In the destiny of these beings, there are, however, rays of hope. The slightest incident serves to transform them; suddenly their hearts begin to beat happily, tears of tenderness moisten their eyes, they vaguely feel the existence of something luminous and good. A profound sensibility, an ardent love of life bursts forth in their souls. (pp. 223-24)

The question is whether Andreyev himself believes in the triumph of the elements of life over the elements of death, the horror of which he excels in portraying for us. (p. 230)

[What] constitutes the essence of Andreyev's talent is an extreme impressionability, a daring in descriptions of the negative sides of reality, melancholy moods and the torments of existence. As he usually portrays general suffering and sickness rather than definite types, his heroes are mostly incarnations and symbols. The very titles of some of his stories indicate the abstract character of his work. Such are: "Silence," "The Thought," and "The Lie." In this respect he has carried on the work of Poe, whose influence on him is incontestable. These two writers have in common a refined and morbid sensibility, a predilection for the horrible and a passion for the study of the same kind of subjects,—solitude, silence, death. But the powerful fantasy of the American author, which does not come in touch with reality, wanders freely through the whole world and through all the centuries of history. . . . Andreyev, on the other hand, but rarely breaks the bounds which unite him to reality. His heroes are living people, who act, and whose banal life ends with a banal death. This realism and this passionate love of truth make the strength and the beauty of all his work.

A certain harmony between the imaginative and the real element is characteristic of the best of Andreyev's productions, especially ["The Red Laugh."] . . . (pp. 231-32)

"The Red Laugh" is the symbol, the incarnation, of the bloody and implacable cynicism of war. . . . The feeling of terror, the somewhat mystical intuition of events which, at times, seem to be paradoxes in the other works of Andreyev, are perfectly adapted to this terribly real representation of the effects of war. (pp. 232-33)

It is principally in the dramas which he has written . . . that Andreyev has developed with most force and clearness his favorite themes: the fear of living and dying, the madness of believing in free-will, and the nonsense of life, the weakness and vanity of which he depicts for us.

The first of these works to appear was "The Life of Man," which is a tragic illustration of this pessimism. (p. 239)

At times, Andreyev tries to find the justification of life, and looks for it in mysticism. He then expounds a doctrine, according to which, truth is individual and perhaps conceived by each man, thanks to direct intuition. Such is the mystical truth which the author tries to affirm in "Anathema." (pp. 241-42)

This admirable play, born of a philosophical conception which relates it to Goethe's "Faust," has been received with particular interest. Andreyev, in writing it, has come very near to solving the question of the meaning of life, and its justification. And, to the person who ponders a while over this work, it will appear that it is not Anathema who entreats "Him who guards the gates" to reveal the mystery [of eternity], but it is Andreyev himself, who, carried away by the force of his genius, has thrown himself, as if at an invincible wall, against this pitiless guardian, the guardian of the solution of the enigma of life. (p. 243)

> Serge Persky, "Leonid Andreyev," in his Contemporary Russian Novelists, *translated by Frederick Eisemann, J. W. Luce and Company, 1913 (and reprinted by Books for Libraries Press, 1968; distributed by Arno Press, Inc.), pp. 199-245.*

THOMAS SELTZER   (essay date 1914)

[With] all his resourcefulness, with all his variety of matter and method, there is one note running through almost all of [Andreyev's] works. In many this one note grows so loud as to drown all the other sounds. Like a Wagnerian motif it is iterated and reiterated until it seizes hold of you and never lets you go. This theme is Death. Tolstoy said of Andreyev: "He wants to frighten me, but I am not frightened." The truth is, he does not want to frighten. He is himself frightened, and because he is frightened with good reason, and because this reason applies equally well to you and to me, his dread is easily communicated to every mortal who has not attained the superhuman serenity of Tolstoy when he made that remark. (pp. 11-12)

He devoted two of his best stories, *Lazarus* and *The Seven Who Were Hanged,* entirely to this theme of death. *Lazarus* is written in Andreyev's usual impressionistic style and is full of symbolism. When Lazarus rises from the grave after having lain dead for three days, he becomes the very embodiment of Death. Whosoever meets his gaze feels its "destructive force." But for Andreyev the terror of death lies not merely in its being the cessation of life; still more horrible is its incomprehensibility, its riddlesomeness, the impenetrable darkness stretching beyond it. (p. 12)

[For all Andreyev's pessimism, however,] death is not always the supreme and final power. Certain forces, at the command of the superman, seem to be capable of coping successfully with it. This idea recurs in Andreyev's works under various forms.

In *The Seven Who Were Hanged,* death is treated in quite a different aspect—not so much in a philosophical presentation of the problem as in a psychologic and realistic study. Five of the seven condemned to death are political offenders; two are common criminals. The theme of the story is the way in which each of them receives the death sentence: what their inner experiences and feelings are in the interval between the sentence and the execution, and how they meet death. In the wonderfully realistic pictures of the seven, Andreyev reveals at length that power of which we catch only occasional glimpses in his other writings. Stripped of his impressionism, Andreyev appears as a master, not of abstractions, not of symbols, as in his other works, but of the individual human character, the individual soul and the concrete personality. *The Seven Who Were Hanged* is a human, a fearfully human story. Though we are introduced to the characters only when they are about to die, we learn to know them intimately and follow their remaining fortunes with interest. Here we have, pure and unadulterated, that Russian realism which finds its highest expression in Tolstoy, and which makes literature so awfully like life. (pp. 14-15)

Another theme which bulks large in Andreyev's books is *Loneliness.* Ever so many of his characters are afflicted with that malady. (p. 15)

We have seen that on the one hand, Andreyev has command over a wide range of subjects and that on the other he seems to be attracted, nay, obsessed, by one or two ideas which appear and reappear in almost all his works. But that involves no contradiction. Despite the variety of his topics there is one point of view from which his work is done, and it is this point of view which, running like a thread through all his creations, unifies them and gives them meaning and significance. It is this point of view also from which his favorite subjects are treated so that through it they assume universal importance. (pp. 16-17)

Andreyev forever asks this question: How shall we make

life livable, how reconcile our feeling of what life ought to be with the evils which fill the world? Andreyev, contrary to the general notion, does not, I think, hate life; he loves it. It is because he loves it that all the misery and wrongs and ills of the world so appall him. He wants to solve the riddle. What does it all mean? Why, after a wretched life, such as the average life is today, such as the life described in his drama *The Life of Man,* comes death? It is not death *per se* then, not a morbid fancy, such as those in which Poe so loved to indulge for their own sake, that preoccupies Andreyev's mind. Andreyev dwells on death because he desires "eternal life," just as he dwells on the horrors of life because he wants "the good." His whole literary activity is an endeavor to solve the conflict between reason which condemns life and feeling which affirms it. Considered in this way Andreyev's works from the first to the last form an organic unit and show a continuous growth along the line of this central thought. (pp. 17-18)

His very first play, *To the Stars . . . ,* turns upon this conflict between life as it is and the refusal of reason to accept it. (p. 18)

Technically, *To the Stars* can scarcely be regarded as a play. It is rather a series of conversations, flowing along easily enough and interestingly enough, but not connected by any action or plot even in the modern sense of the word plot. In fact all the action there is happens elsewhere, not on the stage, and is only talked about in the play. One of the leading characters, Nikolay, never appears in person. All he is and all he does are conveyed indirectly. [His next play,] *Savva,* on the other hand, is a play well knit together. It has plenty of action, all bearing naturally and directly upon the central plot, and the interest grows steadily until the strikingly powerful denouement in the last act. The characters also are carefully drawn. Each stands out as a vivid, well-defined personality, the more important ones . . . revealing themselves in all their strength and weakness, the minor ones drawn in a few broad, masterly strokes. (p. 21)

The Life of Man is one of the boldest and . . . one of the most successful attempts of its kind in dramatic literature. It is abstraction in art raised to the highest conceivable power. Andreyev set himself no less a task than to write in this one play, consisting of five scenes and a prologue, all that the title signifies: The Life of Man, of Everyman. It is meant to comprise all the essential elements that enter into the average human life. Like an algebraic formula, it can be applied to every special case. In fact, in external workmanship it strongly suggests a mathematical formula. It is precise, accurate and stiff as a paradigm. . . . There are no surprises. There must be none, for it is the life of the average man. But the throb of life is there as truly as in a character of Shakespeare or Dickens, or any particular individual of your literary or actual acquaintance. Andreyev has the peculiar power of re-embodying the disembodied, of making the spiritual tangible, the abstract concrete. He himself calls it the "neo-realistic" drama. What peculiar virtue must reside in a name! The "neo-realist" in the character of Andreyev simply goes ahead and quietly does what the "futurist" so loudly professes, but fails to perform. (pp. 22-3)

The play is as compact in structure as it is rich in symbolic meaning. Very curious, as contrasting with the impression of the extreme modernity of the drama, are the crude and primitive methods which Andreyev uses without the least scruple. In the second scene Man's wife indulges in a long monologue to tell the audience the past history of the hero; and in the fourth scene an old servant is conveniently made to talk to herself and blab out all that has happened since the Ball at Man's. But these crudities, far from jarring, seem to fall in quite harmonisouly with the general atmosphere of the play, which is all in the region of the primitive. (pp. 24-5)

[Also evident in Andreyev's work is the need for spiritual victory. The] all-conquering human spirit is to atone for the ills of outer existence. It alone vindicates life and gives it that meaning which is not to be found in the external world of the senses and without which it is intolerable. Some such faith Andreyev must have always had. Traces of it, rather faint, to be sure, are discoverable here and there. It could not have been very strong. It was not a dominating note, but a timid voice of weakly protest in an overpowering chorus of condemnation. For a long time Andreyev seems not to have been able to arrive at a direct affirmative answer to the question of the worth-whileness of life. Apparently he vacillated between his faith and its awful alternative, sometimes leaning to the bright side, sometimes to the gloomy side, though never completely losing hope in the possibility of some favorable solution. In *The Life of Man* the dismal note predominates, and the saving faith scarcely shows itself. In *To the Stars,* on the other hand, despite the scepticism, the other side is given a fair hearing. The justification of life is found in the superman's power to rise superior to the evils of the outer world. . . . But the first time Andreyev meets the question, Is life worth while? with an emphatic and unequivocal Yes, is in his drama *Anathema.* Gradually, by painful struggling and searching, Andreyev appears to have worked his way to this position, and *Anathema* therefore represents the highest and most positive stage in the development of his thought. (pp. 27-8)

Anathema is hardly recognizable as the devil. He bears but slight resemblance to the conventional Spirit of Evil. He is not the tempter in Goethe's Mephistophelian sense, nor in that same sense is he the "Spirit that denies." He is a new creation in literature, an original conception of Satan. He is the spirit of investigation, the scientist. He wants proofs; he wants to be shown; he cannot believe without observation. He is *reason without feeling;* he has no heart and he therefore cannot "feel" his way to faith. He cannot feel that human life justifies itself and is founded upon a rational basis. But he burns with a desire to find out; he is consumed with a passion for truth. Oh, for one peep into eternity! And if he tempts to evil, he does so to gratify this ruling passion, not out of original sin, not out of a desire to destroy. And if he is a skeptic it is also because of his passion for truth, and not from a desire to deny. Andreyev's devil is the passion for truth. (pp. 31-2)

For a picture of the world as a vale of tears there is in the whole of literature scarcely the like of *Anathema.* And when one tries to analyze one hardly knows how the effect is produced. Surely not by the ordinary means of the drama, for it can scarcely be called a drama. It is a succession of pictures, and for the general impression it would make little difference if, with the exception of the prologue and the last scene, their order were reversed. So it is futile to judge the play by ordinary standards. If we did, the verdict of absolute condemnation would be easy and unmistakable. But Andreyev wrings pity from our hearts and touches us with wonderfully warm emotions in behalf of poor humanity. Let not critics step in where angels fear to tread. The pathos of the drama proper is as great as the extraordinary grandeur of the prologue and the finale. (pp. 32-3)

Thomas Seltzer, "Leonid Andreyev," in The Drama, *Vol. IV, No. 13, February, 1914, pp. 5-33.*

EUGENE M. KAYDEN (essay date 1919)

Andreyev belongs to that great fellowship of Russian authors who did not accept the scientific advance of the century with its unquestioning ambition and belief in the saving grace of mere action and work. An unflinching realist seeking truth with a terrible zeal, he divested things of their good nature and gloss, and his chosen themes were the failure of the cultured man in the face of all-pervading coarseness, and the moral decay of middle-class correctness and order. At first he told himself that it was best to live without theories and misgivings, and unheeding joy seemed the solution, which he expressed in *There Was, In Springtime, On the River, A Present, Holiday,* and others. . . . But aloofness was foreign to his nature, and the themes which won undiminished ascendancy in his writings were the problems of man's solitude in the midst of conventional social life, his loneliness before inexplicable fate, and his eager yearning for human solidarity, for a moral—not economic—bond in human existence. In the everyday kingdom of mere things, in contact with our joyless existence and the adamantean wall of social customs and falsehoods, he saw nothing but confusion, madness, death. Not life itself was terrible, but its debasement to meaner ends, our fierce absorption in inconsequential aims and activities, and the employment of intelligence in works that negate civilization, although presumptuously and solemnly undertaken to ameliorate and save. (p. 425)

A pessimist? True. But Andreyev does not end with pessimism. He was not the brilliant author toying with his changeful moods and fancies, but a fiery soul gripped by the world's sorrow, and seeing visions of new worlds and beauty. By temperament a man of combat, he yearned for a wider heaven and real people. Denying life he yet vibrates with love and sorrow of life, convinced that life is great, invincible. Refuting life, he believes in the symbol. The dying will thirsts for the impossible, looking for the miracle in the order of gloom and bestiality. . . . The mysticism which Andreyev accepted was not the comfort of an undisturbed faith, but a mysticism born out of great combat and striving, a mysticism of belief and asseveration. No wonder then that with the revolution of 1905 the cordial swiftness of Andreyev's art and his infinite love for the thwarted hopes and agonies of his people had completely captivated the imagination and the deep worship of his compatriots. No pessimist could have produced in rapid succession the individual and social dramas which followed after 1905: *To the Stars, Savva, King Hunger, Life of Man,* and *Anathema.* In these Andreyev reached the acme of his poetic utterance.

The light which was breaking through the gloom and confusion of Andreyev's early work was the conception of man as the son of eternity, a citizen of countless worlds, a sun-snarer. (pp. 425-26)

Andreyev cannot forget the individual "speck of dust," our common brother who is demanded as a sacrifice to brother-

hood. He tells many stories of the life of the ordinary "gray" men, souls lost and bewildered, and yet dreaming of excellence. He cannot reconcile himself to man doomed to nothing. In *Life of Man* we see him suffering for this gray man of the crowd. He chooses common incidents—poverty, heedless pleasures of youth, ambition, rise to wealth, family happiness, dreams of home and big fireplaces, comfort at maturity, the loss of the only son, and man's bewilderment before misfortune and unknown fate. Imperceptibly we begin to understand that the tragedy of the modern individualist consists in his failure to relate himself organically with the plangent life about him, to establish an immediate bond between himself and the larger social life, in the absence of which personal achievement hangs like a pall that shrouds dullness and vacancy.

But though the soul is lost, and the sick beast defiles man, he is reaching out for indissoluble truth. This is the eternal ageless reality so significant to Andreyev, for it is a power which flouts deformity and laughs at failure. This common concrete circumstance Andreyev traces out divinely on the walls of man's thought. (p. 426)

King Hunger appeared at a moment of universal desperation when the defeat of the revolutionary movement produced a state of chaos in the life and literature of Russia. Andreyev seized the spirit of the desperate condition of the struggle, the tragic spirit of rebellion among the peasants, and the monstrosity of a spiritually barren class in a position of power. The dramatic pictures of *King Hunger* reveal the masterful broad strokes of a great artist's brush. We feel the presence of Stygian shadows; they waver, fading into transparent colossal shapes, incomprehensible and gruesome as the figures of Time, Death, and King Hunger. (p. 427)

Into this fantastic struggle of social forces Andreyev projected the dark mood of The Girl in Black. She represents the best and noblest instincts of the ruling classes, who, confronted with a dreadful social overthrow, and exhausted under the pressure of historic evolution, blindly strive to live with their backward faith. She cannot merge herself with the hopes and struggles of the masses, her princely offering of sympathy is spurned, but she would not "laugh at the fallen." The cruelty and cynicism of her class exasperate her. She feels that their greed and malice have produced delusions and monsters. Moving in a class which can no longer fight for its power as an ideal, she can only advise them "to meet death dancing," to die beautifully. She knows that the growing solidarity of the toiling masses will end all passive submission to the myth of authority. . . . She and her class can only hear voices roaring revenge and poison. Deceived by the immediate utterances of indignation, blind to the deeper and nobler instincts demanding a worthy share in the joys of life whose physical sustenance shall no longer exhaust man's forces in weary service, she and her class mistake the true nature of the great upheaval. (pp. 427-28)

The picture of collective man at work, creating, is not found in Andreyev: he lacked enthusiasm and the strength of a soul willing to give itself to those who blunderingly but earnestly labor for a larger life. Andreyev was not the man to reveal the subterranean ideas and passions generating within life itself. He was never the *conscience* of Russia, with lips touched by divine living fire, as Tolstoy was, but the *mood* of Russia, falling and rising with the dreams and hopes of the struggle. (p. 428)

Eugene M. Kayden, "Leonid Andreyev: 1871-1919," in The Dial *(copyright, 1919, by The Dial Publishing Company, Inc.), Vol. LXVII, November 15, 1919, pp. 425-28.*

MOISSAYE J. OLGIN (essay date 1919)

Andreyev questions the fundamentals of our life. Things taken by mankind for granted he subjects to a sharp scrutiny only to arrive at the conclusion that there is "madness and horror" everywhere. Human existence, human thought, human actions and valuations strike him as full of exasperating problems that allow no rest and no happiness to the inquisitive mind. The simplest of these problems is, perhaps, the problem of the subconscious. Man never knows what he is apt to do in a few minutes. . . . Can there be any prospect of freedom for the individual?

Andreyev creates one work after the other to emphasize this lack of freedom. . . .

Andreyev is engaged in a cruel feud with life, with destiny, with God, with reason. (p. 123)

From the angle of [his] multifarious queries Leonid Andreyev appears to be the most universal writer. From the standpoint of psychological motives and moving social forces, however, Andreyev is intrinsically Russian. It is not an accident that whenever he happens to portray actual life in a realistic manner, he finds nothing but poverty, cruelty, meanness. . . . In the later periods of his creative work Leonid Andreyev seldom resorts to mere description of existing conditions. Yet whenever his problem compels him to glance at life's realities, it seems as if he had opened a trap-door into a cold and dark cavern full of poisonous gases.

This subterranean current, always felt if not always accentuated in Andreyev's colorful and sonorous configurations; this omnipresence of poverty and degradation underneath a thin crust of modern culture, an abysmal apparition that sent a chill through Russian intelligentzia of whatever social or political denomination, makes the "abstract" Andreyev very close to "concrete" Russian life. (pp. 123-24)

Andreyev is not so much interested in . . . events themselves or in their outcome, as in their meaning for the human conscience, in their bearing upon the universal problems of human existence. In this as in all other aspects of his creative activities, Andreyev is the spokesman of the Russian intellectual who was awakened by modern progress from the sluggishness of a patriarchal system to the retaliation of the complexity of life. . . . Andreyev was the writer destined to embody this spirit of intellectual unrest in striking artistic pictures. When he wrote his great question marks, he brought together strong yet unclear currents of thought and emotion diffused through thinking Russia, and out of them created vivid images. The response was vast.

Andreyev is never contented to write a story for the story's sake. Every story or play of his represents a problem. The scheme is somewhat like this: Granted a man is put in certain conditions and made to suffer certain experiences, what would be the spiritual or moral effect? The surroundings and conditions thus become of subordinate importance; the center of gravity is put into the spiritual or moral reaction.

The form itself becomes of subordinate value. None of the Russian writers has so often changed the form of his writings and none is so difficult to put into a class. In his early works (1898-1902) Andreyev is still under the apparent influence of Chekov and may be classed with what is commonly known as the "realistic school." Yet already *The Wall* . . . with its lepers vainly attempting to crush or climb over the implacable and eternally silent Great Wall that stands between them and the unknown, bears all the earmarks of a symbolistic work. . . . [*The Life of Man*] introduced a method christened in Russia as *schematization,* while *King Hunger* and *The Black Marks* . . . are populated by mere allegories. Andreyev's method is never the same in two successive productions, yet Andreyev is everywhere the same with his passionate temperament, with his furious impact, with his fearless piercing of the most painful wounds, with his masterful imagination and with that power of expression which makes even the abstract creations of his mind glow with intense life. . . . It is Andreyev's personality that lends unity to all his productions. (p. 124)

Andreyev's style is the most metallic in all modern Russian literature. His works have to be recited, not read. His prose has a unique rhythm which makes it more musical than many of the free verse creations. "There is a spiral-like impetuousity in the combination of Andreyev's words and phrases," says [Konstantin] Arabazhin. "His words harass, beat, lash your face, they importunately intrude into your soul, they moan and clang, they ring the great alarm bell, they strike your heart like claps of thunder, they rankle in your soul, sometimes they yelp and howl like hungry dogs begging for mercy and attention. Andreyev loves contrasts. His contours are sharp. Everything is thrust on the canvas with crude and bold strokes, sometimes producing a sensational effect." And yet, there is often a beautiful tenderness, an almost bashful love of life and youth in many of Andreyev's works in spite of his heralded objectivism, there is a strain of lyricism vibrating through his thunderous questionings, at times rising to heights of powerful harmony and drowning all other sounds. It is this personal, intimately human quality that lends his writings a peculiar fascination. (pp. 124-25)

Moissaye J. Olgin, "A Wounded Intellect: Leonid Andreyev (1871-1919)," in The New Republic *(© 1919 The New Republic, Inc.), Vol. 21, No. 264, December 24, 1919, pp. 123-25.*

ALEXANDER KAUN (essay date 1924)

Unlike the majority of his predecessors and contemporaries, Leonid Andreyev advocates no definite political or moral creed. His problems are not those of particular individuals under particular conditions. Nearly every story or play of his presents an illustration or postulation of some universal and general philosophic question, the plot and the dramatis personae serving merely as incidental accessories. He is mainly occupied with the problem of life, of its purpose and value, and he approaches his problem with no ready solutions or definite formulas and prescriptions. Everlastingly querying and setting forth questions, he quails before the task of answering them. Usually he leaves them open. Only rarely, and then hesitatingly, does he hint at a possible solution, in a veiled and ambiguous manner. The solution itself does not appear to be of import to the author.

Andreyev fails to give a definite answer because he lacks a fixed philosophic system. To create, or even to embrace

tacks our holiest beliefs. His story, *The Abyss, . . .* aroused a storm of indignation and protest. (p. 200)

The sordidness of the story need not befog the problem it raises. *The Abyss* is the first of Andreyev's attempts at broadening and deepening the range of his themes. Henceforth he will time and again probe our inner self, analyzing our motives and impulses, and endeavoring to gauge the relative strength of our instinct and intellect. . . . Nemovetsky [the protagonist of *The Abyss*] thinks he knows himself, but it is only his intellectual, thinking, reasoning self that he may wager on. He is unaware and therefore horrified at the advent of his dormant self composed of brutal instincts, of animalistic impulses, which slumber under the flimsy mask of intellect and morality, but emerge unexpectedly, and, unleashed, drag him irresistibly into the Abyss. (pp. 201-02)

Nearly all [Andreyev's] works have as their central idea, one might say as their hero, thought. The typical scheme of a story by Andreyev consists of the drab life of a commonplace person suddenly illuminated by a flash of thought, which sublimates gray existence to tragedy. The author seems to regard thought with a mixed feeling of reverence and awe. He sees in it a merciless surgeon apt to destroy the disease together with the body in which it is lodged. He considers it a double-edged sword which may slash the hand that wields it. (p. 204)

In the mental chaos which enveloped Russian society at the end of the nineteenth century, [Andreyev's] critical eye looked at life clear and undimmed as that of a hawk. He observed the everyday existence of his contemporaries and found it sunless, empty, futile. He pronounced this diagnosis without equivocation. He doubted everything, our dearest beliefs and most sacred tenets. . . .

The epitome of his views at that period may be seen in his play, *The Life of Man*. . . . [One] has no difficulty in tracing a definite Schopenhauerian thread through *The Life of Man*. In fact, nearly all of Andreyev's early writings are saturated with Schopenhauerism of the more obvious variety. Misery, squalor, monotony, fear, loneliness, futility, illusion, disillusionment—these are the elements which in the writings discussed previously, compose Andreyev's vale of tears. (p. 207)

The Life of Man presents a disenchanted view of life and man. "Limited in vision and in knowledge," man fussily wriggles during the brief span of his existence, pursuing his small activities, craving for petty, selfish achievements, conceitedly regarding himself as the centre of the universe. Only through suffering does man arrive at the bitter knowledge that his choices and preferences are an illusion, that he is a slave, in bondage to his Will, and that only through destroying this Will, through overcoming life, can he become free. . . . In *The Life of Man*, however, he does not go beyond liberating man from his bondage to will, and terminating his futile struggle in peace eternal—death. It is for this reason that Andreyev's first symbolical play forms a fitting climax for the early period of his writings, the period of unrelieved negation and hopelessness. It sums up his fragmentary indictments against life's monotony, cruelty, stupidity, illusoriness, in one sweeping condemnation of man's existence under the tyranny of his Will. (p. 212)

The last two decades of Russian history, so replete with upheavals, catastrophes, transformations—in a word, so

dramatic, have been reflected profoundly and many-sidedly in Andreyev's works. . . . Andreyev fails to portray these shifting changes, these transient events, these portentous processes, in themselves. Out of these turbulent phenomena he extracts their essence, their absolute significance, their value beyond time or place, thus lending the phenomena a general, universal importance. For this reason his reaction to the Russo-Japanese war becomes a symbolization of war in general, just as his observations of the revolution and of its various concomitants acquire a scope far beyond their local and temporal limits. (p. 215)

Andreyev lacks unity of outlook. He is torn with discordant ideas and with discrepant sentiments. As a result his attitudes appear at times mutually contradictory, particularly with regard to intellect, thought. Explicitly, he disparages human thought, demonstrates its treachery, futility and impotence. . . . At the same time one is aware of his passion for searching, probing, never-resting thought. In presenting the victims of thought, he adorns them, by implication, with the thorny crown of heroes. Defeat does not prove the wrongness of endeavor. . . . [The] duality of Andreyev's attitude toward man's reasoning faculty is not altogether contradictory. He exalts reason in its function of uncompromising quest after ultimate goals and meanings. He rejects reason when it presumes to solve and settle problems dogmatically. The former attitude goads him on to question and doubt, to destroy and overturn, causing him and his readers heartbreaking disappointments and disillusions. (pp. 259-60)

[To Andreyev] suffering is the essence and sense of life. With the greater number of Russian writers, he regards suffering as an ennobling factor, as a redemption from sordidness. . . . Man needs, however irrationally, faith and suffering to fill his life and to lend it meaning.

Thus our reason, though it may wreck the faith of individual persons, proves helpless in face of mass faith, the instinctive, elemental medium for self-protection. But in describing the manifestations of blind faith as a weapon of self-defense in the hands of the masses shrinking before freedom and responsibility . . . , Andreyev is not so resentful as when he attacks beliefs that savor of the head, of the intellect, whether it be in religion or in philosophy or in social conduct. While pitying blind faith . . . , he hates rationalizing faith, all attempts to base beliefs on logic, to explain everything through reason. (pp. 266-68)

Andreyev does not believe in the ability of man to acquire absolute knowledge, either about himself or about life and the world outside of himself. Not one of his fervent seekers achieves his aim. Intellect is a tool and plaything of the will, of the self, and is bound to be defeated in its presumptuous attempt to interpret the cause and source of all. But the attempt in itself, however futile, has an intense charm for Andreyev, who returns to this theme time and again. It is evident from the preceding discussion that intellect, reason, is obnoxious and hateful to Andreyev only when it pretends to have arrived at a definite solution of all questions, when it dictates precise Thou shalt's and Thou shalt not's. In other words, he is opposed to dogmatic reason. But the quest in itself is dear to his heart, and we recognize Andreyev himself in his passionate, often Quixotic, hunters after absolute knowledge and perfect understanding of the universe and its laws. (pp. 275-76)

Alexander Kaun, in his Leonid Andreyev: A Critical Study *(copyright 1924 by B. W. Huebsch, Inc.; reprinted by permission of Viking Penguin Inc.), B. W. Huebsch, 1924, 361 p.*

MAXIM GORKY (essay date 1928)

[Andreev] was a wonderfully interesting talker, inexhaustible, witty. Although his mind always manifested a stubborn tendency to peer into the darkest corners of the soul—nevertheless his thought was so alert, so capriciously individual, that it readily took grotesque and humorous forms. In a conversation among friends he could use his sense of humour flexibly and beautifully, but in his stories he unfortunately lost that capacity, so rare in a Russian.

Although he possessed a lively and sensitive imagination, he was lazy; he was much fonder of talking about literature than of creating it. (pp. 123-24)

Indifferent to facts of actuality, sceptical in his attitude to the mind and will of man—it would seem that the idea of laying down the law, of playing the teacher, ought not to have attracted him. That is a role inevitable for one who is familiar—much too familiar—with reality. But our very first conversation clearly indicated that, whilst possessing all the qualities of a superb artist, he wished to assume the pose of a thinker and of a philosopher as well. This seemed to me dangerous, almost hopeless, chiefly because his stock of knowledge was strangely poor. And one always felt as though he sensed the nearness of an invisible enemy, that he was arguing intensely with someone and wanted to subdue him. (p. 125)

Leonid was talented by nature, organically talented; his intuition was astonishingly keen. In all that touched on the dark side of life, the contradictions in the human soul, the rumblings in the domain of the instincts, he had eerie powers of divination. (p. 128)

To Andreev man appeared poor in spirit, a creature interwoven of irreconcilable contradictions of instinct and intellect, for ever deprived of the possibility of attaining inner harmony. All his works are "vanity of vanities," decay and self-deception. And above all he is the slave of death and all his life long he walks, dragging its chain. (pp. 138-39)

What a pity that he who in conversation was such a master of humour neglected or was afraid to enrich his stories with its play. Evidently he was afraid of spoiling the dark tones of his pictures with the varied colours of humour. (p. 156)

[While] the plans he related were full of colour and substance, he composed carelessly. [For example, in] the first version of his *Judas* several mistakes occurred which indicated that he had not even taken the trouble to read the New Testament. (p. 182)

He behaved to his talent as an indifferent rider treats a superb horse—he galloped it mercilessly, but did not love it, did not tend it. His hand had not the time to draw the intricate designs of his riotous imagination; he did not trouble to develop the power and dexterity of his hand. . . .

He tried to hypnotize the reader by the monotony of his phrasing, but his phrasing was losing the convincing quality of beauty. Wrapping his thought in the cotton wool of monotonously obscure words he only succeeded in revealing it too much, and his stories read like popular dialogues on philosophical subjects. (p. 183)

Maxim Gorky, in his Reminiscences of Leonid Andreev, *translated by Katherine Mansfield and S. S. Koteliansky (reprinted by permission of the translators' literary estates and The Hogarth Press Ltd), C. Gaige, 1928 (and reprinted in his* Reminiscences of Tolstoy, Chekhov and Andreev, *translated by Katherine Mansfield, S. S. Koteliansky, and Leonard Woolf, The Hogarth Press, 1948, pp. 117-91).*

IVAR SPECTOR (essay date 1943)

Up to Andreyev, Russian literature had championed the cause of the oppressed and the persecuted. It had found a niche in its Pantheon for the serf and later for the peasant, for the "poor folk," for the prostitute, the criminal, the "lower depths," and the "possessed." (p. 219)

There was still another group which awaited sympathetic treatment in Russian letters, and that was the persecuted Jewish minority. The champions of the "poor folk," the peasants, and the "lower depths" had so far neglected the Jew, while Slavophilism contributed still further to his misery. This hitherto neglected task fell to the lot of Leonid Andreyev. In *Anathema,* as well as in some of his other works, Andreyev sympathetically portrayed the lot of this persecuted race. (pp. 219-20)

Through the experiences of David-Leizer, he demonstrated to the world, that there are Jews, who, far from being greedy for gain, are ready to share an American fortune with the outcasts and the unfortunate, regardless of nationality, race, rank, or station; that while the David-Leizers become the victims of pogroms, and are stoned to death by the ungrateful mob, their deeds and their sufferings bring them the reward of immortality.

It was this play, *Anathema,* and the message contained therein, that placed Leonid Andreyev among the Russian classical writers. For if we analyze the Golden Age of Russian Literature, we immediately notice that only those writers became immortal, who espoused the cause of the weak, the insulted, and the injured. The others, in spite of material contributions along other lines, were seldom classed with the mighty. One play of this type was sufficient to raise the other works of Andreyev to the ranks of the classics. (p. 221)

While *Anathema* was the first sympathetic plea for the Jewish minority in Russia, it also reflected the disappointment, the bitterness, and the disillusionment of the Russian intelligentsia after the Revolution of 1905. . . .

Anathema was Andreyev's attempt to find out whether it was worth struggling, not necessarily living, for a better life and a better social order. Like Anathema himself, Andreyev's inquisitive mind sought to penetrate the iron gates of uncertainty (eternal mystery), of baffling obscurity (eternal silence), and to establish whether or not there was even a faint ray of hope for the future. Like many of his contemporaries, his reason demanded knowledge rather than blind faith, in order to cope with insuperable obstacles. The message of Anathema was, that in spite of the mob's ingratitude, in spite of the seeming futility of his unselfish efforts to help mankind, David-Leizer nevertheless obtained immortality. Even while he admitted the difficulty, for him the practical impossibility, of grasping the secret of the world order and the justice of its rewards and punishments, he reached the conclusion that a good cause was worth while. (p. 222)

Ivar Spector, "Leonid Nikolayevitch Andreyev: 1871-1919," in his The Golden Age of Russian Literature (copyright 1939, 1943 by Ivar Spector), revised edition, Caxton Printers, Ltd., 1943, pp. 212-23.

JANKO LAVRIN (essay date 1954)

In each literature there are authors the symptomatic significance of whose works is often greater than their artistic value. Typical not so much of their own epoch as a whole but rather of some of its conspicuous single facets, they are usually overrated during their life-time, and underestimated once they are dead. Such, at any rate, was the fate of Leonid Andreyev ... who, between 1902 and 1910, was one of the most discussed writers in Russia and, for a time, rivalled in popularity even Gorky himself. . . . While Gorky worked for a new era, a new community and a new set of readers, Andreyev preferred to hitch his talent to the decaying bourgeois intelligentsia in order to reflect, as in a magnifying and also somewhat crooked mirror, their consciousness during the last few years before their passing out of history. (p. 254)

Apart from his early stories, the majority of Andreyev's writings deal with rather "big" subjects, treated in that hasty quasimodernist style which, for all its pretentious garb, is generally accessible and therefore likely to flatter the vanity of the less tutored readers by giving them the illusion of being "highbrows." (pp. 255-56)

In his early stories the echoes of Chekhov, Korolenko, and Gorky are noticeable. Soon the influences of Dostoevsky and Tolstoy were added, and later also that of Edgar Allan Poe. The writings of his early period are realistic, with a social or humanitarian undercurrent, but invariably ending in a minor key. (p. 256)

Two of Andreyev's best early stories, Once there Lived . . . and In the Fog . . . were partly inspired by Tolstoy—the first by The Death of Ivan Ilyich, and the second by The Kreutzer Sonata. Once there Lived takes place in a clinic where there are several patients knowing that they are doomed, but the atmosphere of death is handled with Chekhov's technique and, what is more, with Chekhovian understatement—a rare thing in Andreyev's writings. A different propensity is noticeable in In the Fog. Here Andreyev tackled the tragedy of awakened sex in a schoolboy who has contracted a venereal disease and eventually murders a prostitute and commits suicide. The story caused much uproar and can serve as a proof of the author's growing hankering for sensational themes, worked out in a dramatic (or melodramatic) manner. This was particularly the case when he came under the spell of Dostoevsky's themes and problems. As the latter were often much bigger than his talent, he tried to make up for it by raising his tone and filling his pages with would-be symbolistic clichés, designed to surprise, or rather to stun his readers also by means of paradoxical logic. This brought, however, a forced, not to say false note into his writings, and its pretence increased in the ratio in which he abandoned the straightforward realistic method for the sake of stilted pseudo-symbolism. This genre was clearly anticipated in stories such as Silence, The Wall, The Tocsin, The Abyss, and The Thought—all of them written . . . in a mood of futility. Chekhov's pathetic blind-alley was taken up by Andreyev with relish, but he turned it into a substitute for religion, with its theology of "mystical anarchism," its

solemnly hollow rites and incantations, the only genuine element in which was his fear of life. The apotheosis of this fear became Andreyev's "purpose" (one could almost say —moral purpose) which he piously cultivated as the very essence of his own aesthetic modernism.

Always an individualist, Andreyev was strongly attracted by the heroic pose of a modern and anti-philistine. But as he felt more and more the fascination of Dostoevsky's metaphysical rebels, he too became one of them without even believing in metaphysics. He prostrated himself before the principle of negation which he pushed to the verge of grotesqueness. Like some of Dostoevsky's heroes he saw (or forced himself to see) in life only a "vaudeville of the devils"; but instead of searching for something beyond it, as Dostoevsky did, he derived from the very hopelessness of such a disposition—into which he often worked himself by means of alcohol—a peculiar and almost ecstatic pleasure. (pp. 257-58)

[Senselessness is] canonized   Andreyev's story, Phantoms . . .—obviously a literal descendant of Chekhov's Ward No. 6, with the action taking place in a lunatic asylum. The author analyzes the imaginary phantom existence of the inmates in whose minds the boundary line between the normal and abnormal has been obliterated. But life outside the asylum . . . is implied to be equally phantom-like; so there is not much to choose between the two. . . . (p. 259)

Yet if his "metaphysical" themes often outsprip his talent, Andreyev fares much better when concentrating mainly on psychology. One of his best stories of this kind, The Governor . . . , is told with restraint and with almost Tolstoyan matter-of-factness. . . . As psychologist Andreyev had learned a great deal from Dostoevsky. At his best he also succeeded in skilfully combining psychological observations with some deeper thought which added to the value of the story. In his Christians . . . , for example, he unmasks with unflagging irony the hypocritical character of our Christianity, seen from the angle of a prostitute who obstinately refuses to take a Christian oath, to the indignation of the no-less-prostituted but otherwise respectable and respected citizens—a mark of Tolstoy's influence. (p. 260)

Andreyev can be good, even excellent, only when he is less preoccupied with his nihilistic outlook than with the story as such, provided he tells it without affectations. The two of his longer though widely different narratives of this kind are Judas Iscariot and Others . . . and The Seven that Were Hanged. . . . (p. 261)

Like his stories, [Andreyev's plays] can be divided into a realistic and a philosophic group, with the addition of a few pot-boilers of the kind that are sure to please the public. And like his stories again, they all reflect Andreyev's problem-hunting and nihilism à outrance. (p. 264)

His realistic Savva and his abstractly "expressionist" morality-play, The Life of Man . . . , testify to an even greater despair over man and life than his stories. . . . Savva is soaked in that negative revolutionary mood which wants to destroy mainly for the sake of destruction. Since history and civilization have proved such a flop, then the best we can do is to scrap the whole of it and start afresh— perhaps with more success. Also the drama, King Hunger, is revolutionary in its protest against the capitalistic minority. The enslaved workers who rebel are crushed by the technocratic (or for that matter—"managerial") elite, but the muffled threats of the slain to come back do not augur well for the future of that elite. On the whole, this is one of Andreyev's weakest plays. As in *The Life of Man,* or even more so, he mistakes here allegory for symbolism, especially in the last scene the forced artificiality of which is positively painful. (pp. 264-65)

> *Janko Lavrin, "Leonid Andreyev," in his* Russian Writers: Their Lives and Literature *(copyright, 1954, by D. Van Nostrand Company, Inc.; reprinted by permission of the author), D. Van Nostrand, 1954, pp. 254-66.*

D. S. MIRSKY   (essay date 1955)

Old-fashioned critics and readers of the older generation of the orthodox radical (and, still more, of the conservative) school were scarcely able to distinguish between Andréyev and the symbolists. Both were to them equally detestable malformations. In reality there is very little in common between the two beyond the common tendency away from accepted standards and a decided inclination towards the grandiose and the ultimate. Both the symbolists and Andréyev are always somewhat stiltedly serious and solemn and distinctly lack a sense of humor. But the differences are far more important. The symbolists were united by a high degree of conscientious craftsmanship; Andréyev dealt in ready-made clichés and was simply no craftsman. Secondly, the symbolists were men of superior culture and played a principal part in the great cultural renaissance of the Russian intelligentsia; Andréyev, on the contrary, lacked culture as much as he despised it. At last—and this is the most important point—the symbolists stood on a foundation of a realistic (in the mediaeval sense of the word) metaphysics, and even if they were pessimists of life, they were optimists of death—that is to say, mystics. . . . Andréyev and Artsybáshev proceeded from a scientific agnosticism and were strangers to all mystical optimism—theirs was an all-round and absolute pessimism—a pessimism of death as well as of life. It may be said, in short (with a degree of simplification), that while the symbolists proceed from Dostoyévsky, Andréyev proceeds from Tolstóy. The negation of culture and the intense consciousness of the elemental realities of life—death and sex—are the essence of Tolstoyism, and they reappear in the philosophy of Andréyev and of Artsybáshev. As for the purely literary influence of Tolstóy over these two writers, it can hardly be exaggerated. (p. 395)

> *D. S. Mirsky, "Prose Fiction after Chékhov: Andréyev," in his* A History of Russian Literature, *edited by Francis J. Whitefield (copyright 1926, 1927, 1949, © 1958 by Alfred A. Knopf, Inc.; reprinted by permission of Alfred A. Knopf, Inc.), revised edition, Knopf, 1955, pp. 394-401.*

RUTH DAVIES   (essay date 1968)

During his lifetime Andreyev's fame probably depended more on his plays than on his stories. More recently, however, the plays have been nearly forgotten—bloodless relics of a period almost lost in oblivion. They usually deal, even in the several attempts at realism, with destruction or negation. Their subject matter is repetitious, their effect impotent. They have none of the sense of life with which the dramas of Chekhov are charged to quivering intensity. Andreyev apparently had no talent for integrating scenes

into a powerful dramatic structure or for creating memorable and individualized characters. The confused symbolism is an external manifestation of the inner darkness of the plays. Still, they have some authenticity as interpretations of the alienation of the intelligentsia, who had nothing to substitute for their lost faith. The catastrophe Dostoevsky feared had come to pass. Divorced from their belief in man and God, the intellectuals had become Nihilists, atheists, dilettantes, and lost souls. The only one of the plays widely known in America, *He Who Gets Slapped,* is actually one of the least interesting. But the title is a fitting clue to Andreyev's concept of man. "He" gets slapped by other people and by various dark forces "he" cannot name. "He" hides an anguished spirit behind the grease-painted mask-face of a clown. Andreyev's characters often belong to the fraternity of the dispossessed. They are the precursors of those who are waiting for Godot—or just waiting. Existential man peers forth from the eyes of most of them. (pp. 349-50)

The detachment and spiritual decadence of the wealthy and the intellectual and the reaching upward of the poor, who would not continue forever to endure their suffering—these are the recurring themes in the dramas of Andreyev which give their author claim to attention as a commentator during the first decade of the twentieth century in Russia.

More memorable than any of the dramas and more clearly related to the outline of the future are two of Andreyev's narratives [*The Red Laugh* and *The Seven That Were Hanged*]. Both added immensely to the author's prestige at the time of their publication. From the vantage point of more than half a century later they are interesting chiefly because of the accuracy of their prophecy. Although it would be an exaggeration to attribute to Andreyev the prophetic insight of Dostoevsky, the fact remains that these two narratives were heavy with portent. They offered a preview of two of the primary phenomena of the present century. (pp. 350-51)

> *Ruth Davies, "Interim: Andreyev and 'The Red Laugh'," in her* The Great Books of Russia *(copyright 1968 by the University of Oklahoma Press), University of Oklahoma Press, 1968, pp. 346-63.*

JAMES B. WOODWARD   (essay date 1969)

Regarded by the majority of his contemporaries as one of Russia's most original and talented writers, Andreyev displayed in his works almost from the outset an overriding preoccupation with problems of an abstract, philosophical nature and an artistic method or technique which at once distinguished him from other writers of the period. To no one else could the term 'realist', in the conventional sense of the term, be applied so inappropriately. Indeed, not the least of Andreyev's claims to our attention is the leading role which he played in promoting and reinforcing a counterbalancing romantic element in Russian narrative fiction and drama of the early twentieth century. (p. v)

Almost from the beginning his works show a dualistic conception of reality, a polarization of metaphysical unity and harmony and phenomenal diversity and discord. (p. 29)

His belief in the existence of an ulterior, truer reality beyond the concrete reality in which we live certainly gave him an affinity with so undoubted a mystic as Maeterlinck; moreover, an undeniably mystical element manifests itself in his works from 1899 (*The Grand Slam*) onward. But decidedly uncharacteristic of Andreyev is the mystic's spiritual self-withdrawal from contingent life; on the contrary, his overriding concern is always with the *malaise* of the contingent world, with the detachment of the 'first reality' from the ulterior unity and harmony, with the reconciliation of man and nature, consciousness and unconsciousness. (p. 30)

It was Andreyev's belief that if man is to achieve well-being and spiritual freedom in his empirical life he must live in obedience to the promptings of his subconscious, which is possible only if he is aware of its infinitely superior wisdom to that of his intellect—in short, if he recognizes his own subconscious as part of the spirit which informs the whole of nature, and thought as merely a faculty of his ephemeral individuality. (p. 31)

It was [Andreyev's] first concern, however, to unmask the monstrosity of bourgeois life, to display to his readers the chains with which they bound themselves, and to trace for them the consequences of their actions. (p. 46)

[Andreyev's first fictional portrayal of a 'fugitive from life' is the civil servant Andrey Nikolaevich, the protagonist of *By the Window*,] who sits out his days by the window of his room, rarely trespassing beyond its threshold. . . . The self-incarceration of the hero signifies an attempt to escape from the element of 'accidentality' in life, from life as a multitude of unforeseeable combinations of events. (pp. 46-7)

In his work as a civil servant, which involves the mechanical repetition of identical functions, and in the stereotyped pattern of a life spent at his window Andrey Nikolaevich feels himself to be master of the situation. Every healthy impulse, every warm sentiment and pleasant sensation he meets . . . with the destructive questions: Why? Whence? What will come of it? But though he succeeds in reducing his conscious life to a rigid circle of experience, his subconscious perpetually disturbs his peace with demands which find no gratification within this circle. . . . His stifled instincts call for life and shatter his peace of mind with recollections of the one romance in his life, the fields, mown hay and the red disc of the moon. The work is punctuated with notes of alarm denoting the author's hostility to his hero, his determination to allow him no rest. . . . The story begins and ends, for example, with the detail of the flapping shutter on the other side of the street, which repeatedly breaks the silence. This simple detail is symbolic of the whole 'idea' of the work. Again, particularly disturbing for Andrey Nikolaevich is the time when the painters and carpenters proceed to transform the appearance of the aristocratic dwelling directly opposite his window, the centrepiece of his artificial cosmos, thus destroying momentarily his faith in the calculability of his vista. . . . In many of his early stories Andreyev . . . made it his task precisely to instil this note of alarm into the world of the 'depersonified' fugitive from life. (pp. 47-8)

The contrast between reality and the barely hinted ideal is present in one form or another in most of [the] early stories of Andreyev. . . . The transcendence of egoism usually reveals itself in one of two inseparably related forms: in simple altruism or in attachment to a large, abstract, supraindividualistic unit. Those works which pivot on simple acts of altruism . . . inevitably seem sentimental; there is a distinct artificiality, for instance, in the coincidence of the

'resurrections' of Garas'ka and Kacherin, the hero of *A Holiday* . . ., with the Easter festival. . . . [It] should still be noted that altruism and respect for man were implicit in [Andreyev's] whole philosophical conception of life. (pp. 56-7)

[By] 1902 Andreyev had described the entire arc which extends from the social-psychological *malaise* of 'depersonification' through individualistic rebellion to the transcendence of narrow individualism and resultant reconciliation with life. This arc is a prefiguration in miniature of the whole chronological development of his thought as expressed in his fiction. Conspicuous is the artistic inferiority of those works of this early period in which acts of altruism and self-transcendence constitute the philosophical and thematic nucleus; Andreyev was subsequently to refer to them with contempt. (p. 58)

Though Andreyev was not saturated with European culture as the symbolists were, . . . he was by no means unacquainted with the foreign sources of 'modernism'—in particular, idealistic philosophy. . . . But the conception of the function of form with which he entered literature remained basically unaffected by these influences throughout his literary career. Though his works are rich in metaphor and evocative devices, the formal element never becomes one with the idea which it clothes in the sense in which such a fusion was understood by the symbolists. He never creates symbols in the narrow, specific, symbolistic sense of the term. (pp. 123-24)

[For example, Andreyev's purpose in the play *The Life of Man* was neither to probe into the 'mystery of life', nor to portray a 'universal man',] although Man is indeed in his creator's view representative of the overwhelming majority. The playwright had a specific type of man in mind—the man who describes the 'circle of iron predestination', the man who recognizes nothing higher than the dictates of his individual will and regards life as a war of individual wills, each seeking to subdue the other in the quest for personal well-being. . . . The capital letter with which the name of the protagonist begins is an indication not so much of universality as of Andreyev's conviction of the prevalence of the pattern of life which he presents in schematic form and of the scope of his indictment. For the greater part of the play his Man emerges as a generalization of the outstanding type produced by contemporary Russian and European society. . . . [The] life of Man is not a generalization of life, but a 'crude carcase' of true life. . . . (pp. 152-53)

[Similarly, the dominant motif of *He Who Gets Slapped*] is the contrast and antipathy between 'here' and 'there', the circus and the world without, which are identified respectively with talent and culture. Throughout the work the antithesis has distinct moral implications, talent being associated with innocence and culture with corruption. Within the circus company itself Andreyev distinguishes between varying degrees of spiritual proximity to 'here'. . . . The happiest are those who live in ignorance of the existence of the outside world, those whose minds are uninfected by the 'contagion' of books. . . . (p. 249)

From 'there' suddenly appears 'He' with the plea that he be accepted in the circus as a clown. Greeted as a being from an alien and hostile world, as a 'phantom', he eventually gains his wish by the sheer force of his enthusiasm and is allotted the role of the clown whom the other clowns slap.

His real identity is never disclosed, though we learn that he is an intellectual of renown. The significance of and motives for his action do not become completely clear until mid-way through the play, when he is confronted by 'The Man', the embodiment of the quintessence of 'there'. 'He', we discover, comes to the circus robbed by 'The Man' not only of his wife, but also of his ideas, which have been vulgarized for popular consumption. Culture is branded as the vulgarization of talent. Moreover, the mere existence of talent is a source of profound embarrassment to the purveyors of culture, and 'The Man' implores 'He' to vow that he will never return 'there'. 'He's' agreement to this request carries the same force as the curse of Man.

Various attempts have been made to understand the symbolic significance of the role which 'He' performs as a clown. Sologub took it to be symbolic of the act of Christ: 'He who gets slapped,' he writes, 'has taken on himself . . . the sinfulness of the world.' Alternatively, Andreyev might have had in mind the 'underground man's' words on the particular kind of pleasure to be derived from humiliation. . . . Andreyev, however, does not appear to be plumbing these psychological depths; he seems to interpret the role of his hero as a form of vengeance. . . . The submission of 'He' to the slaps of his fellow clowns is a parody of his fate in the external world, a parody of the profanation of his ideas. Society's rejection of his ideas signifies its rejection of those principles which could ennoble and enrich its life; thus, in essence, he is presenting his audience with the spectacle of their profanation of their own lives. (pp. 249-50)

Certainly, Andreyev's frequent inability to combine abstraction with convincing motivation is one of his main weaknesses as a writer, . . . but this very inability is merely further testimony to his overriding preoccupation with abstract, metaphysical concepts. There is no exaggeration in the claim that ideas as such acquire in his fiction a prominence unsurpassed in the works of any other writer of his generation, not only serving as the point of departure in his creative process, but also investing the seemingly discordant mass of his work with an unusually consistent inner unity. (pp. 276-77)

[Andreyev must] be regarded as a wholly unique figure in the literary life of his times. Identifiable with none of the numerous contemporary literary groups, he followed his own independent path with remarkable perseverance, and the solitude which he continually lamented was the price which he paid for it. Yet no less remarkable, as stated, is the degree to which he summed up in his person and in his art so much that was typical of the age in which he lived. The isolation and rootlessness of the intellectual in contemporary Russian society, the intrinsic perils of a predominantly rationalistic culture, the inevitable bankruptcy of an assertive individualistic philosophy of life, the irreconcilability of abstract ideals and mundane reality, the relation of man to his neighbour and to the universe as a whole—these are the problems to which his thoughts were constantly directed, problems which had inspired some of the best-known works of nineteenth-century Russian literature, but which from the turn of the century to 1917 acquired an unparalleled ascendancy in Russian intellectual life. And the level of abstraction to which he raised them was in itself symptomatic of that renewed concern with the metaphysical, as distinct from the social-political, dimension of life

which was an important contributing factor in the birth of Russian symbolism and in the general renaissance of art and letters in the two decades before the Revolution, and which, tragically for the future of Russian literature, proved incompatible with Bolshevik aesthetics. The excitement and controversy which greeted almost his every work is evidence of the extent to which Andreyev was inwardly attuned to the spirit of his times. Nor was this a case, as hostile critics have claimed, of a writer pandering to popular taste, for the most salient features of Andreyev's mature art . . . [are] apparent in his earliest stories. He wrote in the only way he knew how on the subjects which dominated his attention, and thereby provided a generation with one of its most representative and intriguing voices. (pp. 278-79)

James B. Woodward, in his Leonid Andreyev: A Study *(© Oxford University Press 1969; reprinted by permission of Oxford University Press), Oxford University Press, Oxford, 1969, 290 p.*

JOSEPHINE M. NEWCOMBE   (essay date 1973)

[It is] common in Andreyev's stories for the hero not to be able to achieve any sort of escape from his isolation and unhappiness, and this is one reason why critics soon began to call Andreyev a pessimist, although there is no evidence that he held the view that suffering was inevitable—a way out is usually implied. (p. 26)

Andreyev is more concerned with expressing the intensity of his characters' experience, and by placing them in extreme situations, he tests them. If they prove themselves to be weak, it is partly the fault of society for not equipping them to deal with these situations and partly a failure to understand the force of the unconscious part of their minds. (p. 38)

Andreyev was always sincere in his attempts to bring home to his readers the dangers he thought they were facing. He chose fantastic or horrible situations and dramatic, hyperbolic language in order to convey his passionately held beliefs to the reader. He may be considered a precursor of the expressionist movement, which rebelled against conventional descriptions in literature and painting, seeking a fresh, new inner vision. (p. 105)

Josephine M. Newcombe, in her Leonid Andreyev *(copyright © 1972, 1973 by Josephine M. Newcombe), Frederick Ungar Publishing Co., 1973, 118 p.*

HAROLD B. SEGEL   (essay date 1979)

A Neo-Romantic only marginally related to the Symbolists . . . , Andreev succeeded where the Symbolists failed at devising a theatrically plausible and at times even effective type of allegorical rather than symbolistic "cosmic" drama that demonstrates perhaps better than the plays of any of his contemporaries the impact on Russian drama of Maeterlinck's ideas on static drama and metaphysical tragedy (which Andreev later repudiated). (p. 78)

[*The Life of Man*] deserves to be considered a high-water mark of Russian dramatic symbolism, although Andreev's detractors have been quick to dismiss it as inflated and pretentious. Andreev, to be sure, is often overblown and pretentious in his "philosophical" plays; but in the case of *The Life of Man* the overly negative assessment is the result, to a great extent, of a common misinterpretation of the play as a derivative Maeterlinckian tragedy in allegorical style about the universal human condition.

In five acts undivided into scenes, Andreev dramatizes his conception of the five periods of a common—if not necessarily universal—life cycle: birth (I), marriage and the hardships of a beginning career (II), success and fame (III), misfortune and decline (IV), and death (V). The vision of man's earthly sojourn is personal and grim yet consonant with the Neo-Romantic *Weltanschauung:* there is no pleasure that is not accompanied or followed by pain, no attainment without loss. The joy of birth is tempered by the terrible pains of the mother in labor; the happiness of love and marriage is offset by the misery of poverty; success brings fame and riches but also sycophantic fawning and envy; worldly success and material wealth are followed by failure and loss . . . , death, when it finally comes to Man himself, claims its victim in loneliness and despair. And beyond death, what? Andreev is silent. (p. 80)

Light sets the mood of the play; a chiaroscuro extends from the synoptic Prologue to the final curtain. Figures move from darkness or a grayness into a dim, hazy light, or into the flickering light of a candle or, conversely, from bright warm light into an ever encroaching darkness. Apart from the second act, when Man and his wife early in their marriage take refuge from the reality of their poverty in a game-and flower-filled private world of dreams and illusions, the stiff, jerky, puppetlike movements of the characters correspond to the artificial, highly stylized rhythms of the language. This is best seen in Act III when Andreev uses a ball scene, with music and dance, to convey the sumptuousness of Man's life style after the attainment of material success and the shallowness and insincerity of personal relationships. (p. 81)

[Many critics have made an] erroneous reading of *The Life of Man* as a universal statement of the human condition; through the character of Man, it was believed, Andreev sought to generalize all human life experience. Not only that, but in view of the somberness and pessimism of the play it was assumed that Andreev intended a repudiation of life itself. By failing to appreciate that in *The Life of Man* Andreev is not repudiating man himself, that is *being,* but a certain quality of life, a life style, the entire ethos, in fact, of bourgeois philistinism, his critics simply missed the point of the work. In a Schopenhauerian sense, Andreev does depict man's life on earth as forever accompanied by pain and misery, forever doomed to frustration in its quest for the fulfillment of all desires. But Andreev's gloom is qualified. Man is capable of rebellion: he can rise up against a universal pattern of life and its values and assert his dignity and even nobility as man through rebellion, whatever the outcome. . . .

In [a] long letter to Andreev about *The Life of Man* Gorky mentions the old women of Act I reminding him of Maeterlinck's *The Intruder.* (p. 83)

The association works up to a point. Andreev was certainly no less susceptible to the Belgian's influence than most of the other dramatists of his time who were inclined to symbolism. But a play such as *The Life of Man,* whatever the Maeterlinckian reminiscences, cannot be defined merely by reference to the type of dramaturgy for which Maeterlinck won greatest renown. Andreev shares with the Belgian a generally pessimistic view of life. Death figures prominently in the plays of both. Language—and often gesture—are stylized, and light, sound, and silence are important in establishing a quality of mood. But Andreev goes beyond the evocation of the mystery and dread of unseen and unknowable forces, beyond the sinister insinuation of the presence of death. *The Life of Man* is a dramatic symbol of a way of life repugnant to Andreev for its essential debasement of the inherent dignity of man. The somberness and pervasive mood of Maeterlinckian drama realize Andreev's point of view, but resemblance vaporizes beyond this level. (pp. 83-4)

Generally speaking, the Neo-Romantics disdained subjects drawn from contemporary life. They were either hostile or indifferent to the society around them and they preferred to look to the classical past, to the Middle Ages, to the Romantic era, to distant, exotic cultures, or to their own dreams and fantasies, rather than at the real, everyday world. Their repudiation of realism and naturalism and their quest for new forms of dramatic expression tended to militate against plays with contemporary settings.

There were exceptions, of course, and Neo-Romantic plays set in the late nineteenth and early twentieth centuries did appear from time to time. (p. 118)

One Russian Neo-Romantic dramatist whose *oeuvre* includes several plays with contemporary settings was Leonid Andreev. . . . While all of these plays have caused misunderstanding and controversy, the one which has endured and has become something of an international classic is *He Who Gets Slapped.* It is the only play of Andreev's many that a reader may sometime actually have a chance to see on a stage. (pp. 118-19)

We have here a familiar Neo-Romantic situation involving a sensitive person who is infringed upon and finally overwhelmed by a less sensitive and less scrupulous person, someone, in short, whom the author uses to represent the hypocrisy and venality of bourgeois society. . . . He seeks only a temporary and imperfect refuge in the circus, where for the moment he can strike back at the society he has fled through the character he has assumed, the clown who is slapped. The slaps he receives represent a grotesque reenactment of the real plunder of his personal dignity. However, by his reaction to the slaps in the arena, he returns the humiliation to the public itself. Symbolically, the public, here representing the other world, is connected with the ultimate responsibility for He's dispossession, flight, and self-abasement. But the satisfaction this provides He is brief; the refuge of the circus is illusory and finally He takes his own life.

From the beginning of *He Who Gets Slapped* Andreev's pessimism is inescapable. The world depicted is one in which there is no escape from the crass, the vulgar, and the hypocritical. Actually, the circus in which He seeks a haven is a microcosm of the society beyond; both are filled with pettiness, materialism, banality, and squabbling. (p. 121)

Although myth and circus combine in *He Who Gets Slapped* to produce a theatrically appealing work and one of the most durable plays of the Russian Neo-Romantics as a whole, the pervasive pessimism of the work must be noted. Although outwardly escapist, *He Who Gets Slapped* should perhaps best be regarded as a refutation of the notion of escape, as a dramatization of the futility of escape. . . .

With *He Who Gets Slapped*, Andreev appears to oppose the romantic-escapist trend within neo-romanticism by showing the futility of flight. What makes the pessimism of the play so striking is not simply that its subject is the death of nobility and beauty, but that the theme of inescapability from society is etched with such venom. That nobility and beauty perish by poison in *He Who Gets Slapped* is no mere coincidence; to Andreev the other world acts on whatever comes within its grasp like a poison spreading throughout the whole system. (p. 123)

> *Harold B. Segel, "The Revolt against Naturalism: Symbolism, Neo-Romanticism, and Theatricalism," in his* Twentieth-Century Russian Drama: From Gorky to the Present *(copyright © 1979 Columbia University Press; reprinted by permission of the publisher), Columbia University Press, 1979, pp. 50-146.**

BIBLIOGRAPHY

Jackson, Robert Louis. "Leonid Andreyev and *Notes from the Underground*." In his *Dostoevsky's Underground Man in Russian Literature*, pp. 84-101. The Hague: Mouton & Co., 1958.
> Close study of several of Andreyev's stories which compares his protagonists to the protagonist of *Notes from the Underground*.

Kaun, Alexander. "The End of Andreyev." *The New Republic* XXVI, No. 395 (28 June 1922): 133-35.
> Brief examination of Andreyev's political opinions illustrated by extracts from his letters.

King, Henry Hall. *Dostoevsky and Andreyev: Gazers upon the Abyss*. Ithaca: The Cornell Alumni News Corp., 1936, 88 p.*
> Exhaustively catalogs the preoccupations of Andreyev's work and contrasts his pessimistic vision of life with Dostoevsky's optimistic one.

Shotton, M. H. Introduction to *Selected Stories*, by Leonid Andreev, pp. 5-16. Letchworth, England: Bradda Books, 1969.
> Largely negative assessment of Andreyev's stylistic and thematic inconsistencies, which finds his greatest stories to be those that most nearly approximate Chekhov's.

Turkevich, Ludmilla B. "Andreev and the Mask." *Russian Literature Triquarterly*, No. 7 (1973): 267-84.
> Study of Andreyev's use of masks including a close reading of *He Who Gets Slapped*.

Woodward, James B. "Devices of Emphasis and Amplification in the Style of Leonid Andreev." *Slavic and East European Journal* 9, No. 3 (1965): 247-56.
> Examination of Andreyev's use of rhetorical devices such as repetition.

Woodward, James B. "The Theme and Structural Significance of Leonid Andreev's *The Black Masks*." *Modern Drama* 10, No. 1 (May 1967): 95-103.
> Study of *The Black Masks* which views it as a dramatization of its protagonist's psychic conflict, after the manner of Poe's *The Haunted Palace* and *William Wilson*.

Guillaume Apollinaire

1880-1918

(Pseudonym of Wilhelm Apollinaris de Kostrowitzki; also Kostrowitski, or Kostrowitzky) French poet, dramatist, critic, short story writer, and novelist.

A quintessential modernist, Apollinaire was one of the most important poets of the early twentieth century. His career, despite its brevity, spanned such nineteenth-century literary movements as symbolism and such twentieth-century movements as surrealism and cubism. During various periods his work shows affinities with each of these movements. Apollinaire was, however, more than an artist formed by trends and traditions, for he himself helped to shape the modernist schools that followed him.

There is a significant relationship between Apollinaire's life and his work. According to most sources, he was born in Rome, the illegitimate son of a Polish mother, and spent much of his youth traveling around Europe before finally settling in Paris. With such a background he developed a cosmopolitan outlook and became fascinated with a variety of studies. His interest in art, for example, led to his becoming a significant critic and early promoter of the Cubists. He mixed with a bohemian group of artists including Picasso and Marcel Duchamp, and he became himself an offbeat model of the definitive bohemian. Apollinaire had always lived somewhere on the fringe of a stable society, and at one point he was unjustly imprisoned in connection with the theft of the *Mona Lisa*. This experience was expressed through a series of poems written during his incarceration, one example of the autobiographical element in his writing. Another example of the relationship between Apollinaire's art and life is the wartime poetry chronicling his duty at the front during World War I. After a head wound sent him back to Paris, Apollinaire saw the staging of his *Les mamelles de Tirésias*, which he called a *drame surréaliste*. This epithet was later adopted by the surrealists to describe their delirium-like approach to art and experience. Apollinaire's two major collections of poetry, *Alcools* and *Calligrammes*, also exhibit the experimental and enigmatical qualities that led the surrealists to claim him as one of their predecessors.

Undoubtedly, the most outstanding characteristic of Apollinaire was his constant vitality and consequent willingness to take risks. It is perhaps this spirit that makes Apollinaire's name synonymous with literary innovation.

PRINCIPAL WORKS

L'Enchanteur pourrissant   (short stories)   1909
L'Hérésiarque et cie   (short stories)   1910
  [*The Heresiarch and Co.*, 1965; published in England as
  The Wandering Jew, and Other Stories, 1967]
Le Bestiaire; ou, Cortège d'Orphée   (poetry)   1911
Alcools: Pòemes, 1898-1913   (poetry)   1913
  [*Alcools: Poems, 1898-1913*, 1964]
Méditations esthétiques: Les Peintres cubistes   (art
  criticism)   1913
  [*The Cubist Painters: Aesthetic Meditations, 1913*, 1944]
Le Poète assassiné   (novel)   1916
  [*The Poet Assassinated*, 1923]
Vitam impedere amori: Poèmes et dessins   (poetry)   1917
*Calligrammes: Poèmes de la paix et de la guerre (1913-
  1916)*   (poetry)   1918
  [*Calligrams*, 1970]
L'Esprit nouveau et les poètes   (essay)   1918
*Les Mamelles de Tirésias: Drame surréaliste en deux actes
  et un prologue*   (drama)   1918
  [*The Breasts of Tiresias* published in journal *Odyssey*,
  1961]
La Femme assise   (novel)   1920
Il y a   (poetry)   1925
Les Onze mille verges   (novel)   1948
  [*The Debauched Hospodar*, 1953]
Couleur de temps: Drame en trois actes et en vers
  (drama)   1949

(essay date 1924)

This Rabelaisian extravaganza in prose [*The Poet Assassinated*] by one of the most important of modern French poets begins better than it ends. The procreation, gestation, birth, and education of the hero Croniamantal are narrated with superb spirit, but his later quarrels with relatively insignificant Parisian poets do not make very exciting reading this many miles away from the Seine. On the whole, however, an amusing and reckless book by a diabolically gifted writer.

"*Books in Brief: 'The Poet Assassinated'*," *in* The Nation (*copyright 1924 The Nation Associates,*

Inc.), Vol. CXVIIII, No. 3066, April 9, 1924, p. 404.

MALCOLM COWLEY (essay date 1924)

There is no attempt to present [Croniamantal in "The Poet Assassinated"] as a real person, for Apollinaire wrote the novel as a defiance to all the conventions of realism. He detested the sort of book which recounts the adventures of mean people in a mean way and of which the ultimate praise is to call it just as tiresome as the life it represents. When a character of Apollinaire's grew boring he killed the man promptly. When narration wearied him, he introduced dramatic dialogue, investing birds and fountains with speech. He swung backwards and forwards in time, and returned suddenly from centuries to make the inhabitants of salon or bordello repeat their accustomed words; or rather their words made emptier, more vapid than in life, for even where he has the air of describing faithfully Apollinaire is never realistic, but a super-realist. One reads him to be amused and surprised.

When he was first published one read him to be frightened or to imitate. The influence of "The Poet Assassinated" is one explanation of why a whole generation of French writers have taken to writing novels in which facts are sacrificed to imagination and fantasy. [Jean Giraudoux, Paul Morand, Joseph Delteil, André Salmon] . . . owe a considerable debt to the book which Apollinaire compiled during the war out of the legend he wished to perpetuate and the fragments of a score of novels he had outlined during his youth. . . .

Unlike Apollinaire's poems ("Alcools" and "Calligrammes"), ["The Poet Assassinated"] fails of being a great book. It will, however, continue to be read when more pretentious volumes are forgotten.

Malcolm Cowley, "St. Apollinaire," in Literary Review, *Vol. 4, No. 43, June 21, 1924, p. 835.*

ROGER SHATTUCK (essay date 1948)

The amazing reputation of Apollinaire—and its frequent inaccuracy and one-sidedness—require that any evaluation of him as a poet be very carefully made. He is probably the first truly European poet since Goethe, and his spirit and his work is widely known on the continent from which he drew his themes. His poems are never content to speak of France alone; their prophecies and conversations and descriptions are of all Europe. But his reputation seldom encompasses the whole man. He is known as the sensitive lyric poet, as the mystifying entertainer who could twist verse to his own unpredictable purposes, or as an erratic Paris bohemian. None of these is complete.

[The evaluation of his poetry according to the standard of a tension between mystery and clarity] gives him considerable stature as a poet. Clarity resides in the uncomplicated mechanics of his composition and in the familiarity of the objects to which he turned his sensibilities in order to transform them. The mystery resides in the world of new unities and relationships, of fresh experiences, which this transformation produced, and in the conviction with which he presented that world as real. It is the world he would teach us to inhabit. The descriptions he gives us of Paris, of Europe, of love, of war, and of all of life are clear in the realism of their detail; however, from the unobserved intervals between these details emanates the aura of magic and meta-

morphosis to which Apollinaire was so sensitive. This tension is most delicately established in his best poems: "Un Fantóme de Nuées", "Crépuscule", "Le Pont Mirabeau", "Saltimbanques", and sections from "Zone", "La Chanson du Mal-Aimé", "Les Collines", and "Le Bestiaire". One learns from a reading of these poems that physical reality is not a limit for the senses. It is rather a kind of screen, beautiful but really impalpable, through which we can pass to find unpredictable wonders beyond.

It is helpful in examining the submerged aspects of Apollinaire's work to consider the concept of *distortion*. . . . By distortion I mean any representation which violates the conventions upon which traditional representation is based. In an absolute sense any representation, any work of art, is a distortion of the world. However, by becoming accustomed to conventions of painting . . . and of poetry . . . , we accept as normal what are nevertheless artificial representations of nature. (pp. 47-8)

Apollinaire used distortion in order to include in one composition the states of gaiety and despair which alternately resulted from his quest for himself. In making this combination he took the final step toward discovering himself. Ordinary poetic images could not transform the world sufficiently for it to carry the meaning he desired. Therefore, in the natural fecundity of his imagination, he cultivated and arrived at surrealist distortion. By this means he surpassed in certain poems the intermittences of his emotions and combined the tragic and the comic into a new awareness where we feel the pull of both poles. It is not a hesitation between the two, not an indecision. It is so positive and so forceful an assertion of both attitudes that their contradictions fuse into fresh values. Apollinaire's particular technique of distortion . . . [encompasses] the animation of dead objects, the defiance of time and place, the most rash and distant of associations, and the gratuitous combination of things in order to produce unforeseen meanings. The usual logic both of reason and of our feelings is put aside in order to find the value of paradox insisted upon so tenaciously that it becomes a simple, positive fact. (p. 49)

Magic recurs a great deal, its incantations, the names of its great figures, and above all its supernatural powers of divination, resuscitation, conjuring, changing of appearance, and the like. But more than magic, mysticism is the tone of surrealism to which Apollinaire gave strong impetus. The absurd elements of the world are picked out to demonstrate their relevance to the understanding life. In physical objects and relationships are found all the enchantment and inspiration of supernatural belief. It becomes increasingly clear that Apollinaire felt no need or inclination to posit "another world" to which living spirits attain. Rather the material world itself, if manipulated and exploited to the full without the restraints normally observed upon absurdity, contradiction, and paradox, contains all the mystic promise of the future and of timelessness. (pp. 49-50)

The bravura association of physical objects will always extend the dimensions of the world, and it is according to this principle that we must approach the casual composition of Apollinaire's "poèmes conversations". They are similar to the automatic writing in works like *Les Champs Magnétiques* which Breton and Soupault were to produce in a few years. They also anticipate the methods of surrealist painters like Tanguy, Seligmann, Ernst, and especially de Chirico (before 1920) and Dali. With the utmost clarity and meticulousness of painting technique they describe objects whose juxtaposition is both absurd and mysteriously suggestive. The emotional content of these poems is either nil or, if the spectator finds he can respond, explosive. (p. 50)

I am stressing Apollinaire's surrealist solution of the modern quest for identity because it seems to have been far more satisfying than his brief acceptance of other roles and because it is important in its influence on subsequent developments in literature. Literary exploration today too often is unable to escape the ageing principles of surrealism. Before we can pass beyond the meshes of this doctrine, it must be thoroughly understood and assimilated. Apollinaire's boldly affirmative solution of the question which haunts all modern artists provides an early manifestation of surrealism where its qualities are still pure. In answer to the question: Who am I? he states that he is not only what he chooses to be or what he thinks himself to be, but also everything that he is shown to be by dream and hazard and past and future and every object in the physical world. (pp. 51-2)

> *Roger Shattuck, "Apollinaire, Hero-Poet" (1948), in* Selected Writings of Guillaume Apollinaire *by Guillaume Apollinaire, translated by Roger Shattuck (copyright © 1971 by Roger Shattuck; all rights reserved; reprinted by permission of New Directions Publishing Corporation),* New Directions, *1950, pp. 3-54.*

C. M. BOWRA   (essay date 1949)

Apollinaire's unerring eye for the right means to a given end can be seen from his use of metres. At a time when *vers libre* was widely vaunted, he kept his head and used both old and new metres, allowing his subject to dictate the rhythm which was best suited to it. The result is that he is a master of most forms from classical alexandrines to long unrhymed lines of varying rhythm. In each case we can almost see why he chooses a form and why, having begun with it, he changes to another. When he writes in impeccable alexandrines, he speaks solemnly with an air of dignity and needs the resources of authority behind him. In shorter metres, especially in a regular five-lined stanza in which the third and fifth lines rhyme with the first, he conveys the play of his mind as it turns round a subject and looks at it from different angles. At times he even bursts into lyrical song, as in the ravishingly melancholy *Le Pont Mirabeau,* and, more artfully, in *Les Saisons* where a haunting refrain breaks the realism and solemnity of the heavier, more formal verses. When he felt the need for free verse, he indulged it inventively. (p. 67)

Apollinaire's vocabulary shows the same care and delicacy as his choice of rhythms. He did not invent new words or revive obsolete ones. If at times he uses words of Greek origin like "pyraustes", "argyraspides", or "dendrophores", it is exceptional and no doubt rises from his love of recondite information. Normally he writes with exceptional ease and clarity, goes straight to the point and has the rare gift of saying all that he wants so succinctly that it seems impossible to say it otherwise. But the wonder of this ease is that is so full of poetry. The plain statements are charged with intense significance: there is no suspicion of artificial simplicity. (p. 68)

Apollinaire found no difficulty in expressing his thoughts and feelings by appropriate images. He was quick to notice resemblances between one thing and another and turn such relations to immediate profit. The boy who had thought of the ascending Christ as a bird or an aeroplane grew into a man who was never at a loss to make his meaning vivid through some unexpected and apt comparison. In his earlier poems this gift sometimes leads to strange results. Apollinaire seems not always to have cared what an image was so long as it was surprising and reasonably appropriate, and, partly inspired by a desire to shock, he allowed himself an occasional indulgence which detracts from the gravity of his work. (p. 70)

It is a small step from imagery to myth, from conveying one aspect of a situation to portraying a whole situation in a mythical tale which emphasises its essential character. By throwing into the objective form of a story something which he knows in himself, Apollinaire suggests that it has a much wider significance. Wherever he found his myths, he set so new a character on them that their origins are of little importance. Once, for instance, he drew on the Arthurian cycle, and wrote *Merlin et la vieille Femme,* in which the ostensible subject is Merlin's love for Vivian and the effect which this has on him when he remembers it by an accident in old age. The story becomes the myth of the creative life. We may need love and win it, but more powerful than love is the sudden violent memory of it, the chance return of an apparently lost moment in a flood of inspiring beauty.... [All] Apollinaire's myths have their own existence and their own appeal as stories—so full are they of delicate observations and life—but their special strength is that through the interest which they arouse they call to wider and less noticed issues which are his fundamental concern. (pp. 74-5)

[In] Apollinaire's work, there are many startling effects. He seems to have written in a frenzy of creative energy, and a first reading does not suggest that he took much care about construction. No great effort is needed to understand him, but his details are so provocative that we may think that Apollinaire was no great architect in building a poem. Actually he was more careful than is often admitted. He built his verses into fine patterns and shaped quite long poems out of them, so that even when he seems to be at his most ecstatic he is really in control of his material and imposes a noble order on it. (p. 75)

In *La Chanson du Mal-Aimé* Apollinaire's youthful gifts found their finest form. There is not a line in it which is not indubitably poetry and does not shine with a peculiar radiance. Though Apollinaire does not explain the situation and often passes unexpectedly from one image or idea to another, there is no real obscurity. Each image and each idea stands out so clearly that we know at once what it means to him. The words are all perfectly familiar, except when Apollinaire wishes them to be unusual, and even then they cause no trouble. There is a great concentration of power in the short sentences, and each achieves its own kind of effect. Indeed there seem to be few effects which Apollinaire cannot achieve.... His comparisons of himself to characters so varied as the burghers of Calais or the prince-regent of Bavaria may astonish us, but they fit with perfect ease into his varied, vivid pattern. Into this poem Apollinaire flung the riches of his reading and his observation, and it remains a consummate masterpiece in which a regular, carefully considered form encloses an experience deeply felt and seen with the full resources of a powerful imagination. (pp. 79-80)

[While in prison] Apollinaire composed *A la Santé,* in which six short poems maintain all his style and elegance as he laments his fate. If we compare these with what Verlaine wrote in prison, we see how much closer Apollinaire was to ordinary life, how intimately his surroundings affected him and what significance he found in the routine of prison. The stripping of his clothes, the daylight coming past the bars, the sound of footsteps overhead, the daily walk in the yard, a fly on the wall, and the noises from the world outside, all touch him with a poignant intimacy and stress the horror of his isolation. There is no rhetoric in this poetry. Apollinaire notes what happens and shows what meanings it has for him.

Deep though Apollinaire's distress was, it did not prevent him from writing with his usual balance or from discovering moments of illumination in his plight. (p. 84)

His experience at the front [in World War I] helped Apollinaire to advance his technique and use imagery in a new way suited to his new surroundings. War creates a dual personality in those who take part in it. On the one hand, it is always and insistently present. There is no escape from the abnormal conditions which it imposes on its victims. On the other hand, in it the soldier's thoughts turn inevitably to what is normal and familiar, to his affections and his loves at home. In this double condition his thoughts are shot simultaneously by vivid recollections of home and by an awareness no less vivid of his present state: the themes of the one life are inextricably mingled with the themes of the other. Apollinaire understood this dual state; for it was his own. No one appreciated more keenly the life which he had left behind him in Paris or the strange, unnatural existence which war forced on him. Sometimes he portrays it quite simply, as in *Simultanéités,* where a German prisoner enters the French lines with all his thoughts on his mistress, or in *Un Oiseau chante,* where Apollinaire hears a bird singing and imagines that is the soul of his Madeleine awakening. From such simple beginnings he moves to more elaborate effects. . . . [By] use of imagery Apollinaire identifies one set of experiences in his divided self with another and shows how the scene of war penetrates his thoughts of love and is transformed by them into something more significant.

This method opened the way to new successes. The violence of battle is identified with the violence of love, and in *Chef de Section* Apollinaire uses the language of the attack to stress the power of his passion. . . . This is the way in which the poet who is also a soldier turns his experiences to profit. It is more than a metaphor: it is the reflection of a dual state of mind. (pp. 88-9)

What Apollinaire gives in his poetry is not in the least narrow or affected or esoteric. Of all poets in this century he is perhaps the closest to natural man in his straightforward love of simple things and his delighted acceptance of what life has to offer. Whether he writes about love or war or Parisian life, he shares the tastes of other men, and his special claim is that he interprets their feelings with the intensity of genius and so transforms experience into something new and extraordinarily exciting. (p. 92)

> C. M. Bowra, *"Order and Adventure in Guillaume Apollinaire,"* in his The Creative Experiment *(reprinted by permission of Macmillan, London and Basingstoke), Macmillan, 1949, pp. 61-93.*

WALLACE FOWLIE   (essay date 1950)

[Apollinaire's poetry] is fantasy in the deepest sense of the word. It is lawful fantasy: its images rightfully conceal and communicate at the same time the emotions he experienced.

His poetic fantasy was, first, that of revolt, by which he always remained precious and close to the surrealists. He broke with the familiar patterns of thought, with the poetic clichés and literariness of the Parnassians and Symbolists, and with the familiar units and rules of syntax. His poetry comes together in a great freedom of composition, as if he allowed the images and emotions to compose themselves. In his poetry, phantoms, wanderers, mythic characters bearing sonorous names, appear and disappear as the laws of syntax and prosody do. His verse is not literary in any strict sense, and in that, he marks a revolt against the poetic research and endeavor of the entire preceding period. (p. 88)

It was quite appropriate that Apollinaire, coming after the highly self-conscious and studied literary school of symbolism, would, in rebellion against such artifice, seek to return to the most primitive sources of lyricism. I have a feeling that only because such a fully developed literary tradition was in him, as a part of his background, was he able to allow in his verse the seemingly spontaneous mixture of emotion and irony, of nostalgia and cynicism. Both by the form and content of his poetry, he seems to be making a kind of plea or defence for moral disorder, or moral relaxation. (p. 89)

The practical example of Apollinaire's poetry is a warning against the two most dangerous temptations of poetry, the two traps everlastingly set to stifle its life vigor: first, didacticism or moral preaching; and secondly, overconscious intent or exaggerated artifice. When poetry avoids these two pitfalls, as Apollinaire's does, it is able to become a complete and autonomous universe, capable of encircling us and assailing us. When we read this kind of poetry, we know that a world is being organized and constructed around us. It gradually becomes so ordered and achieved that we end by recognizing this new country and end by recognizing ourselves in it.

The universe of great poetry is always composed of passions and images: passions which are the experiences of suffering and therefore of knowing; and images which in their rhythmical form are the unique way a poet has to express his passion. Apollinaire's volume, *Alcools,* . . . is this kind of universe. The poems have the quality of folk-lore and fairy tales. . . . Critics have pointed out that Apollinaire is the only one of the major poets who never sounds the theme of mysticism, who, unlike a Péguy or a Claudel or an Eliot, seems impervious to the religious problem in any form. This critical statement seems to me too absolute because of the primitive mystical quality in magic. There is no true or matured mysticism in Apollinaire's poetry, that is certain, but the way between the mysterious and the mystical is not very far. The poet Apollinaire is like a mystical child, enchanted but not inspired, too humble and too fearful, too wondrously imaginative to consider or need the experience of religious ecstasy. (pp. 90-1)

In such a poem as *Zone* and the other earlier poems of Apollinaire which follow it in *Alcools,* one can sense the revolutionary use to which poetry is being put. The strong

19th century poetic tradition was hard to kill. Apollinaire opposed to its formalized emotion and rhetoric, a poetry of irony and paradox and indirectness. All the familiar childhood and religious nostalgia is still there in his poetry, but it is treated in a new freshness and humor. In referring, for example, to the Ascension of Christ, Apollinaire says that He goes up to the sky better than aviators. . . . (pp. 92-3)

The profoundest lesson of surrealism has to do with unity or unification, and Apollinaire's poetry may be considered a transcendent part of this lesson. A true poem, according to this doctrine, should reveal some aspect of the original unity of the universe. This seems to signify that poetry, which is created out of suffering (as the world itself was created out of chaos), preserves the memory of suffering (as the world preserves the memory of chaos), teaches man how to bear it and weaves a marvellous myth which then becomes a part of all the myths of mankind.

The surrealist is hereby stating a thesis not at all unfamiliar: that poetry is a method of knowledge, a way of knowing. . . . Apollinaire, without possessing the poetic genius of a Mallarmé or a Rimbaud, was very necessary in the unfolding of this poetic theory. He was able to bring poetry back from its Mallarmean hermeticism and Rimbaldian violence to tenderness and nostalgia, to the gentleness of the clown. With Apollinaire's period the clown became the most sensitive of the modern heroes, the living receptacle for all dramas, the hero who refused to see them as tragedies. The surrealist hero is visibly the clown. . . . (pp. 99-100)

> Wallace Fowlie, "Apollinaire: The Poet," in his Age of Surrealism *(copyright 1950 by Wallace Fowlie; copyright © 1960 by Indiana University Press; reprinted by permission of the author), The Swallow Press, Inc., 1950 (and reprinted by Indiana University Press, 1960, pp. 83-101).*

WARREN RAMSEY (essay date 1964)

Alcools is a remarkably ambitious book. Like the title itself, the longer and later poems show how much the author wanted to get into it: nothing less than the whole burden of poetic enthusiasm as expressed by Plato in the *Ion*. Apollinaire is inviting his readers to be drunken—on the spiritual air of Nietzschean high places. Better prepared and more resilient than Crane, if somewhat less intensely imaginative, Apollinaire came equally close to voicing the affirmations of a time. The mode is the psychological notation of the Rimbaldian Symbolists. . . . (p. xi)

Apollinaire cannot be said to have realized some revolutionary or Futurist dream of *pensers nouveaux* in verse. Such a task lay beyond even his capacities, and it was open to his misgivings. There is something heroically outsize about "Vendémiaire," with its debt to Whitman and the poetic mode that was being called Hegelian at about this time. Parts of the poem are a trifle too praiseful and all-encompassing to be quite convincing, except as a bold rhetorical conclusion to an important book. They suggest a kind of poetry Apollinaire might have written had he been a complete Cubo-Futurist. He was not, and we have the brief masterpieces, rather lower pitched.

A number of these are to be found in *Alcools*. Among the Romantic lyrics are "Cors de Chasse" and "Automne malade." "La Tzigane" and "Saltimbanques" renew late nineteenth-century themes in a way endlessly stimulating to twentieth-century readers and writers. "Marizibill" is another of the brief episodic poems finding the symmetries of a dramatic lyric. Its title, a sort of inspired exercise in phonetic spelling, brings the poem closer to the time and place of its conception by the change of a few letters (from "Marie-Sybille"). Here too, growing out of prison desolation, the end of the love affair with Marie Laurencin, and a medieval *chanson de toile,* is "Le Pont Mirabeau."

Equally to the poetic point are longer episodic poems. An early one, "Le Larron," with its Chorus, Thief, Old Man, and Actor, is an incipient parable play. Apollinaire is best remembered, however, for two other lines of development. Episodes are sometimes connected by a conceit, as in "Le Brasier" or "Les Fiançailles." The poet elaborates on the theme of casting previous selves into the crucible, toward discovery of an authentic self. Or he loafs and invites his soul to reconciliation with fully apprehended objects. . . . (pp. xii-xiii)

Not the least of Apollinaire's functions was that of reminding other poets of the traditional resources of French verse. His poetry has its "Vergers," a little like those of Rilke's French verse, reflecting devotion to past periods and styles. Into those green hereditary precincts he introduced objects sometimes rich and strange, almost invariably curious and interesting. "Paupières" . . . is compact with the poetic future. It is not the inevitable word within its pattern; but it anticipates the Surrealist reshuffling to come.

"Zone," the rather hurriedly prefixed poetic preface to Apollinaire's book, caused excitement from Prague to San Francisco and can still do so. This is all the more remarkable because it is compounded of several well-known poetic styles, not even excluding a few lines in the manner of Charles Péguy. (p. xv)

"Zone" and other late poems grapple determinedly with features of the modern landscape, however remote and magical the world preceding the Great War may now appear. Here the poetic result is achieved by letting objects hang suspended in the blue distance of a pastoral. Baudelaire, whose modern reputation Apollinaire the critic would do much to establish, had shown the way. But Apollinaire's *églogues de la cité* go much further. And it is chiefly in its paradoxically pastoral tone that "Zone" differs from a work which it resembles and possibly owes to, Blaise Cendrars' "Pâques à New-York." The modern malaise of the latter poem is without letup. "Zone" is less insistent. (p. xvi)

The fluid octosyllabics of Apollinaire's first really notable poem, "La Chanson du Mal-Aimé," cover bewildering variety, yet the theme is the well-tried one of striving after the absolute. This finds its statement in imagery having the drained-white hue familiar from Melville and other American writers, as well as the poets whom Apollinaire knew. . . . (p. xix)

[Apollinaire was] the theorist of the two ways supposedly hardest to navigate: that of "poetry" and that of "truth," the imaginary and the real, the invented and the raw residue of fact. "The plastic virtues: purity, unity and truth," he wrote, apropos of the Cubists. The Symbolists before him had paid due heed to the cathartic and unitive values of the creative process. For them, too, purity and unity were plastic virtues. They had, however, and here Paul Valéry was to follow them, minimized the mimetic function of art. Apollinaire is still the poet who has stated most forcefully the twentieth-century view that art is also a search for truth, a lever of discovery, adding like other cognitive acts to the sum of what is known.

The "false windows," as Valéry called them, remain—the lines and masses added or adding themselves, for balance, helping to order experience in the work of art. But they exist only by virtue of their opposition to the real windows, as heresies, we are told, have only the life they borrow from a parent faith. Without real windows the simulated ones do not exist. (pp. xxiv-xxv)

[A] little like Dostoevsky after the Siberian exile, [Apollinaire] took to identifying somewhat uncritically, enthusiastically, with contradictory manifestations and values of the society in which he found himself. We may call this his Futurism. Or we may call it a quest for identity culminating in his war service—as cavalryman, then, by his own wish, as infantryman—his head wound and his death from Spanish influenza. It makes, in any case, for one of the meaningful personal histories in the tangled, dark-brown-spotted web of twentieth-century events. It makes for poetry representing, if not quite the highest pitch of artistic accomplishment, something close to it, and for the triumph of a temperament. (p. xxvi)

Warren Ramsey, "Foreword" (1964), in Alcools *by Guillaume Apollinaire, translated by Anne Hyde Greet (copyright © 1965 by The Regents of the University of California; reprinted by permission of the University of California Press), University of California Press, 1965, pp. v-xxvi.*

MICHEL BUTOR   (essay date 1965)

Reading [*Qu'vlo'v'?*] indicates one of the fundamental aspects of Apollinaire's art, one that will permit him to appear, after the torment of 1914, as the "modern" poet *par excellence*, as the very type of poet who, though inspired to an extraordinary degree by literature, and even for this reason, manages not to be "literary"; in other words, the overpowering awareness he has always retained of the physical reality of language; it is as if he has made poetry fall back out of the sky and down to earth in his admirable incapacity to forget that words are first of all something you hear and see. This intense concentration on what he hears spoken or sung in the streets, in the inns, in the fields and woods, closely links two regions of his poetry, which for many critics even today seem contrary: the folkloric poem and the conversational poem.

As a matter of fact, the one derives quite naturally from the other, and we may even find a remarkable intermediary in a poem like *Les Femmes*. (p. 190)

Apollinaire's prosody, departing from that of the romantics which was based on syllable-count, returns to the much older prosody which regards the line of verse as a unit of utterance.

In the recording he made in 1914 for the Sorbonne of *Marie, Le Pont Mirabeau* and, in fact, *Le Voyageur*, Apollinaire deliberately isolates each line.

It follows that the suppression of punctuation in *Alcools* is the direct consequence of this state of things. Whereas punctuation is indispensable in the broken, crannied versification of a Hugo, the internal silences in the lines often

being longer than those which separate the lines, the introduction of punctuation marks in the first strophe of *La Chanson du Mal Aimé* is not only futile but harmful: it risks provoking considerable errors of intonation. . . . (p. 191)

Thus the line of verse in his practice once again becomes that "perfect line" Mallarmé spoke of. An auditory or oral unit is naturally transposed into "volume" in a visual unit, a reading unit. The typographic arrangement of the poem recovers its origin.

This suppression has the further value of preserving a certain number of the words' properties which they have when heard and which generally lose when printed, at least in the West, particularly grammatical ambiguities. (pp. 191-92)

[The] advantages of punctuation in the control not only of grammar but of intonation are tremendous and so obvious that the radical solution adopted by Apollinaire and by so many poets after him: total supression, is necessarily provisional, so many opportunities being accessible when we combine the two systems; but it has had an eminent value as a manifesto, a proclamation, and has obliged us to become aware once again of what punctuation really was, of its value and its function, as well as of what verse was, and its arrangement on the page. If we can today explore the entire realm which extends from Apollinaire's non-punctuation to the punctuation of classical prose, it is indeed to him that we owe the fact, and the experiments which he conducted in this realm deserve the closest study. (p. 194)

Michel Butor, "Apollinaire" (originally published as "Monument of Nothing for Apollinaire," translated by Richard Howard, in Tri-Quarterly, *No. 4, 1965), in* Inventory: Essays by Michel Butor, *edited by Richard Howard (copyright © 1968 by, Simon & Schuster, Inc.; reprinted by permission of Simon & Schuster, a Division of Gulf & Western Corporation), Simon & Schuster, 1968, pp. 185-208.*

SCOTT BATES   (essay date 1967)

"One Evening" [from *Alcools*] serves as an introduction to Apollinaire's nature myths. On a visual level, the eagle descending seems to represent the setting sun, which in turn suggests the eclipse of Christ the sun god and Christian faith. In keeping with an ancient poetic tradition, Apollinaire usually represented the death of love as taking place in evening (and autumn) whereas spring was often his time of creation and rebirth.

A great mastery of poetic technique is revealed in the poem. (p. 21)

[The] main themes of "One Evening" are the end of the old world and Christian faith; the secular second coming with its divinization of beauty and love and its canonization of the poet-prophet-worshiper; and the presence of a marvelous iron pastoral of modern urbanity full of despair and hope, death and resurrection, and the legendary ghosts of the past. (p. 22)

"The Thief" is the most direct and violent attack Apollinaire ever made on Christ and Christianity's Jewish patrimony; it is a barbarous, clanging poem, full of dissonances and ambiguities, erotic puns, drunken verbalisms, and an extraordinary compendium of the pagan marvelous culled from his already considerable knowledge of ancient lore. (p. 29)

Although it would have been natural for the young Apollinaire . . . to draw upon his earlier religious ideas and his own traits for some of the features of a poetic Christian-thief, and although it is undoubtedly true that "the man protesteth too much," his revolt like Baudelaire's or Rimbaud's denoting hidden ambivalence and spiritual torment, I feel reasonably certain that the thief is Jesus and that the poem is an anti-Christian, pro-pagan (primarily, pro-Pythagorean) satire. (pp. 31-2)

More than any other Apollinaire character Merlin [in *L'Enchanteur pourrissant (The Putrescent Enchanter)*] is the antithesis of Christ. The son of a virgin and a devil, he is nonetheless baptized (like Jesus, Simon Magus, and Apollinaire) as he retains mastery over all the diabolical powers of the underworld. He takes after his father, Satan. He extols suicide and revolution before his six immortal visitors. . . . He is buried underground by a sterile, ignorant love, in contrast to Saint Simeon Stylite's pillar "which leaps to the sky." His solitary nature as a poet leads him to hate crowds, while "God loves those who meet together." He places man higher than Christ. Yet he would be an angel were he not baptized, perhaps one of the marvelous host described in "Simon Magus."

As in "The Thief," Apollinaire satirizes divine birth and resurrection in *L'Enchanteur pourrissant,* this time in scenes of a "funereal Christmas" and a "voluntary damnation." (p. 36)

[In] "The Hermit" . . . [Apollinaire] carries his revolt from the Church to a summit of burlesque in the caricature of a lecherous old ascetic who, fleeing his self-inflicted sufferings for God, finds minor but satisfactory salvation outside the Lord. (p. 37)

The hermit is Apollinaire's most pathetic, bedraggled Antichrist: his problem is that he can be neither spiritual savior nor pagan lover. Like Saint Simeon Stylites in *The Putrescent Enchanter* "assailed by temptations according to the temperature," he suffers a new kind of fleshly Passion-in-reverse by *not* sweating the bloody sweat, the hematidrosis (in French, *hématidroses*); *not* perceiving the comforting angel on his Mount of Olives; *not* having his unleavened bread consecrated (a pun on his enforced sterility). Nor does a transcendent Magdalen, his mysterious *Unknown,* arrive. Half-crucified by his libidinous desires, his sole ascension that of his anxious flesh, he finds nothing but the cruel passion of owls nailed to impure peasants' huts. His salvation is achieved only when he abandons the desert for a counseling job in the city, as he discovers like Saint Jerome a kind of purity in the vicarious sexual activity of the confessor.

If "The Thief" is not Apollinaire as I believe—the poet is rather the thief's pagan interrogators—I think that there can be little doubt that the hermit, like Merlin, is he. (pp. 37-8)

How conscious Apollinaire became of what Freudians would now term the Oedipal import of his inheritance is evident in several passages in his writings. In *The Putrescent Enchanter,* for example, the forty-year-old heroine Angelica (Apollinaire's mother, Angélique de Kostrowitsky, was in her forties at the time of writing) is raped, murdered, damned, and then freed in a kind of incestuous episode which redeems the entombed (wombed) Merlin-Apollinaire; in the pornographic novel [*Les Onze mille verges*] *The Eleven Thousand Rods* . . . the most sadistic

ghoul-queen of a whole succession of bacchantes is a lovely Polish aristocrat, a "madonna," with a *face angélique.* In "Touch at a Distance," on the other hand, the adventurous Antichrist shot by Apollinaire-Christ has a name which was originally based on that of his erstwhile father. (pp. 40-1)

Violence, usually misogynic and masochistic, is the keynote of Apollinaire's fiction. (p. 47)

Castration and purity (sublimation) motifs, finally, like those in "The Hermit" are found everywhere in his work. . . . The pull and counterpull of Eros and Anteros, desire and the death wish, are beautifully portrayed in Chapter 12 of [*Le Poète assassiné*] *The Assassinated Poet,* where Croniamantal leaves his love momentarily "to die of thirst by the spring"; in "The Women" where cozy indoor comfort is contrasted with the cold German winter; and in the gay, apocalyptic poem "The House of the Dead" where the poet finds a refuge from love in his glaciers of memory and in the past. . . . Romantic madness caused by the death of love, a sort of mental suicide, is ambivalently feared and willed by the author of "The Passerby of Prague" and "The Rose of Hildesheim." Both the suicide and madness themes are related to the theme of the Superman . . . who is at the same time master and slave of his destiny. The tormented sun could set heroically: Merlin praised cremation as well as suicide in *The Putrescent Enchanter,* and Apollinaire discussed the nobility of beheading in his first version of "The Dancing Girl." . . . (pp. 47-8)

A glance over the poems of *Alcools* which were conceived before 1908, reveals the importance of the Sun-Night theme. . . . [In "The Night Wind"] the dramatic emasculation of Atys—son and lover of Cybele, the Mother of the gods—in one of his emblematic pines is mockingly contrasted to the creative meditations of the physically sterile, virgins, old people, and poets, after the sun has set and the lights gone out. The virile armies have fled; and the contrast between creativity and sterility, flight and fall, is pointed up by the Manichaean whiteness and darkness of the last line. . . . (pp. 48-9)

["La chanson du mal-aimé" ("The Song of the Poorly Beloved")] is] one of literature's most beautiful complaints, a modern elegy to rank with love lyrics of Catullus, Ronsard, and Verlaine. . . . Yet this terribly twentieth-century poem, chronologically the first in *Alcools* to describe the "heap of broken images" (Apollinaire's "water bad to drink") which the lost contemporary poet meets on his wanderings and the first to set a tone for the most recent poetic cries of distress, owes almost entirely its imagery, prosody, vocabulary, ideas, and references to the medieval and Symbolist literature Apollinaire studied in his adolescence. In thus successfully bringing old themes in an old garb to a modern *ethos* Apollinaire reveals himself for the first time one of the world's great poets.

This miracle he accomplished mainly, I think, by his faith in his myth, his transcendent belief that he was in no way inferior to the tragic poets and heroes of history. Like T. S. Eliot he hungered for cultural unity and significance; but unlike Eliot, he felt no personal inadequacy before the great shades of the past lost in the sterile wasteland of the present. (pp. 51-2)

As in "The Thief" and *The Putrescent Enchanter* the past in "The Song of the Poorly Beloved" is contemporary: a seventeenth-century Cossacks' curse against the Turkish

Sultan becomes the frustrated lover's imprecation; the goal of Columbus becomes the beloved; and the mythology of the ancient world mixes with medieval demons and unicorns to being another fabulous cortege to life. But no longer is this literary framework a symbolic, enchanted world of its own, replacing a pale, lifeless Christianity; rather, it is determined by a powerful psychological line running through the poem, the poet's chaotic yet logical emotions of hope, despair, desire, madness, melancholy, jealousy, and hatred caused by the death of love. (p. 52)

[All] the popular sources and the most careful construction cannot account for the poem's rich self-sufficiency and personal music. Apollinaire's vaulting egoism combined all that he had learned poetically with the acuity of his feelings —whether remembered in tranquillity or not—to place him not only at the summit of contemporary French lyricism but in the ranks of the kings and heroes of the past. The main myth of "The Song of the Poorly Beloved"—and of all the body of poetry of which it forms a part, in the final analysis —is his own. (p. 57)

Apollinaire set as the highest goal for life its divine creation through art, and join the "life for art's sake" writers of the nineteenth century—Baudelaire, Flaubert, Rimbaud, and Mallarmé—to say nothing of Yeats, Rilke, and Proust, with whose writings he was not acquainted. Like many of the works of those other authors, his two complementary Orphic poems "The Brazier" and "The Betrothal" prove that the subject matter of the poem-object—that microcosm of the universe—can only be itself, its description of its own voyage to itself, its own creation of itself. It is thus an absolute, an eternal unity of form and matter, constantly renewed with each new reading, the most significant absolute the poet-explorer can discover. He creates Byzantium by sailing poetically to it.

Apollinaire's joyful voyage to the godhead of pure poetry in "The Brazier" is at the same time mobile and immobile, horizontal and vertical, like the voyages of Dante and Mallarmé's Igitur: he travels both upward toward the Empyrean and outward toward Désirade—while remaining firmly pinned to a bank of the Seine. Dividing the poem into the symbolic three parts, which . . . [represent] renunciation, renewal, and elevation, he relates both the poem's and the poet's voluntary martyrdom and final ascension. (pp. 84-5)

"The Betrothal" is more biographical than "The Brazier" and recounts Apollinaire's Passion in more detail; but it is the same journey to the same divinely phallic pyre of creation. It picks up the search for a new love just touched upon in the last section of its complementary poem, and carries a betrothal theme to its consummation on three levels: profane love, sacred love, and divine poetry. (pp. 87-8)

Whatever the obscurities, I believe I can affirm with a reasonable amount of certainty that the last section of "The Betrothal" is one more example of the erotic solar cycle. In it Apollinaire brings together Christian and pagan symbols of death and resurrection to form another unified poem-star; his flame again represents purity, unity, and truth. With "The Brazier" at the summit of his symbolism and at the most penetrating depth of his inner voyages, it reveals that he has been able . . . to place order in his universe. He has found it good. (p. 94)

Each work of fiction and poetry that Apollinaire published

established a different myth for the poet. In *The Putrescent Enchanter* he was the Antichrist Merlin, buried by love but still creating a marvelous world of enchantment. In [*Le Bestiaire; ou, Cortège d'Orphée*] *The Bestiary, or Cortege of Orpheus*, a "divine" masterpiece like "The Brazier" of the 1908-9 period, he was Orpheus, in command of nature, turning bird and beast into symbols of his poetic aspirations. In [*L'Hérésiarque et cie*] *The Heresiarch and Company*, that "Cortege of Orfei," he was Benedetto Orfei himself, the epicurean Italian heresiarch of the title story with his mystical eroticism and his sainted vision of what true religion really is, that is, marvelous science fiction. He was also the heresiarch's company, the picturesque band of wanderers and Antichrists he knew so well from his travels through literature and Europe. (p. 95)

The myth of the Wanderer is never better expressed than in "The Traveler." . . . Like the protagonist of Walter de la Mare's famous poem "The Listeners," Apollinaire, too, knocks on a moonlit door as he seeks the key of closed eyes: "Open this door on which I knock weeping." Thus he touches on the more Germanic side of the Symbolist current, a side which often surfaces in modern French poetry, wherein life is regarded as a marvelous, enigmatic dream, made significant only by art.

As in "The Betrothal" the search in "The Traveler" is the only discovery, but here the search is not so much for the self's creative transcendency as it is for a meaning of self outside the artistic experience. Poetic technique is accordingly reversed: instead of following a fairly exact chronological and dialectical progression which turned images from experience into trinitarian symbols of the creative process, here the poet takes memories out of his past and *disorders* them—or, better, brings them to the poem in their natural disorder—thumbing through old travel photographs out of sequence in order to discover their secret significance. (pp. 100-01)

An examination of the main themes and symbols takes us closer into the heart of [the organic myth of a poet]. The negative Sun-Night theme of the crepuscular poems before 1908 is now completed and brought to a full cycle by the positive phoenix theme of "The Betrothal," the epigraph of "The Song of the Poorly Beloved," the last stanza of "Twilight," and the dawn of "Vendémiaire." In a countercycle, the beloved's ascension at sunset in "One Evening" is transcended in "The Betrothal" and "The Brazier" and ended in "Zone." The theme of the death of love in autumn remains a strong one, with, however, a new emphasis: in new poems "Marie" and "Hunting Horns," images of reluctant acceptance, of the melancholy enjoyment of dying sounds and passing waves, replace those of sterility and suicide. "Zone" is an exception, of course; but it in turn is balanced by the autumnal victory of "Vendémiaire." Particularly does the eternal, cyclical river beome an important symbol of the passing of time and love, replacing the murderous sea in "The Traveler," "Clotilde," "Mirabeau Bridge," "Marie," and "Zone." The poet has become more of a pathetic, fated hero—in spite of what he says in "Hunting Horns"—than a tragic victim. Only in "Zone" does he sorrowfully set when a bloody sun rises; but this poem with its admiration for its wounded hero and its description of the counterrise of the century serves as an excellent introduction to all the rising and falling themes in *Alcools,* day and night, light and shadow, the joys and grief of a poet-errant. . . . (pp. 103-04)

Light and shadow form one of the four principal categories of symbols in *Alcools;* the others are liquids, plants and animals, and the human body. All are interdependent and part of the poet's psyche.... Above everything else, fire is primary: Apollinaire, a poet of growth and movement like Shelley, makes the flame the source of all things. In this, he reflects the philosophy of Heraclitus "who saw in fire the symbol of general life, the emblem of the organizing and dissolving force."

After light and fire, liquids are most frequently alluded to in *Alcools*.... The external world of nature is everywhere, with about fifty species of animals taken primarily from literary references, and forty plants and trees, mainly from the poet's own personal observation, knowledge, and love. But there is scarcely a natural phenomenon or object, plant, stone, or animal that is not personified, just as in the animistic view of his philosophy, nature is made up of slumbering gods and demons to be aroused by the poet. (p. 104)

Thus the symbolism of *Alcools* forms itself inevitably into the pantheistic triad, the creation myth, of Apollinaire's esthetics: marvelous external reality unites with inner vision to form a new universe of art. External reality for him is a world of multiple relationships, or, to use Baudelaire's term, *correspondances,* between the symbols of other worlds in this one (the sea, shadow, masks, destiny, dreams, magic, mirrors, legendary plants and animals, legendary and historical characters) and symbols of contemporary reality (rivers, light, houses, streets, cities, countries, clothes, games, the body, the dance, seasons, animate and inanimate nature, contemporary personages). The inner vision is that of the poet as Eros and Christ and Anteros and Antichrist, a wandering god betrothed to Psyche and the Virgin, undergoing the death-birth cycle of love and life in melancholy and joy. Both visions, the inner and outer, combine like Ixion mating with his vision of reality, and the result is *Alcools,* a balanced, clear-obscure, mysterious-realistic, bittersweet, Dyonisian-Apollonian dance of life, represented by its three major symbols, fire, shadow, and *alcools.* (p. 105)

> *Scott Bates, in his* Guillaume Apollinaire *(copyright © 1967 by Twayne Publishers, Inc.; reprinted with the permission of Twayne Publishers, A Division of G. K. Hall & Co., Boston), Twayne, 1967, 204 p.*

J. LEGH-JONES   (essay date 1968)

[In *L'Hérésiarque et Cie*] we see revealed with astonishing clarity the pleasure-guilt complex which tortured so many of the apparently thoroughly amoral and 'emancipated' men of the 1890s and the early years of this century. Apollinaire seemed quite unaware of the psychological implications of these tales, but they show with remarkable directness that all the logic, learning and worldly wisdom of a gifted young Frenchman of the modern world were still insufficient to overcome the restrictive, fire-and-brimstone doctrine of his Catholic background.

The story of *The Wandering Jew* is especially interesting from the psychological viewpoint.... (p. 318)

The author's attitude to the Wandering Jew, with whom he describes a meeting one evening in Prague, is ambiguous: the narrator thinks of him in the traditional light of the wicked man punished by Jesus with the typically mediaeval punishment-concept of eternal life on this hellish earth, but

Ahasuerus represents Apollinaire's pagan, purely instinctive desire for life, more life at all costs, and escape from death. Ahasuerus-Apollinaire tries to justify and reassure himself that his impiety will not be punished, was actually an admirably independent act....

The author's reason rejects the possibility of the Wandering Jew's existence (note his stilted, highly literary conversation, more like a learned treatise than the words of a man), but his fear, not only of the possibility of God's revengeful existence but of inevitable annihilation if death is really the end, makes him cling to the possibility of immortality of the body, not even limited to Ahasuerus. (p. 319)

[The] author subconsciously fears retribution of some sort for his defiantly anti-clerical attitude. Ahasuerus' remark concerning the advantages of the immortal lover that 'fortunately, no-one ever attaches himself to me. So I never have time to make a habit of the experience which engenders jealousy', is clearly a *cri de coeur* from the depths of a lonely man who feels himself alienated from his fellows and strangely apart from reality, incapable of participating fully in ordinary joys, much as he would like to. Apollinaire himself is Ahasuerus, condemned to a spiritual loneliness, engendered by guilt, which he tries to exalt as true freedom and independence by his irreverent, over-analytical attitude to life, by which he dissects everything to the point where it becomes mechanical and dead. This paralyses his chances of decisive action and prevents the possibility of a normal relationship, shutting him out from the presence of God while sumultaneously denying him the pleasures of the Devil. He is in danger of becoming a zombie. His anguish lies in the fact that he sees perfectly clearly that this type of death, the emotional and spiritual rather than the physical, is every bit as bad. The acute consciousness of his helpless position results in the tense, anxious atmosphere of the story.... (p. 320)

> *J. Legh-Jones, "Sin and Salvation: The Moral Conflict in Guillaume Apollinaire," in* Contemporary Review, *Vol. 213, No. 1235, December, 1968, pp. 318-21.*

MARTIN TURNELL   (essay date 1969)

Apollinaire's debt to the Symbolists, both metrically and in other ways, was a large one. Now he differs in one respect from most poets who become famous. It is impossible to point to a single one of his predecessors and describe him as Apollinaire's master.... Apollinaire was never tired of insisting on his "modernism" as though this implied some intrinsic merit. When we compare him with his predecessors we observe one very significant fact. He went round borrowing or adapting every one of their individual innovations: themes, verse forms, and what I have called in another place the "shock image" or modern equivalent of the seventeenth-century conceit. The theme of the poet's vocation was introduced by Baudelaire, pushed to extremes by Mallarmé, and taken up by Apollinaire. Although usually more discreet, there was plenty in Mallarmé to encourage Apollinaire's sophisticated eroticism. *Un Coup de dés,* with its typographical novelties, must surely have played a major part in one of the least fruitful manifestations of "l'Esprit Nouveau": the "ideograms" in *Calligrammes.* (pp. 956-57)

[Comparison] with Verlaine is of particular interest. There was in Verlaine both a genuine folk-poet and an innovator whose experiments with language often went further than those of any of his contemporaries. In Apollinaire popular and modern, "tradition" and "invention," are frequently present in the same poem, as they are in "La Chanson du Mal-Aimé"; but like Verlaine he also wrote complete poems which one is tempted to describe as folk-poems. The obvious example is "Le Pont Mirabeau." . . . (p. 958)

Although it is usually concealed beneath an elaborate web of immensely sophisticated imagery and learned allusion, Apollinaire's sentimentality is basic and central in his poetry. The right comparison, indeed, is not with Villon or Verlaine or the great García Lorca who was almost Apollinaire's contemporary . . . but with the Aragon of "Les Lilas et les Roses" which possesses the same immediate attraction and the same weaknesses.

The fact is that the figure of the "Mal-Aimé" is a projection of the poet's own naively sentimental attitude to women, a persona who haunts a vast number of the poems and is plainly the speaker in "Zone." (p. 959)

In placing ["Zone"] at the beginning of [*Alcools*] the poet clearly intended it to be a manifesto. . . . [It is] one of his most characteristic poems because in it he employs all the main devices that he had learned from his predecessors. It is an account of a stroll through Paris, or rather the stroll through Paris which represents the contemporary urban world is the thread or theme that holds the poem together. In this way it provides the background for a series of meditations on the poet's main interests—his experiences with women and his vocation as a poet mingled somewhat unexpectedly in this poem with religion—which are grafted on to what might be called the holding theme. The free verse with its lines of varying lengths reflects the movements of the *flâneur* who will stop from time to time to watch a street scene, then move on, lost in his private dream until something else turns up to bring him back to earth. (p. 962)

[The] image of "Christ the Aviator" [in "Zone"] invites comparison with the use of a religious image in a different medium. Whatever the cinéaste's personal beliefs, the statue of Christ the Worker sailing above Rome suspended from a helicopter at the beginning of Fellini's film, *La Dolce Vita,* does provide a comment on what is to come. . . . The point is that while Fellini's religious images are woven into the film and possess a moral value, the image of "Christ the Aviator" and the flippant remark about "the world record for altitude" do not possess the same force. It is surprising and amusing, but instead of forming part of the texture of the poem it sticks out and has something of the effect of a comic strip.

The poet indulges in the kind of free association which bears the mark of Surrealism. The image of "Christ the Aviator" becomes the pretext for a digression on flying which ranges from the mythical figure of Icarus to Simon Magus, Enoch, Elijah, and Apollonius of Tyana who are described as "hovering near the original aeroplane." It then passes into the realm of birds and concludes with a reference to eagles, phoenixes, and pihis "fraternizing with the flying machines." The transition from aeroplanes to birds is managed ingeniously by the spectacle of an aeroplane landing "without folding its wings." (pp. 964-65)

Comparisons between Apollinaire's poem and film are of particular relevance. There is a sense in which the texture of the whole poem might be described as cinematic with its constant shift and change of scene and angle and its "cuts." (p. 965)

The cinematic "cuts" multiply in the second half of the poem. Paris and the sufferings of the lovesick poet vanish. He finds himself in the more relaxed and congenial atmosphere of the Mediterranean. . . .

Other "cuts" take him to Prague, Marseilles, Coblenz, Rome. There is a switch from the Holy City where he has been basking under a "Japanese medlar tree" to Amsterdam where the circumstances are somewhat different. . . . (p. 966)

[Although] Apollinaire's image of "Christ the Aviator" does not possess the effectiveness of Fellini's image of Christ the Worker, the poem can be divided roughly into two halves. In the first the poet is concerned with *ascents:* in the second with *descents.* The brief glimpses of the places where for a short time he was happy are no more than interludes: the last part of the poem records a steady downward movement which began with the spectacle of the devils in their "abyss" jeering at "Christ the flyer." The poet goes rapidly down in the human scale until he finds himself an outcast among other outcasts in Paris: emigrants who can no longer "take it," prostitutes of every description. Descent in the human scale is compared with descent in the religious scale: the outcasts are identified with the adherents of inferior religions—"Lesser Christs of dim aspirations." (p. 967)

For me "Zone" is Apollinaire's most successful, most characteristic, and most entertaining poem. At the same time it illustrates most of his shortcomings: his sentimentality and the disappointing use he made of devices like the "shock image" that he had learned from other poets. A great poet borrows from his predecessors, but he develops what he borrows, adapts it to his particular needs, turns it into something new, makes it his own. That is where Apollinaire failed. His borrowings always give the impression of somehow being put in from outside; innovations cease to be innovations; instead of being developed and adapted, they are reduced to the level of amusing gimmicks. . . . A typical example of the gimmick was the decision, taken at the time of publishing *Alcools,* to remove all punctuation from the poems. It added nothing to them except a specious appearance of "modernity" and made them more difficult to read. The most striking example in "Zone" is the cinematic texture. In a good film or a good poem the diverse images combine to form a pattern and that pattern is its meaning. It happens in Laforgue's *Derniers vers* which probably provided Apollinaire with his model. In Laforgue the images are woven into a pattern as surely as in Fellini's film. In "Zone" there is no coherent pattern; there is a succession of startling but largely unrelated images which have the effect of dissipating instead of concentrating emotion, undermining instead of creating unity, with the result that the poem dissolves into a series of incidents, memories, reflections—some amusing, some painful, others shocking or humiliating. The close is a brilliant tour de force, a dazzling image which so far from bringing the poem to a triumphant conclusion drives home the fundamental lack of unity.

Any discussion of Apollinaire's poetry must include some account of his particular brand of obscurity. . . . [The] opening of "La Chanson du Mal-Aimé" [is] an example of the poet's lyrical gift, the compulsive rhythms that we not infrequently find in his verse. It is evident, however, that even in the opening verses a certain kind of obscurity is rife. (pp. 968-69)

[There are] different kinds of obscurity that we find in Apollinaire's work: personal reminiscences, learned or sometimes erratic allusions, puns, invented words and various devices for conveying covertly erotic details which could not be openly described. (p. 970)

The particular forms of obscurity exemplified by his poetry are naturally a temptation to the academic mind because they can be resolved in the main by the methods of the crossword puzzle expert and do not call for actual involvement in the poet's experience. His obscurity is also one of the clearest signs of Apollinaire's shortcomings as a poet. The complexity of his work is essentially a surface complexity; the complicated allusions, the puns, the coined words, the sensational imagery conceal, and the straightforward syntax reveals, an attitude which was basically a simple one. He was misled by his own passion for "l'Esprit Nouveau." His mistake was to equate modernism with poetic merit while disparaging one of the greatest of all moderns and playing down others. . . .

The truth is that in Apollinaire there is no vision; there is a feverish poetic activity in which he uses all the tricks of the trade to create the illusion of a vision which is not there. He does not widen or deepen or transform our experience: he is simply a high class entertainer whose skillful manipulation of words, images, and rhythm is interesting and amusing, but seldom penetrates our defenses. (p. 975)

> *Martin Turnell, "The Poetry of Guillaume Apollinaire" (copyright, 1969, by Martin Turnell), in* The Southern Review, *n.s. Vol. 5, No. 4, Autumn, 1969, pp. 953-75.*

LEROY C. BREUNIG   (essay date 1969)

Apollinaire was above all a lyric poet. . . . The elusiveness of the self and the emotions it excites constitute a dominant theme. Indeed he was one of the first and the most lucid among the hordes of writers—and readers—engaged in the search for their indefinable identities in this twentieth century.

His rootlessness generated an exhilarating sense of freedom. He felt bound by no traditions, no taboos. Whether or not he inspired the character of Lafcadio in Gide's *Les Caves du Vatican,* as has been claimed, Apollinaire was a fine example of Gidean "disponibilité," that total willingness to experience new sensations and beliefs. But noninvolvement can weigh heavily, and just as often we find him thirsting after more binding ties. (pp. 6-7)

Such oscillation in turn reveals a deeper trait in Apollinaire, his congenital indecisiveness. Coming from no direction, he knew not what direction to go. A recurrent image in his poetry is the compass pointing in all four directions at once. In one of his little quatrains of *Le Bestiaire,* entitled "L'Ecrevisse," he apostrophizes "incertitude," calling it his delight and adding that "you and I" go along like the crayfish, "backwards." Aimlessness explains the workings of his mind as well, which was apparently unable to follow a neatly developed chain of reasoning. His thought proceeded by free association, hopping at random from one notion or image to another. The prose writing suffers from this fault. The two novels, *Le Poète assassiné* and *La Femme assise,* fail to achieve the coherence which this genre demands. The art criticism is inferior to Baudelaire's because it lacks the cogent expository style of the essays in *Curiosités esthétiques.*

Apollinaire might well have disintegrated into an inert mass of neutralizing contradictions but for his vigor and his lucidity. . . . Thanks to his lucidity he came to realize that in the very weakness of his undirected thought processes lay his strength and originality as a modern poet. He had only to transform "primitive disorder" (if we may adapt the terms of Kenneth Rexroth) into "sophisticated disorder."

It is obvious, of course, that during that fruitful prewar decade in Paris Apollinaire did make a choice—in favor of modernism. As spokesman for the new trends in painting and poetry in both the daily press and the little magazines he regularly defended whatever was the newest. This took a powerful lot of legerdemain, since Paris had never been so heady with "isms." (pp. 7-8)

What Apollinaire really espoused was avant-gardism. More important than the contents of this or that manifesto was the fact that what he championed was new. His most earnest desire was to form a common front in the fight against traditionalism, and his acrobatics with labels represent successive efforts by stretching the meaning of this or that "ism" to designate the over-all trends of the moment. The last label he sought to impose, without much success in spite of its greater accuracy, was simply "l'esprit nouveau." (p. 9)

Unfortunately the new has the bad habit of never staying that way. The calligram of an automobile in "La Petite Auto" definitely betrays its 1914 lines, and Apollinaire's modernism, when only that, is paradoxically the element of his poetry that has aged most quickly, sounding at times like a not so felicitous mixture of Whitman and Marinetti. The spurts of old-fashioned optimism and the hopes in a bright future where the union of the spiritual and the technological will ensure the felicity of mankind seem woefully passé, and Apollinaire would be forgotten today were he merely the voice of the "Counter-Decadence" of the first decade and a half of the century.

His very rootlessness saved him, however, for among the contradictions it inspired was a fascination with the past just as intense as the anticipation of the future. A simple pirouette, and the Eiffel Tower becomes the Tower of Pisa. (p. 10)

[Apollinaire's] spiritual ubiquity . . . made him feel a deep affinity with the "fourth dimension" as he defines it in *Les Peintres cubistes:* "It figures the immensity of space eternalizing itself in all directions at a given moment." That this is hardly a scientific definition is beside the point; for Apollinaire it reflects in his poetry the constant effort to perfect a multidirectional style so as to express the intense radiation of his compass-boxing emotions. It is the stages of this effort that make up the chapters of Apollinaire's biography as a poet.

His first two known pieces, written at seventeen, are signed "Guillaume Macabre," and indeed much of the early verse has the morbid tone of the *fin de siècle* which we associate with the symbolist movement. In symbolism Apollinaire also found nourishment for his love of out-of-the-way myths and fairy tales which he had had since childhood. Greek, Hebrew, and Celtic lodge side by side in these youthful efforts as they will in his first prose work, *L'Enchanteur pourrissant.* The death of Pan, the metamorphosis of Lilith into an osprey, the imprisonment of Merlin the magician under a crystal bell by the fairy Vivian, these are some of the rather decadent themes of this period. (pp. 11-12)

["Merlin et la vieille femme," "Le Larron," and "L'Ermite"] are among the most enigmatic poems Apollinaire wrote. The obscurity comes in part from the strangeness of the three legendary characters (Merlin is the only one named): a hermit, a thief, and a magician, all of them representing of course the Poet. They are isolated figures who seem to exist out of time and place. The lack of localization recalls the symbolist manner which creates "landscapes of the soul" through the filtering process of the poet's memory.

Yet these pieces differ from the typical symbolist poem which seeks through a "medley of metaphors" (Edmund Wilson) to communicate a certain mood, an "état d'âme" which no matter how ineffable is nonetheless coherent and consistent. What strikes one here, however, is the incongruity of the juxtapositions and the disconcerting shifts of tone. (pp. 12-13)

[During the German period] Apollinaire was seeking an accommodation between a form of lyricism anchored in reality, whether urban or rural, and the symbolist notion of the poem as an enigma. This involved turning some of the techniques he had tried during his apprenticeship in a new direction and with more subtlety than the purely mechanical juxtapositions of "Au Prolétaire." The imagery becomes more direct. Clearly stated similes replace tenuous metaphors based on synesthesia and other "correspondances," so that the enigmatic quality derives less from the images in themselves than from the arrangement of the lines in which they lie. Two closely related devices predominate: structural ellipsis inherited from the symbolists, and free association, more peculiar to Apollinaire. (p. 16)

Free association is an extreme form of structural ellipsis in which the link may be hidden or not there at all. In such cases one is not sure whether a line is mysterious or simply mystifying. In "Les Colchiques" the poisonous flowers resemble mothers, "daughters of their daughters." Is there a cryptic connection between an imaginary cyclical process uniting generations and the circle around the eyes with which the flower has already been compared? And does this "eternal return" suggest the fatality of the poet's poisoned love? Or is Apollinaire simply enjoying the repetition of the word "filles" for its own sake? His fantasy can often be quite gratuitous, and it would be a mistake to attempt to explicate him as though he were Mallarmé or Valéry. (p. 17)

One has only to recall the single, fixed décor of the most celebrated French love poem of the nineteenth century, Lamartine's "Le Lac," to appreciate the tremendous diversity of material in "La Chanson du Mal-Aimé." Disparate blocks of imagination jostle each other between the two terminal points which pin down the poem in reality. Discontinuity of course is a risky technique which can easily become the enemy of coherence. The problem for Apollinaire was to create an effect of disorder reflecting the turbulence of the poet-lover's distraught soul while imposing enough order to make the poem aesthetically valid. Hence the necessity for a compromise with the devices of continuity: the regular verse form, the more or less symmetrical architecture (avoiding at all costs the coldly mathematical), the transitional stanzas uniting certain but by no means all of the sections. Thanks to these compromises the lyric sentiment is at once multifaceted and single. Projected into the vastness of history and legend it retains at the same time all the intimacy of the subjective self. Much of the power of "La Chanson du Mal-Aimé" derives from the delicate balance it achieves between "Order" and "Adventure," the Apollonian and the Dionysian. (p. 23)

[If] neo-symbolism and nascent cubism were the accoucheurs of "Les Fiançailles," the birth pangs were Apollinaire's own. It is the first poem in which he confides so openly about his ecstasies and sufferings as a poet. He tells of his grandiose projects as a youth, and in fact the first two of the nine sections are fragments from two long 1902 poems, one pastoral, one urban, like exhibits on display exemplifying two distinct styles which the poet now intends to fuse. He tells how he sought for absolute purity but realizes now that perfection lies in the moment, that poetry is a state of mind rather than a work. He confesses the "torments" of silence that he has just suffered. At times he sees himself as a divine stellar force: it is toward *his* eyes that Icarus rises. Then again he glimpses only his mortal self with death rushing upon him "like a hurricane." He proclaims his omniscience—only to ask forgiveness for his ignorance. The single constant in these fluctuations seems to be his love, a love so all-inclusive that it must embrace the totality of life.

"Les Fiançailles" ends triumphantly with a phoenixlike regeneration of the poet's spirit. More specifically—and here perhaps lies the key to an understanding of this very obscure poem—it is his "incertitude" that is reborn out of its own ashes. In this one word Apollinaire sums up all the oscillations and indecisions of his mercurial character which were constantly threatening to make a jumble of inconsistencies of his rootless existence. "Les Fiançailles" is thus the dramatization of a decision, not the decision to choose from among the conflicting forces within him, since this would mean suppressing others—and on what basis could the choice be made?—but rather the decision to embrace them all by fully recognizing their simultaneous existence. Of "incertitude" itself he would make a principle and a source of plenitude, bringing his life and his poetry into focus as through a single lens.

Rereading the poem with this in mind one discovers that its very style illustrates this sense of totality. Whether one calls this "cubism" or more accurately "simultanism" (with a broader connotation than that of the 1912 school which Apollinaire himself attempted to incorporate in his term "orphism") it consists of the interlocking of opposites in new syntheses through the use of words and images with multiple meanings placed in discontinuous lines and sections in an effort to nullify the flow of time and thus achieve an effect of ambivalent immediacy.

The trouble with "Les Fiançailles" is its very excess of riches. Intoxicated by this revelation the author has packed the poem with a bewildering profusion of ambiguities, fused dichotomies, shifting images with shifting meanings, collages that only he can recognize, and secret allusions to which he holds the keys. Although "Le Brasier" grew out of the same drafts it is more coherent because, as the title indicates, it centers upon the single element of fire. One of the main traits of Apollinaire's imagery in general is its volatility. Objects visually perceived and simple in themselves constantly melt into one another. . . . (pp. 25-6)

["Zone"] is perhaps the masterpiece of what one might call Apollinaire's peripatetic poetry. . . . (p. 31)

"Zone" is particularly successful as a "poème-promenade" because the "peripatetic" motion governs the form throughout. The title suggests both the Parisian term for the suburbs surrounding the city and etymologically the somewhat beltlike or circular direction of the walk, which continues from one morning to the next, interrupted by several stops (the Gare Saint-Lazare, a bar, a restaurant, a brothel) before the poet returns at sunrise to his apartment in the suburb of Auteuil. The correlation between the ever increasing fatigue of the walk and the despondency of the poet is implied all along.

Within this framework, which shows the real city unfolding before him, the poet introduces a series of memories from the various stages of his past life, and it soon becomes apparent that he is endeavoring to reconcile present and past time on a single plane or more precisely to reconcile his conflicting feelings toward two sets of opposites in time. The opening lines seek to proclaim enthusiastically the rejection of the past in its obvious connotation of "old" in favor of the present as "new." (pp. 32-3)

As an attempt to deal with the contradictions implicit in the concept of time, "Zone" is the poetic counterpart in miniature of a novel which began to appear the same year: *A la recherche du temps perdu*. Both seek to surpass the division between past and present in a new synthesis which, thanks to memory, would resurrect "lost time" in all its resplendence. Unlike Proust, Apollinaire sought the palingenesis through religious faith, which makes the confession of his failure all the more poignant. His compassion for the outcasts toward the end of the poem is certainly a Christian virtue, but Faith and Hope have gone. Only Charity remains.

Its stark ending did not prevent "Zone" from becoming the great avant-garde banner of the "Counter-Decadence," and it is usually cited as the "cubist" poem par excellence. No doubt it produces a fragmented, multidimensional effect through such devices as the telescoping of syntax, the almost exclusive use of the present tense, the rapid shifting of personal pronouns, the abrupt changes of locale, and the suppression of connectives and of course of punctuation. As we have seen, however, its basic structure remains sequential rather than simultaneous. If cubism is indeed a "sum of destructions" as Picasso claimed, in the sense that the fragmented elements of reality are rearranged so as to create a state of tension between the opposing forces of unity and multiplicity, then both the structure and the greater degree of polyvalence in "Les Fiançailles" and "Le Voyageur" make them more truly "cubist" than "Zone," which for all its zigzags flows along in time like "La Chanson du Mal-Aimé." (pp. 34-5)

In general the 1912-14 poems [including *Calligrammes*] push the cubist principle of fragmentation to the extreme. The "blocks" become shorter, the images and statements more heterogeneous. Notations replace complete sentences. Free, blank verse becomes the rule. Like the futurist *parole in libertà* the lines, if not always the actual words, have declared their independence. Has coherence become taboo? Is the reader who earnestly seeks some elusive "objective correlative" making a fool of himself? That depends upon the poem. In some, no doubt, chance plays

the dominant role. The "poèmes-conversations" like "Lundi rue Christine" record the haphazard flow of real scraps of conversation around the pivotal point of the poet. In "Liens," on the other hand, the diverse images all relate to the theme of bonds or ties announced by the title, and the poem's coherence derives from the harmonious fusion of the techniques of simultanism in the form and the ambivalent feelings toward interdependence which they express. (p. 36)

Apollinaire's victory as a poet sprang from the maze of contradictions within him as a man. Poets have understood at least since Heraclitus that "of everything that is true, the converse also is true," and time and again they have sought to pronounce "Odi et amo" in one breath. Yet the fact that the word "ambivalence" was not coined until 1916 is sufficient indication that the general acceptance of this concept is predominantly a twentieth-century acquisition. It is in this sense and not simply because he sang of the Eiffel Tower that Apollinaire is profoundly modern. (p. 46)

Leroy C. Breunig, in his Guillaume Apollinaire *(Columbia Essays on Modern Writers Pamphlet No. 46; copyright © 1969 Columbia University Press; reprinted by permission of the publisher), Columbia University Press, 1969, 48 p.*

OCTAVIO PAZ (essay date 1970)

"Le Musicien de Saint-Merry" is one of Apollinaire's most disturbing and mysterious poems. It also—along with "Zone," "Les Fenêtres," "Lundi rue Christine," and a few others—prefigures many of the forms that a few years later will be adopted by twentieth-century art, poetry as well as the novel and painting. Interest in "Le Musicien de Saint-Merry" is twofold: on one hand, it is one of Apollinaire's best poems; on the other, it is an example of the possibilites and limitations of a poetics founded on the simultaneous expression of realities, separated in space or in time, that the poet brings together in order to show us that the "already seen" (*déjà vu*) is the "never been seen before" (*jamais vu*). (p. 277)

"Le Musicien de Saint-Merry" is a complex poem, although not in the sense that Mallarmé's are. I mention this poet for two reasons: first, because he is Apollinaire's immediate antecedent: second, because his work is the touchstone for all modern French, even universal poetry. In the case of Mallarmé, obscurity is inseparable from the poem; his poetic method, he said several times, is that of *transposition*, and it consists of replacing perceived reality with a word which without specifically naming that reality elicits another, equivalent, reality. . . . Apollinaire also begins with an anecdote, one or another reality, but he does not erase it: he separates it into fragments that he brings together according to a new order: this shock, or confrontation, is the poem—the true reality. Mallarmé proposes to abolish the object, to the benefit of the language, abolish language to benefit the idea, which in turn resolves into an absolute which is identical to nothingness. Thus, his poem does not present things to us, but words, or more exactly, rhythmic signs. Apollinaire intends to destroy and reconstruct the object through language; the word continues to be a means of allowing us to see things in their instantaneous vivacity. There is no transposition of reality, rather, transfiguration. Mallarmé's method approximates music, Apollinaire's, painting, especially the cubist esthetic.

"Le Musicien de Saint-Merry" brings together two kinds of realities, spatial and temporal. The first—there, over there, closer, more distant—does not take place in a "here" but in a "now," that fragment of time that is an afternoon on the 21st of May in 1913. The diverse verbal times—classical antiquity, the end of the Middle Ages, the sixteenth and seventeenth centuries, our own time—are conjugated in a "here": the old church of Saint-Merry and the district that surrounds it. Poetry is a temporal art: in painting, the signs (lines, colors) are presented together, at one time; in poetry, some after others. In painting the composition is atemporal; in poetry, sequential. The *simultaneity* of Apollinaire is not something we *see* as we do in painting, but something we *convoke*. (p. 278)

In truth, we do not see things happen: we see things happen through the poet—who is also "happening." The "I" of the poet, whether he uses first person or third, is the space in which things happen, a space that is itself time. The poem of Apollinaire is not the presentation of a reality, it is the presentation of a poet in his reality. It is objective lyric poetry, if I may express it this way. For that reason, his poetry resolves into theatre—grotesque, sentimental, marvelous, and realistic—and into myth. "Le Musicien de Saint-Merry" contains both elements: the tragicomedy of "pauvre Guillaume" and the figure of the visionary poet.... (p. 279)

> *Octavio Paz, "'The Musician of Saint-Merry' by Apollinaire: A Translation and a Study," in L'-Esprit Créateur (copyright © 1970 by L'Esprit Createur), Vol. X, No. 4, Winter, 1970, pp. 269-84.*

ROGER LITTLE (essay date 1976)

Alcools is Apollinaire's scrapbook pasted up anew to give variety. Like most scrapbooks it is the record of a person and a period and holds most interest for the compiler's friends when anecdotal material accompanies its presentation. But this one contains some treasures which need no anecdotes to survive both the poet and his friends. (p. 34)

While *Alcools* is a medley on the dominant theme of the self with particular reference to love's labours lost and creativity, *Calligrammes* is unified in several ways. Firstly, its presentation is essentially chronological: its sub-title, *Poèmes de la paix et de la guerre (1913-1916),* is both a note of the period of composition, as in *Alcools: Poèmes 1898-1913,* and an indication that the volume forms a direct sequel to the earlier one. But in addition the sub-title gives a definition of subject-matter: the collection is directly linked with external events of the period, notably the First World War, in which Apollinaire along with many other millions of men took part until he was invalided out in 1916. Such a shared experience helps avoid the private element of *Alcools*. Secondly the war imposes a thematic unity on most of the volume. To this Apollinaire adds a further unifying factor, brought forward from *Alcools:* his continued preoccupation with love. No longer is love lost through any fault of the poet's: now it is absent love that obsesses him.... There is, finally, greater stylistic unity than in *Alcools,* despite the appearance of the picture-poems.... In no sense was Apollinaire a metaphysical poet: he revelled in immediacy, and that is both his main limitation and his main attraction.

Undoubtedly the most striking and disorientating feature of *Calligrammes* is the inclusion of what Apollinaire at first called 'idéogrammes lyriques' and subsequently 'calligrammes', in which his lyrical vision turned to visual lyricism.... (pp. 35-6)

Apollinaire came to an unsatisfactory compromise between the two media since his ideograms ... ignore a factor fundamental to the literary use of language, namely rhythm. They are amusing doodles. Apollinaire cannot take their visual aspect beyond a stylised representation of the object evoked.... Nor can he prevent the picture disappearing as we decipher the text. Nor, with rare exceptions, is the text *per se* paid sufficient attention by the poet to retain intrinsic interest as literature. Instead of bridging a gap successfully, the calligrammes fall between two stools.

Their double aim of surprise and simultanity nonetheless allows of other forms of expression which are more satisfactory because more integrated.... (p. 38)

That humour, even the slightest of word-play, should be an integral part of Apollinaire's most serious new experiment is both infuriating and exciting. It necessarily frustrates the critic trying to categorise his work and excites the reader who feels that since everything is valid material for poetry humour has the right to be included. (p. 42)

[In *Le Bestiaire ou Cortège d'Orphée*] a number of Apollinairean themes and features are adumbrated: metamorphoses created by the magus, syncretism, travelling, past and fleeting time, the difficulty of living, pride in poetry, the importance of the presence of friends and the pleasures of carnal love. One feature not to reappear in any but a thoroughly modified form is the apparently unquestioning acceptance of Christian terminology.... (p. 64)

Vitam impendere amori groups six brief poems written in octosyllabic quatrains on the topic of time and love gone by. Strictly limited to the tone of regret and self-pity they never catch fire: the images remain too general to be personalised and the language is unexciting. (p. 66)

[The heteroclite collection entitled *Il y a*] is very uneven.... The early pieces show elements of pastiche and are also traditional technical exercises in stanzaic form and borrowed voice, mixing elegant if slight conceits to sing the lady's praises. A cavalier approach to the alexandrine is already in evidence, and lessons in *enjambement* have clearly been learnt from the Symbolists. Yet at root it is the Renaissance that pervades these early works, and it is interesting to reflect that even in 'Per te praesentit aruspex' ... one hears the shade of Ronsard celebrating another love affair or the ghost of Du Bellay, sad and sardonic as ever. The later poems mostly evoke places or people without adding resonances to those familiar from *Alcools* and *Calligrammes;* they are loose-textured, largely circumstantial, and memorable only when humour, irony or concision comes into play, for those qualities bring a lightness of touch or tone which strains neither poet nor reader and seems to characterise the former's dominant key. (pp. 66-7)

Critical images of Apollinaire are so varied that it is as if each reader fills the void in his own way. Yet if Apollinaire was suggestible he is also multiply suggestive. Like the paintings of the cubists he befriended, he is a simultaneous multiplicity of facets. Yet because he reflects so many influences, I see him rather as a broken mirror, precariously held together in its frame, longing to be resilvered and made whole. For in his quest for a new order incorporating the innovations of his time into the perspective of his acquired culture, he stands ironically as a landmark in the fragmentation of that culture. (p. 117)

Roger Little, in his Guillaume Apollinaire *(© Roger Little 1976), The Athlone Press, 1976, 145 p.*

BIBLIOGRAPHY

Breunig, LeRoy C. "The Chronology of Apollinaire's *Alcools*." *PMLA* LXVII, No. 7 (December 1952): 907-23.
Attempts to regroup the poems of *Alcools* in their original order of composition, using biographical, stylistic, and thematic clues in establishing chronology. It is an interesting piece of scholarly detection and in addition to dating the poems also defines five distinct creative periods subsumed in the larger eras of Apollinaire's work.

Carmody, Francis J. *The Evolution of Apollinaire's Poetics, 1901-1914.* Berkeley: University of California Press, 1963, 130 p.
Technical philological analysis of Apollinaire's work.

Davies, Margaret. *Apollinaire.* London: Oliver & Boyd, 1964, 312 p.
A study that has well-integrated critical and biographical material on Apollinaire.

George, Emery E. "Calligrams in Apollinaire and in Trakl: A Psycho-stylistic Study." *Language and Style* 1, No. 1 (Winter 1968): 131-93.*
Technical linguistic study of the way Apollinaire and Georg Trakl, among others, form words into shapes to create and reinforce poetic meaning.

Greet, Anne Hyde. "Wordplay in Apollinaire's *Calligrammes*." *L'Esprit Createur* X, No. 4 (Winter 1970): 296-307.
Discusses puns, word associations, and other verbal overtones in Apollinaire's war poems.

Lawler, James R. "Music and Poetry in Apollinaire." *French Studies* X, No. 4 (October 1956): 339-46.
Draws parallels between Apollinaire's poetry and musical rhythms and structures. The essay contains an interesting section that analyzes as music a recording Apollinaire made of some of his poems.

Lawler, James R. "Rimbaud and Apollinaire." *French Studies* XIX, No. 3 (July 1965): 266-77.*

Attempts to document Apollinaire's knowledge of Rimbaud, and to present evidence for Rimbaud's influence on the later poet's work. The essay admits to being a brief exploratory investigation, though it does offer much useful substantiation toward its thesis.

Mackworth, Cecily. *Guillaume Apollinaire and the Cubist Life.* New York: Horizon Press, 1964, 244 p.
Literary biography of Apollinaire, focusing on his social and professional relationships with figures in the Cubist movement. The author's work is not treated critically in this study.

Porter, Laurence M. "The Fragmented Self of Apollinaire's 'Zone'." *L'Esprit Createur* X, No. 4 (Winter 1970): 285-95.
Sees the linguistic and thematic extremes exhibited by "Zone" as reflecting various crises in Apollinaire's life.

Rinsler, Norma. "The War Poems of Apollinaire." *French Studies* XXV, No. 2 (April 1971): 169-86.
Discusses Apollinaire's war experiences and the poems that resulted, which were published in *Calligrammes*. Apollinaire's war poems are compared to those of other poets of wartime.

St. Onge, Ronald Rene. "The Accursed Families of Apollinaire." *Kentucky Romance Quarterly* XXII, No. 1 (Winter 1975): 3-14.
Discusses Apollinaire's negative depictions of family relationships in his work, and looks at the author's own hectic upbringing as a partial prototype for these "accursed families."

Shattuck, Roger. "Guillaume Apollinaire, 1880-1918." In his *The Banquet Years: The Arts in France, 1885-1918,* pp. 195-248. New York: Harcourt, Brace and Co., 1955.
Anecdotal essay discussing Apollinaire's position in the artistic society of his time.

Steegmuller, Francis. *Apollinaire: Poet among Painters.* New York: Farrar, Straus and Co., 1963, 305 p.
Biography of Apollinaire that traces many autobiographical references in the author's work, though is not strictly speaking a critical study.

Sullivan, Dennis G. "On Time and Poetry: A Reading of Apollinaire." *Modern Language Notes* 88, No. 4 (May 1973): 811-37.
Highly philosophical approach to Apollinaire's poetic theory as it is articulated in his critical writing and implied in his poems.

Urdang, Constance. "The Hills of Guillaume Apollinaire." *Western Review* 22, No. 2 (Winter 1958): 117-23.
The critic argues for the thematic unity of Apollinaire's "Les collines," saying that this unified structure distinguishes it from the disjointed poetry of surrealism.

Antonin Artaud

1896-1948

(Also wrote under pseudonym of Le Révélé) French essayist, dramatist, poet, novelist, screenwriter, and translator.

Artaud, an important influence in the development of modern drama, extended the possibilities of theatrical presentation with his vision of a new theater. His theories of a Theater of Cruelty, as outlined in *Le Théâtre et son double*, repudiate Western theatrical traditions in favor of an antirationalist spectacle meant to act upon the collective unconscious of his audience.

Artaud deplored the psychological drama of character and proposed a theater of symbolic gestures, mime, incantations, and sounds which would have the power of a primitive rite in releasing the audience's repressed emotions. His concept of cruelty did not involve sadism, but rather was meant to explore the metaphysical cruelty of the implacable forces which control man. Critics find his influence in the work of Ionesco, Genet, and The Happenings. However, his various theories have never been realized in a single production: *Les Cenci*, his only attempt at a Theater of Cruelty production, was a failure.

Artaud was apparently mentally ill for most of his adult life and spent nine of his last eleven years in mental asylums. Some critics utilize this fact to dismiss his work as illogical and contradictory. It is just as often noted, however, that he had no use for formal logic but sought instead to develop the emotive powers of his work. Artaud's illness, drug addiction, and alienation have caused him to be linked with poets such as Rimbaud and Nerval as a cult hero of the avant-garde. Like his predecessors, his poetry is an often deeply moving portrait of a tortured mind.

PRINCIPAL WORKS

Tric-trac du ciel (poetry) 1923
L'ombilic des limbes (poetry, essays, and dramatic dialogues, includes *Le Jet de sang*) 1925
Le pèse nerfs (poetry) 1925
Correspondance avec Jacques Rivière (letters) 1927
  [*Artaud-Rivière Correspondence* published in journal *Exodus*, 1960]
L'art et la mort (essays) 1929
Héliogabale; ou, L'anarchiste couronné (novel) 1934
Les nouvelles révélations de l'etre [as Le Révéle] (essays) 1937

Le théâtre et son double (essays) 1938
  [*The Theater and Its Double*, 1958]
D'un voyage au pays des Tarahumaras (essays) 1945
  [*Concerning a Journey to the Land of Tarahumaras* published in *City Lights Journal*, 1964]
Artaud le mômo (poetry) 1947
  [*Artaud the Momo*, 1976]
Ci-gît, précédé de la culture indienne (poetry) 1947
Van Gogh: Le suicidé de la société (essay) 1947
  [*Van Gogh: The Man Suicided by Society* published in *The Trembling Lamb*, 1959?]
Lettres de Rodez (letters) 1948
Supplément aux lettres de Rodez, suivi de Coleridge, le traître (letters and essay) 1949
Oeuvres complètes. Vols. 1-7 (essays, poetry, drama, novel, letters, sketches, dramatic dialogues, dramatic sketches, interviews, screenplays, and diaries) 1956-1967
Antonin Artaud Anthology (essays, poetry, and drama) 1965
Collected Works. Vols. 1-3 (essays, poetry, drama, dramatic sketches, dramatic dialogues, letters, and interviews) 1968-1972
The Cenci (drama) 1969
Love Is a Tree that Always is High: An Artaud Anthology (poetry, drama, and essays) 1972
Selected Writings (essays, poetry, drama, letters, dramatic dialogues, screenplay, interview, and diaries) 1976

WALLACE FOWLIE   (essay date 1959)

Artaud's name is associated with a fundamental revolt against insincerity. His most cherished dream was to found a new kind of theatre in France which would be, not an artistic spectacle, but a communion between spectators and actors. As in primitive societies it would be a theatre of magic, a mass participation in which the entire culture would find its vitality and its truest expression. . . . He wanted for the theatre the same kind of frenzy and moving violence which he found in the paintings of Van Gogh. He claimed that a new kind of civilization was needed, one that would consummate a break with the sensitivity and the logical mentality of the 19th century. Thunderingly he denounced his age for having failed to understand the principal message of Arthur Rimbaud. (pp. 645-46)

Artaud divides humanity into the primitive or prelogical group and the civilized or logical group. The roots of the real theatre are to be found in the first group.... A dramatic presentation should be an act of initiation during which the spectator will be awed and even terrified—and to such a degree that he will lose control of his reason. During that experience of terror or frenzy, instigated by the dramatic action, the spectator will be in a position to understand a new set of truths, superhuman in quality.

The method Artaud proposes by which this will be brought about is to associate the theatre with danger and cruelty.... Words spoken on the stage will then have the power they possess in dreams. Language will become an incantation.... Action will remain the center of the play, but its purpose is to reveal the presence of extraordinary forces in man.... It is a power able to move the spectator closer to the absolute. The theatre is not a direct copy of reality, it is another kind of dangerous reality where the principles of life are always just disappearing from beyond our vision, like dolphins who, as soon as they show their heads above the surface of the water, plunge down into the depths.... Artaud has acknowledged that in this conception of the theatre, he is calling upon an elementary magical idea used by modern psychoanalysis wherein the patient is cured by making him take an exterior attitude of the very state which he should recover or discover. A play which contains the repressed forces of man will liberate him from them. By plastic graphic means, the stage production will appeal to the spectators, will even bewitch them and induce them into a kind of trance. Artaud would like to see stage gesticulations elevated to the rank of exorcisms. In keeping with the principal theories of surrealism, Artaud would claim that art is a real experience which goes far beyond human understanding and attempts to reach a metaphysical truth. (pp. 647-48)

> *Wallace Fowlie, "The New French Theatre: Artaud, Beckett, Genet, Ionesco," in* The Sewanee Review *(reprinted by permission of the editor; © 1959 by The University of the South), Vol. LXVII, No. 4, Autumn, 1959, pp. 643-57.**

GEORGE E. WELLWARTH (essay date 1963)

The contemporary avant-garde theatre—the theatre of Ionesco, Beckett, Adamov, and Genet—is for most people a theatre of mystification.... Much of the confusion caused by these apparently wilfully obscure playwrights might be cleared up by a study of the source of the ideas which animate them. All of the plays of the current avant-garde experimental drama have a common source in the theories of Antonin Artaud.... (p. 276)

The avant-garde drama is the comedy of nihilism and despair. (p. 277)

As Artaud saw it, what was wrong with drama, as well as with all the other arts, was culture. By "culture" Artaud meant the overlay of artificialities which civilization had imposed upon human nature.... Artaud perceived that men are now, as they always have been, basically barbaric, that the thick protective wall of urbane, civilized behavior which they have acquired through centuries of hiding from psychological self-realization is easily crumbled by a forceful appeal to irrational emotion. (pp. 277-78)

The function of the drama, according to Artaud, is twofold: it must protest against the artificial hierarchy of values imposed by culture by being consistently uninhibited, and it must demonstrate the true reality of the human soul and the mercilessly relentless conditions under which it lives by a "drama of cruelty."

The manner in which this violent attack on the everyday is to be accomplished involves a fantastic, larger-than-life callousness which enables the characters to disregard the amenities of social behavior, and a rejection of speech as a means of communication. Speech, according to Artaud, is non-theatrical; therefore, strictly speaking, it has no place in the theatre. The paradox that forms the basis of Artaud's system of theatrical practice is that instead of clarifying the meaning of drama, instead of using the various elements of the theatre (the scenery, the lighting, the costumes, the stage movement, etc.) to make the plays easier to understand, it is necessary to make the plays less easy to understand in order to make them the more accessible to instinctive human emotion. (pp. 278-79)

Artaud felt that the theatre had originally been the medium through which men expressed their innermost, unconscious, instinctual feelings—the mysterious, undefinable, non-rational essence of their beings. Through the ages the true essence of the theatre had become obscured because of the necessity of conforming to the demands of society. Gradually theatre became something national, even local, reflecting the current mores and points of view of individual societies instead of striking through to the root of universal human feeling.... Artaud's theatre was therefore a return to the original purity of drama. (pp. 279-80)

His reason for going back to the original form of drama was his conviction that the drama was a religious expression of man's state. Unlike the ceremonies of religious worship, in which man abased himself before a superior power with the object of propitiating it, the ritual of the drama was man's assertion of his dignity and independence and was therefore a defiance and *protest* against the superior power. (p. 280)

[The cruelty Artaud] referred to is the impersonal, mindless —and therefore implacable—cruelty to which all men are subject. The universe with its violent natural forces was cruel in Artaud's eyes, and this cruelty, he felt, was the one single most important fact of which man must be aware. This cruelty must, of course, at least to some extent take the form of cruelty and viciousness between human beings. Such scenes must be presented in a manner calculated to purge the spectator of the corresponding emotions in him rather than to arouse in him the desire to imitate. At the same time, the spectator must be made aware of the violence dormant within him and the omnipotence of the forces outside him: each theatrical performance must shatter the foundations of the spectator's existence. Artaud is motivated in this solely by a desire to make men aware of their position. He is not a reformer because he believes that neither improvement nor amelioration of man's situation is possible.... The theatre must give the spectator an impression of his own helplessness in the presence of the awesome and ineluctable forces that control the world. Artaud's theatre must be *ecstatic*. It must crush and hypnotize the onlooker's sense....

The natural consequence of all this is that theatre must be spontaneous. (p. 281)

If, then, theatre is to be spontaneous, it must use only works inspired by the emotion of the moment. In his essay, "No More Masterpieces," Artaud explained that all the so-called masterpieces of dramatic literature must either be eliminated or brought up to date. The scholar's slavish cringing before the classics and their automatically respectful, if bored, reception by the layman have no place in the new theatre. Artaud maintained that there is no reason whatever to suppose that a work can be equally valid at all times.... Even if a work deals with a theme that is still as valid as it was in the time the work was written, the structure of the work must be altered to bring it into closer harmony with the feelings of a contemporary audience.... Form as such has no meaning for [Artaud]. All that matters is the theme of the play and the technique by which it can be presented most effectively. Plays must be changed in form and language in order to make them clear to the public. The only objection that might be made against this is that form is self-evidently an integral part of a work of art. Change the form of *Oedipus Rex* and you no longer have *Oedipus Rex*. What you have is a different play on the same theme, like the modern re-interpretations of the classical drama by Sartre, Giraudoux, and Anouilh. Artaud's answer to this would be that if modernizing a play means destroying it, then it must be destroyed. In short, Artaud sees drama as a set of important themes floating around amorphously, ready to be shaped into whatever form the all-powerful *metteur en scène* (a combination of producer, director, and author in Artaud's system) wishes to give them. (pp. 282-83)

In the drama of Artaud the *metteur en scène* is responsible both for the text and for the manner of its presentation. The text as written has no authority whatsoever, and the *metteur en scène* is perfectly free to alter it at will. It is his business to transform the text into a set of animated hieroglyphs which will involve everyone's emotions. Artaud suggested that this can best be done by a technique of interpenetration of action and audience. That is to say, the old partition between action and audience, which was achieved by the artificial dividing line of the proscenium arch or the barrier of the front-row seats, must be eliminated. The stage will continue to exist, but a great part of the action will be carried on *in* the audience and all around it. Instead of the auditorium being lined up in front of the stage, as in the theatre of conventional design, or around the stage, as in the arena theatre, *the stage will surround the audience.* In this way, the audience, seated on swivel chairs, will be encompassed by the action and will feel itself to be part of it instead of being separated from it or hovering over it like students at a surgical demonstration.... Artaud's only opportunity to put his theories into practice with absolute freedom came between 1927 and 1929, when he and Roger Vitrac ran their own theatre, significantly named the Théâtre Alfred Jarry. Here he produced *Les Cenci,* which he adapted from the Shelley and Stendahl versions, several of Vitrac's plays, Strindberg's *Dream Play,* the third act of Claudel's *Partage de Midi* (acted as a farce), and several other things. But Artaud is not important as a mere transformer of other men's work. He was the catalytic agent for an entirely new drama which used the complex resources of the modern theatre to express the age-old cry of fear and protest which has been the most elemental human impulse from the most primitive man to the present.... Artaud continued to define a drama denuded of all the excess and

essentially non-dramatic elements which had accumulated round the art of the theatre through the ages. Artaud's drama may be compared to the bare trunk of a tree stripped of all the shrubbery which usually obscures its reality.... From this tree sprang the modern avant-garde drama—the plays of Beckett, Ionesco, [Arthur Adamov, Jean Genet, Jacques Audiberti, and Jean Vauthier,] ... of Jean Tardieu, Carl Laszlo, and all the other avant-garde playwrights. All of the plays of these modern avant-garde writers are concerned with man's subjection to a malignant fate, all of them discard sociology and psychology as media for building characters, and all of them move in a purely theatrical "unreal" ... dreamlike atmosphere. This dreamlike atmosphere ... is not accidental, but is rather the key to the whole technique. Artaud felt that men see themselves clearly only in dreams; and that it was through dreams that men could reach back to the primeval past when drama was born as the ritual observance of the myths whose creation is coeval with the beginning of human thought itself. Artaud's theory of the dream is allied to the Jungian theory, in which dreams bind men together through their demonstration of an inherited collective unconscious. (pp. 284-86)

The use of the dream technique is basic to Artaud's drama. It enabled him to use speech in a purely theatrical and non-literary manner; and it enabled him to justify his use of visual communication through hieroglyphic symbols, which is the method by which dream communication takes place. It was through the use of the dream technique, too, that Artaud could present the apparitions, effigies, and other "shocks and surprises" which could bring the audience into the desired mystic union with each other, with the action, and with the cruel, primeval, juggernaut-like forces which govern the world. (pp. 286-87)

George E. Wellwarth, "Antonin Artaud: Prophet of the Avant-Garde Theatre," in Drama Survey *(copyright 1963 by The Bolingbroke Society, Inc.), Vol. 2, No. 3, February, 1963, pp. 276-87.*

ALAN SEYMOUR (essay date 1964)

It is obviously easy to make fun of Artaud. He *was* deranged.... His rhetoric did become obscure and self-contradictory. Much of it is patently juvenile and hysterical. Like all prophets he is naïve.... In his hatred of the local norm he over-values the exotically unfamiliar and rambles on for pages about the unlimited possibilities of the Balinese theatre until we suspect he saw it not often enough to become bored by the obvious limitations of all (otherwise delightful) Asian theatre: a lack of the intellectual enquiry which, rightly or wrongly, has characterized Occidental theatre for over 2,000 years. (p. 60)

His concept of the inevitability of cruelty and his claim that constant exposure to cruelty in the theatre will not brutalize us are the two fundamental ideas which betray his philosophical and political view....

It is a reactionary view that in venting our simple impulse to hate, to hurt, to kill, we are somehow returning to a purer natural state. It is impossible to return to a purer natural state.... [Calls] to universal anarchy, though temporarily intoxicating, are, as they have always been, useless. Artaud's alternative suggestion that we act out our blood-thirstiness in the theatre seems to me unconvincing. It is not practical, either economically—for to mount his mass spectacle one would need companies with huge casts and unlimited subsidies; or socially—for it presupposes a universal society which adopts such a theatre holus-bolus. (p. 61)

The only society in which this overtly bloody theatre could take place would be one in which a gangster government had waived all concepts of legality. Of which recent twentieth-century society does that remind you? (p. 62)

To investigate him without sympathy is to end up making fun of him. And then to feel ashamed. He was a man of piercing visions, of profound mental agonies. . . . In his iconoclastic rending of the Western theatre's ills he touched on so many raw nerves. Now, looking back at the bourgeois theatre he attacked and glad of the broadening which has little by little come into the theatre since, we can understand that again and again in his criticism he was right. My only request is that we read him with as much discrimination as possible, accept what is clearly good and bracing, and reject what is bad . . . because what is bad is dangerous. . . . Taken at his own value Artaud and his concept would lead us to a 'philosophy' in which brutality was glorified as a 'necessity'. . . . [People] are so likely to become habituated to casual violence as a means of solving problems that they accept it as inevitable and *right* and become ultimately insensitive in their responses to other human beings. (pp. 62-3)

Art, and especially the theatre . . . has been the one continuing force for making us not less but more sensitive to the dilemmas of human existence. (pp. 63-4)

Alan Seymour, "Artaud's Cruelty," in London Magazine (© London Magazine 1964), Vol. 3, No. 12, March, 1964, pp. 59-64.

ROBERT BRUSTEIN (essay date 1964)

Like the kind of theatre it propagates, *The Theatre and Its Double* has the quality of an exotic and frenzied dream, throwing out flashes of illumination with that hypnotic lucidity which is the hallmark of Artaud's powerful style. A gifted poet himself, Artaud introduces into the theatre the feverish intoxication of the *poètes maudits*, Baudelaire, Rimbaud, Lautrèamont. Like theirs, his poetic ecstasy is very close to madness. . . . Despite the disordered quality of his career and the fragmentary nature of his contribution, however, Artaud exercises a tremendous impact upon the modern French imagination, belonging, in the words of Jacques Guicharnaud, "to that breed of seers who leave trails of fire behind them as they pass through the world." The most important of these fiery passages leads to the theatre of cruelty, even in its embryonic stage one of the most original movements in the modern drama. Yet, Artaud did not live to see it realized. In this movement, Artaud plays the role of a prophetic Aristotle, writing the *Poetics* of an imaginary theatre which Jean Genet, his posthumous Sophocles, will not begin to execute until after his death. (pp. 363-64)

Artaud was associated with both the Dadaists and the Surrealists early in his career, and he shares their loathing of traditional art, of modern industrial life, and of Western civilization. But he turns these negative attitudes into positive acts, transforming the nihilism, sterility, and buffoonery of his predecessors into profoundly revolutionary theory. Artaud's revolt is so radical, and so deadly serious, that it leads him into messianic conclusions. A Romantic who tol-

erates no boundaries, a prophet of rebellion who preaches "extreme action, pushed beyond all limits," Artaud demands nothing less than a total transformation of the existing structure. And this revolution will begin in the theatre. (p. 366)

Artaud's ideas about the theatre are inseparable from his feelings about the world in which he lives. Behind every theory he advances lies his messianic desire to change the face of the West. Artaud does not merely relax into alienation, like the Dadaist and Surrealists. His revolt is so acute that it has brought him full circle into a vision of communion. (p. 367)

In the course of his exegesis, Artaud supplies us with the kind of myth he has in mind, in that provocative essay where he compares the effect of his theatre to that of a plague. For Artaud, the beauty of the plague is its destruction of repressive social forms. Order collapses, authority evaporates, anarchy prevails; and man gives vent to all the disordered impulses which lie buried in his soul. It is this delirium—so similar to Rimbaud's "disordering of all the senses"—that Artaud wishes to introduce into the theatre. . . . Thus, the theatre will be able to evoke that lost world of anarchy and danger without which there is neither humor nor poetry, without which freedom is a chimera and delusion prevails. "That is why," declares Artaud, "I propose a theatre of cruelty. . . . We are not free. And the sky can still fall on our heads. And the theatre has been created to teach us that first of all."

Artaud immediately proceeds to explain that by "cruelty" he does not mean "blood." Nevertheless, his proposals have been widely misunderstood, expecially in Anglo-Saxon countries where Artaud has remained a suspect and unwelcome, if not largely unknown, figure. To cultures which prefer their sadism and masochism disguised (for example, in wars, prizefights, gangster movies, and television), the openly sado-masochistic thrust of Artaud's thought has seemed pathological and perverse. Still, Artaud's assumptions are no more unhealthy than Freud's in *Civilization and Its Discontents;* both assume that men created neurosis when they suppressed their sex and aggression to live together in society. (pp. 368-69)

Artaud himself never advocates perversity, sadism, or violence in daily life. What he proposes is that the theatre serve as a harmless "outlet for repressions," in much the same manner as the analyst's couch. . . . Thus, Artaud would purge the spectator of those bloody impulses he usually turns on others in the name of patriotism, religion, or love.

The primary function of Artaud's theatre, then, is the exorcism of fantasies. Similar to the Great Mysteries—the Orphic and Eleusinian rites—it is based on sacrifice and revolves around crime; but in exteriorizing the spectator's desire for crime, it acts as a catharsis, and drains his violence. . . . His theatre is a double, because it duplicates not everyday reality but rather "another archetypal and dangerous reality." It is a kind of mirror held up to the unconscious. . . . But the meaning of all these analogies is that the Artaudian theatre will be an outwardly illusory world evoking an inner reality—the kind of reality usually revealed in dreams. For it is in the cruel content of dreams that Artaud's theatre will find its true material. . . . (pp. 369-71)

Artaud's attack on language is the most radical part of his theory and—some would say—the least influential, since even the most experimental French drama continues, to this day, to be a drama of words. (p. 373)

Artaud's idea of theatre is primarily visual. It is a theatre in which character, plot, and diction are subordinated to *mise en scène,* or spectacle. Artaud's *Poetics* eliminates, in consequence, the conceptualizing playwright and substitutes the visualizing director—not the conventional traffic cop or actor's coach of Western theatre but rather a "manager of magic, a master of sacred ceremonies." (p. 374)

Aside from these suggestions, however, and the few plays Artaud staged before and after writing his essays, he left no practical applications of his theories. His theatre remained in his head, a vision he could transcribe only to the written page; and he died before its impact was really felt. (pp. 375-76)

> Robert Brustein, "Antonin Artaud and Jean Genet: The Theatre of Cruelty," in his The Theatre of Revolt: An Approach to the Modern Drama *(copyright © 1962, 1963, 1964 by Robert Brustein; reprinted by permission of Little, Brown and Company in association with the Atlantic Monthly Press), Atlantic-Little, Brown, 1964, pp. 361-412.*

STEPHEN KOCH (essay date 1966)

[In Artaud's] development of the modernist relation between spectacle and spectator, the audience is obliged to be [passive].... It is acted upon. Artaud does not regard his spectator as a thinking man, to be instructed, cajoled, seduced. Rather, the spectator is an organism, an exalted nervous system to be set free of itself through shock. In the Theater of Cruelty, the spectator is a hieratic victim. (p. 30)

As an artist and as a man, [Artaud] was thrashing around in the unspeakable.... To express himself at all, Artaud had to wrench language out of its rationalized poetic forms and put it in direct contact with a turbulent psychic flux that had not been expressed before. No formal ideal could precede or determine this contact. Artaud wishes to rely exclusively on immediate associations between impulse and physical images. (pp. 32-3)

While Artaud's language—particularly in the early work—has the advantage of rendering the physical and the ideal simultaneously ("flesh naked with all the intellectual deepening of this spectacle of pure flesh") it hardly prohibits a quite conventional poetic assimilation of what is being said. Most of Artaud's written work is finally that of an intellectual, a theorist, rather than a poet—at least the poet he wanted to be. This dilemma seems to have been forced on him by the purity of his artistic ambition in conspiracy with language itself. Language can be rendered abstract through formal objectification. Or words can be violently flung around like things. But only a voice can throw them, and a voice must be coherent. Artaud was entirely aware of this, and consequently had no interest in, say, automatic writing. True, he did not find it necessary either to abandon the written word or to return to conventional form as a solution. But he was forced into a kind of compromise, particularly in the early part of his career. The works in *le Pèse Nerfs* and *l'Ombilic des Limbes,* ... are essentially in the tradition of Baudelaire's *Spleen,* and they subdue their vile imagery of derangement to the rhythms of Baudelairian vision.

Finally, the realization of Artaud's intuitively ordered chaos was impossible. The very idea is a contradiction, assuming as it does that a violent mental flux can be made ideal, and brought to rest, like an object. But beyond the formal incapacity of language to embody this contradiction, there was something in Artaud's illness itself that annihilated thought on the verge of expression. His descriptions of this hysterical crumbling of the imagination are among the most remarkable and moving things in his work. (pp. 33-4)

This pathological asphyxiation of the expressive capacity mirrors—is the double of—the poetic inconsistency that defines all of Artaud's work. It is impossible to know, of course, whether the Theater of Cruelty, had he been able to establish it, would have been maimed in the same way. He obviously did not think so. But since the unity he sought, whether formal or intuitive, could never be made wholly immanent on the page, Artaud was reduced to the practice of poetry as process; a series of fragmentary Pyrrhic victories over his imaginative isolation.... (p. 34)

Few poets of any period have more successfully completed the identification of sense experience (and ultimately, mind) with the nervous system, with protoplasm, than did Artaud. But the poems in *l'Ombilic des Limbes* and *le Pèse Nerfs* are not simply about pain, exhaustion, hysteria, nervous decay, and the rest. They are surreal images *of* these things. Thus, they have a reflective awareness of themselves, they look upon themselves with a kind of consciousness that is the true locus of pain. Just as important, only their surreality permits this identification of feeling—all feeling, including thought—with the organism....

Artaud was not content to be a poet. I have called the formal unity of his early works the result of a compromise—which suggests that some "purer" alternative was open to him. But Artaud's imagination in its "pure" form destroyed itself. Thus, the unity of *le Pèse Nerfs* was inevitably false to his own sensibility, though it is only through a peculiarly modern perspective that it is called false rather than transcendent. As we all know, ecstasy has turned out to be ambiguity, and Artaud is one of that group of ecstatic poets *manqué,* such as Sade and Rimbaud, who eventually chose for themselves and against literature. (p. 35)

[Artaud's] later work—"Journey to the Land of the Tarahumaras," "Artaud le Momo," "Ci-Git," "Shit to the Spirit," the essays on Van Gogh, Coleridge, Lautréamont—resemble the screams heard in the most up-to-date hospitals. They are assaults, and when really read, they are almost unendurable. In them, Artaud abandons all the formal modifications to which he had subjected his early work, in order to exert only that shock from which he gained the richness and relief. But in this new capacity, the shock which Artaud wishes to inflict cannot be assimilated.

Now, the charge of hermeticism cannot be brought against Artaud's work at any point. *L'Ombilic des Limbes* and *Pèse Nerfs* are accessible, if difficult, works, and rather than seek an entirely private existence, the later writings attempt to *make contact* in violent good faith. Indeed, they have a quality more properly attributed to discourse than to poetry, for theirs is a voice that speaks solely to and for others. Their intonation is that of announcement, explanation, abuse, seduction, sneering, coyness, raving. In them, Artaud has entirely rejected the Word as something self-contained. They are a "revolt against poetry."

Still, they are not discourse, for they don't participate in any kind of dialectic. This means two things. They are entirely un-self-aware—many are, simply, ravings. Secondly, their ideas are unstable, unassimilable, and probably intended to be that way. That self-awareness which in most poetry creates the knowledge of the voices meaning to itself, has here been made into knowledge of the voices meaning to something, someone, wholly other and alien. This is poetry determined by an advanced stage of paranoia, directed against a loathed and invincible threat—a threat created, true enough, by Artaud himself, but nonetheless seen as external. Because it is alien, Artaud speaks to make contact with it; because it is loathed, he speaks with violence; because it is invincible, his awareness is limited to an unconfessed sense of futility which renders his expression both incomplete and unremitting. Thus these works do not, properly speaking, have a form: like the discourse to which they are phenomenologically related, they are potentially interminable. . . . What remains—their unremitting violence, their incompletion, their voice—is felt, from the reader's side, as it was doubtless intended to be felt: constant contact with a sensibility that regards one as alien, and which is itself, in consequence, alien. (p. 36)

At a certain point, he abandoned the attempt to embody or transcend the monster that loomed on the ruined landscape of his mind. Instead—it was his most radical gesture—he changed the metaphor. He externalized his entirely modern intellect, attributed to it everything loathsome usually associated with the body, and assaulted it in a hitherto unknown poetry of the human voice as pure action. Perhaps this new metaphor—the mind as loathed physicality—is the most important aspect of Artaud's writing. (p. 37)

Stephen Koch, "On Artaud," in Tri-Quarterly *(© 1966 by* Tri-Quarterly*), No. 6, 1966, pp. 29-37.*

BETTINA L. KNAPP (essay date 1969)

Artaud was unable to adapt to life; he could not relate to others; he was not even certain of his own identity.

Such an attitude of "rootlessness" or of "suspension", was by no means a façade or a pose; it was rather the direct result of a smouldering and festering disease which was slowly eating away at Artaud's very being. (p. 17)

The poems in *Tric Trac du Ciel* focus around several themes: the genesis of the creative process, the conflict between inner and outer reality, and the fear of the void.

The violence of the imagery as well as the auditory qualities of these verses can be used as a barometer to measure the highs and the lows of the author's emotional state. Fire and flames (hot images) express activity, the fervent onrush of ideas as in the poem "Organ Grinder" and "Romance"; ice and snow (cold images) denote passivity and sterility as in "Snow" and "The Organ and the Vitriol." The almost constant juxtaposition of images takes on metaphysical significance: it indicates eternal flux and by extension the perpetual metamorphosis of all elements within the universe. Therefore, "blankness" or "whiteness" does not necessarily mean the end of the creative forces within the individual, it signifies only a change in direction. "The Trappist," for example, shows that what was once unfit food for poetry can in time turn into a delectable dish. A haunting cosmic quality is achieved by a depletion of imagery and a slowing down of pace as in "Moon," an exquisite little

poem in which the author ponders the question of reality and its mirror image. The auditory sense frequently assumes greater importance in these verses than does the visual. *Prière*, which depicts the author's fright of the void, is accompanied by a whole series of tumultuous sounds. (p. 20)

Artaud's anxieties concerning his mental state . . . are expressed in metaphysical terms in "The Umbilicus of Limbo" (*L'Ombilic des Limbes*). The title itself is an indication of the mood and meaning of the work. The navel is the point of creation and this scar or hole or abyss, by extension, is the only physical remembrance of that other life or of *primordial unity*. "Limbo" is the abode of souls barred from heaven through no fault of their own, souls of men who died before the coming of Christ or unbaptized infants. It is, therefore, a place of confinement, a state of neglect or of oblivion.

The umbilicus is a physical attribute; limbo, a condition existing in the mind, a spiritual concept. Artaud unites these opposites, the spiritual and the physical. He does so primarily because of his inability, at times, to differentiate between them. (pp. 23-4)

Artaud was in essence constructing an entire metaphysical system around his sickness, or, if you will, entering the realm of the mystic via his own disease. The focal point of his universe was himself and everything radiated from *him* outward. To explicate himself, he reasoned, would enable him to understand the collective, the spiritual, the physical, life, death, and so relate to them. . . . "Umbilicus of Limbo" was intended to "derange man," to take people on a journey "where they would never have consented to go." Artaud was going to open the door on to his *reality*, take his readers down the damp corridors of time, into recesses riddled with strange beasts and grotesque phantoms, display his inner world, the source of creative energy itself, where black suns sparkle and blue flames congeal.

What Artaud revealed during the course of his inner pilgrimage and how he described these discoveries makes for one of the most thrilling, horrifying, and absorbing documents since Dante's *Inferno*. By means of Artaud's peregrinations through the mystical *spheres* of his heavens and his hells of existence, or the various layers of his unconscious, he succeeds in contacting the most primitive elements within himself and within all men. . . .

Artaud's voyage inward can be divided into three distinct phases: the journey itself, fraught with all sorts of hazards; the initiation, a painful rite; the partial attainment of his goal. (p. 24)

Artaud was like a man possessed and pursued. . . . [He felt] the pain one must know as part of an initiation process which permits one to cross from one world to another.

Such a crisis or initiation process is referred to by certain mystics as a "break-through" from one aspect of life to another, from self consciousness to cosmic consciousness. When this "break-through" occurs, the inner Abyss or Nothingness, that gaping hole or void which Artaud so feared and at the same time so longed for, would be experienced. (pp. 27-8)

Artaud did see the Abyss—but for seconds only. At these moments, he spoke in terms of "gel" and "clarity," implying that from these icy impersonal depths, the clarity and purity of absolute Being, or the Deity was revealed. To penetrate this new realm had its dangers. In this undifferentiated state or sphere of Being, one risked being sucked down into those limitless waters of the unconscious world, of never returning to a differentiated or conscious existence. Artaud, therefore, experienced ambivalent feelings toward his quest: fright and joy; love and hate. . . .

Added to his dolor was the terrifying reality of being severed from his *Self,* doomed to a state of oblivion in limbo, fully communing neither with his inner world nor with the world about him. (p. 28)

His nightmarish existence takes on dramatic form in ''The Jet of Blood'' (*Le Jet de sang*). . . . (p. 31)

''The Jet of Blood'' is a short play which attacks the political, social, sexual and religious attitudes of the day in a half-mocking, derisive manner; one which is suffused with a sense of dread and despair. Far more than a criticism of society, it is a revelation, of course, of Artaud's inner life: this time, the difficulties he had in making his adjustments as he grew from boy to man, and the bloody struggle to make some connection between inner and outer reality. What Artaud sets before his viewers, however, is anything but personal. It is, on the contrary, an anonymous collective world, detached and objective. Even the cast is impersonal, each character appearing as a function rather than by name: the young man, the young girl, the nurse, etc.

''The Jet of Blood'' not only stands as a landmark in Artaud's development, but also as a bizarre and highly original theatrical concoction which has gone a long way in influencing the writers of the *absurd*. (p. 32)

Strangely enough, Artaud's [theatrical] innovations, for the most part, arose directly as a result of his malady. An inability to think in a cartesian manner and an overly sensitive and high-strung nature, had led him to opt for a theatre which worked on the nerves and the senses, and reject one which sought to speak to the intellect alone. Artaud's theatre, therefore, would be militantly anti-rational as well as hugely emotional; it would attempt to spew forth venom —to scathe—all those with whom it would come into contact. (p. 45)

The spectator must be shocked, react violently to the ''unprecedented eruption of a world'' on stage; he must feel that he is seeing the essence of his own being before him, that his life is unfolding within the bodies of others. If a theatrical production is to be considered effective, the spectator must experience anguish, be immensely and intensely involved; so deeply affected, in effect, that his whole organism is shaken into participation.

Since Artaud's ideas concerning the dramatic arts were born from his sickness, he looked upon the theatre as a curative agent; a means whereby the individual could come to the theatre to be dissected, split and cut open first, and then healed. (pp. 45-6)

Artaud reveals his system in a series of disparate lectures, manifestoes, letters, and essays written from 1931 to 1935. . . . (p. 93)

[In these works] Artaud voiced his most profound ideas, *all* of which had emerged—not from any intellectual concepts —but rather from his own personal agony, like drops of blood staining the earth's surface. Artaud's ideas

throughout these works are never expressed in a cartesian manner, but seem to topple forth, helter-skelter—each as a result of some association or sensation which acts as a releasing agent for a torrential blast of new formulations. Such insights as are expressed by Artaud throughout these pages are revealed frequently by means of strikingly colored images: nightmarish and ghoulish figures scampering across its pages; cutting and brittle enunciations, onomatopoeias; cacophonous and deafening phrases. The reader, spellbound, tingling all over, his sensations aroused to the breaking point, as he makes his way through this labyrinth, this tremendously stirring and hyper-magnetised field of action, can actually feel Artaud's flashes of intuition, his heaving sighs of sorrow, his bursts of joy and hatreds, as he yields to revelation upon revelation. Artaud's super and sustained emotionalism, his psychic fire which he unleashes with stinging intensity, propels the reader on one of the most traumatic voyages ever taken; it also leaves him gasping for breath, bewildered, numb, trying to penetrate, to *see* into Artaud's exquisitely and intricately chiseled world of mosaic thought-patterns. (pp. 93-4)

In ''Van Gogh: the Man Suicided by Society,'' Artaud brought new depths of vision to the field of art criticism. He looked upon the plastic arts as an externalization of self; painting, as a device by which man's mythical heritage could be renewed and made to live again, where unconscious archetypal images could be made to dance their dance of the hours, confronting, stifling, crippling, or unburdening the heart of the spectator. Painting for Artaud was a material manifestation of an immaterial myth, the stating of an intangible *reality*. To interpret such a mythical reality, Artaud declared, requires genius, and this is just what Van Gogh possessed.

Furthermore, painting was a manifestation of the occult, a hypnotic agent. Each object on a canvas, each color, each line and stroke was looked upon by Artaud as a ''talisman'', a force serving to draw the viewer's vision *inward*. This altered vision, plus the viewer's intuition, imagination, and feeling, created a new state of being, a fresh world with a just-born sense of self.

In ''Van Gogh: the Man Suicided by Society,'' Artaud maintained that Van Gogh was endowed with powers beyond the average. He was a man of extraordinary vision, and therefore, his personality differed from that of others. Artists who see things in a different light cannot function according to the dictates of society and cannot be expected to follow the behavior patterns of the so-called *normal* human being. (p. 125)

Artaud certainly, unconsciously or deliberately, identified with Van Gogh. Both men were victims of society's indifference to and incomprehension of their gifts. Both men found their deepest release in their creative work. (p. 182)

Artaud's contribution to the field of art criticism cannot be unduly stressed. He made it live at a time when this art had disintegrated to an unbelievable degree: it had become an academic exercise, not even that, a superficial and unintelligible retort. (p. 186)

One reason for his failure during his lifetime may have been that the fulgurating insights of his genius were frequently obscured by a chaotic and repetitious writing style. But the fundamental cause of this phenomenon is more likely that what had been Artaud's individual situation in the 1920's and 1930's had become a collective malady a generation later. In his time, he was a man alienated from his society, divided within himself, a victim of inner and outer forces beyond his control—and he remained isolated in an indifferent world. The tidal force of his imagination and the urgency of his therapeutic quest were disregarded and cast aside as the ravings of a madman. Today, things have changed. (pp. 200-01)

In a word, modern man can respond to Artaud now because they share so many psychological similarities and affinities. (p. 201)

Bettina L. Knapp, in her Antonin Artaud: Man of Vision *(copyright © 1969, 1980 by Bettina L. Knapp; reprinted by permission of Ohio University Press, Athens), David Lewis, 1969 (and reprinted by Ohio University Press, 1980), 233 p.*

SANCHE de GRAMONT (essay date 1970)

Two French doctors who have written about Artaud see him as a classic illustration of schizophrenia. . . .

The two doctors interpret Artaud's creative achievements as a form of therapy, as an activity that brought relief from his mental illness and allowed him, at the same time, to keep a grip on reality.

But Artaud never wanted to be cured. If he was mad, he welcomed his madness. He did not hope that writing and acting would help make him well. On the contrary, he felt that it was only because he was ill that he was able to create and that his illness gave his work a special quality. Much of his writing was an inquiry into the limits and definition of his madness. . . . To him the rational world was deficient; he welcomed the hallucinations that abolished reason and gave meaning to his alienation. He purposely placed himself outside the limits in which sanity and madness can be opposed, and gave himself up to a private world of magic and irrational visions. (p. 50)

[Artaud] devoted himself to his own vision of the theatre. (p. 51)

The closest Artaud came to staging the Theatre of Cruelty was his . . . production of *The Cenci*, a melodrama of murder and incest in an Italian Renaissance family that was derived from Shelley's tragedy and from the *Italian Chronicles* of Stendhal. Artaud himself said that there was as much difference between *The Cenci* and the Theatre of Cruelty as there was between a water fountain and a thunderstorm. . . . Artaud practiced his theories concerning screams, gestures, and the use of lighting as a language, but the critics were not impressed. They repeated what had already been said of Alfred Jarry: "He may have genius, too bad he has no talent." (p. 53)

A year before his death [Artaud] gave his last major performance. . . . The two Andrés were there, Breton and Gide, as well as Albert Camus and a score of other writers whose presence showed that Artaud's books, although published in small numbers, were steadily making their way. But much of the audience had probably been drawn by the promise of seeing a freak, like the man with the crocodile skin or the tattooed lady in the circus.

Artaud did indeed look like a fugitive from a side show, a grimacing phantom of a man—toothless, emaciated, ragged, his disorderly hair tumbling about his shoulders, his eyes

filled with the same panic that he had simulated years before in the part of the shell-shocked soldier. But once he began to speak, those present realized that they were not going to be entertained, but that Artaud had placed them in the uncomfortable position of watching a man live out his torment. This was the Theatre of Cruelty: to see Artaud stutter, sob, and shout as he told about his treatment in asylums and made them reflect on a society that could produce an individual at once so lucid and so demented. Suddenly he stopped, the fire subsided, and he said very calmly: "I put myself in your place and I see that what I am saying is devoid of interest—how can I be really sincere?" . . .

More than twenty years later Artaud endures as a cult figure. . . . [The] Theatre of Cruelty continues to inspire a certain kind of modern drama, and madness itself is understood in some circles today as a form of artistic sensibility. (p. 55)

Sanche de Gramont, "A Vocation for Madness," in Horizon *(© 1970 American Heritage Publishing Company, Inc.; reprinted by permission), Vol. XII, No. 2, Spring, 1970, pp. 49-55.*

NAOMI GREENE (essay date 1970)

[Artaud] was drawn to the Surrealists' rejection of rational, logical thought, and to their quest for a reality beyond that of the everyday world. Convinced that our conventional perception of the world had to be destroyed in order to find this reality, the Surrealists turned to drugs, dreams, automatic writing, and hallucination. Even madness was regarded as an acceptable way of furthering this process of destruction. (p. 92)

Artaud shared the Surrealist dream of establishing contact with another reality, one far surpassing the world of ordinary logic and natural law. Such contacts could be effected only in "surrealistic" states during which a man apparently loses control of his being but, in fact, experiences a different kind of control, one that "prevents contact with ordinary reality and allows these subtler and more rarefied contacts." . . . (p. 93)

Artaud was drawn to mysticism and to Surrealism by the characteristic the two had in common: The subsidiary role accorded rational thought in Eastern religion coincides perfectly with the Surrealists' rejection of Western logic and reason. Surrealism could even be called "mystical" insofar as it insists that true reality cannot be perceived by the logical mind.

The mark of Eastern mysticism is particularly evident in the articles Artaud published anonymously in *la Révolution surréaliste.* (pp. 107-08)

At first glance, what Artaud wrote in the 1930's appears to mark a radical departure from his earlier work. No direct mention of his own problems is found in the major works of this period: *Le théâtre et son double,* . . . *Héliogabale, Les nouvelles révélations de l'être,* and *D'un voyage au pays des Tarahumaras.* However, many of the themes which dominate his earlier writings are also found in these books, albeit in veiled form. Although Artaud no longer speaks in subjective terms, it soon becomes clear that he remains obsessed with sexuality and fearful of his own subconscious instincts, while his rejection of normal discursive language and his dislike of Western society, with its traditional faith in the power of logic and rationality, have grown stronger than ever. For the first time though—and this is what distinguishes these writings from the earlier ones—Artaud's fears and desires are expressed in universal terms. In an attempt to transcend, or perhaps to justify, his own problems, Artaud seeks to demonstrate that those fears and desires haunt all of Western civilization. (p. 113)

The element most characteristic of Artaud's work during the 30's is violence, a violence often bringing in its wake perverted sexuality. Artaud's fascination with the more savage aspects of human life no doubt stems, in part, from his experience with the Surrealists. (p. 114)

Artaud wants to project man's violent instincts—lust, vengeance, the drive for power—onto the stage where they will be transformed into symbols. (p. 116)

Any mention of violence in Artaud's work is inevitably accompanied by another word—cruelty. . . . Afraid lest his readers equate cruelty with physical violence, Artaud sought to make it clear that the cruelty he had in mind was not brutal and sadistic but cosmic and metaphysical. The task of the theater, he maintained, is to show that life itself is cruel because metaphysical forces are constantly at work to deprive man of his freedom. (p. 117)

Artaud's belief that life is cruel also seems related to his own problems, for whenever he attempts to prove or justify that belief, the reasons he advances are less than convincing. On a few occasions, he hints at the personal connotations that the word "cruelty" has for him. In one such passage, he introduces a key word, "evil." "In the flame of life, in the appetite for life, in the irrational impulsion to live, there is a kind of initial malice. . . . In the manifested world, metaphysically speaking, evil is the permanent law." . . . Artaud's use of the word "evil" is revealing; while life can conceivably be called "cruel," it cannot be said to be "evil." Evil is a concept which belongs to an entirely different realm—the realm of morality and religion wherein reside absolute good and absolute bad. The notion of evil can play no role in a world of impersonal metaphysical forces. But since Artaud appears to use "cruel" and "evil" interchangeably, the question is not why Artaud considers life to be cruel, but why he thinks it is evil. . . . Artaud obviously believes that life is evil (or cruel) because it cannot escape from matter. Conversely, he praises the theater for its capacity to release us from the inertia of matter weighing us down. . . . Upon examination, Artaud's grand notion of cruelty is based on slender philosophical ground: life can be called cruel only if we assume that matter is basically evil. (pp. 118-19)

The fundamental ambiguity characterizing Artaud's concept of cruelty was also evident whenever he proposed ways of presenting violence and cruelty on stage. While he continually asserted that the cruelty he envisioned was cosmic and was not to be equated with physical violence, all the plays he suggested producing were permeated by blood and gore. (p. 119)

This attempt at justification is well illustrated in *Les Cenci*, the only play Artaud completed. The play deals with a Renaissance nobleman, a monster named Cenci who rapes his daughter and is killed, in turn, by assassins she has hired. Far from regretting his vicious nature, Cenci glories in the evil deeds he has committed. . . . Artaud tries to infuse a feeling of cosmic cruelty into the play by having Cenci represent the evil forces of nature, not unlike the plague. . . .

[Intentions] such as this, however, pale alongside scenes of murder, rape, and torture. (p. 120)

The sexual perversions found in *Les Cenci* occur, in one form or another, in virtually everything Artaud wrote during the 1930's. In his description of the plague, for example, Artaud does not fail to mention that the disease heightens eroticism, adding that many recovered victims, instead of fleeing the city, attempt to find pleasure with the dying, or even with the dead. At one point in *Le théâtre et son double* he implies that all our violent instincts are sexual in nature. Although he does not fully understand the link between sexuality on the one hand and violence and evil on the other, Artaud is convinced that such a link exists. (p. 121)

[Most] of the books Artaud wrote during the 1930's reflect his ever-growing fascination with primitive religions whose cosmologies explain the world's genesis in terms of masculine and feminine principles. Artaud expounds upon the fact that primitive societies have always been violently torn by the struggle between the two sexual principles. He apparently hopes to prove that violence has always been the handmaiden of sex. (pp. 125-26)

At times, Artaud banishes discursive language from the theater by declaring that words must be used for their sound rather than for their meaning. Once stripped of their rational significance, words would serve the same function as musical notes or different shades of light and color. Artaud was convinced that the pitch of the voice, the repetition of certain syllables, could affect our nervous system and so influence us emotionally. If sounds, noises and cries are chosen first for their vibratory quality and only secondly for their meaning, language will communicate physically—not intellectually, and therefore superficially. (pp. 148-49)

From 1946 until his death in 1948 [Artaud] devoted all his energies to poetry, with the notable exception of his book on Van Gogh. For many readers of Artaud these poems constitute the most important part of his career. No longer does Artaud make use of universal terms to camouflage, or justify, his own problems, as he did in *Le théâtre et son double*. . . . Nor is there an effort to analyze the mechanism of his thoughts and the dilemma of his being, as he attempted to do at the outset of his career. His desperate attempts to dissect the nature of his problems have come to an end. Completely disillusioned with the value of intellectual analysis, he now seeks only to convey to us the intensity of his sufferings. His lifelong fears and hatreds, more intense than ever, are voiced in violent and often brutal terms. (p. 160)

[All] of his later poems are strongly marked by the presence of the body: vivid metaphors of brutal physical sensations give to his poems a directness and a violence unequaled elsewhere in his work. Formerly, Artaud analyzed his reactions in intellectual terms. Now, however, his problems can no longer be *understood*, only *felt*. And, for the first time, his own work seems to meet his lifelong demand that literature have the power to move us viscerally rather than intellectually.

All his old obsessive anxieties are now revealed through metaphors. Instead of informing us, for example, that his being is menaced (as he would have done twenty years earlier), he evokes this sensation with physical, concrete images. (p. 172)

The horror Artaud experiences when he contemplates the loss of his being is frequently expressed by metaphors involving holes. . . . Holes, or voids, represent the non-being, the nothingness, the utter disintegration that terrified Artaud. And, in its ultimate form, such disintegration is death. (p. 180)

The holes which occupy Artaud most are those constituting the body's orifices. The Freudian overtones which this suggests are rendered more explicit by Artaud's fear that man will lose his being through these orifices and consequently die. . . .

Artaud's dread of bodily orifices is but another aspect of his lifelong hatred of all the animal functions and instinctual drives within him. As always, chief among the instincts he despises is sexuality, which, he now declares, is at the root of all our other animal functions. (p. 181)

Artaud's fear of external hostile forces leads him to denounce with particular relish all those bodily functions—such as eating and copulating—which involve other people or things. If need be, he would destroy all the organs which traffic with the outside world. (p. 183)

His repeated insistence that he was not born like other men reflects not only Artaud's abhorrence of sex but also an intense desire to create himself. He wants to be alone responsible for his existence. (p. 186)

While the sound of words plays an extremely important role in Artaud's later poetry, it is highly doubtful that these poems accomplish the aims Artaud himself had in mind. He wanted to create a *new* language which would both coincide with the author's being and affect the listener in a physical way. Even Artaud's most fervent admirers could scarcely maintain that he was successful in these objectives. His language is not new and, far from having a physical effect, the poems demand all the resources of the reader's intellectual and mental ingenuity. (p. 197)

However difficult Artaud's poems may be, many readers consider them to be the finest portion of his work. Although Artaud could never eliminate traditional language, nor make language coincide with being, he, like other important contemporary writers, did push language to a breaking point. Had he gone further, had he wrenched language out of its traditional patterns any more than he did, any communication would have been impossible. As it is, many passages in his later poems are partially, if not totally, incomprehensible. (p. 199)

Thus far, no mention has been made of the incantatory passages strewn throughout Artaud's later poems. Most of his critics believe that these passages reflect the importance he placed upon sounds. . . . Although Artaud's incantations are undeniably related to his preoccupation with sound, it seems highly probable that they are motivated by something more fundamental. (pp. 210-11)

The belief that every word possesses physical strength is at the base of the verbal magic and incantatory rites of primitive peoples. Since Artaud shares this belief it follows that he would attribute magical powers to incantation. Convinced that demonic spirits were casting spells upon him, he fought magic with magic. Through incantations he hoped to exorcize himself of the things he dreaded and despised. (p. 212)

Although the incantations and the violent passages in Artaud's poems are probably the most original and personal element in his work, by no means do they constitute a new language. Like all of Artaud's puns and word games, they are meaningful only because, in one way or another, they are related to discursive language. Artaud could no more create a new language than he could render language real. (pp. 216-17)

Artaud did not create new theatrical concepts, he had the undeniable genius to make them come alive in the burning language of poetry. . . . It must not be forgotten that, above all, Artaud was a *poet* who wrote of the theater. (p. 220)

> *Naomi Greene, in her* Antonin Artaud: Poet without Words *(copyright © 1970 by, Naomi Greene; reprinted by permission of Simon and Schuster, a Division of Gulf & Western Corporation), Simon & Schuster, 1970, 256 p.*

SUSAN SONTAG   (essay date 1976)

Both in his work and in his life, Artaud failed. . . . What he bequeathed was not achieved works of art but a singular presence, a poetics, an aesthetics of thought, a theology of culture, and a phenomenology of suffering.

In Artaud, the artist as seer crystallizes, for the first time, into the figure of the artist as pure victim of his consciousness. What is prefigured in Baudelaire's prose poetry of spleen and Rimbaud's record of a season in hell becomes Artaud's statement of his unremitting, agonizing awareness of the inadequacy of his own consciousness to itself—the torments of a sensibility that judges itself to be irreparably estranged from thought. Thinking and using language become a perpetual calvary. (pp. xix-xx)

The consequence of Artaud's verdict upon himself—his conviction of his chronic alienation from his own consciousness—is that his mental deficit becomes, directly or indirectly, the dominant, inexhaustible subject of his writings. Some of Artaud's accounts of his Passion of thought are almost too painful to read. He elaborates little on his emotions—panic, confusion, rage, dread. His gift was not for psychological understanding (which, not being good at it, he dismissed as trivial) but for a more original mode of description, a kind of physiological phenomenology of his unending desolation. Artaud's claim in *The Nerve Meter* that no one has ever so accurately charted his "intimate" self is not an exaggeration. Nowhere in the entire history of writing in the first person is there as tireless and detailed a record of the microstructure of mental pain. (p. xxi)

Artaud appears to have been afflicted with an extraordinary inner life, in which the intricacy and clamorous pitch of his physical sensations and the convulsive intuitions of his nervous system seemed permanently at odds with his ability to give them verbal form. This clash between facility and impotence, between extravagant verbal gifts and a sense of intellectual paralysis, is the psychodramatic plot of everything Artaud wrote; and to keep that contest dramatically valid calls for the repeated exorcising of the respectability attached to writing.

Thus, Artaud does not so much free writing as place it under permanent suspicion by treating it as the mirror of consciousness—so that the range of what can be written is made coextensive with consciousness itself, and the truth of any statement is made to depend on the vitality and wholeness of the consciousness in which it originates. Against all hierarchical, or Platonizing, theories of mind, which make one part of consciousness superior to another part, Artaud upholds the democracy of mental claims, the right of every level, tendency, and quality of the mind to be heard: "We can do anything in the mind, we can speak in any tone of voice, *even one that is unsuitable*." Artaud refuses to exclude any perception as too trivial or crude. (p. xxiii)

Struggling to embody live thought, Artaud composed in feverish, irregular blocks; writing abruptly breaks off and then starts again. Any single "work" has a mixed form; for instance, between an expository text and an oneiric description he frequently inserts a letter—a letter to an imaginary correspondent, or a real letter that omits the name of the addressee. Changing forms, he changes breath. Writing is conceived of as unleashing an unpredictable flow of searing energy; knowledge must explode in the reader's nerves. The details of Artaud's stylistics follow directly from his notion of consciousness as a morass of difficulty and suffering. His determination to crack the carapace of "literature"—at least, to violate the self-protective distance between reader and text—is scarcely a new ambition in the history of literary modernism. But Artaud may have come closer than any other author to actually doing it—by the violent discontinuity of his discourse, by the extremity of his emotion, by the purity of his moral purpose, by the excruciating carnality of the account he gives of his mental life, by the genuineness and grandeur of the ordeal he endured in order to use language at all. (pp. xxiv-xxv)

The Umbilicus of Limbo, The Nerve Meter, and *Art and Death*—which may be read as prose poems, more splendid than anything that Artaud did formally as a poet, show him to be the greatest prose poet in the French language since the Rimbaud of *Illuminations* and *A Season in Hell.* Yet it would be incorrect to separate what is most accomplished as literature from his other writings.

Artaud's work denies that there is any difference between art and thought, between poetry and truth. Despite the breaks in exposition and the varying of "forms" within each work, everything he wrote advances a line of argument. Artaud is always didactic. He never ceased insulting, complaining, exhorting, denouncing—even in the poetry written after he emerged from the insane asylum in Rodez, in 1946, in which language becomes partly unintelligible; that is, an unmediated physical presence. All his writing is in the first person, and is a mode of address in the mixed voices of incantation and discursive explanation. His activities are simultaneously art and reflections on art. (p. xxxv)

Despite Artaud's passionate rejection of Surrealism [after his split from the Surrealist movement], his taste was Surrealist—and remained so. His disdain for "realism" as a collection of bourgeois banalities is Surrealist, and so are his enthusiasms for the art of the mad and the non-professional, for that which comes from the Orient, for whatever is extreme, fantastic, gothic. Artaud's contempt for the dramatic repertory of his time, for the play devoted to exploring the psychology of individual characters—a contempt basic to the argument of the manifestos in "The Theatre and Its Double," . . .—starts from a position identical with the one from which Breton dismisses the novel in the first "Manifesto of Surrealism" (1924). But Artaud makes a wholly different use of the enthusiasms and the aesthetic prejudices he shares with Breton. The Surrealists are connoisseurs of joy, freedom, pleasure. Artaud is a connoisseur of despair and moral struggle. While the Surrealists explicitly refuse to accord art an autonomous value, they perceive no conflict between moral longings and aesthetic ones, and in that sense Artaud is quite right in saying that their program is "aesthetic"—merely aesthetic, he means. Artaud does perceive such a conflict, and demands that art justify itself by the standards of moral seriousness. (pp. xxvii-xxviii)

The parameters of Artaud's work in all the arts are identical with the different critical distances he maintains from the idea of an art that is language only—with the diverse forms of his lifelong "revolt against poetry." . . . The dimensions of the poetry he was capable of writing in the twenties were too small for what Artaud intuited to be the scale of a master art. In the early poems, his breath is short; the compact lyric form he employs provides no outlet for his discursive and narrative imagination. Not until the great outburst of writing in the period between 1945 and 1948, in the last three years of his life, did Artaud, by then indifferent to the idea of poetry as a closed lyric statement, find a long-breathed voice that was adequate to the range of his imaginative needs—a voice that was free of established forms and open-ended, like the poetry of Pound. Poetry as Artaud conceived it in the twenties had none of these possibilities or adequacies. It was small, and a total art had to be, to feel, large; it had to be a multi-voiced performance, not a singular lyrical object. (p. xxx)

Artaud's search for a total art form centered upon the theatre. Unlike poetry, an art made out of one material (words), theatre uses a plurality of materials: words, light, music, bodies, furniture, clothes. (p. xxxi)

[Upon theatre Artaud] has had an impact so profound that the course of all recent serious theatre in Western Europe and the Americas can be said to divide into two periods—before Artaud and after Artaud. No one who works in the theatre now is untouched by the impact of Artaud's specific ideas about the actor's body and voice, the use of music, the role of the written text, the interplay between the space occupied by the spectacle and the audience's space. Artaud changed the understanding of what was serious, what was worth doing. Brecht is the century's only other writer on the theatre whose importance and profundity conceivably rival Artaud's. But Artaud did not succeed in affecting the conscience of the modern theatre by himself being, as Brecht was, a great director. (p. xxxviii)

All Artaud's work is about salvation, theatre being the means of saving souls which he meditated upon most deeply. . . . In Artaud's Theatre of Cruelty, it is the audience that will be twice-born—an untested claim, since Artaud never made his theatre work. . . . (p. xlii)

What Artaud did on the stage as a director and as a leading actor in his productions was too idiosyncratic, narrow, and hysterical to persuade. He has exerted influence through his ideas about the theatre, a constituent part of the authority of these ideas being precisely his inability to put them into practice. (p. xliii)

Artaud wandered in the labyrinth of a specific type of religious sensibility, the Gnostic one. . . . The leading energies of Gnosticism come from metaphysical anxiety and acute psychological distress—the sense of being abandoned, of being an alien, of being possessed by demonic powers which prey on the human spirit in a cosmos vacated by the divine. The cosmos is itself a battlefield, and each human life exhibits the conflict between the repressive, persecuting forces from without and the feverish, afflicted individual spirit seeking redemption. (pp. xlv-xlvi)

Artaud's thought reproduces most of the Gnostic themes.... Throughout his writings, Artaud speaks of being persecuted, invaded, and defiled by alien powers; his work focusses on the vicissitudes of the spirit as it constantly discovers its lack of liberty in its very condition of being "matter." Artaud is obsessed with physical matter.... Artaud's prose and poetry depict a world clogged with matter (shit, blood, sperm), a defiled world. (pp. xlvi-xlvii)

Both the obstacle to and the locus of freedom, for Artaud, lie in the body. His attitude covers the familiar Gnostic thematic range: the affirmation of the body, the revulsion from the body, the wish to transcend the body, the quest for the redeemed body. "Nothing touches me, nothing interests me," he writes, "except what addresses itself *directly* to my flesh." But the body is always a problem. Artaud never defines the body in terms of its capacity for sensuous pleasure but always in terms of its electric capacity for intelligence and for pain.... In Artaud's imagery of distress, body and spirit prevent each other from being intelligent. He speaks of the "intellectual cries" that come from his flesh, source of the only knowledge he trusts. Body has a mind. "There is a mind in the flesh," he writes, "a mind quick as lightning."

It is what Artaud expects intellectually from the body that leads to his recoil from the body—the ignorant body. Indeed, each attitude implies the other. Many of the poems express a profound revulsion from the body, and accumulate loathsome evocations of sex. "A true man has no sex," Artaud writes in a text published in December 1947. "He ignores this hideousness, this stupefying sin." "Art and Death" is perhaps the most sex-obsessed of all his works, but Artaud demonized sexuality in everything he wrote. The most common presence is a monstrous, obscene body —this unusable body made out of meat and crazy sperm," he calls it in *Here Lies*. Against this fallen body, defiled by matter, he sets the fantasied attainment of a pure body— divested of organs and vertiginous lusts. Even while insisting that he is nothing but his body, Artaud expresses a fervent longing to transcend it altogether, to abandon his sexuality. In other imagery, the body must be made intelligent, respiritualized. Recoiling from the defiled body, he appeals to the redeemed body in which thought and flesh will be unified.... (pp. xlviii-xlix)

[His] last works, in their mounting obsession with the body and their ever more explicit loathing of sex, still stand in a direct line with the early writings, in which there is, parallel to the mentalization of the body, a corresponding sexualization of consciousness. What Artaud wrote between 1946 and 1948 only extends metaphors he used throughout the nineteen-twenties—of mind as a body that never allows itself to be "possessed," and of the body as a kind of demonic, writhing, brilliant mind. In Artaud's fierce battle to transcend the body, everything is eventually turned into the body. In his fierce battle to transcend language, everything is eventually turned into language. (p. lii)

The language Artaud used at the end of his life, in passages in *Artaud le Momo, Here Lies,* and *To Have Done with the Judgement of God,* verges on an incandescent declamatory speech beyond sense. "All true language is incomprehensible," Artaud says in *Here Lies....* The unintelligible parts of Artaud's late writings are supposed to remain obscure—to be directly apprehended as sound....

Artaud offers the greatest *quantity* of suffering in the history of literature. So drastic and pitiable are the numerous descriptions he gives of his pain that readers, overwhelmed, may be tempted to distance themselves by remembering that Artaud was crazy. (p. liii)

But simply to judge Artaud mad—reinstating the reductive psychiatric wisdom—means to reject Artaud's argument....

The task of the reader of Artaud is not to react with [distance]..., as if madness and sanity could communicate with each other only on sanity's own ground, in the language of reason. The values of sanity are not eternal or "natural," any more than there is a self-evident, common-sense meaning to the condition of being insane. (p. liv)

The insane person has a dual identity in Artaud's works: the ultimate victim, and the bearer of a subversive wisdom.... Artaud suggests the existence of a natural affinity between genius and madness in a far more precise sense than the romantics did. But while denouncing the society that imprisons the mad, and affirming madness as the outward sign of a profound spiritual exile, he never suggests that there is anything liberating in losing one's mind. (p. lvi)

To read Artaud through is nothing less than an ordeal. Understandably, readers seek to protect themselves with reductions and applications of his work. It demands a special stamina, a special sensitivity, and a special tact to read Artaud properly. It is not a question of giving one's assent to Artaud—this would be shallow—or even of neutrally "understanding" him and his relevance. What is there to assent to? How could anyone assent to Artaud's ideas unless one was already in the demonic state of siege that he was in? Those ideas were emitted under the intolerable pressure of his own situation. Not only is Artaud's position not tenable; it is not a "position" at all.

Artaud's thought is organically part of that singular, haunted, impotent, savagely intelligent consciousness. Artaud is one of the great, daring mapmakers of consciousness *in extremis*. (pp. lvi-lvii)

[The] experience of his work remains profoundly private. Artaud is someone who has made a spiritual trip for us—a shaman. It would be presumptuous to reduce the geography of Artaud's trip to what can be colonized. Its authority lies in the parts that yield nothing for the reader except intense discomfort of the imagination. (p. lviii)

Unknown outside a small circle of admirers ten years ago, Artaud is a classic today. He is an example of a willed classic—an author whom the culture attempts to assimilate but who remains profoundly indigestible.... Certain authors become literary or intellectual classics because they are *not* read, being in some intrinsic way unreadable....

Like Sade and Reich, Artaud is relevant and understandable, a cultural monument, as long as one mainly refers to his ideas without reading much of his work. For anyone who reads Artaud through, he remains fiercely out of reach, an unassimilable voice and presence. (p. lix)

Susan Sontag, "Introduction" (originally published in a different form as "Approaching Artaud" in The New Yorker, *Vol. XLIX, No. 13, May 19, 1973; reprinted by permission of Farrar, Straus & Giroux, Inc.; copyright © 1973, 1976 by Susan Sontag), in* Selected Writings by Antonin Artaud, *edited by Susan Sontag and translated by Helen Weaver, Farrar, Straus & Giroux, 1976, pp. xvii-lix.*

ROGER SHATTUCK   (essay date 1976)

[Artaud's] early writings show little attempt to master his own suffering—physical and metaphysical; instead, he exacerbated it to the point of frenzy. Correspondingly the Theater of Cruelty aims at provoking collective delirium.... [André] Breton puts his finger on the right word. "Finally I distrusted a certain paroxysm that Artaud was clearly aiming for." But the point is that what Artaud sought was *sustained* paroxysm, a form of permanent intensity that would leave behind the fluctuations of consciousness....

In Artaud one finds none of the attitudes that could keep him firmly within the domain of the human. He lacks any sense of scale or limit to contain time short of eternity, to contain individual consciousness short of megalomania. He lacks the capacity to doubt the authority of his own immediate sensations. He lacks the third ear of humor, which can detect one's own voice becoming obsessed or grandiloquent. (p. 20)

Compared to the self-pity and wavering diction in the early poems, the free verse/prose compositions of the 1940s resound with pronouncements of a stentorian ego seeking untrammeled self-performance. One begins to hear echoes of Victor Hugo. These declamatory texts rely increasingly on two elements: a scatological vision of the universe, and invented words apparently used for sonorous effect as if they were physical entities, not mental signs. (p. 21)

What shall we do, then, with this whirling dervish of self-performance, with this poet anathematizing poetry and proclaiming contradictions at the top of his voice? We cannot dismiss him as merely mad. He had too much talent and perverse intelligence.... Addressing herself to these questions.... Susan Sontag has written a fine exposition of Artaud's thought. Her long essay has greater reach than the three other books on him in English, and she remains more clear-sighted than most of the French critics who have now taken him up....

[According to Sontag his] failure as a writer was due to his alienation from language and to the agony he experienced in writing.

I must disagree with both reasons. Artaud reveled in language: the evidence indicates that he found writing one of his few available links with reality and with the joy of accomplishment. Furthermore, Artaud was deluding himself and his readers when he claimed that the only form he would write in was the personal letter. His chosen format was the public lecture, a one-man theater, solo performance for an audience—even in writing to one person.... Thus he commandeered and suppressed true theater. Artaud was

not an intimate letter writer but an incorrigible public preacher, more histrionic finally than gnostic. (pp. 22-3)

Roger Shattuck, "Artaud Possessed," in The New York Review of Books *(reprinted with permission from* The New York Review of Books; *copyright © 1976 Nyrev, Inc.), Vol. XXIII, No. 18, November 11, 1976, pp. 17-23.*

MARTIN ESSLIN   (essay date 1977)

[Artaud] shaped his image deliberately, fully conscious of what he was doing. Between the face of the soulful young monk of 1928 and the toothless, ravaged martyr's visage of 1948 there lies a lifetime of suffering which Artaud regarded as his ultimate artistic achievement.... He designed his life, took upon himself and endured his suffering as a deliberate creation, a work of art. And the double image which remains with us compresses and sums up his whole existence, *is,* in a certain sense, that work of art, or at least a metaphor for it. (p. 4)

Any attempt to present or understand Artaud must, therefore, take his life as its starting point. He is the true existential hero: What he did, what happened to him, what he suffered, what he *was,* is infinitely more important than anything he said or wrote. (p. 6)

There is an inner logic and consistency in his creation of his youthful image in films like *La Passion de Jeanne d'Arc* to provide a stunning and heart-rending contrast with that of the wizened martyr of society's rejection and contempt which became the image of his final epiphany. And there is a similar deep inner consistency in his gradual abandonment of the conventional objectives of the artist in pursuit of public recognition and fame, the discovery of himself as his supreme subject matter in the correspondence with [Jacques] Rivière, his brief adherence to surrealism, and his final apogee as the poet of utter spontaneity, scattering along his way writings which are no longer craftily wrought artifacts but bleeding pieces of flesh torn from his living, suffering body. There is even a satisfying meaningfulness in Artaud, the man of the theater, kept out of the promised land of rebirth and renewal but, like Moses, proclaiming its future laws while glimpsing it from afar, a tragic prophet. But, above all, there is perfection of design in his final descent into madness (if madness it should be called rather than a plumbing of the ultimate depths of human suffering and existential anguish).... (p. 67)

Artaud was not a systematic thinker and never formulated his views on language in a fully developed theory. Yet it is possible to reconstruct the pattern of his thought on the subject.

Basically this amounts to the conviction that it was a profound mistake to equate all human consciousness with that part osion. Our consciousness is made up of a multitude of elements only a few of which are capable of being directly formulated in words. What we see with our eyes, for example, is constantly within our consciousness, yet is very rarely actually put into words or thought about verbally. (p. 73)

To a poet, Artaud would argue, it is precisely that nonverbal element of consciousness which is of supreme importance. For it is closely bound up with the very stuff and matter of poetry: human emotion. (p. 74)

That is why the three words "I am cold" seemed to Artaud

incapable of conveying what he actually experienced when he felt cold. To communicate emotion, which is the stuff of poetry, abstract words were not enough. That is why poetry makes use of concrete aspects of language which directly communicate to the body, elements such as the musical quality of the words, the sensual nature of the sounds they are made of, the rhythmic quality of the poem which directly activates the body's own rhythms—the beat of the blood—and the vast multitude of nonverbal associations inherent in language and activated by words.

The formula "I am cold," which abstracts all the body sensation, all the actual and complex feelings connected with one individual's experience of such a physical state, exemplified for Artaud the manner in which too glib a use of language desiccates experience and eventually makes people who rely on such modes of communication and thought lose contact with life itself. They seemed to him to substitute the mathematical formula, the abstract blueprint of experience for the complex fullness of the surging flood of existence in all its richness and complexity.

"The theater is the only place in the world and the last general means left to us to reach the organism directly and, in the period of neurosis and low sensuality into which we are about to plunge, to attack that low sensuality by physical means which it will not resist." . . . This is how Artaud put his realization, at which he had arrived by the mid-1930s, that the poetry he wanted to deal in transcended the merely verbal; and that the human body was both the instrument to be used in conveying his kind of poetry and the recipient of that poetry, to be exposed to it so as properly to experience its impact. (pp. 74-5)

The new language of the theater, a superior instrument of communication beyond the mere discursive use of concepts, language, and words, would establish a link through which the totality of emotion could freely flow from body to body, from actor to spectator. And this breaking down of the barriers between human beings, enabling them to partake in each others' most shattering emotions, would achieve no less than a new communion of mankind, a total transformation of society, and give to all human existence a greater richness and higher quality.

It is a grandiose vision, powered—one can feel this in the prophetic sweep of the essays in *The Theater and Its Double*—by the rage and fury of frustration accumulated through his desperate efforts to bridge the gap between his feeling and its verbal expression. It is as though Artaud wanted to unleash the pent-up energies of this frustration in a vast liberating outburst of violence, of aggression against an unfeeling outside world, visualized as a mass of complacent, apathetic spectators in the theater who would find themselves engulfed, overwhelmed, and compelled to feel, to suffer as deeply as he himself, Antonin Artaud, had suffered. . . . (pp. 76-7)

And yet the hopes that Artaud had pinned on the theater and his own ability to create a new language of physically embodied poetry came to nought. It is a tragic irony that it was through this collapse of his expectations and the breakdown it caused that he eventually bridged the chasm that had yawned between his emotion and its transmutation into words, and that he found his very own poetic language, a mode of utterance so powerful and direct that it was indeed capable of fully conveying the poet's emotion right down to the physical level of body sensations. (p. 78)

The breathless frenzy with which he proclaimed his mission to save the world from impending doom imbues a text like that of *Les Nouvelles Révélations de l'Etre,* never intended to be poetry, with a sweep and intensity of vision which transmutes its language into that of a sublime poem, a poem, moreover, which, in its power to stir the imagination and the senses, is far superior to anything Artaud ever was able to achieve in the theater. . . .

[In the last two years of his life] Artaud produced an unceasing output in the form of essays, letters, personal confessions, rhythmic prose, glossolalia, and inarticulated combinations of consonants. It is difficult to decide which of these writings should be classified as poems, for all are deeply poetic, simply because they are direct and unalloyed expressions of profound emotion and triumphantly succeed in communicating that emotion through language. (p. 79)

It is difficult to analyze the means by which Artaud's writings at this period have their effect. *What* they say (the discursive or conceptual element) is so wildly outside the customary bounds of reason that it contributes as much to their physical effect (through the sheer amazement or terror such descriptions inspire) as the *way* they say it, the furious discordance and variation of the rhythms, the abrupt transitions, the intensity evoked by repetition and accumulation of words, all combining to communicate the rage, anguish, and deep commitment which underlie them. Here language truly reaches its utmost limit. (pp. 80-1)

Like Bergson, Shaw, or Nietzsche, Artaud was a romantic vitalist, a believer in the healing power of the life force, the power of man's natural instinct as against dry-as-dust rationalism and logical reasoning based on linguistic subtlety; he supported the heart against the head, the body and its emotions against the rarefied abstractions of the mind. But while Nietzsche in *The Birth of Tragedy* had proclaimed his conviction that the basis of the theater is the spirit of Dionysos, dark, violent, turbulent, passionate, inarticulate in its musical ecstasy, but tempered and tamed by Apollonian clarity, measure, and reason, Artaud rejected the Apollonian element altogether and put his trust in the dark forces of Dionysian vitality with all their violence and mystery. If these forces could be activated through the theater, incarnated by the theater, Artaud hoped that mankind might be diverted from the disastrous path that led toward increasing atrophy of the instincts, which amounted to the death of vitality and to eventual extinction. (p. 87)

The theater, as seen by Artaud in *The Theater and Its Double,* is essentially a religious ritual. . . . And by making the full force of a full emotional life, the whole gamut of human suffering and joy, again active in multitudes of human beings, the theater could change their basic attitude to life and institutions, their ways of thinking, their entire consciousness, and thus transform society and the world. (pp. 90-1)

The cases in which the *personality* rather than the *oeuvre* or achievement of an important figure continues to increase in its impact are very rare. . . . As he did not aim to create an *oeuvre* so much as to make his own life his supreme work of art and thus to incarnate his ideas rather than merely express them, [Artaud] engenders, not the appreciation given to great artists, but the devotion due to a beloved individual. And the very contradictoriness, dissociation, even incoherence of his ideas merely strengthen such primarily emotional devotion, which must ultimately lead to a cult. (p. 129)

[Artaud] himself saw himself as one of a long line of *poètes maudits:* Hölderlin, Baudelaire, Nerval, Lautréamont, Nietzsche. And he was undoubtedly right. Yet none of these has left as full and enlightening a documentation of himself as that which Artaud has left to posterity.

But Artaud transcends the category of the *poètes maudits* as well as that of the great self-revealers [Pepys, Casanova, the Marquis de Sade, the Marquise de Sevigné, Boswell, Horace Walpole]. For he provides an immense wealth of detailed insights into a human type of the utmost importance in history. Artaud's life was a fascinating anachronism in our times but all the more valuable through the material it furnishes us with about this crucially influential kind of character: the character, that is, of the "Holy Fool." It was Artaud's misfortune that he was born into an epoch which consigns individuals of this stamp to lunatic asylums. In other epochs he might have been a shaman, a prophet, an alchemist, an oracle, a saint, a gnostic teacher, or, indeed, the founder of a new religion. (pp. 130-31)

Martin Esslin, in his Antonin Artaud *(copyright © 1976 by Martin Esslin; reprinted by permission of Viking Penguin Inc.), Penguin Books, 1977, 148 p.*

ALBERT BERMEL (essay date 1977)

It is often said that Artaud wishes to destroy dialogue, or at least to tame it and subordinate it to his theatrical business. This notion is refuted by two of his plays, *The Fountain of Blood* (*Le Jet de sang*) and *The Cenci,* in which the quantity of dialogue outweighs the quantity of stage directions. Spoken lines are not merely important in Artaud: because he is frugal with them they take on unusual significance. If he objects to conventional dialogue, what he dislikes in it is its conversational or argumentative tone. He wants his spoken material to be explosive in sound, equivocal in meaning, and unnatural in its delivery—that is, as theatrical as the physical activities—and he often specifies these requirements.

A short play that runs to only about five pages of text, *The Fountain of Blood* is not a scenario or outline, but a completed work. (pp. 62-3)

The play amounts to a nightmarish, comic story in miniature of the creation of the world and its desecration by people, especially by women. It starts with the Boy and Girl in a state of bliss; when the Girl revives at the end it is as though a new cycle of creation is beginning.

The action contains two distinct elements. Side by side are a set of personal scenes written with dialogue, and a set of impersonal scenes, the cataclysmic happenings, expressed wholly in stage directions. . . . All in all, *The Fountain of Blood* is a tragic, repulsive, impassioned farce, a marvelous wellspring for speculation, and a unique contribution to the history of the drama. (p. 64)

The play *There is No More Firmament* is Artaud's unfinished symphony. . . . The composition is musical throughout, themes and variations in the dialogue and stage effects, with music employed more freely than in any of his other works. The form suits the material. This is an account of a natural (that is, unnatural) catastrophe, treated at greater length than are the ones in *The Fountain of Blood.* The ca-

tastrophe is recounted in language and images that remind one of some passages in "The Theatre and the Plague." . . . The few people alluded to separately in the text have generic titles, not names: a Woman, a Policeman, the Doctor, the Inventor, and so on. This depersonalizing gives the impression that mere people are helpless before the onslaught of the catastrophe, during which the sky is "physically abolished" and the Dog Star, Sirius, is located "only a minute away" from Earth. (pp. 66-7)

Yet the play's theoretical statements mean little when divorced from the theatrical means Artaud hoped to use and the strictly theatrical dividends they could bring. In this play, sometimes considered surrealistic, he has actually borrowed a great many formal devices from the Expressionists. . . . Indeed, *There Is No More Firmament* is the only out-and-out example I can recall of French Expressionism. Its massed characters with titles instead of names, its caricatures, its vehement rhetoric, its scathing of machinery and scientific discovery, its cinematic overlapping and cross-fading of scenes, and above all its portrait of modern civilization as a morass of insanity—these are all characteristics we associate with the turbulent writings of [Expressionists]. . . . Yet the play is Artaudian through and through: extravagant, authoritative, and an open-ended quest. (pp. 69-70)

Bernard Shaw prophetically said more than once that the theatre of the twentieth century would go in one of two directions: it would follow Richard Wagner's example of drama with music toward a predominantly sensuous "total theatre," or it would fall into line with the "drama of thought," which had acquired its most striking modern forms from Ibsen. . . . Artaud's Theatre of Cruelty aligns itself more with Wagner than with Ibsen. It is a romantic, evocative theatre of the senses, colored by dramatic overstatement, and it lacks irony, that favored device of the intellectual playwright. Although it operates by visual and auditory shock tactics, rather than by the accretion of mellifluous sounds and moods, its extravagance and spellbinding have Wagnerian affiliations. (p. 89)

Artaud's theatre stands at the opposite pole from Brecht's. In an ideal Brechtian performance the spectator receives intellectual signals that keep him alert. . . . This didactic theatre does not openly prescribe remedies for social ills and inequities, but it does foster a critical attitude. (p. 90)

Brecht's theatre is reformist, if not revolutionary, in intent. Artaud's is antireformist; it puts on theatre a burden it cannot sustain. By pretending to purge its audiences of their potentially violent "ideas of war, riot, and blatant murder," by first arousing that violence and then appeasing it, canceling it out, it substitutes itself for political activity. The Artaudian transfiguration leaves itself open to Brecht's charge against the Aristotelian catharsis: it militates against active social change by inducing a spirit of acquiescence. (pp. 90-1)

Most of the best-known troupes and directors who borrowed from Artaud's theories . . . have not lost sight of the Brechtian ideal: theatre that sharpens an audience's political consciousness. Their showings have repeatedly leveled political criticism at modern societies. They have not muffled the criticism by processing it through a catharsis. (p. 91)

In tempering Artaud with Brecht, these artists have demonstrated that the Theatre of Cruelty, which Artaud did not himself accomplish as a codified plan, can be broken down into separable ideas and techniques. As these component parts, Artaud's theories have given the contemporary theatre a series of life-awakening jolts. (p. 92)

> *Albert Bermel, in his* Artaud's Theatre of Cruelty *(copyright © 1977 by Albert Bermel; published by Taplinger Publishing Co., Inc., New York; reprinted by permission), Taplinger, 1977, 128 p.*

JULIA F. COSTICH (essay date 1978)

[*Héliogabale, ou l'anarchiste couronné,* the] "historical novel" which Artaud wrote . . . on the life of the Roman emperor Heliogabalus is unusual in the context of Artaud's work and in the range of historiography. (p. 58)

A perpetual schism in the text between Artaud as creative historian and Artaud as narrator of himself leads to a fusion of subject and object and creates a unity in the text which reflects the evanescent and exalted unity in the life of Heliogabalus. *Héliogabale* may, therefore, be compared with *Les Cenci,* in which Artaud is likewise the author . . . of a character, Count Cenci, who is manifestly not the writer himself and yet who serves as a vehicle for Artaud's own ideas of cruelty and destiny. Hence, the life of Heliogabalus is a striking example of Theater of Cruelty transposed to life, for it retains a quality of manipulation and vicious humor which further allies it with theater. (p. 59)

The two premises of the central chapter are that principles have real existence and that these principles war against one another. . . . Beyond this epistemological duality, there is a synthesis: ". . . the human spirit remains the dominant element even in this union. In the sustained frenzy of Heliogabalus's reign, this point may have been attained. To the conflict of spirit and matter within man corresponds the duality of the human and the divine. . . . In its furthest extreme, this religious unity is expressed in the king, who traces his parentage to the gods and who proclaims his complete participation in both divine and human states. Just as the summit of humanity is the fusion of matter and spirit, so the highest perception of divinity is the great Whole which is Nothing. . . . While the divine dialectic exists on a more abstract and grandiose plane than the human one, it still risks sliding into a perceptual void without the complementary synthesis in man. Human identity and divine otherness are aspects of a single indissoluble unity; neither can exist in the text of history without the other.

Nevertheless, it is neither on the plane of humanity nor on that of absolute divinity that the perpetual war of principles takes place. The combat zone is double: within the celebration of the divine, Artaud reveals a war of effigies; within the human world, this battle is doubled by a war between races which stand for the two cosmic principles, the male and the female. The situation represented by this war is erotic when the principles exist as separate, interacting entities, and it becomes androgynous when they fuse. But war only becomes violent when it is religious, when supernatural forces are explicitly engaged in human combat. The case of Heliogabalus, the pederast king who wanted to be a woman but who was also a priest of masculine deities, represents the archetypal war carried on within the human being itself. Every detail of Artaud's account reinforces this image of the individual *psychomachia* as a microcosmic example of the conflicts that occur on a universal scale.

Although in a strange and terrifying way Heliogabalus is a unity and represents the phantasmagorical specter of unity to his subjects, his actions are characterized by incessant duality. His behavior displays the unsettling quality of paradox. . . . However, the unity of Heliogabalus's world is such that these [paradoxes] are not contradictory: order and disorder participate in the same inferior level of action, unity is perceived through the generous and cruel operation of anarchy, and so forth. As in the case of Artaud's theatrical theory, new criteria for judgment are posited, and what is apparently contradictory becomes a vital fusion in the new unity. (pp. 59-61)

> *Julia F. Costich, "Occult Explorations," in her* Antonin Artaud *(copyright © 1978 by G. K. Hall & Co.; reprinted with the permission of Twayne Publishers, A Division of G. K. Hall & Co., Boston), Twayne, 1978, pp. 55-64.*

BIBLIOGRAPHY

Bermel, Albert. "Artaud as Playwright: *The Fountain of Blood (Le Jet de Sang)."* *Boston University Journal* 20, No. iii (Autumn 1972): 8-15.
  Study of the metaphoric characterizations of *The Fountain of Blood* and how they symbolically embody the story of the Creation.

Bersani, Leo. "Artaud, Birth, and Defecation." *Partisan Review* 43, No. 3 (1976): 438-52.
  Study which attributes Artaud's desire for a non-psychological theater to his own fears of loss of self. Bersani contends that Artaud's theories derive from an antirationalist vision of life.

Brustein, Robert. "No More Masterpieces." *Michigan Quarterly Review* 6, No. 3 (Summer 1967): 185-92.
  Survey of modern theatrical productions that embody Artaud's concepts of an antitraditional theater.

Chiaromonte, Nicola. "Antonin Artaud." *Encounter* XXIX, No. 2 (August 1967): 44-50.
  A study which examines the deficiencies inherent in Artaud's theater and the conflicting elements of his theatrical principles.

Demaitre, Ann. "The Theater of Cruelty and Alchemy: Artaud and Le Grand Oeuvre." *Journal of the History of Ideas* XXXIII, No. 2 (April-June 1972): 237-50.
  Study comparing Artaud's theater to alchemy as two processes aimed at transmuting the physical and discovering a higher reality.

Finkielkraut, Alain. "Desire in Autobiography." *Genre* VI, No. 2 (June 1973): 220-32.
  Psychological study of Artaud's letters to Jacques Rivière.

Gattnig, Charles, Jr. "Artaud and the Participatory Drama of the Now Generation." *Educational Theatre Journal* XX, No. 4 (December 1968): 485-91.
  Discussion of the ways in which Artaud's dramatic theories were embraced by avant-garde theatrical groups of the 1960s.

Jacobs, Carol. "The Assimilating Harmony: A Reading of Antonin Artaud's *Héliogabale."* *Sub-Stance,* No. 17 (1977): 115-38.
  Close reading of *Héliogabale* which focuses on Artaud's use of physical imagery.

Labelle, Maurice M. "Artaud's Use of Language, Sound, and Tone." *Modern Drama* 15, No. 4 (March 1973): 383-90.
  Study of Artaud's use of innovative language in his poetry and plays.

Roose-Evans, James. "The Theatre of Ecstasy—Artaud, Okhlopkov, Théâtre Panique." In his *Experimental Theatre from Stanis-*

lavsky to Today, rev. ed., pp. 55-63. New York: Universe Books, 1973.*

   Survey of the theatrical movements which preceded Artaud showing by historical precedent that Artaud's theater was neither new nor revolutionary. The author also discusses the Théâter Panique as an example of Artaud's theories.

Sellin, Eric. *The Dramatic Concepts of Antonin Artaud.* Chicago: The University of Chicago Press, 1968, 190 p.

   Survey of the major cultural and dramatic influences on Artaud's theories, followed by a summary of his theories and discussion of his staging devices.

Sellin, Eric. "Artaud." *Diacritics* 1, No. 2 (Winter 1971): 21-2, 24, 26.

   A review of Bettina Knapp's *Antonin Artaud, Man of Vision* and Naomi Greene's *Antonin Artaud, Poet without Words,* both of which are excerpted above. Sellin's belief that Artaud was merely an indicator of the mood of his time and not an important influence on drama informs his approach to the two books.

Thevenin, Paule. "A Letter on Artaud." *The Tulane Drama Review* 9, No. 3 (Spring 1965): 99-117.

   Reminiscence of Artaud's last years by a personal friend, an actress who was instrumental in his release from the Rodez sanatorium.

Versteeg, Robert. "Images of Man in the Theatre of Cruelty." *The Southern Humanities Review* 9, No. 1 (Winter 1975): 17-28.*

   A study which uses *The Cenci* to demonstrate the essential problems of Artaud's Theater of Cruelty.

Sholem Asch

1880-1957

(Also transliterated as Schalom, Shalom, or Sholom; also Ash) Polish-born Yiddish novelist, dramatist, short story writer, and journalist.

Asch, a prolific and popular writer, is the foremost Yiddish novelist of the early twentieth century.

After traditional Hebrew schooling in Poland, Asch moved to Warsaw in 1899 where he became exposed to contemporary European literature and decided to become a writer. Under the influence of Isaac Leib Peretz, Asch began writing in Yiddish in order to reach a world-wide Jewish audience. His early novels and dramas were characterized by a blend of eroticism and spirituality. Asch's crafting of these themes reached a zenith in *The God of Vengeance*. This, his best known and most controversial play, banned in Russia, but staged in Berlin, Paris, London, and New York, brought him international fame.

Asch lived and worked in several European countries as well as the United States and Israel during his lifetime. His portrayal of Jewish life was correspondingly wide-ranged, covering the Jew in Europe and America and in historical and contemporary times. The theme central to all his works is the power of faith to free one from sin and suffering. Asch's Christological trilogy, *The Nazarene, The Apostle*, and *Mary* —the first two published during the Holocaust—brought angered charges from some Jewish readers that he had become an apostate and was inciting further hatred of Jews. Asch denied these accusations, stating that in his works he was attempting to reconcile Jews and Christians.

Asch remains one of the best known figures of modern Yiddish literature and his novels, with their enduring qualities of warmth and humor and their concern for the everyday activities of ordinary people, are still loved.

PRINCIPAL WORKS

Dos shtetl (novel) 1904
Tsurikgekumen (drama) 1904
Der got fun nekomeh (drama) 1907
  [*The God of Vengeance*, 1918]
Sabbatai zewi: Tragödie in drei akten (sechs bildern) mit einem vorspiel und einem nachspiel (drama) 1908
  [*Sabbatai Zevi: A Tragedy in Three Acts and Six Scenes with a Prologue and an Epilogue*, 1930]
Die familie Grossglück: Komodie in drei akten (drama) 1909

Amerika (essays) 1911
  [*America*, 1918]
Der bund der schwachen: Drama (drama) 1913
  [*The League of the Weak*, 1913]
Reb Shloyme nogid (novel) 1913
Motke ganev (novel) 1916
  [Published in England as *Mottke the Vagabond (Mottke ganev)*, 1917; published in the United States as *Mottke the Thief*, 1935]
Onkel Moses (novel) 1918
  [*Uncle Moses: A Novel*, 1920]
Kiddush ha-Shem (novel) 1919
  [*Kiddush ha-Shem: An Epic of 1648*, 1926]
Di muter (novel) 1925
  [*The Mother*, 1930]
Die kinder Abrahams: Novellen aus America (short stories) 1931
  [*Children of Abraham: The Short Stories of Sholem Asch*, 1942]
Farn mabul (novels, includes *Petersburg, Warsaw*, and *Moscow*) 1933
  [*Three Cities: A Trilogy*, 1933]
Der tehillim yid (novel) 1934
  [*Salvation*, 1934]
Auf'n opgrunt (novel) 1936
  [*The War Goes On*, 1936; published in England as *The Calf of Paper: A Novel*, 1936]
Dos gezang fun tol (novel) 1938
  [*The Song of the Valley*, 1939]
Der man vun Notzeres (novel) 1939
  [*The Nazarene*, 1939]
Paulus (novel) 1943
  [*The Apostle*, 1943]
Ist River (novel) 1946
  [*East River: A Novel*, 1946]
Maria (novel) 1949
  [*Mary*, 1949]
Moshe (novel) 1951
  [*Moses*, 1951]
A Passage in the Night (novel) 1953
Ha-navi (novel) 1955
  [*The Prophet*, 1955]

ABRAHAM CAHAN (essay date 1918)

[Sholom Ash's] narratives and plays are alive with a spirit of poetic realism, with a stronger leaning toward the poetic than toward reality, perhaps, but always throbbing with dramatic force and beauty. Sholom Ash's passion for color and melody manifests itself as much in his rich, ravishing style as in the picturesque images it evokes. The "jargon of servant maids" becomes music in his hands.

His "God of Vengeance," which is his strongest play, is one of the best things he has written in any form. Absorbingly interesting and instinct with human sympathy, it mounts to a natural climax of cataclysmal force and great spiritual beauty. (p. v)

Himself a creature of the gutter, Yekel Tchaftchovitch, the central figure of "The God of Vengeance," is stirred by the noblest ambition known to a father in the world of orthodox Judaism. Imbedded in the slime that fills Yekel's soul is a jewel of sparkling beauty. But the very income by which he seeks to secure his daughter's spiritual splendor contains the germs of her loathsome fall and of this own crushing defeat.

The clash between Yekel's revolting career and his paternal idealism, and the catastrophe to which it inevitably leads form one of the strongest and most fascinating situations known to the modern drama (p. vi)

> *Abraham Cahan, in his preface to* The God of Vengeance: Drama in Three Acts *by Sholom Asch (copyright 1918 The Stratford Co., Publishers), Stratford, 1918, pp. iii-vii.*

ISAAC GOLDBERG (essay date 1918)

It is interesting to consider Ash's "The God of Vengeance" in connection with a play like "Mrs. Warren's Profession." To be sure, there is no technical resemblance between the two dramas; nor, despite an external similarity in backgrounds, is there any real identity of purpose. Shaw's play is essentially sociological, and is a drama of disillusionment. Ash's piece glows with poetic realism and recounts an individual tragedy not without symbolic power. Yet the essentially (though not conventionally) moral earnestness of both Shaw and Ash brings the circles of their themes in a sense tangent to each other. (p. ix)

"The God of Vengeance," despite conclusions too easily drawn, is not a sex play. When Ash wishes to deal with sex as sex he is not afraid to handle the subject with all the poetry and power at his command. Such a play as his "Jephthah's Daughter" treats the elemental urge of sex with daring, beauty and Dionysiac abandon. Here, too, a golden symbolism wafts through the piece. Again, in his powerful novel "Mottke the Vagabond," Ash has given us scenes from the underworld of Warsaw that are unparalleled for unflinching truth to detail. "The God of Vengeance," however, despite the sordid environment in which the play takes place, possesses a certain moral beauty,—a beauty much dimmed, perhaps, by the repellant human beings who are its carriers, but a beauty none the less. Its symbolism and its poetry lift it far above the brothel in which it takes place. And what a strong conception is the Holy Scroll, itself one of the chief characters, and how frightfully eloquent in the mysterious, religious power that the dramatist has woven around it! (p. xi)

> *Isaac Goldberg, in his introduction to* The God of Vengeance: Drama in Three Acts *by Sholom Asch (copyright 1918 The Stratford Co., Publishers), Stratford, 1918, pp. ix-xiv.*

JOHAN J. SMERTENKO (essay date 1923)

As artist, Asch is a modern, rather to be classed with the Russian novelists than with any of his Yiddish contemporaries. Naturally he derives much from the Hebrew of Talmud and Bible, but it is his peculiar privilege to be one of the founders of the literature to which he is contributing. He has been called the Jewish Maupassant, which is altogether unintelligible; he is nearest to Gorky in novel and sketch and play; but for an analogy to his position and his share in the formation of a Yiddish literature one must seek among the poets of the Elizabethan period and among the essayists in the age of Queen Anne. (p. 180)

His salient characteristic is a Rabelaisian amplitude. In "Mottke the Vagabond," undoubtedly his masterpiece, the fulness of his scenes is as breath-taking as the Paradise of Tintoretto. And with this amplitude goes an equally Rabelaisian downrightness and mirth. There is the heavy fragrance of the primitive in the recounting of Mottke's birth in a crowded, dirty cellar, of Mottke besieging the synagogue with his troop of dogs, of Mottke's initiation into sex, of the murder, and of the trial scene. There is a shocking simplicity in sentences like "the result was that the child either died or pulled through the crucial period" and "he was now fourteen years old and had experienced every sensation of life except murder."

Asch is at his best as a novelist. He needs the ease and the elasticity of this medium to get the Rembrandt richness of his characters and the Corot placidity of his environment. And he has tried every form of narrative from historical romance to sociological study. "I am a romanticist. But don't confuse me with those who sentimentalize over and falsify reality," he hastens to add. "I mean that I insist on finding the romance and beauty of life." But this statement, too, needs modification. He does not always mean the beauty of patriarchal Jews going to synagogue services; he also means the beauty in the dreams and passions of the girls in a brothel. . . .

[Whatever] his theme, there is a unity of style. Asch uses the large stroke. He is content to evoke the symbol of his character and omit the color of hair. It is not necessarily a simple symbol yet it is always intelligible. One senses it as well as comprehends it. And this feeling is communicated by the nervous, sonorous rhythms of the Scriptures—his earliest work was written in Hebrew—by the Oriental felicity of metaphor, and by the passionate relationship between author and subject. Nevertheless Asch will not recognize style per se. . . .

Whether consciously or not, he has sought new modes— and unsuccessfully; he has wandered in the paths of symbolism and expressionism, and out again. For Asch unquestionably recognizes that the beauty and poetry of his early work in novel and sketch are due to a certain literary naivete which enabled him to express himself most completely. Moreover, it is precisely his style, or rather, the inability to suit his style to the demands of drama which makes his plays inferior to the other work. Here again the only analogy is to be found in the Elizabethan drama, for here, I believe, the state of Yiddish literature as well as the character of the man is responsible. Again we have an unsophisticated public and fertile, unbroken ground; and again the result is an exuberance which ignores the limits of a stage. Yiddish drama has as yet no Jonson to urge restraint, no Dryden to practice it, no Racine to sublime it; and Asch is no Shakespeare to transcend it.

Still, it should be distinctly understood that Asch is a dramatist, a dramatist who takes great liberties with his form, to be sure, who lacks perfection as a craftsman, but withal one who has the requisite elements of the art. He builds, he convinces, he moves. Here, too, he is versatile and prolific. He has written comedies of manners like "Die Familie Grossglück" and "Der Bund der Schwachen," powerful social pieces like "The God of Vengeance," poetic dramas like the symbolic sex play, "Jephthahs Tochter," and Biblical and historical plays—his weakest work, loose jointed, careless of fact, and inclined to rant—like "Shabbethai Zebi." In all, however, are his characters essentially dramatic, not simply histrionic like Barrymore's Hamlet. They err with their author on the side of the spectacular, for to portray emotion they must gesture—often dirk or ax or whip in hand; at least, they do not grunt and sob and wheeze like a herd of porkers going through the slaughterhouse. They are too human for that.

I doubt whether this unabashed humanity of Sholom Asch's creations will be stomached by American readers and audiences. The Yiddish author, even more than the Russians, is talking to people in the lower depths. Life there is an open book. Crowded within the Pale of Russia and confined to Ghettoes within that Pale are all manifestations of life, and they must be seen. The rabbi's daughter—that conventional symbol of virgin innocence—and the bawd must meet; brothel and hive of thieves are on the same street as respectable home and growing children. Thus the Yiddish public as well as the artist has learned to face the nasty facts. The average American, on the other hand, is not forced to live in his tenderloin district. He will probably be shocked and disgusted. But at least he will understand whence comes this all-embracing sympathy for the under dog. And he will marvel that the artist's idealism remains unshaken by this degrading environment. (p. 181)

> Johan J. Smertenko, "Sholom Asch," in The Nation (copyright 1923 by the Nation Associates, Inc.), Vol. CXVI, No. 3006, February 14, 1923, pp. 180-82.

HERBERT S. GORMAN   (essay date 1923)

It was in Warsaw that [Asch] began to write. The short story, the sketch, first absorbed his attention. He felt that through this medium he could best give the multitude of thoughts and moods that were seething in him. Always he has been a close observer of his own people, and his work is, from first to last, essentially realistic. (p. 145)

If we except a number of sketches, several one-act plays . . . , a book of essays called "America," now out of print and difficult to procure, the fame of Sholom Asch can manifest itself to English readers only through two novels and a single play. Both of these novels are distinguished in quality, although they possess flaws, and the play was sufficiently important to achieve production by Reinhardt in his Berlin theatre.

The first novel by Sholom Asch to be translated into English was "Mottke, the Vagabond," which was brought out a number of years ago. "Gonef," the word from which "Vagabond" is fashioned in the title, literally means a gangster. Mottke is the child of misfortune, a thief who runs wild from his earliest youth, is terribly beaten and abused, and becomes the natural enemy of those in authority. The first six chapters of the book, describing the early boyhood of Mottke, are superbly written; and the character under clever handling shapes itself consistently and in high literary fashion for the reader. After that the book, which was written as a serial, grows erratic and almost picaresque in quality. . . . The book becomes a horrible description of the very lowest forms of life. But, strangely enough, it holds the reader, for flashing through the sordidness and emphatic insistence upon gross reality are frequent bursts of beauty, lyrical interludes that remain in the memory. One feels that Mottke is the victim of adverse circumstances. He is a primitive creature, swayed by passions, and wholly oblivious to the endless shibboleths of civilized communities; at the same time, fate is always against him. He is a criminal, but he is a dreamer as well. The vivid qualities of this novel have undoubtedly been strengthened by the careful study of underground Warsaw and life among the poorer classes of Jews in Poland. It is a painful book, but it is a sincere book, also.

"Uncle Moses," written but a few years ago, is in quite another vein. There is sordidness here of a sort, but there is no degeneracy. The idea that occasioned the book, according to Asch, was a true happening. Uncle Moses is a Polish Jew who comes to America, eventually establishes a sweatshop in the Bowery, and then sends back to his native village for workers. At home he was but a poor hanger-on; in America he is a power to be reckoned with. Small group by small group, he brings over the people of his native village, and it is not long before he has practically all of them, mayor, merchant, and miller, at work in his unsanitary slave-driven shop. . . . Then follows a remarkable psychological exposition of the degeneration of Uncle Moses from the once proud sweatshop owner to a vagabond. Almost pitiful in his attempts to win the affection of the woman he married against her will, Uncle Moses forsakes his business, his assistant cleverly steals it, and the mark of fate is set on the perplexed man. Asch has done an exceptionally fine piece of work in this novel. His characterizations are the result of more than meticulous observation. He breathes souls, sometimes tormented, into them. And the book, as a whole, becomes a valuable picture of certain aspects of Jewish life in New York.

["The God of Vengeance" is] Asch's one full-length play to be translated . . . Its theme is such as only a continental writer could handle. The reader is given the spectacle of a man bringing up his daughter in dewy innocence and having a Holy Scroll carefully copied out for her while he runs a brothel in the cellar beneath his house. . . . Vengeance is directed at the maddened brothel keeper through the destruction of the child's innocence. The play is tragic in quality, and over it hover the dark wings of impending fate.

These three books are sufficient to intimate rather well the qualities of Sholom Asch as a writer. The Jewish religion is an overwhelming part of his inspiration always. It is because he writes so well about Jews and knows their hearts so clearly, their famished desires and indestructible dreams, that he has become so important to them in any consideration of their contemporary literature. He is untamed at moments in a literary way, and sometimes loses that fine restraint that is so much a part of authentic achievement; but he is indubitably a born story teller, the chief requisite of a Jewish writer if he is to be popular among his own people. (pp. 149-54)

> Herbert S. Gorman, "Yiddish Literature, and the Case of Sholom Asch," in his The Procession of Masks (copyright, 1923 by B. J. Brimmer Company), Brimmer, 1923, pp. 139-54.

A. A. ROBACK (essay date 1940)

There can be no two opinions about the place of Sholem Asch . . . as one of the foremost novelists in contemporary literature. Fired with ambition and teeming with imaginative leads, he made the first stir in the Yiddish literary world with his portrayal, in pastel colors, of the Yiddish townlet [*A Town*] with its tradition and charm, balmy evenings and social, as well as religious, functions. The poet that was Asch, revealed in this idyll, a shining example of romanticism at its best, has never again appeared in this nostalgic light. It was probably the first piece of impressionistic writing in Yiddish. . . . (p. 216)

Asch remained, on the whole, a romanticist, but his horizons were not narrowed. He not only picked up his themes wherever he could, but evinced a catholic curiosity about everything, and thus introduced new *motifs* in the literature of which he was destined to become the coryphaeus. His early short stories contain some of the choicest morsels of word-painting and a resilience of expression which are not duplicated in his later works. These sketches, or rather pictures, deal with a multitudinous array of situations, from the sublime to the degenerate. (pp. 216-17)

It is not likely that Asch intended either to depreciate or to extol his People. As an artist he is neutral, an impartial spectator, waiting for the theme to develop out of his unconscious. Possibly, too, a cyclothymic temperament causes him to move from one extreme to the other, in the manner of the pendulum. It is this mixture in him of the realistic and the idealistic, the sensuous and the spiritual, that causes the effervescence which is so much in evidence in his writings. (p. 219)

Asch's development is from Main Street to the metropolitan Broadways, from the tender lyricism of the ghetto to the epic events which have fashioned history, from the peephole of the microcosm to the purview of the macrocosm, but the artist has made, in the interim, a number of intermediate stops. He has touched on the symbolic in such dramatic fragments as "The Sinner" or the exquisite tale "In a Carnival Night"; he has brought out the beauties of the past in his historical pilgrimages (*Sabbatai Tzvi* and *The Sorceress of Castille*); he has retold the stories of the Bible in the quaint language of our great-grandmothers, lending them an ingenuous and wholesome flavor, suitable for juvenile consumption. (pp. 220-21)

It was *The Nazarene* which marked the peak of his success, although not of his art. In his previous fiction, he would turn successively, psychologist, sociologist, chronicler, and historian. He now chose to play the rôle of archaeologist, theologian, and biographer of Jesus. (pp. 221-22)

> A. A. Roback, "The Epigones As Masters: Sholem Asch," in his The Story of Yiddish Literature (copyright, 1940 Yiddish Scientific Institute—YIVO), Yiddish Scientific Institute—YIVO, 1940, pp. 216-23.

HARRY SLOCHOWER (essay date 1945)

Three Cities is a kind of Jewish *War and Peace*. Like Tolstoy's novel, it is the story not so much of individuals as of a collectivity, of families, tribes and groups. And while Zachary, the Jew, is a paler version of the massive Russian Pierre, both are dissatisfied with and estranged from the reigning symbols of authority. Both are inwardly at war during the peaceful period, and both achieve stability through the wars of their societies by identifying themselves with the anonymous masses. The contrast lies in the different status of the main characters which determines their final stages. Tolstoy's Pierre is nearer to the center of his community and at the end is shown happily married, content in the daily round of household routine. Zachary Mirkin finds only the formal categories for security. At the close he is still in quest of social integration. (pp. 237-38)

The first book, "Petersburg," has the feeling of solid, heavy timber. It is like a dark, thick wood in which one discerns giant trees dominating and choking the growth of the forest. "Warsaw" has the character of a vast and deep ocean where numberless human families move and huddle together. Petersburg exhibited power; Warsaw exudes warmth and generosity. It has the cohesion of water particles.

In Warsaw, Zachary meets various shades of Jewish aspirations, from those who argue for "Enlightenment" to Zionists, orthodox Jews and socialists. However, it is not any one doctrine which captures Zachary's heart but rather the communal body of the Jewish masses. . . . What draws Zachary to these masses is the "essential communism" of their life. Precisely because these Jews belong to none of the warring classes, they have salvaged a sense of "classlessness"; because they are outcasts, they have drawn together. And in the daily routine, and in hours of need, Zachary finds a warm readiness to help, finds an attitude of universal kinship. It is in their midst . . . that he knows happiness at last and through them hopes to find salvation. (pp. 238-39)

When the Russian Revolution breaks out, we find Zachary in Moscow fighting with the Bolsheviks. . . . He supports the Revolution for its ethical goal to liberate the communal striving in man. "Moscow" appears to him the means of actualizing and universalizing the coöperative spirit he saw struggling in "Warsaw." (p. 239)

(It is interesting to note that the third book, "Moscow," lacks the personalization of events which characterizes the other books. Its "metaphor" is neither the static density of "Petersburg" nor the oceanic flow of "Warsaw," but rather the punctuating sound of machine-guns.) (p. 240)

Zachary's way from Petersburg to Warsaw to Moscow and back to Warsaw appears as a circular route. In Warsaw Zachary came to the conclusion that the only way the Jewish masses could be restored to health was by enclosing them within the productive life of modern industry, run on a coöperative basis—the goal which Moscow aimed at. Asch closes the story with Zachary's arrival in Warsaw, leaving the reader to wonder what kind of activity, aside from that of a Samaritan nature, is open to Zachary. (p. 241)

Harry Slochower, "Spiritual Judaism: The Yearning for Status: Sholem Asch," in his No Voice Is Wholly Lost . . . : Writers and Thinkers in War and Peace *(reprinted by permission of Farrar, Straus & Giroux, Inc.; copyright 1945 by Harry Slochower), Creative Age Press, Inc., 1945, pp. 237-42.*

EDMUND FULLER   (essay date 1949)

["Mary"] stands in an interesting relation to the two fine novels that have preceded it. For it seems to me that "The Apostle," and now "Mary," have each marked a perceptible deepening of the sense of mystical celebration of [Asch's] theme. "The Nazarene" had a cryptic quality, emphasized probably by the elaborate narrative devices employed in it. This was gone in "The Apostle," giving way to affirmation. Now, in this last work, the mystic, the ecstatic are uppermost.

In some aspects "Mary" could be called the best of the three as a work of art. It is altogether free of the cumbersome framework burdening "The Nazarene"; it has a greater unity than the massive novelizing of The Acts of the Apostles. . . .

Telling the story of the mother of Jesus is a perilous enterprise because of the many pitfalls of sentimentality or sectarian overtones for the author to fall into. Asch avoids these almost—if not quite—entirely. The basic story-telling obligations of the undertaking lead him, at times, to assign a degree of crucial importance to Mary's role in her Divine Son's mission exceeding that which many readers of the New Testament would grant. But this portrayal of Miriam —as he calls her—is perceptive and tender and rich in intuitive insights into the heart of the devout young girl who finds herself marked for the glorious but terrifying role of which every Jewish girl dreamed—that of bearing the Messiah. (p. 19)

However great the changes in stress, and in selection of detail, there is a certain amount of repetition from "The Nazarene." Enough, in fact, to suggest what Asch might vehemently reject, the desire to restate and reexamine elements in the former book free of any cryptic reservations it may have contained. In any event, he tells a part of his chosen story twice. . . . His finished trilogy is an epic work in the grand tradition, intellectually, spiritually, and in literary stature. Among Biblical re-creations only Thomas Mann's is its equal, with Gladys Schmitt's "David the King" deserving honorable mention.

By contrast with the nearly fool-proof elements in the drama of Jesus, "The Apostle" is the grandest in scale, the most difficult, probably the most notable achievement of Asch's trilogy. "Mary," however, in its simplicity and tenderness, is likely to move its readers the most deeply. (p. 20)

Edmund Fuller, "Mother of Christ," in The Saturday Review of Literature *(copyright © 1949 by Saturday Review; all rights reserved; reprinted by permission), Vol. 32, No. 41, October 8, 1949, pp. 19-20.*

OSCAR CARGILL   (essay date 1950)

The works of Sholem Asch fall conveniently into three categories: (1) plays, short stories, and novels on the lot of the Jew in Europe; (2) short stories and novels on Jewish life in New York City; and (3) tracts and a fictional trilogy to establish the common cultural and moral matrix of the Jewish and Christian faiths. The only book that will not yield to this patterning is *Song of the Valley* . . . , which tells of the heartbreaking struggle of a band of pioneers, largely Muscovite Jews, to drain a portion of the great Jordan swamp in Palestine and to establish a community there. Asch is not a propagandist for Zionism in this slight novel; on the contrary, his objectivity is notable and suggests a sympathy for those already committed to the movement rather than a desire to make converts. . . .

Of the works in English with a European setting, . . . *Mottke the Thief, Salvation, Three Cities,* and *The War Goes On* appear to be the most rewarding for the American reader. . . . Notable for its picture of the Warsaw slums, *Mottke the Thief* raised some indignation among the Jews because of the portrayal of its protagonist. It was contended that no Jew could be like Mottke or, for that matter, like Yekel, the father in *The God of Vengeance.* Asch has never commented on the relative amount of villainy among his people, but he has always found scoundrels enough to counterpoise his better motivated characters, and he has not hesitated to use them. This was one of his special merits as a writer when he was addressing only a Jewish audience. In this sense he is almost as anti-Semitic as Shakespeare.

Salvation . . . contains one of Asch's best character studies, that of the holy Jew, Jechiel, rabbi of the Psalm Fellowship. The story is set in Poland and covers approximately the middle fifty years of the nineteenth century. (pp. 69-70)

Beautifully patterned with its two Reisels [female characters] and its duplicate window episodes, equally capable of mystical or realistic interpretation, minutely detailed in all respects, alive with a score of vivid characters, and unified by the ever fine presence of Jechiel, whose self-scanning is microscopic but never unwholesome, *Salvation* is one of Sholem Asch's finest novels, and one of the few convincing pictures of a truly religious person in fiction.

Three Cities (a trilogy composed of *Petersburg, Warsaw,* and *Moscow*) has not the tightness and good design of *Salvation*. One character, Zachary Mirkin, supplies a sort of unity, since he is the focal character in the work; but he is a rather weak young man of good will, whose intellectual meanderings are somewhat less interesting than his physical. . . . Asch has done better elsewhere with his [depictions of the] ghetto, but his pictures of pre-revolutionary St. Petersburg, with its sycophancy and its loose morality, and of revolutionary Moscow, with its calculated crime in the name of the proletariat, are memorable. Zachary's father, the multimillionaire Gabriel Mirkin, and the irrepressible posturer Solomon Ossipovitch Halperin are triumphs of characterization. (p. 71)

Sholem Asch's *Uncle Moses* . . . belongs to a further past, probably, than does his novel *Salvation*, for the relations between men in the latter novel are such as are always being resumed, whereas those that existed between Moses Melnik and the men who worked for him belonged to a special era and a brief one in our history, now closed forever. Melnik was "Uncle Moses" because he was the friend and patron of every Jew who arrived in New York from Kusmin, Poland, and who regularly began his career in Uncle Moses' clothing establishment, for Melnik preferred workers from no other town or district but his own. . . . Asch had the materials here for a better story than he has written: it is necessary to make Uncle Moses even more of a dated figure than he does; it is necessary for us to see more of the man's own struggles and kindnesses, if we are to feel the pathos of his position. As it is, *Uncle Moses* is now chiefly useful as a historical document of the era when *Landsmann* organizations flourished. In this book all the Kusminites cleave together; Uncles Moses even furthers this by promising them a prayer-house of their own. They make a society resistant to the New World and more readily exploited by it. (p. 72)

Asch makes far better use of the emotions in *The Mother* . . . , a story in which the poor, hard-worked daughter of a Jewish family, after a brief fling in which she is the childless mistress of a young sculptor, gives him up to a woman of another faith—a woman with beauty, and culture, and money—and returns to the drudgery to which, it seems, from birth she has been fated. *The Mother* is one of the author's better novels. Dvoyrelè, the heroine and model for her lover's masterpiece "The Mother," is drawn with great sympathy, and only a gentle irony plays over the unfitness of her father—who had been glorious at cantillating the Book of Esther in Poland. Bucholz, the sculptor, is the acme of Bohemian selfishness.

Unless he surpasses it with another, *East River* . . . will probably be regarded as Sholem Asch's best book with New York as its locale. . . . [A] great variety of characters, clearly delineated, swarm the pages—the presence of the improvident and devout grocer, Moshe Wolf Davidowsky, one of the outstanding figures among Sholem Asch's many fine portraits of old men, lingers after the reader is done with the book. But despite its many excellencies, *East River* is not quite a convincing novel. (pp. 72-3)

It should be understood . . . that the primary object which Asch had in view in writing [*The Nazarene, The Apostle,* and *Mary*] was to pay reverence to the goodness in Christianity, not to subscribe to it or to settle theological questions. And, because this was his purpose, he may be suspected of another subordinate but equally valid purpose, that is, to show how much of the Christian faith is derived from the Hebrew. (p. 73)

Following the Gospels closely, save that Asch provides Jesus with four brothers and a sister, he gives us a minutely detailed picture of the life and times of Jesus in *The Nazarene, The Apostle,* and *Mary,* but he is no naturalist in the sense that Zola is a naturalist. He accepts annunciations, revelations, and miracles, because the majority of Christians accept them—they are a part of *their* faith. Hence no one can object that Jesus, as Asch draws him, is not divinely appointed—the Messiah of the Christians. Yet adherence to the Gospels does not limit the imagination, which displays itself in two ways: in the poetry of the scenes of spiritual rapture and in the invention of nonbiblical characters, like Taddi, the tanner, simple friend of Joseph and later follower of Jesus. (pp. 73-4)

The Nazarene is the best [novel of Asch's Christological trilogy] with an ingenious framework and a fascinating background. . . . By contrast, *The Apostle,* which centers on the life of Paul, seems somewhat labored and dull. The novel *Mary,* dealing chiefly with her son, is admirable in its treatment of the boyhood of Jesus, after which the author

plainly tired and skipped to the climactic scenes of his life. But the trilogy may be read by either Jew or Christian with profit—and with no damage to his faith. (p. 74)

Oscar Cargill, "Sholem Asch: Still Immigrant and Alien," in College English *(copyright © 1950 by the National Council of Teachers of English; reprinted by permission of the publisher and the author), Vol. 12, No. 2, November, 1950, pp. 67-74.*

RALPH W. GEORGE   (essay date 1950-51)

The power of Sholem Asch has numerous roots. One of these is a certain subtle humor. One might judge from his writings of the past decade, tinged as they often are by the consciousness of his people's tragedies, that he lacks any such feeling. Yet among the tales in the collection, *Children of Abraham,* is one called "From the Beyond." Here an elfish glee delights and fascinates the reader. The story concerns one Boruch Mordecai, who was thought to have died. But when the undertaker arrived, Boruch suddenly roused from his coma, sneezed, and to the consternation of everyone demanded that his wife produce a bowl of grits and milk. Somewhat later, when it had been explained to Boruch that he was supposed to have passed on, he decided to agree. (pp. 106-07)

Another source of Sholem Asch's power lies in his use of materials familiar to him but unfamiliar to his American readers. His early novels have their roots largely in the life of Eastern Europe—Poland particularly, and Russia—as in the case of *Three Cities. Salvation,* a novel of Poland in the late nineteenth century, is a good example of the way in which our artist weaves together the colors and sounds which he had known in childhood. It is a story of life in a small, isolated town, unfolding a modified feudalism and a core of folklore and superstition which have now passed away forever. (p. 107)

In addition to [*Salvation*'s] other qualities, one catches here the undertone of a purpose more compelling than that of an author who is simply writing to earn a living. For this tale is a study in religious tensions. (p. 108)

[Asch] does not stoop to the vulgarity and profanity of a Steinbeck or a Hemingway. Sholem Asch belongs to the classic tradition in literature, to the school of Dickens and Thackeray and Scott. Indeed, so far as an incomplete but wide reading of his works can discover, only one of his novels plays up the sex instinct to any degree. Yet even in this tale, *The Mother,* he does not begin to touch the depths sounded by our so-called realists. The fact is, Sholem Asch is a true son of Israel, not to be identified too closely with any one of its groupings—Orthodox, Conservative, or Reform—but a devout Jew for whom the Third Commandment is as sacred a word as was ever written. (p. 109)

In the trilogy comprised of *The Nazarene, The Apostle,* and *Mary,* the purpose which has become increasingly dominant in our author's thinking stands out clearly. It is that of reconciling, if possible, the Jewish and the Christian cultures. *The Nazarene* is the story of Jesus in novel form. It is presented by means of an unusual device, that of first-person narratives by three very unlike characters: a Roman officer, Judas the disciple, and a young man of Jerusalem who appears as a student of Nicodemus. The first chronicle, by the officer Cornelius, provides us with a sweeping panorama of the Jerusalem of 2,000 years ago. In this account we visit Herod at his summer palace, witness the dance of Salome, and watch her as she is presented with the head of John the Baptist. Even in these necessarily sordid lines the author makes us feel the spiritual power of the Nazarene. Part Two is a magnificent piece of cadenced prose which suggests that the betrayal of Jesus was simply an act of misguided loyalty. And Part Three is a highly dramatic record in which the author places the blame for the crucifixion not on the Jews as a people, not on the Pharisees who are sympathetically portrayed, but on the selfish Sadducees and the Roman officials.

Here surely is a volume which none of us can afford to overlook. For *The Nazarene* is a vivid, artistic, and satisfying work, as brilliant as it is accurate. It has been said by some critics that no one but Sholem Asch possesses both the technical knowledge and the literary skill to write such a book. This statement might well be true also of *The Apostle,* with its 800 pages set forth in the grand tradition of the heroic novel. In his research, our author has scanned the Book of Acts, the Epistles, and contemporary secular literature for every shred of available evidence. . . . Religion, politics, and social customs are subjected to the most minute and detailed treatment.

Paul himself is presented to us as a divided personality—a schizophrenic. For the technique of the novelist, this theory of a split personality provides the basis for a plot: how could the hero's unity be secured? To the credit of Sholem Asch it must be said that although he does not allow his hero to find mental healing until just before his death, yet he does show his transformation as being due to the influence of Christ. A tense, dominating man grows patient and tolerant, finds a moving faith, and joins the mystics in his consciousness of oneness with God through Christ. And this is a great admission on the part of any Jew.

In his beautifully written story, *Mary,* our author concludes the trilogy begun in *The Nazarene* and *The Apostle.* It is, in fact, both prelude and postlude to his history of the beginnings of Christianity. As in the other works of this group, the environment of the main character is depicted with meticulous care. Only in this instance we find not a city with all its malformations but a village, Palestinian in every detail. . . . Nazareth becomes a living reality as Sholem Asch describes the village characters together with their social and religious customs. (pp. 110-11)

Two contributions in particular are made by this novel to our understanding of the greatest of all mothers. First, it answers some of the questions which New Testament scholars have often raised. . . . How could a human and a divine nature be embodied in one personality? This man of letters answers with a picture of a normal physical body united to a consciousness devoid of every evil passion. Secondly, this story opens the door to the self-consciousness of Mary herself in which agonizing fear is followed by calm resolve, only to be succeeded again by fresh apprehensions. Quite aside from all its theological implications, this narrative is one of literature's most exquisite and daring delineations of the human spirit.

This trilogy—*The Nazarene, The Apostle,* and *Mary*—more than any other group of his works, allows us to peer into Sholem Asch's mind. As he [has stated], the horrors of the past fifteen or twenty years have convinced him that only one force can save our world—that of a union of the Jewish

and Christian religions and cultures. For the consummation of this end he must himself become a prophet, vehement and passionate. (pp. 111-12)

Ralph W. George, "Sholem Asch—Man of Letters and Prophet" (originally a speech presented before the Itinerants' Club of Boston), in Religion in Life *(copyright © 1950 by Abingdon Press), Vol. XX, No. 1, Winter, 1950-51, pp. 106-13.*

JOSEPH C. LANDIS   (essay date 1966)

Asch is a writer of great scope and wide interests. His subjects range from Moses to the present, from Eastern Europe and Israel to America, from the small towns to the world's great cities. He writes of Jews and gentiles, of prophets and peasants; of the respectable middle class, of the tough butchers and draymen without social status, and of the world of thieves and prostitutes. He has an eager eye for externals, for sharp contrasts, dramatic situations, panoramic vistas, and masses in motion; he is less interested in details. Of the themes that run through his works, the most frequent is probably faith; yet it is a faith that is not precisely defined, a faith in miracles, in Judaism, in the reality of a common Judeo-Christian tradition, in the common man and his yearning for morality, in life. It is the drama, the color, the sentiment, the mystical surface of faith that intrigues him rather than its substance, as it was the dramatic situation of the Messiah and the martyr that attracted him all his life—the loyalty and the mystic ecstasy of their ordeal, not the inner struggle or the anguish. Though he admires Jewish—which is more than Stoic—endurance of suffering, he is also intrigued by violence, and he finds a fusion of the two in the violent endurance and the endurance of violence that constitute martyrdom. He has a great enthusiasm for what he admires that leads him to idealize it, to paint it in glowing color and idyllic form. He admires all who have faith or are faithful to a vision of goodness, and these include not only Messiahs and martyrs but virtuous matrons, chaste maidens, young lovers, and harmonious worlds that are past—and owners of brothels. Two types appear in his works with great frequency—one, the traditional pious Jew, who has a disdain for the bestializing and brutalizing effect of violence and an admiration for gentleness, morality, study, and observance; the other, the rough, tough man whose physical work, while it relegates him to a low position in the social scale, endows him with muscle and with the ability to give as well as take a blow. Asch admires them both, but there is no conflict in his admiration, for his men of muscle, though unlearned and unrefined, remain loyal to the ideals and the defense of their people and to the traditions of learning. (pp. 69-70)

Joseph C. Landis, in his introduction to "God of Vengeance" by Sholem Asch, in "The Dybbuk" and Other Great Yiddish Plays, *edited and translated by Joseph C. Landis (copyright © 1966 by Bantam Books, Inc.), Bantam, 1966, pp. 69-72.*

CHARLES A. MADISON   (essay date 1968)

A Town immediately placed Asch in the front rank of Yiddish writers. It is in essence a long prose poem. Saturated from early childhood with the passionate piety of a Hasidic environment permeated with the wholesomeness and earthiness of nature, pastoral in its simplicity, and almost primitive in its lusty animality—Asch described this medieval milieu with the ecstasy of first love. In contrast to the sordid and squalid life in the Warsaw ghetto, where he then lived, the simple Hasidim of his childhood memory appeared in his imagination as an idyllic folk: firmly founded in the revered faith of their fathers, inured to their static social customs and economic practices, endowed with the carnal robustness of their peasant neighbors, yet childlike in their placid innocence. In this story they therefore appear quite unlike the Jews met with in the Polish towns of the late 19th century and described by [several other writers]. . . .

Indeed, they emanated from a nostalgic self-love that visualized these Jews in Asch's own romantic image. In depicting them as pulsating with pristine potency he also revealed a love of nature as novel to his Yiddish readers as his romanticized townsmen. He was the first Yiddish writer to portray the out-of-doors with pagan exuberance, to luxuriate in the description of sensuous beauty for its own sake.

Asch . . . began to experiment with the dramatic form. In 1904 his two-act play, originally named *The Return* and later retitled *Downstream,* was produced in Polish in Cracow. It dealt with the skepticism which began to gnaw at the minds of young Talmudic students in the 1870's. (pp. 222-23)

Asch propounded the self-evident truth that once one is infected with doubt, faith is doomed—even where there is nothing to replace it. Yet the drama is wanting in conviction, having been developed more by means of rhetoric than action. Moreover, David [the protagonist] is hardly representative of the emancipated intellectuals of his generation. Most of them were no weaklings; having broken the gyves of orthodoxy, they found faith in Zionism, radicalism, scholarship, or mammon. (pp. 223-24)

The theme of [*The God of Vengeance*] is essentially spurious drama. The action concerns Yekel Shabshevitz's attempt to strike a bargain with God to preserve his daughter Rivkele's moral purity. The absurdity of Yekel's behavior is immediately obvious. (p. 225)

Yekel fails to become a tragic figure because he is the creation of Asch the moralist. In life Yekel, eager to protect his only daughter from the influence of the brothel, would either have abandoned the bawdyhouse altogether and given her a respectable home, or sent her away to some distant place where she would remain unaffected by his immoral activities. If, after he had done either of these two things, Rivkele nevertheless took the path trodden by her mother, Yekel's frustration would have assumed a tragic aspect. Asch, however, compels him to keep Rivkele in his apartment over the brothel, within easy reach of temptation. . . .

[Yekel's ranting against God's vengeance], under the circumstances, sounds hollow and sentimental, as if spoken not by a man in deep anguish but by a character in a brash melodrama. That the play achieved a certain notoriety was due largely to the novelty of the setting and to its moral overtones. Also in its favor are the vigorous and vivacious brothel scenes and the poetic tenderness of the lesbian affection between Manka and Rivkele. (p. 226)

Wealthy Reb Shlome [*Reb Shloyme nogid*] is a more mature and variegated portrayal than *A Town.* In neither story is action of much consequence, but in the later work character becomes a more positive factor. Reb Shlome, patterned after the elder Asch, is imbued with the glow of

romantic reality. From the moment he enters the narrative on his return home for the Sabbath, until he celebrates the betrothal of his son to the daughter of his favored rabbi, Reb Shlome lives by virtue of his positive personality. (p. 228)

Milieu, rather than character, assumes first importance in this work. The market square, the synagogue, Reb Shlome's open house, the Vistula River, the soil and its products, Jews and peasants, all play their poetic parts in this idyllic symphony. Each day has its own significance, every season its special character. (p. 229)

Asch depicted these village scenes with romantic gusto. Drawing upon authentic memories of his early youth, he invested the narrative with epical breadth and beauty. He endowed his rustics with pristine appeal, and the magic of his glowing prose transformed their homely environment into an idealized community. . . . Asch's idyllic sensuousness impregnated Jewish life with the simple charm of the pastoral. (pp. 229-30)

The first major work he completed in the United States . . . was *Mottke the Thief.* Here Asch contrasts the simple and static life of the Jewish poor in a Polish village with the gaudy and grimy sordidness of the Warsaw slum. The first half is written with inspired gusto, the character of the youthful Mottke drawn with Rabelaisian strokes. Red Zlatke, Blind Layb, Blind Pearl, Burck the trick dog, the acrobat troupe, and numerous others are delineated with realistic clarity. The strong elemental attachment between Mottke and his harassed mother is etched with rare tenderness and insight.

The life of the poor is portrayed almost epically. In their midst the youthful Mottke is evoked with gargantuan vividness. (pp. 231-32)

Asch's fertile and quick imagination could not but be stimulated by the teeming life of New York's East Side. He was especially affected by the pathetic attempts of Jewish immigrants to adapt themselves to American ways and practices. . . .

Uncle Moses . . . makes painfully clear that in their attempts to gain a footing in their new and alien environment, many Jewish immigrants unavoidably relinquished or deliberately discarded the traditions and faith of their fathers. (p. 233)

The novel begs comparison with *Wealthy Reb Shlome.* In both stories the people have a similar rustic origin, and interest in each is centered in the potent leader of the communal group. In writing about the Jews in their native patriarchal setting, where they were ready to defend their faith with their very lives and endured the week for the serene pleasure of the Sabbath. Asch tended to wax idyllic and give his words the glow of lyric gusto. In describing the drab and dreary existence in their sweatshop environment of the same Jews—to whom the bliss of the Sabbath has become a troubled memory, whose religious orthodoxy was being devitalized by the vulgarities of a leveling freedom, and whose weary minds were of necessity concentrating on the economics of the factory—he could only write with the bluntness of uninspired irony. Moreover, serializing the story in a popular newspaper, he found it necessary to concoct a palatable plot, so that while many pages contain cogent writing, the narrative ends melodramatically.

The persecutions and pogroms in Eastern Europe during and immediately following World War I, causing death and destruction in scores of Jewish towns, profoundly perturbed Sholom Asch. . . . In his effort to comfort his people he turned his mind to these and earlier calamities, and wrote about them to exalt the spiritual faith and perseverance of the victims. (pp. 233-34)

[*The Sanctification of the Name,* for example,] delineates Jewish life in Poland during the bloody massacres perpetrated by Bogdan Khmelnitski and his kossaks in the decade following 1648. The Jews were then, even more than in 1918-1919, on the brink of annihilation. Asch wished to indicate that, as before, the undying faith of the Jews would keep them from extinction. (p. 235)

[*The Mother*] is a loosely told story. The first half concerns the vicissitudes of a Jewish family as it leaves its native Poland and strives to establish a footing in New York's strange and squalid East Side; the remainder concentrates on Jewish Bohemian life, particularly Bucholtz's struggle for artistic recognition. The novel is thus dichotomous and without inner interrelation. Nor are the main characters fully realized. Soreh Rivke lacks the robust earthiness of Asch's other mothers despite the wonders she achieves with her "magic pots"; by stressing her instinctive motherliness rather than her unique personality he tends to attenuate her essential appeal. Even more negative is her daughter Deborah, to whom Asch also ascribes the "secret mission" of motherhood, and whose self-sacrifice . . . is hardly credible. And the towering, uncouth Bucholtz, to whom sculpting is as natural and vital as breathing, often acts too much the boorish clown to arouse one's sympathy. What saves the novel from mediocrity is the realistic insight which quickens the chapters dealing with the provocations and tribulations of the immigrant family in the effort to get established in its new home. (pp. 236-37)

[*The War Goes On* pursues] the story of social upheaval from the savage civil strife on the Russian border in 1918 to the economic and spiritual collapse in Germany five years later. The early chapters add little to development of the main theme, and Aron Yudkewitch's undue prominence deprives Hans Bodenheimer of his rightful place as chief protagonist; moreover, the portraits of several prominent characters emerge flat and flaccid. Yet the book towers as a work of historical fiction. It depicts with notable clarity and acuteness the suffering, pathos, chaos, and most of all the unmitigated despair which spawned the Nazi rulers of Germany. Again and again the narrative flares forth with the passion of the proud Jew; over the whole hovers the artist's wistful and compassionate insight into human vicissitude. (p. 242)

Asch is at his keenest in describing the pathos of a haughty people made desperate by defeat. He makes painfully clear the terrible postwar conditions which forced the truculent and recalcitrant Germans to nurse delusions of grandeur, to make the small Jewish minority their needed scapegoat—to fall like overripe fruit into the lap of "Death's Prophet." Simultaneously he dissects and exposes the crooked roots of hatred of which the Jews become the outraged victims. His objective and perspicacious treatment makes the indictment all the more crushing. (p. 243)

Jewish piety, whole-souled adoration of Jehovah, and devout observance of the 613 precepts had from childhood

fascinated Asch's romantic imagination, and he tended to write about it with the ardent tenderness of lyric love. Composing *Salvation* as an antidote to Hitlerism, he stressed the moral beauty of Jewish piety, as if urging his readers to "seek the ideal, the noble, and the beautiful in our historic past." (p. 245)

The lyric beauty of the prose imbues the narrative with artistic authenticity. Asch's delineation of the piety and mystical aspirations of ordinary Jews is as vivid and veracious as if he were describing his own inmost emotions. Their pathetic and at times pathological behavior assumes inherent reality in their sincere yearning for spiritual beatitude. Their implicit faith is set off throughout against the poverty and earthiness of their daily lives. Their supreme representative is Jekhiel, who believes that not erudition but faith leads to salvation, that the love of God ennobles man's spirit. He naturally cleaves to God with all his soul. He believes that man is a chip of God: a soul sojourning on earth but longing to rejoin his Maker. Hunger and suffering in others so wring his heart that soon the magic of his words gives bread to the hungry and comfort to the sick. Asch, confronted by Nazi brutality, concluded the book with the pious hope that "each generation will see its own righteous man. For is it not written that the righteous man is the cornerstone of the world?"

Another visit to Palestine, primarily to gather material and saturate himself with its atmosphere for his next major work, led Asch to write the brief novel, *The Song of the Valley* . . . , dealing with the efforts of young pioneers to redeem the inert and swampy plains of Israel. (pp. 246-47)

Writing the book in painful awareness of Hitler's intensified ruthlessness, Asch tended to exalt the courage and heroism of the Zionistic youths. Ready to risk their lives for the success of the colony, they meet each hardship with a song and undertake onerous tasks with fanatical enthusiasm. The vision of a thriving Jewish Palestine is ever before them, and how they seek to realize their dream is developed with idyllic simplicity. (p. 247)

In the last decade of his life, Asch, *Mary* excepted, returned to his Jewish setting. *East River* . . . and *A Passage in the Night* . . . concern Jews in the United States who are already well established and Americanized. In the first he poses the problem of antagonism among peoples, nations, and religions, and suggests that amicable relations are possible among them. The question of intermarriage is treated sympathetically, and he implies that not religion but character is basic to human amity. The novel lacks the freshness and lyricism of his earlier work, although it is more deftly conceived. In the second story Grossman, the protagonist, had in his youth stolen a wallet from a Polish peasant, and its content enabled him to start his climb to considerable wealth. In his old age he becomes eager to find the Pole and compensate him generously. In both narratives three generations are contrasted and their interrelationships described in detail. Both works are in a minor key, but evidence the literary dexterity of the mature novelist: the characterization is firm and the motivation lyrical and persuasive. (p. 257)

[In *Moses*], as in the Christological volumes, he adheres to the religious sources, adding legendary and mythological as well as anthropological embellishments to provide a psychologically sympathetic portrait of Moses as a revolutionary and prophet. Like Jesus, he emerges as through a misted glass mystically: a noble human being, a seeker of truth and justice, but no Son of God. (p. 258)

Asch dwells lovingly on his human qualities and spiritual afflatus, ennobling him as the founder of Judaism and Jehovah's exalted prophet.

For his next book Asch chose Deutero-Isaiah, the humble prophet who sang God's word because he could not silence the voice within him. Isaiah in *The Prophet* . . . , like Jekhiel in *Salvation,* is from boyhood possessed by consuming love of God. The Babylonian exile preys on his youthful mind. So eager is he, dwelling with his parents in the outskirts of Jerusalem, for the return of his people and restoration of the Temple that he soon begins to hear God's voice in his heart, and is impelled by an irrepressible urge to journey to Babylon to preach the word of God to the exiled Jews. (p. 259)

[Later], sick and starved, [Isaiah] suffers grievously at the hands of his rich and powerful tomentors. Yet he persists in his inspired preaching and prophesying, and his life is saved by the poor who believe in him. . . . [The intimation at the end of *The Prophet*] of the advent of Jesus, as well as of Israel's place in the world, is in keeping with Asch's continued belief that the salvation of mankind lies in the recognition of Judeo-Christian concord. (pp. 259-60)

> *Charles A. Madison, "Sholem Asch: Novelist of Lyric Intensity," in his* Yiddish Literature: Its Scope and Major Writers *(copyright © 1968 by Frederick Ungar Publishing Co., Inc.), Ungar, 1968, pp. 221-61.*

BIBLIOGRAPHY

Lieberman, Chaim. *The Christianity of Sholem Asch: An Appraisal from the Jewish Viewpoint.* Translated by Abraham Burstein. New York: Philosophical Library, 1953, 276 p.
  Critical attack on Asch, his Christological trilogy, and *Moses.*

Liptzin, Sol. "Sholem Asch." In his *The Flowering of Yiddish Literature,* pp. 178-89. New York: Thomas Yoseloff, Publisher, 1963.
  Traces Asch's literary development, focusing on the theme of the Jew in both historic and contemporary times.

Mariano Azuela

1873-1952

(Also wrote under pseudonym of Beleño) Mexican novelist, short story writer, and biographer.

Azuela is one of the foremost Mexican novelists of the twentieth century and his *Los de abajo* is considered by many critics to be the premier novel of the Mexican revolution. Azuela's novels provide a documentary portrait of Mexican society before, during, and after the revolution. They have been likened to the murals of Diego Rivera and José Clemente Orozco for their panoramic portrayal of the changing face of modern Mexico.

A doctor in his poor rural village or in the slums of Mexico City for most of his adult life, Azuela was concerned throughout his career with the poor. His experience as a doctor for Pancho Villa's troops and as a minor politician after the revolution was integral to his work. He depicted the moral ambivalence and self-serving nature of all political persuasions with satire that grew increasingly pessimistic as he witnessed the corruption of the ideals of the revolution.

Azuela was greatly influenced by French realism and naturalism. Not all of his work was straightforwardly realistic, however, and his experimentation with literary techniques in some of his work has influenced many subsequent Mexican novelists.

PRINCIPAL WORKS

María Luisa (novel) 1907
Los fracasados (novel) 1908
Mala yerba (novel) 1909
  [*Marcela: A Mexican Love Story*, 1932]
Andrés Pérez, maderista (novel) 1911
Sin amor (novel) 1912
Los de abajo (novel) 1916
  [*The Under Dogs*, 1929]
Los caciques (novel) 1917
  [*The Bosses*, 1956]
Domitilo quiere ser diputado (novella) 1918
Las moscas (novella) 1918
  [*The Flies*, 1956]
Las tribulaciones de una familia decente (novel) 1918
  [*The Trials of a Respectable Family*, 1963]
La Malhora (novel) 1923
El desquite (novel) 1925
La luciérnaga (novel) 1932

El camarada Pantoja: Novela (novel) 1937
San Gabriel de Valdivias, comunidad indígena (novel) 1938
Regina Landa (novel) 1939
Avanzada: Novela (novel) 1940
Nueva burguesía: Novela (novel) 1941
La marchanta: Novela (novel) 1944
La mujer domada: Novela (novel) 1946
Sendas perdidas (novel) 1949
La maldición: Novela (novel) 1955
Esa sangre (novel) 1956
Madero: Biografía novelada (novel) 1958-60; published in *Obras Completas*

CARLETON BEALS (essay date 1929)

The revolution is crude, the revolution is loud; it is battle and cannon-fire and stentorian hopes, futility, and false creeds, land-seizures and strikes, bastard ambitions and strutting generals. All of this has gone into the Mexican mill. . . .

To keep pace with this turmoil, the literature of Mexico has had to slug hard and quick. . . .

And so expressionism—in poetry and in the novel. . . . [In] the novel, and to some extent in poetry, there have stepped forward the Noise-makers—the Estridentistas! They have to shout to be heard. They have shouted. Hence *Estridentismo*. "Noisyism!" they have shouted. (p. 280)

The Under Dogs gives none of the broader outlines of the Mexican Revolution; it is close-up photography of day-by-day struggle. . . .

The scenes have the brutality of Gorki. Azuela is the Mexican Chekhov only in so much as he is a doctor; in all else he is closer to Gorki, with a touch of Gorki's terrific pessimism and none of Gorki's revolutionary optimism. The style is crisp; it burns like the flash of a gun-muzzle close to the skin. Azuela knows the Under Dogs. He has seen the revolution; he has smelled it; he has felt it. His language is the language of reality, the patois of the Nickelmen, crude, often vile, truculent, fiendish. (p. 282)

Demetrio [protagonist of *The Under Dogs*] is a humbler,

less grandiose type than the famous Sarmiento's *Facundo*. Nevertheless, in some ways this novel surpasses the masterpiece of the Argentinian. All in all Azuela bids fair to become the novelist of the Mexican Revolution. His books mount up, and they form a broad canvas of the dark events of the past eighteen years. (p. 283)

> Carleton Beals, "The Noise-Makers: The 'Estridentistas' and Other Writers of Revolutionary Mexico," in The Bookman, Vol. LXIX, No. 3, May, 1929, pp. 280-85.*

WALDO FRANK (essay date 1929)

[*Los de Abajo*] has been called photographic realism; but Homer and Cervantes antedated Daguerre, wherefore I consider the description ill-chosen. [Azuela's] portrayal of the blind whirl of revolution has been called bitterly satiric; it seems to me rather to be merely faithful and humbly clairvoyant. If you look with an intelligent eye at men in business—or at men in civil war—you are likely to judge that they are fools. But if you are an artist, you will find that there is beauty in them. And if you are a great artist, you will find (even if you have never heard of Spinosa and utterly reject the Epistles of Saint Paul) that they are divine. Doctor Azuela is intelligent, and a great artist. He is a silent man, and his hands and heart are busy all the day, healing the plagues of the lowly. He does not talk about what he saw in the Mexican revolution. Probably, even to himself he is not confiding. But his pages reveal his complete and therefore prophetic vision. He saw the folly of men, and the divinity. His book is significant, because both these qualities are in it; the beauty, the tenderness, the vital splendor, the immaculate life of this Mexico of his tale are important, precisely because these traits reside within and emanate from the cruelty, the sordidness, the filth and desperation of the Mexico he portrays.

Moreover, the book is well joined as a Greek ode. A story of indespicable confusion, it has the body of an inner order —an order not in the least intellectual or studied; an order that is organic. And this too is important. The terrible materials of this chaos which Azuela describes are integrally related: seen as a whole, they fall into place, its esthetic form proves that this chaos is on the way to being an organic world; the book depicts the ignorance and horror of the Mexican struggle; but within them, plainly, is wisdom and revelation. (pp. 275-76)

> Waldo Frank, "The Mexican Invasion," in The New Republic (© 1929 The New Republic, Inc.), Vol. 60, No. 777, October 23, 1929, pp. 275-76.*

JOHN E. ENGLEKIRK and LAWRENCE B. KIDDLE (essay date 1939)

[Azuela] is fighting for a cause. Social conflict is his theme. In his earlier works, he points accusingly to social conditions that bespeak the tyrannical oppression of *los de arriba;* later, when caught up in the ruthless brutality of the Revolution itself, he boldly condemns those guilty of having plunged his people into a class war without any clearly defined program of social reform; and, later still, he paints a somber picture of post-Revolutionary society, more corrupt and degenerate than before, for the Revolution had unleashed new forces of evil hitherto held in check through fear of a powerful centralized control. (p. xvii)

Azuela's penchant for contrasting opposite types is already

apparent [in *María Luisa*]. . . . [His] confrontation of conservatives and liberals [is] exemplified in the *seminaristas* and in Pancho, the medical student. He fills in his canvas with many other familiar provincial types—no one completely escapes his caustic scrutiny. He is outspoken in his anticlerical feeling and his criticism of religious education. And in this first novel there is much of the fatalism of *Los de abajo* and the same concern for the future of his people. (p. xviii)

Mala yerba is Azuela's first important work and must be classed among the best of his novels. Though melodramatic and none too original in plot, it offers splendid characterization and a vigorous, artistic portrayal of rural customs and types. And for the first time Azuela assigns nature an inescapable and effective role in the setting and in the lives of his protagonists. Although given to overdrawing his principal characters because of the intensity with which he flays the feudal scene, Azuela is especially adept in his delineation of minor types. . . . The barbed satire and heavily charged pessimism that prevail throughout are momentarily relieved by Azuela's avowal of faith in Mexican womanhood, an avowal he will voice more artistically and with even greater conviction in *La luciérnaga*. *Mala yerba* is not without its blemishes, but it is a forceful novel, compelling in its interest. (pp. xix-xx)

[*Andrés Pérez, maderista*] is Azuela's first novel of the Revolution. Artistically it is a decidedly inferior work, overly sententious, poorly and hurriedly written, at times difficult to follow; but ideologically it is one of his most significant novels. Conceived during those very months when Azuela already foresaw the tragic turn the revolt of the idealist Madero was soon to take, . . . it is the work of one who boldly, fearlessly, and prophetically [decried the Revolution]. . . . (p. xx)

But the Revolution was not all horror, lust, and bloodshed, as many would believe; as Azuela says [in *Los de abajo*] in the words of Solís, the idealist, "How beautiful the Revolution is, even in its very barbarism!" And so, artist that he was, Azuela softened the harsh, brutal realism of his canvas with many a lyric touch; in striking contrast to the sordid primitiveness of most of his characters, the natural background is awe-inspiring in its grandeur and serenity. The language, sometimes racy and virile, sometimes poetic and subdued, is in every instance in perfect accord with the mood and character of the story. Apparently as aimless as the Revolution itself, the novel unfolds easily and naturally. Just as out of the chaos of guerrilla warfare and the clash of human pawns is born the primal, well-defined motif of the movement it has indelibly engraved for all time, so too out of the individual scenes that are here brought together there springs an artistic unity that only one who had experienced them could have achieved. (pp. xxiii-xxiv)

[*Las tribulaciones de una familia decente*] is Azuela's firsthand account of the tragic struggle of the Vázquez Prado family [to begin life anew]. . . . The family itself, symbolic of the Revolution and of the nation, is torn between conflicting ideologies. (p. xxvi)

[The first part of the novel] is narrated by César. . . . Characterized to the point of caricature, César provides genuine entertainment in many a scene of clever satire; César is anything but a "Caesar"; cowardly, weak, effeminate, spineless, he is the pitiful offspring of a too long pampered, degenerate social class. César's death prepares the way for the second part of the novel, "El triunfo de Procopio" ["The Triumph of Procopio"]. The ensuing shift in emphasis and narrative technique lends added meaning to Procopio's moral stature and exemplary conduct.

The novel abounds in penetrating, prophetic observations on the nature and course of the Revolution; it is also a remarkable document of the manners and types of middle class Mexican society of the period. Unquestionably, the novel is one of Azuela's most effective pieces of satire, and of those works dealing with the years 1910-1917, it stands second only to *Los de abajo*. (p. xxvii)

In style the novelette [*La Malhora*] represents a radical departure from Azuela's earlier work. . . . It is by no means easy reading; many lines and some passages must be read again and again before their complete meaning and symbolic strength can be fully appreciated. Azuela abides by no accepted standards of sentence structure or style: substantives and adjectives are endowed with verbal power; adjectives are given unexpected and amazingly suggestive meanings; recondite images, often one upon another, dazzle one into incomprehension; there is occasionally an excessive grouping of adjectives, not always to the best effect. The obvious narrative thread is repeatedly interrupted and definitely subordinated to a more profound and more suggestive one which knits together the many soliloquies that illumine the intricate psychological pattern of subconscious forces motivating the surface action. This baffling but provocative style places *La Malhora* among the best of the earliest attempts to elaborate new novelistic techniques in the America of that day. (pp. xxviii-xxix)

[*El desquite*] follows the stylistic and structural pattern of *La Malhora*, but is far less artistically done. Azuela's striving for inordinate effects has definitely marred the work. Psychological bits of retrospect, too frequently interspersed, nearly obliterate the main narrative and impede and distort character portrayal; the imagery is challenging but too often obscure. The novel suffers from hasty composition and from a blurred conception at the outset of just how the rather involved theme—especially complex because of structure and style—was to be carried to a logical end.

The picture Azuela paints for us here is a somber one indeed, distinctly Zolaesque in the sordidness and the physical and mental degeneracy it portrays. It is the tragedy of a woman who married beneath her in spiritual and moral dignity. . . . (p. xxix)

[*La luciérnaga*] testifies to Azuela's liberation from forced and unfortunate stylistic techniques that marred *El desquite* and that made the reading of *La Malhora* a marked intellectual challenge. Azuela was never a slave to any literary movement; he might have been attracted for a time by the mood and manner of the day, but he was too vigorous a writer not to emerge soon with a style decidedly his own. For example, Azuela became an avid reader of Proust during the years immediately preceding the publication of *La luciérnaga*, and he who will can find occasional echoes of the French writer in Azuela's novel. But there is no servility, either here or in any of his writing. . . .

La luciérnaga is a psychological study of two brothers, a study again in contrasts: Dionisio, who left the provinces with his family and with his share of the inheritance to con-

quer the capital, and José María, who remains behind with his money—not all rightfully his—and with his remorse to argue himself into believing, in a convincing display of casuistry, that his soul will be saved. (p. xxx)

The opening chapter is a brilliant piece of concise exposition and psychological portrayal. Through his masterful depiction of the thought processes of the *pulque*-soaked, drug-befuddled brain of Dionisio and his studied treatment of the sophistry of José María, Azuela introduces naturally and artistically those elements of the narrative that, had they been presented in any other way, would have impeded and distorted the development of the story. In style *La luciérnaga* ranks with *La Malhora* as the best of Azuela's experimental work.

Azuela's flirtation with modern novelistic techniques was brash but brief. (p. xxxi)

Certain features are common to all of [Azuela's last six novels: *La Marchanta*, *La mujer domada*, *Sendas perdidas*, *La maldición*, *Esa sangre*, and *Madero: Biografía novelada*]. Gone, for example, is the old urge to speak out sharply against sociopolitical ills and injustices, and no longer is there any pronounced, purposeful indictment of the on-going social revolution or of the political party in power. Rather, the emphasis now shifts to individual man, and the action is less explicitly grounded in the Mexican scene. This is especially marked in the city novels in which modern attitudes and manners have cast off the colorful garb of the older provincial way of life. In keeping with this emphasis, the settings incline heavily toward the urban. However, there is also a tendency to shift scenes frequently, and disconcertingly, from city to country and back again, often to the detriment of sound plot development. Azuela's loyalties to realism are at play here; he had observed teeming urban living at close hand for well over a quarter century, yet happily nurtured memories of his earlier years continued to well up as vividly as they had in a rapidly receding past. And as a result there is also in these latter novels a reiteration of his belief in the superior moral fiber of provincial Mexico and a reaffirmation of his preference for the rural scene and the rural way of life. (p. xxxvii)

John E. Englekirk and Lawrence B. Kiddle, "Introduction: Mariano Azuela (1873-1952)," in Los de abajo: Novela de la Revolución Mexícana *by Mariano Azuela, edited by John E. Englekirk and Lawrence B. Kiddle (© 1939; reprinted by permission of Prentice-Hall, Inc., Englewood Cliffs, New Jersey), F. S. Crofts & Co., 1939 (and reprinted by Prentice-Hall, Inc., 1971, pp. xi-xl).*

JEFFERSON REA SPELL   (essay date 1944)

While Azuela's youthful sketches are rather puerile, they reveal his interests and attitude at the time and certain literary tendencies that are characteristic of his first longer works. They express first of all a vital concern for the poor and oppressed, for the less favored in the scheme of life that existed in the Díaz régime. (p. 69)

As in his sketches, Azuela expresses in his first group of novels his discontent with existing social conditions. While on the whole sentimental, with very little commendable in either plot or characterization, they depict admirably certain types and portray vividly certain aspects of Mexican society of the first decade of the twentieth century. The background in the four novels is varied: student life in

Guadalajara in *María Luisa;* small town life in *Los Fracasados* and *Sin Amor;* and life on a country estate in *Mala Yerba*.

María Luisa, which Azuela developed into a novel from his early sketch, centers about a beautiful young woman who, as the story opens, was debating whether she would continue her humdrum existence in a factory or become the mistress of Pancho, a young medical student. (p. 70)

Whatever charm this novelette has lies outside of the commonplace story of seduction, which fails to arouse pity. Of greater artistic worth are the interlarded essays that portray certain aspects of life in Guadalajara. . . . Also well done are the portraits of certain social types—María Luisa's mother, who kept a boarding-house; her old cousin, the falsely pious Doña Juana; Esther and her mother, somewhat light of virtue; and their protector Don Pedro. Not less interesting is the piquant dialogue, Azuela's principal stylistic forte, in which these personages express themselves. Nevertheless the work, done at the outset of his career, presents the chief weaknesses of Azuela as a novelist—his inability to tell an interesting and well-balanced story, and to integrate harmoniously the various elements of which fiction consists.

Likewise in *Los Fracasados* Azuela was less concerned with telling a story than with exposing the iniquity of certain inhabitants of Alamos, which has been identified with his native Lagos. The folk of Alamos of some thirty-odd years ago that are mirrored in this book are unforgettable. . . . (pp. 70-1)

The setting in which the characters move, the town of Alamos, is developed fully from every angle. Even in the purely descriptive passages, for which Azuela's fiction is in general not remarkable, *Los Fracasados* is admirable. . . . The social background itself, the most distinctive element in the book, is attained through a series of essays in which provincial life—with all of its foibles, jealousies, hatreds, and bickerings—is satirically but effectively pilloried. (pp. 71-2)

In all this detail, sight is often lost of the visionary and unselfish Reséndez, the protagonist who voices the ideas and sentiments of Azuela himself. (p. 72)

While *Los Fracasados* lacks much as a novel from a technical and artistic point of view, it is significant in that it portrays the intolerable conditions in a Mexican town that gave rise to the brutality of the underlings when they rose a few years later against their masters. The pessimistic tone found not only here but consistently in most of Azuela's novels, evidently voices his own attitude. . . .

Also set in a small town is another thesis novel, *Sin Amor,* . . . which portrays more pleasingly the same bourgeoise society. The bare mention of the new government under Madero suggests that no radical change had as yet occurred in Mexican social life. The well-developed narrative is decidedly a source of interest; the protagonist, a young woman, in comparison with Azuela's other characters who are generally of one fiber, is more complex; and the milieu, while amply set forth, is not overdone. (p. 73)

In *Sin Amor* there is less portrayal, for their own sake, of manners and customs than in *Los Fracasados,* yet the philosophy of life of the social group common to both the novels—the middle-class folk of a fair degree of culture—is

effectively revealed. One senses the great gulf between those that have and those that have not; the resentment of the latter toward the former; and the scorn of the wealthy for the poor. Both the men and the women are represented as uncharitable and mercenary; the latter are hypocritical, sharp of tongue, backbiting; and the men, who spend most of their time in the public bars and houses of prostitution, are debauched. Some of the minor figures embody in a high degree vices that are more or less characteristic of the entire social group. . . . (pp. 74-5)

The accuracy of the settings of both these novels shows that Azuela's knowledge of small town life resulted from first-hand observation. Equally intimate was his acquaintance with rural folk. . . . (p. 75)

The most distinctive feature of [*Mala Yerba*] is the excellent interpretation of the two types of people that it presents: the landed proprietors and the peasants on their estates. (p. 76)

In brief but effective passages, Azuela throws in descriptions of the countryside itself. . . . In the dialogue, in which as always he excels, the peasants speak in colloquial language. Various phases of the social life of the region . . . all enter into the picture.

In these stories Azuela has sketched the background of the Revolution; in the novelettes and short stories of the next decade, in which the portrayal of groups or of types rather than of individuals is also characteristic, he is to portray the Revolution itself. The first of these, *Andrés Pérez, Maderista,* gives a picture of life on an hacienda when the Revolution was brewing, and analyzes the motives of some of the participants. (pp. 76-7)

The stir and confusion of the first armed struggles is well portrayed, and the varying motives of the *Maderistas* effectively contrasted—Reyes, honest and altruistic; Vicente, who had been robbed of his property; and Hernández, concerned only with securing high rank with the successful faction. (p. 78)

The pessimism with which *Los Caciques* [a novelette about small town capitalists] is imbued—its sense of despair for the future—is that of Azuela when he wrote it. Yet, through the injustice that it lays bare, the book affords a vindication, in a measure, of those who committed the most shocking atrocities against the lives and property of the privileged classes when the Revolution broke. From the standpoint of good storytelling, not much can be said for *Los Caciques;* it lacks singleness of purpose and coherence. It does however present many scenes which throw light on the thoughts and attitudes of the shopkeeping and other middle-class elements in a small Mexican town. Types, too, of this society are excellently drawn. . . .

It is the absence of idealism or principles in politicians and government employees that Azuela satirizes in *Las Moscas* and *Domitilo quiere ser Diputado.* (p. 79)

From a literary standpoint, these two sketches deserve a high place in Azuela's works. Essays rather than short stories, their title page rightfully describes them as "scenes and sketches of the Revolution," but it is their theme, not their narrative element, that is important. The technique employed is loose and discursive; the satire is keen and clever; but, without abuse or sentimentality, Azuela lets his characters condemn themselves through their own words and actions—lets them reveal their lack of principles or of loyalty to either party or leader, once their personal interests are endangered. It is this aspect of the Mexican Revolution that Azuela makes plain. Both sketches contain, too, some excellent descriptive passages. (pp. 80-1)

[The trials during the Revolution of the Vázquez Prados, a family of landed proprietors, is] recounted in Azuela's *Las Tribulaciones de una Familia decente.* (p. 81)

This novel will probably live, not for its story or its character delineation, although they are to be counted among Azuela's best, but for its depiction of certain phases of life in Mexico City in those unsettled years following the downfall of Huerta—the desperate condition of those formerly wealthy; the invasion of the capital by savage hordes; the rise of Villa to power; and finally the corruption and excesses of the Carranza régime. The novel voices one of Azuela's best messages—his praise of labor; for in individuals like Procopio, he sees the only salvation for such people as the Vázquez Prado. (p. 82)

That [*Los de abajo*] will continue to [be considered a classic] is more than probable, for its masterly interpretation of a certain phase of the Revolution combined with its literary excellence insure it a permanent place in literature. Among the qualities which contribute to its excellence is its intense and varied emotive power, for while the author arouses pity for the downtrodden peasants, he also horrifies the reader with the crimes that some of them, in their ignorance and bestiality, commit. Then, too, *Los de Abajo,* which was conceived and largely written in a period of great despair in the author's own life, is lyric in its expression of pessimism and hopelessness over the situation that existed in his country. Besides, the book is in general poetic rather than either historical or realistic. . . . A further poetic charm of *Los de Abajo* is to be found in the language itself, which, despite its simplicity, its short and elliptical periods, its predominantly colloquial or vulgar tone, is decidedly rhythmical.

The characteristic that distinguishes Azuela as a literary artist in *Los de Abajo,* both in regard to the work as a whole and to its component parts, is his mastery of the art of selection and condensation. This method, whether he is describing nature, persons, or the man-made world, is to emphasize a few well-chosen characteristics concerning each. (pp. 85-6)

Within the various scenes or sketches that compose the story, Azuela compresses into a short paragraph incidents of a narrative nature that other writers would treat far more extensively. (p. 86)

Certain stylistic qualities that distinguish *Los de Abajo* as a work of art—the fresh and striking imagery in regard to nature, the elliptical and suggestive, rather than direct, manner of narration, which makes heavy demands on the reader's imagination and factual knowledge—are often carried to the point of exaggeration in his next two novelettes, *La Malhora* and *El Desquite,* and in a longer work, *La Luciérnaga,* all of which portray some aspect of the Mexican society produced by the Revolution. (p. 88)

Between Azuela's first four novels and the group consisting of *La Malhora, El Desquite,* and *La Luciérnaga* there is a basic change in his technique. Those of the latter group are, in varying degrees, more or less obscure. Suggestive rather than direct in manner, they are subtle and tenuous; in spite of their brevity, they incline to discursiveness; and they are marked by an affected, over-wrought style whose extreme singularity attracts attention. These characteristics, except type of style, are less prominent in *La Malhora,* which in its singleness of purpose . . . is the most unified of the three. It is also enhanced by strong contrasts in both characters and settings: the denizens of the underworld and their rendezvous, the "pulque shop," on the one hand; and respectable folk and their environment, on the other. In *El Desquite* there are also excellent descriptive touches, but as a whole it falls far short of being a well-knit work. What there is of a plot seems to be purposely concealed, so embedded is it in irrelevancies. In *La Luciérnaga,* the most pretentious work of the group, the description of the small town Cieneguilla and the impressionistic portrayal of certain parts of Mexico City are charmingly done. But this work, although to a far less degree than *El Desquite,* lacks proportion, singleness of effect, and compression. . . . The style of the three works is poetic and rhythmic, but the dialogue is often exaggerated and not in keeping with the characters. (pp. 90-1)

Of the outright bandit, who has at least the virtue of being true to himself, Azuela is more tolerant than of that dishonest politician who, although his name be engraved on the national monuments of bronze and stone, has been untrue to the ideals he professed. It is the problem created by this type of individual—who, as Azuela sees it, has used his power solely for self-aggrandizement and thus frustrated the ideals of the Revolution—that figures conspicuously in [a group of five novels which includes *El Camarada Pantojo, San Gabrielde Valdivias, Regina Landa, Avanzada,* and *La nueva Burguesía*]. (pp. 93-4)

Azuela brought to *La nueva Burguesía* and the four novels that preceded it many years of observation and experience with disease; his diagnosis of the ills of his country is profound, but he knows no remedy. The disease from which Mexico suffers is still, like malignant cancer, incurable. He writes of it in these, as in all of his works, with a tone of hopelessness but with an earnestness of conviction that leaves no doubt as to his sincerity. On account of their theses these last novels have an especial interest. Yet, aside from their sociological interest, they have, decidedly, an artistic value. That lies—and what is said now applies in varying degrees to Azuela's work as a whole—not in the plots of his novels, which are rather formless, nor in any great character creations, although there is a very full gallery of excellent character types, nor in a realistically portrayed background, but in the fact that the author was able, at various periods throughout his own life, to analyze the motives which gave rise to the conflicts about him, to penetrate to the depths of the souls of the contenders, and to give to his findings both dramatic and lyric expression.

In spite of the fact that Azuela's fiction has a sociological and ethical basis, its poetic quality is its most distinguishing characteristic. For, except in the realistic detail of his earliest novels, he did not retain Balzac and Zola, for whom he admits a passion in his youth, as his models. On the contrary, his technique or approach to novel writing is far closer to that of the poet than of the purely realistic or naturalistic novelist. This is best exemplified in his masterpiece *Los de Abajo.* In many of his works he is both personal and imaginative, and the artistic use of language is often with him an end in itself. Like the poet, he centers on the points of high interest, leaving much to the imagination; as a result, the plots of his novels—consisting as they often do of sections almost complete in themselves—are in general difficult to follow. (pp. 99-100)

Jefferson Rea Spell, "Mariano Azuela, Portrayer of the Mexican Revolution," in his Contemporary Spanish-American Fiction *(copyright, 1944, by The University of North Carolina Press), University of North Carolina Press, 1944 (and reprinted by Biblo and Tannen, 1968), pp. 64-100.*

JOHN E. ENGLEKIRK (essay date 1953)

Several of Azuela's less significant novels have already been deservedly forgotten and in all probability others that are still read for the light they shed on the contemporary scene will also lose in stature for want of sustaining literary strength as time removes them from the glow of the present. Much of Azuela's work suffers from defects inherent in the conditions under which it was written: unevenness—moments of true artistic inspiration, others of distorted, ineffectual expression; much hasty, careless composition; moments when passion and concern either tainted the work with an excess of pessimism and negation or prevented the attainment of artistic unity of subject and style, these are the natural concomitants of an art that is the product of an uninhibited outburst of deep-seated emotions. In its chaotic spontaneity of structure *Andrés Pérez, maderista* may well reveal the total absence of any orderliness or plan in the social conflict that suddenly burst over the country. To deny, however, that the novel is poorly done on the grounds that, as it stands, it does reflect the attitude of the author at that given historic moment, would be to invite absolute lawlessness in the realm of literary criticism. The point is that Azuela would not have given us *Andrés Pérez, maderista*, nor *Las moscas*, nor *Los de abajo*, in fact none of his writing—with the possible exception of his *estridentista* novels and the historical sketches—had he deliberately curbed his pen in observance of the rules of "punto y coma" [periods and commas]. . . . (pp. 132-33)

John E. Englekirk, "Mariano Azuela: A Summing Up (1873-1952)," in South Atlantic Studies for Sturgis E. Leavitt, *edited by Thomas B. Stroup and Sterling A. Stoudemire (copyright 1953 by the South Atlantic Modern Language Association), Scarecrow Press, 1953, pp. 127-35.*

LESLEY BYRD SIMPSON (essay date 1956)

[*The Bosses* (*Los Caciques*) and *The Flies* (*Las Moscas*)] have been undeservedly neglected, probably because of the impact of *The Underdogs*. They are, nevertheless, very much worth reading, being, so to speak, pages from a journal written hotly from life. (p. vii)

The action of *The Flies* opens during a panic in a railway station of Mexico City. . . . [All those] who had short-sightedly thrown in with Villa are striving desperately to escape their imagined death at the hands of Obregón's Yaqui Indian troops, who enjoyed a well-earned reputation for ferocity. The frightened refugees crowd into a hospital car, where throughout the night we listen to their wild surmises.

Azuela's style in this story, staccato or even telegraphic, is admirably suited to suggest the jerky movement of the train, the nervousness of the fugitives, their naked fear. The choppy, fragmentary dialogue, the abrupt shifts, the callousness of some, the maudlin drunkenness of others, and the prodigious silliness of the frightened mother and her gold-digging family, together give us an etching of civil war not easily forgotten.

The somber tone of *The Bosses* is as remote as possible from the raucous gaiety of *The Flies*. . . . The action takes place in a small western city which is dominated and virtually owned by a merchant-banker-landlord family of parasites, the Del Llanos (the *caciques,* or bosses), who had risen to power and affluence under Porfirio Díaz and who now boggle at no measure, however low or violent, to maintain their privileges. (pp. viii-ix)

It is difficult for us at this distance to accept the monstrosities of the Del Llano family—the cynical priest, Father Jeremiah, and the cold-blooded Don Ignacio; but Azuela is writing in white-hot anger against the cruelty and injustice of a system and uses the effective device of extreme caricature to point up his thesis, much as José Clemente Orozco pilloried the Mexican middle class in his frescoes later on. Azuela's scalding humor boils over most of all on the jackals and stool pigeons in the pay of the caciques.

The rest of the cast is treated gently. The grocer, Juan Viñas, a kind of Mexican Poor Richard, his saintly wife, Elena, and his two children, Esperanza and Juanito, victims of the system, are necessarily the opposites of the caciques. The author here runs the risk of oversimplification, of drawing a naive black-and-white picture, but he accepts the risk and through his art makes his picture plausible. He does so by employing the same technique that was so successful in *The Flies*, by allowing his characters to portray themselves with all their human failings. (pp. ix-x)

Lesley Byrd Simpson, in her preface to Two Novels of Mexico: 'The Flies', 'The Bosses' *by Mariano Azuela, translated by Lesley Byrd Simpson (copyright © 1956 by The Regents of the University of California; reprinted by permission of the University of California Press), University of California Press, 1956, pp. v-xiii.*

FRANCES KELLAM HENDRICKS (essay date 1963)

The Trials of a Respectable Family reveals new aspects of Azuela's literary gifts and of his ability to reflect the age in which he lived. In this novel the force and action of the Revolution are in the wings of the stage. The author centers attention on the impact of the Revolution on the people of the middle class and their reactions to their trials and tribulations. Seized with panic engendered by reports of the excesses of the revolutionaries, people of means fled to seek safety in the capital city. There through successive stages they descended to penury and hardship. Azuela undertakes to explore the ways in which the altered conditions affected the individuals concerned and how they reacted—how they revealed themselves.

His primary theme, he wrote, is as old as time but inexhaustible: that pain and suffering are the most fruitful source of noble deeds. (p. xxv)

Azuela indulges freely in this work in a propensity for satire and caricature, especially in his depiction of the unsympathetic characters. Though the effect is sometimes humorous, the principal consequence is to make them hardly believable as human beings, but admirably suited to demonstrate the despicable nature of the traits and attitudes he uses them to typify. In Procopio, the protagonist, he creates a distinctive personality who is more than a conveyance for Azuela's thoughts, though he serves that purpose, too. (p. xxvi)

Azuela's warmth of spirit, his affection for the simple life, and his moral fervor are essential ingredients of *The Trials of a Respectable Family*. The worth of the work lies not only in the force with which he displays his indignation at outrages against human rights and the effectiveness with which he explores his central theme, but as well in its character as a social document of the Revolution. (p. xxvii)

> *Frances Kellam Hendricks, in her introduction to* Two Novels of the Mexican Revolution: "The Trials of a Respectable Family" and "The Underdogs" *by Mariano Azuela, translated by Frances Kellam Hendricks and Beatrice Berler (copyright by Principia Press of Trinity University), Principia Press, 1963 (and reprinted in* Three Novels: "The Trials of a Respectable Family," "The Underdogs," *and* "The Firefly" *by Mariano Azuela, translated by Frances Kellam Hendricks and Beatrice Berler, Trinity University Press, 1979, xvii-xxv).*

HARRIET de ONÍS   (essay date 1963)

In spite of the abundance of his subsequent writings, Azuela's fame rests on *The Underdogs*. It is not only that in it he gives us his vivid firsthand impressions of the Revolution long before any other writer had employed the theme, transmitting them with the intensity of the moment in which he experienced them, but also that he so quickly sensed the problems inherent in its triumph. The strength of the work lies in its terseness and rapidity; the characters live with indomitable vitality, and throughout the book one feels the pulsating breath of beings who are heroes, or at any rate can behave heroically, without being aware of it.

"If one were to select a single note characteristic of all Azuela's work," says González de Mendoza, "it would be this: he fought generously and gallantly against stupid evil and injustice. Unfortunately, the struggle between intelligence and stupidity, as between rectitude and iniquity, will probably last as long as mankind endures upon the earth." (p. x)

> *Harriet de Onís, "Foreword" (copyright © 1962 by The New American Library of World Literature, Inc.; reprinted by arrangement with The New American Library, Inc., New York, New York), in* The Underdogs: A Novel of the Mexican Revolution *by Mariano Azuela, translated by E. Munguía, Jr., New American Library, 1963, pp. v-xi.*

LUIS LEAL   (essay date 1971)

It is typical of Azuela's technique to intermingle with the human environment descriptions of nature. These passages are always short, well integrated into the narrative, and in consonance with the nature of the characters. The fusion of man and landscape is characteristic of his style, as there is always an intimate relation between man and nature, and in nature between the landscape and animal life. As a rule, nature is humanized, which makes human actions appear either insignificant or ennobled. . . .

This humanizing of the lower forms of life makes ferocious human acts appear much more inhuman. When Azuela describes a cockfight he tells the reader that the struggle has "an almost human ferocity." . . . (p. 98)

Azuela learned the technique of characterization in the novels of the French realists and naturalists of the nineteenth century: Balzac, Zola, and Maupassant. Following Zola's dictum, he copied directly from life. . . . (p. 100)

In the novels published before *Los de abajo*, characterization is weak due to Azuela's insistence on creating characters in opposition representing good and evil; the good characters are flawless and the evil ones are all evil. As a revolutionary and in contact with people from all social classes and from all regions, Azuela made a great discovery. He wrote: "Men who are all good or all bad exist only in novels." . . . From here on he forgot the French models and created characters that are a true reflection of men, neither thoroughly good nor thoroughly evil. (p. 101)

Characterization in Azuela's novels is based on the use of the portrait, giving emphasis to the physical characteristics, supplemented by realistic dialogue and significant actions. In *La Luciérnaga*, however, the technique differs somewhat. Here the author makes an effort to analyze the psychology of the characters. The reader is placed in the minds of Dionisio and José María and is able to follow their thinking and become acquainted with the motives that make them act the way they do. Unfortunately, Azuela does not follow the same technique in the novels written after *La Luciérnaga*, in which he returns to the well-tried method used previously. He firmly believed that by avoiding the psychological portrait and creating flat, plain characters he could reach a larger reading public, who, he thought, would not be interested in new techniques. But even so, he was a master at creating characters by providing only a few outstanding features.

Azuela was able to breathe life into his creations by immediately giving the reader the outstanding individual features by means of which the character could be recognized and remembered. This technique has its drawbacks, as often the portrait turns out to be a caricature, especially in cases where the novelist paints persons he detested. To them he often gave animal features, perhaps due to the influences of the Naturalistic novelists. (pp. 103-04)

Often, when Azuela wanted to present a person in a ridiculous light, instead of comparing him to an animal, he attributed to him some characteristic pertaining to the plant kingdom. (p. 104)

In characterizing, Azuela paid special attention to the tone of voice of his characters. He went out of his way to look for adjectives and adjectival phrases to describe a voice. . . . As important as the physical portrait is the characterization accomplished, always with great effect, through dialogue. Azuela knew well the characteristic speech of each social class and used speech effectively in each character according to his social class, his region, and his profession. (p. 105)

All this may give the impression that Azuela's characterizations are always done in negative terms, but this is not so. There are persons in his novels drawn with sympathy. Normal characters are as common as the abnormal or queer. It seems, however, that his genius for characterizing shines when the drawing is negative. In both cases he had the ability to select the details necessary to give the reader, in a few lines, a precise idea of the character. (p. 106)

[In] Azuela's novels, background and characters stand out, while plot and structure are weak. His works are usually structured around characters. The novel can begin without the author having a definite plan in mind. The interesting point for him is character development, often at the cost of neglecting the unfolding of the plot. (p. 107)

Azuela's early novels reflect an interest in personal illness and in personal maladjustments. Beginning with *Los caciques* there is a change from this interest in individual cases to an interest in group behavior, and finally to social change and national problems: the revolution, the downfall of the feudal regime, the creation of a new social class.

In the novels of his last period Azuela's interest changes again. Instead of being an objective recorder of social change, he becomes a stern critic of the new social order and is thus less effective as a novelist.

Of all the elements that go into the making of a novel, Azuela paid least attention to its structure. This is perhaps the weakest point in his narrative technique. He very seldom had a plan of the whole novel before he sat down to write it. (pp. 107-08)

From the point of view of its structure, *Los de abajo* can be considered as Azuela's best planned novel. Divided into three symmetrical parts (21, 14, and 7 chapters), the novel opens with a scene in the Cañón de Juchipila. From here until the end of the second part the action increases progressively, both in violence and in dramatic intensity. . . . The novel ends with his death in the same Cañón de Juchipila where he had so soundly beaten the enemy in the opening scenes. The wheel of fortune has completed its full circle. "Los de abajo" return to their position, both physically and socially, from which they had started. This closed structure is similar to a *bola*, a ball, which makes the reader think of a revolution, called *la bola* in Mexico.

The novel's structure does not have the precise planning found in other great Latin American novels. It is not, like Romulo Gallegos' *Doña Bárbara*, a novel with a logical structure, with its thesis, antithesis, and synthesis. Rather than logical, the structure of *The Underdogs* is organic. Although it may be a chaotic story (a well-ordered picture of a revolution is unthinkable), the structure is very well suited to the theme, and thus Azuela is able to lift the work to an esthetic plane where, under an apparent disorder, the reader finds an internal, organic order in which there are no loose scenes, no actions without a proper function in the apparently dissonant whole. As an organism, the novel is characterized by its dynamic essence, which is to be found not only in the plot, but also in the style, in the painting of nature, and in the violent quality of the scenes, not too far distant from those painted by José Clemente Orozco.

The structure of *Los de abajo* is an innovation in Spanish American narrative. Azuela, either consciously or unconsciously, created a new form for the Latin American novel, a form that for the first time reflects the nature of the world where it was born. For the first time the novelist forgets the European forms and writes a novel in which the theme and structure complement each other. Azuela's work begins a new trend in the development of the Spanish American novel. (pp. 110-11)

In the writing of his first novels Azuela tried to imitate the style of the French and Spanish Naturalists. Gradually he began to create his own style, characterized by simplicity in sentence structure, brief descriptions of the landscape, and increased use of dialogue. His style is the result of his concept of the novel. For him it was not necessary to be a great stylist in order to be a good novelist, and he believed that the novelist who is overly conscious of style loses other essential qualities necessary in the good novel. For this reason he would never sacrifice a clear description of reality for the sake of style. . . . Azuela refused to write in [a] bombastic style and preferred simple, straightforward, clear expression.

This simplicity does not imply that Azuela's style is childish or primitive. On the contrary, it reveals a great effort on his part to write clearly and without stylish mannerisms. (p. 115)

Azuela obtains simplicity by avoiding the use of learned, unfamiliar words. Nevertheless, he never lacks the proper words to convey his thoughts to the reader or to describe things vividly. . . . [The] novelist used in his writings the popular speech he had learned directly from experience, whether at home, on the farm, or in the city slums. Since his main preoccupation was to capture in his novels the flavor of the Mexican scene, this popular speech was sufficient, and he could afford the luxury of avoiding literary language. Thus, one of the striking stylistic features in Azuela is the large number of words, idioms, and expressions taken from the popular speech of the people, that is, from Mexican Spanish. He believed that through speech, people reveal their souls and innermost ways of being.

Azuela's sentence structure is characterized by its straightforward nature, obtained by eliminating or reducing the use of subordinate clauses. The majority of his sentences are short, without complicated syntactical elaborations. His rule seems to be to follow the shortest path in the building of the sentence. This syntactical brevity, which imparts a great force to his style, was what made the French critic Larbaud think of Tacitus when reading Azuela.

In *Los de abajo*, the novel in which Azuela reached his highest stylistic accomplishment, the reader can best observe the several techniques which the novelist used to give his style a seal of its own. There he will find the use of very short paragraphs, the predominance of dialogue over description, the use of expressions typical of the Spanish of Mexico, the brief, almost schematic, descriptions of the landscape, and the use of a rhythmical pattern that reflects the violent nature of the subject matter. This style, which is to be found in other novels of Azuela, especially in those written during this period in his development as a novelist, is the most original and the one that reader associates with his name. (pp. 115-16)

Since his novels of the revolution, and indeed all his novels, had been ignored by the critics, Azuela decided to experiment with a new style. (p. 116)

The style Azuela used in his new novels does not show as radical a departure from the old style as he himself thought. Certainly there is a greater novelty in the structure of these novels than in the style, which seems to be a logical development of the one used in *Los de abajo*. . . . The stylistic innovations consist of the use of distorted sentences, the omission of the main verb in the sentence, and the use of indirect discourse. (p. 117)

After *La Luciérnaga* Azuela abandoned this distorted manner of writing and returned to the style of his first period. (p. 118)

The novels Azuela wrote after *La Luciérnaga*, in which he used a straightforward style, often writing carelessly, do not add anything to his stature as a stylist or as a novelist. With the possible exception of *Nueva burguesía*, these novels present no novelty whatsoever. (p. 119)

Although there are pronounced differences in the style of the . . . novels that Azuela wrote, certain characteristics that recur frequently give continuity to his development as a writer. . . . [Some of these characteristics are]: the use of words peculiar to the Spanish of Mexico; the predominance of dialogue over description; the quick brushstroke of words to paint a scene; the short, staccato sentence to give his style a nervous, dynamic impact. Other characteristics peculiar to his style are the use of certain key words, of images that reflect an interest in his native soil, of metaphors based on the association of the several levels of life (animal, vegetable, human), and a very personal use of certain adjectives. His style, it can be said, reflects his personal interests, his personal likes and dislikes, and his preoccupations in life, which were centered around rural Mexico, medicine, and life among the poor city dwellers.

The influences of his profession upon his style can be found in the use of medical terminology and in the creation of images derived from that field. He often speaks about voices that have a cold, of eyes that are vitrified, of consumptive thick lips, of mangy pity, of neurotic asceticism, of semi-idiotic happiness. Figures of speech are often derived from the field of medicine: a guitar sheds nitroglycerine tears, Factor Street is compared to an enormous esophagus, and the *pitahayo* plant has branches like the fingers of a giant suffering from ankylosis. (pp. 119-20)

In [the novels of Azuela] the reader finds not only the portrait of a country in transition but also absorbing stories well told, for Azuela was a born novelist. He had the ability to make the reader identify with his characters and to censure, or sympathize with, their ambitions and weaknesses. Azuela's world is a contemporary one, beset with innumerable social and political problems, but the novelist never turns his back on those problems, and he never turns away from those of the common people. Reading Azuela's novels is the best way to get a profile of modern Mexico and the best way to become acquainted with the Mexican people, of which he himself was an excellent representative. (p. 122)

> *Luis Leal, in his* Mariano Azuela *(copyright © 1971 by Twayne Publishers, Inc.; reprinted with the permission of Twayne Publishers, A Division of G. K. Hall & Co., Boston), Twayne, 1971, 145 p.*

KURT L. LEVY (essay date 1972)

[*La luciérnaga*] is essentially a probing of the individual conscience and . . . Azuela selected his title to fit his sensitive *leitmotif*. . . . [Azuela imposed] through *leitmotif* and narrative technique a marked unity of structure on a superficial variety of character and incident.

From the very beginning of the novel Azuela leaves no doubt about his focus of interest. As Dionisio staggers away from the scene of the accident which he has caused and mingles with the crowd, all of a sudden a pair of eyes stare at him. . . . [Becoming multiplied,] the eyes stalk him re-

lentlessly. . . . Evidently, there is no escape from his pangs of conscience, which is made abundantly clear even before the reasons are explained. (p. 322)

Despite the apparent acquittal which he achieves with the aid of that eloquent "family attorney" named inner dialectics, the array of accusing eyes . . . continues to molest Dionisio in section IV. If anything, the assault of his conscience becomes intensified, turning into an obsession. Eyes are no longer an isolated phenomenon; there is a whole sequence of them to poison Dionisio's existence. . . .

[Section III] lays bare the dilemma of the "man of conscience" who struggles against the challenge of his conscience. Here, as in the opening section of the novel, we witness a progressive lighting-up process, as the author breaks down the most elaborate defenses that his character creation can devise. If section I unfolds in the shadow of Dionisio's guilt complex, section III scrutinizes the successive responses of José María's conscience when confronted by a series of demands. (p. 323)

[Section V focuses on the moral dilemma of Conchita.] In accordance with the dictates of her conscience, she reverses her earlier stand and returns to Dionisio, who receives her and the children outside of the hospital, smiling. . . . The melancholy reunion, which to me does not offer the slightest suggestion that Dionisio's "regeneration" is imminent, takes place against the bright morning sun outlining in vivid detail the squalid human setting. I can find no ground for idealizing Dionisio or glorifying Conchita. The final glimpse of Dionisio indicates—and this I think is one of Azuela's great artistic and psychological achievements— that he remains true to his wretched self. (pp. 325-26)

The method which Azuela applies to his literary creations in *La luciérnaga* with such stimulating results is reminiscent of the psychiatrist who inexorably explores the total conscience of the patient reclining on his couch. Resist as he may, the patient is finally made to relax, "unfold" his inhibitions, and lay bare his impulses, including the hidden crevices. . . .

The thoughts of some of the characters become increasingly "inconexos y confusos" [unconnected and confused] under the strain of circumstances and sickness. The literary definition of Dionisio, José María, or Conchita could not be clearer. The author achieves the total view of their human substance by applying his literary scalpel with equal intensity to physical portrait, psychological profile, and subconscious echoes. . . . (p. 327)

Listening to life's dictation, the novelist imposes an unmistakable rhythm upon the latter and supplements scenes of outer chaos with a genuine concern for inner anguish. In *La luciérnaga*, even more than in *Los de abajo*, life's dictation is enhanced by structural discipline which confers aesthetic status on realistic scenes, turbulent emotions, and picturesque types. . . . If, in *Los de abajo*, one human being holds the novel together and three distinct *leitmotif* moods reflect its architectural pattern, the process is reversed in *La luciérnaga* where one single *leitmotif* is scrutinized in three human beings.

Azuela's consistent probing into the role of the moral conscience, "la luciérnaga cintilando" [sparkling firefly], and his apt and imaginative choice of an appropriate medium, show the inadequacy of the term "truco" [clever trick].

They testify not only to the novelist's insight into the inner workings of humanity, in both its negative and positive responses, but also to his profound awareness of narrative harmony. They account for the structural unity of *La luciérnaga:* in the context of this unity the novel and its title assume their most comprehensive artistic and human significance. (pp. 327-28)

> *Kurt L. Levy, "'La luciernaga': Title, Leitmotif, and Structural Unity," in* Philological Quarterly *(copyright 1972 by The University of Iowa), Vol. 51, No. 1, January, 1972, pp. 321-28.*

BIBLIOGRAPHY

Dulsey, Bernard [M.] "The Mexican Revolution as Mirrored in the Novels of Mariano Azuela." *Modern Language Journal* XXXV, No. 5 (May 1951): 382-86.
  Discusses the presentation of social change in Azuela's novels.

Dulsey, Bernard M. "Azuela Revisited." *Hispania* XXXV, No. 1 (February 1952): 331-32.
  Briefly corrects minor misreadings of Azuela's texts made by the critics Englekirk, Spell, and Beals.

Englekirk, John E. "The 'Discovery' of *Los de abajo.*" *Hispania* XVIII, No. 1 (February 1935): 53-62.
  Literary history concerned with the public recognition and response to *Los de abajo.*

Gamboa de Camino, Berta. "The Novel of the Mexican Revolution." In *Renascent Mexico*, edited by Hubert Herring and Herbert Weinstock, pp. 258-74. New York: Covici, Friede, Publishers, 1935.*
  A survey of the general characteristics of novels concerned with the Mexican Revolution.

Luckey, Robert E. "Mariano Azuela: 1873-1952." *Books Abroad* 27, No. 4 (Autumn 1953): 368-70.
  A brief biograhical survey of Azuela's career.

Mullen, E. J. "Towards a Prototype of Mariano Azuela's *La Luciérnaga.*" *Romance Notes* II, No. 3 (Spring 1970): 518-21.
  A comparison of the two published versions of *La Luciérnaga* which contends that the version published in book form is less stylistically innovative than the initial magazine publication.

Spell, Jefferson Rea. "Mexican Society of the Twentieth Century as Portrayed by Mariano Azuela." In *Inter-American Intellectual Interchange*, pp. 49-61. Austin: The University of Texas Press, 1943.
  A sketchy summary of Azuela's career which praises his ability to analyze the passions which gave rise to the conflicts within Mexican society.

David Belasco

1853-1931

American producer and playwright.

Belasco is better remembered as a leader of the theater than as a playwright, and prominent in his career was his successful attempt to curb the power of the Theatrical Syndicate, a monopoly tightly controlling theater booking.

Belasco's devotion to the theater started at an early age. As a boy in San Francisco he gave dramatic readings to his school chums; he became a stagehand in the San Francisco theater, then an actor, manager, producer, and at the height of his career, an independent producer with his own playhouse. Dubbed the "bishop of Broadway," Belasco added to his theatrical aura by his clerical demeanor and ecclesiastical appearance: a stand-up collar, black ascot, and dark suit.

Belasco, a highly emotional man, was an indefatigable worker with prodigious energy. His goal was to entertain and he brought to the stage a mastery of technique, an eye for realistic detail, and an unflagging romanticism. He so excelled at stagecraft that Alexander Woollcott called him "the great Wizard."

Belasco was responsible for cultivating the star system in the American theater: it was through his diligence that Leslie Carter, Blanche Bates, and David Warfield enjoyed successful stage careers. Belasco's contribution as a playwright, however, is not significant. The plays he wrote were tailormade for the stock company and later for his stars. Probably his best-known work is *Madame Butterfly*, a play he adapted from the story by John Luther Long which Giacomo Puccini later made into his famous opera.

Though his style of theatricalism was superseded by the naturalistic theater of O'Neill and Ibsen, Belasco's reputation is secure as an important producer in the American theater.

PRINCIPAL WORKS

Zaza [adapted from a play by Pierre Berton and Charles Simon] (unpublished drama, first performed in 1899)
Sweet Kitty Bellairs [adapted from a novel by Agnes and Egerton Castle] (unpublished drama, first performed in 1903)
The Girl of the Golden West: A Play in Four Acts (drama) 1915
The Return of Peter Grimm: A Play in Three Acts (drama) 1915

The Rose of the Rancho: A Play in Three Acts [with Richard Walton Tully] (drama) 1915
The Son-Daughter [with George Scarborough] (unpublished drama, first performed in 1919)
The Theatre through Its Stage Door (essays) 1919
Six Plays (dramas, includes *Madame Butterfly* [adapted from a story by John Luther Long], *DuBarry*, *The Darling of the Gods* [with John Luther Long], *Adrea* [with John Luther Long]) 1928
The Heart of Maryland and Other Plays (dramas, includes *The Girl I Left behind Me* [with Franklin Fyles]) 1941
The Plays of Henry C. DeMille, Written in Collaboration with David Belasco (dramas, includes *The Charity Ball*, *Lord Chumley*, *Men and Women*, *The Wife*) 1941

GEORGE BERNARD SHAW (essay date 1898)

We have been suffering of late years in England from a wave of blackguardism. . . . My objection to this sort of folly is by no means purely humanitarian. I am quite prepared to waive the humanitarian point altogether, and to accept, for the sake of argument, the position that we must destroy or be destroyed. But I do not believe in the destructive force of a combination of descriptive talent with delirium tremens. (pp. 287-88)

The question for the dramatic critic is, how is it possible to knock all this blood-and-thunder folly out of the head of the British playgoer? Satire would be useless: sense still more out of the question. Mr Charles Frohman [the American producer of Mr David Belasco's *The Heart of Maryland*] seems to me to have solved the problem. You cannot make the Britisher see that his own bunkum is contemptible. But shew him the bunkum of any other nation, and he sees through it promptly enough. And that is what Mr Frohman is doing. *The Heart of Maryland* is an American melodrama of the Civil War. As usual, all the Southern commanders are Northern spies, and all the Northern commanders Southern spies—at least that is the general impression produced. . . . [The villain has been] drummed out of the Northern army for infamous conduct. The villain joins the Southerns, who, in recognition no doubt of his high character and remarkable record, at once make him a colonel, especially as he is addicted to heavy drinking. Naturally, he is politically impartial, and, as he says to the hysterical Northerner (who is, of course, the hero of the piece), fights for his own hand. "But the United States!" pleads the hysterical one feebly. "Damn the United States" replies the villain. Instantly the outraged patriot assaults him furiously, shouting "Take back that. Take it back." The villain prudently takes it back; and the honor of America is vindicated. This is clearly the point at which the audiences should burst into frantic applause. No doubt American audiences do. Perhaps the Adelphi audience would too if the line were altered to "Damn the United Kingdom." But we are sensible enough about other people's follies; and the incontinent schoolboyishness of the hero is received with the coolest contempt. This, then, is the moral mission of Mr Charles Frohman. He is snatching the fool's cap from the London playgoer and shewing it to him on the head of an American. Meanwhile, our foolish plays are going to America to return the compliment. In the end, perhaps, we shall get melodramas in which the heroism is not despicable, puerile, and blackguardly, nor the villainy mere mechanical criminality.

For the rest, *The Heart of Maryland* is not a bad specimen of the American machine-made melodrama. (pp. 289-90)

> *George Bernard Shaw, "Mr Charles Frohman's Mission" (1898), in* Shaw's Dramatic Criticism, *selected by John F. Matthews (copyright © 1959 by the Public Trustee as Executor of the Estate of George Bernard Shaw; reprinted by permission of the Society of Authors on behalf of the Bernard Shaw Estate), Hill & Wang, 1959, pp. 287-90.*

MONTROSE J. MOSES (essay date 1917)

[The] art of the drama is the art of all arts, where proportion, perspective and color accumulate for a given effect. No one has studied this fact to greater purpose than David Belasco, in whom the instinct of the painter before his canvas is the dominant characteristic,—an instinct which must assuredly prompt the mechanism of any art theatre we may ever hope to have. When the story of scenic realism is told, he will occupy a distinctive position. (pp. 111-12)

It is not always essential for a dramatist to penetrate deeply into life, but one cannot deny that Mr. Belasco's glance has taken the details in thoroughly. He has had the experience which should come to all writers of plays; he has been thrown against the strong contrasts of living which are usually to be found in a mining camp; he has lurked in the highways and byways of existence, unconsciously gathering those elemental stuffs which are the essential ingredients in all passion. These he has in most cases toned down, but the brutal elements in "Du Barry" and in "Adrea" indicate to what uses experience of this kind is brought.

There is the ascetic streak in David Belasco, colored by a pronounced spiritual and contrasting sentimental *verve;* there is the tinge of morbidity which is always attendant upon a clinical analysis of psychological phenomena. (p. 113)

"The Heart of Maryland" . . . was one of the first of his dramas stamped by a large piece of stage technique, such as the swinging bell, with the heroine holding to the clapper; "Zaza" . . . indicates the deftness with which his translation quite eclipsed the real author of the French original, and his training of Mrs. Carter in the title *rôle* exemplifies the wonderful illuminative power with which he can, in his instruction, carry an actress to the heart of a character and bring out, as a photographer does on a negative, those fine lines which are never evident in the first moments. (p. 121)

What are the elements that mark Mr. Belasco, or it would be more in order to say on what special elements does Mr. Belasco place the stamp of his own temperament and genius? I have been fortunate in having before me the stage copies of his important dramas, and I cannot but marvel at the strokes which are made by his unerring eye, unerring in the sense that his strokes seem always to fulfil the special requirement which he at the moment needs. The intricate movement in the first act of "Zaza," the filmy threads of broken dialogue, the minute directions of the dressing-room scene, where, not for a moment, even in the reading, is the imagination left in doubt as to the details of business. . . . (p. 123)

I do not contend that light plots, and property plots, and calcium plots entitle a man to the distinction of playwright, but the power to conjure up the effective contrasts of high light and shadow is as much to Mr. Belasco's credit as it is to the artist who paints upon a large canvas. The stage settings, sometimes overrich in detail, are nevertheless almost always unfailing in their atmospheric effects. The courtesan, *Du Barry,* is given a setting which balances the savage abandon of her nature with the licentious terrorism of the period. "Adrea," barbaric throughout, does not fail to create a disgust which is too strong to be counteracted by the moment of sacrifice in the end. These are not characteristics which are new to Mr. Belasco; they were evident in him long before, even though they were not fully developed. (p. 124)

Not one of our present-day managers has so profited by the response of the electric switchboard to human psychology as Mr. Belasco; in his hands it is the very essence of atmosphere, the very indicator of the scene's tone. Whether it be the enervating blaze of sunlight in the opening act of "The Rose of the Rancho," or the cold gray dawn after the night's anguish in "Madame Butterfly," the result represents no mechanical accident. Once, not so long ago, effect used to be entirely artificial; the villain's entrance was heralded by dark, restless music from a few violins, and by the roll of a kettledrum. But to-day, Mr. Belasco has driven incidental sentimentality from the orchestra by the dependence upon the switchboard.

What do we mean by the psychology of stage lighting? Simply that every emotional effect of large import results in a corresponding direction being given to the electrician. (pp. 125-26)

In his studio, Mr. Belasco first imagines his canvas; he then places his "light plots" in the hands of his electrician for fulfilment. At rehearsal he adds to, modifies, rejects, fusing the whole as a painter does with his brush. His stage directions at first become mere skeleton notes of transitory feeling. His assistant stands near, pencil in hand, watching the restless move of the manager, searching among the lights for what he wants. The switchboard is taxed to its uttermost, mixing color to accord with a certain quality of shadow in Mr. Belasco's mind. (p. 126)

In the matter of the switchboard, Mr. Belasco stands in a new light. He is not the conventional stage manager; he is a lover of nature, having felt the close of day on the plains, and seen the first streak of dawn in Italy. He has been an investigator of all phases of the physical as well as of the emotional. He is not merely satisfied with reaching the eye, but he must strike the heart; his lights are always accessories; they are made to reinforce or to counteract; they must serve a purpose, otherwise be discarded. (p. 128)

[David Belasco] is the creative manager who writes his plays by acting them; who, faced by two stenographers, evolves his characters and situations in actual movement, now thinking of a speech which he pins up somewhere for his last act, again jotting down some business, some note about this act or that, but always moving surely toward the completion of the first draft, so as to begin rehearsals. Were some of his plays published just as they are typewritten for the stage, they would be invaluable texts for the amateur playwright; they would point to the platitudinous but none the less absolute fact that the theatre, taken as a whole, demands that the playwright must be master of more than one set of tools. (p. 134)

> Montrose J. Moses, "David Belasco and the Psychology of the Switchboard," in his The American Dramatist (copyright © 1911, 1917 by Little, Brown, & Company; reprinted by permission of Mrs. Leah Moses, executrix of The Estate of Montrose J. Moses), revised edition, Little, Brown, 1917, pp. 111-34.

WILLIAM WINTER   (essay date 1918)

[While] Belasco has not invented any new style of acting he has done great service to the Stage, and his name is written imperishably on the scroll of theatrical achievement in America. As an actor his experience has been ample and widely diversified. He possesses a complete mastery of the technicalities of histrionic art. As a stage manager he is competent in every particular and has no equal in this country to-day. His judgment, taste, and expert skill in creating appropriate environment, background, and atmosphere for a play and the actors in it are marvellous. His attention to detail is scrupulous; and his decision is prompt and usually unerring. No theatrical director within my observation,—which has been vigilant and has extended over many years,—has surpassed him in the exercise of that genius which consists in the resolute, tireless capability of taking infinite pains. Many of the performances which have been given under his direction are worthy to be remembered as examples of almost perfect histrionic art. As a dramatist he is essentially the product of that old style of writing which produced "Venice Preserved," "Fazio," "The Apostate," "The Clandestine Marriage," "The Jealous Wife," etc.,—a style with which his mind was early and completely saturated,—and of the example and influence of Dion Boucicault, whose expertness in construction, felicity in fashioning crisp dialogue, and exceptional skill in creating vivid dramatic effect he has always much and rightly admired. He has written many plays and he has colabored with other authors in the writing of many more. He has exerted a powerful influence upon the Stage in every part of our country. He has battled successfully against the iniquitous Theatrical Trust and in a great measure contributed to the curtailment of its oppressive power. He has developed and made efficient several stars who, without his assistance, would never have gained the prominence which, with it, they have attained. He has established and now (1917) maintains one of the finest theatres in the world. To

have done all this,—to have raised himself from indigence and obscurity to honorable distinction and actual leadership in an intellectual calling, to have made his way by force of character, native talent, indomitable resolution, patient, continuous, indefatigable labor; to have borne, with unshaken fortitude, hardships, trials, disappointment, enmity, and calumny, and to have risen above all the vicissitudes of fortune,—this surely is to have shown the steadfast man of the old Roman poet and to have merited the reward of prosperity and the laurel of fame. (pp. 159-61)

> William Winter, "The Nature of Belasco's Talents and Services, in his The Life of David Belasco, Vol. I (copyright, 1918, by Jefferson Winter), Moffat, Yard, and Company, 1918, pp. 159-62.

WILLIAM WINTER   (essay date 1918)

Careful study of the plays of Belasco has convinced me that, much as he has accomplished, he has not yet fully developed his powers or fully expressed himself as a dramatist. There is ample evidence in his writings that he abundantly possesses the natural faculty of dramatic expression. (p. 332)

Belasco, when he began to write, was a poor boy, imperfectly educated, in a disorderly environment, subject to all sorts of distractions and impediments, and throughout the whole of his career he has struggled onward under the sharp spur of necessity, without leisure or peace. In scarcely one of his many dramas is it possible to discern an *unforced* dramatic impulse, spontaneously creative of an exposition of diversified characters, acting and reacting upon circumstances, in dramatic situations, and constituting an authentic picture of human nature and life. In many of those dramas the *existence* of that impulse is perceptible, but almost invariably the growth of it is checked and the sway of it is impeded by the necessity of haste, or of conformity to the demand of some arbitrary occasion or of deference to the requirement of some individual actor, or to weariness and dejection. Fine bits of characterization appear; flashes of fancy frequently irradiate dialogue; imagination imparts a splendid glow to striking situations,—as in "The Darling of the Gods" and "The Girl I Left Behind Me,"—and pathos is often elicited by simple means; but sometimes probability is wrested from its rightful place, and extravagance of embellishment mingles with verbosity to cause prolixity and embarrass movement. In a word, a sense of *effort*, a strenuous urgency for the attainment of violent *effect,* is largely perceptible in Belasco's plays,—as, indeed, it is in nearly the entire bulk of modern American Drama. (pp. 333-34)

He has adapted or rewritten more than 200-odd plays, has collaborated with other writers in making twenty-odd new ones, and is himself the sole author of about thirty more, most of which have been acted but several of which have not. The wonder is not that his writings exhibit some defects, but that, at their best, they contain so much truthful portrayal of character, pictorial reflection of life, fine dramatic situation, and compelling power to thrill the imagination and touch the heart. The time, it seems to me, has not yet come for attempting a comprehensive and final estimate of his faculty and achievement as a dramatist. . . . He has pursued a course natural to himself, and he has created much in Drama that is both original and beautiful. If he had written nothing but "The Girl of the Golden West" and

"The Return of Peter Grimm" his name would live as that of one of the best dramatists who have arisen in America. (pp. 335-36)

William Winter, *"Belasco as Dramatist–A Fragment,"* in his *The Life of David Belasco, Vol. II (copyright, 1918, by Jefferson Winter), Moffat, Yard and Company, 1918, pp. 332-36.*

GEORGE JEAN NATHAN (essay date 1921)

Highly venerated by the Broadway hazlitts as a *tour de force* in the realistic producing method, Belasco's production of "The Son-Daughter" actually achieved its most telling coup in the impressionistic producing method. The first act and the second act of the play, staged in the familiar Belasco extra-realistic manner, were—even by the word of this hazlittry—not impressive. But the undeniable melodramatic effectiveness of the last act of the play was—in the two particular scenes most frequently commented upon in the daily journals—wholly and entirely due to Belasco's temporary rejection of realism and his reliance, instead, upon impressionism or, perhaps more accurately, relative impressionism or modified realism. In the first of these two scenes, a Chinese den, Belasco literally took a leaf from Gordon Craig and by the adroit employment of simple curtains and lights gained a far more remarkable effect of scenic depth, darkness and mystery than he had hitherto ever gained with his tons of Fourth Avenue delicatessen. The picture, disregarding the crude and idiotic traffic that passed within it, was dramatic in the extreme. And so with the one moment in the succeeding scene where the comparatively impressionistic method was permitted to take the place of the realistic. This second scene, depicting a Chinese wedding chamber, was heavy with all the Belasco extravagant "realism." A million dollars' worth of scenery cluttered up the stage. All that the scenery needed, so suggested the spectator's mind, was Al Jolson and a chorus. The action transpiring within this gaudy suite failed to move the audience until—suddenly—Belasco divested his stage of its glaring literality, moved his protagonists behind partly transparent curtains, dramatized the lighting, and swung his action against the Appia-Lert silhouette-shadow frame. The effect was electric. The audience was held fascinated. In this second instance, of course, the impressionistic method was impressionistic not in the way the first instance was, but purely by comparison with what directly preceded and followed it. Yet it was by virtue of its relative impressionistic quality that it achieved the very effect believed by the local lessings to be due to the stereotyped Belasco realism. (pp. 216-18)

George Jean Nathan, *"Belasco Sees the Light?"* in his *The Theatre, the Drama, the Girls (copyright © 1921 by Alfred A. Knopf; reprinted by permission of Alfred A. Knopf, Inc. Associated University Presses, Inc.), Alfred A. Knopf, Inc., 1921, pp. 216-18.*

WALTER PRICHARD EATON (essay date 1936)

[In his early years Belasco] had forced what effects he could out of sensational or sentimental melodrama and had learned to lean heavily on "situation"—which was, indeed, in such a theatre the rock of salvation. But in manipulating situations on the stage he had shown a flair for realistic illusion and had displayed a creative ingenuity which set him apart. (p.175)

[Belasco] read a story by John Luther Long, turned it into a one-act drama, and on March 5th, 1900, at the Herald Square Theatre, *Madame Butterfly* was produced and David Belasco came into his own. . . . In this wistful little tragedy—if anything so fragile can be called tragedy—there was full opportunity for that obvious sentiment Belasco had seen affect audiences all his life and no opportunity for sensationalism. The story was simple and direct. There was, however, unlimited opportunity for atmospheric stage effect, for Oriental color, exotic charm, and the creation of mood and emotion by picture and light—especially light. No one who saw that production will ever forget the extraordinary feat Belasco performed when he placed Butterfly, the servant, and the child at their peep holes to watch for the arrival of the ship and then, without lowering the curtain, let night come on, the stars come out, the long vigil pass, the dawn flush creep into the sky, the bird voices break out, the sun rise, now revealing two figures fast asleep on the floor but Butterfly still at her vigil. For fourteen minutes by the watch he held an audience in perfect hush—and not one word was spoken on the stage! Here was a correlation of all the elements of dramatic production under perfect control and manipulated by a master. Here was authentic atmosphere, beauty, suspense, human emotion, all obviously the result of infinite care and high theatrical intelligence. Belasco became "the Wizard" from that night. (pp. 176-77)

[*The Darling of the Gods*] which grew out of the success of *Madame Butterfly* and his association with John Luther Long was written in active cooperation with Mr. Long and carried Japanese atmosphere to its extreme limits. It told the story of a Samurai revolt in old Japan and the love of the Princess for one of the Samurai, how she betrayed his companions to save him from torture and how he died to redeem his honor but forgave her in the world to come. There were cherry blossoms and exotic silks, moonlit gardens and Samurai swords, pictures of rare beauty illusively composed of authentic furniture and costumes and paint and light. And there were "situations." The climax was reached when . . . the menacing War Minister compelled . . . the Princess to look down into the red glare of a pit to witness (and hear!) her lover's torture. . . . Reality of set, beauty and poetry of atmosphere, could not disguise the fact that the story was "devised," and devised to make assault upon our emotion through sheer situation. (pp. 177-78)

In 1905 came the production of his play, *The Girl of the Golden West. . . .* Here was a play about a life he knew, a land he loved—his golden and romantic California. Here was a bar and a dance hall in a mining town, authentic to the last detail and filled with characters and motion which recreated a period. And here was a gambling sheriff out of Bret Harte and a girl who saved her road-agent lover by a card trick—and of course then redeemed him from a life of crime. Here was atmosphere of unmistakable sincerity, a glow of nostalgic and romantic affection for a vanished corner of America—and unblushing (though at the time and under Belasco's spell highly effective) trick melodrama. The following year another play of the West, containing a girl and a bad man, was produced in New York, William Vaughn Moody's *Great Divide*. And the two dramas were separated by a gulf as deep as the Grand Canyon. The one was a romantic situation play . . .; the other was the illumination of a profound spiritual problem. The meaning of modern drama was beginning to come home to us and thereafter the realism of "the Wizard" began to break down, on critical examination, into paints and properties and lights and carefully trained acting. (pp. 178-79)

A lust for perfection of detail and a pride of accomplishment and place drove [Belasco] on. His mind grasped all phases of a production, just as his vision saw the whole, and thanks to his years of practical training he was able to realize, as few ever have, the ideal of the theatre—a single intelligence which can create or at least definitely control text, scenery, and lights, can train and direct the players, and can therefore achieve a complete and unique unity. He thus established in our theatre a standard of artistic accomplishment which was tonic and enduring. His instinct, too, early told him that the way to greater illusion for his age led through a better and more artful use of mechanical devices, especially of electric light, and a more careful imitation of nature in acting. He was here a child of his times. Illusion was what he sought and realism pointed the way. Atmosphere must come through realism handled with imagination.

But he had another instinct which must possess every successful theatre artist—the urge to rouse emotional excitement in an audience. Without that the theatre cannot long endure. In most of the plays he staged in his youth and younger middle years that emotion was raised by easily understood "situations." If he had to write a play hastily and throw it on the stage as he so often did he inevitably grabbed situations out of the bag to get his play across. By nature a romantically sentimental man he saw his beloved theatre as a place of escape from drabness and in the eager response of audiences to "situation" in a day when the tentative new drama bored or bewildered them he would have found self-justification, had he felt any need for it. . . . His realism remained always one of surface. And *that* he carried to a point of such dramatic effect and beauty that the next step (which he was too old to take) would have been into significant simplification. The drama, even as he reached his prime, was starting to sweep beyond him into a realism deeper than surface. His contrived situations became hollow to us and his plays (save *Madame Butterfly*) have passed away. (pp. 180-81)

[Belasco] had a passion for artistic unity and perfection and a capacity for unremitting labor in their attainment which made him one of the most influential men in the entire history of our theatre. He was not influential as a dramatist; neither his early training nor his type of intelligence fitted him to grasp post-Ibsen developments. But in most things that concern bringing a drama to life on the modern stage he was pioneer and perfecter; he taught our crude theatre the lesson of detailed discipline; he brought to it mood and atmosphere and sensuous beauty; above all he showed us that to achieve a final effectiveness one guiding intelligence must rule a theatre. He taught us how to unify the diversified arts of the modern playhouse and make them one art. (pp. 181-82)

Walter Prichard Eaton, "Madame Butterfly's Cocoon: A Sketch of David Belasco," in The American Scholar *(copyright © 1936 by the United Chapters of Phi Beta Kappa; reprinted by permission of the publishers), Vol. 5, No. 2, Spring, 1936, pp. 172-82.*

GLENN HUGHES and GEORGE SAVAGE (essay date 1941)

David Belasco . . . is, and for a considerable time will remain, an intriguing figure to the student of American drama. His life was colorful and in some respects enigmatical; his contributions to the technique of theatrical production were numerous and influential; his work as a playwright offers to the historian a bewildering *mélange* of originality, collaboration and adaptation. (p. ix)

Belasco's characteristics as a producer are familiar to all students of the contemporary theater: his lavishness in the matter of stage settings, costumes and properties; his meticulous attention to detail in the training of actors and the creation of stage business; his fanatical quest for perfection in lighting effects; his emphasis on the emotional rather than the intellectual. Those who scorned him insisted he was superficial, but not even his bitterest detractors could deny his genius. The worst epithet they could hurl at him was master of hocus-pocus, and there was admiration in that phrase.

As a playwright Belasco had his training in a rough-and-ready school, where action and strong, simple motives were dominant. Although in the course of his life he passed through many phases, and although he adapted himself somewhat to changing styles and points of view, he never relinquished his fundamental belief in simplicity of motive and strength of situation as the basic factors in drama. A direct approach to the human heart was his chosen path, and from that path he never strayed. Many of his plays disclosed a love of the morbid, but his morbidity was natural, not decadent. Even his sensuousness escaped the charge of perversion.

Realistic effect was his forte. Knowing that, he could indulge his fancy, for to a showman like Belasco the theater is primarily a place where the implausible is made plausible. In print many of his plays seem today too implausible, but plausibility in the theater is a variable thing, and in their day, presented by the hand of the master, they were plausible. History is consistent on that point.

It was Belasco's magic touch, as playwright and producer, which brought many other writers to his door. And the fact that most of his collaborators failed in their independent efforts indicates to what extent they were indebted to Belasco. In many cases, it may be assumed, he played a major rôle in the composition; in others his contribution was smaller. But it was always vital. (pp. x-xi)

Glenn Hughes and George Savage, in their introduction to The Heart of Maryland & Other Plays *by David Belasco, edited by Glenn Hughes and George Savage (copyright © 1941 by Princeton University Press; reprinted by permission of Indiana University Press), Princeton University Press, 1941, (and reprinted by Indiana University Press, 1965), pp. ix-xii.*

ROBERT HAMILTON BALL (essay date 1941)

The De Mille-Belasco collaborations [*The Main Line, The Wife, Lord Chumley, The Charity Ball,* and *Men and Women*] were playwrought before they were playwritten. Except for experimental snatches, dialogue was held in abeyance until character had been conceived and developed and situations devised and arranged in elaborate detail. Most of the actual writing was done by DeMille, most of the planning and dramatic construction by Belasco. The preliminary discussions over and the development of the action clear in their minds, the two men repaired to the theater and staged the play. DeMille sat at a table in the front row of the orchestra; Belasco on the stage impersonated all the characters in the situations which had been plotted. Such dialogue as had been written down was primarily a point of departure, a means by which the situations were set in motion. The dialogue which emerged in final form sprang less from the preliminary speeches than from the situations in action; the determining factor was stage effectiveness. DeMille would read a few lines; Belasco would set them in motion, suggest alterations, omissions, and enlargements to fit stage business. Lines were written not to be acted but to suit the acting. For example, since entrances and exits had already been carefully timed, Belasco would come upon the stage in character at R.2.E. as planned, start across to stage L., see an imaginary character down C., and come slowly downstage. DeMille would then devise a speech to fit the given situation, which would allow the character Belasco was impersonating to make these transitions. This done, and always bearing in mind the actor who was to play that part, Belasco would try it on the stage, time it, and approve or suggest changes. The speech finally determined upon was the result of this kind of collaboration. After this manner were all the DeMille-Belasco plays wrought, DeMille's literary ability combining with Belasco's almost miraculous stage management to form the completed scripts. (pp. xii-xiii)

> *Robert Hamilton Ball, in his introduction to* The Plays of Henry C. DeMille, Written in Collaboration with David Belasco, *edited by Robert Hamilton Ball (copyright © 1941 by Princeton University Press; reprinted by permission of Indiana University Press), Princeton University Press, 1941, (and reprinted by Indiana University Press, 1965), pp. ix-xxv.*

STARK YOUNG (essay date 1948)

Mr. Belasco has long been a kind of landmark in our theatre, and the course of his career has many meanings.

The theatre trick, the contagious presentation of the matter to be shown, is more or less the same in all epochs. One epoch plays up the romantic, one the social-serious, another sexual audacity, and so on; but in all epochs and all theatrical talents this instinct for persuasion, magnetism, diversities in glamor, whether low or superb, persists and is the basic element. Mr. Belasco will snatch at any or all of these preferences and elements, with whatever taste, or lack of taste, understanding or what not possible to him and will push them as far into theatricality as he can get them. (pp. 43-4)

It goes without saying that Mr. Belasco has no supreme gift of any sort. As a showman he has an eye for effective plays and effective moments. His taste, though luxurious and enthusiastic, is uncertain, to say the least; uncertain to the point of vulgarity— some of which anyhow is merely a matter of being out of style— at times. As to the acting, the play, and their relation to sincerity of purpose and artistic aim, he stands on no high, impressive plane. Amid the new movements, foreign influences, themes, et cetera, he has kept his ear to the ground, his eye on the theatrical chance. What he has not learned was not in his nature to learn. At least one kind of sincerity cannot be denied him, and that is theatrical sincerity. Events, people, passions, the arts, his private and personal experience, his joys and sorrows he

can see in only one light; without footlights, in sum, without footlights he is blind. He trembles all through his being with a thousand echoes, despairing silences and warm applauding hands, invisibly awaited. And this in the theatrical faculty is a kind of genius. (p. 44)

> *Stark Young, "The Passionate Pilgrim," in his* Immortal Shadows: A Book of Dramatic Criticism *(abridged by permission of Charles Scribner's Sons; copyright 1948 Charles Scribner's Sons), Scribner's, 1948, pp. 41-4.**

CRAIG TIMBERLAKE (essay date 1954)

Throughout his life Belasco evinced a remarkable interest in wayward womankind. His preoccupation with the aberrant feminine personality prompted his interest in and development of the career of Mrs. Leslie Carter, influenced his choice of plays for that lady and other stars, and explained, in part at least, his absorption in scenes of domestic strife, murder and other crimes of violence whose lurid details were set forth in the pages of the yellow journals. For him these were the important elements of which real drama was compounded. (p. 191)

During the first decade of the twentieth century, Belascoism had been thoroughly sold to the American public as the quintessence of all that was fine and admirable in the American theater. (p. 309)

In the second decade of the century it became obvious even to the dullards that other managers were producing better plays by better authors and investing them with skill and imagination equal to, and at times greater, than that displayed by the Wizard himself. (p. 310)

If Belasco had been less the pretender and posturer, undoubtedly he would have escaped much of the abuse that was heaped upon him by detractors who penetrated his pretentiousness. He assailed commercialism as the disease of the theater and then produced plays so flagrantly commercial and catch-penny in nature that his condemnation of others had about as much efficacy as a public denunciation of demon rum by the town drunk. He decried the star system as the stumbling block and downfall of the budding playwright, but he himself carefully tailored his scripts to the precise fit of the personalities in his entourage and encouraged the authors who came under his influence to do likewise. He cluttered his scenes with excessive detail and engaged his audience's attention with excursive stunts and tricks which masked the defects of bad plays but also robbed good ones of their spiritual essence. He pressed this artistic fallacy to such a point that he was accused of retarding the development of public taste for worthwhile drama and was openly indicted in *Current Opinion*, February 1915, as "the evil genius" of the American theater.

From the seasons of 1909-10 to 1919-20, Belasco produced thirty-two plays in New York City, which submit to the following admittedly arbitrary classification: ten melodramas, half a dozen comedies and an equal number of farces, three revivals of the serio-comic plays of David Warfield, one fantasy, one costume play, a play on the evils of drink, one dealing with spiritualism and another with the psychic phenomenon of dual personality, and two "domestic" dramas dealing with maladjustments occasioned by incompatability in the station and temperament of the leading male and female characters. Of these plays, only one was written by a dramatist of real distinction; not more than half a dozen were the work of competent "play carpenters," the rest were adaptations of varying quality of inferior or slight originals, a number of which Belasco welded into solid commercial successes. (pp. 310-11)

> *Craig Timberlake, in his* The Bishop of Broadway: The Life & Work of David Belasco *(copyright, 1954, by Library Publishers), Library Publishers, 1954, 491 p.*

LISE-LONE MARKER   (essay date 1975)

[The] legend of the Bishop of Broadway carefully and methodically disseminated by critics of the twenties such as Stark Young and [George Jean] Nathan [see excerpts above] has been perpetuated in subsequent, generally cursory, evaluations of Belasco, obscuring his contributions to the theatre and the nature of his scenic art. (p. 4)

David Belasco's productions should be viewed against the background of the conventions and techniques of stage naturalism: ensemble playing, detailed psychological motivations and objectives, realistic stage atmosphere, and, first and foremost, directorial autocracy. Some elements of Belasco's production style contrast sharply with Continental interpretations of naturalism, while others have direct European parallels. (p. 5)

The plays which Belasco produced were chosen or written by him with a keen sense of the practical theatre as his guide. His repertoire cannot be called remarkable for its purely literary value. But his passion for artistic unity and perfection and his capacity for uncompromising labor to attain these goals made him one of the most influential men in the history of the American theatre. (p. 6)

In terms of actual theatrical practice, the naturalistic emphasis upon the deterministic role played by each significant, verisimilar detail implied a central guiding principle: the necessary integration of the various elements of play production—setting, lighting, costumes, and acting—in a meaningful, unified whole. In achieving this integration, the figure of the director emerged as a power hitherto unequalled in the theatre. It is through no coincidence that the names associated with the establishment of naturalism are frequently those of directors: André Antoine in France, Otto Brahm in Germany, Constantin Stanislavski in Russia, William Bloch in Scandinavia, and David Belasco in America. In the English speaking countries the traditional actor manager was replaced during this period by the figure of the producer-director. (pp. 10-11)

Belasco's talent lay first and foremost in his eminent ability to exercise theatrical persuasion. The plays he produced were chosen or written by him with a sharp sense of the practical theatre and a concrete image of that theatre invariably in mind. His repertoire consisted not of literary masterpieces but chiefly of romantic, sentimental "well-made plays" and melodramas. Belasco himself was keenly aware of their primarily theatrical value. It was his deep conviction that the terms "literature" and "theatre" had very little in common with each other. (p. 46)

The repertory which Belasco presented as a New York director falls into at least three distinct categories. Following his early collaboration with DeMille on the plays depicting a typical New York society milieu, his taste swung toward plays more closely related to the environment and the repertory he had known during his years on the West Coast. Thus vivid, colorful panoramas of Western life in America—[*The Girl I Left behind Me, The Heart of Maryland, The Rose of the Ranch,* and *The Girl of the Golden West*] . . .—constitute one important category in his repertory and his scenic style.

This type of play was supplemented by a second group of exotic or historical romances and extravaganzas, starting with [*Madame Butterfly, DuBarry, The Darling of the Gods, Sweet Kitty Bellairs,* and *Adrea*]. (p. 48)

Meanwhile, Belasco also continued the line of domestic milieu dramas with such productions as Lee Arthur and Charles Klein's [*The Auctioneer,* Klein's *The Music Master,* and his own *The Return of Peter Grimm*]. Within this category of contemporary domestic dramas, those oriented toward an outspoken social realism, chiefly *Zaza . . .,* adapted by Belasco from a French play by Pierre Berton and Charles Simon, and Eugene Walter's *The Easiest Way . . .,* hold particular interest. (pp. 48-9)

As a theorist Belasco was, as his selection of a dramatic repertoire suggests, deeply anchored in the most solidly entrenched ideas of the nineteenth century. As a practical theatre man, however, he was distinctly a spirit of progress. An analysis of phases of his scenic technique, his technical discoveries, and not least his experiments with stage lighting points clearly forward towards a period which is considered revolutionary in American theatre, the period of the emergence of the New Stagecraft in the 1920s. It is in this context that his artistic contributions must be viewed. (pp. 49-50)

As a rule his plays centered about feelings, moods, or situations, and not about moral, social, or ethical questions. Hence it was possible for champions of an artistic and social realism unencumbered by the artificial conflicts of the "well-made play" to raise numerous objections to the dramas he presented. (p. 51)

Belasco epitomizes a period in American theatre in which theatrical effectiveness took precedence over all other considerations for a dramatist. He frequently expressed the view that from the very outset he had felt obliged to write parts in his plays which would reflect the talents of the actors engaged to appear in their presentation. (p. 54)

A sense of the harmonious and the conciliatory lay deeply rooted in Belasco, a sense that appears everywhere in his work and comes to expression in all phases of his theatrical activity.

Characteristic of these attitudes is the description of his creation of *The Return of Peter Grimm,* a play which represents both a high point in his writing career and an illustration of his special ability to plan dramatic action on the basis of theatrical values. (p. 56)

The drama deals, in Belasco's own words, with "the persistent survival of personality, or, as some people would have it, a ghost." The action and the main idea of the play necessitate the fact that the spirit of its title figure, a Dutch greenhouse owner, becomes visible to one of the characters. Peter Grimm returns to repair a mistake he has committed in life which has blighted the romance and threatens to destroy the happiness of his niece. A note in the program for the production stressed the fact that the play was not intended to advance any theory regarding the probability of the return of the main character. (p. 57)

Belasco's efforts in connection with *The Return of Peter Grimm* were directed wholly toward the relation of the dramatic story in realistically plausible scenic terms. In presenting the return of Peter's spirit, he first introduced a seance scene with a female medium, but at rehearsals this method struck him as ridiculous. Experiments with numerous other possibilities followed, none of which succeeded in satisfying him, until he hit upon the idea of introducing a new character into the play: a small eight-year- old boy who, when he dies at the close of the play, sees the presence of Peter's spirit and brings his message to the others. Belasco sought to ameliorate the painful effect which the little boy's death scene might have on the audience by including an effective contrast in the opening scene. Here, a circus parade passes the house where the action takes place, a circus band playing and clowns singing, to the delight of the small boy standing at the window and watching the procession go by. One of the clowns suddenly leaps through the open window and dances about with little Willem. Peter Grimm sends the lad off with the clown to buy tickets to the circus. . . . (pp. 57-8)

Because the basic principle behind Belasco's method of interpretative lighting involved constant, subtle changes expressive of the shifting moods of his productions, he did not operate with a static and unchanging lighting design. (p. 82)

Through his lighting of *Peter Grimm*, Belasco solved a major problem of interpretation regarding the drama. He was keenly aware of the scenic difficulties involved in treating the physical presence of a spirit among mortals. Peter Grimm had to be in the same room with other people without, however, being visible to them. They were to sense his influence without seeing him. Yet Belasco wished to maintain his character free of anything "supernatural." Instead of relying on stereotyped eerie lights or fantastic makeup, then, he depicted Grimm in an entirely natural and normal manner, with only a differentiating light around him. In the production he seemed always to be moving about in shadow, while the other characters were always in a bright light. In reality, however, he was as well lighted as the others and every one of his facial expressions was clearly visible. The extremely detailed light plot from Belasco's production book presents the manner in which he accomplished his task: footlights were abolished and the faces of the other characters were illuminated with individual baby spots of a faint rosy hue while a cold, gray light was thrown on Peter Grimm's face. This imaginative use of suggestive realism projected the desired impression of Grimm, as a strong, returning, yet human force. Technically such a system of lighting also entailed the necessity of locating each character upon his entrance with an individual shaft of light, and then continuing to adjust to his movements about the stage without ever allowing the light surrounding him to spill over into the colder light which surrounded Grimm. (pp. 83-4)

Belasco was personally convinced that the aesthetic satisfaction which audiences derived from his productions was due as much to their manipulation of light, colors, and costumes as to the content of the plays themselves. (p. 86)

[*The Girl of the Golden West*] grew out of memories and experiences from his past, the tall tales and taller adventures of the primitive, transient mining centers in California that he knew. For outward visualization in the play, he called upon every technical resource of the theatre at his command. His whole attitude toward the theatre had been formed at a time when audiences looked to the stage for some form of vicarious romantic adventure, presented in the guise of stirring spectacle, atmospheric effects, and general scenic opulence. The romantic penchant for the picturesque, for the sublime and overpowering aspects of nature, and for the romance of commonplace events permeated *The Girl of the Golden West,* set in the fabled period of the California gold rush of 1849. Within the play's broadly romantic design, however, Belasco incorporated a multitude of realistic details—visual, aural, and behavioristic—in a meticulously integrated and illusionistic totality. (pp. 139-40)

For Belasco, . . . the theatre was "a composite of *all* the arts; literature, music, the dance, painting, sculpture—even architecture, for it is three-dimensional." (p. 207)

[The] obvious Achilles heel [of Belasco's theatrical art], given the wisdom of our critical hindsight, was the less than distinguished repertory upon which its power was sometimes lavished. Its great strength was its magic—that is, intensified and sharply focused—realism and its vigorous totality. Belasco intended his art to be no spiritless copy of reality, but a reinvention of reality that started with reality itself in order to be able to transpose and amplify it in telling his story. His theatre was one of fundamental consistency, firmly bound by a single style and thus acquiring its own truth, its own peculiar meaning and poignancy. Herein lies the source of its great success in its own time as well as the seeds, once the tastes and ideals of that time had altered, of its subsequent decline. (pp. 208-09)

Lise-Lone Marker, in her David Belasco: Naturalism in the American Theatre *(copyright © 1975 by Princeton University Press; reprinted by permission of Princeton University Press), Princeton University Press, 1975, 248 p.*

BIBLIOGRAPHY

Brown, John Mason. "David Belasco." In his *Upstage: The American Theatre in Performance,* pp. 183-90. Port Washington, N Y : Kennikat Press, 1969.
    Insightful essay in which Brown challenges the label of Belasco as a realist. Belasco's realism, says Brown, is limited to his stage production and does not refer to his portrayal of human nature.

Gagey, Edmond M. "Maguire and Belasco, 1873-1882." In his *The. San Francisco Stage: A History,* pp. 126-64. New York: Columbia University Press, 1950.*
    A history of the San Francisco theater during the "reign" of Tom Maguire, including Belasco's beginnings as actor, manager, and producer at Maguire's Baldwin Theater.

Morehouse, Ward. "Belasco, Fitch, Gillette, and C. F." In his *Matinee Tomorrow: Fifty Years of Our Theater,* pp. 14-23. New York: Whittlesey House, 1949.*
    Brief character sketch of Belasco as theater man summarized in the statement: "a showman without an appreciation of writing."

Moses, Montrose J. Notes to *Six Plays: Madame Butterfly, Du Barry, The Darling of the Gods, Adrea, The Girl of the Golden West, The Return of Peter Grimm,* by David Belasco, pp. 3-8, 33-5, 141-44, 225-29, 307-09, 405-08. Boston: Little, Brown, and Co., 1928.
    A history of each of the plays from conception to dramatization with little critical comment.

Jacinto Benavente (y Martinez)

1866-1954

Spanish dramatist, essayist, poet, short story writer, translator, and journalist.

Jacinto Benavente, who was awarded the Nobel Prize in 1922, is credited with introducing European modernist trends into the Spanish theater. His intelligent, verbally elegant plays, which are characteristically bereft of action, created a new movement in a theater which had been dominated by portentous melodramas. Benavente sought his models outside the traditional Spanish stage, and was influenced not only by contemporary European playwrights, but also by the comedy of manners and the works of Shakespeare and Molière, which he translated into Spanish.

Benavente's subjective dramas show the influence of cubism in their subtle examination of multifaceted problems. His plays were meant to be performed to an intellectual and social elite, and therefore Madrid's upper classes and aristocracy constitute the world of most of his works. His are dramas of character, not action, in which dialogue, not plot, is of primary importance. Many critics feel that his experience as an actor aided him in creating actable characters in what are essentially static plays.

Benavente's view of life is an essentially Christian doctrine of kindness, self-sacrifice, and love which tempers his sharp dissection of the weaknesses of human nature and Spanish society. Moral tolerance is celebrated in his plays by the satirization of the inflexible. His early work was ironically satiric without overt moralizing, but through the years he adopted a more consistently moral tone, and his later work often degenerated into doctrinaire tracts. Benavente's dramas have also been variously criticized as being overly intellectual, indifferent, or excessively poetic. The venom he directed against characters he detested and his verbal brilliance have led to comparisons with George Bernard Shaw. Benavente has been termed a feminist for his excellent presentation of female characters who usually have more moral substance than his men. Though his work was extremely popular during his lifetime it is generally conceded that only a handful of his nearly 200 dramatic works will survive.

PRINCIPAL WORKS

Cartas de mujeres (fictional letters) 1893
El nido ajeno: Comedia en tres actos (drama) 1894
Gente conocida (drama) 1896

Figulinas (sketches) 1898
Cuento do amor (drama) 1899
Lo cursi: Comedia en tres actos (drama) 1901
La gobernadora: Comedia en tres actos (drama) 1901
Sacrificios (drama) 1901
Alma triunfante: Drama en tres actos (drama) 1902
El automóvil (drama) 1902
El hombrecito (drama) 1903
La noche del Sábado: Novela escénica en cinco cuadros (drama) 1903
Por que se ama (drama) 1903
El dragón de fuego (drama) 1904
Los Malhechores del bien: Comedia en dos actos (drama) 1905
Rosas de otono (drama) 1905
Vilanos (sketches) 1905
Más fuerte que el amor (drama) 1906
La Princesa Bebé (drama) 1906
Los intereses creados: Comedia de polichinelas en dos actos, tres cuadros y un prólogo (drama) 1907
El marido de su viuda: Comedia en un acto (drama) 1908
Señora Ama (drama) 1908
La escuela de las princesas: Comedia en tres actos y en prosa (drama) 1909
Por las nubes (drama) 1909
El principe que todo lo apprendió en los libros: Cuento en dos actos y siete cuadros (drama) 1909
La malquerida (drama) 1913
El collar de estrellas: Comedia en cuatro actos, en prosa (drama) 1915
La propia estimación (drama) 1915
Campo de armiño: Comedia en tres actos (drama) 1916
La ciudad alegre y confiada: Comedia en tres cuadros y un prólogo considerados como tres actos (drama) 1916
Plays (dramas, includes *His Widow's Husband, The Bonds of Interest, The Evil Doers of Good, La Malquerida*) 1917
Plays: Second Series (dramas, includes *No Smoking, Princess Bebé, The Governor's Wife, Autumnal Roses*) 1919
Una pobre mujer (drama) 1920
Una señora (drama) 1920
Plays: Third Series (dramas, includes *The Prince Who Learned Everything Out of Books, Saturday Night, In the Clouds, The Truth*) 1923

Plays: Fourth Series (dramas, includes *The School of Princesses, A Lady, The Magic of an Hour, Field of Ermine*) 1924

Obras Completas (dramas, letters, sketches, essays, and short stories) 1940-58

*The dates given are first performance dates.

JULIUS BROUTA (essay date 1915)

Benavente possesses an astonishing richness in style, for he writes indiscriminately in verse and prose, treating tragedy and comedy with the same master hand; the flexibility of his genius lends itself equally to the deepest tenderness and emotion, to the most cruel irony and incisive sarcasm, and to the greatest poetry. (p. 555)

[Benavente's early play, *Gente conocida (Familiar Faces)*] is a biting satire upon the customs of the upper classes. . . . The play introduced an unprecedented note, rich, spontaneous, and of a poetic realism, without false pathos and melodramatic effect; it was potent with philosophic flashes which searched out the most obscure corners of conscience.

Avoiding excesses of artifice, Benavente aims at a simple structure, actions which are consequences of sentiments, education, *milieu,* and customs; neither more nor less poetic charm than life itself affords, for to reduce it is unhealthy pessimism, and to pretend to augment it is a task both useless and deceptive. He carefully avoids what is called dramatic conflict, complexity, intrigue, the so-called cumulative situation, scenic effect, and artificially sustained characters—which in reality are emptiness itself and dependent upon circumstances. He shuns all those elements which astonish and deceive and are stimulants of childish curiosity, elements which, in defiance of truth, reach their highest grade of dismal completeness in the works of the French writer, Victorien Sardou.

[If this early] work published by Benavente bears all the marks of maturity and is therefore difficult to distinguish from those which follow, this is doubtless due to the fact that it was the fruit of a sustained preparation and self-criticism. . . . (pp. 557-58)

Benavente is, in many respects, the Bernard Shaw of Spain. Like Shaw, he is a disciple of Ibsen; like him, an iconoclast, a reformer, a teacher, a preacher, and his dialectics are hardly less efficient or his spirit less brilliant. (pp. 558-59)

Benavente depicts the world of elegance, not in a parody, as generally is the case in the majority of modern plays, but as a palpable reality, and his mordant observations are frequently of such a character as to make a great part of his audience most uneasy, for there are attitudes and postures in which nobody likes to be photographed.

Benavente, above all, is a serious writer, without any parade of bad taste, with no trace of crudeness, with an irony similar to that of Anatole France, and a comprehension of woman's heart (see his *Ladies' Letter Writer*) equalling that of de Maupassant and Prévost. . . . (pp. 559-60)

But Benavente is not only an acute critic of feminine malice and subterfuge, he is also a great admirer and lover of woman in the most noble acceptance of the word. In many of his works he has stoutly espoused the rights of woman, the idea of the equality of the sexes, and pointed out the moral obligation which matrimony imposes upon man. Love stands forth prominently in Benavente as the principal dynamic factor, love toward every cause of human freedom and justice. . . . (p. 560)

> Julius Brouta, "Spain's Greatest Dramatist," in The Drama, *Vol. V, No. 20, November, 1915, pp. 555-66.*

JOHN GARRETT UNDERHILL (essay date 1917)

[Benavente has] tried his hand at almost every *genre,* and he has been successful in them all—peasant drama and the tragedy of blood, so long associated with Spain in the minds of foreigners, satires of provincial and metropolitan society, of the aristocracy, dramas of the middle class, court comedy in the most subtle and refined of forms, in which by birth and breeding the personages are all royal. He has written romantic comedies and dramas, rococo spectacles, imaginative fairy plays of genuine poetic worth. Only the play in verse has remained unattempted, implying, as it no doubt does, through its diction a certain artificiality in the very processes of thought. In all these different *genres* he has moved with consummate ease, without the suggestion of effort, until the drama of character has seemed the most facile and casual of arts. (pp. xiv-xv)

["His Widow's Husband"] is a comedy of provincial life, and as such was received with a certain disfavor by the more precious critics. . . . In structure a farce, it is primarily an adventure in provincial psychology, and condenses into effectiveness the provincial atmosphere—the town itself, its society, its intellectual status. The characters seem to have no mentality; their minds are atrophied and slow. We become conscious of the outward feel of things, of the streets of the city as they appear to the eye; the personages seem to be present before us in the body, through which the retarded action of their thoughts struggles to the surface with effort. It is astonishing that one of the most spirituelle of writers should be capable of conveying such a vivid sense of crass reality. More closely considered, this Protean quality is implicit in his method. Benavente never describes characters; he has no inclination to serve them as tailor, nor does he give their ages away. In his plays there is no description either of persons or of locale. He does not set his scenes—the settings are implied, and the effect attained by an acute perception of mental processes which in themselves suggest the environment. Herein lies the secret of his versatility, in the highest art of description, which finds most perfect expression in *Señora Ama,* wherein the Castilian plains are painted in human terms, their bright, hard lights and vast, treeless distances being projected from the austere poverty of the minds of the *aldeanos,* or peasants, whose voices seem to break upon the surrounding void and are heard in the great silences of space.

In *La Malquerida* the process is carried even further from the point of view of drama. . . . The detail is of the most meagre. We are shown a small town, apparently ill lighted or not at all. A brook, or *arroyo,* runs near by. Evidently the country is a rolling one. There are fields, a grove, a mill in the river bottom, a long road with a crucifix beside it, and mountains in the distance—"those mountains"—to which no adjective is ever applied. On the mountains there are brambles, thickets, and rocks. This is all. The drama is an emotional one in which the landscape and action are exteriorized from the realm of character and conscience, and partake of its nature, vague and blurred of outline, seemingly painted in broad but ill-defined strokes, which harmonize with a pervading sense of doubt and uncertainty, bewilderment of conscience and impending doom. The subject is the struggle of the individual conscience against the conscience of the mass, which is embodied in the talk of the town. . . . (pp. xv-xvi)

"The Evil Doers of Good" is a comedy of manners, according to the classification of the schools. It is obviously a satire of complacency, of those fruits of religion which are not things of the spirit. . . . Yet "The Evil Doers of Good," for all its wit, was in fact directed neither against piety nor organized beneficence. Benavente does not satirize individuals; he puts his finger instead upon inherent inconsistencies which need only to be presented in their native contradiction to appear what they are. His is a civilizing rather than a destructive or reforming force. In this comedy, character and environment react upon each other in the domain of the will. . . . In the domain of experience every problem is a special problem, to be determined by the condition of the individual and his relation to his environment. The suggestion of this conflict is always present in Benavente, in terms of feeling and the heart. It prevents his most acrid satire from becoming artificial. As his plays unfold, slowly, imperceptibly it wells up in them—where, we can scarcely say, nor how—until at last we find ourselves afloat upon the drama of human experience, of which the author seems not until then to have been conscious, and whose development he has had no part in determining. The effect of some of the plays is optimistic, of others pessimistic, according to the degree in which the conditions of life they present are susceptible of domination or are immutably cruel. (pp. xvii-xviii)

A satire primarily psychological must in the end lead to some sort of generalization. The moral factor is explicit in such comedies as "The Evil Doers of Good" and "Autumnal Roses," and in the more recent serious plays, "The Graveyard of Dreams" and "His Proper Self," it assumes a dominant place. However, these are in no sense problem plays, nor may they be considered as expositions of themes. Always and in whatever form the drama of Benavente is a drama of character, never of character in its superficial aspects, its eccentricities, but in the human motives which underlie and determine its individual manifestations, without which it would be otherwise or cease to be. This is the source both of his unity and his complexity, which partake of the multifariousness of the modern world. (p. xxiii)

The subject of Jacinto Benavente is the struggle of love against poverty, of obligation against desire, of imputed virtue against the consciousness of sin. His point of attack is where the individual and the social problem join. Upon these frontiers of the social life—which are also frontiers of the moral life—he is completely at home, in those fateful moments when society touches the individual to the quick, and he ceases to be his conventional self, and becomes for a brief space a free agent to make the decision which sets in motion again the wheels of the social organism which is to crush him or to carry him along. (p. xxiv)

John Garrett Underhill, in his introduction to Plays, first series *by Jacinto Benavente, translated by John Garrett Underhill (abridged by permission of Charles Scribner's Sons; copyright 1917 by John Garrett Underhill; renewal copyright 1945 by John Garrett Underhill), Scribner's, 1917, pp. vii-xxv.*

JOHN VAN HORNE   (essay date 1918)

Between 1894 and 1901 Benavente produced eighteen plays on the Madrid stage. They represent, in a general way, the first phase of his dramatic career. The element that characterizes them most conspicuously is satire. Benavente holds up to scorn Spanish aristocratic society of the present day. He introduces to his audiences a succession of types whose failings and foibles are displayed with merciless precision. (p. xvi)

[There] is not a strong element of plot in these plays of Spanish society. The object is rather delineation of character. (p. xvii)

As we pass beyond the year 1901, we realize that a change is taking place. This does not mean that pictures of life in the upper classes are to constitute an unimportant part of Benavente's *teatro.* . . . [They] are especially congenial to his artistic sense. However, the later periods of his career give evidence of ever-expanding powers and of increasing versatility. The early type of play does not disappear, but it becomes only one of a number of different *genres,* all of which are connected by their author's keenness of observation, fidelity to life, genius for irony and universal human interest. (p. xviii)

Those who are familiar only with Benavente's earlier manner can scarcely conceive of him as the author of a problem or thesis drama. A tendency to deny the presence of a thesis may be observed on the part of certain reviewers and critics. But careful reading of the plays and consideration of their chronological development disclose that at one period in his career Benavente's mind was busy with the problems of married life in such a way that he produced something very close to the drama with a purpose. We may trace the beginning of this tendency back to some of the first plays in which a strong woman is introduced as a foil to her worthless companions. Later, *Alma triunfante* is a glorification of a woman's generosity of soul, and *Por qué se ama* describes the influence of compassion in causing a woman to cling through thick and thin to the object of her affection.

In 1905 and 1906 appeared the plays that best illustrate a purposeful treatment of conjugal relations. Benavente's prime object is to idealize feminine love and constancy. A second theme, second in prominence only to the first, is a glorification of true love itself. (p. xxi)

Prepared as a reader might be, after perusal of the problem plays, to anticipate further changes, he could scarcely expect from Benavente's pen simple sketches written with no other aim than to uphold humble virtues. Yet in some cases that is exactly what we find. A definite moral tone is observable in a large portion of Benavente's recent output. (p. xxiii)

[But the] keynote of *El collar de estrellas, La propia estimación,* and *Campo de armiño* [still] seems to be the building of character. Nowhere else, perhaps, is the author quite so insistent in setting a standard of human virtue. As a natural consequence he paints some personages who come perilously close to being angels or villains. The tendency is quite in line with the progressive development of Benavente's dramatic and intellectual life. Possibly his art has suffered slightly from a desire to exert a good moral influence, but his reflections have become correspondingly more profound and valuable. (p. xxviii)

[Benavente's] mind is encumbered by few, if any, illusions. He is both satirical and practical. Irony and hatred for Spanish abuses do not prevent him from exhibiting a pure and noble patriotism. Cosmopolitan as he may be in theories, his nature is essentially and intensely Spanish. It is a genuine comfort to find that the scientific observer of human nature, the man who can make acute comments on the most diversified subjects, can occasionally give way to a noble passion, and even to a pardonable prejudice; not too often, but just often enough to prove that he is human. One cannot turn away from Benavente without feeling that he has been enriched by communion with a master spirit and benefited by association with a broad, clear-thinking, sympathetic nature. (pp. xxx-xxxi)

> *John Van Horne, in his introduction to* Tres Comedias: 'Sin querer,' 'De pequeñas causas ...,' 'Los intereses creados' *by Jacinto Benavente, edited by John Van Horne (copyright, 1918, by D. C. Heath & Co.), Heath, 1918, pp. xi-xxxi.*

JOHN GARRETT UNDERHILL (essay date 1919)

For all its seeming simplicity, [Benavente's] style is one of the most complex and highly personal in literature. Primarily, it is suggestive. With the thought, he contrives to convey the implication. The direct meaning is not of chief concern, but its connotations in the mind which harbors it. It is a style built upon contrast, seizing upon the inconsistencies in which human nature is most intimately revealed. Given one point, the spectator is led to infer another, so that, without visible means, or the appearance of doing so, the playwright turns his characters inside out, till we view them with him from all sides at once, while at the same time we see through them. He shows us not only what his people think, but how they feel when they think it, their doubts and accompanying reservations. His theatre has been called a theatre of ideas, and it is a theatre of ideas in so far as ideas are an expression of intense intellectual activity. But Benavente is not concerned with ideas, he is concerned with thought as it formulates itself—with ideas in the making. Thus his comedy stimulates the mind to an extraordinary degree, in which it is possible for him to communicate to an audience what under more usual circumstances it would fail to perceive. . . . His style may best be compared to a rational cubist art, in which the elements are all valid and intelligible in themselves, but which surrender their true significance only when taken in juxtaposition.

With Benavente, the story is never of predominant importance, nor in the beginning was his treatment of it unusual, or markedly individual. His plots unfolded symmetrically and were sufficient to sustain the interest through the customary sequence of situations and climaxes. Yet as his dialogue matured in fertility of suggestion, obviously a purely objective plot, a chain of circumstance and outward fact, with laws of its own, became an unsuitable vehicle for its transmission. The tendency of Benavente's art is away from the plastic toward the insubstantial, the transparent. A

fresh adjustment became imperative. What he had accomplished with satire he next essays with plot, turning his attention to its secondary and suggestive values, transferring the emphasis from the events to the inferences which wait upon them, and the atmosphere which they create, either directly or through collocation. . . . A similar extension of plot had been attempted by the symbolists, through the imposition of parallel meanings upon the action. With Benavente, on the other hand, the events induce their own meaning, while, in order to permit them to do this, he deprives the story of definite form. . . . [The] drama is removed from the domain of structural regularity, until it depends for its effect upon the impressions derived from a panorama of incident and of situation in which the story is swallowed up and upon occasion lost from view. These dramas may be considered the romantic outburst, the ungovernable adventure of the Benaventian theatre, by very lack of restraint stimulating the imagination to a perception, at once restless and inchoate, of the awe and majesty of life.

Variety so kaleidoscopic precludes, of course, unity of impression. At best, fact is inexpressive, and Benavente seems to have felt that, independently developed, whatever its transcendence, it was susceptible only of the broadest effects. . . . Instead, he subordinates the story; it ceases to be the prime factor in the dramatic fabric, or, in any proper sense of the word, the action. Henceforward the story becomes subservient wholly to the main action, which thus is unified, and this action is entirely psychological and subjective. In life as upon the stage, says Princess Bebé, the real entertainment goes on behind the scenes. ''The Bonds of Interest'' provides a typical example of this new dramaturgy. Rather than the outward history of the characters, the story becomes the window through which they may be seen, as they react upon each other, and so interpret themselves. The old values are present, but they are changed. The danger which besets the reader of Benavente is not that he will fail to appreciate him, but that he will fail to appreciate him at his proper worth. His drama is a drama of character, not because it is occupied with character, but because it takes place within it, and the conflict is joined in the play and interplay of thought and emotion, of volition and inhibition, of impulse and desire, as they are colored and predetermined by tradition, by heredity, by convention, by education, and all the confused network of motive and prejudice of which conscious assertion of personality is but a part. (pp. viii-x)

> *John Garrett Underhill, ''Benaventiana,'' in* Plays, second series *by Jacinto Benavente, translated by John Garrett Underhill (abridged by permission of Charles Scribner's Sons; copyright 1919 by John Garrett Underhill; renewal copyright 1947 by John Garrett Underhill, Jr.), Scribner's, 1919, pp. vii-xviii.*

STORM JAMESON (essay date 1920)

The work of Jacinto Benavente is in the highest tradition of the Spanish drama, and a symbol of its promise. The creative genius of Lope de Vega informed his vision of reality with the fullest active and emotional life. To his country's drama he left a tradition of suppleness; skilful construction; splendour of movement and music; living, distinctive characters. (p. 239)

His comedies have exquisite fantasy, poetic grace, technical perfection, and intellectual distinction. Where they fail is in an occasional careless handling of their finest qualities: poetry becomes sounding verse, fantasy overshadows reality, to the marring of dramatic proportion. Take *Los Intereses Creados*, played in London as *The Bias of the World*. The atmosphere is perfectly suggested. An ironical side-glance at life gives depth and colour to the charm of the fantasy. Behind Harlequin and Columbine, the Captain and Punchinello, a countless multitude of mocking, graceful shadows grow more dim and stately as thought follows them down the years. The picaresque novel has given of its life and movement to the figure of Crispin, valet, vagabond, philosopher, weaver of subtle stratagems to save his own and his master's skin. He is the intellect of the play, his introspective genius its criticism of life. Passion here is not allowed to shatter the delicate form: the bitter-sweet love-making of Leandro and Silvia is subdued to the imaginative beauty of the whole. (pp. 239-40)

[The dialogue is exquisite, but the play] is more than exquisite dialogue, more than fantasy in perfect form: it is an artistic criticism of life, the highest form of comedy; a criticism of the world in which the noble must needs save himself by the baser, where love and morality are pawns in the game of the masters of life. And through it all, beneath the grace in which it clothes itself, is the pulse of creative life.

In his tragedies, Benavente, the fierce enemy of false thinking, the reformer and iconoclast, cannot always hold his naked hate and anger from tearing in pieces the dramatic fitness of speech and character. The short measure of the dramatist is filled up by the preacher. So that not all the radiant beauty of style, nor the clear deep of passion, nor the tenderness, can carry his tragedies to the peaks that first catch the sun. (pp. 241-42)

His first play—*Gente Conocida* (*Familiar Faces*)—was a satire on the habits of the upper classes. The words have the thrust and glint which marks his dialogue throughout. This early work is not blurred by crudeness, and already he is very nearly master of the irony and philosophic insight that light up not one aspect of life alone, but all life and all the striving of men. *Los Malhechores del Bien* (*Evil-doers of good*), an attack on the hypocrisy and pietic froth of the clergy is at once more bitter and more sure. In all his plays the satire is a terrible sword, beaten and tempered by his fierce indignation, and used without fear or shrinking. (p. 242)

The other side of the dramatist's passionate indignation is love, love towards the oppressed, the thwarted and the maimed of life. As he hates injustice so he loves justice and freedom. He sees the world set free through the power of love, touching all things that suffer with pitiful fingers. But pain and injustice are not only for wailing or mad outcry. In the crowding life of his plays they take their place as one of the burdens that man's stupidity binds heavier on his fellows even as he struggles to free himself. Men are to be pitied, but they are also to be loved. Through the dynamic force of love they will be set free, not from pain, but from despair and the isolation of defeat. (p. 243)

It must be said that there is in Benavente a divine sanity which does not often allow the poet to overwhelm the dramatist, and insists always that it is better to understand life, even if to understand be to suffer, than to take her loveliness to build a dead city of the arts.

This is his power: the artistic activity that criticises life in creating it. (p. 244)

> *Storm Jameson, "The Drama of Italy and Spain," in his* Modern Drama in Europe *(copyright 1920; reprinted by permission of A D Peters & Co Ltd), W. Collins Sons & Co. Ltd., 1920, pp. 221-70.**

JOHN DOS PASSOS (essay date 1921)

Benavente is the last *madrileño. Tiene el sentido de lo castizo.* (pp. 226-27)

Lo castizo is the essence of the local, of the regional, the last stronghold of Castilian arrogance. It refers not to the empty shell of traditional observances, but to the very core and fragrance of them. . . .

In the flood of industrialism of the last twenty years that has obliterated landmarks and brought all the world to the same level of nickel-plated dulness, the theatre in Madrid has been the refuge of *lo castizo.* It has been a theatre of manners and local types and customs, of observation and natural history, where a rather specialized, well-trained audience accustomed to satire as the tone of daily conversation, was tickled by any portrayal of its quips and cranks. A tradition of character acting grew up nearer that of the Yiddish theatre than of any other stage we know in America. Benavente and the brothers Quintero have been the most successful playwrights of this school that has been in vogue pretty much since the going out of the *drame passionné* style of Echegaray. At present Benavente, as director of the Teatro Nacional, is unquestionably the leading figure. Therefore it is very fitting that he should be, in life and works, of all *madrileños* the most *castizo.* (p. 227)

Benavente's plays . . . acquire double significance as the summing up and the chief expression of a movement that has reached its heyday, from which the sap has already been cut off. It is, indeed, the thing to disparage them for their very finest quality, the vividness with which they express the texture of Madrid, the animated humorous mordant conversation about café tables: *lo castizo.* (p. 229)

[On the] willingness to play the game of wit, even of abuse, without too much rancor, which is the unction to ease social intercourse, is founded all the popularity of Benavente's writing. Somewhere in Hugo's Spanish grammar . . . is a proverb to the effect that the wind of Madrid is so subtle that it will kill a man without putting out a candle. The same, at their best, can be said of Benavente's satiric comedies. . . . (p. 230)

> *John Dos Passos, "Benavente's Madrid," in* The Bookman, *Vol. LIII, No. 3, May, 1921, pp. 226-30.*

GEORGE JEAN NATHAN (essay date 1921)

The propaganda in behalf of Jacinto Benavente's sublimity, its lethargic flanks assiduously spurred and whacked on by the indefatigable Señor Underhill [see excerpts above], fails to move me. . . . To Underhill, every Spanish playwright is a *maestro.* . . . To the ebullient Underhill there isn't a Sammie Shipman in the whole Spanish theatre. . . . (p. 106)

In behalf of Benavente, in particular, doth the effervescent Underhill spread himself. Benavente, according to our

Underhill, is the very crême de la crême . . . of modern dramatists. (p. 107)

Another of this towering genius' *opera,* "La Malquerida," was recently imported to these shores. It discloses itself to be an ably constructed but perfectly empty piece of stage writing. . . . His characters are developed not in the manner of imaginative photography with its careful study, its careful adjustment of lights and shadows, its careful development and printing, but in the manner of snapshots. He is a serviceable technician of the stage, but he builds with the hand and the mind of a [Victorian] Sardou. The other plays of his with which I am acquainted—I know the bulk of his dramatic writing fairly well—do not persuade me much more greatly. He is, at his best, a distinctly inferior [José] Echegaray. He is, at his worst, a distinctly inferior amateur playwright of the London Play Actors' experimental stage brand. He is, in general, an imitator: in "The Bonds of Interest" of the methods of [Giuseppe] Giacosa, in certain of his other satires of the methods of Shaw (much diluted), in "La Malquerida" of the methods of [Angel] Guiméra, in "Sacrifice" and "The Victor Soul" of the methods of [Henri] Lavedan and French dramatists of his stripe, in "The Evil Doers of Good" of the methods of the German satirical comedy school that sprang to life in the wake of Shaw. . . . He writes nimbly, but he writes other men's ideas. (pp. 109-10)

George Jean Nathan, "Benavente," in his The Theatre, the Drama, the Girls *(copyright © 1921 by Alfred A. Knopf, Inc.; reprinted by permission of Associated University Presses, Inc.), Alfred A. Knopf, Inc., 1921, pp. 106-10.*

ISAAC GOLDBERG (essay date 1922)

There is, in [Benavente's] most characteristic labors, a sophistication that almost militates against depth of passion; whether he weeps or he cries, he is never so absorbed that he cannot pause for introspection, for self-analysis. It is no accident that his beginnings, toward the end of the nineteenth century, are made in satire, and that his most famous work, *Los Intereses Creados* (played in the United States as *The Bonds of Interest* and in England as *The Bias of the World*) is satire so sublimated that, from viewing mankind as a tangled string of puppets, it takes the logical step of converting them frankly into puppet figures upon the stage. Remember that Benavente's plays . . . are centrifugal; they proceed from a common center, but do not return; they elude ready classification because they were born of a spirit hostile to the artificial ease of order. There is neither morality nor immorality in Benavente, who is amoral. . . . To characterize the man's work—as apart from whatever artistic values we may assign to it—one needs words that do not stand still, that mock, that snicker, that brood, that shift forever restlessly like the colored glass of the kaleidoscope, into patterns new and alluring. (pp. 102-03)

The characteristic Benavente is to be found rather in such arresting performances as . . . [*La Gobernadora, La Noche del Sabado, La Princesa Bebé, Los Intereses Creados,* and *La Malquerida*]. In these his satire, his irony, are at their most pungent; his wit is at its sharpest, his skill at suggesting psychology through a minimum of words and actions most fine. Around these, and the few others that might be grouped with them, are clustered a score of minor works, illuminative of his best rather than illustrative of it.

As, for example, *El Automóvil.* . . . If I mention *The Automobile* at all, it is because in this fairly clever farce I seem to find a sort of "rehearsal" for the writing of the widely acclaimed *Bonds of Interest* of five years later. . . . [The] distance between this and *The Bonds of Interest* is continental; in *The Automobile* the persons are largely puppets; in *Los Intereses Creados,* the puppets are more than persons, living a life that is their own and a symbolic life dependent not upon arbitrary, parallel meanings, but upon the significance that radiates from all genuine personalities. (p. 107)

[Let] us return to the salient series that starts with *La Gobernadora.* In these one imagines one discovers Benavente in the core, not upon the rim, of his work. The satire and the irony in them are not the detached commentary that may be found in his lesser social pieces; they are the overtones of the action and the personages, vibrating with the fundamental tone and coloring its timbre. The very frames merge with the pictures they contain until they dissolve in the variegated detail. . . . Far more versatile than Pirandello, [Benavente] more resembles [Shaw] in his radiant technical insouciance, his ventilation of current notions, his ready wit, his intellectual curiosity. One looks in vain through Benavente, however, for Barbaras, Candidas, predacious Anns and their life-force brood. One looks in vain for meticulous stage-directions, which Benavente avoids, and logorrheic prefaces. The Spaniard lacks almost entirely the Irishman's ethical preoccupations, though, curiously enough, no one has come away from Shaw with a hampered sense of personal liberty. Benavente's is not a discursive world; it is rather a compact, pyrotechnic institution where the rockets glare, the wheels spin a while, and then the display is over. He dazzles the mind and leaves the heart curiously indifferent,—perhaps because he is himself an indifferent spectator. (pp. 107-08)

Benavente's fecundity is qualitative as well as quantitative. Echegaray stamped ready-made ideas into the prevailing dramatic forms; Benavente's intellectual resiliency created its own amorphous ambient. Yet, something in the man's intellect seems to suppress the emotional fervor that alone could nourish living creatures rather than sublimated symbols. His plays, with their thin fables and their rich dialogues, suggest those pages of the Talmud in which islets of text are submerged in an ocean of commentary. Not so much excess of emotion, as Jameson would have it [see excerpt above], but excess of intellectuality, interferes with the dramatic fitness of speech and character. (pp. 120-21)

Isaac Goldberg, "Jacinto Benavente," in his The Drama of Transition: Native and Exotic Playcraft *(copyright, 1922, by Stewart Kidd Company), Stewart Kidd, 1922, pp. 96-121.*

WALTER STARKIE (essay date 1924)

It is impossible to think of [Benavente] apart from his contemporaries for his literary personality is made up of tendencies of the late nineties. Nor can he be looked on as a typical Spaniard. He is in reality the most cosmopolitan writer in Spain and many of his enemies have made it an accusation against him that he introduced foreign ideals which caused the decline of true Spanish art. To those, however, who examine carefully Benavente's drama, it will become plain that foreign influences did not altogether hide the Spanish dramatist who counted back his literary descent to Lope de Vega. (p. 19)

Benavente is an example of the complete dramatist. . . .
Under his guidance we shall find that most of the conventions dear to former writers disappeared. He destroyed the
aside and the soliloquy, introducing in their stead the quick,
jerky dialogue of ordinary speech. But Benavente's mission
was a deeper one; he wanted to get away from the old romantic love story and draw nearer to the presentation of
modern life as it is. . . . [Most] of his plays deal with the
problems of married life. (p. 21)

Cartas de Mujeres—'Women's letters' . . . is the first work
which shows that the foundation of Benavente's work is
feminist. In these letters he tries to plumb the depths of the
Spanish woman's soul. (p. 28)

Cartas de Mujeres is first of all important for its style. It
was the harbinger of the new methods of literature that
were coming into Spain. These, with reference to Benavente, might be summed up in one word—simplicity. . . .
Into [an] atmosphere overladen with thought, Benavente's
scintillating prose came like a ray of sunshine; what others
had taken a chapter to say he now said in an epigram. This
feminine correspondence is simple and colloquial in style,
but with what deep knowledge of psychology he reveals the
complex character of his heroines! (pp. 28-9)

Benavente has no illusions about his heroines, but analyses
them with strict impartiality. Many of the supposed writers
of these letters are frivolous and empty-headed, and in a
few words they confess their inanity. (p. 30)

The first period of Benavente's production may be called
satiric. From 1894, when he produced *El Nido Ajeno,* down
to 1901, dramatic ideas came to him armed with the Toledo
blade of satire. The bloated, complacent society which had
evolved in the years of Spain's misfortunes at the end of the
century was ready material to this modern Molière. At first,
he attacks the society of Madrid and afterwards turns his
attention to provincial life. (pp. 33-4)

In 1901 we notice the gradual evolution of Benavente's
style onwards from Satire. The play *Sacrificios,* which was
produced in that year, opens a new period. In this second
period might be included all the plays written between 1901
and 1914. . . .

In the years 1901 to 1914 Benavente's genius reaches its
highest development and in consequence we find the utmost variety in the type of play produced. The satiric tendency of his style mellows and becomes humour—that
spirit whose laugh is always a grave one. The critic examining those plays is in great difficulty in the matter of subdivisions for the master's spirit eludes like quicksilver. At
one moment he produces a comedy of middle-class life, at
another a pageant play. (p. 36)

Benavente seems always to write and develop his theme
with difficulty, and he needs many characters with whom to
conceal the springs of his action. The first acts of his plays
are generally full of movement and bustle. The first act of
La Gobernadora is a good example. It is very long and yet
nothing definite happens. We see the square at Moraleda
and watch the people wandering about. Little by little we
get to know the chief persons of the town, and from the
waiter we hear all the gossip. Many first acts of the author
are like that. His method centred in dialogue, and by scraps
of conversation bandied about from lip to lip, he explained
the characters in the play. Often the true plot does not

begin until the second act, and the first performs the functions of an overture to create the atmosphere. In many
plays it is a pity that he was not able to follow more closely
the economy of French drama, but there is no doubt that
dullness is avoided by the introduction of secondary characters who by means of varied episodes rouse the interest
of the audience. (pp. 64-5)

It is in dialogue, however, that we notice the wonderful
skill of the early satiric plays. The running fire of epigrams
and smart sallies in *Gente Conocida* or *Lo Cursi* is worthy
of Oscar Wilde at his best. Benavente, like the great English wit, was able to throw off at a minute's notice the most
profound aphorisms on life. It is a tendency natural to the
Spaniard who has inherited from centuries of ancestors the
love of the 'phrase'. The effect of Benavente's satire in
these plays is nearly always obtained by lightning flashes of
wit—but often the cascade of epigrams has very little to do
with the situation in the play. We often feel that the young
Benaventian wits are straining like the young men of our
Restoration comedy for effect, and would willingly lose
their honour for a *mot.* We notice also in the plays after
1901 a tendency towards euphuistic expression that was
afterwards to spoil much of Benavente's work. Spanish,
like English, drama, has always suffered from affected conceits of language. (pp. 65-6)

Benavente's laughter in these more mature comedies often
touches on the tragic. Instead of skimming the surface of
life as he saw it, he now tries to probe the hidden depths of
society, to reach the fundamental causes of the great problems of life. Society appears to him as it did to Ibsen to be
supported by pillars that stand on a foundation of lying and
corruption. Benavente, however, has not the *saeva indignatio* of Ibsen—but rather a grey, misty pessimism from
which he takes refuge in his doctrine of renunciation. Ibsen
had faith in the regeneration of man by truth, and he rises
like a giant in glorious rebellion against the falsity of society. Benavente . . . can never rise from humdrum existence to breathe the rarer air on mountain tops. He shows
the falsity of the conventions of society, the egoism of men,
the cruel logic of modern life, but he offers no real solution.
(p. 67)

[An example of just such a play is *El Hombrecito.*] It would
be difficult in all Benavente's works to discover a play that
ends on a tone of deeper pessimism than this one. The
satire that had seemed so brisk in this play becomes tragic.
In this drama of a girl's soul smothered by life we no longer
see the author as an ironic, passionless god, contemplating
his creatures from the security of divine aloofness; rather
does Benavente's spirit resemble that harsh, elfin humour
of Pirandello which maliciously pulls to pieces the mechanism of any image raised by sentiment, in order to see how
it is made. And after pulling to pieces Nené's soul he forces
her to creep back maimed and cowed to join in the farce of
society. (p. 70)

It is easy to understand why . . . criticism of Benavente
should arise in Spain which of all countries has admired in
literature and art the presentation of the 'man of flesh and
bones'. . . .

Benavente is the very antithesis to the spirit which produced such art: instead of the massiveness of marble we
find in him the daintiness of porcelain, instead of passionate
exaltation, the cold smile of the cynic. Instead of fashioning

a mighty statue he has rather followed the boudoir-sculptors of modern times, chiselling out numerous figurines that delight by their miniature graces. (p. 88)

Two qualities [in Benavente] dominate all the others: irony and fantastic imagination. Ironical paradox constitutes the characteristic of his literary form, and to these paradoxes he adds his wonderful gift for drawing mental pictures. (p. 121)

[*La Noche del Sábado* and *Princessa Bebé*] derive their brilliant qualities from Benavente's satire. With Satanic glee he takes infinite pains to tear down the filmy veil of fantasy in which he enveloped his royal characters, and show us in detail their pretty faults, their lack of ideals, their false, tinsel vices. But when he tries to make these disillusioned puppets fit into a scheme of philosophy he fails as a dramatist. Yet Benavente is determined . . . to introduce on the stage a critical philosophy of life. Thus gradually the harsh grin of satire softens into the benevolent smile of the worldly philosopher who accepts society and its failings, and his later works become manuals of tolerance, holy bibles of benignity. Benavente believes with Anatole France that evil is necessary. If it did not exist neither would good. And so we understand why the author describes so complacently scenes of vice. (p. 137)

Benavente in all his plays gives us a picture of our modern life that varies every instant at the dictates of emotion and will. We find thus a fundamental dualism in his works: on the one hand, the ebb and flow of life that is ever tossed about and uncertain, always renewing itself from instant to instant; on the other hand, society with its masks and conventions that have grown up from our desire to crystallize the ever-changing. The essence of drama thus exists in the struggle between the primitive life and the clothes and masks by which men try to conceal its nakedness. No play of Benavente shows this idea more completely than *Los Intereses Creados,* and indeed the play may be taken as the progenitor of the brilliant *teatro grottesco* that sprang up in Italy during the Great War, through the instrumentality of Chiarelli and Pirandello. (pp. 152-53)

Leandro [in *Los Intereses Creados*] is not worthy of Silvia; he is said to symbolize the ideal part of man, but yet it cannot be said that he ever becomes inspired. In the love scenes it is always Silvia who uses the beautiful phrases. In the scenes with Crispín he fades altogether into insignificance, and becomes shy and shamefaced before the other characters. There seems to be a slight trace of Benaventian irony in this character chosen to symbolize a poet. He belongs to those dreamers who call themselves poets, but who, owing to their lack of energy and action, never compose anything. (p. 162)

In this subtle play perhaps more than in any other it is possible to see Benavente's complete development. His plays are baffling in their complexity and open up different vistas to the interpreter. It has been said that he is always to be found at the scales, and this is particularly true in this play where there is continual antithesis. He has a particular aversion to definite statements, for his art is mainly one of parenthesis. His dialogue is not the frank and open conversation of former dramatists, when only one meaning could be interpreted; in plays such as *La Noche del Sábado* and *Los Intereses Creados* there is a dialogue of inference where every idea causes another contrasting idea to spring

up by inevitable antithesis. This psychological method Benavente employed many years before it was adopted by the writers of Grotesques. (p. 166)

Benavente, like Socrates, concludes his argumentative conversations by some fanciful symbol which mythlike caps the teaching of the play. In *Collar de Estrellas* Don Pablo, the hero, invokes the starry necklace in the sky as a symbol of the family. In *Campo de Armiño,* Irene, the marchioness, will place on the ermine field of her armorial shield a lily symbolizing the redemption of her soul. Benavente, by the insertion of those little allegories, renders more palatable to the public his moral treatises. It is probable that this symbolical tendency he derived not from Plato, but from Ibsen, who intensifies his drama and stamps it indelibly on the mind of the audience by some picturesque parable. (p. 174)

In the last period, since 1914, Benavente has tried . . . to rise above the dust of contemporary life, but he has lost his hold on the realities of life and gives the impression of writing from memories that are fading. His heroes and heroines in most cases tend to become mere mechanical symbols of an abstract thought. In many cases also he falls into sentimentality, and mistakes rhetoric for art. . . . Benavente in the majority of these plays tries to show a moral purpose. Their construction from a dramatic point of view is sometimes very faulty, and often it appears as if he had intended to make them philosophical dialogues. Experience of the vast world has made him the ironist, kinder towards men. Indeed it may be said that sentimental kindness has killed his inspiration. (pp. 192-93)

In Benavente's theatre cultivated woman is the cynosure of all eyes. The subtle delicacy of his style evoked faint sylphlike heroines that seem to be faint echoes of Desdemona, Ophelia, and Helena reaching our ears down the centuries. (p. 203)

Let us not ask from this exquisite ironist whose figures have the dainty delicacy of fine porcelain, for the rude shocks of tragedy, for the kingly stature demanded by Aristotle. In his tragedies the characters make haste to throw off the cothurnus: nor can they stare rough passion in the face, but gaze at it diminished through the mist of their fantasy. Benavente in his supreme mood resembles some subtle modern musician like Debussy or Ravel, who evokes old popular melodies of his country—rugged, passionate tunes sprung from the soil, but in such a way that they float wistfully to our ears down the course of centuries. (pp. 210-11)

Walter Starkie, in his Jacinto Benavente *(reprinted by permission of Oxford University Press), Oxford University Press, London, 1924, 218 p.*

L. A. WARREN   (essay date 1929)

Jacinto Benavente, the leading twentieth-century Spanish dramatist, is almost in opposition to the main tendencies of his country's theatre as it has manifested itself throughout history. The Spanish stage is crude and violent, providing fare for a primitive populace. Benavente is fine, polished and thoughtful, producing plays for an over-civilized and decadent audience. The Madrid theatre is full of melodrama, action, strife, passions. In Benavente there is no action, he offers no situations, is almost non-dramatic. The Spanish drama is extremely idealistic with poetic flights and high sentiments. Benavente is poetic neither in form nor feeling, is essentially a prose writer, not in the sense of writing dull, heavy, leaden sentences, but in the manner of La Rochefoucauld; his prose is witty, cynical, sarcastic. In pointed, vivid realism, Benavente is Spanish; but on the whole Spanish drama has been more idealistic than realistic, the realism for which the Spanish mind is celebrated having shown itself more in the novel than on the stage. The Castilian temperament has shown itself in the theatre by a dramatic instinct for action combined with an idealism of poetic form and noble sentiments. . . . He is more of a European writer than a Spanish one. He is a man of his time. He represents the theatre of ideas of the last years of the nineteenth century. His concreteness has prevented him from achieving success in the Maeterlinck manner of dream, suggestion and weird intangibility; just the contrary, his Castilian temperament has furnished him with his two great qualities, wit and realism. . . . (pp. 556-57)

Benavente's method is to take a philosophical or social idea and build his play around it. He produces a set of people to discuss and illustrate this idea; it is hardly drama at all, more like an essay, in a series of dialogues; being put in dramatic form sharpens, condenses and makes vivid the ideas; putting his ideas in the form of realistic dialogues gets rid of the necessity of coherence, orderly development and sticking to the point—dreadful stumbling-blocks to the average Spanish essayist. (p. 559)

Benavente's theatre is one for the discussion and illustration of ideas. What then are his ideas? He has two main ones closely connected, and both derived from Ibsen. His main idea is liberal anarchism, an idea suited to the individualism of the Iberian race, that every person should be free to develop their own character, to be spontaneous and natural, free from the trammels and fetters of an artificial, corrupt society. His second theme is that of a feminist. His liberal anarchism is the subject of *La Princesa Bebé*. He starts with his philosophical point and writes a thesis on that. The Princess has been brought up in a narrow, stiff court life, and is not free to develop herself and her character, to be spontaneous, to be human, to be natural. . . . The Princess, therefore, throws over the traces and breaks loose; mixes in the life of showy swindlers, sham nobles and wealthy *roués* on the Riviera—and instead of finding them free and natural finds them equally artificial and prejudiced.

The play is modern in both construction and sentiment. There is but little dramatic action, and when the situation is such that the scene might be made striking we have long conversations, even moralizing harangues. It is true that the plot or dénouement, whether the heroine will go off with her lover or renounce him, is concealed to the very end; and when we come to the crisis it is solved in a long and rather dull conversation and the decision is neither one thing nor the other but an unsatisfactory compromise. All this is deliberate on the part of Benavente. His is a drama of ideas and not of action. There is nothing of the briskness of mid-nineteenth-century drama. He does not brim over with cheerful spirits, there is no frolic of lively incidents not intended to be taken seriously. He is deadly serious; he preaches morality, even harangues. . . . He has new values to set up. His heroine is the new woman, and he requires of women that they should be more than kittenish playthings that lead in luxury a life of amorous intrigue. They are to be grave and serious. (pp. 562-63)

The professional love-maker to other men's wives, the Don Juan, whose business and glory it is to seduce as many women as possible, dominates the nineteenth-century Spanish stage, and swamps the literature. Benavente never tires of jibing at this creature. He flaunts into prominence the cynical immorality of husbands which he contrasts with the lifelong sacrifices of the wives. However, although in some of his plays he sermonizes, and in others tends towards the didactic, generally he does not preach but discuss, and is usually content to illustrate the corruptness of fashionable life. His defects all come from the abstract world of intellect, where the Spanish talent is at its weakest, his merits from the concrete world of actuality, where the Spanish genius is at its best.

His finest plays are those in which the discourses are few and the harangues short, where he does not give us his views on all that is going on, but is content to stay outside the plays and with keen eyes to see that which is around him, with sharp ears to take in all that is said and then to set it all down vividly. Such a play is *La Gobernadora*. Here are noted down the appearance, behaviour and sayings of all the chief people and prominent types of a provincial town; the types are satirically caricatured but with such deftness and ironic wit as to avoid the farcical, and the background has been filled in with minor figures in vivid detail; the pity is that Benavente is apt to break down over his leading characters by stuffing them with discourse. For the most part he observes with genial humour and records the result of his observation with suave irony with but a slight flavour of the bitter, yet has at command fierce anger and biting sarcasm. He is a master of irony, which comes from keeping back one's anger till it has cooled and then reflecting upon it. (p. 564)

> *L. A. Warren, "Modernists: Benavente," in his* Modern Spanish Literature: A Comprehensive Survey of the Novelists, Poets, Dramatists and Essayists from the Eighteenth Century to the Present Day, *Vol. II, Brentano's Ltd., 1929, pp. 556-65.*

ROBERTO G. SÁNCHEZ   (essay date 1955)

There are indeed plenty of reasons to find fault with the work of Benavente. His plays cannot stand close analysis, and yet he was clever enough to deceive many intelligent people. (p. 41)

Benavente has been called "the Bernard Shaw of Spain." There is no doubt that he would have liked to live up to the title, but Spain, even the Spain of that earlier era, offered no climate for Shaws. The Spanish dramatist wrote to the day of his death . . . , but unlike Shaw he had his say, if he had anything really worth saying, by 1900. In short, Benavente was no thinker.

All this may seem harsh, but fair critics of Benavente have based their censure on it. There is little that can be opposed to their argument. But if Benavente was no thinker he was a sensitive man of the theater and a magnificent craftsman. This is something too often ignored by his critics and not examined with enough care by his followers. It was he who brought to the Spanish stage all the currents of the European theater of that first quarter of the century. In most of his works . . . he may have practiced a quick formula, as many claim, but he is the author of three unquestionably fine plays: *Señora Ama* is sensitive and admirably constructed; the theatricality of *The Bonds of Interest* is ingenious and charming; and no one can deny that *La Malquerida* (produced in New York as *The Passion Flower*) is a powerful and fascinating melodrama, a landmark in the modern Spanish theater. The censure, however, has continued, and on different grounds. His political shifting has infuriated some . . . but this is more a criticism of the man than his work. (pp. 41-2)

[The Spanish critic] Pérez de Ayala attacked the falseness, the superficiality of Benavente's plays. He found his skepticism and cynicism irritating. He believed him to be acute in a satire that delighted in pointing out the weaknesses of others and incapable of a true moral satire, one that, having in mind a norm of perfection, tries to correct those very weaknesses. In short, Pérez de Ayala touched upon that sensitive Benaventine sore spot: the dramatist's lack of depth. . . .

[Jose Vila Selma] carries still further Pérez de Ayala's comments on the ready-made sentimentality of the plays. He show how these characters, self-centered and worshippers of the cult of the individual, confuse the heart with the mind, feeling with reason. To Vila this feeling, or *sentimiento*, is one that remains irreligious because it has chosen man as its focus, and he finds this spiritual barrenness something impossible to tolerate. His observations are carefully thought out and documented. In fact, there is much that is penetrating and just in his comments, but the spirit of intolerance that accompanies them always destroys their effect. To him this is all wrong not because it is a frivolous and empty way of life but because it is unorthodox. Benavente should be burned at the stake, not for being superficial but for being a heretic. (p. 42)

If most of Benavente's theater is frail as literature, it is rich as a mirror of a particular spiritual and social confusion. Therefore today, when the changing values of Liberalism are being examined, when what we have come to know as "modern ideas" are coming under careful scrutiny, the Spain of Benavente's plays offers a fascinating picture of a society lost between faith and nihilism. (p. 43)

> *Roberto G. Sánchez, "Not in the Reviews: Jacinto Benavente, 1866-1954," in* Books Abroad *(copyright 1955 by the University of Oklahoma Press), Vol. 29, No. 1, Winter, 1955, pp. 41-3.*

ALFREDO MARQUERIE   (essay date 1968)

Benavente's theatre is devoid of ideological conceptions or philosophical observations. The dramatist's thoughts revolve on the period, on impulses, experience, circumstances. Although some of his productions contain flashes of fatality or the bitterness of pessimism, these are not the key-note of his art. In a simple and natural way, or with the use of subtle paradox (which earned for him his fame as an author of "ingenious and ironic phrases"), what he preached through the lips of many of his fictional characters —from his drawing-room comedies . . . to his allegorical farces . . .—was generosity, understanding, forgiveness, love of art, truth, and beauty, the supremacy of mind over matter, the expiating value of sacrifice, and the sublime quality of maternal love, to which cult he devoted much attention. He was no inventor of metaphysical systems—for they have no place in the theatre—but he rejected the virus of anarchy and the germs of destructiveness. (p. 33)

One of the most marked literary and theatrical preoccupations of Benavente is presenting a vehicle of shock and dispute which has strong links with the themes and enigmas of Pirandello. . . . This conflict originates in what the characters are and what others, the rest of humanity, the world in general, think of them. It is the conception of existence as a battle between the pure, naked truth to which human beings aspire, and distorted reality, which casts a dim and indistinct reflection of itself, for practically no one really wants to see things as they are but as he would like to see them. Too often, this caprice conceals gross presumptions and wicked or malicious suspicions. (p. 34)

Benavente, who had much in common with Oscar Wilde and Bernard Shaw, particularly in the game of dialectics and irony, anticipated many points of surrealist evasion or subconscious evasion in works . . . in which the characters disclose their thoughts in a newly justified monologue, brought up to date in O'Neill's *Strange Interlude* and certain plays by Bertold Brecht. (p. 35)

> *Alfredo Marquerie, "A Centenary of Spanish Theatre," in* Topic *(copyright, Washington and Jefferson College 1968), Vol. VIII, No. 15, Spring, 1968, pp. 30-8.*

BIBLIOGRAPHY

Dial, John E. "Benavente: The Dramatist on Stage." *Revista de Estudios Hispánicos* VIII, No. 2 (May 1974): 211-18.
   A study which discusses Benavente's use of fictional playwrights as characters in his plays.

Rehder, Ernest C. "The Obscure Motives of Rubio in Benavente's *La Malquerida.*" *South Atlantic Bulletin* XLI, No. 1 (January 1976): 16-21.
   Interesting in-depth study of the character Rubio and his dramatic role.

Schwartz, Kessel. "Benavente on Shakespearean Characters." *Modern Drama* IV, No. 1 (May 1961): 60-2.
   Summary of Benavente's remarks on Shakespeare's plays and characterizations.

"Benavente and Chehov." *The Times Literary Supplement*, No. 1183 (18 September 1924): 572.*
   A short study which discusses the similarities and differences in the presentation of character and atmosphere by the two playwrights.

Underhill, John Garrett. "Theory and Criticism: Notes on the Plays." In *Plays, third series*, by Jacinto Benavente, translated by John Garrett Underhill, pp. vii-xxv. New York: Charles Scribner's Sons, 1923.
   Discussion of the three major stages of Benavente's career and the overall scheme of his dramaturgy.

Underhill, John Garrett. "On Theatre and Antitheatre." In *Plays, fourth series*, by Jacinto Benavente, translated by John Garrett Underhill, pp. v-xx. New York: Charles Scribner's Sons, 1924.
   Surveys the history of modern drama and Benavente's place in it.

Young, Raymond A. "Benavente and the Emancipation of Spanish Women." *Modern Languages* XLIX, No. 4 (December 1968): 157-60.
   Sees Benavente as portraying women realistically thus freeing them from the dramatic stereotypes of the Spanish theater.

Zdenek, Joseph W. "Psychical Conflicts in Benavente's *La Malquerida.*" *Romance Notes* XIX, No. 2 (Winter 1978): 183-89.

Psychological portrait of the character Acacia which utilizes
Freud's concepts of id, ego, and superego.

Gottfried Benn

1886-1956

German poet, essayist, short story writer, and critic.

Benn is considered by many to be the most influential German poet of this century, but the strength of his influence lies more in his theories of poetry than in his poetry itself. An early devotee of expressionism, Benn promoted an art for art's sake ideal of absolute poetry and viewed the work of art as the only indestructible object of truth. With his first book of poems, *Morgue*, Benn was considered an original voice in expressionism. Many critics feel, however, that he was most successful in his later poetry, when his expressionist technique was tempered with classical structure. Benn's clinical descriptions of death and decay reflect his lifelong experience as a practicing physician who dealt extensively with autopsies and venereal diseases. They also convey his important poetic theme: "disintegration of the self." His work understandably makes much use of medical, scientific, and anthropological jargon and theories.

Benn's personal life cannot be considered happy. His first wife died, his second wife and a mistress committed suicide, and he was estranged from his children. These personal crises were expressed in a shockingly cool and pessimistic prose in the form of an alter-ego, the character Dr. Rönne, who is thoroughly isolated and unable to communicate with others.

Benn felt that none of the traditional solutions to the problems of life were viable, and embraced primitivism as an attempt to reestablish harmony with the world. He was thus vulnerable to the primitively racist Nazi ideology, which he endorsed much to the consternation of his literary compatriots, most of whom emigrated during the Nazi regime. Benn defended his position in several published letters and essays, revealing that he sought in Nazism a regression to primal man and spontaneous action as opposed to the intellectual torpor of modern man. His defense, however, did not protect him from attacks in the Nazi press as a decadent writer. Publication of his work was banned by the Nazis in 1938 and he was not published again until after the war. Among the works released then was his autobiography, *Dopelleben*, in which he explained his acceptance and subsequent disillusionment with Nazism. *Dopelleben* won him great popularity for its reflection of the growing cynicism of the German people.

Benn's poetic theories, especially his belief that art and form were the only cultural values worth preserving, were expressed in *Probleme der Lyrik*. This work was influential among the young postwar poets, who applauded his intellectual honesty and strict adherence to apolitical artistic purity in poetry. The difficulty of effective translation has been an important factor in Benn's lack of popularity outside his country. Yet, unique in German literature, he is considered one of the great German poets since Rilke.

PRINCIPAL WORKS

Morgue und andere Gedichte (poetry) 1912
Ithaka (dramatic sketch) 1914; published in journal *Weisse Blätter*
Söhne (poetry) 1914
Gehirne (short stories) 1916
Fleisch (poetry) 1917
Spaltung (poetry) 1925
Fazit der Perspektiven (essays) 1930
Das Unaufhörliche (poetry) 1931
Nach dem Nihilismus (essays) 1932
Der neue Staat und die Intellektuellen (essays) 1933
Kunst und Macht (essays) 1934
Statische Gedichte (poetry) 1948
Drei alte Männer: Gesprache (dramatic sketches) 1949
Der Ptölemäer (novellas) 1949
Dopelleben: Zwei Selbstdarstellungen (autobiography) 1950
Fragmente: Neue Gedichte (poetry) 1951
Probleme der Lyrik (essays) 1951
Die Stimme hinter dem Vorhang (dramatic sketches) 1952
Destillationen: Neue Gedichte (poetry) 1953
Aprèslude (poetry) 1955
Gesammelte Werke in vier Bänden. Band 2: Prosa und Szenen (short stories and dramatic sketches) 1958
Gesammelte Werke in vier Bänden. Band 1: Essays, Reden, Vortrage (essays) 1959
Gesammelte Werke in vier Bänden. Band 3: Gedichte (poetry) 1960
Primal Vision: Selected Writings of Gottfried Benn (poetry, essays, dramatic sketches, and short stories) 1960
Gesammelte Werke in vier Bänden. Band 4: Autobiographische und vermischte Schriften (autobiography) 1961

FRANCIS GOLFFING   (essay date 1952)

[The poems of *Morgue* are] brutal clinical pieces, in precision of language and to some extent in imagery not unlike the early poems of Mina Loy. The rhythmic mode was a clipped free verse, handled with more than competence; the drive behind the poetry radical from the start, torturing every ounce of meaning out of a timely medium. Later a concern with sonority supervened, becoming more marked as time wore on, but the fierce earnestness, the determination to say all and say it as economically as possible, were still there. So was the nihilist's—never the cynic's, as some thought and still do—sombreness: no longer exercised on the concrete horrors of operating room and dissecting table but on the abstract shame of mankind at large, specifically the white race. The professional physician and surgeon developed into the amateur, and not wholly amateur, anthropologist, biologist, sociologist of the mature essays. Benn's poetry, while always uneven, profited not a little from the change. Scientific axioms and technological details now jostled Parmenidean or Minoan memories; primordial incantations, ultra-modern slang—and all this in stanzas whose formal beauty was nothing short of amazing, sometimes flawless; whose music was as haunting as that of [Rainer Maria] Rilke or [Stefan] George at their best.

The essays of that period (1920 to 1932) . . . proved even to the most skeptical Benn's unusual philosophical and expository gifts; and though his later prose-pieces may be considered simply as variations on certain themes stated with great power by the youth, they show no appreciable decline in either verve or acumen. There is indeed something very impressive about the constancy of these themes; also, perhaps, a touch of monomania. Practically all Benn's prose deals with the problem of biological and conceptual mutations and with man's tragic rôle in the universe; each new essay represents yet another attempt to fuse archaic and chthonic notions with the most differentiated notions of the contemporary metropolitan mind. (pp. 271-72)

I am confident that Benn's work will survive as long as there are readers to appreciate a poetry both difficult and moving; a prose that—if high-flown at times from excess of oratorical skill—manages again and again to touch bedrock. (p. 275)

Francis Golffing, "A Note on Gottfried Benn," in
Poetry (© *1952 by The Modern Poetry Association; reprinted by permission of the Editor of* Poetry), *Vol. 80, No. 4, July, 1952, pp. 271-75.*

EDGAR LOHNER   (essay date 1953)

[Benn's] work is open to comparison with that of such Anglo-American lyric-reflective writers as T. S. Eliot, Ezra Pound, W. H. Auden and Wallace Stevens. [In a footnote Lohner expands this point: With Eliot in scrupulousness of style, with Pound in scope, with Auden in formal invention and use of the vernacular, with Stevens in content (ideas on the value of poetry and expression).] (p. 39)

Between [the] two poles, scientific rigor of thinking and exactitude of thought, on the one hand, and on the other a mixture of ecstasy, biologism and "Südlichem," fall [Benn's] fundamental concerns: his idea of the absolute reality of the poem, his idea of the disintegration of pseudo-ideal European concepts and beliefs, his disavowal of history as the space within which mankind can find salvation, his concept of "regression", that is a tendency away from the mathematical and categorical towards the creative and intuitive. (p. 40)

As one of the most ruthless expressionists [Benn] laid bare pretentious modesty, perversity and morbidity. He uncovered the lemurian existence of the bourgeois and recreated what went on in cancer-wards and sanatoriums. Nearly all of Benn's early poems [*Morgue, Söhne,* and *Fleisch*] . . . were pieced together in the dissecting room, in anatomical and pathological laboratories; lyrics of medical perceptiveness, they are a collection of *documents humains,* ghastly, acid and uncanny. They . . . reveal the bestiality of our world. . . .

[The poems of *Morgue*] are the poems of a doctor-poet under whose hands hundreds of corpses have passed. . . . Man in these early poems is thought of as a nauseating, sick, dying figure, a creature of only brain and sex. . . . [These are expressionistic poems], a return to reality with a vengeance, and [are] marked by a union of naturalistic detail and impressionistic sensitivity. . . . Benn does not tire of depicting the horror and decay of modern life in images of disease, of the human garbage-pile, of rats. Undoubtedly, Benn works with hyperbole in these poems, and he does so intentionally. He is bitter. The needs of mankind in its confusion are felt most acutely and shared. Everything is brought to the lowest common denominator. Yet the cynicism and the experience of pain so obvious in these poems give evidence of his fundamental concern with the nature of man. . . . (pp. 41-2)

These early poems represent a world in which not love, sympathy and the moon-valley landscape are important, but deep perplexity about the chaotic state of the human soul. Benn is the depersonalized authority of the world of death. His words are scalpel gesticulations and expression; the transformation of strong convulsive emotions into language is his passionate instrument. (pp. 42-3)

What is this world of expression, this "Ausdruckswelt"? . . . From the nihilistic point of view, from the viewpoint of modern man asking what remains, the world of expression is set against the historical world and against the world of causality as a world of form with definitive structures.

Thus Benn sees the "Ausdruckswelt" as the only possible and real affirmation capable of persisting through change. Art is the center of things and within art the poem is the ultimate and greatest achievement and, within the poem, the word. (p. 48)

[Benn] believes that there are heuristic states of weakness in which he finds, through words, new ways of experience, new insights. Through words he comes to grips with what really matters: that a thing impinges upon us by its very character, its self-existence, without reference to any other thing. The consuming scepticism and the self-enveloping irony which Benn's incisive intelligence wreaks upon any idea are a presupposition, but they lead to a sphere of creating expression.

Philosophically speaking, the experience Benn depicts here comes very close to what Henri Bergson called the intuitive process. . . . (p. 50)

The creative act is "die Stunde, die eint," the harmonious, unifying hour with the eternal stream of life; it is the glance behind the veils where the demiurge creates and destroys the worlds. . . . [This describes], however, only the emotional-intuitive side of the creative process of establishing the world of expression. But there is also another element, which is a new and particularly characteristic quality of modern poetry that Benn calls the artistic element. . . . [It emphasizes] the necessity of the greatest possible intellectual awareness while writing. This attitude implies that observation of self, of the personality of the poet, is an element in the creative process; to paraphrase Wallace Stevens, by process of the personality we mean to select what may seem the incident of the nervous sensitiveness of the poet in the act of creating a poem and, generally speaking, the physical and mental factors that condition him as an individual. This new and decisive quality in poetry . . . is realized and seriously considered by Benn for the first time in German literature. . . . The result of this "twofold" process, the emotional-intuitive and the artistic-fabricative, is the poem, the center of Benn's "Ausdruckswelt." (pp. 50-1)

The poem that results from these insights initiates a new type of lyric poetry in German literature. It is no longer written to sing of bush, valley and moon; it does not exist to confirm moral, political or religious views and sentiments. It is amoral, it is beyond time and space. It is in itself and beyond all adjectival classifications. (p. 52)

The early Benn celebrated decay, the mere decline of the Self. The later Benn shifts the accent to what paradoxically originates from decisive awareness of decay: the poem. This poem of Benn's, the absolute form of a poem, a poem without faith, without hope, addressed to nobody, a poem made out of words, ideas, expressions, this poem may well again gain for the German poem world-wide recognition. (p. 54)

> Edgar Lohner, "The Development of Gottfried Benn's Idea of Expression as Value," in The German Quarterly (copyright © 1953 by the American Association of Teachers of German), Vol. 26, No. 1, January, 1953, pp. 39-54.

T. S. ELIOT (essay date 1953)

I shall explain at once what I mean by the "three voices" [of poetry]. The first is the voice of the poet talking to himself—or to nobody. The second is the voice of the poet addressing an audience, whether large or small. The third is the voice of the poet when he attempts to create a dramatic character speaking in verse; when he is saying, not what he would say in his own person, but only what he can say within the limits of one imaginary character addressing another imaginary character. The distinction between the first and the second voice, between the poet speaking to himself and the poet speaking to other people, points to the problem of poetic communication; the distinction between the poet addressing other people in either his own voice or an assumed voice, and the poet inventing speech in which imaginary characters address each other, points to the problem of the difference between dramatic, quasi-dramatic, and non-dramatic verse. (p. 4)

Now, what about the poetry of the first voice—that which is not primarily an attempt to communicate with anyone at all?

I must make the point that this poetry is not necessarily what we call loosely "lyric poetry". (p. 15)

It is obviously the lyric in the sense of a poem "directly expressing the poet's own thoughts and sentiments". . . . It is in this sense that the German poet Gottfried Benn, in a very interesting lecture entitled *Probleme der Lyrik,* thinks of lyric as the poetry of the first voice. . . . Where he speaks of "lyric poetry", then, I should prefer to say "meditative verse".

What, asks Herr Benn in this lecture, does the writer of such a poem, "addressed to no one", start with? There is first, he says, an inert embryo or "creative germ" . . . and, on the other hand, the Language, the resources of the words at the poet's command. He has something germinating in him for which he must find words; but he cannot know what words he wants until he has found the words; he cannot identify this embryo until it has been transformed into an arrangement of the right words in the right order. When you have the words for it, the "thing" for which the words had to be found has disappeared, replaced by a poem. . . . I agree with Gottfried Benn, and I would go a little further. In a poem which is neither didactic nor narrative, and not animated by any other social purpose, the poet may be concerned solely with expressing in verse—using all his resources of words, with their history, their connotations, their music—this obscure impulse. He does not know what he has to say until he has said it; and in the effort to say it he is not concerned with making other people understand anything. . . . He is oppressed by a burden which he must bring to birth in order to obtain relief. (pp. 16-18)

I have been speaking, for the sake of simplicity, of the three voices as if they were mutually exclusive: as if the poet, in any particular poem, was speaking *either* to himself or to others, and as if neither of the first two voices was audible in good dramatic verse. And this indeed is the conclusion to which Herr Benn's argument appears to lead him: he speaks as if the poetry of the first voice—which he considers, moreover, to be on the whole a development of our own age—was a totally different kind of poetry from that of the poet addressing an audience. But for me the voices are most often found together—the first and second, I mean, in non-dramatic poetry; and together with the third in dramatic poetry too. Even though, as I have maintained, the author of a poem may have written it primarily without thought of an audience, he will also want to know what the poem which has satisfied *him* will have to say to other people. (pp. 19-20)

> T. S. Eliot, in his The Three Voices of Poetry (originally a lecture delivered at the Central Hall, Westminster, on November 19, 1953), Cambridge University Press, 1953 (and reprinted by Cambridge University Press, 1955), 24 p.

MICHAEL HAMBURGER (essay date 1956)

[Gottfried Benn] is a solitary poet, but his awareness of being so has prevented most of his work from being pure monologue. He is like a man talking to himself in a room full of silly people, trying hard to ignore them but always irritated by their insolent scrutiny; his attitude towards them is one of aggressive self-defence. The trouble, of course, is his own self-consciousness; but since monologue is the only kind of communication which Dr. Benn thinks valid, and since he knows his self-consciousness to be incurable, he has reconciled himself to his paradoxical function, that of an *enfant terrible* as much in demand for his terrible outbursts of scorn and anger as for the aura of his self-absorption. (p. 275)

[Though] Benn has much to say of his generation and of Expressionism, Benn's later development was strongly influenced by a reaction against the excesses of the later Expressionists, and especially against that desperate optimism which took the form of political agitation: and, from the start, Dr. Benn's poetic practice differed essentially from that of all his contemporaries. (pp. 275-76)

Benn's premises go back to two definitions by Nietzsche which he is fond of quoting: "The world as an aesthetic phenomenon" and "Art as the last metaphysical activity within European nihilism." Gottfried Benn accepts this nihilism as one accepts the weather. . . . Benn believes that nihilism is the inevitable frame of mind of every contemporary European whose intellect is highly developed; but, in later years especially, he also speaks of "transcending nihilism", and this is done by setting up new values to take the place of those no longer tenable—much as Nietzsche spoke of the "revaluation of all values." At one time, the particular mode of "transcendence" which Benn recommended was a brutal vitalism; since he identified nihilism with a highly developed intellect, sometimes even with consciousness itself, the only way to "transcend" it was to glorify crude energy, to drug the conscious mind and release subconscious impulses. (pp. 276-77)

What is least clear about Benn's thought is his grounds for assuming the inevitability of nihilism in our time. The reasons he gives for this assumption have varied greatly, according to Benn's momentary pre-occupations; and they are neither consistent nor convincing. Sometimes he bases his determinism on biological factors, sometimes on psychological ones—though he tends to treat psychology as a sub-category of biology—sometimes historical. . . . The truth may well be that Benn's belief in nihilism amounts to a blind faith. Artistically, this faith permits him to travel light; to be as inconsistent as he pleases, to abandon himself to the moment, to experiment freely with words and ideas. (p. 277)

All his theories, aesthetic, metaphysical and political, derive from his sense of the disharmony between the part and the whole, inward and outward reality. (p. 278)

It is significant that Benn's first poems were concerned with an aspect of outward reality which repelled him. The bitterness of his first collection, *Morgue,* . . . was in its realism. With one exception, all these poems are a direct reaction to Benn's professional duties. The diction is coarsely colloquial, with compassionate or sentimental undertones which Benn is reluctant to admit. In most of these clinical poems he employs a loose free verse, deliberately empty of tension. . . . Disintegrating bodies . . . were the given reality [of *Morgue*], because Benn had chosen to be a doctor; but of course there was no more need for him to write about corpses than for [Georg] Trakl to write about medicine bottles or Mr. Eliot about bank balances. (pp. 278-81)

Benn's next collection, *Söhne,* is dominated by the theme of revolt that became a commonplace of the Expressionist drama: the conflict of generations, or rather the young man's complaint against the parents who stand for smugness, deceit and corruption. These poems, on the whole, are clumsy and imitative, except where Benn's vitalistic

frenzy breaks through. . . . The diction of these poems takes realism further than in *Morgue;* it brutalizes reality into caricature. . . . Most of the poems in the collections that followed *Söhne*—up to the early 'twenties—were in this vein; they are much more disgusting than Benn's studies of the dead, because the dead are less vulnerable to this pseudo-scientific mode of vision. In the collection called *Fleisch,* Benn sees human beings as so much meat which, while alive, also has the misfortune to be invested with a substance which he calls not "mind" but "brain". Since "thinking is lonely", there is no bond between one human being and another; only one's own ego is real, other people's, at best, are an abstract hypothesis. (pp. 281-83)

Benn has rarely written with any degree of sympathy about anyone but himself. (p. 286)

Strangely enough, Benn has been unable to do without the second person in his poetry. In his later poems he commonly addresses a "you" that is purely functional and therefore even more "mythical" than the form he has tried to eliminate; this later "you" is a part of Benn's own mind, the poetry a kind of schizophrenic soliloquy addressed to himself. (p. 288)

Benn's revival of the doctrine of Art for Art's sake—which he calls *"Artistik"*—is simply another aspect of his denial of "reality", of moral and political institutions, of the importance of history, of all that men achieve by conscious endeavour. (p. 293)

As for his definition of *Artistik,* it is the definition of a vicious circle; for the "general nihilism of values" which he wants Art to transcend has been largely brought about by those who—like himself—are out for the destruction of these values; it is only Benn's wholly specious determinism that allows him to regard nihilism as a biological, historical or otherwise general predicament. . . . *Artistik* is a pathetic attempt on Benn's part to climb out of the nihilistic pit which he has dug for others. (pp. 294-95)

Benn's chief limitation as a poet and critic is that nearly all his thinking is determined by a reaction against one thing or another—against literary or ideological fashions, against a bourgoisie already hard pressed from other directions or against his own better nature; but reaction is only a different sort of dependence. To be always sneering at the vulgar is a sort of vulgarity. (p. 299)

Benn's prose writings are not an exploration of other minds, but comments on his own practice and justifications of his own attitude. . . . His belief in "absolute" prose and poetry—that is, in prose and poetry written for their own sake, without a primarily didactic purpose—has had the very salutary effect of opposing the tendency . . . to think that poetry is only a matter of expressing sublime sentiments in regular stanzas. He has made up for the early Expressionists' indifference to questions of form and diction; but he has done so with an exclusive emphasis on art as self-expression—or rather as self-indulgence—which may well have repelled readers more squeamish than he.

Benn's writings are highly exhilarating and abysmally depressing in turn, as befits an intoxicant. They can induce a euphoria of infinite possibilities, which results from the total release of energy from the bonds of reason; and a corresponding hangover, when Benn returns to himself and reminds us that despair is the mother of all his inventions.

Self-pity is the chink in Benn's armour, as in Nietzsche's, who also dramatised his solitude, though with more justification than Benn; for in spite of his claim to the contrary, Benn's solitude is less extreme than Nietzsche's, if only because Nietzsche had already charted the place. (p. 300)

It is probably too early to say what will remain of Benn's work.... Almost every one of his collections contain pieces that are not only grossly inferior to his best work, but simply unformed—cerebral jottings in loose free verse or mechanical rhyme that all too clearly communicate something—Benn's concern with his own ego or with ideas not realized poetically. (p. 301)

The poems of Benn's best period, the early 'twenties, are almost consistently remarkable; but only two or three of them are faultless. The difference has to do with truth as much as with style; for the fault is always due to the intrusion of irrelevant ideas and inessential phenomena into a poem that ought to have been purely imaginative; and these ideas and phenomena always appertain to Benn's immediate environment. The most blatant of these faults is the introduction of abstract neologisms and scientific terms—witty, and therefore self-conscious—where they have no business to occur.... Benn's most outstanding collection of poems [is] his *Spaltung*.... Of the 28 poems in this book, only one is wholly free from such satirical irrelevances; and one or two more are successful in spite of them, because the tension between myth and modernity is essential to them.

These poems, unfortunately, are untranslatable, precisely because they are the nearest possible approximation to Benn's ideal of "absolute poetry".... Benn has never written with greater mastery than at this time and in this medium—poems in trochaic or sprung rhythms, in short lines with alternating feminine and masculine rhymes.... Benn summed up his purpose at the time in the phrase *trunken cerebral,* (drunkenly cerebral); his poems break down where they become cerebral without being drunken. (pp. 302-03)

Statische Gedichte, a collection of poems written mainly between 1937 and 1947, contains poems in at least three distinct styles: the incantatory style of *Palau,* a more sober neo-classical style—sometimes clearly derivative from Goethe's later lyrics, as in the poem *Ach, der Erhabene*—and a self-consciously "modern" style mainly confined to poems in loose free verse. These three styles recur in Benn's more recent collections. (p. 307)

Of Benn's three styles in his collections of the 'fifties, the one best suited to what he now has to say is the neo-classical, a neutral, impersonal style almost wholly purged of modernist idiosyncracies; all the best poems in *Fragmente* and *Destillationen* belong to this category. These poems contradict the theories which Benn continues to expound. (p. 310)

The modernist poems in free verse, on the other hand, read like jottings from a private note-book. Whereas Benn could once afford to throw away poetry disguised as prose, he now reverses the process: part of the poem *Spät* (in *Destillationen*) corresponds word for word with a [prose] passage in *Die Stimme Hinter dem Vorhang.* These poems are feeble because they render undigested phenomena and fragments of personal experience rejected by the imagination.... Under the cover of this and similar exercises in free verse, Benn has been quietly retreating from modernism; since the battle is already over—as Benn has proved by writing real poems in a neo-classical style, poems like *Der Dunkle, Jener* and *Eingeengt*—there is little point in exposing the ineffectiveness of the stratagem. (pp. 310-11)

[Benn] has written the "six or eight consummate poems" which he believes to be all a contemporary poet can achieve; and, more often than not, even his failures have the fascination of uninhabitable regions. (p. 312)

Michael Hamburger, "Gottfried Benn" (1956), in his Reason and Energy: Studies in German Literature *(reprinted by permission of Grove Press, Inc.; copyright © 1957 by Grove Press, Inc.), Grove Press, 1957, pp. 275-312.*

WALTER H. SOKEL (essay date 1959)

[Next] to Kafka probably the greatest and most influential Expressionist [is Gottfried Benn]. (p. 89)

[Whereas] Rimbaud, the Surrealists, and Expressionists like [Georg Trakl, Stefan Heym, and] Kafka emphasize the image or dreamlike scene as the building stone of their compositions, [Stéphane] Mallarmé, [Paul] Valéry, T. S. Eliot, Benn, and the Expressionists of the *Sturm* circle make the single word (in Benn's case a noun like "Ithaca," for example), and the universe of associations buried in its sound effects and multiple meanings, the basic unit of their "magic." ... In Benn's poetry the *parole essentielle* of Mallarmé assumes the place of the *image essentielle* of the visionary Expressionists.... Benn's finest poems, like "Die Dänin" ("The Danish Girl") or "Das verlorene Ich" ("The Lost Self") consist of strategic nouns (not strategic metaphors as in the visionary poetry of Trakl and Kafka), strung together in musical compositions. The basic chords of these compositions are cultural associations and evocations rather than dreamlike metaphors. This method connects Benn with T. S. Eliot. Both produce poetic effects by means of a highly Alexandrian learning, an Alexandrianism that the title of Benn's chief prose work, *The Ptolemaic,* deliberately underlines. Benn's word "Ithaca" is an early example of his method. This single noun evokes, like Eliot's quotations and allusions, a whole world of cultural, historical, mythological, and literary associations for poet and reader. Yet despite its learned connotations, it is a "magic word," a *parole essentielle* in Mallarmé's sense. It achieves the same kind of hypnotic and concentrated effect as the dreamlike metaphoric visualizations of Kafka or Trakl. Its use and effect are musical. It evokes a magic contrast, a counterpoint of bliss and freedom to the main theme, the wretchedness and frustration of the "brain-eaten" modern self. If properly used, the single noun acts like an incantation. It enables the poet to conjure an atavistic surreality which redeems him from his monstrous modernity. (pp. 92-3)

His method of evoking a magic surreality by richly connotative words like "Ithaca," although already encompassing a much greater range of cultural-social reality than the private dreamlike images of Trakl and Kafka, evolved in his later period much further in the direction of an Alexandrian poetry of learned allusions and so arrived, completely independent of them, at the kind of intellectual poetry practiced by Eliot and Pound. However, ... Benn ironically offsets, and thereby underscores, with the lilting melody of his verse, the harsh and bitter dissonances produced by the cultural-historical contrasts which he evokes in his poems. (p. 113)

[The] whole history of civilization serves him now as hospital and morgue had served him in the beginning. Spirit and form have remained the same: the evocation of the fundamental dissonance of existence witnessed and recorded by an agonized, impotent, and cynical consciousness. This poetry is at once ironic and elegiac; and this combination, plus Alexandrian learning and musical artistry, relates Benn to Eliot, a kinship which Eliot acknowledged when he paraphrased Benn at length in his "Three Voices of Poetry" [see excerpt above]. . . . Benn, who, unlike Eliot, cannot find his way back to tradition of Church and country, raises his own "pure form," his own process of formulation and expression, to the Absolute and source of salvation.

Creation, according to Benn, is nothing but the concentrated effort to conceal one's despair. (pp. 113-14)

The concept of "constructive mind" with which Benn seeks to overcome nihilism is nothing else but the principle of artistic creation. However, Benn's concept of art has nothing in common with the traditional view of art as representation of reality or as a confession of experience. . . . The type of art of which Benn thinks is not the psychological novel or the drama of individual characters; he rejects "psychological complications, causality, milieu-tracing." The ideal art which he envisions has no content; it is nothing but form. It is to embody the complete triumph of mental organization over the resistance of matter. The raw material, the "data" given by nature—and nature includes human nature—should be sucked up and made to disappear in the formal structure of the work. . . . The "constructive mind" thinks only in functional terms. Facts, things, feelings, and persons do not exist for it in their own right, but only as parts in a working relationship to other parts. Even as content gives way to form, the concept of "being" yields to the concept of "functioning." This is the Expressionist ideal of the "desubstantivation of the world" . . . which Benn formulated and elaborated with a consistency and tenacity lacking in the other Expressionists. Substance is transferred into process and function; the noun bows to the verb; content becomes method; active *expression* replaces passive *experience*. With these ideas, German Expressionism is completely at one with European modernism. The theories of . . . [the *Sturm* poets and] Benn cannot be distinguished from those of [Vasili] Kandinsky or Valéry. This kinship allows us to see the modernist "musicalization of the arts" in a new light. (pp. 115-16)

Walter H. Sokel, "The Thorn of Socrates," in his The Writer in Extremis: Expressionism in Twentieth-Century German Literature *(copyright © 1959 by the Board of Trustees of the Leland Stanford Junior University; with the permission of the publishers, Stanford University Press), Stanford University Press, 1959, pp. 83-118.**

W. D. SNODGRASS (essay date 1961)

Reading Gottfried Benn for the first time, I am startled to find myself interested not in his poetry, but in his prose—and interested not because of its success, but because of the meaning of its failures. Insofar as I can understand German poetry, which isn't far, Benn's poetry seems suc-

cessful but not very interesting; not as good, say, as Eliot; perhaps as good as Pound. . . .

The prose is another matter. Nearly all these essays are, in some sense, autobiographical; they all attack, philosophically, anthropologically, literarily, or politically the problems of meaninglessness and vacancy which permeated his thought—because they dogged and determined his life.

There was a curious emptiness and degradation to his career. . . . His early poetry concerns the physical decay he saw as a young physician; his early prose, a corresponding intellectual and psychological decomposition. (p. 118)

The problem which (in one disguise or another) constantly dogged Benn's life and thought, which gives him a crucial place in our intellectual history, was a deep distrust of substance, an open disbelief in the reality of matter. . . .

Benn was born just at the time when matter (or, sometimes, metaphorically, "substance") was being broken down into energy: first by the painters, like Manet, Van Gogh, Matisse; by the poets, like Rimbaud (whose objects are not only surcharged with energy, but in the process, lose their identity as objects); by the musicians like Debussy (who dissolves the solid matter of form and tonality into a vague and luminous energy not unlike that of Monet), and by the more savagely energetic atonalists. (p. 119)

It is his relation to this dissolution of matter which makes Benn's work so interesting. For the fact is that he never believed in the reality of matter, the solidity of substance. Never did a sense of unreality leave him. . . .

This distrust of external reality is intimately interwoven with a distrust of Nature, a preference for the city and the artificial. . . . The artificial, however, may [also] mean the conceptual. . . . (p. 120)

The same feeling may be expressed by what Benn, somewhat inconsistently, calls "nihilism":

> This is the law: Nothing is, if anything ever was; nothing will be. . . . There is nothing that can be turned into reality.

This last statement, though, is subject to an ambiguity: art, as we shall see later, can and does turn this nothing into a something, into a reality. . . . (p. 121)

[In] the place of vacuum, he proposed (as did many artists of his generation) to erect art. Again and again, he declared that art is the only thing that will create form, the only real reality. . . . Finally, art is not only to replace substance in the world, but negation (the rejection of substance) becomes a way of reaching art. . . . That, of course, is somewhat shaky reasoning: there is no matter unless we create art; also, we must reject matter to create art. Benn's thought on such matters has much, also, of the god-creator sort of *hubris* so common in such esthetic theories. . . .

Yet inside this world of creation, Benn did excel and created much. And for one who refused to recognize it, he certainly crammed his essays full of external reality. One strikes on passage after passage of most brilliantly captured physical detail. . . . (p. 122)

Like most of the poets of his generation—Pound, Eliot—Benn shows that longing for the past, for myths, the church, the State, for some external authority. As soon as he found it, he rebelled against it. Yet he did not really rebel: rather he stayed in Berlin, in the Army, and complained. . . .

This conflict led, as Benn knew only too well, to an abrupt split in his life—a complete dichotomy between act and belief. (p. 124)

[It] is scarcely chance that placed Gottfried Benn in Berlin; he chose to stay and serve a group of men he recognized as idiots and monsters. Now, however, he pretends that there was no choice, to excuse himself for not choosing what would have been difficult. For like the Beats, what he wants is, over and over, to put himself at the mercy of those very authorities he abominates; to return again and again to Berlin, or to the Army.

Thus, in his "defense of error" what he defends is not his own actions, his refusal to emigrate, or even his right to error, but his passivity. He merely recognizes that he would do the same again. For, in his wishful thinking, he simply will not credit the outside world; he will flee again and again to the city of his childhood or to those parental institutions against whose nylon fur he can burrow in and dream an existence for himself. . . . Small wonder Benn has become popular. And with readymade dreams so available (here's the paper, there's the television), why should any of us bother with thought at all? (p. 126)

> W. D. Snodgrass, "Gottfried Benn: The Dissolution of Matter," in The Hudson Review (copyright © 1961 by The Hudson Review, Inc.; reprinted by permission), Vol. XIV, No. 1, Spring, 1961, pp. 118-26.

IAN HILTON (essay date 1964)

Gehirne, [Benn's first attempt in prose] written 1915-16 in the period of Benn's military experiences in Brussels, is a short story collection of an autobiographical nature recording the loss and destruction of "reality" as experienced by the central character, a Dr. Rönne. (p. 132)

Rönne has a desire to contact man, envying the ordinary man his ability to communicate even on trivialities, and going to great lengths to get included into the social circle. . . . [His] problem is one of excessive cerebralism. For theoretical mentality cannot attain spontaneous communication. . . . Rönne, with his disintegrated personality, with his hatred of the "Self" . . . has to query every fresh experience he undergoes. It is a mechanical process which leads to reverie and isolation (as for example in the barber's shop episode in *Die Eroberung*). (p. 133)

Reason is useless, Benn argues, for it only leads to a "dead terrain" and banalisation of the world. Consequently he longs for primal vision as a radical reaction to cerebralism, seeking contact with a deeper layer of life. The struggle for reality becomes in effect that between the outer world of consciousness and the inner world of the unconscious. And in this struggle the dream becomes a means of communication. For although a dream may be an illogical sequence (but: "nur das Sinnlose ist Realität", writes Benn elsewhere), it provides a form of security and at the same time a freedom from frustration and the fulfilment of erotic desires (all in all Benn shows himself to be aware of Freud's interpretation of dreams). . . . The dream is a trance of forgetting and longing. The South offers him bliss, colour and excitement; the warmth of the sun, the scent of flowers, the blue of the sea—ethereal blue providing, as it were, a form

of transcendence of harsh reality on the one hand, and on the other an affirmation of life. This "southern complex" is a continually recurrent theme in Benn's work; one need but think of the well-known poems *Palau* or *D-Zug,* or in prose of the Rönne stories. (pp. 133-34)

Dreams may give Rönne confidence, but happiness is only fleeting and the tensions of the mind are relieved but momentarily. This southern complex is a substitute reality, it is not reality. . . . Rönne, however, is forced back to the harshness of real life, and with this comes the admittance of defeat. . . . In the end the doctor sinks back into apathy, unable or unwilling to do anything constructive about anything because of his disintegrated personality. (pp. 134-35)

The fear of progressive cerebration is very great and is one which besets Benn's heroes. . . . The murder of the professor in *Ithaka* is seen as a way to regeneration from this progressive cerebration. But this more "positive" approach as hinted at in *Ithaka* is far from maintained in Benn's immediately subsequent writings, as has been seen. Indeed, what one finds really is a gradual change from vitalism to an intellectual abstraction. (p. 135)

[The poems of *Statische Gedichte*] represent something permanent against the decline and fall of man. Each poem is static because it appears as a complete image or work of art, static because, although it may well be stylistically dynamic, it has a form which is objective and is to be contrasted with the senseless process of perpetual change in life. This basic hatred of change and its futility has caused Benn to seek something which is lasting. Thus he seeks "Sein" (the static), not "Werden" (the process of change). Hence his love of the archaic world, his longing to return to the amoeba. . . . Hence his love of the sea and of darkness. Benn likes the city because it is real and concrete, something he can cling to in the transience of life. Thus can one begin to understand phrases which abound in Benn's writing like: "Kunst ist statisch" and "Kunst ist Sein im Strom des Vergehens". (pp. 138-39)

But any "message" that one thinks to find here in the work is certainly not directed at man in general. Benn is the isolated artist who is writing for himself, expressing his own thoughts and sentiments, addressing no one or nothing other than his own mind. . . . Benn's art is his personal answer to the loss of communication with the substance. He denies the necessity of viewing and interpreting art politically and socially. . . . (pp. 140-41)

Benn commenced his literary activities as an Expressionist and critics have been wont to declare that he remained an Expressionist throughout his career. This is important in the sense that Expressionism started off after all as a movement of style rather than of content . . . and throughout Benn has been solely concerned with the method of expression. . . . As for Baudelaire, so too for Benn does art act as a counter to the world around, not just as an idealisation or imitation of it. Benn is not interested in presenting in his work pure description of milieu, for example, or psychological problems. He has no wish to express the obvious. And so Benn's prose is not merely a logical sequence of words in the generally accepted fashion, but becomes, as it were, a series of newspaper headlines . . . , to correspond to the accelerated tempo of life. There is a condensation of language to the bare essentials (one of his verse collections is entitled *Destillationen*), which creates an air of allusiveness as part of the technique of implication and demands from the reader both the power of concentration and interpretation to appreciate the tremendous thought associations (which have a special beauty in their richness) implied in just one word. . . .

For Benn the individual word is the key to inspiration and the world of expression, the basis of his style. . . . (p. 142)

The matter of key words existing in Benn's work corresponds to his interesting innovations in style as seen, for example, in the novel form. The novel for Benn is not one logical sequence of events and thoughts, as normally encountered, but is seen as something fragmentary. . . . The process involved Benn describes in *Absolute Prosa:* he calls the ''novel'' a ''sequence of factually and psychologically disconnected parts'' and it is built up ''in the shape of an orange'', by which he means that the individual segments have a separate being as they stand side by side, yet at the same time they all tend to the centre, to the ''existential''. . . . And so, since there are no real characters, there is not much action as such either in the prose or in the dramatic sketches. The characters in these works, characters like Rönne and Pameelen, are not really convincing people of flesh and blood who ''develop''. Rather are they to be considered as types, mouthpieces for Benn himself. . . . It is no chance, incidentally, that Benn should readily turn to the essay form in the way and to the extent that he does, for although the essay may be written more with an audience in mind, yet is it closely bound to the personality of the essayist himself and so comes near to the monologue.

But behind all this innovation of form and experimentation in language that one encounters in Benn's work, the note of deliberateness is to be observed throughout. . . . Benn's mastery of this is evident from a survey of his literary production. Style and language match the mood of the content throughout. . . . [For example] the longing for order in life in *Gesänge* is complemented by Benn's application of a regular rhyme and metrical pattern. . . . The same diversity of approach is likewise evident in Benn's prose which overall can be seen as a kaleidoscope of countless allusions and streams of consciousness and intellectual dissertations with learned references; a so-called montage-art of visionary and cerebral sequences in a prose ranging from journalistic jargon and slang . . . to lyrical dynamism. . . . (pp. 143-44)

Undeniably Benn is a complex character to understand because of paradoxes inherent in his nature and his work. He is a creative artist and a theoretical programmatic writer, but it is far more rewarding to read his imaginative works than his critical writings. For Benn is an erratic thinker. He is the artist who demands the retention of his independence, yet at the same time wishes for a measure of identification with and acceptance by his fellow beings. . . . He is the person who, while supposedly seeking the complete loss of ''Self'', is wholly preoccupied with his personal position. (pp. 144-45)

And this stark dichotomy appears throughout Benn's work, in the way that the brain and intellect is suddenly countered by flights of fancy to the South, or myth is treated in scientific terms; in the contrast of the concepts of time and timelessness, the conscious and the unconscious; in the individual words: Schutt, Chaos, Trümmer, Hirn, Geist, as against Süden, Meer, Rausch, Traum, Leben. (p. 145)

Benn, therefore, is to be seen as an exciting innovator whose prose (as well as his verse, for which he is at present better known) will stand the test of time. (p. 146)

Ian Hilton, ''Gottfried Benn,'' in German Men of Letters, Vol. III, *edited by Alex Natan (© 1964 Oswald Wolff (Publishers) Limited), Oswald Wolff, 1964, pp. 129-50.*

M. R. TOWNSON   (essay date 1966)

It is possible to distinguish three categories of montage in Benn's lyric; firstly there is *collage,* secondly the mixing of vocabulary taken from different spheres and thirdly the introduction of foreign words. (p. 157)

Strictly speaking, collage is a term taken from the pictorial arts, and it can be regarded as the pictorial equivalent of montage. . . . In its application to poetry the word is taken here to describe a . . . process whereby the poet takes not single words, expressions or concepts and joins them together . . . , but varied episodes, facts and the description of complete events from a variety of sources which are in some way relevant to the central theme of the poem, and joins these together, the only link between them often being simply their relevance to the central subject or in the associations which the poet attaches to them. . . .

[An example of this technique is the poem *1886* from *Doppelleben.*] The poem is . . . intended to give a picture of the world in 1886, which, if one is expecting a reasonably composite chronicle, is precisely what it does not do. It consists of a series of random facts and events joined together piecemeal. (p. 158)

Altogether the poem presents nearly forty events arranged for the most part in an arbitrary manner, and at the end one is not really left any the wiser about the year 1886 than one was at the beginning of the poem: most of the information given is of dubious significance, and any piece of news which might be important has its importance reduced by being placed in a banal context.

This being the case, what is the reason for Benn's use of the collage technique? It is suggested that, particularly in view of the material Benn has employed, his intention was firstly to show that the year 1886 was of no particular importance and, by extension from this, to show further what little regard he had for formal history anyway.

This impression is conveyed by two means: firstly by the actual choice of material employed and secondly by the style and structure of the poem, which in this case makes no attempt to form any kind of meaningful pattern or give an overall picture. Thus the style of the poem, particularly the fragmentation of the material, plays a large part in carrying the idea which the poet wishes to present. (p. 159)

[A quite different example is the poem *Chaos.*] As the title might already lead one to suspect, this poem presents a complete disintegration of normal syntactic structure and also of logical thought patterns. It is impossible to observe any unity behind the poem, whether of theme or syntactic structure. In the forty lines of the poem there are only eleven main verbs, three of which are imperatives, of which two are joined together in one phrase, and one of which is in a question. As for the others, none of the thoughts they express is logically developed—the sentences in which they are placed remain fragmentary. They often have no connexion with the preceding or succeeding sentence; in one particular section a sentence is even split by the insertion of the first half of a parallel sentence, which in its turn is split by the second half of the original sentence. . . . (p. 164)

Despite the chaotic style and arrangement of material, however, this poem fits into a strict formal pattern. It is composed of four eight-line stanzas, the stanzas being cross-rhymed. In addition a frame is set round the poem by the final four lines being a slight variation on the first four lines, and sharing the same rhyme scheme. Although there is a dissolution of logical thought and speech patterns the poem is subjected to the poetic discipline of rhyme and consistent stanza structure. The collage technique is not, therefore, as arbitrary and haphazard as it might seem, but does in fact still require discipline on the part of the artist. Furthermore, there is a system of order and form which can survive and contain a collapse of conventional syntax. (p. 165)

[Benn also makes use of effects based upon the mixture of vocabulary.] Under this heading come instances where words and phrases taken from different levels of vocabulary and style are used in conjunction with each other; there could, for example, be a juxtaposition of slang terms and mythical references. . . . The question here is more one of a single stylistic feature than of the poem as a complete and total formal entity. (p. 168)

[Benn also utilizes a third montage technique, the insertion of] foreign words into his verses. The foreign word obviously stands out very clearly from its German surroundings and thus provides an extreme example of the mixture of vocabulary from a variety of different spheres, for these alien insertions are truly alien as they are taken from a foreign language. (p. 173)

[There] are two main reasons for Benn's use of foreign words in his lyric. The first is that foreign words are used either because there is no German equivalent or because the equivalent German term does not convey the same impression as the foreign word, and the second that by using foreign words or phrases, even where there is a corresponding German equivalent, he can create a certain atmosphere or effect. In both these categories foreign words are used for a definite stylistic purpose and not just for show or affectation. (pp. 173-74)

By his use of the collage technique and also, to a lesser extent, by the mixture of vocabulary, Benn forges new linguistic links and relationships, in the operation of which association plays an important part. In so doing he makes the arrangement of his material carry great expressive power. . . . The new linguistic patterns and systems which he forms represent a turning-away from conventional grammatic and syntactic relationships and the attempt to form a new mode of language in which the language pattern is dictated by the poem and the poet and not arbitrarily imposed from outside.

Benn also manages to transcend conventional linguistic usage by simultaneously using vocabulary taken from a variety of spheres. The main artistic effect achieved, however, is an accuracy and fineness of expression and the ability to achieve special linguistic effects, both of which are shown particularly well in the case of foreign words. In *Probleme der Lyrik* Benn regarded poetic language as having a national character and limitation, with seemingly

equivalent words in different languages carrying different associations and shades of meaning. He is, however, prepared to go outside the bounds of his own language to incorporate these subtleties of meaning. Also, by using a foreign language for its quality of foreignness Benn achieves certain special effects which would have been impossible had he kept solely to German. . . . (p. 180)

> *M. R. Townson, "The Montage-Technique in Gottfried Benn's Lyric," in* Orbis Litterarum, *Vol. 21, No. 1, 1966, pp. 154-80.*

MARION ADAMS (essay date 1969)

[From the time Benn] began to publish in 1910 he had tried to establish principles of thought which would support the practice of his art. Theoretical passages accompany, form part of, and predate his poetry and novellas. . . .

Benn always insisted on the organic basis of thought and art, and he was inclined to look for the source of consciousness and psychic events in sensations and physical states. He also assumed initially the existence of substance.

Substance is defined as a permanent, independent, irreducible substratum underlying changes in time and space. (p. 7)

As a consequence of his persistent physicalism Benn always stressed links between art and organic life. (p. 29)

Highly physical too is his much-admired image of the poet as a type of sea-urchin, which he advanced in 1923 and quoted in his address "Probleme der Lyrik". . . . The poet's sensitivity to language is compared with the capillary hairs by which a lower-order sea creature apprehends its world. . . . (p. 31)

In what has been described as his primarily physicalist system, which stresses identities between thought and basic biological organization, Benn found it easier to account for sameness than for difference or change. If life and human consciousness are explicable in terms of cells and cell patterns, the variety of life and experience requires explanation. . . . Throughout his writing he brings forward several principles, including some irrational principles, to explain change, movement and events in thought and life. (p. 32)

[Most] of the possibilities that Benn raised to explain in a large way organization and movement in the world depend on the dynamism introduced by Hegel into metaphysics. Hegel asserted change as reality, and as in no way inferior to permanence, and established negation as the main driving force in thought.

These two closely-related ideas are basic to Benn's writing. He came increasingly to identify intellect with analysis by negation. . . .

Benn is thus provided with proper licence for the strong flow which has been so often noted in his poetry. He sometimes invokes this dynamism directly as an abstract, as well as reflecting it in the movement of the verse. . . . (p. 34)

Benn also sometimes shows flux as an inner reality, an inward "melody" and a sustaining psychological force. . . . Here, as wherever flux is understood as the stream of experiences and memories that enriches consciousness, it is synthesizing and positive. . . . In [the poem] "Ein See" he thinks of the constant renewal of a lake from rivers, and connects this with human tears, which also flow endlessly but become part of the natural flux and are in a sense preserved in it. . . . (pp. 35-6)

Despair over transience and incoherence is a consequence of Benn's principle of flux, just as despair over mortality is a consequence of his stress on the biological basis of thought. Flux tends to break down into universal anarchy, acceptance of which means the abandonment of thought. Benn could and did say that he was a nihilist, and that chaos is what the universe is like, but an active thinker like Benn will propose other solutions. (pp. 36-7)

The main theory of change that Benn found at hand around 1910 was *Entwicklung,* a concept of slow and steady growth that can include a certain amount of interruption, decline and violence, but thinks in terms of a more stable larger process, and is optimistic because it seems to have time on its side. . . . Benn was not satisfied with it, and [his ideas of flux, rhythm, recurrence, mutation and catastrophe] are attempts to find alternatives. (p. 49)

Because Benn wrote on the whole at a high level of generality, he naturally had to group and arrange ideas and facts. But the way he did this points once again to the materialist basis of his thought and its latent determinism. All too often he binds achievement and attitudes to constitution, sex, race and to what he sees as intellectual types. He also divides mankind rather too readily into fixed categories.

He was always inclined to limit intellectual possibilities according to sex. In his early poems and novellas women represent a relaxed warm animality, they are associated with odours, flowers and the dance, and because of their close contact with universal flux their role in thought is the path they provide for men to achieve insights about reality. . . . In these years Benn often represents alert consciousness as a state of misery which women are spared and from which sex offers an escape. But he could also evaluate consciousness and masculinity differently. . . . Benn's affirmation of mind is not a late development, as we are so often told by his critics; identified as a masculine principle it was always there.

In the 'twenties and 'thirties he occasionally refers to the man's special grasp of cosmic events and of fatality. . . . [In the long poetic work *Das Unaufhörliche* the man represents science and learning] and is opposed to the woman as an anti-life principle, and capable of nihilism as woman is not. . . . This masculine intellectuality is described as a fragile human achievement endangered by the preference within organic life for female or bi-sexual forms. . . . (pp. 53-5)

After 1940, however, Benn's attitude towards women in his writings is less reactionary and more conciliatory. His essay "Pallas" of 1943 even uses a female figure, Pallas Athena, as a symbol of the intellectual qualities he admires —clarity, objectivity, aggressiveness, and contempt for uncritical affirmation of the life-force. . . . His essay "Feminismus", also written about this time, is an even more generous tribute, because here he equates the social dominance of women with certain periods of high culture. (p. 56)

Benn's primitivism is the historical counterpart of his metaphysic. Just as he assumed that a material or psychic substance should exist to account for the world or for thought, and that the loss of these had resulted in nihilism, so he also believed that human life and intellectual effort had been intact at some point in the past, compared with which the present represents decline.

The intention of Benn's primitivism is not only anti-modernist but anti-materialistic. He enlisted primitivism against optimistic 19th-century evolutionary theories, as well as against aspects of his own society. But just as his thought remained in a number of respects tied to materialism, he was unaware too that modern primitivism starts from and constantly relates itself to materialistic assumptions, such as a marked biological monism. (p. 84)

Benn was not a nationalist primitivist. He did not romanticize the Germanic past, or the peasant, or the German landscape, or any form of humble or low life. There are one or two bows in this direction in his publications of 1933 and 1934, which however also contain some criticism of this tendency, and in his subsequent private writings it is satirized. He was not a moral primitivist, with a special response to virtues like innocence and candour. He was not a political primitivist; in fact he rejected political nihilism and anarchism, even certain idealistic aspects of democracy, because of their Rousseauistic, anti-institutionalist basis. In his controversy with the Marxists around 1930 he appears as a realist like George Orwell, although even gloomier about the prospects for society.

Benn's primitivism takes three main forms: first, what was called earlier his organic fundamentalism; secondly, his evocation of certain sorts of landscape; thirdly, his interest in 'the primitive mind' and its achievements. (pp. 86-7)

[Organic fundamentalism is a concern with the reversion to lower-order matter and] is part of the subject of Benn's poem . . . "Fleisch". To aid human regression even below the animal level, which is too painfully advanced along the organic scale, he imagines the eyes stitched and the brain removed and replaced by . . . vegetable matter. . . . [Benn's sensational opening poem in his first collection, "Kleine Aster" in *Morgue,*] in which organs are cut from a body and replaced by a flower, is no doubt another example of this inversion of values on the organic scale. Nietzsche had argued that we should not assume the superiority of one level of organic life over another, or even of organic over inorganic forms, which have at least superior durability. . . . (p. 88)

Because Benn started from the idea of substance, and always had it in mind, even if only often to criticize it, he was inclined to think of unity and uniformity as primal, and of difference, division and individuation as later developments. This is a common idea, in which metaphysics overlaps with creation myths which describe individual things and beings as emerging from an original flux. (pp. 88-9)

Primitivism meant therefore to Benn, as he was quite well aware, recovery of an original undifferentiated totality. (p. 89)

Benn's early exoticism includes the conventional German response to the Mediterranean south, with the difference that the sea, islands and beaches are more important than the usual tributes to Italian cities, with their cultural associations; and Benn's response is strongest to an archaic Mediterranean landscape, sometimes containing bacchantes or ritual processions but more often solitary, deserted of people. . . .

The anti-social, or at least anti-urban character of Benn's

primitivism is more marked in his non-Mediterranean landscapes. (p. 93)

Benn's final preference was for the South Seas rather than the Mediterranean world. In his essay "Dorische Welt" . . . he magnifies the archaic Dorian as against the Attic contribution, but points to the brutality and treachery endemic in all Greek civilization. . . . The whole post-Doric Mediterranean world, he says, is degenerate; the true aesthetic source is now the Pacific. . . .

A lasting aspect of Benn's primitivism was his belief that early man had a certain sort of mind and a certain valuable effortless harmonious relation to the world which today only primitive peoples have retained. . . .

The concept is due to the convergence around 1910 of three areas of study: depth psychology; prehistory and palaeontology; and anthropology and comparative religion. The synthesizers whose works Benn knew best were Freud, Jung, and the French scholar Lucien Lévy-Brühl. (p. 99)

These modern descriptive studies reinforced the sceptical relativism that Benn found argued for on other grounds by Nietzsche.

They also reinforced his indifference to ethics. As he said several times in his last years, humanitarian ideals are not universal among primitive peoples or even in high cultures. . . . The only social role that Benn would therefore ever admit for the artist was special concentration on the memories of the race. . . . (pp. 104-05)

What is behind primitivism then, or what it leads to, is nihilism. There is the same relation between primitivism and nihilism as between materialism and nihilism. Materialism assumes an underlying substance, primitivism assumes intact substance in the past; and the result of the assumption in each case is nihilism. Benn himself declared that the dependence of modern artists on the primitive world is a consequence of nihilism. (p. 107)

Benn's theory of art is altogether a logical development from nihilism of substance. It makes out of art a shell or husk from which substance is progressively abstracted. But since he understands this husk also as a timeless sphere separate from flux in nature and in man, he is able to be both a primitivist, castigating modern decline, and a modernist, championing formalism and on the whole excepting art from the general decline.

However, in this scheme art too seems frail and threatened, and is a rather precarious absolute. Inevitably, Benn prophesies the end of art. (pp. 128-29)

There is a corresponding slackness in some of Benn's poetry. In the 'thirties he began to write some very accomplished but academic poems: "Astern", "Anemone", "V. Jahrhundert", "Welle der Nacht" are examples. They are among his most popular poems and represent him in some anthologies. Interpretations of the last two poems have appeared which make them out as something like the summit of Benn's achievement. But they are conventional in their reverential attitude towards classical Greece and in their symbolism. They could be by some other poet; it did not take Benn at his best to write them. (pp. 129-30)

[The] early and lasting basis of Benn's thought is materialism, against which he was however from an early point in reaction. Although in violent opposition to much 19th-cen-

tury thought Benn retained and was in some respects confined by some of its assumptions. (p. 147)

The three main counter-movements to materialism in which he involved himself were vitalism, primitivism, and formalism. Vitalism admitted unpredictability and an irrationally creative chaos. It thus provided an alternative to any deterministic scheme and also to Kant's rational metaphysic of nature. But Benn was somewhat contemptuous of its glorification of life forms and the life force. Primitivism enriched Benn's poetry and prose with expanded perspectives in space and time, expressed mainly as an intense response to remote landscapes. It also provided him with an ideal type of thought against which modern achievement could be satirically measured. This primitivism merged with Benn's physicalism, because it located recollections of the remote past in the brain structure of modern man, and put a positive value on low-level states of consciousness which could be provoked physically. Formalism took Benn farthest from his early organic bias.

There is no clear chronology for these various positions. One cannot say that in any year or period Benn changed over or shifted emphasis from preoccupation with biological substance to preoccupation with non-organic forms. His attitudes were fixed by about 1916, and included primitivism and formalism as well as the physicalist bias evident earlier in "Gespräch". (p. 148)

Benn can be put alongside the other great German poets of the 20th century, who are Brecht, Trakl, Mombert and Else Lasker-Schüler. No poet writing in English in this century has achieved the rank of any of these. (p. 149)

> *Marion Adams, in her* Gottfried Benn's Critique of Substance, *Van Gorcum & Comp. N.V., Dr. H. J. Prakke & H.M.G. Prakke, 1969, 156 p.*

J. M. RITCHIE (essay date 1972)

Benn has rarely if ever been read for purely aesthetic reasons. This is not surprising for his poetry was rarely absolute and his essays never. In fact his work constantly forces the reader to confront the problem of ideology and art. He is after all a reflective poet like Eliot, Pound and Yeats, all of whom have at various times raised similar obstacles to appreciation. What is the reader's proper approach to the work of a poet of whose religious, political and philosophical ideas he strongly disapproves? None of the poets named raise the issue as clearly as Benn, for none of them was associated with a political movement so brutally mindless as National Socialism. Certainly in Germany Benn was the only poet who raised such issues. (p. 36)

What made the ideological conflict so acute was the presence of Brecht in Berlin. In effect the battles of the thirties between nihilism and dialectical materialism were still being fought in the fifties round the figures of Benn and Brecht. These two men seemed a key to the mentality of a divided Germany, and reading them together showed not only how far apart they were both ideologically and aesthetically, but also how close they were in so many respects. . . . Similarities between Benn and Brecht were, of course, not always immediately apparent for both produced highly individual theories and critical terminology which were often greater barriers than they were aids to comprehension. However, similarities there were, not least in their mutual obsession with the problem of alienation. Brecht, of course, is famous for his simple poetry and use of popular art forms, while Benn is notorious for his formalism and linguistic obscurity. Yet they meet in their shared fondness for colloquial speech and aphoristic conciseness and precision. Both share the Expressionist generation's fascination with all things Chinese and in their poetry constantly strive after Chinese simplicity and wisdom. And with both poets it is impossible to remain unaware of the basic philosophy which informs their poetry. Benn's nihilism is as inescapable as Brecht's dialectical materialism. (pp. 36-7)

At no time can [Benn] be said to have been a great dramatic talent, but it was a form he found useful to express violently opposing concepts and ideas. This is noticeable already in the earliest of them all, *Ithaca*. The setting, as so often with the early Benn, is medical, indeed pathological. The focus for discussion is the brain, or to be more exact the cervical cortex. The professor's first speech is a *reductio ad absurdum* of a scientific method which leaves everyone concerned still a long way away from any understanding of 'the vast complex of forces which control the universe'. Science refuses to draw conclusions, leaving the theologians and mystics to do that. But what Rönne and the medical students really react violently against is the insistence on regulating experimental conditions and destroying the simple self-contained naïveté of things as they are, the individual case! They reject the mere collecting and systematising of knowledge as a puerile activity, they reject the positivistic hunt for data as meaningless fact-grubbing and pour ridicule even on the practical and humane arguments in favour of medical science. . . . As Rönne himself puts it, thinking and logic mean the destruction of the universe. All that they leave is 'words and the brain'. This is the cross he is nailed to: the brain! God and the natural world have been destroyed by thought. . . . The experience to which Rönne and his contemporaries is giving expression is the classic twentieth-century loss of centre . . . , and these are the very words he uses: 'What centre is there for us to gather round?' Yet the possible means of escape from the affliction of thought are also adumbrated. One is the Romantic path of inwardness, turning in upon oneself to where strange associations are found and mysterious processes take place. Another is the path of regression to a primeval harmony. . . . (pp. 43-5)

For such an early work *Ithaca* shows a remarkable number of elements, which were to remain constant throughout Benn's later work. But the real key seems to lie in the words: 'And once the mists had cleared what was left? Words and the brain.' There are always obscurities and difficulties in Benn's thinking, but these are the central concepts to which he always returns. (p. 46)

The poem 'The Singer' . . . reads like a statement of [Benn's] concept of the poet and indeed being so 'self'-centred Benn does in fact often write about the problems of poetic creation. The striking feature of this poem is the vocabulary Benn is prepared to use, not simply *paroles essentielles* . . . , but very scientific, technical words like hyperaemia and azimuth. Such 'unpoetic' language has a certain shock effect, but once its meaning has been grasped and its potential for poetry admitted, it can be seen that Benn is once again widening the range of his lyrical expressivity. The basic technique of the poem seems akin to the Expressionistic one of *montage*, whereby a series of substantives are placed in explosive proximity to each other.

(There are very few adjectives: a poem of this kind is not striving for shades of meaning or fine nuances.) Similarly there are very few finite verbs. Any suggestion of action, movement or direction is carefully avoided. Already such poems tend towards the 'static', one of the key concepts for Benn's later poetry. When the various substantives in the poem are examined, they are seen to have been all carefully chosen to spark off their own world of associations. Hence although in the expressionistic manner the poem is very condensed and concentrated it is also capable of vast scope. (pp. 58-9)

In his lecture 'Problems of Lyrical Poetry' he was later to discourse at length on the ideal poem as he saw it and this was definitely not poetry for any faith or political party. He spoke of 'the absolute poem, the poem without faith, the poem without hope, the poem addressed to no one, the poem made of words assembled in a fascinating way'. It may be seriously questioned whether Benn or any other modern poet has ever realised this ideal, but one or two examples of sheer magic like 'Wave of the Night' . . . and 'One Word' . . . force the reader to stop looking for the meaning (though the poems are of course not devoid of meaning) and experience the rhythm, the rhyme, the formal excellence and the lucidity of the images, whether Mediterranean or cosmic, captured by the power of the poetic word. (pp. 64-5)

The later Benn is characterised by [a] gradual abandoning of Expressionistic extremes and a return to almost traditional elegiac forms and tones. (p. 68)

There is no escaping now the note of tired acceptance which the poems of the older Benn exude, a note decidedly more pleasing than his pose of heroic isolation in the face of the void. He no longer sees himself as the nihilistic superman of superhuman suffering. . . . The really pressing question [in his later poetry] is why do we try to express anything? . . . This is the question Benn's work poses. This compulsion to write poems is what gives his life substance. Did it make him a great poet? Probably not. A great thinker? Certainly not. He was a man who followed many spiritual leaders: [Christian] Hebbel, Nietzsche, Flaubert, Heinrich Mann, and others. Perhaps he came nearest to Chopin, the musician whom he admired most, who:

> Never composed an opera,
> Not one symphony,
> only these tragic progressions
> from artistic conviction
> and with a tiny hand.

(pp. 69-70)

J. M. Ritchie, "Monograph," in his Gottfried Benn: The Unreconstructed Expressionist (© *1972 Oswald Wolff (Publishers) Limited), Oswald Wolff, 1972, pp. 11-70.*

BIBLIOGRAPHY

Alter, Reinhard. *Gottfried Benn: The Artist and Politics (1910-1934)*. Bern: Herbert Lang, 1976, 149 p.
   A study of the relationship between Benn's artistic theories and his political beliefs.

Ashton, E. B. Introduction to *Primal Vision: Selected Writings of Gottfried Benn*, by Gottfried Benn, edited by E. B. Ashton, pp. vii-xxvi. New York: New Directions, 1960.

A biographical introduction to Benn in the first American publication of his work.

Casper, M. Kent. "The Circle and the Centre: Symbols of Totality in Gottfried Benn." *German Life and Letters* XXVI, No. 26 (July 1973): 288-97.
A psychological and philosophical examination of Benn's concept of regression.

Hamburger, Michael. "A Proliferation of Prophets" and "De-Demonization." In his *From Prophecy to Exorcism: The Premisses of Modern German Literature,* pp. 54-70, pp. 140-62. London: Longmans, 1965.*
A brief summary of Benn's political beliefs and Nietzschean allusions.

Hannum, Hunter G. "George and Benn: The Autumnal Vision." *PMLA* LXXVIII, No. 3 (June 1963): 271-79.*
A close textual examination of the divergent techniques of Benn and Stefan George in two representative lyric poems.

Hannum, Hunter G. "Gottfried Benn's Music." *The Germanic Review* 40, No. 3 (May 1965): 225-39.
A study of the musical elements and allusions in Benn's poetry.

Jolas, Eugene. "Gottfried Benn." *Transition* 5 (September 1927): 146-49.
An early review in English which examines Benn's vision of cosmic loneliness.

Wodtke, Friedrich Wilhelm. Introduction to *Gottfried Benn: Selected Poems,* by Gottfried Benn, edited by Friedrich Wilhelm Wodtke, pp. 9-41. London: Oxford University Press, 1970.
A summary of Benn's life and poetic works.

Wood, Frank. "Gottfried Benn's Attic Triptych." *The Germanic Review* XXXVI, No. 4 (December 1961): 298-307.
A study of classical Greek allusions in Benn's triptych of poems "V. Jahrhundert."

(Paul Louis) Georges Bernanos

1888-1948

French novelist, essayist, journalist, screenwriter, poet, and short story writer.

Bernanos is remembered for his moralistic novels replete with intense hatred of the corrupting power of evil and love of innocent virtue.

Bernanos was born in Paris and educated by Jesuits, and he saw action as a soldier in the First World War. He was a politically conservative young man, and an outspoken member of the monarchist Action Française. Bernanos's extreme right-wing inclinations gave way to anti-bourgeois, anti-cleric Roman Catholicism after firsthand exposure to Francoist brutality during the Spanish Civil War. From his wartime experiences in the Balearic Islands, Bernanos came to believe that the Roman Catholic Church needed a spiritual cleansing, and that a transformed Church held the solutions for the world's problems. His *Journal d'un curé de campagne*, considered by many to be his master work, came out of this period.

Just before the disastrous Munich agreement of 1938, Bernanos moved with his family to Brazil. During the war he was a supporter of de Gaulle's Free French, and wrote pamphlets and articles for the allied cause. With the final surrender of the Reich, Bernanos returned briefly to France, and settled in Tunisia, where he spent the last years of his life. During the postwar years Bernanos wrote several important works, among them his screenplay *Dialogues des Carmélites*, an interpretation of Gertrude von Le Fort's novel concerning the beheading of Carmelite nuns during the French Revolution, *Die letzte am schafott*. At the time of his death Bernanos was at work on a life of Jesus.

Critics have noted that although Bernanos was a prolific author, he hated the practice of writing for financial gain. He wrote because he felt compelled by God to convey messages to humankind.

PRINCIPAL WORKS

Sous le soleil de Satan   (novel)   1926
  [*The Star of Satan*, 1927]
L'imposture   (novel)   1927
Jeanne: Relapse et sainte   (essay)   1929
  [*Sanctity Will Out*, 1947]
La joie   (novel)   1929
  [*Joy*, 1946]

La grande peur des bien-pensants, Edouard Drumont
  (essay)   1931
Un crime   (novel)   1935
  [*A Crime*, 1936]
Journal d'un curé de campagne   (novel)   1936
  [*The Diary of a Country Priest*, 1937]
Nouvelle histoire de Mouchette   (novella)   1937
  [*Mouchette*, 1966]
Les grandes cimetières sous la lune   (essays)   1938
  [*A Diary of My Times*, 1938]
Nous autres Français   (essays)   1939
Scandale de la verité   (essays)   1939
Lettre aux Anglais   (letters)   1942
  [*Plea for Liberty: Letters to the English, the Americans, the Europeans*, 1944]
Le chemin de la Croix-des-Ames   (essays)   1943
Monsieur Ouine   (novel)   1943
  [*The Open Mind*, 1945]
France contre les robots   (essay)   1947
Dialogues des Carmélites   (screenplay)   1949
  [*The Carmelites*, 1961]
Les enfants humiliés: Journal 1939-1940   (essays)   1949
Tradition of Freedom   (essays)   1950
Un mauvais rêve   (novel)   1951
  [*Night is Darkest*, 1953]

BEN RAY REDMAN   (essay date 1938)

[Georges Bernanos is], judging from this book which was published in France as "Les Grands Cimetières sous la Lune," a much harassed and somewhat bewildered man. He is bewildered because, like all men of good will today, he finds himself surrounded by enemies and is compelled to fight on a dozen fronts at once. As a result, he is often breathless and even incoherent; but he is always on the side of the angels. It is a fairly lonely position, as assumed by M. Bernanos, for ignorance and stupidity and cowardice are as abhorrent to him as overt evil; even his fellow royalists seem to disgust him for the most part, and the chief battle which he wages in these latest pages is against fellow Catholics—the priests and bishops and cardinals and simple church-goers who have approved of the Spanish counter-revolution as a holy crusade and who have endorsed a reign of terror. . . .

When he writes of what he saw in and around Palma . . . he is at his best. There were three thousand political murders committed on the island in seven months, and he makes them real to us. He makes us feel the grisliness of a reign of terror, during which every man was subject to denunciation by his neighbor. . . .

When he rises from the particulars of personal experience to generalization and argument, he is still stimulating; but his arguments are discursive and fragmentary and unorganized; and the reader of English suffers from the disadvantage of reading him in a language that ill serves his style, for it is a style native to French controversy—high-pitched and magniloquent.

And, at the last, when he looks about him for the means whereby the current forces of evil are to be overcome, he has little to say that is heartening to those who are not of his faith. He tells us that he believes in "the war of Men of Good Will," and he also adjures us to become as little children and to seek salvation in Christ. Who would not, if he could? But many will find it easier to follow him when he writes: "A man of good will has no longer any party. I am wondering if he will soon have any country."

> *Ben Ray Redman, "Indignant Royalist," in* The Saturday Review of Literature *(copyright © 1938 by Saturday Review; all rights reserved; reprinted by permission), Vol. 19, No. 5, November 26, 1938, p. 11.*

CHARLES P. BRUEHL   (essay date 1939)

It is in the rôle of . . . a prophet that Mr. Bernanos appears before us [in *A Diary of My Times*]. An exceptionally harassing emotional experience, as he tells us himself, has produced in his mind a violent revulsion of sentiment: "The spectacle of injustice shatters me." . . . This frank statement at once explains the temper of the book and indicates where we must look for its possible shortcomings. We are reading an indictment written under great emotional stress and such a presentation will naturally have, as the Frenchman so well says, the defects of its qualities. Emotion renders vision keen and myopic but it distorts the perspective that gives to the objects their proper place and setting.

The title of the original, "Great Cemeteries under the Moon," is more illuminating than that of the translation and suggests the particular event which has so deeply touched the author's soul and alienated his sympathies from the Nationalist movement. Living in Majorca at the outbreak of the Spanish counter-revolution he has seen piled up in the cemeteries of the neighborhood the corpses of thousands who were slain by the Insurgents. In his estimation these killings were unjustified yet officially sanctioned and even winked at by the clergy of Nationalist Spain. His chief grievance is that the campaign of the Nationalists has been dignified by the name of a Crusade or Holy War.

We are justified in applying to the assertions made by Mr. Bernanos the principles of inner criticism which judges a document by its own inherent character. Viewed from this angle the general impression cannot but be unfavorable. Testimony delivered in the manner of Mr. Bernanos can impossibly inspire confidence; its credibility is seriously damaged by the uncontrolled and passionate vehemence of its utterances. Its tenor is not that of an objective report of facts. For all that, the sincerity of the man need not be impugned, for the wrath born in his breast may have beclouded his vision and led him to see things out of focus and grotesquely exaggerated. (p. 515)

If we gage Mr. Bernanos's sentiments correctly, he was not meant to write a book against the Church, and this may be the reason why his violent denunciations of churchmen have not been fully exploited in an unfriendly sense. On the other hand, it is not yet apparent whether he has rendered the Church a service by the publication of this strange volume in spite of the inspiring passages which it contains. On the constructive side the book is rather weak and offers only the vaguest generalities for, if it advocates "the war of men of good-will," we are left completely in the dark as to the nature of the warfare and as to who these good men are. On the author's own showing the number of these men of good-will is discouragingly small and no criterion is given by which they might be identified; we do not know who comes under this class, outside of himself, the old soldiers, for whom like Joseph de Maistre he cherishes the tenderest affection, and the little children. (p. 517)

> *Charles P. Bruehl, "A Censor of His Age," in* Commonweal *(copyright © 1939 Commonweal Publishing Co., Inc.; reprinted by permission of Commonweal Publishing Co., Inc.), Vol. XXIX, No. 19, March 3, 1939, pp. 515-18.*

PIERRE DIDIER   (essay date 1951)

The action of Bernanos' novels always presents a limited number of people, who, because they have been drawn from the same social strata, end up by becoming stereotypes. One can expect to meet representatives of the traditional *états* of the French society: the clergy, the nobility, the *bourgeoisie*, and the peasantry. We might mention in passing that the working class, established after the French Revolution, has practically no place in Bernanos' society. However, the setting of the novels does not favor its inclusion. The little Artois village of Bernanos' novel is completely isolated from the large cities with which one has contact only rarely and only when absolutely necessary.

More exactly, this community is a parish rather than a village, for the essentially lay *commune* hardly receives the attention of Bernanos except when he ridicules it in the person of Arsène, the pathetic mayor of Fenouille. Arsène has no family name, no personal existence; Arsène is just Arsène. The country priest always has the leading role in a Bernanos novel, but he does not always reveal himself as a leader of men, an honored and respected pastor. He complains incessantly that his parish is dying before his eyes and that he has to be present during its interminable agony. His awkward build leaves him open to the poorly concealed mockery of his flock. His inopportune efforts only compromise him further. He would like to convince everyone of his complete selflessness, of his burning charity, but no one seems to pay any attention to him except to dismiss his attempts with a snicker or a scornful sneer. (pp. 101-02)

The deference which the country people refuse their pastor and the local gentry they accord to the doctor, the representative of Science, which they worship superstitiously, paying to it, with a fearful reverence, the homage they deny to the God of their childhood. And Bernanos presents us with finely chiseled silhouettes of pretentious public health officers or practitioners who possess a common aptitude for turning pompous and empty phrases, for saying nice words which easily convince their outclassed adversaries. These doctors are redoubtable opponents of the poor parish priests, for they are the high priests of a new religion, worshipped in bewilderment and terror, the pretentious ministers of a cult which dazzles with its strangely shaped instruments of shining nickel and chromium.

Vaguely uneasy in the face of the wonders of science, which at the same time frighten them, incapable of freeing themselves from the traditions which form the basis of their humble existence, the peasants often fall back on a stubborn and secretive silence, thus limiting themselves to outer appearance and the materialism of life which has lost all significance. (pp. 102-03)

And this is why Bernanos has pronounced such a terrible sentence upon our modern world: because in this world the three theological virtues [of faith, hope, and love] no longer occupy their former place of importance. A lively faith requires a respectful attitude, a sense of the sacredness of things. But the traditional values have been submitted to a destructive criticism which has shaken their foundations and led to a general leveling-down. This leveling, while debunking some idols, has nevertheless left us in a state of disillusionment, turmoil, and bitterness. (p. 103)

Bernanos, who strongly doubts that the message of Christianity reaches man, has striven to present it in such a manner that it stirs his readers. By so doing, Bernanos is following in the footsteps of all those apologists who since Pascal have sought first to create a feeling of unrest. He has sought a modern transposition of Christ's earthly mission; thus we may consider his priests as being faithful disciples of Christ, the leaven in the bread, whose role is to bear the sins of the world and to interpret the sufferings of this poor godless people. He has boldly chosen them from the ranks of poor country priests who, according to the Dean of Blangermont, are very seldom saints. To judge by their outward appearance they hardly differ from their city brothers who are more or less comfortably ensconced in their daily routine. However, one quality clearly distinguishes them: they have the gift of second sight whereby they see through the most hidden schemes and read the darkest of minds. Moreover they possess an extraordinary capacity for suffering, both physical and spiritual. They abhor sin, particularly in its most hideous form, human lust, which dulls the spirit of generosity and smothers man's highest aspirations.

It is easy, but probably useless to go on identifying all characters in Bernanos' novels with people in the New Testament: doctors with Pharisees, scribes and lawyers, the mayor of Fenouille with the centurion. Although this little game may be entertaining, suffice it to say that the Scriptures always underlie the novel. And perhaps it was Bernanos' intention to write Biblical tales adapted to the modern taste for action, adventure and sensational events, such as murders or suicides, somewhat like the Flemish masters who introduced contemporary people in their religious paintings and went as far as to dress up Biblical figures in the garb of the noble ladies and gallant knights of their times. It is a naive representation to be sure, but a superb idea, and we may ask if any better solution could be devised to recall the Biblical tragedy to our minds than a dramatization of this unforgettable story in which the various roles are played by people like ourselves. (pp. 106-07)

Pierre Didier, "Bernanos' World," *in* Yale French Studies *(copyright © Yale French Studies 1951), No. 8, 1951, pp. 101-07.*

THOMAS MOLNAR (essay date 1956)

The world of Bernanos' novels reflects his main preoccupation: what is the position of the saint in the midst of a world teeming with the most complicated, the most sophisticated forms of evil? But, first of all, who is a saint? and what is evil? What happens when these two poles of spirituality come into contact? These are the problems that Bernanos pursues in all his works, and in his political writings no less than in his novels. The spiritual man is not a strictly religious apparition: he is, rather, the man with a positive life whose whole being is heavy with the weight of God in him. . . .

Bernanos' sinners are all in a state of advanced corruption. The soul, absorbed in self-contemplation, shrinks continually until it is stripped of all the elements which composed originally its mysterious chemistry. This is a half-conscious process, but the victim turns away wilfully from the spectacle he offers. Even when he no longer can deceive himself, when, panic-stricken, he finds himself in the cold night of unbelief, he does not give up. (p. 246)

Cénabre, the central character of *L'Imposture*, is a priest and a man of superior intellect. The drama, in his case, erupts with a particular force; his imposture spreads with the speed of an infectious disease, and before us who follow the progress of the poison in his system, he disintegrates spiritually, intellectually, even physically. The book he writes no longer has the qualities that the world used to admire; he becomes listless and negligent, his formerly meticulous neatness yields to a sudden desire for external degradation.

Or take Monsieur de Clergerie, the pedantic historian in *La Joie,* whose sole great ambition is to be elected to the Academy. Does he defy God? By no means. But in the words of the saintly Abbé Chevance, he is "opaque": God is not visible through him. His little manias, his constant complaints about the heat and about his nerves, etc. are innocent only in appearance; in fact, he had let a young wife die of despair at his side, and now prepares to sacrifice a daughter to a second marriage which would promote his election. He surrounds himself with souls as dry as his own, and with vicious servants who thrive in the ambiguous atmosphere of the house. As one of them remarks: "Nobody here has the courage of good or evil." (p. 247)

The examples could be multiplied, but the central preoccupation is always the same: the priest as a saint (Donissan in *Sous le soleil de Satan,* the curé d'Ambricourt in *Journal* . . ., Abbé Chevance in *L'Imposture*), then the negative priest, the anti-priest, the whited sepulchre: Cénabre, Monsieur Ouine, Doctor La Pérouse, etc. No other author has treated the figure of the priest in such a deep, yet nuanced manner. As a Balzac of the sacerdotal world, Bernanos explores the priest's life, his inner conflicts and external conditions, his place at the crossroads where the ways of God and men's ways meet.

To the unity of the characters there corresponds, in Bernanos' novels, a certain unity of the topic. The desiccated soul of one man infects the souls and actions of others; sin is a dynamic reality, living a life of its own, eating itself into the tissue of being. It has such an impact that only a saint may force it to a halt, and eventually reverse it. The economy of salvation functions as a well-ordered plan.

God's man makes his presence manifest by the extraordinary *lucidity* he possesses. The young curé of Ambricourt, the Abbé Chevance, or Chantal de Clergerie are people with little experience of the world. They are shy and disarmingly naive, they stumble along the path of everyday routine where even a child would walk unguided. Abbé Chevance, an elderly man, had not even been entrusted with a parish after his awkwardness in the first. The curé in the *Diary of a Country Priest* is an idealistic freshman among the tough and suspicious peasants who obstruct his well-meaning enterprises. And Chantal is but an extremely young girl, exhausted by the tasks of running a household. They know no evil; they could say, with the curé d'Ars, that all they know about sin is what they learned from the lips of sinners.

Yet these three are capable of forcing the most hardened carapace to break and uncover the palpitating soul underneath. Cénabre before Chevance, the psychiatrist La Pérouse in Chantal's presence, the countess cornered by the curé of Ambricourt become like fragile children bathed in a mother's strict but immense charity. In these scenes of confrontation, which are, beyond any doubt, Bernanos' best, the sinner has all the advantages of intelligence, fame, authority. That he yields, step by step, is nothing if not the work of living faith unfurling itself as a victorious flag. Under the reader's eyes an incredible transformation takes place: the young priest or the young girl seem to grow gradually old and weary, as if they were struggling with a tremendous burden, taken off the other's back; but they never weaken. Their purity absorbs the world's wickedness without a trace. They carry out "the saint's duty, the duty for which he was born: the salvation of weak souls." (pp. 247-48)

Thomas Molnar, "Anatomy of Evil," in Commonweal *(copyright © 1956 Commonweal Publishing Co., Inc.; reprinted by permission of Commonweal Publishing Co., Inc.), Vol. LXV, No. 10, December 7, 1956, pp. 246-48.*

GERMAINE BRÉE and MARGARET GUITON (essay date 1957)

It has been said that Bernanos's world is a Manichaean world in which the priest, the representative of God, fights a terrible battle against Satan, who, in the eyes of Bernanos, now almost totally possesses our earth. This Manichaean world is more concretely a medieval world of monsters and gargoyles, of moral weaknesses or vices incarnate, against which the writer-priest, Bernanos, wages *his* desperate battle. It is a world doomed, were it not for that courageous figure in black, the priest. And this image is surely symbolic of the faith that sustained Bernanos against all odds and kept him sane through many a personal descent into Hell. "For your peace of mind," he wrote a young novelist, "give, give names and faces and adventures to your demons . . . your beasts."

Bernanos's vision of our time coincided with his own inner struggle: He could not come to terms with an age of spiritual and physical breakup in which men butcher each other anonymously and smother in the oozing mud of trenches. This latter aspect of World War I haunts Bernanos's fictional world. Hell, for Bernanos, is often mud, a mud in

which the human being slithers and slides until he is swallowed up.

The moral atmosphere and the inner coherence of Bernanos's world go back to his childhood, a childhood he defends against the aggressions of an adult world. . . . The sin without remission is, for Bernanos, the sin against childhood. Humiliated children, betrayed, unloved, brutalized, raped, murdered, driven to despair and suicide, are present in all his novels. The ever-repeated crime we encounter is the murder of a child, or, as in *Journal d'un curé de campagne (The Diary of a Country Priest)*, the indirect murder by universal conspiracy of a young priest, little more than a child. Each novel is an indictment, a cry of horror for the world that kills childhood, the spirit of childhood in mankind. And here again the inner world of Bernanos's obsessions and his personal view of the tragedy of our time coincide: The good priest is the knight-errant, the defender of divine innocence; the same is true of Bernanos, who is defending his child's world against the inroads of bitter experience, like that of war. (pp. 123-26)

The scenes of the novels are taken from Bernanos's childhood environment, but this flat, northern countryside is transformed according to the spiritual significance it has in the different novels. Ambricourt, the village of the country priest, lies in wait for him avidly under its layer of dust, the dust of accumulated boredom. The "dead parish" of M. Ouine is soaked in water; it is a marshy land in which all the characters flounder; water oozes everywhere; a sort of wet Dantesque hell. In the *Nouvelle Histoire de Mouchette* a violent, hallucinating deluge beats down on the forest.

Nowhere in any of the novels do we find a trace of what might be the France of our time. Bernanos no doubt intended to portray the various layers of French society. His novels are actually concerned with a few very limited elements of this society: the village, the château, the church with its priest, the mayor sometimes, and the village artisans. The priest is at the heart of this world and in his relation to the parish gives meaning and poetry to the apparently chaotic, formless events. His fate and that of the human beings he encounters are inextricably linked; for the priest must enter into communion with the evil in his parishioners before he can snatch them from the living death in which Satan has plunged them. All Bernanos's novels have in common this recurring theme. But they show a marked transformation in the novelist's art and in his use of his fundamental novelistic elements. (p. 126)

Sous le Soleil de Satan interweaves two stories. The first is the story of Mouchette, a rejected and unloved girl who, sinking into despair and suicide, is finally possessed by Satan. Satan also plays a part in the second story, the story of l'Abbé Donissan. Satan tempts Donissan, as he tempted Christ on the Mountain, but with the worst of all temptations in the view of Bernanos: despair. The encounter with Satan is physical. Donissan meets Satan himself, then recognizes his presence in the pale hard face of Mouchette, whose path he crosses by chance. Donissan triumphs over Satan, and his victory is linked to the gift of seeing the state of a soul. This gift makes a saint of Donissan, and saves Mouchette by breaking through the wall of her despair before she dies. Before his own death, Donissan, as the Saint of Lumbres, will have to go through a moment of despair and solitude as terrible as Mouchette's, whose destitution is a prefiguration of his own. Donissan's life as a saint, his trials and his death, are closely connected to those of a real priest, the Curé of Ars. The novel as a whole shows the inexperience of the writer, but, fairly traditional in technique if not in content, it is a good introduction to the peculiar world of Bernanos.

L'Imposture and *La Joie* form a sort of diptych: the story of a damnation and the story of a redemption through a child saint, Chantal de Clergerie. L'Abbé Cénabre is the impostor, the false priest who, though he has lost his faith, continues to perform the empty rituals of his sacred office and lives in daily inner betrayal of his God. Cénabre is a living lie, and all that is around him turns into an empty shell. Evil for Bernanos is precisely the empty imitation of what is real, and Satan is the mock appearance of God. Chantal, the heroine of *La Joie,* lives in the radiance of her total surrender to God. Her clear-sighted charity sheds its light on her mediocre entourage. But the forces of evil combine to destroy her, and she is murdered by Fiodor, the sinister valet who haunts her footsteps. At her death bed Cénabre loses his mind; but he regains his faith, becoming as childlike as Chantal's former confessor, the innocent, almost imbecile saint, Chevance.

The outline of these stories gives only a poor idea of their significance. For Bernanos each was a spiritual adventure, and, as he said, "all spiritual adventures are calvaries." For the eventual victory of light over darkness, the price paid is the price Christ paid upon the Cross, and Donissan, like Chevance or Chantal, must go through the anguish of the Passion and cry out, as Christ cried out to his Father: "Why hast Thou forsaken me?"

In Bernanos's first books the spiritual and physical adventures do not quite coincide, and the satanic element is too apparent, too individualized to be altogether convincing. With the *Journal d'un curé de campagne* and, still more, with *Monsieur Ouine,* Bernanos moves toward a mastery of the novel and a real innovation of technique. These two novels, written in most part at the same time, are also companion pieces. The first tells the story of a young, sick, poor and awkward priest's day-by-day encounter with his parish. Indolent, somnolent and bored, in a sort of collective indifference to life, the parish is gradually being destroyed by the cancer of evil. . . . It is the task of the poor country priest to fight for their spiritual survival, to reach the walled-up sources of their souls and save them from the annihilation threatening them. (pp. 127-28)

The Curé of Ambricourt, Bernanos's favorite character, is humble, awkward, innocent and inept in all the material aspects of life. But he has one gift, the same as Donissan's. He sees not the body but the soul, and as he undergoes his humble calvary, he accomplishes his mission. "All is grace" are his last words. His story is that of a parish saved. The priest has day by day assumed the burden of the evil he eradicates from others. Grace in the world of Bernanos does not mean peace but the courage to bear the cross of human suffering.

In the *Journal d'un curé de campagne* the inner and external events adhere closely one to the other. The humble external event suggests a spiritual reality but never exactly delineates what is taking place as the figure of the priest, by its very existence, dislocates the superficial order of the parish.

This technique is still more apparent in the strange and unique *Monsieur Ouine,* a novel in which Bernanos abandons his passionate use of rhetoric and ceases to fight for his ideas under the cover of his creatures. The whole story revolves around the murder of a little cowherd. Neither the circumstances of his death nor the identity of his murderer is ever known. The murder is nevertheless at the core of the organic dislocation of a world, a "dead parish." The whole parish slides into hallucination, madness and death, under the eyes of an adolescent, Philippe, who watches this disintegration with cold detachment. (pp. 128-29)

Monsieur Ouine has been considered chaotic, and rightly so, for it deals with a nightmarish and seemingly unrelated series of experiences. Yet Bernanos worked on it for several years and composed it with apparent care according to a formula of his own. What we read is not a story in the simple sense of the word. We are caught, like Philippe, in the collective metamorphosis of a parish that is turning into a subhuman, incoherent, fast-dissolving animal world. This metamorphosis, unlike Kafka's, has many different parts, each one an aspect of the whole terrible transfiguration of the world with which Bernanos started. The characters do not know what is happening to them or to others around them. Each is plunged in his own obscure adventure, and zones of darkness separate the episodes in which they encounter each other. This is the reason for the imprecise contours, the strange lighting of the scene, the mysterious, irrational quality of events and, more particularly, of relationships. In this instance, at least, Bernanos may well be the precursor of a new approach to the novel, an innovation produced by the sheer intensity of vision on which his world rests. (pp. 129-30)

Germaine Brée and Margaret Guiton, "Private Worlds," in their An Age of Fiction: The French Novel from Gide to Camus *(copyright © 1957 by Rutgers, The State University; reprinted by permission of Rutgers University Press), Rutgers, 1957, pp. 98-131.**

ALBERT SONNENFELD (essay date 1964)

No reader of Bernanos' work can fail to discern its Dostoevskian resonances, and indeed the major Bernanos critics . . . have linked the two writers. But their comparisons have remained almost entirely conjectural, theoretical and non-literary. Typically, a recent American study of the novelists maintains that one cannot know whether Bernanos had even read Dostoevsky, that all one can safely assert is that Dostoevsky was "in the air." (p. 83)

[A] fruitful approach to Bernanos' work is to consider it as his attempt to offer a Roman Catholic illumination of the shadowy souls of "the possessed." And the clairvoyant Curé d'Ars of Bernanos' hypothesis, the priest who, as he was fond of saying, learned of sin only from the mouths of sinners, is variously represented by Father Donissan, Abbé Chevance and the Curé d'Ambricourt, Catholic sacerdotal modulations of Dostoevsky's secular saints, Shatov, Prince Myshkin and Alyosha Karamazov. . . . As Myshkin reads faces, so do Donissan and the Curé d'Ambricourt read the souls of Mouchette and Chantal; and their own simplicity and innocence match "The Idiot."

The possessed who are to be succoured by Bernanos' Curé d'Ars figures are remarkably Dostoevskian too. The most tragic manifestation of the demonic presence, that is, of becoming possessed, can be found when innocent, holy creatures are violated by one who is already among the possessed. . . . [Hysterical laughter] is the surest sign of the diabolic presence (in both *The Brothers Karamazov* and *Sous le Soleil de Satan,* when the devil appears he is laughing). . . . (p. 84)

The importance of laughter as a recurring symbol of the satanic in the works of the two novelists can be traced to a fundamental kinship of psychological vision. Both Bernanos and Dostoevsky create an imposing roster of characters who when humiliated or contaminated spiritually or physically react perversely, rebelling against the integrity of their own personality. "We're ashamed," Mouchette says, "But between us, since the first day, have we been looking for anything else?" Dostoevsky calls them "self-lacerators." They frenetically debase themselves in public, but their suffering originates in pathological pride and fear, not in true humility. It is unregenerative suffering. . . . The use of the double motif is also common to both novelists: Cénabre's walk with the beggar cannot help but recall Stavrogin's meeting with Fedka. The self-lacerators are usually just on this side of insanity and often do indeed lapse into madness or suicide. The madness of Cénabre at the end of *La Joie* or of Olivier Mainville in *Un Mauvais Rêve* is no less symbolic of spiritual corruption than the brain fever of Stavrogin and Ivan Karamazov. And psychiatry is not the remedy to purify the tainted soul. . . . The psychiatrists in Bernanos' novels, Lipotte and Lapérouse, are . . . ineffectual, though they are equipped with the latest theories. For Dostoevsky and Bernanos, Alyosha's kiss to Ivan and Father Donissan's absolution of Mouchette provide the only form of redemptive therapy.

Another symptom of the self-lacerator is his uncontrolled, almost hysterical verbalizing. For both our novelists, saintly figures are essentially silent listeners. (pp. 85-6)

Drugs have been mentioned in connection with Simone Alfieri. In his essay, *La Liberté pour quoi faire,* Bernanos calls toxicomania "that perverse form of escape, of fleeing one's own personality." If the Bernanos novels include among the most notable addicts La Pérouse in *La Joie,* Dr. Laville in the *Journal,* Dr. Lipotte, Philippe, Olivier and Simone in *Un Mauvais Rêve,* a list of the drunkards in Dostoevsky's works (for alcohol serves an analogous function for the Russian) would be impossibly long. . . . For both novelists, the desperate attempt to escape one's self ultimately leads to a far more tragic confrontation. It is no accident that Mouchette kills herself in front of a mirror. (p. 86)

If I were to point out the one trait which most clearly marks Dostoevsky and Bernanos as fraternal novelists, it would be their fundamentally Romantic mistrust of the intellect. . . . For both writers, the intellectual almost by definition is the first to succumb to the temptation of knowledge; the picking of the forbidden fruit is what Donat O'Donnell calls the religious Faust motif. . . . Monsieur Ouine, a professor of Modern Languages, is consistently portrayed as an anti-priest reigning over a dead parish which is the image of a living hell. Both novelists reserve the most strident satiric tones of their lyre for intellectuals. Dostoevsky's hatred of a Ratikin or a Lebeziatnikov is matched only by Bernanos' disdain for a Monsieur de Clergerie or a La Pérouse. Neither novelist hesitates to judge his characters personally. Moreover, both draw savagely caricatural portraits of writers, and one could develop at length a compar-

ison of Antoine Saint-Marin, the ruler of the kingdom of irony, in *Sous le Soleil de Satan,* with Stepan Verkhovensky and, above all, Kamarazinov in *The Possessed.* In each case, the writer has betrayed not only religion but his country. Interestingly, Anatole France and Turgeniev, models for Saint-Marin and Karamazinov respectively, are both essentially cosmopolitan and ironic. (pp. 86-7)

[Though Bernanos' priest-heroes] illuminate the tormented souls of the possessed, it has been the function of the novelist himself to provide the coherent diagnosis. But Bernanos' stated intention to redo Dostoevsky's *Possessed* from a Catholic point of view leads him to transform the Russian's saint-like figures, Shatov, Prince Myshkin, Alyosha Karamazov, into specifically Roman Catholic expressions: Donissan, Chevance, Chantal de Clergerie, the Curé d'Ambricourt. The consanguinity of these childlike, holy creatures has often been pointed out. They all neglect the sacraments in favor of person-to-person soul fishing; they are all religious modulations of the alienated Romantic post-hero. Their natural habitat is the monastery, even the sanatorium; in the infernal world their best-intentioned actions go astray and, typically, the intervention of a Donissan and a Myshkin has equally nefarious results. There is an important distinction between the Dostoevsky and Bernanos saint figures, however, one which shows that the Frenchman has indeed met his self-imposed challenge of Catholicizing Dostoevsky. For Dostoevsky, the only path toward the regeneration of the sinner leads through suffering, and those of his novels where redemption remains a possibility are open-ended, projecting into an unwritten future episode, as in the epilogue to *Crime and Punishment* or in the conjecture as to Dmitri Karamazov's eventual return to Russia and acceptance of the cross. Bernanos, on the other hand, believes in the sudden, mystical intervention of Grace, effected in part by the sacrificial act of the Saint ("sacrifice," etymologically, means *making holy*). Myshkin returns to his sanatorium in Switzerland, but Chantal de Clergerie's murder may have led Cénabre back to God; Shatov's death does not redeem his murderers or even Stavrogin, but the Curé d'Ambricourt's death may have restored a measure of faith to the defrocked priest, Monsieur Dufréty, who gives him absolution. If the word which best represents Sonya Marmeladov as she accompanies the sinner to Siberia on the stations of his long itinerary of redemption is compassion (that is, *suffering with*), the word for the Bernanosian Saint as he imitates Christ by dying as a scape-goat (all of the priest-heroes of Bernanos die) is passion. (pp. 87-8)

Albert Sonnenfeld, "A Sharing of Darkness: Bernanos and Dostoevsky," in Renascence (© copyright, 1964, Marquette University Press), Vol. XVII, No. 2, Winter, 1964, pp. 82-8.*

RIMA DRELL RECK (essay date 1965)

Georges Bernanos' novels revolve about two central themes, sin and death. . . . As abstractions these ideas meant nothing to him. To speak of sin, of the temptation of evil, Bernanos put characters into situations. Indeed, according to [his] creative method . . . it would be more accurate to say that Bernanos' characters lived out these themes, each in his own way, as the novelist recorded the resultant spiritual adventures. (p. 626)

In his first novel, *Sous le soleil de Satan,* the Devil appears to one of his characters, and at this point the three apparently disparate sections of the book are united. [Here], the visual, the concrete illustration serves to convey Bernanos' thought, while the abstract idea seems to elude him.

Evil finds other concretizations in Bernanos. The curé in the *Journal* is slowly killed by a tumor, which appears almost a physical manifestation of evil in the world. (p. 627)

In Bernanos' novels, sin is best expressed by the solitude which inevitably accompanies it. As his characters plunge further into sin, they are more completely cut off from the human world. "Misery . . . closes in upon itself. It is walled in, like Hell." In *M. Ouine,* which is in fact a novel about Hell on earth, the characters are unable to experience anything resembling love. (pp. 627-28)

Death, the other major theme in Bernanos' work, is also the answer to some of the questions arising out of his preoccupation with sin and evil. . . . [He looked] on death as the highest, most mysterious and most personal form of human experience. The death of his characters is often their only instant of self-realization; frequently it appears as the goal of their existences which they discover for the first time. (p. 628)

> Rima Drell Reck, "George Bernanos: A Novelist and His Art," in The French Review (copyright 1965 by the American Association of Teachers of French), Vol. XXXVIII, No. 5, April, 1965, pp. 619-29.

PETER HEBBLETHWAITE, S.J.   (essay date 1965)

Dénouement, in Bernanos, means death. His novels drive on inexorably towards the death-agony, the act of dying, which alone completes and expresses a life. Few important characters outlive his novels. . . . But this apparently headlong course towards death is not the only point of reference in Bernanos' novels. Equally important is the recalling of childhood, especially at the approach of death. . . . There is hardly an important character in any of Bernanos' novels of whose childhood we are not given a revealing glimpse. This is true of those like Cénabre and Simone Alfieri, to whom dissimulation has become second nature, and it is found in those, like Ganse and Ouine, who have failed their lives. The evocation of childhood in all these cases momentarily wins sympathy for these unadmirable characters because it suggests a psychological explanation for their adult unpleasantness; it takes the reader back to the point in time when the character was poised, not yet hardened, potentially a different sort of person. . . . Bernanos does not romanticise childhood—one has only to think of Séraphita Dumouchel in *Journal d'un curé de campagne* to recognise that—but at least childhood represents, if it does not always embody, candour, an absence of either suspicion or bad faith. There are two periods in life when sincerity can be expected, childhood and the death agony, and that is why Bernanos links these two moments.

The evocation of childhood is thus neither a nostalgic memory of something long since disposed of nor merely a psychological explanation. Childhood—or the possibility of recalling it—constitutes the *durée intérieure* of a Bernanos character. Time, in his novels, does not move in one direction only towards inevitable death, it ranges backwards towards childhood, which is never entirely disposed of, finished with. . . . Bernanos does not view childhood simply as a prelude to the serious business of living. The adult, in Bernanos, has hope in so far as he has preserved something

of childhood, and as long as the memory, the active memory, of 'the child he once was' remains alive in him.

Dialogues des Carmélites provides the most explicit statement of his view of childhood. The Prioress is explaining what it is to be a nun, and she recognises that for one who does not believe in prayer, nuns must be either impostors or parasites; but, she goes on, prayer is a need, a hunger, and human solidarity is such that we can pray not only for each other, but in place of each other. . . . In a sense there is nothing surprising in Bernanos' use of the theme of childhood in his saints. After all, as a Christian, he had to try to understand the gospel text, 'I tell you, whoever does not accept the kingdom of God like a child will never enter it.' What is perhaps surprising, and more interesting, is the survival of childhood where one least expects it, in characters like Cénabre and Ouine, Ganse and Simone Alfieri.

Cénabre's childhood is like an underground stream steadily undermining the wall of security he imagines he has built round his life. This is the meaning of the episode, so often regarded as a digression, which makes up Part III of *L'-Imposture.* Cénabre meets a beggar who follows him round Paris at night for upwards of an hour. He dismisses the conventional heart-rending stories and tries to squeeze the truth out of the man. But below the surface of Cénabre's conscious intentions there are stirrings which elude the control of the will, and the image of the underground stream expresses this. . . . He questions the beggar about his childhood, about how he came to be in his present destitute state. The questions make little sense to the beggar, who anyway is not very sober.

In fact, Cénabre is addressing them to himself, and it is the truth about himself that he is obscurely trying to discover through his interrogation. . . . As long as the slain ghosts of childhood remain there, even potentially, Cénabre is not irremediably lost. He is, in the strictest sense, judged by his childhood, and as long as childhood memories are present, no matter how repressed they are, he may be saved. If Cénabre is to be saved it will not be by the recovery of lost innocence—for the innocence of a child is a pre-moral innocence and it cannot be recovered—but by the partial restoration of the truth and candour of the child he once was, now buried deep within him. The habit of hypocrisy has been with him for so long that when, in *La Joie,* he is brought into contact with the childlike saint, Chantal, he loses his reason, but only after uttering, *d'une voix surhumaine,* the words, *Our Father.* The night of insurrection has become a reality. Cénabre, in other words, was never quite so far in the land of unbelief as he thought; underground forces were patiently at work. It would be a mistake to think of them as purely psychological, but equally mistaken to think that these touches of grace ignore psychology. From the *ténèbres* gleams obscurely the grace of childhood remembered.

The character of Cénabre is a kind of challenge offered to *la douce pitié de Dieu.* It is as though Bernanos said: find something redeemable, something not totally superficial in this character who has replaced love by curiosity. That something is the child he once was. In Cénabre there is a breach. (pp. 87-92)

Bernanos is obsessed with the survival of childlike—or simply human—values into adult life. Inevitably, therefore, another theme occupies him: the transition from adolescence to adulthood. The intransigeance of youth, its sense of risk and adventure, its need for a love that will be absolute, come into depressing collision with the compromises and equivocations of the grown-up world. The result of the clash is disappointment. The girl-saint, Joan of Arc, standing before her eminently respectable judges and invited to deny what she knows to be true, provides an exemplary pattern. From Joan to the second Mouchette may seem a violent imaginative leap, but Bernanos' sense of the Communion of Saints makes it possible.

In *Nouvelle histoire de Mouchette*, Bernanos' last novel, there is no saving intervention within the story, no mention at all of grace or God. It is as though Bernanos had at last accepted Léon Daudet's advice and eliminated the soutane. But the sacerdotal role, defined by compassionate insight, is taken over by the narrator himself, to make this one of the most remarkable of his novels. It is certainly the most lyrical. . . . (pp. 96-7)

[It is also] the most daring and compassionate of Bernanos' novels; and it was inspired by a political event. This last remark is important because Bernanos not only explores the childhood of his fictional characters but widens his analysis to include the political figures of his own time. . . . But childhood is not always lost, even where it appears to be, and the evocation of childhood in Bernanos is a source of hope. It is not an attempt to perpetuate a Peter Pan state, still less an attempt to put back the clock; nor is it simply an explanation in the manner of Freud. Childhood, in Bernanos, is an image of the supernatural condition; though past, it can still beckon to us from the future, it has still to be achieved. . . . Bernanos' saints have maintained contact, and in them childhood values have grown to maturity; but his other characters are not lost as long as contact, however difficult, is still possible. (pp. 101-02)

> Peter Hebblethwaite, S.J., ''Childhood,'' in his Bernanos: An Introduction *(reprinted by permission of Humanities Press, New Jersey), Hillary House Publishers Ltd, 1965, pp. 86-103.*

ALBERT SONNENFELD   (essay date 1966)

When we first meet Mouchette [in the prologue to *Sous le Soleil de Satan*] she has just entered the Malorthy home bearing a bucket of fresh milk. Almost immediately thereafter she faints, and her parents soon guess that she is pregnant. This initial vision is of crucial significance, for the story of Mouchette is that of the corruption of a completely natural being, a wild thing, a child, by Satan himself and by the Satanic forces of modern life represented by Malorthy, the Marquis and Dr. Gallet. Like Rimbaud . . . , Mouchette's adolescent imagination leads her to desperate rebellion against the straightjacket of bourgeois conventionality, to a thirst for freedom, adventure and love. Three times she will be imprisoned by her implacable foes: her father's house is likened to a cage; the Marquis locks her in his living room, the doctor in his study. Twice she will escape; finally, flight from physical confinement is no longer enough. Mouchette must then escape from reality into madness and ultimately from life into death. She herself has become a Satanic creature, but one in whom vestiges of childhood purity (Bernanos constantly describes her with the adjective ''petite'') remain. Moreover, her complete devotion to evil paradoxically endows her with a vigorous and primitive integrity: she, not her tormentors, is destined

for possible salvation. The pattern is a familiar one in Christian novels, from *Crime and Punishment* to *The Power and the Glory*. (pp. 142-43)

Bernanos creates a complex network of imagery to emphasize poetically both the predatory quality of Cadignan's relationship with Mouchette and the untamed ferocity which results from the defilement of her innocence. When she escapes from the paternal clutches, she is likened to a young female animal. . . . During the course of her story she is variously described as a young wolf, lithe stealthy . . . , a light doe . . . , a supple beast. . . . There are constant allusions to her curled-back lips and her sharp little teeth . . . , the references becoming more frequent as her angry rebellion deepens. In her voice, one detects an animal pride. . . . This richness of imagery, combined with the author's interventions in describing her emotions, endows Mouchette with the complex dimensions of a genuine novelistic character. In contrast, the Marquis is a mere shell precisely because Bernanos is determined to dramatize the basic emptiness of an aristocrat who is no longer aristocratic. Cadignan has no deep emotions; he speaks largely in the jargon of the hunter. . . . (p. 144)

Mouchette is made of the stuff of poets, heroes and fictional criminals. She is willing to dare, to take risks, to live, to face the world of the unknown. . . . In her [childhood] fantasies, Mouchette had already been an intrepid traveler. Unlike Columbus, Bernanos writes, for whom the round earth had meant the possibility of return, she had sought an endless road, one leading nowhere except to freedom. The road will itself become one of Bernanos' favorite images for the exhilaration of risk in adventure. . . . [After] Malorthy's angry order to leave the house, her dream of the open road becomes a reality. . . . Her freedom will be tragically short-lived, however. After killing Cadignan she returns under the family roof: what had been a cage ironically becomes a refuge from the law. The *worm* of boredom devours her youthful dreams . . . , and she is on the inner road to despair. She now becomes Dr. Gallet's mistress, meeting him secretly. Her love for Cadignan had been her ''first secret'' (her predilection for this word is itself a sign of her childishness): her new secrets (the murder of Cadignan and her affair with Gallet) measure the change in her. . . . (p. 147)

The concluding episode of ''Histoire de Mouchette'' has few rivals for brilliance of execution in all of Bernanos' work. It is as memorable as Cénabre's walk with the beggar in *L'Imposture* and the visit to the countess in *Journal d'un Curé de Campagne*. In this scene between Mouchette and Gallet there are unmistakable echoes of her earlier interview with the marquis. In both cases, she has ostensibly come to announce her pregnancy and to find, by lying if necessary, an influential protector. Each time, she encounters misunderstanding and an unwillingness to take the slightest risk in her behalf. Violence becomes inevitable, though it will take appropriately different forms. In both scenes, she expresses her rage [with] unearthly sounds. . . . If [her] sounds recall the cry of a wild animal in a cage, there is a radical difference which is reflected in a change in imagery. Mouchette is no longer the graceful wild creature of the earlier scene; [in this scene] she compares herself and her lover to odd centipedes who diving in the pond leave a cloud of mud. . . . Bernanos . . . has not forgotten the monster of the novel's opening paragraph.

Mouchette is desperately in need of the ministrations of the "curé du républicain," as Malorthy called the doctor, since no other priest is available. The rapid accumulations of symptoms of impending mental breakdown are a mute and unconscious appeal for help; so is her confession. But the doctor is incapable of understanding. . . . [Only] the supernatural insight of a Donissan can illuminate the dark recesses of a tortured soul. What Bernanos implies here is that no mere psychic disturbance is responsible for Mouchette's disintegration, that insanity is but the surface reflection of the ineffable workings of Satan. When she is released from a rest home as "completely cured" at the end of the prologue, her most acute crisis is still to come. Similarly, Father Donissan himself will be remanded for psychiatric treatment at the end of "La Tentation du Désespoir" by well-meaning Church authorities who are as uncomprehending as the bogus curate Dr. Gallet. Mystical experiences, be they Satanic or angelic, have always been suspect in an age of positivism. (pp. 147-49)

Albert Sonnenfeld, "The Art of Georges Bernanos: The Prologue to 'Sous le soleil de Satan'," in Orbis Litterarum, Vol. 21, No. 2, 1966, pp. 133-53.

C. W. NETTELBECK (essay date 1966)

His first book, *Sous le soleil de Satan*, contains, at least potentially, almost every idea and technique that Bernanos exploits in the seven following novels, from the setting of the action in his native Artois to the types of character so familiar to his readers: the rebellious adolescent, the priest, the doctors, the decadent nobleman, and so on. The deeper themes that characterize his work—revolt, anguish, death—are also there. From novel to novel, the problems he sets himself remain the same, he works them out through the same kinds of characters, for the most part in the same sort of country village in which he himself grew up.

Why did he write more than one novel? (p. 241)

[Perhaps] the dream world shut up inside him like some prisoner or wild animal demanding release is the key to the compulsive nature of his inspiration. It did not find its liberation in *Sous le soleil de Satan*, and Bernanos had to try again.

Before examining the content of this dream world, we must note that Bernanos thought of it as an indivisible whole: it is the *total* dream that each book attempts to 'liberate'. *L'Imposture* and *La Joie*, for example, were to have been a single novel. . . . [So were] *Un Crime* and *Un Mauvais Rêve*. Bernanos had begun the former as a pure detective story to make some quick money, but in writing developed it into a full-scale work that was rejected by his editor. He rewrote the second part and used the rejected material as the base for *Un Mauvais Rêve*. Together, these novels may have represented a unified vision, but as separate works, they are just two more fragments of the dream already more completely expressed in *Sous le soleil de Satan*.

This series of failures to achieve unity of expression is epitomized by *M. Ouine* and the *Journal d'un curé de campagne*. Daniel Pezeril has shown that Bernanos abandoned *M. Ouine* . . . in order to begin the *Journal*. Most critics agree that the latter is the novelist's finest work, and that it reaches the total expression he was seeking. In some ways, however, this is not so. The *Journal* is a less intensely dramatic work than any of the first three or *M. Ouine*. The

culminating scene, for example, when the priest breaks the countess's revolt against God, never reaches the heights of Donissan's encounter with Mouchette (*Sous le soleil de Satan*), or of Chevance's with Cénabre (*L'Imposture*). This is simply because the countess is not as full or imposing a figure as Mouchette or Cénabre. Certainly the destiny of the curé d'Ambricourt is a striking example of spiritual acceptation; and the 'tout est grâce' which closes the novel can be interpreted as referring not only to the hero's adventure but to the author as well. But as we shall see, there are elements in the Bernanos dream world that are not susceptible to reconciliation, and the very fact that the novelist went on to finish *M. Ouine,* which is a vast fresco of a disintegrated world, is perhaps the best proof that the solution he had reached in the *Journal* was not entirely satisfying. These two novels, like *L'Imposture* and *La Joie,* or *Un Crime* and *Un Mauvais Rêve*, are, in fact, complementary, each [of] them representing one of the two main facets of Bernanos's vision: on the one hand satanic evil, on the other omnipotent Grace. (pp. 241-42)

To portray this in fiction . . . is an awkward task for the writer is dealing with the psychology of human beings; and whereas he may effectively present, as Bernanos does with the curé d'Ambricourt, a dominating figure of good, it is almost impossible to confront such a personage with others who, while having the same psychological stature, indicate the presence of evil in a position of defeat. (pp. 242-43)

Bernanos maintains orthodoxy at the expense of unity, and the dream world, as he communicates it in his last two novels, is split into two parts, related but different, and artistically less disconcerting than the unintentionally chaotic structure of *Sous le soleil de Satan*. To grasp fully the import of this novelist's work, it is therefore necessary to attempt what Claude-Edmonde Magny calls 'une critique de restitution', to elucidate the kind of synthesis that Bernanos reaches only if the reader is willing to consider *L'Imposture* and *La Joie* or the *Journal d'un curé* and *M. Ouine* as two aspects of the same thing. We shall do this by analysing first the importance of the setting of the novels, and then the recurring figures who assume the value of myths.

The action of almost all the novels takes place in the villages and countryside of Artois, where Bernanos spent his childhood and adolescence. . . . The communities that inhabit the region are . . . evoked by suggestion rather than detailed description. But Bernanos is careful, here, to portray the *structure* of the community by creating representatives of its two co-existing ways of life: on the one hand, the centuries-old traditional society, embodied in the local nobility and the priest with his parishioners; on the other, the newly emerged bourgeois society of the Third Republic, represented by the mayor or his deputy, the schoolteacher, the doctor, the merchants. The two ways of life are in deep, if silent, conflict, each involving not just a separate political ideology, but a whole different conception of the world. (pp. 243-44)

Bernanos's vision transcends its vehicle. As Albert Béguin has pointed out, the country village is a microcosm of all of French society and even of all that was once the Christian world, now disappearing in the wake of a fast-moving new society. A monarchist and a catholic all his life, the novelist, longing for an unquestionable order, compulsively returns to the places that still contain vestiges of the old traditions. Yet he is aware that the surviving framework is hollow. The curé de Fenouille pronounces his parish dead, and the curé d'Ambricourt perceives in his a devouring boredom which prevents him from reaching the souls of his flock. The efforts of these priests and of their counterparts in other novels stir up fierce hostility, enough to show that, though Christianity may be surviving, Christendom, as a secular reality, has fallen into dust.

The aristocratic traditions are worse off still. Their representatives—such as Cadignan in *Sous le soleil de Satan*, M. de Clergerie in *L'Imposture* and *La Joie*, Mme. de Néréis (Jambe-de-Laine) in *M. Ouine*, and the count in the *Journal*—are all symbols of decadence and mediocrity. (pp. 244-45)

The other aspect of the village society is viewed in just as sombre a light. The novelist sets before us *Républicains* who are depressingly unsuited to any kind of leadership, and odiously selfish. (p. 245)

The presence of evil in the lives of men is an age-old preoccupation of literature, and the identifying of evil with a supernatural spirit (or spirits) is far from new, but to find Satan in a twentieth-century novel comes as a shock. It is to Satan, however, that Bernanos's search for the causes of disintegration leads him, and beyond the more evident social and psychological evils it is Satan who is seen as the ultimate adversary.

As its title suggests, the action of *Sous le soleil de Satan*, with its two protagonists, Mouchette and Donissan, is played out in 'the land of the devil's promise'. Mouchette first, then Donissan: these two figures are the prototypes of all the central figures Bernanos creates thereafter. Together, they form the very nucleus of his imagined world, and their combined adventures are at the heart of his most stubborn obsession.

L'Histoire de Mouchette is above all a study of different levels of revolt and acceptance. For Mouchette to accept the circumstances into which she has been born would mean denying all her inner life-forces, so that her initial rebellion, against her boorish family, is inevitable and necessary. But as the story progresses, we see that the outward movement towards liberation, as long as it is confined to the human level, is gradually turned back on itself. From the love affair with Cadignan, through the debasing relationship with Gallet, to her eventual fit of madness, her search for freedom evolves into a total alienation of herself within herself. Just as her pregnancy by Cadignan symbolizes the hope and promise of fruitfulness in her revolt, her still-born child in the asylum is the image of her abortive first efforts to free herself. The introduction of a supernatural dimension at this point, in the person of the priest, Donissan, is thus crucial: it provides not only an explanation of her failure—the presence of Satan in her life—but the only chance of salvation. On this level, however, there is a reversal of values. Whereas in the natural world resignation to her condition meant sterility, and revolt the only hope of freedom, on the supernatural plane, rebellion is a snare, and acceptation of her destiny complete liberation. In fact, the question of her actual salvation or perdition remains ambiguous. What is important for Bernanos is that her destiny has been placed in a context where salvation is possible.

Either all or a good part of the structure of the Mouchette story is to be found again in the adventures of several other characters: Cénabre, in *L'Imposture* and *La Joie*, Evangéline and André in *Un Crime*, Simone Alfieri and Philippe in *Un Mauvais Rêve*, Chantal and the countess in the *Journal*, the heroine of the *Nouvelle Histoire de Mouchette*, and Philippe (Steeny) in *M. Ouine*. There are, of course, modulations. . . . But the basic pattern is always the same, and to multiply examples would be superfluous. (pp. 246-47)

The real significance of Mouchette can only be seen against the background discussed earlier. In a society where identification with the collectivity means stagnation for the individual soul, Mouchette's savage rebellion is a ray of hope. Her tremendous vitality is a call to the generation of young people threatened by despair. She is also the novelist's image of this generation. It can hardly be a coincidence that Mouchette, in her search for self-discovery, turns first to Cadignan, who symbolises the decadence of traditional values, and then to Gallet, the doctor-politician who represents modern republican society with its faith in numbers and its concomitant mediocrity. This must be seen as an allegory of the new generation of French youth, looking first to the past, then to the present for an answer to its innermost hopes. Neither being worthy of its spirit or capable of making free men, Bernanos is, through Mouchette, inviting the young to revolt, to reject everything, past and present, that might diminish their humanity. . . . As to what ends the revolt should accomplish, the novelist never provides any real indication, beyond the liberation of the individual. He offers no plan of social reform, no ideas for a new kind of community, no picture of a Utopia. His realization that revolt is not an end in itself leads him to seek a way out only for the individual, and even here, as we have seen, the solution is a spiritual one: the Christian doctrine of Redemption. His pessimism is deeply scored into the adventures of all his diverse Mouchette figures, and their attempts to resolve in human terms the conflict between themselves and their environment all end, seemingly inevitably, in despair. There is only one exception to this pattern and, significantly enough, it is Bernanos's last Mouchette figure, Steeny. His inner strength is such that he survives his humiliating frequentation of Ouine, the very heart of evil, with his spirit of rebellion not only unbroken, but untarnished. His destiny is left in suspense *before* he reaches a point of despair. This indicates a hope in *man* not apparent anywhere else in the novelist's work. Why this should be so is not entirely conjectural, for Steeny, although ostensibly belonging to the same period as his predecessors—the action of *M. Ouine* takes place just after the first World War—is in fact of a later generation. Bernanos finished this novel during World War II, and in suspending judgment on Steeny, he doubtless had in mind those young men who, like his own sons, were fighting for the Free French, and who inspired the cautious optimism that permeates the war-time essays. (pp. 247-48)

Without Mouchette, the creation of the priest figures would have been, if not impossible, at least unnecessary. . . . She stands at the very centre of Bernanos's dream world, and it is hardly an exaggeration to say that she is the *raison d'être* of all its other elements. It must be emphasized that there is no conscious symbolic process. For Bernanos, Mouchette is an active participant in his recurring nightmare, a spontaneous imaginative creation of his unconscious mind, spontaneous because absolutely necessary to the dialogue that every artist must engage in. If she appears as a being who organically needs salvation, it is not because Bernanos has artificially injected her with this need, but because his Christian convictions are so deep as to inform all his creative activity, even that which stems, as Mouchette does, from the furthest reaches of his mind. On this level, she is the image of the novelist's own deepest tendency to despair. She is the Eve in him, the part of his being which, because it has once rebelled against God (through original sin), has become permanently vulnerable to the temptations of Satan, needing constant exorcism if contact with hope is to be maintained.

The agent of exorcism and Redemption will be the priest, provided, at least, that he is true to his vocation as a man of God and a disciple of Christ. (p. 249)

Mouchette exists in a world where all ties with family, society, in fact any external reality, have been severed. To reach this world is beyond the mediocre, chained by their own petty preoccupations to everything that Mouchette has rejected. Nor can the well-balanced pastors, Menou-Segrais or Torcy, release themselves from the care of their flock. The saintly priest, because of his background, his personality, and his crisis, is the only one capable of meeting Mouchette on her own ground. He alone is able to achieve the total self-effacement that is necessary to penetrate another's solitude. (It should also be pointed out that Mouchette's inner world is the only one in which the priest's presence can be effective: he has been totally ostracized by society, and any attempt on his part to reach the collectivity—such as when the curé de Fenouille tries to save the half-crazed mayor—must fail.)

The mechanism of reconciliation is very delicate. Mouchette recognizes in the priest the image of her own solitude, and thus offers no defence against a personage she would in other circumstances have avoided. During this brief moment the priest takes the upper hand. Conscious only of Mouchette's soul, he brings his entire lucidity to bear on it, and addresses himself, beyond everything that she is, to Satan. Strong with the knowledge that he is the instrument of Grace, he assumes, before God, responsibility for this soul, whatever may happen. For Mouchette, this means liberation. The magic circle is broken and her future acts will be free. For the priest, the encounter is his fulfilment as a servant of Christ; he has been given a specific task, and through it has understood the meaning and direction of his destiny. (pp. 251-52)

The priest's death eliminates any possibility of his completing his task as Redeemer. For Mouchette—the myth that haunted Bernanos's soul, not one or other of its fictional representations—to be fully exorcised would mean following the priest beyond death to the resurrection, which is patently impossible. As things stand, even the curé d'-Ambricourt's 'Tout est gráce', which is a perfect expression of faith and hope, does not prevent Mouchette, this time in Steeny in *M. Ouine*, from being left behind to face life with all the same question marks before her as in her previous 'incarnations'.

Bernanos's dream world explains both why he wrote more than one novel and why he abandoned fiction after *M. Ouine*. Until his last novels, he believed he could achieve total expression in a single work, but with the *Journal* and *M. Ouine*, by far his best works *technically*, the two poles of his ambivalent vision, for being more clearly fixed, are all the more clearly set apart. These works contain the complete reflection of the artist's vision of the crumbling society and institutions of western civilization, but above all, they prevent a sharp image of the deepest contradictions of his own soul. It is because he [could] never communicate himself in a more unified manner that Bernanos [turned] his back on fiction [during the last years of his life]. (pp. 252-53)

C. W. Nettelbeck, "The Obsessional Dream World of Georges Bernanos," in AUMLA, No. 26, November, 1966, pp. 241-53.

GRAHAM GREENE   (essay date 1968)

Sous Le Soleil de Satan, the first novel of Bernanos, is stamped in deep wax with the very personal seal which he never lost. Technically it is full of faults, faults many of them that he never troubled to amend in his later books. He was a writer rather than a novelist; in the impatience and even the fury of his creation he seems to have snatched at fiction because it was nearest to his hand. He belongs in the company of Leon Bloy rather than of François Mauriac, who has patiently through the years pruned and perfected his style and learned his method. Bernanos belongs to the world of angry men, to a tradition of religious writing that stretches back to Dante, 'who loved well because he hated'.

Bloy wrote in an essay on the Danish writer Joergensen, 'It will always be known that he wrote for the glory of God . . . and I know it well, that terrible profession.' Bernanos could have made the same claim. There is no catharsis in his work; his stories are open wounds which refuse, like the stigmata, to heal. (p. 122)

It is a weakness, I think, in the novel that it begins with the story of Mouchette, a melodramatic nineteenth-century plot even though seen through Bernanos's timeless eyes, and if we judge the book strictly as a novel, we have to deplore the intrusions of the author who occasionally mounts the pulpit to draw a lesson which we would have preferred to discover for ourselves. . . . Perhaps only in *Journal d'un Curé,* where a stricter method was imposed by his use of the first person, did Bernanos allow his characters to speak for themselves without explanation or annotation by the author. He never discovered the cunning method of disguised commentary employed by Mauriac who conceals the author's voice in a simile or an unexpected adjective, like a film director who makes his personal comment with a camera angle.

And yet . . . are we, when all this has been said, only trying to impose arbitrary laws which have no authority higher than Flaubert's? Even what sometimes seem to be clumsy or undramatized interventions by the author are the very characteristics which give the story of the curé of Lumbres its odd authenticity. It is as though Bernanos were a biographer rather than a novelist. True that on occasion he takes on the tone of a hagiographer, but a work of hagiology has been written about a real saint, and the very faults of Bernanos's first novel become virtues and authenticate the character of the curé—this is not fiction, we tell ourselves: the curé exists in the same historic world as the Curé d'Ars and his parish with him. (pp. 124-25)

With what astonishment, in this novel unlike all novels hitherto, [the first readers of *Sous Le Soleil de Satan*] must have encountered *le tueur d'ames* when he intercepted the curé on the dark road to Boulaincourt in the guise of a little lubricious horse-dealer with his sinister gaiety and his horrible affection and his grotesque playfulness.

This is surely one of the great scenes in literature, the scenes which suddenly enlarge the whole scope of fiction and like new discoveries in science alter the future and correct the past. (pp. 125-26)

> *Graham Greene, "Bernanos, the Beginner" (1968), in his* Collected Essays *(copyright © 1966, 1968, 1969 by Graham Greene; reprinted by permission of Viking Penguin Inc.; in Canada by Laurence Pollinger Ltd. for The Bodley Head, Ltd.),* Viking Penguin, 1969, pp. 122-26.

WILLIAM BUSH   (essay date 1969)

Bernanos' non-fiction can be divided into three categories: first, that represented by four biographical essays ...; secondly, political essays, books written to deal with particular historic issues and situations; thirdly, the compilations —books made up of his lectures, articles and unpublished pieces. As a source of information concerning the man behind the fictional world, these books are essential. (p. 121)

[The four biographical] essays deal, in order of composition, with St. Dominic, St. Joan of Arc, Edouard Drumont and Martin Luther, respectively. Of these, the first is certainly the least interesting in that it gives little insight into Bernanos' thought. Published in the *Revue Universelle* in 1926, the article is of a rather routine sort, written at a time when the Dominican order was very much in the forefront with the "Catholic revival" in literature. Although Bernanos does discuss certain ideas on sanctity, none of them bespeaks the fervent personal conviction which, eight years later, was to resound in his short study of Joan of Arc.

The original title, *Jeanne, relapse et sainte,* translated as *Sanctity will Out,* points to the issue at stake in this essay: a relapsed heretic, officially proclaimed such by the Church and delivered to the secular forces for execution, was actually a saint. Bernanos seems to have enjoyed this contradiction and he exploits it to the full. The much-vaunted appeal to the pope, he reminds the reader, was completely out of order since the papal legate was already officially present and his signature figures on the condemnation beside that of the Bishop of Beauvais. Moreover, Bernanos saw a particular pathos in Joan's abjuring, denying her voices for fear of the flames and of that eternal hell to which the ecclesiastics assured her she was destined if she persisted in not abjuring. Thus, in this essay as in his novels, Bernanos underlines the theme of the humiliated adolescent. (pp. 122-23)

Provided one is prepared to read a book written to praise the author of *La France juive,* the very long biographical essay on Edouard Drumont, *La Grande peur des bien-pensants,* is of great richness and no mean depth. (p. 123)

What is in question in *La Grande peur des bien-pensants,* is the extent to which the Jews, having abandoned their spiritual pact with God, now apply their great gifts to mere temporal ends. This question, a basic one for every Christian and Jew, cannot, perhaps, be answered; but there are temporal powers which the Jews, according to Bernanos, do control, almost as if these powers were a recompense to them for having broken the ancient pact with God.

In *La Grande peur des bien-pensants* Bernanos also went far in showing the essential evil of modern society which has been formed by the conservative spirit. This is the society which has created a new kind of misery, a misery the like of which, according to Bernanos, man has never seen before. *La Grande peur des bien-pensants* thus joins the writings of Péguy in its uncompromising condemnation of the forces controlling modern society, seeing within them the mark and sign of infernal powers which aim at snuffing out grace and man's dignity of being created in the image of God.

The last of Bernanos' biographical essays, "Brother Martin," consists of a few pages on Martin Luther, an historic personage for whom Bernanos had great sympathy. He supposedly had envisaged an entire book on the German reformer and, if the pages left today are any indication of what the whole work would have been, it would have proven extraordinary. (pp. 125-26)

In spite of his great sympathy for Luther, there is no doubt that Bernanos here arrives at a point of seeing very lucidly the dangers and the futility of any reformer who willfully breaks completely with the immediate past.

The first and, perhaps, the greatest of the political essays is *The Diary of My Times,* Bernanos' book on the Spanish Civil War of 1936. (p. 126)

Living on the Spanish island of Majorca when the conflict broke, Bernanos saw the passions of both sides. As he revealed in his book, he saw also far beyond both sides into the heart of modern man whose one aim is not freedom, but totalitarian order at no matter what price. (p. 127)

At the heart of this volume ... is a remarkable diatribe against the contemporary Christian. Bernanos imagines a non-believer climbing the steps to the pulpit on the feast of St. Thérèse of Lisieux and telling a congregation of typical parishioners what the whole world awaits from them, the believers, those who have received the gift of faith. He upbraids them for hiding their joy—or perhaps the truth is that they just haven't got any joy? He pleads with them to renew that fresh evangelical spirit of childhood, taught by the saint being celebrated that day, so that the world may not only be saved from the spirit of old age, but simply saved. Childhood's spirit of joyful acceptance must not only oppose the conservative spirit of calculation and intrigue, but must also tip the balance in its favor if the world is to be saved.

Of especial importance in *A Diary of My Times* is the preface. In this, one of the most frequently quoted sources used to explain both Bernanos and his work, he speaks beautifully of childhood and of the language of childhood which he has tried, again and again, to capture in his books. (pp. 127-28)

Both *Nous autres Français* and *Scandale de la vérité* date from the immediate pre-war period. ... Both are centered on the problems raised in Bernanos' mind by the Munich pact and the political position of [Charles] Maurras and the *Action française* in regard to the resulting political climate. That Maurras should sympathize with Mussolini and the barbaric, fiery suppression of helpless Ethiopian peasants indicated to Bernanos how opportunist had become the politics of his former master.

The presence of Péguy frequently cuts through the pages of these two volumes, not only in *Scandale de la vérité* where

Bernanos makes generous quotes from the essays of the poet he admired so much, but in Bernanos' text itself, almost as if he had submerged himself in the style and thought of the founder of the *Cahiers de la Quinzaine*. Indeed, Péguy is chosen by Bernanos as a pole of opposition to the position of Maurras and his followers. (pp. 128-29)

The opportunism of the Church is, needless to say, hardly passed over in silence in these two books. The eternal combination of the conservatives and the ecclesiastical hierarchy, now supported and no longer opposed by Maurras, is attacked and declared neither French nor Christian. (p. 129)

Les Enfants humiliés is a long meditation on the meaning of the lost victory of 1918 and, indeed, on the meaning of the First World War, now that the second one was upon the world. Bernanos bitterly attacks the "home front" as the "rear" with the full force of the double meaning that might be given that word.

But Bernanos' meditation carries him much farther than a bitter attack on the "rear." He meditates on such unusual things as Hitler's motivations and what this frightening master had suffered as a child. And, as usual, Bernanos sees the poor and the "children" as related, concluding this book with a long and very beautiful discourse on the meaning of the poor and on their hope which is so essential to the human race.

Although less fiery than *A Diary of My Times*, *Les Enfants humiliés* is nonetheless one of the most important of Bernanos' volumes of non-fiction. It is surely not to be neglected by any reader wishing to grasp the basic theme of "humiliated adolescence" so prominent in the fiction, since this work gives the essential historic setting in which Bernanos learned many of his truths on this, his favorite theme.

This book is more "literary" than the other political essays in the sense that there is more of a unifying vision perceptible in the organization of its contents. Nor is it limited by some of the more parochial arguments of the other political books. Bernanos' ideas on the modern state, on the Church and on political attitudes remain the same here as elsewhere, but *Les Enfants humiliés* provides us with a very controlled and carefully worked literary exposé of them. (pp. 130-31)

Plea for Liberty, in French entitled *Lettre aux Anglais*, consists, in fact, of seven "letters" dated December, 1940, and March, May, July, August, September and November, 1941. It came into being as the result of a request in 1940 from the editors of the *Dublin Review* who asked Bernanos to supply them with an article. The article written, Bernanos found great appeal in the idea of exposing his own ideals of French honor to that "little island and great people" who stood alone against the forces of the Axis. *Plea for Liberty* resulted.

Here, as always, the theme of childhood emerges, and Bernanos articulates for all foreigners the genius of France and her part in the world scene. He honors and admires the English position as much as he bemoans his own country's disaster in the Armistice. When he hears that French soldiers, incorporated in the German war effort in Libya, are confronting the English soldiers, he concludes that, following the Armistice, all opportunities for death are good for a young Frenchman. (pp. 131-32)

[An] interesting aspect of *Plea for Liberty* is the fact that one can there detect a somewhat new tone, that which will especially be enunciated in Bernanos' post-war lectures and writings, a tone of hope that France will once again take her place at the head of free men as she had done ever since the Revolution of 1789. This time the difference will be that the new revolution will be one of the Spirit, establishing the reign of free men and having done, once and for all, with the conservatives. (p. 132)

This book thus stands at a crossroads in Bernanos' non-fiction. With France defeated, he had nothing left to do but search for reasons to justify his country and plead pardon for her defeat as he addressed himself to those who had been her friends and allies.

Bernanos' last political book, *Tradition of Freedom*, was written in 1945 as the European war drew to a close. Here Bernanos becomes more aggressive, attacking the *imbéciles* of the modern world on every possible occasion. The themes are essentially the same as in his other writings of this period, but now he shows a hurt pride, for example, in the fact that the French language was not to be used at the San Francisco conference in 1945 to found the United Nations. Bernanos sees therein a proof that the conference itself was simply an utilitarian affair which had no interest in the part of the language of Rabelais, Montaigne and Pascal.

Of all Bernanos' political essays, this one seems the most likely to offend, probably simply because it is a tirade against the civilization of the *imbéciles*. Bernanos obviously classified his reader in that category. The agony of Pétain's Armistice and the Vichy French is touched on here, as in most of these works. (pp. 132-33)

The largest and earliest published of the compilations is the volume entitled *Le Chemin de la Croix-des-Ames*. It contains articles which Bernanos wrote between May, 1940, and May, 1945. (p. 133)

A final note in regard to a certain similarity with Léon Bloy is in order before leaving *Le Chemin de la Croix-des-Ames*. In a few of Bernanos' titles one detects a certain rapport with *Exégèse des lieux communs* wherein Bloy gave his own, inimitable exegeses of such overworked proverbs as "Business is business." When Bernanos chooses a topic such as "Hunger goes well with shame" and writes around it, using it as a point of departure, one easily recalls Bloy's earlier work. In the final analysis, this method may be considered a clever device of journalism; yet there is, perhaps, something a bit more substantial in the point of view being expressed by these two *visionnaires* than that expressed by the average journalist under an equally clever headline. (p. 134)

William Bush, "The Non-Fiction," in his Georges Bernanos *(copyright © 1969 by Twayne Publishers, Inc.; reprinted with the permission of Twayne Publishers, A Division of G. K. Hall & Co., Boston), Twayne, 1969, pp. 121-37.*

H. A. BOURAOUI (essay date 1971)

Georges Bernanos' *Journal d'un curé de campagne* is, first of all, a novel in the form of a diary kept by the hero. This obvious fact has been frequently overlooked by readers and critics who see in it primarily a treatise on Catholic theology or a document typifying a resurgence of Catholic intellectualism between the two wars. . . . However illuminating or rewarding such a theological study might be, the purpose of the present article is to set in relief the relationship between the formal elements of the narrative technique, exemplified by the diary itself, and the themes treated by the curé and his creator Bernanos.

One aspect of the diary is particularly puzzling, and reveals that it is not simply a straightforward philosophic debate on the human condition. That aspect is its silence: at crucial moments the curé erases lines or whole pages which even he himself seems unwilling to face. Yet, at the end of the novel, all seems resolved by the curé's dying exclamation, "Tout est grâce!" Nothing in the diary, with its hesitancies, incoherences, and silences, seems to prepare us for this final mood of joyous acceptance. (p. 181)

One might suspect that if the ending is indeed unconvincing, it is because of a tension in Bernanos himself, as well as in his hero, between the religious and aesthetic commitments. The curé's triumphs as a priest are, in fact, largely aesthetic. His whole aim in life is to communicate his faith, his vision of the world, to his parish, a village which is dying of boredom and indifference to any spiritual preoccupations. The one person to whom he succeeds in communicating his faith is the Comtesse.... He succeeds in penetrating her wall of reserve not in the way he consciously intends, but through the force of his passions, because he speaks better than he knows, because, finally, he awakens her maternal sympathies. It is the artist's power to touch the emotions, not the theologian's to touch the intellect or faith, that gives him the power of persuasion over other human beings. When we read the "Tout est grâce" of the ending, we cannot help wondering whether Bernanos himself is trying to force the work back into the religious framework because he is afraid to recognize the implication that the artist's power can be truer and more efficacious than the priest's. (pp. 181-82)

The diary ... is the receptacle for thoughts [the priest] dare not or cannot communicate to the village.... We sense from time to time that, if it contains thoughts he cannot reveal to his parishioners, it also contains half-formed thoughts which he cannot quite communicate to God either. His long preamble or apologia for undertaking the work makes us suspicious of the relationship in which he thinks it may place him with God. He is determined to write, but is ambivalent about the diary, admitting that his long reflection over it is only an "alibi." ... At one point he claims that he conceives of it as a private conversation with God, ... but in the next breath he admits that he senses at times the presence of another reader.... There is almost a "dédoublement" of characters here, a kind of splitting of his own personality, for this invisible presence is not simply a nameless ideal reader, but [a] kind of ... friend.... (pp. 183-84)

How distinct this nameless friend is from his own personality is a moot question, for the dominant metaphor for the diary is that of the mirror. In looking at the pages of the diary he seems to be examining his own conscience, or, rather, a conscience whose existence he does not quite understand....

The identity of this other self, or other conscience, is probably the central question posed by the novel. The very brief first and third sections, flanking the long central section, underline the curé's obsession with the problem of writing

and with the genesis and ultimate fate of his journal, which seems to take on the role of the other self. (p. 184)

The omissions and erasures from the diary most clearly bear upon his doubts of his priestly function. Some go so far as to question his faith, but none recognizes the identity of the "second self" and the fact that he is more of an artist than a priest. At the end of Part I, he claims that he will record a kind of stream-of-consciousness.... We soon learn, however, that he is exercising both a kind of artistic selection and a censorship of doubts about his vocation.... (p. 185)

The curé's public self is a priest, his private a poet. Both are reflected in the mirror of the diary as well as in the multiple mirrors provided by the other characters. At times, however, the mirror seems to crack, and the fragmentation, reflected by the erasures in the diary, suggests that there are gaps in communication, or communion, even between the public and private selves. (p. 190)

If we can accept the doubling of priest as artist, and recognize that he is himself not fully conscious of the merging (and that he might be horrified by it if he were), the ambiguities of the ending seem to resolve themselves, however abrupt we may find it, however shapeless on the structural level. There is a parallelism between the aesthetic and metaphysical concerns. If the ending is unconvincing in terms of plot, on another level it, like the dual role of the priest, is extremely compelling and persuasive. In death, apparently, the curé finds the ultimate complicity or communication. We are all dying, as is Dufréty, who writes the final letter describing his friend's death. But the ending is also anti-ritualistic, repudiating the necessity for the last rites of the Church visible. They are administered only by a defrocked priest but, as the curé says, "What does it matter? Everything is grace." His last communion is blessed because it is administered by love, and because at the end there is no more unknown double to trouble him. Artist and priest seem to have finally become integrated, because he no longer feels guilt about his own priestly shortcomings which ... can also be viewed as artistic strengths.... (p. 191)

H. A. Bouraoui, "The Face in the Mirror: Bernanos' Hero As Artist in 'Journal d'un curé de campagne'," in Modern Fiction Studies (© copyright 1971 by Purdue Research Foundation, West Lafayette, Indiana), Vol. 17, No. 2, Summer, 1971, pp. 181-92.

BIBLIOGRAPHY

Beaumont, Ernest. "The Supernatural in Dostoyevsky and Bernanos: A Reply to Professor Sonnenfeld." *French Studies* 23, No. 3 (July 1969): 264-71.*
    Examination of the Roman Catholic and Eastern Orthodox elements in the works of Bernanos and Dostoyevsky.

Blumenthal, Gerda. *The Poetic Imagination of Georges Bernanos: An Essay in Interpretation.* Baltimore: The Johns Hopkins University Press, 1965, 154 p.
    Critical interpretation of Bernanos's novels.

Cor, Laurence W. "Mystical Perception in *Journal d'un curé de campagne.*" *Romance Notes* 12, No. 2 (Spring 1971): 244-50.
    Examination of the mystical elements within *Journal d'un curé de campagne.*

Falk, Eugene H. "The Leap to Faith: Two Paths to the Scaffold." *Symposium* 21, No. 3 (Fall 1967): 241-54.*
  Comparison of Bernanos's *Dialogues des Carmélites* with Gertrud von Le Fort's *Die letzte am schafott*.

Field, Frank. "Georges Bernanos and the Kingdom of God." In his *Three French Writers and the Great War: Studies in the Rise of Communism and Fascism*, pp. 139-93. New York: Columbia University Press, 1975.
  Study of the effect Bernanos's wartime experiences had on his concept of evil and good.

Guers-Villate, Yvonne. "Revolt and Submission in Camus and Bernanos." *Renascence* XXIV, No. 4 (Summer 1972): 189-97.*
  Comparison of the beliefs on revolt and submission held by Bernanos and Camus.

Lye, John. "*The Diary of a Country Priest* and the Christian Novel." *Renascence* XXX, No. 1 (Autumn 1977): 19-31.
  Essay on *The Diary of a Country Priest* which examines it as a realistic Christian novel following centuries of religious sentimentality.

Mary Sandra, Sister. "The Priest-Hero in Modern Fiction." *The Personalist* XLVI, No. 4 (October 1965): 527-42.*
  Essay on *The Diary of a Country Priest*.

Molnar, Thomas. "The Political Thought of Bernanos." *The Review of Politics* 20, No. 2 (April 1958): 225-42.
  Study of Bernanos's political ideas, their reflection in his work, and how they evolved during his lifetime.

Noth, Ernst Erich. "Georges Bernanos 1888-1948." *Books Abroad* 23, No. 1 (Winter 1949): 19-24.
  A biographical tribute to Bernanos.

Weinstein, Arnold L. "Vision As Feeling: Bernanos and Faulkner." In his *Vision and Response in Modern Fiction*, pp. 91-153. Ithaca: Cornell University Press, 1974.*
  Critical examination of Bernanos's *Monsieur Ouine* and Faulkner's *The Sound and the Fury*.

James Bridie

1888-1951

(Pseudonym of Osborne Henry Mavor; also wrote under pseudonyms of Mary Henderson and Archibald P. Kellock) Scottish dramatist.

Bridie, Scotland's first modern, native playwright, was the moving force behind the minor revival of Scottish theater in this century.

Bridie, an established physician, ventured into the theater in his forties. His medical background served him well in many of his plays, notably *The Anatomist,* his first London play, and *The Sleeping Clergyman,* which Bridie considered his best work.

Bridie was extremely loyal to Scotland. Unlike his fellow Scot, dramatist J. M. Barrie, Bridie refused to attach himself to the London theater or to live in London. Instead, he established in Glasgow a repertory theater, the Glasgow Citizens' Theatre, and encouraged younger writers.

Bridie has been compared most often to Shaw and does show the same interest in ideas, love of argument, and penchant for witty dialogue. His concerns, however, are more nationalistic and moralistic than Shaw's, centering around good and evil, the ambiguity of human values, and divine intervention. Religious myth figures greatly throughout his works, especially in his biblical, apocryphal plays. *Tobias and the Angel* is considered his most successful in this genre.

Bridie charmed his audiences with his humor and delightful use of farce and fantasy. In his later plays he effectively combined poetic and realistic drama. Though not well known outside Great Britain, Bridie is assured a place as a minor writer for his contribution to Scottish theater in modern times.

PRINCIPAL WORKS

The Switchback, The Pardoner's Tale, The Sunlight Sonata: A Comedy, a Morality, a Farce-Morality (dramas) 1930
The Anatomist and Other Plays (dramas, includes *Tobias and the Angel* and *The Amazed Evangelist*) 1931
*Jonah and the Whale (drama) 1932
A Sleeping Clergyman: A Play in Two Acts (drama) 1933
Colonel Wotherspoon and Other Plays (dramas, includes *What It Is to Be Young* and *The Dancing Bear*) 1934

Marriage Is No Joke: A Melodrama (drama) 1934
The Black Eye: A Comedy (drama) 1935
Babes in the Wood: A Quiet Farce (drama) 1938
The King of Nowhere; A Play in Three Acts (drama) 1938
The Last Trump (drama) 1938
"Equilibrium" (essay) 1939, published in *The London Mercury*
What Say They? A Play in Two Acts (drama) 1939
Susannah and the Elders, and Other Plays (dramas, includes *The Golden Legend of Shults* and *The Kitchen Comedy*) 1940
Plays for Plain People (dramas, includes *Lancelot, Mr. Bolfry, Jonah 3, The Sign of the Prophet Jonah, The Dragon and the Dove*) 1944
Gog and MacGog (unpublished drama, first performed in 1948)
It Depends What You Mean: An Improvisation for the Glockenspiel (drama) 1948
Daphne Laureola: A Play in Four Acts (drama) 1949
John Knox, and Other Plays (dramas, includes *Dr. Angelus* and *The Forrigan Reel*) 1949
Mr. Gillie: A Play in Two Acts (drama) 1950
The Queen's Comedy: A Homeric Fragment (drama) 1950
The Baikie Charivari; or, The Seven Prophets: A Miracle Play (drama) 1953
Meeting at Night (drama) 1956

*This drama was rewritten as his radio play, *The Sign of the Prophet Jonah,* in 1942; also rewritten in a third version *Jonah 3* published in *Plays for Plain People,* 1944.

ERIC LINKLATER (essay date 1947)

Mr. Bolfry is an excellent introduction to the mind of Mr. Bridie, who is a serious man with an exuberant and fantastic sense of humour. But his humour is arbitrary and unpredictable. He once wrote a play about a successful young novelist, a poor play, and to show there was nothing in it—or so I think—he called it *Colonel Wotherspoon;* because among its characters there was no such person as Colonel Wotherspoon. And he wrote a play called *Marriage is No Joke,* a title that suggests a trim, tidy, well-contrived domestic comedy; but the play, in fact, was a sprawling, romantic gallimaufry in which the scene shifted from drunken brawling in a Scotch public-house to battle in northern Persia, with Cossacks in the distance, while a deadly Russian adventuress embraced the hero, and thence to roguery in London and back-stage intrigue in a theatre—all to prove what he clearly stated in the title, and what is a recurrent theme in his work, that marriage is no joke. (p. 31)

His first professional play was entitled *The Sunlight Sonata,* and in this, as in *Mr. Bolfry,* one of the principal characters is the Devil, who with the help of the Seven Deadly Sins comes to harass a picnic-party on the shore of Loch Lomond. Mr. Bridie's high regard for the Devil is a facet of his prevailing interest in the old contest between Good and Evil; whose ancient, enormous, and eternal rivalry he regards with the eye, not I think of a moralist, but rather of a biologist—an optimistic biologist. . . . Mr. Bridie is neither frivolous nor sentimental, and his biological optimism is derived from a fundamental Calvinistical belief that the world was created for a predetermined end by a Creator who, though beyond knowledge or explanation, must be essentially benevolent. This belief is apparent in a play called *A Sleeping Clergyman,* which is certainly his most serious work, and one of three or four that might be chosen as his best. (p. 35)

[Mr. Bridie's] serious, though not solemn, concern with theology has several times led him to find subjects for the stage in the Old Testament. One that he discovered, very much to his taste and more agreeable in the new shape he gave to it, was the story of the prophet Jonah. Early in the play, however, there is a remark that does not reveal Jonah so much as Mr. Bridie himself. 'Argument', says one of the characters, 'is an interesting and a beautiful exercise.' Here, quite certainly, is one of Mr. Bridie's dearest beliefs. Argument is among his prime accomplishments, and an argument is the basic structure of many of his plays. They often resemble an intellectual wrestling-match, and his typical wrestlers are agile, brawny, and urbane. But in addition to the principal or basic argument there is always a company of little arguments, of lightweight wrestling-matches, for his conception of dramatic dialogue is a perpetual contest of opponent ideas or rival wits. His characters toss their ideas into the ring, and there they grapple and throw each other about in the liveliest manner, until they are succeeded by another pair. (p. 38)

It is, I believe, his conception of drama-as-argument that has led to a loose-thinking but common complaint against Mr. Bridie. It has often been said that he has a tendency to lose interest in the conclusion of his plays, and bring down his final curtain either before he has wound up the story, or just as he is beginning to unroll a new one. But this complaint comes from critics who, because they are looking for a purely dramatic *dénouement,* have lost sight of the argument. The plays finish when the argument is finished. (pp. 38-9)

[While Mr. Bridie] is a dramatist with a great deal to say, it is difficult to foretell in what circumstances he will say it next. He is copious as well as witty, he is imaginative as well as inventive; and his dialogue is not merely good dramatic speech, but admirable writing that can accommodate a full thought as well as a happy answer. But he has, on the other side of the account, prejudices that can impede him, scruples that hinder. (p. 42)

Eric Linklater, "James Bridie" (a revision of a speech originally delivered on behalf of the British Council, in Norway, Sweden, and Finland, in Spring, 1946), in his The Art of Adventure *(reprinted by permission of A D Peters & Co Ltd), Macmillan, 1947, pp. 25-43.*

MARGARET MARSHALL (essay date 1950)

Mr. Bridie uses as [the base of "Daphne Laureola"] the myth of Daphne, who when she was pursued by Apollo prayed to be turned into a laurel tree and was granted her request. "Daphne Laureola" explores, in contemporary terms, the consequences of Daphne's choice.

Now the consequences of such choices are interesting enough. The trouble is that, in the theater, they constitute third act and epilogue—the real drama, the dynamic development, has gone before. The incidents illustrating the consequences may be fascinating, and some are dramatic in themselves, but all are part of a situation which is an ending, not a beginning or a middle, and therefore basically static. "Daphne Laureola" is all third act and epilogue. . . . And this fact creates another hazard. What has gone before must somehow be made clear—which makes for long stretches of analysis and reporting that may, again, be interesting but are not intrinsically dramatic.

Aside from this basic flaw, "Daphne Laureola" has other defects. The young Pole who is the foil for Lady Pitts, the Daphne of the story, is highly unconvincing, more ludicrous than touching, as he is supposed to be. And the minor characters—a group of people whom Lady Pitts picks up in a drunken moment and invites to her house for tea—come to seem very tiresome because they are merely types in the first place and in the second have no integral part in the story. Finally, even as a study Mr. Bridie's exploration does not come off, because his main, and potentially powerful, theme is obscured and weakened by other minor themes.

Margaret Marshall, "Drama: 'Daphne Laureola'," in The Nation *(copyright 1950 by the Nation Associates, Inc.), Vol. CLXXI, No. 14, September 30, 1950, p. 295.*

GEORGE JEAN NATHAN (essay date 1951)

Daphne Laureola without Edith Evans . . . would be very close to *rigor mortis.* (p. 30)

Bridie's play is of the general sort that the reviewers are in the habit of letting down as "amiable," in the sense, one supposes, that a confidence man who swindles one out of one's money with an ingratiating smile is. Though I am told by his friends that the late, eminent Scot doctor was personally a fellow of wit, charm, and educated humor, the plays he confected—and this one in particular—often stubbornly suggest a fundamentally sedate mind out for a lark with the boys, and just a little self-conscious and uncomfortable about it. The plays are further as unsatisfying as a dinner, even when presided over by an expert waiter, which skips from the cocktail to the dessert and fails to provide an entrée. They have a beginning and an end, sometimes fair enough, but no middle.

This latest comedy, about a brandy guzzling eccentric who upon her widowhood marries her manservant, resembles such a dinner and the comments that might be attendant upon it. One's eyes are solicitously on the waiter rather than on the table, which is largely bare. (pp. 30-1)

This Bridie, like Priestley in England and Saroyan in America, seemed to write a play almost every other day. Whenever I chanced to pick up a London newspaper, a new one had either just been produced or was about to be. I shall not make the obvious remark that I do not see where, in view of his various other interests, he got the time, since time isn't a factor with anyone who can toss off plays so rapidly. In fact, judging from the nature of a large number of them, I don't see why he could not toss off twice as many as he did. As in the case of Priestley and Saroyan, however, one might wish he would have wasted a little time and dawdled over his scripts a bit longer. It is evident that, like the playwrights mentioned, he was a man of ideas and talent but his assembly line activity did not allow him to do justice to them. There is about most of his work an unmeditated air and slapdash preparation that give it the sense of a first draft. All through this *Daphne Laureola* one feels it, together with its lapses and confusions. Shreds of the fantastic and whimsical mix awkwardly with patches of conventional polite comedy and the pseudo-philosophical. The recognizable and believable collide with the farfetched and silly. And on the whole you have an ill-assorted grab-bag out of which the art of Miss Evans pulls a piece of tinsel in the guise of a silver necklace. (p. 32)

Like the majority of plays tailored to a star, Bridie's neglects most of the other characters and leaves them in their underdrawers. As if conscious of the fact and a little troubled by it, the playwright tries to trick his negligence into acceptance by embroidering the underdrawers here and there with quaint designs. But it doesn't work, except maybe with nine-tenths of the audience. (pp. 32-3)

> George Jean Nathan, "'Daphne Laureola'," in his The Theatre Book of the Year 1950-1951: Record and an Interpretation (copyright © by permission of Alfred A. Knopf, Inc.; reprinted by permission of Associated University Presses, Inc.), Alfred A. Knopf, Inc., 1951, pp. 30-5.

AUDREY WILLIAMSON (essay date 1951)

Tobias and the Angel is the most enjoyable of Bridie's Bible-into-modern-language experiments: its quiet wit flickers, like a tongue in the cheek, over the simple narrative and characters.... The tale of Tobias's journey from timidity to a difficult marriage, with the Archangel Raphael as his incognito companion, is set along lines of domesticated comedy, and even the affair of the daemon Asmoday, Sara and her seven strangled bridegrooms only hints at a psychiatrical tragedy. The real charm of the tale lies in its characterisation, and most of all in Tobias's aged blind father, Tobit, a philosophical chatterbox of the utmost purity and kindness of heart.... (p. 76)

Bridie's command of the stage is curiously capricious; at his best he has the roots of the matter in him, at his worst he can still entertain and exasperate at the same time. (pp. 77-8)

In even the slightest of [his] plays there has been wit and a reasoned intellect, although credibility of plot is not always Bridie's strongest characteristic. His finest play remains *The Sleeping Clergyman*, a study of heredity over three generations, embracing tuberculosis, seduction, murder and blackmail, yet sustaining in the end Bridie's theory that though the worst characteristics may be passed genealogically to succeeding generations, the qualities of genius may equally emerge and eventually save mankind. It is a bold play on a bold theme, and one which not only brilliantly paints that passion for science that already, in *The Anatomist,* Bridie had made the driving motive in an individual character, but also reveals something more which we less frequently find in his plays: an understanding of other forms of human passion, and an ability to depict people in the round. His Charles Cameron the First, the reckless, tuberculosis-ridden student who is at once blackguard and medical genius, is a superbly-drawn character, who appears in only one short scene but haunts the play like a ghost through his descendants. His illegitimate daughter who murders her lover has, too, a splendid passion for living and experience, in spite of the bad qualities she has inherited. The grandson Charles, in whom the first Charles lives with a new irresponsible charm and a scientific genius carried to fruition, and his twin sister Hope, who combines their ancestor's defective lungs with an original strain of community service, round off the play with qualities of their own. (p. 79)

The weakness of this family biography, if we must seek it, is Bridie's usual one of fantasy and incredibility. The Great Plague which sweeps the world in the last scene is too obviously invented to enable Charles Cameron the Second to prove his medical genius, save mankind, and thus justify Dr. Marshall's biological theory. Nevertheless the play grips and stirs: its characters are flesh and blood. It is, altogether, Bridie's most intellectually coherent, well-constructed and dramatic work. (p. 80)

> Audrey Williamson, "The Thistle and the Leek," in her Theatre of Two Decades (copyright by Audrey Williamson 1951), Rockliff Publishing Corporation Ltd., 1951, pp. 75-91.*

T. C. WORSLEY (essay date 1952)

[*The Baikie Charivari*] belongs to the class of [Bridie's] intellectual fantasias, a form which he very much fancied, though, truth to tell, he never managed to get control of it.... *The Baikie Charivari* is filled with amusing passages but it is also filled with false starts and dropped herrings. It is continually entertaining, but finally unsatisfying. It provides a far more enjoyable evening in the theatre than most playwrights give us, yet leaves us feeling provoked that its author could never be induced to discipline his talent more severely.

The play sets off, as commonly with this kind of Bridie, on a thoroughly diverting and promising notion. Sir James Pounce-Pellott has retired from a Governorship in India and proposes to settle down at a Clydeside resort, Baikie. He has chosen this place because he has decided to use his retirement to start life afresh. Baikie will provide him with a good cross-section of Scottish life, and this fresh start of his is to be a voyage of discovery. What is life in contemporary Britain really like? What values do people live by, what makes them, as we say, "tick"? So each specimen he picks up he treats as virgin ground and assembles round himself a variegated collection, a Communist councillor, a lady psychiatrist, an anarchical beach boy, the local minister, a lady American publisher on a visit, a self-important Civil Servant. They are woven loosely but convincingly enough into the pattern, which is working up into a Grand Debate.

Any other playwright might have been content with this framework. Not so Bridie. Before we reach the end we have had any number of interruptions to smudge the line. There is the inevitable Bridie Devil, intervening from above from time to time and conjuring up three irrelevant though amusing witches who have read their *Macbeth.* Then the playwright is also, concurrently as the lawyers say, putting over two fancies which he never succeeds in integrating into the play though he obviously feels them important if we may judge from his short preface. "There is a tradition", he tells us, "that the celebrated character of Punch is a projection of Pontius Pilate". Pontius Pilate was also a proconsul and must have at some time retired. Therefore our Sir James Pounce-Pellott is, in some way, a projection of Pontius Pilate-Punch. These are entertaining analogies, but they need very much more thorough working-in than they get here. By stray allusions and veiled hints we know them to be somewhere at work in the play but they tease more than they illuminate, and the main outline remains this cross-section of opinion leading up to a final symposium. This, when eventually it comes, is a little disappointing. (p. 448)

Outlining a Bridie play inevitably reduces it, for it is in the detail that it expands. (p. 449)

T. C. Worsley "The Last Bridie," in The New Statesman & Nation *(© 1952 The Statesman & Nation Publishing Co. Ltd.), n.s., Vol. XLIV, No. 1128, October 18, 1952, pp. 448-49.*

WALTER ELLIOT   (essay date 1953)

[*The Baikie Charivari* is] one of the most noteworthy of the Bridie plays. It is really a companion to another piece, *The Queen's Comedy,* published two years earlier. . . . Bridie, in his own view, had come by this time to the limit of his accomplishments. . . .

The Queen's Comedy is about the Gods. *The Baikie Charivari* is about men; or rather, about man, and therefore also about the Devil, the Opponent of man, who is called in our country sometimes the Enemy of Mankind, sometimes the Adversary, sometimes simply the De'il, according to the aspect which he presents. . . .

[This] theme has always pre-occupied Scottish thought, to the verge of obsession. (p. v)

To come to his problem, Bridie had to clear his stage of the Gods. He did this in *The Queen's Comedy.* (p. vi)

The Baikie Charivari is about mortals, and here the rebels come to the centre of the picture. The hero is Punch, their legendary protagonist. But the play being about mortals, and mortals in Scotland at that, Bridie has to place in the forefront of the action the Devil, the endless enmity to humanity and all its works, which is one of the evident factors in the make-up of our affairs, including the make-up of man himself. (pp. vii-viii)

Bridie uses his device of the old tale told anew. But, as the protagonist has to be a good man as well as a rebel, to be a hero, Punch is incarnated as Sir James MacArthur Pounce-Pellott, K.C.I.E., sometime District Commissioner of Junglipore and other places, an administrator, a maker of order, in his time and place a King and a Priest; who has retired to Baikie, a little seaside resort on the Clyde estuary, to adapt himself, his wife, and daughter, to the 20th century in the West. (p. viii)

Punch, by the way, in stage tradition, is also Pontius Pilate,

so this strand also has been woven into his being; and if you boggle at this for a good man, remember that not only was Pilate, in Bridie's view, an upright administrator and an upholder of the *Pax Romana,* but that he is canonised in the Church of Abyssinia amongst the earliest saints. In any case, the play is about the pursuit, by Evil, of a good man; there is no drama in seeing the Devil collect his own. (pp. viii-ix)

[The] play then moves forward simultaneously on the two planes of fantasy and reality. The reality is that of the little Clydeside town, with its minister, its tradesmen, its doctor —a lady psychologist—and all the rest. . . . It is shot through with the fantasy of the Punch characters; at times there is interference between the one plane and the other; elsewhere, they are wholly independent.

The two planes blend at the play's finish. (p. ix)

[Mr. Punch] has defeated his foes with his stick, and exorcised the Devil with his incantation. He finds himself, for all that, no nearer truth. But he has still the heart to jest again, and the conviction that [his] question has a reply.

This denouement leaves a vast, empty stage; and, though why I do not know, a great satisfaction. After *The Queen's Comedy* and *The Baikie Charivari,* what folly to say that Bridie could not write a last act . . .

You may say this is too fine-drawn, too metaphysical, and obviously too complicated, ever to make a play. Of that, future audiences must judge for themselves. (p. x)

If you do not concede, as some of us do, most wholeheartedly, the word genius, to Bridie, you will agree at least that he possessed a most unexpected and a most original mind. (p. xi)

Walter Elliot, "Bridie's Last Play," in The Baikie Charivari; or, The Seven Prophets: A Miracle Play *by James Bridie, Constable and Company Ltd., 1953, pp. v-xii.*

ERIC BENTLEY   (essay date 1953)

Bridie's [*Gog and MacGog*] everyone agrees, doesn't quite come off. . . . If he can't quite make his wild tale a symbol of human fate . . . it's not for lack of trying. And by trying, I don't mean having highminded intentions outside the play, but seeking after the right theatrical form for the intentions in the play. At those happy moments when Bridie's farce began to mesh with his idea, one glimpsed a bigger sort of drama. . . . We must be thankful for such moments . . . for, if Bridie isn't a very great playwright, he is a genuine one, and the best, apparently, that the British can offer today. (pp. 42-3)

Eric Bentley, "Gentility in London," in his In Search of Theater *(reprinted by permission of Atheneum Publishers; copyright 1953 by Eric Russell Bentley), Knopf, 1953, pp. 38-46.**

WINIFRED BANNISTER   (essay date 1955)

Second only in significance to George Bernard Shaw in modern British drama, Bridie emerges as one of the most fecund and original dramatists of his time and is unique in his period, for he alone of modern dramatists has extended a creative concern with drama itself to theatre organisation on an important scale. I do not think it is too much to say that the all-over pattern of the Bridie achievement is as important to the future of British theatre as Shaw's single-minded thrust for greatness. (pp. 5-6)

Bridie made no claims as an improver of human nature; he satirised it without rancour, with gay impertinence. He made an art, a dramatic art, of laughter and there was no price to pay in terms of propaganda or social criticism of a solemn nature. A Bridie comedy is usually an invitation to the audience to look at itself in the Hall of Mirrors. Bridie was no smooth technician. Barrie, Maugham, Priestley, Coward, indeed most of his contemporaries have made a neater play shape than could Bridie, but he had a capacity for planting interesting hazards on the fairway, for surprising and startling the audience in a variety of ways. His gleeful disregard for conventional technique, for a set order of things, caused him to mix sense and nonsense in arresting argument. It did not always come off, but he often got away with his unorthodox methods because of unique compensations of character or caricature and because of his powers of expression. Dazzling sunbursts of colour; a gleaming frost of wit; a thunder-and-lightning phraseology; laughter leaping phrases—these were Bridie's to command, and he was a born story-teller.

Unfortunately he scattered his gifts carelessly sometimes; or was it that he was simply determined to wander at his own sweet will? (p. 6)

Bridie will not be remembered as a mouthpiece of the common man; he was not the salt, but the sauce of both Scottish and English drama. It was only in his last years that Bridie wrote plays with a vital, common touch. *Mr. Gillie* is the most human of the Bridie volume. He rarely had use for ordinary people in useful surroundings as subject matter, perhaps because he strained away so much from naturalism, towards caricature or fantasy. As a writer the very thought of the common touch made his impish wit yawn and his brilliance fade. He loved extremes, eccentrics, and was at his best with a saint, a murderer, a genius or a man with a crazed thirst; to him there was nothing rich and strange about a man with an empty belly. And yet, as a person his sympathy was quick and genuine for the underprivileged. It was simply that he wanted to highlight the more stimulating, the more amusing and exuberant aspects of man's experience; not to dwell on the struggle for existence. He did, however, powerfully dramatise the struggle between good and evil in man, seeking to engage the tolerant reaction of an audience to human frailty rather than a fierce partisanship to a point of view. What he hated most in life, the kill-joy influences in society, were vividly reflected in his plays. He got up to as much mischief as Molière and frequently threw in as much argument as Shaw, but it was Bridie's own individual way of laughing with human nature at itself that often made the play. (pp. 6-7)

In *Mr. Gillie*, the most unpretentious of all Bridie's plays, there is no audacious invective, no wish to irritate, no display of rhetoric for its own sake. Deep concern for humanity irrigates this steady, unforced drama of the old schoolmaster who has failed to keep a roof over his head but who has sent gifted children singing into life's adventure, and Bridie has so uncharacteristically obeyed the rules that no fault can be found with construction. There is the ironic humour and pity if not the grandeur of tragedy that comes in *The Queen's Comedy* and *The Baikie Charivari*. In these two are grand passages of tragedy, and the finale of each play has a similar solemnity and dramatic impact,

when Bridie forces one to see man as a shivering—not cowardly, but pitifully incapable—traveller towards a dignified civilisation, and in both plays Bridie ends by asking questions rather than answering them—for Bridie himself at this stage of his life was becoming increasingly preoccupied with life's purpose and destination; he still "clowned it" in the pantomimes he wrote latterly, but the reciprocating tragedy pursued him. (pp. 9-10)

I think Bridie's lack of discipline in construction and in the characterisation of supporting characters was partly due to an attempt to avoid comparison with Shaw, an attempt which involved shock tactics, eccentricities and tangents; a way to originality and invention which are often so hard to reconcile with technique of construction. (pp. 10-11)

One of the most significant differences between Shaw and Bridie as dramatists is revealed in their attitudes to the other sex. Shaw had a feminine mind; a grasp of woman's own view of herself. In this he was, of course, an apt pupil of Ibsen. The Ibsen and the Shaw heroines could mingle quite happily. If one could put Hedda Gabler, Candida, Nora, Eliza Doolittle, the Lady from the Sea and the Lady of the Unexpected Isles in one room there would not be any awkward silences. Bridie's Daphne Laureola would hold her own, but the rest of the Bridie female characters would not have the stamina to last out the first rounds of conversation, for Bridie drew women from a standpoint of masculine superiority, a handicap which limits any dramatist at the start; but he could hardly help it, for it is a national characteristic. It is little short of amazing that Bridie, who, like the majority of Scottish dramatists, lacks the capacity and the courage to draw full-scale portraits of women, has become as popular as he is without the enormous advantage of having achieved women rampant or radiant on several canvases. Apart from Daphne Laureola, who is a freak, the women in Bridie's plays are rarely of an arresting nature. (p. 11)

But what Bridie has lost on the swings he seems to have gained on the roundabouts; if he could not see into women (*or* bear to reveal what he did see), he could see through men; Bridie's male portraits in drama are just as surely bound for posterity as Shaw's impressions of women. (p. 15)

[*The Sunlight Sonata*] has flashes of brilliance and passages of sheer silliness. Most of the time it is very amusing and it reveals a satirist of original and genial wit. Bridie described it as a farce-morality. Not satisfied with this provocative description he enumerated its five stages of development as follows: A Prologue; An Interlude; A Demonstration; An Apotheosis and An Epilogue. None of this is overstatement. Bridie was enchanted with himself when writing a play and revelled in introductions and explanations. It was a weakness in himself and sometimes in the play that he gave detailed description of the characters after the cast list. Description should of course be implicit in the dialogue, and *The Sunlight Sonata* needed no introduction to dialogue. The characters were sufficiently well drawn. Nevertheless, as reading matter, these explanations and introductions are lively additions. The two pages describing the characters, (1) the unfortunate mortals, (2) the husky and awe-inspiring Beelzebub, (3) the three priggish Graces, (4) the irrepressible Sins, show Bridie the painter and caricaturist happily at work on a fantastic piece. The play is a satire on that section of the Glasgow middle class whose sins are mainly dyspeptic or costive with caution; the characters have not dated. (p. 49)

Tobias and the Angel is a vivid mural, not an argument, but a journey into splendour by travellers who have simplicity and a Guide who knows all the answers; a play full of colour, it sparkles with a tender mischief. It is a tale of innocence and wonder, of devils slain and a good man rewarded. Bridie has treated the wisdom of the Ancients with honour for all his tripping modern phraseology.

All Bridie's gifts have been brought to this richly dramatised story of how the shy youth Tobias was used as an instrument of reward to his gentle, unworldly father Tobit, who had become poor and even blind through over-generous giving. The dialogue is consistently lively; it has the spontaneity of the thoroughly human play and is at the same time full of poetic feeling despite its modern colloquial phrasing. It is the kind of play that the painter in Bridie loved to handle and here he does find the poetry of painting. (p. 77)

The journey reveals the transformation of the shy, lumpish, but engaging youth Tobias into a dashing traveller and confident lover by Raphael, a being who combines the experience of a man of the world with the high endeavour of the welfare worker. . . . Raphael is at once Bridie's most impressive and most human character, and the dialogue and action between Tobias and Raphael in the desert scenes are the wittiest part of the play. The conquest of the lovely Sara, the defeat of her pursuer, the Devil Asmoday, the triumphal return with the gold, and even the miracle of Tobit regaining his sight, are all what we may expect from an angel at work on an ingenuous boy.

Bridie makes all these events a logical outcome of character without depending on religious effect or moralising. A typical trick of Bridie's this, to make his Devil or Angel, his Mr. Bolfry or Raphael, man's guide to clear thought and enriching experience through a this-worldly rather than the other-worldly background. It is the human qualities of Bridie's Angel that attract and I think it is likely that Bridie made the Devil Asmoday a monster instead of a Mephistopheles for the sake of greater contrast with the Angel.

As reading matter there is not a superfluous word in the play; what is not there to delineate character and describe plot is there for decoration and it all delights the imagination of the reader. But as matter for production it is somewhat long drawn out. (pp. 77-8)

It is perhaps surprising that Bridie, whose male characters are usually so masculine, should have achieved such a feminine mind in Tobit, but apparently the author drew Tobit from his—Bridie's—own mother. Bridie's youngest brother, Mr. Eric Mavor, says that the portrait is very faithful, and I think we can regard Tobit, one of the best-loved of the Bridie characters, as a tribute to his mother. (pp. 79-80)

There is no doubt that Bridie abundantly achieved what he set out to do in this play, to create lovable characters and to portray through them God's reward to the generous and gentle people. Tobit, Anna and Tobias, especially Tobit, make an appealing family group, and the reciprocating excitement of Raphael, Sara and the other dazzling figures charges the domesticity of Tobit's family with a lively dramatic action which makes the play an enchanting experience.

Tobias and the Angel is one of Bridie's best plays. (pp. 80-1)

[There are three versions of the Jonah play:] *Jonah and the Whale . . . , The Sign of the Prophet Jonah* (a broadcast version) and *Jonah 3*. (p. 86)

As great drama, *Jonah* in all its versions falls short—but as a character study of Jonah himself and as a portrayal of the Almighty's sense of humour (has any other writer of religious drama given God a sense of humour?—I think not) the play has quality, a subtle quality that makes it worth while. In attempting to repeat the success of *Tobias and the Angel*, Bridie did not quite bring it off, but he added another charming play to the volume of religious drama. . . .

The production of *A Sleeping Clergyman*, Bridie's tenth full-length play, marked an important stage in the author's development. Like *The Switchback* and *The Anatomist*, it stands out from the others in this first ten as a gale of inspiration. These three plays of spirited attack, all with medical backgrounds, all concern the struggle of the creative urge in man to break through and move mountains, to declare what there is of human advancement in him. . . .

In *A Sleeping Clergyman* the creative urge itself is the central character. (p. 89)

Powerful in content and character though the play is, it must be admitted that it fails in form. . . .

If the *perfect* play must be contained in architecture as good as its content, and I think it must, then Bridie has not achieved a perfect play here. It has the faults of its virtue, powerful, but unshapely. He but rarely found a graceful shape for a play. He would begin well enough, with firm foundation and sturdy walls—following a good design, only to spoil the erection with violent bulges or fanciful detail or a roof which was either flat or eccentrically high.

In *A Sleeping Clergyman* the "roof" tends to flatten. It is a satisfying but not an abundantly dramatic finish. But much may be forgiven a play with such great virtues as this one. It has a powerful theme, and acutely observed character presented in brilliant and spontaneous dialogue. (p. 104)

[*Mr. Gillie,* the] examination of a village schoolmaster's remote and unsung career is probably Mr. Bridie's best play, for here his characteristic brilliance is perfectly mated with humanity. For once he has gone as deep with emotion as he ever went high with wit. The action mounts with a fine sense of form; character here is not to be so replete with cleverness that some sympathy must be sacrificed. As a story, a parable and an example of how a naturalistic, domestic drama should be written, *Mr. Gillie* succeeds abundantly. It is the only one of its kind in his entire collection, it is also the simplest of all his plays. (pp. 179-80)

Every character in the play is beautifully drawn. Mr. Gillie himself is Bridie's most lovable portrait, not excluding the biblical portraits. . . . Mrs. Gillie is a warm-hearted wife, common-sensical, but with enough uncommon common sense to have sensibility. Dr. Watson, Nelly's drunken old humbug of a parent, is a clever study of a selfish, weak, possessive father, and Gordon MacLeod missed none of the cruel sentimentality with which Bridie has invested the portrait. Mr. Gibb, the minister, whose duty it is to dismiss the schoolmaster as an unsuitably experimental guide for the young, is sufficiently conventional and expedient to highlight Mr. Gillie's greater claims to grace. And Tom and Nelly are tremendously alive; they both have the strain of violent egotism which Bridie can handle so well. (pp. 180-81)

While writing this book I have often been asked what I considered to be Bridie's best play. I have frequently asked others the same question and the answer was usually, *A Sleeping Clergyman*. I find it certainly the most absorbing argument, but not the best play. I cannot answer in the singular. The best of the naturalistic plays is surely *Mr. Gillie*. Faultlessly constructed, it is deeply human and exquisitely ironic: it has simplicity. It is first-class social criticism. I choose *The Forrigan Reel* as the best of the Scottish comedies, and I consider *The Baikie Charivari* and *The Queen's Comedy* to be the finest experiments. A special award to *The Dragon and the Dove* for the most beautifully fashioned and most witty satire on a biblical theme in modern theatre. The most powerful character study—Dr. Knox of *The Anatomist*. The most fascinating character—I am torn between Daphne Laureola and Harry Magog. And one could go on, not finding the best play but a company of individuals, each with some kind of claim to be singled out. (pp. 188-89)

Winifred Bannister, in her James Bridie and His Theatre *(copyright by Winifred Bannister), Rockliff, 1955, 262 p.*

J. B. PRIESTLEY (essay date 1956)

[Bridie] had no specific gift for story-telling, never mastered the economy and structure of narrative. We do less than justice to the remarkable qualities he did possess if we endow him with others he never even pretended to possess. (p. viii)

Actually in his work, though capable to the last of dashing off something just for a lark, he was less impudently wilful and wayward—less given to mere "flyting" in the Scots tradition—than he wished to appear to be. Because he started late, out of a very different profession in which he had won decent recognition, because he was at heart both proud (in the best sense) and shy, and dramatic criticism is more ruthless and damaging than any other sort, he made use of this appearance to cover certain defects while trying hard to remedy them. He had a lot of ideas, some of them not good; he was impatient and quickly lost interest in work that did not fulfil its first bright promise; and often he wrote too quickly and refused to have any second thoughts about a hastily finished piece. . . . Even so, he worked harder and longer, and revised more often, than he pretended to do. But he became the victim of his *persona*, the critics too often taking him at his word, telling him he was not taking sufficient trouble to write a sound last act, more than hinting he was careless and lazy.

These critics missed the point. It is true that Bridie created brilliant and memorable scenes and then time after time failed to produce a satisfying whole play. . . . But this was not from lack of patience and application, not from failure to reach the ordinary professional standard of competence. It was usually because Bridie was trying to do something very difficult to bring off successfully in the narrow naturalistic form preferred by most of our playhouses. It is a form admirably suited to a frugal-minded playwright with a trick of neat contrivance. But Bridie was like a tailor cutting awkwardly because he is using a rich brocade and not grey flannel. He was trying to cram a large loose mind and a large loose play into the narrow space of our convention. He was no born story-teller, but he nearly always wanted to tell much more of a story than most contemporary playwrights try to handle. There is enough dramatic stuff in one or two of Bridie's failures to keep neat contrivers like Mr. [Terence] Rattigan and Mr. [John] van Druten successfully going for years and years. (pp. ix-x)

Perhaps if he had had no other profession . . . he would have been able to abandon the naturalistic convention, in which he was always bursting the seams, and would have discovered for himself a new form of dramatic writing peculiarly suited to his needs. (There are signs of it in his later work for the Scottish Theatre.) . . . As it was, Bridie was doomed to be frequently disappointing, especially to those critics and playgoers who are more impressed by tidy construction than by the brilliance or depth of individual scenes. But when he found both a theme and a manner that allowed him to work with some ease within the limitations imposed by the conventional form, ranging from *A Sleeping Clergyman* to *Tobias and the Angel*, we are compelled at once to recognise his size and weight and originality.

Though many of his plays may have left us feeling confused and dubious, his best scenes—and they might occur anywhere—are blazing triumphs. At certain moments of heightened debate, the kind of scene in which Shaw excelled, Bridie at his highest pitch seems to me to excel Shaw. He is both as pointed and as eloquent; he may not have as much wit but he has more humour, a richer and warmer tone; and his characters appear to exist more in their own right than Shaw's. (pp. x-xi)

Bridie of course was very much a Scot. There seems to me far more of Scotland in his work than in [J. M.] Barrie's; at least, more of the masculine genius of the nation. . . . There are signs in his later plays that the feminine principle was at work in him at last—yet another reason why we must regret his comparatively early death—but the bulk of his drama is essentially the creation of a male Scot, happiest . . . away from the women, in a club when the bores (it can happen) have gone home. (p. xii)

Unlike nearly all the successful dramatists of the previous generation, he schemed and laboured and begged to reform the Theatre, to leave it wider open to younger men. (p. xiii)

J. B. Priestley, in his introduction to Meeting at Night *by James Bridie, Constable and Company Ltd., 1956, pp. vi-xiii.*

FREDERICK LUMLEY (essay date 1956)

The plays of James Bridie present an optimist's window on the world; he is a tolerant moralist little concerned . . . with social propaganda. Bridie, an acute observer of man, shows a shrewd sense of character throughout his work, a sense developed, no doubt, by the experience he gained when he was a medical practitioner. At any rate, he delights in poking fun at our foibles without preaching. His characters are without exception interesting people, the good are never too good and the bad are always human. . . . In his characters Bridie has a bond of understanding and sympathy, and transfers this to the audience even for characters they would not normally feel affection for at all (i.e. John Knox, or the Wee Free minister in *Mr. Bolfry*).

Throughout his work—some thirty plays—Bridie shows an

innate sense of theatre, and even in his poorest plays he never bores and even offers just a wee dose of idiosyncrasy which is the signature of Bridie's own civilised intellect. They are always interesting but often slap-dash. It was as if he had so many ideas in his fertile imagination that he rushed on to the next one without doing justice to his last one. As so many critics have complained, a play by Bridie has the appearance of being unfinished. It is more like a first draft, often in urgent need of revision and structural alteration. His refusal to take pains is regrettable, but fortunately a born playwright does not depend on that. (pp. 203-04)

Bridie never gave us a masterpiece by which he may be remembered by succeeding generations, but there is no reason why his themes should date. (p. 204)

Bridie came to the rescue of the English theatre when there was no one left after Shaw who could write the polished and witty conversation pieces which English audiences had grown to admire and demand instead of tragedy. It is ridiculous to call Bridie the Scottish Shavian . . . ; his plays have an atmosphere of their own. But his imagination, the sharpness of his intellect, the flow of language (he often makes his characters slightly tipsy in order to encourage the whirlwind of words to come more naturally!) and the roundness of character surely give Bridie . . . a place of honour in the theatre since Shaw. (p. 205)

> Frederick Lumley, "The State of the Drama," in his Trends in 20th Century Drama: A Survey Since Ibsen and Shaw (copyright 1956 by Frederick Lumley; reprinted by permission of Oxford University Press, Inc.; in Canada by Barrie & Jenkins), Rockliff Publishing Corporation Ltd., 1956, pp. 197-218.*

GERALD WEALES (essay date 1961)

James Bridie, who wrote out of Glasgow and, as often as not, for the Scottish theater, is the playwright who comes closest to Shaw in his use of religious figures and religious idiom in specifically personal terms. Bridie . . . wrote mainly comedies, but comedies in which such harsh realities as death, disease, and drunkenness are accepted and transcended. His penchant for puns and obvious verbal jokes was even more insistent than Shaw's, and he had a sense of fantasy that often shattered conventional play structure and placed his work close in form to the late Shavian extravaganzas. The chief criticism that was aimed at him all through his career was that his plays fell apart before the end or that his ideas were never fully developed. Actually, Bridie preferred to approach an idea skippingly, to run around it rather than to build it slowly and carefully; most of his plays, although they often leap from character to character, from place to place, from reality to fantasy, have a unity that is recognizable as Bridie's approach to life, as his point of view about the meaning and importance of the human being.

Although his career was dogged with comparisons to Shaw, Bridie never had political or religious views that were carefully articulated, as Shaw's were. . . . Bridie's religion, at least on the evidence of the plays, is amorphous; only in two of his last plays—The Queen's Comedy and The Baikie Charivari—did he appear to be working toward some specific statement about religion. For the most part, his plays express a faith in and a fondness for the individual, a dis-

trust of institutions—government and the church—a distaste for social compulsion, a suspicion of the overdedicated man, and a feeling for a God who is distant and impersonal, unconcerned with and uninvolved in the activities of men. This concept of God is best seen in A Sleeping Clergyman . . . , a play in which three generations are manipulated to show that the strain of genius in them overcomes their strain of violence, the operation of a Life Force, more accidental, less purposive than that of Shaw. The title of the play refers to a white-bearded clergyman who dozes in a chair in the Chorus openings to each act, clubroom scenes in which one man tells another the story. Bridie specifically identifies the clergyman and explains why he should sleep through the whole story: "God, who had set it all going, took his ease in an armchair throughout the play." (pp. 79-80)

In Susannah and the Elders . . . , Bridie manages to do two things—to save Susannah from false accusation and, at the same time, to endow the lecherous old men with a pathetic dignity. In Bridie's enlargement of the Aprocryphal story, the two Assyrian judges are self-indulgent old gentlemen, fond of good food, good company, good conversation. . . . They are concerned with form not substance. Having maneuvered Susannah, pure to the point of foolishness, into their garden, they stoop to violence, to lies, to murder (of the young man who comes in answer to her cries for help and whom the judges accuse as her lover). In the court scene, they are easily defeated by Daniel, but in the face of the penalty against them, they manage a dignity that they have not been able to achieve as judges and certainly not as would-be seducers. Daniel is drawn as a bright and angry young Jewish lawyer, defeating the oppressing Assyrians in the name of the oppressed Jews—as he is pictured in a number of the Apocryphal stories. In saving Susannah, Daniel has done what he knows had to be done; yet when one of his admirers suggests that God has spoken through his mouth, Daniel says, "I hope He did, Meschach. I do not know," as though he suspects that in some sense the Lord also spoke through the desires and the unhappiness of the defeated old men. (p. 84)

[In The Queen's Comedy and The Baikie Charivari] Bridie's religious ideas found their most effective dramatic form. The Queen's Comedy is a decidedly free working of Books XIV and XV of the Iliad, the section in which Juno seduces Jupiter (Bridie uses the Roman names) and gives the Greeks a chance to triumph momentarily over the Trojans. As in Homer, the action swings between earth and heaven. Bridie's gods are even more frivolous than those in Homer. The action on earth, except for some Colonel-Blimpish portraits of the Greek officers, is confined to discussions between a medical orderly and a plain foot soldier, conceived unfortunately in the clichés of contemporary colloquialism, and between the nurse Hecamede and the young doctor Machaon. When the four chief human characters are killed after the Greek advance is turned back, they are given a chance to confront the gods. It is the orderly who does the attacking, "Call yourself gods! I've seen savages up in Scythia make better gods in an old clay puddle. . . ." His indictment becomes a plea for the cessation of heavenly intervention, for the sleeping-clergyman concept of God. . . . Jupiter appears and makes a speech, telling how, as a child, he accidentally constructed the Universe and how he has been working on it ever since, not certain where it is to go. In substance, his speech hints at the

Shavian will; in tone, it sets him off from both man and the gods, makes him as distant as an impersonal force. . . . (pp. 86-7)

If *The Queen's Comedy* is Bridie's last clear statement about God, *The Baikie Charivari, or the Seven Prophets* is his last dealing with the devil. In this play, Bridie's most elaborately conceived and most carefully worked out, man triumphs over the devil and his agents. This "Miracle Play," as Bridic calls it, is told on two levels—the realistic and the fantastic—and it runs freely from one to another. The characters in it are real residents of the Scottish village of Baikie; they are also characters out of Punch and Judy and, beyond that, diabolic agents. In the fantasy scenes the play breaks into verse, sometimes rhymed, that achieves an intensity that is not so much the result of verbal ingenuity, as it is of the emotional and intellectual investment of the hero in his search for knowledge in and of the new world in which he finds himself. The action is inaugurated by the De'il who announces his intention to use the seven figures to try the hero. At the end of a career in India, a retired civil servant, named Pounce-Pellott, a combination of Punch and Pontius Pilate, . . . comes to Baikie with his wife (Judy) and his daughter (Baby). He meets an assortment of people and asks them all to dinner. Each of them offers a standard solution for the world's ills. (p. 88)

There is wryness in [Pounce-Pellot's curtain speech to the devil]:

> If you don't know, who knows? Nobody knows.
>   Nobody knows.
> I've killed all those fools who pretended to know.
> And so . . . and so . . .
> With the soothsayers littered about the stage
> That I slew in my rage,
> Who did not know . . . and no more do I . . .
> I must jest again and await my reply . . .
>
> Good-bye.

This end, however, is not defeatist. Pounce-Pellott has accepted his guilt in mankind's guilt and he has rejected easy solutions, the crutches that might protect him without helping him. In wielding his stick, he has also saved his daughter, for, as in Punch and Judy, the Seven Prophets have been after Baby. She decides to marry Toby Messan, the apprentice plumber, the man who does not work with theories. Bridie with a depth and a sadness that does not appear in many of his plays is reminding man that he still must beware the devil who takes so many and such provocative human forms. (pp. 89-90)

> *Gerald Weales, "A Doctrine of Substitution," in his* Religion in Modern English Drama *(copyright © 1961 by Gerald Weales), University of Pennsylvania Press, 1961, pp. 51-90.**

ANNE GREENE (essay date 1964)

In his essay "Equilibrium," Bridie names Calvin, Huxley, and Hegel as three "radio-active" influences on his thinking, and explains the nature of each: From Calvin he absorbed the doctrines of the Absolute, Election, and Predestination; from Huxley he absorbed the idea of man as a step in an evolutionary process; and from Hegel he learned a principle of dialectic—thesis, antithesis, synthesis—by whose means he tried to reconcile the other two. Thus he evolved the concept of a Master Experimenter who is in a

sense his Father, and of man as one of the experiments and a tool of the Experimenter. . . .

In his first play, *The Sunlight Sonata* or *To Meet the Seven Deadly Sins* . . . , the idea of man's heart as innately evil is suggested in the prologue by Beelzebub, a fatherly Devil who stands against a background of Highland scenery brooding over mankind. Beelzebub understands man's little hypocrisies and secret motives, and as he watches a group of Glasgow citizens having a picnic he knows what is in the heart of each. (p. 96)

[In] a sparkling, nonsensical manner the play makes the point that sin is an indispensable part of humanity. When Carmichael loses his pride he loses his usefulness as a minister. When Groundwater loses his avarice he loses the quality which made him a successful business man. . . .

In including among Groundwater's charities the "Do-you-believe-in-fairies Guild," the dramatist is satirizing Barrie, of whose Peter Pan he wrote: "Barrie should have been better grounded in the doctrine of Original Sin than to have invented such a character." (p. 97)

The Amazed Evangelist: A Nightmare . . . approaches the problem of evil from an entirely different standpoint. It tells of a pair of Glasgow newlyweds who fall into the clutches of a Cummer who quickly calls up the Devil. When the couple assert that they do not believe in a Devil, having recently read "A Popular Synopsis of the Views of the Neo-Mechanists," the Devil feels obliged to prove his existence. But he finds that in order to do so he must explain his opposite. . . . Thus God is explained as the evolutionary principle, or progress toward perfection, and evil as whatever hinders that progress.

In *A Sleeping Clergyman* . . . the evolutionary principle is dramatized on the biological level. It tells the story of three generations of Camerons. In the first two, evil hinders progress, but in the third the social impulses harness the antisocial ones, genius takes control, and the wheel moves forward. (p. 98)

Mr. Bolfry . . . makes the point that good and evil are reciprocating opposites on both the individual and the cosmic level, and that both elements are necessary in the process of evolution. Principally, however, it attacks the joyless, repressive influences of Calvinism as Bridie had known them in the Free Kirk, and presents a Blakean-Shavian Devil whose function it is to set the individual free. (p. 100)

[Throughout an evening the Minister, McCrimmon, and the Devil, Mr. Bolfry, carry on their argument.]

Mr. Bolfry represents the vigorous positive qualities which the Minister lacks, his freedom from repression being symbolized by his reaching for the Minister's medicinal whiskey and leaning over occasionally to pat the knee of the maid. The keynote of his philosophy is the freedom of the individual. He refers to the war in Europe and to the "lunatic" who is trying to regiment mankind, but the war that really interests him is a "Holy War"—a war to free man from his load of guilt and his fear of Hell and make him an *individual,* no longer one of a timid, trudging horde of "Christian Soldiers." He says his war is fought also for the freeing of man's genius—for the freedom of the artist and the poet. These points of concern suggest the dramatist's affinity with Shaw, as does Bolfry's emphasis on the creative impulse. (p. 101)

In this encounter the dramatist argues on both sides. Bolfry is his mouthpiece against the Minister's timid, repressive qualities; yet the pride of the dramatist is revealed no less than that of the Minister in McCrimmon's declaration that three hundred years of discipline in body, brain and soul has produced in Scotland "a breed of men that has not died out even in this shauchly generation." As the Minister explains the great principles of Calvinism, his language becomes that of a doctor whose long experience with human frailty has taught him to interpret these mysteries in terms of everyday life. (p. 102)

The portrayal of the Minister is not satire on Calvinism but on what the Free Kirk has made of Calvinism, while the portrayal of Bolfry is a reminder that Calvinism originated in a spirit of freedom and rebellion which animated the sermons of John Knox but has been lost in the Free Kirk. . . . [The] Minister feels Bolfry to be his own heart speaking evil. (pp. 102-03)

Bridie's view of the Devil is kaleidoscopic, however, and changes within the play. Bolfry is not satisfied to be merely the Minister's other self. . . . It is the *struggle* toward purpose that makes for progress rather than the *achievement,* he says. Denying the Minister's accusation that he is a Manichaean, "full of Dualistic sophistications," he identifies himself with that instrument of Providence who afflicted Job's body for the good of his soul; with the enemy who makes progress difficult but without whom there can be no victory. Bolfry thus represents one aspect of the evolutionary concept as defined in *The Amazed Evangelist.* . . .

The Queen's Comedy . . . , based on the fourteenth and fifteenth books of the *Iliad,* is a sharp satire on war, the Greek soldiers being portrayed as British "Tommies" and the Greek generals as British "military brass." . . . It raises the question "What is God and what is man's relation to him?" Until near the end, the answer is summed up in the play's epigraph:

> As flies to wanton boys are we to the Gods:
> They kill us for their sport.

But in Jupiter's last speech there emerges an evolutionary concept in which war is seen as a temporary evil in a long process of development. (p. 103)

The groping and striving and misplaced faith of the Rebels are all the more poignant in the light of the duplicity and frivolity of the gods. The character of Jupiter, however, requires special consideration. . . . Most striking is his duality, a quality suggested by his appearing "in two minds about something" and emphasized in the words of Juno: "It is not possible to understand you. . . . You are . . . the inscrutable Master of all things. The sower, the reaper, the disheveller, the builder-up." . . . Finally, Jupiter speaks in the accents of a Master Experimenter—one who does not himself know the final shape of things but is compelled by his very nature to keep on experimenting. He tells of his restless childhood, and of a day when his mother pulled off a chunk of Chaos from the round on the kitchen dresser and threw it at him. "There," she said, "Sonny, take that into the yard and do whatever you like with it." He tells of moulding his bit of Chaos until it looked "something like an egg and something like a sausage." He called his little toy the Universe. But he found his Universe hard to control because it was full of "mad, meaningless, fighting forces." He kept working, however, until by arranging the forces in

a certain way he got a thing called Life. "Life is very interesting," he says. "I am still working on its permutations and combinations." (pp. 105-06)

This is the concept of a Master Experimenter "who is in a sense my Father" and of man as one of the experiments and a tool of the Experimenter. "I have not nearly completed my Universe," adds Jupiter. "There is plenty of time. Plenty of time. You must have patience."

In *The Baikie Charivari* or *The Seven Prophets* . . . , the evil with which the dramatist is concerned is the disorder in modern society. This disorder is viewed through the eyes and mind of Pounce-Pellott. . . . The play dramatizes the role of Pounce-Pellott as rebel, judge, and truth-seeker as the prophets of confusion pursue him, each on behalf of his ideology. (p. 106)

A major aspect of the play is its satire on the values of the modern world. (p. 108)

But the main interest centers in Pounce-Pellott as he rejects all these forces that would dominate and regulate him. . . . Pounce is not only a rebel; he is a *concerned* rebel—concerned not so much for himself as for the next generation. (pp. 108-09)

As truth-seeker Pounce gets no answer. . . . (p. 109)

[These plays] show Bridie himself as truth-seeker. They show his persistent effort to synthesize the Calvinist idea of God with the Huxleian concept of an evolutionary process. They also show his effort to include in the evolutionary concept both good and evil as reciprocating opposites, thereby denying the idea of a dualistic universe with evil as an independent force. He comes near achieving a complete synthesis of these ideas in *The Queen's Comedy* with the portrayal of Jupiter as a Master Experimenter who combines the functions of creating and destroying and is in a sense his Father, and of man as one of the experiments and a tool of the Experimenter. It must be admitted that the Calvinistic aspect of this portrayal is weak. Frequent references to Calvinistic doctrine and the frequent appearance of fantasy devils reveal the dramatist's profound moral and emotional involvement with Calvinism; but the core of his thought, his experimental approach, and his suspension of final judgement are Huxleian. (p. 110)

Anne Greene, "Bridie's Concept of the Master Experimenter," in Studies in Scottish Literature, *Vol. II, No. 2, October, 1964, pp. 96-110.*

HELEN L. LUYBEN (essay date 1965)

Inconclusiveness, or ambiguity, is inherent in the structure of a Bridie play because the plays are arguments in which the balance of thesis and antithesis is maintained and of which the conclusion is never a resolution. They are arguments about, or searches for, truth, and about truth there is no finality. Even Bridie's fantasies—although he would pass them off as pure entertainment—must be construed as arguments. (p. 24)

Bridie's use of the Adam myth was never . . . as specific as it was in his first play, *The Switchback.* Usually he was simply describing a temptation and loss of innocence—a temptation by daemons to leave a state of innocence . . . in order to realize a potentiality beyond innocence. The New Adams have two choices after their fall. They can attempt to regain their lost innocence, that is they can deny all daemons, can look the other way and go about their house-hold tasks, as Raphael suggests Sara should do. Or they can walk boldly toward a New Eden, to live inspired by their ruling daemon in a land beyond the further temptation of the routed daemon. Mallaby says in the last act of *The Switchback,* "Mankind has many inventions, but only three ways of happiness—Make-believe, Curiosity and Irony. The first two ways I have travelled hopefully on aching feet. They are finished. I'll see what is in the third." Having lived in a state of innocence that was only make-believe, Mallaby "falls" under the temptation of daemons representing opposite forces—in a moment of inspiration or curiosity—and chooses to be led by the victorious daemon into the Land of Irony, beyond further temptation. This is the most general application of the Adam myth, corresponding to its treatment in other plays. But the myth can be applied more specifically in *The Switchback.* . . . (pp. 35-6)

Mrs. Mallaby is an Eve, and Palmyra is Mallaby's new Eden. Mallaby, at the end of the play, is a fallen Adam, tempted by Eve and a pack of serpents out of his innocence, and off to a new Eden in the pursuit of knowledge. Again one can look to situation, characterization, and language to prove Bridie's intention. . . . First of all, Mallaby's characterization has the innocence of Adam—a child-like innocence which reveals itself in emotional instability, egotism, stubbornness, tactlessness, and gullibility. Mallaby hardly needs alcohol to make him lose his inhibitions. (p. 42)

If Mallaby is the traditional Adam, forced to leave Eden because of a first disobedience (eating the fruit of the Tree of Knowledge), and if Craye is an archangel delivering God's orders, Mallaby sins in putting his responsibility to himself above his responsibility to his profession. The fall, then, comes at the end of Act II, when he refuses to publish a disclaimer, having completely submitted to the temptations of Mrs. Mallaby and Burmeister. Symbolically, this triumph of self over social responsibility can be construed as tasting of the fruit of self-knowledge, or leaving a period of self-ignorance (innocence) to enter a period of self-knowledge (experience). (p. 45)

If the heroes of Bridie's early plays . . . are innocent Adams, certainly Pounce-Pellott and all the heroes of the later plays are old or experienced Adams, residents not of the make-believe Garden of Eden but of the Land of Irony. The best of them speak with a godlike distance or irony, in imitation of the voice of the morality operating in all of Bridie's plays. . . .

Among Bridie's early ironic Adams, which all are minor characters, Mr. Samuels, George's savior in *The Black Eye,* is most memorable (the divine Raphael in *Tobias and the Angel,* whose irony is natural and not cultured, cannot be considered in this classification). Of the heroes in the middle plays, only George Prout in *It Depends What You Mean* suggests this kind of distance when he faces the reality that his wife does not spend her life thinking of others (as he believed she did when they met) but is capable of sulking for ten days if he forgets her birthday. The change between Mr. Samuels, a minor, eccentric character, and Pounce-Pellott, a major character of tragic stature, was taking place in Prout. When Bridie, about the time that he wrote *The Baikie Charivari,* attempted to use an ironic Adam in the role of a comic eccentric, a misfit—the char-

acter of George Triple in *Meeting at Night*—most of the fun had gone out. (p. 130)

Lady Katherine Pitts of *Daphne Laureola* . . . is symbolic of something much larger and more significant than a titled London matron misused by the uncivilized persons around her. She seems a symbol of disillusioned innocence, a symbol of England after the Second World War, and by extension, of Western civilization. Yet she is only partly successful as such a symbol, is a much lesser Pounce-Pellott. She is a transitional character between George Prout and Mr. Gillie, her disillusionment rendering her ineffectual like Prout; the two of them, Prout and Lady Pitts, are as ineffectual in their experience as Robert Gillet of *Babes in the Wood* is in his innocence.

Daphne Laureola is transitional in still another sense: It suggests the conscious poetic method which Bridie was to use in his last play. In it Bridie is using the myth of Daphne . . . [Apollo, Edith Hamilton writes,] came upon Daphne hunting in a short dress with her hair "in wild disarray," and he thought, "What would she not look like properly dressed and with her hair nicely arranged?" He pursued her, but she called to her father for help and was changed into a laurel tree, thus escaping violation. (p. 132)

Lady Pitts is in every sense of the word a *fallen* woman. . . . She is bound by no illusions about herself or others; she is anti-romantic and ironic. Ernest is "an excitable. crazy, ignorant, young man" who is in love with himself, who is not interested in *her* but in finding a Beatrice. . . . She is a bad woman, playing at respectability, "a kept woman," she says. . . . She is kept by Sir Joseph . . . , like a jewel in a glass case; she allowed him to buy her ("It's the only way I ever had of getting what I needed," he says) and to make of her a "collector's piece," "Pure bloody Hepplewhite." Ernest would do what Sir Joseph has done; he would make an object of Katherine Pitts in an attempt to attain something of inhuman purity. He would make her a laurel tree, a goddess. That she has had enough of worship is revealed in the final act when she enters the restaurant with Vincent, who could never be accused of putting her on a pedestal. (pp. 135-36)

Certainly Katherine Pitts symbolizes in one sense England in the aftermath of war, rejecting romanticism for realism, illusion for reality. Bridie contrasts the Soho restaurant, cluttered with ladders, ceiling and floor sheets, and only half plastered, with Sir Joseph's secluded garden. . . . (p. 136)

Two structural matters should be noted. First, the play approaches poetic drama, not entirely because of the metaphorical nature of its language but because of the symbolism of its action and characterizations. The minor characters are "types," as Margaret Marshall notes [see excerpt above], but this is intentional; they are only symbols of humanity. The play has a cyclic structure appropriate to its theme: the same people are present in the restaurant in the first and fourth acts; their conversation is essentially unchanged. Acts II and III are the antistrophe, contrasting with strophe both in setting and tone: Lady Pitts in the Soho restaurant—the public self—is invulnerable; the tone she sets is predominantly brittle. Lady Pitts at home reveals a vulnerability which radiates softness. Second, Bridie in *Daphne Laureola* uses to its maximum effect a device which cannot have escaped the reader's notice in his plays; as early as *The Switchback,* when Mallaby, fortified by whisky, faced Sir Anthony Craye, Bridie used intoxication not only as a device for character revelation but also to symbolize inspiration, heightened sensibility, possession by daemons or gods. (p. 139)

What Bridie failed to do dramatically with Lady Pitts he did with Pounce-Pellott in *The Baikie Charivari,* a play similar in theme, tone, and poetic structure yet differing in the final choice it makes. But the resurgence of courage, the resolution beyond Lady Pitts' choice of despair, came first in the realistic play *Mr. Gillie.* (p. 140)

In choosing the way of forlorn hope rather than of acceptance or compromise, Gillie has literally chosen to slay himself to be himself. In choosing survival and Vincent, Lady Pitts has chosen to be to herself enough—that is, she has refused possession by any master, Apollo or otherwise. While seeming to involve herself with humanity by her marriage to her chauffeur, actually she withdraws. But not Gillie, who chooses slavery, possession, involvement. . . . What is important is that Gillie has been mastered by something beyond the self, by literature and art. Yet he is not entirely unlike Lady Pitts, for he also is an ironic Adam, and his muted despair is the most haunting found in all the plays.

Because of the paradox involved in slaying oneself to be oneself, Gillie's behavior is inherently ambiguous. He has chosen the way of slavery or dedication, responsibility or commitment, and selflessness, yet he attacks servility and conventional conceptions of responsibility and is attacked for irresponsibility and selfishness. He is committed to inspiring the human soul and would die rather than fail to perform his duty. . . . (pp. 143-44)

Possessed by the gods, Gillie finally seems to win at life, too—the distance of a seeing Man, an irony which gives him an infinite capacity for taking (that is, bearing) pains. Thus pervading the play is this necessary ambiguity. . . . (p. 148)

Although the action and language of *Mr. Gillie* are meaningful on several levels, the play within the fantastic framework of the heavenly court remains naturalistic. This is not true of *The Baikie Charivari,* which alternates the realistic with the poetic more consistently than the two were alternated in *Daphne Laureola* and without, in this play, use of the device of intoxication to excuse dialogue which is meaningless on the literal level. (pp. 148-49)

What is Bridie's intention in *The Baikie Charivari?* Structurally he intends a miracle play, he says. The play is an intellectual fantasia, as [T. C.] Worsley says [see excerpt above], non-naturalistic, poetic in structure as well as in language because it is poetic in conception; its action interprets one symbol—the internal conflict of a human soul as symbolized by the struggle of Pounce-Pellott against his tempters. [There is] control in the use of the symbol of Pontius Pilate and . . . originality in the use of the characters from the Punch and Judy show. . . . Philosophically Bridie is still concerned with the paradox involved in the impossibility of arriving at absolute truth but the necessity—the moral duty—of choosing and defending if necessary truth and good over evil. In his last story of temptation, he is specifically concerned with man's temptation to be *less* than himself, to become dehumanized and impersonal, to subordinate his individuality and will to some collective

impulse, in an effort to adapt and adjust to an impersonal environment. In Pounce-Pellott, as in Gillie, he creates a character whose soul will not adapt itself to its environment, a character who resists society when it is wrong—not by any absolute standard, but according to his lights.

The Baikie Charivari suggests a summary of Bridie's work, a last word on the themes which teased his mind during the twenty years that followed *The Switchback* and that carried Mallaby to the East and back again. A study of Bridie is completed, then, when the last implication of the play has been explored. If such finality is not entirely possible, it is only further testimony to Bridie's genius. (pp. 164-65)

Helen L. Luyben, in her James Bridie: Clown and Philosopher *(© 1965 by the Trustees of the University of Pennsylvania), University of Pennsylvania Press, 1965, 180 p.*

JAMES A. MICHIE (essay date 1969)

It is a pity that so much twentieth century religious drama lacks the humanizing element of humour. A notable exception is James Bridie. Like the mediaeval dramatists, he did not make the mistake of confusing seriousness with solemnity. In dramatizing the Old Testament story of Jonah, for example, he captured very well the spirit of so many of the Mystery plays, the combination of the sincerely religious with the broadly comic. Of course he did not have to invent the humour; it was there to begin with in the Bible narrative; but he deepened and extended it. Humour, varying from the boisterous to the oblique, from the gently mocking to the astringently ironic, is the powerful solvent of spiritual complacency, ignorant and illiberal narrow-mindedness, and obdurate egoism. It is a humour that stems ultimately from compassion. This, too, was a quality which Bridie shared with the Old Testament author. The affinities between the two writers are unmistakeable, both in attitude and in treatment of their theme. Both obviously hated smug exclusiveness and intolerance; both disliked men whose religion separated them from other people; and both esteemed humility. The author of the book of Jonah clearly implied that the Israelites should realize, with deeper humility, the great honour bestowed on them as the bearer of the message that God is love. Bridie no less clearly indicates that a proper sense of modesty will help a prophet not to confuse his inspired message with his own quite ordinary, fallible self. Being artists, however, both avoid heavy didacticism in conveying their meaning. Thus, instead of arguing about exclusiveness in religion, the Biblical author wrote a tale about it, spun out of his lively inventive mind a story of marvellous events to capture his readers' attention. In adapting this story for the modern theatre Bridie maintained its narrative momentum but broadened its scope and, without overt moralising, brought out its relevance today for all who seek to build walls about their religion. Bridie's God is too big to be imprisoned within the walls of any particular sect or church. The type of prophet who was unwilling to see God's grace extended to the heathen of Nineveh must have seemed to him a proper target for satire, not unmingled with pity. Narrow-mindedness and intolerance were anathema to Bridie. Pomposity, vanity and pretentiousness also come in for a rough time in this and other plays. Certainly it is noticeable that in many of his works some of the wisest utterances come from the lips of the unassuming men and women.

On this occasion, however, the lesson on humility is read by the Whale, a characteristically whimsical touch by the dramatist. Jonah, the son of Amittai, had done great work, it seems, in the little village of Gittah-Hepher. In his not altogether modest way he had been conscious of possessing an impressive personality and considerable magnetism. He had set about the reformation of Gittah-Hepher and in next to no time had the pleasure of seeing it transformed beyond all recognition. In three weeks the ribald songs ceased, the dancing feet trod warily, and the garish garments had given way to decent sackcloth. All of which was very gratifying to the prophet's self-esteem. But now, commissioned by God to go and cry against Nineveh, he flees like a coward to the coast and takes a *single* to Tarshish.

A storm arises. The ship is struck by lightning; she begins to leak like a sieve; the starboard bank of oars is smashed; and she is heading for Davy Jones' locker. (pp. 429-30)

Eventually Jonah, as the cause of all the trouble, is pitched overboard and is consumed by a passing whale. It is no ordinary whale that Bridie gives us. It has a remarkable flair for metaphysics and an exegetical eloquence unlooked for in those quarters. For three days and three nights Jonah is subjected to a ceaseless flow of cetacean rhetoric. During that time the whale attempts to improve and broaden the prophet's mind. The belly of a whale is perhaps as good a place as any to have the edges rubbed off one's provincialism. It is also a fine touch of dramatic irony, since it is a drastic change for Jonah to find himself at the receiving end of a harangue. It is the painful but salutary kind of experience he needs. (p. 430)

In the course of four scenes we have been transported in turn from the gates of Gittah-Hepher, across a blasted heath, to the hustle and bustle of the seaport town of Joppa, and thence to the whale's ample interior, specially illuminated for the occasion. Now, for the fifth scene, we are translated to the King's Palace overlooking Nineveh. His Majesty is heavily oppressed with the tedium of life and requires of the Governor to know some of the celebrated people in town tonight. . . . Jonah is summoned to relate his amazing adventure and at once the King is roused from apathy and sensuality by the dynamic personality of the prophet. To his consternation, Jonah prophesies the total destruction of the city and its inhabitants in forty days; and to such good purpose that the King immediately exhorts his people to repent. Sackcloth and ashes are now the order of the day.

In the sixth and last scene we are taken to a low hill looking across the Tigris to Nineveh. Day after day in the burning sun Jonah waits for his prophecy to come true. He is confident. He knows that his Vindicator liveth. But on the long-awaited day nothing happens. Non cecidit Nineveh. No trumpet sounds in Zion. Jonah, with un-prophet-like petulance, curses the day that ever he saw the light. He will become a mock and a hissing to the uncircumcised. With the salvation of a whole city to his credit he can think only of his own reputation. By sparing the city the Lord, he feels, has let him down. . . .

"How is it," asked the great Jowett, "that some people are so much sterner than God?" How indeed. Bridie's play goes some way towards answering this question and suggesting a remedy. It is a delightful play, one that can be enjoyed simply as a good story. But it would be a pity if the spirit of it, so close to that of the New Testament, were missed in mere amusement at its curious details. (p. 431)

James A. Michie, "Educating the Prophets," in Modern Drama *(copyright © 1969, University of Toronto, Graduate Centre for Study of Drama; with the permission of* Modern Drama*), Vol. 2, February, 1969, pp. 429-31.*

BIBLIOGRAPHY

Brown, Ivor. "Biblical (*Tobias and the Angel*)." In *Specimens of English Dramatic Criticism XVII-XX Centuries,* edited by A. C. Ward, pp. 316-20. London: Oxford University Press, 1945.
    Praises the liveliness of this biblical play and Bridie's modern handling of traditional themes.

Dukes, Ashley. "The English Scene." *Theatre Arts Monthly* xxiii, No. 10 (October 1939): 704-08.
    Brief laudatory comments on *Tobias and the Angel* citing its religious and secular importance.

Krutch, Joseph Wood. "A Fig from Thistles." *The Nation* CXXXIX, No. 3616 (24 October 1934): 486-87.
    A review of *A Sleeping Clergyman* acknowledging Bridie's shortcoming in dramatic construction while appreciating the substance of his play.

Luyben, Helen L. "Bridie's Last Play." *Modern Drama* V, No. 4 (February 1963): 400-14.
    A long look at *Baikie Charivari* as a poetic and symbolic play in structure and language.

Luyben, Helen L. "James Bridie and the Prodigal Son Story." *Modern Drama* VII, No. 1 (May 1964): 35-45.
    An analysis of the prodigal son theme in Bridie's early play *The Black Eye.*

Walter, Marie. "The Grateful Dead: An Old Tale Newly Told." *Southern Folklore Quarterly* XXIII, No. 4 (December 1959): 190-95.
    Essay linking Bridie's twentieth-century Tobias "modernized and Anglicized" to a long tradition in folklore preceding and including the *Book of Tobit* in the *Apocrypha* and originating in the family of stories in The Grateful Dead tradition.

Wittig, Kurt. "Scottish Drama." In his *The Scottish Tradition in Literature,* pp. 318-22. Edinburgh: Oliver and Boyd, 1958.
    Identifies Bridie as characteristically Scottish with his concern about "good and evil, sin and righteousness" and his increasing development of these themes with each new play.

Worsley, T. C. "A Bridie Triumph: *Daphne Laureola*" and "Two New Plays: *Mr. Gillie.*" In his *The Fugitive Art: Dramatic Commentaries 1947-1951,* pp. 69-71, p. 128. London: John Lehmann, 1952.
    Review of *Daphne Laureola* with much praise for performance of Dame Edith Evans and some reference to the literary merit of the play. Also included is a cursory review of *Mr. Gillie.*

Anton (Pavlovich) Chekhov

1860-1904

(Also transliterated as Chekov, Tchehov, Tchekhov, Čechov, Čexov, Čekov, Čechov, Čehov, or Chehov; also wrote under pseudonyms of Antosha Chekhonte, My Brother's Brother, and A Man without a Spleen) Russian dramatist, short story writer, and novelist.

In stature and significance Chekhov is the most prominent Russian author of the literary generation succeeding Tolstoy and Dostoyevsky. He stands pre-eminent for his stylistic innovations in the form of short stories and dramas, and for his depth of insight into the human condition. Although Chekhov was influenced for a time by Tolstoy, his work does not share the variety and vaulting ideological proportions of the older writer's. Instead, Chekhov's stories and dramas are more uniform in mood and narrower in scope, frequently illustrating situations of hardship, boredom, and untragic suffering. The view of Chekhov as an utter pessimist, however, has always met with opposition, particularly from those Soviet critics who see the Russian author as a chronicler of the degenerating land-owner classes during an era of imminent revolution.

The exact relationship between Chekhov and his work has been a matter of interest for critics, and a distinction is sometimes made to isolate the somber spirit of the stories and plays from the personal philosophy of their author. Chekhov in fact expressed optimism with regard to social progress, which he believed would be furthered by scientific advancement.

Trained as a physician, Chekhov derived much practical insight from his experience in medical science, and he wrote his first stories and sketches while attending medical school in Moscow. Though these first writings were pieces of pure humor—his only novel was a satire of the detective genre—Chekhov eventually developed a prose and dramatic style of a completely different tone. His mature artistic method was based upon the ideals of nonmoralizing objectivity in prose and unsensationalized realism in drama. The realism in Chekhov's plays has seemed to some critics as merely a recreation of the oppressively formless and banal quality in everyday existence. Others, however, perceive subtlety of form comparable to the meticulous intricacies of a Henry James novel.

The first performance of *The Sea-Gull* was roundly booed, but the play was successful two years later when director Konstantin Stanislavski emphasized, some critics say over-emphasized, the more dismal aspects of Chekhov's art. Chekhov himself felt his plays suffered from the excessively gloomy interpretations of actors and directors. His early plays included a number of comic farces, and later he subtitled *The Cherry Orchard* "A Comedy," genuinely intending it to be viewed as such. It is the later dramas, including *Uncle Vanya* and *The Three Sisters*, that have led to Chekhov's image as exclusively a portrayer of futile existences and a forerunner of the modernist tradition of the absurd. Critics such as Ronald Hingley have attempted to overcome this view of a pessimistic Chekhov while at the same time trying to avoid the equally erroneous image of a totally optimistic one. The difficulty that critics have had in arriving at a balanced and accurate identity for Chekhov is perhaps one of the most significant indications of an author whose work promises an unending source of interpretive possibilities.

PRINCIPAL WORKS

P'yessa bez nazvaniya (drama) 1881
  [*That Worthless Fellow Plantonov*, 1930]
Pёstrye rasskazy (short stories) 1886
Nevinnye rechi (short stories) 1887
V sumerkakh (short stories) 1887
Ivanov: Drama v chetyryokh deystviyakh (drama) 1889
  [*Ivanoff* published in *Plays*, 1912]
Rasskazy (short stories) 1889
Leshy: Komediya v chetyryokh deystviyakh (drama)
  1890
  [*The Wood Demon: A Comedy in Four Acts*, 1925]
Chayka: Komediya v chetyryokh deystviyakh (drama)
  1896
  [*The Sea-Gull* published in *Plays*, 1912]
*Djadja Vanya: Stseny iz derevenskoy zhizni v chetyryokh
  deystviyakh* (drama) 1897
  [*Uncle Vanya* published in *Plays*, 1912]
Chekhov: Polnoe sobranie sochineniy (short stories and
  dramas) 1900-04
The Black Monk, and Other Stories (short stories) 1903
Visňevyǐ sad (drama) 1904
  [*The Cherry Garden: A Comedy in Four Acts*, 1908]
The Kiss, and Other Stories (short stories) 1908
The Darling, and Other Stories (short stories) 1916
The Duel, and Other Stories (short stories) 1916
The Lady with the Dog, and Other Stories (short stories)
  1917
The Party, and Other Stories (short stories) 1917

MAXIM GORKY (essay date 1906)

Anton Pavlovich in his early stories was already able to reveal in the dim sea of banality its tragic humour; one has only to read his "humorous" stories with attention to see what a lot of cruel and disgusting things, behind the humorous words and situations, had been observed by the author with sorrow and were concealed by him.

He was ingenuously shy; he would not say aloud and openly to people: "Now do be more decent"; he hoped in vain that they would themselves see how necessary it was that they should be more decent. He hated everything banal and foul, and he described the abominations of life in the noble language of a poet, with the humorist's gentle smile, and behind the beautiful form of his stories people scarcely noticed the inner meaning, full of bitter reproach.

The dear public, when it reads his *Daughter of Albion*, laughs and hardly realizes how abominable is the well-fed squire's mockery of a person who is lonely and strange to everyone and everything. In each of his humorous stories I hear the quiet, deep sigh of a pure and human heart, the hopeless sigh of sympathy for men who do not know how to respect human dignity, who submit without any resistance to mere force, live like fish, believe in nothing but the necessity of swallowing every day as much thick soup as possible, and feel nothing but fear that someone, strong and insolent, will give them a hiding.

No one understood as clearly and finely as Anton Chekhov the tragedy of life's trivialities, no one before him showed men with such merciless truth the terrible and shameful picture of their life in the dim chaos of burgeois everyday existence.

His enemy was banality; he fought it all his life long; he ridiculed it, drawing it with a pointed and unimpassioned pen, finding the mustiness of banality even where at the first glance everything seemed to be arranged very nicely, comfortably, and even brilliantly. . . . (pp. 107-09)

Reading Anton Chekhov's stories, one feels oneself in a melancholy day of late autumn, when the air is transparent and the outline of naked trees, narrow houses, greyish people, is sharp. Everything is strange, lonely, motionless, helpless. The horizon, blue and empty, melts into the pale sky, and its breath is terribly cold upon the earth, which is covered with frozen mud. The author's mind, like the autumn sun, shows up in hard outline the monotonous roads, the crooked streets, the little squalid houses in which tiny, miserable people are stifled by boredom and laziness and fill the houses with an unintelligible, drowsy bustle. (pp. 109-10)

There passes before one a long file of men and women, slaves of their love, of their stupidity and idleness, of their greed for the good things of life; there walk the slaves of the dark fear of life; they straggle anxiously along, filling life with incoherent words about the future, feeling that in the present there is no place for them.

At moments out of the grey mass of them one hears the sound of a shot: Ivanov or Treplev has guessed what he ought to do and has died.

Many of them have nice dreams of how pleasant life will be in three hundred years, but it occurs to none of them to ask themselves who will make life pleasant if we only dream.

In front of that dreary, grey crowd of helpless people there passed a great, wise, and observant man; he looked at all these dreary inhabitants of his country, and, with a sad smile, with a tone of gentle but deep reproach, with anguish in his face and in his heart, in a beautiful and sincere voice, he said to them:

"You live badly, my friends. It is shameful to live like that." (p. 111)

> *Maxim Gorky, in his* Reminiscences of Anton Chekhov, *translated by S. S. Koteliansky and Leonard Woolf (reprinted by permission of the translator's literary estates and The Hogarth Press Ltd), B. W. Huebsch, Inc., 1921 (originally published in Russian in 1906; and reprinted as "Anton Chekhov: Fragments of Recollections," in his* Reminiscences of Tolstoy, Chekhov, and Andreev, *translated by Katherine Mansfield, S. S. Koteliansky, and Leonard Woolf, The Hogarth Press, 1948, pp. 91-111).*

MAURICE BARING (essay date 1910)

Tchekov's stories deal for the greater part with the middle classes, the minor landed gentry, the minor officials, and the professional classes. Tolstoy is reported to have said that Tchekov was a photographer, a very talented photographer, it is true, but still only a photographer. But Tchekov has one quality which is difficult to find among photographers, and that is humour. His stories are frequently deliciously droll. They are also often full of pathos, and they invariably possess the peculiarly Russian quality of simplicity and unaffectedness. He never underlines his effects, he never nudges the reader's elbow. Yet there is a certain amount of truth in Tolstoy's criticism. Tchekov does not paint with the great sweeping brush of a Velasquez, his stories have not the great broad colouring of Maupassant, they are like mezzotints; and in some ways they resemble the new triumphs of the latest developments of artistic photography in subtle effects of light and shade, in delicate tones and half-tones, in elusive play of atmosphere.

Apart from its artistic merits or defects, Tchekov's work is historically important and interesting. Tchekov represents the extreme period of stagnation in Russian life and literature. (pp. 263-64)

Tchekov, more than any other writer, has depicted for us the attitude of mind, the nature and the feelings of the whole of this generation. . . . And nowhere can the quality of this frame of mind, and the perfume, as it were, of this period be better felt and apprehended than in the plays of Anton Tchekov; for in his plays we get not only what is most original in his work as an artist, but the quintessence of the atmosphere, the attitude of mind, and the shadow of what the *Zeitgeist* brought to the men of his generation. (p. 265)

Tchekov's discovery is this, that real life, as we see it every day, can be made just as interesting on the stage as the catastrophes or the difficulties which are more or less exceptional, but which are chosen by dramatists as their material because they are dramatic. (p. 271)

He shows us the changes, the revolutions, the vicissitudes, the tragedies, the comedies, the struggles, the conflicts, the catastrophes, that happen in the souls of men, but he goes a step further than other dramatists in the way in which he shows us these things. He shows us these things as we ourselves perceive or guess them in real life, without the help of poetic soliloquies or monologues, without the help of a Greek chorus or a worldly *raisonneur,* and without the aid of startling events which strip people of their masks. He shows us bits of the everyday life of human beings as we see it, and his pictures of ordinary human beings, rooted in certain circumstances, and engaged in certain avocations, reveal to us further glimpses of the life that is going on inside these people. The older dramatists, even when they deal exclusively with the inner life of man, without the aid of any outside action, allow their creations to take off their masks and lay bare their very inmost souls to us.

Tchekov's characters never, of their own accord, take off their masks for the benefit of the audience, but they retain them in exactly the same degree as people retain them in real life; that is to say, we sometimes guess by a word, a phrase, a gesture, the humming of a tune, or the smelling of a flower, what is going on behind the mask; at other times we see the mask momentarily torn off by an outbreak of inward passion, but never by any pressure of an outside and artificial machinery, never owing to the necessity of a situation, the demands of a plot, or the exigencies of a problem; in fact, never by any forces which are not those of life itself. (pp. 273-74)

[Although Tchekov's plays are as interesting to read as the work of any first-rate novelist, they] are a thousand times more interesting to see on the stage than they are to read. A thousand effects which the reader does not suspect make themselves felt on the boards. The reason of this is that Tchekov's plays realise Goethe's definition of what plays should be. "Everything in a play," Goethe said, "should be symbolical, and should lead to something else." By symbolical, of course, he meant morally symbolical,—he did not mean that the play should be full of enigmatic puzzles, but that every event in it should have a meaning and cast a shadow larger than itself.

The atmosphere of Tchekov's plays is laden with gloom, but it is a darkness of the last hour before the dawn begins. His note is not in the least a note of despair: it is a note of invincible trust in the coming day. The burden of his work is this—life is difficult, there is nothing to be done but to work and to continue to work as cheerfully as one can; and his triumph as a playwright is that for the first time he has shown in prose,—for the great poets have done little else,— behind the footlights, what it is that makes life difficult. Life is too tremendous, too cheerful, and too sad a thing to

be condensed into an abstract problem of lines and alphabetical symbols; and those who in writing for the stage attempt to do this, achieve a result which is both artificial and tedious. Tchekov disregarded all theories and all rules which people have hitherto laid down as the indispensable qualities of stage writing; he put on the stage the things which interested him because they were human and true; things great or infinitesimally small; as great as love and as small as a discussion as to what are the best *hors d'oeuvres;* and they interest us for the same reason. (pp. 298-99)

> Maurice Baring, "The Plays of Anton Tchekov," in his Landmarks in Russian Literature, *Methuen & Co. Ltd., 1910 (and reprinted by Methuen, 1916), pp. 263-99.*

WILLIAM LYON PHELPS　(essay date 1911)

Although Chekhov belongs to our day, and represents contemporary Russia, he stands in the middle of the highway of Russian fiction, and in his method of art harks back to the great masters. He perhaps resembles Turgenev more than any other of his predecessors, but he is only a faint echo. He is like Turgenev in the delicacy and in the aloofness of his art. He has at times that combination of the absolutely real with the absolutely fantastic that is so characteristic of Gogol: one of his best stories, *The Black Monk,* might have been written by the author of *The Cloak* and *The Portrait.* He is like Dostoevski in his uncompromising depiction of utter degradation; but he has little of Dostoevski's glowing sympathy and heartpower. He resembles Tolstoi least of all. The two chief features of Tolstoi's work—self-revelation and moral teaching—must have been abhorrent to Chekhov, for his stories tell us almost nothing about himself and his own opinions, and they teach nothing. His art is impersonal, and he is content with mere diagnosis. His only point of contact with Tolstoi is his grim fidelity to detail, the peculiar Russian realism common to every Russian novelist. (pp. 238-39)

Among recent writers Chekhov is at the farthest remove from his friend Gorki, and most akin to Andreev. It is probable that Andreev learned something from him. Unlike Turgenev, both Chekhov and Andreev study mental disease. Their best characters are abnormal; they have some fatal taint in the mind which turns this goodly frame, the earth, into a sterile promontory; this majestical roof fretted with golden fire, into a foul and pestilent congregation of vapours. Neither Chekhov nor Andreev have attempted to lift that black pall of despair that hangs over Russian fiction. (pp. 239-40)

Chekhov's position in the main line of Russian literature and his likeness to Turgenev are both evident when we study his analysis of the Russian temperament. His verdict is exactly the same as that given by Turgenev and Sienkiewicz—*slave improductivité.* A majority of his chief characters are Rudins. They suffer from internal injuries, caused by a diseased will. In his story called *On the Way* the hero remarks, "*Nature has set in every Russian an enquiring mind, a tendency to speculation, and extraordinary capacity for belief; but all these are broken into dust against our improvidence, indolence, and fantastic triviality.*"

The novelist who wrote that sentence was a physician as well as a man of letters. It is a professional diagnosis of the national sickness of mind, which produces sickness of heart. (pp. 240-41)

[Chekhov] does not rank among the greatest. He lacks the tremendous force of Tolstoi, the flawless perfection of Turgenev, and the mighty world-embracing sympathy of Greatheart Dostoevski. But he is a faithful interpreter of Russian life, and although his art was objective, one cannot help feeling the essential goodness of the man behind his work, and loving him for it. (p. 247)

> *William Lyon Phelps, "Chekhov," in his* Essays on Russian Novelists *(reprinted with permission of Macmillan Publishing Co., Inc.; copyright 1911 by Macmillan Publishing Co., Inc.; renewed 1939 by William Lyon Phelps), Macmillan, 1911 (and reprinted by Macmillan, 1922), pp. 234-47.*

ASHLEY DUKES   (essay date 1912)

Tchekhov's plays are the most interesting that modern Russia has as yet produced. A certain questioning of life is all that they have in common with the work of Tolstoy and Gorky. Tolstoy sought the meaning of life among the peasantry, Gorky among the city slums and the lower bourgeois class, Tchekhov among "the intelligence." . . . His types belong to an aristocracy of thought, and, further (since intellect alone can be of little service to the dramatist), to an aristocracy of feeling. They possess the capacity for great drama because they are at once highly sensitive and highly differentiated among themselves. The capacity for great drama, be it noted; not necessarily its achievement. (pp. 190-91)

It must be said at once that Tchekhov can by no stretch of imagination be called a great dramatist. He cried "Open Sesame!" to actuality, but the reality behind was only vaguely outlined, and he died before he could perfect the new dramatic form which he attempted to create. His plays are a series of original experiments rather than a finished whole. . . . ["The Seagull"] is full of the atmosphere of the Russian "intelligence." It depends altogether upon elusive moods, and only by entering very fully into these moods can the spectator find its tragedy even remotely credible. The weakness of Tchekhov's strikingly original technique is that his characterisation depends so much more upon what the characters say than upon what they do. They seem at first sight the most irrelevant people that any dramatist could devise. They stroll casually upon the stage, talking about the weather, their supper, their ailments, their preferences, their views, their philosophy; and from this fluid mass of conversation there crystallises very gradually the conception of each individual as a separate entity. The conversation is always extraordinarily good, and so the individual conception which emerges, without having the rigidity of the theatrical "type," is always clearly defined.

Tchekhov retains the form of the four-act play, dealing throughout with the same group of persons. He is concerned with ideas only as the means of drama, and what he lacks is sense of the theatre rather than dramatic sense. As to the ideas themselves, he has clearly used the young poet Constantine in "The Seagull" as his mouthpiece. (pp. 192-93)

["The Three Sisters" is] another tragedy of disillusionment. (p. 207)

If this play were unrelieved, it would be intolerable. It is relieved by its note of revolt, by its distinction of dialogue, and by its plea (more insistent even than in "The Seagull") that comfort and civilisation alone can give no dignity to

existence. To the cry of "Life is vulgar, therefore art is debased," Tchekhov replies with "Art is debased, therefore life is vulgar." His demand is for a standard of living rather than for a standard of life. Individuality, with him, comes first.

And so with all his plays. It is as if the author said: "We live in a civilisation accessible only to the few. Here are the few. I show them to you for an hour, with their culture, their books, their plays, their theatres within the theatre, their learning and their wit. Their existence represents the last word in modernity. They are dissatisfied, unhappy, often dulled and broken. What is the meaning of it all? What is modernity? An episode. The motive of life? A mystery to which every individual has potentially the key. I give you the picture-puzzle of existence in fragments. Seat yourself here in the prison cell, and piece them together as you please. (I write only for those who want to understand. Life and art—those two must be placed side by side.) Yes, go on. You have discovered a part of the secret. You are building, creating. More fragments here and there—the scheme grows clearer. Now hold it up to the light . . . See, you have made a window of stained glass."

That is the drama of Tchekhov. (pp. 209-10)

> *Ashley Dukes, "Russia," in his* Modern Dramatists, *Charles H. Sergel and Co., 1912, pp. 181-210.**

LEV SHESTOV   (essay date 1916)

Tchekhov was the poet of hopelessness. Stubbornly, sadly, monotonously, during all the years of his literary activity, nearly a quarter of a century long, Tchekhov was doing one thing alone: by one means or another he was killing human hopes. Herein, I hold, lies the essence of his creation. (pp. 4-5)

Take Tchekhov's stories, each one separately, or better still, all together; look at him at work. He is constantly, as it were, in ambush, to watch and waylay human hopes. He will not miss a single one of them, not one of them will escape its fate. Art, science, love, inspiration, ideals—choose out all the words with which humanity is wont, or has been in the past, to be consoled or to be amused—Tchekhov has only to touch them and they instantly wither and die. (pp. 6-7)

[In] his earlier work Tchekhov is most unlike the Tchekhov to whom we became accustomed in late years. The young Tchekhov is gay and careless, perhaps even like a flying bird. . . . But in 1888 and 1889, when he was only twenty-seven and twenty-eight years old, there appeared *The Tedious Story* and the drama *Ivanov,* two pieces of work which laid the foundations of a new creation. Obviously a sharp and sudden change had taken place in him, which was completely reflected in his works. (p. 7)

Ivanov and *The Tedious Story* seem to me the most autobiographical of all his works. In them almost every line is a sob; and it is hard to suppose that a man could sob so, looking only at another's grief. And it is plain that his grief is a new one, unexpected as though it had fallen from the sky. Here it is, it will endure for ever, and he does not know how to fight against it.

In *Ivanov* the hero compares himself to an overstrained labourer. I do not believe we shall be mistaken if we apply this comparison to the author of the drama as well. There can be practically no doubt that Tchekhov had overstrained himself. And the overstrain came not from hard and heavy labour; no mighty overpowering exploit broke him: he stumbled and fell, he slipped. (p. 8)

The hero of *The Tedious Story* is an old professor; the hero of *Ivanov* a young landlord. But the theme of both works is the same. The professor had overstrained himself, and thereby cut himself off from his past life and from the possibility of taking an active part in human affairs. Ivanov also had overstrained himself and become a superfluous, useless person. Had life been so arranged that death should supervene simultaneously with the loss of health, strength and capacity, then the old professor and young Ivanov could not have lived for one single hour. Even a blind man could see that they are both broken and are unfit for life. (pp. 9-10)

I would point out a fact which I consider of great importance. In his work Tchekhov was influenced by Tolstoi, and particularly by Tolstoi's later writings. It is important, because thus a part of Tchekhov's 'guilt' falls upon the great writer of the Russian land. I think that had there been no *Death of Ivan Ilyich*, there would have been no *Ivanov*, and no *Tedious Story*, nor many others of Tchekhov's most remarkable works. But this by no means implies that Tchekhov borrowed a single word from his great predecessor. Tchekhov had enough material of his own: in that respect he needed no help. But a young writer would hardly dare to come forward at his own risk with the thoughts that make the content of *The Tedious Story*. (p. 11)

[The] longer Tchekhov lives, the weaker grows the power of lofty words over him, in spite of his own reason and his conscious will. Finally, he frees himself entirely from ideas of every kind, and loses even the notion of connection between the happenings of life. Herein lies the most important and original characteristic of his creation. . . . I would here point to his comedy, *The Sea-Gull*, where, in defiance of all literary principles, the basis of action appears to be not the logical development of passions, or the inevitable connection between cause and effect, but naked accident, ostentatiously nude. As one reads the play, it seems at times that one has before one a copy of a newspaper with an endless series of news paragraphs, heaped upon one another, without order and without previous plan. Sovereign accident reigns everywhere and in everything, this time boldly throwing the gauntlet to all conceptions. In this, I repeat, is Tchekhov's greatest originality, and this, strangely enough, is the source of his most bitter experiences. (pp. 12-13)

'A man cannot reconcile himself to the accomplished fact; neither can he refuse so to reconcile himself: and there is no third course. Under such conditions "action" is impossible. He can only fall down and weep and beat his head against the floor.' So Tchekhov speaks of one of his heroes; but he might say the same of them all, without exception. The author takes care to put them in such a situation that only one thing is left for them,—to fall down and beat their heads against the floor. With strange, mysterious obstinacy they refuse all the accepted means of salvation. (p. 14)

[The] real, the only hero of Tchekhov, is the hopeless man. He has absolutely no *action* left for him in life, save to beat his head against the stones. It is not surprising that such a man should be intolerable to his neighbours. Everywhere

he brings death and destruction with him. He himself is aware of it, but he has not the power to go apart from men. With all his soul he endeavours to tear himself out of his horrible condition. Above all he is attracted to fresh, young, untouched beings; with their help he hopes to recover his right to life which he has lost. The hope is vain. The beginning of decay always appears, all-conquering, and at the end Tchekhov's hero is left to himself alone. He has nothing, he must create everything for himself. And this 'creation out of the void,' or more truly the possibility of this creation, is the only problem which can occupy and inspire Tchekhov. When he has stripped his hero of the last shred, when nothing is left for him but to beat his head against the wall, Tchekhov begins to feel something like satisfaction, a strange fire lights in his burnt-out eyes. . . . (pp. 35-6)

Tchekhov knew what conclusions he had reached in *The Tedious Story* and *Ivanov*. Some of his critics also knew, and told him so. I cannot venture to say what was the cause —whether fear of public opinion, or his horror at his own discoveries, or both together—but evidently there came a moment to Tchekhov when he decided at all costs to surrender his position and retreat. The fruit of this decision was *Ward No. 6*. (pp. 39-40)

The critics could consider themselves quite satisfied. Tchekhov had openly repented and renounced the theory of non-resistance; and, I believe, *Ward No. 6* met with a sympathetic reception at the time. (p. 42)

Indeed, the construction of this story leaves no doubt in the mind. Tchekhov wished to compromise, and he compromised. He had come to feel how intolerable was hopelessness, how impossible the creation from a void. . . . Tchekhov joined the choir of Russian writers, and began to praise the idea. But not for long. His very next story, *The Duel*, has a different character. Its conclusion is also apparently idealistic, but only in appearance. The principal hero Layevsky is a parasite like all Tchekhov's heroes. He does nothing, can do nothing, does not even wish to do anything, lives chiefly at others' expense, runs up debts, seduces women. . . . His condition is intolerable. (pp. 42-3)

For contrast's sake Tchekhov brings Layevsky into collision with the zoologist, Von Koren. . . . Von Koren, as one may see from his name, is of German origin, and therefore deliberately represented as a healthy, normal, clean man, the grandchild of Goncharov's Stolz, the direct opposite of Layevsky, who on his side is nearly related to our old friend Oblomov. . . . To reconcile them is impossible. The more they meet, the deeper, the more merciless, the more implacable is their hatred for each other. It is impossible that they should live together on the earth. It must be one or the other: either the normal Von Koren, or the degenerate decadent Layevsky. Of course, all the external, material force is on Von Koren's side in the struggle. He is always in the right, always victorious, always triumphant—in act no less than in theory. It is curious that Tchekhov, the irreconcilable enemy of all kinds of philosophy—not one of his heroes philosophises, or if he does, his philosophising is unsuccessful, ridiculous, weak and unconvincing—makes an exception for Von Koren, a typical representative of the positive, materialistic school. His words breathe vigour and conviction. . . . Von Koren's speech has the stroke of a hammer, and each blow strikes not Layevsky but Tchekhov himself on his wounds. He gives more and more strength to

Von Koren's arm, he puts himself in the way of his blows. For what reason? Decide as you may. Perhaps Tchekhov cherished a secret hope that self-inflicted torment might be the one road to a new life? He has not told us so. Perhaps he did not know the reason himself, and perhaps he was afraid to offend the positive idealism which held such undisputed sway over contemporary literature. (pp. 43-6)

Tchekhov's last rebellious work is *Uncle Vanya*. Like the old professor and like Ivanov, Uncle Vanya raises the alarm and makes an incredible pother about his ruined life. He, too, in a voice not his own, fills the stage with his cries: 'Life is over, life is over,'—as though indeed any of these about him, any one in the whole world, could be responsible for his misfortune. . . . 'Your life is over—you have yourself to thank for it: you are a human being no more, all human things are alien to you. Your neighbours are no more neighbours to you, but strangers. You have no right either to help others or to expect help from them. Your destiny is—absolute loneliness.' Little by little Tchekhov becomes convinced of this truth: *Uncle Vanya* is the last trial of loud public protest, of a vigorous 'declaration of rights.' (pp. 48-9)

In *The Black Monk* Tchekhov tells of a new reality, and in a tone which suggests that he is himself at a loss to say where the reality ends and the phantasmagoria begins. The black monk leads the young scholar into some mysterious remoteness, where the best dreams of mankind shall be realised. The people about call the monk a hallucination and fight him with medicines—drugs, better foods and milk. Kovrin himself does not know who is right. When he is speaking to the monk, it seems to him that the monk is right; when he sees before him his weeping wife and the serious, anxious faces of the doctors, he confesses that he is under the influence of fixed ideas, which lead him straight to lunacy. Finally the black monk is victorious. Kovrin has not the power to support the banality which surrounds him; he breaks with his wife and her relations, who appear like inquisitors in his eyes, and goes away somewhere—but in our sight he arrives nowhere. At the end of the story he dies in order to give the author the right to make an end. This is always the case: when the author does not know what to do with his hero he kills him. . . . The matter is exhausted—stop the tale short, even though it be on a half-word. Tchekhov did so sometimes, but only sometimes. In most cases he preferred to satisfy the traditional demands and to supply his readers with an end. This habit is not so unimportant as at first sight it may seem. Consider even *The Black Monk*. The death of the hero is as it were an indication that abnormality must, in Tchekhov's opinion, necessarily lead through an absurd life to an absurd death: but this was hardly Tchekhov's firm conviction. It is clear that he expected something from abnormality, and therefore gave no deep attention to men who had left the common track. True, he came to no firm or definite conclusions, for all the tense effort of his creation. He became so firmly convinced that there was no issue from the entangled labyrinth, that the labyrinth with its infinite wanderings, its perpetual hesitations and strayings, its uncaused griefs and joys uncaused—in brief, all things which normal men so fear and shun—became the very essence of his life. Of this and this alone must a man tell. Not of our invention is normal life, nor abnormal. Why then should the first alone be considered as the real reality?

The Sea-Gull must be considered one of the most characteristic, and therefore one of the most remarkable of Tchekhov's works. Therein the artist's true attitude to life received its most complete expression. Here all the characters are either blind, and afraid to move from their seats in case they lose the way home, or half-mad, struggling and tossing about to no end nor purpose. (pp. 54-6)

[The] strange fate of Tchekhov's heroes is that they strain to the last limit of their inward powers, but there are no visible results at all. They are all pitiable. The woman takes snuff, dresses slovenly, wears her hair loose, is uninteresting. The man is irritable, grumbling, takes to drink, bores every one about him. They act, they speak—always out of season. They cannot, I would even say they do not want to, adapt the outer world to themselves. Matter and energy unite according to their own laws—people live according to their own, as though matter and energy had no existence at all. In this Tchekhov's intellectuals do not differ from illiterate peasants and the half-educated bourgeois. Life in the manor is the same as in the valley farm, the same as in the village. Not one believes that by changing his outward conditions he would change his fate as well. Everywhere reigns an unconscious but deep and ineradicable conviction that our will must be directed towards ends which have nothing in common with the organised life of mankind. Worse still, the organisation appears to be the enemy of the will and of man. One must spoil, devour, destroy, ruin. To think out things quietly, to anticipate the future—that is impossible. One must beat one's head, beat one's head eternally against the wall. (pp. 59-60)

Lev Shestov, "Anton Tchekhov: Creation from the Void," in his Anton Tchekhov and Other Essays, *translated by S. Koteliansky and J. M. Murry, Maunsel and Co. Ltd., 1916 (and reprinted by University of Michigan Press, 1966), pp. 3-60.*

L. S. WOOLF (essay date 1917)

[Tchehov] more than any other writer challenges one to ask those ultimate questions about Art and his art. For nine out of ten of his stories end for the reader upon several notes of interrogation. You cannot put down the book after reading, say, the story of *The Lady with the Dog* or *A Doctor's Visit* without asking a great many questions about the author, about art, and about life. (p. 446)

His stories raise over and over again that oldest of questions about ̶r̶e̶a̶l̶i̶s̶m̶. For Tchehov, as Mrs. [Constance] Garnett and many others have remarked, belongs most obviously to the Maupassant school of "unflinching realists." But that after all does not take us very far, and we may and do legitimately ask about the realist what he is attempting to do with this unflinching realism. The answer is easy in the case of the old photographic and cinematographic realist. Carefully and accurately to convey a piece of bleak and naked life into the covers of a book was to him enough: that *was* the object of his art and of Art. . . . But if Tchehov is an unflinching realist, his object is most certainly not unflinching realism. It is true that many of his shortest short stories seem at first sight to be the work of a man who has delicately, fastidiously, and ironically picked up with the extreme tips of his fingers a little piece of real life, and then with minute care and skill pinned it by means of words into a book. Thus in *The Head of the Family* he gives us in barely six pages the description of a meal at which the father, a family bully, tortures his wife, his son, and the governess, not physically, but mentally. And having made the reader feel acutely himself the exquisite and sordid torture of the nagging bully, Tchehov leaves him: but he leaves him not as Zola and his school did, or at least obviously intended to do, with a sense of solidity and finality and explanation, but with a sense of incompleteness, of there being surely something on the other side of the page, a feeling of puzzled interrogation. And in many of the other stories this effect is intensified by the fact that the story itself is in the form of an unanswered question. (pp. 446-47)

But this incompleteness, this sense of questioning to which there is no answer, is not in the accidental facts of the stories, it is present because it is part of Tchehov's mind and art. It is present even when the story is rounded off with the completest of finalities, death. Even when the Black Monk appears again to Kovrin and whispers that he is a genius, and Kovrin dies with a "blissful smile upon his face," the reader still feels that for him "the most complicated and difficult part of it is only just beginning."

There is, in fact, in Tchehov's writings a most curious and not immediately obvious contradiction, a contradiction which explains why with all his powers he so often just fails of the highest achievement. At first sight there seems to be a completeness and certainty about his art which only belongs to writers of the very first quality. Dealing with the subtleties of emotions and human relations, he is able with a few words, a single sentence, to place his scenes with all their subtleties vivid and clear-cut before his reader's eyes. Without hesitation or hurry, he picks a word here, a sentence there, and with that contemptuous aloofness which accompanies the certainty of great skill—you can see it at its best in conjurers and billiard players—produces from under the handkerchief a little definite and rounded piece of real life in the form of a short story. That is why so much is made of his "unflinching realism." He has the air of a man who with extreme detachment is going to show you exactly what a little piece of real life is like, and show it to you without comment, without feeling, without any of the tiresome moralisations or bestowal of praise and blame. And yet at the critical moment, when the achievement seems to be most definite, and rounded, and complete, the sensitive reader will, if he be attentive, feel a slight wobble, a tiny tremor of the conjurer's hand. And if he look a little more closely he will see that Tchehov is one of those people who, to change the metaphor, suffer from a bad mental stammer. (p. 447)

The precision of Tchehov's realism masks the mental stammer which afflicted him when he contemplated life. One notable characteristic in all his work is the extraordinary aloofness of the writer. As Mr. [Edward] Garnett has remarked he does not, as Dostoievsky does, identify himself with his characters: he stands by their side, "watching them quietly, and registering their circumstances and feelings with such finality that to pass judgment on them appears supererogatory." Now a method of this sort is extraordinarily effective within a limited range. The subtlest ironies of life and human relations lend themselves peculiarly to its treatment, and over and over again Tchehov turns to that field of human comedy and tragedy. But the "finality" is a distinctly limited finality. . . . Tchehov's "finality" is the finality of irony, of the man who stands a little aside from life and almost caresses its absurdities. And that is where his mental stammer comes in. His one keen and

persistent emotion towards life is bewilderment. He seems to be literally stammering with unanswered questions as to the meaning of these grotesque comedies and tragedies of the human mind, these absurdities and cruelties, passions and pains and exaltations and boredoms of human relationship. And the perpetual and delicious irony, the amazing and refreshing aloofness, the cool precision and the cold realism are the methods by which Tchehov controls his bewilderment and prevents himself overwhelming his reader with a torrent of "Why's" and "What's." (pp. 447-48)

L. S. Woolf, "Miscellany: Tchehov," in New Statesman *(© 1917 The Statesman Publishing Co. Ltd.), Vol. IX, No. 227, August 11, 1917, pp. 446-48.*

J. MIDDLETON MURRY (essay date 1920)

Tchehov is not what he is so often assumed to be, an impressionist. Consciously or unconsciously he had taken the step—the veritable *salto mortale*—by which the great literary artist moves out of the ranks of the minor writers. He had slowly shifted his angle of vision until he could discern a unity in multiplicity. Unity of this rare kind cannot be imposed as, for instance, Zola attempted to impose it. It is an emanation from life which can be distinguished only by the most sensitive contemplation. (pp. 76-7)

What is most peculiar to Tchehov's unity is that it is far more nakedly aesthetic than that of most of the great writers before him. Other writers of a rank equal to his—and there are not so very many—have felt the need to shift their angle of vision until they could perceive an all-embracing unity; but they were not satisfied with this. They felt, and obeyed, the further need of taking an attitude towards the unity they saw. They approved or disapproved, accepted or rejected it. It would be perhaps more accurate to say that they gave or refused their endorsement. They appealed to some other element than their own sense of beauty for the final verdict on their discovery; they asked whether it was just or good.

The distinguishing mark of Tchehov is that he is satisfied with the unity he discovers. Its uniqueness is sufficient for him. It does not occur to (im to demand that it should be otherwise or better. The act of comprehension is accompanied by an instantaneous act of acceptance. He is like a man who contemplates a perfect work of art; but the work of creation has been his, and has consisted in the gradual adjustment of his vision until he could see the frustration of human destinies and the arbitrary infliction of pain as processes no less inevitable, natural, and beautiful than the flowering of a plant. Not that Tchehov is a greater artist than any of his great predecessors; he is merely more wholly an artist, which is a very different thing. There is in him less admixture of preoccupations that are not purely aesthetic, and probably for this reason he has less creative vigour than any other artist of equal rank. It seems as though artists, like cattle and fruit trees, need a good deal of crossing with substantial foreign elements, in order to be very vigorous and very fruitful. Tchehov has the virtues and the shortcomings of the pure case.

I do not wish to be understood as saying that Tchehov is a manifestation of *l'art pour l'art*, because in any commonly accepted sense of that phrase, he is not. Still, he might be considered as an exemplification of what the phrase might be made to mean. But instead of being diverted into a barren dispute over terminologies, one may endeavour to bring into prominence an aspect of Tchehov which has an immediate interest—his modernity. Again, the word is awkward. It suggests that he is fashionable, or up to date. Tchehov is, in fact, a good many phases in advance of all that is habitually described as modern in the art of literature. The artistic problem which he faced and solved is one that is, at most, partially present to the consciousness of the modern writer—to reconcile the greatest possible diversity of content with the greatest possible unity of aesthetic impression. Diversity of content we are beginning to find in profusion . . . but how rarely do we see even a glimmering recognition of the necessity of a unified aesthetic impression! (pp. 77-9)

Tchehov, we believe, attempted a treatment radically new. To make use again of our former image in his maturer writing, he chose a different string to let down into the saturated solution of consciousness. In a sense he began at the other end. He had decided on the quality of aesthetic impression he wished to produce, not by an arbitrary decision, but by one which followed naturally from the contemplative unity of life which he had achieved. The essential quality he discerned and desired to represent was his argument, his string. Everything that heightened and completed this quality accumulated about it, quite independently of whether it would have been repelled by the old criterion of plot and argument. There is a magnificent example of his method in . . . 'The Steppe.' The quality is dominant throughout, and by some strange compulsion it makes heterogeneous things one; it is reinforced by the incident. Tiny events—the peasant who eats minnows alive, the Jewish innkeeper's brother who burned his six thousand roubles— take on a character of portent, except that the word is too harsh for so delicate a distortion of normal vision; rather it is a sense of incalculability that haunts us. The emphases have all been slightly shifted, but shifted according to a valid scheme. (pp. 80-1)

To-day we begin to feel how intimately Tchehov belongs to us; to-morrow we may feel how infinitely he is still in advance of us. A genius will always be in advance of a talent, and in so far as we are concerned with the genius of Tchehov we must accept the inevitable. We must analyse and seek to understand it; we must, above all, make up our minds that since Tchehov has written and his writings have been made accessible to us, a vast amount of our modern literary production is simply unpardonable. Writers who would be modern and ignore Tchehov's achievement are, however much they may persuade themselves that they are devoted artists, merely engaged in satisfying their vanity or in the exercise of a profession like any other; for Tchehov is a standard by which modern literary effort must be measured, and the writer of prose or poetry who is not sufficiently single-minded to apply the standard to himself is of no particular account. (pp. 84-5)

[The] supreme interest of Tchehov is that he is the only great modern artist in prose. He belongs, as we have said, to us. If he is great, then he is great not least in virtue of qualities which we may aspire to possess; if he is an ideal, he is an ideal to which we can refer ourselves. He had been saturated in all the disillusions which we regard as peculiarly our own, and every quality which is distinctive of the epoch of consciousness in which we are living now is re-

flected in him—and yet, miracle of miracles, he was a great artist. He did not rub his cheeks to produce a spurious colour of health; he did not profess beliefs which he could not maintain; he did not seek a reputation for universal wisdom, or indulge himself in self-gratifying dreams of a millennium which he alone had the ability to control. He was and wanted to be nothing in particular, and yet, as we read these letters of his, we feel gradually form within ourselves the conviction that he was a hero—more than that, *the* hero of our time. (p. 85)

> *J. Middleton Murry, "Thoughts on Tchehov," in his* Aspects of Literature *(reprinted by permission of The Society of Authors as the literary representative of The Estate of John Middleton Murry), W. Collins Sons & Co. Ltd., 1920, pp. 76-90.*

N. BRYLLION FAGIN (essay date 1921)

Chekhov is essentially a humorist. His is not the quiet, genial humor of an Addison or a Washington Irving nor the more subtle, often boisterous humor of a Mark Twain. His is rather the cynical chuckle of a grown-up watching a child assume grimaces of deep earnestness and self-importance. In his earlier stories the laughable, and it is a more or less cheerful laugh, with little of the serious behind it, often predominates. But as the stories grow more in volume, the undercurrent of gloom and a stifled groan of pain become more and more audible, until, in the later volumes, his laugh quite eloquently suggests the ominous combination of submission to Fate and Mephistophelian despair. (pp. 417-18)

[In] vain would we look for an exaggeration or an untruthful note in his works. We feel, with that instinctive perception which is higher than knowledge, that it is all too true; that the people he pictures live and act in reality just as they do in his works. For Chekhov as artist is flawless. No detail of any importance ever escapes his knowing eye. . . .

And this verisimilitude is attained not by voluminous description—Chekhov fortunately seems to have been ignorant of the verbose methods of a Wells, for instance—but by a judicious stroke here and there, a word, a short phrase, a mere mention of a peculiar characteristic. Most of his stories are very short—only two or three pages. Yet within these two or three pages a real live man or woman, or both, or a whole group, live through life, each with his peculiar characteristics, environment, dreams, yearning, struggles, sufferings, victories and defeats, always ending with defeat—a logical sequence with Chekhov. (p. 418)

[While] Chekhov quarrels primarily with the representative class—composed of the middle and upper classes—yet he plainly indicates his opinions of the lower class—the peasant, servant, workman—to be no better. In the few stories in which he deals with this lower class, he frankly shows that he is quite remote from his predecessors, as he was also from his successors, the idealistic group of Russian writers, who held up the common people as an ideal. Chekhov's common people are as base and dull as their educated masters. They are cunning and selfish, capable of hypocritical flattery and hideous humbleness to attain their petty ends.

In *The Simulators* the peasants flock to the general's wife whose hobby is homeopathic medicine. They praise and flatter and bless her for the wonderful cure she has effected of all their ills. At the same time they complain of their poverty and receive from her presents of hay, seeds, etc. On leaving her they throw the medicine away, and next week come again to praise and bless her for her magic remedies. . . . (pp. 420-21)

But there is still another side to Chekhov. It is that touch of pity for the wretched people of his stories which is sometimes felt through his flippancy and scorn and contempt in his early works and which becomes the dominant note in his later ones. With age he becomes more serious, and gradually his scathing sarcasm becomes softened and in its place appears a more benevolent tone. After all, these people are helpless. And helpless and cowardly they are merely because life is so hard and every thing in it so deadening! They imbibe it with the air they breathe! (p. 421)

And even man's cruelty and selfishness are not entirely man's fault. It is the grayness, the monotony of life, the defeat of all dreams and aspirations that give him his mold. There is nothing left but to kill that awful creeper—Time—and to forget. Hence, long live vodka! (pp. 421-22)

Of the great masters of realism none perhaps have plumbed the depths of woman's soul—Goethe's *Das ewig Weibliche* —with more perfection of touch than Chekhov. The outstanding feature of all Russian literature is its search for a motive of life. Chekhov's efforts were compensated in his finding but the ancient motive of love as the guiding-star of woman's life, her supreme motive, the highest expression of her soul, the alpha and omega of her being.

And it is in this field of love that Chekhov's women lose their equilibrium. One by one they start out on their quest, cheerfully, hopefully, courageously, and one by one they return, bloodless and lifeless, carrying but burnt embers in their hearts. Some, like Katya in a *Tiresome Story* are killed outright. Others like Sinaida in *The Story of an Unknown Person* still show faint traces of possible life—the last lingering rays of a setting sun. . . .

But after all, what is the difference between Katya and Sinaida? Both have taken their hearts and souls, their very lives, and have thrown them at the altar of love—and have thrown them away. . . . Both are modern women, daring women, ready to trample on all barriers they might encounter on their way and both have been hurled back cruelly into the abyss of hopelessness never to rise again. And back they come defeated because they live in the enchanted pool of polluted and indifferent waters—in a pale, drab world where nothing, not even love, is worth a pebble; where man is brutally selfish and cannot be trusted; where the stronger woman is destined to become cynical, distrustful and unattractive (*Three Years*). In such a world woman must pay along with man, and often more than man.

And woman does pay—not only in blood and tears and anguish of heart, but in a lowering of ideal values; in degeneration of conception of motive. (p. 423)

Such is the message of this great Russian writer; an endless chain of gray people, passing through a gray life, thinking, building, striving; fighting for the space of a lifetime a battle which they have not chance of winning; then stepping aside to drink of the waters of Lethe.

And yet this message has found fertile soil not only in Russia but wherever modern man dreams and struggles and suffers. Chekhov has come to occupy a place among the world's great writers because, in striking the chords of Russian life, he struck, with that silver touch which is the magic of genius, the elemental chords of universal life. . . .

[Chekhov's spirit], despite its morbid tone, is virile, beautiful, and rich. What if he did sing but the Tristan and Isolde of life? What if he painted but the gray dusk? There is a charm and a beauty of its own in it, for by the sickly tint of the sun fading in the west we learn to see its glory when it appears in the east on the morrow. (p. 424)

> *N. Bryllion Fagin, "Anton Chekhov: The Master of the Gray Short-Story," in* Poet Lore *(copyright, 1921, by Poet Lore, Inc.), Vol. XXXII, Autumn, 1921, pp. 416-24.*

EDWARD GARNETT   (essay date 1922)

Wherein is [Tchehov] so "modern"? It was the conjunction of his peculiarly independent flexibility of mind with his keen scientific outlook that equipped him for seizing and judging modern life from fresh angles. While representative of the changing horizons and complexity of the social organism of the new Russia (1885-1904) Tchehov's vision fused the detached impartial attitude of the modern scientist with the deep humanism, the psychological insight, the caressing tenderness and the gay humour of his sensitive temperament. It would be wrong to exaggerate this "scientific" strain in Tchehov's art, but it is sublimated in the soft, rich depths of his aesthetic consciousness, and is constantly inspiring or reinforcing his critical attitude. . . . Tchehov indeed is in advance of us by the way in which his scientific knowledge corrects or sharpens ordinary insight and his humanity corrects scientific narrowness. In England, America and Europe generally scientific men are apt to be cribbed, cabined and confined by their work of specializing. Their scientific horizon stops short of the humanities. But with Tchehov science broadens the humanities, and both reconcile themselves with art. . . . [A] good example of this fusion of artistic and scientific insight is to be found in that brilliant and fascinating social picture "The Party," a story which for atmospheric truth and subtle inflections of tone leaves most of contemporary art in the shade. (pp. 52-5)

[Life's] processes in Tchehov are very intricate, very elusive in pattern, and in "My Life" we have a wonderfully rich arrangement of the human muddle with all its cares, sorrows, brutalities and cheats intertwined with its compensating hopes, gratifications and fleeting gains. We must note here that one of the most vital features of Tchehov's art, as in the case of his great Russian predecessors, is that the background of his pictures nearly always breathes of the vast ocean of humanity, the peasant masses, and that this vision of secret depths lifts the picture out of the petty, restricted class plane of fiction in Western Europe. It is so in "My Life" which is non-European in its social atmosphere. It is so in "The Coach-house," "The Schoolmistress," "Misery," "Sorrow," "The Cattle-Dealers," "On Official Duty," to take only one volume of Tchehov's tales. It is this background of the vast, haunting sea of human life, appealing and tragic, from which is born the Russian breadth of vision, and the Russian scale of emotional apprehensions, of moral valuations so distinct from our own. (pp. 58-9)

People in the mass, everywhere, are the same in all grades; at root there is the same stupidity, cruelty and dishonesty at work in the press and the politicians as in the peasants; and the evils of human life can only be opposed by "love and work, study and will." The one thing essential is that we should understand, and *it is the artist's job to show people what they are*. Sympathy and knowledge, insight and charity, these are the corner-stones of Tchehov's morality and also of his art. "I thought people already knew that horse-stealing was wrong; but what's essential is to show the motives, the nature, the how and why of people's actions" is Tchehov's attitude. So in "In the Ravine," the cruel triumph of the hard, sly, unscrupulous Aksinya over her mild, sweet sister-in-law, Lipa, is recorded remorselessly. Aksinya gets all the family power and property into her own hands, and even turns her old father-in-law out of doors. Hers is the success of the harsh, strong, callous world. But what is there left to offset this unceasing triumph of human greed and human stupidity? Only, in Tchehov's view, beauty and truth. "And however great was wickedness still the night was calm and beautiful, and everything on earth is only waiting to be made one with truth and justice, even as the moonlight is blended with the night." It is this element, the element of tenderness and sweetness of understanding that forms the spiritual background of so many of Tchehov's Tales, and dominates invisibly the coarse web of the human struggle and the petty network of human egoism. . . . It is not merely the individual life however, with its broken, shifting tangle of yearnings and regrets that calls forth Tchehov's wistful compassionateness, but his recognition disentangles the irony in the very texture of life. Time's revenges or the irony of satisfied desires are treated in "Ionitch," "A Teacher of Literature" and "The Lady with the Dog." Yet one cannot say that Tchehov himself is "disillusioned." His sense of spiritual beauty is too strong, and his depth of acceptation of life's patterns forms, as it were, an aura enveloping his subject. This spiritual aura hovers about it and enwraps the gloomiest, greyest, most sardonic facts of life: death itself cannot diminish it. Examine "Gusev," a sketch of the death of two worn out soldiers on board a steamer, when returning from the East, a sketch that is so "modern" in its all-embracing outlook and bold acceptations as to shame nearly all the writers of today. It is so humanly broad, so tender, so infallibly true in its spiritual lightings, and it conveys the mystery of nature and all her transitory processes with sharp precision. In "Gusev" there is a sharper consciousness of life's pulsating forces, of its inescapable laws, and evasive rhythms than in any other "modern." Compare it with Tolstoy's wonderful "Three Deaths" and note how the tinge of "science" that faintly colours "Gusev" marks the advance of a new generation. The fluid, emotional receptivity of the Russian nature, which we have noted above, is seen here, like a wave, to gather force in its onward sweep. (pp. 61-5)

Tchehov's aesthetic charm culminates in "The Steppe," a tale where his tender, fluid consciousness, infinitely delicate, mirrors in its pellucid depths the whole mirage of nature, variegated, wild and stern, elusive in its changing breath, in the vast bosom of the steppes. This consummate piece of art is not "modern," save in a few recurring notes. It is a record, seen through the magic glass of boyish memories, of the passing life of travelling merchants and wayfarers, journeying in old world conditions; Tchehov is here looking backward, away from the new currents and atmospheres that his vision caught and reflected from the great ocean of contemporary life within Russia's boundaries. But when he looked forward he caught and reflected with equal

subtlety, with equal precision the new vistas of our modern emotions and apprehensions; the new "values" moral and intellectual of our modern vision. (pp. 65-6)

Edward Garnett, "Tchehov and His Art," in his Friday Nights: Literary Criticisms and Appreciations *(copyright 1922 and renewed 1950 by David Garnett; reprinted by permission of Alfred A. Knopf, Inc.), Knopf, 1922, pp. 39-66.*

WILLIAM GERHARDI (essay date 1923)

I do not presume that I could give the whole of Chehov's outlook in a nutshell. But if pressed to do so, I would rather say that Chehov's outlook in a nutshell was that he thoroughly distrusted nutshells. His intellectual attitude was inconclusive. After he has said his say, there is still the implication that he reserves the right to leave his further thoughts unsaid, even unthought. . . . He ends upon an inconclusive note: indeed, so far as it is his aim to demonstrate that truth is in its very nature inconclusive, he ends on a conclusive note. (pp. 38-9)

Chehov's realism is the natural development of the realism of Gogol, Turgenev, Dostoevski, and Tolstoy; and it differs from the older realism in that he has found for it a new and more consistent form. (p. 104)

[The essential difference] between the old tradition and the new one (of which Chehov is the pioneer), is that, whereas of old the fluidness of life as it is really lived and felt was all but overlooked and sometimes forced in order to round off the form and to sharpen the outline of a particular story, in Chehov it is just the fluidness of life that is in fact at once the form and context of his stories, the vitality of form depending on the clarity with which he shows us that the fusion of form and context is deliberate. (p. 108)

How did he do it? Not by dispensing with plot, but by using a totally different kind of plot, the tissues of which, as in life, lie below the surface of events, and, unobtrusive, shape our destiny. Thus he all but overlooks the event-plot; more, he deliberately lets it be as casual as it is in real life. Before Chehov realism was no more than a convention. . . . To Chehov literature is life made intelligible by the discovery of form—the form that is invisible in life but which is seen when, mentally, you step aside to get a better view of life. Life, because it has aspects innumerable, seems blurred and devoid of all form. And since literature must have form, and life has none, realists of the past thought that they could not paint life in the aggregate and preserve form, and thus saw fit to express one aspect of life at a time. Until a wholly new aspect occurred to Chehov—that of life in the aggregate: which aspect, in truth, is his form. (pp. 111-12)

Chehov does not give us a cross-section of a lump of life taken, as it were, at random by merely registering the irrelevant perceptions which make it up. Chehov—because he is an artist as well as a psychologist—discriminates in his choice of those seeming irrelevancies which in literature go to the making of the illusion of real life, for he feels that by economising in dullness he heightens our delight; and he does it all by killing as many birds as possible with one stone. (p. 133)

Chehov excels in group emotions. In his plays this is particularly noticeable. The company on the stage, as indeed in life, is to all purposes an *ensemble* of solitary souls. That no individual can wholly and continuously understand the mood of another individual at the time, because he is more particularly concerned with his own, is a favoured theme of Chehov's. When he advised writers to be cool in their presentation of emotional effects, he knew what he was doing: he wanted a contrasting background against which to reveal the more clearly the tenderness of the emotion. When, as in real life, one sensibility falls on deaf ears, that is, on a momentarily different sensibility, then they both together, or severally, shine brighter. He plays off one mood against another, and so creates a group mood—his own, which he transfers to the audience. This is one of the differences between life and art: in life the group mood is casual; in art, intentional. In Chehov it is intentionally casual; but the intention is hidden from us: this is good art. When we perceive how well it is hidden, we say: "But this is superb art!" For it is at once like life and like art. (pp. 184-85)

> *William Gerhardi, in his* Anton Chehov: A Critical Study *(copyright, 1923, by Duffield & Company), Duffield, 1923, 207 p.*

D. S. MIRSKY (essay date 1925)

[There] can be no doubt as to the greatness of Chekhov. Without going to the length of comparing him with Shakespeare, as some English critics have done, without putting him on a level with Russia's greatest writers—Pushkin, Gogol, Tolstoy, and Dostoevsky—we must recognize that he was the greatest writer of his age and of his class. Whatever the order of his greatness, he was a perfect artist, and achieved in full what he was called to achieve. There were no lost possibilities in him and what he could do he did. This is high praise and one which cannot always be assigned to greater men, not for instance to Gogol or Dostoevsky. Nor was Chekhov precisely typical of his age. Being a great artist, he could not be typical, and being a perfect artist, he lacked the chief feature of his contemporaries—ineffectiveness. But, being a realist, he chose his age for his subject and gave it permanent life in his art. (p. 85)

Chekhov in a very broad sense continues the tradition of Turgenev, but he is no imitator, nor even in any strict sense of the word a disciple. He has in common with Turgenev the method which may be called the poetical or suggestive method, as opposed to the analytical method of Tolstoy and Dostoevsky. He does not indulge in direct descriptions of his characters' feelings, but by appropriate detail tries to create sympathetic emotions in the reader. Chekhov is a singularly even writer. If one excepts his early and lighter writings, it is very hard to choose between his stories: they are all on the same level of perfection. Every one of them is a perfect bit of work, which holds together from beginning to end, and which can neither be added to, nor taken away from. He is the supreme *artist* of Russian fiction, the creator of the most perfectly made objects. In this respect he is superior to Turgenev, who possessed this sense of proportion and wholeness in an inferior degree, and whose stories do not produce that impression of everything necessary and nothing superfluous which is the essence of Chekhov's art. On the other hand, Turgenev's Russian is superior to Chekhov's. Chekhov lived in a time when the spoken language was losing its organic raciness, and his is consequently more level and less rich. This makes Chekhov the least difficult of Russian writers to translate. But Chekhov had not the easy mellifluousness of Turgenev. . . . (pp. 87-8)

Unlike most of the great Russian writers, Chekhov is not a creator of characters. None of his people is alive with the independent and three-dimensional life of Bazarov, of Anna Karenina, of Stavrogin, or even of the men and women of Goncharov and Ostrovsky. Chekhov's is a more general and less individualized humanity. He deals in that which is common to people, not in that which is peculiar to them. All his characters may really be reduced to two types: the gentle and ineffective dreamer, and the vulgar and efficient man of action. There are infinite gradations in these; but the ineffective people, if sometimes funny, are invariably lovable, and the efficient people are vulgar. Nowhere is this contrast more marked than in *The Cherry Orchard,* between the old proprietors and the *nouveau riche* Lopakhin, who has all the virtues, but is successful, and for that reason alone detestable. For every foolishness and every absurdity Chekhov has an immense treasure of sympathetic pity and understanding, but not for success. This dread of success again links him to Turgenev. But he outdoes Turgenev in the cult of inefficiency. He hated the man who *deserves* success quite as much as the man who commands it undeservingly. Inefficiency is for him the cardinal virtue, and defeat the only halo. This attitude has been believed by some to be essentially Russian, but in its extreme expression it is certainly quite personal to Chekhov. (pp. 88-9)

The cult of inefficiency goes far to explain the general atmosphere of pity for impotent, ridiculous, but lovable mankind which pervades the whole of Chekhov's work. For he is a poet of atmosphere, of the vague thing they called in Russian *nastroenie* and in German *Stimmung,* but for which there is no adequate word in English, except this meteorological metaphor. But Chekhov's art is by no means confined to atmosphere. On the contrary he is one of the most constructive writers of Russian prose. His stories are stories of situation, to which the characters play an entirely subordinate part. In this he has hardly any predecessor in Russian literature, except perhaps Lermontov, whose *Taman* Chekhov thought the best short story in the language. The situations of his stories are not dramatic, but subtly psychological. They are stated not in terms of character, but in terms of humanity. And the means of expression is not analysis, but suggestion. Chekhov found numerous disciples, but none of any worth in Russia. . . . (p. 89)

The history of Chekhov's plays repeats the broad outline of his tales. There are the early light comedies comparable to the humorous stories, and there are the wonderful dramas written after 1895. But here there is a more distinct line of progress. The first of his long plays, *Ivanov* . . . , is a failure; the *Seagull* and *Uncle Vania* each mark stages forward; in *The Three Sisters* and in *The Cherry Orchard* he attains the perfection of the genre. This last play . . . has been proclaimed by an English critic the greatest play since Shakespeare. However this may be, Chekhov created a new kind of drama, and in this new kind of drama produced masterpieces which are not likely to be surpassed. Chekhov inherited the tradition of the Russian stage of Ostrovsky and still more of Turgenev (*A Month in the Country*) in deliberately eliminating that element which was thought to be essential to the drama, the element of plot, and in removing from his plays all theatrical effect. Only he went much further in this direction. He made his theatre as untheatrical as possible. . . . Chekhov's plays are not progressively developed plots, but 'slices of life' arranged and set together with a poetical, rather than with a dramatic, purpose. What has been said of his tales applies fully to his plays. The effect is attained by absolute and suggestive reality. The construction is not narrative but subtly psychological, or, if the metaphor be allowed, musical. They are calculated to arouse certain sympathetic 'nastroenies', a certain lyrical atmosphere, and in bringing about this effect Chekhov shows a sovereign mastery over his material. In the contrast between the trivial and sordid material he works in and the intensely poetical or musical effect derived from it lies the great charm and originality of Chekhov. Like his tales, his last plays are perfect, with all that is necessary and nothing superfluous in them, instruments of marvellously calculated precision. But to imitate his dramatic system or even to learn from him is obviously impossible. Those who, like Gorky and Andreev, have tried to do so, have failed piteously, and Russian dramatic literature after Chekhov's death is one unrelieved desert.

The work of Chekhov marks the crest of a second wave in the history of Russian Realism. But it is a lesser wave than the one that carried Turgenev, Tolstoy, and Dostoevsky. The age of Chekhov is an Age of Silver. Of its writers Chekhov alone may be compared to the elder ones. (pp. 90-1)

> *D. S. Mirsky, "Chekhov and After," in his* Modern Russian Literature *(reprinted by permission of Oxford University Press), Oxford University Press, London, 1925, pp. 82-100.**

NINA ANDRONIKOVA TOUMANOVA (essay date 1937)

Chekhov's plays occupy a special place in the history of the theatre. Believing that life should be so interpreted that the audience would divine the inner and greater realities born in the mind of the author, Chekhov expressed the subtle aspects of human nature: its complete aloneness, the disintegration that overtakes a human soul immersed in its own agony. His unheroic heroes, who live in a strange world of keyed-up emotions, are, like himself, perpetually puzzled by life. The dramatic dialogue disappears, to give place to a peculiar form of speech built along two parallel lines that never meet. One is constantly aware of an undertone of sorrow and pain expressed in detached, inconsistent, often incoherent words. Long pauses and reticence create an odd feeling that important things, indeed the most important ones, have never been said and never will be said. The actions of his heroes are as surprisingly inadequate as their conversation. Often in the midst of a desperate situation they smile and cling to hope, for hope is the only resource of those charming misfits. They are never able to fight.

The form of Chekhov's plays is essentially static. He has interwoven symbols into their outwardly realistic structure, not only as a rebellion against the artificiality and the platitudes of his time, but as the means of creating a misty autumnal mood, his favorite artistic effect. Moonbeams on the lake, fallen leaves, abandoned gardens, empty houses, an odd stillness interrupted only by "a sound sad and strange, as if coming from the sky" form an appropriate autumnal setting for his forlorn heroes, with their tears, their longing for the unattainable, and their final partings which are as tragic as death.

This strange mixture of symbolism and reality, of hope and despair . . . created that peculiar "Chekhovian mood" which began a new page in the literary history of crepuscular Russia. (pp. 6-8)

Indeed, it was in a queer world of silvery twilight and dark shadows that the gentle soul of Chekhov took refuge, in a desperate fear of life. (p. 8)

> *Nina Andronikova Toumanova, in her introduction to her* Anton Chekhov: The Voice of Twilight Russia *(copyright 1937 Columbia University Press; reprinted by permission of the publisher), Columbia University Press, 1937, pp. 3-8.*

V. S. PRITCHETT (essay date 1943)

After I had read Chehov's *My Life* . . . and had reflected on the enormous difference that lies between him and the Soviet writers of the last twenty years, I came to the conclusion that it is disadvantageous for a writer to have been a doctor. The advantages are, of course, enviable and notorious. . . . The disadvantages seem to me to be two: first, he sees the world only when it is sick. Life is a patient lying passively before him. Secondly, he is caught by the habit of diagnosis, a habit which encourages a static conception of life and human nature. The doctor is plainly at work in this way in Chehov's stories. We see him isolating the pattern in the lives of his characters and diagnosing the case. To this pattern the poet in Chehov fits the natural cadence—a comic or elegiac music which is appropriate to the sight of human beings caught, ridiculously or unhappily, in patterns that are fixed. The weakness of this static conception of life and character is obvious. The assumption is that there is a definite point outside of life and outside of society from which one can contemplate them.

I see no reason why a writer should not make this assumption or any other; in literature one is justified by results and the peculiar cadence of Chehov's stories enabled him triumphantly to dispense with plot in a form of writing which seemed entirely to depend on formal exactitude. But when we read a story like *My Life* we are bound to notice that by the end of the tale none of the characters has changed. They spend their time going round in circles. The same can be said of *The Darling* or *The Lady With the Dog*. There is essential change in neither character nor situation. The doctor has said bronchitis or kidney trouble and bronchitis and kidney trouble it is until the end of the time, and one can only go away murmuring, as so often Chehov's characters do murmur: "How sad life is." Of course, all kinds of events occur in these stories: the young man in *My Life* marries, his sister is seduced. And all kind of moods and ideas come to these people. In *My Life* Chehov drew, in that somehow arid, pen-and-watercolour detail of his, a scathing picture of corrupt and pushing people in an awful provincial town and linked it all with the social and spiritual problems of their time. . . .

Yet all the people, events and ideas which we have seen displayed with such exciting limpidity in *My Life* lack a vital substance. One feels they are caught not in the toils of a story but in the wayward meshes of a mood. The things which occur to the two chief characters are like the wind soughing in the branches of two trees in winter. The branches bend and sway; they toss and struggle; but once the wind has died away they come to rest and form once more their familiar pattern against the sky. Life is something which passes through them like a sigh; it does not grow out of them. Their story has been that epidemic agitation which came from no one knows where and as mysteriously departs. When I say that the agitation comes from nowhere I mean to stress, for a moment, what is perhaps

Chehov's greatest quality—his sense of the mystery and elusiveness of living. But in fact Chehov both knows and does not know the source of his particular drama. *My Life* is especially readable to-day because it shows Chehov's acute knowledge of the social conditions of his time and his great indignation. He sees, as a doctor, the force of environment. But he is like those doctors who see environment merely as a widening of the personal pattern. The problem is larger, too large for us. Before it the doctor-artist can do no more than state the problem correctly; he cannot solve it. His duty is to preserve his integrity. It is easy enough to show the relation of this point of view to the stagnant political conditions in Russia during Chehov's lifetime. Chehov himself has written about that in his letters and has set down—in a passage of perhaps too sweeping self-criticism—the opinion that greatness is denied his contemporaries and himself because the sense of "going somewhere," the impetus of moral purpose and the desire to suggest life as it might be as well as life as it is, has been denied them. Chehov would hardly perceive that his own work has that inescapable nostalgia for the future which is one of the characteristic notes of Russian literature. Between the lines of his stories—and he is, I would say, unsurpassed in the power of suggestion that lies between one sentence and the next—Chehov has no lack of purpose: his plea for personal integrity is joined to the wider plea for compassion. And the hero of *My Life* cannot be accused of regarding integrity as a private exercise. But the interesting thing is to see how this attitude of Chehov's affected his stories. It does not matter how energetic, successful and dynamic some of his characters are—no one can accuse the newly rich engineer in *My Life* of being sapless—they are Chehov's only while they are his patients. They are cases. They are fixed patterns. They are still because they are seen from the outside. We see all the incalculable things in a human being; we do not see the calculable dynamism of the will. And it will be noticed that we never see Chehov's characters acquiring their character. The young man in *My Life* has started his rebellion before the story begins. What started the rebellion? What incident started it? Chehov does not show us. Surely some inner force in that character or in the society which produced him. In that force Chehov is not interested.

V. S. Pritchett, "Books in General: 'My Life'," in The New Statesman & Nation (© 1943 The Statesman & Nation Publishing Co. Ltd.), Vol. XXV, No. 631, March 27, 1943, p. 209.

ERIC BENTLEY (essay date 1946)

Chekhov's earlier version [of *Uncle Vanya*]—*The Wood Demon*—is what Hollywood would call a Comedy Drama: that is, a farce spiced with melodrama. (p. 323)

The Wood Demon is a conventional play trying, so to speak, to be something else. In *Uncle Vanya*, rewritten it succeeds. Perhaps Chekhov began by retouching his ending and was led back and back into his play until he had revised everything but the initial situation. (p. 324)

Chekhov's theatre, like Ibsen's, is psychological. If Chekhov changed his story, it must be either because he later felt that his old characters would act differently or because he wanted to create more interesting characters. The four people who emerge in the later version as the protagonists are different from their prototypes in *The Wood Demon*, and are differently situated. Although Sonya still loves As-

trov, her love is not returned. This fact is one among many that make the later ending Chekhovian: Sonya and Astrov resign themselves to lives of labor without romance. Vanya is not resolute enough for suicide. His discontent takes form as resentment against the author of his misery. And yet, if his missing his aim at such close quarters be an accident, it is surely one of those unconsciously willed accidents that Freud wrote of. Vanya is no murderer. His outburst is rightly dismissed as a tantrum by his fellows, none of whom dreams of calling the police. Just as Vanya is the kind of man who does not kill, Yelena is the kind of woman who does not run away from her husband, even temporarily.

In the earlier version the fates of the characters are settled; in the later they are unsettled. In the earlier version they are settled, moreover, not by their own nature or by force of circumstance, but by theatrical convention. In the later, their fate is unsettled because that is Chekhov's view of the truth. Nobody dies. Nobody is paired off. And the general point is clear: life knows no endings, happy or tragic. (Shaw once congratulated Chekhov on the discovery that the tragedy of the Hedda Gablers is, in real life, precisely that they do *not* shoot themselves.) The special satiric point is also familiar: Chekhov's Russians are chronically indecisive people. What is perhaps not so easy to grasp is the effect of a more mature psychology upon dramaturgy. Chekhov has destroyed the climax in his third act and the happy consummation in his fourth. These two alterations alone demand a radically different dramatic form.

The framework of the new play is the attractive pattern of arrival and departure: the action is what happens in the short space of time between the arrival of the Professor and his wife on their country estate and their departure from it. The unity of the play is discovered by asking the question: what effect has the visit upon the visited—that is, upon Vanya, Sonya, and Astrov? This question as it stands could not be asked of *The Wood Demon*, for in that play the Professor and Yelena do not depart and Vanya is dead before the end. As to the effect of the Professor's arrival, it is to change and spoil everything. His big moment—the moment when he announces his intention to sell the estate—leads to reversal in Aristotle's sense, the decisive point at which the whole direction of the narrative turns about. This is Uncle Vanya's suicide. Vanya's futile shots, in the later version, are a kind of mock reversal. It cannot even be said that they make the Professor change his mind, for he had begun to change it already—as soon as Vanya protested. Mechanical, classroom analysis would no doubt locate the climax of the play in the shooting. But the climax is an anticlimax. If one of our script-writers went to work on it, his "rewrite" would be *The Wood Demon* all over again, his principle of revision being exactly the opposite of Chekhov's. What Chekhov is after, I think, is not reversal but recognition—also in Aristotle's sense, "the change from ignorance to knowledge." In Aristotle's sense, but with a Chekhovian application.

In the Greeks, in much French drama, and in Ibsen, recognition means the discovery of a secret which reveals that things are not what all these years they have seemed to be. In *Uncle Vanya*, recognition means that what all these years seemed to be so, though one hesitated to believe it, really is so and will remain so. This is Vanya's discovery and gradually (in the course of the ensuing last act) that of the others. Thus Chekhov has created a kind of recognition that is all his own. In Ibsen the terrible thing is that the quotidian surface of life is a smooth deception. In Chekhov the terrible thing is that the quotidian surface of everyday life is itself a kind of tragedy. In Ibsen the whole surface of life is suddenly burst by volcanic eruption. In Chekhov the crust is all too firm; the volcanic energies of men have no chance of emerging. *Uncle Vanya* opens with a rather rhetorical suggestion that this *might* be so. It ends with the knowledge that it certainly *is* so, a knowledge shared by all the characters who are capable of knowledge—Astrov, Vanya, Sonya, and Yelena. This growth from ignorance to knowledge is, perhaps, our cardinal experience of the play (the moment of recognition, or experimental proof, being Vanya's outburst *before* the shooting).

Aristotle says that the change from ignorance to knowledge produces "love or hate between the persons destined by the poet for good or bad fortune." But only in *The Wood Demon,* where there is no real change from ignorance to knowledge, could the outcome be stated in such round terms. Nobody's fortune at the end of *Uncle Vanya* is as good or bad as it might be; nobody is very conclusively loving or hating. Here again Chekhov is avoiding the black and the white, the tragic and the comic, and is attempting the halftone, the tragi-comic.

If, as has been suggested, the action consists in the effect of the presence of the Professor and Yelena upon Sonya, Vanya, and Astrov, we naturally ask: what *was* that effect? To answer this question for the subtlest of the characters—Astrov—is to see far into Chekhov's art. In *The Wood Demon* the effect is nil. The Action has not yet been unified. It lies buried in the chaos of Chekhov's materials. In *Uncle Vanya,* however, there is a thread of continuity. We are first told that Astrov is a man with no time for women. We then learn (and there is no trace of this in *The Wood Demon*) that he is infatuated with Yelena. In *The Wood Demon,* Sonya gets Astrov in the end. In *Uncle Vanya,* when Astrov gives up Yelena, he resigns himself to his old role of living without love. The old routine—in this as in other respects—resumes its sway. (pp. 325-27)

The Might-Have-Been is Chekhov's *idée fixe.* His people do not dream only of what could never be, or what could come only after thousands of years; they dream of what their lives actually could have been. They spring from a conviction of human potentiality—which is what separates Chekhov from the real misanthropes of modern literature. Astrov moves us because we can readily feel how fully human he might have been, how he was dwindled, under the influence of "country life," from a thinker to a crank, from a man of feeling to a philanderer. "It is strange somehow," he says to Yelena in the last scene, "we have got to know each other, and all at once for some reason—we shall never meet again. So it is with everything in this world." Such lines might be found in any piece of sentimental theater. But why is it that Chekhov's famous "elegiac note" is, in the full context, deeply moving? Is it not because the sense of death is accompanied with so rich a sense of life and the possible worth of living.

Chekhov had a feeling for the unity of a drama, yet his sense of the richness of life kept him clear of formalism. He enriched his dramas in ways that belong to no school and that, at least in their effect, are peculiar to himself. While others tried to revive poetic drama by putting symbolist

verse in the mouths of their characters, or simply by imitating the verse drama of the past, Chekhov found poetry within the world of realism. By this is meant not only that he used symbols. . . . It is rather the use to which Chekhov puts the symbol that is remarkable. We have seen, for instance, what he makes of his "wood demon." This is not merely a matter of Astrov's character. Chekhov's symbols spread themselves, like Ibsen's, over a large territory. They are a path to the imagination and to those deeper passions which in our latter-day drama are seldom worn on the sleeve. Thus if a symbol in Chekhov is explained—in the manner of the *raisonneur*—the explanation blazes like a denunciation. (pp. 329-30)

What a paradox: our playwrights who plump for the passions (like O'Neill) are superficial, and Chekhov, who pretends to show us only the surface (who, as I have said, writes the tragedy of the surface) is passionate and deep! No modern playwright has presented elemental passions more truly. Both versions of *Uncle Vanya* are the battleground of two conflicting impulses—the impulse to destroy and the impulse to create. (p. 331)

Chekhov does tell a story—the gifts of one of the greatest raconteurs are not in abeyance in his plays—but his method is to let both his narrative and his situation leak out, so to speak, through domestic gatherings, formal and casual. This is his principle of motion. (p. 333)

Chekhov's development as a playwright is quite different from that of Ibsen, Strindberg, or any of the other first-rate moderns. While they pushed tempestuously forward, transforming old modes and inventing new ones, perpetually changing their approach, endlessly inventing new forms, Chekhov moved quietly, slowly, and along one straight road. He used only one full-length structure: the four-act drama; and one set of materials: the rural middle class. For all that, the line that stretches from *Ivanov* . . . to *The Cherry Orchard* . . . is of great interest.

The development is from farce and melodrama to the mature Chekhovian *drame.* The three early plays are violent and a little pretentious. Each presents a protagonist (there is no protagonist in the four subsequent plays) who is a modern variant upon a great type or symbol. Ivanov is referred to as a Hamlet, Platonov as a Don Juan, Astrov as a Wood Demon. In each case it is a "Russian" variant that Chekhov shows—Chekhov's "Russians" like Ibsen's "Norwegian" Peer Gynt and Shaw's "Englishman" representing modern men in general. Those who find Chekhov's plays static should read the three early pieces: they are the proof that, if the later Chekhov eschewed certain kinds of action, it was not for lack of dramatic sense in the most popular meaning of the term. Chekhov was born a melodramatist and farceur; only by discipline and development did he become the kind of playwright the world thinks it knows him to be. (p. 341)

In the later plays life is seen in softer colors; Chekhov is no longer eager to be the author of a Russian *Hamlet* or *Don Juan.* The homely Uncle Vanya succeeds on the title page the oversuggestive Wood Demon, and Chekhov forgoes the melodrama of a forest fire. Even more revealing: over-explicit themes are deleted. (p. 342)

Chekhov does not tone things down because he is afraid of giving himself away. He is not prim or precious. Restraint is for him as positive an idea as temperance was for the

Greeks. In Chekhov the toned-down picture . . . surpasses the hectic color scheme of melodrama, not only in documentary truth, but also in the deeper truth of poetic vision. And the truth of Chekhov's colors has much to do with the delicacy of his forms. Chekhov once wrote in a letter: "When a man spends the least possible number of movements over some definite action, that is grace"; and one of his critics speaks of a "'trigger' process, the release of enormous forces by some tiny movement." The Chekhovian form as we find it in the final version of *Uncle Vanya* grew from a profound sense of what might be called the *economy* of art.

[While] this form does not by any means eliminate narrative and suspense, it reintroduces another equally respectable principle of motion—the progress from ignorance to knowledge. Each scene is another stage in our discovery of Chekhov's people and Chekhov's situation; also in their discovering of themselves and their situation (in so far as they are capable of doing so). The apparent casualness of the encounters and discussions on the stage is Chekhov linking himself to "the least possible number of movements." But as there is a "definite action," as "large forces have been brought into play," we are not cheated of drama. The "trigger effect" is as dramatic in its way as the "buried secret" pattern of Sophocles and Ibsen. Of course, there will be people who see the tininess of the movements and do not notice the enormousness of the forces released—who see the trigger-finger move and do not hear the shot. To them, Chekhov remains a mere manufacturer of atmosphere, a mere contriver of nuance. To the others, he seems a master of dramatic form unsurpassed in modern times. (p. 343)

> Eric Bentley, "Craftsmanship in 'Uncle Vanya'" *(1946), in his* In Search of Theater *(reprinted by permission of Atheneum Publishers; copyright 1946, 1953 by Eric Russell Bentley), Vintage Books, 1957, pp. 322-43.*

FRANCIS FERGUSSON (essay date 1949)

The Cherry Orchard is often accused of having no plot whatever, and it is true that the story gives little indication of the play's content or meaning; nothing happens, as the Broadway reviewers so often point out. Nor does it have a thesis, though many attempts have been made to attribute a thesis to it, to make it into a Marxian tract, or into a nostalgic defense of the old regime. The play does not have much of a plot in either of these accepted meanings of the word, for it is not addressed to the rationalizing mind but to the poetic and histrionic sensibility. It is an imitation of an action in the strictest sense, and it is plotted according to the first meaning of this word which I have distinguished in other contexts: the incidents are selected and arranged to define an action in a certain mode; a complete action, with a beginning, middle, and end in time. Its freedom from the mechanical order of the thesis or the intrigue is the sign of the perfection of Chekhov's realistic art. And its apparently casual incidents are actually composed with most elaborate and conscious skill to reveal the underlying life, and the natural, objective form of the play as a whole. (pp. 161-62)

[*The Cherry Orchard*] is a drama "of pathetic motivation," a theater-poem of the suffering of change; and this mode of action and awareness is much closer to the skeptical basis of modern realism, and to the histrionic basis of all realism. Direct perception before predication is always true, says

Aristotle; and the extraordinary feat of Chekhov is to predicate nothing. This he achieves by means of his plot; he selects only those incidents, those moments in his characters' lives, between their rationalized efforts, when they sense their situation and destiny most directly. So he contrives to show the action of the play as a whole—the unsuccessful attempt to cling to the Cherry Orchard—in many diverse reflectors and without propounding any thesis about it. (p. 162)

The play may be briefly described as a realistic ensemble pathos: the characters all suffer the passing of the estate in different ways, thus adumbrating this change at a deeper and more generally significant level than that of any individual's experience. The action which they all share by analogy, and which informs the suffering of the destined change of the Cherry Orchard, is "to save the Cherry Orchard": that is, each character sees some value in it—economic, sentimental, social, cultural—which he wishes to keep. By means of his plot, Chekhov always focuses attention on the general action: his crowded stage, full of the characters I have mentioned as well as half a dozen hangers-on, is like an implicit discussion of the fatality which concerns them all; but Chekhov does not believe in their ideas, and the interplay he shows among his *dramatis personae* is not so much the play of thought as the alternation of his characters' perceptions of their situation, as the moods shift and the time for decision comes and goes.

Though the action which Chekhov chooses to show onstage is "pathetic," i.e., suffering and perception, it is complete: the Cherry Orchard is constituted before our eyes, and then dissolved. The first act is a prologue: it is the occasion of Lyubov's return from Paris to try to resume her old life. Through her eyes and those of her daughter Anya, as well as from the complementary perspectives of Lopahin and Trofimov, we see the estate as it were in the round, in its many possible meanings. The second act corresponds to the agon; it is in this act that we become aware of the conflicting values of all the characters, and of the efforts they make (off-stage) to save each one *his* Orchard. The third act corresponds to the pathos and peripety of the traditional tragic form. The occasion is a rather hysterical party which Lyubov gives while her estate is being sold at auction in the nearby town; it ends with Lopahin's announcement, in pride and the bitterness of guilt, that he was the purchaser. The last act is the epiphany: we see the action, now completed, in a new and ironic light. The occasion is the departure of the family: the windows are boarded up, the furniture piled in the corners, and the bags packed. All the characters feel, and the audience sees in a thousand ways, that the wish to save the Orchard has amounted in fact to destroying it; the gathering of its denizens to separation; the homecoming to departure. What this "means" we are not told. But the action is completed, and the poem of the suffering of change concludes in a new and final perception, and a rich chord of feeling. (pp. 163-64)

Chekhov does not demand the intellectual scope, the ultimate meanings, which Ibsen demanded, and to some critics Chekhov does not look like a real dramatist but merely an overdeveloped mime, a stage virtuoso. But the theater of modern realism did not afford what Ibsen demanded, and Chekhov is much the more perfect master of its little scene. If Chekhov drastically reduced the dramatic art, he did so in full consciousness, and in obedience both to artistic scruples and to a strict sense of reality. He reduced the dramatic art to its ancient root, from which new growths are possible. (p. 177)

> *Francis Fergusson, "'Ghosts' and 'The Cherry Orchard': The Theater of Modern Realism," in his The Idea of a Theater: A Study of Ten Plays; The Art of Drama in Changing Perspective (copyright 1949 © 1977 by Princeton University Press; Princeton Paperback, 1968; reprinted by permission of Princeton University Press), Princeton University Press, 1949, pp. 146-77.**

EDMUND WILSON (essay date 1952)

[The] humor that runs all through Chekhov is but one of a number of features that the foreigner may miss or misunderstand. If Chekhov has been baffling to Russians, it has been only because they wanted to pin him down to a definite political position, which he always refused to take. His work is not vague but compact and dense, all made up of hard detail and larded with allusions to specific things. Yet his stories as well as his plays, which have fascinated Western readers, have often left them puzzled or blank. To such readers—though, as much as Flaubert, as much as Ibsen or Shaw, these fictions are nailed to their time and place—they have seemed to occur in a realm of dream. "They are not lit [Chekhov's characters]," writes Mr. Somerset Maugham, . . . "by the hard light of common day but suffused in a mysterious grayness. They move in this as though they were disembodied spirits. It is their souls that you seem to see. The subconscious seems to come to the surface and they communicate with one another directly, without the impediment of speech. Strange, futile creatures, with descriptions of their outward seeming tacked on them like a card on an exhibit in a museum, they move as mysteriously as the tortured souls who crowded about Dante when he walked in Hell. You have the feeling of a vast, gray, lost throng wandering aimless in some dim underworld." We cannot, I think, entirely blame pale translations for the misty effect that Chekhov produces on Mr. Maugham. . . . Chekhov's writing, though it sometimes lacks color, is never blurred in Russian; it gives rather the impression of the tight-strung lines of a masterly steel engraving. (pp. 55-6)

[There] is no question that Western readers have been seriously handicapped with Chekhov even more than with the other Russian writers by their unfamiliarity with the cultural and social background of the world that he is writing about. He is much more limited and local than Tolstoy or Dostoevski, and we do not always catch his allusions or understand the points he is trying to make. Though Chekhov is always specific, always quite sure and sharp, we think him elusive and vague. . . . Nor are the full social implications of Chekhov's characters grasped. . . . [It is] in the Russian tradition to deal critically with Russia's specific problems, and Chekhov was no exception to this. He did not have a religious message, as Dostoevski and Tolstoy did, and he deliberately kept clear of politics, but, after all, his story "Ward No. 6" was one of the contemporary writings that most aroused Lenin in his youth, and his whole work is a social document of a powerful if largely negative kind. (pp. 57-8)

If we follow his line of development, we see that, beginning with satirical jokes, Chekhov goes on to master the art of the ironic anecdote, so often pathetic or tragic (it would hardly, one would think, be possible to complain of a good many of these that one did not understand the point); these, in turn, begin to expand into something more rounded-out (the dense but concise study of character and situation) and eventually—in what Mr. Hingley calls Chekhov's Tolstoyan period ("A Nervous Breakdown," for example)—take on a new moral interest or attain, as in his "clinical" one ("The Black Monk"), a new psychological depth. These studies become more comprehensive—"The Steppe," "A Dreary Story," "Ward No. 6"—in such a way as to cover a whole life *en raccourci* or an experience in fuller detail. Such pieces are not short stories but what Henry James called *nouvelles*. (The earlier "Shooting Party" was Chekhov's only real novel.) Then Chekhov enters his final phase, which extends from 1894 to his death in 1904, and which it seems to me possible to date from the story called "A Woman's Kingdom," which immediately follows "The Black Monk." The "Monk" had been a masterpiece of a kind different from any of these later ones: a story of the supernatural that had something in common with Hawthorne, though it was also a "clinical" story of a psychiatric case; and all through the stories before this, even when they were dealing with lives that were sordid or uneventful, there had run a certain vein of the grotesque, of something not always quite plausible: an element of satiric relief, of comic exaggeration—even, in certain cases, of fable and fairy tale. But there is nothing of this in "A Woman's Kingdom," which simply describes a day in the household of an unmarried woman—a chronicle of domestic incident, solidly and soberly treated, in which the rise of the industrial middle class (the theme of a number of his later stories) is given its first intensive treatment. The method here changes as well as the scale. We now rarely get a single situation—as in "Ward No. 6"—carried through to an ironic climax.

This final series of stories, of which Chekhov managed to produce only a few a year, become more and more complex, involving a number of characters and presenting, as his plays of these years do, a whole social microcosm. These are really compressed novels, and we soon come to see that Chekhov is composing, in this latest period, a kind of "Comédie Humaine" in miniature. He is covering contemporary Russia in a sequence of significant studies, each one or each group of which aims to deal with—and for the purposes of the author more or less to exhaust—some clearly defined milieu. He is certainly concentrating here on an anatomy of Russian society rather than on appraising the soundness, as Virginia Woolf found him doing, of this or that individual soul. In "A Woman's Kingdom," and later on in "A Doctor's Visit" and "The New Villa," it is the recently arrived *bourgeoisie*, who have grown up with modern factories and modern engineering and now find themselves cut off from the people, from whom they have sprung. In "Three Years," it is the old Moscow merchant world, almost as self-contained as a ghetto, in which the strength of the older generation, bigoted, harsh, and oppressive, is at last undermined by the defection of its sons, who are marrying into the gentry or attempting, as intelligentsia, to escape to a world of more freedom and more sophistication; but these latter do not pan out, they cannot adapt themselves, and the wife of the brother who has stayed with the business—a woman from a "county" family, who has suffered a good deal from her boorish inlaws—comes to feel in the long run that her husband has chosen the better part. In "The Murder," it is a family of inn-keepers who have learned to read the Bible and are possessed by fanatical religious ideas—a form of illumination that does not save them from benighted savagery. "The Peasants" is a study of the peasant world, which Chekhov is far from idealizing, as Tolstoy liked to do, or sentimentalizing, as Turgenev sometimes did.... In "The Bishop," the next-to-last story that Chekhov lived to complete, he fixes on his slide a specimen of the not quite diseased yet not very vigorous tissue of the Greek Orthodox Church: a dying peasant priest, who has risen above the level of his parents but now finds he has nobody close to him; who has been turned into a professional churchman, caught up in the routine of his duties, without ever having experienced a moment of genuine religious feeling; who should clearly have been a lay intellectual but has never had the chance of becoming one. In these, and in the stories that immediately precede them, are presented a variety of other types of peasants, ex-peasants, and the lower middle class that were called in Russia *meshchane,* together with doctors, professors, petty provincial officials, and—given the full-scale treatment in "The Duel" of 1891—the pretentious and inept intelligentsia.

It should be noted that in his stories of this period Chekhov gives us no comparable picture of the decaying landowner class that is the subject of three of his later plays, and that this class, when it does appear—the story called in English "An Artist's Story" is the only possible exception—figures usually, as in "My Life," in only an incidental role and is shown as degenerate to the point of squalor. There are here no lakes with symbolic gulls, no cherry orchards in bloom.... [The] lower-class man who is on the make is the central figure in Chekhov. This is the theme—transposed into terms of a variety of milieux—of every one of the stories mentioned above. And it is much to the point at the present time to inquire how Chekhov judged these characters. For it was people of this kind who came to the top with the success of the Russian Revolution. (pp. 59-62, 64)

[What] did Chekhov think of these people, of whom he had been one himself and from whose cowardices, servilities, hypocrisies he prided himself ... on having delivered himself, declaring that he had succeeded in finally "squeezing out of myself every drop of servile blood" and becoming "a real human being." He seemed to be well aware that the future belongs to them. (pp. 64-5)

> Edmund Wilson, "Seeing Chekhov Plain" (originally published in The New Yorker, *Vol. XXVIII, No. 40, November 22, 1952), in his* A Window on Russia *(reprinted by permission of Farrar, Straus & Giroux, Inc.; copyright © 1952 by Edmund Wilson; copyright renewed © 1980 by Helen Miranda Wilson), Farrar, Straus & Giroux, 1978, pp. 52-68.*

THOMAS MANN (essay date 1959)

The question "What's to be done?" keeps cropping up in a deliberately confused manner throughout Chekhov's work; the strange, helpless, stilted way in which his characters hold forth on the problem of existence almost borders on the ludicrous. I can no longer remember in which story, but somewhere a lady appears and says: "Life should be observed as through a prism—that's to say, it should be seen in refractions, should be divided into its simplest elements, and then each element studied separately." His short sto-

ries and plays seethe with this kind of dialogue. In part it may be just a satirical description of the Russian love for the interminable and fruitless philosophical discussion—a kind of persiflage that can also be found in other Russian writers. But in Chekhov's case it has a very special background, a specific, disconcertingly comical artistic function. (pp. 189-90)

"What can we do?" The uneasiness caused by this question haunts numerous characters in Chekhov's stories. In "A Doctor's Visit" he coined the phrase "honorable sleeplessness." In this story Doctor Korolyov has been summoned to the intelligent, unhappy young lady, heiress to a million rubles and some factories, because she suffers from nervous fits and insomnia. "It's not that I feel ill," she says herself, "I am just uneasy and filled with anxiety, because it has to be like this and cannot be otherwise." It is quite clear to the doctor what he ought to tell her: Give up the five factories and the million as soon as possible and cast that devil out! And it is equally clear to him that she thinks the same, but is simply waiting to have it confirmed by someone she trusts. But how can he put it to her? One shrinks from asking a condemned man why he has been condemned, and it is also painful to ask the wealthy why they need so much money, why they make such poor use of their wealth, why they don't give it away, even when they realize it is the cause of their unhappiness. And once this kind of conversation is begun it invariably becomes embarrassing, painful, and boring. This is why he answers her frankly but in a consolatory tone: "It's in your role as factory-owner and wealthy heiress that you are dissatisfied; you don't feel entitled to wealth, so you cannot sleep. This is preferable, of course, to your being satisfied, to sleeping well and believing that all is as it should be. *You are suffering from an honorable sleeplessness....*" (pp. 196-97)

One has to face the fact that man is a failure. His conscience, which belongs to the spirit, will probably never be brought into harmony with his nature, his reality, his social condition, and there will always be "honorable sleeplessness" for those who for some unfathomable reason feel responsible for human fate and life. If anyone ever suffered from this, it was Chekhov the artist. All his work was honorable sleeplessness, a search for the right, redeeming word in answer to the question: "What are we to do?" The word was difficult, if not impossible, to find. The only thing he knew for certain was that idleness is the worst, that man has to work because idleness means letting others work for him, means exploitation and oppression. In his last story, "Betrothed," Sasha—who, like Chekhov, is consumptive and soon to die—says to Nadya, another girl unable to sleep: "Please understand that if your mother and grandmother do nothing, it means that others are working for them, that they are usurping someone else's life. Do you think this is decent? Isn't there something wrong? ... Dear, sweet Nadya, go away! Show them that you are sick of this stagnant, gray, sinful life! Prove it to yourself! I swear you won't regret it. You will go away; you will study and let yourself be guided by your fate. As soon as you have taken your life into your own hands, everything will be different. What matters most is to break out of the rut; everything else is unimportant. Now, shall we leave tomorrow?" And Nadya really does go. She leaves her family, her ineffectual fiancé, renounces marriage, and escapes. It is a flight from the shackles of class, from a way of life felt to be out of date, false, and "sinful," which keeps recurring in Chekhov's work, the same flight on which the aged Tolstoy embarked at the last moment. (pp. 197-98)

[Chekhov's] last story was "Betrothed" . . . , his last play *The Cherry Orchard*. In both works a spirit, facing dissolution with composure and making no fuss even about illness and death, sowed a seed of hope on the very brink of the grave. His life's work, although it laid no claim to the monumental proportions of the epic, nevertheless encompassed the whole of Russia, that vast country's natural landscape forming the background to the appallingly unnatural conditions of its pre-revolutionary era. "The impudence and idleness of the strong, the ignorance and animal submission of the weak, everywhere unbelievable poverty, oppression, degeneracy, alcoholism, hypocrisy, and dishonesty . . .". Yet the nearer his end approached, the more movingly an inner light of faith in the future flowed round the dark picture, the more fervently the poet's loving eye looked forward to a coming community of human beings, proud, free, and active, to "a new, dignified, and sensible way of life on whose threshold we may already be standing, of whose appearance we occasionally get a glimpse."

"Good-by, my dear, dear Sasha," says Nadya, the "Betrothed," to the dead man who has persuaded her to flee from a false existence. "And before her mind there rose a vision of a new life, wide and free, and this new life, still obscure and full of mystery, called to her and beckoned her." A dying man wrote those lines shortly before his end —and perhaps it was nothing but the mystery of death that was calling and beckoning. Or may we believe that the passionate longing of a poet can actually alter life? (pp. 201-02)

Thomas Mann, "Chekhov," translated by Tania and James Stern, in Last Essays by Thomas Mann (copyright © 1958 by Alfred A. Knopf, Inc.; reprinted by permission of Alfred A. Knopf, Inc.), Knopf, 1959, pp. 178-203.

FRANK O'CONNOR   (essay date 1960)

I know enough about the business of storytelling to be able to put my finger on certain devices that maintain the astonishing freshness of [Chekhov's] stories. The devices are not unlike those that [Toulouse-Lautrec] and Degas used; ultimately, they can all be traced to the naturalistic theory about describing what you see—the simplest artistic theory in the world until you begin to ask yourself what you *do* see. As in Degas' "L'Absinthe" the figures are not placed solidly in the center of the picture and the figure of the man trails off inexplicably behind the frame, so in Chekhov there is always a deliberate artlessness of composition— people walk on and off, and sometimes a fascinating character is described and then dropped. Men are always being caught buttoning their trousers and women pulling up their stockings, and their outraged glances as we catch them at it are always part of the total ironic effect. But any satirist can demolish a pose in that way, and nothing fades so fast as satire. There is a great deal more to Chekhov than his ironic attitude. (p. 1)

If one really wants to understand Chekhov, one must realize that he was the moralist of the venial sin, the man who laid it down that a soul is damned not for murder, adultery or embezzlement but for the small, unrecognized sins of ill-temper, untruthfulness, stinginess and disloyalty. The woman in the "Grasshopper" who is unfaithful to her dull doctor husband with a flashy painter is not going to be damned for adultery; she will be damned and damned thoroughly for the supercilious way in which she addressed her husband in company. As in Degas and Lautrec the whole beautiful theory of the art schools is blown sky-high, so in Chekhov the whole nineteenth-century conception of morals is blown sky-high. This is not morality as anyone from Jane Austen to Trollope would have recognized it, though I suspect that an orthodox theologian might have something very interest to say about it. . . .

For the benefit of orthodox theologians the weakness of Chekhov's morality is that it is almost a branch of esthetics. Sin to him is ultimately a lack of refinement, the inability to get through a badly cooked meal without a scene. But at the same time one can say that his esthetic is moral as Katherine Mansfield's and Joyce's are not. All the casualness is only apparent. When Laevsky in "The Duel" says "The same thing every day. Why not have cabbage soup?" somebody is in great danger of being damned for it. . . .

I am not sure but some orthodox theologians would agree with me that Chekhov was the greatest moralist of them all. I am not even sure that my theologian would make too much fuss about the fact that Chekhov believed that a remark like "The same thing every day" was the outward and visible sign of an inward lack of grace, meaning in Chekhov's sense of the word refinement—Chekhov's notion of the horror that Adam and Eve and the Apple first brought into the world. (p. 24)

Frank O'Connor, "A Writer Who Refused to Pretend," in The New York Times Book Review (© 1960 by The New York Times Company; reprinted by permission), January 17, 1960, pp. 1, 24.

DAVID MAGARSHACK   (essay date 1960)

[Chekhov's dramatic] work can be divided into two main periods. The plays belonging to one period differ from the plays belonging to the other, both in their structure and their final aim. There is an interval of about seven years between them during which Chekhov evolved the original type of drama which has made him famous. The first period includes four full-length plays, of which two have been preserved, and eleven one-act plays, eight of which are light comedies. All of them are characteristically direct-action plays, that is, plays in which the main dramatic action takes place on the stage in full view of the audience. The four plays of the second period, on the other hand, are indirect-action plays, that is, plays in which the main dramatic action takes place off stage and in which the action that does take place on the stage is mainly "inner action".

The Wood Demon does not strictly speaking belong to either of these categories and represents Chekhov's first attempt to write an indirect-action play or, as he first called it, a "lyrical" play. (p. 53)

The Wood Demon is essentially a morality play on Tolstoyan lines: it is not a play in which virtue triumphs over vice, but in which vice is converted to virtue. In this play Chekhov deals with the great theme of the reconciliation of good and evil by letting his vicious characters first defeat his virtuous ones and then realise the heinousness of their offence. At the same time, however, Chekhov wished to challenge the generally accepted view that stage characters ought to be "dramatically effective". He wished to show life on the stage as it really was and not as it was invariably contrived by the professional playwright. But, not surprisingly perhaps in view of the essentially "theatrical" nature of the main theme of *The Wood Demon,* what he finally produced was a revival of a romantic convention of a bygone age with all its incongruous crudities. And he did so chiefly because he failed to realise that the drama of indirect action he was attempting to write had its own laws which could be ignored only at the price of complete failure. When he discovered those laws, he transformed the crude melodrama he had written into a great stage masterpiece. (pp. 121-22)

[There are two] characteristic features of Chekhov's indirect-action plays that must be considered. The first concerns the difference between the dialogue of Chekhov's early plays and that of his late ones. The dialogue of the early plays is remarkable for the directness of its appeal to the audience, while in the late plays its appeal is indirect and, mainly, evocative. (pp. 159-60)

[Chekhov's dialogue is] a very subtle instrument for evoking the right mood in the audience and in this way preparing it for the development of the action of the play. It is no longer the colloquial prose Chekhov used in his early plays and in *The Wood Demon,* but a prose that is highly charged with emotional undertones, or, in other words, a poetic prose.... Tension in an indirect-action play is ... one of the main motive forces of action.... [Chekhov conveyed tension] to his audience at the very beginning of the play. He did it by showing one of his main characters in a state of high nervous tension, like, for instance, Konstantin in the opening scenes of *The Seagull* or Voynitsky in the opening scenes of *Uncle Vanya.* (pp. 162-63)

Another powerful impetus to action and movement is provided in an indirect-action play by the presence of "invisible" characters.... For instance, Nina's parents in *The Seagull,* Protopopov in *The Three Sisters,* and Mrs. Ranevsky's aunt and her Paris lover in *The Cherry Orchard.* In a play of direct action they would be allowed to take an active part on the stage, for they all occupy an important place in the plot and without them the final dénouement would be impossible. In an indirect action play, however, it is necessary that they, like the supernatural powers in a Greek play, should remain invisible, for their function is to supply a motive force for the action which is all the more powerful because the audience never sees them but is made to *imagine* them. (pp. 163-64)

The main elements through which action is expressed in an indirect-action play are: the "messenger" element, the function of which is to keep the audience informed about the chief dramatic incidents which takes place off state (in a direct-action play this element is, as a rule, a structural flaw); the arrival and departure of the characters in the play round which the chief incidents that take place on the stage are grouped; the presence of a chorus which, as Aristotle points out, "forms an integral part of the whole play and shares in the action"; peripetia, that is, the reversal of the situation leading up to the dénouement, which Aristotle defines as "a change by which the action veers round to its opposite, subject always to the rule of probability and necessity", and which is the most powerful element of emotional interest in indirect-action plays and their main instrument for sustaining suspense and arousing surprise; and, lastly, background which lends depth to such plays. (p. 164)

[The most] remarkable thing about *The Seagull* is that in it Chekhov has achieved a complete synthesis of theme and character, and that the action of the play flows logically and naturally out of the interplay of the themes and characters upon each other. So complete is this synthesis that an illusion of real life is created, while in fact nothing could be further from reality than the events that happen in this play, or the situations out of which Chekhov so cunningly contrives its climaxes. Where in life would one come across such an absolute agglomeration of love triangles as in Chekhov's comedy? ... And yet the love theme does not play any important, or any decisive part in the play: it is an ancillary theme introduced to give point to the comic elements in the play, though it is not the main comic element in it by any means. (p. 187)

Uncle Vanya is of course an adaptation of *The Wood Demon,* but Chekhov always maintained that it was an entirely new play, and to it is in spite of the fact that the second and third acts of two plays are practically identical. For what did Checkhov do? He took one of the main themes of *The Wood Demon* and built an entirely different play round it. What must have struck him forcibly when he exhumed *The Wood Demon* six years after he had decided to bury it for good was that the dramatic relationships in that play were all wrong, mainly because they did not develop naturally, but were most commonly contrived by the playwright himself. Now that he had mastered the technique of the indirect-action play he could see clearly why it was so. The action, for one thing, did not unwind itself *inevitably* because it lacked the elements through which it is expressed in a play which depends for its final effect on the inner workings of the minds and hearts of its characters. The messenger element was most grossly mishandled; the chorus element was submerged in a flood of irrelevant detail because the playwright was too anxious to *copy* instead of *creating* it; the most vital peripetia element was not there at all, so that the dramatic movement of the play did not follow one single line of development, thus creating a most chaotic impression and resulting in a most unconvincing ending. Only the Serebryakov-Voynitsky incident seemed to hang together, and even that came to an abrupt end by Voynitsky's suicide. The play had therefore to be first of all disencumbered of all irrelevant matter and its action firmly based on the peripetia element. All unnecessary characters had to be dropped.... [A] vital change in the plot [changing a suicide to a bungled attempted murder] at once supplied Chekhov with the peripetia element of the new play: the whole action now centred round the reversal of the situation as it existed at the beginning of the play (pp. 204-06)

The Cherry Orchard has been so consistently misunderstood and misrepresented by producer and critic alike that it is only by a complete dissociation from the current misconceptions about the play that it is possible to appreciate Chekhov's repeated assertions that he had written not a tragedy but "a comedy, and in places even a farce." Structurally, this last play of Chekhov's is the most perfect example of an indirect-action play, for in it all the elements are given equal scope for the development of the action. And in no other play is the peripetia element so important for a proper understanding of situation and character without which any appreciation of the comic nature of the play is impossible. (p. 264)

[In declaring] that there was not a single pistol shot in *The Cherry Orchard*, Chekhov overlooked another remarkable feature which distinguishes his last play from all his other plays, namely that there is not a single love triangle in it, either. Indeed, Chekhov seems to have been so anxious that nothing should obscure the essentially comic character of the play that he eliminated everything from it that might introduce any deeper emotional undercurrents. The play, it is true, has plenty of emotional undercurrents, but they are all of a "comic" nature, that is to say, the ludicrous element is never missing from them. *The Cherry Orchard,* in fact, conforms entirely to Aristotle's definition of comedy as "an imitation of characters of a lower type who are not bad in themselves but whose faults possess something ludicrous in them". (p. 272)

The misinterpretation of *The Cherry Orchard* as a tragedy . . . is mainly due to a misunderstanding of the nature of a comic character. A "comic" character is generally supposed to keep an audience in fits of laughter, but that is not always so. No one would deny that Falstaff is essentially a comic character, but his fall from favour is one of the most moving incidents in *Henry IV*. Don Quixote, too, is essentially a comic character, but what has made him immortal is his creator's ability to arouse the compassion and the sympathy of the reader for him. The same is true of the chief characters of *The Cherry Orchard:* the sympathy and compassion they arouse in the spectator should not be allowed to blind him to the fact that they are essentially comic characters. (p. 273)

The main theme of the play is generally taken to be the passing of the old order, symbolised by the sale of the cherry orchard. But that theme was stale by the time Chekhov wrote his play. . . . What is new about this theme is the comic twist Chekhov gave it. (p. 274)

The symbolism of the cherry orchard, then, has nothing to do with its sale. All it expresses is one of the recurrent themes in Chekhov's plays: the destruction of beauty by those who are utterly blind to it. . . . The cherry orchard indeed is a purely aesthetic symbol which its owners with the traditions of an old culture behind them fully understand; to Firs it merely means the cartloads of dried cherries sent off to town in the good old days, and to Lopakhin it is only an excellent site for "development."

That the sale of the cherry orchard does not form the main theme of the play can also be deduced from the fact that the peripetia element has very little, if anything, to do with it. Indeed, the moment its owners appear on the stage, it ought to become clear to the discerning playgoer that they are certainly not going to save it. The whole dramatic interest of the play is therefore centred on Lopakhin, the future owner of the cherry orchard. (pp. 274-75)

Lopakhin can well afford to buy the estate on which his father has been a serf, but it never occurs to him to do so. At first he is absolutely genuine in trying to save the estate for its owners, but in the end it is he who becomes the owner of the estate—a complete reversal of the situation. It is the inner conflict between the son of the former serf and the rich business man round which the peripetia element in the play revolves. At the very beginning of the play Chekhov makes use of a device he used with equal effect in *The Three Sisters,* the device of the chorus element which gives the audience a vague hint of what the development of the

plot is going to be while leaving the characters themselves completely in the dark. In *The Three Sisters* this device is associated with Protopopov and the two lines about the bear from Krylov's fable. In *The Cherry Orchard* it is more openly comic in character (p. 276)

The contention, so frequently repeated and so firmly held, that Chekhov's favourite theme was disillusionment and that, moreover, he was, as [one critic] expressed it, "the poet and apologist of ineffectualness," appears in the light of the foregoing argument to be wholly untenable. Nothing, indeed, could be further from the truth than the opinion expressed by Bernard Shaw in his Preface to *Heartbreak House* in a reference to *The Cherry Orchard,* an opinion, incidentally, that has probably shaped the attitude to Chekhov in England more than any other critical appraisal of his plays. "Chekhov," Shaw wrote, "more of a fatalist than Tolstoy, had no faith in these charming people extricating themselves. They would, he thought, be sold up and sent adrift by the bailiffs; therefore, he had no scruple in exploiting and flattering their charm." Now, Chekhov was certainly not a fatalist, nor did he dream of exploiting and flattering the charm of his characters; that is done by the producers and actors who find themselves entirely at sea in face of a drama that seems to defy every canon of stage-craft and yet contains such wonderful stage material; therefore, they fall back on the more obvious and dramatically insignificant details, the mere bricks and mortar of a Chekhov play which, without its steel frame, is more of a picturesque ruin than an enduring monument to a great creative artist. (pp. 286-87)

> *David Magarshack, in his* Chekhov the Dramatist *(reprinted by permission of Hill & Wang, a division of Farrar, Straus & Giroux, Inc.; copyright © 1960 by David Magarshack), Hill & Wang, 1960, 301 p.*

MAURICE VALENCY   (essay date 1966)

Platonov is a very poor play, but it repays study. It indicates, among other things, that at this stage of his career, at least, Chekhov had no idea of doing anything new. The theme he settled on was the most popular theme of the day. In developing it he followed assiduously the practice of successful playwrights. For a beginner, he was as sensible as could be. *Platonov* is entirely conventional. (p. 48)

What Chekhov had in mind was a depiction of the spiritual plight of the landowning class during the period of transition following the emancipation of the serfs. It is substantially the theme of *The Cherry Orchard.* Unlike *The Cherry Orchard,* of course, *Platonov* is full of plot and artifice. It is more than generous in theatrical effects, and is obviously journeyman's work. But the importance of the theme for Chekhov may be inferred from the persistence with which he returned to it throughout his dramatic career. For Chekhov, Platonov was a character of exceptional significance. (pp. 48-9)

Obviously this play, such as it is, has many romantic elements; indeed, it has as much in this line as a play could possibly have. There are two Satanic characters, one male, one female; there is the woman who is resolved to ruin her lover, and the one who is determined to save him at all costs; there is the innocent wife, and the no-nonsense type of girl who is really more vulnerable than the rest; finally, there is the irresolute, impulsive, and introspective hero, by turns brutal and masochistic, who attempts to sum up in himself the illness of the age. One might say that from the standpoint of characterization, Chekhov covered the ground. (p. 51)

[Platonov] has unexpected universality. He speaks not only for the lost generation of the 1880's, but for all those who periodically find it possible to rationalize their ineptitude in terms of a tragic sense of the world's absurdity. If he speaks badly, it is because Chekhov did not as yet know how to make him speak well; but it is not difficult to see in Platonov an early example of the angry young men of a later age. . . .

[Platonov] clearly represents the matrix from which so much of Chekhov's later drama was drawn. Its protagonist was, in fact, surprisingly well conceived. It is in the telling of the story that Chekhov demonstrated his lack of skill. Platonov compensates for his failure as a man by exerting his power over women. His Don Juanism is the sign of his weakness, and the principal symptom of his disease, and it is fitting that it should be the cause of his death. He is, to use the Freudian phrase, neither *arbeits-* nor *liebesfähig,* and he is socially dangerous. In the circumstances there is nothing much to be done about him but to have him shot.

Ivanov, in Chekhov's later play, is evidently much the same man. Though shorn of the excessive sexuality of his predecessor, he has the grace to shoot himself. Uncle Vanya is a much later development. In his first version, he too shoots himself. But in *The Cherry Orchard* it is quite unnecessary to shoot Gayev. He is ineffectual, but no longer dangerous. He has retired gracefully from the fray, and taken refuge in a dream. In the evolution of this character it is perhaps possible to gauge with some accuracy the development of Chekhov as a realist. (p. 52)

The Duel is a great masterpiece. Its tone is by turns moody and comic. It has no melodrama and no theatricalism. There are no suicides in it and no dramatic speeches. On the contrary, in *The Duel* all is understated. The climaxes are quiet. The emotion current runs deep and still. Whatever sentimentality there is in it is touched with humor. *The Duel,* as a reworking of *Ivanov,* demonstrates clearly that Chekhov was at this time primarily a storyteller, accustomed to working in a free medium which he himself developed to a kind of perfection. He became a dramatist only when he gave up the technique of the stage. It was when, toward the end of his life, he quite abandoned the rules of playwrighting, and began to write for the theatre in his own natural medium, that he achieved greatness as a playwright. (pp. 99-100)

The action [of *The Wood Demon*] is embarrassingly inept. There is something undeniably mealy-mouthed and moralistic about the play, but apart from the fact that some of the characters are shown the error of their ways, there is in it little or nothing to justify its qualification as Tolstoyan. *The Wood Demon* is certainly not conceived as a conflict of good and evil forces, nor is there any indication that, in the end, good triumphs over evil. Nor is the ending truly happy. On the contrary, the evil relationship between the old professor and his young wife, which is central in the action, is perpetuated at the end, and there is no suggestion that this conflict is soluble.

It is possible to estimate the degree of Chekhov's development as a playwright . . . by comparing the birthday party

with which *The Wood Demon* begins with the birthday party in *Ivanov.* In that scene the people are grotesque puppets; and the party is a bore. The people in corresponding scenes of *The Wood Demon* are alive and interesting, witty and genial. They abuse each other freely, but their abuse demonstrates the closeness of their relationship. It is a group of dear friends who detest one another. (pp. 106-07)

The Wood Demon is a play about waste. In Russia, it is said, everything is wasted, forests, people, lives, intellect. The peasants waste the trees out of sheer thoughtlessness. The gentry waste each other out of sheer boredom. Voynitsky has wasted his life toiling on the farm to support Serebryakov, whom he once idolized. Serebryakov wasted the life of his first wife, Voynitsky's sister; now he is wasting Elena's youth and beauty. He wastes the timber of the estate in order to get himself a little ready money. He has wasted his own talent, senselessly hashing over other men's thoughts. Fyodor and Zheltukhin are wasting their inheritance through gambling and drink. All is waste, senseless and stupid.

The theme of waste was evidently obsessive with Chekhov. Brought up in poverty, he was a frugal soul, and he knew how difficult it is for a poor man to earn in the sweat of his brow what the rich toss away recklessly. The idea of waste, universal waste—since, obviously, nature is infinitely more wasteful than man—troubled Chekhov deeply. The theme is renewed in *The Sea Gull.* Its various aspects are developed further in *The Three Sisters,* and further still in *The Cherry Orchard.* All his drama, in some sense, involves this idea; for Chekhov, as for A. C. Bradley, the Shakespearean critic, the sense of waste is the prime source of the sense of tragedy.

The Wood Demon is, however, a comedy. The second act takes place at night in the Serebryakov's dining-room, where the professor is sitting up late, sharing his arthritis with his family. We understand that he is, in reality, a pathetic old man who has worked too hard all his life; that he is cruelly bored in the country; and that he longs for fame and the admiration of his students, his only pleasures. He feels, rightly, that nobody loves him; and he takes the occasion to explain himself at length, thereby impeding the flow of the action. . . . All the characters in *The Wood Demon* are at pains to depict in detail their states of mind. It was much later in his career that Chekhov learned how important it was for his characters to keep their counsel. In *The Three Sisters* all the characters, even the most voluble, are essentially reserved. In *The Wood Demon,* the characters elbow one another in their haste to uncover their inmost souls. (pp. 108-09)

The Wood Demon was no doubt intended as a comedy of manners. But in the absence of evidence, it is difficult to decide whether the author was not yet quite sure of how gentlefolk acted in these circumstances, or whether he intended to give a realistic picture of the brutal coarseness of upper class life in the provinces. Both are possible; but it is not unreasonable to suppose that the former was the case. (p. 111)

The Wood Demon ends in most unsatisfactory fashion. Khrushchov, who is never reticent throughout the play, reveals himself in the end as its *raisonneur.* He explains the title of the comedy, and, in some sense, defines the theme. . . . (p. 115)

The Wood Demon marked a low point in Chekhov's fortunes as a dramatist, but it contained some very good things. . . . (p. 117)

[Chekhov] was primarily an ironist, and his plays were, on the whole, comedically conceived. But Chekhov was taking the pulse of a dying world. It died well, with courage and gayety; nevertheless, the description of its agony could not be altogether funny. His plays are full of laughter, but in each we hear the sound of the breaking string; and from the contrast between what seems, from one viewpoint, comic, but tragic from another, Chekhov developed a form of drama, a dramatic polyphony, which is unparalleled in the history of the theatre. (p. 290)

> *Maurice Valency, in his* The Breaking String: The Plays of Anton Chekhov *(copyright © 1966 by Maurice Valency; reprinted by permission of Oxford University Press, Inc.), Oxford University Press, New York, 1966, 324 p.*

RONALD HINGLEY (essay date 1966)

[In some ways Chekhov] worked within a limited range compared with many other writers of similar importance. This was due, not to a lack of enterprise on his part, but to a wish to concentrate on something which he regarded as of overriding importance. 'Real life' was the criterion which he repeatedly applied to literature, and accordingly the words 'such things do not happen in real life' often have the ring of absolute condemnation when related by him to a story or play. (p. 206)

[*The Teacher of Literature*] describes the courtship and early married life of a young schoolmaster, Nikitin. All that happens is that Nikitin falls in love with a girl called Masha, proposes, gets married and gradually falls out of love. The entire action of the story is seen through the young man's eyes, and Chekhov conveys with his usual complete authenticity the texture and flavour of the portion of life experienced by his hero.

A complicated series of thoughts and sensations passes through Nikitin's brain. Some of them are important—his marriage plans and love for Masha; the majority are trivial and concern certain smells, sights and sounds of everyday life which unaccountably detach themselves as significant and vaguely disturbing. They succeed each other in apparently haphazard order—just as such sensations always do in real life. It would perhaps have been difficult for Chekhov himself to say just why he selected for mention at one moment the silhouette of a brewery, at another the purring of a cat, or the sound of a band in the park. Many of these themes recur several times, an aspect of Chekhov's stories which has led some critics to compare their construction with that of a piece of music—it has even been said that they have *leit-motivs* like a Wagnerian opera. (pp. 206-07)

Chekhov's method was selective. He did not attempt a comprehensive catalogue of all his hero's sensations, such as has been known to fill novels of several hundred pages with the events of a single day, but merely picked out a few individual items. These might not all have any immediately obvious logical relevance, but they had a peculiar quality of evoking the atmosphere of the whole. . . .

D. S. Mirsky's phrase 'biographies of a mood' remains one of the few successful attempts to find a portmanteau description of these stories. Chekhov had, of course, been producing such 'biographies' long before he wrote *The Teacher of Literature,* and the mood, or *nastroenie,* evoked in some of his early serious stories was seen to have a special quality. This quality was developed to perfection in Chekhov's later fiction, and will always be recognized as one of his greatest and most distinctive charms as a writer. (p. 207)

His method of describing nature had not altered in essentials since he wrote *The Steppe,* and he still relied on flashes of vivid detail to bring a whole scene before the reader's eyes. More than ever nature-descriptions were now relevant to the mood of one or other of the characters, and Chekhov still found it useful to stress this link by attributing human reactions to natural phenomena. Thus, in *The Teacher of Literature,* it is quite characteristic that the flowers in Masha's garden should participate emotionally in the proposal scene which they witness: 'in the dark grass, dimly lit by the moon, were sleepy tulips and irises, which seemed themselves to be awaiting a confession of love from somebody.'

Nature is also called into play in this story to help Chekhov to execute a neat and thorough Chekhovian figure, to which Mirsky first drew attention. During the first half of the story Chekhov sets a course in a straight line towards an apparently predictable goal. The straight line is Nikitin's courtship of Masha, which develops so delightfully that the reader begins to anticipate a conventional magazine-story ending. At a certain point, however, Chekhov's course begins, imperceptibly at first, to curve away from the line, and before very long it is proceeding in an entirely different direction. The curve is traced with such subtlety that it is hard to determine the exact point at which it begins. Nevertheless this point can be found if one looks for it, and it is typical that it should coincide with a description of nature.

One interesting feature in the production of atmosphere is the way in which Chekhov regularly provides hints calculated to link his scenes with the past and the future. He believed that a writer should make his readers feel, in addition to the personalities described, 'the human mass out of which they have come, the air they breathe and the background perspective—in a word everything.' (pp. 207-08)

Closely allied with this feature of Chekhov's atmosphere-building is his characters' habit of evoking memories and aspirations in their personal lives. Again and again they refer to the sensations of childhood, a period of life which tends above all to be surrounded with an aura of suggestive and intangible beauty. . . . (p. 209)

Chekhov recognized the great importance of love interest in fiction when he said of his own *Ward No. 6:* 'I am finishing a story which is very boring, because women and the element of love are quite lacking in it. I don't like that sort of story.' He certainly made up for the deficiency elsewhere. (p. 210)

The most obvious feature of love as portrayed by Chekhov is that it almost never works out to the satisfaction of either party, and *The Darling* would seem to contain the only exceptions to this rule in the whole of his later fiction. If Chekhov believed in the possibility of happy married life he certainly left little trace of this belief in his work. He seems to have regarded young love as an illusion, but an illusion so beautiful that he repeatedly used it for the evocation of atmosphere. His young men in love are liable to meet with one of three different fates, none of them enviable. Either their love is not returned, or they are separated from their beloved by circumstances, or, finally, they get married and the illusion ends in inevitable disillusion. All these experiences involve emotions and memories which, however frustrating to the participants, make ideal material for the construction of atmosphere.

It is not possible to do more than indicate the importance of this theme in Chekhov's stories. Love, it would seem, was the subject which fascinated him above all others, and he was concerned to present it, like all his themes, exactly as he saw it. There was certainly no problem to which he was less likely to pretend to have found a solution. . . . (pp. 210-11)

Chekhov's characters do not fall into ready-made patterns, and are almost entirely free from the tendency to repetiton of which he accused Turgenev's heroines. The production of this amazingly wide and diverse range of living figures can be claimed as one of his main achievements, and it was natural that he should have thought that any attempt to theorize about them robbed them of life and colour. However, there are some general points which it is interesting to bear in mind when reading the stories. Among these is a tendency for each character to enjoy the author's sympathy in so far as he possesses the quality of sensitivity. This is especially fascinating in stories like *Ionych,* where the hero starts off with a high degree of this quality and can be observed progressively shedding it with the passage of years. This process can be seen in reverse in *Betrothed* and *The Teacher of Literature* in which Chekhov describes its awakening where it has hitherto been dormant. In the latter story the birth-pangs of sensitivity in Nikitin were attended with a growing feeling of unhappiness, and this is in accordance with Chekhov's normal practice, for there is among his characters a high degree of correlation between sensitivity and unhappiness. These qualities often (though by no means always) go together with a lack of will power and a tendency to drift, which Chekhov describes with sympathy and a pleasing undercurrent of humour. (pp. 212-13)

Chekhov's method of introducing his characters and bringing them to life for his readers has something in common with his technique of nature-description, for it exhibits a similar concentration on brevity and compactness. Again it is possible to contrast the method of Turgenev, who often settles down to a set-piece character study of important characters, expounding in detail their habits, temperaments and biographical background. Chekhov succeeded in dispensing with this, and usually managed with a few brief indications, often enlivened by an emphasis on some eccentricity typical of the person described. In the sphere of character-drawing he again revealed his unerring instinct for suggestive detail. Just as he believed that he could make his reader visualize a moonlit night by mentioning the glitter of light on a broken bottle, so he often found it possible to conjure up the personality of a man by insisting on some detail, such as his way of mispronouncing the letter R or his method of wrinkling his eyes when he smiled.

Chekhov often reverted in his later stories to the type of humorous caricature which he had perfected as *Antosha Chekhonte.* His humour was never very far from the surface, and continually imparted a lightness of touch, even to his most sombre studies. Even *Ward No. 6* contains funny scenes—for example, the occasion when Doctor Ragin appears before a group of local officials who make a series of rudimentary tests of his sanity. One character in the story, the preposterous Mikhail Averyanych, is almost wholly comic, especially in the ridiculous scene in Warsaw where he borrows Ragin's last savings to pay his gambling debts, with a cry of 'Honour before everything!' (pp. 213-14)

Quite often a reader unfamiliar with Russian literature may wonder whether he is expected to laugh or cry when reading certain scenes of Chekhov. How, for example, is one expected to react to the pathetic figure of the heroine's father in *'Anna on the Neck'*? He is a poverty-stricken old schoolmaster who is steadily going to the bad, and who is continually threatened with dismissal because of his 'weakness'—a fondness for the bottle. His two small sons have to follow him everywhere in order to stop him from misbehaving himself, and their pathetic cries of 'Don't, Daddy, don't!' recur in the story as a repeated motif. The Russian reader, who knew his Gogol and Dostoevsky, was used to scenes of this type, where one might be expected to smile and weep at the same time, and to which the critical formula 'laughter through tears'—popularized by Gogol—was often applied. Again and again Chekhov evokes this mingled reaction, which is one of the most subtle effects at his disposal. (p. 214)

It is perhaps a commonplace to say that the qualities of simplicity and straightforwardness, which appear at their best in Chekhov's prose, are often the most difficult of attainment for a writer, and the most satisfying to his readers when attained. Chekhov seemed to find that his language acquired elegance and grace in so far as it became absolutely appropriate to his meaning; he described the quality he was looking for—which he knew could only be attained by a laborious process of re-writing and correcting—as 'musical'. Jarring notes must be avoided. . . .

It would be doing less than justice to Chekhov's own style to describe it as one which merely avoided such obvious errors as undue repetition and the use of ugly-sounding words. His descriptive passages are models of harmoniously-constructed Russian, beautiful and subtly evocative in spite of its simplicity. (p. 215)

[The] quality of Chekhov's plays, so charged with emotional significance in spite of their surface innocence, has stimulated Russian critics to look for a suitable name to describe his technique. His drama has been called 'lyrical'; it has been called 'internal', as opposed to the earlier, 'external' variety, and it has also been called the 'drama of the under-water current', since the operative dramatic stresses are so often submerged. The most common description is 'the drama of *nastroenie*', a concept already discussed in relation to the stories, where it was shown that 'mood' or 'atmosphere' are the best English equivalents.

An examination of the plays shows that Chekhov's methods of presenting *nastroenie* are similar to those employed in the stories. The same use is made of memories of the past, hopes for the future, and the state of mind associated with unsuccessful love. Chekhov often chose to present situations particularly calculated to throw such sensations into relief. Leave-takings were very suitable for the purpose—for example, those involved in the departure of the regiment at the end of *Three Sisters.* It had been stationed for some years in the provincial town where the action takes place, so that, when it came to leave, intimate associations had to be broken off, with little prospect of them ever being renewed. The emotions attendant on such an occasion blended harmoniously into the Chekhov mood. Similar emotionally-charged partings are to be found in *Uncle Vanya* and *The Cherry Orchard*. (pp. 236-37)

In the plays, as in the stories, Chekhov also makes use of the beauties of nature in building up atmosphere. For example, the audience is not long allowed to forget the lake which figures so prominently in *The Seagull* that it has even been suggested that Chekhov regarded it as one of the *dramatis personae*. The cherry orchard plays an even more important part in conditioning the mood of the play to which it gives its name. (p. 237)

Only a small minority of Chekhov's personages are satisfied with their fate, and even these are usually people whose futility is patent to amost everybody else but themselves. . . . (p. 239)

The characters lose few opportunities for airing their frustrations. The younger people usually want something in the future, and nearly always it is something which they do not look like getting. . . . With the older characters frustration often takes the form of laments over a wasted life and lost opportunities. (p. 240)

Among the sources of frustration in Chekhov's plays love occupies pride of place. Broadly speaking no one is allowed to be in love with anyone who is in love with them, and on the rare occasions when this rule is broken some external circumstances can be relied upon to create an effective obstacle. In *The Seagull* the love-pattern presents a remarkably complicated picture. . . .

It is obvious that anyone prepared to identify Chekhov with his own characters could find abundant evidence in the plays to support the 'Chekhov legend'. During his lifetime the idea sometimes did arise in Russia that Chekhov himself was a sort of Uncle Vanya, but this impression dissolved as his work and biography became better known. It was seen that Chekhov, far from identifying himself with his gloomier heroes, was often laughing at them, and it even began to be thought that he conceived his plays as scathing satires directed against the futility and morbid self-pity of intellectuals belonging to his generation. This view was almost equally mistaken. Perhaps Chekhov's attitude was puzzling because it was so simple. He was merely following his usual policy of putting on the stage ordinary people in an everyday environment. He might ridicule them or sympathize with them (very often he seems to have been doing both simulataneously) but his general attitude was not one of wholesale condemnation or approval. (p. 241)

The element of humour became more noticeable with each play that Chekhov wrote, and it is most prominent in *The Cherry Orchard*. (p. 243)

Chekhov himself was seriously convinced that *The Cherry Orchard* and—what is more surprising—*The Three Sisters* were 'gay comedies, almost vaudevilles'. . . . Neither Chekhov himself nor the 'sorrowful tragedy' school of thought seem to have expressed the true position on the subject. The plays are not comedies or tragedies in the accepted sense of either word, nor are they exclusively gay or sorrowful. They contain rather an extremely subtle blend of both elements. That the evocative atmosphere peculiar to Chekhov should combine harmoniously with broad farce is perhaps a surprising fact, but *The Cherry Orchard* is there to prove the possibility of such a combination. (p. 244)

Ronald Hingley, "Chekhov's Approach to Fiction" and "Chekhov's Last Years: His Approach to Drama," in his Chekhov: A Biographical and Critical Study *(© George Allen & Unwin Ltd, 1966), revised edition, George Allen & Unwin Ltd, 1966, pp. 196-218, 219-44.*

JOHN GASSNER (essay date 1967)

Two diametrically opposed interpretations of Chekhov have appeared in the English-speaking world, and they have been proclaimed with special fervor in the world of the theater. The first dominant view, while conceding his talent for vaudeville humor in a number of short stage pieces, lauded an artist of half-lights, a laureate of well-marinated futility, and a master of tragic sensibility even if his work failed to conform to classic standards of tragedy. This view came to be challenged with considerable vigor in England and America after World War II, particularly in the academic world. Without any ideological impetus, such as one could expect in Eastern Europe, to favor a new image of Chekhov as the prophet of a new society, there arose a tendency to discard the old image in favor of a tinsel view of Chekhov as a paragon of breezy extroversion. Young academicians were particularly eager to divest him of the atmosphere of gloom and soulfulness ("Slavic soulfulness," at that!) which he had accumulated in Western criticism and stage productions. Moreover, so many journalistic sources gave their support to proponents of this view that it became the prevailing one whether or not it was applicable to any particular work in whole or in part.

It must become evident, though, upon reflection, that this view has its inadequacies, if not indeed dangers—inadequacies even with respect to a brief humorous story such as the often-printed "A Work of Art," in which a physician is embarrassed in his provincial milieu by the gift of a nude statuette, let alone with respect to the great plays upon which rests much of Chekhov's reputation in the West. The advocates of a blithely extrovert interpretation or the image of a Chekhov purified of "Chekhovianism" are constrained to omit or at least play down too many facets, not to mention nuances, of his work to make it conform to a simplistic definition of comedy; the work thus becomes too thin and clemeary, and would therefore have to be rated as little more than clever second-rate histrionics. The proponents of this recently "discovered" image have not known what to make of their extroverted Chekhov, just as their predecessors didn't quite know what to make of their introverted one. (pp. 175-76)

What the old tendency in Chekhovian production failed to perceive . . . was that Chekhov himself was not dispirited even if a good many of his characters are, and that even the latter are not altogether willing to wallow in hopelessness. If this old-guard view of Chekhov had been entirely tenable, it would have been easy to advance claims for him as one of the progenitors of the Theater of the Absurd, and it is perhaps significant that no such claims have been advanced. What the "new-generation" view of the extrovert-Chekhov has failed to take into account is precisely the large area of stalemate against which Chekhov rebelled, and the fact that what he exposed in his plays plainly existed in turn-of-the-century provincial life. It was pervasive and oppressive enough, in fact, to arouse his scorn and indignation. It comprised a world abundantly present in his plays and stories, for a good writer does not launch an attack on something that lacks reality and he also does not tilt against anything to which he has failed to give existence as an artist. And Chekhov could not have done what he did if he had been a wholly detached naturalist, an intellectual snob, a blithely sneering sophisticate, or a superficial propagandist thundering against a crumbling *ancien régime*. It is absurd to assume that he had no empathy with his stalemated characters, no share in the sensibility that makes them so alive and appealing, as it would be to claim that he felt no ambivalence in portraying them sensitively or even sympathetically.

It is ambivalence translated into art (and that means into *artistic reality*) that distinguishes the writer even in laughter from the nonartist and that separates the poet from the poetaster. Chekhov's sensibility for stalemate as well as his attack on it is an important element in his artistry. . . . (pp. 176-77)

Most important of all, however, is the fact that both our old-generation and new-generation viewpoints have tended to fail on the very same ground. They have been almost equally remiss in overlooking the positive element in his work, which has its basis not simply in the natural buoyancy of his character, but in his *positivist* outlook as a physician and as a "man of the people" to whom "soul-sickness" seems largely self-indulgence and suffering seems essentially the result of individual and societal bumbling. Chekhov was surely the most positivist and least Dostoevskian of the Russian literary masters. The *old* generation of Chekhov admirers in the English-speaking theater tended to ignore or glide over this fact. The *new* generation, which became articulate after World War II, has tended to overlook the same fact in the very process of raising paeans to him as a writer of comedies. To publicize him without substantial qualification as a humorist is an insult to his engaged intelligence and passionateness.

Chekhov is passionate in both his scorn and his sympathy even when he displays a cool surface of detachment, a surface of naturalistic objectivity. This is often only his literary façade, so to speak. If anyone undertakes to appraise Chekhov seriously, he will, it is true, find much humor in the major works of fiction and drama. Chekhov may be a comic master, though hardly that alone (only ignorance of such works as "The Peasants" and "Ward No. 6" could allow such an unqualified generalization); he is far from being one of those clever jesters for whom a jest of any consequence is not, in Shaw's famous words, "an earnest in the womb of time." Only when this is realized can the critic do justice to Chekhov as a major figure of the literary world. Only then, too, can a theatrical production of a major Chekhov play find the necessary mean between its farcicality and tragicality. (pp. 177-78)

[Chekhov] transcended the superficiality that often adheres to optimistic literature and at the same time escaped the morbidity that besets pessimistic profundity; and he kept a characteristic balance in other important respects. He stood virtually alone among the modern literary masters after 1890 in being complex without some mystique and subtle without obscurity. He was, so to speak, Olympian and yet also thoroughly companionable. It is chiefly by bearing these polarities in mind, and remembering especially the

plain yet somehow elusive fact that there was ever sympathy in his comedy and some degree of comedy in his sympathy, that we may hope to bring his plays authentically to the stage. (p. 183)

John Gassner, "The Duality of Chekhov" (a revision of a speech originally delivered at Brooklyn College in 1960; copyright © 1967 by Prentice-Hall, Inc.; reprinted by permission of Mollie Gassner, the Executrix for the Estate of John Gassner), in Chekhov: A Collection of Critical Essays, *edited by Robert Louis Jackson, Prentice-Hall, 1967, pp. 175-83.*

RUTH DAVIES   (essay date 1968)

[The] much heralded objectivity of Chekhov is a factor in the spirit and style of his writing. To Chekhov human beings were neither villains nor heroes, and he made no effort to interpret life on the grand scale. He saw it honestly and realistically, without sugar-coating; he saw both shadow and sunlight. The dark blots did not provoke his censure or disdain; he did not indulge in the luxury of passing judgment. Instead, he looked at human life against its background of nature and recorded what he saw. "To a chemist," he wrote a friend, "nothing on earth is unclean. A writer must be as objective as a chemist, he must lay aside his personal subjective standpoint and must understand that muck heaps play a very respectable part in a landscape, and that the evil passions are as inherent in life as the good ones." . . . Even though the objectivity in Chekhov's writing is obvious, it is only part of the pattern. Whatever his intentions, he could not be only a "chemist." He did not judge people or events, but he did see them through his own prism. The subtle blend of the subjective elements with his objectivity is what gives his work its distinctive flavor.

One of the highly personal characteristics apparent in all Chekhov's writing is the lack of heroic proportions. Turgenev, Dostoevsky, and Tolstoy all sought leaders and looked for the splendor in mankind which might be the motive force to organize and move the mighty, yet slumbering, potentials of Russia. . . . With Chekhov the dimensions are contracted. In his writing everything is small in scope—small stories, short plays—except for the few full-length plays made up, as it were, of a succession of small moments, flashes of life. His view of mankind is correspondingly small.

Chekhov's students are not Bazarovs or Raskolnikovs struggling to be "extraordinary," but insignificant young men who ride in the darkness on the mail wagon, unable to communicate with others ("The Poet"); or who end their cramped existences with bullets ("Volodya"); or who walk home from shooting ("The Student"), numbed by the wind and cold. . . . (pp. 324-26)

In many of the stories man is particularly paltry in comparison with the majesty and harmony of nature, which Chekhov felt deeply and used so perfectly as background for his characters that when he wrote of nature, it was as if he had at his command all the instruments of a symphony. (p. 327)

Perhaps no other story gives more memorable expression to [the] unheroic, petty quality of human experience than "Gooseberries." It tells of a man who devotes his life to the realization of a dream: he wants a country estate, with a house, servants' quarters, kitchen-garden, and gooseberry bushes. He slaves, scrimps, and sacrifices everything that might have given meaning to life, until at last he gets all he wants. "Then he put one gooseberry into his mouth, looked at me with the triumph of a child who has at last received his favourite toy, and said: 'How delicious!' . . . They were sour and unripe." The sight of the man, now lazy and dull, his spirit extinguished by complacency, plunges his brother into despair. The latter is aware only of the bitterness of the fruit. Chekhov saw many men trading their souls for gooseberries!

Another of the most pervasive elements in the writing of Chekhov is irony, especially the irony of unfulfillment. Chekhov was not concerned with salvation, but he was acutely aware of frustration. (pp. 327-28)

One form this irony takes is the realization that achievement, arriving at one's goal, seldom brings satisfaction. The bishop, in the narrative of that name, finds nothing but loneliness in his high position. He is not a success in his own estimation, and to others is only someone to fear. Irony is also expressed in the failure to realize hopes, in the pursuit of what proves to be a will-o'-the-wisp, and in lack of awareness of what the present offers. (p. 328)

To Chekhov marriage was not an idyllic relationship, but usually an unavailing struggle between two people to achieve compatibility. In "The Wife" the married couple, both well intentioned, can endure each other only by remaining apart; the wife lives upstairs, the husband down. Their only common language is quarreling, recrimination, and threats. (p. 329)

Chekhov sensed acutely and expressed the isolation of the human spirit. Like the husband and wife in "The Party," who love each other but cannot confess their love, people try in vain to communicate. (p. 330)

Pettiness, disappointment, loneliness, and alienation—these are the elements of Chekhov's gray view of man's life. He saw what Thomas Hardy has called "life's little ironies" on all sides. This recognition did not cause him to rebel or even to despair; it caused instead a gentle melancholy which is marked by peace as well as pain—the peace that comes from not expecting much from life. This is the twilight tone in Chekhov's writings which blended so harmoniously into a twilight period in the history of Russia.

The stories to which reference has been made are only an intimation of the panorama of characters and moments produced by the inexhaustible resources of Chekhov's perceptive and creative powers. There is nothing to equal them in the whole range of the short story. No one has ever been able to surpass Chekhov in showing man as a laughable creature. Still, he was polite enough to make us laugh at ourselves more quickly than at others: he laughs with us instead of at us. Sudden moments of recognition are more likely to provoke a chuckle than a guffaw, but there is an occasional jab of robust humor. Chekhov was a master of the combination of understatement with anticlimax. He had a droll sense of the ridiculous, and his timing was perfect. He knew how to open the door just a crack; the hint stands for the whole.

An extremely significant element in the writings of Chekhov is his interpretation of the peasants. After the rising scale of adulation beginning in Turgenev's *Sportsman's Sketches,* progressing through Dostoevsky, and reaching a climax in Tolstoy's *Anna Karenina* and many of his late stories, it is something of a shock to find the Russian peasants presented impersonally and with no glorification. In Chekhov's tales there is little evidence of the peasants' humility and dignity, their reservoirs of inner strength, and their patient endurance or longing for a better life. Nor is there any of the Tolstoyan conception of the peasants as personifying the spirit of the Beatitudes. Chekhov's view of them was more realistic. He said, "Peasant blood flows in my veins, and you cannot astound me with the virtues of the peasantry." He showed even the idealist who went back to the people as being disconcerted by their lack of response. Chekhov recognized with regret that for the most part "the people" were not waiting with outstretched arms to come out of the mire. (pp. 330-31)

Chekhov's great plays repeat many of the same themes, although the irony is subtler, the interplay of relationships more complicated. The longing is painted on a broader canvas, but the tone is much the same as that of the best stories. Chekhov's plays reveal more clearly than the stories a deepening and maturing of his views. In order to understand the plays, one must be aware that as he began to make serious use of his talent, the objectivity for which Chekhov had always striven was no longer enough to satisfy him. He recognized that if he were to say anything significant as a writer he must be more than objective. (p. 333)

It would be inaccurate to imply that Chekhov had been without aims in writing his stories. Many of them were obviously intended to show up the dreariness and ugliness, the waste and apathy, and the ignorance and brutality of Russian life. . . . But because of their brevity and their dramatic intensity the stories have a static quality almost photographic in nature. The reader comes away from them with a mood rather than an idea.

Unfortunately, the same thing has been too often true of the effect of the plays. . . . (pp. 334-35)

On the surface [*The Seagull*] appears to be a chain of futility which tightens around a group of sensitive individuals. It seems to begin in hope and end in desolation. But this is only the surface impression of the play. Chekhov did not intend to depict characters who were victims of circumstances that bruised and battered them. He intended to show most of them as empty, useless, self-centered people, victims primarily of their own selfishness and aimlessness. The characters in this play accept no responsibility for their deeds. Chekhov does not accuse them, but neither does he excuse them. By exposing their weaknesses he ceased to be neutral.

The fact that Chekhov considered and called this play a comedy has always been mystifying, especially to English and American audiences and readers. Obviously it is not a comedy in the conventional sense, but it is not tragedy either, by anybody's definition. When Chekhov used the term "comedy," he was not considering the frustration which permeates the play or the death which concludes it; he was considering the small natures of the characters. (p. 336)

The seagull is a symbol of the potential of man who is meant to soar. The death of the bird symbolizes the useless and wanton destruction of this potential. In this play and in the plays which follow Chekhov implies that being decorative is not enough and that melancholy is not a substitute for determination and honest effort.

In *Uncle Vanya* destructive forces are again at work in the personalities of the characters, but there is at least a beginning of vitality. (p. 337)

In this play a positive element appears in the personality of Astrov. This man is an indefatigable worker. He is both a conscientious doctor and a passionate advocate of the conservation of natural resources. It is as if Chekhov had shown in Astrov a part of his own nature which he respected, as Trigorin in the earlier play represented the part he condemned. Astrov is an admirable man, yet there is something missing. He is convinced that nothing is or can ever be satisfying or pleasant in his personal life, and he has no other hope than "that when we are asleep in our graves we may, perhaps, be visited by pleasant visions." He says he loves life, but there is an irreconcilable ambivalence within his nature: he loves life and hates it at the same time. He lacks faith, buoyancy, and eagerness. Astrov is probably more autobiographical than Chekhov knew or intended, but Chekhov had scant patience with Astrov's inclination to submit.

When Astrov asserted that he could not endure the routine provincial life in Russia, he had, of course, ample justification for his dislike. His description of the district in which he lived gave Chekhov a chance to explain what was wrong with Russia. It also, perhaps unintentionally, expresses the mood of the gray period out of which Chekhov was writing. . . . (p. 338)

The Three Sisters is the most subtle, complicated, and in some ways the most painful of Chekhov's plays. Tolstoy would not finish reading it; he and others called Chekhov cruel and unfeeling. How little they understood him. It was precisely his being the opposite of cruel and unfeeling that made Chekhov conscious of the sadness of existence. He well knew how precious life is . . . , but he saw that few people manage to live it to the full or sense its preciousness until too late. Chekhov's last three plays are all remarkable for the degree to which they produce the impression of reality, but *The Three Sisters* accomplishes this end best of all. Its unanswered questions and unsatisfied longings bear the haunting image of truth.

In this play the forces of destruction and decay are again shown in conflict with dreams and idealism, and stultification in conflict with aspiration. There are two happy characters. The first, Chebutykin, is happy because he has lost touch with life. The second, Tusenbach, has to pay for his happiness and his goodness by dying when he is on the eve of realizing his hopes. Solyony and Natasha are ruthless egotists. Anyone who gets in their way is marked for disaster. So Tusenbach is destroyed by Solyony, and Andrey and his three sisters have no chance against Natasha. Is life like that? Does evil triumph over good? Chekhov implies that such is the case.

The drama is not, however, a simple morality play in black and white. There is another basic motif. Though Andrey and his sisters are not evil, they are unfulfilled. They are all looking for something—in vain. For all of them that elusive something is epitomized in the idea of Moscow. "To Moscow, to Moscow" is the refrain that rings through their lives. But if they did go to Moscow, it would make no difference. The dream would then change; they would want something else. (pp. 339-40)

Yet Chekhov was apparently determined that his plays would not end in negation and that his characters would not be only empty or ineffectual. At the end the three sisters all make affirmative pronouncements. Masha suddenly asserts that, in spite of her stodgy husband and her lost love, "We must live." Irina has given up the hope of a great passion and decided to serve those who need her; she will find salvation in work. Olga will go on being a headmistress; she assures her sisters that their lives are not yet finished. Both Irina and Olga express the hope that some day they may know why they suffer. So Chekhov asked and left unanswered one of the basic questions of life.

The positive note which relieves the bleakness of *Uncle Vanya* and *The Three Sisters* is faith in work—Chekhov's personal faith which he communicates to some of his characters. In *Uncle Vanya,* Dr. Astrov is always preaching the gospel of work, and the disappointed Sonia concludes the play by avowing that they must work for the future. In *The Three Sisters* the lonely but gallant Vershinin is the apostle of work. If they work enough he says, happiness will be the portion of their descendants. He is sure the time will come when everything will be changed for the better—will be as they want it to be.

The theme of work carries over to *The Cherry Orchard*. In this play the student Trofimov is Chekhov's spokesman. Trofimov is a rarity among Chekhov's characters: he is buoyant, enthusiastic, and filled with hope. "Humanity progresses," he says, "perfecting its powers. Everything that is beyond its ken now will one day become familiar and comprehensible; only we must work." Chekhov knew that improvement in Russia would come slowly and with difficulty. (p. 341)

With this play the curtain went down irrevocably on the nineteenth century, and the prologue of the twentieth century was spoken. (p. 345)

> *Ruth Davies, "Chekhov: The Axe to the Tree," in her* The Great Books of Russia *(copyright 1968 by the University of Oklahoma Press), University of Oklahoma Press, 1968, pp. 309-45.*

PENELOPE CURTIS   (essay date 1972)

As one learns to know [Chekhov's] plays, one comes to find in them especial forms of freedom, ordinarily not given to created, fictional characters; one finds, too, an unusually comprehensive sense of life as something not just social, but communal; and one finds a treatment of gesture, of conscious or unconscious physical movement, which does not embellish, or illustrate, or replace dialogue, but somehow at once makes visible, and shows one how to understand, the spoken words. One learns from Chekhov a language of unconscious gesture which is used in life, but one finds it used best, most expressively, in his own plays. The point is important, since the verbal language comes to us in translation, and that is a peculiar disadvantage for an artist as delicate as Chekhov. For he gives each of his characters autonomy, a way of moving and speaking direct from the centre of his or her own life; and yet he articulates their movements and gestures in continuously unfolding, multiple relations. Everything that is said or done in his three last and greatest plays is implicitly analyzed: but that in no way inhibits its life. 'People eat their dinner, just eat their dinner, and all the time their happiness is being established or their lives are being broken up.' Chekhov's 'naturalism' has often been interpreted in a very limiting way. In fact, however, he is able to suggest the structure of the happiness being established, or the most privately felt rhythms of the lives being broken up. Life, for him, is movement, process, change: but it has rhythms which, when they are revealed, also disclose the hidden structures of what is disappearing or coming into being between people. (p. 13)

Three Sisters is his greatest play. Two matters are, I think, most fully comprehended in *Three Sisters:* the mystery of personal and psychic freedom, and the more than collaborative, the communal nature of the human reality. These concerns are also present, in a more specialized form, in *The Cherry Orchard,* but a third is perhaps more prominent there: Chekhov's sense of the points at which articulate communication fails, gives way to gesture, and produces farce. One might see a model for the kind of thing I mean in Freud's work. The example, the Freudian view of man may be seen as in some ways very deterministic; but, looked at in another light, it does allow each man the *right,* as it were, to a highly complex motivation. People who might have otherwise been found inarticulate, therefore stupid, therefore inconsiderable, may instead be seen as speaking a highly complex, partly wordless, language: as expressing wishes, feelings, sufferings, intentions, in a symbolic language at once highly regulated and, in its particular combination, each man's own.

Chekhov, in *The Cherry Orchard,* articulates a view of man not unlike this: except that he is able to show men as being at once the more free, and the more bound up with others, in living in a communal, a more than social, way. (p. 14)

Chekhov's creative method has the effect of subtly freeing his characters, freeing their personalities and the atmosphere around them; and the further effect of freeing them to act out their own natures and bring about their 'misfortune', their doom. Yet though they bring about their doom with such rapidity and ease, with such unarguable naturalness, the impression of free-moving personalities persists so long as there are actually people on the stage. (p. 15)

His characters are robustly selfish, and yet capable of poignant sympathies when they notice one another at all. Consider this speech of Irena, in Act I of *Three Sisters:* 'Tell me, why is it I'm so happy today? Just as if I were sailing along in a boat with big white sails, and above me the wide, blue sky, and in the sky great white birds floating around?' To which the old doctor replies, kissing her hands, 'My little white bird!' a sympathetic and tender response, but one notes the way Irena's 'great white birds' have become 'My' and 'little', for no two people can share quite the same perception. Such declarations of feeling tend to go half-heard and half-understood; each person inhabits an intense inner world which only partly impinges on the consciousness of others. Chekhov's achievement is that he discovers the extent and the quality of his people's separateness, even when he is suggesting moments of intense sympathy between them. He actually goes much further than Ibsen in suggesting private, half-articulate, regions of feeling, but he does so by maintaining the rich and variable social context in which both separateness and mutual feeling are experienced. . . .

The kind of social context varies from play to play with the stable centre of its community. *Uncle Vanya* opens in a garden with a gathering around a samovar, and, despite

Astrov's preference for vodka and the Professor's withdrawal to his study, the tea-drinking ceremony does offer an image of a freely functioning, traditional group. At the close, Astrov's defection, and the Professor's, are confirmed, but we still find Marina, Sonia, Vania, working quietly in a domestic interior, an image of continuity and God's will. A comparable group is seen at the opening and close of *Three Sisters.* Again the serving of tea attests some kind of communal existence, despite the lonely doctor's embarrassing birthday present of a silver samovar, which cannot bear the significance he wants it to; and despite the fact that Vershinin's thirst is never satisfied in Act II: he is forced back to his own familial centre ('My wife's taken poison again.'). The centre of *The Cherry Orchard* is again a family, but one which has already known dispersal: the group re-collects around Liubov Andryeevna and her Parisian coffee-drinking in Act I, only to experience a violent mutual revulsion and rift of destinies in Act III. (p. 16)

Chekhov's is a social vision in a special way: and by 'social vision' I mean something that is at once a stage-convention and an unique way of seeing human lives. Again and again he sets his scenes in formal social gatherings: a play, a picnic, an arrival or departure, or, most often, a party. These gatherings are in some sense formal, but they also always contain an uncertain and even an explosive component. There are always irregularities. (pp. 16-17)

The most striking irregularity—or movement of withdrawal, protest, uncontainment—is, of course, a suicide, which recurs throughout the plays like a motif. A suicide not only expresses some self-destructive force within the group, but seems to be the sole effective means of leaving it: everyone has to live in a society or group even if, like Soliony in *Three Sisters,* he can only disrupt and suffer in it. In the last three plays, we find consciously ironic suicide-substitutes: Vania shoots at, and misses, his ex-hero; Soliony kills the only man with whom he has made contact or with whom he has anything in common; while in *The Cherry Orchard* Yepihodov keeps failing to shoot himself, and dropping his cue, and we also find a symbolic suicide of the whole group at the end when it disperses, and when that which was best in it, its fine creation and victim, Feers, abandons the will to live and lies down motionless and dumb. Before he does so, though, he speaks not for himself, but for the family that has already disappeared. He voices the *group* experience of dissolution and death.

Every disturbance in the plays is a movement which expresses life and brings death closer. Feers' last action is, I think, a closing movement for the whole Chekhovian oeuvre. All sense of community is relinquished in that implicit death.

Of all Chekhov's plays, *Three Sisters* is most completely about its title-subject, or, to put it another way, the one play in which the main symbol is identical with, and not just a focus for, the subject. . . . If that were not so, if Chekhov's tragic attention were not on the sisters for, and as, themselves, we might suspect him of being somehow partisan in their struggle against deadening and destructive forces. But, in fact, he is not interested in a case-study at all. He is less interested in what the sisters represent than in what they are: in a quality of life they share and communicate, and in the social group of which they are the nucleus. *In extremis,* they are that social group. (p. 17)

Nothing is fixed, in his plays: there are no definite units which we might call 'scenes'. The social group keeps altering: it depends for its existence and quality on the physical presence of its members, and hence it is subject to constant renewal and change, as people come and go. The tone and drift of conversation alters with each unobtrusive entrance: but not casually; the effect of such changes is to intensify preoccupation. One of the commonest exchanges in Chekhov's plays is the following:

> 'I love you.'
> 'Sh! Someone's coming.'

A private exchange is broken off; one person seeks an intimate relationship which another repudiates; a social situation is suddenly altered by the arrival of someone new. Always we feel an imbalance between people: we are left with things unfinished, loose ends, private attachments half-declared, half-listened to, and a sense of the arbitrary dynamism of social situations and the ties formed within them. (p. 19)

> Penelope Curtis, "Chekhov," in Quadrant (reprinted by permission of Quadrant, Sydney, Australia), Vol. XVI, No. 3, May-June, 1972, pp. 13-22.

HARVEY PITCHER   (essay date 1973)

What each character brings to the Chekhov play may be described as a particular set of emotional preoccupations. Chekhov presents his characters in terms of what they feel about themselves and other people, about their situation in life and about life in general. It is true, of course, that the characters can also be distinguished from one another by virtue of certain individual qualities. Of the three sisters it may be said that Olga is considerate, Masha outspoken and Irina dreamy. But if asked what was important about this trio, it is unlikely that we should start by isolating these qualities. We are more likely to say that what stands out about them, what seems to *define* them, is their longing for a better life, their longing for 'Moscow'. What Chekhov's characters *do* is important only in so far as their actions (or in the sisters' case, inaction) illustrate these emotional preoccupations, and in particular, as the expression of some inner emotional crisis: 'A shot, after all, is not a drama, but an incident.' What the characters *say* is likewise primarily important as an indication of what they are feeling.

In practice, Chekhov's important characters are to be defined in terms of such emotions as their hopes, longings, yearnings, aspirations, optimism about the future, nostalgia for the past, regrets, frustrations, disappointments and disillusionments. There is a peculiar quality about all these emotions. On the face of it, they are not in the least dramatic. . . . [The] emotions that Chekhov portrays are the undramatic, long-term ones. They do not appear and vanish suddenly but remain largely unresolved, persisting perhaps for a lifetime and being momentarily highlighted during the course of the play. And they are pervasive emotions, in the sense that they do not take sudden and exclusive possession of a person, but tend to colour the whole of his behaviour in a much more subtle and pervasive manner. To depict these pervasive long-term emotions, Chekhov did not have recourse to unfamiliar settings but took his material from life round him, so that there is nothing esoteric about the emotions he presents. Just as the outstanding quality of his best short stories is their ability to generalize, to take a simple story about a handful of people and to make it seem relevant and important to everyone, so too in the Chekhov play the kind of emotions portrayed are never just of importance to those involved, but can always be widely recognized and appreciated.

What happens in the course of the Chekhov play is that the characters are shown responding and reacting to one another on the emotional level: Chekhov creates among them what may be called an emotional network, in which it is not the interplay of character but the interplay of emotion that holds the attention of the audience. . . . A kind of electric field exists among all the persons in a Chekhovian group. No one has ever matched his ability to put on stage the infectiousness of a mood. It may be a mood of youthful gaiety, as in the first act of *Three Sisters,* when even the usually staid schoolmaster, Kulygin, and the middle-aged Colonel Vershinin are affected by what is going on around them, and start to behave like schoolboys; or it may be a mood of contemplation, as in Act II of *The Cherry Orchard,* when even the ebullient Ranyevskaya is affected by the general atmosphere and falls silent, and all the characters hear in the distance the mysterious sound of 'a breaking string'.

But it is not only when a large group is assembled that these 'vibrations' of the emotional network begin to operate. Emotional preoccupations in the Chekhov play do not remain private and submerged, but are brought to the surface as the characters intermingle and become emotionally involved with one another. This as it were activates the emotional network, and emotions may come to vibrate between particular individuals. At one extreme, these emotional vibrations may be full of tension and disharmony: as when one person is seeking from another an emotional response that is not forthcoming, or when a character feels that someone else is standing in the way of the fulfilment of his desires. At the other extreme, there are occasions when emotions vibrate with unusual sympathy and harmony: as when individuals come to share a common outlook, a common yearning or a common grief. It is on occasions such as these, when the emotional network is vibrating with an unusually high degree of harmony or disharmony, that the characters' emotional preoccupations are likely to be most clearly revealed.

There is one more feature of the Chekhov play that is very distinctive and deserves to be pointed out. . . . I mentioned above that Chekhov presents his characters not only in terms of what they feel about themselves (their emotional preoccupations) and about other people (the emotional network), but also in terms of what they feel about their situation in life and about life in general. Characters like Astrov in *Uncle Vanya* and especially Vershinin in *Three Sisters* react to their situation by evolving for themselves a 'philosophy of life'; and this philosophy of life can best be described as a way of coming to terms with life emotionally. When a Chekhov character is philosophizing, it is likely that he will be expressing what he *feels* about life. When characters are philosophizing together, it is likely that they will be comparing what they feel—comparing notes, as it were, about life, trying to discover whether their feelings have anything in common. This philosophizing involves the individual in the need to look beyond his private life and fortunes, to forget about his *own* problems, and to speculate on the significance of his life within the scheme of human life as a whole. These philosophies of life do not however stand outside the emotional network of the plays. On the contrary, they may acquire within the network a special importance: for other characters respond emotionally to the philosophy that is being put forward and may come to share it (as happens in the case of the three sisters and Vershinin), so attaining an unusual degree of emotional harmony. (pp. 9-13)

[The] Chekhov play may be described as subtly and deeply concerned with emotion, whether in respect of the playwright's approach to his characters, or of what happens in the course of the plays, or of the likely responses of the audience. More than any other dramatist before or since, Chekhov is the dramatist of the emotional side of man's nature. (p. 13)

> *Harvey Pitcher, "The Chekhov Play," in his* The Chekhov Play: A New Interpretation *(© Harvey Pitcher 1973), Chatto & Windus, 1973, pp. 1-34.*

RICHARD GILMAN (essay date 1974)

[It] is no mistake to see Chekhov as a precursor of theatrical absurdity, less obviously than Strindberg but with as much force; it isn't silly to regard *The Three Sisters*, for instance, as being very close in spirit and even in technique to a play like *Waiting for Godot*. For whatever the differences in their work of utterance, gesture, and *mise en scène*, the geniuses of Chekhov and Beckett share some common grounds and intentions: they will not make theater as they have seen it being made; they will present new relationships and not new tales; they will use the stage for the creation of consciousness and not for its reflection; and they will offer neither solutions nor prescriptions, not even heightened emotion, but mercilessly stripped artifacts of the imagination that will present our deepest "story." (p. 123)

[Chekhov's most] radical change from the standpoint of the history of the theater was the alteration in . . . dramatic construction. . . . For Chekhov [created] a dramatic style, its major lineaments first fully if a little tentatively on display in *The Seagull*, in which crucial action of a physical kind takes place almost entirely offstage and in which the activities that do occur onstage are oblique, heavily verbal, and without resolution. . . . (pp. 133-34)

The Seagull is a play about art. In being about art, it is about the creative self and more specifically about the ways this self can sustain itself in relation to physical and social necessities and the contrary ways it can go under. The crux of the drama is in the opposing beings of Konstantin and Nina, the one enacting his career as a writer in a spirit of self-pity and romantic literary illusion, the other hers as an actress with devotion, clear-headedness, and, above all, stamina. Chekhov is saying that Konstantin goes down to defeat (his offstage suicide is simply the sign of his prior inadequacy) because he cannot accept his freedom and the responsibility that goes with it, wanting to be taken out of himself and to be nurtured by destiny, while Nina triumphs through a recognition that an artist survives neither by means of inspiration nor favorable circumstances but by persistence.

Such a truth is paradigmatic of life itself; . . . Chekhov uses the artist's fate as a perspective on wider existence. For in the artist's task and situation one can see in their purest,

most conscious form the conditions of experience in which all are held. . . . Beneath our ideas and values, our ambitions and dreams, lies fact, the rock-hard actuality of what we are and must do. It is Nina's awareness of necessity that keeps her from self-pity and self-delusion. . . . (pp. 134-35)

The Seagull demonstrates once again how form is a function of idea and perception and in turn modifies them. In placing offstage what might ordinarily be considered the play's major events, the happenings that ought to make for its "drama"—Nina's love affair with Trigorin, Konstantin's suicide—Chekhov accomplished a quiet revolution in our notions of action on the stage. For it was Chekhov's genius to see that those events, situated in the full light, would not have made for drama but for melodrama. (p. 135)

The Three Sisters is one of the greatest of all plays, a drama as inexhaustible in its way as *Oedipus Rex* and *Hamlet* and *Lear* are in theirs. (p. 146)

That they do not go, with its implication that they are fated to a "lesser" life, is generally considered their tragedy, but in fact their tragedy, if it really is one, lies elsewhere. It ought to be seen that nothing physically (or morally, for that matter) prevents them from leaving, nothing in the objective situation requires them to remain mired in the provinces. At the same time, they aren't weak or ineffectual, they don't lack will in the ordinary sense. Why then do they stay?

Everything suggests that they stay because to remain is the meaning of their lives, the condition of their existence . . . ; staying is synonymous with their being alive, and everything exists beyond categories such as tragedy or its opposite and beyond alternatives like despair or hope. They stay, finally, because in this play, which is not a re-creation of actual lives but a creation exhibiting what it is like to be alive *whatever the circumstances*, Chekhov wishes to reveal how time, as we experience it, is always and only the present, how the future is always illusion, the past always absence or loss. The painfulness of the play is the suffering, at its deepest levels ontological and not simply social or psychic, of all of us, creatures whom time erodes while it is simultaneously promising us fullness.

The eroding action of time is most subtly manifested in *The Three Sisters* by forgetting. Andrey forgets his ambitions, the doctor his medical knowledge, Vershinin people's faces, Masha the title and author of the song she is humming. . . . But there are more material or substantial losses. Love is lost to Masha and Vershinin, dignity to Andrey, her unloved but respected future husband to Irina, and, by implication, their house itself to the Prozorovs.

As they are consumed by the present, the characters yearn toward the future, all, that is, but the old servants, in whom desire is simple and meek, and the doctor, who is aging too but, more than that, emptied of pride. But the future, as we have said, is illusory, a matter for speculation, for talk which however passionate and "sincere" will not bring it about in its desired shape. The speeches in *The Three Sisters* about the new age to come, especially those of Vershinin and Tuzenbach about a future of honorable work and usefulness for all, are even more grandiloquent and extensive than those in *Uncle Vanya*, but they have the same function. And this is to deny themselves, to exist as evidence that the present is all we can know of life, all we can be truthful about.

It's worth noticing that the sisters' talk about the future is much less abstract, less socio-political than the men's. For them the future beckons in personal ways and promises love, or at least some element of palpable beauty. Chekhov is never obvious about it, but in all his major plays he gives to female characters a kind of stewardship of immediate bodily life, sometimes moving into the erotic and always having as its governing idea the principle of persistence that runs through *The Seagull* and *Uncle Vanya*. Whether or not he is objectively accurate, for the purposes of his art Chekhov thinks of women as being freer than men of the capacity for self-delusion through theorizing and literary constructions, and so more physically accepting.

[At the same time, however,] a woman, Natasha in *The Three Sisters*, is unquestionably Chekhov's most villainous character. Working mostly on the fringes of the play, she devours the family's possessions like an "animal," as they come to regard her. But she is really much more complex than that. Like the play's other evil or negative character, Solyony, she is an incarnation of aggression and acquisitiveness deriving from an incomplete sense of self.... Both [are aggressive] out of feelings of powerlessness that can only be appeased by possessions, bulwarks against the void, and both think only of themselves, craving their "due."

That the other characters, especially the sisters, seem to bow to Natasha's depredations like helpless victims has led to a reading of the play as, on at least one level, a social and ethical drama in which a rising, aggressively insensitive but historically inevitable bourgeoisie pushes out a morally noble but enervated aristocracy. But this is once again to read Chekhov within the tradition of a theater of opposites, dramatic clashes; it is to read the play as a melancholy tale of materialism overcoming the spirit or of goodness bowing before brute strength.

But the play is one in which no such decisive encounters are allowed to take place, so that the reason the sisters don't oppose Natasha is that Chekhov, for the most stringent of artistic purposes, doesn't want them to. It is a condition of human life as the play exhibits it that rapaciousness of Natasha's kind be present in the world, but it is not the purpose of *The Three Sisters* to seek any large truth about human fate in that presence. Natasha is there, she is one of the conditions of the sisters' lives, they must survive her as they survive all other inroads and losses. And in the end, when the three women embrace one another in that last painful, loving communion and Olga's words about someday knowing "why we live, why we suffer" echo in our consciousness, we are aware of their victory, the only one Chekhov in his marvelous refusal of the world's hierarchies of success and failure, tragedy and triumph, will permit.

Yet such is his artistic quietness that even this fragile victory is hemmed in and denied full resonance. In that final scene the doctor, sitting apart from the sisters, reads a newspaper, murmurs the most frivolous song, and mutters, "What's the difference, anyway," as a counterstatement to Olga's closing expression of hope in the future. The play ends on a note of absolute non-resolution; the ambiguity and uncertainty remain.... (pp. 149-52)

This closing scene is a splendid demonstration of Chekhov's dramaturgy of indirection and what we might call

lateral construction. There is no encounter or confrontation between Chebutykin and the women; they simply occupy the stage together, saying *what each has to say*, without the coercion by plot, the necessities of storytelling that in most naturalistic drama results in dialogue being linearly progressive, a question eliciting an answer, a comment a related one, a piece of information another.

One can even say that there is very little true dialogue in *The Three Sisters* but a series of utterances designed to fill out a world, to create it.... At times Chekhov's characters do speak directly to one another, to be sure, but much more often and even in many apparently straightforward conversations their words are as though momentarily suspended—for the time it takes to hear them—in an atmosphere which all breathe but where there is no obligation to "communicate."

The communication, that is to say, resides much more in the relations of the various speeches to each other and to the non-verbal elements of the play, in the texture of what is being composed, than in their substantive "meanings." When the doctor, sitting apart once again, mutters something he has just read in the newspaper—"Balzac was married in Berdichev"—the utterance exists with no discernible connection to what the others have been saying; it works in the play precisely to exhibit how such a fact, so useless a bit of information, has as much or as little significance as any other statement, as the grand descriptions of the future, for example. (pp. 152-53)

This world goes forward in time, as that of any drama must: *The Three Sisters* covers a period of about four years and, in the dimension of "real" time, takes perhaps an hour to read and two and a half to perform. Within these physical restrictions it was Chekhov's whole effort ... to try to overcome the sense of progression which is an ineradicable aspect of drama. This is both a thematic and a technical matter. For if, as has been argued, Chekhov's very subject is the "timelessness" of time, the necessity of living in the present together with the unreality of the future, then it became incumbent on him so to construct his play as to make each scene or unit of action live independently, as free as possible from causal relationships with what precedes and follows it. And in fact nearly every scene in *The Three Sisters* does exist in this way, moving through time but appearing, or being absorbed in our consciousness, like paintings, which is not to say they are static pictures, *tableaux vivants*, but that at any moment we can grasp the chief elements of the work.

The first act, which is one long scene, a gathering of the characters into the Prozorovs' house and ambience, contains everything it is essential to know; what will happen afterward isn't so much development as the making of fullness. (pp. 153-54)

It is all done with astonishing economy, an economy that isn't simply a matter of restraint but an active structural principle. "When a man spends the least possible number of movements over some definite action, that is grace," Chekhov had once written. This is one of the secrets of his method of indirection and helps to explain the elisions, the gaps between speeches and within them, the questions not replied to and the points not taken up, which many people have mistaken for a theme of "non-communication." Chekhov's characters communicate as much as any in dramatic literature—it is almost all they do—but only what he wants them to, only what the consciousness reigning in this imagined world requires.

An especially illuminating example of this is the scene in which the doctor drops and breaks a clock . . . , mutters in confusion and guilt a bitter pseudo-philosophical apologia—"Maybe I didn't break it but it only looks like I broke it. Maybe it only looks like we exist, and really we don't"—then abruptly, as a way of being "real" and in connection, says to the others, "Natasha is having an affair with Protopopov, and you don't see that. You sit there and see nothing and Natasha's having an affair with Protopopov." He goes out, upon which Vershinin says, "Yes . . . *(He laughs.)* How strange all this is. . . . When the fire started I rushed home . . ." and the matter-of-fact conversation picks up and goes on.

It isn't that they haven't heard Chebutykin or haven't noticed the affair before this, nor is it that they are repressing an unpleasant truth. Their failure to respond, Vershinin's changing the subject, is due to their *decision* not to allow Natasha's affair to concern them directly. It is there, a factor in their lives, part of their weather, but there is nothing to be done about it, they will not intrude into it with judgments, moral interference. And Chekhov will not allow the affair, potentially so rich in melodramatic energy, to move from the edges of the play, where its shadowy presence will be real but where it cannot draw attention to itself at the expense of subtler things.

One can discover at almost every moment of *The Three Sisters* Chekhov's marvelous capacity for making his dramas yield exactly the consciousness he wants, which is a power to exclude whatever would be false or irrelevant, what would disturb the balance of his world. (pp. 154-55)

> *Richard Gilman, "Chekhov," in his* The Making of Modern Drama: A Study of Büchner, Ibsen, Strindberg, Chekhov, Pirandello, Brecht, Beckett, Handke *(reprinted by permission of Farrar, Straus & Giroux, Inc.; copyright © 1972, 1973, 1974 by Richard Gilman), Farrar, Straus & Giroux, 1974, pp. 116-56.*

HOWARD MOSS (essay date 1977-78)

[In *Three Sisters*] the inability to act becomes the action of the play. How to make stasis dramatic is its problem and Chekhov solves it by a gradual deepening of insight rather than by the play of event. The grandeur of great gestures and magnificent speeches remains a Shakespearian possibility—a diminishing one. Most often, we get to know people through the accretion of small details—minute responses, tiny actions, little gauze screens being lifted in the day-to-day pressure of relationships. In most plays, action builds toward a major crisis. In *Three Sisters*, it might be compared to the drip of a faucet in a water basin; a continuous process wears away the enamel of facade. (p. 525)

Three Sisters is the most musical of all of Chekhov's plays in construction, the one that depends most heavily on the repetition of motifs. And it uses music throughout: marching bands, hummed tunes, "the faint sound of an accordion coming from the street," a guitar, a piano, the human voice raised in song.

Yet too much can be made of the "music" of the play at the expense of its command of narrative style. Private con-

frontation and social conflict are handled with equal authority, and a symbolism still amateur in *The Seagull,* written five years earlier, has matured and gone underground to permeate the texture of the work. No dead bird is brought onstage weighted with meaning. No ideas are embalmed in objects. What we have instead is a kind of geometric structure, one angle of each story fitting into the triangular figure of another, and, overlaying that, a subtle web of connected images and words. Seemingly artless, it is made of steel. (pp. 525-26)

Compared to *The Seagull* and *Uncle Vanya,* a technical advance occurs in *Three Sisters* that may account for a greater sounding of the depths. Chekhov's mastery of the techniques of playwriting may be measured by his use of the gun; it is farther offstage here than before—not in the next room but at the edge of town, which suggests that it might, finally, be dispensed with, as it is in *The Cherry Orchard,* where the only sound we hear, ultimately, is an ax cutting down trees. As he went on, Chekhov let go of the trigger, his one concession to the merciless demands of the stage. The gunshot in *Three Sisters,* unlike the shot in *Vanya,* is terminal. But Tuzenbach's death has further implications; it is partly the result of, and the price paid for Irena's lack of love. (pp. 530-31)

Three Sisters is enigmatic—it would be hard to say just how the last speeches should be played—sadly, bitterly?—as a kind of cosmic, ridiculous joke? Realistically?—as if in the face of hopelessness it were possible to conceive a Utopia? Only *Hamlet* offers so many unresolved possibilities. . . . There are overtones and undertows. More clearly than in any of Chekhov's other plays, fantasy imbues consciousness with a strength similar to the power of dreams in the unconscious. The play teeters on an ambiguity: if coming to terms with reality is a sign of psychological maturity, philosophy offers a contrary alternative: in letting go of an ideal, the sisters may be depriving themselves—or being deprived—of the one thing that makes life worth living.

These positive-negative aspects of the play are not easily resolved. Ambivalence enriches the action but fogs the ending. The problems *Three Sisters* raises have been presented to us with a complexity that allows for no easy solutions. Yet the curtain has to come down, the audience depart. And Chekhov, almost up to the last moment, keeps adding complications. In spite of its faultless construction, or because of it, the play is full of surprises. . . . (pp. 541-42)

> *Howard Moss, "'Three Sisters'," in* The Hudson Review *(copyright © 1977 by The Hudson Review, Inc.; reprinted by permission), Vol. XXX, No. 4, Winter 1977-78, pp. 525-43.*

BIBLIOGRAPHY

Beckerman, Bernard. "The Artifice of 'Reality' in Chekhov and Pinter." *Modern Drama* XXI, No. 2 (June 1978): 153-61.*
> Explains how Chekhov creates a sense of dramatic "reality" in terms distinct from those of conventionally naturalistic theater.

Bruford, W.H. *Anton Chekhov.* New Haven: Yale University Press, 1957, 62 p.
> Examines Chekhov's work in relation to the social and political climate of the Russia of his time.

Bunin, Ivan. "Chekhov." *Atlantic Monthly* 188, No. 1 (July 1951): 59-63.
Memories of the Russian novelist Bunin concerning his friendship with Chekhov.

Debreczeny, Paul, and Eeckman, Thomas, eds. *Chekhov's Art of Writing: A Collection of Critical Essays.* Columbus: Slavica Publishers, 1977, 199 p.
Essays from a predominantly formalist-structuralist critical perspective.

Farrell, James T. "On the Letters of Anton Chekhov." In his *The League of Frightened Philistines and Other Papers,* pp. 60-71. New York: The Vanguard Press, 1945.
Sketch of Chekhov's life and opinions through his letters.

Gifford, Henry. "Chekhov the Humanist." In his *The Novel in Russia: From Pushkin to Pasternak,* pp. 125-34. London: Hutchinson University Library, 1964.
Introductory level overview and biographical sketch.

Hahn, Beverly. *Chekhov: A Study of the Major Stories and Plays.* Cambridge: Cambridge University Press, 1977, 350 p.
Sees Chekhov's work as highly psychological and claims he is "a more positive writer than even his strongest supporters often contend."

Hingley, Ronald. *A New Life of Chekhov.* New York: Alfred A. Knopf, 1976, 352 p.
Much significant documentary material used which became available since publication of Hingley's *Chekhov: A Biographical and Critical Study* (see excerpt above).

Jackson, Robert Louis, ed. *Chekhov: A Collection of Critical Essays.* Englewood Cliffs, N.J.: Prentice-Hall, 1967, 213 p.
Collection composed primarily of essays translated from Russian, German, and French specifically for this appearance. Of particular interest are a number of essays by Russian scholars and critics, including Boris Eichenbaum, V. Yermilov, S. D. Balukhaty, G. Berdinov, A. Skaftymov, Vsevolod Meyerhold, and Dmitri Chizhevsky.

Jarrell, Randall. "Six Russian Short Novels." In his *The Third Book of Criticism,* pp. 235-75. New York: Farrar, Straus & Giroux, 1969.*
Reprint of an introduction to an anthology of Russian novellas, including *Ward No. 6.* The pages devoted to this story give a plot summary and some background information.

Kazin, Alfred. "Writing for Magazines." In his *Contemporaries,* pp. 469-74. Boston: Little, Brown and Co., 1962.
General evaluation praising Chekhov for showing "that prose could be as profound . . . an intimation of human existence as poetry."

Laffitte, Sophie. *Chekhov 1860-1904.* Translated by Moura Budberg and Gordon Latta. New York: Charles Scribner's Sons, 1973, 246 p.
Literary biography with an introduction that outlines major themes in Chekhov scholarship.

Magarshack, David. Introductions in *The Real Chekhov: An Introduction to Chekhov's Last Plays,* by Anton Chekhov, pp. 9-18, 21-3, 79-81, 125-26, 187-96. London: George Allen & Unwin, 1972.
Criticizes translators and directors of Chekhov's plays for their misinterpretation of Chekhov as an artist who deliberately promoted despair. The introductions to *The Seagull, Uncle Vanya, The Three Sisters,* and *The Cherry Orchard* give biographical and literary background, including a long section from Chekhov's letters concerning the writing of *The Cherry Orchard.*

Matual, David. "Chekhov's 'Black Monk' and Byron's 'Black Friar'." *International Fiction Review* 5, No. 1 (January 1978): 46-51.*
Provides autobiographical documentation from Chekhov to substantiate Byron's influence on him.

Mirsky, D. S. "The Eighties and Early Nineties." In his *A History of Russian Literature,* pp. 333-67. New York: Alfred A. Knopf, 1955.*
Biographical sketch and introductory overview of Chekhov's work.

O'Connor, Frank. "The Slave's Son." In his *The Lonely Voice: A Study of the Short Story,* pp. 78-98. Cleveland: The World Publishing Co., 1963.
Thematic analysis of several plots of the short stories.

Rayfield, Donald. *Chekhov: The Evolution of His Art.* New York: Barnes & Noble, 1975, 266 p.
Traces the development of Chekhov's literary career, dealing with dominant themes running throughout the author's work and attempting to reconcile seemingly contradictory facets of his art.

Slonim, Marc. "The Beginnings of the Moscow Art Theater." In his *Russian Theater: From the Empire to the Soviets,* pp. 100-32. Cleveland: The World Publishing Co., 1961.*
Plot outlines and theatrical history of the major dramas.

Smith, Virginia Llewellyn. *Anton Chekhov and the Lady with the Dog.* London: Oxford University Press, 1973, 249 p.
Study finding deprecatory attitudes towards women, sex, and love permeating Chekhov's work.

Speirs, Logan. "Chekhov: The Stories" and "Chekhov: The Plays." In his *Tolstoy and Chekhov,* pp. 137-82, 185-223. Cambridge: Cambridge University Press, 1971.
Sees the major similarity between Tolstoy and Chekhov in their realistic recreation in literature of the world around them, and their major difference in their divergent philosophical outlooks, Tolstoy's that of dogmatic religiosity and Chekhov's that of agnostic materialism.

Winner, Thomas G. "Myth as a Device in the Works of Chekhov." In *Myth and Symbol: Critical Approaches and Applications,* edited by Bernice Slote, pp. 71-8. Lincoln: University of Nebraska, 1963.
Points out archetypal patterns and characters in Chekhov's work drawn from classical mythology.

Winner, Thomas [G]. *Chekhov and His Prose.* New York: Holt, Rinehart and Winston, 1966, 263 p.
Critical study of the short stories divided into sections which analyze Chekhov's themes, styles, and development as an author, as well as his relationship to the artistic and social world of nineteenth-century Russia.

Yermilov, Vladimir. *Anton Pavlovich Chekhov, 1860-1904.* Moscow: Foreign Languages Publishing House, 1956, 415 p.
Biography with an emphasis on developmental factors significant to Chekhov's evolution as an author.

Young, Stark. "Gulls and Chekhov." *Theatre Arts Monthly* XXII, No. 10 (October 1938): 737-42.
Criticizes and corrects some English translations of *The Sea-Gull.* The critic also attempts to remedy Chekhov's widespread image as an artist of gloom and morbidity.

Lion Feuchtwanger

1884-1958

(Also wrote under pseudonym of J. L. Wetcheek) German novelist, dramatist, essayist, and translator.

Feuchtwanger is known primarily for his historical novels and is often acknowledged as having broadened the range of the historical romance by giving it the psychological reality of the modern novel. Though extremely popular in his lifetime, some critics now feel that his work is dated. Even his admirers admit that his novels are often verbose and read like pulp fiction.

Feuchtwanger began his career as a fairly successful playwright. An active member of the Berlin avant-garde of the 1920s and 30s, Feuchtwanger's greatest contribution to the drama was his discovery and promotion of the young Bertolt Brecht, with whom he collaborated on several dramatic works. The success of his first historical novel, *Die hassliche Herzogin*, changed his direction and thereafter he only dabbled in drama.

Feuchtwanger, being more concerned with his work as fiction than as historical pageantry, would often distort facts for the purposes of characterization and narrative development. He constantly used his historical works to examine contemporary problems and a primary theme in his novels, coming from his experience as a Jew in Nazi Germany, is the antithesis of power and the intellect. The dichotomy is typically embodied in a Jewish intellectual who is an exile in an alien culture. This theme was developed most powerfully in his *Josephus* trilogy (*Der jüdische Krieg, Die Söhne*, and *Der Tag wird Kommen*), which many critics consider his best work.

Feuchtwanger also used the techniques of the historical novel to treat contemporary events. The trilogy *Der Wartesaal* (*Erfolg, Die Geschwister Oppermann*, and *Exil*) chronicled in fictional form German life from 1918-1939 and provided a contemporary examination of the development of a fascist state. In that sense Feuchtwanger was a political writer, for he was most concerned with the analogies to contemporary problems that could be found in the past.

Feuchtwanger left Germany for exile in France in 1933 and was interned by the Nazis when France fell in 1940 but, dressed as a woman, he made a dramatic escape to the United States via Portugal. He spent the rest of his life in California. Feuchtwanger's novels were so successful in the United States that some of his last works appeared first in English translation.

PRINCIPAL WORKS

Warren Hastings, Gouverneur von Indien (drama) 1916
Jud Süss (drama) 1918
Thomas Wendt (drama) 1919
  [*1918* published in *Three Plays: Prisoners of War, 1918, The Dutch Merchant*, 1934]
Die hässliche Herzogin (novel) 1923
  [*The Ugly Duchess: A Historical Romance*, 1927]
Jud Süss (novel) 1925
  [*Power*, 1926; published in England as *Jew Süss*, 1926]
Kalkutta, 4. Mai. [with Bertolt Brecht] (drama) 1927
  [*Warren Hastings* published in *Two Anglo Saxon Plays: The Oil Islands, Warren Hastings*, 1928]
Die Petroleuminseln (drama) 1927; published with *Wird Hill amnestiert?* in *Drei angelsächsische Stücke*)
  [*The Oil Islands* published in *Two Anglo Saxon Plays: The Oil Islands, Warren Hastings*, 1928]
Pep: J. L. Wetcheek's amerkanisches Liederbuch [as J. L. Wetcheek] (verse) 1928
  [*Pep: J. L. Wetcheek's American Song Book*, 1929]
Erfolg: Drei jahre Geschichte einer Provinz (novel) 1930
  [*Success: A Novel*, 1930]
**Der jüdische Krieg* (novel) 1932
  [*Josephus*, 1932]
***Die Geschwister Oppermann: Roman* (novel) 1933
  [*The Oppermanns*, 1933]
**Die Söhne: Roman* (novel) 1935
  [*The Jew of Rome: A Historical Romance*, 1935]
Der falsche Nero: Roman (novel) 1936
  [*The Pretender*, 1937]
Exil (novel) 1939
  [*Paris Gazette*, 1940]
Unholdes Frankreich (autobiographical narratives) 1942; also published as *Der Teufel in Frankreich: Erlebnisse*, 1954
  [*The Devil in France*, 1941]
Simone: Roman (novel) 1944
  [*Simone: A Novel*, 1944]
**Der Tag wird kommen: Roman* (novel) 1945
  [*Josephus and the Emperor*, 1942]
Waffen für Amerika (novel) 1947
  [*Proud Destiny: A Novel*, 1947]
Goya; oder, Der arge Weg der Erkenntnis: Roman (novel) 1951
  [*This is the Hour*, 1951]

Narrenweisheit; oder, Tod und Verkïarung des Jean-Jacques Rousseau: Roman (novel) 1952
['*Tis Folly to Be Wise; or, Death and Transfiguration of Jean-Jacques Rousseau: A Novel*, 1953]
Spanische Ballade: Roman (novel) 1955
[*Raquel, the Jewess of Toledo*, 1956]
Jefta und Seine Tochter: Roman (novel) 1957
[*Jephta and His Daughter*, 1958]

*This play is a revision of *Warren Hastings*.

**These volumes were collected under the title *Josephus Trilogie* in 1952.

***This was originally published as *Die Geschwister Oppenheim* in accordance with German censorship policy.

LION FEUCHTWANGER (essay date 1940)

["Paris Gazette"] was planned as a historical novel; and now that events have definitely put an end to the period with which it deals, no one could mistake it for anything else.

It forms the third part of a cycle of novels, the first two parts of which [are] "Success" and "The Oppermanns." The whole trilogy is to be called: "The Waiting-Room."

"The Waiting-Room," then, covers the period between the wars of 1914 and 1939, taking as its subject-matter the course of events in Germany: that is to say, the resurgence of barbarism in Germany and the temporary eclipse of reason. The aim of the trilogy is to document for posterity these dreadful years of suspense.... For posterity will be baffled by the fact that we put up with such a state of things for so long; posterity will find it difficult to understand why we should have waited so long before drawing the only valid conclusion, namely, that the rule of force and unreason must be ended by force and replaced by a reasonable social order. (p. 5)

One word more about the technique of these three novels. Perhaps I was over-confident when I set out to write the first of them as if I were writing in the year 2000. And I probably went to the other extreme in the second novel, allowing myself in certain chapters to be too strongly influenced by immediate impressions, so that these chapters became too naturalistic, too photographic for the kind of composition I had in mind. This novel consequently ("The Oppermanns") is the least successful of the three from my point of view; it shows the fewest traces of that historical character which every good contemporary novel should possess. In "Paris Gazette," however, I think I have struck the happy medium between the over-confidence of "Success" and the timidity which made me content with long passages of naturalistic description in "The Oppermanns." (p. 17)

> *Lion Feuchtwanger, "'Paris Gazette': As the Author Sees It," in* The Saturday Review of Literature *(copyright © 1940 by Saturday Review; all rights reserved; reprinted by permission), Vol. 22, No. 1, April 27, 1940, pp. 5, 16-17.*

LOUIS UNTERMEYER (essay date 1940)

Lion Feuchtwanger has always displayed an extraordinary

sense of traveling through toppling civilizations: his novels have been time-machines carrying the breathless readers into the decaying eighteenth century world of "Power," the middle European clash of dynasties in "The Ugly Duchess," the florid Rome of "Josephus." While his native Germany was returning to old barbarisms, Feuchtwanger was turning to old cultures, to the fruits of Western imperialism and Oriental decadence. "Success" was the first of his novels devoted to the modern scene. And now, in "Paris Gazette," Feuchtwanger has synthesized his gifts: he has written his most timely interpretation and his finest story.

It is a lengthy but not overlong tale of suffering humanity caught in one corner of a world which was, until recently, the boast of civilization. With little of the detachment which characterized his historical novels, Feuchtwanger has pictured the Paris of a few years ago, a Paris as unknown to the casual American traveler as it is to the average Frenchman. It is neither the enchanting tourist city, nor the haunt of idle men and lightly accessible women, nor the center of art, epicureanism and escape, but a city within a city: a haven for German refugees and a hunting ground for German officials. Enormously complicated in its ramifications, Feuchtwanger never allows the story to lose itself in its involvements; the plot is devious but never obscured.

Perhaps the explanation of Feuchtwanger's clarity in the midst of confusion is that his work is not so much a study of cultures and conditions (although it may well claim to be that) as it is a book of people. Here is an astonishing portrait gallery of exiles and spies, patriots and patrioteers, poets and musicians, editors and diplomats, badgered housewives and arrogant prodigies. They assume importance beyond their physical existence; the poorest of them are larger than life.... (p. 5)

Strands of all these lives are interwoven, and it is the journal of the refugees, the "Paris Gazette," which tangles and untangles them. They are twisted in party cabals and personal intrigues, in fine-spun subtlety and sudden action. Too intricate to outline, the book is full of incidents which are overwhelmingly tragic and incredibly ironic, events which are grotesque, and flashes which are superbly comic.... Feuchtwanger has created his most dramatic work: an epic *in petto;* an agitated panorama on a small but vividly crowded canvas. (p. 15)

> *Louis Untermeyer, "'Paris Gazette': As the Reviewer Sees It," in* The Saturday Review of Literature *(copyright © 1940 by Saturday Review; all rights reserved; reprinted by permission), Vol. 22, No. 1, April 27, 1940, pp. 5, 15.*

F. S. GROSSHUT (essay date 1960)

The writer Lion Feuchtwanger is best characterized by his passion for reason. His novels fulfil a sociological function: They convey insight. (p. 9)

The study of Feuchtwanger's work reveals his endeavor to renew the historical novel. The earlier German novels were essentially novels of development.... Their center was the *hero;* the reader experienced the hero's development, his fate, growth, years of conflict, his sufferings and transformation.... The plot was invented for the hero's sake.... [The] plot became egocentric, it distorted life and led to romantic sentimentalities; the danger of black-and-white characterization arose.

This tendency was most hazardous when applied to the historical novel; for the historical novel demands an adequate account of an era, it demands a measure of historical truth and reality. (pp. 9-10)

Here Lion Feuchtwanger stepped in. Out of the German historical novel he created the European historical novel. Insight and awareness became the center of the higher historical truth. History has meaning, history moves forward, it may move slowly and at random, but the progress toward reason and enlightenment is visible. . . . Feuchtwanger believed in the meaning of human history. His works manifest his militant humanism against injustice and violence.

Feuchtwanger discovered a polar tension in the history of the peoples. Inherent in it are the contradictions of life. . . . Here it becomes clearly evident that there are certain forces behind the acting characters which decisively influence the trend of human development. They are the expression of certain ideas. These ideas are of an antagonistic nature, and they arc in conflict. The destiny of mankind depends on the victory of the one or the other.

What is this polar tension? What are these forces and conflicting ideas? According to Feuchtwanger it is the antithesis of *power* and *reason*. In all his novels the turning point is the showdown between power and reason. Usually the representatives of power turn out to be political gamblers. . . .

Here the writer Lion Feuchtwanger arose. He warned against underestimating violence and revealed its sinister stature: the anti-social hostility of the great and the small political gamblers, beginning with the ancient Caesars to the modern Führer-dictators. (p. 10)

Against the image of violence in the hands of power, Feuchtwanger put the image of reason. Against falsehood he put knowledge and truth. He did it clearly, calmly, factually. . . .

And the outstanding merit of Lion Feuchtwanger is the fact that he applied the law of the *drama* to the historical novel. . . . This is how Lion Feuchtwanger revived and renewed the German historical novel, beginning with *Power* and *Success*. He adjusted it to the tradition of significant world literature. . . .

[Feutchwanger's] novels teach the meaning of history without pathos or romanticism, in the service of truth. They give evidence of doubts and experiments. Some of his friends raised objections against Feuchtwanger's allegedly exaggerated fairness toward figures of the counterpart, King Louis XVI for instance or Marie Antoinette in the novel *Proud Destiny*. But the great art of unbiased empathy for all the characters is a main virtue of significant epics. . . .

[Feuchtwanger's work] will endure. It has greatness, truth, and human dignity, the consolation of the creative word, the uplift of the spiritual deed. (p. 12)

> *F. S. Grosshut, "Lion Feuchtwanger and the Historical Novel," in* Books Abroad *(copyright 1960 by the University of Oklahoma Press), Vol. 34, No. 1, Winter, 1960, pp. 9-12.*

GEORG LUKÁCS (essay date 1962)

[In both *Jud Süss (Jew Süss)* and *Die hassliche Herzogin*

(The Ugly Duchess)] history is no more than a decorative costume for specifically modern psychological problems. The fate of the Tyrol in the struggles for power between the Luxemburgs, Habsburgs and Wittelsbachs has very little to do with the individual love tragedy of Margarete Maultasch. The tragedy of the gifted, but ugly woman, which constitutes the human interest of this novel—for there is very little in the actual political power intrigues that could interest the present-day reader from a historical-human angle —is woven into the plot of political intrigue with great skill, but humanly has hardly anything to do with it. It is a similar case with *Jew Süss*. The main theme here is also a specifically modern psychological conflict, a clash of outlooks. Feuchtwanger himself says of his subject: "For years now I have wanted to show a man's path from doing to not-doing, from action to contemplation, from a European to an Indian outlook. There was an obvious example of this development in our own times: Walther Rathenau. I attempted it: I failed. I transferred the subject two centuries back and attempted to portray the path of the Jew Süss Oppenheimer: I came nearer my goal."

Feuchtwanger's mistake is very instructive. He says that his failure with Rathenau and success with the Württemburg Jew proves the suitability of historical themes for the embodiment of abstract-intellectual collisions. We think that it was neither the proximity nor the unfavourableness of contemporary material which caused Feuchtwanger's failure with the Rathenau theme, but the fact that his collision has little to do with the inner tragedy of Rathenau. Thus the familiar personality of the latter and the well-known circumstances of his life strongly and successfully resisted the writer's attempted "introjection". Rathenau's Jewishness certainly plays an important part in his tragedy and there is some kind of split between activity and comtemplation. But Rathenau's real tragedy is the tragedy of the liberal bourgeoisie of Germany. . . . The doing notdoing theme could only form an episodic abstraction from this vast subject; it certainly could not master it.

Feuchtwanger realizes his aim in *Jew Süss,* because he is able to do what he likes with this remote historical figure. However, as far as the story as a whole is concerned he is not successful, nor could he be. His aim was to take the Jew Süss from action to inaction. Action meant the fearful exploitation of Württemburg with the help of a minor branch of the dynasty which had come to power. Now when the turning-point occurs and Feuchtwanger's hero takes the "Indian path", everything which has preceded it is made to appear a chain of aberrations, incidental and episodic. This, however, produces a grotesque and distorted perspective in which the fate of a whole country and of millions of people appears as an irrelevant stage background to the spiritual conversion of a Jewish usurer. (pp. 288-89)

Yet Feuchtwanger is passionately concerned with historical and human concreteness; he chooses a type for whom the problem of action and inaction is a real one, arising from the actual conditions of his life, namely those of a Jewish financier and usurer of the seventeenth century scarcely out of the ghetto. The direct juxtaposition of extortionate money mainpulations and religious mysticism corresponds to social and historical truth. Considered in himself, the hero is both psychogically and historically true to life. Feuchtwanger departs from inner historical truth and hence artistic truth in two ways. First, in the disproportion between the action itself and the twist he gives to it. A writer who deals with history cannot chop and change with his material as he likes. Events and destinies have their natural, objective weight, their natural, objective proportion. If a writer succeeds in producing a story which correctly reproduces these relationships and proportions, then human and artistic truth will emerge alongside the historical. If, on the other hand, his story distorts these proportions, then it will distort the artistic picture as well. Thus it offends if the suffering of an entire people during a decade should appear as a "pretext" for the spiritual conversion of a none-too-important individual.

The other way in which Feuchtwanger offends against proportion and artistic truth is by surrounding his hero's conversion with an "eternal", "timeless" halo as if it has resolved some universal human destiny. The conversion of a seventeenth century Jew to the mysticism of the Cabbala is socially and psychologically understandable and portrayed by Feuchtwanger with sensitive psychological insight. But the underlying philosophy—the abandonment of fickle, practical Europe for the contemplative heights of the orient, where the deceptive illusions of action and history dissolve into nothingness—is but a voice of a past period in literature. It was Schopenhauer who discovered for Germany that Indian philosophy was the appropriate antidote to Hegel's "superficial" view of human progress. And since then this theory has been re-echoed in every possible variation in the philosophy and literature of the German intelligentsia and the intelligentsia of other countries. (p. 290)

In the case of a progressive writer and fighter of Feuchtwanger's rank this position stands in harmful contradiction to his work. For a decadent, who was only interested in décor and psychology, everything preceding the conversion in *Jew Süss* would indeed be no more than a pretext for the latter. Such a writer would have presented all this in decorative abbreviation, unlike Feuchtwanger, who aims at a genuine realism. The structure could thus have been more unified—but Feuchtwanger's importance lies in the fact that the "pretext", the fate of the people of Württemburg, grips him deeply as a writer and a man. He portrays it in vigorous, realistic colours, but precisely by so doing reveals the eccentricity of his final statement. Feuchtwanger is too honest a humanist and too realistic a writer to be able to master this theme adequately.

Hence the step which Feuchtwanger takes in his Josephus Flavius novels is a vitally necessary one.... [The] general theme of these novels, the antithesis between nationalism and internationalism, really grows out of the historical material itself. For this reason alone the proportions here between Feuchtwanger's general-humanist ideas and the historical events and figures he portrays are quite different and much more correct. The big collision is no longer tranferred *into* past history, it is developed *out* of it. This is an extremely big step forward towards a real historical novel.... (pp. 290-91)

[One can often observe a] "triumph of realism" in Feuchtwanger. One can criticize in many ways the conception of Fascism both in *Erfolg (Success)* and in *Die Geschwister Oppenheim (The Oppenheims)*. And it would be interesting to show how these false conceptions of Fascism have been enlarged and vulgarized in his historical novels. But this is not so important for us as the fact that Feuchtwanger has created really living and really popular characters in these novels, who express plastically and convincingly all that is best in the popular forces rebelling against Fascist barbarism. Characters such as Johanna Krain in *Erfolg* or the young grammar school boy Bernard Oppenheim are nowhere to be found in Feuchtwanger's historical novels. In these characters especially, but also in many other of his contemporary novels, Feuchtwanger's outstanding talents emerge unobscured by false theories and contemporary prejudices. He is converted to the historical novel because its self-contained material seems to promise lighter artistic labour and easier success. It seems to us that this "lightness", this insufficient resistance of the historical material to false constructions is one of the sources of the shortcomings of these novels, whereas the contradictory hardness of the living life of the present wrests from the writer his highest artistic talents. (p. 342)

Georg Lukács, "The Historical Novel of Democratic Humanism: Popular Character and the True Spirit of History" and "The Historical Novel of Democratic Humanism: Prospects for the Development of the New Humanism in the Historical Novel," in his The Historical Novel, *translated by Hannah Mitchell and Stanley Mitchell (translation copyright © 1962 by Merlin Press Ltd.; originally published as* Der historische Roman, *Merlin Press, 1962; English translation copyright © 1962 by Merlin Press Ltd), Merlin Press, 1962, pp. 282-99, 332-50.*

LION FEUCHTWANGER   (essay date 1963)

Readers and critics who wish to laud historical literature frequently say that the author has succeeded in lending life to the period he has portrayed. They obviously regard this as the ultimate purpose of historical literature, and that is a mistake. Academicians who have authored historical novels may well have had that in mind as their principal purpose. But the creative writers desire only to treat contemporary matters even in those of their creations which have history as their subject. Such writers want only to discuss their relation to their own time, their own personal experience, and how much of the past has continued into the present. (p. 129)

If my assumption is correct that the writers of historical literature desire really only to express themselves about contemporary problems, then everyone is immediately entitled to ask: Why then do you writers not use contemporary costumes, props, and locutions? ... Historical disguise often enables an author to express truths, notably those of a political or daringly erotic kind, he would fear or be incapable of stating in a contemporary setting. (p. 133)

A genuine artist is really not too concerned about the choice of his materials. "Reach into life, it is a teeming ocean!" Story material is interesting to an artist only as a means for expressing his experiences. The material is never of interest to him for its own sake. He is conscious of the fact, however, that his story or play must have a firm skeleton or outline. And most historical materials offer that kind of skeleton. Historical themes present a given beginning and a given end with specific milestones in between. (p. 138)

A genuine artist is moved to the choice of an historical setting by much more profound considerations. Wittingly or no, he chooses an historical framework simply to avoid an uncomfortable proximity to the theme he wants to treat. He wants to enhance his theme by giving it perspective and he knows that he can accomplish this only by means of distance. One can appreciate the outlines of a mountain much better from a distance than from the center of the mountain itself. To portray successfully a contemporary view of the world, an author must move it into vaster areas of time and space. The author is not re-creating history for its own sake but uses the costume or disguise of history as the simplest stylistic means for achieving the illusion of reality. He compels himself and his reader to step back and view the forest rather than the trees, to envision the immediate environment in perspective. (p. 140)

> *Lion Feuchtwanger, in his* The House of Desdemona; or, The Laurels and Limitations of Historical Fiction, *translated by Harold A. Basilius (reprinted by permission of the Wayne State University Press; copyright © 1963 by Wayne State University Press), Wayne State University Press, 1963, 236 p.*

W. E. YUILL   (essay date 1964)

It was some time before Feuchtwanger's bent for the historical novel emerged, for it was not until after the First World War that he turned to the genre that was to make his reputation. His earliest work was written for the theatre and . . . was marked by the aestheticism and over-sophisticated psychology of the day. (p. 180)

[In two dramas written during the First World War,] *Warren Hastings* and *Jud Süss*, a . . . profound and characteristic theme begins to emerge, a theme which in one form or another features in nearly all of the author's works: this is the conflict of "Macht und Geist", of authority and free intellect. In these two plays the conflict is seen under the particular aspect of the active and the contemplative life, the restless, thrusting, questing ethos of the West in conflict with the tranquil, passive wisdom of the East; a conflict epitomised in the philosophies of Nietzsche and Buddha. (p. 181)

A modification of this theme, the gulf between insight and action, idea and deed, morality and expediency, is illustrated in *Thomas Wendt*. This is a work which reflects the collapse of the revolutionary régime in Germany in 1918, and which in its form—"dramatic novel"—marks Feuchtwanger's transition to the epic genre. (p. 182)

While in the main stream of his work Feuchtwanger was reconstructing and interpreting the past and incidentally expressing an individual philosophy, he was also writing in a satirical vein about contemporary society. The coolness and intellectuality of his approach in these minor works makes a strange contrast with the predominant sultriness of his historical novels, and in fact the satirical was a vein which seems to have petered out fairly rapidly. Its prominence at this time is perhaps a consequence of Feuchtwanger's friendship with Brecht. Both men seem to have been fascinated and repelled by the image of American capitalism and the Transatlantic influences in Germany. This preoccupation may be seen in such plays as . . . [Feuchtwanger's] *Die Petroleum-Inseln* and the comedy *Wird Hill amnestiert?*, in which the allegedly class-ridden justice of the United States is attacked. The satirical note also sounds in Feuchtwanger's lyric of the period. *PEP, J. L. Wetcheeks amerikanisches Liederbuch*, which purports to be a translation from American, mocks the vulgarity and

philistinism of B. W. Smith, the type of the American businessman, who discovers to his disgust that his money will not buy intangibles—the beauties of nature or the things of the mind. . . . (p. 186)

Feuchtwanger is not a particularly gifted satirist, and this note soon fades from his work. The pattern of parallel development—historical study on the one hand, study of contemporary society on the other—remains, however, and becomes, in fact, more marked in the central phase of his career, the years from 1930 to 1942. This phase is dominated by the two trilogies. *Der Wartesaal* (*Erfolg, Die Geschwister Oppenheim*, later *Oppermann*, and *Exil*) and *Josephus* (*Der jüdische Krieg, Die Söhne* and *Der Tag wird kommen*). The *Wartesaal-Trilogie*, more diffuse and loosely articulated than the other, describes the genesis of the Nazi movement and traces the typical fate of a number of Jewish families. The Josephus trilogy is dominated by the figure of the Jewish historian Flavius Josephus (born A.D. 37) and deals with the ambiguous situation of the Jew in Western civilisation—an elaboration of the *Jud Süss* theme, in fact. (p. 187)

Erfolg is a lightly camouflaged account of events in Bavaria between the years 1921 and 1924. It is a work of great complexity, a veritable kaleidoscope of personalities and parties. In the midst of this turmoil Feuchtwanger lays bare what he believes to be the roots of Nazism: a reactionary administrative machine, a greedy and demoralised middle class, a few fanatical demagogues exploiting the masses and used in their turn by cool-headed industrial and agrarian magnates. (p. 188)

Around the central characters of *Erfolg* there is a whole throng of secondary figures, some purely episodic, others reappearing in a thematic way, but all of them sketched firmly and clearly, even where, in pursuit of typical truth, the writer alters particular features. (pp. 188-89)

The narrative chapters of the work are interspersed with blocks of statistics; it is in the laconic comments accompanying these data that a satirical vein may still be observed. "The materially underprivileged", writes Feuchtwanger in mock-historical style, "were mostly organised in the parties of the Left, the mentally underprivileged in those of the Right." . . .

Apart from the satirical intent, it is by such arrays of statistics and by the reporting of historical events like the murder of Kurt Eisner that Feuchtwanger seeks to achieve the effect of an historical account, to place a distance between the reader and events which were practically contemporary, as well as to fulfil his obligation to future generations. One might almost speak here—in view of Feuchtwanger's association with Brecht—of an alienation effect applied to the novel. One of the consequences of this technique here is a striking contrast between the detachment of the statistical sections and the descriptions of the pullulating life of Munich beercellars, the emotionally charged atmosphere of the courts or the grey squalor of a prison-cell.

The other two volumes of the trilogy show an increasing concentration as well as a manifest autobiographical bias. *Die Geschwister Oppermann* describes the fate of a Jewish family in the weeks before and after Hitler's accession to power. The sufferings of these distinguished people—a writer, a doctor, two businessmen—and their dependants are described with compassion, but seen nevertheless as a consequence of their disdainful indifference to politics: they have tried to preserve the intellectual and contemplative life in circumstances which call for determined action. Ultimately they are brought to realise that the intellectuals' abdication of responsibility leaves power automatically in the hands of brutal men of action. This is clearest in the figure of the writer, Gustav Oppermann, who—no doubt like Feuchtwanger himself—comes to realise the futility of the aesthetic attitude in these circumstances. . . . (p. 189)

The development from the view of Jacques Tüverlin in *Erfolg* represented in the action—ineffectual as it is—of Gustav Oppermann, no doubt indicates a further movement in Feuchtwanger's own mind towards the idea of commitment, a movement away from the ideal of contemplation. With Oppermann, too, another notion is introduced—the artist's solidarity with the masses. . . .

Exil concerns itself ever more intensively with the dilemma of the artist in times of political repression. The central character, in this case a musician, Sepp Trautwein, is required to take over the editorship of a newspaper for German emigrants in Paris when the original editor is abducted by Nazi agents. Trautwein sees his involvement in politics as an unpleasant temporary necessity, as the price he must pay for the freedom to practise his art in the future. . . . The relevance to Feuchtwanger's own development is clear. There is perhaps an element of personal confession, too, in the reservations which Trautwein has about the Socialist doctrine. . . . (p. 190)

The ambivalent situation of the artist and intellectual, bound to the past and dedicated to the future, is summed up in the epilogue to the trilogy. . . .

The problem of the artistic individual's dedication to the mass movement of Socialism continues to echo through the works of Feuchtwanger's later life. (p. 191)

The Josephus trilogy, the other great branch of Feuchtwanger's work in this period, has the organic unity of the hero's life. Not that it is a simple biography: Flavius Josephus is a symbolic figure who embodies in his character and fate conflicts and contradictions that not only concern Feuchtwanger personally but are also typical of his race. Like Süss, Josephus is a Jew in a Gentile environment, he is both thinker and man of action, soldier and historian; he is torn between ideals of Jewish nationalism and cosmopolitanism, acting now by reason, now by feeling—"this Joseph, however, was rational and emotional at one and the same time, a rare mixture". (pp. 191-92)

Josephus, as Feuchtwanger represents him, was a man in advance of his age—and in advance of ours. The story of his life is the most problematic of Feuchtwanger's works; there is a sense of perplexity about it which raises it artistically above works like *Waffen für Amerika* and *Narrenweisheit* which are more doctrinaire in their approach.

These two great trilogies, the two main lines of Feuchtwangers' work, are brought together by the author's universalising tendency: on the one hand he seeks to give historical perspective to contemporary events; on the other, he describes the Roman Empire in the terms of a modern dictatorship, taking characteristically modern account of economic factors. (p. 194)

The completion of the two trilogies, and of the shorter novels which are appendages to them, more or less marks the close of a phase in Feuchtwanger's work. From 1945 until 1952 his attention turns from Germany and the ancient world to France and to Spain. Here, too, the parallelism of his approach is in a sense sustained; on the one hand, historical novels—*Waffen für Amerika, Goya* and *Narrenweisheit*—on the other, topical works—*Simone,* a novel about a latter-day Saint Joan, perhaps better known in the theatrical version by Brecht, and *Der Teufel in Frankreich,* an account of Feuchtwanger's personal experiences in a French internment camp. In this phase, however, the centre of gravity has moved to the historical novel. The central event is the French Revolution, and the three novels form a kind of trilogy: *Waffen für Amerika* sees the American War of Independence as a prologue to the French Revolution; *Narrenweisheit* describes the Revolution and the Terror; *Goya* involves the repercussions of the Revolution in Spain. (p. 195)

Feuchtwanger's conception of history [as demonstrated in *Waffen für Amerika*] has changed somewhat since the days of *Die hässliche Herzogin* and *Jud Süss:* no longer does he see the destiny of society as dependent upon human vices and virtues, upon the whim of colourful individuals. Men are driven by forces over which they have no control; this deterministic view tends to erode the impression of human greatness and implied tragedy that is discernible in figures like Josephus, and to that extent it is not an aesthetic advance. There are striking characters in *Waffen für Amerika,* resolute men and fascinating women, but the real "hero" of the novel is an abstraction . . . ["progress"]. (pp. 196-97)

From *Narrenweisheit* it is clear that "progress" now means unequivocally the Marxist doctrine of dictatorship of the proletariat. Here, the individual is eclipsed, absorbed into the mass. (p. 197)

[In] satirical drawings of Goya, Feuchtwanger sees the way in which the power of the intellect can be brought to bear against authority: it is the way of art. The mind need not abdicate in the face of force, it can still attack under the cloak of art. . . . (p. 198)

The portrait of the artist in *Goya* is perhaps the best feature of the novel: the painter is a man outwardly coarse, sullen and sturdy, inwardly hypersensitive, plagued by moods of despair verging on madness and by a host of melancholy phantoms: a peasant and a visionary. . . .

Although not the last of Feuchtwanger's novels, *Waffen für Amerika, Goya* and *Narrenweishert* are in the nature of a political testament. The two works of his final period [*Spanische Ballade* and *Jefta und seine Tochter*] revert to less specifically doctrinaire problems and to more personal preoccupations; in particular they show the obsession with sacrifice which lies behind so many of his novels. It is possibly significant that these last two novels leave the field of recorded history for that of legend. . . . [Jehuda, the central figure of *Spanische Ballade,*] combines in character and situation the features of Süss and Josephus. Like the former, he rises to power and influence in a Gentile state; like the latter he dreams of wedding the wisdom of the East to the energy of the West. (p. 199)

In this novel again, as in *Die hässliche Herzogin,* Feuchtwanger tries to depict an age of transition in which the knight is giving way to the artisan, fanaticism to reason. (pp. 199-200)

In the last of his novels, *Jefta und seine Tochter*, Feuchtwanger finds his way back to the primitive beginnings of his race, to the story of the judge in Israel who, by the sacrifice of his daughter, saved his people.... *Jefta* is Feuchtwanger's ultimate, and perhaps his most difficult, exercise in historical empathy, an attempt to evoke in a legendary theme the sense of circumstance and of progression that raises historian and reader out of the limitations of the present and thus helps them to understand their own age. (p. 200)

It is this constant endeavour to comprehend and to communicate, to make the reader understand human nature and the progress of the human race which most impresses us when we look back on the long catalogue of Feuchtwanger's published works. It is certain that he has his weaknesses both as a writer and as a thinker. His voice is often too strident.... His view of past ages is often naïve and tendentious, his devotion to reason is undermined at times by a kind of temperamental nihilism. There is in much of his work a strong suggestion of sadism—lurid scenes of torture and death abound.... There is, too, an intermittent salaciousness, a fondness for erotic scenes that is disturbing. These features, together with a general leaning towards the sensational and a style that is sometimes prolix and undistinguished, may debar him from the company of the greatest German writers of today. In spite of such defects, however, Feuchtwanger has considerable qualities as a novelist: vivid imagination, very considerable erudition and a sense of literary form. But perhaps what is most attractive about his work at its best is the impression of a vehement temperament—the strong emotional impulse behind the philosophy of reasonableness. It is this which will make at least some of his novels retain their attraction, for, as Josephus says: "The living Word is born wherever feeling and knowledge come together." (pp. 200-01)

> *W. E. Yuill, "Lion Feuchtwanger," in* German Men of Letters, *Volume III, edited by Alex Natan (© 1964 Oswald Wolff (Publishers) Limited), Osward Wolff, 1964, pp. 179-206.*

LOTHAR KAHN   (essay date 1968)

Lionel Trilling once remarked that he could not understand why Feuchtwanger was not a great writer. The answer may well lie in the unevenness of his later work and the mediocre prestige enjoyed by the historical novel. At his worst, Feuchtwanger's erudition subordinated characterization and movement, shoving aside the novel's focal points, and resulting in a length that invited skipping and slurring. But the best of Feuchtwanger will be remembered. *Jud Süss* will live as will his Josephus trilogy; *The Oppermanns* merits rereading as does *Paris Gazette* and *Success*. Significantly, all four are concerned with the basic Jewish situation in the Diaspora.

It is on this theme that Feuchtwanger wrote with consistent understanding and compassion. Here, too, he managed more circumspectly to curb his tendency to write history at the expense of novel. Moreover, Feuchtwanger established an identity with his Jewish protagonists which he did not build with all his characters. (p. 96)

> *Lothar Kahn, "Lion Feuchtwanger: Historical Judaism," in his* Mirrors of the Jewish Mind: A Gallery of Portraits of European Jewish Writers of Our Time *(reprinted by permission of the pub-*

lisher; copyright © 1968 by A. S. Barnes & Company, Inc.; all rights reserved), Thomas Yoseloff, 1968, pp. 95-110.

WERNER JAHN   (essay date 1972)

Clearly, Feuchtwanger wished to present his main characters ... as influenced in their thoughts, desires, and actions by an invisible co-actor—progress—without being aware of its presence or of their dependence. But does this not rob them of that very individuality which interests us, the readers, most of all? Does not this invisible "hero," progress, reduce all the other characters from subjects to mere objects of history? (p. 51)

In *Jud Süss* and Feuchtwanger's other early novels, historical change, though already present, is still unrelated to the plot of the novel, still not perceived as something dynamic, still without an important function within the whole, and still completely concealed by the human constants. Why then, we must ask ourselves, did historical change—and "progress as hero"— become so overwhelmingly important in Feuchtwanger's late work? (pp. 53-4)

In *Josephus* progress is by no means the "hero" of the work; what we have instead are two intellectuals who exchange reflections on man's destiny against the background of the all-powerful Roman Empire—historical pressure has not become yet the driving force in the development of the plot. (pp. 55-6)

What does Feuchtwanger see differently in his *Waffen für Amerika* or his *Goya*? One might almost say that no new positions or ideas have actually developed; instead we find a greater decisiveness and consistency. First there is the greater depth and breadth of the social panorama he spreads before us. We see a society in motion, full of dynamism, and with the awareness of new possibilities and decisions which must be made.... Once again, intellectuals, particularly writers, artists, and politicians, are placed in the center of historical conflict, but now art itself gains an active role. Once enlisted in such conflict, art's provocative, transforming effect is suddenly freed on a vast scale, strengthening the force of reason in a way the artist himself might find unlikely. (p. 57)

Yet as he turned from the individual to mankind in history, order and direction became visible: "I am also continually struck by the realization that in the confusion of a million accidents a particular direction—'progress' toward more highly developed reason—becomes evident." (p. 59)

In *Waffen für Amerika* and *Goya* the struggle for progress was presented primarily as a struggle of ideas. In *Narrenweisheit* these ideas are not only confronted by resistant reality, they themselves are to become reality as the revolution sets in motion a process by which theory presumably will become social practice....

Where does progress lead us? Did Feuchtwanger leave us any sketch or plan of a future society based on reason? No; rather he focused on the recognizable progressive tendencies and strivings of the present. His use of the past was to trace the growth of insight, to show unreason losing. (p. 61)

Feuchtwanger's concept of progress is not utopian. It is firmly anchored in psychological and historical realities. Feuchtwanger recognizes the need to base one's commitment to progress on awareness of history's complexity: on awareness, too, of individual fallibility, of the necessity of patience, but also of the individual need to struggle in the cause of reason and justice. Thus skepticism and hope are two modes of one view: skepticism in light of the burden of the past, the world's heritage of tyranny and inequality, exploitation and injustice, as deep as the ancient aggressions and repressions of the psyche; hope, in view of the growing supremacy of man over nature and over himself through reason. Feuchtwanger did not yield to the temptation of presenting a philosophical-historical panorama. The color and drama of human lives forces philosophy into the background. The poet always outwitted the historian. Real men, with their potentialities and weaknesses, always supplanted the shades of history. Feuchtwanger's hope is above all the wise hope for man in both his grandeur and his misery, in his dreams, his possibilities and his fears: a hope that frankly measured the resistance of the majority to the prerequisite of truly conscious progress—the will to change. (p. 64)

> Werner Jahn, "The Meaning of 'Progress' in the Work of Lion Feuchtwanger," in Lion Feuchtwanger: The Man, His Ideas, His Work—A Collection of Critical Essays, *edited by John M. Spalek (copyright © 1972 by Hennessey & Ingalls, Inc.; used by permission), Hennessey & Ingalls, 1972, pp. 51-65.*

UWE KARL FAULHABER (essay date 1972)

Feuchtwanger took care not to allow spectacle to obscure content. Even the untrained reader must repeatedly come to terms with the philosophical problems Feuchtwanger presented. Although the *Josephus* trilogy is replete with detailed descriptions of the grandeur of the Roman Empire, from its emperors to its masses, the three novels continually deal with the question of the survival of an exclusive religious minority, the Jews, within the dominant military society of the Empire. This question arises within the continuing argument between two historians of the era. Justus of Tiberias asserts that the Jewish nation rebelled against Rome out of economic necessity. Flavius Josephus, on the other hand, insists that the uprising grew out of ideological conflict. Not content to allow his readers to accept blindly one man's answer, Feuchtwanger did not resolve the argument. The reader must project the problem beyond the scope of its historical setting, perhaps toward a possible conclusion suggested in the title of the third novel: *Der Tag wird kommen.*

The title *Der Tag wird kommen* is one manifestation of a recurring motif in Feuchtwanger's novels. It is his prime lesson to his readers. He saw history as an eternal struggle between reason and stupidity. . . . For Feuchtwanger, the ultimate outcome of this struggle would see insight triumphant over instinct.

Feuchtwanger based this optimistic conclusion on two major decisions he had reached in his extensive study of history. He first posited that there must be some order in history, even if, as Lessing demonstrated, this order is created by man confronting a hostile world. (p. 71)

Feuchtwanger's second decision was that there must be progress in history, indeed that progress is the guiding force in history. . . . In other words, Feuchtwanger wished to emphasize that history, although eternally the same, is not static, that it has specific direction. . . . Thus Feucht-

wanger's assumption that there must be direction in history is less a statement of empirical deduction than a profession of faith in the ultimate triumph of rationality. (p. 72)

Feuchtwanger pared his works down to a minimum of material and a maximum of relevancy, selecting only those facts needed to trace the events to their logical outcome. Structure is therefore usually sequential, the plots following one strand of causally related events. Feuchtwanger seldom enhanced or embellished the plot by extended use of flashbacks or foreshadowing of events, though the characters within the novel may frequently reflect on the past or future. He enforces the strictest historical perspective, no event is out of place, and indeed he becomes at times almost too austerely efficient in streamlining his plots. In the second volume of the *Josephus* trilogy, Demetrius Liban, the actor, drowns on his return from Israel and is never heard of again, never even mentioned by any of his close friends. Although the *Josephus* trilogy is an extensive work, this disappearance of Demetrius can hardly be an oversight on the part of the author. Demetrius Liban had served his purpose.

Feuchtwanger's overriding attention to historical perspective also affected his delineation of characters. When the reader meets Josephus, Franklin, or Süss, he learns little or nothing about their prior life, their development up to that point. How they came to be the characters they are is irrelevant, since Feuchtwanger was interested in only that segment of their lives when they gained historical and therefore exemplary significance.

By maintaining a measured distance, Feuchtwanger was able to emphasize the underlying epochal forces which play a major role in his novels. He embraced the Hegelian concept of the evolution of history. Thus the past, as well as the present and future, was for him a giant field of ideological forces disrupted periodically by change. During major change the historical forces are starkly magnified and devoid of all the superfluous elements attending their development. Looking back on these forces displayed during times of flux, Feuchtwanger could then clearly visualize them.

Feuchtwanger's desire to portray these forces at a peak led him to set most of his novels in times of crisis. His novels usually begin at a point when a new order is about to supplant the old. (pp. 73-4)

The historical forces themselves form merely one element of the lesson Feuchtwanger wished to convey. The lesson is complete only when the reader recognizes man's relationship to these forces. The individual himself is swept along, reduced to utter helplessness by forces he cannot control. To emphasize man's relative impotence, Feuchtwanger generally chose men of high social standing and historical significance. Not even the Emperors in the *Josephus* trilogy are immune to historical necessity. (pp. 75-6)

Thus many of the characters in Feuchtwanger's novels appear as passive heroes. As in Hebbel's dramas, they act as tools of history, unaware that they are not guiding, but rather are being guided. . . .

Since man has little free choice in the shaping of large events and courses, the significance, meaning, and purpose of history must lie not in the individual but in history itself. (p. 76)

All these lessons about man's place in history are insubstantial unless they reflect the present. Feuchtwanger repeatedly stated that historical novels must essentially be of the present. He insisted that the content, i.e. the essential theme, be the same whether a novel portrays the seventeenth century or the twentieth. . . .

Aside from content in this sense, Feuchtwanger employed two techniques to ensure contemporaneity: one affects delineation of character, the other the use of language. Each of the main characters must meet three demands of historical fiction: they must be simultaneously unique, typical and contemporary. A character is unique by virtue of that aspect of character which sets each off from all the others in the novel. A character becomes unique through correct costuming, individual appearance and a particular emphasis on his foibles. Feuchtwanger often delighted in exaggerating peculiarities in his characters. . . . These very quirks give the character a three-dimensional aspect. Upon these weaknesses of the characters depends their verisimilitude in the eyes of the reader.

The uniqueness of a character must not obscure his significance as a type. The individual character embodies the characteristics of a certain recognizable type of person who lived in the era which the novel portrays. (p. 77)

While being unique and typical, the main characters must also be contemporary. They must wrestle with problems which are as acute today as they were at the time in which these historical characters existed. Josephus seeks a solution to the problem of Jewish identity. He wants to consider himself both a Jew and a Roman, but finds himself alienated on either side. His plight parallels the predicament of any cultural or ideological minority.

Feuchtwanger intensified the apparent modernity of his characters in the *Josephus* trilogy by using a twentieth century idiom in the dialogue. When Vespasian says to his spouse, "Well, old girl, now we've made it. From now on you can't get me going, no matter how high you lift your leg," it is as if a crude German farmer of the present were speaking, not the unrefined provincial Roman nobleman who became emperor.

The prerequisites of uniqueness, type and contemporaneity hold true only for the main characters in Feuchtwanger's novels. When dealing with minor characters, Feuchtwanger relinquished all requirements but that of type. Almost all minor characters in his novels defy substantiation in the form of historical research, because they are composite figures of all characteristics of their class. . . . Because they are types, these minor characters quite often remain one-dimensional. Nonetheless, they serve a dual purpose in the novels: they are instrumental in the development of the plot, and they contribute to the delicate balance between historicity and contemporaneity. (p. 78)

Feuchtwanger enlarged the scope of the historical novel . . . by including insights into the nature of the processes which governs all events, past and present. In doing so, he shifted the emphasis from inner to outer conflict. Instead of penetrating the psyches of key personalities, he concentrated on the external forces which guided or moved these men. He presented a character's thoughts only when those thoughts reflected either his own philosophy of history, as in the case of Dr. Franklin, or the historical tensions which surrounded that character, as in the case of Josephus. By expanding the role of history in the historical novel, Feucht-

wanger sometimes lost the balance between plot and character, and some of his novels virtually became elaborate philosophical constructions. Although his theoretical didacticism may at times be distracting or heavy, Feuchtwanger did nevertheless raise the historical novel from its position as popular literature to the level of a serious genre.

Feuchtwanger's use of the serious historical novel was didactic: he purposed to convey the lessons of history. Each novel was meant to proclaim the eventual victory of reason over unreason. Feuchtwanger indicated in various prologues and epilogues to his novels that the basic concept was the final enlightenment of man. Because Feuchtwanger treated man as dependent on overriding historical forces, thereby transmitting what might appear to be a fatalistic view, he tended to obscure the sense of the triumph of the individual. Instead of deriving from Feuchtwanger's novels the author's actual optimism regarding the future, the modern reader is faced with a dilemma. He must choose between futile activity in the present and faith in a future paradise which he may not be able to enjoy. It is significant that the popularity of Feuchtwanger's novels reached an acme at a time when inaction meant tacit resignation to Nazi madness, when even futile action was preferable to merely witnessing. As with any urgent statement of faith, these novels have their greatest appeal to men overwhelmed by a sense of inadequacy in the face of inhumanity. (p. 79)

> Uwe Karl Faulhaber, *"Lion Feuchtwanger's Theory of the Historical Novel,"* in Lion Feuchtwanger: The Man, His Ideas, His Work—A Collection of Critical Essays, *edited by John M. Spalek (copyright © 1972 by Hennessey & Ingalls, Inc.; used by permission), Hennessey & Ingalls, 1972, pp. 67-81.*

DENNIS MUELLER   (essay date 1972)

Feuchtwanger's apprenticeship as a dramatist left its mark in many ways. The former playwright in him is most evident in his frequent employment of dialogue and interior monologue as opposed to narration. (p. 99)

Feuchtwanger's choice of archetypal figures adds a new dimension to characterization, for characters function both as conveyors of the theme and also as its human representatives. (p. 101)

Feuchtwanger's theory that an author seeks an objective recreation of the personal past in his novels is borne out in his own works. His novels elaborate one basic theme: the problems the social outsider encounters in his attempt to adapt or oppose himself to hostile surroundings. The hero of each of the above novels is at some point in his life an outcast, and each faces a difficult confrontation with society. It is always the same theme with certain variations. Frequently the outsider is a Jew in a non-Jewish milieu. . . . One major theme is related to that of the socially excluded: the tension between ruler and subject. . . . The ruler is pictured as an uncouth barbarian devoid of self-control . . . , while the subject is refined, intelligent, rational and yet passionate. It is in essence a case of brute strength pitted against cultured reason. One other theme is of prime importance in several of the novels: the role of the mediator who tries to intervene between extreme factions. . . . (pp. 102-03)

The first work which brought Feuchtwanger international

fame was *Jud Süss*. The protagonist is the financier Josef Süss Oppenheimer. In *Jud Süss*, as in all his novels, Feuchtwanger reveals the hero's nature through contrasts with other characters. The first such contrast is between Süss and the wealthy Jewish business man, Isaac Landauer. (p. 103)

Among the several themes in this novel one is dominant: the theme of how the social outsider comes to terms with an adverse world. Süss, determined to make his mark in the world despite his background and religion, does not hide the fact that he is a Jew, but he also does not parade it in his dress and action as Landauer does. (p. 104)

In *Erfolg*, as in *Jud Süss*, Feuchtwanger reveals the personality of the protagonist through a series of character contrasts. Krüger is first clearly differentiated in his choices from his friend, Kaspar Pröckl, modeled after Feuchtwanger's friend, Bertolt Brecht. Krüger and Pröckl are opposites in almost every respect. (p. 105)

Josef Süss has a great deal in common with Krüger. Both men are vain, both are highly cultured, both place their professional aims above everything else in life and both are unjustly imprisoned; even the descriptions of their actions in prison are strikingly similar. But whereas Süss is steadfast in his drive for power and money, Krüger tends to bend and compromise. He is ready to surrender in all matters but one: for art he is adamant. The main theme conveyed through Martin Krüger is also akin to that of the earlier novel: the fate of the exceptional individual who does not conform to the accepted patterns of society. Tüverlin's relatively complaisant course exemplifies the path an outsider must follow to achieve survival. He must at least be financially independent, as Krüger was not. (p. 106)

The character types depicted in *Jud Süss* in the persons of Süss himself, the Duke, Landauer, Weissensee, Naemi and Magdalen Sibylle reappear regularly in the later novels, down even to *Jefta und seine Tochter*. . . . [The] setting of the novel hardly affects the recurrence of symbolic likenesses, since *Jefta und seine Tochter* is set in Old Testament Judea, the *Josephus* trilogy in Rome of the first century A.D., *Spanische Ballade* in 12th century Spain, *Jud Süss* in 18th century Germany and the *Wartesaal* trilogy in contemporary Europe, and yet there are no essential differences in the life patterns or struggles of the bearers of any given heroic type. . . . Feuchtwanger conscientiously followed his own basic rules for the historical novel: he does not portray history for its own sake, but always for the higher end of presenting universal human experiences; he never loses sight of his end by stressing too heavily the plot or action of the story; and he uses the characters in his novels as a medium for achieving his end. The characters fulfill their dual function of conveying the theme and serving as symbolic representatives of the theme. The theme itself is basically the same in all of the novels we have discussed: the portrayal of Feuchtwanger's personal experience as a social outsider. (pp. 110-11)

Dennis Mueller, "Characterization of Types in Feuchtwanger's Novels," in Lion Feuchtwanger: The Man, His Ideas, His Work—A Collection of Critical Essays, edited by John M. Spalek (copyright © 1972 by Hennessey & Ingalls, Inc.; used by permission), Hennessey & Ingalls, 1972, pp. 99-111.

W. E. YUILL (essay date 1972)

[Süss, the protagonist of *Jud Süss,* is] caught in triple crosscurrents—his own inborn lust for wealth and financial success, the self-assertive arrogant mystic megalomania that makes Karl Alexander identify himself with his land and the asceticism of Rabbi Gabriel—but it is above all the conflict of the restless Western ethos and the passive Nirvana of the East, ruthless materialism and renunciation that is acted out in his heart and mind. . . .

The psychological conflict in Süss between spiritual aspiration and animal appetite is represented in the novel by his relation to the mystic Cabbalist Rabbi Gabriel, on the one hand, and the brutish Duke, repeatedly referred to as an animal, on the other. In visionary moments Süss and the Duke see themselves pacing through a phantom quadrille hand in hand with Rabbi Gabriel. . . . (p. 119)

In the evolution of Feuchtwanger's work *Jud Süss* may be seen as representing a transition from the psychological study of an essentially modern character in historical costume such as we have in *Die hässliche Herzogin* to the later historical novels like *Waffen für Amerika* or *Narrenweishert,* in which broad historical perspectives are manipulated in a politically tendentious sense. In *Jud Süss* Feuchtwanger seems still to be fascinated by the drama of individual lives on the one hand, the conflict of universal moral attitudes on the other. The detailed political, social and economic implications of a given historical incident seem only to be dawning on him, and the parallels with contemporary life which he draws are very tentative indeed. Apparently he required the first-hand study of contemporary events embodied in the *Zeitromane* before he could fully exploit the potential of the historical novel as a comment on the current pattern of events and, in a sense, a vehicle of prophecy. (p. 121)

The double perspective implied by such parallels is underlined by the contrast between the period setting, particularly the pastiche of eighteenth-century speech, and the modishly breathless style of the narrator. Feuchtwanger's naturally nervous style of writing seems to be rendered even terser here by certain almost spastic expressionistic mannerisms of the time. There are traces of affectation in the use of idiosyncratic forms—simplex instead of compound . . . , [the coining of unusual compounds or variants, and rare adjectives]. . . . The use of slightly outlandish words is by no means always a haphazard affectation, however; they can be used to form a kind of background pattern that engages the reader's attention almost subconsciously. For example, the threat of violence and disruption implicit in the characters and action of the novel is conveyed through the striking number of verbs compounded with *zer-*, many of them Feuchtwanger's own coinings. . . . (p. 123)

Feuchtwanger's syntax is here compressed and almost convulsive, its rhythm choppy and closely knit; it is a style devoid of sostenuto. Conventional word order is disrupted, often to create an ejaculatory effect, but sometimes merely as a mannerism without rhetorical effect. Characteristic is the accumulation of verbs or adjectives in staccato rhythmic series, frequently linked by assonance and alliteration. . . . Drastic monosyllabic adjectives—often linked in alliterative couples—are a favorite device in characterization. . . . Such groups of adjectives are associated repeatedly with individual characters, not as leitmotifs but more in the manner of the deft strokes with which the strip cartoon artist creates again and again the recognizable likenesses of his characters. In Feuchtwanger's case the technique is obviously more apparent with the less complex secondary characters: the attributes of such characters are shuffled and re-arranged on successive appearances, but they are always recognizably labelled. (pp. 123-24)

Events, too, are often sketched in equally laconic terms, in the manner of captions or interjection. . . . This hectic style is sometimes used to suggest the subjective impressions of characters in the novel. . . .

Even those few passages in the novel which have some kind of lyrical or atmospheric intention have little amplitude or resonance. Although they are brief and rarely sustained by repetition over any distance, these passages have a kind of hypnotic sing-song intonation. . . .

The overall effect is of contours and salient features heavily delineated and of hectic movement. The relatively few salient ideas are underscored by repetition. The narrator allows himself little in the way of coherent reflection, developed argument or extended description; there is little repose either in the pace of the narrative or in the minds of the characters, whose obsessive or tumultous thoughts occupy so much of the book. It is in many ways a primitive style, but it is racily effective and imposes its patterns with exaggerated clarity on the mind of the reader. (p. 124)

[*Jud Süss*] is hardly the best of Feuchtwanger's novels when seen in the perspective of his work as a whole: in acuteness of social observation and political insight it cannot compare with the *Zeitromane* of the *Wartesaal* trilogy; in intellectual substance and the circumstantial evocation of a past age it is surely inferior to the *Josephus* trilogy; as an exercise in historical double perspective it is not as ingenious as *Der falsche Nero*. . . . In spite of such limitations *Jud Süss* represents a masterly achievement in the choice and exploitation of a historical theme. The period and setting, and particularly the erotic element in the story undoubtedly had an intrinsic appeal, and Feuchtwanger exploits to the full the piquant contrast of glamour and squalor, elegance and brutality characteristic of life at a rococo court. He does this not by elaborate cultural or historical digression but by judicious use of documents and linguistic pastiche; the local color is applied thinly but invariably in the right locality. For the fastidious there might seem to be about *Jud Süss* more than a touch of Hollywood and even a whiff of that gamey kind of Kitsch now known as "camp," but behind the historical trappings there are individuals and human relationships that strike us as authentic and cogent. The psychology of the central figures is devious but comprehensible; it is clearly represented in inner monologues which may not perhaps reflect the mode of thought of the eighteenth century but which do strike a chord in the modern reader. It is perhaps this gift for detecting "human interest," along with the verve of his style, that accounts above all for Feuchtwanger's success.

As a work of philosophical thought *Jud Süss* occupies only a modest place and obviously cannot compare in this respect with its contemporary, *Der Zauberberg;* its pattern of thought is relatively coarse-grained. The surrender of Süss to his fate is ultimately problematic, fraught with masoch-

ism, more of an individual than an exemplary act. Nevertheless, the moral lesson of the story, the vanity of power . . . is conveyed with typical masterly clarity that may have found a special response in the immediate post-war years.

It is not only in its characterization that *Jud Süss* is reminiscent of a well-drawn strip-cartoon. It is constructed from a series of scenes in which the background is simply but clearly sketched and the foreground dominated by colorful characters stylized for instant recognition. Superimposed on these scenes rather than integrated in narrative or description are blocks of dialogue or inner monologue. It is hardly surprising that the story has the compulsive legibility of such a cartoon, and an era that finds high aesthetic merit in the work of Roy Lichtenstein may be able to appreciate *Jud Süss* as a work of art rather than simply as a piece of popular fiction. (pp. 125-26)

> *W. E. Yuill, "'Jud Süss': Anatomy of a Best-Seller," in* Lion Feuchtwanger: The Man, His Ideas, His Work—A Collection of Critical Essays, *edited by John M. Spalek (copyright © 1972 by Hennessey & Ingalls, Inc.; used by permission), Hennessey & Ingalls, 1972, pp. 114-29.*

LOTHAR KAHN (essay date 1975)

Feuchtwanger's conception of historical process encompasses such diversity of motivation as to suggest faithfully the complexity of human life. Economic greed and caste consciousness join ego cravings, sexual need, pure dream, and equally pure chance in bringing about the mighty events in man's history. A high political and worldly wisdom is one of the trademarks of a Feuchtwanger novel, as is the rare fusion of a heartening optimism and a derisive skepticism.

Feuchtwanger possessed an unrivaled talent for spinning most intricate social and political plots, but not even during his Marxist period did he ever permit his views to take charge of his story. His fiction is rarely doctrinaire or even didactic, and it never deteriorates into a political tract. A thesis, it is true, is built into all his fiction, but through dialectical tension it always contains its antithesis. Meticulously woven into the narrative, it is happily supported by a more than sufficient imagination. The works, however, are so subtle in their ideas that a historical novel *à la* Feuchtwanger is truly an intellectual historical novel, divorced from the romantic species of the early nineteenth century and the pseudo-scientific variety more popular in subsequent decades. (p. 19)

But Feuchtwanger's modernity transcends thematic concerns. His work is a veritable course in the dynamics of top-level decision-making, the maneuverings behind the subtitles of history books or the headlines of newspapers. Feuchtwanger is uncommonly skillful in picturing the backstage jugglery of international finance. He is a master of the subtle dialogue in which a suddenly raised eyebrow or a change in inflection provide a hint that enemies can become bedmates and allies turn into enemies. Feuchtwanger had few peers in sketching intelligent men and women whose intelligence was humbled or nullified again and again by the frailties of their human nature and the perversities of chance. Upon conquerors and victims alike, Feuchtwanger smiles with gentle irony, wit, and compassion. (p. 20)

Success was Feuchtwanger's first novel on a contemporary subject. As he explained in a *Nachwort* (epilogue) to a later edition, he wanted to bring to the present-day subject the distancing techniques he had learned with the historical novel. By regarding the present from the vantage point of the future, that is, as the events of a dead past, he hoped to provide a clearer, more incisive perspective. Lion was not altogether successful in using this device; he changed distance too frequently and thus detracted from the seriousness of his intent. (p. 138)

In several regards, the time covered (1920-23) and the themes—especially the dialectical insight and action, doing and writing, commitment and evasion—*Success* represents a veritable sequel to *Thomas Wendt*. The dialectic is played out for the most part by the writer Jacques Tüverlin, who clearly mirrors Feuchtwanger's positions, and the Communist engineer Kaspar Pröckl, a thinly disguised Bert Brecht. Pröckl keeps urging Tüverlin to create "activist, political, revolutionary" literature, entertains grave doubts that aesthetics and art are meritorious contributions, bombards him with Marxist interpretations of various phenomena. Tüverlin listens tolerantly to Pröckl's explanations, some ludicrous, others capable of startling Tüverlin into a reassessment of his own position. . . . While he is at times swayed by argument, Tüverlin . . . does not substantively change his humanist values and visions of an author's independence. (pp. 140-41)

Though Tüverlin moves gradually toward greater commitment in the novel, he never even remotely approximates Kaspar Pröckl's. In the final analysis, his commitment consists exactly of what he said earlier it should be: of writing, of explaining, of interpreting an event. (p. 141)

The dichotomy Tüverlin-Pröckl will be narrowed, but never removed nor satisfactorily bridged. In one form or another, the dilemma of the liberal intellectual, the writer who is heir to the Enlightenment, will be posed again and again, though never conclusively resolved.

Its vast scope, which yet sacrifices little in depth, places *Success* in the forefront of major panoramic social novels. Essentially conservative in form, despite daring but fitting innovations—the units of catalogued, encyclopedic facts concerning the humanity, the Germany, and the Bavaria of the 1920s—it blends plausibly the tangled issues that invaded Bavarian society in the fear-ridden postwar years; justice politicized, Fascism or radical conservativism as the trusted legatee of the values of the past, the role of the writer-artist in a time of convulsion, the threat and promise of Marxist revolution. Yes, despite his criticisms of the province and its people, an unmistakable affection is still evident.

Though his subject is deadly serious, Feuchtwanger gives it a light, deft touch. The novel does not arouse fear or terror, partly because the author does not carry his own analysis of an ailing society to its probable conclusion of doom. But the sense of ill-omen is also dissolved by the mature fusion

of a light irony, stoic calm, and tolerant appreciation of the contradictions that constitute life itself. (p. 142)

Paris Gazette was decidedly one of his better works and a panoramic novel of depth and scope. The terrifying experiences of the thirties were all present in one form or another. . . . Old themes are conjoined to new ones and become broadly reflective of the times: contemplation and action, conciliation and confrontation, political and economic democracy. . . . As a *Zeitroman, Paris Gazette* ranks second only to *Success* in overall achievement. (p. 223)

Paris Gazette deploys a broad range of emotions, a skillfully devised set of actions, none contrived and many founded on actual incidents, and above all a vast array of characters, nearly all removed from their native soil. Even the outright Nazis and their more subtle and treacherous fellow-travelers manage to become men of flesh and blood and not merely stereotyped political villains. (p. 224)

> *Lothar Kahn, in his* Insight and Action: The Life and Work of Lion Feuchtwanger *(© 1975 by Associated University Presses, Inc.), Fairleigh Dickinson University Press, 1975, 392 p.*

BIBLIOGRAPHY

Burkhard, Arthur. "Thomas Becket and Josef Süsz Oppenheimer as Fathers." *Germanic Review* VI, No. 2 (April 1931): 144-53.*
     A comparison of Conrad Ferdinand Meyer's *Der Heilige* with Feuchtwanger's *Jud Süss* that notes the similarities of character and situation and proposes that Feuchtwanger used Meyer's book as his model.

Kahn, Lothar. "Another Look at Lion Feuchtwanger." *The Chicago Jewish Forum* 27, No. 2 (Winter 1968-69): 98-103.
     A study of Feuchtwanger's treatment of Jews and their role in history which examines Feuchtwanger's use of humanitarian principles and Jewish tradition to link the cultures of East and West.

Raphael, Marc Lee. "An Ancient and Modern Identity Crisis: Lion Feuchtwanger's 'Josephus' Trilogy." *Judaism* 21, No. 4 (Fall 1972): 409-14.
     A study which relates Feuchtwanger's struggle as a Jew fleeing Nazi Germany with his character Josephus's struggle as a Jew in ancient Rome.

Spalek, John M., ed. *Lion Feuchtwanger: The Man, His Ideas, His Work.* Los Angeles: Hennessey & Ingalls, 1972, 330 p.
     A collection of essays that attempts to present a comprehensive survey of Feuchtwanger and his work. Included among the contributors are Werner Jahn, Ulrich Weisstein, Wolfgang Berndt, and Faith G. Norris.

"Exiles." *Time* XXXVI, No. 20 (11 November 1940): 80, 82.*
     An account of the problems encountered rescuing authors from the Nazi regime, with a brief account of Feuchtwanger's escape.

(Hannibal) Hamlin Garland

1860-1940

American short story writer, novelist, playwright, essayist, poet, biographer, and critic.

Garland was one of the literary progeny of realist William Dean Howells, and one of the early debunkers of the utopian rural myth. He was the forerunner of such writers as Edgar Lee Masters and Sherwood Anderson, depicting the Midwest as a wearying and unrewarding frontier.

Garland spent his youth on midwestern farmlands but moved east to Boston when he was twenty-four, where he pursued his education, wrote, and lectured. A return visit to his parents' bleak Dakota farm, coupled with encouragement from Howells, strengthened his desire to write of life on the prairie, and soon his first stories appeared in national magazines.

Many critics feel that his first book of stories, *Main-Travelled Roads,* is one of the most important books in American literary history. Collectively, the stories provide a study of the poverty faced by rural farmers in the age of industrialization, with an eye to the social and economic forces which caused that hardship. A dedicated proponent of various reform movements, in most of his work of this period Garland demonstrated his Populist principles, though his bitterness and pessimism did not endear him to a wide audience.

In this early period Garland promoted and utilized veritism, a form of literary realism, but at the beginning of the twentieth century his veritism gave way to romance as his story settings shifted from the Midwest to the Rocky Mountains. These novels are replete with the stereotypical characters and sentimental situations of popular western fiction, and it was widely believed that Garland was retreating from his principles in favor of fame and wealth. Many critics considered it ironic that Garland, who did so much to dispel the romantic myths of the midwestern farmer, should so romanticize life in the Far West. In recent years, however, these novels have been reevaluated as serious works in which Garland tried to present his political vision within the limits of popular conventions.

After seventeen years of commercial success with novels such as *Her Mountain Lover* and *The Captain of the Gray-Horse Troop,* Garland turned to refined realism with his autobiographical "Middle Border" tetralogy. These works have been highly praised for their entwining of Garland's family history with the history of his region. He received the 1921 Pulitzer Prize in Fiction for *A Daughter of the Middle Border.*

Although Garland is considered one of the pioneers of realism, his realistic works of fiction are regarded more as valuable records of a period in American history than as significant works of art.

PRINCIPAL WORKS

Under the Wheel: A Modern Play in Six Scenes   (drama) 1890

Main-Travelled Roads: Six Mississippi Valley Stories (short stories) 1891

A Member of the Third House: A Dramatic Story   (novel) 1892

A Spoil of Office: A Story of the Modern West   (novel) 1892

Prairie Folks   (short stories)   1893; also published with *Wayside Courtships* as *Other Main-Travelled Roads,* 1910

Prairie Songs: Being Chants Rhymed and Unrhymed of the Level Lands of the Great West   (poetry) 1893

Crumbling Idols: Twelve Essays on Art, Dealing Chiefly with Literature, Painting and the Drama   (essays) 1894

Rose of Dutcher's Coolly   (novel)   1895

Jason Edwards, an Average Man   (novel)   1897

Wayside Courtships   (short stories)   1897; also published with *Prairie Folks* as *Other Main-Travelled Roads,* 1910

Boy Life on the Prairie   (novel)   1899

The Eagle's Heart   (novel)   1900

Her Mountain Lover   (novel)   1901

The Captain of the Gray-Horse Troop: A Novel   (novel) 1902

Hesper: A Novel   (novel)   1903

The Light of the Star: A Novel   (novel)   1904

Cavanagh, Forest Ranger: A Romance of the Mountain West   (novel)   1910

A Son of the Middle Border   (autobiography)   1917

A Daughter of the Middle Border   (autobiography)   1921

The Book of the American Indian   (biography and short stories)   1923

Trail-Makers of the Middle Border   (autobiography)   1926

Back-Trailers from the Middle Border   (autobiography) 1928

Roadside Meetings   (autobiography)   1930

WILLIAM DEAN HOWELLS (essay date 1891)

[The stories in *Main-Travelled Roads*] are full of the bitter and burning dust, the foul and trampled slush of the common avenues of life: the life of the men who hopelessly and cheerlessly make the wealth that enriches the alien and the idler, and impoverishes the producer. If any one is still at a loss to account for that uprising of the farmers in the West, which is the translation of the Peasants' War into modern and republican terms, let him read *Main-Travelled Roads* and he will begin to understand, unless, indeed, Mr. Garland is painting the exceptional rather than the average. The stories are full of those gaunt, grim, sordid, pathetic, ferocious figures, whom our satirists find so easy to caricature as Hayseeds, and whose blind groping for fairer conditions is so grotesque to the newspapers and so menacing to the politicians. They feel that something is wrong, and they know that the wrong is not theirs. The type caught in Mr. Garland's book is not pretty: it is ugly and often ridiculous; but it is heart-breaking in its rude despair. The story of a farm mortgage as it is told in the powerful sketch "Under the Lion's Paw" is a lesson in political economy, as well as a tragedy of the darkest cast. "The Return of the Private" is a satire of the keenest edge, as well as a tender and mournful idyl of the unknown soldier who comes back after the war . . . with no stake in the country he has helped to make safe and rich but the poor man's chance to snatch an uncertain subsistence from the furrows he left for the battle-field. "Up the Coulé," however, is the story which most pitilessly of all accuses our vaunted conditions, wherein every man has the chance to rise above his brother and make himself richer than his fellows. It shows us once for all what the risen man may be, and portrays in his good-natured selfishness and indifference that favorite ideal of our system. . . . [It] is the allegory of the whole world's civilization: the upper dog and the under dog are everywhere, and the under dog nowhere likes it.

But the allegorical effects are not the primary intent of Mr. Garland's work: [*Main-Travelled Roads*] is a work of art, first of all, and we think of fine art; though the material will strike many gentilities as coarse and common. In one of the stories, "Among the Corn Rows," there is a good deal of burly, broad-shouldered humor of a fresh and native kind; in "Mrs. Ripley's Trip" is a delicate touch, like that of Miss Wilkins; but Mr. Garland's touches are his own, here and elsewhere. He has a certain harshness and bluntness, an indifference to the more delicate charms of style; and he has still to learn that though the thistle is full of an unrecognized poetry, the rose has a poetry too, that even over-praise cannot spoil. But he has a fine courage to leave a fact with the reader, ungarnished and unvarnished, which is almost the rarest trait in an Anglo-Saxon writer, so infantile and feeble is the custom of our art; and this attains tragical sublimity in the opening sketch, "A Branch Road," where the lover who has quarrelled with his betrothed comes back to find her mismated and miserable, such a farm wife as Mr. Garland has alone dared to draw, and tempts the broken-hearted drudge away from her loveless home. It is all morally wrong, but the author leaves you to say that yourself. He knows that his business was with those two people, their passions and their probabilities. He shows them such as the newspapers know them. (pp. 639-40)

William Dean Howells, "Editor's Study," in Harper's New Monthly Magazine *(copyright, 1891, by Harper and Brothers), Vol. LXXXIII, No. CCCCXCVI, September, 1891, pp. 638-42.**

(essay date 1892)

The flavor of the soil which Mr. Garland unquestionably succeeds in giving to his stories of Western life is so palpably due to the bludgeon-like quality of his realism that what little charm might be got from the commonplace histories of his Bradley Talcotts and Bert Gearhearts is entirely lost. . . . There is a directness about the telling, however, and an evidence in them that they are true to the facts as the author has seen them, which makes them readable. But being true to facts is not, necessarily, being true to nature. Facts do not make art, nor do they make literature; and if the novelist—who, in telling a story which is a fiction, acknowledges to a certain extent this truism—insists upon furnishing that story with but a setting of bare facts, he must not be disappointed if even their completeness and accuracy fail to entitle his work to be called literature. One notices, too, a certain carelessness in Mr. Garland's workmanship which might lead one to distrust the accuracy of his observations without shaking one's faith in his honesty. (p. 262)

"Recent Novels: 'A Spoil of Office: A Story of the Modern West'," in The Nation *(copyright 1892 The Nation Associates, Inc.), Vol. LV, No. 1423, October 6, 1892, pp. 262-64**

ROYAL CORTISSOZ (essay date 1895)

[*Crumbling Idols*] should have been printed on birch bark and bound in butternut homespun, and should have had for cover design a dynamite bomb, say, with sputtering fire tipped fuse: for the essays which it contained were so many explosions of literary Jingoism and anarchy. In an ill-ordered if forcible way, they presented [Mr. Hamlin Garland's] views of the duty of the coming American writer. This promising young author ought, he said, utterly to abjure all models and masters, all "Good" English, falsely so-called, all rhetorical rules, and be his own spontaneous, untrammeled self. He should be, in short, a literary anarchist. He ought also—although his spontaneous self, if untrammeled, might wish to do quite other things—to saturate himself with local color, and in a new American way and in a new American language celebrate the plain American people. He should be a literary Jingo, and bear ever on his shoulder a banner inscribed, "Our literature—right or wrong." And Mr. Garland was so sure that the coming American writer would be the anarchist he described that, with magnificent *naivete*, he entitled his volume *Crumbling Idols*. (p. 840)

[If] extravagant in manner and trite in substance, *Crumbling Idols* has for the critic the merit of revealing with considerable distinctness what manner of man is behind it. . . . And really, the book reveals a man who, if deficient in critical power and in culture, has certain admirable qualities. True, these are moral rather than literary, but they may mean much to the future of his art. There is revealed, for example, a splendid faith in America as a field for genuine literary art as opposed to literary exploitation, a deeply rooted interest in the common people and love for them, an enthusiastic devotion to what we must yet call his work rather than his art, and an almost Napoleonic self-confidence. He who has those qualities to reinforce a true literary gift—Mr. Garland has that—may hope, if not led by his own self-will and contempt of guidance into futile wanderings in wrong paths, to go far. Pondering these qualities, one begins to understand how the same author could produce so foolish a book as *Crumbling Idols* and so admirable a one as *Main-Travelled Roads*. (p. 841)

Main-Travelled Roads, his first and best book, has faults enough. It is partly his lack of training, partly his scorn of refinements, which make the sturdy, homespun style, generally so effective, always rough, and often perversely incorrect. The same reasons may serve to account for the sometimes unnecessarily frank, sometimes even brutal realism. His own personality explains the prejudiced point of view: the sketches are only too plainly biased by the anger at circumstances felt by a young man, ambitious of the intellectual life, who is forced into hard, uncongenial physical labor. . . . It is difficult to escape the conviction that, in some measure, Mr. Garland has without adequate warrant read into the minds of others the same fierce hatred for the discomforts of the life which he, with his artistic temperament, was bound to feel. The controversial note is also subtly struck in the sketches; the reader has an uneasy, ever-present feeling that they are written not so much for him as at him. "Here is a pretty state of affairs," they seem to say between all their lines, "for which our author holds you personally responsible. What are you going to do about it?" When an argument is thus suggested, the reader loses faith a little. Instinctively he puts himself on his guard, and warns himself that these are the adduced examples of a controversialist, and may accordingly be overcolored. In the work of a less obviously sincere writer, of a writer with less knowledge of his subject and less native power, these faults would work sad havoc. The best proof of the solid merit of *Main-Travelled Roads* is that, in spite of all, it convinces the reader, willy-nilly, of its general fidelity to fact, and lifts him off his critical feet by its sheer brute force. It is his highest achievement, and, ominously, also his first. It shows strikingly what may be done by strong native talent working with the help of a single sound formula for effective composition; for here most emphatically Mr. Garland has written of what he knows. The book is unique in American literature; passionate, vivid, written with absolute certainty of touch, native and virile as the red man.

It is appropriate to return for a moment to *Crumbling Idols*. In that volume, Mr. Garland, with an appearance of infallibility a pope might envy, predicts the future of American fiction. He declares it will not—with the air of one who says it shall not—be national, but local. Each writer will—that is to say, shall—tell what he knows of the special life into which he is born. . . . It is interesting to note that this prophecy of Mr. Garland's, thus found to be supported by fact, is based upon the one sound dictum, "Write of what you know," which is discoverable in his literary philosophy. It is also interesting—although the fact may lack significance—to observe that the prediction was written after the publication of *A Spoil of Office*.

In theme this book—the pun in the title is pitiable—is magnificent. He who will embody in a noble fiction, as Mr. Garland has here tried to do, the career of a Western farmhand, from the time of his early struggles for an education to the time of his election to the national legislature, will achieve, as nearly as any one, the great American novel. No career could be more typically American. None needs

for its description a wider range of intimate knowledge of American life, a greater degree or maturity of literary power. There the theme lies, obvious, tempting, impossible, awaiting, like Arthur's sword, the hand of the master. Mr. Garland has attempted it. He would better have emulated the temerity of angles. There is no need to say he has failed. That he should do so was inevitable. He is too young, too immature in his art, too limited in his knowledge of life, to treat well so all embracing a topic. By his own theory, he should not have undertaken the task. He rails at those authors who write of foreign lands of which, as he says, their knowledge can be only that of tourists. But one may be a tourist in his own country. Mr. Garland knows no more of Washington than the American traveler of an observing habit knows of London, no more of politicians than the traveler of Englishmen. He can write of them only from the outside. As in other instances he has illustrated by his success the value of the one literary truth he has perceived clearly. Write of what you know, so here he illustrates it by his failure. And, with singular accuracy of coincidence, the work begins to grow less. It opens buoyantly and successfully with the easy mastery of detail and the strength of handling so conspicuous in *Main-Travelled Roads*. But where he ceases to deal with the familiar farm, the academy, the life and politics of the county-seat, and tries to carry his hero with as firm and competent a hand into the national legislature at Washington, his sureness of touch vanishes, he begins to be at a loss, he unmistakably fumbles. Denunciation takes the place of delineation. Losing interest in a plot and in characters he can no longer bring bravely off, he yields to his controversial instincts, and makes of his hero—whom he starts with a very distinct personality—a characterless mouthpiece for vague charges of corruption in the "regular parties," for appeals to the farmers to rise and for expositions of the beauties of "populism" and woman suffrage. Plot and characters dissolve, and at the end, the book has no firmer consistency than the weak reveries of a political visionary. (pp. 842-43)

Royal Cortissoz, "New Figures in Literature and Art: Hamlin Garland," in The Atlantic Monthly *(copyright © 1895 by The Atlantic Monthly Company, Boston, Mass.), Vol. LXXVI, No. CCCCLVIII, December, 1895, pp. 840-44.*

H. L. MENCKEN (essay date 1919)

American criticism, which always mistakes a poignant document for esthetic form and organization, greeted [Garland's] moral volumes as works of art, and so Garland found himself an accepted artist. No more grotesque miscasting of a diligent and worthy man is recorded in profane history. He had no more feeling for the intrinsic dignity of beauty, no more comprehension of it as a thing in itself, than a policeman. He was a moralist endeavoring ineptly to translate his messianic passion into esthetic terms, and always failing. "A Son of the Middle Border," undoubtedly the best of all his books, projects his failure brilliantly. It is, in substance, a document of considerable value—a naïve and often highly illuminating contribution to the history of the American peasantry. It is, in form, a thoroughly third-rate piece of writing—amateurish, flat, banal, repellent. Garland got facts into it; he got the relentless sincerity of the rustic Puritan; he got a sort of evangelical passion. But he couldn't get any charm. He couldn't get any beauty.

In such a career, as in such a book, there is something profoundly pathetic. One follows the progress of the man with a constant sense that he was steering by faulty compasses, that fate led him into paths too steep and rocky—nay, too dark and lovely—for him. An awareness of beauty was there, and a wistful desire to embrace it, but the confident gusto of the artist was always lacking. What one encountered in its place was the enthusiasm of the pedagogue, the desire to yank the world up to the soaring Methodist level, the hot yearning to displace old ideas with new ideas, and usually much worse ideas. . . . The natural goal of the man was the evangelical stump. . . . He should have gone back to the saleratus belt, taken to the chautauquas, preached his foreordained perunas, got himself into Congress, and so helped to save the Republic from the demons that beset it. What a gladiator he would have made against the White Slave Traffic, the Rum Demon, the Kaiser! (pp. 498-99)

> *H. L. Mencken, "Hamlin Garland" (originally published as "Six Members of the Institute," in his* Prejudices: First Series, Knopf, 1919), in his A Mencken Chrestomathy *(copyright 1920 by Alfred A. Knopf, Inc.; and renewed 1948 by H. L. Mencken; reprinted by permission of Alfred A. Knopf, Inc.),* Knopf, 1949, pp. 498-500).

CARL VAN DOREN (essay date 1922)

[Before the 1880s,] the prairies and the plains had depended almost wholly upon romance—and that often of the cheapest sort—for their literary reputation; Mr. Garland, who had tested at first hand the innumerable hardships of such a life, became articulate through his dissent from average notions about the pioneer. (p. 39)

It throws a strong light upon the progress of American society and literature during the past generation to point out that the service recently performed by *Main Street* was, in its fashion, performed thirty years ago by *Main-Travelled Roads*. Each book challenges the myth of the rural beauties and the rural virtues; but whereas Sinclair Lewis, in an intellectual and satiric age, charges that the villagers are dull, Mr. Garland, in a moral and pathetic age, charged that the farmers were oppressed. His men wrestle fearfully with sod and mud and drought and blizzard, goaded by mortgages which may at almost any moment snatch away all that labor and parsimony have stored up. His women, endowed with no matter what initial hopes or charms, are sacrificed to overwork and deprivations and drag out maturity and old age on the weariest treadmill. The pressure of life is simply too heavy to be borne except by the ruthless or the crafty. Mr. Garland, though nourished on the popular legend of the frontier, had come to feel that the "song of emigration had been, in effect, the hymn of fugitives." Illusion no less than reality had tempted Americans toward their far frontiers, and the enormous mass, once under way, had rolled stubbornly westward, crushing all its members who might desire to hesitate or to reflect.

The romancers had studied the progress of the frontier in the lives of its victors; Mr. Garland studied it in the lives of its victims. . . . Mr. Garland told his early stories in the strong, level, ominous language of a man who had observed much but chose to write little. Not his words but the overtones vibrating through them cry out that the earth and the fruits of the earth belong to all men and yet a few of them have turned tiger or dog or jackal and snatched what is precious for themselves while their fellows starve and freeze. Insoluble as are the dilemmas he propounded and tense and unrelieved as were his accusations, he stood in his methods

nearer, say, to the humane Millet than to the angry Zola. There is a clear, high splendor about his landscapes; youth and love on his desolate plains, as well as anywhere, can find glory in the most difficult existence; he might strip particular lives relentlessly bare but he no less relentlessly clung to the conviction that human life has an inalienable dignity which is deeper than any glamor goes and can survive the loss of all its trappings.

Why did Mr. Garland not equal the intellectual and artistic success of *Main-Travelled Roads, Prairie Folks,* and *Rose of Dutcher's Coolly* for a quarter of a century? At the outset he had passion, knowledge, industry, doctrine, approbation, and he labored hard at enlarging the sagas of which these books were the center. Yet *Jason Edwards, A Spoil of Office, A Member of the Third House* are dim names and the Far Western tales which succeeded them grow too rapidly less impressive as they grow older. . . . In that first brilliant cycle of stories this downright pioneer worked with the material which of all materials he knew best and over which his imagination played most eagerly. From them, however, he turned to pleas for the single tax and to exposures of legislative corruption and imbecility about which he neither knew nor cared so much as he knew and cared about the actual lives of working farmers. His imagination, whatever his zeal might do in these different surroundings, would not come to the old point of incandescence.

Instead, however, of diagnosing his case correctly Mr. Garland followed the false light of local color to the Rocky Mountains and began the series of romantic narratives which further interrupted his true growth and, gradually, his true fame. He who had grimly refused to lend his voice to the chorus chanting the popular legend of the frontier in which he had grown up and who had studied the deceptive picture not as a visitor but as a native, now became himself a visiting enthusiast for the "high trails" and let himself be roused by a fervor sufficiently like that from which he had earlier dissented. (pp. 40-4)

[The] prime penalty of his [new] school overtook him: he came to lay so much emphasis upon outward manners that he let his plots and characters fall into routine and formula. The novels of his middle period—such as *Her Mountain Lover, The Captain of the Gray-Horse Troop, Hesper, The Light of the Star, Cavanagh, Forest Ranger*—too frequently recur to the romantic theme of a love uniting some powerful, uneducated frontiersman and some girl from a politer neighborhood. Pioneer and lady are always almost the same pair in varying costumes; the stories harp upon the praise of plains and mountains and the scorn of cities and civilization. These romances, much value as they have as documents and will long continue to have, must be said to exhibit the frontier as self-conscious, obstreperous, given to insisting upon its difference from the rest of the world. In ordinary human intercourse such insistence eventually becomes tiresome; in literature no less than in life there is a time to remember local traits and a time to forget them in concerns more universal.

What concerns of Mr. Garland's were universal became evident when he published *A Son of the Middle Border.* His enthusiasms might be romantic but his imagination was not; it was indissolubly married to his memory of actual events. The formulas of his mountain romances, having been the inventions of a mind not essentially inventive, had been at best no more than sectional; the realities of his autobiography, taking him back again to *Main-Travelled Roads* and its cycle, were personal, lyrical, and consequently universal. (pp. 44-5)

In a sense *A Son of the Middle Border* supersedes the fictive versions of the same material; they are the original documents and the *Son* the final redaction and commentary. Veracious still, the son of that border appears no longer vexed as formerly. Memory, parent of art, has at once sweetened and enlarged the scene. What has been lost of pungent vividness has its compensation in a broader, a more philosophic interpretation of the old frontier, which in this record grows to epic meanings and dimensions. Its savage hardships, though never minimized, take their due place in its powerful history; the defeat which the victims underwent cannot rob the victors of their many claims to glory. If there was little contentment in this border there was still much rapture. Such things Mr. Garland reveals without saying them too plainly: the epic qualities of his book—as in Mark Twain's *Life on the Mississippi*—lie in its implications; the tale itself is a candid narrative of his own adventures through childhood, youth, and his first literary period.

This autobiographic method, applied with success in *A Daughter of the Middle Border* to his later life in Chicago and all the regions which he visited, brings into play his higher gifts and excludes his lower. Under slight obligation to imagine, he runs slight risk of succumbing to those conventionalisms which often stiffen his work when he trusts to his imagination. Avowedly dealing with his own opinions and experiences, he is not tempted to project them, as in the novels he does somewhat too frequently, into the careers of his heroes. Dealing chiefly with action not with thought, he does not tend so much as elsewhere to solve speculative problems with sentiment instead of with reflection. In the *Son* and the *Daughter* he has the fullest chance to be autobiographic without disguise.

Here lies his best province and here appears his best art. It is an art, as he employs it, no less subtle than humane. Warm, firm flesh covers the bones of his chronology. He imparts reality to this or that occasion, like a novelist, by reciting conversation which must come from something besides bare memory. He rounds out the characters of the persons he remembers with a fulness and grace which, lifelike as his persons are, betray the habit of creating characters. He enriches his analysis of the Middle Border with sensitive descriptions of the "large, unconscious scenery" in which it transacted its affairs. If it is difficult to overprize the documentary value of his saga of the Garlands and the McClintocks and of their son who turned back on the trail, so is it difficult to overpraise the sincerity and tenderness and beauty with which the chronicle was set down. (pp. 45-7)

> *Carl Van Doren, "Argument: Hamlin Garland," in his* Contemporary American Novelists: 1900-1920 *(reprinted with permission of the Estate of Carl Van Doren; © 1922 by Macmillan Publishing Co., Inc.), Macmillan, 1922, pp. 38-47.*

VERNON LOUIS PARRINGTON (essay date 1930)

The romance was fading from the prairies when [Hamlin Garland] took up his pen. The Golden West of Mark Twain and the bucolic West of Whitcomb Riley had both slipped into the past and the day that was rising was to bring its discouragements that seared men's hopes as the hot winds seared the fields of rustling corn. The burdens of the western farmer were heavy on his shoulders and he could foresee no time when they would be lighter. . . . This was his land and his people. The blight laid upon men and women and children by the drab pioneer life was a familiar fact to him. . . . It was a life without grace or beauty or homely charm—a treadmill existence that got nowhere. If this were the Valley of Democracy then the democracy was a mean thing and hopeless. . . . In the completeness of his disillusion the glamour of romance was swept away and he proposed to set down in honest plain words the manner of life lived by these Middle Border folk, and the sort of earnings won by their toil. He would speak frankly out of the common bitter experience. The way to truth was the way of realism.

To a later generation that never knew the pioneer hardships of the Middle Border, Hamlin Garland seems strangely remote and old-fashioned; yet his intellectual antecedents are both ancient and honorable. At bottom he is an idealist of the old Jeffersonian breed, an earnest soul devoid of humor, who loves beauty and is mightily concerned about justice, and who, discovering little beauty and finding scant justice in the world where fate first set him, turned rebel and threw in his lot with the poor and the exploited. As a young man, consumed with a desire to speak for his people, he espoused a somber realism, for only by and through the truth could he hope to dislodge from men's minds the misconceptions that stood in the way of justice. (pp. 290-91)

And yet in the light of his total work one hesitates to call Garland a realist. Perhaps more justly he might be called a thwarted romantic, and his early rebellious realism be traced to its source in a passionate refusal to be denied the beauty that should be a portion of any rational way of living; for when later he found himself in a land of nobler horizons, unsoiled as yet by crude frontier exploitation, when he looked out upon vast mountain ranges and felt the warm sun on the gray plains, he discovered there the romance of his dreams and fell to describing the strange splendors with the gusto of a naïve romantic. *Main-Travelled Roads* and *Prairie Folks* are the protest of one oppressed with the meanness of a world that takes such heavy toll of human happiness; *Her Mountain Lover* is the expression of a frank romantic who glories in the nobility of nature's noblemen; and *The Captain of the Gray-Horse Troop* is a tale in which romance is justified by ethics and the hero discovers in the protection of a weaker race the deepest satisfactions of life. Beauty is excellent, but beauty should walk hand in hand with service—not art for art's sake, but art subdued to the higher good of humanity.

Between these extremes of a stark realism and an ethical romanticism, stand two books, separated by many years and great changes, that embody in more finished form the theme which after all was the master passion of Garland's life—the Middle Border and the rebellions it bred. *Rose of Dutcher's Coolly* is a full-length portrait of an idealist in revolt against the narrowness of farm life, and *A Son of the Middle Border* is an idyll of the past, autobiography done in mellower years when the passions of youth have been subdued to less exigent demands. These books, together with the sketches of *Main-Travelled Roads* and the militant critical theory of *Crumbling Idols*, contain pretty much the whole of Hamlin Garland that after years have cared to remember—the saga of the Middle Border in the days of its great rebellion when the earlier hopes of boundless prosperity were turning to ashes in the mouth. (pp. 291-92)

It is the agrarian background of Garland's mind that makes him seem old-fashioned to a generation that has forgotten the agrarian roots of our past growth. He was so deeply colored by this earlier native America that he never outgrew it; and when the Populistic revolt had died down, when this last organized agrarian rebellion against the exploiting middle class had become only an episode in our history, he had outlived his day. He was too deeply stirred by Whitman's romantic faith in democracy, too narrowly a disciple of Henry George's Jeffersonian economics, to fit into an industrializing America. Despite his discipleship to European realism he refused to go with the group of young left-wing naturalists who were boldly venturing on new ways of fiction. He would not follow the path of naturalism. . . . [He] would reject the somber, mechanistic background of naturalist thought. He had learned his science of the Victorian evolutionists, with their grandiose conception of a far-flung beneficent progress from the homogeneous to the heterogeneous, and the backgrounds of his mind were radiant with promise. Neither a mechanistic science nor a regimented industrialism had risen in his outlook to bank the fires of his hope. No impersonal determinism had chilled his belief in man as a free-will agent in a moral universe. . . . Like a French romantic of a hundred years before, he remained a confirmed optimist who believed that the future will correct the mistakes of the past, and the peace and beauty for which the human race longs lie immediately ahead. The art of the young man was becoming old-fashioned in the world of Stephen Crane; his ideals were Victorian. . . . And so after the agrarian revolt had failed and America lay fat and contented in the lap of McKinley prosperity, he found himself a man without a country, an alien in an industrializing order, and he turned away to the newer West and the romance he had always sought. While America was driving towards regimentation he traveled backward in time to recover a vanishing world of individualism, and the distance rapidly widened between them.

In those romantic wanderings through Colorado and California and into the far Northwest he found a new interest in the frontiersman's exploitation of the Indian, and in *The Captain of the Gray-Horse Troop* and *The Eagle Heart* he has wedded his social ethics to French romanticism, and endowed man in a state of nature with exalted social responsibilities. The old theme is dressed in new clothes and Captain Curtis of the Gray-Horse Troop becomes an Indian agent fighting the lawless and cruel encroachment of the frontiersmen upon the Indian rights; but the theme remains. Garland hated the frontier as fiercely as Cooper hated it, and like him he loved the clean free spaces; but when after his long and somewhat futile rambles he returned to the Middle Border, he found there a new light upon the familiar fields and in that light he wrote his saga of the Garlands and the McClintocks. This was to be his great bequest to American letters. To have sought the spirit of the Middle Border in its hopes and its defeat, to have written the history of the generation that swept across the western prairies, is to compress within covers a great movement and a great experience—one of the significant chapters in our total American history. (pp. 299-300)

Vernon Louis Parrington, "Literature and the Middle Border," in his Main Currents in American Thought: The Beginnings of Critical Realism in America, 1860-1920, *Vol. 3 (copyright 1930 by Harcourt Brace Jovanovich; reprinted by permission of the publisher), Harcourt, 1930, pp. 288-300.**

SINCLAIR LEWIS (essay date 1930)

It was with the emergence of William Dean Howells that we first began to have something like a [national literary] standard, and a very bad standard it was.

Mr. Howells was one of the gentlest, sweetest, and most honest of men, but he had the code of a pious old maid whose greatest delight was to have tea at the vicarage. He abhorred not only profanity and obscenity but all of what H. G. Wells has called "the jolly coarseness of life." In his fantastic vision of life, which he innocently conceived to be realistic, farmers and seamen and factory-hands might exist, but the farmer must never be covered with muck, the seaman must never roll out bawdy chanteys, the factory-hand must be thankful to his good employer, and all of them must long for the opportunity to visit Florence and smile gently at the quaintness of the beggars. (pp. 14-15)

He was actually able to tame Mark Twain, perhaps the greatest of our writers, and to put that fiery old savage into an intellectual frock coat and top hat. His influence is not altogether gone today. He is still worshipped by Hamlin Garland, an author who should in every way have been greater than Howells but who under Howells' influence was changed from a harsh and magnificent realist into a genial and insignificant lecturer. Mr. Garland is, so far as we have one, the dean of American letters today, and as our dean, he is alarmed by all of the younger writers who are so lacking in taste as to suggest that men and women do not always love in accordance with the prayer-book, and that common people sometimes use language which would be inappropriate at a women's literary club on Main Street. Yet this same Hamlin Garland, as a young man, before he had gone to Boston and become cultured and Howellized, wrote two most valiant and revelatory works of realism, *Main-Travelled Roads* and *Rose of Dutcher's Coolly.*

I read them as a boy in a prairie village in Minnesota—just such an environment as was described in Mr. Garland's tales. They were vastly exciting to me. I had realized in reading Balzac and Dickens that it was possible to describe French and English common people as one actually saw them. But it had never occurred to me that one might without indecency write of the people of Sauk Centre, Minnesota, as one felt about them. Our fictional tradition, you see, was that all of us in Midwestern villages were altogether noble and happy; that not one of us would exchange the neighborly bliss of living on Main Street for the heathen gaudiness of New York or Paris or Stockholm. But in Mr. Garland's *Main-Travelled Roads* I discovered that there was one man who believed that Midwestern peasants were sometimes bewildered and hungry and vile—and heroic. And, given this vision, I was released; I could write of life as living life.

I am afraid that Mr. Garland would not be pleased but acutely annoyed to know that he made it possible for me to write of America as I see it, and not as Mr. William Dean Howells so sunnily saw it. And it is his tragedy, it is a completely revelatory American tragedy, that in our land of freedom, men like Garland, who first blast the roads to freedom, become themselves the most bound. (pp. 15-16)

> *Sinclair Lewis, "The American Fear in Literature" (originally his Nobel Prize address, 1930), in his* The Man from Main Street: Selected Essays and Other Writings, 1904-1950, *edited by Harry E. Maule and Melville H. Cane (copyright © 1953 by the Estate of Sinclair Lewis; reprinted by permission of Random House, Inc.), Random House, 1953, pp. 3-17.**

ALFRED KAZIN   (essay date 1942)

Garland, who was in a sense the victim of his own reputation, gloried in the illusion that he was an "artist," a "veritist." The word flowed easily; he even dedicated his *Crumbling Idols* to "the men and women of America who have the courage to be artists." Yet what a depressing career Garland's was! With his talk of "veritism," his aggressive intensity, his passionate espousal of realism long before the word became fashionable, he performed yeoman labor; but to the end of his life, when he had ceased to write his interminable autobiography and sat in the Hollywood sun composing books on spiritualism, he was essentially a half-writer, a sloganeer of literature who had worked himself so snugly into the formative history of realism that one could barely distinguish between his place in the movement and his palpable contributions to it. He was to an extraordinary degree the Theodore Roosevelt of modern literature, the booster who campaigned so fiercely for freedom, identified himself with realism so completely, that whatever his campaign services, his manifesto, his friendships, his eagerness, one forgot that Garland had a dreary mind and a pedestrian talent.

What gave Garland his importance from the first was the remarkable—and perhaps once justified—extent to which he had dramatized his own life in terms of the battle for realism. To the nineties he became the "realistic young man," the active protagonist of the new spirit.... Garland's work became one long autobiography, and as it became explicit autobiography it lost the explicit intention which lies at the base of art. That is not to say that he contributed less than others in his generation; he contributed more; but his work became increasingly irrelevant to the art of realism and suggested that his service had been to identify himself with the creed and the courage of realism. For Garland's was surely not the imagination of a mature artist; his novels were often embarrassing, and his now famous first short stories painstakingly honest but narrow. He was not a critic, not a polemicist, not a teacher; *Crumbling Idols* . . . is one of the windiest critical documents of the new era. Yet precisely because it was hortatory and shrill, Garland acted as the bandmaster of realism. His service was to announce its coming, to suggest its emotional importance and its sterling Americanism, to open the common mind to vistas of nationalism, freedom, and democracy in which Lincoln and Ibsen, Howells and the Declaration of Independence, were somehow commingled.

Unlike Howells and Frank Norris, the other two pioneer theorists of American realism, Garland had very little knowledge of its European counterpart and was not above vulgar references to "imitative English sensationalism and sterile French sexualism." What he saw in realism was utterly remote from its possibilities as a craft, or even as a

philosophy of letters. He believed it to be a guide to action, a kind of Utopian literary Socialism, a rhetorical device by which to awaken the dormant energies of writers to the native life they knew. The significance of Garland's career is a nationalistic one; he had an expansive Whitmanesque sense of democratic solidarity in literature.... In his mind realism was not a literary counterpart of Populism; it actually was Populism. He reduced the innumerable complexities of taste and form and experience to a class struggle between the burly West and the decadent East. Realism stood for "progress"; romanticism—how much of a romanticist Garland was himself he never knew—for reaction; realism signified democracy, romanticism aristocracy. So the American tyro who had everything to learn from the European example ended by denouncing in vague incendiary belligerence the subtleties and insights he needed most. (pp. 36-7)

> *Alfred Kazin, "The Opening Struggle for Realism," in his* On Native Grounds: An Interpretation of Modern American Prose Literature *(copyright 1942, 1970, by Alfred Kazin; reprinted by permission of Harcourt Brace Jovanovich, Inc.), Reynal & Hitchcock, 1942, pp. 3-50.**

ROBERT E. SPILLER   (essay date 1952)

[With the manifesto *Crumbling Idols*,] Garland joined a distinguished company. His was but one more of those declarations of independence by which American literary history has consistently marked out its course. Emerson's "American Scholar" address and Whitman's first preface to *Leaves of Grass* were by then already classic. The voices of later literary radicals like H. L. Mencken, Van Wyck Brooks, and Thomas Wolfe were yet to be heard. Like all these others, past and to come, Garland saw the central issues of his time clearly and stated them bluntly, without benefit of logic and with enough repetition for emphasis. His *Crumbling Idols* defines clearly the beginning of that literary movement which appeared first in the 1890's, paused for a decade, and reached its climax in the 1920's.

Garland's revolt was the perennial protest of youth against age, of the future against the past; but in 1893, when the nation was stretching out culturally as well as economically to its full continental limits, it was also the West in revolt from the East. The literary radicals of the 1890's could set the terms of their quarrel on any one or more of a number of levels: as the Middle Border *vs.* the effete Atlantic Seaboard, as realism *vs.* romanticism, as a provincialism that delighted in "local color" *vs.* a colonialism that forever remembered Britain, or as the evolutionary determinism of Spencer *vs.* the idealism of Emerson. Garland's protest was on all of these levels at once. (pp. ii-iii)

[Garland] saw man as a product of environmental forces beyond his control, but he also believed that, by identifying himself with social change, the writer could regain his lost individualism. He had already allied himself with the current radical movements—the granger, populist, and feminist —and was writing stories to illustrate their principles. Individualism in the old and absolute sense of Thoreau and Emerson was virtually dead because the romantic principles upon which it was based had become obsolete; the new individualism was to be relativist, open-minded, exploratory, realistic. (pp. iii-iv)

[Garland recognized] the inadequacy of a literary philosophy that left the artist a passive recorder of objective facts. In Véron's *Aesthetics* the younger man had found a new term which seemed more nearly adequate to his needs: "Veritism," or the faithful recording of *truth* rather than mere fact. The difference between realism and veritism in literature was exactly that between realism and impressionism in painting, and much of the value of Garland's essay lies in his comparative treatment of the movement in the two arts. In realism the artist is faithfully recording a set of facts outside his personal jurisdiction; in impressionism, the artist is giving full rein to his perceptions and sensibilities and is recording, equally faithfully, his subjective response to a set of apparent facts which might or might not be universally true. With the transfer of the right of choice from the material to the artist, modern art assumed that it was approaching closer to the core of truth, but it was actually taking a long step toward the complete divorce from life which the abstractionist art of today has achieved. It was exactly on this point that Garland and [William Dean] Howells differed. Garland's plea for impressionism in literature and art (we can safely forget his alternative term, veritism) was answered by the tales of Stephen Crane and Henry James with much more artistry than he himself could manage, but no one at that time defined the issue as sharply as he did.

The subjective and analytic character of much twentieth-century literature can be understood much more fully if it is related to impressionism and the movement toward abstraction rather than only to a supposedly deepening and expanding "realism." Apparently the young radical did not realize the full import of his radicalism, for his subsequent literary career is the history of a return to the idols which for him did not crumble. What happened to Garland later is not important; in time the idols did crumble for American writers, and the subjective symbolism of O'Neill, Eliot, Hemingway, and Faulkner created a literary movement that went far beyond anything the young Garland dreamed, even though it followed, in the main, the path which his book suggested. (pp. iv-vi)

> *Robert E. Spiller, in his introduction to* Crumbling
> Idols *by Hamlin Garland, Scholars' Facsimiles &
> Reprints, 1952, pp. i-viii.*

CHARLES CHILD WALCUTT   (essay date 1956)

Garland struggled with inadequate technique and irreconcilable ideas in a manner that is both interesting and painful to behold. (p. 54)

Garland's early sketches [collected in *Main-Traveled Roads* and *Prairie Folks*] deal with the influence of environment in the lives of frontier farmers. They present the effects of long hours, grim toil, and spiritual barrenness on people who live without benefit of culture.... The foil against which these hard gems of determinism shine is the moral order in which Garland angrily lives. Somebody, we feel, is to blame for these wasted lives.... Something should be done by the rich East to ease the burden on those who win the West.... Men should not have to suffer such privation. And so on. There is a quality of reproach and indignation in every line.

Whenever we see a powerful assertion of determinism we know that the writer is working under emotional stress. Determinism is not, in fiction, objective, although it certainly is objective in theory. These early sketches put the reader in an emotional straitjacket. Every line asserts the need to be free. They press out against the confining determinism in which they are phrased. There is emotional appropriateness in this condition, moreover, for the confinement of the sketches, conveyed through a sense of tension and exasperation, expresses the writer's revolt against whatever order permits such conditions.

These sketches are tight and confining in the further sense that they do not move, and their aesthetic effect lies in this painful constriction, it expresses a sort of outraged, speechless indignation that such things can be. They do not move because the effect of environment has already asserted itself; the characters are trapped. The content is retrospective, looking back on what has happened, on the one chance to escape that was missed ten years ago, on the aspirations of youth now lost. The future is confined by a blank wall. The form of such a piece is perfect; it creates and it embodies its meaning.

But what happens when Garland introduces, as he occasionally does, movement? Then we have something like "A Branch Road," a story in which the hero loses his fiancée because of his own bad temper in prolonging a misunderstanding, disappears into the West for seven years, and returns to find the girl married to a brutal and tyrannical oaf. The bitterness of her life and the sense of tragic destiny which forges a dark chain of necessity from a single error are powerfully evoked. Garland has an insight here which could be left to speak for itself as a tragic fact of experience, but he cannot stop. The returning lover paints a dazzling word-picture of love, travel, luxury, Europe (he has of course made his fortune in the intervening years), and while the vicious husband is driving his old father to church the hero carries off the wife and her babe to a brave new world of bliss.

It is scarcely necessary to say that we expect some degree of wisdom, rather than daydreams, from a serious artist; we expect that he will pursue the logic of his situations to the bitter end. Garland's determinism, however, is pure protest; it is his mode of defining the injustice that has scarred his own soul; and it is not surprising that he should jump from definition to defiance by writing a story in which the iron chain is broken.

A more consistent working out of a situation appears in "Under the Lion's Paw," from *Main-Traveled Roads*. This, Garland's best known short story, deals with a tenant farmer who works like a galley slave for three years improving a run-down farm which he hopes to buy for twenty-five hundred dollars. When his heroic labors have brought him to the point of being successful, the owner of the farm tells him that the price is now fifty-five hundred dollars: "It was all run down then; now it's in good shape. You've laid out fifteen hundred dollars in improvements, according to your own story."... [The] effect of the story is not controlled by its "naturalism" because the closing scene makes the landowner unnaturally vicious. He is not forced by economic necessity to ruin the poor farmer's life.... He squeezes his victim, it appears, because he is an innately evil man, a hateful character who enjoys making others suffer. A modern psychologist would undertake to account for this landowner's personality, perhaps as a product of the same grinding and rapacious milieu which makes his victim so appallingly energetic, but Garland only gives him to us as a bad man who must be indignantly denounced.

The reader is confused by the emotional and logical inconsistencies of this story; the idea of very good and very bad people is not placed in any clear relation to the notion of economic determinism, and one is uncertain how to react. (pp. 54-7)

The exposure of Garland's inconsistencies will not appear uncharitable if the reader sees in them the impassable abyss that yawned between the genteel tradition and the first stirrings of naturalistic theory in our literature. Because writers like Garland were unsophisticated and therefore completely at the mercy of the literary techniques which they absorbed from their Victorian world, it is understandable that they could not integrate the new ideas into a fictional structure.... [If] the action that is used comes from the literary forms and attitudes of a sentimental tradition, it will inevitably, as it has with Garland, determine the quality of its subject matter. Garland's rather pathetic failures are painful first tries to break away from the genteel tradition, attempts to cross the abyss that had to be made by someone. Garland had the idea, if not the style and technique to make them live. (pp. 62-3)

> *Charles Child Walcutt, "Adumbrations: Harold Frederic and Hamlin Garland," in his* American Literary Naturalism, a Divided Stream *(© 1956, University of Minnesota), University of Minnesota Press, Minneapolis, 1956, pp. 45-65.**

CARLIN T. KINDILIEN (essay date 1956)

In 1887, after three years in the East, Hamlin Garland returned to South Dakota to visit his parents and to be awakened to the meanness of the life in which he had grown up.... It was this West which furnished the material for his best writing ... and it was this West which was responsible for the finest volume of poems written about the region during the Nineties—Garland's *Prairie Songs*.... The background of this book was the mixture of the poet's love of the prairies and his hatred of the existence which they supported: a personal balance which he tried to maintain in his most effective stories. The paradoxical scheme of values which troubled Garland grew out of the pattern of his boyhood.... He saw the conflict between his father's frontier optimism and his mother's wasting drudgery and he acquired his one great theme. The honest and sharp impressions of the farm life he had led were at the center of *Main-Travelled Roads* and *Prairie Songs*. In these songs, Garland exploited the poverty and hardship of his life as well as the zest of blue skies and open prairies, and he recorded the spirit of the western pioneers and the disintegration of the myth that had settled the West. For the poles of midwestern life during the Nineties, a modern reader can turn to the sentimental Indiana of James Whitcomb Riley and to the realistic Dakotas of Hamlin Garland. (p. 137)

Unfortunately, Garland's songs turned into sentimental hack work in a few efforts. He scraped the contemporary tear barrel to write of old veterans recalling the War, of a farmer homesick in the city, and even of an old man being forced out of his son's home. But these verses amount to little in the one hundred and fifty pages in which he set down his impressions of the West and its problems. It would be difficult to claim high rank for Garland as a craftsman in poetry, and it would be equally difficult to deny the significance of his poetry as a most important medium in which a modern reader can study the idyllic and terrifying American West.

The paradox of *Prairie Songs* was its blending of nostalgic and realistic moods. His nostalgia was reserved for the natural beauty of the prairie country; his realism was directed to the human beings who worked its hard dirt. When Garland wrote of the rains and the winds, the snows and dry heat, the sunsets and the fires that transformed the prairies, he wrote the best descriptive poetry of the region. The scenes which went into his poetry were ones of manifold sensory appeals.... The prairies had gone before the plows when Garland wrote, but his recollections of the scenes in which he had grown up remained intact. He reproduced these scenes in a series of descriptive poems which illustrated again the value of traditional forms in the hands of a poet who would not be a mere copyist.

For a half century Americans had reacted to the magnet of the West. A land had been settled by the pioneers who moved ever farther westward in their quest of an American Eden—a garden spot, a fulfillment of the dream as old as Plato.... Garland wrote in his poetry of the end of this romantic and savage drama.... [The] Eden had turned into a dust bowl; the myth of the garden vanished before the reality of mountains, floods, deserts, and "the fierce suns".... In the mood of *Main-Travelled Roads*, joined with a Crane-like imagery, Garland exposed the actualities of the farming life he knew. His songs became cries for the men who killed themselves in the dust on "hot red mornings" and for women who "scrubbed, suffered and died." Although Garland wanted to curb the indignation that he was expressing in his prose, he could not exclude—even in a book of "verses"—his real feelings. (pp. 138-41)

No midwestern poet of the Nineties accomplished more than Hamlin Garland. In his descriptive poetry he recorded the prairie region with a fidelity and an immediacy that set his work apart. When he turned from his own experience he wrote sentimental claptrap; when he correlated his own impressions of his region and its state of mind with an adequate form he presented a valuable poetry. In the Nineties, he was the major commentator in poetry on the social problems of the midwestern farmers. (p. 141)

> *Carlin T. Kindilien, "The Poet-Critics of Society and Religion," in his* American Poetry in the Eighteen Nineties: A Study of American Verse, 1890-1899 *(copyright 1956 by Brown University), Brown University Press, 1956, pp. 123-68.**

DONALD PIZER (essay date 1960)

During the relatively brief period of his early career Hamlin Garland produced his most distinctive work, notwithstanding the excellence of two later autobiographies, *A Son of the Middle Border* ... and *Roadside Meetings*.... A few of his short stories written during 1884-1895 will always live in American literature; a larger portion of his fiction and prose continues to be readable. But all Garland's work of his early career, published and unpublished, is of permanent value to the historian of American life and letters. For Garland was one of those in the history of literature whose ideas and activities are ultimately of more interest and worth than their literary achievements. Neither an outstanding artist nor an original mind, he had rather the capacity to reflect the most cogent intellectual, social, and aesthetic ideas of his own day while concomitantly representing the continuity of American radical individualism.

Three of the main currents of late nineteenth-century American thought appear in Garland's work and career. The theory of evolution was influencing every phase of belief; social protest was rising to meet the threat of uncontrolled industrialism and monopolism to American ideals; and local color, realism, and an increasing subjectivism were occupying the leading literary figures of the time. Garland's literary and social ideas had an evolutionary foundation. Much of his writing was affected by his participation in several of the great reform movements of the 'eighties and 'nineties. He was a major spokesman and the only aesthetician of local color, though of a local color influenced by impressionistic and realistic critical ideas.

The emotional center of reference of Garland's thought in each of these fields was the romantic individualism characteristic of a major segment of the nineteenth-century American mind. . . . Garland represents the continuation, though channeled into new patterns and practiced with new means, of this individualism. And because the freedom of the individual is perennially being oppressed or threatened or ignored, Garland was a radical, a reformer, just as Emerson and Whitman were in the same sense reformers and radicals in their attempts to state and to advocate individualistic philosophies.

Garland wanted to set men free and he strove to do so. He seized upon the evolutionary ideas of Herbert Spencer, which made individual freedom the most important product of evolutionary progress, and used them as the foundation for his social, economic-political, and aesthetic ideas. In social affairs he sought to express the right of the individual to be free from economic and social oppression in order that he might achieve the humanistic ideal of the full life. Garland was directly involved in two reform movements which epitomized the late nineteenth-century struggle for freedom of the individual—the single tax and woman's rights. In aesthetics he attempted to free the artist from the domination of the standards and the masters of the past and to encourage him to express his own emotions and beliefs. He worked out a local-color critical system which was heavily laden with impressionistic ideas and which called for the free and full expression of each artist's individuality. In all, Garland crudely, yet forcefully and coherently, adopted the currents of thought and expression vital and applicable in his own day . . . to give voice to the American dream, to the faith in individual freedom, in the capability and need of the individual to make his own way in life as fully and as best he could. (pp. 1-3)

> *Donald Pizer, in his introduction to his* Hamlin
> Garland's Early Work and Career, *University of
> California Publications in English Studies, Vol. 22
> (reprinted by permission of the University of California Press), University of California Press,
> 1960, pp. 1-3.*

H. WAYNE MORGAN   (essay date 1965)

[In *Rose of Dutcher's Coolly* Garland] showed America in microcosm in her pilgrimage from country to city, from a kind of mental slavery to the independence proclaimed by the whole generation of thinkers and reformers. He took Rose from a rustic coolly in Wisconsin to Chicago, from the intellectual poverty of rural life to an awakening to the city's riches and splendor. In her journey he developed artistically a fine fictional character and showed again, but in subtler form, the social and intellectual problems facing America. . . .

Rose of Dutcher's Coolly was filled with the tensions of adolescence, and spoke of sexual matters that Howells and other Realists shunned. Garland did not blink at rural life's seamier side. Rose knew of sex, felt it stir within her, vaguely understood that her compatriots knew it too. But the snickers, scrawlings, and innuendoes that accompanied it repelled her. (p. 96)

Determined to escape country life and the grim existence that awaited most girls, Rose went to the University of Wisconsin. One year's study showed her the distance between what she could become and what she had been. (pp. 96-7)

The last half of *Rose* dealt with her problems in adjusting to city life, of realizing that she had forsaken not merely her way of life but her family. (p. 97)

Rose of Dutcher's Coolly deserves to be better known. Though it breaks in half and is in essence two novels, its first part contains some finely constructed narrative and well-developed characters. It evokes not only a past America, but a time of life. It is full of the tensions, yearnings, and frustrations of youth and adolescence. It touches upon the force of sex in life, a surprising venture for Garland. When Garland left his milieu in the book's second half, it ceased to be real. His tone became tired and character development faltered. If *Main-Travelled Roads* was bitter, *Rose* was bittersweet. Garland was at the end of his viable career as a realistic writer. (pp. 97-8)

> *H. Wayne Morgan, "Hamlin Garland: The Rebel
> As Escapist," in his* American Writers in Rebellion: From Mark Twain to Dreiser *(reprinted by
> permission of Hill & Wang, a division of Farrar,
> Straus & Giroux, Inc.; copyright © 1965 by H.
> Wayne Morgan), Hill and Wang, 1965, pp. 76-103.*

DONALD PIZER   (essay date 1966)

A Son of the Middle Border is about the relationship of a young man to his parents, with that relationship significant not only for his personal development but for his self-discovery as a writer and for his understanding of his epoch. The conflict in the narrative is that of Garland's love for his mother and his rebellion against his father. As Garland grows to young manhood, his father represents to him pioneering and the hard work of the farm ("west" and the "plow"), while his mother represents the established life of a settled area and an appreciation of Garland's expanding intellect and ambitions ("east" and the "pen"). *A Son of the Middle Border* dramatizes Garland's polarization of his experience into opposites symbolized by his parents. The thematic strength and suggestiveness of the work derive not only from Garland's symbolic use of a pervasive family conflict but from the "plot" which grows out of this conflict. Seeking to escape from his father's dominion and from his father's ideals of the West and the plow, Garland "deserts" his mother, leaving her to his father and to the difficult life of a Western pioneer wife while he pursues a career as a student and writer in the East. Gradually he is overcome by guilt until his life in the East is controlled by his drive to "rescue" his mother—to rescue her from further hardship and, in a sense, from his father. Garland's changing relationship with his parents, from rebellion and desertion to guilt and rescue, is the narrative and emotional center of the book.

The two other primary themes of the work stem from this

center. The first deals with Garland's discovery of himself as an artist. He finds that the West is his basic subject, despite his desertion of it, and that his depiction of the West is inseparable from his rebellion against it and his guilt toward it. The second theme deals with Garland's discovery of himself as a Westerner. As the son of a pioneer, he occasionally shares in the westering spirit. But as the member of a particular pioneer family, he associates his family's failure in the West with the end of the pioneering era. Garland therefore expands his personal autobiography into an account of an epoch. He does this not by writing about the epoch but by infusing an interpretation of his age into the story of his life. (pp. 448-50)

A Son of the Middle Border contains much of the traditional subject matter of autobiography, and since the life depicted is principally that of a farmboy, and since the style and form are not difficult, the casual reader is apt to think that the work is obvious and direct. But in reality it is a book of considerable complexity, its intertwined themes becoming constantly more suggestive as the youth grows and as his mind and his world change both in reality and in his understanding of them. Part of the depth of the work lies in the fact that its themes represent some of the basic paradoxes in the relationship of most artists to their families and to their areas. Garland is the son of a pioneer who has rejected his father and his father's goals and who has deserted his mother, yet who has translated rejection and desertion into self-discovery and success. He is a Westerner who has deserted his land, yet who has discovered that he cannot and does not wish to desert it. He is the plowboy longing for books and schooling who learns that education leads him back to the subject matter of the plow. So the themes of the work turn on themselves, and one realizes at last . . . that the notes of melancholy and somberness which appear throughout the book are products of Garland's recognition that self-discovery is not happiness, though it may serve as the basis for art. . . .

A Son of the Middle Border tells not only of a son of a middle borderer. It presents history as an aspect of family history and thus invests the first with emotional depth and the second with significance. It is the work of a minor writer who had the good fortune to undertake his one major theme when his skill and insight were equal to the theme and the task. (p. 459)

> Donald Pizer, "Hamlin Garland's 'A Son of the Middle Border': An Appreciation," in South Atlantic Quarterly *(reprinted by permission of the Publisher; copyright 1966 by Duke University Press, Durham, North Carolina), Vol. 65, No. 4, Autumn, 1966, pp. 448-59.*

LARZER ZIFF   (essay date 1966)

Main-Travelled Roads was Garland's first and best book, but in its uncertain use of language it revealed the elements of its author's incapacity for the literary work he was pursuing. The lunch served the lonely farm wife in "A Day's Pleasure" is a moving symbol of the human community regularly denied her, but Garland insists on helping out the contrast inherent in the scene by calling it a "dainty luncheon." The false ring of the phrase works against the desired effect, just as, on a larger scale, does the uneven play of narration and dialogue in "A Branch Road" when Garland says of the returned lover, "As he went on his argument rose to the level of Browning's philosophy"—only

to offer as a representative statement: "God don't expect a toad to stay in a stump and starve if it can get out." The author's characterization of such homely dialogue is ludicrous not because it debases Browning's philosophy (if one happens to admire it), but because it belittles the ability of his simple tortured characters to represent their own woes and their own dignities in their own words and gestures.

In almost all his work Garland's settings and characters are resistant to the creeds he seeks to lodge with them, so that in his works of social protest he is left stating rather than dramatizing. He was seldom sure of his language. Though he could grasp the vernacular . . . he distrusted its respectability and betrayed his awe of a genteel culture by constantly resorting to constructions designed to show he was not limited by the life of which he wrote but had mastered a wider experience. So frequently Garland says not that his characters ate, but rather that they "ate of" food; and things are not like other things, they are "like unto" them. After *Main-Travelled Roads,* regardless of what else happens in a Garland fiction, the language constantly betrays the realistic subject matter by coming to its aid with injections of loftiness. When finally, in the mid-nineties, Garland settled into writing romances about life in the Rockies, this was not so much a betrayal of his promise as an acceptance of the themes for which his language was better suited. (p. 99)

> Larzer Ziff, "Crushed Yet Complacent: Hamlin Garland and Henry Blake Fuller," in his The American 1890s: Life and Times of a Lost Generation *(copyright © 1966 by Larzer Ziff; reprinted by permission of Viking Penguin Inc.),* Viking Penguin, *1966, pp. 93-119.**

JAMES K. FOLSOM   (essay date 1966)

In many ways Hamlin Garland's Indian studies are a transition between traditional and modern literary treatments of the Indian. Both "The Silent Eaters"—a fictionalized biography of Sitting Bull—and the short stories which together make up *The Book of the American Indian* . . . are written out of a feeling of indignation over unjust treatment of the Indian; and both as well have a very definite social reference which, in the weakest of the stories, deteriorates into a thinly disguised program of social action. Yet this program is significantly different from earlier fictional discussions of the Indian problem; for, as Garland sees, the problem itself has changed. No longer is it conceived in terms of how best to defeat the Indians; rather it has become the question of how best to rehabilitate a defeated enemy. (p. 149)

This is most clearly seen in "The Silent Eaters," which in format most closely resembles the escapist plot. In this biographical account of the Sioux chief Sitting Bull, Garland presents an expanded metaphor for the decline of the Sioux nation, from its early proud self-sufficiency to its final utter dependence upon the whites. Garland tells his story with considerable skill, especially when he succeeds in generalizing the character of Sitting Bull from that of a conventional "bad" Indian into a sympathetic type of the Sioux nation in general. And just here is the focus of Garland's story; for "The Silent Eaters" universalizes the particular figure of Sitting Bull into a general statement of the nature of that historic process which has inevitably ended with the triumph of the whites and the subjugation of the Indians.

Such a focus enables Garland to establish a double point of view toward his material. While he can admire Sitting Bull's courage, resourcefulness, and so on, at the same time he may consistently condemn these qualities as out of place in the white world inevitably to come. Hence Sitting Bull can be personally admired, but at the same time the position for which he stands need not be affirmed. (pp. 149-50)

The general philosophical burden of these various tales [in *The Book of the American Indian*] is that, like it or not, the Indian must change. This is emphasized by a recurrent image which is made explicit in a number of the stories, that the Indian's trial has ended, and that the white man's road is the only one left for the Indians to follow. (p. 151)

Garland's insistence upon the inevitability of change relieves him from the fictional necessity to choose sides and accept either white or red ways without qualification; he need not categorically defend or excuse either whites or Indians. Hence villains as well as heroes can be either white or red, and in fact there are many white villains in *The Book of the American Indian*. As a general rule, these white villains are missionaries, for whom Garland has little respect. . . .

Garland's white heroes are usually Indian agents and schoolteachers, whose tolerance and kindliness stand in none too subtle contrast to missionary bigotry. The agents and schoolteachers are sympathetic to those Indian ways which are not immediately harmful and do not stand in the way of the Indians' education. They view the process of education as basically one of training the Indians in the use of unfamiliar skills which he will need to survive in the white man's world. (p. 153)

Ultimately Garland's point is that the Indian can and should be allowed to have the best of both white and red worlds. . . .

This is true of all the stories in *The Book of the American Indian* with the exception of the best one, "The Story of Howling Wolf." In this somber tale the often complacent "long view" of history which justifies particular present hardship is subjected to serious qualification. When the story opens Howling Wolf hates white men because his brother had been killed for sport by cowboys seven years before. He has never forgiven the whites and has taken a vow to kill the men responsible for his brother's death, but the Indian agent manages to talk him out of his lust for vengeance. Howling Wolf is strongly influenced by the example of the Indian agent, with whom he makes friends, and, renouncing his savage ways, determines to turn himself into the kind of Indian white men will respect. (p. 154)

Howling Wolf does what a sober, industrious Indian should and gets a job hauling hides. But when he transports a wagonload of hides to town the whites laugh at him and spurn his offers of friendship. A cowboy picks a fight with him and fires a wild shot which hits another white man in the knee. The outraged citizenry assume that Howling Wolf has fired the shot, and are all for lynching him. . . . The agent's efforts to have Howling Wolf released are futile. One day Howling Wolf, who has borne up patiently throughout the whole affair, is taken from jail by the sheriff, who wants to attend a baseball game and is afraid to leave the Indian unattended. Howling Wolf thinks he is being taken to his execution, so he tries to escape; but he is apprehended by a group of cowboys who lasso him and drag him behind their horses for amusement. . . . Howling Wolf's attempt to civilize himself has ended disastrously. (pp. 154-55)

The most sobering aspect of "The Story of Howling Wolf" and what sets it apart from the other stories is Garland's conception of the limited possibilities for goodness in the nature of man. In the brutal and savage "civilized" world to which Howling Wolf is introduced, there is little room for the optimism which Garland elsewhere shows. Evil in this story is not a product of the conflict between different social values, a conflict which, the other stories lead us to believe, can be smoothed away when one set of social values disappears; rather evil is understood as an expression of the bestiality in man, and social values are not its causes but the ways in which it is made manifest in the world. To such a view history cannot possibly appear optimistic; for all hopes of meliorating human life depend upon the assumption that man's character can be changed for the better. In "The Story of Howling Wolf" such is simply not the case. The parable of history in this story resembles that in the Leatherstocking Tales. Change is certain, but it does not represent progress; history records the frustration of hope. (p. 155)

James K. Folsom, "The Vanishing American," in his The American Western Novel *(copyright © 1966 by College and University Press Services, Inc.), College & University Press, 1966, pp. 141-76.**

JAY MARTIN (essay date 1967)

[Garland shows] the characteristic tension of the regional writer—between his sense of a lost past and a present so debased that it shows no resemblance to that heroic past from which it has been severed. Garland thus, by nature and training, wrote two kinds of stories. In the one, he asserts that the present is corrupted, but, hypothesizing progress and amelioration, writes fiction of a strongly reforming character. In his other kind of writing, he rejects the present (and thus the future) in reverie for a golden day long past. With the one hand he is a realist, with the other a romanticist. These are aspects of the double vision of all regional literature. The depth of the writer's romanticism drives him to realism, in a rage to reorder his antiromantic age. Contrary to the claims of many critics that Garland fell into romance after an earlier realistic recognition of social problems in the West, it is clear that from the very beginning of his career both impulses are present and operate sometimes simultaneously, sometimes separately, in his work. (p. 125)

Jay Martin, "Paradises Lost," in his Harvests of Change: American Literature, 1865-1914 *(copyright © 1967 by Prentice-Hall, Inc.; reprinted by permission of the author), Prentice-Hall, 1967, pp. 81-164.**

EBERHARD ALSEN (essay date 1969)

A Spoil of Office is one of Hamlin Garland's least known and least appreciated works. Only a few critics have taken the trouble to analyze it, and what they have had to say about the book certainly does not encourage anyone to read it. The novel is usually described as a political tract and an artistic failure. But its flaws have been both exaggerated and misrepresented. (p. 91)

There seems to be general agreement among the book's critics . . . that *A Spoil of Office* fails for two reasons: First, because Garland was more interested in its political than in its artistic success, and second, because Garland's realism becomes unconvincing as soon as he leaves the environment of his successful middle border stories. A closer study of the book will show, however, that both charges miss the mark, and that the book's chief shortcomings lie elsewhere. Moreover, it will become apparent that *A Spoil of Office* is put together with much more thought and subtlety than its critics have been willing to see and that this somewhat offsets its shortcomings.

Too much has been made of the political propaganda in the book. As any objective reader will find, the didacticism actually does not become obtrusive until the last three chapters. . . . What moves the plot of the novel are not the political issues but Bradley Talcott's courtship of Ida Wilbur and his "rise" from hired hand to congressman.

The central theme of the novel, the success story of Bradley Talcott, is throughout connected with and dependent on the love story. It is, in fact, the love interest that gets the plot of the novel started. (pp. 96-7)

Throughout his gradual rise in politics, Bradley is actually motivated more by his desire to gain Ida's approval than by firm political convictions.

Nevertheless it is in politics that Bradley becomes a success, and this gives Garland the opportunity to take a stand on political issues. He does so for the most part without becoming overtly didactic, for he hardly ever makes Bradley his mouthpiece. Instead he expresses his political ideas through Ida Wilbur (who is, after all, a political agitator) and through other secondary characters such as Judge Brown, Cargill, and Radbourne. (pp. 97-8)

Bradley's rise in politics is, as Garland emphasizes, only an "apparent success." For it is accompanied by his gradual disenchantment with the country's political system which does not help the oppressed but rather insures the perpetuation of their misery. Bradley has risen within the structure of this system only to find that he "can't do anything" for the people he represents. His success has brought him personal benefits and he is on the verge of becoming "a spoil of office." His "rise" is therefore really a decline, and this ironic contrast of material rise and moral decline might have been suggested to Garland by Howells' novel *The Rise of Silas Lapham.*

As Garland points out, it is Ida who stops Bradley's decline by winning him over to the cause of the People's Party. . . . And it is at this point that the development of the novel's double-edged central theme reaches its climax. For this . . . also resolves the love interest, because it is here that Bradley wins Ida's love by showing her that he has not become "a spoil of office," that his office as a congressman has not made him forget the concerns of the people. With both of the primary themes thus resolved, Garland would have done well . . . to end his novel after this scene.

But instead Garland tacked on a concluding chapter. This chapter appears rather as an epilogue, since the didactic purpose here clearly overrides the logic and realism of plot and character. Garland skips the wedding of Bradley and Ida. . . . He picks up the narrative ten weeks after their marriage, only to let the newlyweds decide to separate for an indefinite time. (pp. 98-9)

The point that Garland has been trying to make throughout the novel becomes blatantly obvious in this scene when Ida silences Bradley's objections to their separation and admonishes him: "Now, we mustn't be selfish, dear." For according to Garland the misery of millions of hard-working people could be speedily alleviated if it were not for the selfishness of the office-holders and the resulting corruption in the government. And *A Spoil of Office* contrasts this selfishness with the altruism and humanitarianism of Bradley Talcott and Ida Wilbur.

It is Garland's moral idealism, then, which accounts for the weaknesses in the delineation of the characters of the novel's hero and heroine. Although it is in the concluding chapter that both Bradley and Ida become especially unconvincing, their characterization is actually overly idealized from the very beginning. (p. 99)

Bradley's superhuman goodness is matched by that of Ida, who on occasion appears even less real than Bradley. This is probably due to the circumstance that "the most wonderful charm of her personality was," as Garland says, "her complete absorption in thought" and her "ability to rise into the sexless regions of affairs and thoughts." And at one point, when Ida is explaining her theories to Bradley, Garland even suggests that "she had the effect of a statue."

And this is exactly how both central characters come across through much of the novel, as lifeless statues representing what human beings ought to be and not what they really are. It is only in the delineation of minor characters . . . that Garland matches the realism that distinguishes his portraits of the middle border characters in *Main Travelled Roads.* In the characterization of the novel's hero and heroine, however, Garland betrayed his artistic code by sacrificing realism for the sake of didacticism. And this is probably the most serious flaw in *A Spoil of Office.*

The book's lack of realism is then essentially a matter of characterization and plot motivation and not, as some critics contend, of Garland's unfamiliarity with the urban settings that he used in the later chapters. (p. 100)

If the localities and events in the Des Moines and Washington chapters appear somewhat more unreal and remote than those in the earlier Rock River chapters, then this is chiefly the result of Garland's employing Bradley Talcott's perspective as the narrative point of view throughout the novel. (p. 101)

Since Bradley feels a close personal relationship with the natural environment of rural Iowa that provides the background in the first half of *A Spoil of Office,* the descriptions of these settings reflect his attitude and are accordingly very concrete, graphic, and colorful. In Des Moines and Washington, however, Bradley does not have this direct and intimate relationship to his environment or the people associated with it. . . . If therefore many of the descriptions of locales and activities in Des Moines and Washington create an atmosphere of remoteness and unreality and read as if they had been written by someone just passing through, then this effect—intended or not—actually works well to support the thesis that Garland pursues in these chapters, namely that the country's legislature, as Radbourne puts it, "is getting farther and farther away from the people every year."

By stressing that his hero, a simple and upright man from

the rural Midwest, does not feel at home in the urban environment that provides the setting for many of the chapters in the second half of the novel, Garland underlines a theme that is characteristic of much of his fiction. This theme is the contrast and conflict between city and country, between the cultured but corrupt and materialistic city dwellers and the uneducated but honest and frugal farmers. (pp. 101-02)

In Garland's moral scheme of things, and this is evident through most of his work, the city and the East stand for corruption, materialism, and exploitation whereas the country and the West represent integrity, frugality, and productivity. It becomes clear in *A Spoil of Office* that this contrast depends on Garland's essentially romantic conception of the corrupting effects of civilization as opposed to the morally invigorating effects of nature. For according to Garland people that live close to nature are more likely to be moral than those that live away from it. The novel's hero, Bradley Talcott, epitomizes this strikingly Thoreauvian notion.

Bradley is firmly rooted to the soil. For him nature—despite its occasional harshness—is a beneficent force. Throughout the novel its beauty, vigor, and serenity give him the moral strength he needs in periods of stress. This view of nature marks a significant development in Garland's philosophy. For earlier, in the stories of *Main Travelled Roads* and in the play *Under the Wheel*, he portrayed nature as a predominantly cruel and malignant force. (pp. 102-03)

[Garland] realized while writing *A Spoil of Office* that it is chiefly the cruelty and selfishness of men and not the malignancy and hardness of nature that is responsible for the misery of the Midwestern farmers.

As Garland's view of nature in *A Spoil of Office* indicates, his philosophy has begun to develop away from the naturalistic tendencies that characterize much of his earlier work. While they are still essentially realistic, his descriptions of natural scenery in *A Spoil of Office* appear often quite rhapsodic and clearly foreshadow the romantic and often sentimental treatment of nature in his later Western novels. (pp. 104-05)

> Eberhard Alsen, "Hamlin Garland's First Novel: 'A Spoil of Office'," in *Western American Literature, Vol. 4, No. 2, Summer, 1969, pp. 91-105.*

STANLEY R. HARRISON (essay date 1969)

Hamlin Garland presents the vibrations of hope and despair, naturalism's double vision of life and death, in possibly the most complex fashion of all. In the midst of the destructive economic and natural forces that swirl through his short stories, he provides, not one, but three havens of liberation for his prairie folk and main-travelled roaders: they find respite and transcendent wonder in the physical beauty indigenous to the landscape, spiritual satisfaction in their tragic anger and in their own humanity, and hope in the possibility of eventual escape. These well-defined areas of freedom, though elusive, invest his stories with vital dramatic contrast and poignant want; they provide the necessary naturalistic counterpart to total despair and abject surrender.

The life aspect of Garland's shorter works finds an outlet in the release of affections quickened by the sweet freshness, the airy lightness, and the calm enchantment of an untainted natural scene. (p. 549)

Garland complements the vibrations of sound with a canvas of startling color. Purple, orange, and a yellow-green are the prevailing tones of his backdrop, but there is not a flush, no matter how striking in appearance, that is not represented. . . .

Nature, in its magnificence of color and sound, is to Garland what the Mississippi River was to Twain—a testament to life—and Garland utilizes it, as did Twain, to celebrate its wonder and to provide contrast for the infirmities that mar its beauty. His vision alternates between the splendors of the colorfully vibrant scene and the dingy quality, the drab appearance of the humans who people the setting. . . .

"The goodness and glory of God was in the very air, the bitterness and oppression of man in every line of her face," writes Garland; and nowhere is his basic theme, that of the oppression of the individual in the midst of the richness of Western life, more tersely expressed, more dramatically stated. One senses the pathos and dullness reflected by the sordid and squalid structures that house the people. (p. 550)

As striking as the contrast is between the liveliness of nature and the oppressiveness of the atmosphere, between the majesty of nature and the crude hovels of nature's caretakers, Garland's portraits of physical debility in the presence of nature's vigorous force create an even more discordant uneasiness and contribute an even more frightening quality of emotional experience to his landscape. The severity of the farmhands' labors and the meagerness of their compensation combined with an attitude of resignation, an intuition of hopelessness, and an understanding that change and flexibility have no application to their lives effects a premature deadening of the soul and depletion of the body and creates a race of catatonic embodiments. Henry Adams observed that woman, as a force, was unknown in America, that an American Venus would never dare exist. Possibly she would have endeavored if she had only possessed the energy or if her life force had not been previously drained by the agony of labor and the callousness of rejection. Garland's women are thin and weary and bent; their wrists are red, their necks sinewy, their hands gaunt and knotted, worn and discolored; a skeletal appearance further distinguishes them as does the droop of their lips and the glaze of their eyes. (pp. 551-52)

Possibly more distressing than the femininity and sex that are denied the woman is the youth that is denied the young. This is no longer the nostalgic world of Tom Sawyer, wherein the adolescence of youth parallels the immaturity of the nation, and the child is encouraged in his indulgences because early maturing and assumption of responsibility have not yet become necessary to survival. The Civil War has intervened, some fifty years have passed, industrialization has become a fact, mobility and flexibility have undergone stabilization, opportunities have diminished, landlordism has introduced the severities of tenant farming, fertile tracts have long since been laid claim to, wealth has become consolidated, and the adventure of settling the land has given way to the drudgery of cultivating it; progress has introduced hardship and inequity.

The almost premature growth thrust upon the nation and the consequent confusion visited upon the individual make participation in toil by all who are able a requisite for family survival. No longer permitted the pleasures of idle fancy and the opportunities for leisurely adventure, youth has to serve rather than be served, and their energies of dissipation are converted into labors of responsibility. A nightmare of resignation and horror replaces a childish dream of conquest. (pp. 552-53)

Garland's characters find themselves in a pitiful and frustrating situation, for nature's paradise is constantly within their sight; yet they are powerless to reach it. . . . Only those who remain ignorant of their expulsion and oblivious to the closed nature of their universe—and there are some, though few indeed—preserve their hope and find in the act of defiance an outlet for emotional expression. Though no qualitative change is in the offing, the rebellion, short lived and transitory as it is, provides it own purpose and meaning. (p. 553)

The moment of challenge, of tragic conflict, is a human triumph, but it is only a moment; it expends itself and the discontent resolves into an eternity of despair. There is no reaffirmation, only resignation and futility made more pathetic for the awareness of a moment's triumph. (p. 555)

Despair is the property of naturalism and death is its end, but the celebration of life is its counterpoint; and Garland held to this double vision of man's existence throughout his Middle Border years. (p. 556)

> Stanley R. Harrison, "Hamlin Garland and the Double Vision of Naturalism," in Studies in Short Fiction (copyright 1969 by Newberry College), Vol. VI, No. 5, Fall, 1969, pp. 548-56.

WARREN FRENCH   (essay date 1970)

Garland strikes me as one of those comparatively rare figures in literary history whose name has not endured because of his work, but whose works (or more exactly, the recollection of them, for most are out of print) have endured because of his personal activities. Critics have been justified in assuming that the most important thing about Garland is his decline, for he remains important not as an individual artist, but as an example of an American type—the man who made it too quickly and then hung around too long. (p. 283)

What perplexes friendly critics of the "realistic" movement is that during the last decade of the nineteenth century, Garland appeared to be an outspokenly liberal artistic and political leader who championed fresh vision and the "little man" against the machinations of the complacent and bloated plutocracy. After the turn of the century, however, Garland became increasingly conservative, increasingly uninterested in the world around him, and an increasingly garrulous producer of reminiscences of the old days on the Middle Border. (p. 284)

Garland's meditations on life and art during his "progressive" decade are projected through a series of essays that he collected in 1894 under the title *Crumbling Idols.* Although the pronouncements in the book upset some traditionalists at the time, it really contained little that was new. If one eliminates the statements that simply echo Whitman and William Dean Howells, one is left with a very small collection of excerpts. . . . Garland simply jumped on an already rolling bandwagon, shouting "Me, too."

Eleven of the twelve essays comprising the pretentiously titled book (the twelfth, a defense of impressionist painting, is a competent technical treatise only tangentially related to

the others) are really variant treatments at a length that modern readers may find tedious of three subjects—provincialism, which Garland defines not as "local color" but a colonial dependence on models; sincerity, and "veritism", his own lacklustre coinage for the mode of literary treatment that he briefly championed. . . . Garland concisely defines ["veritism"] at the beginning of the second essay: "The secret of every lasting success in art or literature lies, I believe, in a powerful, sincere, emotional concept of life first, and, second, in the acquired power to convey that concept to others." This "acquired" power, however, he maintains somewhat contradictorily in the next sentence, "leads necessarily to individuality in authorship, and to freedom from all past models." From where, one may ask, can it be "acquired," since *acquisition* implies a gain from another source. Garland seems to mean "contrived," but that word might jar with his claims about "sincerity." (pp. 284-85)

I have not seen it suggested before that Garland is to American literature what Bryan is to American politics, yet once one happens upon the analogy it is so obvious that one is surprised it is not a commonplace.

Both men emerged from the Middle West determined to take over effete and corrupt institutions dominated by the East. Both men appeared, for a time in the 1890's, to be dynamic liberals, although it is apparent upon examination of their pronouncements that they were simply masters of "Me-tooism." After others had done the hard work of blazing the trail, Garland and Bryan attracted attention by taking bold stands against already discredited practices. . . . Garland and Bryan are both examples of American opportunist types who do not really expect to be crucified on crosses of gold but to melt the crosses down for the manufacture of achievement medals. (pp. 285-86)

With the appearance of Dreiser, Garland had to put up or shut up as a hawker of "veritism," but he could not reverse his stand on acceptable materials. Again his career parallels Bryan's because the occultism into which Garland retreated is a genteel equivalent of the fundamentalism into which Bryan retreated. Both signify the rejection of the unacceptable degeneracy of the modern world. Curiously, both Garland and Bryan enjoyed their last blazes of glory after the disillusionment resulting from World War I drove many Americans back to a search for "normalcy," defined as the way things were in the horse-and-buggy days. The respect paid both Garland's recollections of the Middle Border and Bryan's performance in the Scopes Trial were indicative of a hopeless quest to recapture the "verities" of an often arduous, but virtuous past. (p. 286)

Despite Garland's pronouncements to the contrary, he was not the augur of a new age, but the last gasp of an old. . . . Garland's "decline" can be seen not as a unique phenomenon but as a classic example of the inability of the mind steeped in the genteel cliches of the nineteenth century to cope with the uncompromising vision of the twentieth-century students of behavior. The reason that Garland remains important is not his individuality, but his typicality. (p. 289)

> Warren French, "What Shall We Do about Hamlin Garland?" in American Literary Realism (copyright © 1970 by the Department of English, The University of Texas at Arlington), Vol. 3, No. 4, Fall, 1970, pp. 283-89.

JOHN C. McGREIVEY (essay date 1976)

There are several good reasons for leaving Hamlin Garland's best-selling romance, *The Captain of the Gray-Horse Troop*, in the justly earned oblivion of the numerous romances he produced between the late 1890's and World War I. Despite Garland's deft manipulation of a more complex plot than he had attempted previously, or was to attempt afterwards, *The Captain* duplicates faults of his other novels. Its major characters are the ubiquitous stereotypes of turn-of-the-century popular western fiction, and some of its subsidiary ones have strangely oblique connections to the novel's theme and plot. In addition, Garland distracts the reader's attention from the serious issues contained in the novel by his penchant for sentimentality, genteelisms, comment rather than dramatization, and his timidity in developing (or in *perceiving*?) the sexuality latent in the motives and relationships of his characters. But there are equally good reasons for not allowing *The Captain* to sink completely out of sight. First, *The Captain* reminds us that Garland consistently conceived of fiction primarily as a vehicle for social, economic, and political ideas, and only secondarily as a means of rendering reality. Thus ... it may be that his desire to disseminate his ideas to the widest audience possible—an understandable aim for a reformer— led him to conclude that the genre of popular romance would best serve his reformist purposes—as well as make him money. Second, in contrast to most of his novels and the bulk of his short stories, *The Captain* still retains some of its original relevance, for the issue it examines remains, unhappily, with us—the issue of how the American Indian can preserve his identity when he is surrounded by an alien culture which, for numerous reasons, wishes to destroy that identity. Third, and most importantly, the novel is worth examining because it was Garland's most successful attempt at the difficult artistic task he set for himself in the middle stage of his career—the task of combining the rigid conventions of character and plot of the popular romance with an exploration of an important social issue. (pp. 52-3)

The Captain, for example, contains three characters who seem superfluous to the novel's plot. All, however, are important to Garland's attempt to work out certain ideas about the Indian and the West within the framework of a romance. The first of these characters is Captain George Curtis's sister, Jennie. Why Garland bothers to give Curtis a sister is, at first, not clear. ... But if Jennie is something of a loose end in the plot, she does have a function in the novel's ideological objectives, for she serves as a model for what the heroine, Elsie Brisbane, should become—an adherent to the "western view," which means devoting one's self to duty, becoming an aficionado of the western landscape, and, above all, accepting the Indian as a fellow human being who possesses a culture worthy of preservation.

Similarly, Osborne Lawson, the ethnologist ..., presents another puzzle in regard to both the theme and the plot. While he does provide a third to the inevitable love triangle, this role could have been filled by one of the ranchers.... But if he seems to be excess baggage for the plot and theme, he plays an important part in Garland's strategy for making his ideas clear. As an ethnologist, he provides objective, "scientific" authority to bolster Curtis's more instinctive insights into the Indian and, in effect, gives Garland two personas through which to speak. Curtis is the intelligent man of action whose sympathetic understanding

and good judgment lead him unerringly in the right direction in his administration of the reservation; Lawson, on the other hand, is the contemplative man who gives Curtis's Indian policies the aura of intellectual authority, even if Garland's poor ear for speech rhythms makes it difficult to distinguish one from the other when they are speaking. (p. 53)

Cal Streeter is another character who seems not too neatly disposed of in the novel's romantic plot, but who is firmly integrated into the novel's ideas.... [Representing] the ideas of the changing values of the white westerner, Cal demonstrates the possibility of the whites and Indians living side by side in a harmony achieved through understanding, magnanimity, and justice. Even his failure to rescue [an Indian from a lynch mob], a puzzling incident when placed against Garland's adherence to the conventions of the western romance, is part of his ideological role. To allow him to save the Indian would have suggested the efficacy of the individual, whereas the novel as a whole suggests that even the hero, Curtis, can only be victorious when he acts in concert with others. (pp. 53-4)

Of course, the two main characters, Captain Curtis and Elsie Brisbane, are most crucial both to the novel's plot and to Garland's development of his ideas. Strangely, they are also the least interesting of the novel's characters. Of the two, Curtis is the most unoriginal. Cut from the conventional pattern expected of the hero of a western romance, Curtis is eastern born, but chooses to live in the West. At home on the trail and in an Indian tepee, he is equally at ease in an eastern drawing room. Contemptuous of a life not lived in service to "duty" (his major value), he frequently protests his inarticulateness, but speaks schoolmarmish English. In common with several other heroes of Garland's novels, he reads Herbert Spencer. He even dabbles in ethnological studies in odd moments. His principal thematic function—as opposed to his role as the hero of the romantic plot—is to represent the mingling of the best values of the East and the West. He is, however, pretty much of a bore, possibly because he has to spend so much time tying together the disparate threads of the plot and theme by incessant speech-making that he has little opportunity to develop as a character.

Compared to Curtis, Elsie Brisbane is a fully developed fictional character.... [She] is the only character in the novel who is allowed to change in response to her experiences and, consequently, to exist as more than either a simple functionary of the plot or as a vehicle for Garland's ideas. True, the transformation Garland has her undergo is the conventional one; like Wister's schoolmarm and countless other heroines of western romances, Elsie comes to understand that genuine self-realization as a woman can be achieved only among the honest folk and great open spaces of the West....

Garland works out her transformation in terms of the theory of literary impressionism he called "veritism." In doing this, he attempts to blend his love story, his ideas about the Indians, and his idiosyncratic brand of realism.... Elsie has been attempting to paint the Indians according to impressionistic and art-for-art's sake notions she has picked up in France. But her paintings of the Indians are failures in all but technique because she does not understand that *true* impressionism (i.e. "veritism") ... stems from the artist's emotional identification with the subject—

an identification which reveals the ethical dimensions of the subject as well as its literal "reality." The result is that both the artist and the viewer are moved to moral and social action. Thus, except for his more careful circumscribing of the limits of simple local color, Garland repeats in *The Captain* the theory of art and literature he had argued in *Crumbling Idols* in 1894. . . . To Garland, the accuracy of the impressions received by the artist is less important than art's potential for stimulating reform. (p. 54)

Garland's attempt to work out the ingredients of a romantic western in terms of his theory of realism is linked to his examination of the Indian. Just as Elsie has to become a veritist before she can become either Curtis's lover or a first-rate artist, so the problem of the Indian can not be solved until the white man comes to view the Indian as he really is. To do so, Garland makes it clear that the so-called "Indian problem" is really the white man's problem with himself and that it is imperative for the white man to change his attitude both for his own good as well as for the good of the Indian. (p. 55)

Garland had many limitations as an artist and as a thinker, but he was neither totally naive nor stupid—although [thematic] inconsistencies may suggest that he was these and more. But if the image of Garland as an opportunistic country bumpkin out to make good as a "literary fella" is put aside and *The Captain* examined on its own terms rather than against his early stories or in light of contemporary racial and social thinking, the cause of these inconsistencies may be traced to the simplistic conventions of romance that he was trying to use for his reformist ends. For one thing, the convention that the hero must be faultless and, consequently, absolutely right in all of his thoughts and acts, placed a limitation upon the density of Garland's fictional presentation of the Indian problem. In other words, the conventions did not allow Garland to distance himself enough from his protagonist to allow Curtis to be humanly fallible. Then too, the reformer in Garland gained the upper hand over the artist. Consequently, the novel's characters talk so much before they act that Garland forces the reader to evaluate their actions in the light of their talk. All this talk tends to make even the relatively simple actions which comprise *The Captain*'s plot to become muddled in their meanings. Finally, his conformity to the conventions of romance forced him to give the appearance of a happy ending to the Indian issue as well as to the love story. He may have known better (and his non-fiction writing on the Indian shows that he did), but by choosing to work *within* the conventions instead of *with* them, he ends by satisfying the reader instead of disturbing him. Consequently, the novel tends to neutralize the very reformist aims that generated it.

If the modern reader is unable to read *The Captain of the Gray-Horse Troop* either as a satisfactory work of art— even "veritistic" art—or as a completely satisfactory exploration of the problems of the Indian, he is, however, left with something more than a dreadfully dated novel and an impression of Garland as a callous seeker after public favor and financial success. Instead, the picture of Garland that emerges from the novel is that of a basically decent man

and a limited but serious writer hampered by the literary conventions of his time—conventions, it should be remembered, that hampered writers of far greater genius than Garland during the period in which Garland was writing. (pp. 57-8)

> John C. McGreivey, "Art and Ideas in Garland's 'The Captain of the Gray-Horse Troop'," in The Markham Review (© Wagner College 1976), Vol. 5 (Spring), 1976, pp. 52-8.

BIBLIOGRAPHY

Åhnebrink, Lars. *The Beginnings of Naturalism in American Fiction: A Study of the Works of Hamlin Garland, Stephen Crane, and Frank Norris with Special Reference to Some European Influences; 1891-1903*. Essays and Studies on American Language and Literature, edited by S. B. Liljegren, vol. IX. New York: Russell & Russell, 1961, 505 p.*
  Brief but thorough study of Garland's career that presents his relationship to social problems of the time, his importance as an early forerunner of American naturalism, and the literary theories he held which led him to that style.

Brooks, Van Wyck. "The Middle West." In his *The Confident Years: 1885-1915*, pp. 63-83. New York: E. P. Dutton & Co., 1952.*
  Biographical sketch that also discusses the environment of the postbellum Midwest.

Carter, Joseph L. "Hamlin Garland's Liberated Woman." *American Literary Realism* 6, No. 3 (Summer 1973): 255-58.
  Study of Garland's feminist sympathies and their reflection in several of his works.

Duffey, Bernard L. "Hamlin Garland's 'Decline' from Realism." *American Literature* 25, No. 1 (March 1953): 69-74.
  Discussion of possible motives for Garland's changing writing style.

Gish, Robert. *Hamlin Garland: The Far West*. Boise State University Western Writers Series, edited by Wayne Chatterton, James H. Maguire, and Dale K. Boyer, no. 24. Boise, ID: Boise State University, 1976, 48 p.
  Good critical overview of Garland's western romances.

Holloway, Jean. *Hamlin Garland: A Biography*. Austin: University of Texas Press, 1960, 346 p.
  Biography which also includes contemporary criticism of Garland's works.

McElderry, B. R., Jr. Introduction to *Boy Life on the Prairie*, by Hamlin Garland, pp. v-xvi. Lincoln: University of Nebraska Press, 1961.
  Study which examines the importance of *Boy Life on the Prairie* as a document of 19th century boyhood, and laments the neglect the book has suffered.

Pilkington, John. "Fuller, Garland, Taft, and the Art of the West." *Papers on Language and Literature* VIII, supp. (Fall 1972): 39-56.*
  Account of the friendship of Garland, satirist Henry Blake Fuller, and sculptor Lorado Taft, and of Fuller's mocking treatment of Garland's veritism in several short stories.

Saum, Lewis O. "Hamlin Garland and Reform." *South Dakota Review* 10, No. 4 (Winter 1972-73): 36-62.
  Study of the political and social concerns of Garland's early work.

(Sir) W(illiam) S(chwenck) Gilbert

1836-1911

(Also wrote under pseudonym of Bab) English librettist, dramatist, poet, journalist, and short story writer.

Gilbert is most memorable for his collaboration on a series of operas with Sir Arthur Sullivan, and the efforts of this famous partnership still endure as one of the definitive features of the Victorian age. In his librettos Gilbert satirically treated many of the social, moral, and political attitudes of his times, giving the works a quality that critics call characteristically English. It is Gilbert's humor and pure verbal inventiveness, however, as much as his satirical comment, that constitutes his literary significance.

Gilbert's father was a moderately successful novelist, and the young Gilbert always harbored literary ambitions, his first plays being performed by his schoolmates. His first professional appearance, though, was postponed by an intervening career as a clerk in government service and a brief time studying and practicing law. This training, with its legal and logical complexities, later became the substance of the farcical situations in works like *Trial by Jury* and *The Mikado*.

Gilbert initially gained recognition writing comic verses in *Fun* magazine using his childhood nickname "Bab." Later these controversial verses and drawings were published as *The "Bab" Ballads*. These are primarily poems of fanciful nonsense in the tradition of Edward Lear and Lewis Carroll, and one of them, "My Dream," describes the kind of upside-down mirror-world that is recognized as the dominant tool of Gilbertian parody. Through the portrayal of fantastic topsy-turvy realities Gilbert was able to effectively lampoon manners, movements, and institutions in a way that was entertainingly good-natured and, as some critics contend, essentially serious. The dramas of Gilbert in which he deliberately set out to deal with a serious subject in a serious manner are considered artistically less interesting than the operas and never achieved the same kind of success, much to the author's unending frustration. Plays such as *Gretchen* and *Broken Hearts*, among the many he had written before meeting Sullivan, are the works Gilbert would have preferred his peers and posterity to know him by, but in the judgment of many critics it was only as the librettist of the Savoy operas (produced at the Savoy Theatre) that Gilbert's full genius was at work; even his writing for other composers never approached the artistic mastery he achieved with Sullivan. Their creative affiliation lasted more than twenty years, though it was not without conflicts and occasional separations.

Gilbert's biographers describe him as an often demanding and despotic figure in his professional relationships. He exercised control over his works at every step from creation through stage production and demanded high theatrical standards. This emphasis on artistic excellence helped bring the English theater out of a particularly sterile era in its history and the operas enjoy a continued popularity.

PRINCIPAL WORKS

Dulcumara; or, The Little Duck and the Great Quack: A New and Original Extravaganza (drama) 1866

The "Bab" Ballads: Much Sound and Little Sense (poetry) 1869

The Palace of Truth: A Fairy Comedy, in Three Acts (drama) 1871

Thespis; or, The Gods Grown Old: An Entirely Original Grotesque Opera, in Two Acts (opera libretto) 1871?

Creatures of Impulse: A Musical Fairy Tale, in One Act (opera libretto) 1872

Pygmalion and Galatea: An Entirely Original Mythological Comedy, in Three Acts (drama) 1872

The Wicked World: An Entirely Original Fairy Comedy, in Three Acts and One Scene (drama) 1873

Broken Hearts: An Entirely Original Fairy Play, in Three Acts (drama) 1875

Trial by Jury: A Novel and Original Dramatic Cantata (opera libretto) 1875

Dan'l Druce, Blacksmith: A New and Original Drama, in Three Acts (drama) 1876

"Engaged": An Entirely Original Farcical Comedy, in Three Acts (drama) 1877

The Sorcerer: An Entirely Original Modern Comic Opera, in Two Acts (opera libretto) 1877

H.M.S. Pinafore; or, The Lass That Loved a Sailor: An Entirely Original Nautical Comic Opera (opera libretto) 1878

Sweethearts: An Original Dramatic Contrast in Two Acts (drama) 1878

"Gretchen": A Play, in Four Acts (drama) 1879

Charity: An Entirely Original Play, in Four Acts (drama) 187?

The Pirates of Penzance; or, The Slave of Duty: An Entirely Original Comic Opera in Two Acts (opera libretto) 1880

Tom Cobb; or, Fortune's Toy: An Entirely Original Farcical Comedy, in Three Acts (drama) 1880

Foggerty's Fairy: A Fairy Comedy (drama) 1881

Patience; or, Bunthorne's Bride: An Entirely New and Original Aesthetic Opera, in Two Acts (opera libretto) 1881

Iolanthe; or, The Peer and the Peri: A New and Original Comic Opera in Two Acts (opera libretto) 1882

Princess Ida; or, Castle Adamant: A Respectful Operatic Per-version of Tennyson's "Princess," in Three Acts (opera libretto) 1884

The Mikado; or, The Town of Titipu: An Entirely New and Original Japanese Opera, in Two Acts (opera libretto) 1885

Ruddigore; or, The Witch's Curse: An Entirely Original Supernatural Opera, in Two Acts (opera libretto) 1887

The Yeomen of the Guard; or, The Merryman and His Maid: A New and Original Opera, in Two Acts (opera libretto) 1888

The Gondoliers; or, The King of Barataria: An Entirely Original Comic Opera, in Two Acts (opera libretto) 1889

The Mountebanks: An Entirely Original Comic Opera, in Two Acts (opera libretto) 1891

Utopia, Limited; or, The Flowers of Progress: An Original Comic Opera (opera libretto) 1893

The Grand Duke; or, The Statutory Duel: A Comic Opera in Two Acts (opera libretto) 1896

The Fairy's Dilemma: A Domestic Pantomime (drama) 1904

The Hooligan: A Character Study (drama) 1911

(essay date 1869)

These "Bab Ballads" are the dreariest and dullest fun we ever met with; they have no real humour nor geniality, nor have they the broad farce of burlesque; they are wooden, both in the verses and in the illustrations; the jokes are entirely destitute of flavour. To have real fun you must have a real human heart, for fun requires sympathy quite as much as sentiment. Humour quaint and whimsical, like Charles Lamb's or Hood's, requires an insight into the most contradictory moods and tenses of human nature, and a power of love for all human things inspiring and underlying the sense of whimsicality. The "Bab Ballads" do not contain a single thread of interest, nor a spark of feeling. (p. 3)

> *"Two Reviews of 'The Bab Ballads': Part I," in* The Athenaeum, *No. 2163, April 10, 1869 (and reprinted in* W. S. Gilbert: A Century of Scholarship and Commentary, *edited by John Bush Jones, New York University Press, 1970, pp. 3-4).*

M. B. (essay date 1869)

[*The Bab Ballads*] the key-note of which is struck by the vignette of the baby thumping the piano-keys at baby-random—appear to be entirely without pretension. It is a curious fact that they read better at a second or third glance than they do at first, and that, utterly trivial and mechanical as they appear, a certain truthfulness of workmanship does after a time disclose itself to those who look at them more than once. This, of course, no one will do who is impatient

of sheer punchinello nonsense, with sheer commonplace for the raw material of the fun. But genuine fun there assuredly is in the "Bab Ballads," while some of the little wood-cuts, from the author's own hand, are almost better than the verses. . . . In one or two cases, the drawings are simply unpleasant, and the serious ballads are not successful. . . . (pp. 4-5)

> *M. B., "Two Reviews of 'The Bab Ballads': Part II" (originally published under a different title, in* The Contemporary Review, *Vol. XI, May, 1869), in* W. S. Gilbert: A Century of Scholarship and Commentary, *edited by John Bush Jones (copyright 1970 by New York University), New York University Press, 1970, pp. 4-5.*

WILLIAM ARCHER (essay date 1882)

I wish to emphasize at the outset my respect for [Mr. Gilbert] as the most striking individuality, the most original character our theatre of to-day can boast. He is not a mere spinner of verbal humour. He is not a mere constructor or adapter of comic or pathetic situations. Other dramatists have qualities which he has not, or has only in a minor degree; but in all his work we feel that there is an "awakened" intellect, a thinking brain behind it. He impresses us as a man who has looked at life with his own eyes, and has looked below the surface. There is a certain irony in his treatment of it, and that not only, nor even mainly, when he is professedly ironical. His so-called cynicism is shallow enough, but even it is genuine in so far as it proceeds from a genuine temperament. In short, he is not merely *l'homme sensuel moyen,* . . . who has more or less turn for making jokes, and more or less eye for superficial eccentricities of character, which he looks at through spectacles borrowed from Charles Dickens. This is the ordinary English dramatist, but this is not Mr. Gilbert, and therefore in my opinion he is the most interesting figure in our dramatic literature. (pp. 148-49)

[Mr. Gilbert] is not a dramatist. He is essentially a humorist whom circumstances have led to write for the stage. Long habit, and no doubt a certain natural bent, have given him a mastery of stage technique, but he has never created a character or written a drama. In two or three instances he has chanced upon a truly dramatic subject, and has treated it seriously, and in a measure successfully. But in none of his plays is there the growth and development, the action and reaction of character and incident, in short, the creative and inventive force which go to make a true drama. (pp. 150-51)

"Dan'l Druce" is Mr. Gilbert's nearest approach to a drama. Its motive, taken from "Silas Marner," is exquisitely conceived, but it remains a play of lost opportunities. . . . The first act is a little play in itself, and should have been called a prologue, to use a word often abused, but precisely fitted for the present case. . . . The prologue over, there remains matter for a full and rounded drama, in three or even more acts, not merely for the incident in two acts which Mr. Gilbert gives us. (pp. 151-52)

The love-scene in "Dan'l Druce" is one of the prettiest bits of writing Mr. Gilbert has done, and Dorothy is a theatrically effective character; yet it is perhaps she who proves most plainly how far Mr. Gilbert's mechanical skill falls short of the true dramatic gift. The fact that her dialect is precisely that of the Bible may be passed over, though I see no reason to suppose that a village girl in the reign of Charles II. would speak exactly as certain divines wrote in the reign of his grandfather. (p. 153)

The fact that he does not appreciate the value of silence is one evidence of the undramatic quality of Mr. Gilbert's talent. He leaves nothing to divination or even to action. He never gets into those depths of human nature where words are useless, or if he ever gets there he does not know it. . . .

["Dan'l Druce,"] seems to me a typical play. It illustrates admirably the limitations of Mr. Gilbert's talent on its serious side. He might have given its action the beautiful, natural curve of a rocket—the resultant between the impetus of dramatic circumstance and gravitation in the shape of the universal forces of human nature. He has chosen instead to make it a cracker—its course an arbitrary zigzag, accentuted by irrelevant explosions. (p. 154)

Mr. Gilbert is of opinion that Goethe's "Faust" is not a stage play, but a philosophical treatise upon human nature written in dramatic form. . . . The result [in "Gretchen"] is that he has transmuted the marvellous legend into a commonplace and painful seduction-story. (pp. 157-58)

His Faustus is not the weary student who has "durchaus studirt" all the world's wisdom, and after all knows only that he can know nothing. He is a blasé young man whose mistress has played him false, and who has consequently turned monk. A more utterly shallow character was never conceived, unless perhaps it be that of Mephisto—for this is the name of Mr. Gilbert's fiend, shorn of his tail in more senses than one. He is a sort of long-winded Dick Deadeye, only that his cynicism is good-humoured instead of snarling. . . . His influence on the character of Faustus is nil. . . . [But it is in] his character of Gretchen that one can least forgive Mr. Gilbert. He may say that we have no right to compare her with Goethe's Margarete, but, right or no right, we cannot help it. If she were even the faintest reflex of that exquisite incarnation of "das Ewig-Weibliche," she would be tolerable. But her ingenuousness is modern throughout, and perfectly self-conscious. Mr. Gilbert is responsible for the paradox, not I. She is a moral—I mean a moralizing, Gretchen. She is tolerant, not ignorant, of evil. (pp. 158-59)

[There] is not a breath of freshness, not a throb of life about her. No drop of warm blood runs in her veins, no thought of nature's teaching grows, flower-like, in her mind. To make up for this she can put all her thoughts into words, very precise and well-chosen words, and plenty of them. (pp. 159-60)

I seem to find more humanity in [Goethe's] lines than in all "Gretchen" put together—and yet "Gretchen" is a drama and "Faust" is a "philosophical treatise!" The death-scene is as verbose and conventional as the rest of the play—epithets which are too often applicable to Mr. Gilbert's pathos. It leaves us unmoved and cold. (pp. 160-61)

[But in "The Palace of Truth"], the keynote of Mr. Gilbert's peculiar talent is struck, his style of satire is epitomized. His most successful works have all for their scene an imaginary Palace of Truth, where people naively reveal their inmost thoughts, unconscious of their egotism, vanity, baseness, or cruelty. Touches of this peculiar mannerism are apparent in earlier works, . . . but it was first consis-

tently adopted in "The Palace of Truth." The comedy is constructed and written with a good deal of ingenuity. It is so thoroughly fantastic, both in motive and treatment, that its cynicism does not become repulsive. The spotless Lady Mirza is a well-conceived figure, and her downfall an extremely effective touch. Altogether, the play is in itself one of Mr. Gilbert's best pieces of work; but it acquires double importance from the fact that since he discovered "The Palace of Truth," he has hardly ever succeeded in freeing himself from its enchantment. He conceives the whole world as subject to the spell. He seldom cares to use the talisman which frees him from its influence, and when he wants to use it, he sometimes seems to have mislaid it. It was the magic of "The Palace of Truth," for instance, that spoiled the semblance of nature in "Charity," and contributed largely to its failure.

That he has touched nothing which he has not adorned cannot, unfortunately, be said of Mr. Gilbert. As he vulgarized the legend of Faust, so he vulgarized in an even greater degree the legend of Pygmalion and Galatea. His initial mistake lay in giving the sculptor [Pygmalion] a wife, and introducing the element of jealousy in a very modern and commonplace form. But even if we accept this as a necessary device for giving the story interest and consistency on the stage, it is impossible to accept his development of the theme in detail. It is remarkable that Mr. Gilbert, whose peculiar form of humour is based upon a strong logical faculty, should work out the problem of psychology presented by a vivified statue [Galatea] in a peculiarly illogical form; and it is also remarkable that he, who as a librettist has so successfully steered clear of vulgarity, should have treated this theme in a peculiarly vulgar fashion. (pp. 164-66)

He regulates Galatea's state of consciousness by the fluctuating exigencies of dialogue whose comedy is levelled straight at the heads of the old Haymarket pit—never in the least over them. (p. 166)

"Engaged" is a repulsive, vulgar, and—extremely amusing play. It shows us eight personages all actuated by the most unblushingly mercenary motives, who confess these motives in the most unblushing way, and with the air of uttering the noblest sentiments. The intrigue is really ingenious in its absurdity. (p. 172)

That it is extremely funny cannot be denied, especially when it is played with the business-like earnestness which Mr. Gilbert manages to impart to his interpreters. But it leaves a bitter taste in the mouth. It is as unpleasant and degrading as "Gulliver's Travels," without their deep human truth. Its cynicism is as irrelevant as it is exaggerated.

A much pleasanter, if not much cleverer work, is "Tom Cobb." It is a delicious piece of absurdity, very neat in its conception, and without a dull scene in its short, crisp action. The satire now and then takes a deeper grasp than is usual with Mr. Gilbert. . . . Perhaps my preference is exaggerated, but this play, trifling as it is, seems to me the happiest of all Mr. Gilbert's works,—that in which the maximum of effect is attained with the minimum of (apparent) effort. (p. 176)

Only Mr. Gilbert could have written "The Pirates of Penzance," whereas we have several playwrights who could have written "Dan'l Druce," and one or two who might have been perpetrated "Gretchen." As for the farces we might have had in their stead, it seems to me that the operas are fully equal in point of quaint humour to anything Mr. Gilbert has done. (p. 179)

The humour of the operas is a thing by itself. . . . There is a good deal of the Palace of Truth mannerism in it, but this is not the whole secret. Indeed the operas are more closely akin to the "Bab Ballads" than to "The Palace of Truth," Mr. Gilbert having actually, with the frugality of true genius, worked up several ideas from those early productions. A strong logical faculty is the basis of this humour. *Reductio ad absurdum* is its favourite method of procedure. Maxims of morality carried to their logical extreme and developed into paradoxes are its chosen playthings. In "Pinafore," for instance, much of the fun is extracted from the logical development of the modern idea of consideration for inferiors, or rather the broader principle of essential equality modified by accidental distinctions of rank and office. In "The Pirates," material is found in pushing to its logical extreme the idea of duty. In "Patience," much of the action turns upon the absurdities which may be deduced from a literal acceptance of common maxims on love and unselfishness. . . . The "contrast yet kinship," to use Mr. Carlyle's phrase, between the every-day common-sense application of these principles and Mr. Gilbert's apparently logical deductions from them, forms the basis of our enjoyment. There is a general inclination to attribute to these operas, or at any rate to the last three, a serious satiric purpose. Nothing could be more mistaken. Not even "Patience" is to be taken as a satire. It is an extravaganza, pure and simple, and so are its predecessors. Genuinely satiric touches are no doubt interspersed, but we are no more meant to conclude from "Patience" that Mr. Gilbert believes "aestheticism" as a whole to be a sham and a craze, than we are to conclude from "The Pirates" that he believes our police as a body to be arrant cowards. That they are not satires in the true sense of the term is proved by the fact that they leave every one's "withers unwrung." Satire which meets with universal acquiescence is unworthy of the name. (pp. 179-80)

I have no hesitation in calling these operas the most characteristic productions of our contemporary English stage. Their humour . . . is original if not profound, their literary workmanship is thorough, and they are . . . all in excellent taste. I do not mean to say that occasional speeches do not occur, which the most rigid fastidiousness might wish eliminated. . . . But such cases are very rare, and quite unimportant. They do not affect the broad fact that Mr. Gilbert, as author and stage-manager, has succeeded in producing a style of entertainment fitted *virginibus puerisque,* yet capable of affording to intelligent men amusement not altogether despicable in its intellectual quality. (pp. 180-81)

William Archer, "Mr. W. S. Gilbert," in his English Dramatists of To-day, *Sampson Low, Marston, Searle, & Rivington, 1882, pp. 148-81.*

MAX BEERBOHM (essay date 1904)

["The Fairy's Dilemma"] is, in scheme, a very good specimen of what is commonly called Gilbertian humour—that later humour of carefully calculated extravagance, such as we find in the Savoy pieces. But, good specimen though it is, I must confess that I don't rejoice in it. . . . Mr. Gilbert is a popular classic; and I may be frank without compunction. The only compunction were in pretending to confuse

what bores me with that in which my soul revels. Frankly "The Fairy's Dilemma" bored me. Had it happened to be an opera, with music by Sullivan, I daresay I should not have been bored at all. But without the music, the machinery of the humour creaked for me, audibly. Perhaps, even without the music, I should have heard no creaking if Mr. Gilbert had written the play in verse. His humour and his versification are inextricably connected; for his sense of rhyme and rhythm are as humorous as his ideas. Take any favourite stanza from the "Bab Ballads", and translate it into prose, and see how poor a thing it will seem in comparison. It will still, indeed, be funny. Many writers of humorous verse are men whose humour lies wholly in their technique; and they, when they write in prose, surprise one by their deadly dulness. "Bab", on the other hand, is full of intrinsically humorous ideas. . . .

Mr. Gilbert's prose is, and has always been, peculiarly dull and heavy. . . . Mr. Gilbert's one notion of humorous prose is to use as many long words and as many formal constructions as possible—a most tedious trick, much practised by other mid-Victorian writers. . . . In "The Fairy's Dilemma" all the characters talk rather like that, except the Demon Alcohol and the Fairy Rosebud, who talk mostly in verse. What a relief those two are! . . .

Yes, assuredly the whole play should have been in verse. Even so, however, it would not have quite "come off". Verse is not the only thing that it ought to have been written in; it ought also to have been written in the 'seventies. For in the 'seventies pantomime was flourishing still. Demon King and Fairy Queen, transformation scene and harlequinade, were familiar and popular things. But to satirise them now, in the 'noughts, as Mr. Gilbert does, is to shoot at a target long since removed from the range of vision. Mr. Gilbert once wrote a delightful parody of Martin Tupper. Surely he would not now sit down and write another parody of Martin Tupper. Indeed, he evidently does recognise, to some extent, the need to be contemporaneous in parody; for he has a shot at the criticisms in the "Times". But this skit, like the references to motor-cars and other recent things, seems queerly out of key with the play as a whole. For the mortal characters "date" not less obviously than the fairies. There *are* no mild young curates, with side-whiskers, and with a horror of the stage, nowadays. There *are* no young military baronets who compose love-verses and sing them with a piano-accompaniment, nowadays. There *are* no ladies who sit at their toilet-tables combing tresses of false hair, nowadays. . . . Had "The Fairy's Dilemma" been written and produced in the 'seventies, and were this production of it a revival, then the satire in it would seem to us all (as the satire in 1880's "Patience" lately seemed) quite fresh and vital. But the novelty of the thing is fatal. (p. 620)

Max Beerbohm, "Mr. Gilbert's Rentrée (and Mine)," in The Saturday Review, *Vol. 97, No. 2533, May 14, 1904, pp. 619-20.*

WALTER SICHEL (essay date 1911)

Our English Aristophanes [Sir William Gilbert] was eminently a stylist and constructor. He was a master of the comic and lyric stage in nearly all their departments. His rhymes and his rhythms harmonise even the most extravagant of his capers and caprices, and, while they dance hand and foot with them, they restrain their antics almost severely. He is the most critical of creators, the most creative of critics in an atmosphere which he may be said to have rediscovered. For that atmosphere, despite the centuries, *is*, after all, the atmosphere of Aristophanes. Their world is one not of nonsense but of sense upside down. It laughs thought into us. (p. 681)

Gilbert may have regarded himself as mainly a poet. A poet he was by instinct, with a charming lyrical gift, and, throughout, a topsy-turvy pathos which transforms tears to laughter. But his very restrictions accentuate the originality of his works. Combined in their varied fulness they find no parallel in our language. Compared with kindred whimsies they stand out supreme, while in metrical grace and fantastic flexibility Aristophanes himself does not surpass him. (p. 682)

Gilbert, like Aristophanes, was an artist to the core. His feeling for symmetry and proportion was native and needed no emphasis. In one faculty, indeed, he may be said to have excelled Aristophanes himself—in concentration. Not only is Gilbert's phrasing terse and trenchant, but his lyrical comedies are of the kind that leave an impression of length without ever being long—intaglios reduced from statues, or, to vary the metaphor, miniatures with the quality of pictures. They are his own *Bab Ballads* dramatised, acted epigrams. Rarely do they exceed some forty pages of print; indeed, *Pinafore* falls short of thirty pages, while the *Sorcerer* and the *Pirates of Penzance* occupy little over that amount. Yet how spacious these are in the hearing, how their plot distends, how excellently they read! Their facets gleam in the setting of the study as effectively as they do under the limelights. He is lambent. This art of condensation concerns the very gestures of the persons that emphasise the fantastic world which surrounds them. Their topsy-turvydom is written in italics, yet it is never mis-shapen. It is, in fact, *character*—the character of inversion. The inversion is often a toy inversion, but their character is no toy and it breeds familiarity. The persons are humanised elfs or elfinised mortals with momentary motives and glimpses of actions that, none the less, lend us the feeling of protracted acquaintance. They pass from mouth to mouth, and memory to memory, till they become types and proverbs. That is surely a mark of creative genius. They are normal in their abnormality. Their very child's play is grown-up, and though the artist only draws fleeting profiles, the beholder takes away with him the genuine expressiveness of life at full length. They are never perversions; they are versions, and lively versions. Fantasies in shadowland, they are not phantoms; and so it happens that inside all their gossamer vagaries their solid substance begets human intimacy attracting general welcome, and workaday acceptance. That is why they in no sense resemble some of those bizarre and bloodless ephemerals who serve a newer satire as pegs for passing paradox, and are debarred from stature and the vitality of quotation. Gilbert's characters, it must be insisted, breathe. They are no marionettes to be danced on the wires of a dramatic essayist. Nor are they ever morbid. Their madness is sane, and their follies are sympathetic. Still less are they merely intellectual figments. They feel as well as think. And so Gilbert's works form a sort of *scherzo serioso* relating him, however gaily, to the tragi-comedy of existence. Two characteristics in this connection he shares with Sheridan and with Thackeray. He is a sentimentalist tilting at sentiment, and he has what is hardly found outside Eng-

lish literature—the true schoolboy's love of fun. (pp. 683-84)

In *Foggerty's Fairy* Gilbert started his peculiar prose-fairyland with its romance and realism alike upside down. The fairy "Rebecca," who causes the complications besetting the path of the perplexed little hero, is a practical and entirely English fay. . . . She is, indeed, less a fairy than a glorified *figurante*. By recklessly invoking her aid to wipe out an embarrassing incident in his past, Foggerty has also accepted the condition of obliterating all the possible consequences of that incident, and so he only finds himself plunged from one hopeless dilemma into others more hopeless. . . . And the whim is worked out with an algebraical exactness, and with strict adherence to character, since the motives are always true, however feigned may be the positions and actions. Nowhere is a better example of his union of the practical and the poetical. . . . This logic of fantasy stamps his pathos also. (p. 687)

Irony always makes the great and the little, the masks of Comedy and of Tragedy, exchange places. But Gilbert makes them exchange and re-exchange places again and again, and with an infinite network of involution defying disentanglement. So much so that at length we can scarcely escape from the Chinese puzzle, and give credence to illusion within illusion—all mutually destructive—just as if each were an isolated matter of fact. This is why a farcical pathos is always possible to him. . . . (p. 690)

[*Pygmalion and Galatea*] brings us to close quarters with Gilbert's attitude towards the sexes. I have said that he was a sentimentalist tilting against sentiment, and the statement is borne out by nearly all his stage-heroes and heroines. No one had a deeper reverence for manly manhood and womanly womanhood; none a more piercing scorn for their affectations or the reversal of their types. The whole of *Engaged* forms a satirical homily on this theme. But Gilbert also seems to have held that the theory of affinities verged perilously on nonsense. He thought that under normal conditions any normal man would suit any normal woman, and he delights in the whimsical application of this cynical common sense. "Cynical" is perhaps hardly the epithet, yet what is the cynic but the denuder of the superimposed —the microscope of motives? Woman was made, not for competition, but marriage. (p. 692)

[Gilbert] exalted order and freedom and discipline. He abominated the greed of monopoly whether it styled itself Socialism, or Finance, or the Cabinet. He dragged down the pretenders from their thrones, and unmasked them with a quip or a moral. (p. 696)

Gilbert has left England more than a legacy of pure and lasting laughter, though this is much indeed. He has bequeathed an inheritance of melody as well as of mirth, of thought, and criticism, as well as of whim and fantasy. These are not evanescent, and "another morn" will dawn on them, though it is always hard to prophesy the permanence of words wedded to music. But as literature the librettos will endure. The great Englishman, like the greater Greek, will long outlive the surroundings that his irony brought into such sharp yet such joyous relief. (p. 704)

Walter Sichel, "The English Aristophanes," in The Fortnightly Review, *Vol. 96, No. DXXXVIII, October 2, 1911, pp. 681-704.*

MAURICE BARING (essay date 1922)

The Gilbert of the operas has been compared to Aristophanes; and the comparison has been said to be a wild one. To place Gilbert in the same rank as Aristophanes, it is said, would mean he should have written lyrics as beautiful as those of Shakespeare. But to compare Gilbert and Sullivan with Aristophanes is not, I think, a wild comparison, for the lyrical beauty which is to be found in the choruses of the Greek poet, is supplied, and plentifully, by the music of Sullivan. . . . For its purpose not even Aristophanes could have improved on it, because the point about Gilbert's lyrics and Gilbert's verse is that it is just sufficiently neat, lyrical and poetical, besides being always cunningly incomparably rhythmical, to allow the composer to fill in the firm outline he has traced with surprising and appropriate colour. (p. 424)

If Gilbert had been a greater verbal poet, a poet like Shelley or Swinburne, there would have been no room for the music; the words would have been complete in themselves; their subtle overtones and intangible suggestions would have been drowned by any music, however beautiful. As it is, the words have just enough suggestive beauty, and are always unerringly rhythmical, and this is just the combination needed to enable the composer to display his astonishing musical gift. (pp. 424-25)

Another important factor in Gilbert's work is the quality of his satire. Some people detest it. It affects them like bitter aloes. But it owes its enduring permanence, not to bitterness, for it is never really bitter, but to a certain breadth and force which has two cardinal merits. Firstly, that of being dramatic, of getting over the footlights, of appealing to the component parts of a large and mixed audience, so that the stalls will smile at one line and the gallery be convulsed at another, and all will be pleased; and, secondly, of being general enough to apply to the taste and understanding of succeeding generations. Gilbert's satire, although directed at the phenomena of his own time, had a Molière-like quality of broad generalisation, which applied not only to the fashions and follies of one epoch, but to the eternal weaknesses of unchanging human nature. (p. 429)

But although Gilbert's satire is not bitter, it is undeniable that it sometimes has an element not only of downrightness, but of harshness in it. It is not savage, like that of Juvenal or Swift, but it is not too squeamish for a knock-out blow. This may sometimes, and does sometimes, ruffle and jar upon the sensitive. But these easily ruffled persons should remember that Gilbert's harshness is an ingredient which is to be found in all the great comic writers; in Aristophanes, in Cervantes, in Molière, and indeed in any comic writer whose work endures for more than one generation. It is a kind of salt which causes the soil of comedy to renew itself; and in Gilbert's case it arises from his formidable commonsense. He never took his paradoxes seriously as so many of his successors did. He is as sensible as Dr. Johnson, and sometimes as harsh. Gilbert has often been blamed for gibing at the old. It is true that his jokes on the subject of the loss of female looks are sometimes fierce and uncompromising. But they are mild indeed compared with those of Aristophanes, Horace, and Molière; and on closer inspection, we find it is not really at the old he is gibing, but at the old who pretend to be young. . . . What is exceptional in

Gilbert's satire is that he combined with this downright strong commonsense and almost brutal punching power a vein of whimsical nonsense and ethereal fancy which generally goes with more gentle and flexible temperaments.

The third cardinal quality of Gilbert's work is almost too obvious to dwell upon, namely his wit, both in prose and in rhyme; his neat hitting of the nail on the head, his incomparable verbal felicity and dexterity; and the peculiar thing about Gilbert's verbal felicity is its conversational fluency. He uses the words, the phrases and the very accent and turn of ordinary everyday conversation and yet invests them with a sure, certain and infectious rhythm, the pattest of rhythm; and rhymes that are always inevitable, however fantastic and far-fetched. (pp. 429-30)

Another remarkable fact about Gilbert's satire is this: Just those subjects which, when he treated them, were thought to be the most local and ephemeral, have turned out, as treated by him, to be the most perennial and enduring. Take *Patience*, for instance. *Patience* was a satire on the aesthetic craze of the 'eighties. It was produced in 1881. It was aimed at the follies and exaggerations of the aesthetic school—the greenery-yallery, Grosvenor-gallery, foot-in-the-grave, hollow-cheeked, long-necked and long-haired brood of devotees of blue china and peacocks' feathers and sunflowers, who were the imitators, the hangers-on and the parasites of a group of real artists and innovators, such as Whistler, Burne-Jones and Rossetti. (pp. 430-31)

But in writing this satire, Gilbert, if he magnified the follies of his contemporaries, hit the bull's eye of a wider target. He struck the heart of artistic sham, so that his satire is appropriate to any time and any place. (p. 431)

I should not be in the least surprised if, in ages to come, people will talk of the age of Gilbert and Sullivan, as they talk of the age of Pericles. Perhaps they will confuse fact with fiction, and the children of the future will think that trials by jury in that amusing age were conducted to music; that pirates and policemen hob-nobbed at Penzance; that Strephon, the Arcadian Shepherd brought about the reform of the House of Lords; that the Bolshevik Revolution took place in Barataria; and the Suffragist movement happened at Castle Adamant. (p. 436)

Maurice Baring, "Gilbert and Sullivan," in The Fortnightly Review, *Vol. 112, n.s., No. DCLXIX, September 1, 1922, pp. 422-36.*

A. H. GODWIN (essay date 1927)

Gilbert, it has often been said, never spoilt his stage women by any excessive flattery. Not only do I hold this to be true, but it has seemed to me that the weakness of his characterisation of women is a flaw in the operas, inasmuch as it stamps them with an age that the freshness of the story . . . disguises. Gilbert's women are terribly Victorian. Ko-Ko, Pooh-Bah, . . . and many other male characters are clear-cut types, each distinctive and definite, and as such they belong to the stage. It never occurs to us to classify them as belonging to the past or the present. But it is not so with the ladies. They are all so much of a pattern. They "date" themselves—and the operas with them—as the relics of a past generation.

Speaking generally, Gilbert drew his women-folk from two models only, and in real life their types are almost forgotten. You cannot escape from his simpering innocents or from his man-trapping spinsters. They positively litter the ground. The younger ones have little personality and less self-dependence.... [How] terribly conventional they are and how exasperatingly "according to plan"! Empty-headed creatures most of them are, just casting a demure eye when a possible husband appears on the scene, and looking as if they might faint becomingly when the silly fellow seems inclined to propose. (pp. 123-24)

Why is it that Gilbert, with his inventive fund of humour, so often makes a mock of those pitiable creatures who are, and sometimes plainly announce that they are, on the bargain-counters of marriage? . . . [Lady Jane is] the best or the worst of those sorry examples. Lady Jane's chase after Bunthorne is not edifying comedy, and the words put into her mouth are a trifle cheap.... My own Victorian recollections do not tell me that maiden ladies used to flaunt their caps with such flagrant despair. (pp. 124-25)

> *A. H. Godwin, "Concerning the Ladies," in his* Gilbert & Sullivan: A Critical Appreciation of the "Savoy Operas," *J M Dent & Sons Limited, 1927, pp. 123-29.*

HENRY TEN EYCK PERRY (essay date 1928)

It may seem odd to think of W. S. Gilbert as an important representative of Victorianism.... Tennyson and Browning took their Victorianism seriously; Gilbert did not openly attack contemporary civilization, like Samuel Butler, but he treated it more gaily than the great poets did. He was able to make mild fun of its shortcomings in adroit paradoxes and sly understatements at the same time that, with delightful whimsicality, he glorified its major premises. The lines that fall from the lips of his characters cannot safely be taken as literal expressions of his own point of view; but the bewildering variety of Gilbert's comic inventiveness does not obscure the fact that has basic ideas were those of a conservative Victorian. (p. 302)

[Gilbert] saw the absurdities, if not the perils, of much in the Victorian régime, but he was content to accept life as it was going on about him on its own terms. He valued British institutions for the good that they were achieving and criticized only their less significant features; his adverse criticism is of the limited kind permitted by Englishmen to Englishmen, not to outsiders. (p. 303)

Gilbert himself loves the whole structure of English society, with all its faults, just this side idolatry. (pp. 303-04)

Trial by Jury is a significant document in Gilbert's treatment of sex; the casual way in which the Judge succumbs to the charms of the Plaintiff suggests not only a carelessness as to the sanctity of law, but also a lack of violent physical attraction on either side. One need not take this lack too seriously, as the comic opera tradition demands a general pairing off of all the characters at the final curtain. Still there is an indication throughout Gilbert's work that he did not consider the relation between the sexes as a vital matter. (p. 305)

Love must be upheld because it leads to marriage and children and the home, dearest of Victorian institutions; love as a spiritual factor in life is beyond Gilbert's ken, and the same holds true of his attitude towards beauty, art, and poetry. (p. 306)

In politics, as in love-making, Gilbert seems to say radical changes are of no avail; whatever is, is right.

He definitely repudiates the philosophic ideal in such a play as *The Palace of Truth*, where a justification of falsehood is implied, and his partial notion of perfection is aptly summed up in the title, *Utopia, Limited*. This piece . . . does not contain the creative exuberance of his early work, but in it his creed is not obscured by unessentials.... Utopia seems about to decay of dry rot until Party Government is introduced as a certain panacea, "because one party will assuredly undo all that the other party has done." From this time on, "Utopia will no longer be a Monarchy (Limited), but, what is a great deal better, a Limited Monarchy!"

This apotheosis of an ideal state until it becomes "England —with improvements" is characteristically Gilbertian. It implies that England is not perfect as it is, but that it is progressing on the right track to a heaven upon earth. (pp. 307-08)

Complacency is a deathblow to great art, and complacency was the outstanding characteristic of the Victorian age. Gilbert had his share of this quality; it underlies all his literary work. That is why, although his comedies occasionally appeal to the critical faculty, they always leave us with a pleasant feeling of universal well-being. And that is why, delightful as Gilbert's phantasies are, they pale before the works of that author to which they have so often been compared. When Gilbert is termed "a *Victorian* Aristophanes", the much abused adjective takes on a renewed sting. (p. 309)

> *Henry Ten Eyck Perry, "The Victorianism of W. S. Gilbert," in* The Sewanee Review *(reprinted by permission of the editor; © 1928 by The University of the South), Vol. XXXVI, No. 3, Summer, 1928, pp. 302-09.*

CHARLES E. LAUTERBACH (essay date 1956)

Gilbert described "The [Bab] Ballads" as "much sound and little sense." By a curious quirk of circumstance it was this non-sense, not his sense, which made him famous. He might well be called the King of Topsy-turvy-dom.... But it is questionable science to "psychologize" him as sadistic and infantile because of the behavior of his nonsense characters. It is more probable that his good common sense led him to a vein of popular interest which he then mined for all it was worth.

It might be supposed that continued indulgence in utter nonsense would become monotonous. There are at least two reasons why Gilbert's doesn't. One is the wide range of his inventiveness. Kings, princes, generals, lieutenant colonels, majors, captains, bishops, curates, ogres, ghosts, precocious infants, and modest maidens throng his pages without a vestige of logic or a shred of dignity. His characters possess a sort of primitive universality that keeps them from growing stale. That the clever "Bab" drawings contribute to their effectiveness is generally acknowledged. They also cancel his anonymity wherever they appear and identify much of his unsigned writing.

Another circumstance which prevents "The Ballads" from becoming wearisome is the great variety of verse and stanza form in which they are written. The predominant meter is iambic but the anapaest also appears, as in "Old Paul and Old Tim." . . . Nor is the trochee slighted. It is in trochaic dimeters and trimeters that Georgie of "The Fairy Curate" resolves to join the clergy. . . . (pp. 196-97)

The length of verse varies from this airy dimeter and tri-meter to the protracted Ogden Nashery of "Lost Mr. Blake." . . .

The length of the stanza is as variable as the verse form, ranging from the couplet of "Fernando and Elvira" through stanzas of three lines, four lines, five lines, and so on, to the twelve-line stanza of "The Fairy Curate." All of which helps keep "The Ballads" out of the rut and makes each one a refreshing adventure. (p. 197)

> *Charles E. Lauterbach, "Taking Gilbert's Mea-sure," in* The Huntington Library Quarterly *(©️ 1956 by The Henry E. Huntington Library and Art Gallery), Vol. XIX, No. 2, February, 1956, pp. 196-202.*

ROBERT A. HALL, JR. (essay date 1958)

The Yeomen of the Guard does not fit into the general pat-tern of the Savoy operas. Most critics formulate the differ-ence between the *Yeomen* and the other Gilbert and Sul-livan operettas by saying that in it, Gilbert eschewed his customary satirical vein of humour and Gilbertian "topsy-turveydom." Yet discussions of the *Yeomen* in general sen-timentalize it and thereby obscure its true significance. To regard the *Yeomen,* as some do, as a "tender little romance which mingles laughter and tears," or as "the romantic, somewhat relenting exception" to Gilbert's satire, will not suffice to explain its peculiar effect on the spectator. To an audience expecting Gilbert's rollicking cheerfulness, it of-fers a mood hovering between wry jest and serious drama; and instead of a final solution of all difficulties, it presents an ending in which an apparently "happy" outcome is marred by the discomfiture . . . [of several characters]. The sensitive spectator leaves a performance of the *Yeomen,* not cheered, but saddened. . . . (pp. 492-93)

The key to an understanding of Gilbert's "normal" characters—i.e. those who live in Gilbertian "topsy-turveydom"—has been furnished by Clarence Day, Jr., in a penetrating analysis. He points out that Gilbertian charac-ters derive their special characteristics from the unusual and incongruous emotional fortitude which they manifest in wildly improbable situations. . . . (pp. 493-94)

Apply this conception to the characters of the *Yeomen,* however, and what do we find? A group of people, all of whom are quite ordinary, and all but two of whom are un-heroic, un-generous, and the very opposite of the Gilbertian "frontiersmen of emotion." It is as if Gilbert had decided for once to show how a group of people, similar to his stock characters but without their emotional strength and resil-ience, would react in a melodramatic situation of the type he was fond of parodying. The result is a sorry mess. . . .

To see the *Yeomen* in this light—which I believe to be the true one—we must revise the currently prevalent view of a number of the personages of the play, a view which unduly sentimentalises and distorts them. Jack Point most of all. The appeal of this character, particularly in "I have a song to sing, O!" and in his final collapse, has led most critics to idealise him: he has been referred to as "the prince of jest-ers," the play's "chief source of wit and philosophy," "a merryman of infinite wit," who is no ordinary strolling player but has a taste for pretty wit and nimble repartee. Various critics have seen in Point a reflection of Gilbert's own personality, his "essential self" and an "idealised Gil-bert," and have considered the *Yeomen* to be Gilbert's

"spiritual testament." These estimates of Point are based primarily on the philosophy of professional humour ex-pressed in [two] songs. . . . But the philosophy of these two songs is at variance with Point's actual behaviour; basing our analysis purely on the internal evidence of the dialogue, we must come to a quite different estimate of his character. From his first appearance in the play, he is in a sorry state, not merely because he has been "down on his luck," but because he is in fact a failure, professionally and person-ally. (pp. 494-95)

Physically, Point is anything but heroic, as evidenced in his dealing with the angry crowd at his first entrance; in his personal relations he is indecisive and selfish. . . . When he has definitely lost her, however, he is suddenly torn by self-pity, which grows throughout the second act until he falls insensible at Elsie's feet at the end of the play, through a sorrow which he has brought on himself by his earlier indif-ference to her and his eagerness to make a hundred crowns quickly and effortlessly. (pp. 495-96)

Satire there is in the *Yeomen,* and in plenty; but it is the bit-terest of all satire, that of a man mocking his own work. The *Yeomen* is, in other words, Gilbert's satire on Gilber-tian tomfoolery, and as such does indeed occupy a special place in the series of the Savoy operas, but in a different sense from the interpretation that has customarily been given to it. It confirms, in a direct artistic manifestation, what we are told [by H. Pearson in his *Gilbert and Sullivan: A Biography*] concerning Gilbert's attitude towards his "topsy-turveydom": "Gilbert had an extremely high opinion of his contribution to what he believed to be the higher drama, and while Sullivan turned to comic opera with relief, Gilbert turned to it with regret." (p. 497)

> *Robert A. Hall, Jr., "The Satire of 'The Yeomen of the Guard'," in* Modern Language Notes *(©️ copyright 1958 by The Johns Hopkins University Press), Vol. LXXIII, No. 7, 1958, pp. 492-97.*

DAVID CECIL (essay date 1962)

[The] Savoy Operas are unique in our literature. . . . The special Savoy flavour comes from the blending of two in-gredients. Fantasy is added to satire, fantasy of the comic, preposterous, nonsensical kind. The characteristic Gilber-tian world is a wonderland where everything is topsy-turvy and incongruous, where likely boys are legally apprenticed to pirates and fairies appear in Parliament Square. Like [Lewis] Carroll's, too, Gilbert's is what may be called log-ical nonsense; it depends on the strict logical working out of a preposterous hypothesis. Thus the son of a fairy and a mortal is fairy to the waist and mortal below, or a child born on the 29th of February in leap year has to live eighty-four years before it legally becomes of age. (pp. vii-viii)

Gilbert's moments of sentiment never [last for long]. He realized that if they continued, they would jar with the pre-vailing mood of the piece: in . . . succeeding scenes he takes care to deflate them. Such deflation is a characteristic device of his. He uses it in detail as well as in general de-sign. (p. viii)

Sentimentality is also incompatible with the second ingre-dient in the Savoy flavour, satire. . . . *Ruddigore* makes fun of Victorian melodrama with its wronged maidens and wicked baronets: the plot of *The Gondoliers* parodies the typical plot of the then fashionable Italian opera by Bellini or Donizetti, with its recognition scenes and its story of the child changed at birth. There is some similar operatic parody in *Iolanthe* and *Pinafore;* but the laughter in these is primarily directed elsewhere, at the parliamentary system in *Iolanthe,* at the Navy in *Pinafore.* Gilbert satirizes the feminist movement in *Princess Ida,* the aesthetic movement in *Patience,* and the legal profession in *Trial by Jury.* He takes a side kick at egalitarianism in *The Gondoliers,* at the extravagances of romantic love in *The Sorcerer,* and, in *Utopia Limited,* at the new capitalism. *Utopia Limited* also mocks English institutions in general. Now and again Gilbert sets out to make us laugh at individual types, the offensive busybody like Gama, the clerical lady's man like Dr. Daly; and he parades for our derision a whole procession of ladies of doubtful age and waning charms relentlessly in pursuit of husbands.

Thackeray made fun of these last two types. Gilbert often recalls Thackeray. Alike in his matter and manner he was a satirist in the Thackeray tradition. (pp. viii-ix)

Indeed, there was an affinity between the two men. They both laughed at their fellows from the same point of view: that of a typical masculine representative of the liberal middle class that gave the tone to Victorian England—sensible, sharp-eyed, worldly-wise, but conventional, philistine, and suspicious of anything abnormal or immoderate. Such a point of view inevitably distrusted feminism; a normal reasonable girl, it thought, must want to settle down with a good husband. Or aestheticism; a normal reasonable man does not devote his life to blue china and Botticelli. Political extremes were no better. The idea of absolute equality was ridiculous. . . . On the other hand, there was something highly comical about the hereditary artistocracy with their garters and coronets and bland brainless assumption of superiority. . . . Gilbert, too, was civilian in sentiment. The Victorian citizen, hard-working and in sober broadcloth, could not help smiling at the sight of a guardsman standing about apparently doing nothing, in scarlet and bearskin and with twirled moustaches. Further, though deeply insular, he had the Liberal impatience with any florid manifestation of patriotism. . . . Gilbert, it is to be noted, looked back to the age of Thackeray not forward to the age of Kipling.

Respectable and domestic Victorians of this time were also prudish. So are the Savoy Operas. Gilbert made it a rule that no man or woman should appear in the costume of the other sex; Sullivan never allowed the voluptuous rhythms of the waltz to defile his chaste scores. (pp. ix-xi)

It was the fact that they were so typical of their age that made these operas immediately and extraordinarily popular. They plattered the average Englishman of the period in all his pet prejudices against lords and aesthetes, and democrats and feminists, and slippery lawyers and blustering generals. How pleasant it was to find clever Mr. Gilbert equally against them, but able to laugh at them with a wit beyond his powers! It is true Mr. Gilbert sometimes laughed at the average Englishman too: but never in such a way as to disturb him; and, anyway, was it not one of the Englishman's peculiar glories to be able to see a joke against himself? (p. xi)

Sullivan has lasted better than Gilbert. His tunes are still played everywhere while few people read Gilbert's words. This is not wholly Gilbert's fault; there are a hundred

people who enjoy a pleasant tune for one who likes verbal wit. But it is also true that Sullivan in his own line was an artist of the first order. . . . (p. xii)

Gilbert does not maintain the same level. On the contrary, unhelped by the charm of Sullivan's tunes, the libretti show up as very unequal. The prose dialogue in particular is often stilted and facetious: Gilbert was one of those who suffered under the delusion that to say a simple thing in long words is to make it laughable. Further, his touch on fantasy is uncertain. He was not a man of imagination in the sense that Carroll or Lear were; so that he cannot manage the same flights of inspired extravagant nonsense. When he tries, he is liable to degenerate into a mechanical whimsicality. . . . Gilbert's paradoxes can be mechanical too. He sometimes labours them too long, pursuing their implications long after the last drop of spontaneous fun has been squeezed out of them.

Along with imaginative weakness goes insensitiveness of taste, especially apparent when he aspires to be graceful and gallant. . . . Alas, Gilbert was no cavalier but a middle-class Victorian with the characteristic defects of his type. Though prudish, he was not refined. Indeed, his prudery emphasizes his lack of refinement; for it meant that whenever he came near the subject of sex he became embarrassed and then tried to hide his embarrassment under a jaunty jocular archness. The only result of this is to embarrass his readers.

He has also been called cruel. Certainly he was more light-hearted than kind-hearted. He laughed uproariously and without compunction at ugliness and awkwardness and advancing years; and he never could resist a joke about an execution. But should these things be counted against him? Jokes do not have to be kindly. They are often more amusing if they are not. Gilbert's are. . . . Moreover, his malice saves his fun from the risk of insipidity created by its prudishness: it provides the spice to his gaiety . . . and it serves still further to sharpen the gleaming cutting-edge of his satirical wit.

For if his fantasy is relatively weak, his satire, most of it, is brilliantly strong. This is primarily due to his sheer virtuosity as a writer, the audacious triumphant ease with which he juggles with helter-skelter rhythms and complicated rhyme schemes; the sparkling felicity with which he pinpoints a type or a personality in a brief impressionistic phrase. . . . His satire can be penetrating as well as brilliant. Not always; sometimes lack of sympathy makes his approach too external: he is not close enough to the object of his mockery to perceive its true weakness. The anti-feminism of *Princess Ida,* for example, is conventional. Gilbert could not, for good or for ill, bother with intellectual women enough to discover what they were like. Even his delightful satire on the aesthetes is a touch superficial. (pp. xii-xiv)

It is different when he turns his mocking eye on the law, for he had been a lawyer himself. Or on political subjects; for all respectable Victorians were in some degree politicians. The result is that Gilbert's satire on these things pierces through topical reference to expose something permanent and fundamental in English institutions and the English temperament. . . . As for Gilbert's jokes about the class system, they are even more to the point now than when they were written. (p. xv)

The satirical Gilbert, then, is the strong Gilbert. It follows then that his best works are those in which the satire is best and where there is most of it; *Iolanthe, Pinafore, Patience, The Mikado, Trial by Jury. Trial by Jury*, indeed, which is composed of Gilbert's satire at its liveliest and of nothing else at all, is the most perfect thing he ever wrote. Conversely, *The Gondoliers* and the rest, where the satire is not so strong and there is more fantasy, are by comparison weaker; and *The Yeomen of the Guard*, where there is hardly any satire, goes to the bottom of the class. (pp. xv-xvi)

> *David Cecil, "Introduction" (© Oxford University Press 1962; reprinted by permission of Oxford University Press), in* Savoy Operas, Vol. I *by W. S. Gilbert, Oxford University Press, London, 1962, pp. vii-xvii.*

PAUL J. REVITT   (essay date 1965)

In all of Gilbert's libretti, something is topsy-turvy. . . .

Gilbert's endings are either an absurdity which laughs the whole thing off the stage, or a miraculous twist such as Dickens might invent, or an exploitation of some casually mentioned circumstance earlier in the narrative in the manner of H. H. Munro, or a turn-about typical of O. Henry, or a mistaken identity, the common property of the theater since Aristophanes. In any case, Gilbert ends with a surprise and always on a cheerful note. (p. 22)

The serious message, however, is always the same. Beneath the topsy-turvy situations, in spite of their manufactured logic, is the Victorian principle that departure from the established order is fatal. . . .

Satire [in Gilbert's libretti] is based upon obvious flaws in a social convention. Gilbert does not pick at the cracks nor does he even go after a slight blemish. And the truth is that the audience in the theater does not laugh at the satire, but at the situation. It may not be too bold to say that Gilbert does not attack the institutions at all. . . .

Scattered here and there [in *Trial by Jury*,] are lines which show that Gilbert was thinking of something far deeper than a breach-of-promise suit. Edwin, the young blade, defends himself by the argument that he is but obeying the laws of nature, and that nature constantly changes. In a flash, the profound philosophical question concerning the relationship of Natural and Codified Law arises. Moreover, the question of the immutability of Natural Law presents itself. To be sure, "Natural Law" in Edwin's case is not the fullest manifestation of that Divine Order recognized as applicable to mankind, past, present, and future; but nonetheless, while the audience enjoys the courtroom scene, Gilbert is seriously, not satirically, probing the basis of law. (p. 23)

Gilbert's choice of names is as precious as the characters he portrays. Descriptive names such as Dick Deadeye, Bill Bobstay, and Ralph Rackstraw as able seamen in *H.M.S. Pinafore* are as colorful as those found in Dickens. Nanki-Poo, the son of the Mikado and the Heir-Apparent to the throne, is in Titipu disguised as a Second Trombone. What tickles the funnybone here is the implication that Nanki-Poo is disguised, not as the player of the Second Trombone, but the instrument itself. Professionally speaking, it is within the bounds of propriety to address an instrumentalist by the instrument he plays—but during the rehearsal in a non-personal way or with reference to the performing or-

ganization only. Not many in the audience know of this form of address, however, and mirth results by the conjecture of a caricature of a man in the shape of a slide trombone. And the others in the same opera have those euphonious non-sense syllables that actually carry the connotation of the character they represent: Yum-Yum as the delectable young lady in love with Nanki-Poo, Pitti-Sing, and obviously a spoonerism, Peep-Bo, all school companions whose trio is one of the high points of a performance. Of course, Pooh-Bah is onomatopoetic for the blustry, vaunted character around whom the opera centers, and Pish-Tush reveals the questionable intelligence of A Noble Lord as readily as Go-To represents a Man of Few Words. (pp. 24-5)

Gilbert's men are characters. The most colorful is Pooh-Bah, Lord High Everything Else in the town of Titipu. (p. 25)

The very complexity of Pooh-Bah is the seriousness with which Gilbert sees Everyman. In a conversation with Ko-Ko who asks advice about the cost of a court marriage, Pooh-Bah not only reflects the paradoxes confronting the world, but those of the philosopher who sees things too clearly. He gives conflicting advice according to the offices he alternately represents. As Private Secretary, who knows the funds will come from the city treasury, he states that expense is of no consideration. But as Chancellor of the Exchequer, it is of primary consideration. And so on through several court offices. (p. 26)

The ultimate secret of the seriousness in Gilbert and Sullivan is that the texts avoided the distasteful, vulgar, and cheap; the emotions depicted are never hate and revenge. The music reflects this. The well-bred captain of *H.M.S. Pinafore* never—but, being forced by the echoing chorus to be more truthful, admits *hardly ever*—uses a big, big D . . . , whatever the emergency. This is the tone of the Savoy operas. Love is a central theme, and a plot of innocence rather than malicious intrigue moves it along. On the surface, it is clean comedy, it is supple satire; fundamentally, it is significantly serious. (p. 34)

> *Paul J. Revitt, "Gilbert and Sullivan: More Seriousness than Satire," in* Western Humanities Review *(copyright, 1965, University of Utah), Vol. 19, No. 1, Winter, 1965, pp. 19-34.**

JOHN BUSH JONES   (essay date 1968)

Virtually everyone who writes on the Gilbert and Sullivan operas refers to their peculiar brand of humor as "topsy-turvy" and to the many worlds of W. S. Gilbert's creation as "Topsy-turvydom." If these writers go on to define the terms (and many do not), they are usually content to say that topsy-turvydom is the inversion of the world as we know it, and that the humor arises from our seeing convicts become public officials, policemen turn cowards, or gondoliers assume the functions of royalty. The implication is that the humor of topsy-turvydom is the result of cherished ideas and commonplaces turned upside down. It is from the "humor" thus broadly defined that the adjective "Gilbertian" has evolved and worked its way into the dictionary.

And yet, the simple inversion of the world is not necessarily humorous, nor is it the private claim of a single dramatist. *King Lear* presents a world turned upside down—children governing parents, a king made a virtual subject—but the product is certainly not humor. Similarly, in the sphere of comic drama, writers from Aristophanes on down have delighted in distorting the everyday and examining the consequences. If, then, Gilbert's humor merits a distinguishing adjective of its own (as I believe it does), we must look deeper for those characteristics which may rightly be called Gilbertian. (pp. 28-9)

[William Archer] came closest to singling out the distinctive quality of the dramatist's humor [see exerpt above]. Archer maintains that "a strong logical faculty is the basis of this humor. *Reductio ad absurdum* is its favourite method of procedure. Maxims of morality carried to their logical extreme and developed into paradoxes are its chosen playthings. The 'contrast yet kinship,' to use Mr. Carlyle's phrase, between the every-day common-sense application of these principles and Mr. Gilbert's apparently logical deductions from them, forms the basis of our enjoyment." Whereas many later writers only noted Gilbert's inverted world, Archer early discovered *how* that inversion was brought about. The distinguishing feature of Gilbertian humor is the method, not the end product.

In limiting its remarks to Gilbert's treatment of "maxims of morality," Archer's definition remains incomplete. In fact it has, in part, been contradicted. Walter Sichel observed that the humor is "the triumph of hypothesis, resembling one of those systems that proceed logically from a paradox." To Archer, then, Gilbert's humor ends in paradox; to Sichel, it begins in it. Neither conclusion is entirely accurate, for regardless of the absurdity of the initial proposition, Gilbert's logical development of it, unlike paradox, is seldom self-contradictory and never at odds with common sense. Rather, Gilbert uses common sense to carry the premise to its ultimate and often preposterous conclusions.

Furthermore, especially in the plots of the operas, there is a two-stage logical development of the basic premise. The first logical deduction serves to complicate the action; the second—the logic pushed to its farthest limit—functions as the denouement. (p. 29)

The proposition on which the plot of *Ruddigore* is based, is the curse placed on Sir Rupert, the first baronet, and all his descendants.... [The] complicating action proceeds directly and logically from the terms of the curse.

In the concluding moments of the play, all is resolved by logically carrying the first premise to its ultimate conclusion.... Thus, through commonsense reasoning, Gilbert has pushed the *same proposition* that complicated the action to its logical extreme, thereby resolving the plot. (pp. 29-30)

[This denouement and the proposition from which it evolves is] in the realm of pure fantasy, but even within that realm Gilbert follows a course of rigorous logic. If we only accept the fantastic framework and the farfetched initial premise, we can then trace common sense working its way to a comic resolution; everything is consistent, nothing jars.

Occasionally Gilbert slightly varies his method by placing his characters in a rather "real" world, letting them get befuddled because of the faulty use of their reason, and finally bringing them back to reality once again by the inevitable extension of their logic, showing them where they went astray. Such a situation occurs in *Princess Ida*....

Gilbert uses this strictly logical approach not only in the complicating and unraveling of entire plots, but also in the other components of the operas. Character delineation and motivation are often solidly grounded in logic, the result being grotesquely humorous distortions of most aspects of human nature. A good number of characters have implanted in them an idée fixe which they accept as a fundamental and inviolable premise on which they methodically and logically base their actions. In *The Pirates of Penzance* it is Frederic's sense of duty; in *Patience* it is the title character's notion of love as unselfishness. In attempting to run their lives purely on logical deductions from these premises, they either run head-on against conflicts with emotion and feeling or they go so far as to work out even these essentially irrational qualities through closely reasoned logic. (p. 30)

By examining the consequences of logic confronting emotions and values, and by submitting irrational human conduct and character to the rules of logic, Gilbert reveals the humor in aspects of humanity too often taken for granted.

The method of Gilbert's satire and social commentary is also a logical process....

Gilbert was trained as a lawyer, and his familiarity with the law is in evidence in many characters and situations in the operas. But even more striking is the way in which the logical legal mind is constantly in play in the creation of the great bulk of the humor. It has become something of a commonplace disparagement of Gilbert to say that his plots and characters are often mechanical. Indeed they are, but this mechanical quality is the direct result of Gilbert's peculiar mechanism—rigorous and consistent logic.... It is, then, this method of humor-through-logic that is the real basis for that topsy-turvy comic inversion we call Gilbertian. (p. 31)

John Bush Jones, "Gilbertian Humor: Pulling Together a Definition," in The Victorian Newsletter, *No. 33, Spring, 1968, pp. 28-31.*

N. W. HENSHAW (essay date 1973)

Gilbert's world is, admittedly, a narrow one. It cheerfully excludes the consideration of any transcendent agonies or ecstasies of the human condition. Serious questions of philosophy, psychology or morality simply never arise. Perhaps Gilbert intends the sanguine implication that, in any sensibly ordered society, matters which do not bear much looking into are best left to look after themselves. In any case, it is with social phenomena alone that Gilbert concerns himself. His special preoccupation is with the absurdities perpetrated by society's dedication to and dependence on euphemism, equivocation and downright hypocrisy. But all the while Gilbert is exposing society's absurdities, he is simultaneously delighting in the capacity of absurdity to triumph over itself. He absolutely revels in civilized man's propensity for observing rituals of speech and behavior which may have no reference to evident probabilities or even to palpable facts.

Some of the rituals have changed since Gilbert's time, but the use of ritual goes on. Brides, for instance, are always described as lovely, new mothers are always congratulated, people are always delighted to meet one another and always speak well of the dead.... In our world, as in Gilbert's, social interaction requires a certain minimum cushion of falsehood. So, in a certain context, a certain sort of lie may be, for all practical purposes, a certain sort of truth, and here we have the basic Gilbertian paradox of situation.

Consider a case in which the true king's identity is doubtful and both pretenders to the throne are not only unsuitable but reluctant. A third, unexpected pretender turns up, a highly suitable and eager young man who is clearly the best man for the position. The best man for the position is obviously the true king, and if he is the true king, why not say so? Inez, in *The Gondoliers*, does say so and, when it is to everyone's advantage to believe it, why should anyone doubt it?

It is by insistence on and adherence to such logical absurdities as this that Gilbert circumscribes his bright little, tight little, slight little, light little, trim little, prim little world. Gilbert's characters often behave as if false were true, upside-down were right-side-up, mutually exclusive phenomena were peacefully coexistent and nonsense were sense. But since in his world, as in our own, much conventionally accepted sense proves, on examination, to be nonsense, who knows? The best way to face reality, in our world as in his, may sometimes be to stand stalwartly on one's head. (p. 50).

Gilbertian inversion is not unrelated to the logic of real events. . . . The difference between our adjustments and those of Gilbert's characters is only that ours take time and anguish, while theirs take only an inversion of image—as through a glass, brightly. We try to untangle the paradoxes which confront us, they accept and embrace paradox as the basic stuff of life. (pp. 51-2)

Paradox manifests itself in even the smallest units of phrase, action or idea: *"Utopia, Limited,"* "Modified rapture," "with happiness my soul is cloyed," "I once made an affadavit; but it died," "I said often, frequently, only once." Gilbert's puns, incidentally, are not irrelevant frivolities but instances of paradox in microcosm, and they are perfectly integral to their contexts. . . . *Princess Ida* teems with punning passages which are not silly wordplay, but wordplay about silliness. . . . (p. 53)

At least once in every opera we are presented with a delicate diagram of pathos which invites us to be moved if we care to be—in a refined and respectable way, of course. We are provided with a momentary respite from self-deprecation, a token assurance that even an Englishman must cry just once or twice. Deeply involving, individualized emotion would be out of place and unseemly in these cases. It would also be uncalled-for since in the Gilbert and Sullivan world (as often in our own), sound, sensible, normal people do manage to muddle through. Gilbert's characters never cause us to doubt that if they turn enough logical summersaults they will eventually land right-side-up, whichever way that turns out to be. After a sympathetic tear or two, we return, relaxed and refreshed, to invigorating astringency. (p. 58)

Gilbert and Sullivan opera is a minor art form with no pretensions to intellectual eminence or scholarship sublime, let alone emotional profundity. Here is no poignant contrast with human pain, no laughter with overtones of cosmic despair, no complex interweaving of tragic and comic strands in which the ambiguities of existence are ensnared. Here, rather, along with other delights, is the satisfaction of a minor but universal craving for safe and sane sentiment without any sting. (p. 62)

N. W. Henshaw, "Gilbert and Sullivan through a Glass Brightly," in The Texas Quarterly (© *1973 by The University of Texas at Austin), Vol. XVI, No. 4, Winter, 1973, pp. 48-65.**

MAX KEITH SUTTON   (essay date 1975)

[*The Bab Ballads*] convey a bold vision of men's pretenses at having attained order in an unstable world. They expose characters in the act of maintaining this illusion through clinging to a persona, as Simon Magus does in playing the role of a pious clergyman. They show how obsessively people rely upon systems—rituals, laws, rules of ehtics and etiquette—to give life the semblance of order, and thereby neglect the possibility of living freely, even happily, as the two marooned Englishmen lived before being trapped once more by their sense of propriety.

Gilbert's darker poems provide a significant background for the themes of the humorous ones. "At a Pantomime" reads almost like a song of experience, bringing into Bab's world an awareness of facts that loom above the trivial concerns of his comic figures. Though the children at the pantomime "clap and crow," the elders see Father Christmas as a skeleton. . . . Knowing "Starvation,—Poor Law Union Fare," "cold and want and death," "They wearily sit, and grimly long / For the Transformation Scene." Against this serious background, Bab's characters appear all the more absurd by treating etiquette, royalty, or social status as if it were the crucial fact of their existence. Death by itself dwarfs the concerns of an artificial society.

The ballads are also bold in entertaining a view of reality that offers no simplistic sense of providence, no consistent poetic justice, and no assurance of the rightness of one's goals and values. Bab dared to dream of Topsy-Turveydom where "vice is virtue—virtue vice" . . . , and to suggest to those Victorians who put their faith in moral absolutes that this world might be one of moral relativism. Against the vision of the terrestrial globe rolling on its "pathless" course, Bab shows how men persist in investing objects and rules with absolute value and absolute authority. Between the little circles of their awareness and the vast, ignored stage on which they act, such incongruity exists that Bab can offer a comic vision of human rivalries, codes, and ambitions. The vision becomes satiric as well as comic whenever Bab helps us to remember alternatives: Captain Reece does not have to be a slave of duty; Somers and Gray do not have to deprive themselves of companionship and their favorite foods. But in Bab's world, to be natural "is always unbusiness-like," and his comic figures cling to their obsessions unless freedom comes to them . . . in the only way they can respect—by "compulsion." (pp. 46-7)

As a librettist, Gilbert could make the fullest use of his talent for stylizing life. This talent had given distinction to the absurd figures in his comic drawings; stylization allowed him to condense a Victorian melodrama into a one-page parody in *Fun* and to transform a breach-of-promise suit into a page of comic opera, the first version of *Trial by Jury*. Verse could save Gilbert so many words, as anyone can tell by comparing the opening of *H.S. Pinafore*, of *The Mikado* or of *The Gondoliers* with the expositon scenes of his prose plays. The conventions of opera, ridiculous or not, sanctioned sudden expression of feeling ("Oh horror!" "O ciel!"), quick changes of heart, and asides: operatic emotion could be stylized, and conventions provided the formula for it. (p. 85)

Finally, music could add to Gilbert's work what he had tried desperately to "pump up" in *Broken Hearts* and had totally avoided in *Engaged*. Music could stir feeling—joy, sadness, pride, even tenderness—and restore to the operas the emotional vitality that the librettist apparently forfeited by stylization and caricature. . . . In the most unlikely places, it could give the operas sentimental appeal. . . . The right music could intensify the moments of feeling as well as add to the humor in Gilbert's work. (pp. 85-6)

In expressing this conflict, the action of *Thespis*, the first opera with Sullivan, is so simple that it is ritualistic. Actors invade Mount Olympus, usurp the functions of the decrepit gods for a year, and are finally driven away when the gods return. Gilbert was still building on this pattern at the end of the series, when in *The Grand Duke* another dramatic company gains control of Pfennig-Halbphennig and creates fantastic political and social chaos until the rightful duke returns to power. Between these two works, the "invasion motif" is central to *Iolanthe*, where British lords blunder into fairyland and then suffer a retaliatory extension of fairy power into Parliament.

The movement into a kingdom of fantasy, where the intruders make radical innovations, can also be clearly seen in *The Gondoliers* and *Utopia Limited*. Baratarian society becomes hopelessly muddled by the two commoner-kings' ideal of equality, and Utopia almost bursts into revolution because the English political and economic advisers (the "Flowers of Progress") make its institutions too perfect for human nature to endure. By showing the effects of an intrusion the second acts of these operas resemble the second half of a comedy by Aristophanes, where the focus is on the intrusions of imposters and the movement into a fantastic realm of Barataria, or Utopia, follows the pattern of *The Birds*, where characters from the familiar world venture into the Kingdom of the Hoopoe. (p. 89)

Throughout Gilbert's satire, the fantastic worlds are meant to mirror his society. As one of his fairies remarks, "Great Britain is the type of Fairyland!", and Great Britain provides the model for the absurdities of Titipu, Barataria, and Utopia. If absurdity seemed inseparable from social existence in Gilbert's vision, then a program for reforming society through satire or political action would have been unthinkable. When the Utopians complain that military reform has ruined the country by making it so strong that war is impossible, and when they consider the sanitary and legal reforms to be a disaster because doctors and lawyers are now out of work, the only remedy is to gratify their masochistic need for disorder. (p. 92)

Gilbert's skepticism about reform did not mean that he lacked concern about the welfare of British life. The operas supply grotesque images of the ills and weaknesses of the social order, reflecting in miniature a conflict within an established structure of power. Normally, one character represents official authority—the Judge in *Trial by Jury*, Sir Joseph Porter in *H.M.S. Pinafore*, the Lord Chancellor in *Iolanthe*. Because the chorus has such prominence, the action tends to affect the complete society depicted on the stage. . . . The plot is almost never limited to the problems of the main characters: their difficulties are part of some larger predicament, especially in the last three operas where the emphasis becomes more political than personal, and the theme expresses a concern of Aristophanes—the governing of a state. (pp. 92-3)

The vitality of the Savoy Operas, decades and oceans away from their original time and place, suggests an inner strength that is far more potent than topical satire. Part of their life springs from the ritualistic quality they share with the comedies of Aristophanes. The operas appeal to our delight in ceremonial behavior, to the fun of wearing masks, playing games, and watching contests in which the participants must not violate the most inhibiting rules. (p. 94)

The ritual enacted in a typical Gilbert and Sullivan opera involves an intrusion, a resulting crisis, and a resolution marked by a wedding—by weddings *en masse,* to be more exact. Gilbert complicates this pattern in three basic ways. One is by enlisting sympathy for the nominal intruders, as in *The Gondoliers,* where Marco and Giuseppe technically become impostors when they rule Barataria and yet hold the sympathetic interest of the audience. (p. 95)

A second variation is the ironic ending which allows the impostors to stay in power, rather than be driven off as they usually are in Aristophanes. Despite the Major-General's lie, he escapes death, thanks to the Union Jack; and the Machiavellian Judge wins a bride, or perhaps a mistress, at the end of *Trial by Jury*. A third complication is the double invasion—sometimes reciprocal, as in *Iolanthe* and *The Pirates;* sometimes simply additional, as in Act II of *The Grand Duke,* where the Prince of Monte Carlo intrudes into a court that has already been taken over by impostors. Whatever its form, Gilbert's invasion plot calls for marching or dancing intruders—pirates in a Gothic chapel, bold dragoons, peers in full regalia, fairies before Westminster Hall, the Mikado and his court, and Sir Despard and his "evil crew." If drama is basically movement, and if Attic comedy developed from ritual processions, then the Gilbert and Sullivan operas contain the primal dynamic of theatrical art.

Ritualistic motifs give strength to the most popular of the operas. According to Northrop Frye, the vestiges of a sacrifical rite, "the king's son, the mimic death, the executioner, the substituted victim, are far more explicit" in *The Mikado* "than they are in Aristophanes." Frye uses this opera to illustrate his belief that "the element of play" separates art from savagery: Gilbert's plot affords a way of "playing at sacrifice." Such "playing" occurs in most of the operas. (pp. 95-6)

Gilbert handles the motif repeatedly, but in *The Mikado* he dwells upon it with the most spirit and gusto. . . . Human sacrifice is necessitated in *The Mikado* by the conflict of two worlds. One is Titipu, the lax, workaday world of political expediency where everything, somehow, is "quite correct." Here a public official can plan to marry his ward without feeling any of the legal scruples that bother the Lord Chancellor in *Iolanthe;* and all but one of the public offices can be filled by one man, the versatile Pooh-Bah. Here the Mikado's stifling decree against flirting can be circumvented simply by selecting a Lord High Executioner who is already under sentence of death and therefore "'cannot cut off another's head / Until he's cut his own off.'"

Threatening these ingenious makeshift arrangements are two forces: romantic love and legal absolutism. Nanki-Poo embodies the romantic force; his intrusion at the start of the opera threatens but does not in itself disrupt Ko-Ko's plans for marriage. The larger threat comes from the seat of legal authority, the Mikado's court. His decree against premarital flirtation strikes at life itself, threatening the normal relationships of men and women. (p. 96)

The conflicting forces within *The Mikado* appear repeatedly in other operas. In *The Pirates of Penzance* . . . melodrama represents the absolutist world of rigid order; and the burlesque of melodrama becomes one with the satire of legalistic behavior. With its subtitle, *The Slave of Duty,* which names the central theme, *The Pirates* is an exploration of moral law—the Victorian ethic of duty and renunciation. (p. 99)

The action of *The Pirates* develops the conflict between absolutism and relativism. The central event is Frederic's coming of age, ending his apprenticeship to the pirates, and allowing him to re-enter respectable society. While he sees piracy and respectability as opposites, his view is constantly challenged and ridiculed as the opera unfolds. The King warns him of the "cheating world" of Victorian finance. . . . The Major-General demonstrates this point when he lies about being an orphan: he is as dishonest as the outlaws. The first act ends with a symbolic equation between piracy and British society, as the Pirate King unfurls the Jolly Roger and the Major-General waves the Union Jack. (pp. 100-01)

The Pirates shows our world of moral confusion, and it torments the romantic hero by placing him in such a dilemma that he must betray his beloved in order to perform his duty. (p. 101)

The drama of choice is at the heart of *Iolanthe,* the most intricate and perhaps the most brilliant exploration of conflicting worlds in all of Gilbert and Sullivan. Fairyland and British politics are the two alternatives, and almost every element in the opera expresses their opposition. (p. 102)

Psychologically the divisions persist in the chief mortal, the Lord Chancellor, whose mind is like a courtroom in which his romantic self pleads against his official conscience and persona. . . . This complicated being embodies British law, and he must confront the embodiment of another law in the Fairy Queen.

The antagonism between the Queen and the Lord Chancellor, the fairies and the peers, has more solid grounds than fantasy. . . . If *Iolanthe* follows the symbolic implications of *The Wicked World,* the fairies reflect Victorian womanhood; and their conflict with the peers is, in part, a battle of the sexes. (p. 103)

In the most serious work by Gilbert and Sullivan, *The Yeomen of the Guard,* the characters choose, scheme, and suffer beneath a huge symbol of the law—the Tower of London. (p. 106)

Whether interpreted as death or fainting, [Jack Point's] falling "insensible" at the end represents the collapse of his spirit. The jester's mask cannot fit the shape of his grief over losing Elsie.

When he falls, the Tower stands in the background, looming over the one character who is destroyed by the events arising from an unjust imprisonment. The opera ends with ironic contrasts: instead of a public execution, the climactic scene is a wedding celebration, interrupted by a frail jester; the bride and groom embrace as he falls at their feet. The players' folk melody is sung once more before the awe-

some prison, and the "singing farce of the Merryman and his Maid"—which had told of an imagined reunion—now tells of their separation. If there is a secret source for these ironies, it should lie hidden somewhere in the recesses of the Tower. Gilbert made the Tower his most emphatic symbol of something larger than British or Fairy law and something beyond human power to outwit, alter, or fully understand. Its dark presence gives *The Yeomen of the Guard* a final undertone of tragedy. (p. 108)

Gilbert was unsuited for creating realistic characters in two ways. First, his talent in drawing and writing was for stylization: he perceived types more clearly than individuals. Second, his comic view of a world where anything can happen—where characters like Grosvenor in *Patience* and the Reverend Hopley Porter suddenly reverse roles—contrasts with the vision of stern causality in tragic and naturalistic art. Gilbert could prescribe a way to maintain identity in a song—"Be nobody else but you,"—as Mr. Goldberg tells the princesses in *Utopia,* but to represent the struggle for identity in drama that would seem convincing after Ibsen's plays was beyond his power.

Gilbert's success lay in comically exposing compulsive behavior. Through exaggeration and fantasy, he revealed the human penchant for acting like machines. The characters in *Creatures of Impulse* jerk about like tightly wound toys; the Duke, the Colonel, and the Major become esthetic marionettes in *Patience;* Bartolo and Nina become clockwork dolls in *The Mountebanks.* These images bring into focus Gilbert's sense that people seek conformity rather than the responsibilities of free decision. . . . (pp. 122-23)

Unburdened by a constructive program, Gilbert could indulge in parody and satiric ridicule without pausing to explain or defend a "positive" social or economic theory. Anyone who wanted to know his values could find them stated clearly at the end of *Charity* (he did not invent them) and could realize that honesty and a charitable concern for others were the values implied by the ironies of his comic works. (p. 125)

Max Keith Sutton, in his W. S. Gilbert *(copyright © 1975 by G. K. Hall & Co.; reprinted with the permission of Twayne Publishers, A Division of G. K. Hall & Co., Boston), Twayne, 1975, 150 p.*

BIBLIOGRAPHY

Allen, Reginald. "William Schwenk Gilbert: An Anniversary Survey." *Theatre Notebook* 15, No. 4 (Summer 1961): 118-28.
    Informative survey of Gilbert's literary career, including dates of early published works and first performances of plays and operas.

Bargainnier, Earl F. "*Charity:* W. S. Gilbert's 'Problem Play'." *South Atlantic Bulletin* 42, No. 4 (November 1977): 130-38.
    An analysis of Gilbert's melodrama *Charity* which sees the play as anticipating the 1890s drama of Pinero, Jones, and Shaw.

Coe, Charles N. "Wordplay in Gilbert and Sullivan." *Word Study* XXXVII, No. 3 (February 1962): 6-8.*
    Examines Gilbert's uses of rhetorical devices and figures of speech in the Savoy operas.

Cox-Ife, William. *W. S. Gilbert: Stage Director.* London: Dennis Dobson, 1977, 112 p.

History of the Savoy operas, concentrating on Gilbert's production and directing techniques.

Dark, Sidney, and Grey, Rowland. *W. S. Gilbert: His Life and Letters.* London: Methuen & Co., 1924, 269 p.
    Biography of Gilbert, with some critical sections.

Ellis, James. "The Unsung W. S. Gilbert." *Harvard Library Bulletin* XVIII, No. 2 (April 1970): 109-40.
    Traces the genesis and history of Gilbert's "Bab Ballads."

Garson, R. W. "The English Aristophanes." *Revue de Littérature Comparée* XLVI, No. 2 (April-June 1972): 177-93.*
    Interesting comparison of Gilbert's satire with that of Aristophanes.

Goldberg, Isaac. *The Story of Gilbert and Sullivan; or, The 'Compleat' Savoyard.* Rev. ed. New York: Crown Publishers, 1935, 588 p.*
    Thorough study of the musical partnership, of especial interest for its presentation of contemporary reviews of the opera.

Jones, John Bush. "Gilbert and Sullivan's Serious Satire: More Fact than Fancy." *Western Humanities Review* 21, No. 3 (Summer 1967): 211-24.*
    Point by point argument with critic Paul J. Revitt (see excerpt above) intended to clear up "errors" of latter.

Pearson, Hesketh. *Gilbert and Sullivan: A Biography.* London: Hamish Hamilton, 1935, 319 p.*
    Dramatic, strictly biographical study of the famous collaborators, with separate sections covering Gilbert's life before and after Sullivan.

Pearson, Hesketh. *Gilbert: His Life and Strife.* New York: Harper & Brothers, 1957, 276 p.
    Biography that serves as companion work to *Gilbert and Sullivan: A Biography,* filling in the background details to some of the dramatized episodes in the former book.

Smith, Patrick J. "W. S. Gilbert and the Musical." *Yale Theatre* 4, No. 3 (Summer 1973): 20-6.
    Considers Gilbert's innovations in the stage musical form and his affinities with lyricists of the twentieth-century.

Stedman, Jane W. Introduction to *Gilbert Before Sullivan: Six Comic Plays,* by W. S. Gilbert, edited by Jane W. Stedman, pp. 1-51. Chicago: The University of Chicago Press, 1965.
    Critical and theatrical history of Gilbert's comic plays.

Stedman, Jane W. "From Dame to Woman: W. S. Gilbert and Theatrical Transvestism." *Victorian Studies* 14, No. 1 (September 1970): 27-46.
    Discusses the Victorian theatrical convention of one sex playing parts of the other and how this practice functions in Gilbert's early burlesques.

George (Robert) Gissing

1857-1903

British novelist, short story writer, critic, essayist, and travel writer.

Gissing is considered important, along with George Meredith and Arnold Bennett, for achieving a transition between the Victorian and the modern novel. His novels are Victorian in their three-volume, melodramatic style, but modern in their concern for alienated individuals.

Gissing's early work, often characterized as grim and humorless, dealt with the lower social orders whose lot he idealistically wished to improve, but whom he later came to despise for their vulgarity. In many ways the course of his life and work was determined by his early reformist visions. It is generally conceded that Gissing had a superb scholarly mind, and that he destroyed a potentially brilliant academic career by his youthful love for a prostitute. His idealistic notions of redeeming her led to a series of petty thefts to keep her off the streets; his arrest disrupted his plans for completing his education. He later married the woman, the first of two disastrous marriages.

Gissing's work is often concerned with relationships between men and women. His male characters idealize women in typical Victorian fashion. Inevitably disillusioned, they are forced by experience to accept women as fallible human beings. For this reason, Gissing has often been praised for his efforts to present male and female characters honestly.

Forced to live by his pen, Gissing spent his life torn between the necessity of writing commercially acceptable fiction and his desire to create fiction that lived up to his neo-classic ideal of art. His most famous novel, *New Grub Street*, examines this basic division of purpose. Gissing was extremely poor most of his adult life, and a typical situation in his novels involves the dilemma of a sensitive soul forced by poverty to live in squalor among intellectual inferiors.

Although a few of his novels were popular with other authors, his work was long ignored by the critical community. In the past two decades, however, there has been a resurgence of interest in his work. Critics now recognize his importance as a chronicler of English life and the alienated individual's response to it.

PRINCIPAL WORKS

Workers in the Dawn (novel) 1880

The Unclassed (novel) 1884
Demos: A Story of English Socialism (novel) 1886
Isabel Clarendon (novel) 1886
Thyrza: A Tale (novel) 1887
A Life's Morning (novel) 1888
The Nether World: A Novel (novel) 1889
The Emancipated: A Novel (novel) 1890
New Grub Street: A Novel (novel) 1891
Born in Exile: A Novel (novel) 1892
Denzil Quarrier (novel) 1892
The Odd Women (novel) 1893
In the Year of Jubilee: A Novel (novel) 1894
Eve's Ransom: A Novel (novel) 1895
The Whirlpool (novel) 1897
Charles Dickens: A Critical Study (criticism) 1898
Human Odds and Ends: Stories and Sketches (short stories and sketches) 1898
The Town Traveller (novel) 1898
The Crown of Life (novel) 1899
By the Ionian Sea: Notes of a Ramble in Southern Italy (travel essays) 1901
Our Friend the Charlatan: A Novel (novel) 1901
The Private Papers of Henry Ryecroft (novel) 1903
Veranilda: A Romance (unfinished novel) 1904
Will Warburton: A Romance of Real Life (novel) 1905
The House of Cobwebs, and Other Stories (short stories) 1906

HENRY JAMES (essay date 1897)

[For Gissing] I profess, and have professed ever since reading "The New Grub Street," a persistent taste—a taste that triumphs even over the fact that he almost as persistently disappoints me. I fail as yet to make out why exactly it is that going so far he so sturdily refuses to go further. The whole business of distribution and composition he strikes me as having cast to the winds. . . . (p. 438)

"The Whirlpool," I crudely confess, was in a manner a grief to me, but the book has much substance, and there is no light privilege in an emotion so sustained. This emotion perhaps it is that most makes me, to the end, stick to Mr. Gissing—makes me with an almost nervous clutch quite cling to him. I shall not know how to deal with him, however, if I withhold the last outrage of calling him an interesting case. He seems to me above all a case of saturation, and it is mainly his saturation that makes him interesting—I mean especially in the sense of making him singular. The interest would be greater were his art more complete; but we must take what we can get, and Mr. Gissing has a way of his own. The great thing is that his saturation is with elements that, presented to us in contemporary English fiction, affect us as a product of extraordinary oddity and rarity: he reeks with the savour, he is bowed beneath the fruits, of contact with the lower, with the lowest middle-class, and that is sufficient to make him an authority—*the* authority in fact—on a region vast and unexplored.

The English novel has as a general thing kept so desperately, so nervously clear of it, whisking back compromised skirts and bumping frantically against obstacles to retreat, that we welcome as the boldest of adventurers a painter who has faced it and survived. (pp. 438-39)

[Gissing] *is* serious—almost imperturbably—about [his lower-class characters], and, as it turns out, even quite manfully and admirably sad. He has the great thing: his saturation (with the visible and audible common) can project itself, let him get outside of it and walk round it. I scarcely think he stays, as it were, outside quite as much as he might; and on the question of form he certainly strikes me as staying far too little. It is form above all that is talent, and if Mr. Gissing's were proportionate to his knowledge, to what may be called his possession, we should have a larger force to reckon with. (pp. 440-41)

It is impossible not to be affected by the frankness and straightness of Mr. Gissing's feeling for his subject, a subject almost always distinctly remunerative to the ironic and even to the dramatic mind. He has the strongest deepest sense of common humanity, of the general struggle and the general grey grim comedy. He loves the real, he renders it, and though he has a tendency to drift too much with his tide, he gives us, in the great welter of the savourless, an individual manly strain. (p. 443)

> *Henry James, "London Notes, July 1897," in his* Notes on Novelists, with Some Other Notes *(abridged by permission of Charles Scribner's Sons; copyright 1914 by Charles Scribner's Sons; renewal copyright 1942 by Henry James), Scribner's, 1914, pp. 436-45.**

H. G. WELLS (essay date 1897)

The treatment of the work of Mr. Gissing as a progress, an adolescence, is inevitable. In the case of no other important writer does one perceive quite so clearly the steady elimination of immaturities. As a matter of fact his first novels must have been published when he was ridiculously young.

The earlier novelists seem to have shaped their stories almost invariably upon an illustrative moral intention, and to have made a typical individual, whose name was commonly the title of the novel, the structural skeleton, the sustaining interest of the book. . . . About the central character a system of reacting personages and foils was arranged, and the whole was woven together by an ingenious and frequently complicated "plot." . . . The new structural conception was the grouping of characters and incidents . . . [in the novel] about some social influence or some far-reaching movement of humanity. Its first great exponent was Victor Hugo. . . . Zola's "Lourdes" and "Rome," and Tolstoi's

"War and Peace" are admirable examples of this impersonal type of structure. This new and broader conception of novel construction finds its most perfect expression in several of the works of Turgenév. . . . (pp. 192-93)

No English novelists of the first rank have arisen to place beside the great Continental masters in this more spacious development of structural method. . . . Within the last few years, however, three English novelists at least have arisen, who have set themselves to write novels which are neither studies of character essentially, nor essentially series of incidents, but deliberate attempts to present in typical groupings distinct phases of our social order. And of these the most important is certainly Mr. George Gissing.

The "Whirlpool," for instance, Mr. Gissing's latest novel, has for its structural theme the fatal excitement and extravagance of the social life of London. . . . The design has none of the spare severity that makes the novels of Turgenév supreme, but the breadth and power of its conception are indisputable. It is, perhaps, the most vigorously designed of all the remarkable series of novels Mr. Gissing has given us. But the scheme of his "Emancipated" is scarcely less direct, presenting as it does, in an admirably contrived grouping, the more or less complete release from religious and moral restraints of a number of typical characters. "In the Year of Jubilee" is more subtly and less consistently planned. The picture of lower middle-class barbarism, relieved by the appreciative comments of Mr. Samuel Barmby, voracious reader of a latter-day press, was conceived in a fine vein of satire, but the development of the really very unentertaining passions of the genteel Tarrant robs the book of its unity and it breaks up into a froth of intrigue about a foolish will and ends mere novel of a very ordinary kind. (pp. 193-94)

So far as the structural scheme goes there is an increased conventionality of treatment as we pass to Mr. Gissing's earlier novels, to "Thyrza," "Demos," and "The Nether World," and from these the curious may descend still lower to the amiable renunciations in "A Life's Morning." "The Unclassed" has its width of implication mainly in its name; it is a story of by no means typical persons, and with no evident sense of the larger issues. But "The Nether World," for instance, albeit indisputably "plottésque," and with such violent story mechanisms in it as the incredible Clem Peckover and that impossible ancient, Snowdon, does in its title, and here and there in a fine passage, betray already an inkling of the spacious quality of design the late works more and more clearly display. (p. 194)

[He] has been learning life and his art simultaneously. (p. 195)

Through all the novels of Mr. Gissing, fading with their progress, indeed, and yet still evident even in the latest, runs [the] quality of bias, that intervention. Very few of them are without a "most favoured" character. (p. 196)

Apart from their aspect as a diminishing series of blemishes, of artistic disfigurements, the "exponent" characters of Mr. Gissing deserve a careful consideration. If they are, in varying proportion, ideal personages, unstudied invention that is, they are, at any rate, unconventional ideal persons, created to satisfy the author rather than his readers. Taken collectively, the present an interesting and typical development, they display the personal problem with a quality of quite unpremeditated frankness. . . . At the outset we encounter an attitude of mind essentially idealistic, hedonistic, and polite, a mind coming from culture to the study of life, trying life, which is so terrible, so brutal, so sad and so tenderly beautiful, by the clear methodical measurements of an artificial refinement, and expressing even in its earliest utterance a note of disappointment. At first, indeed, the illusion dominates the disappointment.... [The essential fallacy of Mr. Gissing's earlier attitude is that] there are two orders of human beings.... It is evident in a curious frequency of that word "noble" throughout all his works. The suburban streets are ignoble, great London altogether is ignoble, the continent of America also, considered as a whole. This nobility is a complex conception of dignity and space and leisure, of wide, detailed, and complete knowledge, of precision of speech and act without flaw or effort; it is, indeed, the hopeless ideal of a scholarly refinement.

As one passes to the later novels the clearness of vision increases, and the tone of disappointment deepens.... People say that much of Mr. Gissing's work is "depressing," and to a reader who accepts his postulates it is indisputable that it is so. The idealised "noble" women drop out of these later works altogether, the exponent personages no longer marry and prosper, but suffer, and their nobility tarnishes. Yet he clings in the strangest way to his early standards of value, and merely widens his condemnation with a widening experience. In "Eve's Ransom" and "New Grub Street" the stress between an increasingly truthful vision of things and the odd, unaltered conception that life can only be endurable with leisure, with a variety of books, agreeable furniture, service, costume, and refined social functions, finds its acute expression. The exponent character—a very human one—in "New Grub Street," Reardon, is killed by that conflict.... (pp. 197-98)

In the early novels it would seem that the worst evil Mr. Gissing could conceive was crudity, passion, sordidness and pain. But the "Whirlpool" is a novel of the civilised, and a countervailing evil is discovered—sterility. This brilliant refinement spins down to extinction, it is the way of death. London is a great dying-place, and the old stupidness of the homely family are, after all, the right way. That is "The Whirlpool's" implication.... (p. 199)

Mr. Gissing has written a series of extremely significant novels, perhaps the only series of novels in the last decade whose interest has been strictly contemporary.... [Admirable] as his work has been, he is still barely ripening and ... his best has still to come.... (p. 201)

H. G. Wells, "The Novels of Mr. George Gissing," in Contemporary Review, Vol. LXXII, August, 1897, pp. 192-201.

ARNOLD BENNETT (essay date 1899)

[It is the depressing], 'grey' quality of his subjects, so repellent to the public, which specially recommends Mr Gissing's work to the critics.... To take the common grey things which people know and despise, and, without tampering, to disclose their essential grandeur—that is realism, as distinguished from idealism or romanticism. It may scarcely be, it probably is not, the greatest art of all; but it is art, precious and indisputable. Such art has Mr Gissing accomplished. In *The Nether World,* his most characteristic book, the myriad squalid futilities of an industrial quarter of London are gathered up

into a large coherent movement of which the sinister and pathetic beauty is but too stringently apparent.... Sometimes, by a single sentence, Mr Gissing will evoke from the most obscure phenomena a large and ominous idea. The time is six o'clock, and the workshops are emptying. He says: 'It was the hour of the unyoking of men.' A simple enough phrase, but it lends colour to the aspect of a whole quarter, and fills the soul with a vague, beautiful sense of sympathetic trouble. This is a good example of Mr Gissing's faculty of poetical constructive observation—a faculty which in his case is at once a strength and a weakness. He sees the world not bit by bit—a series of isolations—but broadly, in vast wholes. He will not confine himself to a unit, whether of the individual or the family. He must have a plurality, working in and out, mutually influencing, as it were seething. So he obtains an elaborate and complicated reflection of the variety and confusion of life impossible to be got in any other way. So also by grouping similar facts he multiplies their significance into something which cannot be ignored. That is his strength. His weakness is that he seems never to be able to centralise the interest. His pictures have no cynosure for the eye. The defect is apparent in all his books, from *The Unclassed,* a youthful but remarkable work, wherein several separate narratives are connected by a chain of crude coincidences, down to the recently published *Crown of Life,* of which the story loses itself periodically in a maze of episodes each interrupting the others. Out of the fine welter of *The Nether World* nothing emerges paramount. There are a dozen wistful tragedies in this one novel, of which the canvas is as large as that of *Anna Karenina*—a dozen exquisite and moving renunciations with their accompanying brutalities and horror; but the dark grandeur which ought to have resulted from such an accumulation of effects is weakened by a too impartial diffusion of the author's imaginative power. (pp. 362-63)

Mr Gissing has often been called a pessimist: he is not one. He paints in dark tints, for he has looked on the sum of life, those few who have done this are well aware that life is dark.... The average artist stays at home in life; Mr Gissing has travelled far, and brought back strange, troublous tales full of disturbing beauty; and he suffers for his originality.... But Mr Gissing is not thereby constituted a pessimist; he is merely a man who can gaze without blinking; he is not soured; he has, I fancy, the marvellous belief that happiness is evenly distributed among the human race; he may sup on horrors, but he can digest them without a headache the next morning; he is neither gay nor melancholy, but just sober, calm, and proud against the gods; he has seen, he knows, he is unmoved; he defeats fate by accepting it.... This may be grievous, but is not pessimism. (p. 365)

Arnold Bennett, "Mr. George Gissing, an Inquiry" (originally published in Academy, Vol. LVII, No. 1441, December 16, 1899), in Gissing: The Critical Heritage, edited by Pierre Coustillas and Colin Partridge (© Pierre Coustillas and Colin Partridge 1972), Routledge & Kegan Paul, 1972, pp. 361-65.

THOMAS SECCOMBE (essay date 1906)

Upon the larger external rings of the book-reading multitude it is not probable that Gissing will ever succeed in impressing himself. There is an absence of transcendental quality about his work, a failure in humour, a remoteness from actual life, a deficiency in awe and mystery, a shortcoming in emotional power, finally, a lack of the dramatic faculty, not indeed indispensable to a novelist, but almost indispensable as an ingredient in great novels of this particular genre. In temperament and vitality he is palpably inferior to the masters (Dickens, Thackeray, Hugo, Balzac) whom he reverenced with such a cordial admiration and envy. A 'low vitality' may account for what has been referred to as the 'nervous exhaustion' of his style. It were useless to pretend that Gissing belongs of right to the 'first series' of English Men of Letters. (p. ix)

The *Nether World* contains Gissing's most convincing indictment of Poverty; and it also expresses his sense of revolt against the ugliness and cruelty which is propagated like a foul weed by the barbarous life of our reeking slums. Hunger and Want show Religion and Virtue the door with scant politeness in this terrible book. The material had been in his possession for some time, and in part it had been used before in earlier work. It was now utilised with a masterly hand, and the result goes some way, perhaps, to justify the well-meant but erratic comparisions that have been made between Gissing and such writers as Zola, Maupassant and the projector of the *Comédie Humaine*. The savage luck which dogs Kirkwood and Jane, and the worse than savage—the inhuman—cruelty of Clem Peckover, . . . render the book an intensely gloomy one; it ends on a note of poignant misery, which gives a certain colour for once to the oft-repeated charge of morbidity and pessimism. Gissing understood the theory of compensation, but was unable to exhibit it in action. He elevates the cult of refinement to such a pitch that the consolations of temperament, of habit, and of humdrum ideals which are common to the coarsest of mankind, appear to elude his observation. He does not represent men as worse than they are; but he represents them less brave. No social stratum is probably quite so dull as he colours it. There is usually a streak of illusion or a flash of hope somewhere on the horizon. (p. xxvii)

[Gissing] gradually obtained a rare mastery in the delineation of his unlovely *mise en scène*. . . . In all his best books we have evidence of the savage and ironical delight with which he depicted to the shadow of a hair the sordid and vulgar elements by which he had been so cruelly depressed. The aesthetic observer who wanted material for a picture of the blank desolation and ugliness of modern city life could find no better substratum than in the works of George Gissing. Many of his descriptions of typical London scenes . . . are the work of a detached, remorseless, photographic artist realising that ugly sordidness of daily life to which the ordinary observer becomes in the course of time as completely habituated as he does to the smoke-laden air. To a cognate sentiment of revolt I attribute that excessive deference to scholarship and refinement which leads him in so many novels to treat these desirable attributes as if they were ends and objects of life in themselves. It has also misled him but too often into depicting a world of suicides, ignoring or overlooking a secret hobby, or passion, or chimaera which is the one thing that renders existence endurable to so many of the waifs and strays of life. He takes existence sadly—too sadly, it may well be; but his drabs and greys provide an atmosphere that is almost inseparable to some of us from our gaunt London streets. (pp. l-li)

There may be a perceptible lack of virility, a fluctuating vagueness of outline about the characterisation of some of his men. In his treatment of crowds, in his description of a mob, personified as 'some huge beast purring to itself in stupid contentment,' he can have few rivals. In tracing the influence of women over his heroes he evinces no common subtlety; it is here probably that he is at his best. (pp. li-lii)

Gissing was a sedulous artist; some of his books, it is true, are very hurried productions, finished in haste for the market with no great amount either of inspiration or artistic confidence about them. But little slovenly work will be found bearing his name, for he was a thoroughly trained writer; a suave and seductive workmanship had become a second nature to him, and there was always a flavour of scholarly, subacid and quasi-ironical modernity about his style. There is little doubt that his quality as a stylist was better adapted to the studies of modern London life, on its seamier side, which he had observed at first hand, than to stories of the conventional dramatic structure which he too often felt himself bound to adopt. In these his failure to grapple with a big objective, or to rise to some prosperous situation, is often painfully marked. A master of explanation and description rather than of animated narrative or sparkling dialogue, he lacked the wit and humour, the brilliance and energy of a consummate style which might have enabled him to compete with the great scenic masters in fiction, or with craftsmen such as Hardy or Stevenson, or with incomparable wits and conversationalists such as Meredith. It is true, again, that his London-street novels lack certain artistic elements of beauty (though here and there occur glints of rainy or sunset townscape in a half-tone, consummately handled and eminently impressive); and his intense sincerity cannot wholly atone for this loss. Where, however, a quiet refinement and delicacy of style is needed as in those sane and suggestive, atmospheric, critical or introspective studies, such as *By the Ionian Sea*, the unrivalled presentment of *Charles Dickens*, and that gentle masterpiece of softened autobiography, *The Private Papers of Henry Ryecroft* . . . in which he indulged himself during the last and increasingly prosperous years of his life, then Gissing's style is discovered to be a charmed instrument. (pp. lii-liii)

Thomas Seccombe, "The Work of George Gissing," in The House of Cobwebs *by George Gissing, E. P. Dutton & Co., 1906, pp. vii-liv.*

MAY YATES (essay date 1922)

Amidst much that is inconclusive and variable, much that may be interpreted as dramatic rather than personal opinion, there may be traced throughout [Gissing's] novels a fairly consistent attitude to life. The author's beliefs hang well together: he loved the classics; believed in aristocracy; had hopes of education; despised politics; distrusted the press; hated modern civilization; and loathed industrialism, with its logical outcome, war. (p. 16)

The natural bent of Gissing's mind was certainly aristocratic, and the course of his life confirmed it. He passed impressionable years amidst squalor and domestic misery, constantly retreating in self-defence to that inner sanctuary of mind and memory where Greek and Roman polity prevailed. His innate distaste for democracy was thus strengthened, so that he eventually arrived at a frame of mind combining contempt for popular life and opinion with an almost absurd veneration for scholarship and refinement. (pp. 16-17)

Out of the twenty-two novels which Gissing wrote, twenty-one have, at any rate in part, a London background. (p. 31)

[Gissing's London is] a city of dull, drab, wearisome streets seen through an intermittent drizzle of rain. (p. 32)

It is against backgrounds such as these that Gissing's characters play out their parts. The backgrounds themselves are not unfamiliar to the dweller in the industrial north; which, by the way, Gissing neither liked nor understood. What is unfamiliar is the absence of friendliness and good-will; the depressing atmosphere of indifference, suspicion, even hostility. (p. 33)

Slums and tenements with their countless one-roomed houses, lacking the very essentials of decency, privacy and cleanliness, are depicted with unsparing fidelity, yet with restraint and a certain fastidiousness of touch which prevented Gissing from being a realist of the order of the Continent. (p. 35)

Gissing rarely identifies himself with the suffering he is describing; he is always a little aloof, a little detached from the actual life of the workers. He was incapable of such a passionate exhortation to rebellion as Shelley's *Song to the Men of England*, 1819. His attitude shows a curious mixture of pity and contempt. His nature admits of no facile brotherly kindness. He shrinks with disgust from contact with the coarseness, brutality, and ugliness which he describes. His constant protest against the mental and bodily degradation of his fellows is wrung from him by an acute imaginative experience of their woes. Seen through his eyes, their lot is hopeless, their misery unmitigated; but it might not seem so to another observer, or to themselves. Dickens, for example, though some of his London street scenes are sufficiently grim, has always an eye for the redeeming features and for humours. . . . That is the common reaction of the mind against insistent misery, the reaction, probably, of the slum-dwellers themselves. But Gissing absolutely concentrates on the misery he sees and intensifies it a thousandfold in the crucible of his sensitive mind. He makes no allowances; overlooks every compensating feature. Custom has undoubtedly dulled the edge of wretchedness for the majority of slum-dwellers, and though the fact is no argument against social reform, it is an argument against supposing such people to be endowed with acute sensibilities and extraordinary capacity for suffering. . . . Gissing certainly lived in the world he describes—he was never of it; and to this fact we owe the vividness of his descriptions. A more sympathetic observer could never have written the ''Io Saturnalia'' chapter in *The Nether World*. The fine quality of the irony demanded a certain detachment of view. An access of humanity would have spoilt it as literature. (pp. 36-7)

Gissing ultimately realizes something of the communal cheerfulness of crowded city life; something of the fascination of its traffic. (p. 40)

Gissing was far better at portraiture than at landscape, though occasionally in *The Ryecroft Papers* he achieves a precision of glowing colour such as enamels Tennyson's verse. On the whole he is too closely occupied with urban humanity to turn aside for natural description. (p. 43)

[Gissing's] greatest achievement is undoubtedly his delineation of the young man of the period. His heroes are rarely men of action; their tragedies are psychological; thus they fail to achieve popularity, though they bid fair to become a touchstone of criticism both in life and in letters. His portraits of young men are largely autobiographical, and further, they show the workings of the same ''time-spirit'' that influenced Turgenev in the creation of Rudin, and Hardy in the evolution of Jude. In a letter . . . complaining of the obtuseness of contemporary critics, Gissing expressly declares that his books deal with ''a class of young men distinctive of our time: well-educated, fairly-bred, but without money.'' (p. 52)

Gissing's conception of the tragedy of life is largely determined by his reading of Greek literature. His constant theme is one of the oldest in existence—the revolt of man against circumstance—or, to state it in modern terms, the conflict between temperament, heredity, and environment. He takes a fine, sometimes a superfine, nature, a little lacking in moral courage, yet saved from anything approaching baseness by a woven strand of idealism and aspiration; he endows the youth with more than average brains, and less than an average income; he leaves him deficient in self-confidence, then sets him to wrestle with a not-quite-possible task—to force his way, handicapped by birth and breeding, into a higher sphere of society; to achieve success as a novelist, hampered by failing health and hope and an exacting artistic conscience. (pp. 55-6)

Poverty is an artistic necessity in Gissing's strongest work: it supplies that element of contrast without which tragedy cannot take shape. It is the direct cause of suicide in *A Life's Morning*, of misery and misunderstanding in *New Grub Street*, of hypocrisy and concealment in *Born in Exile*. Poverty certainly is a demoralizing circumstance; according to Gissing, it is ''the root of all social ills.'' The peculiarly low key in which his tragedies are pitched is determined by that lack of resilience in his characters directly occasioned by their poverty. (p. 57)

[The] tragedy of his characters is not that they are frustrated and die, but that they are frustrated and live. . . . Gissing absolutely discounts hopefulness as a motive for continued existence in the face of disaster, consequently he has to enter into elaborate psychological explanations to make the conduct of his characters credible. (p. 59)

Gissing's appeal to posterity will probably rest upon his faithful delineation of the struggles of these contemporary young men to whom intellectual and emotional aspiration is at once the safeguard of morality and the substitute for religion. They will remain representative of an age in which ''the fruits of the spirit'' were at a discount.

From first to last Gissing's heroes are idealists where women are concerned. . . . Woman appeals to Gissing as a civilizing, an ennobling, yet at the same time a conservative force, ''the natural safeguard of traditions that have an abiding value.'' In the character of Godwin Peak [the protagonist of *Born in Exile*], Gissing's two idealisms are united: the love of culture for its own sake, and of woman as its highest incarnation. . . . It is no longer woman as woman, but woman as an intellectual equal and companion that Gissing's heroes henceforth profess to desire.

The fact that Godwin Peak can, and does, at one and the same time love Sidwell and speculate about other, though imaginary women, indicates the subtlety of Gissing's psychology of the emotions. This was a state of mind with which he was constantly preoccupied. (pp. 62-5)

Gissing makes one grave mistake, especially in his earlier delineations of women. His idealism will hardly allow that their qualities and motives are just as likely to be mixed as those of men. Women like Maud Enderby in *The Unclassed,* and Emily Hood in *A Life's Morning,* are, quite literally, too good to be true; they leave us cold. There is a tendency for his women to become types rather than individuals; all goodness and graciousness, tenderness and dependence, . . . or all brains and brusquerie, aloofness and independence. . . . (pp. 65-6)

When Gissing devotes his power to the delineation of more complex characters, such as Marion Yule in *New Grub Street,* a girl whose affections and whose intellect are equally responsive, or Beatrice Redwing in *A Life's Morning,* whose warring moods of asceticism and artistic ambition are for the moment harmonized in an act of quixotic devotion, he shows greater penetration, perhaps, than that which allowed Amy Reardon [of *New Grub Street*] scarcely a redeeming feature. Yet she, a woman practically devoid of generous impulse, is one of Gissing's most impressive creations. (p. 68)

[Gissing] is particularly happy in ironical thumb-nail sketches of humanity; an odd line of humour and pathos and a character stands revealed, *e.g.,* Mrs. Yule "with her familiar expression of mental effort," and Mrs. Poppleton, "who could follow nothing but the very macadam of conversation." (p. 71)

Constantly, but not obtrusively, "literary" in his expression, Gissing is yet sparing of quotation, preferring the subtler grace of allusion. (p. 73)

Gissing is particularly happy in throwing a side-light on character by a literary allusion. Thus Godwin Peak, waiting in the theatre queue, tries to console himself with the reflection that he is in the spiritual company of Charles Lamb. (p. 74)

The ease and grace of Gissing's style were not attained without sundry wrestlings with intractable words. . . . (p. 94)

In the words of his favourite, Izaak Walton, his diction was "choicely good." He handles words lovingly, careful not to despoil them of their trailing clouds of glory. In reading his work one continually feels the shock of appreciation caused by sheer felicity of phrasing, or by the perfect union of thought and expression. . . . The peculiarities of his diction are commonly due to the use of words of classical origin or association. We see the pedant at play as he writes of "the future *nigritude*" of Sir Job Whitelaw's statue. . . . But there is a greater art in writing than this simple process of substitution, an art in which Gissing follows Flaubert in his search for *le mot propre.* . . . On the whole, however, Gissing's use of Latin derivatives illustrates his precision of thought rather than his pursuit of beauty. (pp. 94-5)

Gissing's character comes out in his deprecatory habit of phrasing, as if he constantly feared to overstate his case and wished to disarm criticism. He is deficient in self-assertion. This trait is, naturally, most marked in his autobiographical writings. One can hardly turn the pages of *The Ryecroft Papers* without noting phrase after phrase of this kind: "I am no cosmopolite," "I am no botanist," "I am no friend of the people." To describe by negations is the habit of a timid mind. The frequent aspiration of Gissing's

heroes is for "not inadequate leisure" to possess their souls in quiet amongst their beloved books, "a not ignoble ambition." (p. 96)

Gissing has a thin vein of literary humour, not very genial, tending rather to harden into irony. It is the humour of words, not of situations. A purist himself, he delights to pounce upon the misuse of words by the uninitiated. . . . Possibly Gissing regarded his facility in this direction with disdain. His puns are always made by his less distinguished characters. Humour, indeed, is not an integral part of his nature. (pp. 97-8)

What, then, is Gissing's note? What is his special contribution to modern prose? It is the note of the scholar whose appeal is primarily to academic people; by choosing and polishing his diction he has, to some extent, limited his public. He cherishes the classical ideals of lucidity and restraint. His influence should avail to foster the love of letters in an unregenerate age. (p. 99)

> *May Yates, in her* George Gissing: An Appreciation, *Manchester University Press, 1922, 109 p.*

FRANK SWINNERTON (essay date 1923)

[Gissing] did not love his fellow men. He had suffered much, and he was, during the greater part of his life, expressing his suffering in terms of his distaste. For that reason, although he is often mentioned by those who write about novels, he is not very much read by the fashionable; and indeed at the present time I believe the greatest readers of his books are to be found less among those who can appreciate their value than among those who find in the novels an expression of their own bitter, egotistical hostility to life. He is thus, if I am right, helping discontent to arise in the mediocre. It is not that he had any liking for mediocrity—he hated it; nor that his books are addressed to stupid people. But in the nature of things his books will be increasingly read by ill-educated egoists, because they voice numerous dislikes . . . which are capable of flattering a sense of superiority in mis-cultured readers. The ideas he expressed have, as it were, percolated through the strata of intellectual and intelligent people, and they are now food for the agitated lower middle-class. (pp. 19-20)

Being an egoist, he dwelt frequently upon the egoistical temperament, on the point of individual frustration, of individual rebellion. He never in any large sense was a revolutionary, for this reason. His anger with the conditions of life was the anger simply of a man who finds himself out of sympathy with his familiars. It was instinctive, not philosophic, not social. (p. 21)

[He attempted] to generalise his small experiences into a philosophic notion of life. . . . He could not see an incident without spinning from it—not a story, but a series of reflections. He was an essayist, a writer upon moral themes; and he began to write novels. (pp. 41-2)

[It] is very surprising, when one considers the whole of his work, that Gissing should be persistently described as the realistic historian of the lower classes, and particularly of the lower middle-class. Whether he knew anything about the professional and economically-independent classes or not, it is to these that he most often turns in what proves, on the whole, to be his best and most characteristic work. Of clerks, and of the ordinary wage-earning members of the lower middle-class, he seems to have made practically no use in his novels; and where they appear, as in *Eve's Ransom, In the Year of Jubilee,* and *The Town Traveller,* they are generally so eccentric as to give the books no value as social studies. In several of his earlier novels, it is true, a number of the characters belonged to the lower orders; but in only one of them—*The Nether World*—were all the characters by birth proletarian. The bulk of what remains is composed of studies of the modern nervous temperament set against a background of the middle and professional classes. Also, in spite of the fact that Gissing is vaguely labelled a realist by those who suppose realism to connote everything dismal, it is among the studies of abnormal temperament that his most notable successes are to be found. (pp. 49-50)

Gissing was fired, in his early years, to do for English life what Balzac had done for France in the *Comédie Humaine* —an extraordinarily ambitious dream for even the most sanguine young writer. Certainly, his first novel, *Workers in the Dawn,* showed him to be both inexperienced and irresolute, for the book has no Balzacian omniscience and romantic quality. It is a curious mixture of conventionalism, raw philosophy, imperfect observation, imperfect but laborious humour, and imitation of Dickens. (pp. 50-1)

But in spite of the fact that *Workers in the Dawn* represents the crude and youthful Gissing, it has, in view of his later work, very considerable interest for the student. It made a rough attempt to contrast the life of ease and the life of poverty; it allowed Gissing to express many of his various immature philosophical thoughts; and it indicated his inability to imagine life in the warm colours of life itself. It was remote from experience; it revealed a writer who was all his life to lack "intimacy," and who was all his life to write from the head. Gissing was here, even in his first book, the intellectual novelist, . . . endeavouring to frame his characters . . . instead of imagining them. . . . He was too conscious of the defects of his own artistic methods, and too distrustful of the reader's powers of understanding or sympathy, to let the characters explain all. And in the attempt to shape the reader's mind he confessed everything —he confessed that he was writing to the mind, that the characters were mind-created. . . . It was only when his principals took complete hold of him—as they did in *Thyrza* —that the button-holing method, . . . being unnecessary, was cast aside; and then Gissing truly showed his power as a novelist. He was always analytical, scrupulous . . . ; but it was when he trusted himself and the reader that he could also be subtle and convincing. There is every difference between revelation and exposition. (pp. 55-7)

In *The Unclassed,* Gissing the conscious sociologist and artist begins to express himself. We have several declarations upon Art, such as the one that "Art, nowadays, must be the mouthpiece of misery, for misery is the keynote of modern life." It would be impossible to expect a novelist with such a conviction to write otherwise than cheerlessly; and the book is dark with a sense of much evil. But it is a very marked improvement upon *Workers in the Dawn.* We begin to feel the author's power of grasping character. Sometimes that power wavers, and the minor personages are all at the mercy of "characteristic" speeches laid thoughtfully upon them by Gissing. . . . Gissing had not yet achieved the impersonality that he strove after; and the book is again interesting rather in its promise than its performance. (pp. 60-1)

During the next few years, Gissing's observation of the poor grew more exact, until it advanced, from a vague spiritual shame and anger, . . . as exemplified in *Demos,* through humanitarian sentiment, as in *Thyrza,* to the hopelessness of *The Nether World.* Often, in his progress, he almost convinces us of his understanding, only to fall into an exposure of his lack of sympathy with his material. . . . In these early novels about the poor the majority is always hopelessly sprawling in slime, unwashed . . . and repulsive; while, with few exceptions, the virtuous men are agnostic, book-loving, uncultured idealists, fated to unhappiness and useless life. (pp. 63-4)

When we come to *Thyrza,* which I regard as one of Gissing's best books, we shall see that while Thyrza herself is idealised into an almost ethereal person, her sister Lydia is revealed with a sympathy and restraint which is more than commendable. There is, for the first time, an extraordinary subtlety in the method employed. Almost without having our attention drawn to the fact, we are made to realise not only the essential difference between the sisters, but also the attitude towards each of them of every other person in the book. (pp. 68-9)

For the only time in Gissing's lower-class studies we take an active, and not a purely intellectual, interest in the welfare of the persons engaged. This is such a very marked advance for Gissing that it seems to place *Thyrza* easily first among the books of this order, supposing we look first, as we should, for emotion in any work of the imagination. To move by legitimate means is the aim of even the most realistic novelist. (pp. 74-5)

In *The Nether World* the truths of environment are strictly observed. Except that it turns upon the unexpected wealth of a working-class man, and his wish to use this money for the relief of poor people in general, the story is self-supporting. It is easily the ugliest of Gissing's books . . . ; but it is consistent and deserving of respect. (pp. 77-8)

Although as a novel its strength is dissipated by the absence of any clearly defined theme, the quality of the book, judged as a series of chapters, is very high. The characters are finely differentiated, and if that were the sole aim of the novelist it would be achieved here. . . . What the book lacks is that difficult thing, light. It is patient and well reasoned; it is convincing; it simply lacks movement and fire. (pp. 78-9)

Gissing's are all studies of *abnormal* temperament; and, as realism is largely concerned with normality, Gissing's studies are in no way to be regarded (as they have been regarded) as realistic. (p. 86)

New Grub Street is for the first time a book based absolutely on Gissing's personal knowledge of life and living people. Where he has been hitherto a spectator of the classes he has described, he is now writing from experience. . . . The book is convincing as a picture of individuals and, more largely, it is convincing as a picture of a section of life.

The main idea of *New Grub Street* is the contrast between two types of literary man [portrayed by Jasper Milvain and Edward Reardon]. . . . In addition . . . there are the internal affairs of three families . . . which are given in each case with sureness and with proper relation to the rest of the story. Thus the book is well balanced and sane; and while it lacks just that imaginative power which would have made it a great novel—even according to the author's technical ideas, which were old-fashioned—it remains the best picture of middle-class literary life that has been written in English. In every way it is an advance on Gissing's earlier work. . . . By its very "shoppishness" it enables Gissing's purely literary humour (too often that self-conscious irony that degenerates into sarcasm) to have freer play than we shall discover anywhere else in his work. . . . In fact, all Gissing's virtues as a writer have their opportunity of display in this book. (pp. 96-8)

[The] book begins to show, even in twenty years, a slight staleness; but on the whole it is rich in genuine characterisation to an extent unusual with Gissing. (p. 101)

[Born in Exile] is much more pretentious than New Grub Street, because it attempts to give a full-length picture of a man of considerable but perverted talent, who is hampered throughout his life by exclusion from the society to which he aspires. (p. 102)

It is clearly and unashamedly an intellectual novel, based upon a comprehension of the point of view of a powerful personality. Sluggish Born in Exile may be, slow in its machinery, paltry in some of its subterfuges and minor interests; but it moves with a measure, and gains its effects from its own steady, confident growth. It is, in fact, consistent in such a degree as to establish its own importance. For once, Gissing's explanatory method justifies itself; the book makes no attempt to move by means of sentimentality or false reasoning. From the author's brain to the reader's brain its appeal is unhesitatingly made; and the story invites thought and sympathy rather than more emotional response. Yet it has momentum and it is moving. It is more tragic than any other of Gissing's stories, because it is free from self-pity. (pp. 105-06)

Most of the stories in The House of Cobwebs are little narratives, depending hardly at all upon surprise or concentration, and consisting of a series of slight events which may be rounded off into a tale. They are, in short, undramatic. If, without pledging ourselves to any particular definition of what a short story should be, we notice the lack of drama in Gissing's two collections [The House of Cobwebs and Human Odds and Ends], we perceive a particular fact. That fact is, that the dramatic quality is implicit in most effective short stories—either in the sense of surprise, or unexpectedness, or conflict, or incident. When we find the incidents in Gissing's short stories humdrum, or mild, we recognise that we had expected to be stirred in some way, or to be given some precisely poignant moment, whether of suspense or sympathy. The lack of this emotional heightening in the whole of Gissing's work is notable; in his short stories it becomes, according to the dramatic test, a positive defect. It is a defect in the sense that the stories are not, regarded technically, short stories at all, but merely short as contrasted with long. (pp. 129-30)

Yet if we take these short tales for what they are, we shall see how well they illustrate one aspect of Gissing's art—that of characterisation. He had a very keen sense of those slight personal eccentricities which, duly emphasised, may be made to suggest character in a book. His imagining of character, I should say, was not a strong point, because he never had the jolly visualising faculty of a Dickens, nor the detachment of a modern novelist. (p. 131)

Gissing, well-read in the Victorians, had the originality or the misfortune to abandon their benevolent tone, and his temperament was perhaps an additional power in the overthrow of the purely sentimental and moral attitude revealed in their work. But he was still hampered by their methods. In the longer works of the Victorians, continuity was sacrificed to variety of interest, with the result that the art of construction was unknown except in short works or in those where "plot" was important. Gissing despised "plot"; he had the instinct of the true artist in relation to probability and consistency. At the same time, while he built several elaborate structures—none more so than Demos or The Whirlpool—he was Victorian in his notions of construction. Many threads go to make up most of his books, threads interwoven with, for the most part, sincere regard for not improper interrelation. In the control of these threads, he was completely sure and capable: even when his main erections caved in for want of the support of experience he preserved his sense of proportion. . . . But the method which involves a large scheme, embracing a section of life, carries with it a particular defect that is very hard to overcome. It gives the appearance of too greatly diffused interest. Only a novelist with very strong constructive or imaginative power can overcome the defect; and Gissing was too absorbed in care to develop the one or the other. . . . [Lacking] the heroic sense, and without that glow of the imagination which can carry us beyond the consciousness of an author's technical method, Gissing managed somehow to pitch his work in too low a key. He studiously avoided exaggeration and drama (except when his invention of normal incidents failed and led him to the use of conventional expedients), and a climax is instantly smothered in obedience to his sense of veracity. That, so long as the method is successful, could not fail to command our respect: it is where it is unsuccessful that we perceive a fault. It is as unsuccessful in The Whirlpool as it is in The Nether World. (pp. 168-70)

[Gissing's strength] lies primarily in the judgment he displayed in his analyses of situation, in his portraits of women, and in his resolute defiance of low standards of work. He lies between the Victorians and the present day, secure of a certain meagre attention from the public, secure of the respect of all who can appreciate the mental qualities of a novelist. . . . We may grant Gissing many minor qualities as a novelist, in addition to those major ones just detailed; but the fact remains unassailable that for a novelist who is afraid of the world, who possesses none of that marvelling ardour which alone makes the great creative artist, he has received since his death as handsome treatment as could be desired. (pp. 195-96)

Frank Swinnerton, in his George Gissing: A Critical Study (copyright 1923 by George H. Doran and Company; reprinted by permission of Doubleday & Company, Inc.; in Canada by Martin Secker & Warburg Limited), George H. Doran and Co., 1923 (and reprinted by Kennikat Press, third edition, 1966), 200 p.

VIRGINIA WOOLF (essay date 1932)

Gissing is one of those imperfect novelists through whose books one sees the life of the author faintly covered by the lives of fictitious people. With such writers we establish a personal rather than an artistic relationship. We approach them through their lives as much as through their work. . . . (p. 238)

[The] sympathy which identifies the author with his hero is a passion of great intensity; it makes the pages fly; it lends what has perhaps little merit artistically another and momentarily perhaps a keener edge. (p. 240)

We know Gissing thus as we do not know Hardy or George Eliot. Where the great novelist flows in and out of his characters and bathes them in an element which seems to be common to us all, Gissing remains solitary, self-centred, apart. His is one of those sharp lights beyond whose edges all is vapour and phantom. But mixed with this sharp light is one ray of singular penetration. With all his narrowness of outlook and meagreness of sensibility, Gissing is one of the extremely rare novelists who believes in the power of the mind, who makes his people think. . . . [His books] owe their peculiar grimness to the fact that the people who suffer most are capable of making their suffering part of a reasoned view of life. The thought endures when the feeling has gone. Their unhappiness represents something more lasting than a personal reverse; it becomes part of a view of life. Hence when we have finished one of Gissing's novels we have taken away not a character, nor an incident, but the comment of a thoughtful man upon life as life seemed to him. (pp. 241-42)

> *Virginia Woolf, "George Gissing," in her* The Second Common Reader *(copyright 1932 by Harcourt Brace Jovanovich, Inc.; reprinted by permission of the publisher; in Canada by the Literary Estate of Virginia Woolf and the Hogarth Press Ltd; published in Britain as* The Common Reader, *second series, Hogarth, 1932), Harcourt, 1932, pp. 238-44.*

SAMUEL VOGT GAPP   (essay date 1936)

If it is by *New Grub Street* that [Gissing] is best known, it is nevertheless true that the typical Gissing novel is not so much that chronicle of the lives of poverty-ridden authors as is such a story of the poorest of the poor as *The Nether World* or *Thyrza. The Nether World,* above all others, represents the typical Gissing novel. It is a somewhat unusually type of realism which we have in his best work, a type all the more unusual when we consider its early date. Gissing, after all, set forth with *Workers in the Dawn* in 1880 and *The Unclassed* in 1884, novels whose relentlessness in giving poverty its due have seldom been surpassed. The dates alone are enough to show that his realism was a product of the mid-Victorian period. As such it must be judged, not as a writing of the modern realistic period, however many affinities it may have with modern tendencies. It is because of this fact and because of his frequently expressed admiration for Dickens, that his descriptions of the London poor are so often connected with those of that much greater Victorian, that he is often considered first and foremost a follower of Dickens. This view is not without some justification. There is much in Gissing which reminds one of Dickens, particularly of the technique of Dickens. . . . The class of life pictured is much the same. In the spirit of his work, however, Gissing has no resemblance to Dickens. The matter can be expressed most simply by saying that Dickens took a cheerful view of the lives of the poor and Gissing a pessimistic view. . . . There is a certain amount of realism in the technical sense in Gissing which never was in Dickens. He had been influenced by Flaubert and Turgenieff and Balzac and Daudet as Dickens had not. It was from such writers that he, among the first of English

novelists to do so, obtained many an idea that he developed in his own individual fashion. . . . He believed that [realism] involves artistic sincerity in the portrayal of contemporary life, a willingness to give the "ignobly decent" side of life just as it is, without either drama or humor, . . . In Gissing's case it amounted to the photographic portrayal of the life of the poor as he saw it, in all honesty and sincerity, but without propaganda or any indication of a remedy for the evils of modern poverty. It becomes unsensational, undramatic, even uninteresting in its efforts to present the ordinary course of life; perhaps that is why Gissing is so little read. (pp. 1-4)

[He] took no pleasure in such observational work as was necessary for his novels. Scholarship to him was the study of literature, not the study of life; it was the scholarship of the intellectual élite, not that of the economist or the reformer. This shows itself in the very tone of the novels; they are novels of the poor written from the aristocratic point of view. . . . [His] heroes, almost without exception, are people of pronounced intellectual interests, and they are his heroes because they have such interests. (pp. 4-5)

Now the scholarly interests of Gissing are not merely those of a student of the literature of his own nation or of his own time. Again and again we notice that his intellectual interests are centered in a time long past, in the literature of Greece and Rome, in the ages of Pericles and Augustus. This is evident in the most realistic of his novels, in those which are most properly slum novels. Reference after reference to things classic is made, references which only one brought up in the classic tradition would appreciate. (p. 5)

An exact parallel to this unusual duplicity of interests is somewhat hard to find elsewhere in literature. The writers who have combined the study of the classics with the writing of slum novels have been few indeed. (p. 7)

The most obvious case of classic influence on Gissing's novels is that of the direct or indirect use of classic reference. It is a fixed feature of his style, present in the slum novels no less than in those other works where it might be expected. In these novels it appears most often on the part of the author; one could not expect the characters of such works to know their Latin or their Greek. Most often, I believe, he uses the classic by way of descriptive simile—as, for example, in his descriptions of a man's hat as in form "exactly that of the old petasus." . . . (pp. 158-59)

The cultured hero as protagonist is . . . the typical Gissing character. His want of success in the struggle for existence is almost without exception. This usually results from his over-sensitiveness, his lack of social background, the fact that his intellectual approach to life is not shared by the people he meets, particularly the women, his inability to cope with the practical difficulties and small irritations of existence, his unwillingness to compromise with ideals that are not realizable in the conditions of modern life and the consequent poverty. It is a formidable list of disqualifications which the scholar, as Gissing conceived him, had to face. Biffen and Reardon, Milvain and Godwin Peak are examples of this type of character. . . . (p. 163)

It is rather difficult to say much about the influence of Gissing's classic studies upon his style without merely being vague. It is present, though, and none the less important because it is intangible. His style is evidently that of a student. It is somewhat formal; in his earlier books it is even ornate, rather loaded down with classic references and full of difficult and unusual words. It is quiet and subdued, seldom robust, vigorous, or forceful except when he is expressing a dislike for something. The descriptive and reflective parts rather over-balance the action, and Gissing is too fond of a rather irritating apostrophe to the reader. The most classic feature of his style is probably its carefulness, its attention to the rhythm of the sentence.... It is certainly in his sentence construction, in the details of the work, and not in the organization of the work as a whole or in the technique of the novel, that we are to look for traces of any classic influence. (pp. 169-70)

The most evident stylistic trace of his classic studies is his diction. Even in writing of the most uncultured of men he uses the diction of the scholar. These unusual, Latinate words are used so often, in fact, that he sometimes seems pedantic. At times this is deliberately done; when Gissing chooses to be sarcastic, one can always expect words which smell of the dictionary. (p. 171)

[However, the] most important influence of the classics upon his novels is in the realm of ideas. His classic studies have lent to the novels their tone and their point of view. I refer, of course, to the aristocratic point of view, to the ideals of gentility, of bookish leisure, of withdrawal from the everyday world which form so obvious an anomaly in works whose material is drawn from the poorest classes of society. Gissing is no true novelist of revolt; he speaks often as a conservative country squire might speak.... Gissing shared to the full such ideals and never, as far as I can make out, deserted them, although he had every excuse to do so. He may have detested the conventions of morals, society's set of values; he did not question the right of established society to be what it was, nor did he believe that much good would come from its overthrow. (pp. 171-72)

> Samuel Vogt Gapp, "Introduction" and "Influence of the Classic on His Life and Writings," in his George Gissing: Classicist, University of Pennsylvania Press, 1936 (and reprinted by The Folcroft Press, Inc., 1969), pp. 1-11, 158-98.

GRANVILLE HICKS (essay date 1939)

Workers in the Dawn suffers from a plot too complicated for the author to handle. The irony is usually feeble, and the attempt to reproduce Dickens' humor, especially in the portrayal of the Rev. Mr. Whiffle, is distressing. Bathos and melodrama are common, reaching a climax when, in a livid passage, the despairing hero plunges into Niagara Falls.... Yet from the opening description of Saturday night in the London slums the reader knows that here is a man who is trying to do something new and important, and in some measure succeeding. Earlier authors, and primarily Dickens, of whose example Gissing was always conscious, had portrayed the ghastly material conditions of the poor, but they had never shown what poverty did to the mind. (p. 181)

Gissing's own poverty lasted until whatever sweetness his mind may have had was thoroughly spoiled. The more he saw of the poor, the more he feared that he might sink to their level, and the more he clung to everything in himself that set him apart from them. The danger of being lost was in his mind far more than the hope of saving others, and gradually he convinced himself that there was no such hope. Indeed, he convinced himself that the poor did not

deserve to be saved, and he began to look on them with contempt. (pp. 185-86)

His novels naturally followed the course of his changing opinions. (p. 186)

[Isabel Clarendon] was Gissing's first attempt to abandon the world to which he had pledged himself when he wrote Workers in the Dawn. (pp. 187-88)

On the whole, Isabel Clarendon is a revelation of ignorance, as Meredith must have realized, for after reading it, he advised Gissing to keep to "the low-life scenes." Gissing took the advice, dealing in A Life's Morning, and often to good effect, with the poverty of a scholar such as himself. Then in Demos he returned to the slums. But in what a different spirit! Demos, he wrote his brother, "will be a rather savage attack on working-class aims and capacities." It was all of that. Gissing had obviously reached the point at which his abandonment of radicalism had to be justified, and Demos was the book in which he tried to defend himself. For plot it draws upon the old argument that, if a Socialist came into money, he would soon lose his Socialism. (p. 188)

Gissing says as much as usual about the brutality of the poor, but now has nothing to say about its causes. He decries popular education as vulgar, and regards his sincere upper-class idealists as ignorant. (p. 189)

Demos proved to be the bitterest of all Gissing's novels, for, though he did not modify his opinions thereafter, he was content to express them less violently. In the two novels he subsequently wrote about the working class, [Thyrza and The Nether World], he chose characters of whom he could approve, and hence he could allow his sympathies play without making concessions of which he was afraid. (p. 190)

[After New Grub Street] he was forced to deal more and more with the upper classes in his novels, for there was nothing more for him to say about the nether world, and he could not go on writing about writers. In some of his later novels, such as Eve's Ransom and The Town Traveller, he showed a lightness of touch of which he had not previously been capable, and all of the novels of the nineties are put together with a certain craftsmanlike precision. But on the whole nothing that he wrote between The New Grub Street and The Private Papers of Henry Ryecroft has much importance. He addressed himself, rather pretentiously, to a series of middle-class problems. (pp. 192-93)

Neither his tastes nor his experiences fitted Gissing to write about the middle and upper classes, nor had he anything important to say about their problems. The problems, indeed, seldom seem to interest him deeply; they are simply available themes for marketable books. There is little of the passion that went into the early novels and less of the first-hand knowledge. Only in a reflective book such as Henry Ryecroft could he do anything with the talents that were left him....

Gissing has seldom been ranked high among men of letters, but few students of English literature ignore him. He seems more important than any one of his books, in a sense more important than his whole literary achievement, for one feels that he almost gave British literature a new direction.... He began as a disciple of Dickens who, because of his particular experiences, knew there was something Dickens had failed to do and wanted to do it. The Victorian novel was his starting point, wherever he might go or fail to go. (p. 194)

He was not restrained by the "great heart" that, he felt, kept Dickens from portraying the slum-dwellers as they really were. Dickens had sentimentalized and softened, but Gissing . . . was determined to depict the slum "as Truth will paint it and as bards will not." Fear and loathing mingled with devotion to the truth, but he was trying to be a more truthful Dickens. The desire for reform spurred him on, but perhaps the strongest motive was the sense of a literary task that needed to be performed.

For this specific purpose Dickens' work offered the best possible point of departure. In other respects, however, it was a pity that Gissing accepted the conventions of the Victorian novel. (p. 196)

Like Hardy, Gissing discovered at the outset of his career that the middle class wanted plenty of action, but he could not use the complicated plot for his purposes, as Hardy did, and he had none of Dickens' offhand skill in manipulating incidents. In his hands the Dickensian device of a multiplicity of sub-plots, depending on coincidence, violent death, and what an earlier generation called divine intervention, constantly got in the way of the development of character and the portrayal of social conditions that were his real aims. (pp. 196-97)

He was equally troubled by contemporary standards of gentility, and his realism operated within recognizable limits. So far as lower-class characters are concerned, he permits himself to endow them with brutality of act and, within limits, of speech. He even describes, with stated disapproval, their subjection to sexual passion. He also refers to the vices of the rich. But he is frank only when he is dealing with what can be regarded as bestial. He is frank only when he can, at least by implication, condemn what he describes. There is no suggestion that sexual impulses play a part in the lives of ordinary, respectable men and women. . . . *In the Year of Jubilee* contains a seduction, but, like all Victorian seductions, it is incredible, since the heroine is endowed with no emotion to which a seducer could appeal.

For temperamental reasons Gissing did not adopt the colloquial tone so popular from Fielding's time to his own, but he was no more objective, in the formal sense, than his predecessors. In the earlier novels he speaks in his own person, presents characters formally to the reader, and delivers homilies. . . . And Gissing, though he avoided mere chattiness, was like his fellow-writers in not being able to resist the temptation to accompany presentation with commentary.

Gissing, then, was still a Victorian novelist. But within the limits of the Victorian novel he was doing something new. (pp. 197-98)

When he abandoned the poor, he found himself compelled to write about a kind of life that he knew only superficially. Because he had turned his back on all proposals for social change, he had to concern himself with more or less trivial problems, in which he took only a slight interest and about which he had nothing significant to say. Finally, the withering of humanitarian feeling in the course of his struggle to save himself had robbed him of intellectual as well as emotional vitality. In his earlier novels one feels a mind at work

—and this, as Virginia Woolf points out [see excerpt above], is enough to distinguish him among British writers. But in the later fiction, though there are problems, there is little thought. Having himself surrendered intellectually, as the price he had to pay to escape a radicalism that he found unbearable in its implications, he could no longer create thinking human beings. (p. 201)

Though he had gained in craftsmanship, he had lost in sincerity. Not that he was false to himself; he showed life its image as he beheld it, but he did not behold it as clearly as he once had. *The New Grub Street* was probably the last novel in which he set forth a vision of life that he confidently believed to be true and important. In trying to deal with problems of marriage, education, and politics as they presented themselves to well-bred ladies and gentlemen, he was handicapped by indifference as well as ignorance. (p. 202)

We come back to Gissing's achievement in *Workers in the Dawn, The Unclassed, Thyrza, The Nether World,* and *The New Grub Street,* which, though it was repeatedly marred by defects of an uncommon grossness, was substantial. Gissing contributed something, as Hardy and Butler and others were doing, to the emancipation of literature. But far more important was the sense he gave of great possibilities in new themes. . . . Gissing, we now see, was showing the way, though he himself did not follow it very long. (p. 203)

> *Granville Hicks, "The Changing Novel," in his* Figures of Transition: A Study of British Literature at the End of the Nineteenth Century *(reprinted by permission of Russell & Volkening, as agents for the author; copyright © 1939 by Macmillan Publishing Co., Inc.), Macmillan, 1939, pp. 177-216.**

WILLIAM PLOMER (essay date 1946)

[The central point of Gissing's work] is largely an indictment of the period in which he lived, and particularly of its economic structure, which, in his opinion, too often thwarted the growth of the finer man and woman, and of the finer traits in the more ordinary man and woman. The drawing up of this indictment involved an exposition of suffering, which was identified with the contemporary bogy of 'realism.' . . . Zola was regarded as the arch-realist, and often as shocking or salacious; Gissing, whom insular taboos and native fastidiousness deprived of equal candour, was sometimes regarded as a kind of cleaner Zola. (p. 12)

[Gissing's] style has been called scholarly, and so it is: his sentences are properly formed and free from extravagance or vulgarity, but they lack also the piercing precision, the intensity, the touch of strangeness to be found in writers, even prose-writers, with a poetic inventiveness or epigrammatic skill. Gissing's pages have steadiness and shapeliness, not brilliancy or exuberance; they are never dull or careless. (p. 13)

In that careful, often oddly formal style of his, he has caught and fixed in countless forms the vulgarity, the materialism, and the social injustice of his late-Victorian days in a manner and on a scale attempted by nobody else. . . .

Gissing poses in his own way the great and familiar problem which has grown and grown ever since the Industrial Revolution—whether the values of earlier times must be destroyed, and whether man must be reduced by the machine-age to a level unworthy of the better traditions he has inherited. (p. 14)

The Private Papers of Henry Ryecroft, which has been the most popular of Gissing's books, is by no means the least revealing: it is a blend of autobiography, rumination, and the escape-dream. Ryecroft, if you like, is an ostrich who buries his head in the nice warm sand because he doesn't like the look of the weather; or he is the sage—of modestly independent means—who chooses detachment and simple pleasures. . . . I think it became popular because, like Fitzgerald's *Omar Khayyam,* it appealed to a combined fatalism and love of pleasure which is deeply set in the English character but has been strongly repressed by Puritanism and industrialisation. (p. 15)

History, says Ryecroft, is a long moan of anguish, a long record of injustice; but unlike Hardy, who questioned Providence, Gissing questions mankind itself about its follies and miseries. (p. 16)

If one were asked which is Gissing's best novel, one might reply that he cannot be judged by any single novel, partly because some of his work is below his best level. A fair estimate of his achievement as a novelist could be formed by reading, besides *A Life's Morning,* at least the two great 'proletarian' novels, *Demos* and *The Nether World;* the tender *Thyrza; New Grub Street,* so true to its title; *Born in Exile; The Odd Women* and *In the Year of Jubilee,* if only for their portraits of women; *The Whirlpool,* which a little foreshadows *Howard's End;* and *The Crown of Life.* (pp. 16-17)

William Plomer, "Introduction" (1946), in A Life's Morning *by George Gissing, Home & Van Thal, 1947, pp. 5-21.*

V. S. PRITCHETT   (essay date 1953)

[Gissing's] failure is the source of his persistent fame; he is one of those novelists who are neither discarded nor made immortal, but whose reputation drags its heavy-footed way in a kind of perpetual purgatory. His lack of humour, his lack of fantasy—that essence of the English novel—leave him worrying unattended on the pavement of his anxieties and his scholar's dreams. Take books of his at random: *Thyrza, Eve's Ransom, Denzil Quarrier, Odd Women, The Unclassed*—they are well, but stiffly written, without individuality, but as Mr. Plomer says [see excerpt above], in the sound conventional prose of the scholar; their psychological passages are acutely argued but the words never fly, never leave the ground. The dialogue is stilted, though the reported speech of the slums is alive. Their plots groan. Their characters . . . are weighed down by self-pity or moan under an excess of good intention, and only when we break through this encasement do we find how real they are. There is . . . a fundamental sentimentality and more than a touch of conceit and pretence. Gissing was a novelist in error, for he lacked the gift of melting life and pouring it into the mould of artifice. Life and artifice stand side by side in his novels like some ill-assorted couple.

If these very grave criticisms are true why do we read Gissing? The answer is that at certain points in nearly all his novels, he speaks seriously about matters which no other novelist has taken so seriously. . . . Snobbery, priggishness have been subjects for wit and gregarious laughter to the other English novelists. Injustice has aroused pas-

sion, but these novelists end by coming round to the sociable view. Gissing conserves the lonely, the private personal opinion. He is a thinking person thinking for himself; and his contribution as a novelist—as Virginia Woolf suggested [see excerpt above]—is the thinking of ordinary people who so far had not been credited with thought. . . . This discovery that in all character there sits a mind, and that the mind of the dullest is not dull because, at its very lowest, it will at least reflect the social dilemma into which it was born, is arresting.

Where the discovery is most fruitful is in Gissing's portraits of women. Women were known to have feelings. They were known to be shrewd. But who supposed them to have thoughts beyond themselves! The fact is that Gissing realised women were ladies, and now that the modern novel since D. H. Lawrence has presented them as sexual combatants and aggressors, it is refreshing to discover again their thoughts about their social condition. . . . I would go further and say that no English novelist of the realistic kind has drawn women so variously and so intimately. In this sense Gissing's feminist novel, *Odd Women,* is one of his most interesting. It is a picture of loneliness in urban life. Once one has broken the back of the first chapter or two, one's impatience with Gissing's old-fashioned methods of narrative goes. Life shows its teeth. . . . Gissing analyses the fanatical [feminist] Rhoda Nunn and he prepares for her the most delicate psychological drama. (One understands, after this portrait, the admiration Henry James had for Gissing's work.) He finds for Rhoda Nunn a man of the world whom she converts to her feminism, and having done so, she is made to realise that vanity not love has impelled them. Her brain has deceived her; she is obliged to behave unjustly and irrationally like any "silly" woman; and wrecking her own happiness, returns to loneliness and feminism again. She has passed through the strict spiritual test to which Gissing put all his women—for that, he felt, is what the minds of so many women fear and desire—and is left matured by the test but, of course, unhappy. Gissing despised happiness. He had the masochistic imagination of the adolescent.

In life and in literature Gissing's method was severely to criticise women in order to be gratified all the more by the discovery of their graces. This led, of course, to being overgratified and to self-deception in life, but it led to balance in literature where he could be ironical and urbane. (pp. 210-13)

The attempt to revive Gissing is desirable, for we are less likely to be depressed by his novels and to misjudge him than his contemporaries were. By a long detour through the wilderness of literary reputation he arrives at our door. But this revival will confirm, I am afraid, his substantial failure as a novelist. The shadow of Ryecroftism . . . is often dank upon his work; in short he lacks the quality of self-disregard which is essential to novelists. It has been complained justly that his novels have the very amateur fault of being without focus or central plot. Precisely: Ryecroft's shadow takes its place. That unshaped ego is blobbed over his tales. But Gissing is a store-house for novelists. One of his books, the study of Dickens, is a translucent piece of criticism. For the rest, he foreshadows a type which has become commoner: the uprooted intellectual of a later generation, cut off by education from his own class and by economic and social conditions from any other place in society. (p. 214)

V. S. Pritchett, "Poor Gissing," in his Books in General *(copyright © 1953 by V. S. Pritchett; reprinted by permission of Literistic, Ltd.; in Canada by A D Peters & Co Ltd), Chatto & Windus Ltd., 1953, pp. 209-15.*

MABEL COLLINS DONNELLY (essay date 1954)

The fact that Gissing did learn many lessons is not fully appreciated even by his admirers. They continue to prefer their favorite novel, even if it is from the point of view of craftsmanship one of the weaker books. The moral can only be that a strong personality will hold a reader even if the hold has all the subtlety of a hammer lock. Gissing has the attraction most people feel in the spectacle of a frail man bullied by adversaries, a spectacle that Gissing presented, with varying degrees of skill, time and again. (p. 215)

Thoughtful Gissing was always . . . but he learned only gradually to distinguish between thoughtfulness and polemics. In *Workers in the Dawn,* his first novel, *The Nether World* of the eighties or even *In the Year of Jubilee* of the nineties, he insists upon interrupting, like a shrill conductor on a tour of the slums, to make sure that his point is not overlooked. The insistence constitutes the comment of a thoughtful man, but is not welcome reading. To the observer of Gissing, therefore, one of the first signs of maturity is diminution of shrillness, and by the time of *Eve's Ransom,* stridency has almost disappeared. The reader makes inferences about characters and their problems and Gissing merely tells the story.

The major achievement of Gissing is that he learned to move his story easily, no simple feat, for the novelist steeped in the Victorian tradition of plot and subplot hardly recognized the clean sweep of a story. One of the signs of the more skilled novels of Gissing is, then, the "clean" story line. (p. 216)

The design that Gissing used most often was the solitary figure, a little more than life-size, forced into a succession of relationships consisting usually of a central intimate relationship and a multiplicity of ephemeral relationships. The juxtaposition is often arranged so that the intimate relationship constitutes the only security for the chief character, the only permanence in a world of flux. Thus, when the "permanent" relationship is shown to deteriorate the devastation of the protagonist is complete, for the world now seems all motion and force, hostile to him. . . . Gissing's novels, in spite of grandiloquent asides, are essentially domestic novels of a narrow range, and they fare best when the scene is not cluttered and the conflicts of the protagonist are clearly defined.

The most skilled novels of this design are *New Grub Street, Born in Exile, The Whirlpool,* and *Our Friend the Charlatan.* In each of these novels the construction is simple, the focus indisputable. (p. 217)

There are, unfortunately, several novels in which the central design is lost, in which Gissing is so seduced by competing characters that he forgets the "story line." These are the novels that most readily show themselves obsolescent. *Workers in the Dawn* is a book of scattered interest in which the picaresque story of a waif in the tradition of *Great Expectations* could have been poignant if it had been less cluttered and less shrill. . . . [In] *The Odd Women* he deliberately avoids concentration upon a central character and tries his best to give a clinical picture of a family, only to lose the narrative in complicated intrigue involving a character originally intended to be secondary.

The sheep are not difficult to separate from the goats, but several novels are difficult to classify, for by any careful test of design they are shown to be deficient. Nevertheless, as in *Demos,* in which the author adulates the character whom most readers find a sham, or as in *Thyrza* and *The Nether World* when subplots get out of hand—a few novels survive by brute passion rather than by skill. These are the novels in which one endures some tedium for the sake of a fresh or daring conception of character. These are the novels in which one is at once most rewarded and most disappointed. (pp. 217-18)

Mabel Collins Donnelly, "Retrospect," in her George Gissing: Grave Comedian *(copyright © 1954 by the President and Fellows of Harvard College; excerpted by permission of the author and publishers), Cambridge, Mass.: Harvard University Press, 1954 (and reprinted by Kraus Reprint Corporation, 1973), pp. 214-22.*

A. C. WARD (essay date 1959)

The semi-autobiographical *Private Papers of Henry Ryecroft* is the most consciously stylized of Gissing's books, and nowhere else among his works is a reader so aware of a deliciously cultivated artifice of natural description—lingering echoes of Theocritus and Virgil. . . . Even if austere contemporary taste should disapprove the occasional mannered touches . . . or declare that the style is too pervasively mellifluous, *Ryecroft* is nevertheless . . . unstaled and secure; the only one of Gissing's books that has remained in unbroken demand.

While much that is admirable can be found in Gissing's other works, *Ryecroft* is unique among them in arousing affection, or even love. It is one of those rare books that can be read again and again and again without lessening of enthusiasm: an elderly reader finds that the years have not dimmed the enjoyment given by *Ryecroft* in long-past adolescence. Though it is one of the shortest of Gissing's works, it is the richest and widest-ranging in content. Since there is no theme—other than Life in its manifold variety—it is free to conform to the meditations of a liberal and well-stored mind and to the responses of a sensitive heart. (pp. 22-4)

Nowhere else in Gissing's writings can so much of the whole man be found. Without *The Private Papers of Henry Ryecroft* we could deduce from the novels much of the author's circumstances and external life, but much less of his spirit. From *Ryecroft* alone, however, without other aid, we can reach an understanding of the essential Gissing, a man of infinite variety when released from the imprisoning pressure of 'the squalid profession'. . . . Here, in *Ryecroft,* is the lover of England as well as the lover of Italy and Greece. (pp. 24-5)

A. C. Ward, in his Gissing *(© A. C. Ward, 1959; Longman Group, Ltd., for the British Council), British Council, 1959, 43 p.*

J. MIDDLETON MURRY (essay date 1959)

Those who acquire a taste for Gissing's novels find it enduring: astringent, perhaps even harsh, but distinct and unforgettable.

Above all, they are memorable for their portraits of women. Gissing's range in this respect was extraordinary. The ideal, the ambiguous, the sinister—all are alive, and all are thought-provoking. We feel that, whether in imagination or direct experience, he was continually exercised by the mystery of woman. (pp. 24-5)

There are three main types of women in Gissing's fascinating gallery: the ideal of love and loyalty and faithfulness; the horrible opposite of animal cruelty, egoism and destructiveness; and a sort of middle creature—*la femme moyenne*—whose instinctive effort in love is to achieve material security. These main types are admirably individualised, so that they at times shade into one another. But with the clear emergence of *la femme moyenne* as the central figure of his fiction, the urgency and passion and incisiveness go out of it. The conclusion seems unescapable: that Gissing was able to exert his full power as a novelist, to reveal his peculiar strength, when he was suffering the utmost conflict between the reality and the ideal. When the pressure is lifted, the power of imaginatively realising the ideal also departs; and with it the power, or the desire, to depict the horror of the real. (pp. 58-9)

One feels that Gissing had experienced, speculated on, dreamed about woman with an intensity that falls to few. Is it possible or desirable to summarise his findings? On the whole it is probably worth making the attempt.

Speaking roughly, then, we may say that Gissing's finding reduces to this: that except in the case of authentic love, which is as rare as it is precious, the egoistic female will is always lurking beneath the surface of woman. It is a question of breeding and education, or of the pressure of economic circumstance, how far below the surface it hides, or whether it hides at all, except in the woman capable of genuine love. That alone is self-transcendent. In any lesser relation of woman and man, the female will threaten disaster to the sensitive man. Only the man who is prepared to use physical force can hope to emerge unscathed. The choice is simple: he must either dominate or be dominated. And the woman incapable of love does not, when it comes to the test, object to being brought to heel. The fatal thing is for the man to show weakness or compunction. Gissing would have agreed with D. H. Lawrence that 'Woman is the nemesis of doubting man'. (p. 59)

[In Amy Reardon, of *New Grub Street,* Gissing created a woman who embodied] the 'cynical naturalism' that disturbed him. Whereas Reardon genuinely idealises her, she sees in him the instrument of her elegant ambition. Yet, though Gissing is ironical about her, he does not fail to make her sympathetic. She marks, not exactly an advance, but an important change in his portraiture of woman. Previous to her his women had been divided into angels and devils—mostly quite credible angels and alas only too credible devils. With Amy there enters *la femme moyenne.* . . . Under kindly circumstances she can be kind, under adverse ones she can be hard and ruthless in her selfishness. What she cannot do is to make a real surrender of herself. That is reserved for the rare woman who is capable of genuine love, and finds a fit object for it. What *la femme moyenne* can and will often do is to pretend to surrender. She will take advantage of the sexual attraction she sets herself to exercise and trade it for her material ends—or Nature's biological purposes—while still 'tenacious of spiritual interpretations' of her behaviour. It is all very natural, and with

l'homme moyen sensuel, who meets *la femme moyenne* on the same instinctive plane, it works well enough. But when the idealistic and sensitive man falls a victim to her sexual charm, and his eager imagination invests her with spiritual graces she does not possess, disaster is almost certain. The very unselfishness of his pursuit of ideal ends arouses her secret cynicism: indulgent if it does not really jeopardise her security, pitiless if it does. (pp. 62-3)

In general [Gissing's] ideal women are given; they are ideal by natural endowment, born ideal, so to speak. They are perfectly convincing in the sense in which Shakespeare's ideal women, at one level, or Trollope's at another, are convincing; while Dickens's are not. Only their frequency is not in accord with Gissing's private conviction that the capacity for love is very rare in actual life. (p. 63)

[Gissing imagined the demonic female to be] as coeval with the prehistorical emergence of woman. And if it was something more than fantasy which made him wonder why she had not been eliminated by the stone axe of primitive man, one simple answer might be: that she was the specifically female manifestation of universal evil, or—to use the phrase without theological implication—of original sin. The potentiality of evil lurks in every human being: and when it is not suppressed or transcended, it comes to fruition. The most intimate of all human relations—the permanent sexual relation which is marriage—gives it unique opportunity. For here a man and a woman are each in the other's power. The power to humiliate, to wound, to injure, to destroy is as infinite as is the power to encourage, to comfort, to cherish and to edify. (pp. 65-6)

[It] is possible, perhaps probable, in many cases that the demonic behaviour of [the offensive wife] . . . is at bottom, sexually provocative. Constant irritation, wild denunciation, open contempt for the inner sanctities of the man's soul, carried to the point at which his self-control suddenly breaks down, and he is possessed by a fury of violence against the demonic female, does establish a primitive emotional and physical contact bordering on the sexual. . . . And, very often indeed, the reconciliation which follows upon such violence, is consummated in a sexual union which the spiritually sensitive man feels as a degradation; a fearsome corruption of love by hatred. This Gissing came as near as he dared to implying in *In the Year of Jubilee.* . . .

This process, constantly repeated, leads to . . . disintegration. Love and hatred become indistinguishable. Human existence becomes demonic. (p. 67)

It is possible therefore that female demonism is a survival of the primitive animal relation between the sexes, and that it may be eventually eradicated by a process which may be called education. But the education must be an education into love, conceived and experienced as an identity or interfusion of the spiritual and the physical. Gissing, I think, was perfectly clear in his own mind about this; but he was inhibited by the moral conventions of his time, on obedience to which his meagre livelihood as a novelist depended, from giving full expression to his convictions in his own fiction. But this was only part of the trouble. The religion of love, as formulated for the woman in *A Life's Morning;* the intelligence of the heart, as formulated for the man in *The Crown of Life,* are descriptions of the same ideal. But formulation is one thing; embodiment is another: and embodiment is the novelist's particular business. And, though this religion of love is obviously just as valid for man as woman, Gissing was never nearly so successful in presenting it in his men as in his women. With the possible exception of Ross Mallard in *The Emancipated,* there is not one of his heroes who has the same solidity, at the ideal level, as his women. Of all the rest, those who may be said to be capable of the religion of love, if they are not shadowy, are disappointed. (p. 68)

> *J. Middleton Murry, "George Gissing," in his* Katherine Mansfield and Other Literary Studies *(© 1959 by Mary Middleton Murry; reprinted by permission of the Society of Authors as the literary representative of the estate of John Middleton Murry), Constable, 1959, pp. 1-68.*

JACOB KORG   (essay date 1963)

The Unclassed is primarily a novel of love and character, though it is heavily charged with social awareness. (p. 64)

Technically, *The Unclassed* represents a considerable advance over *Workers in the Dawn.* Though he is still awkward at managing the ample proportions of the three-volume novel, Gissing is fairly successful in fixing his attention upon a group of central characters. Esthetic idealism, now relegated to the position of a spiritual failing in a figure of secondary importance . . . no longer prevents him from achieving some significant characterizations. . . . *The Unclassed* presents many features that came to be typical of Gissing's novels. Julian Casti, though he does not occupy the role of the protagonist, is a good representative of the tormented and ineffectual man who is the characteristic Gissing hero. The hearty man-to-man conversations about literature, classical languages, and the deplorable state of the contemporary world that take place between Casti and Waymark are the forerunners of many such scenes in later novels. (p. 66)

Like nearly all of Gissing's social novels, *The Unclassed* fails to adopt a coherent attitude toward social problems. Having introduced the horrors of slum life through descriptions of Elm Court and Litany Lane, it offers no better remedy for them than the private philanthropies of Ida Starr. . . .

The provocative subject matter and opinions of *The Unclassed* aroused much criticism, and Gissing felt again, as he had after the publication of *Workers in the Dawn,* that his readers were ignoring the artistic aspects of his novel for the sake of attacking the opinions expressed by the characters. (p. 67)

The conflict between esthetic and moral intentions that is so clear in *The Unclassed* continued to embarrass Gissing. He had to make the choice anew with every novel, and yet the choice was never really made. It may be that one of the reasons why he found it so painful to reread his books in later years was the realization that he had failed to achieve the objectivity for which he had struggled so hard. (p. 69)

There are many points of resemblance between Gissing's and George Eliot's novels. His books were essentially the expressions of an enlightened didacticism directed to an ideological end. Like George Eliot, he devoted great attention to the intellectual and emotional development of mature characters. He felt the need for clearly realizing and explaining subtle shifts of feeling or attitude, and for pro-

viding sound motivations for the actions of his characters. Every incident of the plot justified its occurrence, ideally, by some important effect, often a psychological one. The cause-effect relationships in the minds of the characters are often analyzed at length and evaluated by instructive references to general experience. The fullness of description and detail, the elaborate compound plots, the passages of authorial commentary, and the slow and sometimes ponderous thoroughness of the narration in Gissing's novels are all imitations of George Eliot. As he strove for greater directness and economy of style, Gissing eliminated some of these characteristics from his work, but he continued to think of the novel as a form suited to the serious treatment of ideas through the narration of psychological experiences. (p. 259)

Like all novelists influenced by the example of George Eliot, Gissing brought to fiction a new conception of its responsibilities. The development of the English novel can be expressed in terms of two gradual tendencies: a turning from motives of entertainment and propaganda to the illumination of genuinely controversial moral issues, and an expansion of the social and psychological areas in which it could feel at home. Both of these developments arrived at new thresholds with George Eliot. (p. 260)

If Gissing's novels can be said to have a dominant theme, it is the destruction of human character in the crushing mill of social evils. He found that the social institutions men worked so hard to create and to maintain were, after all, hostile to dignity, honor, intellect, and sensibility. His opinions were varied and even inconsistent, but he felt clearly that the remedy for the evils he described lay in a change of the spirit of society rather than its form, and that the most advanced reform theories of his time missed that fact. His novels are indecisive because he was denied a vision of life as a well-ordered whole. He had convictions and perceptions, but they were isolated, disjointed, baffling even to himself. Instead of enabling him to arrive at coherent conclusions about the problems that troubled him, they delivered him into a nightmare of conflicting aims. (p. 261)

Paradoxically, Gissing's inability to make up his mind about social issues was an advantage to him as a novelist. He used this failing as one of his literary talents. His active dislike of the poor sharpened his eye for details of their lives and manners; his doubts about cosmic problems gave him insight into crises of the soul; and his indecision about the civilization of his day led him to present it as a complex entity rich in minor characteristics. (p. 262)

> *Jacob Korg, "The Palace of Art" and "Sequels," in his* George Gissing: A Critical Biography *(copyright © 1963 by the University of Washington Press), University of Washington Press, 1963, pp. 43-72, 253-65.*

IRVING HOWE   (essay date 1963)

Alone among Gissing's books *New Grub Street* survives as a classic, a work of abiding value and power. Its historical interest is large, but the claim it makes upon our attention is primarily that of a work of art. (p. 183)

New Grub Street satisfies few of the standards which modern criticism brings to the study of fiction. It is cast within the heavy frame of the three-volume Victorian novel —all too often, with Gissing, the cause of padding, but now used to present a copious portrait of English literary life.

The writing itself lacks that aggressive and flaunting brilliance we often associate with modern fiction. The techniques of modern novelists—foreshortening of plot to allow for dramatic concentration, placing biased and implicated observers close to the center of action in order to make for complexity of perspective, jumbling narrative sequences to involve the reader in a struggle for the meaning of events—these do not figure in Gissing's books. They are books that move along at an even, almost sluggish pace; he relies heavily upon long patches of dialogue; and the events are usually registered through an omniscient observer standing, or pretending to stand, at a considerable remove.

Gissing's treatment of character is also conventional. While there is a strong sense of reality behind his every page, he does not provide the burrowing psychological analysis we have come to expect from modern fiction. He allows the reader to infer the inner life of his characters from what can be seen and heard of them, or he provides brief summaries of his own. His characters are usually treated as if they were fixed and synthetic entities, even if open to changes of impulse and mood; the modern tendency to dissolve character into a stream of psychological notation is not yet at work in his novels. *New Grub Street* remains in structure a Victorian novel, but the subject and informing vision are post-Victorian: the setting of his drama is the modern city, that jungle of loneliness and strife. The book is not at all difficult, it is transparent, and to subject it to a "close reading" in the current academic fashion would be tiresome. What *New Grub Street* asks from the reader is not some feat of analysis, but a considered fullness of response, a readiness to assent to, even if not agree with, its vision of defeat. (pp. 183-85)

Gissing is a master of place, weather, atmosphere. No English novelist except Dickens so fully captures the greyness of a London winter, the greyness of lives spent under its pall, the greyness of the people who wander its streets. . . . [We] encounter not merely the depressing aura of a late-nineteenth-century city, but also the visible effects of that city as a social institution, an agency of inhumane human relations. An air of tiredness and staleness hangs over the world of *New Grub Street,* as if everyone were working too hard, not eating well, living badly. Among English writers Gissing is the poet of fatigue.

New Grub Street is a large novel, but not a shapeless or a sprawling one. Its somber impressiveness depends on a balance struck by Gissing between the needs of dramatic representation and those of thematic rigor. Everything is controlled by Gissing's personal vision of life, yet neither characters nor events are allowed to stiffen into mere illustrations of ideas. . . . In *New Grub Street* we are aware of the presence of a mature mind shaping the contours of the plot but also allowing the characters a measure of autonomy and idiosyncratic existence.

Throughout *New Grub Street* persons and destinies are so balanced that one stands in tragic or ironic juxtaposition to the other, and all together embody the vision of human waste which is Gissing's dominant perception. Abstractly, these contrasts may seem obvious, but Gissing handles them with an objectivity and restraint that gives the novel its aura of profound moral seriousness. (pp. 186-87)

Such contrasts and balances of character help create the over-all "architecture" of the book. Its local vividness of portrayal, chapter by chapter, is due to something else: the remarkable, almost Hardyesque tolerance, a blend of accurate judgment and humane forbearance, Gissing shows toward his characters. It is the tolerance not of a writer who has compromised his standards or surrendered to a sleazy sort of worldliness, but of a writer with a profound reserve of experience behind him, which enables him to grasp how *difficult* it is for men simply to get by. Only novelists who know something about the enormity of social pain are likely to preserve a decent restraint in moral judgment. And because in this book Gissing commands both the knowledge and restraint, his treatment of character is admirably free and plastic. (p. 189)

One last word about Gissing's capacities as a novelist. Somewhat like Hardy, he commands in *New Grub Street* a notable gift for symbolic condensation through fragments of incident, bits and pieces of action, that seem to contain the meaning of the book in a few words or gestures. (p. 190)

Such details are put to the service of the vision that works its way through the whole of the novel, concluding in the bitter ironies of the scene in which Amy and Milvain, no longer troubled by the memory of Reardon, bask and coo in their genteel success. It is a vision of disenchantment with the values of modern life and, more deeply, it asserts the power of that "injustice which triumphs so flagrantly in the destinies of men." This, to be sure, is far from all of the human story, just as Gissing is far from the only kind of novelist we should accept. But from the limits of what he saw, Gissing drew that power of rejection which makes *New Grub Street* a work approaching greatness. There was much in our existence he did not see; about suffering he was seldom wrong. (p. 191)

> *Irving Howe, "George Gissing: Poet of Fatigue,"*
> *in his* A World More Attractive: A View of
> Modern Literature and Politics *(© 1963, reprinted*
> *by permission of the publisher, Horizon Press,*
> *New York), Horizon, 1963, pp. 169-91.*

PIERRE COUSTILLAS   (essay date 1969)

Isabel Clarendon occupies a special position among Gissing's twenty-two novels. In the collector's eye it enjoys the entirely deserved reputation, undisputed even by *Workers in the Dawn,* of being the scarcest title. From the point of view of the biographer, it contains elements which throw light on a period which saw the novelist divided between two worlds and equally unhappy in each. As for the critic, he is, according to his culture and sensibility, likely to detect in it influences as unconnected as those of Turgenev's "country-house and garden atmosphere", Schopenhauer's pessimism, Henry James's technique and occasional touches of Dickens-like characterization. On rereading the novel one discovers something quasi-protean about it. It has a richness of which no stock has yet been taken, for its scarcity has inevitably stemmed the curiosity of critics and, if fresh peeps at *New Grub Street* or *The Private Papers of Henry Ryecroft* have been taken in recent years, *Isabel Clarendon* still awaits a systematic and coherent examination. (p. xv)

Isabel Clarendon was to be his fourth published novel and like most novelists when they reach that stage, he felt the need to renew. (p. xvi)

Isabel Clarendon is the first of several novels to which Gissing tried to give a subtly cosmopolitan atmosphere. He sends his characters abroad with [off-handedness] . . . , this gives the action a certain spaciousness tinted with romantic preoccupations which are quite in keeping with the central love-story . . . Robert Asquith, whom one sees travelling in the East and in America, has the ease and discreet seductive air of those lovers who can afford to play a waiting game in a love affair without suffering any heart sorrows. Whether in travel or in love, he remains on the surface, watches from afar and returns as swiftly as he had gone. (pp. xxxvii-xxxviii)

The only point which seems to me regrettable in the manner of *Isabel Clarendon* is the author's occasional address to the reader, a habit which was as old as the novel itself but which was on the wane when the book first appeared. (p. xli)

The novel, in spite of these mannerisms, testifies to a permanent concern for art, and—here contrasting with *Workers in the Dawn* and *The Unclassed*—to a noteworthy resolve to be discreet in the narrative. . . . Under the influence of Henry James, Gissing had come to appreciate the virtues of suggestion after succumbing to the charms of explanation and long-winded comment. Many times in the story we feel the author deliberately leaving things unsaid and this gives the book, if compared with its two immediate successors, *A Life's Morning* and *Demos,* a misleading air of poverty. Here he delights in ambiguity. (pp. xli-xlii)

Henry James, in spite of his "persistent taste for Gissing", deplored the fact that his fellow novelist struck him "as having cast to the winds the whole business of distribution and composition." . . . Almost certainly he did not have *Isabel Clarendon* in mind when he wrote this in 1897—and it is very doubtful whether he ever read the book—but at all events it could by no means apply to it. On the contrary Gissing shows in his novel a fine care for distribution. (p. xliii)

To try and distinguish signs of influences as varied as those of Meredith, Turgenev and Schopenhauer could amount to a quartering of the novel; even though we can spot traces of each of them here and there these traces are well fused into the fabric of the novel and form but a part of a number of literary devices which contribute to the creation of the general atmosphere. Gissing varied his effects enough to offer his critics a wide choice of elements to be explained as well as the possibility to see but a part of the whole. An attempt must be made to take in the different tones of the book: humorous, as in a conversation on pigs . . . ; jocular, with the disquisition on Thomas Meres' trousers . . . , ironical whenever the Strattons appear, lyrical in the scene describing Kingcote's and Isabel's declaration of love, impressively sober where Mrs. Bolt's sickening conduct is exposed, quaintly romantic with the legend of Knightswell and Kingcote's readings to Percy Vissian, oppressive in the passages depicting the ugliness of Victorian homes . . . , refreshing in the description of the rural scenery. (p. lii)

Acknowledging its absorbing complexity, sensitive also to its atmosphere of reverie and confession, I shall personally avoid all superlatives and be content to say that, whether viewed among Gissing's novels or considered against the background of Victorian fiction, *Isabel Clarendon* is a novel that deserves to live. (p. lx)

> *Pierre Coustillas, "Introduction" (© Pierre Coustillas 1969), in* Isabel Clarendon, Vol. I *by George*

> *Gissing, edited by Pierre Coustillas, The Harvester Press, Brighton, Sussex, 1969, pp. xv-lx.*

GILLIAN TINDALL   (essay date 1974)

Gissing, simply, appeals to people. He touches them. Despite his nineteenth-century themes, his personal obsessions, his blind spots, we often feel near to him. We feel, perhaps, that pressing desire to reach the reader; that 'craving for sympathy' which his friend Edward Clodd noted in the man is perceptible also in his work, taking craving (as surely Clodd himself intended) not in the vulgar modern sense of 'wanting people to be sorry for him', but rather in the sense of wanting understanding, wanting warmth—wanting, in fact, a reciprocation of those feelings he so often and so readily extended towards others. Gissing has been labelled, usually by people who know little of his work, a 'depressing' writer. While it is evident that he was, in the medical sense, a depressive personality, 'depressing' seems an absurdly inept term to apply to a man whose work contains such bountiful evidence of an unquenchable idealism and a desire to love and help others. Several themes occur and reoccur in Gissing's novels with an obsessional frequency. One, certainly, is the malignity of Fate, but another, almost as omnipresent, is the joy of giving. Daydreams of giving—helping—assisting—educating—appear in book after book. The sympathy that Gissing craved from others, he also longed to offer. (pp. 22-3)

[While] it should never be assumed that Gissing 'put his life' and the lives of others straight into his books, in an unworked, unprocessed form, it is certainly fair to say that he is one of those novelists whose books are closely associated with his life, and act therefore as a running commentary on it. Sometimes, if taken too literally, they distort and mislead: the widespread misinterpretation of his pseudo-autobiography *The Private Papers of Henry Ryecroft* provides a classic example of this. But sometimes they appear to embody a more faithful, sensitive and perceptive view of his world than do his personal papers. In diaries and letters we are all of us myopic and over-preoccupied with immediate events and moods to the exclusion of long-term themes. In fiction, the view is longer, the perspective better. The judgement—of personalities and situations—is often keener. Gissing is by no means the only novelist who appears to know with his pen things which, in his daily life, he singularly failed to grasp. (p. 25)

> *Gillian Tindall, in her introduction to her* The Born Exile: George Gissing *(© 1974 Gillian Tindall; reprinted by permission of Harcourt Brace Jovanovich, Inc.; in Canada by Maurice Temple Smith),* Temple Smith, 1974, pp. 19-25.

BIBLIOGRAPHY

Bergonzi, Bernard. "The Novelist as Hero." *The Twentieth Century* 164, No. 981 (November 1958): 444-55.
    Study of *New Grub Street* which concentrates on its autobiographical nature.

Collie, Michael. *George Gissing: A Biography.* Folkstone, England: Wm. Dawson & Sons, 1977, 189 p.
    Explores anew the life and writings of Gissing, interpreting his novels in light of his life. Collie sees Gissing's detachment from society and his secretive personality as evidence that he was a repressed bohemian.

Cope, Jackson I. "Definition as Structure in Gissing's 'Ryecroft Papers'." *Modern Fiction Studies* III, No. 2 (Summer 1957): 127-40.

Close reading of *The Private Papers of Henry Ryecroft* which examines it as an amalgam of the autobiographical novel and essay forms.

Coustillas, Pierre. "Gissing's Feminine Portraiture." *English Literature in Transition* 6, No. 3 (1963): 130-41.

Study of Gissing's relationships with women and how those relationships affected his fictional portrayal of women. Coustillas sees Gissing embroiled in a battle between his ideal vision of womanhood and the reality of the individual natures of the women he encountered.

Coustillas, Pierre, ed. *Collected Articles on George Gissing.* London: Frank Cass & Co., 1968, 186 p.

A critical retrospective of Gissing's work including essays by George Orwell, Jacob Korg, and Irving Howe.

Halperin, John. "The Gissing Revival, 1961-1974." *Studies in the Novel* VIII, No. 1 (Spring 1976): 103-20.

Examination of Gissing criticism and a discussion of the resurgence of interest in his work.

Harris, W. V. "An Approach to Gissing's Short Stories." *Studies in Short Fiction* II, No. 2 (Winter 1965): 137-44.

Survey of Gissing's short stories which stresses his use of the conventions typically associated with the popular magazine story.

Keech, James M. "Gissing's *New Grub Street* and the 'Triple Headed Monster'." *Serif* 7, No. 1 (March 1970): 20-4.

Examination of the widespread use of the three-volume format in Victorian novels. Keech feels that Gissing's *New Grub Street* exhibits all the deficiencies of that format.

Kirk, Russell. "Who Knows George Gissing?" *The Western Humanities Review* IV, No. 3 (Summer 1950): 213-22.

Discusses aspects of Gissing's life as presented in his works and finds him to be an example of his age.

Lelchuk, Alan. "*Demos*: The Ordeal of the Two Gissings." *Victorian Studies* XII, No. 3 (March 1969): 357-74.

Close reading of *Demos* concerned with Gissing's early socialist commitment, his explorations of the British working class, and subsequent disillusion with socialist ideals.

McKay, Ruth Capers. *George Gissing and His Critic Frank Swinnerton.* Folcroft, PA: The Folcroft Press, 1969, 111 p.

Thorough point by point disputation of many of Swinnerton's criticisms of Gissing (see excerpt above).

Orwell, George, "George Gissing." In *In Front of Your Nose: 1945-1950. The Collected Essays, Journalism and Letters of George Orwell, Vol. IV,* edited by Sonia Orwell and Ian Angus, pp. 428-36. New York: Harcourt Brace Jovanovich, 1968.

An excellent brief study of Gissing's protest against "the form of self-torture that goes by the name of respectability."

Poole, Adrian. *Gissing in Context.* Totowa, NJ: Rowman and Littlefield, 1975, 231 p.

Excellent study of the shared concerns of Victorian novelists which places Gissing squarely within the line stretching from Charlotte Brontë to Arnold Bennett. Poole's examination of Gissing's individual novels stresses the relationships between his work and the thought and concerns of his time.

Roberts, Morley. *The Private Life of Henry Maitland.* New York: Hodder & Stoughton, George H. Doran, Co., 1912, 319 p.

Controversial and sensational fictional biography of Gissing by a friend.

Selig, Robert L. "A Sad Heart at the Late-Victorian Culture Market: George Gissing's *In the Year of the Jubilee*." *Studies in English Literature 1500-1900* IX, No. 4 (Autumn 1969): 703-20.

Study of *In the Year of the Jubilee* which examines Gissing's concern for the education of women, and his belief that elements of popular culture such as songs and advertisements were used to keep women satisfied with their subsidiary role.

Spiers, John and Coustillas, Pierre, eds. *The Rediscovery of George Gissing: A Reader's Guide.* London: National Book League, 1971, 163 p.

Excellent guide to Gissing prepared to accompany the 1971 Gissing Exhibition in London. The editors have included throughout much biographic and bibliographic information as well as quotes from Gissing's letters and diaries.

James Weldon Johnson

1871-1938

American novelist, poet, essayist, and translator.

Johnson, known primarily for *The Autobiography of an Ex-Colored Man,* is now regarded as the principal forerunner of the Harlem Renaissance, as well as such modern black writers as Ralph Ellison and Richard Wright. Though Johnson did not make his living by writing, his work does show him to be an accomplished dabbler in many literary realms: the novel, conventional and experimental poetry, popular songs, literary and social criticism, informal history, and autobiography.

Johnson's achievements were as varied as his literary productions. He was, among other things, a school principal, the first black individual admitted to the Florida bar, a successful Broadway songwriter whose song "Lift Every Voice and Sing" was adopted as the Negro national anthem, the U.S. consul to Venezuela and Nicaragua, a newspaper editor, university professor, and the executive secretary of the NAACP. Johnson was undoubtedly one of the most prominent black leaders of his time.

In his literary work Johnson was most concerned with the black man's conception of himself and his role in society. He promoted a conservative approach to change, stressing education and legislation, for which later and more militant generations would label him an Uncle Tom. Early criticism dealt with his work primarily as social documents, but a major critical reassessment during the 1960s stressed his artistic achievement. For example, in *God's Trombones,* regarded as his most impressive poetic work, Johnson captured the black voice in standard English by developing the rhythms and metaphors of a black preacher rather than using the minstrel show dialect prominent at that time. *The Autobiography of an Ex-Colored Man* is similarly now recognized for its psychological insights and ironic portrayal of a man fleeing from self-understanding, and not simply the story of one man's desire to be white.

Although he did not publish a great many works, Johnson's innovations contributed greatly to the development of a black voice in American literature.

PRINCIPAL WORKS

The Autobiography of an Ex-Colored Man (novel) 1912
Fifty Years and Other Poems (poetry) 1917
The Book of American Negro Poetry [editor] (poetry) 1922

God's Trombones (poetry) 1927
Black Manhattan (history) 1930
Along This Way: The Autobiography of James Weldon Johnson (autobiography) 1933
**St. Peter Relates an Incident: Selected Poems* (poetry) 1935

**Saint Peter Relates an Incident of the Resurrection Day* was published in a private, limited edition in 1930.

BRANDER MATTHEWS (essay date 1917)

In poetry, especially in the lyric, wherein the soul is free to find full expression for its innerlost emotions, [the American Negroes'] attempts have been, for the most part, divisible into two classes. In the first of these may be grouped the verses in which the lyrist put forth sentiments common to all mankind and in no wise specifically those of his own race. . . . Whatever their merits might be, these verses cast little or no light upon the deeper racial sentiments of the people to whom the poets themselves belonged. But in the lyrics to be grouped in the second of these classes there was a racial quality. This contained the dialect verses in which there was an avowed purpose of recapturing the color, the flavor, the movement of life in "the quarters," in the cotton field and in the canebrake. (pp. xii-xiii)

In [*Fifty Years and Other Poems*] Mr. James Weldon Johnson conforms to both of these traditions. He gathers together a group of lyrics, delicate in workmanship, fragrant with sentiment, and phrased in pure and unexceptionable English. Then he has another group of dialect verses, racy of the soil, pungent in flavor, swinging in rhythm and adroit in rhyme. But where he shows himself a pioneer is the half-dozen larger and bolder poems, of a loftier strain, in which he has been nobly successful in expressing the higher aspirations of his own people. It is in uttering this cry for recognition, for sympathy, for understanding, and above all, for justice, that Mr. Johnson is most original and most powerful. In the superb and soaring stanzas of "Fifty Years" (published exactly half-a-century after the signing of the Emancipation Proclamation) he has given us one of the noblest commemorative poems yet written by any

American,—a poem sonorous in its diction, vigorous in its workmanship, elevated in its imagination and sincere in its emotion. In it speaks the voice of his race; and the race is fortunate in its spokesman. In it a fine theme has been finely treated. (pp. xiii-xiv)

> *Brander Matthews, in his introduction to* Fifty Years & Other Poems *by James Weldon Johnson, The Cornhill Company, 1917, pp. xi-xiv.*

COUNTEE CULLEN (essay date 1927)

James Weldon Johnson has blown the true spirit and the pentecostal trumpeting of the dark Joshuas of the race in "God's Trombones", composed of seven sermon-poems and a prayer. The seven sermons are like the seven blasts blown by Joshua at Jericho.

An experiment and an intention lie behind these poems. It will be remembered that in "The Book of American Negro Poetry" Mr. Johnson spoke of the limitations of dialect, which he compared to an organ having but two stops, one of humor and one of pathos. He felt that the Negro poet needed to discover some medium of expression with a latitude capable of embracing the Negro experience. These poems were written with that purpose in view, as well as to guarantee a measure of permanence in man's most forgetful mind to that highly romantic and fast disappearing character, the old time Negro preacher.

The poet here has admirably risen to his intentions and his needs; entombed in this bright mausoleum the Negro preacher of an older day can never pass entirely deathward. Dialect could never have been synthesized into the rich mortar necessary for these sturdy unrhymed exhortations. Mr. Johnson has captured that peculiar flavor of speech by which the black sons of Zebedee, lacking academic education, but grounded through their religious intensity in the purest marshalling of the English language (the King James' version of the Bible) must have astounded men more obviously letter-trained. . . .

There is a universality of appeal and appreciation in these poems that raises them, despite the fact that they are labeled "Seven Negro Sermons in Verse" . . . far above a relegation to any particular group or people. (p. 221)

In considering these poems one must pay unlimited respect to the voice Mr. Johnson has recorded, and to the pliable and agony-racked audience to whom those great black trombones blared their apocalyptic revelations, and their terrible condemnation of the world, the flesh, and the devil. Theirs was a poetic idiom saved, by sincerity and the heritage of a colorful imagination, from triteness. (pp. 221-22)

[Certain] technical crudities and dissonances can be explained away. The interpolation here and there of a definitely rhymed couplet among the lines of this vigorous free and easy poetry will not jar, when one reflects that if poetry is the language of inspiration, then these black trumpeters . . . could well be expected to fly now and then beyond their own language barriers into the realms of poetic refinements of which they knew nothing, save by intuitive inspiration. And if on occasion the preacher ascended from *you* and *your* to *thee* and *thou*, this too is in keeping with his character. (p. 222)

> *Countee Cullen, "And the Walls Came Tumblin' Down," in* The Bookman, *Vol. LXVI, No. 2, October, 1927, pp. 221-22.*

CARL VAN VECHTEN (essay date 1927)

The Autobiography of an Ex-Coloured Man is, I am convinced, a remarkable book. . . . [When first published it] stood almost alone as an inclusive survey of racial accomplishments and traits, as an interpretation of the feelings of the Negro towards the white man and towards the members of his own race. (p. v)

The *Autobiography,* of course, in the matter of specific incident, has little enough to do with Mr. Johnson's own life. . . . It would be truer, perhaps, to say that it reads like a composite autobiography of the Negro race in the United States in modern times. (pp. v-vi)

When I was writing *Nigger Heaven* I discovered the *Autobiography* to be an invaluable source-book for the study of Negro psychology. I believe it will be a long time before anybody can write about the Negro without consulting Mr. Johnson's pages to advantage. Naturally, the *Autobiography* had its precursors. Booker T. Washington's *Up from Slavery* (1900) is a splendid example of autobiography, but the limitations of his subject matter made it impossible for Dr. Washington to survey the field as broadly as Mr. Johnson, setting himself no limitations, could. Dr. Du Bois's important work, *The Souls of Black Folk* (1903) does, certainly, explore a wide territory, but these essays lack the insinuating influence of Mr. Johnson's calm, dispassionate tone, and they do not offer, in certain important respects, so revealing a portrait of Negro character. (p. vii)

Mr. Johnson, however, chose an all-embracing scheme. His young hero, the ostensible author, either discusses (or lives) pretty nearly every phase of Negro life, North and South and even in Europe, available to him at that period. That he "passes" the title indicates. Miscegenation in its slave and also its more modern aspects, both casual and marital, is competently treated. The ability of the Negro to mask his real feelings with a joke or a laugh in the presence of the inimical white man is here noted, for the first time in print, I should imagine. Negro adaptability, touchiness, and jealousy are referred to in an unself-conscious manner, totally novel in Negro writing at the time this book originally appeared. . . . Colour snobbery within the race is freely spoken of, together with the economic pressure from without which creates this false condition. (pp. vii-viii)

New readers, I am confident, will examine this book with interest: some to acquire through its mellow pages a new conception of how a coloured man lives and feels, others simply to follow the course of its fascinating story. (p. x)

> *Carl Van Vechten, in his introduction to* The Autobiography of an Ex-Colored Man *by James Weldon Johnson (copyright 1927 by Alfred A. Knopf, Inc.; renewal copyright 1955 by Carl Van Vechten; reprinted by permission of Alfred A. Knopf, Inc.), Knopf, 1927 (and reprinted by Knopf, 1961), pp. vi-x.*

EDMUND WILSON (essay date 1928)

Despite the importance of ["The Autobiography of an Ex-Colored Man"] as a human and sociological document, its value as a piece of literature is not equally great. In this book, though not in some of his other writings, Mr. Johnson lacks the power to convince one emotionally of the stark, hard truth of the scenes which he presents. He fumbles his climaxes, even when the material offers him superb opportunities. Moreover, he does not distinguish with sufficient clearness between the trivial and the supremely relevant. One could spare much of the long account of the hero's youth, but of the psychological reactions which accompany the phenomenon of "passing" one is told only too little. The "Autobiography" is an excellent, honest piece of work. One wishes that it were even better. (p. 304)

> *Edmund Wilson, "An Ex-Colored Man" (reprinted by permission of Farrar, Straus & Giroux, Inc.), in* The New Republic, *Vol. 53, No. 687, February 1, 1928, pp. 303-04.*

HAROLD ROSENBERG   (essay date 1936)

[*Saint Peter Relates an Incident*] is the author's expression, in satirical terms, of the indignation he felt on reading in the newspaper of a morning in 1930 that the U.S. government was sending a group of gold-star mothers to France to visit the graves of their sons slain in the World War, and that the Negro gold-star mothers would not be allowed to travel with the white, but would be sent over later on a second-class ship. (p. 49)

It is grievous to report that the outrageous act of public discrimination against his race which inspired Mr. Johnson to write his poem strikes very little fire in the poem itself. Naturally, the blurb on the book tries to capitalize on the genius of the Negro people by claiming for the poem "something of the simple charm of Negro lore." As a matter of fact, however, the Saint Peter poem, as well as the rest of the volume, is less typical of the poetry produced out of the labor, anguish, courage, and awakening consciousness of the Negro race in America, than of the literary products of the conservative upper-class nationalist of any race or nation. Mr. Johnson is a Negro poet only in the sense that he applies his academic art to the situation of the American Negro. So far as literary qualities are concerned, a conservative Chinese nationalist, a conservative Zionist, a conservative Hindu nationalist, a conservative celebrator of American accomplishment, all resemble Mr. Johnson in their comfortable idealization of nature-sentiments, their reliant appeals to abstract Justice, their self-solacing trust in an after-death rectification of what their people have suffered. Amid the most brutal assaults upon the lives and liberties of their beloved people, these patriots manage to remain aloft and dignified, the official mourners, the official voices of hope in the future. With respect to nationality, they exist as Chinese, Jews, Hindus, Americans; with respect to poetry, they are all one thing—academicians: an internationalism of mediocrity forever seeking to disguise itself under racial and geographic borderlines.

Whatever part it may play in the social and political progress of the people it aims to represent, the official gesture is irreconcilable with good poetry. The chemistry of interaction between experience, imagination, and language is completely unknown to the stencil-designer of monumental shadows of good will. (pp. 49-50)

> *Harold Rosenberg, "Truth and the Academic Style," in* Poetry (© *by the estate of Harold Rosenberg; reprinted by permission of the Editor of* Poetry), *Vol. XLIX, No. 1, October, 1936, pp. 49-51.*

STERLING BROWN   (essay date 1937)

According to William Stanley Braithwaite, *Fifty Years and*

Other Poems by James Weldon Johnson "brought the first intellectual substance to the content of our poetry, and a craftsmanship . . . less spontaneous than Dunbar's, but more balanced and precise." Although containing lyrics of quiet sincerity such as "Beauty That Is Never Old," "The Glory of The Day Was In Her Face" and "Mother Night," this volume will probably be remembered longest for its poems of race-consciousness. . . . [The] most vigorous poem of protest from any Negro poet up to his time is "Brothers." Reminiscent of Markham's "The Man With The Hoe," this poem describes with grim detail a lynching, refusing to urge the innocence of the victim, but attempting to explain how he had become brutalized. . . . And the last muttered words of the brute to the lynchers stated what the America of his day had not often heard:

> Brothers in spirit, brothers in deed are we. . . .

Where the southern tradition could see only the sentimental side, Johnson points out in "The Black Mammy" what was really a tragic experience. In "Black and Unknown Bards" he gives very high praise to the slave-creators of the spirituals. One of Johnson's earlier poems is "Lift Every Voice And Sing"; set to music by his brother, J. Rosamond Johnson, this has been accepted as the Negro National Anthem. Johnson's poems of this period were largely expressions of race pride or defense, protesting with vigor, but trusting unfailingly in God and the future. (pp. 50-1)

> *Sterling Brown, "Dunbar and the Romantic Tradition," in his* The Negro in American Fiction (*copyright 1937 by the Associates in Negro Folk Education*), *Associates in Negro Folk Education, 1937 (and reprinted in his* Negro Poetry and Drama and the Negro in American Fiction, *Atheneum, 1972, pp. 45-59).**

J. SAUNDERS REDDING   (essay date 1939)

[*God's Trombones*] made a return to the primitive heritage [of Negro expression]. . . . "The Creation" and "Go Down Death," two of the seven sermons, are among the most moving poems in the language and certainly rank with the best things done by American Negro poets. (p. 120)

God's Trombones [is] a brilliant example of the maturing of [Johnson's] thoughts on folk material and dialect. Aside from the beauty of the poems, the essay which prefaces them is of the first importance for it definitely hails back from the urban and sophisticated to the earthy exuberance of the Negro's kinship with the earth, the fields, the suns and rains of the South. Discarding the "mutilations of dialect," Mr. Johnson yet retains the speech forms, the idea patterns, and the rich racial flavor.

> O Lord, we come this morning
> Knee-bowed and body-bent
> Before thy throne of grace.
>
>   (p. 121)

[Most important] is Mr. Johnson's acknowledgment of his debt to the folk material, the primitive sermons, and the influence of the spirituals. . . . (p. 122)

> *J. Saunders Redding, "Emergence of the New Negro," in his* To Make a Poet Black (*copyright © 1939 by the University of North Carolina Press*), *University of North Carolina Press, 1939 (and reprinted by McGrath Publishing Company, 1968), pp. 93-126.**

HUGH M. GLOSTER (essay date 1948)

The Autobiography of an Ex-Coloured Man is noteworthy because of its restraint, its comprehensiveness, and its adumbration of the Negro Renascence of the 1920's. At a time when most Negro fictionists were giving blow for blow and painting extravagantly favorable pictures of members of the race, Johnson set out neither to glorify Negroes nor to malign whites but to interpret men and conditions as he knew them. . . .

Besides being more detached than any preceding novel of American Negro life, *The Autobiography of an Ex-Coloured Man* is ground-breaking in its introduction of a well-realized cosmopolitan milieu. Unlike most earlier Negro fiction, it is not localized in the South but moves out into the broader field of European and Northern urban life. (p. 79)

In a word, *The Autobiography of an Ex-Coloured Man* signalizes the liberation of the Negro novelist from the habitual practice of using the South as a principal setting. . . .

In addition to being more impartial and more comprehensive than any earlier novel of American Negro life, *The Autobiography of an Ex-Coloured Man* is a milestone because of its forthright presentation of racial thought. Admitting the dual personality which some Negroes assume—one role among their own group and the other in the presence of whites—Johnson is himself not guilty of such a two-sided character. Not attempting to "wear the mask," he gives a calm, dispassionate treatment of people and situations as he sees them. (p. 80)

> Hugh M. Gloster, "Negro Fiction to World War I," in his Negro Voices in American Fiction (copyright 1948 by the University of North Carolina Press), University of North Carolina Press, 1948 (and reprinted by Russell & Russell, Inc., 1965), pp. 23-100.*

ROBERT A. BONE (essay date 1958)

Johnson is the only true artist among the early Negro novelists. His superior craftsmanship is undoubtedly due to his early training in the musical comedy field. . . . Johnson's seven years as a "conscious artist" in musical comedy proved to be an invaluable apprenticeship. He acquired a skill with words in this exacting medium, and entered a sophisticated world which helped him to attain a cosmopolitan outlook.

The Autobiography of an Ex-Colored Man, simply by virtue of its form, demanded a discipline and restraint hitherto unknown in the Negro novel. It is written in the first person, and as the title indicates it purports to be an autobiography. Johnson, let it be noted, deliberately fostered this illusion by publishing the book anonymously. So well did he succeed in his deception that most of the early reviewers accepted the book at face value. Even after Johnson revealed his identity, he was so beset by readers who thought it was the story of his life that he was forced to write a real autobiography in self-defense.

The narrative structure of the novel consists of a series of episodes which runs the gamut of Negro life in America. (p. 46)

The theme that runs persistently through this narrative is the moral cowardice of the protagonist. A dramatic tension develops between his boyhood resolve "to be a great col-

ored man" and the tragic flaw which prevents him from realizing this ambition. At every crisis in his life he takes the line of least resistance, allowing circumstance to determine his fate.

In spite of his ironical success as a white businessman, the protagonist is a failure on his own terms. Overpowered by life, he becomes a symbol of man's universal failure to fulfill his highest destiny. . . . (p. 47)

Much of the novel's meaning is conveyed by its tone, which is a subtle blend of tragedy and irony. This tone flows naturally from the life of the protagonist, which has both tragic and ironic aspects. . . . He avoids self-pity, however, through an attitude of ironic detachment. (p. 48)

Because of his sympathetic portrayal of Bohemian life, Johnson has been widely regarded as a precursor of the Harlem School. It is certainly true that he is the first Negro novelist to show overt sympathy for this aspect of racial life. He champions ragtime music and the cakewalk, for example, as accomplishments of which the race should be proud rather than ashamed. Nevertheless, in terms of the structure of the novel, the Bohemian episode is presented as an evasion of the protagonist's higher responsibility. A transitional figure, Johnson is no Claude McKay; the low-life milieu of the Harlem School is hardly his natural habitat.

Johnson indisputably anticipates the Harlem School by subordinating racial protest to artistic considerations. For the most part, the racial overtones of the novel form an organic part of its aesthetic structure. While in one sense the racial identity of the protagonist is the central fact of his existence, in another, it is almost irrelevant. The protagonist faces a series of situations from which he flees; his flight into the white race is merely the crowning instance of his cowardice. To be sure, his tragedy is heightened because there are good objective reasons for his final flight, but these reasons in no sense constitute a justification. The focus of the novel is not on the objective situation but on the subjective human tragedy.

Compared to the typical propaganda tract of the period, *The Autobiography of an Ex-Colored Man* is a model of artistic detachment. Yet even Johnson cannot wholly repress a desire to educate the white folks. Artificially contrived discussions of the race problem mar the novel, and at times the author is needlessly defensive. But despite an occasional lapse, he retains a basic respect for his function as an artist. (pp. 48-9)

> Robert A. Bone, "Novels of the Talented Tenth: James Weldon Johnson," in his The Negro Novel in America (copyright © 1958 by Yale University Press), Yale University Press, 1958, pp. 45-49.

EUGENIA W. COLLIER (essay date 1960)

At the turn of the twentieth century the American reading and listening public was amusing itself with a fascinating literary toy. The toy was Negro dialect poetry, popularized by white local colorists after the Civil War, and perpetuated by a young Negro poet, Paul Laurence Dunbar, and his imitators. Poetry in Negro dialect consisted mainly of rhymed and metrical misspelling; its subject matter seldom rose above the stereotype of the black-faced buffoon. . . .

Later a subtle change began to occur in America's literary

taste.... In this change, dialect became more flexible in rhythmic pattern and rhyme scheme; folk experience as expressed in spirituals, jazz, and the blues was basic to the new dialect; folk idioms and speech patterns rather than mere misspellings were fundamental. At its best the new dialect, in subject matter and in form, reached a level of artistry never attained by the best of the Dunbar school.

The change in the handling of folk material in poetry by Negro writers, from traditional dialect to an imitation of the idiom, is most apparent in the work of James Weldon Johnson.... In his dialect poetry Johnson never had Dunbar's facility for sophisticated rhythm and rhyme; he did, however, have an artistic integrity, a more faithful rendition of social truth as he saw it, which is seldom evident in Dunbar's plantation tradition poems. (p. 351)

Most of [*Fifty Years and Other Poems*] consists of adequate (but for the most part, unremarkable) standard English poems; one section, "Jingles and Croons," contains Johnson's dialect poetry. The dialect is written in the Dunbar tradition in form and in subject matter. It is not nearly so polished as Dunbar's; rather, it is quite artificial and occasionally almost clumsy. The attempt at imagery is not nearly so successful as Dunbar's, and the rhythm is often faulty. (p. 352)

The subject matter of "Jingles and Croons," then, follows the Dunbar school: lovers, lullabies, simple pleasures, sentiment, faith—a faith in which one prays for a Christmas turkey rather than for the more basic needs of life. This was the sort of treatment which the "eye dialect" of the Dunbarists seemed best able to portray. Yet there is even in these poems a subtle difference from Dunbar, the beginnings of the use of dialect to express something more than the surface pleasures and pains of a simple people. For Johnson tells of a bacchanal which is held not for the purpose of a little innocent fun, but for the purpose of forgetting very real troubles. (p. 353)

To James Weldon Johnson two things became evident: that folk experience was a rich source of poetic material, a source virtually untouched by colored writers; and that traditional dialect with its emphasis on mispronunciation and its adherence to strict metre and rhyme had not been used as a successful means of interpreting the folk....

For several years Johnson had recognized the poetic possibilities of the "old-time Negro sermon" and had planned to use this subject matter in a way similar to a composer's use of folk music as a theme for serious musical expression. (p. 354)

In *God's Trombones* Johnson discarded conventional dialect....

Compare Johnson's treatment of death in his earlier traditional dialect with his treatment of the same theme in an old-time sermon from *God's Trombones*. "De Little Pickaninny's Gone to Sleep" resembles Dunbar's "Two Little Boots" in its saccharine sentiment as well as in its inaccurate rendering of pronunciation; Dunbar's poem, however, is more skillfully done. Johnson's "Go Down Death" has much more dignity than "De Little Pickaninny" and is much more effective in its rendition of actual speech. (p. 355)

In the language of *God's Trombones* Johnson found a much more flexible medium than Dunbar dialect for the interpre-

tation of folk material. Traditional dialect attempts (sometimes unsuccessfully) a strict infidelity in metre and in rhyme scheme; Johnson adapted to an artistic form the rhythms of an actual sermon, the accents of actual speech and intonation. He freed himself from the necessity to rhyme, thus subordinating strict poetic form to the artistic interpretation of his subject matter. In *God's Trombones* Johnson approximated the vivid imagery of the folk, an imagery far superior to any he attained in the *Fifty Years* dialect poems and certainly an imagery which rivaled the best of Dunbar's. Johnson used all the tricks of the folk preacher's trade—hyperbole, repetition, juxtaposition, personal appeal to his listeners, the knack of making Biblical happenings have an intense meaning to current life. Johnson even used punctuation and capitalization to achieve his effect—dashes to indicate the frequent and dramatic pauses, capitalization to emphasize important words, such as "Old Earth" and "Great White Throne." The sensitive reader cannot fail to hear the rantings of the fire-and-brimstone preacher; the extremely sensitive reader may even hear the unwritten "Amens" of the congregation. Johnson does this without misspellings. (pp. 358-59)

James Weldon Johnson reflected the change from stilted poetics to the more natural poetry of living, a change which was taking place in Negro poetry as well as in American poetry in general. (p. 359)

> *Eugenia W. Collier, "James Weldon Johnson: Mirror of Change," in* PHYLON: The Atlanta University Review of Race and Culture *(copyright, 1960, by Atlanta University; reprinted by permission of* PHYLON*), Vol. XXI, No. 4, Fourth Quarter (December, 1960), pp. 351-59.*

JEAN WAGNER (essay date 1962)

[Johnson's poems] suffer from a major blemish, their impersonal character.... Only rarely did he show himself capable of the limitless abandon without which there can be no real poetic emotion. His verses reveal nothing or almost nothing of his own intimate depths, and may even seek to hide them from us. Johnson can hardly be classed as a lyric poet, since he is too often satisfied with a borrowed or purely conventional lyricism. Compared with [Claude] McKay's earliest American poems, those making up Johnson's first collection, which came out that same year, resemble less the work of a forerunner than of a man trailing behind his time.

His chief contribution to the poetic harvest of the Renaissance was *God's Trombones,* Negro sermons in verse in which, availing himself of the example of his contemporary John Millington Synge, he tried to carry over, into a more respectable idiom than the rough Negro dialect, the essentials of the naïve, clumsy religious lyricism of the oldtime Negro preacher. (pp. 351-52)

Under the collective title of "Jingles and Croons," the dialect poems make up one-third of [*Fifty Years and Other Poems*], some of them previously having been popular hits.... [They] are all basically commercial pieces, put together with every necessary precaution to ensure monetary success. (p. 356)

In most of these poems Johnson rather unimaginatively follows [Paul Laurence] Dunbar's themes and manner; he does not always even bother to change the title of the imitated poems or the names of the characters. Here to be found once again are all the types of song that had been in circulation twenty-five years earlier: the naïve, sugary love song, the cradle song with which the black mammy lulls her picaninny to sleep, the story of the rival rural swains, the fable that pays homage to Brer Rabbit, and even, on occasion, a discreet hymning of the good old days and of good oldtime Georgia. Johnson's portrait of the Negro, in its main lines, still adheres to the minstrel tradition. He is carefree and optimistic, plays the banjo, eats watermelon and 'possum, and steals chickens and turkeys—all traits necessary to arouse an easy sense of superiority in the white public. (p. 357)

In the domain of dialect poetry, it was hard to do better than, or even as well as, Dunbar, and in "Jingles and Croons" Johnson never attains the spontaneity of expression, the vivacious rhythm, or the melodiousness of his distinguished forerunner. (p. 358)

[Johnson] does not seem to have thought that the hostility dividing black and whites disproved the fact that they were destined to be brothers—quarreling brothers, perhaps, but brothers all the same. How else could he have given the title "Brothers" to a poem on lynching which, according to Sterling Brown, is "the most vigorous poem of protest from any Negro poet up to his time"? How else could he have put these last words in the mouth of the Negro, as he dies at the hands of his lynchers:

"Brothers in spirit, brothers in deed are we"?

To behold the poet thus unflinchingly manifesting his faith in racial brotherhood leaves one divided between admiration for his idealism and awareness of a certain incoherence in the sequence of episodes that make up this "American drama." The most authentic and gripping part of the poem is the forceful, realistic description of the lynching—which is the first of its kind in American poetry. With greater audacity than Dunbar in "The Haunted Oak," Johnson piles up the macabre details, depicts the flesh of the victim blistering in the flames and falling away in strips, and stresses the sadism of the killers who, when it threatens to end all too rapidly, throw water on the fire to slow it down, so that they may still revel in this ghastly spectacle. We may also admire the poet's notion of having the victim's last words arouse anguish in the minds of the lynchers. He does not, however, anticipate Cullen by suggesting to us that there is a parallel between this burning and the death of Christ on the cross, though he does eloquently suggest the victim's spiritual triumph and the moral defeat of triumphant brute force.

But how clumsily this powerful scene is introduced! It follows immediately, without the least psychological motivation, upon a no less implausible dialogue between the mob and the Negro they have seized. Doubtless it was Johnson's intention to demonstrate by concrete example that many lynchings had not a shadow of justification, and three lines before the end there is some mention of a "fiendish crime" the victim is said to have committed. But this does not eliminate the incoherence, which actually is double—for the lynching scene, to which is grafted the idea of brotherhood heralded by the title, has no organic connection with the first forty lines or so, which could have been utilized in a separate poem. (pp. 367-68)

Johnson presents [the theme of brotherhood] much more satisfactorily in another poem, "The Black Mammy."

Frankly departing from the sentimentality the plantation tradition had attached to every mention of this figure, who often received a somewhat hypocritical veneration in the great families of the South, the poet is interested in and illuminates only the tragic aspect of the black nurse's situation. She must lavish the same generosity on her own child and on the other, who may one day crush him. . . . (p. 369)

If Johnson rang so many changes on the theme of the hostile brothers, the reason is that this concept's internal contradiction, with its elements suggesting both fraternal love and the opposite, no doubt provided him with a fitting symbol for that other contradiction falsifying relations between blacks and whites who, though the children of the same fatherland and proclaiming the same ideal of liberty, nevertheless are divided by history and by descent.

Johnson hits upon the same contradiction once more, in different form, when he takes up the theme of interracial love in "The White Witch." This is probably the best poem in the volume, as it assuredly is the most "modern."

Yet, at first glance, the symbolism here may seem bewildering. (pp. 369-70)

The white witch stands, in the first place, for the eternal feminine. As early as the second stanza the poet forthrightly declares that this is no old, toothless creature who terrifies little children; quite the contrary, she is adorned with all the charms of youth. Yet she is as old as the world. Thus her bewitching nature is principally that of love.

This portrait is rendered more complex by the racial context into which it is introduced, for the white witch is also the incarnation of the Aryan racial type with blue eyes, fair hair, and lily-white skin. At the same time she symbolizes the white purity which racist America is intent on defending against any admixture of black blood. Such, at all events, is the official doctrine, for in reality the attraction she possesses for the Negro is equaled only by the attraction she feels for him. Since she sees the Negro as closer to the state of nature than the white man, because he is still in close contact with the earth from which, like Antaeus, he derives his strength, the white woman rightly or wrongly attributes to him a greater sexual potency, and initially she expects him to reveal carnal delights hitherto unknown. . . .

Yet the witch of the poem is not only a passionate lover; she has also [an] undeniably maleficent character. . . . (p. 370)

It would still be necessary to specify the danger against which Johnson warns his racial brothers. This is the very point at which the poem moves to the symbolic level. There is no question of the traditional punishment meted out to the Negro whose love for a white woman has become known. The danger is bound up, rather, with another feature in the portrait of the white witch. The poet, who tells us that he has already yielded to her charms, has learned that beneath the fascinating exterior of the woman passionately in love she hides her vampire-like nature, and that in the sexual embrace she seeks to rob of his substance the prey who lets himself be entrapped by her wiles. . . .

Thus the poem's meaning reaches far beyond the theme of interracial love on which it is based, and in the last resort the white witch stands for the whole world of the white man. The reciprocal attraction between the two races is not only of the flesh; it is also felt throughout the many forms of civilization and culture, and in this lies, for the Negro, the chief risk of emasculation. By giving in to the powerful attraction the majority culture exerts on him, the Negro runs the risk of losing his own personality, together with his weapons of defense against the basic hostility of the white world. That is why Johnson advises him to seek safety only in flight. (p. 371)

At any level, consequently, at the heart of this poem—as was true also for the theme of the hostile brothers—is the association of those two opposites, love and enmity. . . . Johnson does no more than state the terms of the antithesis. It will remain for others to raise the level of the debate and to strive for a synthesis. But the fact remains that Johnson broke truly fresh ground by endeavoring to elucidate, via this symbol, the extent of the basic contradiction keeping the races apart. Especially if one bears in mind the inadequacy of the few poems he published in [his later collection, *St. Peter Relates an Incident*], it is no exaggeration to assert that his genuinely creative poetic effort is contained in its entirety in [*Fifty Years and Other Poems*]. (pp. 371-72)

In Johnson's poem ["St. Peter Relates an Incident of the Resurrection Day"], which sets out to be humorous, Saint Peter tells the angels, long after time has ended, how on Resurrection Day all the American patriotic groups came in a body to witness the resurrection of the unknown soldier, and to escort him into paradise. But when the tombstone was raised the unknown soldier, amid universal consternation, turned out to be a Negro. . . . While this was an original idea, it was frittered away in this poorly structured poem. There is a shocking imbalance between the central theme, which extends over 56 lines of the fourth part, and the far too long introductory section of 68 lines, often uninteresting and in dubious taste. . . . But the poem fails above all because Johnson is simply not a humorist. (n., p. 372)

[Johnson's] intent in writing *God's Trombones* is succinctly expressed in these two sentences from the preface: "The old-time Negro preacher is rapidly passing. I have here tried sincerely to fix something of him." . . .

The conventionality of these eight poems is already apparent from the fact that they are monologues, whereas in reality a part of the sermon, at least, would have consisted of a dialogue between preacher and congregation. Here the presence of the latter is not even suggested, as it might have been by appropriate monologue technique—for example, by using the repeated question, as [others] had done. Nor is the monologue able to reproduce the oratorical gestures, always so important for the Negro preacher, who is equally actor and orator. (p. 378)

In principle, the language of *God's Trombones* is normal English, not Negro dialect, but here and there it is possible to note a few minor deviations from the norm. True, the dialect or familiar forms that creep in are for the most part American rather than specifically Negro. They include, for example, the intermittent usage of the double negation and of the gerundive preceded by the preposition "a"—except, however, in these two lines of "Noah Built the Ark," in which "a-going" is not just typically Negro but directly borrowed from the first line of a spiritual. . . . But such forms are exceptional, no more than two or three dozen of them are to be noted in the more than 900 lines of *God's Trombones*, and their contribution to the effect Johnson was aiming at is but subsidiary.

Much more effective in giving these sermons their Negro character are the countless, more or less extensive echoes of actual spirituals with which they are studded. Sometimes a mere word or expression that has long been familiar crops up in the sermon and by its own power suddenly evokes in the reader's mind the whole naïve imagery that makes up the religious context of the spirituals, to which the preacher untiringly returns to find subject matter for his sermon. There are the pearly gates and golden streets of the New Jerusalem, mentioned in Revelation; the custom of calling Jesus "Mary's Baby," and the warning words to sinners and backsliders that they should repent before it is too late. (pp. 378-80)

Johnson gives a correct idea of the preacher's technique, designed to move rather than convince his audience, alternately raising the congregation's hopes and filling them with terror, and arousing their pity by presenting scenes from Holy Writ as though these were taking place before their eyes. (p. 381)

The most personal aspect of the preacher's art is what he creates out of his own fantasy with the aim of stirring the imaginations of his hearers. A ready fabulist, he constantly interpolates in order to supplement the bareness of the biblical narrative. Thus the creation of the world is unfolded before the eyes of the astounded congregation as though it were a fairy tale or a child's game. . . . His preaching ever relies on the concrete, with an anthropomorphism that brings down to the human level the Eternal Father, who is addressed as one would speak to a friendly neighbor. . . . Naïve, homely, and extravagant in turn, but always direct and forceful, these images have no compunction about blending in with those of the Bible so unexpectedly at times as to be almost grotesque. . . . (pp. 381-82)

If allowance is made for his borrowings from the Bible, from the spirituals, and from the Negro sermons he had heard, what then is the poet's share in *God's Trombones*? Johnson was certainly not the creator of these sermons but, as Synge remarked of his own indebtedness to the Irish people, every work of art results from a collaboration. In *God's Trombones*, the artist is clearly present on every page, and he gives even while he receives. The simplicity and clarity, so striking in these poems, are the fruits of his efforts. His musical sense is manifested in the choice of sonorities for the free-verse line which, in his hands, becomes docile and supple, and adjusts to the preacher's rhythm as well as to the rise and fall of his voice. Taking what were, after all, the heterogeneous elements of his raw materials, the poet has marked them with the unity and the stamp of his own genius, so that these sermons, as they come from his hands, have undeniably become his own to some degree.

If he deserves any reproach, it might be for his excessive zeal in idealizing and refining—or, in other words, for having thought it necessary to impose too much respectability on essentially popular material whose crudity is one of its charms, as it is also a voucher for its authenticity. His sermons are still folklore, perhaps, but stylized folklore. (p. 383)

Jean Wagner, "James Weldon Johnson," in his Black Poets of the United States: From Paul Laurence Dunbar to Langston Hughes, *translated by Kenneth Doublas (translation copyright 1973 by The Board of Trustees of the University of Illinois;*

reprinted by permission of the author; originally published as Les Poètes Nègres des Etats-Unis, *Librairie Istra, 1962), University of Illinois Press, 1973, pp. 351-84.*

HAROLD CRUSE (essay date 1967)

The three writers who wrote specifically about the Harlem Renaissance, and were also representative of it—Langston Hughes, James Weldon Johnson, and Claude McKay—all failed to render the kind of analysis the movement demanded. (pp. 32-3)

James Weldon Johnson, older than most of the Harlem Renaissance intellectuals, and with more insight into Negro cultural forms, also saw the renaissance somewhat more clearly.... Johnson's main literary contribution was in poetry, yet today, when everything about the American Negro must be seen in its historical perspective, Johnson's descriptive history, *Black Manhattan,* and his autobiography, *Along This Way* ..., emerge as his most important writing. These two works give us practically the entire panorama of Negro cultural history in America by a man who participated in that history from the 1890's—the decade that marked the actual beginning of the modern Negro cultural movement—until his death in 1938. (pp. 33-4)

Harold Cruse, "Harlem Background—The Rise of Economic Nationalism and Origins of Cultural Revolution," in his The Crisis of the Negro Intellectual *(copyright © 1967 by Harold Cruse; abridged by permission of William Morrow & Company, Inc.), William Morrow, 1967, pp. 11-63.**

ALLAN H. SPEAR (essay date 1968)

Black Manhattan is a document of the 1920's—a celebration, with reservations, of both the artistic renaissance of the era and the dream of a black metropolis. Although set in a broader context, it is not, as its author tells us, "in any strict sense a history." ... Nevertheless, much of *Black Manhattan* remains of lasting value. The heart of the book is an impressionistic evocation of the Harlem of the 1920's by an astute and knowledgeable observer. Its most important contribution is its informed and frequently perceptive analysis of the changing role of Negro artists in music, literature and, especially, the theater. (p. viii)

Johnson was a transitional figure in the history of Negro culture. The product of a late-nineteenth-century upbringing, he came of age at a time when the genteel tradition still held a firm grip on both white and black creative artists. But although his world view was always anchored in the Victorian values of the black bourgeoisie, he himself was part of the movement to create a positive and vital culture rooted in the folk experience of the Negro people. His Broadway career made him deeply aware of the dilemma of the black artist. In the nineteenth century, the only commercially successful Negro songwriters and performers had been those who tailored their work to the demands of white stereotypes. They had operated within the minstrel tradition, playing the role of the irresponsible but lovable "darky" that white audiences expected of them. By the turn of the century, however, the best of the black vaudevillians began to rebel against such blatant pandering to white tastes and attempted to create a more three-dimensional portrait of Negro life.... In *Black Manhattan,* Johnson writes with feeling and perception about this

"middle period of the development of the Negro in the American theater." (pp. ix-x)

[Johnson's creative writing] stands midway between the genteel literary works of the early Negro novelists and poets and the celebrations of Negro "low life" that characterized the Harlem renaissance of the 1920's. (p. x)

In *Black Manhattan,* Johnson views the Harlem renaissance as a close observer and sympathetic supporter—but as a man who is himself too much the Victorian gentleman to wholeheartedly participate. He is impressed by the powerful poetry of Claude McKay, Countee Cullen and Langston Hughes, the music of the great jazz figures of the 1920's, and the joyous song and dance of the black revues and variety shows. But he occasionally feels obliged to apologize for their primitiveness, to praise works for their vitality *despite* their concern with the "low life." He clearly retains the Victorian notion that "serious"—i.e., respectable—literature stands at the apex of cultural achievement.

If as a cultural critic Johnson emerges as a *haut-bourgeois* making a valiant, if not quite successful, attempt to understand the *avant garde,* so too as a social thinker he stands midway between conservatives and radicals. (p. xi)

Johnson's vision of Harlem was more a dream than a reality. Before World War I, Harlem had been, to be sure, a community of great promise, the finest neighborhood that Negroes had ever occupied in an American city. By 1930, however, conditions had badly deteriorated.... Rather than a black metropolis, Harlem was a black ghetto. (pp. xiii-xiv)

Johnson's failure to see the realities of ghetto life was the result of his own world view and of the racial ideology to which he subscribed.... A proper Victorian gentleman, he was frequently blind to the unpleasant aspects of life. He shared his optimism with many Negro leaders of the 1920's who found in the artistic ferment of the decade, in the new interest of white intellectuals in Negro creative activities, and in the dream of a black metropolis, sources of hope for a better future. Ironically, Johnson completed *Black Manhattan* on the very eve of the Great Depression. Within months after the publication of the book, the tragedy of Harlem would lie exposed, visible even through the rosiest lenses. For with economic collapse, black Manhattan's tinsely façade was punctured. (p. xiv)

Black Manhattan is in many ways a period piece. Dated almost as soon as it was written, its sanguine tone seems naïve today. Yet it does evoke an era in Negro life and thought, an era in which a new and better life for black Americans seemed just beyond the horizon. It reveals a great deal about the mind of a man who made a major contribution to both Negro literature and Negro organizational activities. It provides us with an intimate account of the black theatrical and musical world of which Johnson had been a part. And it raises searching questions about the black man's struggle to find his identity. Johnson's formulations may seem out of date, but the central problem with which he grapples is not. (p. xv)

Allan H. Spear, "Preface" (reprinted by permission of Atheneum Publishers; copyright © 1968 by Allan H. Spear), in Black Manhattan *by James Weldon Johnson, Atheneum, 1968, pp. v-xv.*

CLARENCE A. AMANN (essay date 1970)

If [*The Autobiography of an Ex-Colored Man*] is the best of James Weldon Johnson, he has little to recommend him as an artist. (p. 113)

[One] must summon a reluctant "professional" objectivity to sympathize with the effort of James Weldon Johnson in *The Autobiography of an Ex-Colored Man*. Written as if it [were] an autobiographical initiation story, it emerges rather as the paranoid wailing of a bohemian wastrel. . . .

Autobiography is an initiation story. And as an initiation story, it portrays the life of one very *exceptional* Negro individual, a potential *virtuoso* in music frustrated by his own lack of responsibility. The story happens only sketchily and briefly if colorfully upon several typical areas of Negro-American life and culture. It attempts to depict the scenes of Negro Bohemia in New York City and it comes off as superficial. It attempts to represent the attitudes of Negroes in selected enclaves, mostly Bohemian also, about the European continent, and again it deteriorates into a tragicomic dirge that fails to convince. . . .

Beyond the fact that some aspects of the Negro milieu were illumined by this story of "passing" as a white, it is difficult to discover much to recommend it. Were it all we had to define this phenomenon in the early twentieth century, it might be helpful; it would also be dangerous in its inadequacy. One sided (perhaps consciously so) and professedly a story of a wasted life, it seems so unpenetrating, so surface, that it cannot satisfy. . . .

Suffice it to say that in Johnson, in this specimen at least, the genuine initiation process loses its thrust and emotional force in the distraction of inept form. (p. 116)

Little more need be said of the form of James Weldon Johnson's text. Perhaps this reviewer has missed some more subtle intention that makes the work an effective union of form and content. It must seem to me sketchy and superficial. It fails to probe the psyche of its too often surly first person narrator even shallowly. It seems ill-controlled and fragmented and only occasionally gives faint promise of moving. Even then, as in the case of his "love affairs" and his mother's death, the meeting and loss of friends, and the like, he depends too often on trite devices. When he becomes original to attempt the dramatic, it becomes a grotesque and incompleted "deus ex machina," . . . or a shocking shooting or man-burning that lacks sufficient and deft preparation and detail to bring off the emotional impact he essays. It should be pointed out that Johnson is consistent in this fault throughout the book. That is to say, we discover all too abruptly and finally that he's a Negro, that his father is the visitor, that his mother has died, and the like. Yet we are given no insight at all to even the most superficial soul searching one might in the least expect regarding his reluctance to remain a Negro. It makes all his actions seem thoughtless and precipitous, and as such arouse little real sympathy in the reader. (p. 117)

Clarence A. Amann, "Three Negro Classics: An Estimate," in Negro American Literature Forum (© Indiana State University 1970), Vol. 4, No. 4, Winter, 1970, pp. 113-19.*

ROBERT E. FLEMING (essay date 1971)

[*The Autobiography of an Ex-Coloured Man*] has frequently been lauded for its objective presentation of Negro manners in various parts of the country, from rural Georgia to New York City. While this recognition of the novel's sociological importance is merited, it has tended to draw attention from the artistic elements of the work; those critics who admire the novel often do so for the wrong reasons. . . . *The Autobiography* is not so much a panoramic novel presenting race relations throughout America as it is a deeply ironic character study of a marginal man who narrates the story of his own life without fully realizing the significance of what he tells his readers.

It is the irony of *The Autobiography* which sets it apart from a number of novels which deal with a similar theme, for it belongs to a class of novels which was by no means new in 1912. The general theme of the tragic mulatto who fits into neither culture had been employed by [many others]. . . . *The Autobiography* . . . features a protagonist-narrator born after the emancipation of slaves and so light that he may choose the race to which he will belong. External difficulties such as the fear of discovery are almost nonexistent; rather, emotional conflicts become the major concern of the novelist. Johnson's ironic technique is well-suited to such material. (pp. 83-4)

The narrator's first paragraph gives the reader the impression of a self-assured man with a rather objective, analytical approach to what promises to be a searching and honest account of his life. However, the second and last paragraphs alert the reader to the fact that the narrator-protagonist is in reality disturbed, torn by doubt; therefore, his statements should be examined carefully to determine the psychological facts concealed by superficial meanings. The unreliable nature of the narrator is thus suggested, and the reader who keeps this in mind will appreciate *The Autobiography* as a novel rather than as a guidebook to Negro life, as an account of emotional and psychological responses rather than as a mere history of the protagonist's social and financial rise in the world.

The main character's relationship with his father and mother, treated mainly in chapters 1 through 3, illustrates Johnson's ironic use of the unreliable narrator. An examination of what the narrator tells us suggests that he harbors an unrealized resentment toward each of his parents. The father, in particular, is treated harshly, although he is not overtly criticized for his treatment of the narrator and his mother. The narrator's earliest memories of his father center not on traits of character or physique but on the material objects associated with him. . . . When the father is about to send his mistress and son north so that his white fiancée will not learn about them, he drills a hole in a gold piece and ties it around his son's neck. . . . This flawed gold piece serves as a fitting symbol for most gifts the white man has given the black as well as for the white man's materialistic values, values which the protagonist later adopts as his own. The father's action evokes suggestions of slavery, and his choice of a going-away present is another example of his substitution of material gifts for overt recognition. Another suggestion of a master-slave relationship occurs later when the father comes to visit: he addresses his son as "boy" and the son responds, "yes, sir." . . . Thus the reader is prepared to recognize the irony in the mother's statement to her son that his father is "a great man, a fine gentleman" who loves them both very much . . . ; moreover, there is a sort of double-edged irony in her assertion that "the best blood of the South" is in her son. . . . The relationship between father and son is epitomized in one incident: the father sends his son a new upright piano; however, the boy wonders why the gift was not a grand piano. Clearly, although the narrator tells of his father's kindness and his own emotional indifference in purely objective terms, the suggestiveness of the illustrative details and the psychologically revealing nature of apparently casual remarks make the reader aware of the protagonist's true feelings—resentment toward the father and his strictly materialistic expressions of affection. (pp. 85-6)

Johnson's most notable irony is reserved for the narrator's comments about himself. It is significant that passages which deal with his reactions and feelings are characterized by a neoromantic style, by sentimental and rather inflated diction. The narrator views himself in romantic terms, as a tragic hero whose flaw is the black blood he has inherited from his beloved mother. Yet the reader, responding to the irony which undercuts the romantic pose, is more likely to view him as an antiheroic or pathetic character, frequently indulging in self-pity and unable to accept his total identity and assume his position in a race for which he feels little sympathy or admiration. (p. 87)

From time to time throughout the novel, the narrator interrupts the movement of the story to generalize about Negro life and experience, and the reader can hardly help being struck by the objective tone of his observations.... Although the protagonist has apparently accepted his membership in the race he is describing, his attitude toward black people is curiously aloof. In the next section of the novel, chapters 4 through 10, the main character's experiences provide him with opportunities to observe many facets of Negro life, but he consistently views that life as an outsider might and constantly reverts to white values, attitudes, and responses. The fact that the narrator's observations of black life in America have been so highly praised by readers and critics adds an element of irony that Johnson may not have foreseen. (p. 89)

[There are many instances of his sociological observations. Once, for example,] adopting that clinical tone so characteristic of his comments on the black race, he analyzes the socioeconomic classes of black people in the South and points out the curious relationships between the three classes and the white Southerner.... Objective analyses like this one ... have encouraged readers and critics to consider *The Autobiography* a sociological guidebook with only a suggestion of plot; but such disgressions tell us something about the narrator as well. He is able to view "his" race in detached sociological terms because he never feels a part of it. He never succeeds in his attempts to find his identity within the race to which the country's laws and customs consign him, the race which he embraced because it was his mother's. This ability to step outside the race is a reminder of the ironic gap between his true character and the flattering self-portrait the narrator draws of a man earnestly attempting to do what he knows is right. However, beneath his air of detachment, the reader is allowed to glimpse an individual whose racial identity changes because he bases his life on unstable principles. The protagonist's vacillating principles as well as his changing "color" were emphasized by Johnson's alternate title for the novel, *The Chameleon.* (pp. 90-1)

The incident to which the main character attributes his decision to pass for white is indeed traumatic. After a suc-cessful trip through the rural South, during which he collects lyrics and music and observes the spontaneous reactions of Negroes at camp meetings, the narrator witnesses a burning. Unable to help or to leave the scene, he watches as the whites chain their victim to a stake, pile wood around him, and ignite the fuel with coal oil. The narrator's reaction is notable for two reasons: he seems to feel no pity for the victim, yet for himself he feels humiliation and shame.... Thus he decides to take the step toward which he has unconsciously been moving from the beginning, but there is bitter irony in the fact that the narrator chooses to ally himself with the persecutors rather than the persecuted, to be one of those who can, without shame or remorse, treat other human beings as animals. (pp. 94-5)

For a time he enjoys the sensation of playing a practical joke on white society and thinks how surprised his new acquaintances would be if he revealed his true identity. However, the joke recoils on him when he falls in love [with a white girl and reveals his secret to her].... She bursts into tears, and the narrator sums up his own feelings by confessing, "This was the only time in my life that I ever felt absolute regret at being coloured, that I cursed the drops of African blood in my veins and wished that I were really white." ... This statement, as the reader has had ample opportunity to see, is false. From the time he was first called "nigger" by his schoolmates, the main character has fought against being classified as a Negro. It is only at this point, however, that he permits himself to recognize the revulsion against his black blood, his inheritance from his beloved mother.

Eventually the girl accepts the protagonist as he is (something he has never been able to do himself) and marries him.... However, the happiness of being a successful white man now seems insufficient recompense for his unfulfilled dreams of contributing to Negro musical achievement. Self-realization has come at last, if only reluctantly and tentatively, and the ex-colored man fears that he has been the real victim of the practical joke he has played on society. The low keyed ending of the novel is much more effective and realistic than the melodramatic conclusions so typical of earlier black novels on the "tragic mulatto" theme.

Although Johnson wrote no other novels, his achievement in *The Autobiography of an Ex-Coloured Man* deserves recognition. The book has a significant place in black literature because it overthrows the stereotyped black character, employed even by early black writers, in favor of one that is complex and many-sided. Johnson gains depth and subtlety by using the first-person point of view rather than the third-person favored by his contemporaries. Moreover, his skill in using an unreliable narrator who reveals more than he intends—indeed, more than he knows—adds important psychological dimensions to the main character and his story. Finally, Johnson's skill in conveying his vision of black life in America through irony rather than by means of the heavy-handed propagandistic techniques of his predecessors marks a new, more artistic direction for the black novelist. (pp. 95-6)

Robert E. Fleming, "Irony As a Key to Johnson's 'The Autobiography of an Ex-Coloured Man'," in American Literature *(reprinted by permission of the Publisher; copyright 1971 by Duke University Press, Durham, North Carolina), Vol. 43, No. 1, March, 1971, pp. 83-96.*

STEPHEN M. ROSS (essay date 1974)

[Critics like Marvin Garrett and Robert Fleming (see excerpt above) have argued that *The Autobiography of an Ex-Coloured Man*] gains its deepest effects from the irony directed at the unreliable narrator who provides the so-called impartial view of Negro life.... Johnson's purpose, according to this interpretation, is to reveal the ex-coloured man's hypocrisy in abandoning his race for the sake of wealth and security.

Such an analysis has much to recommend it, for the novel is indeed more artfully constructed than any mere sociological survey of Negro life. The narrator is treated ironically, revealing more about his motives than he wishes to. Yet to label him a hypocrite, to see the irony as directed primarily *at* the narrator, gainsays the compassion with which Johnson treats his protagonist. As the victim of a tragic situation, emotionally and physically, the narrator does perceive many if not all of the implications of his actions—it is the narrator himself, after all, who questions the shallow white life he has chosen. I would suggest that instead of directing his irony at the ex-coloured man, Johnson attacks a hypothetical white audience; the narrator is unreliable not because he is obtuse or hypocritical, but because Johnson wants us to see him as betrayed by a white, upper-class value system he cannot escape. (pp. 198-99)

Johnson elicits the otherwise unwilling sympathy of his white reader by creating his protagonist's story out of conventional fictional situations; then, through careful irony, he demonstrates that the psychological impulses and moral values underlying those conventions are themselves the cause of the hero's tragedy. He encourages the reader to wish for his narrator's success in conventional terms, though the narrator is engaged in the unconventional endeavor of successfully "passing" and committing miscegenation. And when the wished-for success is undercut by irony, the reader is left in the same ambiguous position as the narrator, not knowing what "success" really means in a world so divided between Black and White; the reader is thus forced to share the genuinely tragic "unsatisfaction" of the narrator. (p. 200)

To establish [the] burden of whiteness which his protagonist must bear (a kind of Black man's burden), without at the same time overtly alienating his white readers' sympathies, Johnson uses, in ironic fashion, two other literary conventions, the genteel tradition's tale of class, and the popular sentimental love story. His narrator becomes the genteel hero struggling to retain his hold on respectability with its accompanying wealth and status; and he becomes the sentimental lover who supposedly discovers, when he wins the fair heroine, that love reigns supreme, soothing all ills and surmounting all hardships. It is at these conventions, at the values they embody and the audience which responds to them, that Johnson directs his harshest ironic condemnation—not at his narrator, for in acting out the role of respectable romantic hero, the ex-coloured man discovers that he has become a tragic hero indeed. (pp. 200-01)

[If] we regard the narrator, as I think we must, as a tool of judgement which reaches beyond him to white standards, then his commentaries do not violate his characterization. In looking back over his life the ex-coloured man is capable of perceiving much of the irony of circumstance which leads him to join and then flee the Negro race; his confession is not simply a pose of self-justification. Johnson as author was by no means immune from the desire to educate his white readers by direct appeal to reason; thus he allows his protagonist to describe "conditions" accurately and in a straightforward fashion—indeed, his credibility as a spokesman renders his tragedy the more poignant, and the condemnation of the white conventions he is enslaved to all the stronger. (pp. 204-05)

> *Stephen M. Ross, "Audience and Irony in Johnson's 'The Autobiography of an Ex-Coloured Man'," in* CLA *Journal (copyright, 1974 by the College Language Association), Vol. XVIII, No. 2, December, 1974, pp. 198-210.*

BIBLIOGRAPHY

Aptheker, Herbert. "Du Bois on James Weldon Johnson." *Journal of Negro History* LII, No. 3 (July 1967): 224-27.
> A testimonial detailing Johnson's accomplishments in everything but literature.

Baker, Houston A., Jr. "A Forgotten Prototype: *The Autobiography of an Ex-Coloured Man* and *Invisible Man*." *The Virginia Quarterly Review* 49, No. 3 (Summer 1973): 433-49.*
> A comparison of the two novels which shows Johnson to be Ellison's forerunner in many aspects of theme and technique.

Baldwin, Roger N. "The Dean of Negro Letters." *The New Republic* LXXVIII, No. 1003 (21 February 1934): 54-5.
> A review of *Along This Way* which praises Johnson's rare gifts of reflection and action.

Bontemps, Arna. Introduction to *The Autobiography of an Ex-Coloured Man,* by James Weldon Johnson, pp. v-ix. New York: Hill and Wang, 1960.
> A biographical introduction to Johnson and a brief survey of the high points of the Harlem Renaissance.

Braithwaite, William S. "The Poems of James Weldon Johnson." *Boston Evening Transcript* (12 December 1917): Part 2, p. 9.
> Praises Johnson's verse as being intellectually superior to Dunbar's and free of the latter poet's sensuality.

Collier, Eugenia. "The Endless Journey of an Ex-Coloured Man." *Phylon* XXXII, No. 4 (Winter 1971): 365-73.
> An explication of *The Autobiography of an Ex-Coloured Man* tracing the twin motifs of physical and psychological journeys.

Fleming, Robert E. "Contemporary Themes in Johnson's *Autobiography of an Ex-Coloured Man*." *Negro American Literature Forum* 4, No. 4 (Winter 1970): 120-24, 141.
> A brief synopsis of the themes in Johnson's novel which have a recurring place in black literature.

Garrett, Marvin P. "Early Recollections and Structural Irony in *The Autobiography of an Ex-Colored Man*." *Critique* XIII, No. 2 (December 1971): 5-14.
> Analyzes the self-serving posturings of the narrator of *The Autobiography* and reads the book as the study of a weak individual rather than as the study of a subjugated race.

Levy, Eugene. "Ragtime and Race Pride: The Career of James Weldon Johnson." *Journal of Popular Culture* 1, No. 4 (Spring 1968): 357-70.
> Concerned with Johnson's composition of ragtime and show songs and his attempts to give a more refined tone to what were labeled "coon songs."

Levy, Eugene. *James Weldon Johnson: Black Leader, Black Voice.* Chicago: The University of Chicago Press, 1973, 380 p.
> An excellent biography of Johnson.

Long, Richard A. "A Weapon of My Song: The Poetry of James Weldon Johnson." *Phylon* XXXII, No. 4 (Winter 1971): 374-82.
    A general overview of Johnson's poetry stressing his development from dialect to free verse.

Rubin, Louis D., Jr. "The Search for a Language, 1746-1923." In *Black Poetry in America: Two Essays in Historical Interpretation,* by Blyden Jackson and Louis D. Rubin, Jr., pp. 1-36. Baton Rouge: Louisiana State University Press, 1974.
    A survey of black American poetry that stresses Johnson's ground breaking discovery of standard English traditions for black verse.

James (Augustine Aloysius) Joyce
1882-1941

Irish novelist, short story writer, poet, and dramatist.

Joyce is the most prominent literary figure of the first half of the twentieth century. Many critics feel that his virtuoso experiments in prose both redefined the limits of language and recreated the form of the modern novel. Joyce's prose is often praised for its richness and many critics feel that his verbal facility equals that of Shakespeare or Milton.

Joyce's work spans the extremes of naturalism and symbolism, from the spare style of *Dubliners* to the verbal richness of *Finnegans Wake*. *Dubliners*, a naturalistic group of stories concerned with the intellectual and spiritual torpor of Ireland, is the first product of his lifelong preoccupation with Dublin life. Though so disgusted by the narrowness and provincialism of Ireland that he spent most of his life in self-imposed exile, Joyce nevertheless made Ireland and the Irish the subject of all his fiction. These stories are also important as examples of his theory of epiphany in fiction; each is concerned with a sudden revelation of truth about life inspired by a seemingly trivial incident.

Joyce's first novel, *A Portrait of the Artist as a Young Man*, is at once a portrayal of the maturation of the artist, a study of the vanity of rebelliousness, and an examination of the self-deception of adolescent ego. The novel is often considered a study of the author's early life. Originally entitled *Stephen Hero* and conceived as an epic of autobiography, *Portrait* was thoroughly rewritten to provide an objective account of its protagonist's consciousness. Many critics feel that it is the most perfectly structured of Joyce's works.

However, most critics agree that *Ulysses* is the novel in which all of Joyce's considerable talents are fully realized. Fashioned after Homer's *Odyssey*, Joyce utilizes the structure of that epic to universalize Dublin life and to serve as an heroic counterpart to its anti-heroic protagonist, Leopold Bloom. Joyce created *Ulysses* from a complex of various techniques and experiments, one chapter, for example, being a parody of every English prose style from Anglo-Saxon to the present. In *Ulysses*, and later in *Finnegans Wake*, he developed the stream of consciousness technique further than any previous novelist.

Using *Ulysses* as a case in point, many critics have remarked on Joyce's limitations of thought and concluded that his talent was essentially technical. But Joyce is not concerned with presenting a consistent vision of life. In lieu of a philosophy, he explores the interrelationships of life and literature in extremely allusive prose. His comic sense of life saves his work from being merely pedantic; in fact, his comic gift and stylistic experiments place *Ulysses* in the same category as the works of Rabelais and Laurence Sterne.

Like those predecessors, *Ulysses* is frequently bawdy, and was banned in the United States due to its alleged pornographic content. The subsequent trial led to a landmark interpretation of the first amendment which allowed publication in 1933.

Joyce worked on his next book, *Finnegans Wake*, for seventeen years. Throughout that time portions of the book appeared in magazines as "Work in Progress." Unsure just how to characterize the completed work, critics hesitantly call it a novel. Meant to be the subconscious flow of thought of a sleeping Everyman named H. C. Earwicker, *Finnegans Wake* is literally a recreation of the English language. In this masterpiece of allusions, puns, foreign languages, and word combinations, Joyce attempted to compress the history of mankind into one night's dream. Admittedly a work for a select few, a mass of critical exegesis has grown up around the book. Joyce was probably serious when he remarked that a person should spend a lifetime reading it.

In addition to his major works of fiction, Joyce also produced two volumes of lyric poems and a drama, *Exiles*. Although his lyrics demonstrate his mastery of that form and *Exiles* sheds light on his personal life, neither adds much to his literary reputation.

Joyce devoted his life to his art, overcoming obstacles such as poverty, reluctant publishers, and near blindness. His life has come to be a symbol for the spiritual alienation of the modern artist, and his work has spawned numerous imitations. A complicated artistic genius, he created a body of work worthy of comparison with the masterpieces of English literature.

PRINCIPAL WORKS

Chamber Music (poetry) 1907
Dubliners (short stories) 1914
A Portrait of the Artist as a Young Man (novel) 1916
Exiles (drama) 1918
Ulysses (novel) 1922
Pomes Penyeach (poetry) 1927
Collected Poems (poetry) 1936
Finnegans Wake (novel) 1939

Stephen Hero (unfinished novel) 1944

*This novel was originally written in 1901-06 though unpublished until 1944.

H. G. WELLS (essay date 1917)

Like some of the best novels in the world [*A Portrait of the Artist as a Young Man*] is the story of an education; it is by far the most living and convincing picture that exists of an Irish Catholic upbringing. It is a mosaic of jagged fragments that does altogether render with extreme completeness the growth of a rather secretive, imaginative boy in Dublin. The technique is startling, but on the whole it succeeds. Like so many Irish writers from Sterne to Shaw Mr. Joyce is a bold experimentalist with paragraph and punctuation. He breaks away from scene to scene without a hint of the change of time and place; at the end he passes suddenly from the third person to the first; he uses no inverted commas to mark off his speeches. The first trick I found sometimes tiresome here and there, but then my own disposition, perhaps acquired at the blackboard, is to mark off and underline rather fussily, and I do not know whether I was so much put off the thing myself as anxious, which after all is not my business, about its effect on those others; the second trick, I will admit, seems entirely justified in this particular instance by its success; the third reduces Mr. Joyce to a free use of dashes. One conversation in this book is a superb success, the one in which Mr. Dedalus carves the Christmas turkey; I write with all due deliberation that Sterne himself could not have done it better; but most of the talk flickers blindingly with these dashes, one has the same wincing feeling of being flicked at that one used to have in the early cinema shows. I think Mr. Joyce has failed to discredit the inverted comma.

The interest of the book depends entirely upon its quintessential and unfailing reality. One believes in Stephen Dedalus as one believes in few characters in fiction. (pp. 344-45)

> *H. G. Wells, "James Joyce" (originally published in* The New Republic, *March 10, 1917), in* Novelists on Novelists, *edited by Louis Kronenberger (copyright © 1962 by Louis Kronenberger; reprinted by permission of Doubleday & Co., Inc.), Doubleday, 1962, pp. 343-46.*

EZRA POUND (essay date 1918)

On almost every page of Joyce you will find . . . swift alternation of subjective beauty and external shabbiness, squalor, and sordidness. It is the bass and treble of his method. And he has his scope beyond that of the novelists his contemporaries, in just so far as whole stretches of his keyboard are utterly out of their compass. (p. 205)

In the three hundred pages of "A Portrait of the Artist as a Young Man" there is no omission; there is nothing in life so beautiful that Joyce cannot touch it without profanation—without, above all, the profanations of sentiment and sentimentality—and there is nothing so sordid that he cannot treat it with his metallic exactitude. (p. 206)

His earlier book, "Dubliners," contained several well-constructed stories, several sketches rather lacking in form. It

was a definite promise of what was to come. There is very little to be said in praise of it which would not apply with greater force to "A Portrait." I find that whoever reads one book inevitably sets out in search of the other. (pp. 206-07)

We have [in "Chamber Music"] the lyric in some of its best traditions, and one pardons certain trifling inversions, much against the taste of the moment, for the sake of the clean-cut ivory finish, and for the interest of the rhythms, the cross run of the beat and the word, as of a stiff wind cutting the ripple-tops of bright water.

The wording is Elizabethan, the metres at times suggesting Herrick, but in no case have I been able to find a poem which is not in some way Joyce's own, even though he would seem, and that most markedly, to shun apparent originality. . . . (p. 207)

[In] nearly every poem, the motif is so slight that the poem scarcely exists until one thinks of it as set to music; and the workmanship is so delicate that out of twenty readers scarce one will notice its fineness. (p. 208)

The book is an excellent antidote for those who find Mr. Joyce's prose "disagreeable" and who [like H. G. Wells] at once fly to conclusions about Mr. Joyce's "cloacal obsessions." I have yet to find in Joyce's published works a violent or malodorous phrase which does not justify itself not only by its verity, but by its heightening of some opposite effect, by the poignancy which it imparts to some emotion or to some thwarted desire for beauty. Disgust with the sordid is but another expression of a sensitiveness to the finer thing. There is no perception of beauty without a corresponding disgust. If the price for such artists as James Joyce is exceeding heavy, it is the artist himself who pays, and if Armageddon has taught us anything it should have taught us to abominate the half-truth, and the tellers of the half-truth in literature. (p. 210)

> *Ezra Pound, "Joyce" (originally published in* The Future, *May, 1918), in his* Instigations, *Boni & Liveright, 1920 (and reprinted by Books for Libraries Press, 1969), pp. 203-10.*

T. S. ELIOT (essay date 1923)

I hold [*Ulysses*] to be the most important expression which the present age has found; it is a book to which we are all indebted, and from which none of us can escape. (p. 198)

Mr. Joyce's parallel use of the *Odyssey* has a great importance. It has the importance of a scientific discovery. No one else has built a novel upon such a foundation before: it has never before been necessary. I am not begging the question in calling *Ulysses* a "novel"; and if you call it an epic it will not matter. If it is not a novel, that is simply because the novel is a form which will no longer serve; it is because the novel, instead of being a form, was simply the expression of an age which had not sufficiently lost all form to feel the need of something stricter. . . . The novel ended with Flaubert and with James. . . .

In using the myth, in manipulating a continuous parallel between contemporaneity and antiquity, Mr. Joyce is pursuing a method which others must pursue after him. They will not be imitators, any more than the scientist who uses the discoveries of an Einstein in pursuing his own, independent, further investigations. It is simply a way of controlling, of ordering, of giving a shape and a significance to the immense panorama of futility and anarchy which is contemporary history. (p. 201)

T. S. Eliot, "Ulysses, Order, and Myth" (originally published in Dial, *Vol. 75, No. 5, November, 1923), in* James Joyce: Two Decades of Criticism, *edited by Seon Givens (copyright 1948; copyright © renewed 1975 by Seon Givens Manley; reprinted by permission of the publisher, Vanguard Press, Inc.), Vanguard, 1963, pp. 198-202.*

WYNDHAM LEWIS (essay date 1928)

I regard *Ulysses* as a *time-book;* and by that I mean that it lays its emphasis upon, for choice manipulates, and in a doctrinaire manner, the self-conscious time-sense, that has now been erected into a universal philosophy. This it does beneath the spell of a similar creative impulse to that by which Proust worked. The classical unities of time and place are buried beneath its scale, however, and in this All-life-in-a-day scheme there is small place for them. Yet at the outset they are solemnly insisted on as a guiding principle to be fanatically observed. And certainly some barbarous version of the classical formula is at work throughout, like a conserted *daimon* attending the author, to keep him obsessionally faithful to the time-place, or space-time, programme. . . .

That Joyce and Proust are both dedicated to Time is generally appreciated, of course; Joyce is often compared to Proust on that score. Both Proust and Joyce exhibit, it is said, the exasperated time-sense of the contemporary man of the industrial age; which is undeniable, if the outward form of their respective work is alone considered. (p. 84)

Yet that the time-sense is really exasperated in Joyce in the fashion that it is in Proust, Dada, Pound or Miss Stein, may be doubted. He has a very keen preoccupation with the Past, it is certain; he does lay things down side by side, carefully dated; and added to that, he has some rather loosely and romantically held notion of periodicity. But I believe what all these things amount to with him is this: as a careful, even meticulous, craftsman, with a long training of doctrinaire naturalism, the detail—the time-detail as much as anything else—assumes an exaggerated importance for him. And I am sure that he would be put to his trumps to say how came by much of the time-machinery that he possesses. Until he was told, I dare say that he did not know he had it, even; for he is 'an instinctive,' like Pound, in that respect; there is not very much reflection going on at any time inside the head of Mr. James Joyce. That is indeed the characteristic condition of *the craftsman,* pure and simple.

And that is what Joyce is above all things, essentially the craftsman. It is a thing more common, perhaps, in painting or the plastic arts than in literature. I do not mean by this that he works harder or more thoroughly than other people, but that he is not so much an inventive intelligence as an executant. He is certainly very 'shoppy,' and professional to a fault, though in the midst of the amateurism of the day it is a fault that can easily be forgiven.

What stimulates him is *ways of doing things,* and technical processes, and not *things to be done.* Between the various things to be done he shows a true craftsman's impartiality. He is become so much a writing-specialist that it matters very little to him *what* he writes, or what idea or world-view he expresses, so long as he is trying his hand at this

manner and that, and displaying his enjoyable virtuosity. Strictly speaking, he has none at all, no special point of view, or none worth mentioning. (pp. 89-90)

The method that underlies *Ulysses* is known as the 'telling from the inside.' As that description denotes, it is psychological. Carried out in the particular manner used in *Ulysses,* it lands the reader inside an Aladdin's cave of incredible bric-à-brac in which a dense mass of dead stuff is collected, from 1901 toothpaste, a bar or two of Sweet Rosie O'Grady, to prenordic architecture. An immense *nature-morte is the result.* This ensues from the method of confining the reader in a circumscribed psychological space into which several encyclopaedias have been emptied. It results from the constipation induced in the movement of the narrative.

The amount of *stuff*—unorganized brute material—that the more active principle of drama has to wade through, under the circumstances, slows it down to the pace at which, inevitably, the sluggish tide of the author's bric-à-brac passes the observer, at the saluting post, or in this case, the reader. It is a suffocating, moeotic expanse of objects, all of them lifeless, the sewage of a Past twenty years old, all neatly arranged in a meticulous sequence. . . .

At the end of a long reading of *Ulysses* you feel that it is the very nightmare of the naturalistic method that you have been experiencing. Much as you may cherish the merely physical enthusiasm that expresses itself in this stupendous outpouring of *matter,* or *stuff,* you wish, on the spot, to be transported to some more abstract region for a time, where the dates of the various toothpastes, the brewery and laundry receipts [assume less importance]. . . . (p. 91)

The nineteenth-century naturalism of that obsessional, fanatical order is what you find on the one hand in *Ulysses.* On the other, you have a great variety of recent influences enabling Mr. Joyce to use it in the way that he did. (p. 92)

Mr. Joyce could never have performed this particular feat if he had not been, in his make-up, extremely immobile; and yet, in contradiction to that, very open to new technical influences. It is the *craftsman* in Joyce that is progressive; but the *man* has not moved since his early days in Dublin. He is on that side a 'young man' in some way embalmed. His technical adventures do not, apparently, stimulate him to think. On the contrary, what he thinks seems to be of a conventional and fixed order, as though perhaps not to embarrass the neighbouring evolution of his highly progressive and eclectic craftsmanship.

So he collected like a cistern in his youth the last stagnant pumpings of victorian anglo-irish life. This he held steadfastly intact for fifteen years or more—then when he was ripe, as it were, he discharged it, in a dense mass, to his eternal glory. That was *Ulysses.* Had the twenty-year-old Joyce of the *Dubliners* not remained almost miraculously intact, we should never have witnessed this peculiar spectacle.

That is, I believe, the true account of how this creative event occurred with Joyce; and, if that is so, it will be evident that we are in the presence of a very different phenomenon from Proust. Proust *returned* to the *temps perdu.* Joyce never left it. He discharged it as freshly as though the time he wrote about were still present, because it was his present. It rolled out with all the aplomb and vivacity of a contemporary experience, assisted in its slick discharge by the latest technical devices.

So though Joyce has written a time-book, he has done it, I believe, to some extent, by accident. Proust, on the contrary, was stimulated to all his efforts precisely by the thought of compassing a specifically time-creation—the *Recherche du Temps Perdu*. The unconscious artist has, in this case, the best of it, to my mind. Proust, on the other hand, romanticizes his Past, where Joyce (whose Present it is) does not. (pp. 92-3)

In *Ulysses*, if you strip away the technical complexities that envelop it, the surprises of style and unconventional attitudes that prevail in it, the figures underneath are of a remarkable simplicity, and of the most orthodoxly comic outline. Indeed, it is not too much to say that they are, most of them, walking clichés. So much is this the case, that your attention is inevitably drawn to the evident paradox that ensues; namely, that of an intelligence so alive to purely verbal clichés that it hunts them like fleas, with remarkable success, and yet that leaves the most gigantic ready-made and well-worn dummies enthroned everywhere, in the form of the actual personnel of the book. . . .

If you examine for a moment the figures presented to you in the opening of *Ulysses*, you will at once see what is meant by these remarks. The admirable writing will seduce you, perhaps, from attending too closely, at first, to the characterization. But what in fact you are given there, in the way of character, is the most conventional stuff in the world. . . . (p. 96)

Haines is a stage-'Saxon,' Mulligan is a stage-Irishman; that on one side and the other of the Irish Channel such figures could be found is certain enough; but they are the material of broad comedy; not that of a subtle or average reality at all. . . .But if they are clichés, Stephan Dedalus is a worse or a far more glaring one. He is the really wooden figure. He is 'the poet' to an uncomfortable, a dismal, a ridiculous, even a pulverizing degree. . . . [His characterization] has to be read to be believed—but read, of course, with a deaf ear to the really charming workmanship with which it is presented. *Written* on a level with its conception, and it would be as dull stuff as you could easily find. (p. 97)

It would be difficult, I think, to find a more lifeless, irritating, principal figure than the deplorable hero of the *Portrait of the Artist* and of *Ulysses*. (p. 99)

What induced Joyce to place in the centre of his very large canvas this grotesque figure, Stephan Dedalus? Or having done so, to make it worse by contrasting it the whole time (as typifying 'the ideal') with the gross 'materialism' of the Jew, Bloom? . . . [The] answer to that, I believe, is that things *grew* in that way, quite outside of Joyce's control; and it is an effect, merely, of a confusion of method.

Joyce is fundamentally autobiographical, it must be recalled; not in the way that most writers to some extent are, but scrupulously and naturalistically so. Or at least that is how we started. The *Portrait of the Aritist as a Young Man* was supposed to give you a neat, carefully-drawn picture of Joyce from babyhood upwards, in the result like an enlarged figure from the *Dubliners*. You get an accurate enough account, thereupon, of a physically-feeble, timid, pompous, ill-tempered, very conceited little boy. It is interesting, honest, even sometimes to naïveté—though not

often that; but it is not promising material for anything but the small, neat naturalism of *Dubliners*. It seems as unlikely, in short, that this little fellow will grow into the protagonist of a battle between the mighty principles of Spirit and Matter, Good and Evil, or White and Black, as that the author of the little, neat, reasonable, unadventurous *Dubliners* would one day become the author of the big blustering *Ulysses*.

The effort to show Stephan Dedalus in a favourable, heightened light throughout, destroys the naturalism, and at the same time certainly fails to achieve the heroic. Yet the temper of *Ulysses* is to some extent an heroical one. So you are left with a neat little naturalist 'hero,' of the sort that swarms humorously in Chekov, tiptoeing to play his part in the fluid canvas of an ambitious *Ulysses*, unexpectedly expanding beneath his feet; urged by his author to rise to the occasion and live up to the rôle of the incarnation of the immaterial, and so be top-dog to Poldy Bloom. As it is, of course, the author, thinly disguised as a middle-aged Jew tout (Mr. Leopold Bloom), wins the reader's sympathy every time he appears; and he never is confronted with the less and less satisfactory Dedalus (in the beau rôle) without the latter losing trick after trick to his disreputable rival; and so, to the dismay of the conscientious reader, betraying the principles he represents. It is a sad affair, altogether, on that side.

Turning to Mr. Bloom, we find an unsatisfactory figure, too, but of an opposite sort and in a very different degree. He possesses all the recognized theatrical properties of 'the Jew' . . . but such a Jew as Bloom, taken altogether, has never been seen outside the pages of Mr. Joyce's book. And he is not even a Jew most of the time, but his talented irish author.

In reality there is no Mr. Bloom at all, of course, except at certain moments. Usually the author, carelessly disguised beneath what other people have observed about Jews, or yet other people have believed that they have seen, is alone performing before us. . . . He has merely out of books and conversations collected facts, witticisms and generalizations about Jews, and wrapped up his own kindly person with these, till he has bloated himself into a thousand pages of heterogeneous, peculiarly unjewish, matter. (pp. 100-01)

This inability to observe directly, a habit of always looking at people through other people's eyes and not through his own, is deeply rooted with Joyce. Where a multitude of little details or some obvious idiosyncrasy are concerned, he may be said to be observant; but the secret of an *entire* organism escapes him. Not being observant where entire people (that is, people at all) are concerned, he depicts them conventionally always, under some general label. For it is in the fragmentation of a personality—by isolating some characteristic weakness, mood, or time-self—that you arrive at the mechanical and abstract, the opposite of the living. This, however, leaves him free to achieve with a mass of detail a superficial appearance of life; and also to exercise his imitative talents without check where the technical problem is concerned. (pp. 101-02)

The claim to be employing the 'impersonal' method of science in the presentment of the personnel of *Ulysses* can be entirely disregarded. If there were any definite and carefully demarcated personality—except in the case of Dedalus, or here and there where we see a casual person for a moment—it would be worth while examining that claim. But as there are no persons to speak of for the author to be 'impersonal' about, that can at once be dismissed. *Ulysses* is a highly romantic self-portrait of the mature Joyce (disguised as a Jew) and of his adolescent self—of Bloom and Dedalus. (pp. 103-04)

Another thing that can be dismissed even more summarily is the claim that Bloom is a creation, a great *homme moyen sensuel* of fiction. That side of Bloom would never have existed had it not been for the Bouvard and Pécuchet of Flaubert, which very intense creation Joyce merely takes over, spins out, and translates into the relaxed medium of anglo-irish humour. Where Bloom is being Bouvard and Pécuchet, it is a translation, nothing more. (p. 104)

> *Wyndham Lewis, "An Analysis of the Mind of James Joyce," in his* Time and Western Man *(© by the estate of the late Mrs. G. A. Wyndham; reprinted by permission), Harcourt Brace Jovanovich, Inc., 1928, pp. 75-113.*

SAMUEL BECKETT (essay date 1929)

['*Work in Progress*'] is direct expression—pages and pages of it. And if you don't understand it, Ladies and Gentlemen, it is because you are too decadent to receive it. You are not satisfied unless form is so strictly divorced from content that you can comprehend the one almost without bothering to read the other. This rapid skimming and absorption of the scant cream of sense is made possible by what I may call a continuous process of copious intellectual salivation. The form that is an arbitrary and independent phenomenon can fulfil no higher function than that of stimulus for a tertiary or quartary conditioned reflex of dribbling comprehension. (p. 13)

Here form *is* content, content *is* form. You complain that this stuff is not written in English. It is not written at all. It is not to be read—or rather it is not only to be read. It is to be looked at and listened to. His writing is not *about* something; *it is that something itself*. . . . When the sense is sleep, the words go to sleep. (See the end of '*Anna Livia*') When the sense is dancing, the words dance. . . . How can we qualify this general esthetic vigilance without which we cannot hope to snare the sense which is for ever rising to the surface of the form and becoming the form itself? . . . Perhaps 'apprehension' is the most satisfactory English word. Stephen says to Lynch: 'Temporal or spatial, the esthetic image is first luminously apprehended as self-bounded and selfcontained upon the immeasurable background of space or time which is not it. . . . You apprehend its wholeness.' There is one point to make clear: the Beauty of '*Work in Progress*' is not presented in space alone, since its adequate apprehension depends as much on its visibility as on its àudibility. There is a temporal as well as a spatial unity to be apprehended. Substitute 'and' for 'or' in the quotation, and it becomes obvious why it is . . . inadequate to speak of 'reading' '*Work in Progress*'. . . . Mr. Joyce has desophisticated language. And it is worth while remarking that no language is so sophisticated as English. It is abstracted to death. Take the word 'doubt': it gives us hardly any sensuous suggestion of hesitancy, of the necessity for choice, of static irresolution. . . . Mr. Joyce recognises how inadequate 'doubt' is to express a state of extreme uncertainty, and replaces it by 'in twosome twiminds'. Nor is he by any means the first to recognize the importance of treating words as something more than mere polite sym-

bols. Shakespeare uses fat, greasy words to express corruption. . . . We hear the ooze squelching all through Dickens's description of the Thames in '*Great Expectations*'. This writing that you find so obscure is a quintessential extraction of language and painting and gesture, with all the inevitable clarity of the old inarticulation. Here is the savage economy of hieroglyphics. Here words are not the polite contortions of 20th century printer's ink. They are alive. They elbow their way on to the page, and glow and blaze and fade and disappear. (pp. 14-16)

> *Samuel Beckett, "Dante . . . Bruno. Vico. . Joyce," in* Our Exagmination Round His Factification for Incamination of Work in Progress *(copyright 1929 by Sylvia Beach), Shakespeare and Company, 1929 (and reprinted by New Directions Books, 1972, pp. 1-22).*

MORTON DAUWEN ZABEL (essay date 1930)

Throughout his career Joyce has been regarded in many quarters as fundamentally a poet. When *Ulysses* appeared in 1922, its first readers and critics, encountering problems for which their earlier experiences with revolutionary forms of art had not prepared them, at once sought refuge behind the large assumptions that go disguised under the name of poetry. Most of the early notices called it "essentially a poem," "a poet's concept," etc. . . . (p. 206)

In spite of this testimony, we have little evidence that Joyce is not fundamentally a genius in prose. . . . [Conventional] definitions apart, his novels lack specific poetic elements, as well as poetry's absolute sublimation of experience. It is equally apparent that his lyrics are the marginal fragments of his art, minor in theme and too often, for all their precise and orderly felicities, undecided in quality. (p. 207)

The verse in *Chamber Music* has not the finality of single intention. Its deficiencies have been ascribed to the fact that, where it does not reflect the vaporous mysticism of the early Yeats, Æ, and the other Irish revivalists, it is a patent imitation of the Elizabethan song-books. (p. 208)

It is clear that in such poems one has, instead of direct and unequivocal poetic compulsion, a deliberate archaism and a kind of fawning studiousness which attempt to disguise the absence of profounder elements. Yet the archaism . . . was converted into Joyce's own material in two or three lyrics which, for spiritual suavity and logic, approach the minor work of Crashaw. . . . (p. 209)

The later lyrics in *Pomes Penyeach* go so far in integrating [Joyce's disparate influences that he] achieved in the little booklet his own poetic character for the first time. The sedulous understudy which kept him from attaining intimacy or a unifying personality in his earlier work is largely avoided. . . . Archaisms are still present, and the humid emotionalism of impressionist verse still prevails in *Alone* and *Bahnhofstrasse*. But the pattern is constricted by severer form, the lyric accent gains edge, and the emotional content is more secure in its power. Ultimately the tragic surge and wrath of *Ulysses* finds voice in *A Prayer* and in *A Memory of the Players in a Mirror at Midnight*. . . . (pp. 211-12)

Even within this narrow range, Joyce's eclecticism, the long reach of his artistic interests, is revealed. Yet one sees likewise the limitations which have kept his lyric output small. The real functions of free-verse have escaped him, and his lyric ideas must otherwise submit to conventional stanzaic formalities. Diffusion mars the outline of many poems, and unnatural sobriety and caution hinder the spontaneity of others. But in four or five pages he has achieved a complete fusion of rapture and lucidity, and written with mastery. *Simples* must rank as one of the purest lyrics of our time. . . . (p. 212)

The lyric motive and discipline have not been forgotten by Joyce among the problems and ingenuities of his prose epics. Wherever *Ulysses* avoids parody or satire, it is likely to soar in a lyric utterance. . . . Yet the poetic temper which has played an indubitable part in his career has given us, by the way, a small offering of exquisite poems, valuable both as diversions of one of the first literary geniuses of our day, and as lyrics which at their best have the mark of classic beauty upon them. (p. 213)

Morton Dauwen Zabel, "The Lyrics of James Joyce," in Poetry (© 1930 by The Modern Poetry Association; reprinted by permission of the Editor of Poetry), Vol. XXXVI, No. IV, July, 1930, pp. 206-13.

EDMUND WILSON (essay date 1931)

"Ulysses" is, I suppose, the most completely "written" novel since Flaubert. The example of the great prose poet of Naturalism has profoundly influenced Joyce—in his attitude toward the modern bourgeois world and in the contrast implied by the Homeric parallel of "Ulysses" between our own and the ancient world, as well as in an ideal of rigorous objectivity and of adaptation of style to subject. . . . But Joyce has undertaken in "Ulysses" not merely to render, with the last accuracy and beauty, the actual sights and sounds among which his people move, but, showing us the world as his characters perceive it, to find the unique vocabulary and rhythm which will represent the thoughts of each. (p. 203)

[Joyce takes us] directly into the consciousness of his characters, and in order to do so, he has availed himself of methods of which Flaubert never dreamed—of the methods of Symbolism. He has, in "Ulysses," exploited together, as no writer had thought to do before, the resources both of Symbolism and of Naturalism. (p. 204)

[Of] each of his episodes Joyce has tried to make an independent unit which shall blend the different sets of elements of each—the minds of the characters, the place where they are, the atmosphere about them, the feeling of the time of day. Joyce had already, in "A Portrait of the Artist," experimented, as Proust had done, in varying the form and style of the different sections to fit the different ages and phases of his hero—from the infantile fragments of childhood impressions, through the ecstatic revelations and the terrifying nightmares of adolescence, to the self-possessed notations of young manhood. But in "A Portrait of the Artist," Joyce was presenting everything from the point of view of a single particular character, Dedalus; whereas in "Ulysses" he is occupied with a number of different personalities, of whom Dedalus is no longer the centre, and his method, furthermore, of enabling us to live in their world is not always merely a matter of making us shift from the point of view of one to the point of view of another. (p. 206)

[Joyce has achieved] by different methods, a relativism like that of Proust: he is reproducing in literature the different aspects, the different proportions and textures, which things and people take on at different times and under different circumstances. (p. 208)

[It is] characteristic of Joyce to neglect action, narrative, drama, of the usual kind, even the direct impact on one another of the characters as we get it in the ordinary novel, for a sort of psychological portraiture. There is tremendous vitality in Joyce, but very little movement. Like Proust, he is symphonic rather than narrative. His fiction has its progressions, its developments, but they are musical rather than dramatic. (p. 209)

The world of "Ulysses" is animated by a complex inexhaustible life: we revisit it as we do a city, where we come more and more to recognize faces, to understand personalities, to grasp relations, currents and interests. . . . More than any other work of fiction, unless perhaps the "Comédie Humaine," "Ulysses" creates the illusion of a living social organism. (p. 210)

[The] Homeric parallel in "Ulysses" is in general pointedly and charmingly carried out and justifies itself: it does help to give the story a universal significance and it enables Joyce to show us in the actions and the relations of his characters meanings which he perhaps could not easily have indicated in any other way—since the characters themselves must be largely unaware of these meanings and since Joyce has adopted the strict objective method, in which the author must not comment on the action. And we may even accept [the motifs of] the arts and sciences and the organs of the human body as making the book complete and comprehensive, if a little laboriously systematic—the whole of man's experience in a day. But when we get all these things together and further complicated by the virtuosity of the technical devices, the result is sometimes baffling or confusing. We become aware, as we examine the outline, that when we went through "Ulysses" for the first time, it was these organs and arts and sciences and Homeric correspondences which sometimes so discouraged our interest. We had been climbing over these obstacles without knowing it, in our attempts to follow Dedalus and Bloom. The trouble was that, beyond the ostensible subject and, as it were, beneath the surface of the narrative, too many other subjects and too many different orders of subjects were being proposed to our attention. (pp. 213-14)

[Joyce has] half-buried his story under the virtuosity of his technical devices. It is almost as if he had elaborated it so much and worked over it so long that he had forgotten, in the amusement of writing parodies, the drama which he had originally intended to stage; or as if he were trying to divert and overwhelm us by irrelevant entertainments and feats in order that we might not be dissatisfied with the flatness—except for the drunken scene—of Dedalus's final meeting with Bloom; or even perhaps as if he did not, after all, quite want us to understand his story, as if he had, not quite conscious of what he was doing, ended by throwing up between us and it a fortification of solemn burlesque prose—as if he were shy and solicitous about it, and wanted to protect it from us. . . .

[One] of the most remarkable features of "Ulysses" is its interest as an investigation into the nature of human consciousness and behavior. Its importance from the point of view of psychology has never, it seems to me, been properly appreciated—though its influence on other books and, in consequence, upon our ideas about ourselves, has already been profound. Joyce has attempted in "Ulysses" to render as exhaustively, as precisely and as directly as it is possible in words to do, what our participation in life is like —or rather, what it seems to us like as from moment to moment we live.... Joyce has studied what we are accustomed to consider the dirty, the trivial and the base elements in our lives with the relentlessness of a modern psychologist; and he has also—what the contemporary Naturalist has seldom been poet enough for—done justice to all those elements in our lives which we have been in the habit of describing by such names as love, nobility, truth and beauty. (p. 219)

[The] more we read "Ulysses," the more we are convinced of its psychological truth, and the more we are amazed at Joyce's genius in mastering and in presenting, not through analysis or generalization, but by the complete recreation of life in the process of being lived, the relations of human beings to their environment and to each other; the nature of their perception of what goes on about them and of what goes on within themselves; and the interdependence of their intellectual, their physical, their professional and their emotional lives. To have traced all these interdependences, to have given each of these elements its value, yet never to have lost sight of the moral through preoccupation with the physical, nor to have forgotten the general in the particular; to have exhibited ordinary humanity without either satirizing it or sentimentalizing it—this would already have been sufficiently remarkable; but to have subdued all this material to the uses of a supremely finished and disciplined work of art is a feat which has hardly been equalled in the literature of our time. (pp. 219-20)

Joyce's characters [are not] merely the sum of the particles into which their experience has been dissociated: we come to imagine them as solidly, to feel their personalities as unmistakably, as we do with any characters in fiction; and we realize finally that they are also symbols. Bloom himself is in one of his aspects the typical modern man; Joyce has made him a Jew, one supposes, partly in order that he may be conceived equally well as an inhabitant of any provincial city of the European or Europeanized world. He makes a living by petty business, he leads the ordinary middle-class life.... But Bloom is surpassed and illuminated from above by Stephen, who represents the intellect, the creative imagination; and he is upheld by Mrs. Bloom, who represents the body, the earth. Bloom leaves with us in the long run the impression that he is something both better and worse than either of them; for Stephen sins through pride, the sin of the intellect; and Molly is at the mercy of the flesh; but Bloom, though a less powerful personality than either, has the strength of humility. (pp. 222-23)

Both [Stephen and Molly] are capable of rising to heights which Bloom can never reach. (p. 224)

[They] seem to me—the soaring silver prose of the one, the deep embedded pulse of the other—among the supreme expressions in literature of the creative powers of humanity: they are, respectively, the justifications of the woman and the man. (pp. 224-25)

Edmund Wilson, "James Joyce," in his Axel's Castle: A Study in the Imaginative Literature of 1870-1930 (abridged by permission of Charles Scribner's Sons; copyright 1931 by Charles Scribner's Sons; renewal copyright © 1959 by Edmund Wilson), Scribner's, 1931, pp. 191-236.

JOSEPH WARREN BEACH (essay date 1932)

[*Ulysses*] has the most amazing air of reality, and, except for one thing, gives as strong an impression of life as any novel in the English tongue. The one thing lacking is passionate motivation of action. The principal characters are intimately known, their past history, their habits, mental and physical, even their motivation from moment to moment. But whatever it is they are after—and this too we know in a general way if we are very discerning readers—it is never brought to a head in dramatic action or issue. No one commits murder or feels impelled to do so; no one robs a bank; no one tries to get the better of another by trickery or force. The passion or sentiment of love is almost nowhere represented, in spite of certain protoplasmic phenomena of a sexual character.

The nearest approach to story is the striking up of a kind of friendship between Stephen Dedalus and Leopold Bloom. Stephen's father in the flesh is an unsatisfactory person; and Bloom's dearly loved son had died in early childhood; so that each one has need for his psychological complement in the father-son relation. (pp. 404-05)

But after all, the acquaintanceship of Bloom and Stephen is but one of dozens of strands out of which this multifarious web is woven. And, having in mind the whole narrative, it would be absurd to say that the ruling passion of Stephen Dedalus is the craving for a father, or that of Bloom the craving for a son. There is no suggestion that Stephen actually finds in Bloom the makings of a satisfactory father, and very little more indication that Bloom feels strongly drawn toward Stephen with paternal sentiment. (p. 405)

[Joyce] is concerned very little with action, and very much with what goes on in the consciousness of Bloom and Stephen. And it is not to explain their action that he displays their souls; it is their souls themselves that interest him—or, rather, the flux of sensation and thought that constitutes the identity of each. (p. 410)

Joseph Warren Beach, "Post-Impressionism: Joyce," in his The Twentieth Century Novel: Studies in Technique (© 1960; reprinted by permission of Prentice-Hall, Inc., Englewood Cliffs, New Jersey), Appleton-Century-Crofts, Inc., 1932, pp. 403-24.

C. G. JUNG (essay date 1934)

[Is *Ulysses*] perhaps one single, immensely long, and excessively complicated Strindbergian pronouncement upon the essence of human life—a pronouncement which, to the reader's dismay, is never finished? Possibly it does touch upon the essence, but quite certainly it reflects life's ten thousand facets and their hundred thousand gradations of colour. So far as I can see, there are in those seven hundred and thirty-five pages no obvious repetitions, and not a single blessed island where the long-suffering reader may come to rest.... The pitiless stream rolls on without a break, and its velocity or viscosity increases in the last forty pages till it sweeps away even the punctuation marks. Here the suffocating emptiness becomes so unbearably tense that it reaches the bursting point. This utterly hopeless emptiness is the dominant note of the whole book. It not only begins and ends in nothingness, but it consists of nothing but nothingness. It is all infernally nugatory. As a piece of technical virtuosity it is a brilliant and hellish monster-birth. (pp. 109-10)

The incredible versatility of Joyce's style has a monotonous and hypnotic effect. Nothing comes to meet the reader, everything turns away from him leaving him gaping after it. The book is always up and away, dissatisfied with itself, ironic, sardonic, virulent, contemptuous, sad, despairing and bitter. It plays on the reader's sympathies to his own undoing unless sleep kindly intervenes and puts a stop to this drain of energy. Arrived at page 135, after making several heroic efforts to get at the book, to "do it justice," as the phrase goes, I fell at last into a profound slumber. When I awoke quite a while later, my views had undergone such a clarification that I started to read the book backwards. This method proved as good as the usual one; the book can just as well be read backwards, for it has no back and no front, no top and no bottom. Everything could easily have happened before, or might have happened afterwards. You can read any of the conversations just as pleasurably backwards, for you don't miss the point of the gags. Every sentence is a gag, but taken together they make no point. You can also stop in the middle of a sentence—the first half still makes sense enough to live by itself, or at least seems to. The whole work has the character of a worm cut in half, that can grow a new head or a new tail as required. (pp. 111-12)

Surely a book has a content, represents something; but I suspect that Joyce did not wish to "represent" anything. Does it by any chance represent *him*—does that explain this solipsistic isolation, this drama without eyewitnesses, this infuriating disdain for the assiduous reader? Joyce has aroused my ill will. One should never rub the reader's nose into his own stupidity, but that is just what *Ulysses* does. (p. 113)

[What] richness—and what boredom! Joyce bores me to tears, but it is a vicious dangerous boredom such as not even the worst banality could induce.... Everything is desouled, every particle of warm blood has been chilled, events unroll in icy egoism. In all the book there is nothing pleasing, nothing refreshing, nothing hopeful, but only things that are grey, grisly, gruesome or pathetic, tragic [and] ironic.... (p. 114)

[But one] should not be misled into thinking that because Joyce reveals a world that is horribly bleak and bereft of gods, it is inconceivable that anyone should derive the slightest comfort from his book.... Even though the evil and destructive elements predominate, they are far more valuable than the "good" that has come down to us from the past and proves in reality to be a ruthless tyrant, an illusory system of prejudices that robs life of its richness, emasculates it, and enforces a moral compulsion which in the end is unendurable. (p. 121)

But the shattering thing about *Ulysses* is that behind the thousand veils nothing lies hidden; it turns neither to the world nor to the spirit but, cold as the moon looking on from cosmic space, leaves the comedy of genesis and decay to pursue its course. I sincerely hope that *Ulysses* is not symbolic, for [if it were it would have failed in its purpose.] What kind of anxiously guarded secret might it be that is hidden with matchless care under seven hundred and thirty-five unendurable pages? It is better not to waste one's time and energy on a fruitless treasure hunt. Indeed, there *ought not* to be anything symbolic behind the book, for if there were our consciousness would be dragged back into world and spirit, perpetuating Messrs. Bloom and Dedalus to all

eternity, befooled by the ten thousand facets of life. This is just what *Ulysses* seeks to prevent: it wants to be an eye of the moon, a consciousness detached from the object, in thrall neither to the gods nor to sensuality, and bound neither by love nor by hate, neither by conviction nor by prejudice. *Ulysses* does not preach this but practises it—detachment of consciousness is the goal that shimmers through the fog of this book. (p. 124)

Ulysses is the creator-god in Joyce, a true demiurge who has freed himself from entanglement in the physical and mental world and contemplates them with detached consciousness. He is for Joyce what Faust was for Goethe, or Zarathustra for Nietzsche. He is the higher self who returns to his divine home after blind entanglement in *Samsara*. In the whole book no Ulysses appears; the book itself is Ulysses, a microcosm of James Joyce, the world of the self and the self of the world in one. Ulysses can return home only when he has turned his back on the world of mind and matter. This is surely the message underlying that sixteenth day of June 1904, the everyday of everyman, on which persons of no importance restlessly do and say things without beginning or aim—a shadowy picture, dreamlike, infernal, sardonic, negative, ugly, devilish, but true. A picture that could give one bad dreams or induce the mood of a cosmic Ash Wednesday.... (p. 127)

It seems to me now that all that is negative in Joyce's work, all that is cold-blooded, bizarre and banal, grotesque and devilish, is a positive virtue for which it deserves praise. Joyce's inexpressibly rich and myriad-faceted language unfolds itself in passages that creep along tapeworm fashion, terribly boring and monotonous, but the very boredom and monotony of it attain an epic grandeur that truly makes the book a *Mahabbarata* of the world's futility and squalor. (p. 128)

C.G. Jung, "'Ulysses': A Monologue" (originally published under a different title in his Wirklickleit der Seele, Rascher, 1934), in *The Collected Works of C. G. Jung: The Spirit in Man, Art, and Literature, Vol. 15, Bollingen Series XX, translated by R.F.C. Hull, William McGuire, Executive Editor (copyright © 1966 by Princeton University Press; reprinted by permission of Princeton University Press), Princeton University Press, 1966, pp. 109-34.*

DAVID DAICHES   (essay date 1935)

[We] know absolutely everything about Bloom; his whole nature lies completely revealed to us; he is, in fact, one of the most rounded characters in literature. Now Joyce gives no objective description of Bloom's character, yet in this account of his hero during one day's normal activity he reveals him completely. How is it done?

It is done by several means, but largely by his brilliant use of the time dimension. He takes Bloom in one day's action—but that action includes *thought, retrospect* and *anticipation*. It can scarcely be doubted that any man in any day of his life has thoughts which refer back to his past and ahead to his contemplated future, but more especially to his past. Such thoughts, if given adequate expression and interpretation, will reveal the man completely with all his physical, mental, and emotional history.... Joyce seems to be the first who has grasped the significance of this fact for literature.... Consciousness, after all, is in a sense independent of time; retrospect and anticipation are the very stuff of its being. It is the realisation of this on Joyce's part which makes him able to give such a completely rounded picture of his hero. . . . This is a point of technique in which Joyce shows himself as great an innovator as any canonised founder of a new literary school. (pp. 71-3)

[Joyce aims] to select and unite aspects of experience which together will give an appearance of completeness. (p. 75)

It is Bloom's book and Dublin's book now and anything that is relevant, however remotely, at once to Bloom, to Dublin, and to this particular day in 1904 finds its way naturally into *Ulysses*. (p. 77)

One can understand why Joyce deliberately refrains from explaining in normal objective description the particular scene of a given part of the action. It is because nothing must come between the reader and the consciousness of the characters. That is part of Joyce's technique. He wishes the characters to take control, not in the conventional sense in which critics use that phrase, but in the sense that only what comes into the plane of consciousness of one of his characters is allowed entrance. It is not the subconscious, as some critics have maintained; nothing is treated until it has made itself felt on the conscious level, however dimly. There is, of course, a danger in this lack of interference by the author. The reader may get bewildered, he may lose track of where he is, and so fail to make any sense out of whole scenes. This is indeed a real weakness in Joyce's method; the activity of a man's body and mind is only comprehensible when we know their environment, and as this environment is only shown in the reactions of the characters to it, it sometimes takes a certain amount of hard brainwork on the reader's part to deduce where he is. (p. 78)

[The importance of *Ulysses*] is threefold. It shows a new technique in the building up of character in fiction, it provides a brilliant method of escape from the dimensional limitations of the chronological time-sequence, and it marks the beginning of a new and dangerous treatment of language as a medium. All three characteristics give the work interest; the first two give it greatness. (pp. 81-2)

> *David Daiches, "The Importance of 'Ulysses'" (1935), in his* New Literary Values: Studies in Modern Literature, *Oliver & Boyd Ltd., 1936 (and reprinted by Books for Libraries Press, 1968), pp. 69-82.*

WILLIAM TROY   (essay date 1939)

The first and most obvious of the problems [in interpreting *Finnegans Wake*] is, of course, that of communication. Here the most simple-minded explanation that can be offered is that Joyce is reducing language to "pure music." . . . It depends for its movement pretty consistently on a recognizable unit of verse-structure. This is the pattern of movement established by the three-syllable foot, dactylic or anapestic, with its possibility of almost infinite variation within the line through the substitution of other shorter feet. . . . The predominant foot throughout the work, however, is the more lilting, caressing anapest because of its closer correspondence to theme and subject. As Samuel Beckett points out [see excerpt above] . . . , the work is "not *about* something; *it is that something itself.*" And if the anapest is used so often, it is because it is the inevitable movement for rendering the babbling and the bubbling of the "gossipaceous" Anna Livia that is the river of Time. . . . (pp. 303-04)

But this is still not to give justification to the charge that Joyce has reduced language to pure sound, which is to betray an unawareness of the functional interrelationship that always exists between sound and meaning in poetry. . . . [In] poetry, where the individual unit of expression is the word, sound is the *medium* or vehicle of meaning. (p. 304)

In the extraordinary richness and variety of musical effect in his writing, therefore, Joyce is simply pushing to a high degree of development qualities that we find in all authentic poetry. (p. 305)

Several of Joyce's reviewers have been content to [describe Joyce's use of language as punning]. . . . But there are obviously puns and puns; we say that some are pointless, some make sense. Undoubtedly, Joyce allows a certain number of the pointless variety to creep into his book—if for no other reason than that pointlessness is one of the inherent capacities of the human mind. . . . [For] the kind of pun that accomplishes a meaningful fusion between disparate things we have the term metaphor. The important difference between the ordinary or mechanical pun and the metaphor is that where the first is content with the purely intellectual perception of the accidental formal resemblances between words the second is concerned not only with more essential resemblances but with putting these together into a new whole. The first is the work of the abstract intellect, the second of the imagination. (pp. 307-08)

> *William Troy, "Notes on 'Finnegans Wake'," in* Partisan Review *(copyright © 1939 by Partisan Review, Inc.), Vol. VI, No. 4, Summer 1939 (and reprinted in* James Joyce: Two Decades of Criticism, *edited by Seon Givens, Vanguard Press, 1963, pp. 302-18).*

ALFRED KAZIN   (essay date 1941)

I am not sure that [Joyce] was as satisfying a novelist as Thomas Mann or as great a spirit as Lawrence; but Lawrence and Mann, like Dickens and Fielding before them, imposed their gifts upon a conception of the novel which, compared with the progress of poetry, had been relatively uniform. Joyce riddled that conception and hence transformed the novel for others. He threw off the fear of science which had haunted the literary imagination for a hundred years and so adroitly incorporated science into the novel that he proved it to be as illimitable a type of inquiry into human life as any science has furnished. He dissolved mechanism in literature as effectively as Einstein destroyed it in physics. Of so great an innovator in the novel as Zola one can say that he forced writers after him to work with new tools; of Joyce, that he taught them to see experience itself with new eyes. That had been done long before in painting; it had not been attempted in literature since Blake and Wordsworth. (pp. 4-5)

He proved, like Henry James . . . that the novel demanded as much seriousness as poetry, as precise an attention and as scrupulous a sense of form. From those first twilit sketches in *Dubliners* to the subterranean sleep-tossed world of *Finnegans Wake* he showed that the material of fiction could rest upon as tense a distribution and as delicate a balance of its parts as any poem.

Joyce's passion for form, in fact, is the secret of his progress as a novelist. He sought to bring the largest possible quantity of human life under the discipline of the observing mind, and the mark of his success is that he gave an epic form to what remains invisible to most novelists. That passion was deceptive in its energy, but it was as austere and unremitting as Flaubert's. Hence, though his own poetry was juvenilia and sentimental, he restored poetry to the novel not by lacquering it with "poetic" phrases, like Pater or Wilde or some Irish novelists one could name, but by imagining the very context of his novel in poetic terms. (pp. 5-6)

Joyce means many things to different people; for me his importance has always been primarily a moral one. He was, perhaps, the last man in Europe who wrote as if art were worth a human life. He entered literature at a time when science and the brutalization of common life had made the writer's function ambiguous; he stopped writing at a time when literature itself had vanished from Europe and the most elementary intellectual discrimination and activity had become dangerous on a fascist continent. Yet, from first to last he asserted the writer's claim to sovereignty as stubbornly as he illustrated the value of the writer's need to exist. Hence, the greatness of his service: he at once mirrored the disintegration of our world and proved himself superior to it. By living for his art he may yet have given others a belief in art worth living for. (p. 8)

Alfred Kazin, "The Death of James Joyce" (1941), in his The Inmost Leaf: A Selection of Essays *(copyright 1947 by Alfred Kazin; reprinted by permission of Harcourt Brace Jovanovich, Inc.), Harcourt, 1955, pp. 3-8.*

EDMUND WILSON (essay date 1941)

[*Finnegans Wake* is an] attempt to render the dream fantasies and the half-unconscious sensations experienced by a single person in the course of a night's sleep. (p. 190)

But it is Joyce's further aim to create, through Earwicker's mythopoeic dream, a set of symbols even more general and basic. He has had the idea of making Earwicker, resolved into his elemental components, include the whole of humanity. The river, with its feminine personality, Anna Livia Plurabelle, comes to represent the feminine principle itself. At one time or another all the women who figure in Earwicker's fantasy are merged into this stream of life which, always renewed, never pausing, flows through the world built by men. (pp. 201-02)

And if Earwicker is animated in sleep by the principles of both the sexes, he has also a double existence in the roles of both Youth and Old Age. (p. 202)

Finnegans Wake, in conception as well as in execution, is one of the boldest books ever written. (p. 207)

[But there is a] serious difficulty to be got over. We are continually being distracted from identifying and following Earwicker, the humble proprietor of a public house, who is to encompass the whole microcosm of the dream, by the intrusion of all sorts of elements—foreign languages, literary allusions, historical information—which could not possibly have been in Earwicker's mind. The principle on which Joyce is operating may evidently be stated as follows. If the artist is to render directly all the feelings and fancies of a sleeper, primitive, inarticulate, infinitely imprecise as they are, he must create a literary medium of unexampled richness and freedom. Now it is also Joyce's purpose in *Finnegans Wake* to bring out in Earwicker's consciousness the processes of universal history: the lan-

guages, the cycles of society, the typical relationships of legend, are, he is trying to show us, all implicit in every human being. He has . . . been careful to hook up his hero realistically with the main themes of his universal fantasia: the Bible stories, the Battle of Waterloo, Tristram and Iseult, and so forth. But since Earwicker's implications *are* shown to be universal, the author has the right to summon all the resources of his superior knowledge in order to supply a vehicle which will carry this experience of sleep. . . . Why shouldn't H. C. Earwicker be allowed to dream in a language which draws flexibility and variety from the author's enormous reservoir of colloquial and literary speech, of technical jargons and foreign tongues? (pp. 208-09)

[Joyce] has created a whole new poetry, a whole new humor and pathos, of sentences and words that go wrong. The special kind of equivocal and prismatic effects aimed at by the symbolist poets have here been achieved by a new method and on psychological principles which give them a new basis in humanity. But the trouble is, it seems to me, that Joyce has somewhat overdone it. His method of giving words multiple meanings allows him to go on indefinitely introducing new ideas. (p. 211)

Finnegans Wake, in the actual reading, seems to me for two thirds of its length not really to bring off what it attempts. Nor do I think it possible to defend the procedure of Joyce on the basis of an analogy with music. (p. 216)

I believe that the miscarriage of *Finnegans Wake,* in so far as it does miscarry, is due primarily to two tendencies of Joyce's which were already in evidence in *Ulysses:* the impulse, in the absence of dramatic power, to work up an epic impressiveness by multiplying and complicating detail, by filling in abstract diagrams and laying on intellectual conceits, till the organic effort at which he aims has been spoiled by too much that is synthetic; and a curious shrinking solicitude to conceal from the reader his real subjects. These subjects are always awkward and distressing: they have to do with the kind of feelings which people themselves conceal and which it takes courage in the artist to handle. And the more daring Joyce's subjects become, the more he tends to swathe them about with the fancywork of his literary virtuosity. It is as if it were not merely Earwicker who was frightened by the state of his emotions but as if Joyce were embarrassed, too.

Yet, with all this, *Finnegans Wake* has achieved certain amazing successes. Joyce has caught the psychology of sleep as no one else has ever caught it, laying hold on states of mind which it is difficult for the waking intellect to recreate, and distinguishing with marvelous delicacy between the different levels of dormant consciousness. (p. 217)

The finest thing in the book, and one of the finest things Joyce has done, is the passage at the end where Anna, the wife, is for the first time allowed to speak with her full and mature voice. (pp. 219-20)

In these wonderful closing pages, Joyce has put over all he means with poetry of an originality, a purity, and an emotional power, such as to raise *Finnegans Wake,* for all its excesses, to the rank of a great work of literature. (p. 221)

Edmund Wilson, "The Dream of H. C. Earwicker," in his The Wound and the Bow: Seven Studies in Literature *(reprinted by permission of Farrar, Straus & Giroux, Inc.; copyright © 1939 by Edmund Wilson; copyright renewed © 1967 by Edmund Wilson), Houghton Mifflin Company, 1941 (and reprinted by Farrar, Straus & Giroux, 1978, pp. 198-222).*

LOUISE BOGAN (essay date 1944)

Joyce, the parodist, in *Ulysses* always effectively colored matter with manner. The number of styles parodied in *Finnegans Wake* is prodigious. But these present parodies differ somewhat from their predecessors; they are actually more limited. The punning language in which they are framed gives them all a mocking or burlesque edge (the prose poems, only, excepted). This limitation and defeat of purpose—for an immense book written in two main modes only is sure to grow monotonous—is the first symptom to strike the reader of the malady, to be later defined, which cripples *Finnegans Wake*.

Thus equipped, then, with his private vernacular, Joyce proceeds to attack what certainly seems to be every written or oral style known to man. (pp. 144-45)

The "auditive faculty" of Stephen Dedalus has been expanded so that the functions of the other senses become subsidiary to it. Joyce has put down everything he has heard for the last seventeen years. (p. 145)

[Of the dream itself, there] is nothing whatever to indicate that Joyce has any real knowledge of the workings of the subconscious, in sleep or otherwise.... There are no sustained passages which give, for example, the feeling of nightmare. The punning style, as a matter of fact, precludes this. It is as though Joyce wished to be superior to the unconscious.... At one point he brings in a long apologia for his own method and language.... The most frightening thing about the book is the feeling, which steadily grows in the reader, that Joyce himself does not know what he is doing; and how, in spite of all his efforts, he is giving himself away. Full control is being exercised over the minor details and the main structure, but the compulsion toward a private universe is very strong.... Joyce's delight in reducing man's learning, passion, and religion to a hash is also disturbing.... The book cannot rise into the region of true evocation—the region where Molly Bloom's soliloquy exists immortally—because it has no human base. Emotion is deleted, or burlesqued, throughout. The vicious atmosphere of a closed world, whose creator can manage and distort all that is humanly valuable and profound (cunningly, with God-like slyness) becomes stifling.... *Ulysses* was based on a verifiable theme: the search for the father. The theme, or themes, of *Finnegans Wake* are retrogressive, as the language is retrogressive. The style retrogresses back to the conundrum. To read the book over a long period of time gives one the impression of watching intemperance become addiction, become debauch.

The book's great beauties, its wonderful passages of wit, its variety, its marks of genius and immense learning, are undeniable. It has another virtue: in the future "writers will not need to search for a compromise." But whatever it says of man's past, it has nothing to do with man's future, which, we can only hope, will lie in the direction of more humanity rather than less. (pp. 147-48)

Louise Bogan, "'Finnegans Wake'" (1944), in her Selected Criticism: Poetry and Prose *(copyright © 1955 by Louise Bogan), The Noonday Press, 1955, pp. 142-53.*

JOSEPH CAMPBELL and HENRY MORTON ROBINSON (essay date 1944)

Running riddle and fluid answer, *Finnegans Wake* is a mighty allegory of the fall and resurrection of mankind. It is a strange book, a compound of fable, symphony, and nightmare—a monstrous enigma beckoning imperiously from the shadowy pits of sleep. Its mechanics resemble those of a dream, a dream which has freed the author from the necessities of common logic and has enabled him to compress all periods of history, all phases of individual and racial development, into a circular design, of which every part is beginning, middle, and end.

In a gigantic wheeling rebus, dim effigies rumble past, disappear into foggy horizons, and are replaced by other images, vague but half-consciously familiar. On this revolving stage, mythological heroes and events of remotest antiquity occupy the same spatial and temporal planes as modern personages and contemporary happenings. All time occurs simultaneously.... (p. 3)

The first clue to the method and mystery of the book is found in its title, *Finnegans Wake*. Tim Finnegan of the old vaudeville song is an Irish hod carrier who gets drunk, falls off a ladder, and is apparently killed. His friends hold a deathwatch over his coffin; during the festivities someone splashes him with whisky, at which Finnegan comes to life again and joins in the general dance. On this comedy-song foundation, Joyce bases the title of his work. But there is more, much more, to the story. Finnegan the hod carrier is identifiable first with Finn MacCool, captain for two hundred years of Ireland's warrior-heroes, and most famous of Dublin's early giants. Finn typifies *all* heroes—Thor, Prometheus, Osiris, Christ, the Buddha—in whose life and through whose inspiration the race lives. It is by Finn's coming again (Finn-agin)—in other words, by the reappearance of the hero—that strength and hope are provided for mankind.

By his death and resurrection, hod carrier Finnegan comically refigures the solemn mystery of the hero-god whose flesh and blood furnish the race with spirit-fructifying meat and drink. (p. 4)

Finnegan's fall from the ladder is hugely symbolic: it is Lucifer's fall, Adam's fall, the setting sun that will rise again, the fall of Rome, a Wall Street crash.... And it is every man's daily recurring fall from grace. These various fallings (implying, as they do, corresponding resurrections) cause a liberation of energy that keeps the universe turning like a water wheel, and provide the dynamic which sets in motion the four-part cycle of universal history.

But why a "four-part" cycle? This reference is to a conception of the eighteenth-century Italian philosopher Giambattista Vico, whose *La Scienza Nuova* provides the philosophic loom on which Joyce weaves his historical allegory. Essentially, Vico's notion is that history passes through four phases: theocratic, aristocratic, democratic, and chaotic. The last phase is characterized (like our own) by individualism and sterility, and represents the nadir of man's fall. It is terminated by a thunderclap, which terrifies and reawakens mankind to the claims of the supernatural, and thus starts the cycle rolling again with a return to primeval theocracy.

In Joyce's composition, the comical Finnegan episode is only the prologue to the major action.... In *Finnegans*

Wake the transition from the earlier to the later hero takes place ... [when] the company at the wake forcibly hold Finnegan down and bid him rest in peace. They tell him that a newcomer, his successor, has just sailed into Dublin Bay. This newcomer is HCE, or more specifically, Humphrey Chimpden Earwicker, who thereafter dominates the work. ... Joyce refers to him under various names, such as Here Comes Everybody and Haveth Childers Everywhere—indications of his universality and his role as the great progenitor. (pp. 5-6)

As in *Ulysses,* the principal action takes place in Dublin and its environs. We are introduced at once to Howth Castle, Phoenix Park, the River Liffey, Wellington Monument, Guinness's Brewery, and other important landmarks, all of which have allegorical significance. Phoenix Park, for example, is reminiscent of the Garden of Eden. And the product of Guinness's Brewery is the magic elixir of life, the immortal drink of heroes and gods. Many an allusion is clarified by consulting a detailed map of Dublin. (pp. 6-7)

But to return to HCE. He is a man who has won his place in society, a place not of high distinction but of decent repute. He is a candidate in a local election. Gossip, however, undoes his campaign and his reputation as well. (p. 7)

[Earwicker's] predicament is of the nature of Original Sin: he shares the shadowy guilt that Adam experienced after eating the apple. It is akin also to the bewilderment and confusion that paralyze Hamlet, and is cognate with the neurotic misease of modern times. Stephen Dedalus, who suffers from an analogous malady in *Ulysses,* calls it the "agenbite of inwit," the incessant gnawing of rat-toothed remorse. Earwicker, suffering from this taint, yet aware of his claims to decency, is torn between shame and aggressive self-satisfaction, conscious of himself both as bug and as man (an earwig is a beetlelike insect, popularly supposed to creep into the human ear). Worm before God and giant among men, he is a living, aching arena of cosmic dissonance, tortured by all the cuts and thrusts of guilt and conscience. (pp. 7-8)

Although Earwicker is a citizen of Dublin, he is resented by the populace as an intruder, even a usurper. Why? Because, springing from Germanic rather than Celtic stock, he typifies all the invaders who have overrun Ireland—Danes, Norsemen, Normans, and English. The clash of arms that resounds through the first pages of the book recalls the battles of all Irish history and furnishes a background to the battlefields of the tavern—and the battlefields of Earwicker's own soul. (p. 8)

[The] universal judgment against HCE is but a reflection of his own obsessive guilt; and conversely, the sin which others condemn in him is but a conspicuous public example of the general, universally human, original sin, privately effective within themselves. Thus, throughout the work, there is a continual intermelting of the accused and his accusers. All these characters, moving around and against one another, are but facets of some prodigious unity and are at last profoundly identical—each, as it were, a figure in the dream complex of all the others. (pp. 9-10)

Earwicker has a wife, the psyche of the book—bewitching, everchanging, animating, all-pervading. She appears typically under the name of Anna Livia Plurabelle, abbreviated to ALP. Just as Earwicker is metamorphosed into Adam, Noah, Lord Nelson, a mountain, or a tree, so ALP becomes by subtle transposition, Eve, Isis, Iseult, a passing cloud, a flowing stream. She is the eternally fructive and love-bearing principle in the world. ...

But above all, Anna is a river, always changing yet ever the same, the Heraclitean flux which bears all life on its current. (p. 10)

Earwicker and his wife have two sons, called in their symbolic aspect Shem and Shaun. ... They are the carriers of a great Brother Battle theme that throbs through the entire work. Just as HCE and ALP represent a primordial male-female polarity, which is basic to all life, so Shem and Shaun represent a subordinate, exclusively masculine battle polarity which is basic to all history. (p. 11)

What, finally, is *Finnegans Wake* all about? Stripping away its accidental features, the book may be said to be all compact of *mutually supplementary antagonisms:* male-and-female, age-and-youth, life-and-death, love-and-hate; these, by their attraction, conflicts, and repulsions, supply polar energies that spin the universe. Wherever Joyce looks in history or human life, he discovers the operation of these basic polarities. Under the seeming aspect of diversity—in the individual, the family, the state, the atom, or the cosmos—these constants remain unchanged. Amid trivia and tumult, by prodigious symbol and mystic sign, obliquely and obscurely (because these manifestations are both oblique and obscure), James Joyce presents, develops, amplifies and recondenses nothing more nor less than the eternal dynamic implicit in birth, conflict, death, and resurrection. (p. 14)

> *Joseph Campbell and Henry Morton Robinson, in their* A Skeleton Key to "Finnegans Wake" *(copyright 1944 by Joseph Campbell and Henry Morton Robinson; renewed 1972 by Joseph Campbell and Vivian L. Robinson; reprinted by permission of Harcourt Brace Jovanovich, Inc.), Harcourt, 1944, 365 p.*

FRANCIS FERGUSSON   (essay date 1945)

[In *Exiles,* Joyce] paused for a last look at the soul which Stephen Daedalus had been impiously constructing, a vehicle winged for the exploration of new and perhaps forbidden realms, a fresh "conscience of his race." The *Portrait* shows us the process of construction; *Exiles* gives us the completed masterpiece. The timeless artifact of Richard Rowan is an image on the mind's eye ... , a work of art as Stephen Daedalus defines art. *Exiles* is thus at once, and by the same token, a singularly elegant and self-conscious piece of dramaturgy, and a brilliant image of the ethical being of the young Joyce. When the author finished it and returned to his labors on *Ulysses* he lost interest for good in the "artist as man," and his vitality passed into the narrative itself and its characters. Joyce himself is henceforth lost to sight behind or beyond his work.

Exiles is thus important for the understanding both of Joyce and of modern drama between *Peer Gynt,* say, and *Murder in the Cathedral;* but it has been studied less than any of the other works in the canon. The more obvious wealth and virtuosity of *Ulysses* and the more explicit discursive clarity of *A Portrait of the Artist* have eclipsed it. It is in itself an austere and difficult work. Being naturalistic drama, it represents in its three acts as much life and thought as we are accustomed to getting in the looser bulk of a long novel. The reader must let his thought and imagination play over the characters and their stories a long time if he is to appreciate the weight of experience which they can convey. (pp. v-vi)

Richard Rowan's complete rejection of "the mob in himself," as Mr. T. S. Eliot has put it, makes his agony very much like that of the "purely heroic" drama of French Seventeenth Century Rationalism. Undeluded, unsurprisable, fixed on the tragic split between freedom and intellectual integrity on one side and love on the other, he is own brother to the heroes of Racine and Corneille who face without flinching the irreconcilable conflict of Reason and Duty against Love or Passion. (p. xiii)

It is in his relation to Bertha that the split between his intellectual integrity and love—never, in any of its forms, quite digestible by the intellect; always, in our experience, somewhat ambiguous—becomes truly tragic. The scenes between Richard and Bertha, especially the last one, are as beautiful as any love scenes in modern drama. In their quietness, their tender refusal of a passion which is always present, they are like the grave farewells of Racine's monarchs, who are poised for five acts on that point of vibrant stillness, that motionless turn from love to duty. Yet they differ from Racine's scenes in one important respect: Richard is the only character on or off stage who understands the issues, while in Racine or Corneille the characters and the audience are all supposed to share the common light and glory of Reason. . . . The neoclassic hero's integrity is identical with his place, his responsibility, and his *gloire;* but Richard's is presented as the law of his own nature only, and hence as his exile and his invisibility. . . . [The] freedom which Richard has, attaches and subjects Bertha, because she cannot understand it. The "reasons of his heart" she grasps, but the reasons of his reason, which he always obeys, she does not see; and between his intellectual integrity and her love she is held prisoner more completely than she could have been by the ritual sacrifice of the conventional marriage promise. . . . (pp. xiv-xv)

> *Francis Fergusson, "A Reading of 'Exiles'," in* Exiles *by James Joyce (copyright 1918 by B. W. Huebsch; copyright 1945 by Nora Joyce; all rights reserved; reprinted by permission of the author), New Directions, 1945, pp. v-xviii.*

FREDERICK F. HOFFMAN (essay date 1945)

Though Joyce did not need any study of psychoanalysis in order to represent [the nighttown scene in *Ulysses*], he has obviously availed himself here of several psychoanalytical facts. The scene is not simply "black magic"; its use of filial-sexual themes, of burdens of conscience, of masochism in the Bello-Bloom incident, all point to an understanding of the Unconscious, and a literary representation of repressed materials which subsist within it.

Molly Bloom's forty-four page revery, on the other hand, does not approximate the language of the Unconscious. Indeed, she is very much awake and very much alive. But it should be noted that, for her, the dividing line between wish and its conscious satisfaction is slight and ineffective. She may be regarded as a literary demonstration of naïve desire, whose ease of satisfaction argues a freedom from restraint uncommon in society but secretly longed for by many. The absence of punctuation points to a release from the slight hold which the social amenities ordinarily have upon her. In contrast to Bloom's pizzicato musings Molly's

mind flows through present and past without pause. It is readily fed by the sights and sounds of the night, and only when she has finally settled down for a night's sleep does it relax from the holds of her bodily interests. Hence, though the device of one continuous, loose sentence is admirably suited to the moment, there is nothing particularly unusual about the style; nor is it difficult to follow the trend of her thought, since the one theme, the "universal Yes" dominates it at all times. (pp. 137-38)

Finnegans Wake is no mere transcript of a dream. In fact, it is a whole series of dreams, varying in their psychic intensity, changing their object repeatedly and encompassing the entire life of man. The materials of H.C.E.'s "dream day" are only a small part of the whole. Joyce's store of learning and his preoccupation with the exile themes of his entire life allow one to believe that Joyce himself shares the dream state with Earwicker: actually, Joyce is Jerry, the "penman" twin of Kevin. The inclusion of so much material which could not have been the part of even such an exceptional tavernkeeper as Earwicker is explained on two accounts: (1) The dream bears reference to certain primitive symbolic survivals in the Unconscious, archaic symbols which persist through the centuries and are the common heritage of all peoples. This is a convenient peg on which to hang (2) the cyclical theory of history, which is Vico's contribution to Earwicker's dream.

In other words, Earwicker is the common representative of all men, "Here Comes Everybody," whose unconscious dream life proceeds "In the name of the former and of the latter and of their holocaust. All-men." The "Vico road" which this dream takes—here the reference is to an actual road near the site of Earwicker's place of business—corresponds to a historical pattern of three cycles, in which man passes from primitive to complex life to dissolution and thence back to his primitive beginnings. . . . Hence the author has justifiably taken liberties with the dream only so far as he has imposed an alien theory upon the mind of an average man—only to prove that this average man is, when least disturbed by the incidents of his average day, a prototype for all men. For the psychological basis of this blending of myth with dream content, Joyce has gone to Jung's concept of the "collective unconscious"; for the mechanisms of the dream mind he relies entirely upon Freud. As in the case of *Ulysses,* Joyce has scattered clues which enable the reader to mark his course. One such is Earwicker's stammering; another, the incessant play on the word *Guinness;* a third, a series of refrains which though constantly distorted in the course of the dream work, retain their original connection with the whole.

This, then, is the stream of unconsciousness method in its most thorough literary application. . . . [The] latent dream content (the unconscious source of dream thoughts and wishes) goes through a wide variety of changes and disguises as it seeks expression in the manifest dream. The devices of condensation, displacement, and dramatization are all present here, but the real emphasis is upon the *power of words* to evoke dream images and to stand in the place of the visual content, so strong and so necessary in the actual dream. In the "Circe" episode of *Ulysses,* the repressed wishes and fears of Stephen and Bloom are dramatized; stage directions furnish the latent content with adequate visual emphasis. Here *words* are treated as *things,* and sounds take the place of visual images in all cases in which the latter are not sufficiently served by the dream situation itself. Here also Joyce's immense learning in foreign languages comes to his aid. It affords him an opportunity to subscribe to one of the dream's language habits— the tendency to substitute the etymological meaning of a word for its present meaning, if the latter is too abstract for adequate representation. (pp. 138-40)

The linguistic habits of the dream-life, united under the terms *condensation* and *displacement,* are all abundantly revealed in Joyce's work. The ambiguity of a word serves the purposes of condensation, and the manifest dream is therefore likely to contain many examples of what [has been] . . . called "polysemantic verbalism." Puns and portmanteau words are no strangers to the dream, as Freud has abundantly shown; they constitute one of Joyce's chief devices. . . . (p. 141)

Joyce is not enchained or imprisoned by the power of his unconscious life. He is a very careful, painstaking, "conscious" artist, aware of modern psychology and interested in it, yet after all independent of it as well. We would be doing violence to the integrity of the aesthetic consciousness, either to criticize Joyce for employing psychoanalysis inaccurately or to condemn him for using it at all. The true measure of his art is not the judgment of any scientist but the analysis of his use of what materials he considered aesthetically attractive and suitable. In such an analysis a knowledge of psychoanalysis is helpful both to the reader and the critic. (p. 148)

> *Frederick F. Hoffman, "Infroyce," in his* Freudianism and the Literary Mind *(copyright 1945 by the Louisiana State University Press), Louisiana State University Press, 1945, pp. 114-48.*

PHILIP TOYNBEE   (essay date 1948)

In the early passages of *Ulysses* we have seen that there are already two distinct styles; there is the "high" language of Stephen, rich, supple, and poetical, and there is the "low" language of Bloom, earthy, colloquial, and disjointed. Now, admirable though the language of Bloom may be, it is admirable rather as a contrast than in its own right. Taking the styles out of their contexts . . . there is no doubt that Stephen's style is superior. By this I do not simply mean that the language is more beautiful; I mean that it moves us at a greater variety of levels. Both the matter and the manner are Joyce extended to his utmost, using all the resources of his spirit. In Bloom's soliloquies, on the other hand, we are conscious of a brilliant tour de force; we are inevitably conscious of something almost patronizing in the author's choice of a suitable medium for an *inferior* being. Joyce has done everything in his power to avoid giving this impression, and he has come nearer to succeeding than any writer of any time could have done. But he could not quite succeed.

His recognition of this is shown by the tactic which he adopted in the main body of the book. He resolutely rejected the conception of a writer's function which demands that he be always aiming at his own highest possibility. He moved back from the page before him and aimed at a *total* impression in a way which no novelist had done before. Each page was to be, not a thing of individual excellence, but the most potent contribution to the whole. (pp. 271-72)

[The] great disadvantage of the novel is the simple sad fact

that time must elapse in reading it. A total and instantaneous impression cannot be made. . . . To circumvent this difficulty (it cannot be overcome) the older novelists had tried to make each single moment as palatable as possible, to make each brief passage a self-sufficient artistic whole. In this way a total impression was hoped for, but, should it fail through the failing memories of the readers, at least a succession of impressions would have been made. With great pride and integrity Joyce rejected this palliative. When, for example, it is necessary to be dull, he deliberately bores us and at great length. If we are too bored to read what he has written for us to read, then it is so much the worse for us. We shall miss the total impression even more widely than if we had read but forgotten. In any case Joyce will not sugar our pill. It is not true, of course, that none of the independent passages in the middle and later pages of *Ulysses* have any independent merit. It would be a lamentable plan which jealously forbade any value to its components, and many of these later passages are masterpieces in their own right. But they remain subordinate masterpieces.

The stylistic problem was solved in this way. Different styles were apportioned to different passages, strictly on their relevance and not at all on their abstract merit. *No style was bad unless it was unsuitable. No style which was unsuitable was good.* (pp. 273-74)

My own conservative and perhaps cowardly feeling is that Joyce's whole theory was wrong. It was a brilliant theory, bravely executed, but he carried it to doctrinaire extremes which often made its practice intolerable. . . .

So, although there is one sort of courage in Joyce's refusal to compromise, there is also cowardice in his fear of sullying his hands with the dirty work. For the pill *must* be sweetened; the individual passage must have a merit of its own which is not dependent merely on its context in the whole. . . . We cannot achieve the distant view which Joyce demands of us when we are plunged into the thick of his absorbing detail. The whole and the parts, the retrospective and the immediate view, remain distinct, and Joyce has not been able to cure us of the distinction. (p. 275)

The total, the architectural impression [of *Ulysses*] is overwhelming. Indeed, this book is almost unique in the retrospective satisfaction which it gives in spite of the frequent irritation and weariness which one has felt while reading it. The superfluities seem to fall away, and the vivid unforgetable passages (which constantly recur in the most unpromising surroundings) come together in a supreme pattern. Had every part been worthy of the tremendous whole, this would have been the greatest prose work ever written. (p. 284)

> *Philip Toynbee, "A Study of James Joyce's 'Ulysses'" (originally published in a different form as "A Study of 'Ulysses',"* in *Polemic, Nos. 7 & 8, March, 1947), in* James Joyce: Two Decades of Criticism, *edited by Seon Givens (copyright 1948, copyright © renewed 1975 by Seon Givens Manley; reprinted by permission of Vanguard Press, Inc.), Vanguard, 1948 (and reprinted by Vanguard, 1963, pp. 243-84).*

GILBERT HIGHET   (essay date 1949)

The parallelism between details of *Ulysses* and the *Odyssey* is close but artistically pointless. What Joyce wanted from the epic was its structural plan, and that, except in the barest outline, he failed to take. The plot of the *Odyssey* has, with justice, been admired by most of its readers. With superb skill and yet with apparently effortless ease Homer solves the problems of bringing Odysseus and his son Telemachus closer and closer together in their quest without letting them meet until just before the climax. . . . But Joyce has rearranged the incidents of the epic into eighteen sections which have a far looser connecting structure, and most of which are united only by that weakest of bonds, coincidence. For pages and pages he reports events only because they happened to occur in Dublin on the 16th of June 1904. . . . The same criticism applies to the plot, and to the treatment of the characters. The *Odyssey* is the story of a quest. . . . *Ulysses* is not the story of a quest. Bloom and Dedalus merely wander through Dublin, unguided by any single purpose. They do not know each other and belong to dissimilar worlds. When they meet, Dedalus is too drunk to understand what has happened; he, not Ulysses-Bloom, occupies the centre of attention throughout; and their chance association can never grow into a real father-son relationship. Thus, the climax of the book is that Dedalus rejects his true mother and is found by a false father. This rambling inconclusive story-line is responsible for much of the disappointment *Ulysses* causes to its readers. For the rest, Joyce's lack of selectivity can be blamed. The book begins by centring attention on 'stately, plump Buck Mulligan', who drops out of sight after a few chapters; it continues through brilliantly vivid descriptions of unimportant people and things; and then, after an unreadable chapter in the form of question-and-answer, meant to represent the gradual focusing of the mind after a bout of drunkenness, ends with a vast irrelevant monologue by Mrs. Bloom, who has never appeared and is almost as unknown to us as she is to Dedalus. (pp. 506-07)

Most artists have used myths to ennoble contemporary life. . . . But the symbolists sometimes use Greek myths (that is, the stories as distinct from the figures) to degrade life: to show, by contrast with the heroism or beauty of classical legend, how sordid the men and women of to-day have made themselves. That is the chief purpose of the epic parallel in *Ulysses*. It contrasts the strong, noble, statuesque past with the nasty, poor, brutish present, in which everything is dirt and humiliation, even sexual love, even the courage of combat. . . . *Ulysses* is not mock-heroic like *Tom Jones*, but anti-heroic. No one who has read it can doubt its power. It has been called an explosion in a sewer. The commonest criticism of it is that its filth is exaggerated; but few of those who offer this criticism have spent the first twenty years of their lives in a large industrial city. The truth is not that the filth is exaggerated, but that it is not balanced by the gaiety, vigour, and native wholesomeness which are part of man's life, even in Dublins and even in slums; and that it underestimates the power of chance, even in squalid surroundings, to provide moments of fun and pauses of beauty. Its model, the *Odyssey,* is better balanced. (pp. 512-13)

> *Gilbert Highet, "The Symbolist Poets and James Joyce." In his* The Classical Tradition: Greek and Roman Influences on Western Literature *(copyright 1949 by Oxford University Press, Inc.; renewed 1976 by Gilbert Highet; reprinted by permission), Oxford University Press, New York, 1949, pp. 501-19.*

STUART GILBERT   (essay date 1952)

At a first reading of *Ulysses* the average reader is impressed most of all by the striking psychological realism of the narrative. He is apt to attribute this impression to an (apparently) complete lack of reticence in the self-revelation of the personages. . . . But the realism of *Ulysses* strikes far deeper than the mere exercise of verbal frankness; apart from the author's extreme, almost scientific, precision in his handling of words, there are two factors which place Joyce's work in a class apart from all its predecessors, even the most meticulously realistic: firstly, the creator's standpoint to his theme, the unusual angle from which he views his creatures, and, secondly, his use of the "silent monologue" as the exponent not only of their inner and hardly conscious psychological reactions but also of the narrative itself.

In most novels the reader's interest is aroused and his attention held by the presentation of dramatic situations, of problems deriving from conduct or character and the reactions of the fictitious personages among themselves. The personages of *Ulysses* are *not* fictitious and its true significance does not lie in problems of conduct or character. After reading *Ulysses* we do not ask ourselves: "Should Stephen Dedalus have done this? Ought Mr Bloom to have said that? Should Mrs Bloom have refrained?" All these people are as they must be; they act, we see, according to some *lex eterna,* an ineluctable condition of their very existence. Not that they are mere puppets of Necessity or victims, like Tess, of an ironic Olympian. The law of their being is within them, it is a personal heritage, inalienable and autonomous. The meaning of *Ulysses,* for it has a meaning and is not a mere photographic "slice of life"—far from it—is not to be sought in any analysis of the acts of the protagonist or the mental make-up of the characters: it is, rather, implicit in the technique of the various episodes, in nuances of language, in the thousand and one correspondences and allusions with which the book is studded. Thus *Ulysses* is neither pessimist nor optimist in outlook, neither moral nor immoral in the ordinary sense of these words; its affinity is, rather, with an Einstein formula, a Greek temple, an art that lives the more intensely for its repose. *Ulysses* achieves a coherent and integral interpretation of life, a static beauty. . . . (pp. 8-9)

It is curious how few authors in any tongue have written with real detachment. . . . The novelist can rarely conceal his emotive reactions (often, of course, he does not wish to do so), or his indifference is merely feigned. (p. 9)

The attitude of the author of *Ulysses* to his personages and their activities is one of quiet detachment; all is grist to his mill, which, like God's, grinds slowly and exceeding small. (p. 10)

In this detachment, as absolute as the indifference of Nature herself towards her children, we may see one of the causes of the apparent "realism" of *Ulysses*.

Another of Joyce's innovations is the extended use of the unspoken soliloquy or silent monologue, an exact transcription of the stream of consciousness of the individual, which certainly has the air of an untouched photographic record and has, indeed, been compared to the film of a moving-picture. But . . . the superficial disorder of Mr Bloom's and Stephen's meditations, the frequent welling up of subconscious memories and the linking together of ideas by assonance or verbal analogy, all in reality form part of an elaborate scheme, and the movement, chaotic though it seem as life itself, is no more disorderly than the composed confusion of . . . the orchestral score of Stravinsky's *Sacre du Printemps*. (pp. 10-11)

All the action of *Ulysses* takes place in or about the city of Dublin—the unity of place is as thoroughgoing as that of time—and there are many topical allusions to characteristic sights of Dublin streets, to facts and personalities of the Dublin *milieu* of nearly half a century ago, that are incomprehensible for most English and American readers and may become so, in course of time, even to Dubliners. But without such personal touches, these nuances of evanescent local colour, the realism of the silent monologues would have been impaired; their presence in *Ulysses* was indispensable. (p. 16)

[Joyce] introduces political themes because they are inherent in the Dublin scene, and also because they illustrate one of the *motifs* of *Ulysses*, the betrayal or defeat of the man of mettle by the treachery of the hydra-headed rabble. (p. 18)

One of the simpler aspects of [Joyce's technique in *Ulysses*] —a device which, for all its apparent artificiality, exactly resembles Nature's method—is the presentation of fragments of a theme or allusion in different parts of the work; these fragments have to be assimilated in the reader's mind for him to arrive at complete understanding. . . . Moreover, again following Nature's method, Joyce depicts only the present time and place of the times and places that are passing, a rapid flux of images. . . . It is for the reader to assemble the fragments and join the images into a band. (pp. 24-5)

[Each of the 18 episodes of Ulysses,] taken independently, has its internal rhythm; in one of the most remarkable in this respect, the episode of the *Sirens,* there is a specific musical analogy, the *fugue;* in the episode of the *Oxen of the Sun,* where the style is a linguistic counterpart of the development of the embryo, there is a continuously increasing flow of vitality which ends in a word-dance of clipped phrases, *argot,* oaths and ejaculations. . . .

There could be no greater error than to confuse the work of James Joyce with that of the harum-scarum school or the *surréaliste* group . . . whose particular *trouvaille* was a sort of automatic writing, no revision being allowed. To suppose that the subconscious can best be portrayed by direct action of the subconscious—that effectively to depict the state of drunkenness one should oneself be drunk—is mere *naïveté*. (p. 31)

James Joyce is, in fact, in the great tradition which begins with Homer; like his precursors he subjects his work, for all its wild vitality and seeming disorder, to a rule of discipline as severe as that of the Greek dramatists; indeed, the unities of *Ulysses* go far beyond the classic triad, they are as manifold and yet symmetrical as the dædal network of nerves and bloodstreams which pervade the living organism. (p. 32)

> *Stuart Gilbert in his* James Joyce's 'Ulysses': A Study *(copyright 1930, 1952 by Stuart Gilbert; renewed 1958 by Arthur Stuart Gilbert; reprinted by permission of Alfred A. Knopf, Inc.; in Canada by Faber and Faber Ltd), revised edition, Knopf, 1952 (and reprinted by Vintage Books, 1955, 405 p.).*

CAROLINE GORDON   (essay date 1953)

I suspect that [*A Portrait of the Artist as a Young Man*] has been misread by a whole generation. It is not primarily a picture of the artist rebelling against constituted authority. It is, rather, the picture of a soul that is being damned for time and eternity caught in the act of foreseeing and foreknowing its damnation. (p. 140)

Stephen's sin, intellectual pride, like all sin, begets in him a terrible restlessness. He is impelled to leave his home and college and seek a new life. His mother, as she puts his *secondhand* clothes in order, prays that in his own life, away from home and friends, he may learn what the heart is and what it feels, but Joyce has given us to understand that this will never happen. Stephen has told [his classmate] Cranly that he is not afraid to make a mistake, "even a great mistake, a lifelong mistake and perhaps for eternity, too." . . . (p. 143)

These two passages throw considerable light on Joyce's intentions. He was a good classicist and had been steeped in Greek mythology. He was also one of the most conscientious literary craftsmen that ever lived. He was not likely to base his action on a Greek myth without realizing its full implications, nor could he have been guilty of the kind of cheap "modernistic" invention that characterizes Jean-Paul Sartre's play, *Les Mouches.* . . . In Joyce Furies remain Furies. The story follows the myth to its unhappy end. Stephen's father, Dedalus, the artificer, is a man of the nineteenth century. His skepticism and materialism have helped to construct the labyrinth from which both he and his son are trying to escape. Mr. Dedalus escapes through his love of his fellow men. When Stephen goes with his father to his father's college he is amazed at his father's love for his old cronies—there was not one of his set, Simon Dedalus tells his son, who did not have some talent, some merit that lifted him above the ordinary. Stephen, listening, feels that his own heart is as cold as the craters of the moon; the only one of his classmates with whom he is intimate is Cranly and they are intimate only because Cranly feels an almost scientific curiosity about the working of Stephen's mind. Mr. Dedalus escapes from the trap which his own hands have built, as Dedalus escaped of old. But Dedalus' son, Icarus, flies too near the sun. The wings which his father have made for him are only of wax. They melt under the sun's fierce heat and he falls into the sea and is drowned. (pp. 143-44)

> *Caroline Gordon, "Some Readings and Misreadings," in* The Sewanee Review *(reprinted by permission of the editor; © 1953 by The University of the South), Vol. LXI, No. 3, Summer, 1953 (and reprinted in* Joyce's Portrait: Criticisms and Critiques, *edited by Thomas E. Connolly, Appleton-Century-Crofts, 1962, pp. 384-407).*

BREWSTER GHISELIN   (essay date 1956)

The structure of James Joyce's *Dubliners,* long believed to be loose and episodic, is really unitary. (p. 75)

[The structural unity is achieved] by means of a single development, essentially of action, organized in complex detail and in a necessary, meaningful sequence throughout the book. . . . [The] whole unifying development [is] discernible as a sequence of events in a moral drama, an action of the human spirit struggling for survival under peculiar conditions of deprivation, enclosed and disabled by a degenerate environment that provides none of the primary necessities of spiritual life. So understood, *Dubliners* will be seen for what it is, in effect, both a group of short stories and a novel, the separate histories of its protagonists composing one essential history, that of the soul of a people which has confused and weakened its relation to the source of spiritual life and cannot restore it.

In so far as this unifying action is evident in the realistic elements of the book, it appears in the struggle of certain characters to escape the constricting circumstances of existence in Ireland, and especially in Dublin, "the centre of paralysis." As in *A Portrait of the Artist as a Young Man,* an escape is envisaged in traveling eastward from the city, across the seas to the freedom of the open world. In *Dubliners,* none of Joyce's protagonists moves very far on this course, though some aspire to go far. Often their motives are unworthy, their minds are confused. Yet their dreams of escape and the longing of one of them even to "fly away to another country" are suggestive of the intent of Stephen Dedalus in *A Portrait.* . . . Thus, in both books, ideas of enclosure, of arrest, and of movement in space are associated with action of moral purport and with spiritual aspiration and development.

In *Dubliners,* the meaning of movement is further complicated by the thematic import of that symbolic paralysis which Joyce himself referred to, an arrest imposed from within, not by the "nets" of external circumstance, but by a deficiency of impulse and power. The idea of a moral paralysis is expressed sometimes directly in terms of physical arrest, even in the actual paralysis of the priest Father Flynn, whose condition is emphasized by its appearance at the beginning of the book. . . . But sheer physical inaction of any kind is a somewhat crude means of indicating moral paralysis. Joyce has used it sparingly. The frustrations and degradations of his moral paralytics are rarely defined in physical stasis alone, and are sometimes concomitant with vigorous action. Their paralysis is more often expressed in a weakening of their impulse and ability to move forcefully, effectually, far, or in the right direction, especially by their frustration in ranging eastward in the direction of release or by their complete lack of orientation, by their failure to pass more than a little way beyond the outskirts of Dublin, or by the restriction of their movement altogether to the city or to some narrow area within it. (pp. 76-7)

It should be no surprise to discover in a book developing the theme of moral paralysis a fundamental structure of movements and stases, a system of significant motions, countermotions, and arrests, involving every story, making one consecutive narrative of the surge and subsidence of life in Dublin. In the development of the tendency to eastward movement among the characters of *Dubliners,* and in its successive modifications, throughout the book, something of such a system is manifest. It may be characterized briefly as an eastward trend, at first vague, quickly becoming dominant, then wavering, weakening, and at last reversed. Traced in rough outline, the pattern is as follows: in a sequence of six stories, an impulse and movement eastward to the outskirts of the city or beyond; in a single story, an impulse to fly away upward out of a confining situation near the center of Dublin; in a sequence of four stories, a gradual replacement of the impulse eastward by an impulse and movement westward; in three stories, a limited activity confined almost wholly within the central area of Dublin; and in the concluding story a movement eastward to the heart of the city, the exact center of arrest, then, in vision only, far westward into death. (p. 78)

Orientation and easting are rich in symbolic meanings of which Joyce was certainly aware. An erudite Catholic, he must have known of the ancient though not invariable custom of building churches with their heads to the east and placing the high altar against the east wall or eastward against a reredos in the depths of the building, so that the celebrant of the mass faced east, and the people entered the church and approached the altar from the west and remained looking in the same direction as the priest. He knew that in doing so they looked toward Eden, the earthly paradise. . . . Probably he [knew] that Christ returning for the Last Judgment was expected to come from the east. And he must have shared that profound human feeling, older than Christianity, which has made the sunrise immemorially and all but universally an emblem of the return of life and has made the east, therefore, an emblem of beginning and a place of rebirth. . . . He could not have failed, and the evidence of his symbolism in *Dubliners* shows that he did not fail, to see how a multitude of intimations of spiritual meaning affected the eastward aspirations and movements of characters in his book, and what opportunity it afforded of giving to the mere motion of his characters the symbolic import of moral action. (p. 79)

Like the booklong sequence of movements and stases, the various states of the soul in virtue and sin form a pattern of strict design traceable through every story. Each story in *Dubliners* is an action defining amid different circumstances of degradation and difficulty in the environment a frustration or defeat of the soul in a different state of strength or debility. Each state is related to the preceding by conventional associations or by casual connections or by both, and the entire sequence represents the whole course of moral deterioration ending in the death of the soul. Joyce's sense of the incompatibility of salvation with life in Dublin is expressed in a systematic display, one by one in these stories, of the three theological virtues and the four cardinal virtues in suppression, of the seven deadly sins triumphant, and of the deathly consequence, the spiritual death of all the Irish. Far more than his announced intention, of dealing with childhood, adolescence, maturity, and public life, this course of degenerative change in the states of the soul tends to determine the arrangement of the stories in a fixed order and, together with the pattern of motions and arrests, to account for his insistence upon a specific, inalterable sequence. (pp. 80-1)

The pattern of virtues and sins and the spatial pattern of motions and arrests in *Dubliners* are of course concomitant, and they express one development. As sin flourishes and virtue withers, the force of the soul diminishes, and it becomes more and more disoriented, until at the last all the force of its impulse toward the vital east is confused and spent and it inclines wholly to the deathly west. (p. 82)

Brewster Ghiselin, "The Unity of 'Dubliners'" (copyright © 1956 by Brewster Ghiselin; reprinted by permission of the author), in Accent, *Vol. XVI, Nos. 2 and 3, Spring and Summer, 1956, pp. 75-88, 196-213.*

RICHARD ELLMANN (essay date 1956)

In his books Joyce represents heroes who seek freedom,

which is also exile, voluntarily and by compulsion. The question of ultimate responsibility is raised and then dropped without an answer. Joyce's hero is as lonely as Byron's; consequently Joyce obliterated Stephen's brother, Maurice, from the *Portrait* after using him tentatively in *Stephen Hero,* for there must be no adherent, and the home must be a rallying-point of betrayal. A cluster of themes—the sacrilege of Faust, the suffering of Christ, the exile of Dante—reach a focus in the problem of friendship. For if friendship exists, it impugns the quality of exile and of lonely heroism. If the world is not altogether hostile, we may forgive it for having mistreated us, and so be forced into the false position of warriors without adversaries. Joyce allows his hero to sample friendship before discovering its flaws, and then with the theme of broken friendship represents his hero's broken ties with Ireland and the world.

The friendship is invariably between men; here Joyce is very much the Dubliner. A curious aspect of Irish life is that relationships between men seem more vital there than relationships between men and women. It is not easy to know whether this trait is due to a misogynistic bias in Irish Catholicism, or, less impressively, to long hours of pub crawling. Whatever the cause, the trait carries over into the work of Joyce. (p. 62)

To isolate the male friendships in Joyce's novels does not, of course, give a complete account of the novels; but it does them surprisingly little violence. Each book has a special view of friendship, although later developments are lightly prefigured in the earliest, *Stephen Hero*. In *Stephen Hero* Joyce touches upon Stephen's amorous interest in Emma Clery, but shows his relation to her as wary and circumspect when it is not merely blunt. The main interest attaches to his friendship with Cranly, which is much more tender and complex. Cranly's alienation from Stephen is the novel's principal dramatic action. . . . (pp. 63-4)

In *A Portrait of the Artist as a Young Man* the themes introduced in *Stephen Hero* are heightened by the new unifying theme of artistic development. Friendship too is viewed with greater intensity, its collisions are more serious, and at the end of the book it begins to seem an impossibility. (p. 66)

Joyce reserved for his play *Exiles* a saturnalia of the emotions of friendship. (p. 68)

[In *Exiles,* a] friend is someone who wants to possess you mentally and your wife physically, and longs to prove himself your disciple by betraying you. (p. 70)

In *Ulysses* betrayal serves as a countertheme to the main action, which is the coming together of Bloom and Stephen. (p. 71)

Among all [the] betrayals of one man by another, the relationship of Bloom and Stephen stands forth in vivid contrast. Mulligan suspects that Bloom's interest in Stephen is homosexual, but the suspicion is only malicious. The relationship of the two is not friendly, but paternal and filial. Joyce seems to imply that only within the family, or the pseudo-family, can a solid bond be established. (p. 72)

Molly is offered as a pawn not in friendship but in the father-son bond. "Betray me and be my son," Bloom half tells Stephen. Stephen, as usual, ends by committing himself to no one; but Bloom, who has also cast off friendship, is partially at least committed to him and to Molly as father and husband. Joyce perhaps found it easier to picture this triangular relationship in *Ulysses* because he put so much of himself in both his heroes that he was at once betrayer and betrayed.

Moreover, the familial relationship, while not necessarily satisfactory, is at least inevitable. In *Finnegans Wake* Joyce returns to the family situation, and the book contrasts with an early work like *Dubliners,* where most of the relationships are outside the family, or with the *Portrait,* where a break with the family is essential. It is as if, having sampled all varieties of friendship, and in *Ulysses,* foster-kinship, Joyce reverts at last to the fundamental and timeless condition of the family. Betrayal continues: in a famous passage every member of the family is revealed to have illicit relations with every other member. . . . (p. 73)

In the *Portrait* the hero moved away from his father's family to friends, but every friend betrayed him; and now the hero reverts to the family, this time a family of his own making. In the family betrayal continues, yet here all the members of the family seem principally aspects of Joyce's imaginative life, alternately embracing and rejecting each other, but bound as indissolubly as the cortexes of the brain. He is the wooer and the wooed, the slayer and the slain. (p. 74)

> Richard Ellmann, "A Portrait of the Artist as Friend" (originally published in Kenyon Review, Vol. XVIII, No. 1, Winter, 1956), in Society and Self in the Novel, edited by Mark Schorer (© 1958 Richard Ellmann; reprinted by permission of the author), Columbia University Press, 1956, pp. 60-77.

HUGH KENNER (essay date 1956)

People do things in *Dubliners,* but their reasons for what they do are obscured among cadences: obscured, that is, from themselves. The plots of these stories are unexpectedly difficult to paraphrase intelligibly. One can put down what happens, but the motivation of the characters is elusive. On inspecting the stories we find that each phase of action is infallibly preceded by passages of introspection or exhortation whose connection with the action is profound but seldom logical. (p. 14)

[In *Finnegans Wake*] reality is monopolized by the precise but inscrutable products of crossbred words, semantic spooks as necessary and as puzzling as *pi* and the root of minus one, peopling a coherent world that isn't there but that speaks with a Dublin accent. Joyce had suspected as a child, and known as a young man that Dublin's civic reality was contained in its language alone; and through book after book had winnowed that truth until in *Finnegans Wake* he could project in language the generic Dubliner's image: a cataleptic dreaming of the waking world, all his reality a dream and a dream made out of words, the stones of Dublin, its smells, its sunlight, everything but its language taken away. (p. 18)

Every detail of Joyce's aesthetic speculations is oriented toward the epiphany—toward the criterion of intelligibility. The artifact is a supremely intelligible object. The plot, when employed, has ontological consistency, not merely the rationalistic consistency which it may or may not exhibit but which the fortuitous always exhibits. The real plot of *Finnegans Wake* is the emergence of light, imaged by the daybreak at the end through chapel windows: the gradual subsumption of particulars into an intelligible order; so is the plot of a story in *Dubliners*. The breaking of this light upon the mind leads, Joyce saw, to comedy. The proper object of comedy is not desire, "the feeling which urges us to go to something," but Joy, "the feeling which the possession of some good excites in us." (p. 156)

While we no longer suppose, with an early reviewer, that "Mr. Joyce transfers the product of his unconscious mind to paper without submitting it to his conscious mind," we have been encouraged to think that reading [*Ulysses*] amounts to determining why one notion of Bloom's follows another. Joyce's interest in this kind of *consonantia* is however much more sardonic than scientific. While he takes care that Bloom's thought shall be, at Bloom's level, continuous, he takes even greater care that the work as a whole shall be, at Joyce's level, intelligible. Dublin is being presented in a hundred simultaneous perspectives, with the aid of numerous controlling images.

One of the major perspectives is the analogy of Bloom and Stephen; it is an analogy much more than it is a contrast. Parallels between their meditations proliferate; if these are not too readily dismissed (or admired) as tokens of Joyce's concern for "structure" they will yield a great deal of the book's meaning.

This means reading Bloom's reveries fairly closely, with an eye on the progression of motif from motif. It is Stephen who tends to get the close reading, but the higher potential of Stephen's thought is more apparent than real; the Stephen monologues are a highly original pastiche of the decadent sensibility, with a tang of smoking lamps and relished corruption. Bloom's mind, if he could manage to do something with it, is far more inventive. Bloom, amid his associative driftings, is ironically oblivious to the patterns in which his thoughts are cast.... Each strives uselessly towards an ideal conceived in pathetic circumscription— Bloom strives to function as a romantic artist; the romantic artist Stephen strives towards hierophantic power, a Solomon's facility at reading the signatures of all things; the artist whom Stephen cannot be strives towards a prelapsarian efficacy, imposing names according to the essences of things and functioning in a freedom contingent but quasi-divine amid the luminous forms of an inexhaustibly intelligible world. It is from this multiple perspective of inadequacy that the swooning pathos of the latter half of the Nausicaa episode derives. (pp. 198-99)

Joyce's irony goes deep indeed. Not only does Bloom not know that he is Ulysses (the meaning of his own actions); he does not know that he is an analogue of Christ inhabiting a sacramental universe (the meaning of his own thoughts). Stephen on the other hand is aware that he is Hamlet, but his awareness is put to the wrong uses. It provides him with no insight. It merely feeds his morbidity. It is a role in which he is imprisoned. He is constantly aware of an infinitely extending perspective of future selves to be traversed and assimilated. (p. 209)

The career of Joyce is that of a man enacting all the romantic patterns—mother-guilt, Byronic exile, infant as anarch, poet as heresiarch—in order to find out and exhibit what they mean. It is precisely because his "characters" are of the most conventional outline ... that they are so efficacious. The same is true of his situations, chiefly an-

titheses taken from the worst discoverable operas and melodramas. Joyce's perpetual assumption of roles is equally central to his work: Byronic hero, Zolaesque novel, Shelleyan stream-of-images, Carrollean infantilism are phases traversed by him and his artist's consciousness; phases, analogically, traversed by his work. He contains all these things, and he explicates them. His work is the mimetic and cathartic gesture that brings the nineteenth century, with its nightworld in every sense, to an end. After him, every romantic seems spurious.

Portrait-Ulysses-Finnegan: nature as dream and mirror, nature as arena for confrontations with the not-self, nature as matrix of *vestigiae Dei* to be traversed in traversing oneself drop by drop. The history and catharsis of the Romantic Movement is there. (p. 299)

> *Hugh Kenner, in his* Dublin's Joyce, *Indiana University Press, 1956, 372 p.*

E. M. W. TILLYARD (essay date 1958)

[*Ulysses*] is as richly ancestored as any other would-be epic, though the ancestry may be uncommonly miscellaneous. [Giorgio Melchiori in his essay on Joyce in *The Tightrope Walkers*] is right in thinking that it goes behind the main conventions of nineteenth-century prose fiction to the more fluid and experimental conditions of the eighteenth century, when prose fiction included things as unlike the fiction of the nineteenth century as *Gulliver's Travels* and *Tristram Shandy,* while Smollett in *Humphry Clinker* anticipated, through the distortions of Winifred Jenkins's epistolary language, many of Joyce's linguistic habits. Joyce is also the child of the nineteenth century, but through its poetical or poeticising sides. If he broke violently with the current tradition of prose fiction, if he was utterly at odds with the realism of Bennett and Wells and Galsworthy, he compensated by developing, in his prose, methods that had existed, at least embryonically, in the poetry or poetical prose of the last hundred years or more. If Pater gave him the hint of how to manipulate fiction with extreme sophistication and fastidiousness the poets had displayed the art of passing abruptly from one style to another. (pp. 187-88)

There is a vast variety of matter in *Ulysses,* a lavishness which at once satisfies a part of one epic essential. It might be objected that the variety, however dazzling, leaves all kinds of things untouched. Indeed Joyce has been narrowed into a "great destructive satirist" and *Ulysses* into a book that serves to show up the "moral failures of modern civilization". But there is a good deal besides destruction and a good deal of morality which, though it is often in difficulties, cannot be described as a failure. While Joyce does not mitigate a single shortcoming in Leopold and Marion Bloom, he allows them positive qualities and is devoid of satire in so doing. . . . And if Joyce pitilessly mauls a bogus kind of Irish patriotism through embodying it in the violent and ridiculous figure of the Citizen in the Cyclops episode he presents in all sincerity, lucidity, and fear the ineluctable dilemma of the genuine Irish patriot through the visions that Stephen has of his own country and of its overshadowing and overbearing neighbour. Granted that epic is possible when dealt with from the side of comedy, satire, and farce, *Ulysses* does not fall short in point of sheer substance.

There is no need to quarrel with the high value that competent readers generally have put on what Joyce has made of parts of that substance. At his best he can heighten the trivial as successfully as Chaucer and Cervantes. True, he often inflates and bores as well as heightens. . . . The Eumaeus scene in the cabmen's shelter, written in quintessential ditch-water of the stalest English, becomes hideously boring. But it has the quality of the bore who hypnotises his victim and it ends by overpowering all opposition. (pp. 188-89)

It is when the reader scans the whole that doubts begin. Can he honestly believe that this whole is greater than the sum of its parts? (p. 189)

[If] *Ulysses* is ever to represent itself to readers as an accomplished whole, it will be from a side . . . not concerned with subject-matter and parallels of episodes but with matters of form and pervasive, ruling sensations, with matters closer to music than to the representational arts. If such a side *can* be developed it will account, for instance, for the greatly increased length of the episodes that form the second half. It always remains possible that *Ulysses* is organised through a governing rightness difficult to divine and perceptible only after prolonged acquaintance, through a tact in making this episode follow that and lead up to the other that satisfies some very profound instict for order, the kind of tact that I guess unconsciously guided Spenser when he ordered the *Fairie Queene* as he did. . . . (pp. 193-94)

Actually I think those right who hold that the quest for unity is vain and that we should approximate Joyce not to the authors of single great works whose significance lies largely in the union of abundant matter and rigorous shaping but to the great fantasts and exuberants, to Rabelais, Sterne, and the Goethe of the second part of *Faust*. . . .

It is the richness of presentation that first matters in *Ulysses,* and that richness includes much that has very properly been called poetry. . . . (p. 194)

Since *Ulysses* suffers from an unusual amount of fashion-bred, hypocritical adulation, it is not easy to detect the true cause of its appeal. Part of it consists in the technical innovations. However well ancestored *Ulysses* may be, it went back violently and explosively on the prevailing technique of the novel. It gave the revolutionary thrill. Secondly, if it failed to speak for a nation, it had a great deal to say about what have been vulgarly called the disinherited mind and the displaced person. Stephen Daedalus fits the first phrase pretty well, and Leopold Bloom the second. Stephen hopes to gain an inheritance through art and Bloom achieves a precarious attachment to an alien society, but the strength of their appeal consists less in any positive qualities they may own than in being misfits. It could be maintained that *Ulysses* speaks for all those who today feel themselves exiles from the society in which they are set. (p. 195)

> E.M.W. Tillyard, "Joyce: 'Ulysses'," in his The Epic Strain in the English Novel (© E.M.W. Tillyard 1958), Chatto & Windus, 1958, pp. 187-96.

HERBERT HOWARTH (essay date 1958)

The autobiographical elements in *Dubliners* were severely controlled into objective documents of public corruption. In *A Portrait* the autobiography is overt and dominates the narrative. In *Ulysses* and *Finnegans Wake* it is combined with non-autobiographical material so that the critic and the subjects of his criticism are shown and explained simultaneously and equally. Joyce had so complete a conviction of his heroic stature that it seemed natural to him from the start that he should write his story. He thought, what [George] Moore was soon to lay down as a principle, that an autobiography is a perfectly possible form for a sacred book. The last pages of *A Portrait* frankly claim a Messianic mission. He conceives his friend Cranley as John the Baptist. He goes, like Mohammed, into exile "to forge in the smithy of my soul the uncreated conscience of my race". By writing his own story he says three things to the Irish: let me show you how backward you look to me; let me show you how I have fortified and sharpened myself, imitate me; see how I have sacrificed myself for you. If the name Daedalus is a claim of intellect and creativeness, the name Stephen is a claim of a sacrificial Christ-function. In the Irish celebration of St. Stephen's Day, a wren was killed and carried about the town hung on a stick. The theme of the crucified king of the birds later runs through *Finnegans Wake* as one of the mutating motifs, Joyce examining his early claim from all angles favourable and adverse. In *A Portrait* the claims are simple and arrogant. (pp. 254-55)

The *Stephen Hero* draft, the foundation on which *A Portrait* was raised, contains much non-symbolic plain argumentation about the shortcomings of Ireland and her nationalist ideology, very little of which was retained in *A Portrait,* not because Joyce had changed his opinions but because he had decided to jettison the scaffolding by which he had reared his symbols. In his early career he valued clarity. To sculpt clear outlines, free of jagged fringes, obscurities and uncertainties; to eliminate distractions and shape the residue into concord; that was his first consideration during his twenties and early thirties. That was the process that produced the poems of *Chamber Music* and the paragraphs of *A Portrait.* At the beginning of *Ulysses* there are passages that still derive from it. The early passage that describes the *Rosevean* coming up the Liffey is beautiful, but too beautiful; its over-perfection, though intended to write a period to Part I, disturbs. The extension of Joyce's art lay through the abdication of autonomous perfection in favour of complex structures within which no part need be self-explanatory. During heavy composition of *Ulysses* Joyce observed "I fear I have little imagination". If imagination means inventing, this is right; his art was to organise with exacting intricacy. (p. 257)

Joyce's complexity was a necessity to him, and it doubled the force of his feelings by channelling them; and he found an additional purpose for it in *Ulysses*—he proffered it as a decoy. . . . The first generation of critics enjoyed the tabulation of his tricks, and read the novel more as if it were the Greek than the Dublin *Odyssey.* But the Dublin reality and Joyce's feelings about it matter more. He made out of his private problems a story which integrated them with the national problems of Ireland, and permanent problems of man. What is most amazing in the end is not the ingenuity which the critics love . . . , but the power which makes Stephen and Bloom so important to us that we think with them for days after a reading, trying to understand some phrase they throw up in their introspecting—as if the mystery of human experience lay in their memories, and if we could draw the cloud away we should know more about the human drama than ever before. (pp. 258-59)

Joyce was the culmination of the Irish literary movement. He had observed it with distaste in 1900, criticised the senility of the folk-art it praised, scorned the shapelessness of the epics it revived, denounced its submission to the rabblement. He had disliked and feared involvement in it or its political counterpart, had removed himself from its influence, and wrote to efface it by doing differently and better. His achievement, however, was built on it; he took up and completed its work. (p. 285)

[The writers of the movement] had meant to make the world see the dignity and charm of Ireland. He began by telling of her indignity, but gradually broadened to take in all she had, a licentious vitality which the others had omitted until Synge's experiments. Going far beyond Synge, he detailed her oddest oddities and produced the Irish *Comédie Humaine* that Yeats once thought of but could not even design, still less write; it is curious how Yeats and Joyce each had skills beyond the other. By the unflattering completeness of his picture Joyce did more to make the world Ireland-conscious than the dignity-mongering and charm-mongering had done (though they had done something). (p. 286)

Driven by a determination to prove himself above mediocrity, he wrote the epic of the mediocre, incorporating the popular and the banal because they fascinated him, not because he courted popularity. A characteristic of his art is to use popular conventions and codes, ideals, language and toys, in a form accessible only to those who have otherwise turned away from them. . . . Joyce out of his passion for the popular drew it into his intricate designs, careless whether it found an immediate audience or not, though confident that this very indifference to any order but his own would eventually assure a fit audience. (pp. 286-87)

> *Herbert Howarth, "James Augustine Joyce," in his* The Irish Writers 1880-1940: Literature under Parnell's Star *(© 1958 by Herbert Howarth), Rockliff, 1958, pp. 245-87.*

EDMUND FULLER   (essay date 1958)

[Joyce's] works have a kind of maniacal brilliance . . . but, as a conception of man in his nature and life, like John Randolph's famous rotten mackerel in the moonlight, they shine and stink. A derisive distaste for man, self and other than self, permeates them. They culminate in a gigantic mockery, conscious and controlled on the artistic level, but less so, I think, in their sources and motivation. The Joyce cultists insist that *Ulysses* and *Finnegans Wake* are "genial," humor-filled books, but their grin is a *risus sardonicus.* They are, Gogarty claims, "a gigantic hoax, one of the most enormous leg-pulls in history." It is a claim that need not be settled for the purposes of this discussion. (p. 123)

Joyce has been elevated into a figure who has been seized upon by many writers as inspiration and justification for that whole wing of fiction and drama that has repudiated man and extolled unman. That is the truest sense in which he is the founder of a movement.

Few men have said more eloquent things about art, beauty, and the special dedications of the artist than some of the lines in *A Portrait of the Artist as a Young Man.* It is to the priesthood of art and the esthetic that Stephen dedicates himself, in terms of his namesake, Dedalus, the "old artificer," not an artist but the inventor of wings. The philo-

sophic pitfall is in the glib assumption that devotion to art is a dedication to a religion not capable of coexistence or reconciliation with any other religion—an assumption which overlooks or would negate an immense volume of humanity's greatest artistic achievements in every field. Actually, the religion that Stephen embraces is not at all a religion of art—it is a religion of Man. The premise of this remarkable novel seems to be that man, to fulfill himself, must worship his own creativity, and that to worship God is to deny himself. (pp. 123-24)

This high priest of man portrays demented man. Joyce has created a religion with an insane god. The obscene eucharist celebrated in the brothel scene of *Ulysses* is its expression. The image of man visible in Joyce had been sketched graphically before his time in the Fantasies of Peter Breughel and in the Capriccios of Goya. They harmonize perfectly with the famous scene in Bella Cohen's brothel, or the Molly Bloom interior monologue, in *Ulysses,* as well as with *Finnegans Wake.* Both Breughel and Goya castigated in nightmare fury the sometime malignancy and viciousness of man. Joyce accepts these grotesques in broad daylight with the mocking pretension that they are the lords of creation. The affirmation that there is nothing greater than these creatures in the universe is seen by Joyce not as a source of anger or of pride, but of derisive laughter. (p. 125)

The irony is that Joyce, whose rebellion was in the name of individuality, who is acclaimed by his admirers as a prophet of individuality, through his crudely literal early-Freudianism stepped onto the path that leads to the death of the individual, submerging him in bestiality and determinism, which we see graphically in much of the contemporary fiction, triple-fathered (like one of Shaw's characters) by Marx, Freud, and Joyce. (p. 126)

[The purported total reality of *Ulysses* and *Finnegans Wake*] is above all things preoccupied with the Freudian sexual symbols and the grosser bodily functions. The mind and creativity of man presumably are celebrated in *A Portrait of the Artist,* but only in the limited terms of Stephen's esoteric estheticism. The spiritual life of man is represented only in the obscenities of the later books, the grotesque, mockingly blasphemous parodies of liturgy and creed which dominate both big volumes. (p. 127)

I share some of the cult's admiration for the sheer ingenuity seen in the books. But I think that the world of Joyce is a world of stink and death. I think that Joyce saw it exactly as he set it down. And I think that his body of work together with the body of exegesis that has sprung up around it are a perfect and terrifying example of the disintegrative process in the mind that has pinned its utter faith upon its own intellectual, rational, and creative powers to the exclusion of all else.

Joyce insisted upon regarding man as *prime creator* instead of accepting him as that quite sufficient marvel: *creative creature.* He cast himself as Dedalus the "artificer." Perhaps he is more that rash son of Dedalus, that Icarus, who, against the counsel of the artificer, flew too near the sun on wings he had not made. (p. 132)

> *Edmund Fuller, "Joyce: Dedalus or Icarus?" in his* Man in Modern Fiction: Some Minority Opinions on Contemporary American Writing *(copyright © 1949, 1957, 1958, by Edmund Fuller; re-*

printed by permission of Random House, Inc.),
Random House, 1958, pp. 122-32.

HENRY MILLER (essay date 1959)

The story of *Ulysses* is the story of a lost hero recounting a lost myth; frustrated and forlorn the Janus-faced hero wanders through the labyrinth of the deserted temple, seeking for the holy place but never finding it. . . . Through his chaos and obscenity, his obsessions and complexes, his perpetual, frantic search for God, Joyce reveals the desperate plight of the modern man who, lashing about in his steel and concrete cage, admits finally that there is no way out. (p. 206)

With Joyce there is no world-view. Man returns to the primordial elements; he is washed away in a cosmological flux. Parts of him may be thrown up on foreign shores, in alien climes, in some future time. But the whole man, the vital, spiritual ensemble, is dissolved. This is the dissolution of the body and soul, a sort of cellular immortality in which life survives chemically. (p. 207)

Life to Joyce, as one of his admirers says, is a mere tautology. Precisely. We have here the clue to the whole symbolism of defeat. And, whether he is interested in history or not, Joyce *is* the history of our time, of this age which is sliding into darkness. Joyce is the blind Milton of our day. But whereas Milton glorified Satan, Joyce, because his sense of vision has atrophied, merely surrenders to the powers of darkness. . . . Joyce is the lost soul of this soulless world; his interest is not in life, in men and deeds, not in history, not in God, but in the dead dust of books. He is the high priest of the lifeless literature of today. He writes a hieratic script which not even his admirers and disciples can decipher. He is burying himself under an obelisk for whose script there will be no key. (p. 210)

Joyce is not a realist, nor even a psychologist; there is no attempt to build up character—there are caricatures of humanity only, *types* which enable him to vent his satire, his hatred, to lampoon, to vilify. For at bottom there is in Joyce a profound hatred for humanity—the scholar's hatred. One realizes that he has the neurotic's fear of entering the living world, the world of men and women in which he is powerless to function. He is in revolt not against institutions, but against mankind. Man to him is pitiable, ridiculous, grotesque. And even more so are man's ideas—not that he is without understanding of them, but that they have no validity for him; they are ideas which would connect him with a world from which he has divorced himself. His is a medieval mind born too late: he has the taste of the recluse, the morals of an anchorite, with all the masturbative machinery which such a life entrains. A Romantic who wished to embrace life realistically, an idealist whose ideals were bankrupt, he was faced with a dilemma which he was incapable of resolving. There was only one way out—to plunge into the collective realm of fantasy. As he spun out the fabric of his dreams he also unloaded the poison that had accumulated in his system. (p. 222)

Henry Miller, in his The Henry Miller Reader, *edited by Lawrence Durrell (copyright © 1959 by Henry Miller; all rights reserved; reprinted by permission of New Directions Publishing Corporation), New Directions, 1959, 397 p.**

J. MITCHELL MORSE (essay date 1959)

It is a cliché among [the critics] that Molly Bloom is an earth-goddess, a nature-goddess, a mother-goddess, a symbol of the irrational but fertile, the witless but somehow creative, the amoral but somehow good, force of nature. She is spontaneity, they tell us. . . . They ask us to admire her; they ask us to believe that Joyce considered stupidity a necessary concomitant of fertility, creativity, freedom, kindness, and honesty. (p. 139)

I see no evidence in the text for the prevailing view. Molly is not honest, she is not kind, she is not creative, she is not free, she hasn't enough *élan vital* to get dressed before three P.M., and her fertility is subnormal. (pp. 139-40)

What is Joyce's purpose in making one of his chief characters a woman who lacks sufficient energy to be effective in the ordinary tasks of daily life, whose health is declining, whose fertility is below par, whose capacity for sexual enjoyment is questionable, who considers the sexual act dirty and in fact makes it dirty, whose heart is cold, and whose attitude is generally negative and censorious? Who is Molly, what is she, that most of our critics adore her?

The anthropological interpretation of literature as mythography has degenerated into a fatuous ritual; overlooking the obvious in their fond search for occult meanings, our fable-minded critics often myth the point. (pp. 143-44)

[Molly is] not only a faithless figure of faith but also a force of nature that doesn't function: in Dublin even nature is awry, perverse, and moribund. (p. 144)

Joyce never mocked fertility or creativity or love or the joy of life; he mocked instead the ways in which they are falsified and perverted, including the cheap, sentimental, vulgar ways in which they are often celebrated. . . . But a more deadly weapon than mockery is accurate quotation. Molly's soliloquy is the bitterest and deadliest thing Joyce ever wrote. Without exhorting or haranguing his readers, observing strictly his own canon of reticence, he let Molly damn herself as the very center of paralysis. (pp. 148-49)

J. Mitchell Morse, "Molly Bloom Revisited," in A James Joyce Miscellany, *edited by Marvin Magalaner (copyright © 1959 by Southern Illinois University Press; reprinted by permission of Southern Illinois University Press), Southern Illinois University Press, 1959, pp. 139-49.*

HARRY LEVIN (essay date 1960)

It is paradoxical that the *Portrait of the Artist,* so direct in treatment, should be devoted to the problems of art; while *Finnegans Wake,* where the figure of the artist has disappeared into the complexities of his technique, should be concentrated upon the *minutiae* of city life. We shall not be confused by this paradox if we recognize from the outset that Joyce's most protean variations are played upon two obsessive themes—the city and the artist. The connection between these themes is all the more poignant because it is so slight. It is as tenuous and strained as the connection between life and art in our time. The modern metropolis is lacking in beauty; the contemporary writer is without a community. The city finds its obvious vehicle of expression in naturalism. The artist, left to his own devices, turns in the other direction [to symbolism]. *Ulysses* is an attempted synthesis, foredoomed to failure by the very conditions it assumes. (p. 19)

A conscientious pupil of the naturalistic school, Joyce

would not invent his material. He would continue to utilize his own experience, though his imagination was to carry him much farther than the naturalists in interpreting and arranging it. . . . The friends of his student days were quick to sense that he went among them taking notes. "So he recorded under Epiphany," says Dr. Gogarty, "any showing forth of the mind by which he considered one gave oneself away." Here . . . we have a clinical definition of what was to Joyce an essentially mystical concept. The writer, no longer hoping to comprehend modern life in its chaotic fullness, was searching for external clues to its inner meaning. . . .

An epiphany is a spiritual manifestation, more especially the original manifestation of Christ to the Magi. There are such moments in store for all of us, Joyce believed, if we but discern them. Sometimes, amid the most encumbered circumstances, it suddenly happens that the veil is lifted, the burthen of the mystery laid bare, and the ultimate secret of things made manifest. . . . It now seemed to him that the task of the man of letters was to record these delicate and evanescent states of mind, to become a collector of epiphanies. (pp. 27-9)

Such a collection has come down to us by way of *Dubliners*. The doctrine, however, informs all of Joyce's work —the muffled climaxes of the *Portrait of the Artist*, the alcoholic apparitions of *Ulysses*, and the protracted nightmare of *Finnegans Wake*. Listen for the single word that tells the whole story. Look for the simple gesture that reveals a complex set of relationships. . . . His dizzying shifts between mystification and exhibitionism, between linguistic experiment and pornographic confession, between myth and autobiography, between symbolism and naturalism, are attempts to create a literary substitute for the revelations of religion. (p. 29)

In their own way, the tangential sketches of *Dubliners* came as close to Joyce's theme —the estrangement of the artist from the city—as does the systematic cross-section of *Ulysses*. They look more sympathetically into the estranged lives of others. They discriminate subtly between original sin and needless cruelty. (p. 32)

Joyce's own contribution to English prose is to provide a more fluid medium for refracting sensations and impressions through the author's mind—to facilitate the transition from photographic realism to esthetic impressionism. In the introductory pages of the *Portrait of the Artist*, the reader is faced with nothing less than the primary impact of life itself, a presentational continuum of the tastes and smells and sights and sounds of earliest infancy. Emotion is integrated, from first to last, by words. Feelings, as they filter through Stephen's sensory apparatus, become associated with phrases. His conditioned reflexes are literary. (p. 50)

In the critical terminology of Stephen Dedalus, *Ulysses* signalizes a shift from the personal to the epic; it leads the artist away from himself toward an exploration of the mind of the bourgeois. The form progresses, as Stephen has foretold, until the center of emotional gravity is equidistant between himself and the new hero, Mr. Bloom. . . .

Thus *Ulysses* puts the introspective *Portrait of the Artist* against the exterior background of *Dubliners*. It might be described as a desperate effort to reintroduce the artist to his native city. But it also endeavors to subject the citydweller to a process of artistic transfiguration. (p. 67)

The student who demands a philosophy from Joyce will be put off with an inarticulate noise and a skeptical shrug. . . . Association, not logic, is the motive power of Joyce's mentality; he plays with ideas as with words. (p. 74)

Joyce is a consummate master of the music of words, but he is also a master of "the music of ideas," the complex orchestration of associated images which symbolist poets have taught us to appreciate. His innovation is to harmonize the two modes. Now, when you bring discordant sounds and associations together, you have created a pun. If the associations remain irrelevant, it is a bad pun; if they show an unlooked-for relevance, it is better; if the relevant associations are rich enough, it is poetry. The Elizabethans regarded this as a legitimate rhetorical resource. The Victorians degraded it into a parlor trick. Joyce has rehabilitated the pun for literary purposes. (p. 185)

Joyce's books, he was proud to admit, are devoted to the destinies of members of the lower middle class—to the economic decline of the Dedalus family, to Bloom's future on the dole, to Earwicker's bankruptcy.

As his subject-matter reveals the decomposition of the middle class, Joyce's technique passes beyond the limits of realistic fiction. Neither the *Portrait of the Artist* nor *Finnegans Wake* is a novel, strictly speaking, and *Ulysses* is a novel to end all novels. (p. 207)

> *Harry Levin, in his* James Joyce: A Critical Introduction *(copyright 1941, © 1960 by New Directions; all rights reserved; reprinted by permission of New Directions Publishing Corporation), revised edition, New Directions, 1960, 256 p.*

ROBERT MARTIN ADAMS   (essay date 1962)

With his vigorous sense of obscenity and filth [Joyce] combined a characteristically late-nineteenth-century worship of woman as the great redemptive force of modern life. Joyce found in sex a fearful and rapturous experience, the more dramatic because of all the taboos and cosmic rewards he grafted onto it. This combination of extreme attitudes on the subject of sex seems to me rather remote from any attitudes I recognize as wide-spread in the educated sixties. It is remote from healthy-minded "realism," from romantic promiscuity, or from the impersonal, empty mechanism which is the characteristic form of most modern literary sex. Joyce found in woman a doorway to heaven and/or hell; I think historical distance is making it easier to understand this view and less necessary to react for or against it.

Joyce's view of sex . . . is starting to be recognizable as a set of dramatic properties supplied by his social circumstances and personal temperament; much the same thing can be said of his politics, his "philosophy," his esthetics. I don't mean to sound condescending or triumphant here—as if at last, after all these years, we were starting to see around old Joyce. I mean only that, having been distracted all too long by questions about whether Joyce is bad or good for the young, or for Ireland, for the recognition of the truth, or the freedom of the psyche, we are finally coming to judge him as an artist, whose work is a structure of impressions. In building that structure, he came about as close to producing a durable scheme of philosophically impregnable positions as artists usually do. As a matter of fact, he had scruples all his life . . . about his own power to create impressions, and thought himself a forger and a fraud pre-

cisely by virtue of his art. That he was a verbal prestidigi-
tator is not the final truth about Joyce. . . . But it is a real
and inevitable part of the Joyce of the sixties, that the
things he was able to hang people up on in the twenties—
like the theory of epiphany, the bit about Dedalus the maze-
maker, and the great Earth-mother image—are starting to
look a little threadbare. This fact, which inevitably involves
loss as well as gain, still frees us to recognize some interesting things about his art. (pp. 508-09)

When one says that Joyce enriched the speech of English
fiction, there is a natural tendency to think of the various
taboos he violated, the various censorships he knocked
down. The matter is more considerable than this. One has
only to look at the first chapter of *Ulysses,* less than twenty
pages of prose, to sense the dramatic richness, flexibility,
and complexity of the language. The scene moves with elegance and under its own power; the hand of the novelist
does not have to tug it along. Symbols are pervasive, vivid
yet undemanding. The tonality of the chapter is sunlit, yet
under the surface one senses the sulky, resentful power of
Stephen's mind, cuddling its enmity. A complex of energies
is effortlessly set moving in these pages; the economy of
means and richness of achievement mark a genuine imaginative achievement. In the diction of a passage like this,
Joyce worked to standards of subtlety, economy, and exactness by which English novels will be measured for years
to come; his ability to do so was quite independent of technical innovations—stream of consciousness, mythic parallels, multilingual puns, and so forth. (p. 510)

I think we must look for [Joyce] in the figure of a visionary
vulgarist, a man whose extraordinary view of life grew out
of a defeat for, and disillusion with, the conscious, rational
mind. . . . Having tied itself in tighter and tighter knots
throughout [*Ulysses*] rationality blacks out altogether, and
the book culminates, not with the achievement of a symbolic pattern, but with the absorption of all thought in the
endless spinning motion of the blindly appetitive life-force.
Common as dirt, majestic, luminous, and all-embracing, the
sensual life of Molly Bloom is, imaginatively, the beginning
and end of us all. From the dark of "Penelope," Joyce
passed to the deeper darkness of *Finnegans Wake,* and
found there such rewards as, after rationality is defeated,
remain to a great artist—a religion of man which he could
scarcely formulate without deriding it; occult and pantheist
notions which he took only half-seriously; a kind of know-
nothing indifference to all ideas and causes . . . ; an immense and intricate structure of history which he borrowed
from Vico as a frame to hang his artistic patterns on;
language-games, macaronic puns, and lists. These materials
are contemptible neither in themselves nor as the elements
of great art . . . ; but their very nature is evidence of the
fact that Joyce in the last years of his life surrendered structural control over his materials to certain sorts of accident.
(pp. 513-14)

In [*Finnegans Wake*], Joyce has successfully performed the
reduction of the arts to philology, and so far as is possible
re-enacted the creation of the cosmos (a new and private
cosmos) within the proscenium of his peculiar gift. That he
was able to do this using only the junk and litter of the original cosmos is a splendid achievement; but its splendor
need not blind us to its perversity, and its perversity cannot
be judged independently of the age to which it is a response. (p. 517)

What Joyce saw (and it is an inevitable part of my argument
that he saw truly) was an age of bind and smudge; of consciousness and above all of self-consciousness almost infinite in extent but foggy and unformulated in its topography.
A peculiarity of modern feeling, as evident in Franz Kafka
and Jackson Pollock as in *Finnegans Wake,* is loss of horizon, obliteration of perspective. . . . Joyce did not seek or
make a desolation, he found it as in the air we breathe, and
extracted from it the juice of a small and flickering joy. He
is not the greatest modern ironist, he is the only great
modern humorist.

One last speculation. The less we see Joyce's work as an
intricate, logically arranged machinery of glittering, sterile
edges, and the more we emphasize the commonness of his
materials, the more we are likely to think his art itself a
work of magic—one which touches, through intuitive insight, the chords of secret, irrational sympathies. These are
not fashionable concepts in modern criticism, any more
than in modern psychology; but modern criticism and psychology may well be obsolete before *Ulysses* is. (pp. 517-
18)

> Robert Martin Adams, "The Bent Knife Blade:
> Joyce in the 1960's," in Partisan Review (copy-
> right © 1962 by Partisan Review, Inc.), Vol.
> XXIX, No. 4, Fall, 1962, pp. 507-18.

J. I. M. STEWART (essay date 1963)

[*Dubliners*] is a little manifesto of naturalism; but its most
significant phrase is 'moral history'. . . . It is urged upon us
that almost every aspect of Dublin life is horrifying or pitiful or degraded; that everything is nasty and that nothing
nice gets a square deal; and that to the effective asserting of
this the artist must bend all his cunning. Joyce will allow no
half-measures. His book is about paralysis . . . and paralysis is uncompromisingly asserted as something to make
the flesh creep. Each one of the stories cries out against the
frustration and squalor of the priest-ridden, pub-besotted,
culturally decomposing urban lower-middle-class living it
depicts. . . . (pp. 431-32)

[Everywhere] the description and evocation have a precision and economy and sensitiveness which constitute the
substance of the book's style just as the 'scrupulous meanness' constitutes its ironic surface. For the method is essentially ironic. The meanness of language has an air of accepting and taking for granted the meanness of what is
described. It is contrived to expose what it affects to en-
dorse. (p. 433)

It is in the last and longest story in *Dubliners*, 'The Dead',
that Joyce's stature as a writer first declares itself unmistakably. . . . The story mingles naturalism and symbolism
with a new confidence and richness. Tragic ironies play
across it subtly and economically. Its parts are propor-
tioned to each other strangely but with a brilliant effectiveness. And if its artistry looks forward to a great deal in
Joyce's subsequent writing, its charity and compassion are
qualities to which he was never to allow so free a play
again. (pp. 434-35)

The opening of the *Portrait* at once announces a drastic
change of method. The whole effort of *Stephen Hero* had
been towards objectivity. Now our knowledge of Stephen is
going to come to us in terms of the shifting play of his immediate consciousness. That consciousness is to be the

theatre of whatever drama the book attempts to present, and at the same time a territory sufficiently broad for the exercise of the vigorous naturalism which Joyce has been learning from continental masters. Yet with a quite bare naturalism he is no longer to be content. (pp. 442-43)

[The] technique of weaving elusive symbolic themes percurrently through the fabric of his writing is something that Joyce is to exploit more and more, and indeed nobody is likely to follow his work to the end who does not find something congenial in a progressive cryptographic idiosyncrasy. (p. 443)

[*A Portrait of the Artist as a Young Man*] is as much a landmark in English fiction as is *Joseph Andrews* or *Middlemarch* or *The Way of All Flesh*. . . . We have only to think of that fiction's line of representative young men—Roderick Random, Tom Jones, David Copperfield, Arthur Pendennis, Richard Feverel—to realize that Stephen Dedalus . . . is presented to us with a hitherto unexampled intimacy. It is true that Smollett, Fielding, Dickens, Thackeray, and Meredith would probably consider this to have been achieved at some cost to the vitality of Joyce's novel as a whole. Here, as later in parts of *Ulysses,* we are locked up firmly inside Stephen's head, and there are times when we feel like shouting to be let out. Stephen is aware of other people only as they affect his own interior chemistry, so there is something shadowy—as there was not in *Stephen Hero*—about the subsidiary personages in the book. But the picture is always clear and hard in its exhibition of Stephen's successive predicaments. (pp. 444-45)

The book's essential character can be partly analysed in terms of what Joyce preserves, and what abandons, of his earlier method as evidenced in *Stephen Hero*. What he most notably preserves is the refusal to compose or stage-manage his episodes in the interest of conventional construction. . . . What Joyce chiefly abandons in the *Portrait* is that flat and frugal prose, almost artless in itself, out of which he had evolved the highly expressive 'scrupulous meanness' of *Dubliners*. The style of the *Portrait* is rich and resourceful and varied. Vocabulary, syntax, rhythm are so disposed as to accentuate the contours of the underlying emotion. Joyce is beginning to deploy his reserves as a master of imitative form, although his experiments are still all within the received limits of English usage. (pp. 445-46)

When we come to *Ulysses* we shall find a book which, considered in point of style, is virtually a museum, displaying as in a series of show-cases all the old ways of using English and a great many new ones as well. In the *Portrait* there is a diversity of styles pointing forward to this—but at the same time an overriding impression of unity, since each of the styles reflects one facet of Stephen, who is a highly unified creation. (p. 446)

But there is yet another Stephen in the book—the Stephen who ceaselessly communes with himself on solitary walks about Dublin. It is here that the complexity of what Joyce attempts makes the success of the *Portrait* tremble in the balance. There are always two lights at play on Stephen. In the one he is seen as veritably possessing the sanctity and strength he claims—for he has been set aside, not of his own will, to serve an exalted and impersonal purpose. In the other he is only the eldest of Simon Dedalus's neglected children. . . . In the one light he is an artist. In the other he is an adolescent; subject to emotions which may be comi-

cally in excess of their specific precipitating occasions, and to express which he must reach out for maudlin tags, conventional postures, phrases and cadences caught up out of books. It is because he must be seen as thus hovering agonizingly between sublimity and absurdity, hysteria and inspiration, that he is regularly represented in his solitude as outrageously sentimentalizing himself, and as prone to clothe his poignantly felt nakedness in the faded splendours of a bygone poetic rhetoric. To treat even a single sentence of this as a mere indulgence in fine writing on the author's part is entirely to underestimate the art of the book. . . . (pp. 447-48)

[*Ulysses*] begins as if it were a continuation of the *Portrait,* with the thread taken up after the hero's brief absence from Ireland. . . . Unfortunately Stephen as an imaginative creation has been pretty well exhausted before *Ulysses* begins. (p. 451)

Bloom has been written off as a walking cliché, an orthodox comic figure of the simplest outline presented with a vast technical elaboration. It is certainly true that his lifelikeness seems not to proceed from his being very directly observed from the life. He is a highly evolved literary creation. His complexity—for he is complex—is literary. Some aspects of him exist only because a body of Anglo-Irish humour existed; others, only because *Bouvard et Pécuchet* existed. His most important line of derivation is from the mock-heroic tradition. Here is the reason for its being not quite true to say that the *Odyssey* provided Joyce merely with a scaffolding which a reader may disregard. The Homeric correspondences never go deep, but they are regularly exploited to point Bloom's insignificance and ignobility. They are also capable, as in the best mock-heroic, of working the other way, so that Bloom's positive qualities, his representative character, his pathos, all take emphasis from his original. This is one aspect of the elaborate and considered craft with which he is undoubtedly presented to us. Another is to be found in the immense resource and cunning with which the technique of internal monologue, however derived, is developed in his interest. (pp. 452-53)

Ulysses is quite staggeringly full of language. The stuff comes at us in great rollers, breakers, eddies and tumbles of spume and spray. It is exhilarating. It is also rather buffeting, bruising, exhausting long before the end.

What chiefly stands out from this powerful and battering sea of words, what saves it from mere flux, is the steep bold contrast between the content and movement of Stephen's mind and the content and movement of Bloom's. The speculative intellect is ceaselessly at work in Stephen, the practical intellect in Bloom. Stephen's mind hovers, swoops, soars, tumbles in cloud. Bloom's scurries alertly here and there in endless short proliferations. . . . What is new in Joyce's art here is not so much the technique of internal monologue in itself as its development in the direction of a muted drama which culminates when these two minds finally meet in mutual incomprehension and obscure need. (pp. 455-56)

[In *Finnegans Wake* Joyce] is actively imposing upon *language* those sorts of condensation, displacement, and distortion which the mechanisms of dream constantly impose upon *visual images*—impose upon these, we are told, by way of expressing, evading, solving, disguising conflicts. (p. 469)

[However] its pages everywhere suggest degenerative processes at work in the mind which has produced them. Certain of Joyce's specific talents are exhibited in hypertrophy, while much that normally evidences intellectual and imaginative power in an artist has disappeared. What remains constant amid this pervasive shifting of mental balance is an unconquerable comic energy.

The more seriously we take *Finnegans Wake* the more depressing, even saddening, does it appear. In this aspect it is very evidently the work of the man who on being asked 'What do you think of the next life?' replied 'I don't think much of this one'. Correspondingly, the more emphasis we set on the *Wake's* ebullient humour, the better the terms on which we shall get with it, and the less shall we be aware of the large surrounding sterilities and atrophies in which Stephen Dedalus is ending. Here is a great comic work which has gone badly wrong. (p. 481)

It is chiefly when the *vis comica* is at work that we feel Joyce as still an imaginative writer of unimpaired vigour. The section commonly known as Shem the Penman is perhaps the best exemplification of this. Its linguistic texture, while fully representative of Joyce's utmost, his terminal ingenuity, is sufficiently transpicuous to afford a reasonable view of the goings-on behind it. And these—in a common phrase here to be used with entire accuracy—are painfully funny. Joyce's scornful and jeering representation of himself makes a wonderful comic turn. At the same time it is the work of a man who has lived too much alone with his own daemon. Nothing Joyce wrote comes closer to a cry of pain. (p. 483)

> *J.I.M. Stewart, "Joyce," in his* Eight Modern Writers, *(© Oxford University Press 1963; reprinted by permission of Oxford University Press), Oxford University Press, Oxford, 1963, pp. 422-83.*

ELIZABETH DREW   (essay date 1963)

The Dedalus symbol [as used in *A Portrait of the Artist as a Young Man*] is rich and many-faceted. Dedalus is a rebel escaping from the labyrinths and nets of authority; he escapes through his own ingenuity; he is maker, artificer. He escapes by flight, in a double sense—in the meaning of "liberation" and of "soaring above." The wings on which he rises are those of the maker, fashioned from "the sluggish matter of the earth" which appears to hold him down. The wings belong to the sense world, though through them the sense world is transcended, and becomes "a new soaring impalpable imperishable being."

These elements in the symbol are all paralleled in Stephen's story. He has to rebel from the actualities of contemporary Ireland; the captivity of family, nationality and religion. . . . Stephen creates his "wings," as it were, in two ways. On the personal level his intellectual and emotional development fit him finally to assert his own freedom by leaving Ireland; as future artist, he is learning all the time to use *language*, his medium of ingenuity. The new "being" which he finally does create is the book itself, completed ten years after the last events it describes. (p. 251)

It is difficult to know just what Joyce means us to think of Stephen in [the last] chapter. He completed the book when he was a mature man of thirty-two, yet there is little to suggest that he does not regard the priggish and egocentric Stephen with full approval. No doubt by the time he was

writing the end of the book, he had *Ulysses* in mind, and knew that Stephen's next appearance would reveal the emptiness of his prideful self-complacency, and that there he would appear as Icarus, "sea-bedabbled, fallen, weltering." But this final chapter gives no hint of that double vision . . . by which maturity can create youth in all its rawness and yet suggest a further adult standard of judgment. Stephen emerges as a most unattractive figure. . . .

Yet perhaps Joyce's intention may be to suggest that these unpleasant, self-centered qualities in his young self are what made it *possible* for him to take the necessary step toward exile. (p. 255)

The Portrait is, however, so far as I know, the first novel which is enclosed in a sustained symbolic pattern. Recurrent imagery is a feature of the writing of Hawthorne, of Henry James, of Conrad and D. H. Lawrence, but Joyce extends this to pattern the whole theme on the Dedalus myth, and to create its form into a series of "flights" and failures. At the same time he avoids making the outline in any way abstract. The symbolic theme is absorbed into biographical narrative, which includes abrupt transitions from description to dialogue to reverie to diary. In this way Stephen's outer and inner life are presented simultaneously, and we are kept vividly in the immediate, concrete, realistic present, while we watch the growth of inner consciousness and thought processes. Though the story is told in the third person, the author never interrupts with comments of his own, which distinguishes the Joycean method from that of any earlier novelist, even Henry James.

This objective mingling of outer and inner consciousness, especially the revelation of the inner *through* the outer, is the most outstanding feature of Joyce's writing. (p. 258)

> *Elizabeth Drew, "James Joyce: 'A Portrait of the Artist as a Young Man'," in her* The Novel: A Modern Guide to Fifteen English Masterpieces *(© copyright 1963 by Elizabeth Drew; reprinted by permission of Dell Publishing Co., Inc.), Dell, 1963, pp. 245-61.*

CYRIL CONNOLLY   (essay date 1963)

I cannot feel absolutely sure of [Joyce's] greatness, as once I did, because I am now less tolerant of his faults. I feel that so much of *Finnegans Wake* and of *Ulysses*, even when the obscurity has been penetrated, is fundamentally uninteresting that there must be some failure of conception or execution or both, and I think it perhaps springs from Joyce's absolute refusal to let himself mature through the spiritual struggles and intellectual discoveries of his time.

His life is one of the saddest and one of the emptiest except in so far as it was filled by the joys of artistic creation. For he rejected everything—he ignored the war of 1914 and displaced himself from Trieste to Zurich, he ignored the last war and again displaced himself from Paris to Zurich, he ignored the Irish Republic which he had called for in his youth, he ignored Fascism, anti-Fascism and Communism, he despised psychoanalysis, he hated painting, took no interest in architecture or travel or objects, . . . and seems equally immune to modern poetry and literature. His clock had stopped on Bloomsday (June 16th, 1904). (p. 278)

I am not criticizing Joyce from a journalistic or Marxist point of view but I am trying to suggest that he fed his queen bee of a mind with inferior jelly and that from such subject-matter it could not produce the sublime or even the comic effects which were intended. He asks too much of his ideal reader. . . . Perhaps I am the only person to find the plans and keys and clues and commentaries on Joyce's books more exhilarating than the originals. (pp. 278-79)

> Cyril Connolly. "James Joyce: 3," in his Previous Convictions, Hamish Hamilton Ltd., 1963, pp. 277-81.

STEPHEN SPENDER   (essay date 1963)

[James Joyce is often confused with] 'experimentalists'. But although in the long run the tendency of his work was to produce a purely literary language, his aims were as different as possible from theirs, and the difficulties his work offers are of an entirely different kind. The difference between Joyce and Gertrude Stein—with whom he particularly hated to have his work associated—can be summed up by saying that her tendency was to produce a non-language; his tendency was to produce a literary language, extremely difficult to comprehend because it was packed with meanings, the clues to which are almost inaccessible. (pp. 192-93)

The ideal reader of *Finnegans Wake* (a figure whom Joyce had constantly in mind) should be equipped with knowledge including all the referents—languages, places, history, autobiography—to which the work refers. Given all this, he would find *Finnegans Wake* by no means impenetrable. It would appear to him a complex, difficult, translucent and paraphrasable work, as capable of ultimate extensive elucidation as *The Divine Comedy*. Joyce will continue to challenge critics not because he invented an opaque new language but because he combined the available resources of several languages, and of immense learning, and idiosyncrasies of special information, into a whole which, though ultimately transparent, is very difficult to elucidate. The difficulties he presents are of immense complexities of meaning whereas the difficulties of Gertrude Stein's work are of brutish simplicities of meaninglessness.

I think then that the tendency of Joyce is to invent not a language tending to turn writing into music so much as a literary language comprehensible only to specialists. (p. 193)

The Joycean obscurity is the result of the writer [like other moderns] treating his work as a form of specialization. The formula is only communicable to the ideal reader who has devoted his whole life to understanding it, and yet it is about the world which concerns all men, and it may, in its results, shake the world. This means that the language, however much it may exploit current idiom, does so in an esoteric way intelligible only to the most devoted readers. (p. 196)

> Stephen Spender, in his The Struggle of the Modern (copyright © 1963 by Stephen Spender; reprinted by permission of the University of California; in Canada by A D Peters & Co Ltd), University of California Press, 1963, 266 p.

HELMUT BONHEIM   (essay date 1964)

Joyce rebelled against those systems of civilized life—family, church, state, an language—to which most men attach themselves. Yet he too was attached, morbidly attached, to the institutions that obsessed him. (p. 1)

Even in *Portrait of the Artist,* conventionally read as the incarnation of Luciferian naysaying, rebelliousness is an adolescent attribute of its adolescent hero. The young artist's reaction to his seeming oppressors is not merely negative. He seeks attitudes and people, perhaps even institutions, with which he can live, which he can accept. Similarly, one glance at Bloom's and Molly's soliloquies reveals that *Ulysses,* enshrined for a time as the work of a nihilistic rebel, contains characters that positively glitter with Joyce's interest and concern for man, as everyday lives portrayed in literature rarely have. We do not need Molly Bloom's Yes, Yes, to decide that *Ulysses* is not the work of a man psychotically devoted to the principle of opposition. *Finnegans Wake,* too, sparkles with a positive Bloomlike fascination with the world, from stones to stars. . . . (pp. 2-3)

Nevertheless, the flavor of the unconventional views—of the underdog, the anti-authoritarian, and the rebel—effectively pervades every major work that Joyce concocted over a span of almost forty years. (p. 4)

Nonconformity comes to feel comfortable after a while and always yields interesting results, in manner as well as in matter. Iconoclasm is a parasitic mode eternally nourishing. We see its influence not only in the style of the later works. In the other books, too, individualism as a psychological orientation has its political counterpart in anarchy, its religious counterpart in blasphemy and heresy, its aesthetic counterpart in experiment, obscurity, originality. (p. 13)

Joyce is an author of whom it seems particularly reasonable to say that a discussion of his styles is more appropriate to an assessment of what he achieved than is a critique of his ideas. Joyce's manner glitters more than does his matter; the style is more distinctive than the politics. And therefore at first glance his manner is also more important than his thought; it is certainly less derivative and more distinctly *his* contribution. . . . [But] Joyce is not only a literary technician. More likely, matter and manner stand in some vital relation to one another. . . . (p. 14)

Joyce's style is indeed admirably suited to his central theorem: that the more positive and creative aspects of a civilization are developed by those who, by fighting against society as it is, fight for it, by those who envision the future as substantially different from the present. (p. 15)

[The] restless virtuosity of Joyce's styles probably indicates the heterodox thought of their creator, and that the comic effects suggest an artist-comedian who considers himself a little removed and superior to the cosmic circus erected in his work. (p. 16)

As his work grew more difficult, it also became more original, and as it grew more original, it grew more comic. What I am suggesting is that the increasingly complicated nature of Joyce's work is understandable if we view him as a great comic writer, for the difficulties we encounter in Joyce are of the same kind as those displayed by other great comic writers, although different in degree. Comedy has often tended to present difficulties to the reader, to pile up paradox on paradox, as in Rabelais and Shakespeare and Sterne. . . . And often the more paradoxical and multilayered the statement, the funnier it is. (pp. 132-33)

[Of the] works of fiction Joyce wrote, *Dubliners* is the most negative. The "cracked looking-glass" of these stories reflects the miasma only, not the way out, and what comedy the book contains is painful and unconstructive. In *A Portrait* some alternatives are mirrored as well. Religious renunciation of one-upmanship takes over from the ideal of worldly success. If at first you don't succeed, Joyce is saying here, give up the game and say that henceforth you will be one up on yourself rather than on other people, which sounds noble enough. But later the bird-girl epiphany on the beach converts Stephen to a more complex sort of renunciation. (p. 137)

He resolves on a renunciation of authority in general, and more particularly, of community, family, perhaps of love itself. . . . The esthetic ideal is that of the secular saint, whose goal is dissociation, the goal Buddhists recognize as a purification of the self, a goal called "dying to the world" in Christian mysticism. (pp. 137-38)

The new modus vivendi we see explored in *A Portrait* and in *Ulysses* assumes that the old rules are rubbish. Simply to pronounce them in a certain way is to make your audience laugh. If any ambition is to be valued, it is to dissociate from the authority of inconvenient superstitions, such as the abject acceptance of external discipline, and to turn to the pleasures of excelling in the more personal and individual disciplines of art and liberty, in which it is difficult to succeed, but easy to be one up. The artist, at least in his own head, gets at arm's length from the world and learns to laugh at it, at the same time that he still takes part in the picnic. Thus Joyce, in the process of detachment, developed a stance of amused attachment which never left him. So we cannot claim either that Joyce simply rejected or simply accepted his world. His reaction is more complex than that of either acceptance or rejection; it is rather a comic ambivalence which thrives on a juxtaposition of opposites, on a tension which may not be resolved. (p. 138)

> *Helmut Bonheim, in his* Joyce's Benefictions *(copyright © 1964 by The Regents of the University of California; reprinted by permission of the University of California Press), University of California Press, 1964, 144 p.*

EARL JOHN CLARK   (essay date 1968)

[*Exiles* presents] a microcosm of the rebel who finally knows that no man, whatever his qualifications and zeal, can set himself against spiritual, social, and moral values and hope to succeed or even persist without paying a frightful price in terms of the spirit. . . .

Neither the artist nor any one else *can* wholly separate himself from his background; *that* is the solution, albeit a negative answer, to the "problem" the play poses. Richard Rowan is defeated in his attempt. He rather despairingly turns to love and parenthood as one who begins to realize the great force the relationships of man to wife and child have. As Richard could not accomplish the break with tradition and convention, neither could his creator. . . . Joyce's background of strong Catholicism . . . ingrained in [him] a grasp of fundamental attitudes that no amount of denial could wholly escape the ethical teaching of the Catholic Church and Joyce's knowledge of that failure which makes him blasphemous in some of his work. It almost seems as if he were determined to expel traditional beliefs and attitudes by the force of his denials. (p. 75)

In general critics of Joyce regrettably have not examined *Exiles* as a reflection of Joyce himself and have tended to ignore or subordinate it as a commentary on Joyce's biog-

raphy. But *Exiles* gives to the careful reader a deep insight into the problem of Joyce's philosophy, providing an answer to the fact of his long exile more meaningful than any verbiage about the nature of the artist and his need for seclusion. Joyce was in a terrible position. His personality was such that it was repulsed by the teaching of his mother and the Jesuits, but he was unable to extricate himself completely from their influences. Thus his life was a series of paradoxes, which makes of Joyce a figure of tragic interest. His self-imposed exile takes on greater meaning, for in his flight he sought escape from his background and in a sense, from himself. But escape was a sham, a facade. Deep down he was a turmoil of doubts and confusions painted so movingly in the character of Richard Rowan. A return to Ireland and the seat of his tradition brought Rowan's ideational collapse. A similar return by Joyce had to be avoided—and was avoided. . . . Joyce fled Dublin to flee reality and himself. His failure to do so is the story of *Exiles,* a play of great importance as a testimony of the futile quest of its creator. (pp. 77-8)

> *Earl John Clark, "James Joyce's 'Exiles'," in* James Joyce Quarterly, *(copyright, 1968 The University of Tulsa), Vol. 6, No. 1, Fall, 1968, pp. 69-78.*

PATRICIA TOBIN   (essay date 1973)

[*A Portrait of the Artist as a Young Man*] represents the triumph of design: the appropriation of a significant form to embody the feeling of life. It fully satisfies the novel's demands for a coherent narrative structure comprised of a firm sequence of events, both probable and symbolical, which terminate in a climax that confirms the work as a harmonious whole. At the opposite pole, *Stephen Hero,* through its dramatization of the truth that life is a process never at any moment determined or fulfilled, negates the novelistic ideal to affirm the autobiographical: the narration of a life in the world, as that world is encountered by an autobiographical hero too enmeshed in it to make any coherent sense, much less symbolic design, out of its complexities. The great length of the *Hero* manuscript—383 existing pages out of a total of 901—may indicate Joyce's sense of the obligation "to get it all in". . . . (p. 190)

The commanding position within the title of "Portrait" . . . arouses the apprehension of the reader [expecting] autobiography. A portrait is a static product, finished and timeless; whatever it may exhibit of wholeness, harmony, and radiance as an object of art, it lacks the temporal extension within which the dynamic process of becoming must operate. Not only are the temporal rhythms in bondage in *Portrait,* but life's spatial perimeters are also drastically delimited. We know without a doubt what Stephen is *against* in his world, but we do not perceive clearly the world he is *in.* Stephen sits alone for Joyce's *Portrait:* family, priests, and friends merely hover in the shadows outside this one sharp focus. (p. 194)

Autobiography does not celebrate images of permanence, but records the flux of becoming. Freed of the symbolic burden of "artist" and the onerous finality of "adult," Stephen in *Hero* may be presented in the many metamorphoses of the role-playing adolescent who somehow muddles through to a positive identity. Without having acquired the tools and discipline of the mature artist, Stephen nevertheless poses before his peers as the solitary artist/hero;

and while strenuously advocating an aesthetic theory based on emotional stasis, he lives a reality invaded by the most kinetic desire and loathing. This struggle between the outer poise and the inner uncertainty confirms the psychological verities of adolescence, while the vivid scenes of Stephen's encounters with the people of his world render his final withdrawal from them fully credible. (pp. 194-95)

Although Stephen's attempts to extricate himself from a hostile environment evoke the narrator's irony in both books, only the earlier work fully dramatizes the world that entangles Stephen before he rejects it. Nowhere in *Portrait* appear Stephen's dying sister Isabel and his admiring younger brother Maurice or the mother whom he engages in long, frustrating discussions of religion and literature. Emma Clery, who exists in *Portrait* as a sexual object tantalizing Stephen into furious libidinal activity, has six scenes with him in *Hero,* scenes which convey not only the helplessness of the adolescent intellectual before stupid beauty, but also her own dismay at his frantic persistence. Stephen's classmates, characterized by epithet and presented as mere satellites in *Portrait,* are here wholly revealed in their laughter and seriousness. . . .

Beyond the great quantity of content which has been omitted from *Portrait* is a quality that is also missing: "the sense of felt life". . . . One senses that Joyce no longer *feels* what he has rejected. *Stephen Hero,* on the contrary, shows Joyce as sensitive to what Stephen was rejecting as he was insistent upon the act of rejection itself. (p. 196)

A Portrait of the Artist as a Young Man is a better novel for our recognition of the life realities within it—realities, however, which are subordinated to the novelistic values of impersonality, economy, symbolism, and style. Nor is the absence of these values in the earlier work a diminution, for it allows a minimal distraction from the real business of autobiography, which *Stephen Hero* conducts on such a grand and lively scale. The Joyce of 1904 was much less an artistic Jesuit than the Joyce of 1914, and *Stephen Hero* remains his sole testimony to the full humanity that he later submitted to the uses of art. (p. 201)

> Patricia Tobin, "A Portrait of the Artist as Autobiographer: Joyce's 'Stephen Hero'," in Genre (copyright 1973 by Donald E. Billiar, Edward F. Heuston, and Robert L. Vales; reprinted by permission of the University of Oklahoma), Vol. VI, No. 2, June, 1973, pp. 189-201.

ARNOLD L. WEINSTEIN (essay date 1974)

It has been said that all of [Joyce's] writings are supremely autobiographical, but never have the events and details of a life been so converted into the *materials* of literature, the necessary names and faces and places with which to create a world. . . . [In] the last analysis, Joyce's world is both excruciatingly private (necessitating, ideally, a specialized knowledge of his own life and the topography of Dublin) and, paradoxically, entirely surface. The facts that he culls from his own life are never keys to meaning, but rather the elements of a mosaic. This is not to say that Joyce's interest in Ireland, or Stephen's resemblance to himself, are purely superficial; but the enduring dimension of his art, as appears in *Ulysses,* is the malleability of meanings, the manipulation of phenomena into willfully constructed patterns, the unending transformation of details from the realms of fact, thought, and sensation into an aesthetic entity. (p. 169)

[The point here] is whether the integrity of character and/or plot in *Ulysses* survives the masterly treatment Joyce accords them. To what extent is *Ulysses* finally about Bloom, Stephen, and Molly? Surely, we must recognize that the pressures of selection and economy that any "story" imposes on its author are mocked by Joyce, and the Homeric girdle hardly gives a shape to such an inchoate mass of details. Joyce's grid is so large that we are no longer able to say what should or should not be included. His is the true "slice of life," in contrast to the excessive cogency and deterministic pattern of Zola's work. (p. 170)

[In the first part of the novel] Stephen is rendered quite compositely, but the author's arranging hand is felt; above all one feels that these are components, building blocks, used now to depict Stephen but ultimately designed for duty elsewhere as well. The parts do not so much coalesce as they extend outward, betoken things to come, suggest that their propriety is in the overall scheme of things rather than in the domestic organization of Stephen Dedalus. Likewise, Bloom seems more a locus for seemingly random sensory and mental impulses than a defined person. Obviously Joyce doesn't believe in "defined" characters, but there is something voracious and almost faceless in Bloom's recording activities. (p. 172)

If we assume that life is amorphous, then all art cheats through arrangement and selection. My contention is that *Ulysses* cheats more than most works do, but—and this is quintessential—its pattern of selectivity is aesthetic rather than ethical. . . . Joyce, like Eliot and Pound, confronted a vast cultural breakdown and gave it form; unlike Eliot and Pound, Joyce was able to endow his mosaic with incredible human fullness in the portraits of Bloom, Stephen, and Molly. But they remain pieces of the mosaic, somehow lost and unauthoritative amid the bustle of thoughts and sensations they are transmitting. Not only is interaction absent (other than in purely formal terms, such as proximity or parallel or parallax), but the characters are astonishingly (and deviously) egocentric. Doubtless the stream-of-consciousness presentation itself . . . carries a considerable dosage of narcissism with it. Customarily Stephen alone is taxed for self-indulgence and alienation, while Bloom and Molly are celebrated for their openness to life. But is that the case? Bloom's incessant, quasiprogressive chatter (viciously and acutely criticized by the narrative voice of *Cyclops*) is genuinely alert and bubbly, but it is, in every sense, small talk. . . . Only in *Circe* do the repressed or obscured affective bases of Bloom's life come to the fore, but even there they seem to be part of a larger carnival. Such a creation is unquestionably "lifelike," but, before Joyce, he would have been *used* in some fashion (consider, for example, the dramatic use of Homais in *Madame Bovary*). Joyce is, of course, under no obligation to show Bloom in crisis (to show us, in some sense, what his mettle "really" is), but we are correspondingly unable to do much with him. (pp. 173-75)

Joyce made choices; he wrought magnificently, but there were losses too. Along with its achievements, *Ulysses* also registers a waste of human potential. . . . *Ulysses* is not niggardly; there is plenty of life there. But other views of human behavior are possible: Bloom might have seen in Stephen more than possible Italian lessons, in Molly more than a warm bed; Stephen might have felt more than fatigue in his association with Bloom; Molly might have claimed more than "spunk" for Poldy. Joyce might, without changing his view of human nature, have let them respond more to each other. (pp. 176-77)

[For example, the] penultimate chapter, *Ithaca*, with its impersonal, abstract, scientific, interrogatory style, gives us a final image of Bloom that is so distant that the threads of the story disappear in favor of an astronomical, zoological chart. The immensity of the stage, extending, like Pascal's famous dictum, to the infinite in both great and small, provides the narrative focus and effectively obliterates the thinking protagonist. . . . As writing, it is magnificent, filled with puns, alliteration, and great rhetorical effects. . . . But what is it doing? It nullifies the characters, calls into question its own metaphysical content by the weight of its style, effects (as does much of *Ulysses*) a rhetorical overkill. If we take such a framework seriously, individual gesture is inconceivable, for the generic alone prevails. Thus the story embodied in the Odysseus myth, of human trials, of wit and humor and cunning leading to survival and ultimate recognition and union, is transformed into graph. Stephen's "meeting" with Bloom is rendered as a virtual diagram. The discussion between the "father" and the "son" is not so much a failure of communication as a pretext for the real business at hand, the real order to be forged, the rhetorical and grammatical activity of the author. . . . (pp. 178-80)

[The] rhetorical possibilities of the language seem to usurp Joyce's interest as the book continues, and we see the phenomenon of literature shrugging off its subject matter in celebration of its own *modus vivendi*. The living pulse of *Ulysses* is its style, for the pressures and demands of plot and character have been superseded. The term "mosaic" has been used to indicate the strange single-dimensional nature of its texture. Nothing—the autobiographical details, the erudite allusions, the intense sensory and auditory and visual realism—commands authority by sole virtue of its meaning; all the components of the glittering surface, including the human ones, share in stylistic equality. (pp. 182-83)

The coherence of *Ulysses* derives from formal association. It is a world composed solely of building materials, each asserting equal claims, each used for its formal aptness. Joyce's encyclopedic mind delighted in bizarre comparisons and purely figural resemblances. His work frequently offers startling harmonies that are wholly created, but such aesthetic resolution is rarely in the service of human concerns. (p. 184)

For its fullness of character and place, for its flavor of felt experience, *Ulysses* probably has no match in the literature of our age. In formal prowess, nothing (other than *Finnegans Wake*) approaches its overwhelming autonomy, its existence as man-made universe. But—and Joyce typifies our dispossessed age in this—there is a chasm between those two achievements. Not only are the human and the formal dimensions separated, but, as I have tried to show, they are antagonistic and, ultimately, nullifying. (p. 190)

Arnold L. Weinstein, "Eclipse: Kafka, Joyce, and Michel Butor," in his Vision and Response in Modern Fiction *(copyright © 1974 by Cornell University; used by permission of the publisher, Cornell University Press), Cornell University Press, 1974, pp. 154-214.**

HOWARD NEMEROV (essay date 1975)

As far as I have got in [*Finnegans Wake*], I've had every feeling in the book: fascination and despair, pleasure, charm, bitter resentment, resistance to reading one inch farther; great admiration, terrible boredom, simple fury at frustration, childish delight at resolving this or that small trouble, and so on. . . .

Chiefly, though, I am amazed. The energy and geniality of the book are just amazing; there's nothing like it in literature, and comparisons . . . don't seem to mean much. It's a help, too, that so many places are so helplessly funny. . . .

Against that, I keep the sense I began with—that once you've got the idea, the stuff is a good deal easier to write than to read, and maybe even more fun as well. Of course, Joyce had the idea. But it's odd, all the same, that this way of using language never took any real hold among writers; it would seem a natural for people who keep complaining that the center will not hold . . . poets ought to have taken to it right off. . . . [But I guess that if] you disorganized your language in this way you would almost helplessly do so in the same dactylic and anapestic rhythms. Besides, a major point of the book is that there's only one dream; Joyce has dreamed it for us, and we shall have to wait till the end of days for the second coming and the redreamer. . . . (p. 653)

That the book should be so full of shit doesn't seem to be much of a bother, possibly because the leading thematic image of history as a dungheap, garbage midden, tumulus, barrow, and so on is so pleasantly what Kenneth Burke would call a comic corrective to those newspapery notions that confuse the sordid with tragedy. . . .

Similarly, it is ever so easy to acquire a glib familiarity with Viconian cycles, the coincidence of opposites, the reciprocity between death and resurrection; but when you have come to know such things you haven't come to know much more than a set of clichés that in one way and another have been the cant terms of world historians from Augustine to Spengler. (p. 654)

[But I should say] that *Finnegans Wake* is doing one of the things a masterpiece probably ought to do, which is to make me think some thoughts I had not thought before. This is not the same thing as "original thoughts," or "profound thoughts," or "thoughts beyond the reaches of our souls"; only things I had not thought before. . . .

[In] *Finnegans Wake* it is inescapable that language is a bodily thing, having to do somewhat intimately with thought, true, but always as thought by or through the medium of a bodily instrument that is spitting, sputtering, coughing, . . . and saying "um" between words. It is salutary, if humbling, to be made to consider how very many things we do with the voice other than, as we proudly say, "make sense." In this connection I note that Joyce's distortion of words is not always meant to secure a multiplicity of meanings; not infrequently it seems to reach out deliberately for the subhuman, and for the dissolution of meaning entirely for a moment. . . .

Moreover, because all this is happening in a dream there is a further inference to be drawn from the emphasis on the bodily nature of language: whatever the overt subject, with all its ambiguities, may be, the language is liable to be thinking, or enacting, the body's sleep at the same time— the sweatings, the pricklings, the rumbling in the bowels; and some of the most genial comedy of the book comes, too, from the circumstance that at all times the most learned language is but a step from a fart or a snore.

Now I may not think that this circumstance is always a blessing. And on the whole I am just as pleased that Joyce's method has not been widely adapted by novelists, for . . . when the Joycean language fails of genius, and it does even in the hands of genius—when it fails to be genial, it hits the abyss without interval; there's no middle way.

Still, I shall go on, though maybe only a little at a time. What a marvelous book! I even want to find out what happens over again next. And there's a wondrous helpful thing about reading a book you know you don't understand; it may teach you something about all those other books you thought you did. (p. 655)

> Howard Nemerov, "Thoughts on First Passing the Hundredth Page of 'Finnegans Wake'," in The American Scholar (reprinted by permission of the author), Vol. 44, No. 4, Autumn, 1975, pp. 653-55.

MARGOT NORRIS (essay date 1976)

Only by abandoning the novelistic approach to *Finnegans Wake* can readers free themselves from waking conventions and logic enough to enjoy the wholly imaginative reality of a dream-work. . . . By abandoning conventional frames of reference, readers can allow the work to disclose its own meanings, which are lodged in the differences and similarities of its multitudinous elements. (p. 22)

As the Daedalus myth governs *Portrait,* and the Odyssey *Ulysses,* so *Finnegans Wake* is founded on the involuted patterns of the Oedipus myth. Joyce had previously circumscribed the family in his fiction: Stephen's flight and Bloom's travels and return mark the stress of opposing forces that bind the individual uneasily to the home. *Finnegans Wake* explores the nature of the family itself, via a quest for the original sin. All oedipal concerns are plumbed in the process—the mystery of identity, of sexual and social origin, and of the nature of man's relationship to God. If *Portrait* may be called the book of the Son and *Ulysses* the book of the Father, then *Finnegans Wake* is surely the book of the Holy Spirit, the hypostatic bond that unites them.

The quest serves as both form and content in *Finnegans Wake,* as structural principle and theme. Wakean speakers are ever seeking something, asking questions, investigating a mystery, gossiping, or speculating about this and that. Yet these same postures of inquiry and argumentation, slander, and the like perversely reveal the very information that is sought. (p. 28)

A reference to the Oedipus myth helps to clarify the significance of this intricate fusion of form and content. Oedipus, in his quest for the murderer of Laius, seeks to close a discrepancy or gap that exists between what he knows and what he recognizes. He knows all the essential facts at the outset. . . . He has simply failed to put them together, to see their correspondence and thereby recognize himself as the murderer whom he seeks.

Such a discrepancy between knowledge and recognition also constitutes the quest in *Finnegans Wake.* The answers to various riddles in the *Wake,* for example, are invariably contained in the relationship of the figures among whom the riddle is posed. (pp. 28-9)

The search for the original sin leads inevitably to the heart of the family in the complex system of erotic and power relationships that bind the members into a primordially guilty union. . . . In *Finnegans Wake* the quest yields just such guilty sexual and aggressive involvements: father versus son/sons, brother versus brother, father and son competing for sister/mother, brothers competing for sister/mother, as well as homosexual possibilities involving father and sons.

Buried under this disgraceful welter of family loves and hates lies the identity of the individual in society. Insofar as the individual is defined as the locus of numerous familial relationships, the violation of the incest taboo and those laws that ensure the peaceful succession of the son jeopardize the certainty of identity. Oedipus's quest leads from questions of a specific crime and specific guilt to the ultimate question, "Who am I?" The shifting, uncertain nature of characters in *Finnegans Wake* has long been recognized and documented. . . . This pervasive cross-identification of characters, however, is more than simply the reduction of individuals to types. Since the various actions of *Finnegans Wake* precisely portray competition for coveted positions, notably the role of king, father, and subject, rather than object, the confusion of characters and the frequent inability to distinguish between father/son/brother result from the primal crossing of forbidden boundaries in the arena of those primal family relationships that produce identity. (pp. 29-30)

At the mythic heart of *Finnegans Wake* lies the model for all mythic designs—the human family. This family is Freud's oedipal family, a primal, law-governed unit in which the claims of society first impose themselves on the individual and are resisted in the interest of self-possession. (p. 41)

This family theme, which occurs throughout Joyce's works, consists of a series of oppositions in which the conflicting demands of the society and the individual are expressed. The Law is symbolically embodied in the father, actually in the name of the Father, as we shall see. The father's conferral of the birthright on his son preserves the hierarchy of authority that ensures the peaceful transition of the law through the generations. (p. 42)

The son's subordination to the father ensures not only the peaceful transmission of the law, but also the repression of incestuous impulses, which constitutes the primal law of the social order. . . . Just as the son's rebellion against the father disrupts the system of lawful descent, so incest disrupts the social structure by destroying the preordained order of lineages. This rudimentary outline of family function and structure suggests that the conflict between the individual and society resides in the opposition between lawful transference and exchange, and unlawful appropriation. . . .

In *Finnegans Wake* an early preoccupation of Joyce's merges with a mature one. His interest in the problems of selfhood and his later concern with Viconian social theory required a vehicle for the simultaneous expression of psychoanalytic and social processes. This need was aptly filled by the Oedipus myth. . . . In the Oedipus myth, private acts have public consequences, personal crimes become civic crimes, parricide is also regicide, and the quarrels between brothers-in-law threaten to result in civil war. (p. 43)

Civilization requires repression, and Joyce's earlier works explore the consequences of that repression in the spiritual paralysis of *Dubliners,* Stephen's artistic impotence in *Portrait,* and Bloom's sexual impotence in *Ulysses.* The first agency of repression is the family. . . . In the dream world of *Finnegans Wake* the family . . . engages in the gamut of antisocial activities, including war, seduction, kidnapping, murder, invasion, stealing, lying, slander, forgery, and hypocrisy. The teleology of their universe is freedom, and in the enduring struggle between the individual's anarchic psyche and the laws that make civilization possible, the psyche is momentarily triumphant only in the dream. (pp. 43-4)

While the family in *Finnegans Wake* is a complicated psychological constellation, it also serves as the paradigm of a primal social structure. . . . The investigation into the sin in Phoenix Park delves into life's most fundamental mysteries, the mystery of human origin, the mystery of sex fraught with the prohibited oedipal wishes. Yet while incest and parricide are crimes committed in the bosom of the family, they are of all crimes most worthy of public concern, since they strike at the very foundation of the social order. Oedipus's sins jeopardize society and must, therefore, be publicly tried and punished. HCE's family affairs, likewise, become the leaven of a veritable "hubbub . . .". (pp. 54-5)

The Wakean vision of a universe ever hurtling toward chaos is based on the theme of the fallen father. He is named rather than namer. He is uncertain of name and identity, unlocatable rather than a center that fixes, defines, and gives meaning to his cosmos. He is a lawbreaker rather than lawgiver. As head of the family, he is incestuous rather than the source of order in the relations of his lineage. (p. 61)

> *Margot Norris, in her* The Decentered Universe of "Finnegans Wake": A Structural Analysis *(copyright © 1974, 1976 by The Johns Hopkins University Press), The Johns Hopkins University Press, 1976, 151 p.*

BIBLIOGRAPHY

Bandler, Bernard, II. "Joyce's *Exiles.*" *Hound & Horn* VI, No. 2 (January-March 1933): 266-85.
    Study of *Exiles* concerned with the absence of God in the characters' world and the resulting epistemological quests.

Beebe, Maurice. "James Joyce: The Return from Exile." In his *Ivory Towers and Sacred Founts: The Artist as Hero in Fiction from Goethe to Joyce,* pp. 260-95. New York: New York University Press, 1964.
    Discussion of how Joyce converted his own life into a fictional archetype of the artist, Stephen Dedalus.

Beja, Morris. "James Joyce: The Bread of Everyday Life." In his *Epiphany in the Modern Novel,* pp. 71-111. Seattle: University of Washington Press, 1971.
    Study of the development of Joyce's theory of epiphany and of the various types of epiphanies used in his fiction.

Blackmur, R. P. "The Jew in Search of a Son: Joyce's *Ulysses.*" In his *Eleven Essays in the European Novel,* pp. 27-47. New York: Harcourt, Brace & World, 1964.
    Discusses the inaccessibility of the modern novel to the common reader, utilizing an exegesis of *Ulysses* to demonstrate the obstacles in the path of an uninformed reader.

Burgess, Anthony. *ReJoyce.* New York: W.W. Norton & Co., 1965, 272 p.
    An excellent study of Joyce, particularly valuable for its discussion of the development of Joyce's use of language.

Connolly, Thomas E., ed. *Joyce's "Portrait": Criticisms and Critiques.* New York: Appleton-Century-Crofts, 1962, 335 p.
    Very good retrospective of criticism on *Portrait* including among others, Geddes MacGregor on Joyce's artistic theory, Grant Redford on the novel's structure, and Irene Hendry Chayes on Joyce's use of epiphanies.

Eckley, Grace. "Shem Is a Sham but Shaun Is a Ham, or Samuraising the Twins in *Finnegans Wake.*" *Modern Fiction Studies* 20, No. 4 (Winter 1974-75): 469-81.
    Discussion of Joyce's characterization of the twins Shem and Shaun which disagrees with critical theories of a mergence of identity between the two characters.

Edel, Leon. "James Joyce and His New Work." *University of Toronto Quarterly* IX, No. 1 (October 1939): 68-81.
    Argues that Joyce's use of language in *Finnegans Wake* is so intricate that only Joyce himself can fully understand his own achievement.

Ellmann, Richard. *James Joyce.* New York: Oxford University Press, 1959, 842 p.
    Comprehensive biography of Joyce which has become the standard work on his life.

Givens, Seon, ed. *James Joyce: Two Decades of Criticism.* New York: Vanguard Press, 1963, 486 p.
    A retrospective of primary criticism on various aspects of Joyce's work including Hugh Kenner, Stuart Gilbert, and Edmund Wilson, among others.

Goldberg, S. L. *The Classical Temper: A Study of James Joyce's "Ulysses."* London: Chatto and Windus, 1961, 346 p.
    Discussion of Joyce's aesthetic theories, his use of irony, and his reliance upon classical models for the structure of *Ulysses.*

Halper, Nathan. *The Early James Joyce.* New York: Columbia University Press, 1973, 48 p.
    Good survey of Joyce's work through *Portrait.*

Hart, Clive, ed. *James Joyce's "Dubliners": Critical Essays.* New York: Viking Press, 1969, 183 p.
    Valuable collection in which an entire essay is devoted to each story in *Dubliners.*

Hayman, David. "Daedalian Imagery in *A Portrait of the Artist as a Young Man.*" In *Hereditas: Seven Essays on the Modern Experience of the Classical,* edited by Frederic Will, pp. 33-54. Austin: University of Texas Press, 1964.
    How the Daedalus symbol functions in *Portrait* and *Ulysses* and leads to Stephen's understanding of the labyrinthine nature of life.

Kaplan, Harold. "Stroom: The Universal Comedy of James Joyce." In his *The Passive Voice: An Approach to Modern Fiction,* pp. 43-91. Athens: Ohio University Press, 1966.
    How Joyce's comic vision of life informs *Ulysses.*

Levin, Richard, and Shattuck, Charles. "First Flight to Ithaca: A New Reading of Joyce's *Dubliners.*" *Accent* 4, No. 2 (Winter 1944): 75-99.
    Study which examines the thematic and structural resemblances of *Dubliners* to Homer's *Odyssey.*

Mercier, Vivian. "James Joyce and the Irish Tradition of Parody." In his *The Irish Comic Tradition,* pp. 210-36. Oxford: Clarendon Press, 1962.*
    How Joyce parodied epic literature, both Greek and Irish, to create his novels of modern anti-heroes.

Norris, Christopher. "Joyce's Returningties." *Books and Bookmen* 21, No. 5 (February 1976): 22-3.
    Argues that despite the reams of exegesis the value of *Finne-*

gans Wake is found in the sheer exuberance of Joyce's voice and the range of his comic genius.

Prescott, Joseph. *Exploring James Joyce.* Carbondale: Southern Illinois University Press, 1964, 182 p.

Essays discussing Joyce's characterizations, his use of allusion, his verbal facility, and stylistic techniques.

Raisor, Philip. "Grist for the Mill: James Joyce and the Naturalists." *Contemporary Literature* 15, No. 4 (Autumn 1974): 457-73.

Argues that a naturalistic appreciation for detail was as important a component of Joyce's style and vision of life as his classicist appreciation for the universals of human experience.

Senn, Fritz, ed. *New Light on Joyce from the Dublin Symposium.* Bloomington: Indiana University Press, 1972, 208 p.

Papers collected from an international symposium, including, among others, essays by Leslie Fiedler on the nature of Bloom and Darcy O'Brien on Joyce's conception of love.

Tindall, W[illiam] Y[ork]. "Dante and Mrs. Bloom." *Accent* IX, No. 2 (Spring 1951): 85-92.

Discusses the importance of allusions to Dante's *Divine Comedy* in *Ulysses.*

Tindall, William York. *A Reader's Guide to "Finnegans Wake."* New York: Farrar, Straus and Giroux, 1969, 339 p.

Introduction to *Finnegans Wake* that delineates arrangement, allusion, and meaning, often in a very obscure manner.

Alun Lewis

1915-1944

Welsh poet and short story writer.

Lewis's reputation is based on his war poetry, though several critics hold the short story to be his most natural and successful genre. Dylan Thomas named Alun Lewis, Wilfred Owen, and Edward Thomas as "three of the very finest ... of the poets who wrote in the two Great Wars of this century."

Lewis's happy childhood in a warm, close family seems to have taught him the value of human love, for his life and writings were marked by a deep compassion for people. The Welsh mining area where he grew up is the focal point of his early poems and stories. In addition his love for Gweno Ellis, his wife, a great comfort and inspiration in his life, is evidenced in several poems and letters.

Raiders' Dawn, his first book of poetry, marked him as a war poet. This work as well as the stories in *The Last Inspection* are filled with the isolation, frustration, and boredom of the soldier enlisted but not in active duty, the soldier who lived in the "shadow of the war." Lewis wrote from personal experience: he was stationed in England for two years before being sent to India in 1942. His post in India, which exposed him to the poverty and suffering of the Indian peasants, was both disturbing and enlarging. Several of the poems in *Ha! Ha! Among the Trumpets* were inspired by his experiences and observations in India. The most gripping of all his poetic themes was that of the tension between life and death. Lewis's own words best summarize his attitude: "Acceptance seems so spiritless, protest so vain. In between the two I live."

By all reports, Lewis was committed to his men, Welsh compatriots over whom he presided as officer, and he was, in turn, well loved by them. Shortly before his unit was to be removed to active duty, Lewis was offered a position away from the front. He refused, preferring to remain with his men until their command was finished. His subsequent death by accident while on patrol is still shrouded in mystery. The loss to Welsh letters of one with so much promise has been lamented by many critics.

PRINCIPAL WORKS

The Last Inspection   (short stories)   1942
Raiders' Dawn, and Other Poems   (poetry)   1942

Ha! Ha! Among the Trumpets: Poems in Transit   (poetry) 1945
Letters from India   (letters)   1946
In the Green Tree   (letters and short stories)   1948
Selected Poetry and Prose   (poetry and short stories) 1966

ROBERT GRAVES   (essay date 1944)

I was [Lewis's] friend only by correspondence, but from the start became aware of [his] power and knew that it lay in his poetic integrity. In 1941 while he was still stationed in England he wrote to me of the difficulty of reconciling his life as a poet with his life as a soldier, and on the difficulty too of knowing where he stood critically and philosophically in a world that was changing its coat so fast. However, he summed up: 'But at any rate I know where I stand in love'—and love is the orientation of every true poet. (pp. 7-8)

[When] he came to make a collection of his new poems—the ones in [*Ha! Ha! Among the Trumpets*]—he was undecided whether they came up to the standard of accomplishment he had set for them. . . . [He] asked me to read the manuscript and decide for him how much should be included and whether any re-writing was needed. In doubtful cases his wife Gweno was to have the casting vote.

It was an embarrassing charge, but guessing how he felt I accepted it. . . .

His answer to the suggestion I sent him makes a natural foreword to the book. (p. 8)

> Dear Robert,
> I've just sent off the bundle of fifty poems in typescript to England by sea mail, and I'm mentally sitting back and contemplating the bony carcase of the demolished fowl. To steady myself I've got your long list of comments and criticism and this is in the nature of an apology for one thing and another. (pp. 8-9)
>
> For both your purgative criticism and your general *fiat* I am more grateful than I can

say. . . . The degree to which a volume of poems should be autobiographical is always different for different people. For myself I can't claim as much hold on the universal as some poets and consider my poems as expressions of personal experience. (p. 9)

I live a certain rhythm which I'm becoming able to recognize. Periods of spiritual death, periods of neutrality, periods of a sickening normality and insane indifference to the real implications of the present, and then for a brief wonderful space, maybe every six weeks, a nervous and powerful ability moves upward in me. India and the army both tend to fortify and protract the negative and passive phase, and if I am suddenly excited and moved by something I have seen or felt, the excitement merely bounces on the hard unchanging surface like a rubber ball on asphalt. (pp. 9-10)

I've felt a number of things deeply out here; perhaps the jungle has moved me more deeply than anything else, the green wilderness where one has nothing but one's sense of direction and there is no alarm because there is the Sun and there is one's shadow and there is time. . . .

I've taken a sardonic title for the poems from *Job* 39. 'Ha! Ha! among the Trumpets'. You know the beautiful chapter. The liberty of the wild ass, the lovelessness of the ostrich, the intrepidity of the horse. These are the particulars. The infinite, of which I can never be sure, is God the Maker. (p. 10)

I hope, when this reaches you, that I'll be about it and about. . . . So long!
  ALUN. . . .

The 'So long' is the robustness in the core of sadness. The manifest meaning is a robustly casual good-bye; the concealed meaning is a sad comment on the years that he has spent in seeking and not finding, and still seeking. (p. 11)

> *Robert Graves, "Foreword" (1944), in* Ha! Ha! among the Trumpets: Poems in Transit *by Alun Lewis, George Allen & Unwin Ltd, 1945, pp. 7-11.*

A. L. ROWSE (essay date 1946)

Since I came to know [Alun Lewis's] work I have always regarded him as one of the two best poets to be produced by the war: both of them, alas, killed: such losses war brings to our state and literature. And yet one might say, with a sense of fatality, that each of them was chosen by the war: something in the genius of each of them responded to it, was elicited by it, so that they made something out of it by which they transcended the war and its accidents, even death. That was true of Sidney Keyes; it was no less true of Alun Lewis. (p. 9)

The paradox of [Lewis's] work is that it is both complete in itself and yet has promise of even greater things. I think these Letters [from India] show that. It is complete, a perfected art—in spite of the doubts that assailed him, as they assail all poets in the ardours and depressions of writing poetry; the dissatisfactions he felt and sometimes expressed are so much evidence of the standards he set himself.

What is the peculiar value of his poetry? What are its qualities, the source of its strength, the chances of its survival? Why do I rate it so high among all the poetry brought forth by the war? . . . [His poetry is good and strong because it is] so concrete and visual, the general reflection rises naturally out of the observation, out of the particular springs the universal. So much of what his contemporaries write is so cerebral; it is not (as they think) their strength, but their weakness. (pp. 11-12)

I believe that his Welsh roots, the Celtic character of his genius, were a safeguard: that loving observation of detail, the sense of line and pattern and phrase, the attachment to the particular, yet clothed with an imagination sensuous in itself, the brightness of vision with which the object is seen. Those qualities appear in all Celtic art: they are in the instinct of the Celt. (p. 12)

Time was the one thing he was not given; he had everything else: genius, love, happiness, faith in man. (p. 13)

On every page of these Letters we see what a good and conscientious officer he was, willing to do his best at his trade of soldiering, and what an innate and loving sympathy he had for every quirk of human nature, every variety of human being. . . .

Of his own inner struggle, the struggle of any such man caught in such a fatality and so aware of it, these Letters provide, along with his poems and stories and the poems of Keyes, the most direct statement and the most moving evidence I know. (p. 15)

The fruit of all this may be seen in his stories as in his poems; indeed I take his volume, *The Last Inspection and other Stories,* to be the finest to come out of the war, certainly that I know. There are three masterpieces in that book: "They Came," "The Wanderers," "Private Jones," besides much else that is authentic, convincing, true of the soldier's life, of the life of war-time. But it is not confined to that: "The Wanderers" is wholly outside of it and time, a portrait of gipsy life in caravan and country, realist and idyllic, passionate and sensuous, and always with that tenderness of his, seeing straight through to the other side of things. In its rich, dark poetry it is like a Courbet: a most interesting pointer to the future that was in him. His prose —one sees it in these Letters—has a Welsh luxuriance, a Celtic sensuousness: it would be hard to define that specifically, but I think it means a certain sensuousness of the imagination. (pp. 16-17)

Yet these Letters show how the exotic experience of the war and travel in the East was broadening his field of vision and power of reflection. . . . I believe that he had it in him to be a great novelist. He certainly had greatness in him: that moral quality—these Letters show it—such as Milton held it impossible for a great writer to be without. . . . Certainly he had the gifts for it: a deep masculinity of nature along with a sensitive understanding and sympathy for the nature of women: a somewhat rare combination in contemporary literature. It gives us some measure of what we have lost in him.

Of the specific Indian interest of these Letters I am unable to say anything, except what is obvious: how fascinated he was by the Indian scene, its contrasts and colours, its constant surprises, the deep and age-long sense of humanity in the peasant way of life. Here, as always, sympathy and purity of response were the keynotes of his attitude. That is why he is able to give us such vivid and moving transcriptions of things seen, with the spirit of them still fresh in them. In his descriptions of Indian life and landscape he speaks, no doubt, for many thousands of Englishmen, soldiers and others, who have had much the same experience —only he saw with the imagination of the poet, the instinctive understanding of the born novelist. (pp. 17-18)

[These letters have] a double interest, as a rare and fascinating revelation of the process of poetic and aesthetic creation, and as a portrait of a soldier's life. Not, it is true, of the soldier in action, but approaching action, drawing ever nearer and nearer, until the moment of action comes. (p. 19)

I see him in these Letters, as in his poems and stories, with his tart humour, the soldier's "cynicism." . . .

We see him in these Letters occupied more and more, as his term draws near, with the question, What is it that survives?

I never knew him, and yet after reading what he has left us, in his poems and stories, in these Letters especially, I feel that I know all that was essential to him as a man, am in touch with his spirit, all there is of any of us that survives. (p. 20)

A. L. Rowse, in his preface to Letters from India *by Alun Lewis, Cardiff Penmark Press Limited, 1946, pp. 9-20.*

GORDON SYMES (essay date 1947)

Before going overseas, Lewis's poetic development had been taking the pathetically familiar course of nearly all our war-poets: the marking-time and interim speculations of an imagination acutely aware of the terrible tests to come. The poems and poetically informed stories of his *Raiders' Dawn* and *The Last Inspection* have frequent divinations of an impending climax in which his avowed themes of Love and Life and Death would be somehow resolved and integrated. So that when we heard of his arrival in India, we looked forward with excitement to some new mutation this pregnant change of scene and activity might evolve. . . .

Compassion is the outstanding quality which quickens all Lewis's work. It is as clear and unsophisticated as Wilfred Owen's. Sometimes, it is true, it can seem as raw and febrile as an open wound. . . ; sometimes it deteriorates into sentimentality, as in the poem *Goodbye* in the pre-India section of *Ha! Ha! Among the Trumpets*. But mostly it is mellowed with a tender patience and a sense of the healing sacrament of love.

This was another reason why we were anxious to see his new overseas poems. . . .

[Lewis's] Indian poems are remarkably free from political implications of any kind. There is virtually nothing to suggest that his service in India coincided with a period of the most tortured political stress, and, even worse, with the Bengal famine of 1943, which so appalled the world in the very middle of a war. (p. 192)

There is a clue here to the spiritual torpor which seems to have affected Lewis no less than other English writers in India. The forms of misery and want tower up so gigantically naked that the mind is shocked and battered almost into insensibility. . . .

[To] be effective, tragedy must not be too overwhelming. But in India it *is* too overwhelming.

This, I believe, is why Lewis's Indian poems mostly avoid the larger social and political arena. The endeavour to apprehend the physics of that flux beneath India's brilliant, aching surface, to find behind her terrible teeming symbols a unity and meaning in which pity and artistic integrity are reconciled is one which a writer as honest as Lewis would not treat lightly, especially on so brief acquaintance. . . .

Lewis's own comments on specifically Indian scenes are neither very profound nor unusual. . . . Siva and Vishnu make conventional appearances. And the poem *Holi* ends with a too-slick sound of Housman. . . . (p. 193)

He is much more felicitous in his simpler evocations of the Indian panorama. He has a natural poet's eye; observation and image are often exquisitely yoked to produce those haunting vibrations which are one of poetry's greatest charms. *The Jungle* has such memorable moments as

> The bamboos creak like an uneasy house;
> The night is shrill with crickets, cold with space.

And there are other poignant images to be discovered and cherished:

> Dark peasants drag the sun upon their backs;

or

> Daylight had girls tawny as gazelles
> Beating their saris clean in pools and singing.

And yet there is something fragmentary and isolated about such images—or, rather, the glimpses of India which such images illumine. It is almost as if that poet's eye opened to the Indian landscape only at rare moments of waking from a sleepwalking obsessed with the problems and prototypes of a personal cosmology. We see more of Lewis than India. As we read on through the Indian poems, and then reread them, India itself seems to recede and fade. . . . In a word, the chief impact of India on Lewis, as far as we can judge from this handful of poems, was to drive him more and more into himself and his preoccupations with love and death and separation. (pp. 193-94)

There are poems of nostalgia and bereavement, fierce statements of a private faith in love, metaphysical patrols and migrations that parallel his bodily exile. Not many poems have specifically Indian themes, and these, in spite of their pictorial and evocative qualities, are not the best. His most ambitious and significant poem, perhaps, is *The Jungle*. The jungle, he said, had moved him more deeply than anything else. Yet, when he came to write about it, he found that his poem had become a criticism of the western world which he understood; of the jungle he had said nothing. (p. 194)

So that if these poems leave us finally with a feeling of something slender and impermanent . . . we should remember two things. First, that he only lived in India for about a year. Second, that a poet's life is often a stage ahead of his work. That is, the understanding of his own position at any changing-point of life will be most enlightened when he has advanced a little way beyond that point.

In a sense *The Jungle* is only the beginning of such an understanding. Retrospective in mood, it really represents a spiritual gateway to India and a broader vision, because only now had Lewis assimilated the insight of his past. The best Indian poems had yet to be.

As it is, Lewis's poems are still the best to have come out of India during the war and include some of the best war-poetry written in any circumstances. (pp. 194-95)

> *Gordon Symes, "Muse in India: An Aspect of Alun Lewis," in* English, *Vol. VI, No. 34, Spring, 1947, pp. 191-95.*

RALPH HOUSTON (essay date 1951)

From the first few poems of "Raiders' Dawn" it is clear that Lewis, possibly because of his life in the Army, was often unable to recognise the poetry and reject its by-products. Often the reader is almost overwhelmed by a smoky afflatus. . . . (p. 403)

Of the shorter poems towards the end of "Raiders' Dawn" the love poems seem to me the weakest, though good in patches; but generally speaking Lewis does not succeed in controlling his emotion and he was not, apparently, fully aware of the extreme difficulty of writing good love poetry. His "Poems from the Chinese," too, are mostly overshadowed by Pound's, though "The Merchant's Wife" is very well done and can bear comparison. There are, however, several fine short poems among the remainder, especially "The Rhondda" with its powerful Hopkinsian opening. . . . (p. 408)

In turning to "Ha! Ha! Among the Trumpets" the reader may feel some disappointment towards the end; this, I think, is due to the weight of reportage in the poems from India, pleasant reading though much of it makes. As a consequence, these poems suffer by contrast with the earlier work. . . . Lewis was aware of the difficulties inherent in his situation, for he sub-heads the volume "Poems in Transit." . . . Let it be said at once that it was a gallant and far from unsuccessful attempt. But in England Lewis's mythopoetic imagination, his ability to move easily from experience to myth, recreating myth and thereby elevating and recreating experience, seems to have had freer play. (p. 410)

Lewis had many obvious faults and his work could be pruned with advantage. Often he did not know when to stop and he marred many poems by tacking on trite endings; his rhythm sometimes stumbles or collapses into prose; sometimes he appeals to cheap sentiment. But he had had little time to polish his work and I think . . . that he had produced, in a short and harassed poetic life, a not inconsiderable body of good poetry. My title, moreover, implies that I feel he had more to give. . . . [There] were sources of Lewis's power which, I think, would not have failed him.

First, there was his ability to evoke the rural scene, as in "To Edward Thomas," "On Embarkation," "The Mahratta Ghats" and others. In this he provides continuity in our pastoral tradition by taking over from [Edward] Thomas who, in turn bore a close affinity to much of Wordsworth's earlier poetry. Secondly, he had a power to contact, appreciate, absorb and profit by the past in both a historical and poetic sense, as can be seen in "The Captivity," "The Odyssey" and "Threnody on a Starry Night." Thirdly, his mythopoetic imagination, revealed, for example, in "To a Comrade in Arms," "Jason and Medea" and "From a Play" was strong, and, given the chance to exploit it, he might have helped us to penetrate that poetic continent where Blake and Yeats maintain their lonely outposts. (p. 413)

> *Ralph Houston, "The Broken Arch: A Study of the Poetry of Alun Lewis," in* Adelphi, *Vol. 28, No. 1, Fourth Quarter, 1951, pp. 403-13.*

JOHN LEHMANN (essay date 1952)

Alun Lewis had many friends who knew him intimately and loved him, and many who had never met him loved his poetry with an unqualified enthusiasm I could never muster. To all those I offer my apologies for writing as I shall in these pages, but it would be wrong of me to pretend that I thought he was comparable in his poetic achievement with Edward Thomas or Wilfred Owen, the victims of an earlier war, and his own admired masters, or even with some of his own contemporaries who survived the war. It would be unfair to those survivors as well as insincere, because death in battle does not by some mysterious magic immediately make a young man a better poet. But I do think the war, not the bullet that killed him, made Alun Lewis a writer: a writer who was capable of very big things indeed. I had read his volume of stories *The Last Inspection* with the feeling that prose, not verse, might turn out in the end to be his proper medium; and when he sent me from India his story *Ward O 3 (b)*, which is still to me one of the most brilliant stories written by anyone during the war, this feeling became a conviction. (pp. 109-10)

I am more than ever impressed by a quality that runs right through [his works], a natural human warmth, but also something more than that. . . .

It is [his] sureness about the things that matter, above all love, [his] rootedness in life and faith in the sensual world that seem to me so important about Alun Lewis. One of the reasons for this sureness may well have been the unusually happy childhood and home life that he had experienced. (p. 110)

This belief in life and the touchstone of the heart . . . are all too rare today, when literature in so many countries is in danger of being dominated by pseudo-philosophies and the ingenious constructions of the intellect that really deny the heart; and this makes Alun Lewis's death particularly tragic for us. He was always striving to express his faith and vision more clearly and completely in his art. . . . (p. 111)

[He experienced] nostalgia for the elemental simplicities of his Welsh home. This nostalgia saturates many of his early poems and stories: it was so strong an emotion that it was a long time before he got it under control in his art—but he did get it under control, as *Ward O 3 (b)* is there to witness, with its beautiful balance of satiric observation and warm human insight, and what I can only call a kind of poetic wisdom transmuting the violent feelings that his theme must have had for him. (p. 112)

[Even] though I feel almost certain that *as a poet*—that is in the medium of verse—Alun Lewis was not and would not have been the peer of Wilfred Owen, there are many points of similarity in the total personalities of the two soldier writers. And one of them is their sense of comradeship and identity with their men. (p. 113)

Alun Lewis refers in more than one letter to this feeling about not being separated from his men. It was something more complex than liking and the sense of human trust. . . . In his story *The Orange Grove,* he says of one of his characters: 'He was experiencing one of those enlargements of the imagination that come once or perhaps twice to a man, and recreate him subtly and profoundly. . . .' Such an enlargement of the imagination came to Alun Lewis, I feel sure, in India. (pp. 113-14)

[He had] the presentiment that he was on the verge of discovering something far greater than he had lost. All his hints about the search for integrity, and reasoning only from a human standpoint, and the bonds with the men under his command which he found so difficult to analyse, are pointers to that, and pointers too to the role he might have played in literature if he had lived. (p. 115)

John Lehmann, "A Human Standpoint," in his The Open Night, Longmans, Green and Co, 1952, pp. 109-16.

JOHN STUART WILLIAMS (essay date 1964-65)

The themes of [Lewis's] poetry are often paralleled in his stories and their treatment is characterized by a seriousness of purpose even when humour breaks in. He sees man, shaped by his past, attempting to come to terms with himself and his fellow men and with his environment, in spite of the sense of alienation imposed by consciousness of himself as an individual. This alienation becomes in the army stories that of the 'landless soldier lost in war.' . . . The same difficulty, that of relating form and language to subject matter under the pressure of war, which we noticed in his poetry is present but perhaps to a lesser degree in the stories. . . . Some of these stories [in *The Last Inspection*] are not far from reportage, some are character studies; but others are perceptive examinations of crises in relationships arising out of the running together of the lines of circumstance. *Lance Jack,* for example, reads more like a journal than a short-story; *Flick* and *Almost a Gentleman* are studies of a central character, cooler in tone, more objective, perhaps because of the social criticism behind them, and therefore, to me, more acceptable. *Acting Captain* is concerned with the relationships of clearly-defined characters, but even here, in a story which is largely successful, Lewis himself intrudes and tells us what he has failed to imply. Curly Norris in this story sometimes appears to be the author's mouthpiece for making plain what should have been plain in the story itself. Curly, however, is a not unacceptable mouthpiece because he figures as a kind of chorus rather like those characters in the earlier novels of William Faulkner who live on the fringe of the action, at once involved and detached. He is not, like most chorus-figures, impersonally complete, but an imperfect man who understands out of his own imperfections. (pp. 18-19)

The main criticism I have to make of the stories in *The Last Inspection* is, indeed, not that they verge on reportage, not that they are too factual, but that, to quote O'Faolain writing about his own early stories, they are "full of . . . personalizations and sensations which belong to the author rather than to the character." In other words the charge is not of reportage, not of too much objectivity, but of woolliness, of telling too much himself and allowing his characters in their words and by their action or inaction to tell us too little. . . . [In general] it is fair to say that if he wrote out of urgency, that urgency is not always as apparent as he

would have wished. His prose is sometimes too full of qualifying phrases which only confuse the sense and diffuse the focus. His language is often heavy with adjectives, which sometimes result in a rich and satisfying texture, sometimes in a slowing of the pace and slackening of tension. Sometimes, too, it seems self-conscious, as in the opening conversations of *Private Jones,* when his attempt at conveying the idioms of Welsh speech seems almost, but not quite, condescending in a story which is anything but that. That this is the last fault anyone could attribute to Lewis himself suggests an uncertainty of control over language that occasionally disconcerts the reader in an otherwise successful story. (p. 20)

Whatever faults in technique are apparent the honesty of his purpose is never obscured. He writes to know himself and to know others as aspects of humanity and in approaching his subject he is aware of the need for humility. . . . The self-awareness and the awareness, too, of the necessity for understanding is evident in such stories as *They Came, Private Jones, Picnic* and others in *The Last Inspection.* (p. 21)

These last stories [*In the Green Tree*] are for the most part admirable in structure, in the felicitousness of the relation of language to content and in the way in which action, character and imagery are related in the expression of the theme. . . . The simplification of style, this sureness of touch in selecting what is significant, is perhaps related to his mature awareness of the paradox of beauty and ugliness, of life and death. (pp. 21-2)

The 'ripeness' that 'is all' is the dominant theme in most of these stories, but it is more than a passive acceptance of the inevitable. Death and life are seen as together encompassing the circle of being and the tone, with one notable exception, is one of grave compassion and understanding. He has found a secure footing on the point of balance between involvement and detachment. (p. 22)

In *The Orange Grove,* a story rich in association, an officer and his driver are travelling in a truck in an India full of "unrest and rioting." They talk over their attitudes and their personalities grow into contrast. (p. 23)

The driver is killed and Beale's last journey with the body is a spiritual pilgrimage during which he first becomes passionately involved with the life of the dead man, and then moves through sympathy to understanding not only of himself and the driver but of all lost people on the face of the earth. The orange grove [referring to a collective farm the driver had seen in Palestine] is the symbol of perfect belonging, which may or may not be available to any one man in reality, but is profoundly significant even as a symbol alone. In *The Orange Grove* form and content are fused. The language is felicitous, the pattern of character, event, and background is treated with assurance. Narrative and theme are interrelated. It is a short story of unusual quality.

Ward o.3 (b) tells of a group of wounded officers in a convalescent ward in India awaiting a medical board's decision on their futures. Some hope to be sent home, others to return to active service. The hospital itself "is, by 1943 standards, a good place to be in." The backgrounds and foibles of the characters are revealed in their re-action to each other, to the beautiful Sister Normanby (no cardboard heroine this), and to the tension occasioned by the imminence of a decision which will radically alter their lives, with an insight and understanding free from sentimentality. (pp. 23-4)

The story is finely balanced and written with unobtrusive control of technique. I consider it one of his finest achievements. . . . Alun Lewis started with more than facility, he became a poet and a craftsman with something more than talent. He felt confident in his ability at the end. . . . (pp. 24-5)

Ward o.3 (b) and *The Orange Grove* show that confidence to be fully justified. (p. 25)

John Stuart Williams, "The Short Stories of Alun Lewis," in Anglo-Welsh Review, Vol. 14, No. 34, Winter, 1964-65, pp. 16-25.

R. N. CURREY (essay date 1967)

Raiders' Dawn . . . established itself as the first clear statement of the wartime soldier, no longer a student, who saw military training, coastal defence and air-raids against a background of civilian values. The title poem speaks of air-raids—seen from the receiving end—with the dignified epigrammatic brevity that shines out from so many of his poems. (p. 19)

There is a warm acceptance in this book of the human condition, of the essential brotherhood of man, clean and dirty, clever and stupid, which was to enable him to write as no other English poet has done—even Kipling—of the landscape and people of India.

Alun Lewis's second, posthumous, book of poems, *Ha! Ha! Among the Trumpets,* named from the description of the war-horse in the Book of Job—'He saith among the trumpets Ha! Ha!, and he smelleth the battle afar off '—made less impression on the home public than *Raiders' Dawn,* no doubt because a large part of it was about the unfamiliar and hostile landscapes of India and Burma. Yet it was, for this reason, even more widely significant of the Second War. The first part of the book carried on the themes of *Raiders' Dawn.* . . . (p. 21)

It is with war of this kind that the second and third parts of the book deal. He was already the interpreter of the civilian soldier in England: *Ha! Ha! Among the Trumpets* made him the interpreter of the civilian soldier fighting overseas, and more particularly of those who found themselves in the puzzling sub-continent of India. (pp. 21-2)

In these Indian poems he wrote of the aspects of war that came his way. 'Assault Convoy', 'Forward Observation Post', 'Burma Casualty' are among his titles, and in his poem 'To Rilke' he caught vividly the loneliness of the soldier on his first arrival:

> I sit within the tent, within the darkness
> Of India, and the wind disturbs my lamp.
>
> (p. 22)

But it is not in these more obviously 'war poems' that his significant comment about war that ranges the world is made. It is in poems like 'The Journey', 'The Peasants', 'Karanje Village' and 'The Mahratta Ghats' that he brings to bear on the Indian scene his own knowledge of history, and the sharpened perceptions of his generation towards the underprivileged. (pp. 22-3)

No other writer has caught so exactly and sympathetically the grace and dignity and will-to-live of peasants, in mediaeval conditions as dangerous as those of modern war. The quality of poems like 'Karanje Village' and 'Mahratta Ghats' is perhaps less easily apprehended by those who have never seen at first hand peasant life in an under-developed country. (p. 24)

In his poems (and his excellent short stories) he applied Owen's 'pity of war, the pity war distilled' to the waste of exiled years caused by war, to the contrasts of peasant poverty and industrial life which have made the two wars of this century in a real sense world wars. (p. 26)

R. N. Currey, "Second World War," in his Poets of the 1939-1945 War (© R. N. Currey 1960, 1967; reprinted by permission of The British Council), revised edition, Longmans, Green & Co, 1967, pp. 12-41.*

JOHN DAVIES (essay date 1970)

[Lewis's] situation in India heightened his feeling—a feeling and a condition, not an idea or a conclusion merely—of vulnerability in the world. The War, the Army, India, became for Lewis a kind of limbo in which positives and certainties were gradually being eroded. But, if there is a new dimension of experience evident in the later poetry, the central dilemma is essentially that expressed in *Raiders' Dawn.* As a poet and soldier, Lewis had already evoked in this earlier work the strain involved in preserving his essential self, the movements and susceptibilities of the inner man, against pressures from outside himself. His uneasiness in his soldier's strait-jacket, and about his potential role as a killer of men, his consciousness of death, his wariness of the future, and his enforced separation from the woman he loved, most of all his striving as an artist to achieve some measure of emotional synthesis, and of eternal truth (what he was later to call "that which IS") . . . these, basically, are the constituents of the predicament evoked in *Raiders' Dawn.* Now, in India—even further away from his beloved wife and from home, a soldier in an army of occupation—that predicament was intensified. The overwhelming strangeness of India, and his increasing sense of isolation, drove Lewis even further into himself, deeper into the preoccupations he had brought with him from England, and to the climax of his confrontation with the dilemma of "the landless soldier lost in war." The quivering strands of that dilemma meet and cohere in the poet's consistent effort to attain wholeness, integrity, oneness. . . . Those strands are encompassed in the all-pervasive imagery of darkness characteristic of the poetry which Lewis wrote during his Indian experience, and, together, content and style fuse into what is essentially a testament of darkness.

In the first section of *Ha! Ha! Among the Trumpets,* comprising the poems written in England, the darkness of "A Welsh Night" is something which the village wears "like a shroud or shawl." It is "Encirclement," however, another poem written in England, which is more clearly indicative of the significance which the imagery of darkness was to have in the later poetry. Lewis refers here to

> the nameless dugouts and basements
> Of Everyman's darkness.

It is a prophetic allusion, for, in India, the darkness was to become integral to Lewis's world and to his poetry. Sometimes it is the adjective which is utilised, but often the darkness has a presence of its own, either literally as night or as an image of death, of fear of the unknown future, or of uncertainty generally. Uncertainty is everywhere evident in this later poetry. In "Water Music," the lake is as "dark as history," but if the unknown lay behind the poet, it also stalked alongside and towards him.... In "Port of Call: Brazil," written during the voyage to India, he senses already "the heavy-odoured beast / Of darkness." The poem "By the Gateway of India, Bombay" evokes "those darker terrors of the brain" which the poet had brought with him to India, and they add an ominous dimension to the guidebook rhetoric of the title. Lewis sensed what he was to face beyond the gate. What that was he expresses in "Midnight in India" as "the dark compression in my head." ... (pp. 176-77)

He frequently responds sympathetically to the peasants' plight in his poetry, and when he writes of their "dark load," in "The Mahratta Ghats," it is with an awareness of many of those aspects of darkness to which he has alluded elsewhere. He recognises that, like himself, the peasants are at the mercy of forces far beyond their control—of the climate, of fate, history, death. It must be emphasised, however, that such examples of identification are more than offset in *Ha! Ha! Among the Trumpets* by Lewis's recurring sense of the enormous distance which lay between himself and the peasants.

This feeling of separation and isolation exacerbated, and was exacerbated by, the problems which the poet had brought with him from England. The characteristic movement of thought in the poetry which he wrote in India is one inwards, from a brief description of an Indian scene to a close concentration on Lewis's own predicament. In poems such as "A Fragment," "Indian Day," "Karanje Village" and "The Jungle" ("We are the ghosts, and they the denizens"), Lewis's focus closes gradually on his real theme— his own predicament. In the second section of "The Jungle," for example, that focus sharpens perceptibly, closing inwards from the jungle itself, from the West, through the poet's own town and home, to rest finally upon the poet himself. (p. 178)

Most of all, it is death which Lewis evokes by means of the imagery of darkness in *Ha! Ha! Among the Trumpets.* (p. 179)

His preoccupation with death is no neo-romantic indulgence. Lewis's poetry is more directly confessional than that of any of his contemporaries, and his poems are frequently charged with deep-rooted apprehension at, and fascinated expectancy of, a death which is an immediate, not a comfortably distant, possibility. He is fully engaged with the implications of that possibility, integral to which is his concept of a death of one's own which grows organically from a man's character and experience. Thus, in "Burma Casualty," death is viewed as a potentiality inside oneself, carried around by each individual—The "darkness" in "lungs and heart." This concept is also present in "The Sentry" and in "To Edward Thomas" (the "stormy-branchéd dark / Whose fibres are a thread within your hand"), poems in Lewis's earlier volume.... Lewis was constantly aware of death as forcing life into some sort of perspective at the same time that it threatened it. Often, as in "Burma Casualty," the darkness offers a reposeful, fas-

cinating sleep.... Now, this is the mood of Lewis's allusion, in "Burma Casualty," to "all the lads the dark enfolds." At such times, death seems to offer him complete peace, certainty amidst uncertainties, and the "darkness waiting to fold me away" a tempting freedom from responsibility. (It is significant that the Biblical imagery of *Raiders' Dawn* disappears in this later volume.) Allied closely to this response is the poet's preoccupation with death as the imminent, ultimate experience, as a mystery and the final frontier of the artist. Often, death appears to Lewis simply as a menacing prospect, foreshortening earthly experience and the possibility of future joy. In "Observation Post: Forward Area," death is "a darker beast than poverty," whilst "Home Thoughts From Abroad" has "the darkness / Twitch with death." Lewis never completely succumbs to the darkness in his poetry: his fascination is very real, but hedged almost always with reservations. Like his "Burma Casualty," he consistently "refused, refused, the encircling dark." Several of the poems written in India draw on the poet's experience in hospital, in 1943, and this inevitably sharpened his awareness of death. (p. 180)

In one sense, 'dark' and 'darkness' recur as mechanically as a nervous tic—the words appear forty-four times in the thirty-five poems which Lewis wrote on the voyage to India, and in India itself. This, however, is not the best way to appreciate the emphasis: generally the wealth of association which the imagery of darkness accumulates gives resonance to its every successive use. To return to the poem "To Rilke," for example, after reading the other poems written in India, is to realize the full extent of the dilemma it expresses. And in particular the line "I sit within the tent, within the darkness / Of India" becomes poignant with all the implications which the darkness brings with it from other poems. The epithet invariably tells one more of the poet himself than of the scene or situation he is describing. In this instance, the darkness is primarily that of isolation, underlining the poet's physical predicament in an utterly strange environment, but also his mental and spiritual uncertainty. A consideration of such associations, too, gives added meaning to the phrase "our dark belief," in the poem "The Assault Convoy," or to the phrase "The darker terrors of the brain," in "By the Gateway of India, Bombay." Against the darkness Lewis could offer endurance—a fundamental positive in his poetry, involving the will (as he puts it, in "By the Gateway of India, Bombay") to "contest the darkness inch by inch." (p. 181)

To compare his "By the Gateway of India, Bombay" with Bernard Gutteridge's poem "Bombay," written at much the same time, or his "Midnight in India" with Keith Douglas's poem "Egypt," is to realise the full extent to which Lewis's vision was directed inwards. That vision was a rigorous, questioning one, and the poet's uncertainty was characteristic of one who found that the paths from the West "all end in dark" ("Home Thoughts From Abroad"), and who wrote in a letter that, after the war, "some of us will get disability pensions ... others nothing at all except darkness." (p. 182)

His voyage to India was a voyage, self-revealing but inconclusive, into the heart of darkness, and the vigorousness with which he continually reassessed his response to that voyage has resulted in a consistent testament of one man's reaction to an experience which, though in an extreme form, is a universal one. The imagery of darkness—the winter death, the dark night of the soul, the nether darkness, the shade of death—is archetypal, integral for example to Classical and Celtic mythology, and to Christianity.... [The] struggle evoked in *Ha! Ha! Among the Trumpets* is still recognisably that of Everyman and every artist. Part of the value of Alun Lewis's poetry is that, against time and in testing conditions, he fought bravely and honestly to resolve them. (pp. 182-83)

> *John Davies, "The Poetry of Darkness: Alun Lewis's Indian Experience," in* Anglo-Welsh Review, *Vol. 19, No. 43, Autumn, 1970, pp. 176-83.*

ALUN JOHN   (essay date 1970)

Nature was not merely the escape [Lewis] discovered from 'regimental mankind' when he became a soldier. The close recording of natural detail to be found in his schoolboy and undergraduate short stories shows the extent to which it had claimed his attention from his early years onwards.... The third section of his poem "To Edward Thomas" is devoted entirely to natural description. Edward Thomas himself might well have written it for it has the same extended observation, the same lyric quality and the same trick that Edward Thomas had of quietly conveying an awareness of his own presence at the end of the poem. (pp. 9-10)

Alun Lewis certainly admired Edward Thomas and confessed that several of the *Raiders' Dawn* poems had been inspired by what he referred to as the 'Edward Thomas country', but in the same way as Edward Thomas has too often, with only partial accuracy, been referred to as a 'war poet', so it is not entirely true to regard Alun Lewis as a writer who wrote only about war and the confusions and bewilderment it aroused in him. Several of his *Raiders' Dawn* poems were written before September, 1939. The war certainly allowed him to become known as a poet but it did not make him one. His particular concern, eventually, was to record his personal experiences as a soldier and to write about ordinary people caught up in the war. Nature, nevertheless, continues to be woven into his writing. (pp. 10-11)

The poems of the *Ha! Ha! Among the Trumpets* collection are firmer in their poetic quality and more concrete in their realisation than those of *Raiders' Dawn*. Verbally and musically they are also more controlled. Their main appeal, nevertheless, still lies in their lyrical impulse and their quality of truth, gentleness and humanity, qualities that were so much a part of Alun Lewis himself. (p. 77)

The poems and short stories of Alun Lewis may have less immediacy of appeal than when they first appeared in the circumstances of war but the personality of Alun Lewis and his 'writing gift' still make their arresting impact on the reader. Some of his early work may be considered to have faults but these may be attributed to a young writer 'finding his way'. Some of his *Raiders' Dawn* poems may show too easy an indulgence in words, imagery and emotion. Some of his early short stories may perhaps be too moralistic in tone, too sentimental and may approach the level of fictionalised reporting. Intellectually there is possibly an occasional triteness about his work. But overshadowing the faults are the strengths. There is his lyric impulse, his sensitivity and imaginative power and that personal voice of his, quiet and controlled and extremely genuine. The sad tone of some of his poems may manifest itself but there is much

in the poetry to reflect the spirit of Life he declared to be his other main concern.... (pp. 84-5)

With a quarter of a century gone since Alun Lewis was killed, it is possible now to see how his work is related to the main trends of English literature. In his awareness of the power and the shamefulness of War he quite clearly reaffirms the statement made by Wilfred Owen, while the concern he always felt for ordinary people shows him to belong to the social and documentary writers of the 1930's such as George Orwell and the contributors to John Lehmann's *New Writing* and Michael Roberts's *New Country Anthology*. Alun Lewis can be regarded as a poet of Pity for it is pity and compassion, as Gordon Symes has remarked, which 'quickens' all he wrote. (pp. 87-8)

> *Alun John, in his* Alun Lewis *(© University of Wales Press and the Welsh Arts Council, 1970), University of Wales Press, 1970, 98 p.*

JOHN PIKOULIS   (essay date 1972)

Alun Lewis struggled in his too-alterable times to become coherent and then in an environment that was double-edged, both that which fed, sustained, inspired, and that which weakened, irritated and divided....

Death and life were not for him letters on a page or counters of the imagination; they stalked him—or rather their shadows stalked him, for it is a fact that he spent all his time on the periphery of combat, digging trenches, putting up barbed-wire fences, driving tanks, buying pith helmets and drill shorts. This kind of army life is truly betwixt-and-between and is almost certainly more responsive to either the documentary or the comic. It is not readily amenable to poetic creation, but by the time he came to India and became Intelligence Officer, it was succeeded by experiences which yielded the one poem which marks his final maturing into his poetic self and thus defines the nature of his achievement. 'The Way Back' is not only an extraordinarily packed poem but also (because Lewis's dilemma touches the essential matter of a poet's being at several points) a classic paradigm of how the imagination works, an exciting and wholly neglected insight into the nature of literary creation, of the fertilizing tensions which sustain it and which it, in turn, dissolves and reforms. (p. 146)

[The] 'I' of the poem is at once both autobiographical and a creative other self. Moreover, the human being who is a soldier and the human being who is a poet are set off against each other. One man's several selves respond to the equally disparate sources located in the 'you' addressed to the poem: the Indian land, the feminine watery world and the beloved. The poem's fictive task is to bind them all into a compelling unity, to find in the interaction of nature and army life the poet's true creative self. The "you" of the poem offers him a point of harmony, but it co-exists uncomfortably with his soldier's apprehension of death and destruction. The whole poem rests on this confusion or ambiguity and tries to break free from it. The complex rests on the fact that Lewis's is a war poetry; even when it is most private, or relaxed, indirect pressures relate it to the larger effort. The poetry is thus dominated by the tension between the affective man's devotions and the active man's responsibilities. 'The Way Back' is, in this particular sense, the type of Lewis's poetry, an attempt to explore and resolve an unholy interdependence of contrary realities, any one of which is expressed through or by sanction of or in despite of another. It ends with a vision of some tremendous disturbance whereby the essential self, caught up in a physical cataclysm, at last achieves the object of its desires. The cataclysm is half-real, half-imagined, half-loved, half-loathed: the end cannot free itself from the means so that death-wish and life-wish are inextricably wedded. He longs to join the beloved but also the earth. The heavy successive stresses, the accumulating declamations and heightened feeling now seen triumphant cries from the heart, exhilarating and passionately yearning, liberatory, now oppressively emphatic, mechanically inhuman, menacing cries of despair. (pp. 149-50)

'The Orange Grove,' Alun Lewis's finest short story and a luminous work of art, points in a different though related direction. Beale is a conscientious officer limited to the routines and practicalities of army life who is gradually waylaid. He loses his driver, his way, his car, the body of his dead companion. He leaves the main road and his task of reconnaissance to enter a jungle with a troupe of gypsies he meets who speak an unintelligible language and who are making into the unknown. With them, he enters a different dimension of existence; the possibility exists of reaching the springs of life at the end. . . . The gypsies are symbols of the imagination, the opposite of the army and with a little of the peasant about them but with that rootlessness, that capacity for disinterested venturing, that air of mystery, of the semi-human, which was for Alun the essence of poetry. With them is broached the possibility of regeneration, away from the world of political disturbances and murders, the heavy rains and paddy-fields of India, and into that other dimension of existence. Lewis's disenchantment with humanity, the failure of his exaggerated hopes for the political direction of creative effort, is complete. The driver (whose body Beale cares for so punctiliously and which he yields to the gypsies when his truck, the last lifeline of civilization, is stranded in a river) had once been to Palestine and reminisces about an orange grove he saw there and a kibbutz. These are images for Beale of human interdependence, satisfaction and fertility and they contrast painfully with the reminiscences of his barmaid wife and Bible-pushing mother. . . . It is a radiant socialist humanitarianism which is part of the Welsh temper, but Lewis has learnt that the solidarity and idealism of the citizen in war are not identical with the poet's responses. The orange grove must be transformed, though still bearing its salient characteristics, into the jungle, a world less static, less circumscriptive, more troubling. We move from the clean, well-lit, man-made place to the infinite, the chaotic. The good life as conceived by politics, morality and philosophy and as achieved by the practical efforts of men acting daily in their communities *is* good; but the good life as perceived by the imagination (in the exaggerated context here of war's extremities) and realised by the creative struggle of the solitary poet—however broad his sympathies—is something else again. Orange grove and jungle are related, successive stages of Lewis's concept both of life and poetry, true symbols of his quest, and the move from one to another signifies, for the first time, his acceptance of his isolation and the abandonment of the sentimental comforts he had resorted to in order to assuage it. (pp. 160-61)

He who had prided himself in the performance of his army duties and on the recognition of danger-signs is now faintly but distinctly relieved of the responsibility of guarding himself. At intervals throughout the journey, he had passed the gypsies but was more intent on reporting the murder of his driver, to fill in the requisite form, note the date and the time, to care for the

body and the 'integrity' of the man for whose death he felt an uneasy guilt. But at the end he can give his old self up, taking with him the symbolic counters which reveal the significance of the moment. . . . Thus he divests himself of his past self, taking with him only the barest testimony of its earlier existence and bidding farewell to all the rest. He now embarks on the immortal tracks with the anonymous of the earth, joins the eternal round, frees himself to enter the jungle to seek, to reform his selfhood. . . . In the world of 'deep freedom,' he can paradoxically express his love and compassion for 'the common man' in the form of the gypsies, the last wanderers of earth. Especially for a sentimental, pious, shy, serious and sensitive young man as one understands Lewis to have been, the choice was tremendous, even if the manner of it bears the mark of that personality. He approached it through the happiness of such a prophetic poem like 'The Way Back', though he could not have foreseen that the transfiguring moment would not be as dramatic as the last verse of that poem indicates. . . . In 'The Orange Grove', death became rebirth, the isolate self found   a community, a context in which to ground itself. But that does not lessen the value of the poem, whose joy is that of the title of the collection, whose progression is that of the collection's sub-title and whose own title is the direction which the protagonist of 'The Orange Grove' sets out on. . . . And so Beale joins the great nomadic drift through the universe, never to be heard of or from again, as Alun Lewis died in the jungles of Burma. (pp. 162-63)

[There is in Lewis a] profound division between man and it is this which helps give his brief career the significance it has, vitally dependent on but finally beyond all biography and autobiography. It is a significance which has everything to do with the secret recesses of the imagination, its shifting commitments, its sublimely resourceful exactments and rewards. (p. 164)

John Pikoulis, "Alun Lewis: The Way Back" (revised by the author for this publication), in Critical Quarterly, *Vol. 14, No. 2, Summer, 1972, pp. 145-65.*

BIBLIOGRAPHY

Cox, C. B. "Poets at War." *Spectator* 229 No. 7221 (18 November 1966): 654.
Brief mention of Lewis. The critic asserts that Lewis never really found his personal poetic voice.

Hamilton, Ian. Introduction to *Alun Lewis: Selected Poetry and Prose,* by Alun Lewis, pp. 9-59. London: George Allen & Unwin, 1966.
Mainly biographical, weaving the impetus of Lewis's poems and stories with the facts of his life, especially concentrating on his service in the army.

Jones, Gwyn. Postscript to *In the Green Tree,* by Alun Lewis, pp. 137-41. London: George Allen & Unwin, 1948.
Biographical sketch and personal remembrance of the poet, with mention of his increasing craftsmanship and personal maturing through his war time experiences.

Thomas, Dylan. "Welsh Poets." In his *Quite Early One Morning*,
pp. 97-116. New York: New Directions, 1954.*
    Selections of Lewis's poetry with a few introductory remarks.

Lu Hsün

1881-1936

(Also transliterated as Lusin, Lu Hsin, or Lǔ Xùn; pseudonym of Chou Shu-jen also transliterated as Zhōu Shùrén; also wrote under pseudonym of Chou Ch'o) Chinese short story writer and essayist.

Lu Hsün is hailed by many as the leader of China's cultural revolution. Some critics suggest his hunger for the moral regeneration of China had its roots in his childhood. As a youth Lu Hsün lived in a gloomy, failure-ridden atmosphere. The family compound included several unsuccessful uncles addicted to opium. The imprisonment of his grandfather, a government official, together with the sickness and death of his father, exhausted the family fortunes. Lu Hsün's family shame increased his sensitivity to ordinary people despite his birth into the scholarly gentry. Although he first intended to dedicate himself to the revolutionary movement by becoming a doctor Lu Hsün resolved while in medical school, that literature was a more powerful method of effecting change.

Lu Hsün lived in a highly volatile political era. His hope for the October Revolution in 1911 and the overthrow of the Manchu dynasty was soon squelched and Lu Hsün silenced himself for many years. With the May Fourth Movement in 1918 he again became active in the revolution of China, writing stories, and essays. Considered a spokesman for the revolution, Lu Hsün was idolized by leftist writers of China. Chairman Mao Tse-tung paid him this tribute: "The chief commander of China's cultural revolution, he was not only a great man of letters but a great thinker and revolutionary."

Lu Hsün was never formally a communist and his devotion to communist philosophy is still debated. His contribution to the cultural revolution, however, is without question. He spearheaded the move to write in the popular language (pai-hua) rather than the classical language (wen-yen) which had been the standard for generations. Within a few years pai-hua became recognized as the national language, a dramatic change.

Lu Hsün's stories sharply expose the hypocrisy of the old tradition and sensitively portray the upheaval of change. Despite the seriousness of his purpose, Lu Hsün wrote in a charming style rich in imagery. He described writing as painful and labored rigorously for economy of expression.

Lu Hsün holds the distinction of being one of modern China's greatest writers as well as a favorite of the people.

PRINCIPAL WORKS

Huai-chiu (short story) 1913; published in journal *Hsiao-shuo yueh-pao*
[*Remembrances of the Past* published in journal *Tien Hsia Monthly,* 1938]
Na han (short stories) 1923
Chung-kuo hsiao shuo shih lüen (history and criticism) 1924
[*A Brief History of Chinese Fiction,* 1959]
P'ang huang (short stories) 1926
Ku shih hsin pien (short stories) 1936
[*Old Tales Retold,* 1961]
Ah Q and Others: Selected Stories of Lusin (short stories) 1941
Chao hua hsi shih (autobiographical sketches) 1947
[*Dawn Blossoms Plucked at Dusk,* 1976]
Yeh ts'ao (prose poems and sketches) 1953
[*Wild Grass,* 1974]
Selected Stories of Lu Hsün (short stories) 1954
Selected Works of Lu Hsün (short stories, prose poems, reminiscences, and essays) 1956
Lu Hsün jih chi (diaries) 1959
Silent China: Selected Writings of Lu Xun (short stories, reminiscences, poetry, and essays) 1973

LIN YUTANG (essay date 1942)

[Lusin] is one of the most biting satirists of Chinese culture.... Behind some of his short epigrams one gets a glimpse of the gigantic spiritual and mental turmoil of a China in revolt against the past. Lusin represents the Literature of Revolt. But this is in itself a sign of life. (p. 1083)

It must not be forgotten also that the charm he has cast upon his readers is due to his style and his bitter sarcasm and occasional wit, while as a leader of the theory of proletarian literature, his views of ancient Chinese culture, his continual cry of revolt and his strictly Marxian view of the function of literature are eagerly and uncritically accepted as the Bible. That his views of China's culture seem shallow and unsound, especially after the five years of war which have opened the eyes of the leftists themselves to the inner strength of China's ancient ideals, and that a radical young China is willing to take Lusin's word for it when he discourages them from touching ancient books by calling them poison, must be taken as necessary phases of the age of revolt. (pp. 1083-84)

Lusin is a warrior more than a "literary man." It always seems to me that he was happiest when he saw or imagined his face bruised and groggy. And it is his uncompromising, challenging, fighting spirit that so charms his readers, for the public always loves a good fighter. (p. 1084)

He advocates the abolition of Chinese writing, believes in the "Europeanization of Chinese syntax" and is for imitation of foreign grammar. He urges the young men to worship Darwin and Ibsen rather than Confucious and Kuan Yü, and sacrifice to Apollo rather than to the God of Pestilence. These ideas are incredibly naïve and hardly show a sense of discernment either of the East or of the West. They are taken very seriously, and it is a true fact that "leftist professors" advise China's young men not to read Chinese ancient works, though they themselves read them on the sly to improve their style. . . . But China needed a man like Lusin to wake the millions up from the self-complacency and lethargy and accumulated inertia of four thousand years. (pp. 1085-86)

> Lin Yutang, "The Epigrams of Lusin: Introduction," in The Wisdom of China and India, edited by Lin Yutang (copyright 1942 by Random House, Inc.; renewed 1970 by Random House, Inc.; reprinted by permission of Random House, Inc.), Random House, 1942, pp. 1083-86.

FENG HSUEH-FENG (essay date 1956)

In 1918, on the eve of the May Fourth Movement, Lu Hsun [, who had given up literary work in 1909,] started writing again. From this time until his death in 1936, he never rested from his literary work and his revolutionary struggle. In less than twenty years, he made an inestimable contribution to the Chinese revolution, and laid a firm foundation for modern Chinese literature. (p. 34)

A Madman's Diary, Kung I-chi, Medicine and Tomorrow, as well as My Old Home, The True Story of Ah Q, and The New Year's Sacrifice, were all written [to expose certain evils and have them cured]. The chief characters in these stories—the madman, Kung I-chi, Jun-tu, Ah Q and the rest—are all unfortunates in an abnormal society. Lu Hsun made a strong protest against their unhappy fate, and mercilessly exposed and attacked the forces that oppressed them, at the same time giving true expression to their wishes, demands and potential strength. He showed that the only way out was through changing society—through revolution.

For instance, in connection with his immortal work The True Story of Ah Q, Lu Hsun declared that he wanted to portray the "silent soul of the people" which for thousands of years "grew, faded and withered quietly like grass under a great rock." While portraying Ah Q-ism, Lu Hsun is above all pleading for Ah Q and others like him; and through Ah Q he lets readers see the age-long oppression of the Chinese people. It is here that he shows himself such a brilliant realist. He makes it clear that Ah Q's greatest failing is his habit of deceiving himself as well as others whenever he is defeated, by consoling himself with the thought that he has won a moral victory. This is defeatism. Moreover, not only does Ah Q often forget his enemies and

oppressors, he takes revenge on people weaker than he is, assuming the airs of an oppressor himself. Lu Hsun shows us that this is simply the result of thousands of years of feudal rule and a hundred years of foreign aggression. Although the Chinese people have always resisted oppression and fought back, their many defeats have produced defeatism which, combined with the age-old teaching of the feudal ruling class—that a man should submit to his superiors—gave rise to Ah Q's method of winning moral victories, the Ah Q-ism which prevents him from facing up to his oppressors. This is what Lu Hsun tries most to reveal to his readers. (pp. 34-5)

In another significant story, The New Year's Sacrifice, Lu Hsun sketches the life of an ordinary working woman. . . . Through his deep insight into this woman's heart, Lu Hsun makes a profound analysis of society. He shows the layer upon layer of social pressure which surround this widow like a spider's web. The utterly inhuman Confucian morality, much of it pure superstition, is the focal point of all these pressures. . . . The situation revealed here is more horrifying than that exposed in A Madman's Diary. At the end of this story, Lu Hsun's brilliant powers of observation are shown most clearly by his discovery that this woman who has shown such fortitude finally comes to doubt the existence of hell, refuses to go on submitting meekly to her lot, and takes her fate into her own hands.

These stories show Lu Hsun's fearlessness in facing reality and exposing abuses. In the effete China of those days, most men had suffered so much that they were no longer sensitive to pain; but Lu Hsun still heard the cry of agony in the hearts of the oppressed, and felt impelled to express it. His exposure of evil is like a strong beam of light to awaken men. And although he writes soberly, and tries not to let himself be carried away, the more detached he appears the clearer his readers hear the cries of the wretched —cries which come to express awakening and revolt.

In all these stories, Lu Hsun entirely rejects the old way of life and the old society. Readers are convinced that only a complete social revolution can put an end to these evils and the people's agony. A Madman's Diary, My Old Home, The True Story of Ah Q, and The New Year's Sacrifice—all carry this message. (p. 36)

Stories such as In the Wine Shop, The Misanthrope and Regret for the Past describe the disillusionment and struggles of intellectuals at that time. The integrity of characters like Lu Wei-fu, Wei Lien-shu, Chuan-sheng or Tzu-chun depends upon whether or not they believe that society can be reformed. Once they lose this faith, they cease to be true to themselves. Then they have to destroy themselves like Wei Lien-shu, deliberately compromise like Lu Wei-fu, or surrender like Tz-chun, who goes home to die exposed to "the sternness of her father and the icy cold looks of bystanders." What makes them lose their faith? Lu Hsun's analysis is clear: Lu Wei-Fu and Wei Lien-shu are men who were aroused by the tumultuous events preceding the 1911 Revolution. . . . [But when] they came up against all the forces of reaction which this revolution failed to sweep away, they grew disillusioned. This shows the weakness of these intellectuals. Unless these men who were so full of hope before 1911 learned a lesson from the failure of the revolution and linked their fate with that of people like Lao Chuan, who were beginning to become aroused, there was nothing for them but despair. Chuan-sheng and Tzu-chun are two young people awakened by the May Fourth Movement. They fail because they depend only on their own little strength to oppose age-old social pressures. Thus Lu Hsun judged the ideals of intellectuals and young people according to their relationship with the people as a whole.

So Lu Hsun's standpoint and his motive in writing are clearly seen in his stories. (pp. 37-8)

Lu Hsun's essays form the bulk and the most important part of his literary work.

The age in which he lived and his dogged fighting spirit made him look for other weapons besides the short story to enlarge the scope of his struggle on the literary front. . . .

In 1918, a few months after he published his first short story, he wrote *My Views on Chastity and Sutteeism*. From then until his death, he wrote six to seven hundred essays, which provided him with an immense arena, through which he could gallop freely as a pioneer thinker and fighter and give full expression to his artistic genius. (p. 38)

The content of these essays is so diverse as to be virtually all-embracing, ranging from fundamental problems of the revolution to such topics as children's toys. He waged innumerable battles and attacked innumerable enemies: imperialists, warlords, Kuomintang diehards, the men who advocated a return to the past, reactionary writers, "those who trade in revolution," "murderers of the present and future," and "preachers of death." He turned his attention to this great variety of topics because he wanted to indicate and break through to a new way of life for the Chinese people—the democratic revolution which was being carried through and the socialist revolution which was to follow. . . .

It is clear then that the goal which Lu Hsun tried to express and strove for in his stories became more sharply defined in his essays, and he became more confident of its attainment. (p. 39)

Almost every one of these essays bears the imprint of a brilliant mind, and each is clearly the handiwork of a genius in the creation of types and a master of satirical writing; while readers are moved by the passion of a true champion of the people, with his burning love and hate, his blazing anger, and dauntless, invincible might.

It was as a great essayist with his own distinctive style that Lu Hsun became an outstanding polemicist, and a giant in China's cultural revolution who dwarfed all his predecessors. (p. 40)

The scope and profundity of Lu Hsun's thought are paralleled in his art, giving evidence of the most penetrating observation of Chinese society and culture, and the closest links with the people. To describe events or people, Lu Hsun uses a method he calls "drawing the eyes," which implies conveying the spirit of a thing with the utmost conciseness and refinement. (p. 41)

So the salient feature of his style is the accuracy, penetration and vividness with which he depicts a thing, often in a minimum of words. With a few strokes he brings out a man's chief characteristics. Lu Hsun also expresses ideas by means of concrete images, equally penetrating, vivid and compact. With a few sentences, or just one sentence, he can get to the heart of a matter and convey its innermost meaning. This conciseness and refinement, typical of Lu

Hsun's language, are precisely the most striking characteristics of traditional Chinese poetry and prose.

Lu Hsun's vocabulary is very rich. He paid great attention to language. . . . The chief source of his language was the living vernacular of the people, their idioms and colloquialisms, and certain tags from old books and classical allusions; sometimes he also uses expressions translated from foreign words, as well as foreign syntax. Lu Hsun's writing enriched the Chinese language and developed such good features as its conciseness, strength, vividness and wittiness.

Lu Hsun's satire is simply the most concise delineation and criticism of the dark side of society. . . . In Lu Hsun's satire we can find the simple humour and mockery common to Chinese peasants and folk literature. We can also recognize in him the successor of the satirists in classical Chinese literature. Lu Hsun's genius in this field alone wins him an outstanding place in the history of Chinese literature. He developed the humorous wisdom of the Chinese people, and the satiric tradition of both classical and folk literature. (pp. 41-2)

> Feng Hsueh-Feng, "The Trail Blazed by Lu Hsun," in *Chinese Literature, No. 4, April, 1956, pp. 33-42.*

T. A. HSIA (essay date 1964)

[Lu Hsün] loathed the old and hailed the new with too much vehemence to allow his argument to be contained within an entirely rational framework. The power of his rhetoric has much to do with violent contrast between light and darkness, sleep and awakening, between the man who refuses to be eaten and the man who eats men, the human being and the ghost, the single fighter and the hostile forces around him, the contrast between everything the rebel identifies with and everything that oppresses and crushes him. (pp. 195-96)

Lu Hsün became a writer, and a voluminous one at that, almost by accident. He cultivated the craft of writing against his own wishes. Much as he depended on the vocabulary and rhetorical devices of the *wen-yen* for his compositions in *pai-hua* prose, it is his poetry that carries most significantly the paradox of his historical position. Lu Hsün's poetical production was intermittent and never large in quantity, but the excellence of the poems in the old style that he wrote is undeniable. They at least equal his best *pai-hua* prose in terseness, bitterness, sardonic humor, and the strange beauty of "frozen flames" and the "intricate red lines forming patterns like coral beneath the surface of bluish-white ice." But these poems are also traditional literary exercises couched in a language too learned for readers not conversant with classical culture, exercises that served a dubious public function but deflected the energy of both author and reader from "action." In these private compositions, intended to be read by at most only a few friends, he was more than satisfying a whim: he was writing poetry in the manner used by the poets before him. . . .

In spite of his extreme position in the rejection of old China and old Chinese books, he could at times submit himself completely to old Chinese poetry, with all its obscurity and weight of tradition. He could adapt himself to the culture of the traditional élite and derive whatever comfort it might still afford in an age of violent social changes and political revolution.

In contrast with Lu Hsün's accomplishment as a poet in the traditional style, his contribution to *pai-hua* poetry was meagre and indifferent.... But when now and then his creative urge took a poetical turn, he simply resorted to *wen-yen*, a handy vehicle for a man with his cultural upbringing. He was not entirely unhappy within the restriction of the traditional poetical form, which became for him rather a fulfillment and a challenge. As a literary craftsman, he delighted in the *mot juste* and neat phrasing, in excision and compression, in making subtle allusions, in giving surprise by contrast and juxtaposition, and in regulating his emotions according to rhyme, rhythm, and form; he might also have felt the secret gratification of seeing a job well done, a pride in his successful emulation of the masters whom he knew by heart. Meanwhile, he quarrelled with tradition *in toto*. (pp. 197-98)

Lu Hsün left behind a book of unique interest: *Yeh-ts'ao* (*The Wild Grass*). Of the twenty-four pieces included, only one reads like a formal *pai-hua* poem, "A Lament for My Disappointed Love"; but it is a burlesque, not a very clever burlesque either, of the current love poems which Lu Hsün disdained for their cheap facile sentiments and jingling notes. The presence of doggerel among serious poems-in-prose in *The Wild Grass* implies a comment on the sorry condition of *pai-hua* poetry as Lu Hsün saw it. The rest of the book is genuine poetry in embryo: images imbued with strong emotional intensity, flowing and stopping in darkly glowing but oddly shaped lines, like molten metal failing to find a mold. (p. 198)

Lu Hsün's dream world is extremely bare, being composed of nothing but light and darkness and the colorless, half-awake nonentity who helplessly listens to what is said to him and watches things happen to him. This is an experience which requires much greater poetical talent than Lu Hsün possessed to bring out its full meaning. Troubled by dreams like that, Lu Hsün might have carried Chinese poetry, even in its classical form, into a new realm, to give formal rendering to a kind of terror and anxiety, an experience which we might call modern, since it is hardly found among the themes of traditional Chinese poetry, rich as its contents are. Instead, he wrote in prose, but in a style which, highly personal in its jerky rhythm and stark images, had a salutary effect on the *pai-hua*. For he took the *pai-hua* away from the paths guided by the ideals of democratism.... Lu Hsün's rhetorical devices may degenerate into mannerisms, at the hands of his imitators as well as at his own hands, in less felicitous moments; but he let *pai-hua* do things that it had never done before—things not even the best classical writers had ever thought of doing in *wen-yen*. In this sense, Lu Hsün was a truly modern writer. (pp. 198-99)

Those who admire Lu Hsün as a great realist should be reminded of the dimensions of his realism. He began several pieces in *The Wild Grass* with the statement, "I had a dream ..." and those dreams have such a bizarre beauty and delirious terror that they are really nightmares. Even pieces not marked out as dreams have that nightmarish quality of inconsequence and the shock of misplaced reality. In *The Wild Grass*, therefore, Lu Hsün glanced into the unconscious.... His failure to produce a masterpiece using his knowledge of the unconscious mind was probably due to his fear. He was too much occupied with the struggle to shake off the dreams. His beliefs in enlightenment did

not really dispel the darkness; but they served as a shield from the dangerous attraction that darkness exercised. Hope, however illusory, looked lovelier, and it was preferred to the dreams of night.

So it may be said that the gate of darkness for Lu Hsün owes its weight to two forces: one is traditional Chinese literature and culture, the other the writer's troubled psyche. These two forces, oppressive, penetrating, yet unavoidable, were keenly felt by Lu Hsün. One may not agree with his contention that a younger generation could be raised to lead a life free of them, but he uttered the cries of hope in desperation. His heroic stance implies defeat and the position he chose for himself was almost tragic. The very allusion to the legendary hero who was crushed to death suggests Lu Hsün's sense of powerlessness against darkness and his acceptance of sacrifice. It is this sense that gives his body of writings a sadness which marks his genius. (pp. 199-200)

Lu Hsün seemed to be an expert in depicting death's ugliness, not only in his poems-in-prose, but also in his short stories. Many living creatures in his fiction have such a pallid hue, stony stare, and slow, still movements that they seem like corpses even before death finally catches up with them. Funeral rites, graves, executions, especially by beheading, and even sickness are the themes that repeatedly engage his creative imagination. The shadows of death creep over his works in various shapes, ranging from a subtle menace, as in the madman's imaginary fear of death in *The Diary of a Madman*, through the quiet disappearance of Hsiang-lin-sao in *Benediction*, to the real terror: the beheaded martyr and the TB patient in *Medicine*, the old scholar who ran after the illusory white light only to drown himself in the river in *The White Light*, and the corpse with a grim smile on its face in *The Solitary*. The "happy ending" of Ah Q perhaps has its happy side when death comes to the ignorant villager. (p. 200)

So death, like old China, an object of revulsion, has also its fascination. Lu Hsün never made up his mind about the attitude he should adopt towards these two objects of revulsion. (p. 201)

Lu Hsün did not accomplish much in the exploration of this mystery [death]; he was far more pronounced in his angry protest against social evils. But what set him apart from his contemporaries was that he acknowledged the mystery and that he never denied its power. He could even be spellbound by the dark forces in life; he had feelings for individuals in moments of isolation from their social environment, as several of his best short stories, the poems-in-prose of *The Wild Grass,* and some other occasional essays attest. These works are perhaps what will continue to be read after the issue of social reform in China has changed its nature. Indeed, Lu Hsün was not a true representative of the May 4th Movement insofar as that term is understood to mean a popular movement with positive aims to discard the old and adopt the new. He embodied rather the conflict between the old and the new and some deeper conflicts, too, that transcend history. He never attained that state of serenity enjoyed by his contemporaries, Hu Shih and Chou Tso-jen; but he was probably a greater genius than either of them. (pp. 204-05)

Anyway, what was the nature of Lu Hsün's times, even if they are treated as merely a period of transition? It can never fully be comprehended by means of such contrasting metaphors as light and darkness, because there were such an interesting variety of shades of grey. The twilight hours hold ghostly shapes, shadowy whispers and other wonders, and phantasmata which are apt to be dismissed in the impatient waiting for the dawn. As a chronicler of those hours, Lu Hsün wrote with fine perception and a subtlety and profundity of feeling, qualities which were usually lost to him when he spoke as a conscious rebel. (p. 206)

> *T. A. Hsia, "Aspects of the Power of Darkness in Lu Hsün," in* Journal of Asian Studies *(copyright 1964 by the Association for Asian Studies), Vol. XXIII, No. 2, February, 1964, pp. 195-207.*

LAWRENCE W. CHISOLM (essay date 1967)

Lu Hsun, like the madman in his famous story ["Diary of a Madman"], insisted on penetrating the surfaces of pious words to find out what was really happening. His report of what he discovered presented symbolically in this first story raises questions at the outset about the organizing structures of his imaginative world and about the relation of that world to his life and to the course of revolutionary change in China. Why, for example, do images of enclosure and cannibalism introduced in this story recur throughout his best writing? What connections exist between his personal history and the shifting conditions of Chinese culture? (p. 226)

Lu Hsun's skepticism is fundamental. The only certainty which he offers is the certainty of change. Many of his finest stories describe how "you can't go home again," how new experience makes the old accustomed ways no longer comforting, in fact no longer possible. His most complex characters are men uprooted and made wanderers not only by the forces of change but by their own honesty and sensibility. There is little nostalgia for the past in Lu Hsun's fictive world. Nor does he sentimentalize the common people. At best they live by habit, evading unpleasant facts by dreams; at worst they are cruel and credulous, their illusions murderous. . . .

Lu Hsun's sensitive and often scholarly wanderers, by contrast, feel at home nowhere but keep going, surviving somehow for a while, their imaginations alive to contrasts: flowers in the snow, light and darkness, the peppery and the bland, stasis and motion. Even despair becomes a kind of vanity: in the end it is survival that matters and the only hope, if it can be called that, the road itself. To the voyager reflecting back on childhood as he floats down the river, hope is not something absolute which either exists or does not; it is "like the roads that travelers make across the face of the earth where there were none before." Although the past revisited by the voyager in "*Ku Hsiang*" ("My Old Home") cannot be recaptured, it survives as an image connecting the past with the future. (p. 234)

All Lu Hsun's writing is about China and directed at China —even his translations aim to enlarge Chinese consciousness—his mission, to help create forms of written expression through which he and his countrymen might understand their situations, might name their personal and common plights and joys, so that they would no longer be cut off from one another by walls of silence and indifference.

This concern animates his writing as a recurrent theme and also defines the achievements of his style. Through his best

work he released the newly literate into a world complexly imagined yet disciplined so as to heighten perception, neither blurring the mind's newly opened eyes with sentimental plots nor dazzling with eccentric impressions. His chosen instrument was a supple vernacular, clear and economical, a style strong enough to assimilate both classical phrases and foreign ideas, using them to particular effect, embedding the old and the new in the flow of orderly modern consciousness. His short stories introduced the form to Chinese writing and set standards for all who followed; his prose poems combined classical with vernacular in new forms; and in his regular social commentary he developed an influential new style of *tsa wen*, terse pithy essays aimed at specific targets and adaptable across a wide range from satire and polemics to personal impressions and random reflections of all sorts. (p. 235)

Ah Q, Lu Hsun's most famous character, was almost immediately taken into the Chinese language as a symbol of "Ah Q-ism," a set of typical Chinese deficiencies. . . . But Ah Q has other qualities which complicate interpretations of his progress toward death by execution for revolutionary crimes he did not commit during a revolution which did not happen. For example, he is alert to power but not obsequious; he is active rather than passive; and his honesty gets him into as much trouble as his fantasy—in fact, his honesty is what finally kills him. Ah Q totally lacks any past, even a name, and as the story unfolds it becomes evident that he is continually reinvented by others, that he is largely comprised of other people's shifting images of him. Equally striking is the fact that he never learns from experience because he has no continuous interior life of his own. Words fuddle him, especially fragments of old Confucian homilies, and leave him dependent for connection with the world on scattered cues imprinted by threats and ridicule and by animal pain and pleasure. Only when he recognizes that he is on his way to death does he comprehend his feelings and ignore the expectations of the crowd. This nameless man is killed by forces from the past in the name of changes which are unreal partly because left unnamed. But it is also because Ah Q has no past that he dies; in a sense, he has no future because he has no connection to any past, and some kind of continuity remains necessary even in the most extreme situations. (pp. 237-38)

Lu Hsun's sense of the extremity of China's situation and the terrors latent in hopelessness found imaginative integration in recurring images of cannibalism. His first vernacular story hinged on traditional cannibal acts: the central delusion-which-is-truth is the madman's discovery in a book of China's history that although words like "benevolence" and "righteousness" were scrawled over every page, hidden between the lines everywhere were the words "*Ch'ih jen*" ("Eat men"). The theme recurs in Lu Hsun's recollections of Fan Ai-nung: the Chinese patriot from Shaohsing who assassinates the Manchu governor has his heart torn out by his captors, then fried and eaten. In Lu Hsun's symbolic world cannibal acts represent ultimate violent human paradoxes.

Other kinds of death imagery cluster around cannibalism. Images of enclosure—rooms and boxes which hem in, walls which bar the way, ice which is freezing fire, circles which constrict—contribute to a sense of expectancies blocked, of breath stifled, of forces pressing inward toward crises of contained violence, powerfully implosive and apocalyptic in the aggregate. This enclosure imagery intensifies the symbolic implosiveness of cannibal acts imagined as breaking into the core enclosures of the human body.

Several paradoxes converge. Although cannibal acts break through walls which isolate man from man, such acts simultaneously separate man from man: cannibalism simultaneously connects and sunders, nurtures and destroys. In the imagery of group relationships, human nurture, when imagined as a cannibalistic sequence, provides a symbolic model of "partial modernization" applicable to a China "Westernized" in the nineteenth century and, in the process, sliced up like a melon, with the added cut that the slicing was said to be for China's own good—benevolent cannibalism.

Cannibalism can also be considered as symbolizing the terrors of cultural change and suggesting the proper limits of rates of change. New forms which replace old ones too rapidly, which destroy the old completely in the name of the new, are cannibalistic. When the new devours the old, the future is destroying parts of itself which require a nurturing relation to the past in order to survive. This is one of the paradoxes of Ah Q, who was killed by the past because he had no past; it is part of the plight of Lu Hsun's fictional wanderers whose connections with both past and future have been ruptured by rapid change. The paradox is present in creating new forms of written language: as vernacular style displaces and destroys Chinese classical forms, it destroys some of the qualities of conception it needs—latinization breaks even more completely.

Lu Hsun's responses to a series of extreme situations in China's history led his imagination toward comparable symbolic forms, in this case, paradoxes appropriately violent. Toward the end of his life he was driven to fight with a fierceness often thought of as "revolutionary." What made him a revolutionary writer whose news stays news was a symbolic imagination which nurtured continuity as it recognized overwhelming changes and which held on to individual life while sensing universal destruction. (pp. 240-41)

> *Lawrence W. Chisolm, "Lu Hsun and Revolution in Modern China," in* Yale French Studies *(copyright © Yale French Studies 1967), No. 39, 1967, pp. 226-41.*

JAROSLAV PRŮŠEK (essay date 1967)

[The story "Huai-chiu" ("The Past")] was written eight years before the May Fourth Movement began and is thus an isolated phenomenon which cannot be explained in terms of the general tendencies of the time. . . . The story is written in *wen-yen*, the traditional literary language, so that not even in this respect is it comparable with the literature produced under the influence of the May Fourth Movement. Nevertheless, as we read it we feel quite clearly that it is a work entirely of the new modern literature and not the literature of the preceding period. (p. 170)

The first difference between this and traditional stories lies in the structure of the plot. . . . [Traditional stories] are based on a definite plot, the solution of which provides the end of the story. (pp. 170-71)

What is the plot of Lu Hsün's first literary effort? It opens with the narrator recalling an unpleasant teacher under whom he had suffered as a child and describing the bad methods of teaching used. . . . The finishing touch to this portrait of a pedantic and unpleasant creature shows him bending his bald and very shiny head so close to the book that, dampened by his breath, the paper tears. Thus, instead of a plot we have reminiscences of childhood and the evocation of a mood.

Not until well on in this description do we meet with anything that could be called a plot. The lesson is interrupted by the local rich man, a miser no less objectionable than the teacher. . . .

The miser brings frightening news that the "long-haired rebels" are approaching the city. At first the teacher doubts that this can be so, since the T'ai-p'ing rebellion (of the long-haired ones) had been crushed forty years before; but when the rich man declares that he has heard the news from "the third gentleman," the teacher drops his disbelief; he respects "the third gentleman" more than the sages of old.

The rich man and the teacher take counsel how to gain the rebels' favor. (p. 171)

Soon the dramatic action which the rich man's news seemed to have sparked fades out. While servants are retailing horror stories from the days of the T'ai-p'ing rebellion, the terrified teacher appears, followed by the rich man, and announces that it was a false alarm and had been only a band of refugees from famine-stricken parts. (p. 172)

It is clear that Lu Hsün's interest lay elsewhere than in the creation of exciting plots to arouse the fantasy of his readers.

Turning to the central problem of this study, we can consider Lu Hsün's approach to his plot as one of simplification, a reduction of the plot to its simplest components, and an attempt to present his subject without the framework of an explanatory story. The author wants to go right to the heart of his subject without the stepping-stone of a plot. This is what strikes me as the specifically modern feature of the new literature; I would even formulate it as a principle that it is characteristic of the new literature to play down the function of the plot, even to the point of dispensing with it altogether. . . .

There are a number of similar examples in the work of Lu Hsün, so that this weakening of the function of the plot can be considered one of his fundamental principles. (p. 173)

[Lu Hsün] substituted sketches, reminiscences, lyrical descriptions, etc. for the traditional belletristic forms of China and Europe. These tendencies shared by the work of Lu Hsün and that of modern European prose writers could, I believe, be called the penetration of the epic by the lyric and the breaking up of the traditional epic forms. (p. 174)

[The] greatest difference between this story and the traditional form of the Chinese story, however, is to be seen in this recording of insignificant conversation. In the old form of story, dialogue was an important instrument for the development of the plot and determination of the structure. Here the dialogue is quite autonomous, not even serving the purpose of more precise characterization. . . . It is simply a form of presentation of a certain atmosphere, a certain situation, or a set of human relationships, such as we frequently see in the work of such modern writers in the West as Hemingway, Joyce, or Faulkner. Fragments of conversation bring the character before us without any direct description, demonstrating relationships that could not otherwise be described, and revealing the mind of the person, his vacillations and indefinable nuances of thought, in a way straightforward description could never do. Basically it is the principal way of revealing the inner mind of the characters. This makes it all the more interesting to note that in Chinese literature it is Lu Hsün, writing in the old classical language, who sets out in this new direction, one which calls for very sensitive use of living language and the instinctive ability to hear and give expression to every tone and shade of feeling. (pp. 174-75)

> *Jaroslav Průšek, "Lu Hsün's 'Huai Chiu': A Precursor of Modern Chinese Literature" (originally a paper prepared for the Conference of Orientalists at Ann Arbor, Michigan, 1967), in* The Harvard Journal of Asiatic Studies, *Vol. 29, 1969, pp. 169-76.*

JEROME F. SEATON (essay date 1970)

Lu Hsün has been the subject of more scholarly research, criticism, and perhaps even general discussion in China, Japan and the West than any other single modern Chinese literary figure. His popularity in the scholarly world has closely paralleled his popularity in the Chinese literary marketplace. (p. 72)

Lu Hsün was, both in point of time and in personal commitment, artist first and revolutionary only afterward. Even in his earliest works his commitment to his private vision of reality, and the great artfulness with which he realizes this commitment, would seem to mar the satirical effects of his writing. (p. 73)

Though he wrote all of his famous work in a vigorous colloquial style, he retained and used all the values of classical Chinese literature: the value of concision, the uses of motif, the creation of super-logical or super-syntactical connections by means of precise and evocative diction. Lu Hsün's work appears "modern," even Jamesian, in its textures and in its organicness, not because Lu Hsün studied Western models but precisely because he wrote from within the great tradition of Chinese literary art. . . .

Lu Hsün's first short story, *K'uang-jen r-chi* (*Diary of a Madman*), offers prime examples of those features of his work which mark him as a great artist. (p. 74)

In this story, Lu Hsün's precise word choice mimics the mental state of the *Diary*'s supposed author, and at the same time creates a verbal texture which helps to extend the meanings of the mad ramblings within the protagonist's mind into a meaningful relationship with the facts of the Chinese society within which that mind has been set adrift. In the first line of the diary proper, the madman, who suffers from a persecution complex and feels that those about him desire to eat his flesh, slips while writing a very simple character, setting down [the character] *hen,* meaning fierce, for [a similar character] *hen,* which means "very" but which is not a particularly strong modifier. . . . This ploy by the artist sets the tone of the work well. Throughout the story the madman's vision remains fierce, preserved by the artist's choice of fresh and stark objects and images for realistic description. (pp. 74-5)

Diary of a Madman is, then, an extremely well written piece of fiction and on one level at least an effective piece of revolutionary propaganda in its brilliantly poetic description of the evil nature of traditional Chinese society. Yet when one looks closer at the piece, it becomes clear that even here Lu Hsün did not resist the urge to be true to his own vision. The madman ends the diary with a fervent plea to "save the children," who alone have not yet been tainted by the cannibalism of the Chinese social system. The plea seems strong; yet in the light of the introduction to the diary (written in the classical style) in which Lu Hsün pretends to offer the diary itself as an object of scientific interest to psychologists, the whole story becomes at once more terrifying and more sardonically humorous. The reader is told that the "Madman" has recovered from his "illness" and is in another place, awaiting appointment as an official. In short, the man who knew the truth was mad, and no longer mad, no longer knows the truth. . . . Thus the story at once has more of a psychological than a social, hence propagandistic, emphasis, and in large terms, displays a view of human nature too pessimistic to allow much hope of long lasting social change. (p. 76)

The major change evident in Lu Hsün's later work is a turning away from the open satire which made his early works both popular and successful as propaganda despite their essential pessimism. Lu Hsün's art is not noticably reduced in the later works, however, and may appear subtler. *Fei tsao* or *Soap,* the author's last effort, shows the same sort of "technical virtuosity" with which Lu Hsün began his career as artist of the vernacular. . . . The most important incident in the story, Ssu Ming's viewing of a young beggar girl as she is ridiculed by loafers on the street, is acted out off stage and we only know about it from Ssu Ming's own relation of the event. That Ssu Ming's decision to buy soap for his wife is related closely to this experience is clear, but his motivation is perhaps not so simple as his wife believes. At one level Ssu Ming is obviously equating his own wife with the young and the beautiful again. Beneath this, the soap is linked directly with the girl, and Ssu Ming, counter to his traditional values, is in search of illicit pleasure for its own sake, as much as to recapture his lost youth. The foreign Soap and the Cleanliness it brings with it are the symbols of the New China in Ssu Ming's mind, and through the soap Lu Hsün neatly ties together the urge for reform and the equally strong urge for reaction, the universal paradox of man's twofold desires: to remain young, having things always as of old, and yet to dare a future. There is no explicit connection made, and in fact there is no explicit statement of consequence in the story as a whole. The story ends on an ambiguous note, and the very ambiguity of the work as a whole is its strongest point. Ssu Ming's motivations cannot be sorted out or categorized, yet they are recognizably and humanly complex. (p. 77)

Creating a real work on paper with the tools and the care of the writer of classical essays of *fu,* Lu Hsün offers his readers real people and real experience. His characters are almost to a man, or a woman, too complex and too ambiguous to be put in a box and marked "satirical figure." His art is too big to be put in any box at all. (p. 78)

> *Jerome F. Seaton, "On Lu Hsün," in* Critique: Studies in Modern Fiction *(copyright © by Critique, 1970), Vol. XII, No. 1, 1970, pp. 72-8.*

PATRICK HANAN (essay date 1974)

Lu Hsün, in choosing an artistic tradition within which to work, was drawn primarily to Gogol, Sienkiewicz, and Sōseki, with their range of ironic techniques, and only secondarily to Andreev and literary Modernism. . . . The concept of irony, so far left undefined, is thus an appropriate point from which to begin the analysis of Lu Hsün's technique. (p. 75)

Basic or hard-core irony . . . is *the technique of raising something in the audience's estimation while appearing to lower it, or of lowering something in the audience's estimation while appearing to raise it.* . . . In comparison with our notion of irony, "satire" will be taken as indicating both a technique and a purpose. . . . The purpose of satire is ridicule, which it achieves by various techniques of reduction or belittling. The "lowering" techniques of irony may serve this function—in Lu Hsün's fiction they are the primary techniques—but they are not, of course, the only techniques which satire can use. The "raising" techniques of irony do not contribute to satire. (pp. 75-6)

A certain ironic conception is found in Lu Hsün's first piece of fiction, *Looking Back to the Past*, a story written in 1911 on the basis of the current revolution and the Boxer rebellion. The narrator is a man recollecting his childhood, when there were constant rumors of the impending arrival of the rebels. The story is told in part with a nine-year-old boy's understanding; the judgment of the mature man is brought only occasionally into play. His tutor's hypocrisy is given extra force by the artlessness of the narrator's account. The narrator, for example, reflects the conventional view that the tutor, as an educated man, must be superior to the kindly, ignorant servants, but in such a way as to bring the reader to precisely the opposite conclusion. . . . It is significant that in this rather shapeless story, which does not contain some of the other characteristic features of Lu Hsün's writing, irony is already present. Irony is the first, and perhaps the most pronounced, feature of Lu Hsün's fiction.

The closest structural parallel is *K'ung I-chi*, one of Lu Hsün's best stories. . . . The object of irony is the derelict scholar, and the ironic factor the twelve-year-old boy who works in the inn. . . . Although it is represented as a reminiscence, some thirty years after the event, the mature man's judgment is not allowed to condition the boy's naivete. To the boy's mind, K'ung, the butt of jokes by all the regular patrons, is merely a source of amusement in the midst of a dull job, and it is through the boy's dim, uncomprehending mind that we see the casual cruelty in which the derelict lives his life. Unlike *Looking Back to the Past*, this story works according to the irony of raising, not lowering. Precisely because he is the object of derision, the pathos and horror of the old man's end are more convincing than they might have been in any direct portrayal through his own consciousness. Yet that is without doubt the way Andreev would have approached this material, and Sienkiewicz also, probably with the aid of an ironic narrator standing outside the action.

Lu Hsün's first vernacular story, *The Diary of a Madman*, . . . has a different, though still all-embracing, ironic conception. Here a systematic symbolism is applied ironically. The madman's perception symbolizes a set of insights into the traditional social system, but the working of the symbols is ironic. To relegate the symbolic truth about Chinese society to the perception of a madman is, on the surface, to dismiss it as mere raving. In fact, by the working of irony, his perception is given singular force, force such as no *direct* symbolic account would be likely to achieve. (pp. 79-80)

Though remote from the *Diary* in the quality of its irony, *The Story of Hair* has at least this in common with it—a sustained view is cast into an ironic light. This is Lu Hsün's amusing discourse, with its serious implications, on hair as the maleficent factor in modern Chinese history. . . .

The irony which Lu Hsün found in Sienkiewicz and Gogol was presentational irony conveyed by a more or less dramatized narrator standing outside the action. This is the principal method of *Ah Q*, and part of the method of *Tomorrow*, *Storm in a Teacup*, and *The Double Fifth*, in which it is combined with other kinds of irony. In *Ah Q*, the narrator's tone is in violent contrast to the events described; the one is lofty, the other squalid, and the contrast makes the latter ridiculous. There is no need to illustrate this ironic technique, which comes under the broad definition of the mockheroic—the treatment of Ah Q as candidate for a biography, the historical parallels to his pursuit of the servingwoman, and so forth. (p. 81)

The main structure of both *Medicine* and *Tomorrow* is juxtapositional irony. In this case, the ironic factor does not convey information about the object; it affects our opinion of the object by its mere association with it. In *Medicine*, the stories of the two boys run parallel, and the symmetry is sustained at the end of the story in the meeting their mothers have in the graveyard. It is the juxtaposition of the consumptive with the revolutionary, with the consumptive in the foreground, that whole pathetic scene of ignorance and superstition, which heightens the tragedy of the revolutionary. . . . As frequently in Lu Hsün, the inn or teahouse is a natural symbol for heedless frivolity, for the disregard of human tragedy. In *Tomorrow*, the inn is juxtaposed, quite literally, with the widow's house; the two stand side by side, and their association is reinforced by the fact that they are the only two places in town which have lights burning all night long. . . . Drunken song begins the story, punctuates it, and brings it to an end, and the song can be regarded as a commentary on the tragedy next door. The revelers have really very little connection with the widow and her sick child. They mention her once or twice, there is a certain subdued sexual feeling present, and they offer to help after the child's death, but that is all. The inn's function is to stand in ironic contrast to the private tragedy. (p. 83)

Lu Hsün showed a far greater degree of psychological interest in his second collection, an interest manifested particularly in the irony of character, the contrast between the pretension or misperception, on the one hand, and the action or reality, on the other. In this kind of irony, there is no ironic narrator, for both object and factor are located within the character. Such narrators as there are in Lu Hsün's later stories are involved in the action, and their biases form part of the reader's judgment of the story. . . .

The three stories of character irony are *Soap*, *Happy Family*, and *Master Kao*. In each, the ironic contrast between pretension and action is made clear without any obvious ironical comment. (p. 84)

Brothers is another story with some claim to the irony of character. The man who prides himself on his relationship to his brother, who sets himself up as a model for others, is revealed to himself, by a trick of his subconscious, as the prey of selfishness and callousness, even of brutality. But the claim is more apparent than real. The gap between misperception and reality is revealed to the hero, and he is appalled. . . . (p. 86)

Two stories, *Regret for the Past* and *New Year's Sacrifice,* combine presentational irony with character irony in a more complex way than Lu Hsün attempted elsewhere. Both have narrators who are themselves involved in the action, and both narrators—this point is never overtly made—are slightly false, or at least inadequate, personalities. (p. 87)

[For example, in] *Regret for the Past,* the narrator, for all his penitence, does not quite do moral or emotional justice to the lover he has rejected. Although the story contains a good deal of moral ambiguity, it must be remembered that the lover is a social victim, like Ai-ku in *Divorce* or the madman in *The Lamp That Was Kept Alight.* The narrator incurs moral responsibility because he has encouraged her to leave home, like Ibsen's Nora, and has then, for reasons not primarily of his own making, been unable to sustain the relationship. The girl's fate, as she is sent home and dies among unfeeling relatives, emerges with particular poignancy from the narrator's account. (pp. 87-8)

Peking Street Scene illustrates a new kind of all-encompassing ironic conception. It is a brilliant work, on the boundary of prose fiction, an extreme instance of Lu Hsün's interest in ironic structure and conception. A criminal is brought out on the street under guard as a deterrent to the public—this is the significance of the title . . .—and a crowd of onlookers forms. The onlookers jostle for position, wait, and then when they see nothing is about to happen, break ranks to rush away and gape at a rickshaw accident. There is no overt irony beyond a slight touch or two. . . . There is no comment, no center of consciousness, and nobody is even named. Even my précis errs, in ascribing motives. Lu Hsün's narrative is like a camera, moving here and there, picking up this detail and that action, reflecting the surface of things. It is the camera's detachment which constitutes irony. Lu Hsün loathed people's capacity for treating tragic or pathetic scenes as occasions for diversion or curiosity, instead of as matter for conscience and sympathy. (p. 89)

Satire, here defined as the product of a technique (wit, indirection, etc.) and a purpose (ridicule) is, of course, the predominant mode in Lu Hsün's fiction, and the lowering kind of irony is the main technique of his satire. (p. 94)

The ideals implied in Lu Hsün's satire are concerned, in the main, with personal relations in society. This is the area of traditional Confucian ethics, which is no doubt why Lu Hsün seized upon it for his satiric purposes. His first stories, with their obtrusive ironic techniques, were perceived by the public as symbolizing the great schism in contemporary culture, and are consequently the more famous. The concerns of some of the later stories seem, in contrast, rather slight—Lu Hsün's conscience was exceedingly fine-meshed, and these are mostly stories which embody some of his own experience—but they are equally about social morality: relations between husband and wife, father and child, social hypocrisy, and social apathy.

The satiric and realistic modes make different demands and are not easy to reconcile. . . . Satire, with its wit, irony, and so forth, works against the illusion of realism, while realism, with its close imitation of experience, tends to negate the distance or detachment which is essential to satire. . . . Satiric realism, the mode of most of Lu Hsün's short sto-

ries, is therefore a difficult mode to use successfully. Its most natural technique, upon which Lu Hsün's stories and the *Ju-lin wai-shih* both largely depend, is character irony. But even this technique is hard to sustain without a loss of satiric detachment, and it is not surprising to find it used in the short story and the episodic novel.

Lu Hsün's ironic varieties belong to an artistic perception, not a philosophical perception. . . . Finally, irony and detachment are a psychological and artistic necessity for a writer as gripped by moral rage, didactic passion, and private conscience as Lu Hsün evidently was. (pp. 94-6)

Patrick Hanan, "The Technique of Lu Hsün's Fiction," in The Harvard Journal of Asiatic Studies, *Vol. 34, 1974, pp. 53-96.*

WILLIAM A. LYELL, JR. (essay date 1976)

Since we are approaching the stories from the standpoint of Lu Hsün's vision of reality, a useful way of determining the content of that vision will be to take up the stories as a whole and see what kinds of people inhabit Lu Hsün's fictionalized world. The majority of important roles go to intellectuals; women of all kinds come in a close second; third, we have various people in service occupations (boatmen, rickshaw men, and jacks-of-all trades); fourth, rebels, mad and sane; and last, one peasant, Jun-t'u in "Home Town." All these characters act out their roles against a human backdrop which we may appropriately label "ordinary people" and treat as a separate category.

We encounter three types of intellectuals: the traditional, the in-between, and the modern. They can be distinguished primarily by education: traditional intellectuals were trained in private tutorial schools (*ssu-shu*) which prepared them for the civil service examinations, in-betweens in Sino-Western academies (*hsüeh-t'ang*) which prepared them in modern as well as traditional subjects, and moderns in public schools (*hsüeh-hsiao*) which prepared them primarily in modern subjects, while often paying lip service to tradition. . . . Each of the types correlates roughly with a historical period: the traditional intellectual with the Manchu dynasty, the in-between with the period of transition between the end of the dynasty and the establishment of the republic, and the modern with the Republican period.

The traditional intellectuals in Lu Hsün's stories are presented as either the oppressors or the oppressed; there is no middle ground. The first of them, of course, is Master Baldy in "Remembrances of the Past." To the little boy . . . he is merely an old pedant, but to the reader he exemplifies the sterile, restrictive, hypocritical aspects of a superannuated tradition whose chief protectors are scholars and rich men. Freedom, creativity, and fulfillment are to be found among the uneducated (Old Wang and Amah Li), among the criminal (Taiping and other rebels), or out in the unspoiled, burgeoning world of green grasses and chirping insects in the back yard. Indeed one gains the impression that the solution to all problems (perhaps human salvation itself) lies in remaining uneducated, in becoming a rebel, or in escaping to nature. The traditional intellectual fleshes out the accumulated evils of the learning and history of the past. The adult Lu Hsün was painfully aware of what was wrong with the traditions of the past, but, unlike the little boy in "Remembrances of the Past," he had lost the naïveté that would suggest joining the servants or escaping to nature as an alternative. Inability to find a viable alternative probably does much to explain the bittersweet pessimism of Lu Hsün's best work. It is significant that the analysis of the oppressive nature of traditional intellectuals in "Remembrances of the Past" is done primarily through the eyes of a boy who has not yet been assimilated into society: he has not yet fully realized that both birth and circumstances have irrevocably singled him out for the very adult pattern against which he rebels, a fact that is painfully brought to the attention of the narrator of another story, "Home Town." . . . (pp. 140-41)

One of Lu Hsün's lifelong concerns was the discrepancy between name and reality; he had a tendency that bordered on compulsion to look beneath the surface of things. In "Diary of a Madman" the object of this compulsion is nothing less than the whole of traditional China; in "Brothers" it is a single individual vis-à-vis the traditional expectations of fraternal relationships (embodied in the clichés that Yüeh-sheng is forever mouthing at the office). Lu Hsün understood his experiences not as idiosyncratic happenings but rather as threads in the whole fabric of Chinese society and culture. His transformation of experience into fiction is a function of his peculiar ability to understand the general situation of the Chinese people in terms of his own life. It is this ability, in part, that makes him an artist. (p. 196)

With few exceptions, Lu Hsün is much more favorably disposed toward the women in his stories than he is toward the men. If the world is divided into two camps, the oppressors and the oppressed, women clearly belong to the latter group and therefore, given Lu Hsün's way of seeing things, are good. Lu Hsün always sided with the underdog—hierarchically (wives over husbands) and temporally (the young over the old). Those in subordinate ranks have the advantage of not having to justify their positions in society on the basis of religion, morality, or what have you; women, precisely because they occupy such a subordinate status, can afford to see things as they are, free from hypocrisy and without the aid of a pair of distorting glasses borrowed from this or that ideology. They are wholesomely concrete; their men are often hypocritically abstract. (p. 209)

The mirror that Lu Hsün held up to Chinese society was a devil's mirror, the mirror of a Mara poet which reflected the hitherto unnoticed and silent sufferings of oppressed groups. (p. 223)

The rebels against society, though numerically not the most representative, have perhaps the most important role in Lu Hsün's stories. When Lu Hsün addresses his readers directly, in the guise of narrator, more often than not, he does so as social critic or rebel. (pp. 246-47)

Perhaps Lu Hsün sometimes suspected that he was himself . . . a marginal rebel, one who like Wei Lien-shu had not ventured all the way out into the extreme land of open rebellion and madness, but rather had lingered in the in-between stretches of discontent, criticism, and near-neurosis. During the period when he wrote the stories in *Call to Arms* and *Wandering* he was, after all, a respectable government clerk holding down a sinecure in the Ministry of Education —a political moderate who sought to improve society through exhortation and persuasion. (p. 250)

In structure, Lu Hsün's short stories are quite varied; they range from the informality of anecdotes told over a cup of tea to the strict formalism of a classical ballet—from "The Story of Hair" to "A Warning to the People." If we take the stories as a whole, within this diversity a few characteristic structural devices emerge. These are:

Repetition—repetition of phrases, props, and even characters in an incremental, ballad-like fashion as a means of building up the underlying framework of the story.

Use of envelopes—a special instance of repetition in which the repeated elements serve as the opening and final curtains of the entire story or of scenes within it.

Contrasts of sound and silence—contrasts in which sound breaks upon silence to signal a beginning and is returned into silence to signal an end.

Contrasts of stillness and action—contrasts that occur in the mind's eye of the reader so that people and things are jarred into action as the story opens and then are returned into the quiescence from which they came as it ends.

One cannot claim that these elements are present in all of the stories, but they do occur, with modifications, in the majority and can, therefore, be considered as typical. Nor can one claim that the presence or absence of these devices is an absolute gauge of any individual story's worth. In the best of the stories, however, they provide structural clarity, create a certain theatrical quality, and lend poetic overtones. (pp. 263-64)

If, from a structural point of view, we ask what kinds of stories Lu Hsün wrote, we find that an obvious division can be made between the stories that employ a first-person narrator and those that do not. The former may be divided again into two groups: stories whose narrator is a fictional construct, and those whose narrator can be taken to represent the feelings, thoughts, and experiences of Lu Hsün himself. The stories with Lu Hsün as narrator divide further into those which present him in a polemical frame of mind and those (rather atypical and written somewhat under the influence of Eroshenko) which present him in a basically sentimental mood. The various groupings can be exemplified as follows:

Stories told by a fictional narrator—"Diary of a Madman," "K'ung Yi-chi," and "Remorse"

Stories told by Lu Hsün—(i) in a polemical mood: "A Trifling Incident," "The Story of Hair," "Home Town," "The New Year's Sacrifice," "Upstairs in a Wineshop," and "The Isolate"; and (ii) in a sentimental mood: "Some Rabbits and a Cat," "A Comedy of Ducks," and "Village Opera" (p. 267)

As in many of the best stories, in "Soap" Lu Hsün establishes structure through ballad-like, incremental repetition. The dominant repeated elements are two props and a line of dialogue. The story opens as Ssu-ming comes home and presents his wife with a cake of scented soap; it closes with a description of her washing with a second cake of scented soap which she has, apparently, bought on her own. These two cakes of soap provide the typical Lu Hsün envelope, and the cake of soap bought by the husband serves to tie the many incidents of the story together in a thematic unity. (p. 274)

In Taoist fashion, one might say that the language of the stories in *Call to Arms* and *Wandering* achieves the level of excellence that it does precisely because it is so very unimportant. As Lu Hsün himself has indicated, his aim in writing these stories was not to be an artist but to point out the disease he saw in Chinese society, hoping that some abler spiritual physician would attempt to cure it. For him, Chinese realities were of overriding importance, and *language* was only secondary. However, having gotten his priorities straight, he proceeded to present the substance of what he had to say in carefully wrought sentences and phrases that were not equaled by any of his contemporaries. What is more, he said his piece in a language that he was helping to fashion as he wrote—a new colloquial form of writing that was to be the chief vehicle of all intellectual products of the May Fourth period. Lu Hsün's colloquial style was strongly influenced by his wide reading in foreign literatures and by no means a mere continuation of the diction of traditional vernacular literature. Paradoxically, however, the terseness of his style was strongly indebted to the classical diction that the new colloquial language revolution sought to overthrow. Lu Hsün's diction, by no means the language of everyday discourse, was highly literary, despite its being based on colloquial rather than classical Chinese. (p. 288)

The most striking element of Lu Hsün's style is its tone, which is hardly ever neutral. It ranges from hatred to love, from satire to lyricism. One is aware of his tone of voice, and one senses whether he loves or hates the subject at hand. Even in the most objectively presented of his stories, "A Warning to the People," his tone is not neutral. (p. 298)

The dominant tone of Lu Hsün's literary voice is that of a dispassionate news correspondent filing dispatches from Chinese villages and occasionally from the cities. This tone is deceptive. The choice of these seemingly objective news items is highly selective, and their content is always emotionally freighted with the correspondent's point of view. The man behind the voice is lightly touched with melancholy, and his quick, analytic intelligence is held taut by strong emotions which at times drive him to biting sarcasm and satire or loft him to flights of lyric beauty. (p. 301)

[We] ought to remember that his strongest and most heartfelt aspiration . . . was not primarily to be an artist, but rather to change China. (p. 303)

> *William A. Lyell, Jr., in his* Lu Hsün's Vision of Reality *(copyright © 1976 by The Regents of the University of California; reprinted by permission of the University of California Press), University of California Press, 1976, 355 p.*

BIBLIOGRAPHY

Chou, Chien-jen. "Lu Hsün: Pioneer of China's Cultural Revolution." *Literature and Ideology*, No. 12 (1972): 17-30.
> A biographical sketch of Lu Hsün by his brother with a heavy political slant.

Chu, Chiu-pai. "Writing for a Great Cause: Preface to the Selected Essays of Lu Hsün." *Chinese Literature*, No. 5 (May 1959): 40-68.
> Highly emotional and radically political presentation of Lu Hsün with biographical facts interwoven with China's history at the time.

Hsia, Tsi-an. "Lu Hsün and the Dissolution of the League of Leftist Writers." In his *The Gate of Darkness: Studies on the Leftist Literary Movement in China*, pp. 101-45. Seattle: University of Washington Press, 1968.
> Describes Lu Hsün's role in the formation in 1930 of the Chinese League of Leftist Writers, an organization of revolutionaries; his disappointment over the years in its changing policy and slogan, and his eventual split leading a splinter group in 1936.

Huang, Sung-K'ang. *Lu Hsün and the New Culture Movement of Modern China*. Amsterdam: Djambatan, 1957, 158 p.
> Traces the historical development of the New Culture Movement in China, noting Lu Hsün's role as guiding force in the movement.

Kratochvil, P. Introduction to *Three Stories*, by Lu Hsün, pp. ix-xv. Cambridge: Cambridge University Press, 1970.
> Excellent analysis of the emergence of the colloquial *báihuà* language in literature replacing the classical *wényán* and Lu Hsün's role as its foremost pioneer.

Krebsová, Berta. "Lu Hsun and His Collection *Old Tales Retold*." *Archiv Orientální* 28 (1960): 225-81.
> Detailed analysis of each of the stories in Lu Hsün's collection identifying earlier myths and history from which they were drawn.

Wang Chi-Chen. Introduction to *Ah Q and Others: Selected Stories of Lusin*, by Lusin, translated by Chi-Chen Wang, pp. vii-xxvi. New York: Columbia University Press, 1941.
> Explains Lusin's principles of life and holds that Lusin will be remembered for his short stories rather than his essay with "Ah Q" being "the most important single contribution to Chinese literature since the literary revolution."

Weakland, John H. "Lusin's 'Ah Q': A Rejected Image of Chinese Character." *Pacific Spectator* 10, No. 2 (Spring 1956): 137-46.
> Excellent analysis of typical Chinese character traits depicted in the story "Ah Q."

Yang, Gladys. *Introduction to Silent China: Selected Writings of Lu Xun*, by Chou Shu-jen, translated by Gladys Yang, pp. vii-xii. London: Oxford University Press, 1973.
> A biographical sketch of Lu Hsün.

Antonio Machado (y Ruiz)

1875-1939

(Also wrote under pseudonym of Cabellera) Spanish poet and dramatist.

Machado is one of the greatest lyric poets of twentieth-century Spain. Profoundly influenced by Spain's decline, he became a late member of the Generation of 1898 which sought to modernize Spain without undermining its national character.

During his early years in the literary renaissance of Spain, Machado led a bohemian life which included frequent visits to Paris and long conversations in Madrid cafes with other literary figures. In 1907, however, he accepted his first post as teacher in the ancient Castilian province of Soria. The Castilian region with its somber landscape, peopled by shepherds and peasants, was much more the land of Machado's feelings than the lush and colorful region of Andalusia where he was born. It was in Soria that he married his child-bride, Leonor, and experienced happiness previously unknown. Leonor's death three years later reinforced once more the solitary nature of the poet. Machado continued to isolate himself from literary life, preferring the life of a schoolteacher in provincial schools throughout Spain. The themes of decay, stagnation, loneliness, and longing were the soul of his poetry.

In addition to writing poetry, Machado spent a brief period collaborating with his brother, Manuel, writing plays. Though commercially successful, their dramas are not considered lasting literary contributions. It was while writing the plays in Madrid that Machado met the "Guiomar" of his poems. Believed to be the poet Pilar Valderrama, she inspired his elaborations on the idea of love.

In his later years, Machado turned to more metaphysical themes, reminiscent of Unamuno. He expressed these ideas through his aprocryphal teachers, Abel Martín and Juan de Mairena. Machado's early lyric poetry, however, is generally considered to be his best.

Having always supported the Spanish Republic, Machado was deeply distressed at the outbreak of Civil War in 1936. In January of 1939, he crossed the Pyrenees into exile in France. He died the following month.

Though Machado did not approve of the new trends in Spanish poetry, especially the emphasis on concepts rather than intuition, he was much admired by the younger generation of Spanish poets. Machado stands as one who brought to Spain a rebirth in lyric poetry.

PRINCIPAL WORKS

Soledades: Poesías (poetry) 1903
Soledades: Galerías y otros poemas (poetry) 1907
Campos de Castilla (poetry) 1912
Poesías completas (poetry) 1917
Nuevas canciones (poetry) 1924
Poesías completas: 1899-1925 (poetry) 1928
Juan de Mairena: Sentencias, donaires, apuntes y recuerdos de un profesor apócrifo (poetry, essays, and sketches) 1936
  [*Juan de Mairena: Epigrams, Maxims, Memoranda, and Memoirs of an Apocryphal Professor, with an Appendix of Poems from the Apocryphal Songbooks*, 1963]
Poesías completas (poetry) 1936
Eighty Poems of Antonio Machado (poetry) 1959
Castilian Ilexes: Versions from Antonio Machado, 1875-1939 (poetry) 1963
Sunlight and Scarlet: Selected Poems (poetry) 1973

J. B. TREND (essay date 1953)

Antonio Machado is known to everyone who ever read any Spanish: the poet of *Campos de Castilla* and the Elegy on Don Francisco Giner. He wrote earlier and later poems in a very different and more private manner; and invented an apocryphal professor, Juan de Mairena, who, with a still more apocryphal schoolmaster, Abel Martín, was responsible for more verse and some very interesting prose, consisting of reports of what he might have said to his apocryphal pupils. (p. 5)

The poems of *Campos de Castilla* are the corner stone of Antonio Machado's achievement. (p. 20)

[In] *Campos de Castilla* he seemed at last sure of his mastery; his verse took a firmer and longer stride; he learnt to pack his thought and vision more closely. The diffuse images of the earlier poems were telescoped into phrases like that of the branches seeming to smoke with green vapour (for the new leaves), or spring coming like a shudder. (pp. 27-8)

[The *Nuevas Canciones*] have no unity of mood or form,

while the earlier books had both; and when Machado went on to publish his *Cancionero apócrifo,* many readers thought that his fear had come true: the gold had turned to copper . . . and the poet had become an amateur philosopher. The philosophy was obscure; the poems were explained by the author as *complementarios,* mere illustrations to a fragmentary system of thought, and themselves only fragments, showing up the ruins of a poet's mind. . . . Much of the old Machado had gone, though the new poems were full of echoes of themes and images used before . . . , which only seemed to show that he was exhausted, and was picking up the splinters of the magic crystal of his dreams. (pp. 28-9)

The key to Machado's later poetry is in a system of thought, more pervasive, even, than the system of imagery which he was working out in the prose of Martín and Mairena. Except in some of his methods, Machado had nothing really in common with T. S. Eliot, and not much with Yeats. He remained in some ways an old-fashioned poet; yet his development, though not like theirs, might be called parallel. He was conscious, as no other Spaniard was, of the crisis of poetry in the modern world. He realized, in his later years and in his own way, what it was that made Eliot declare that poetry in our time would be difficult. . . . He could not help facing the problem in his thought and his art; for art, to Machado, had always been a revelation of truth: *unas pocas palabras verdaderas.* (p. 34)

To hear the author of *Soledades* saying that personal emotion is no longer interesting is something of a shock, and shows how far he had travelled. Machado's own style, brilliant and beautiful though it was, had died; and in its death he suffered the failure of a whole generation of poets. To Spaniards living in the blaze of the clearest renascence of Spanish poetry since Garcilaso, this sense of failure may have seemed unreal. (p. 36)

War and the waste land were late in coming to Spain; and Machado was the only poet—except the invulnerable Unamuno—who had done some hard political thinking about his own country, not in terms of paper constitutions, but in terms of the people whose lives and faces he knew about the Campos de Castilla and the provincial casinos. And at the end of it he said . . . that the kind of lyric which he used to write was not interesting any more. Instead, he felt the need for a philosophy, on the one hand, which should explain the poet's place in the world; and, on the other hand, for a popular poetry which could speak to others, and why not to all . . . ? (pp. 36-7)

It must be said that Machado's efforts in the style of popular poetry are not successful, though they can be beautiful. He cannot help seeing too much in a landscape: the grey olives, the white roads, and how the sun absorbs the colour of the whole country. . . .

That is all very well; but popular *canciones* do not look at the countryside with such an eye. . . . (p. 37)

Machado was on firmer ground when his fine, penetrating mind began to strike out towards a new philosophy, and particularly a philosophy of love. (pp. 38-9)

His philosophy, expounded by Abel Martín [his apocryphal schoolmaster], was mainly concerned with not-being and the various forms of *nada,* which (he considered) was the one creation of God. One may suspect that these ideas owe too much to the symbolists to be altogether accidental; yet the debt may be unconscious, and the ideas of Antonio Machado and Abel Martín certainly differ from those of the symbolists in many ways. Antonio Machado had in fact rejected the whole symbolist attitude. . . . (p. 39)

[His later poetry] is a poetry of nihilism, perhaps, the expression of an irrationalist outlook on the world; but it reflects the tendency of our times, a tendency which Antonio Machado, the poet, foresaw forty years ago. (p. 43)

> *J. B. Trend, in his* Antonio Machado, *The Dolphin Book Co., Oxford, 1953, 58 p.*

JUAN RAMÓN JIMÉNEZ (essay date 1958)

Even as a child, Antonio Machado sought death, the dead, and decay in every recess of his soul and body. He always held within himself as much of death as of life, halves fused together by ingenuous artistry. (p. 272)

A poet of death, Antonio Machado spent hour after hour meditating upon, perceiving, and preparing for death; I have never known anyone else who so balanced these levels, equal in height or depth, as he did, and who by his living-dying overcame the gap between these existences, paradoxically opposed yet the only ones known to us; existences strongly united even though other men persist in separating, contrasting, and pitting them against each other. . . . Antonio Machado apprehended it in itself, yielded to it in large measure. Possibly, more than a man who was born, he was a man reborn. One proof of this, perhaps, is the mature philosophy of his youth. And possessing the secret of resurrection, he was reborn each day before those of us who saw him then, by natural poetic miracle, in order to look into his other life, that life of ours which he reserved in part also for himself. (pp. 272-73)

> *Juan Ramón Jiménez, "Antonio Machado," in* The Antioch Review *(copyright © 1958 by the Antioch Review Inc.; reprinted by permission of the Editors), Vol. XVIII, No. 3, 1958, pp. 272-74.*

CAROLYN MORROW (essay date 1961)

Antonio Machado attended the classes of Henri Bergson at the Sorbonne and there received one of the most important influences of his life. What resulted from his contact with the French philosopher may perhaps be seen most clearly in "Poema de un día," the poet's first great work after his return from Paris and the death of his wife in August, 1912. . . . The meditations on death, the destiny of man, and time recall *Soledades.* New elements are the poet's concern with philosophy and philosophers and his far more serene attitude toward the peasants. Also new are the work's occasional touches of humor and its rather austere and abbreviated manner. (p. 149)

A central concern of "Poema de un día," and indeed of much of the work of Machado, is that with time. . . . An intermingling of past and present states, basic to Bergson's theory of *la durée,* is revealed in the thoughts of Machado in one of the first poems of *Soledades.* . . . (pp. 149-50)

Like Bergson's *durée,* Machado's time is a stream that never ceases flowing. In "Poema de un día" its continuous passing is symbolized in the parallel sounds of the clock and the raindrops. . . . The repeated mention of the rain and the clock . . . is also a subtle factor in unifying the various parts of the poem.

Machado shares Bergson's belief in an inner self, a fundamental self whose essence is time. . . . For Machado, as for Bergson, the flow of the fundamental self, its intermingling past and present, cannot be measured by the precise movements of the clock's hand. The monotonous tic-tic of the clock is only "el latido de un corazón de metal" and what it measures is "un tiempo vacío," the mathematical, "abstract" time of which the philosopher writes. The poet rebels against the authority of the clock. . . . (pp. 150-51)

Quite unlike Bergson, however, is Machado's feeling of anguish at "la marcha inexorable del tiempo." The thought of a ceaseless, ever-expanding, creative *durée* is one of pleasure and reassurance for the French philosopher, but for Machado the passing of a day means that death has taken from him a precious object. . . . (p. 151)

Machado employs several techniques to emphasize his concern with time. Very obvious is the abundant usage of verb forms in all the tenses, present, past, and future. Often the poet will view objects from all three perspectives—thus affirming once again the linking of past, present, and future in his own mind. . . . In "Poema de un día" appears the same technique of situating an object in all three areas of time. . . . Terms related to time, another device for stressing *el fluir del tiempo,* abound in the poetry of Machado. The divisions of the day, especially *la tarde,* and the seasons of the year are mentioned constantly; in the "Poema" one finds: "tarde gris," "anochece," "es de noche," "luz invernal," "Invierno. Cerca del fuego."

The monotonous tic-tic of the clock and constant fall of the raindrops are also used to emphasize the ceaseless passing of time. The clock makes its appearance in the first poem of *Soledades* and thereafter appears quite often. Usually it only forms part of the background, rarely functioning so importantly as in "Poema de un día." It is curious that in one passage of the "Poema" the message of the clock almost duplicates that of the water in an earlier poem, "Hastío." . . . The most frequent symbol of the passing of time is indeed the flowing water, the water of *la noria, el río, la lluvia,* and, particularly, *la fuente.*

"Poema de un día" thus reveals advances in both the thought and technique of Machado. The influence of Bergson has developed the intuition of time seen in *Soledades* into the profound philosophy of "Poema de un día" and the later works. Machado's interest in philosophy will increase steadily as will the complexity and artistry of his poetry. The rather laconic manner of the "Poema," very unlike that of his earlier works, is a suggestion of the terse refinement to come in the verses of the *Cancionero apócrifo.* Perhaps it is the new ideas initiated by Bergson and then stimulated by the conscientious study of many other philosophers which evoke in Machado this need for a new style. (pp. 151-53)

Carolyn Morrow, "An Analysis of 'Poema de un día': The Philosophy of Bergson in Machado's Concept of Time," in Romance Notes, Vol. II, No. 2, Spring, 1961, pp. 149-53.

HARDIE ST. MARTIN   (essay date 1963)

In Machado's poetry the trimmings are small. The elegances simple, the shadings subtle. But he is *profoundly human,* and *solid internal structure* is important in the makeup of each poem. The poem hangs together by virtue of interior unity and strength. Outer form is not neglected but is generally subdued and just right, never pulling at the center of the poem. Machado therefore prefers assonance to strict rhyme in most of his work, even pretending that alliteration is accidental in his poetry. It is his insistence on the simplest terms, but always the exact word, to carry the central feeling of the poem that saves it from the sort of sentimentality that Verlaine, for instance, often found it difficult to go around.

His simplicity goes hand in hand with his humanity. His recognition of the eternal values of "love, justice, understanding, [and] freedom" drove him, almost from the beginning, to catch the "popular" sound of language, to write what he considered true Castilian. This immersion in the language of the simple man and in the time that surrounded him . . . makes Machado Spanish as no other contemporary poet in Spain has been. His style is so rooted in the Spanish language that it can hardly be deracinated without damage. Perhaps this is the main reason most translators have stayed clear of the work of a poet whose place in the Spanish-speaking world is comparable to that of Yeats in Anglo-American literature.

Machado published various versions of some of his poems and his complex simplicity is successful enough to attract the literary as well as the common reader. Artifice is less obvious in Machado than in Lorca, for example. (Although he admitted the importance of the good poets of Lorca's generation, he objected to the "baroque" in the newer poetry and the intellectual detachment of poets like Guillén and Salinas.) Both poets deliberately adapted the rhythms and subjects of popular Andalusian song, but each was aiming at something else. Lorca recreated the color of the song while Machado looked for the idea more than the obvious play in language. He used the schemes of the "cante" to measure his philosophy. Spain sings in both poets. She is more apparently tragic in Lorca perhaps; as deep and sad, but more sober, in the older poet. (pp. 343-44)

Hardie St. Martin, "The Poetry of Antonio Machado," in Poetry (© 1963 by The Modern Poetry Association; reprinted by permission of the Editor of Poetry), Vol. CI, No. 5, February, 1963, pp. 343-45.

HOWARD T. YOUNG   (essay date 1964)

The reader of Machado's poetry is struck at once by the sparse style and limited vocabulary, both of which deliberately presuppose that language should restrain itself to the expression of emotions and ideas. Words may be beautiful, but they should never be joined in an opulence that outweighs content. (p. 44)

To attain this goal, he borrowed one or two phrases from Bécquer and Verlaine, but mainly relied on a "few true words" . . . of his own. The result is lean and unpretentious poetry. "At times I use words outside of their strict sense, but, when I do, I am aware of my error." He explained that his objective was a classical style, which, for him, meant a noun plus a defining adjective. (pp. 44-5)

Only the flow of water deserves more than one descriptive word. Because water is a symbol of time, Machado always underlined its movements by a liberal use of verbs. Water and the playing children are the sole motion in a static setting. Both are indifferent to the lonely spectator shuffling along the path. Against the background of common words, the old man's exclamation acquires extra poignancy, and the reader suddenly shares the feeling of age in a way that elaborate description would not have accomplished. It is the "deep throbbing spirit . . . in . . . response to the world around it."

By using common words to create an uncommon effect, Machado often achieved a stark realism. "At the Burial of a Friend" piles up concrete, simple detail with an overwhelming effect. . . . (p. 46)

Simplicity of line, limited but fundamental emotions, a sense of life lived without the interruptions of history—these are the goals Machado set for his lean vocabulary. (p. 48)

Thus the most overworked words in the language were revitalized. With care and persistence in poem after poem, Machado repeated his "few true words" until the cumulative effect was one of breathtaking clarity, a "crystal legend." . . . (pp. 49-50)

Within the restrictions of his vocabulary, symbolic meaning plays a fundamental part. His symbols are few, but they are vital, based upon an aching awareness of ebbing life. Among them is the plaza, so important to the Spanish scene. All roads lead to the plaza, especially to the plaza of the small village. There children play, old men dream, and women dressed in black walk to Mass. There, also, the inevitable fountain flows symbolically. The plaza offers a world of memory and illusion, where only grief is steadfast and clear. . . .

> The stone fountain
> spilled its eternal
> crystal legend.
>
> The children were singing
> artless songs
> of something that passes
> and never arrives:
> the story confused,
> the grief clear.

The voices of singing children stand for purity of emotion and lost youth. They hover in the background of many of his poems, their sweet sounds emphasizing the remorseless process of aging, their lingering tone one of memory's chords.

The plaza, however, is not always filled with childish voices and bubbling fountains. It is often a "dead plaza" . . . , where the afternoon foreshadows an ultimate silence, Cupid dreams without love, and life, symbolized by water, is cold and still. . . . (pp. 50-1)

Machado was an inveterate walker, and *el camino* (the road) is another of his favorite symbols. "A labyrinth of streets / leads into the deserted plaza." . . . Along dusty roads in the late afternoon he would dream his way, bemused by the morbid echoes of sun and filled with a poignant sense of something lost. Roads become synonymous with time, and man's reality was defined by his movement on them. . . . (p. 51)

Among the "few true words" of Machado's vocabulary, two of the most cherished are the verb *soñar* (to dream) and its substantive *sueño*. They possess a special radius of meaning in his work, and more than the other tools of his lexicon, enable us to understand the way he looked at reality.

The manifold meanings of *soñar* and *sueño* in Machado's work cannot be compressed into a ready formula, for they are deeply rooted in his character and are as complex to define as character itself. The introspective, melancholy man spent many hours wending his way upon lonely paths, and as his senses peacefully opened to the landscape through which he wandered, he could justifiably begin one of his most famous poems: "I slowly dream the roads / of afternoon." . . . "This dream insomnia of mine," he called it in a later composition. . . .

These are not the daydreams of ordinary mortals, whose senses dilate and who live momentarily at deeper levels of feeling before resuming their mild routine. For Machado, *soñar*—to dream while awake—was a continual state of mind, a means of perception. In a simile reminiscent of Santa Teresa, he likened the mind to a gallery, a series of long winding corridors which remain empty until the winds of memory, blending past and present, fill them with echoes that reverberate in the form of poetry. Then the mind becomes a road of dreams. . . . (p. 53)

Like A. E. Housman's ". . . happy highways where I went / And cannot come again," Machado's road of dreams traces its way from the past through the present to disappear once more into dusk. But Machado insisted upon traveling again those happy highways. *Soñar* unites memory and the actual moment, and expands consciousness by giving it an underlying emotional continuity. When the poet made the fountain ask, "Does my present song / remind you of a distant dream?" . . . , he equated the reality of here and now with the recollection of the past, stating the purpose of his poetry: to sing that which is lost, and, in a sense, to recover it, bathed in a deeper light. His obvious predilection for the evening hour befits that time of penumbra between night and day when visions most easily come and go, and experience is tinged with nostalgia. (pp. 53-4)

A large segment of the poetry of *Soledades* is concerned with the recovery of dreams that have disappeared into memory. The poet delves into the storehouse of the mind and touches the waiting chords which respond with the basic vocabulary of emotional life. . . . (p. 55)

The overwhelming impression of *Soledades* is that all of life is a melancholy dream with poignant moments of beauty woven together by poetry in the lengthening shadows of afternoon. (pp. 55-6)

The people who inhabit the Castilian plain appealed to Machado because of their bare honesty, his own goal in poetry. But he did not idealize them. He remarked their astuteness, suspicious eyes, and high cheekbones. . . . They were not romantic *hidalgos* but laborers, tinged with the curse of Cain, serving a sanguine and fierce Old Testament deity. (p. 60)

The lesson of time and change imparted by [the] beautiful but ruined Castilian cities coincided with the death of his wife. Shortly thereafter, he was beset by a growing sense of decline in his talent. The subjective dreamer of *Solitudes* had tasted of something outside himself. With its disappearance, it seemed likely that the magic of memory and dreams would also fail. . . . (p. 62)

From now on, he was a philosopher-poet. . . .

Bergson's theory of intuition seemed, however vaguely, to reflect a great deal that was present in Machado's poetical use of memory and dreams. (p. 63)

Intuition, which in Bergson's philosophy becomes a means of knowledge, is for Machado the inspirational fount of poetry, the *sueño* of his early days now clothed in garments cut in the style of the Collège de France. As for the intellect, it had never sung, insisted Machado, nor was its mission to sing. (pp. 64-5)

Machado went a step beyond his master, for he saw that to define man philosophically as a creature of time gave terrible confirmation to human finitude. He was too much of a Spaniard to overlook this conclusion, and he emphasized that the themes of poetry written in the stream of time would be unrest, anguish, fear, resignation, hope, and impatience. Gradually he came to accent anguish above other themes, unwittingly aligning himself with European existentialism. But for the moment, he began to reflect an obsessive preoccupation with time. (p. 65)

[Not] every poet can write philosophical verse, and frequently the muse and philosophy make unhappy bedfellows. Machado sensed this, and he restricted his philosophical poetry to a string of ironical, ambiguous, sometimes effective maxims. As for writing philosophy itself, he was even more diffident and hid behind two imaginary professors, whose fragmentary observations he pretended to be collecting.... Critics are not unanimous, but, on the whole, it seems evident that the contact with philosophy was unfortunate for Machado's grave lyric voice, or perhaps merely coincided with the natural decline of the talent that had produced *Soledades* and *Campos de Castilla*. Although he intermittently wrote great poetry until his death, his late verse does not sustain the same level of excellence exhibited by the poetry written between 1901, the date of his first published poem, and 1917. (pp. 68-9)

The artfulness and tentative cast of his aphoristic rhymes conceal an ironic, honest man, committed to no elaborate philosophy and refusing the refuge of dogma. (p. 69)

Weaving in and out of the labyrinth of these playful proverbs, finding in them a fragmentary summary of his views on life and poetry, we renew our admiration for this simple yet profound man. Despite the diffidence and ruling melancholy of his character, the final note is never despairing. He hoped that one day we might all see and speak from the depths of our hearts, and know the deeper levels of life that he had modestly labored to reveal.... (p. 71)

Howard T. Young, "Antonio Machado: A Few True Words," in his The Victorious Expression: A Study of Four Contemporary Spanish Poets *(copyright © 1964 by the Regents of the University of Wisconsin), The University of Wisconsin Press, 1964, pp. 33-73.*

KESSEL SCHWARTZ (essay date 1965)

Machado, in a poem dedicated to Julio Castro, voiced his early admiration for the sea.... This early esteem came to be a poetic preoccupation, as the sea eventually came to represent his destination, an objective, and symbolic end.... Like Unamuno, whom he ardently admired, Machado expresses dread at the loss of identity and the fear of nothingness, becoming as it were a drop of water in the vast sea, an idea which he repeats in many of his poems.... Man is a drop in the ocean, the immensity from which he came and to which he must return. The sea gave him life and claims him again as part of its substance in death.... Man can adopt a positive or negative attitude toward life

and death, for the meaning of both is summed up by the sea. One man thinks of life as an illusion of the sea which must one day end, whereas the dreamer thinks perhaps the final boundary of the sea may be overcome.... (p. 248)

Machado's religious preoccupations are as bound up in the sea as are his existential ones, and at times they appear to be one and the same.... One might go further and affirm that the sea sums up his complete feeling about God. The sea is the substance from which all else, even God, is born. (p. 249)

The ship metaphor to symbolize a safe passage through a dangerous sea occurs in numerous poems dealing with the sea. The latter represented peril and adventure, much as the garden, which Machado also employs symbolically, often represented a feeling of normality and safety....

Nevertheless, the sea symbolizes life or existence in a variety of aspects. (p. 250)

Machado contrasts Extremadura and the sea, Soria and the sea, La Mancha and the sea, and above all Castilla and the sea. (p. 251)

He recalls Leonor whose river of life was swept out to sea, but the past, seared in his memory, brings also hope for the future, and her name will be forever engraved in his heart....

And finally, the sea may give rise to objective descriptions of moods and emotions. The sea may reflect joy, sunshine, merriment, and an ideal.... The sea may represent bitterness and sadness in its grey waves roughened by the wind....

Machado views the sea as great poets have viewed it from time immemorial, as a primitive place of potential power, as an alluring call which is difficult to deny, as unfathomable, desolate, mysterious, terrible, as life and death, God and eternity. Machado's sea serves for every mood and occasion and it may be smiling, sonorous, somber, salty, fierce, tranquil, bitter, or loving. (p. 253)

Kessel Schwartz, "The Sea and Machado," in Hispania *(© 1965 The American Association of Teachers of Spanish and Portuguese, Inc.), Vol. XLVIII, No. 2, May, 1965, pp. 247-54.*

BRUCE W. WARDROPPER (essay date 1965)

Instead of the moans and shrieks, and the obsession with bones and worms which characterized the elegy of their predecessors, contemporary Spanish poets present us with an attempt to salvage from death the meaning of a recently ended life. The old frustration and rage have yielded to a creative attitude towards death. The elegist today protests against death, feels anger or regret at the obliteration of a loved one; but ... he consoles himself by recreating poetically the life that has been destroyed.... He strives—by using to the full the twentieth-century techniques of imprecise symbolism, allusion, juxtaposition, and quotation—to extract from the memory of that life something we might call—poetically, if not in the strictest theology—a soul. By conferring a poetic immortality on that poetic soul he has found a passable substitute for the spiritual immortality in which most poets no longer believe. (p. 164)

[The] short poem by Antonio Machado on the death of Federico García Lorca, *El crimen fue en Granada* [is an example]. This poem is in three sections, or movements. The first one, entitled EL CRIMEN . . . , describes the assassination of the young poet. . . .

The second section, headed EL POETA Y LA MUERTE, is concerned not with more or less objective facts, or the assassination as seen by an observer, but with the way Lorca faced death. It is as though, by some special empathy existing between poets, the poet Machado is able to enter into the feelings, at that moment, of the poet Lorca. The focus shifts to a close-up of the victim in his hour of crisis. (p. 165)

The final section, which lacks a title, is a kind of epitaph. . . .

The poem is not perhaps, in the strictest sense of the word, an elegy. It is as much a political protest as a disengaged lament. The word *crime,* "el crimen," is pinned not on death itself, as it might have been in an older elegy, but on some specific men: on Lorca's betrayers, captors, judges, and executioners. The poem is nevertheless elegiac in tone, and especially in sections II and III. If the first movement contains a protest against a crime committed by an illegal authority for political motives, the remainder of the work consists of reflections on death, imagines and endorses an attitude towards death, and appeals for the reader's assent to this view of death. The main point of the poem, reinforced by its repetition in the title and the refrain, is that Lorca was only incidentally the victim of death, and was essentially the victim of man's inhumanity. (p. 166)

The setting Machado imagines, but with a severely disciplined imagination: a long street, a cold countryside, stars, the end of night, the first crack of dawn, and a volley of bullets. It is the classical scene against which a thousand senseless executions have been carried out. Conventional as is this description, it is tinged with more than the customary pathos. On the one hand, Lorca was innocent; on the other hand, his murderers were hypocritical and inhuman. It is this last detail which moves the reader particularly. The firing squad cannot look their victim in the face, knowing that he is innocent and unafraid. They close their eyes to the horror they are about to commit. But this guilty closing of the eyes dissolves into the closing of eyes in hypocritical prayer. They pray not the usual "May God save your soul" but the perverse "May not even God save you now." The assassination itself is evoked unequivocally: "blood on his brow and lead in his bowels." And then the refrain leads the reader from this objective—prosaic and political—consideration of facts to the affective, pathetic circumstance of the execution: the long street, the cold countryside belong to Granada, the murdered poet's native city. A lamentable Granada it is, since it too is a slave to inhumanity and hypocrisy. It too is an accomplice in this unworthy act of murder.

The second section . . . begins with the same reminder of the fact that there were witnesses of the crime: "se le vio caminar." But, in keeping with the elegiac tone of this *laisse,* the witnesses are now more sensitive to the *poetic* reality which they are observing. If in the first section *they saw him* "caminando entre fusiles," escorted by the firing squad, now they see him "solo con Ella," alone but for the presence of Death.

Machado, if I may return to my generalization about the twentieth-century elegy, recreates the *soul* of this dead

man. He does this by a series of allusions to Lorca's poetry, in much the same way that Lorca in his own elegy, the *Llanto por Ignacio Sánchez Mejías,* recreates the *soul* of the dead bullfighter by imitating the *Coplas* of Jorge Manrique. . . . The essence of Lorca's *soul* . . . was his poetry. Consequently, in the second section of *El crímen fue en Granada,* Machado represents that *soul,* that poetry, by the themes it exploited, and especially by the themes of that classic exploration of death, the *Romancero gitano.*

Death for Lorca is a gipsy woman. She dwells among the Andalusian towers and anvils of his poetry. Because she has appeared so often surrounded by saints and gipsies in the poetic world of his *Romancero gitano,* Lorca treats her with an easy and fearless familiarity. . . . Lorca reminds her of the symbols with which he once created her presence in his poetry and his drama: the clapping of dry palms, the icicles, the silvery blade of her scythe, her macabre appearance. . . . Antonio Machado's Lorca, at the end of this section, unlike Machado himself at the end of the other two sections, refers to no *crime* in Granada. *Death* is all he thinks about, not the circumstances of his death. Machado protests Lorca's death; the poetically recreated Lorca accepts it. The poetic achievement of vanquishing death has merged with the poet's life. The wall separating the two sectors of Lorca's existence has crumbled. The poetry is an adequate preparation for a death which is unexpected only to the observer, not to its victim.

The third section of Machado's poem begins once more with the recalling of witnesses: "Se le vio caminar. . . ." But this time the sentence is broken off before it is completed. The witnesses are urged not to bear witness but to fashion a memorial. Lorca's acceptance of death in the second *laisse* imposes a similar acceptance of his death on the distant observer, Antonio Machado. One is reconciled to another's death when one erects a tombstone and inscribes a suitable epitaph on it. This, in poetry if not in natural stone, Machado does. Since Lorca, in the second section, has accepted his death by recalling the *themes* of his poetry, Machado, in the third, accepts it by recalling its *symbols:* "piedra y sueño" and "una fuente donde llore el agua." Water, stone, and dream are, as we have already noted, recurrent images in Lorca's own great elegy, the *Llanto por Ignacio Sánchez Mejías.* So stone, the natural material for a tomb, is blended with dream, the symbol of a poetic world, and is set near the weeping spring, which is part of the traditional pastoral imagery of lamentation. And by the Alhambra Machado evokes the exotic quality of Lorca's verse, by which he expressed his sympathy for the underdog and the outcast, whether he were Moor, gipsy, or Harlem Negro. . . . Even if Lorca could accept his murder as a natural visit from his companion, death, those who are left must after all dissent. They cannot connive at a murder, the murder of a great poet, a callous political murder, moreover: murder by the poet's fellow-citizens of Granada.

This poem of Antonio Machado's is calculated down to every last effect. This means that the poet's angry grief is under the strictest control; it has been dominated by the very act of poetic creation. In defying Lorca's assassins Machado is trying to recapture from them the man and the artist whom they have sought to obliterate. Poetry has given life where wicked men have dealt death. By recalling, by recreating, Lorca's own poetry after his death Machado has infused his poem with Lorca's poetic personality. It is scarcely a figure of speech to say that Lorca "comes alive" in Machado's poem. (pp. 166-69)

This is poetic creativity at its highest. In Machado's work the elegy has acquired a new impressive status. (p. 170)

> *Bruce W. Wardropper, "The Modern Spanish Elegy: Antonio Machado's Lament for Federico García Lorca," in* Symposium *(copyright © 1965 by Syracuse University Press), Vol. XIX, No. 2, Summer, 1965, pp. 162-70.*

NORMA LOUISE HUTMAN   (essay date 1969)

Since the temporality of life is central to Machado's thought, his poetic expression of every aspect of life reflects this idea. Thus, for him, everything in nature primarily reflects change. It is the familiar, ever varying countryside through which he was accustomed to walk, hour upon hour, which becomes, almost inevitably, the substantial form of his poetic vision: its life process, a projection of his own; and its images, an extended pathetic fallacy. (p. 49)

Machado's critics, in particular Julián Marías, have pointed out his rapport with Azorín in the treatment of the Castilian landscape and the concrete commonplace. This is not, however, the only similarity between them. Both Machado's first book, *Soledades,* and the triology in which Martínez Ruiz creates Azorín are dominated by scenes set in the afternoon and by the authors' recollections of and meditations upon the past. . . . It is precisely their common belief—that man is defined by his relationship to tangible objects and that human understanding is, therefore, bound to sensory reality—which underlies their conclusion: it is always late. Every temporal description is relative: we can define the present only in terms of other specific moments in time. And if the past alone is understood, however imperfectly, then our present is a climax and a limit upon our knowledge.

Tangible things as means of communicating with the past have already appeared in the image of stone fountains. Similarly lemon trees, patios and plazas evoke Seville, as, later in Machado's life, memories of Soria persist in her mountains and craggy hillsides, her dusty oak groves and tenacious herbs. (pp. 76-7)

Thus memories, hopes and images of the physical world are facets of the poet's dialogue with time. The obscurity in which he finds himself, however, and the impermanence of all things lead him to doubt the reality of the dialogue. For conversation requires a something or a someone entirely independent of the speaker. And if only appearances and interpretations exist, then there is no objective reality: no one to whom the poet can address himself: nothing which is not bound to his finitude and, therefore, doomed to expire with it. The dialogue itself becomes a doubt, in which Machado turns first to the object of his memory, Leonor; then to the landscape, visible and present; to his hope and fear; and, finally in the last sonnet of "Los sueños dialogados," to the enigma of reality: that alone which he perceives as existing independent of himself. Because he continues to question, his words do not suggest despair, but desire.

Similarly, aware of Spain's vanquished glories, of her physical and spiritual decay, of her apathy, base passions and empty pride, he does not resign himself to the defects of contemporary society but rather desires that his nation be transformed and challenges his countrymen to join in the task of accomplishing that transformation. (p. 139)

Machado is in certain ways a neoromantic, closer to English than to Spanish romanticism; a formal rather than an extemporizing poet, one whose romanticism makes no pretense to new visions; and an archetypal poet whose myth is nature, viewed not as a sympathetic force but as the reality which yields symbols.

In theme and style his voice resembles many poets of the nineteenth and twentieth centuries. A poet-philosopher, his closest spiritual affinity is with Hölderlin who recognizes with Machado that the two functions are complimentary but opposite voices of the same vision. (p. 142)

Like Baudelaire, Machado is conceptually and verbally, rather than metrically, experimental. His major poems include octosyllables, handecasyllables, one long alexandrine and a sonnet sequence. His free verse and metric experiments are infrequent and not always successful. Borrowing perhaps directly from Baudelaire or more probably from the modernists—whose artistic ancestors were at least fifty per cent French—Machado employs a mingling of sensory imagery. Dawn *sounds* in the East; the crash of waves on the surrealistic shore of "Otro clima" is *green;* the uncertain *white word* ascends from an April fife. The perceived world is altered by our impressions of it and communicated simultaneously as world and as human impression. (p. 145)

With his considerable debt to the modernists and through them to the French symbolists, and his rapport with romanticism, Machado's poetic world is oriented more toward the nineteenth than the twentieth century. Nevertheless he has recently been an inspiration and model for the contemporary generation, not the protest poetry of one contemporary school but the nostalgic, evocative poems which reflect the other face of contemporary Spain. (p. 147)

But essentially Machado is more time-haunted than any writer of recent decades. His temporal consciousness dates from the same age which produced—not by accident—*A la recherche du temps perdu.* Machado too has gone in search of time lost and, except for his own definition (the dialogue with time), no phrase is more descriptive of his work than Proust's title. For Machado, as for Proust, reality is a delicately sustained web of time, interwoven and self-sustaining. (p. 148)

> *Norma Louise Hutman, in her* Machado: A Dialogue with Time: Nature as an Expression of Temporality in the Poetry of Antonio Machado *(© The University of New Mexico Press, 1969), University of New Mexico Press, 1969, 207 p.*

CARL W. COBB   (essay date 1971)

Antonio Machado wrote great poetry in three manners in three fairly well defined periods of his life (and his books tend to follow these periods). . . . Machado created outstanding poetry in all three periods. (pp. 43-4)

While he insists that the two editions of *Solitudes* were in reality "one book", Machado admits that his book was not a "systematic realization" of his aesthetic purposes. We shall have to confess it was not, for no one has succeeded in establishing an entirely convincing organization of *Solitudes,* Machado's own subdivisions being inadequate.

However, the persistent reader of *Solitudes* and some of his later prose finally understands that in general there are two overriding themes which are interrelated. Little by little Antonio Machado himself came to the realization that he was a *poeta en el tiempo,* a poet in time or a poet of time, and that he was also a *poeta en sueños,* a poet of reverie, or memory. In *Solitudes* Machado is a poet of temporality essentially through intuition of time. . . . Machado, as he himself understood, was born into a generation which was the first in Spain to lose the faith in the Church and its promise of eternal life. This loss was critical and profound, and much of the tension in his poetry can be generally traced to the resulting importance attached to temporal existence. (pp. 48-9)

Machado is also the *poeta en sueños,* the poet in dreams. . . . For Machado, to be *en sueños* is a mental state the poet pursued and achieved in his most inspirational waking hours. It is a state of intense reverie, of purposeful daydreaming; the poet looks into his soul and attempts to expand the power of memory, to enhance the remembrance of things past (in Shakespeare's phrase), and in Machado this state usually implies an eternal wait and hope toward the future. (p. 49)

More typical of the mature Machado is a state of reverie in which there is a confusion of opposing elements. Above all, the reverie is not static; the poet's soul itself is usually "upon the road," in constant, seeking movement.

> Upon the bitter earth
> My reverie makes roads
> That wind like labyrinths, torturous paths,
> Parks in bloom, in shadow and in silence;
>
> Deep crypts, and stairways over stars;
> Altarpieces of hopes and of remembrances. . . .
> (p. 50)

As a poet of time and reverie, Machado chose (or his nature chose for him) the late afternoon. The afternoon is the autumn of the day, and autumn's suggestion of melancholy fitted Machado's temperament. In the quiet time of late afternoon, in the clear light, the poet could evoke his intense reveries. "I go along dreaming roads / Of the afternoon" begins a typical poem. Or, "It was a clear afternoon, sad and dreamy / Afternoon of summer." Or, "Twilight was falling / Sad and dust-laden." The afternoon is also the time for meditative walks without a particular destination, and Machado's gradual development as a pensive stroller becomes an important factor in his poetry. (pp. 51-2)

[The] outstanding lyrics from the extensive collection of *Solitudes* can be profitably organized into four loose groupings on another basis. One group utilizes the memories of childhood; another concerns the poet's search for love and lost youth. In a third and very important group, Machado employs the traditional water symbols to express his temporal preoccupations. Finally, toward the end of *Solitudes,* the poet clearly pauses and doubles back, aware of a new concern, generally ethical and religious. . . .

As a poet of memory explored, intensified, and at times almost created, Machado discovered a special richness in the recollections of childhood. As he began to explore his living past, he gradually settled upon a permanent image, that of the patio in Seville, with its fountain and lemon trees and bright flowers. In general, childhood is transmuted into a time of plenitude, of promise, of innocence and joy, al-

though at times a suggestion of monotony intrudes. Somewhere in his past the poet was touched strongly by the evocative power of children chanting or singing in chorus; thus high-pitched voices must have contrasted sharply against the heavy silence of the old Spanish plazas and houses. (p. 52)

In *Solitudes,* as the title suggests, we do not expect the plenitude of love, but certainly the poet is blindly and despairingly seeking, and this search creates a painful tension. Indeed, we cay say the poet is floundering, hardly beginning to hope for love when he suddenly loses hope. Above all, the poet is a painfully reticent figure; he is surely frightened at normal sensuality. Nevertheless, the desire for love is present, even if it is distant. . . .

As Machado continues to explore both past and present in his quest of love, he becomes increasingly disillusioned. In evoking his memories, he is likely to discover mainly childhood memories. His stock of memories of mature love is woefully poor; therefore even intense elaboration and recreation will yield only meager results. And as he stands yearningly before the balconies, he is doomed to defeat almost before he has begun. Thus he begins to dwell upon the realization that his youth, the proper time for love, has passed irrevocably, though he is in fact still a young man. (p. 60)

In *Solitudes* perhaps the poems which evoke the deepest response in our consciousness are those which utilize the water symbols. In his earliest poems Antonio Machado showed a propensity toward the ancient water symbols, and his struggle in *Solitudes* is to capture and express his personal variations around these traditional materials. (p. 61)

In a major poem of *Solitudes* (VI), Machado develops with mature intuition the theme of the flowing fountain as a symbol of time and memory. (p. 63)

By looking inward, into the bottomless "galleries of remembrance," the poet can discover the essentials of life. This "gallery" (*galeria*), which is Machado's symbol of the soul, is understood to be a closed space, possibly immense, into whose immensity the windows let in the light, often as from a distance. (p. 69)

This manner of looking inward, of attempting to feel the deep palpitation of the soul, is essential in Machado. (p. 70)

Antonio Machado ends his poetic venture in *Solitudes* with a confession of defeat, a failure which fortunately proved to be only temporary. (p. 74)

[There are] three themes important to the poet during roughly the years 1905-1924. The first group of poems deals with the theme of the problem and destiny of Spain, generally called the Castilian theme, and of course includes the Soria poems as typical of Castile. The second group are *elogios,* or poems in praise of those Machado considered worthy cultural figures, and a type of poem he sought to establish a first-class status for. The third group traces the history of the poet's love for Leonor in Soria, the shock of the loss of that love, and the persistence and the problems of the memories of it. (p. 76)

The road along the banks of the Duero, which Machado often trod in meditative walks, proved to be the particular place where he meditated upon the essence of Castile and created his poems exploring this theme. (p. 82)

Despite a certain raggedness of structure traceable to the inclusion of poems of somewhat diverse theme and manner . . . , *Fields of Castile* is a solid human document of a type more and more difficult for modern poets to write. It is his effort to look outward toward the real world, toward the Spanish cultural and political problems, and the Castilian landscape, toward the colleagues pursuing the same enterprise, and toward the creation of a personal life. At the same time, it is interesting how this book emphasizes a continuity with *Solitudes*. For example, the symbolic "river" of *Solitudes* he actually discovered in the Duero in Soria, and the symbolic "white road" of *Solitudes* he actually found, winding along the river. Moreover, his preoccupation with temporality is reexpressed in the strong sense of history in Soria as a typical town of Castile. (p. 103)

The third and final period in Antonio Machado's poetic production is complex, difficult, and shot through with paradoxes, but ultimately rewarding to the reader as the culmination of his poetic career. Very early Machado had felt himself wavering between poetry and philosophy, between intuition and conceptual knowledge. *Solitudes* ends in a retreat into the philosophical; the period of *Fields of Castile* also tends to dribble away into philosophical and social concerns. . . .

Machado's attempts to blend the philosophical and the poetic begins in a rather simple way. For a number of years he devoted considerable effort to a long series of "Proverbs and Songs," one-stanza poems which usually present a grain of philosophy in tightly concentrated poetic form. (p. 104)

But the major poems of the third period and the "metaphysical support" in prose for their creation appear in a complex section of the *Complete Works* called finally the *Cancionero apócrifo* (*Apocryphal Songbook*). . . . Just as he turned to drama so as to represent himself in the protagonists of his plays, in his *Apocryphal Songbook* he created a series of *personae* through which to project himself. In the first of the two parts, the *persona* is Abel Martín, poet and philosopher, who supposedly lived from 1840 to 1898. In the second he adds Juan de Mairena, also a figure of the past (1856-1909), who was a student and biographer of Martín. Machado creates also a third *persona* of brief appearance, Jorge Meneses, whose initials indicate that he springs from Mairena, not from Machado directly.

Machado's reasons for creating this profusion of *personae* are fairly clear. He showed reluctance when it came to presenting philosophy under his own name, since he lacked systematic training in this discipline. (p. 105)

The substance of most of Machado's "Proverbs and Songs" concerns his growing skepticism. (p. 106)

Martin develops his idea of love by presenting four sonnets, each followed by further metaphysical discussion. (p. 112)

While stressing the ultimate subjectivity of everything connected with his being or soul, Machado nevertheless felt a persistent urge to overcome that subjectivity by recognizing an incurable yearning toward *Otherness*. In his lyric poetry, this Otherness becomes "erotic" and takes the form of woman, the beloved. In the social sphere, it becomes fraternal love, exemplified clearly in Jesus. In the *Apocryphal Songbook*, the ultimate yearning, religious or metaphysical, is of course toward God. Machado's idea of God is complex, unorthodox, and at times confusing, because he never developed an organized philosophical system. (p. 121)

[For] the third time Antonio Machado marks the end of a period of poetic creation with an expressed defeat. . . . This time his expression of defeat as a poet is almost total, for he predicts nothing less than the disappearance of the lyric poet. He expects nothing from the intellectual poetry then being discussed, and he has only faint hope in a poetry for the masses—or, as he would say, people. For Machado, who matured at a time when belief in lyric poetry was almost an article of faith, it must have been a bitter blow to see another of his worlds collapsing in the later years of his life. Despite the fact that his three journeys into poetry were followed by withdrawals in defeat, his own poetry of course has continued to live, almost as fresh and human as when he dreamed it. (p. 127)

The Machados [Antonio and Manuel] began their collaboration by developing modern adaptations of some well-known Golden Age plays. (p. 146)

We are convinced . . . that the themes and characters of the Machados' theater are essentially Antonio's, while Manuel served importantly in shaping the form of the plays. . . .

[It] is not difficult to interpret most of their plays as Antonio's psychological projections of his difficult relationship with Guiomar. Such an interpretation of course does not affect the critical value of the plays. Further evidence of Antonio's necessity to dramatize himself is found in his insistent creation of *personae*. (p. 147)

[They] modeled their first original play [*The Workings of Fate*] fairly closely after the formula used by the Golden Age dramatists. (p. 151)

As the subject matter is historical, coinciding with the typical Golden Age play, there are certain stylized scenes which could be projected: the court scene, the tavern scene (a sketch of "low life"), the love scene, etc. Perhaps because of the formality and stylization of these scenes, the Machados were able to use their talents in creating poetic dialogue of very convincing quality. Both poets, experienced in handling the popular octosyllable used basically in the dialogue, were able to sustain brisk movement when it was called for, and to achieve a heightened lyrical quality in more intense moments. Moreover, the cast of characters is developed with a completeness perhaps not to be expected in a first play. (pp. 151-52)

But as a modern play written in the twentieth century, *The Workings of Fate* suffers a serious shortcoming. Critics have tended to call it "classical" or "traditional," meaning that it is imitative of the drama of the Golden Age, of Lope de Vega and Calderón. . . . Apparently the Machados were upholding tradition because they objected to the emphasis upon the trivial and the "domestic" in many commercial plays of their day. But it is doubtful that they set out to write an imitation of a Golden Age play; they must have intended to develop elements of their own, of pertinence to their modern audience. Their failure to develop and present their own theme effectively is the shortcoming of the play. In *The Workings of Fate*, the first three acts seem imitative of a Golden Age play, while in the fourth act (this addition of a fourth act violated Golden Age practice), apparently they are trying to project modern subjectivism. . . . This all-consuming type of love is indeed the Machados' theme, but in part they fail with the character who represents it. Julianillo, a traditionally heroic, individualistic character, is not developed in dramatic context, and the whole last act itself seems to dribble away on the stage. This inability to terminate a play with a strong last act became somewhat chronic with the Machados. (pp. 152-53)

In 1929, the Machados achieved their most enduring dramatic success in Madrid working with a traditional theme of the Andalusian *cante jondo* (the deep song) in *La Lola se va a los puertos* (*La Lola Goes off to Sea*). . . . (p. 156)

In this drama, whose substance is mostly Antonio's, the theme is not the usual Andalusian (and universal) one in which the artist discovers life through love; here the artist (La Lola), who shows the way of life to others, must by her destiny lose herself in sublimation, becoming a symbol of her art, the song of the *cante jondo*. (p. 157)

The Machados achieved an example of competent poetic theater in *La Lola*. The success of the play depends largely upon the depth of the two main characters, La Lola and the guitarist Heredia, whose voice is often that of the poet and philosopher Antonio Machado himself. . . . As poets, the Machados were probably guilty of prolonging important speeches and overloading them with lyrically expressed ideas, whereas a craftsman like Benavente would spread his ideas more thinly in the interchange of dialogue, so that the audience could more easily assimilate them. (p. 158)

As would be expected, the Machados' greatest strength was in their creation of poetic dialogue. They modernized somewhat the traditional octosyllabic stanzas by employing more run-on lines to make the dialogue flow more naturally. (p. 162)

The critics of their theater have pointed out their persistent problem in writing a third or final act, without attempting to pursue the underlying reasons. . . . [The] Machados insisted on presenting a real world in the early acts, so that when later their protagonists drifted into illusion, they never quite discovered how to provide a convincing transition between the two worlds. In a sense Antonio is only repeating the general pattern of his poetry: after an engagement with the real world, he tends to drift into a world of *sueño* or illusion. (p. 163)

[While Machado] demonstrated a mastery of form within his essential poems, throughout his career he evidenced a weakness in the organization of his books of poetry, and even in his prose. He was never a prolific or even a consistently inspired poet . . . ; therefore the composition of his books usually covered a period of years, during the course of which his themes and manner tended to change somewhat. . . . Moreover, the quality of his poems is quite uneven. While critics have largely ignored this point, they have proved its validity by returning again and again to a limited number of his outstanding poems, passing over the rest. Surely Machado recognized that some of his poems were of lesser value, but he must have felt that all he chose to preserve in his *Complete Poems* served to fill out the record of his total poetic experience. (p. 168)

As long as our present mood of anguish and alienation endures, undoubtedly Antonio Machado will remain a source of inspiration in Spanish poetry. (p. 172)

Carl W. Cobb, in his Antonio Machado *(copyright © 1971 by Twayne Publishers, Inc., reprinted with the permission of Twayne Publishers, A Division of G. K. Hall & Co., Boston), Twayne, 1971, 188 p.*

NANCY A. NEWTON (essay date 1975)

Most major thinkers, from Plato forward within Western thought, deal with negation, negativity or nothingness. Emphases and perspectives differ greatly, but awareness of the importance of negation has been constant. (p. 236)

[Machado] draws strength from what denies and limits him. In several interlocking processes, the negative constitutes for Machado an essential step in the acquisition of the ideal "conciencia integral." At least four kinds of *via negativa* inform Machado's work; some are mutually dependent and all are subsumed in the underlying psychic structure: (1) the *via negativa* of cognition, wherein reason is the negating power; (2) the *via negativa* of being, or self-actualization, wherein love—in its possessive aspect—is the negating power; (3) the *via negativa* of the creative process, wherein forgetting and distance are the negating powers; (4) the *via negativa* of nature, wherein nature's indifferent otherness is the negating power. Here we shall focus on Machado's awareness of cognitive structuring. (pp. 236-37)

In order for a learner to internalize what he is being exposed to, he must first be shocked into receptive awareness by seeing things as they are *not*. The pattern is that of a *via negativa*. (p. 237)

In Machado's scheme of things, the human invention of the void —*la nada*—is essential to the development of thought, and although it represents the most radical of falsifications of "what is," of reality, it is nevertheless necessary to logic and to reason—tools without which man would be at the mercy of undifferentiated sensation, the chaos of immediate experience. The ability to think abstractly is the ability to remove, separate, put distance between the perceiving sensibility and the thing perceived. (p. 240)

[Machado utilizes] what we shall call [a] reverse "creation myth." . . . [Instead] of "something" being created out of "nothing." Machado's Supreme Being creates "nothing" by a retreat from the surrounding "something" or "thingness," by wilfully blinding himself.

The supreme creative act is accomplished by God wilfully blocking out his vision, a symbolic gesture that provides a rich range of metaphoric possibilities which Machado incorporates in his poetry. The basic metaphors issuing from Machado's "creation myth"—whose presence is of importance throughout Machado's work—are opposed but complementary groupings of images that may be gathered beneath the governing rubrics of "el gran ojo" (intuitive, poetic vision) and "el gran cero" (the blindness of reason). (pp. 240-41)

Machado's insight into the complementarity of negation and creation gives an original dimension to much of his poetry. . . . Thus, the constant oppositions we encounter in Machado's poetry are by no means facile opposites. They do constitute oppositions, but in an overall *complementary* sense. We know day, for example, only by knowing night (or the other way around). In immediate contrast to each other within a single poem-instance, the members of any pair of poetic images can be assigned a plus (+) and a minus (−); but these valences cannot be absolute and unchanging in the poetry as a body because they are mutually dependent. Both the dynamic, constantly changing *fuente* and the static, fixed *piedra* embody a positive quality in that the negative represents an essential step in the acquisition of Machado's ideal "conciencia integral." . . . (pp. 242-43)

"Toda visión requiere distancia, y no hay manera de ver las cosas sin salirse de ellas" [says Juan de Mairena]. This statement encompasses the *via negativa* principle on all its levels of application, and suggests the notion of *visión* as a key image-concept ("el gran ojo") and integrative factor in Machado's thinking. The poet's mission is to see, but Machado makes it clear that the gift of vision is the fruit of a *via negativa*. One important negative way is through the distance of contemplation, through the "removal" inherent to the abstractive process. The result is perspective. But this removal of things from time should serve the purpose of—finally—"seeing" or intuiting them *within* time. In order to see—to achieve "conciencia integral"—one must first be distanced, blinded. (p. 251)

> Nancy A. Newton, "Structures of Cognition: Antonio Machado and the 'Via Negativa'," in MLN (© copyright 1975 by The Johns Hopkins University Press), Vol. 90, No. 2, 1975, pp. 231-51.

BIBLIOGRAPHY

Curry, Richard A. "A Stylistic Analysis of Antonio Machado's 'El hospicio'." *Journal of Spanish Studies* 1, No. 2 (Fall 1973): 85-94.
Close textual study of Machado's poem which elucidates the relationship between his techniques and themes. The critic sees "El hospicio" as a metaphor for Machado's central vision in *Campos de Castilla*.

Fox, Linda C. "The Vision of Cain and Abel in Spain's 'Generation of 1898'." *College Language Association Journal* XXI, No. 4 (June 1978): 499-512.*
Traces the Cain and Abel theme in Machado, finding it a slight motif rather than the major complex assessment of Spanish character seen by other members of the Generation of '98.

Glendinning, Nigel. "The Philosophy of Henri Bergson in the Poetry of Antonio Machado." *Revue de Littérature Comparée* XXXVI, No. 1 (January-March 1962): 50-70.
An in-depth examination of eleven of Machado's poems to establish Bergsonian influence (time vs. space, intuition vs. science). The critic contends these are the only poems where this influence is apparent concluding, "his debt to the French Philosopher has been exaggerated."

Ilie, Paul. "Verlaine and Machado: The Aesthetic Role of Time." *Comparative Literature* XIV, No. 3 (Summer 1962): 261-65.*
Discussion of Machado's "Fué una clara tarde" and Verlaine's sonnet "Apres trois ans," which contrasts the philosophy and sensibility of each poet.

Ilie, Paul. "Antonio Machado and the Grotesque." *Journal of Aesthetics and Art Criticism* XXII, No. 2 (Winter 1963): 209-16.
Places Machado's expression of the grotesque in the Spanish tradition which ranges from the comic and pathetic to the pathological. The critic examines the various techniques Machado used in his poetry which indicate a decline in romanticism and emergence of the absurd as a frame of reference.

Katharine Elaine, Sister. "Man in the Landscape of Antonio Machado." In *Spanish Thought and Letters in the Twentieth Century*, edited by German Bleiberg and E. Inman Fox, pp. 271-86. Nashville: Vanderbilt University Press, 1966.
Interesting study of Machado's concept of the ideal Spaniard in comparison with that proposed by other members of the Generation of '98.

Parker, J. M. "The Poetry of Antonio Machado." *English Studies in Africa* 7, No. 2 (September 1964): 217-26.
Survey of Machado's poetry chronicling his themes and his symbols and concluding Machado is "one of Spain's great modern poets."

Predmore, Michael P. "Antonio Machado." *Contemporary Literature* XI, No. 3 (Summer 1970): 432-34.
Review of the first book-length study on Machado, *Machado: A Dialogue with Time* by Norma Louise Hutman. Predmore finds Hutman's study "severely handicapped": unsystematic, a distortion of Machado's poetic world, and a presentation which confuses Machado the poet and Machado the philosopher.

Predmore, Michael P. "The Nostalgia for Paradise and the Dilemma of Solipsism in the Early Poetry of Antonio Machado." *Revista Hispanica Moderna: Columbia University Hispanic Studies* XXXVIII, Nos. 1-2 (1974-1975): 30-52.
Extensive analysis of themes and symbols in Machado's earliest poetry.

Ribbans, Geoffrey. "Antonio Machado's *Soledades* (1903): A Critical Study." *Hispanic Review* 30, No. 3 (August 1962): 194-215.
Detailed analysis of these early poems centering on Machado's use of various ideas and symbols, e.g., the road, the sunset, the fountain, and especially the river.

Ribbans, Geoffrey. "The Unity of Antonio Machado's 'Campos de Soria'." *Hispanic Review*, Special Issue 41 (1973): 285-96.
Textual analysis of Machado's "most ambitious descriptive poem."

Schulman, Ivan A. "Antonio Machado and Enrique Gonzalez Martinez: A Study in Internal and External Dynamics." *Journal of Spanish Studies Twentieth Century* 4, No. 1 (Spring 1976): 29-46.*
Compares Machado and Martinez at two stages in their poetic careers: "inception and fruition." The critic notes their similarities in tone, imagery, concept, and execution.

Sheets, Jane M. "Symbol and Salvation: Rilke and Machado in Spain." *Comparative Literature* XXIII, No. 4 (Fall 1971): 346-58.*
Compares Machado and Rilke in their use of landscape for images and symbols to express their sense of immanence while they searched for transcendence.

Weiner, Jack. "Machado's Concept of Russia." *Hispania* XLIX, No. 1 (March 1966): 31-5.
Discusses Machado's belief in a social order in which brotherhood and Christianity are the building principles. Machado found these ideals in Russian literature and the Russian soul and expressed this in several essays in his later life.

Maurice Maeterlinck

1862-1949

Belgian dramatist, essayist, poet, translator, and short story writer.

Maeterlinck is considered the major dramatist of the symbolist movement, representing in the theater the philosophy and aesthetics associated with such earlier writers as Paul Verlaine and Stéphane Mallarmé. The influence of the French symbolists is apparent in Maeterlinck's first plays, which signified a rejection of the predominately naturalistic drama in European theater of that time. Rather than following in the "slice of life" tradition which primarily dramatized social themes, Maeterlinck created an other-worldly, often nightmarish reality to explore the inner life of his characters. An example of this style is the allegorical *Pélléas and Mélisande*, which Claude Debussy adapted as the libretto for his noted opera of the same name. The highly allegorical nature of Maeterlinck's dramas led at one point to his dispensing with human actors to write several plays for marionettes, including *The Death of Tintagiles*.

Maeterlinck's first drama, *Princess Maleine*, was described in *Figaro* by the French critic Octave Mirbeau as being superior in beauty to Shakespeare. Later critics generally concurred in judging favorably these early symbolist dramas, and on their strength Maeterlinck was awarded the Nobel Prize in literature in 1911. Though for the most part highly regarded, Maeterlinck has been accused by some critics of cultivating a sense of mystery for its own sake, without the benefit of a structured religious doctrine to support his mysticism. In the initial phases of his career Maeterlinck developed a particular mystical style that rendered, as he stated, "the dread of the unknown that surrounds us." Dramas such as *The Intruder* and *The Blind* portray this vague terror, revealing a philosophical pessimism on the part of their author. Maeterlinck sought to remedy this existential condition through his quest for a metaphysical absolute.

In a second phase of his work, Maeterlinck turned from his previous studies of dream-world anxiety and began composing more markedly realistic and psychological plays, such as *Monna Vanna*. His greatest theatrical success, *The Blue Bird*, is a return to symbolist drama but one in which the allegorical characters and events communicate a new mood of hope based on his studies in the more positive forms of occultism. Maeterlinck's concern with supernatural realms is complemented by his naturalist studied such as *The Life of the Bee*, which lend a scientific dimension to the predominately spiritual character of his work.

Maeterlinck's later works show that any specific spiritual convictions he might have had became less definite toward the end of his life. After a career-long devotion to the varieties of mysticism, Maeterlinck implied in his ultimate metaphysical studies a final abandonment of the pursuit for religious certainty and a lapse into tranquil agnosticism.

PRINCIPAL WORKS

Serres chaudes (poetry) 1889
  [*Serres chaudes* published in *Poems*, 1915]
Les aveugles. L'intreuse (dramas) 1890
  [*Blind. The Intruder*, 1891]
La Princesse Maleine (drama) 1890
  [*The Princess Maleine* published in *The Princess
    Maleine: A Drama in Five Acts, and The Intruder: A
    Drama in One Act*, 1892]
Les sept princesses (drama) 1891
  [*The Seven Princesses: A Play*, 1909]
Pélléas et Mélisande (drama) 1892
  [*Pélléas and Mélisanda* published in *Pélléas and
    Mélisanda and The Sightless: Two Plays*, 1892]
*Alladine et Palomides; Interieur; et La mort de Tintagiles:
    Trois petits drames pour marionettes* (drama) 1894
  [*Alladine and Palomides. Interior. The Death of
    Tintagiles: Three Little Dramas for Marionettes*, 1899]
Aglavaine et Sélysette (drama) 1896
  [*Aglavaine and Selysette: A Drama in Five Acts*, 1897]
Le trésor des humbles (essays) 1896
  [*The Treasure of the Humble*, 1897]
La sagesse et la destinée (essays) 1898
  [*Wisdom and Destiny*, 1898]
Théâtre, Vol. III (dramas, includes *Soeur Beatrice* and
    Ariane et barbe-bleue) 1901
  [*Sister Beatrice and Ardiane and Barbe Bleue*, 1901]
La viè des abeilles (essay) 1901
  [*The Life of the Bee*, 1901]
Monna Vanna: Pièce en trois actes (drama) 1902
  [*Monna Vanna: A Play in Three Acts*, 1903]
Joyzelle: Pièce en cinq actes (drama) 1903
  [*Joyzelle*, 1907]
Le double jardin (essays) 1904
  [*The Double Garden*, 1904]
L'intelligence des fleurs (essays) 1907
  [*The Intelligence of the Flowers*, 1907]

L'oiseau bleu: Féerie en cinq actes et douze tableux (drama) 1909
   [*The Blue Bird: A Fairy Play in Five Acts,* 1909]
Marie-Magdeleine: Pièce en trois actes (drama) 1913
   [*Mary Magdalene: A Play in Three Acts,* 1910]
La mort (essay) 1913
   [*Death,* 1911]
Le Bourgmestre de Stilemonde: Pièce en trois actes (drama) 1919
   [*The Burgomaster of Stilemonde: A Play in Three Acts,* 1918]
Le grand secret (essay) 1921
   [*The Great Secret,* 1922]
Les fiançailles: Féerie en cinq actes et ouze tableaux (drama) 1922
   [*The Betrothal, a Sequel to The Blue Bird: A Fairy Play in Five Acts and Eleven Scenes,* 1918]
Le malheur passe: Pièce inédite en trois actes (drama) 1925
   [*The Cloud That Lifted* published in *The Cloud That Lifted, and The Power of the Dead,* 1923]
La puissance des morts: Pièce en quatre actes (drama) 1927
   [*The Power of the Dead* published in *The Cloud That Lifted, and The Power of the Dead,* 1923]
L'ombre des ailes (essays) 1936
L'autre monde; ou, Le cadran stellaire (essays) 1942

J. W. MACKAIL   (essay date 1897)

M. Maeterlinck is widely known as the inventor of a dramatic method which, with certain obvious imperfections, is vivid, flexible, far-reaching. It is still more important to recognise that this method is the vehicle of a new and strange sense of beauty. . . .

[Maeterlinck's primary impulse is] that of expressing, by such means as the existing arts supply or suggest, the inner meaning and hidden beauty of things as they are freshly felt by a mind which approaches them quite courageously and quite simply. (p. vi)

La Princess Maleine, the earliest and by far the crudest and most fantastic of the plays, is also the one which shows [an] Elizabethan influence in its most direct action and at its highest force. The new thrill which all romantic movements seek is attained in it by the element of undefined supernatural suggestion, which gives *Macbeth* and *Hamlet* their unique horror. . . . (p. vii)

In the two mystery plays—for they should hardly be called dramas—of *L'Intruse* and *Les Aveugles,* the fantastic element, the tragic delirium of the earlier piece was exchanged for a graver, more equable treatment, and for a more or less definite symbolism. The two methods were to a certain extent combined, not perhaps with the most felicitous result, in *Les Sept Princesses,* which followed after a short interval. In these pieces action is reduced to the simplest and most abstract limits. They are, so to speak, the raw stuff, unfixed and unshaped, of a spiritual drama. It is worth noting that in none of them have the persons—if these can be called persons who are rather half-impersonate thoughts or emotions—any names. They flicker on the verge of embodiment, like a flame in the doorway. . . . [In *Les Aveu-*

gles] this method is carried to its most uncompromising conclusions, with a weirdness of effect to which it would not be easy to find a parallel. There is absolutely no action. All the persons who speak at all speak by hints, by touches, by half frozen whispers, scarcely more articulate than the rustle of the dead leaves about them. The terror which grows throughout it is a terror of silence and darkness felt as active presences. The tension of mere situation is so great that the barking of a dog—like the knocking at the gate in the central scene of *Macbeth*—becomes more than the nerves can bear. When at last one of the figures, speechless till then, breaks out into loud weeping, the curtain falls as inevitably on the stoppage of the silence as in an ordinary play it falls on the stoppage of the speech. It would be but a step further to a drama in which the actors should be not only blind, but dumb. (pp. viii-x)

The principle that the highest tragic effect may result from mere passiveness is one which has its instances in the great dramatists. . . . [The Belgian Shakespeare—as M. Maeterlinck has been called in a phrase which was originally meant seriously]—carried this principle almost to the extent of a new dramatic method.

Of a piece with this artifice of structure is the artifice of style in the reiteration and repercussion of phrases, which is one of their most obvious features. In his later plays it is used with extraordinary delicacy and adroitness; in these it has an effect which is now and then almost childish, and often undeniably odd. But in both alike it represents an attempt, no less daring than simple, to use language beyond its normal sphere, so as to produce the emotional effect of music. (pp. x-xi)

In these earlier plays, through which he first arrested the attention of the world, and by which . . . he is perhaps still most widely known, M. Maeterlinck invented, one might almost say, certainly moulded to a very distinct and individual form and use, a dramatic method, subtle, vivid, fantastic, going curiously near to the inner life and heart of things. They touched the springs of pity and terror with extraordinary power. They showed delicate insight, romantic feeling, dramatic force of a high order. They showed a power over language which was akin to a real creative gift. Their faults were no less obvious. . . . The faculty of design, the certain control of beauty, were still to come. (pp. xi-xii)

Of [*Pélléas et Mélisande*], all but faultless in its construction, more than faultless in its beauty, it is difficult to speak with tempered praise, or in words that shall not seem extravagant. In virtue of mere beauty it stands among the masterpieces of literature. All the qualities of the earlier plays are disengaged from their defects. The morbid tone has disappeared; the fantastic element is under control. The symbolism is set back to its proper plane. In the crude form in which it is an uncomfortable quality at best, it only remains in the brief and curiously exciting prologue. The story is one of quite human beauty and sorrow. Pélléas, Golaud, the young wife, the aged king, are no phantasmal types, no reminiscences of some mediaeval portrait gallery. (p. xiii)

The advance in matured power in equally visible in the management of the language. (p. xiv)

The use of language to produce the emotional effect of music, which has been noticed as a distinctive quality of M.

Maeterlinck's work, is carried here to a much higher degree of perfection. The echoes and repetitions of phrase are used with increased skill, more accurately judged and wrought in a freer and larger pattern. . . . In this play the elaboration of the language, notwithstanding its limpid clearness, is commensurate with that of a Greek chorus. (p. xv)

Nor is the dramatic skill less striking than the finished beauty of the language. . . . It would seem to be the only one of M. Maeterlinck's plays in which he has chosen to comply rigorously with the conditions of the modern stage. The three dramatic pieces which appeared in a later volume are significantly described on the title page as *Petits Drames pour Marionnettes,* and revert, though with an increased power and sureness of touch, to the mystical or symbolic treatment of the earlier works.

It is in this later group of plays that the second great English influence which affected M. Maeterlinck's work appears in its full force: that of the Arthurian legend as interpreted anew by the individual genius of two great English artists and thinkers. The number of names transferred or adapted in these plays from the story of the Round Table is only one indication of this influence; Pélléas, Ygraine, Palomides, Tintagiles all come saturated with the associations of the *Mort d'Arthur.* (pp. xvi-xvii)

Almost from the first, M. Maeterlinck seems to have arrived at definite notions as to the stock of scenery which would be sufficient for his stage; and he brings pieces of it out again, when they are needed, with the utmost nonchalance. . . . [Through] all the plays something of the same atmosphere may be felt as a faintly indicated background: old thinly inhabited castles, terraced and moated; trailing canals; trees in long files and avenues; a tower in the middle of a wood, haunted by sea-fowl from the bordering ocean; curtain-like draperies of cloud off a low coast; silent pools suddenly started by the beating of swans' wings in the dusk. (pp. xix-xx)

In the *Trésor des Humbles* M. Maeterlinck appeared as a professed Neo-Platonist, a thinker and mystic, saturated in Emerson, and finding inspiration from Plotinus and Swedenborg. This growing philosophic passion may involve a certain expense of dramatic quality. But there is [in *Aglavaine et Sélysette*] an even higher attainment in delicate insight, and in the power of expressing by simple words some of the subtlest and most elusive shades of emotion.

It has little interplay of action. . . . [Praise] cannot be too high for the fineness and truth of the two principal figures; nor for the consummate skill with which the interest, the sympathy, the beauty are slowly slid from one to the other, as Sélysette unfolds larger and larger, until she blots out her brilliant rival. Nor, given the story with its two actors, is there any inferiority in its dramatic handling. One point beyond all deserves special notice. The artifice of repetition, already applied with such subtle skill to language, is here extended with wonderful effect to action. The doubling of the scene on the tower in the fourth act, led up to by the doubled meeting in the corridor, brings the action itself towards the condition of music. (pp. xxi-xxii)

This inner beauty of human life, of which M. Maeterlinck is so curious and subtle an interpreter, is also its inner truth. (p. xxii)

> *J. W. Mackail, in his introduction to* Aglavaine and Selysette *by Maurice Maeterlinck, translated by Alfred Sutro, Grant Richards, 1897, pp. v-xxiii.*

THOS. FORTEBUS (essay date 1901)

It has been the fashion to call Maeterlinck a dreamer, a mystic. It saves trouble to call him these names. . . . No doubt at his clearest moments Maeterlinck would still be a "mystic" to many; but in his most visionary moods he certainly deserves the epithet, and more. Yet at his best his desire seems to be to show that, though the conventional and commonplace seem wholly to environ us, the eternal flashes through at every turn. (p. 87)

It was unfortunate that such a paper as that entitled *Silence* was placed at the beginning of his first book of essays, *The Treasure of the Humble.* It is not impossible that this has helped to the fashionable depreciation. Readers stumbled at the threshold, as at the entrance of a dark house, and would not go farther. In these few pages, indeed, Maeterlinck reaches depths of obfuscation. "From the moment that we have something to say to each other, we are compelled to hold our peace." . . . Yet there is much of truth in the strange discourse: it seeks to describe the impotence we all feel, at times, to express a sudden sorrow, a passion, a sensation, a confidence. . . . It is these sudden abysses of silence, these flashes into the depths of personality, feeling, confidence, or thought, that to Maeterlinck are the only realities. In this desire to push through the half-seen, the half-intelligible, he reaches a false idealism, and pretends to see the wholly invisible and to understand the wholly unintelligible. . . . With respect to individual character a boundless and inveterate optimism possesses Maeterlinck. . . . But in his later book, *Wisdom and Destiny,* a work of more clarity, where his mind has attained closer to human facts, this optimism is mingled with a splendid stoic acceptation. (pp. 87-8)

[For] every flash of illumination, for every pregnant suggestion there are pages of paradoxes and half-ideas; facts, with the inveterate vice of mysticism, are strained and warped to yield up a meaning he desires, and causes and effects are distorted or magnified. But all is said with so great a charm, so tenderly illusive are his inferences, so gentle is his persuasion, so *naïve* are many thoughts . . . that one's criticism is lulled almost in spite of itself. Sometimes his words take on the measure of a noble chant; at other times his frail meaning is lost in the mass of embroidered prolixity. (p. 88)

Maeterlinck does not speak to the common man; always he addresses himself, with no sense of humour, but with a stupendous seriousness, to the "sage." (p. 89)

In spite of his tenuity, he no doubt has comfort and strength for many. . . . There is an intimate pity for the oppressed; he preaches an abounding charity . . . and he is seized with the passionate wonder of mere existence. . . . Yet these characteristics, in certain passages, seem to be merely the amiability that viciously blinks the truth, and that wishes to see only what it very much desires to believe is the fact. (pp. 89-90)

If Maeterlinck could have been content to respect the far-reaching logic which has discovered the truth he . . . sets out, we should have been spared much lavishness of vague ideas, though our loss would also have included much fragile beauty of phrase and thought. But Maeterlinck, with many others, cannot rest content in the cautiousness that will not assert what it cannot prove, and that relies on merely definite thought. . . . It is this recklessness of the metaphysician that makes Maeterlinck common with a hundred other thinkers possessing not a whit of his charm, his almost womanly beseechment. He is impatient in the confines of the hardly-won outpost of science, and must adventure forth into the dark. He sees visions, and believes they are realities; weaves fancies, and thinks that final truths are revealed to him; and by faith, he is assured, greater knowledge is given to him than science has ever gained by the most laborious, the most worshipful attribute of the mind. (pp. 90-1)

For Maeterlinck too, as for most teachers, there are no unalterable conditions of character. In this he shows his failure logically to follow out all the meaning of the truth he so delicately enunciates. For him, temperament is perfectly plastic, and it is within every one's power to shape himself to the noble ends that he alleges we all consciously carry about us, whether philosopher or criminal, noble woman or prostitute. He has failed to realise that it is not in a man's power to believe what one strain of his complex blend of mind would like to believe, or follow where part of him would like to follow.... (p. 91)

In his "Life of the Bee," the beautiful epic in prose where he mingles observation of apiarian life with a continual reference to human destiny, his reflections have less of the character of the mystic than of the poet who in some measure accepts the spirit of science. He seeks to show how "the little gestures and humble habits" of the dwellers in the hive, "which seem so far away, are yet so nearly akin to our grand passions and arrogant destinies." One cannot help feeling that in presenting his observations Maeterlinck speaks with the emotion of a special pleader. The light by which he perceives the facts of a marvellous life is not the dry light of science; his vision sees them bathed in vivid colours that deepen the mystery which it is his desire to emphasise.... He has no notion of any but a subjective view; he reads human motives into apiarian actions and judges them by the same standard, and he sees Nature as an illogical woman, a combination of sentimentalist, savage, and snob. Yet, however he may misread them, he generally grasps essentials. (pp. 91-2)

[In] Maeterlinck we may have the man that, as his development proceeds, will reveal the unique artist that literature awaits, in whom the spirit of our later science will feed the pure white flame of an emotion that may light the way to the highest achievements of the creative mind. But to become this he will have first to slough off the crude self-deceptions, the facile, almost feminine sentiment, the confused ideas and illogical implications that he has at present in common with the average respectable idealist. (pp. 92-3)

> *Thos. Fortebus, "Maeterlinck," in* The Argosy, *n.s. No. 19, July, 1901, pp. 77-93.*

JAMES HUNEKER (essay date 1905)

When this Belgian poet, dramatist, mystic, became known in America, his plays avowedly written for marionettes, were received with open-eyed wonder or prolonged laughter.

[In time] it was conceded that a mistake had been made just as in Browning's case.... A Belgian Emerson, rather than a Belgian Shakespeare; but an Emerson who had in him much of Edgar Allan Poe. (pp. 367-68)

Maeterlinck began with a volume of poems entitled *Serres Chaudes,* often compared to the unrhymed, loose rhythmic

prose of Walt Whitman. They do bear a certain superficial resemblance to Whitman's effusions, though not in idea. It is rather a cataloguing, aimless apparently, of widely disparate subjects. But the substance derives more from that extraordinary book of an extraordinary poet, *Les Illuminations* by Arthur Rimbaud, than from the ragged, epical lines of Whitman. (p. 368)

[Maeterlinck's first drama] *Princess Maleine* is an undigested compound of *Macbeth, Hamlet, Lear,* and, as Arthur Symons sagely remarks, with more of the Elizabethan violence we find in Webster and Tourneur than in Shakespeare. And its author was only a youth in his twenties.

However, with all its crudities, its imitations, its impossible *mélange* of blood, lust, tears, terror, there are several elements in the crazy play that indicate latent gifts of a high order. The range is narrow and Poe-like. Fear is the theme, and a strange repetition the method of expression. There is a young prince, a Hamlet, who has fed on the art of the modern decadents. He is a spiritual half-brother to Laforgue's Hamlet, shorn of that ironist's humour. (pp. 369-70)

Pestilent and mystic is the atmosphere of *Princess Maleine....* There is much of Poe's dark tarn, of Auber, and the misty mid-region of Weir in the early Maeterlinck. (p. 372)

There are chanting and spectral nuns, lewd beggars, an old Shakespearian nurse, a freakish boy, and the usual scared courtiers. The scenes do not hang together at all—there is no sequence of action, only of moods; or rather the same mood persists throughout. Yet the lines bite at times, and there are great fissures of silence, pauses as deep and as sinister as murky midnight pools. (pp. 372-73)

The ideas, hysterical and few as they are, begin to assume some coherence if compared with the emotional and disconnected experiments of the poems.

Maeterlinck has defined his aesthetic in his prose essays. He played queer pranks upon the nerves with these shadows, these spiritual marionettes, which are pure abstractions typifying various qualities of the temperament. The iteration of his speech is like the dripping of water upon the heads of the condemned. It finally stuns the consciousness, and then, like a performer upon some fantastic instrument with one string, this virtuoso executes variations boasting a solitary theme—the fear of Fear. (pp. 373-74)

[We know that artistically Maeterlinck] springs from the loins of Poe and Hoffmann; ... that by the Belgian's artful scale of words he evoked images in our mind which recall the harmonies of unheard music; that the union of mysticism and freedom of thinking lends to his work peculiar eloquence.... (p. 380)

Upon the anvil of his youthful dreams did Maeterlinck forge his little plays for marionettes. Shadowy they are, brief transcripts of emotion, but valuable in illustrating unity of purpose, of mood, of *tone.* Herein lies their superiority to Browning's more elaborate structures. Before he ventured into the maze of plotting, Maeterlinck was content with simple types of construction. The lyric musician in this poet, the lover of beauty, led him to make his formula a musical one. The dialogue of the first plays seems like new species of musical notation. If there is not rhyme there is rhythm, interior rhythm, and an alluring assonance. Hence we get pages burdened with repetitions and also the "crossing fire" of jewelled words. Apart from their spirit the lines of this poet are sonorously beautiful. In the "purple" mists of his early manner a weaker man might have perished. Not so Maeterlinck. He is first the thinker—a thinker of strange thoughts independent of their verbal settings. He soon escaped preciosity in diction; it was monotony of mood that chained him to his many experimentings. (p. 382)

Maurice Maeterlinck employs the symbol instead of the sword; the psyche is his *panache*. His puppets are all poetic —the same poetry as of old informs their gestures and their speech. He so fashions them of such fragile pure stuff that a phrase maladministered acts as the thrust of a dagger. The Idea of Death slays. . . . (p. 383)

In the beginning Maeterlinck elected to mould poetic moods; later [he became] a moulder of men and women. (p. 384)

Death the Intruder! Always the Intruder. In his first little dramatic *plaque* [*The Intruder*], it is the venerable grandfather who is clairvoyant: Death, protagonist. Almost imperceptibly the shadow steals into the room with the lighted lamp and big Dutch clock. The spiritual evidence is cumulative; a series of cunningly worded affirmations, and lo! Death the Intruder. It is a revelation of the technic of atmosphere. Voice again is the chief character.

The Blind takes us out of doors, though one senses the atmosphere of the charnel-house under the blue bowl of the unvarying sky. This is the most familiar and the most derided of the Maeterlinckian plays. It is hardly necessary to describe that "ancient Nordland forest," with its "eternal look under a sky of deep stars." The stage directions of these poems are matchless. How depict an "eternal look"? These exalted pictures are but the verbal instrumentation of Maeterlinck's motives. They may be imagined, never realized. Yet how the settings enhance the theme! These blind old men and women, with the lame, the halt, the mad and the sad, form a painful tableau in the centre of which sits the dead priest, their keeper, their leader, without whom they are destined to stumble into the slow waters about the island.

Death the Intruder! But in this instance an intruder who has sneaked in unperceived. The discovery is made in semitones that mount solemnly to the apex of a pyramid of woe. This little drama is more "arranged" than *The Intruder;* it does not "happen" so inevitably. *Interior* . . . is of similar *genre* to *The Intruder*. From a coign in an old garden planted with willows we see a window—a symbol; through this window the family may be viewed. Its members are seated. All is vague, dreamy. The dialogue occurs without. An old man and a stranger discuss the garden, the family and—the catastrophe. Most skilfully the poet marshals his facts—hints, pauses, sighs, are the actors in the curious puppet-booth. (pp. 388-90)

The Belgian translates the idea of Death into phrases more hypnotic than Whitman's. His "cool-enfolding Death" is not always "lovely and soothing" for the survivors. His cast of mind is mediæval, and presently comes sailing into the critical consciousness memories of the Pre-Raphaelitic Brotherhood with its strained attitudes, its glories of illuminated glass, its breathless intensity and concentration upon a single theme—above all its apotheosis of the symbol and of Death the Intruder. . . .

The romantic in Maeterlinck began to show itself plainly in *The Seven Princesses*. Death is still the motive, but the picture is ampler, the frame more decorative. . . . Movement, though it be a mere sinister rustling of dead leaves, is more manifest in this transitional period. *The Seven Princesses* is like some ancient morality, with the nervous, sonorous, musical setting of a latter-day composer. (p. 391)

[Mediæval] in its picturesque quality is *The Death of Tintagiles* with its five short acts of despairing sister love. . . . This simple, old-world fairy story—all Maeterlinck has a tang of the supernatural—is treated exquisitely. The arousing of pity for the doomed child is almost Shakespearian. These children of Maeterlinck are his own creation. No one, with the exception of Dostoïevsky and Hauptmann, approaches him in unfolding the artless secrets of the childish heart. Like plucked petals of a white virginal flower, the little soul is exposed. And there is no taint of precocious sexuality as in Dostoïevsky's studies of childhood. . . . (pp. 395-96)

Yet Maeterlinck's *Death of Tintagiles* is in form and style far above his previous efforts. His marionettes are beginning to modulate into flesh and blood. . . . (p. 398)

A study of Maeterlinck's art reveals the evolution of a mystic, the creation of a dream theatre, the master of a mystic positivism. (p. 429)

> James Huneker, "Maurice Maeterlinck," in his Iconoclasts: A Book of Dramatists *(copyright © 1905 Charles Scribner's Sons), Scribner's, 1905, pp. 367-429.*

GEORGETTE LEBLANC-MAETERLINCK   (essay date 1909)

[Aglavaine, Joyzelle, Monna Vanna and Ariane, Maeterlinck's later heroines] are beings of contrast: their pride is made of humility, their liberty of obedience, their gladness of melancholy; and it is rare for them, in the brief space of life, to find in the midst of all these contradictions the equilibrium that gives happiness or the peace that ensures its duration. They are shaken by a thousand doubts, a thousand anxieties: one would believe them to be led by a fierce selfishness, but this selfishness is to their hearts what a cruel armour would be to their delicate flesh; and, while their will refuses to submit to the fatalities of life, they feel harshly the ills of a destiny that scarce throbs beneath the weight of one immense fatality, for they have been born too late or too soon. They outrun the clock!

They stand out in the crowd like the taller flowers that are exposed above a field, maltreated by every wind, overpowered by the light for which they call. The storm strips them and the fine dust of their hearts is scattered at random . . . fruitful and nameless. (p. 49)

[The] fatal powers reign mercilessly over [the earlier heroines,] the unconscious little princesses, crushing their character. Their qualities of gentleness and submissiveness, rather than warding off misfortune, served its purpose. In [Maeterlinck's] second period fatality arouses the characters that blindly seek to struggle against it. The pain of no longer being loved by her betrothed lights up Astolaine's soul and releases its strength. The dread of losing her brother Tintagiles, after all her other kinsfolk, makes an heroic sister of the gentle Ygraine. These are the first wills that we see dawning in the darkness: they are born of misfortune, but powerless to conquer it.

Now, in the third and last period, we come to the characters that create the tragedies by trying to modify the events. The intellects fight against "the human errors and wishes," as we shall now name what before we called "the fatal powers"; and this change is brought about by the very intellects which we propose to study. (pp. 49-50)

It is in this that we find the superiority of Maeterlinck's new heroines. They have a personal character, a personal morality, a will. (p. 50)

Face to face with Aglavaine, what strikes us first of all? It is the new atmosphere, the air, the moral substance which she brings and which will feed all the elements of transformation that really create a world between the drama of *Aglavaine and Sélysette* and its predecessor, *The Death of Tintagiles*.

If we cross the threshold of the castle inhabited by the heroes of this play, we understand that all is changed. It is just a family gathered round the hearth; but this family, for the first time in Maeterlinck's dramas, is composed of reasoning beings, who seek to conduct themselves in accordance with their reason. In the foreground we see the dominating and active intelligence of Aglavaine, which seems incessantly to thrust aside the instincts within and around it. All mystery has now fled. Two beings love each other; another supervenes; and jealousy tangles and disentangles the drama. The world into which we penetrate speaks our language, thinks, feels, loves as we do; all the interest of the poem and all its beauty lie in the manner wherein those beings will act one towards the other. The two women love Mélénare, and yet they love each other and would see each other happy. Aglavaine wishes to raise Sélysette. Sélysette wishes to follow Aglavaine; but the strength of the one acts upon the weakness of the other as sea-air acts upon too frail an organism; it kills instead of invigorating; poor Sélysette will die of it. Sélysette still belongs to the women of the past; and the conflict will arise not only between the two heroines, but between two races of souls; and, when we come to the tragic catastrophe, that is to say, to the triumph of weakness over will, it indeed seems as if the poet himself had solved the problem regretfully, drawn on by the movement of the stage.

Aglavaine is beautiful with a moral beauty but seldom recognised; she seems too bold, she wounds more than she charms. She transcends the circumstances, which seem ordinary beside her; she is new in the face of old conditions, in the midst of beings who are connected with the past; she enters madly upon the struggle with the ancient and eternal instinct of the flesh. What can this new force do, when opposed to it? A clash is bound to come, of which Sélysette will be the victim.

Aglavaine—and by Aglavaine I mean to convey the special will-power of all that new category of women which we are now considering—Aglavaine is too eager in wanting disciples and in testing the laws of a moral system of which she can learn the extent only in proportion to the antipathies and contradictions to which it gives birth. Duty changes with circumstances, but it also changes with characters; and one could almost establish a single law which would be modified with them: duty is that which it costs us most to accomplish. (pp. 50-1)

The martyrdom of Aglavaine will leave behind it a luminous furrow in which her future sisters will walk joyously. . . .

[With] poor Sélysette, the necessary victim, were to die (in Maeterlinck's works) all the adorable princesses, decorative, poetic and delicious images, whose frail grace, however, is inspired by the women who are and always will be, whereas we expect from the genius of poets the pattern of those who will never be anything but exceptions, models necessary to the history, or rather to the formation of the character of women. (p. 53)

[The] new heroines of Maeterlinck were to be patterns. In reality, they all form but one pattern, which is developed through different circumstances and in the poet's very thought; they are born like proofs of one and the same statue, perfecting themselves in an ideal mould. The same figure, after Aglavaine, becomes simplified and purified and gives birth to Joyzelle, to Monna Vanna, to Ariane. Had Aglavaine not existed, we should not understand Ariane, for the faults of the one, better appropriated and differently directed, make the virtues of the other. Aglavaine is the rough cast of Ariane, she is her promise. Between these two heroines, the first and the last of the third part, we shall see the intermediary figures simply in passing.

In the laughing Joyzelle we shall find again the strength and daring of Aglavaine. Joyzelle will struggle to the point of crime to attain her love. . . . But here is the happy Monna Vanna, to whom destiny propounds a problem so beautiful and so simple that no generous soul could have solved it otherwise than she did. I will not insist upon a woman's character so wonderfully called for by circumstances. . . . She was bound to be on the immediate level of the great event that questioned her and bound to reply to it without hesitation. (pp. 53-4)

Ariane does not wait for events to question her: she makes her action burst forth from the very heart of ordinary life, she discerns it where none perceived it. This is her first superiority. Ariane is the apostle of the poet's philosophy. One might call her the deliverer of thought, for her action passes above and beyond life; she does not wish to fight and does not seek to conquer; she wishes to raise, to harmonise, to unite and to deliver not by fighting, but by intelligence. She has no other desire than the passionate love of knowledge; she has all the audacity that provokes love, exerts courage, calls for action; she is led by that divine curiosity which seems to stretch our mind like a bow, to shoot our will beyond the explored boundaries. Ariane is the informed and definite consciousness that seeks to manifest itself, I will even say, to reproduce itself like all things that have accomplished their evolution. Our heroine has all the energy and all the judgment of Aglavaine, all the enlightened simplicity of Monna Vanna, but she uses her qualities as a workman of genius uses his tools; she herself discovers the act to which she can apply the new force of which she disposes; she does not obey this or that conviction; her intelligence simply follows its own laws and responds to the eternal problem of feminine slavery. (pp. 54-5)

The women who charm the most appear in the past like those adorable frescoes which old walls still offer to our eyes, half-discoloured, pale and ideal: frozen in contemplative attitudes, they have the faces of virgins and lilies in their hands. . . . Here are Griselda, the miracle of love and humility, Penelope, the faithful spouse; here all the examples of noble meekness. An abyss seems to separate them from the Aglavaines, the Arianes! And yet these two are

loving handmaids; *but they are the handmaids of the future.*
(p. 56)

Georgette Leblanc-Maeterlinck, "The Later Heroines of Maurice Maeterlinck" (copyright,
U.S.A., by Georgette Leblanc-Maeterlinck, 1909),
part of a lecture delivered in Paris in 1909 (and
reprinted in The Fortnightly Review, Vol. 93, No.
DXVII, January 1, 1910, pp. 48-56).

HOLBROOK JACKSON   (essay date 1910)

Maeterlinck, like Ibsen and Bernard Shaw, is a type of the artist-philosopher. He is a man with a message. He does not trust, however, to the action and symbolism of his drama revealing the whole of his ideas, as Ibsen did, but like Bernard Shaw, he expounds his aims in his essays.

But as a philosopher he is not strikingly original, except in the sense that originality and sincerity are accounted one. He has added little of note to our stock of ideas, but drawing as he has done largely on the wells of the older mystics and some modern sages, he has distilled their thoughts in the alembic of his own temperament and applied the result to life in his own way. His accomplishment amounts to a more intimate revelation of the spirit of man and, in his essays, of animals and flowers. In no other plays do you feel so close to the spiritual essence of life as in the early plays of Maeterlinck; so acutely does he manifest the reality of the soul that you feel at times that he alone among artists has come closest to the unseen and the unknown. The human soul moves through these plays like an actual presence; tragic and tormented it is, to be sure, but it is a vivid reality, more real indeed than the ghostly bodies of his characters, which fade before the fervour of their awakened inner consciousnesses. You feel yourself instinctively pitying their pains; not the pains of the flesh, but, for the first time in a theatre, the pains of the spirit, and this again, as distinct from emotional pain. The creation of such an attitude is Maeterlinck's original contribution to art.

All mystics have been conscious of the soul, but none in quite the same way as Maeterlinck. They have generally looked upon it as a religious counter with a purely formal destiny; he looks upon it with the eye of the naturalist. Where the older mystics are theological Maeterlinck is secular. Consciously or not he has attempted the secularisation of mysticism, but under his touch it is none the less religious in the deeper sense. Everything for him has spiritual significance, yet never for a moment does he pretend to revealed or superhuman knowledge: he is untiring in his watchfulness, but brings no news of final certainty; and although he is sensibly credulous, "I know not" is ever on his lips, punctuating his aspiration with something like pathos. Still, he is never without hope, something may happen at any moment. Humanity after passing through many vicissitudes stands on the threshold of wisdom.

At the same time Maeterlinck anticipates no sudden change; catastrophic revivalism has no place in his outlook; his awakening is progressive, a gradual unrolling, as it were, of the inner vision. (pp. 133-35)

Into this spiritual sensitiveness he weaves his idea of Destiny—the unknown determining force of life. But he gives no detailed scheme of predestination except in the simple symbolism of *The Blue Bird*. Destiny, for Maeterlinck, is immanent and closely related to the will and personal power. Our Destinies are to be guided and controlled

by wisdom, which is love, and truth, and justice. He is progressive both as a fatalist and as a mystic; Destiny is, he believes, constantly being conquered by individuality, by science, by invention, and by every addition to human power. (p. 135)

Maeterlinck, apart from his drama, has become a new type of scientist; his essays reveal something like a marriage between science and poetry. "The Life of the Eze" is perhaps the best example of the work of the new Maeterlinck, for in it he has given us, not only excellent natural history, but social philosophy and mysticism as well, wrapped in a prose which alone would have made his reputation as a writer. And if his dramatic genius no longer dives for pearls in the perilous deep, but is content to investigate the surface of the waters of life, we may be sure that whatever he does will have the quality of great art, and that he has not ceased beating at the doors of mystery. (p. 138)

Holbrook Jackson, "Maurice Maeterlinck"
(1910), in his Romance and Reality: Essays and
Studies (reprinted by permission of The Society of
Authors as the literary representatives of the Estate of Holbrook Jackson), Grant Richards Ltd.,
1911, pp. 127-38.

ARCHIBALD HENDERSON   (essay date 1913)

Maurice Maeterlinck—poet, mystic, transcendentalist—comes with gentle words of wise and aspiring sincerity to impress upon the world the belief that the development and disclosure of the human soul is the ultimate aim and goal of existence. Marking the spiritual reaction from the blatant bestiality of Zolaism, he seeks to realize the infinite, to know the unknowable, to express the inexpressible. "Oh, that this too, too solid flesh would melt!" is his eternal prayer. He is individualistic in the sense that he is unique and essentially modern, not explainable as a product of the age, but rather as a reactionary, hostile to all its materialistic tendencies. He heralds the dawn of a spiritual renascence. (pp. 202-03)

Half conscious of his deep-rooted faith in the meaning of presentiments, the significance of sub-conscious revelations, M. Maeterlinck wrote a number of plays surcharged with the impalpable and imponderable weight of pathos and groping nescience. (p. 214)

In those early plays the interest hangs upon the passage, rather than upon the victim, of fatality; our grief is not excited by the tragedy: we shudder with wide-eyed horror at the argument of the invisible, the evidence of things not seen. By the intuitive apprehensions of the soul, its instinctive gropings, the incomprehensible, disquieting movements in nature, the dark forebodings of dumb, shadowy events—by these means M. Maeterlinck made us aware of the adumbration, the gradual approach, and ultimate presence of the mysterious forces of Fate, Terror, and Death. (pp. 215-16)

The unnamed presence was always Death—Death the intruder. In *L'Intruse* we waited with tense expectancy and strained senses for his coming; in *L'Intérieur* we accompanied him to the scene of the eternal tragedy; in *Les Aveugles* we awaken with a start to find Death in our very midst. Terror lurks behind a half-closed door, and all the poignant mystery of the Universe seems embodied in the figures of seven princesses sleeping in a dim castle beside the sounding sea. There was no escape from the obsession of some dire, inexpressibly dreadful unknown presence. (p. 216)

In all Maeterlinck's love-dramas—*Alladine and Palomides, Pelléas and Mélisande,* and *Aglavaine and Sélysette*—the mood is ever individualistic, symptomatic of the modern thinker. The action, simple to the verge of bareness, is a frail framework through and beyond which we gaze into the depths of the human soul. Maeterlinck seems to throw faint gleams of light into the dark pool where humanity has lost its golden crown. The march of events is but a passing show, life is a tiny oasis in an illimitable desert, a narrow vale between two eternities. The characters do not bring things to pass; they are set in a magic maze of tragic destinies: through them are ever sweeping the impelling forces of the universe. Action is but the seeming; emotion is eternal reality. Deeds are but the evanescent expression of the temporary; feelings are the vital repository of immortal truth.

The realities, the crises of life, are found in silence and in sadness. . . . We see no vital, tremendous, self-captained soul, incarnate with the deep-seated elements of religion and Christian morality. Love is ever the victim, wantonly broken upon the wheel of fate. The supremacy of destiny is solemnly acknowledged, its decrees accepted. The call of soul to soul cannot be disregarded: the forces of Love and Chance conspire in the tragic outcome. (pp. 222-23)

[*Aglavaine and Sélysette*], along with *Sœur Béatrice* and *Ardiane et Barbe Bleu,* marks the actual transition stage in Maeterlinck's art from the drama of fatality, of pity and terror, to the drama of human interests, of real emotions, and of direct volitional activity. *Aglavaine and Sélysette* is an illuminating essay, though seen in a glass darkly, upon ideal possibilities in human relationship in a future state of elevated moral consciousness. (p. 226)

Sœur Béatrice and *Ardiane et Barbe Bleu* serve more clearly to mark the transition in Maeterlinck's attitude towards problems which concern the interpreter of life. *Sœur Béatrice* is the Everywoman of human love—instinctive, sacrificial. She flees the convent with her lover, and though externally besmirched with earthly contacts, she returns in the end to sanctuary to find that the Virgin has kept her place inviolate—a subtle vindication of the sanctity of human impulse. (pp. 227-28)

Monna Vanna is the summit of Maeterlinck's art as a dramatist; and *Joyzelle,* though following it in point of time, in reality is a link between *Monna Vanna* and his earlier works. Indeed, it is a sort of pendant to *Monna Vanna* and should be considered prior to and in connection with it. And I think that the theoretical considerations outlined above may serve to act as commentary upon both plays. *Joyzelle* is more imaginative, poetic and symbolic than *Monna Vanna,* as Maeterlinck himself said, but it is far less coherent and significant, relying upon such obvious symbolism. "It represents," said Maeterlinck, "the triumph of will and love over Destiny, or fatality as against the converse lesson of *Monna Vanna.*" (p. 232)

Original and distinctive as Maeterlinck succeeds in remaining through all his tentatives and experiments, he is perhaps the most impressionable of modern artists. The influences that work in him are lost in the mists of antiquity and find solid ground in the most modern of the moderns. If at times he seems the incarnation of the Stoicism for which

we have to go to Marcus Aurelius to find a parallel, at others he penetrates to the heart of modern problems, and challenges comparison, as moralist, even with Ibsen and Nietzsche. (pp. 234-35)

Monna Vanna is Maeterlinck's great human challenge of mystic morality to the modern world—no fourth-dimensional drama of the spirit, "pinnacled dim in the intense inane," but a drama of flesh and blood, of heart as well as of soul. It bears all the hallmarks of the drama of to-day, even to its ideal spectator, its undulation of emotional process, its classic conflicts of wills. It bears the pure Maeterlinckian stamp as well—but this time the glorious struggle of the ideal morality against the purely human passions of daily life. Monna Vanna is the apotheosis of womanhood—the fine flower of the virginal type become volitional, latent in Aglavaine, just stretching shining pinions in Ardiane. With such high-minded disinterestedness is it conceived that our heart, in turn, goes out to [seven of its characters]. . . . (p. 237)

In *Mary Magdalene,* one divines another illustration of that ethereal mimetic instinct which haunts Maeterlinck in some of the higher flights of his dramatic fancy. In this effort to clothe reality in the garb of mysticism, there is something at once thin, high and remote. (pp. 245-46)

In that sweet, sad vision of *Soeur Béatrice,* the Maeterlinck, who once said that by the side of women "one has at times a momentary but distinct presentiment of a life that does not seem always to run parallel with the life of appearances," revealed a rare power of emotive, intuitive subtlety. In *Mary Magdalene* that power has been elevated to an even higher plane of serenity and wisdom. The Magdalene knows the secret of truth—she has become "the master of reality." Hers is the spiritual divination to see that it profiteth not to gain the whole world, even the salvation of the life of the Master, and lose one's own soul.

The plays which Maeterlinck has produced since the Great War, while marked with many of the characteristics of his individual style, are, with the exception of *The Bethrothal,* lacking in the peculiar quality we have come to associate with his name. . . . *The Cloud That Lifted* [for example] is a play of complex emotions on the theme of the eternal triangle; but it is lacking in any strong dramatic quality. The characters are melodramatic; the emotions overdrawn and ineffectively expressed. *The Power of the Dead,* a modern miracle play, with elaborate setting and well-chosen titles, might prove a success on the film, but the familiar device of the dream is quite outworn for the stage.

Maeterlinck will always hold a place in the history of the stage. But it will not be for plays in this new, unhappy manner. The Maeterlinck we shall cherish is the author of the plays of mystery, pity, and terror, the creative artist who made something new, unique, and strange in the history of dramatic art. (pp. 249-50)

Archibald Henderson, "Maurice Maeterlinck" (1913), in his European Dramatists *(copyright, 1913, 1926, by D. Appleton & Co.; reprinted by permission of Prentice-Hall, Inc., Englewood Cliffs, New Jersey), Appleton, 1926, pp. 199-250.*

EDWIN BJORKMAN   (essay date 1913)

[Maeterlinck's] work abounds with thoughts that are equally sublime in aspect and in scope. Yet he never lets himself be tempted beyond poetic suggestiveness into scientific exhaustiveness. The sense of things still unuttered always remains the final impression. And perhaps it is in this implied abundance, this limitless reserve power, that his main appeal lies. For it is this side of his nature that has enabled him to look at life and death with such imperturbable eyes. (p. 196)

For more than one hundred years, up to the closing decade of the last century, the cry was for action, and for ever more action. From Maeterlinck came the first truly inspired call to rest—but not to rest of the Tolstoyan, life-denying kind. The change foreshadowed by his pregnant words was meant to bring man nearer to life's innermost purpose—which he has himself declared to be perfection—and not away from it. For the mark of civilization is, after all, inhibition rather than stimulation. And by constantly accentuating the need for quiet, subconscious preparation, Maeterlinck has done much to dispose of that vaunted strenuousness which too often in the past degenerated into mere meaningless gyration. Not inaction, but action properly determined, is his gospel. If we follow him, then conflict, which is hastened action, will be reduced to a minimum, while combination and cooperation, which stand for action more fully prepared, will take more and more of the world's energy.

Maeterlinck has been called a poet of the subconscious. . . . But his main discovery and most significant revelation concerning the subconscious rests in the intimate connection which he has established between certain mysterious powers within ourselves and certain equally mysterious powers on the outside. What he shows—or tries to show—is that these two sets of powers are at bottom identical.

Poetically he has accomplished what Bergson has achieved philosophically. Life, so threatening when lying wholly beyond our own selves, becomes homely and familiar when found at work within those same selves. The fear with which man has regarded fate tends thus to change into happy faith—the unknown becomes the partly known—and in dealing with life, destiny, providence, man begins at last to feel as if he were but dealing with another self. . . . Maeterlinck has contributed not only a conception of life as trustworthy, but of death as an integral part of life—and not the unkindliest at that.

Like Tolstoy, like Zola, like so many other men of strong physique and vivid imagination, this dreamer from the Lowlands has been largely preoccupied with the inevitable moment of dissolution that forms the interrogation point at the end of every human career. But while Tolstoy sought to scare men into righteousness by enhancing the terror of that ever-present spectre, one of Maeterlinck's chief tasks has been to breathe the breath of hope and sympathetic comprehension on our terror, and thus to melt it into vanishing mist. Of course, he began by staring at the spectre in open-eyed horror like the rest of us. For years its grim figure stalked through his plays like a veiled angel of darkness. But gradually there came light into his vision, and that vision widened and grew until all creation lay steeped in brightness. It is that vision he has tried to make ours—in "The Blue Bird," for instance. . . . (pp. 196-200)

It is not out of place to give the title of philosopher to Maeterlinck . . . but he is more: a sage. Application lurks back of his most abstract speculations, and what he principally wants us to do is to learn in order to live. (p. 202)

Edwin Bjorkman, "The New Mysticism: Its Poet, Maurice Maeterlinck," in his Voices of Tomorrow: Critical Studies of the New Spirit in Literature *(copyright 1913 by Mitchell Kennerly), Mitchell Kennerley, 1913, pp. 186-204.*

UNA TAYLOR (essay date 1914)

[The paramount inspiration for the poems of *Serres Chaudes*] would seem to be drawn from the besetting spiritual maladies of human existence, in its phase of despondent, enervated mournfulness. (p. 10)

Poem follows poem, the outcome of a melancholy as vaguely sterile as it is incurable; of a grief as drowsy, void, and stifled as that of Coleridge's "Dejection." From the first stanzas to the close of the last page, the poet's imagination dwells in a vision-world of symbolic hallucination. . . . The sequence attains its unbroken unity of impression, visual and pictorial, spiritual and imaginative, bathed, saturated in a vaporous atmosphere where the strings of sensation are muted, where the pulses of life are numbed, its fevers outworn; where the vital tide is ever receding from its shores and passion itself has fallen into the languor of a mortal swoon. (pp. 10-11)

But while the scenes, the symbol-shapes change their masked semblances, the same note is sustained throughout. The sense of stagnation, inertia, impotence, pervades every stanza . . . sentence after sentence accentuates the impression of dolorous quiescence. (p. 12)

The means whereby the æsthetic atmosphere is created and maintained are not far to seek. Master of the resources of his art, Maeterlinck has utilised his gift of language to the full in the achievement of perfect concord between the emotional sentiment and the sound-form of his verse. The scale of the words employed is singularly limited, but he possesses a supersensitive ear. His appreciation of the gradations of significance imparted to one and the same word by its position and rhythmical emphasis in the construction of the phrase is unrivalled. Hence no sense of repetition, reiteration or recurrence obtrudes itself upon the reader's consciousness. The limitation of his vocabulary maintains the intentional monotony of effect, while the predominant use of laggard vowel-sounds in many of the stanzas gives an additional note of languid obsession to the melody of the verse. Few poets have welded together more intimately the emotional sense with the rhythmical cadence. . . . (pp. 16-17)

And finally if the appeal to the ear reinforces the emotional effect, the pictorialism of the poet's method (and there are few lines which do not conjure up a visualised conception) is never allowed to carry the mind's eye beyond the bounds of strictly allegorical suggestion. Analysed, it is a pictorialism rather apparent than real. (pp. 17-18)

The pictorial images of *Serres Chaudes* do not exist for themselves; they are neither descriptive nor narrative; they are merely the outcome of a continuously symbolic exposition of thought and feeling, and the symbol-shape, human or vegetable, is no more than the exhalation emanating from those thoughts and feelings, cast and coloured in a transitive mould borrowed from the semblance of things seen. . . . (p. 18)

For the mystic, from time immemorial, the symbol has served two distinct and converse purposes. It has been the language of the secret-keeper; it has also . . . been the language of the secret-teller. (p. 40)

Maeterlinck has employed the symbol with both intentions. In his lyrics pictorial symbolism is almost exclusively the method and medium of exposition; it is the hieroglyphic script of the ideas; it is the appeal to the understanding through the channel of imaginative vision; it is his formula for the disclosure of thoughts and sensations which elude expression in conventional idiom. In the dramas it serves other ends no less essential to his purpose. With regard to those things pertaining to the region of transcendental vision, his imagery is, or would seem to be, a continued attempt to withdraw the screen, to raise the curtain, which holds the unseen realm of the spirit from view. But conversely, with regard to things tangible, visible, substantial, to what dogmatic materialism is pleased to denominate the real, Maeterlinck utilises the symbol as a mask. (pp. 40-1)

[He] joins the company of the secret-tellers in so far as the symbol in his hands is the only possible language into which he can translate the unknown tongue. . . . It is a cipher he employs, adequately or inadequately, to indicate facts and suggest occurrences passing upon spiritual planes, incapable of direct verbal transcription. On the other hand, he equally applies a symbolic process for the registration of occurrences that take place upon the earth-plane of action and passion; he invests the levels of human existence with a disguise; men wear the aspect of similitudes; their deeds and words are clothed with allegoric significance, they act in parables. The aesthetic outcome of the process is unity of tone. Under the symbol actuality is transcendentalised into harmony with what is above actuality, reality figures as an emblematic representation; under the symbol things spiritual are incarnated, and the invisible takes shape until in a drifting mist the horizon-line between heaven and earth is obliterated, and the symbol which embodies the unseen things of the soul walks hand in hand with the symbol which dematerialises the things of sense. Further, an illusion of distance, of remoteness, is induced, a sense, to adopt Maeterlinck's own image, of the semi-opaqueness of misted glass, interposed between our sight and the workings of human existence. . . . (pp. 41-2)

Life in his plays is a symbol within a symbol. His characters stand in relation to actuality, not so much as types, but as counterfeit presentments of single individualities in whose somewhat blank personality a phase of emotion, for the hour, finds its vivid embodiment, His incidents, often violent to the brink of extravaganza, are but the incidents of a pageantry of shadows, and the pageant itself is no more than a framework within whose bounds emotions perform their mystery play. Episodes, incidents, the living human beings, of his stage, are alike mere threads upon whose tenuous mortal web passion's rosary is momentarily strung. . . . (p. 43)

Behind the scenes of events that pass by, the central figures stand subjected to the inexorable coercion of vast impersonal factors. . . . Likewise we see them subjected to the influence of other passions, emanations from the soul—pity, the self-vision where all other men's sins find pardon, and . . . the love whose pulse is sacrifice.

And each man, each woman, draws to himself or to herself that special catastrophe, emotional or actual, ideal or real, which is in affinity with his or her individual temperament

or with the decree of that inscrutable personality, the soul within the soul, that lies beneath and beyond temperament. (pp. 46-7)

[In] the works of the poet-dramatist, death played, it might almost be said, the title-rôle. Maeterlinck has himself defined the fundamental belief underlying his first presentments of human life, sentiment and action: "a belief in immense powers, invisible and fatalistic, of which no man may know the purpose, but whose intentions the spirit of the dramas assumes to be malevolent." These forces take cognisance of all our actions, are hostile to life, peace, happiness, exercising a jurisdiction of injustice, whose penalties are, maybe, only a manifestation of the caprice of fate. (p. 63)

In the later plays [Maeterlinck] has endeavoured, after a fashion of his own invention, to reconcile the claims of art and those claims of spiritual wisdom we may name . . . ethical morality. . . . (pp. 92-3)

Here, as elsewhere, Maeterlinck is not afraid to allow that if his words have power to incline men towards the "invisible goodness" which, according to his later creed, underlies the outward ill, to dispose them to a gentler tolerance of human defects and to a wiser acquiescence in the secret issues of earth-existence, it is not a matter of indifference to him. Never does he repudiate, even from the aesthetic standpoint, the responsibility of his calling. (pp. 93-4)

Further, he has clearly defined the obligations of the dramatist, as he conceives of them, with the limitations incident to the playwright's art. The lyric poet may remain in some sort a theorist of the unknown. The lyrist may dwell, if it please him, in the realms of abstract ideas; he is not compelled to apply them to practical conclusions. . . . "The dramatist cannot limit himself to such generalisations." He is compelled to transpose into real life, into the life lived day by day, the idea he has fashioned for himself of the unknown. . . . (p. 94)

Read with this key to the artist's deliberate intention, the later plays are closely linked with the essays whose publication they followed, where the medium of exposition is that cadenced prose which it is the despair of even his most accomplished translators to reproduce.

Monna Vanna . . . is a milestone evidencing how far already the dramatist of *Maleine* has travelled upon the road trodden by the moralist of *La Sagesse et la Destinée*.

The change is radical in every respect. Personalities with distinct characterisation supplant the type figures of his early dramas. The atmosphere has lost its haze, the grey-tinted mist has lifted its veil. The filmy glass cupolas of *Serres Chaudes* are shattered. We have emerged from the world of symbols, from a world where shadows cast their similitudes of substance upon the air. Events have divested themselves of their masks, so far as events which have for arena of action the human heart and soul can discard their inevitable disguises. . . . And a yet more fundamental alteration of mental attitude is witnessed to by the substitution of will for destiny. Fate has retired more or less behind the scenes where men's wills and men's actions appear in its stead as determining forces upon whose clash and conflict the dramatic situations depend. Heroes and heroines, in such measure as may be, subordinate doom to volition, fatality is no longer invincible, and . . . character *becomes* destiny.

In accordance with this new ethical scheme youth no longer occupies the forefront in his art. Childhood disappears. For the type of *l'enfant-femme*, of the child-automaton, moved hither and thither by the wind of destiny, the child-serf of passion who worships but one god and him only serves, is substituted the figure of a woman whose actions are premeditated, voluntary, deliberate, of a woman who has entered into her own kingdom of ideas, the violence of whose primitive instincts is appeased, whose heart recognises other lordships than love and the sovereignty of other claims than the impulses of passion. (pp. 95-7)

Una Taylor, in her Maurice Maeterlinck: A Critical Study, *M. Secker, 1914 (and reprinted by Kennikat Press, Inc., 1968), 199 p.*

JOHN FREEMAN (essay date 1916)

The difficulty of dealing closely with Maeterlinck's essays in practical philosophy is shown, as clearly as anywhere, in *The Buried Temple*. The book contains a long essay on *The Mystery of Justice*, and another on *The Evolution of Mystery*, besides two shorter papers. In all of them there is a faint gentle warmth, or at least an *appearance* of fire. Two things, in fact, are conspicuous: the tepidity of the sentiment, and the extreme slowness of the thought. . . . Behind all these essays you are aware of an amiable sincere personality, whose delight it is to reflect upon mysterious things. . . . Easily does he sink into solemnity: you can detect the deliberate clerical tremor in his voice when he talks of grave things, and the tremor is impressive. In this book he speaks of subtle things, and is not himself subtle but elusive, not profound but vague, not penetrating but full of conjecture. He is a swimmer in that stream of tendency which makes for righteousness. Righteousness, justice—the strenuous words are on every page of the first two essays; his aim is as definitely ethical as the aim of the English Positivists.

Look a little closely, however, and you will find nothing positive in Maeterlinck's attitude towards these abstract problems. He speaks for those who do not believe in a unique, all-powerful Judge, but who believe none the less in the existence of Justice. . . .

He remarks that a mystery rarely disappears, but only shifts its ground; and you think this profound until you discover that all that is meant by it is that we re-name our mysteries. "What was once called 'the gods' we now term 'life.' The same quantity of mystery will ever enwrap the world." With a pleasant frugal fancy he pursues the shifting lodgment of the mystery of justice, finding its ultimate abode in the heart of man. This is really one of the few definite thoughts upon which one can take hold, and it yields Maeterlinck a welcome opportunity of impressing as a new thing the precept of a personal justice which is really very old. (pp. 190-92)

In the intimate weakness of personal character does he seek the cause of catastrophe, repudiating supernatural interventions which do not satisfy us to-day. He recapitulates those endless "why's" which always set us agog for explanations; and finds that it is only the fervent believer who will still see in these vital discrepancies between merit and happiness the finger of divine intervention. But Maeterlinck suspects that perfect knowledge of all the circumstances—immediate and remotely contributory—of a tragedy how complex and cruel soever, would make such a tragedy not only less extraordinary but perfectly natural and almost inevitable. Knowledge so intimate and searching is impossible, and so Maeterlinck takes on trust the unverifiable explanation of a mystery rather than the mystery itself. This credulous scepticism is essentially Maeterlinckian. He is, in fact, afraid of being compelled to make some reluctant admission of God. The poet, he concedes, is inclined to personify fatality and justice, but it is not the incomprehensible that crushes us: rather the thought of a possible Power over us, the Immanent Will of Mr. Hardy's *Dynasts*. "What we dread is the presence of a God. . . . it is always a God whom we fear." But he questions whether we are thus brought nearer the truth, and leaves you in doubt of his own station in the advance. (pp. 193-94)

I wish Maeterlinck could have given more clearly his answer to the questions he raises: I am afraid of misrepresenting his opinions. But at any rate he cries clearly enough: Let us not look to the gods, nor to the illimitable laws of the universe, for an explanation. . . . Since we must not look to the gods, he imagines that in ourselves is hidden the key of the mystery. Beneath our conscious existence there hides a profounder unconscious existence, wherein must be sought the meaning of luck. To this invisible consciousness he devotes a page or two of glowing rhetoric; but rhetoric, however profusely tropical, does not help very greatly. (p. 195)

In Wisdom and Destiny Maeterlinck devotes 353 pages to reflections dealing ostensibly with these grave themes, but resolving themselves into Notes for a Manual of Happiness. He is concerned to stimulate and console, and has a religious care for sufferers. If we say that the quest of happiness, too carefully pursued, seems a little weak and childish, it is not meant that Maeterlinck does not utter many true and simple things that are worth remembering. Only, a preoccupation with happiness is like a preoccupation with billiards—pleasant but slightly unworthy. One need not take an unduly solemn view of man's responsibilities, in asserting that personal happiness is such a private and capricious thing that it is best to take it as it comes, and if it comes, and to care not a jot when it goes. What is most conspicuously missing in Maeterlinck's entire conception of life is spontaneousness, instinct. He is always trying to cage the bird, and most earnest when it is most difficult to distinguish the bird from its shadow. (pp. 198-99)

The genius of Maurice Maeterlinck, so far as it is notable and valuable, is an entirely distinct and personal genius. Let this be said clearly, since it would be both unfair and foolish to suggest that his work shows nothing beyond an unusual development of general talent.

Maeterlinck is often called a mystic, and himself uses the word so freely that you might well think it the title he chiefly covets. Perhaps no other word has been more generally or more stupidly abused. . . . Only an unheeding acceptance of impressive words will lead one to accept Maeterlinck as a mystic. He writes mysteriously, but there is nothing mysterious in mysticism. To be vague is not to be mystical, for mysticism often presents things and visions with intolerable sharpness. (pp. 212-13)

When Maeterlinck is called a mystic, I imagine the reason to be that it is not easy to find another equally effective, hasty distinction. In truth, I note in his work very little that points to the spiritual profundity which is thus inadequately named. He has a large and carefully cultivated sense of "the mystery of things," and, for all his explicit disavowal in *The Buried Temple,* is fonder of discovering than of resolving mysteries. He sees the world as a vast perplexity, beauty at odds with misery, life with destiny, and eternity cloud-like enfolding all. Seeing this, he writes beautifully, importantly, sometimes wisely, with infinite qualifications and hesitancies. Nay, more: he writes cheerfully, consolingly, with a constant simple exhortation to happiness. In this, where is there a touch of mysticism? For his plays, he presents a state of impregnable grief, a state of sorrowful love, a state of blindness, a state of loyalty; and these are seen beneath a wonderfully cunning veil of sorrow, loneliness and darkness. But where is there more than a hint of mysticism? (pp. 213-14)

Maeterlinck is as far from being a mystic as he is from being a foreign missionary. He is concerned with the same subjects as the true mystical writers, but his concern moves on a lower plane and is inspired by a fainter energy. It is because he has no faith . . . and because the lack of Faith means the lack of light and foothold among dark places, that he can claim no higher tribute than we yield to a merely influential writer upon serious matters.

In another respect he is distinguished as well from the really profound and noble writers of our day, as from the mystics;—I mean in the quality of his thought. So often it seems to cost him little, and to yield little to the reader. There is a general diffused thoughtfulness over all his work, but it rarely crystallizes into a memorable, precious truth. He occupies the same place among thinkers as among playwriters, or as Anatole France holds among novelists. His work can no better sustain the common comparison with Emerson's than with Plato's; it bears less ripe fruit among all its branches than you may pluck from a single ruddy bough of Meredith. . . . You wander among the frail trammels of his essays, longing for a severer logic and a harder grasp. Maeterlinck's very doubt is as delicate and uncertain as the piety of narrow-minded converts. His essays, with all the frequent fascination of his subject, are hard to understand; to read them is like looking at unfamiliar buildings in a fog. Had he but subjected himself to the sharper exigence of verse-form, he might have given us something as compact and decisive as Pope's steady couplets. Prose exposes his unthrifty faults.

If you turn to his plays, you wonder that plays of so slight a dramatic force should have won so wide an admiration. Not often is there even such heat in them as you may discover in *Pelleas and Melisanda* or *Monna Vanna,* or such tensity as in *Interior.* (pp. 215-16)

What, then, and where, after these large disqualifications, is the distinct and personal genius of Maeterlinck? I find it in the creation of an impression for its own sake, an impression of pure sorrow, love, terror. . . . This is the effect that Maeterlinck prepares; he has this secret of our breasts, this sly key. He turns it, and we are as responsive as children to his slightest movement. He does this inerrably in *Interior,* almost as surely in *Pelleas,* less surely in other plays. It is the chief justification of his claim to be an imaginative writer. This small, narrow, intense power, and this alone of all his powers, is his unique portion. (pp. 217-18)

> *John Freeman, "Maurice Maeterlinck," in his* The Moderns: Essays in Literary Criticism, *R. Scott, 1916 (and reprinted by Books for Li-*

braries Press, 1967; distributed by Arno Press, Inc.), pp. 161-218.

ARTHUR SYMONS (essay date 1919)

The secret of things which is just beyond the most subtle words, the secret of the expressive silences, has always been clearer to Maeterlinck than to most people; and, in his plays, he has elaborated an art of sensitive, taciturn, and at the same time highly ornamental simplicity, which has come nearer than any other art to being the voice of silence. To Maeterlinck the theatre has been, for the most part, no more than one of the disguises by which he can express himself, and with his book of meditations on the inner life, *Le Trésor des Humbles,* he may seem to have dropped his disguise. (p. 84)

Maeterlinck, endeavouring to clothe mystical conceptions in concrete form, has invented a drama so precise, so curt, so arbitrary in its limits, that it can safely be confided to the masks and feigned voices of marionettes. His theatre of artificial beings, who are at once more ghostly and more mechanical than the living actors whom we are accustomed to see, in so curious a parody of life, moving with a certain freedom of action across the stage, may be taken as itself a symbol of the aspect under which what we fantastically term "real life" presents itself to the mystic. (p. 85)

[This drama] is a drama founded on philosophical ideas, apprehended emotionally; on the sense of the mystery of the universe, of the weakness of humanity . . . , with an acute feeling of the pathetic ignorance in which the souls nearest to one another look out upon their neighbours. It is a drama in which the interest is concentrated on vague people, who are little parts of the universal consciousness, their strange names being but the pseudonyms of obscure passions, intimate emotions. They have the fascination which we find in the eyes of certain pictures, so much more real and disquieting, so much more permanent with us, than living people. And they have the touching simplicity of children; they are always children in their ignorance of themselves, of one another, and of fate. And, because they are so disembodied of the more trivial accidents of life, they give themselves without limitation to whatever passionate instinct possesses them. (pp. 86-7)

Maeterlinck has realised, better than any one else, the significance, in life and art, of mystery. He has realised how unsearchable is the darkness out of which we have but just stepped, and the darkness into which we are about to pass. And he has realised how the thought and sense of that twofold darkness invade the little space of light in which, for a moment, we move; the depth to which they shadow our steps, even in that moment's partial escape. But in some of his plays he would seem to have apprehended this mystery as a thing merely or mainly terrifying; the actual physical darkness surrounding blind men, the actual physical approach of death as the intruder; he has shown us people huddled at a window, out of which they are almost afraid to look, or beating at a door, the opening of which they dread. Fear shivers through these plays, creeping across our nerves like a damp mist coiling up out of a valley. And there is beauty, certainly, in this "vague spiritual fear"; but a less obvious kind of beauty than that which gives its profound pathos to *Aglavaine et Sélysette.* . . . Here is mystery, which is also pure beauty, in these delicate approaches of intellectual pathos, in which suffering and death and error become transformed into something almost happy, so full is it of strange light.

And the aim of Maeterlinck, in his plays, is not only to render the soul and the soul's atmosphere, but to reveal this strangeness, pity, and beauty through beautiful pictures. No dramatist has ever been so careful that his scenes should be in themselves beautiful, or has made the actual space of forest, tower, or seashore so emotionally significant. He has realised, after Wagner, that the art of the stage is the art of pictorial beauty, of the correspondence in rhythm between the speakers, their words, and their surroundings. He has seen how, in this way, and in this way alone, the emotion, which it is but a part of the poetic drama to express, can be at once intensified and purified.

It is only after hinting at many of the things which he had to say in these plays, which have, after all, been a kind of subterfuge, that Maeterlinck has cared, or been able, to speak with the direct utterance of the essays. And what may seem curious is that this prose of the essays, which is the prose of a doctrine, is incomparably more beautiful than the prose of the plays, which was the prose of an art. . . . [Maeterlinck] did not admit that beauty of words, or even any expressed beauty of thoughts, had its place in spoken dialogue, even though it was not two living actors speaking to one another on the stage, but a soul speaking to a soul, and imagined speaking through the mouths of marionettes. But that beauty of phrase which makes the profound and sometimes obscure pages of *Axël* shine as with the crossing fire of jewels, rejoices us, though with a softer, a more equable, radiance, in the pages of these essays, in which every sentence has the indwelling beauty of an intellectual emotion, preserved at the same height of tranquil ecstasy from first page to last. There is a sort of religious calm in these deliberate sentences, into which the writer has known how to introduce that divine monotony which is one of the accomplishments of great style. Never has simplicity been more ornate or a fine beauty more visible through its self-concealment. (pp. 87-8)

Belonging, as he does, to the eternal hierarchy, the unbroken succession, of the mystics, Maeterlinck has apprehended what is essential in the mystical doctrine with a more profound comprehension, and thus more systematically, than any mystic of recent times. He has many points of resemblance with Emerson . . . ; but Emerson, who proclaimed the supreme guidance of the inner light, the supreme necessity of trusting instinct, of honouring emotion, did but proclaim all this, not without a certain antimystical vagueness: Maeterlinck has systematised it. A more profound mystic than Emerson, he has greater command of that which comes to him unaware, is less at the mercy of visiting angels. (p. 89)

[Many] mystics have occupied themselves, very profitably, with showing how natural, now explicable on their own terms, are the mysteries of life; the whole aim of Maeterlinck is to show how mysterious all life is, "what an astonishing thing it is, merely to live." What he had pointed out to us, with certain solemn gestures, in his plays, he sets himself now to affirm, slowly, fully, with that "confidence in mystery" of which he speaks. Because "there is not an hour without its familiar miracles and its ineffable suggestions," he sets himself to show us these miracles and these meanings where others have not always sought or found them, in women, in children, in the theatre. (p. 91)

Arthur Symons, "Maeterlinck As a Mystic" (originally published in the United Kingdom and British Commonwealth in the unrevised edition of this book, William Heinemann Limited, 1899), in his The Symbolist Movement in Literature *(copyright, 1919, by E. P. Dutton & Co., Inc.; copyright renewal, 1947, by Nona Hill; reprinted by permission of E. P. Dutton; in Canada by William Heinemann Limited), revised edition, Dutton, 1919 (and reprinted by Dutton, 1958, pp. 84-93).*

PATRICK MAHONY   (essay date 1951)

[The] plays of Maeterlinck are quite extraordinary as regards the time element. They do not attempt to recapture the past but rather take one to places out of space and time, an ineffable cloudland where all things are possible because the world in which we move and have our being is out of sight and mind.

By the same token it is curious how, when reading most of his dramas, the impersonality of the author grows on one. They could have been written by a man living in a period anywhere between 1750 to 1950; and I firmly believe they will present this riddle in the year 2000 and later. This is due to his brilliant abstention from playing privy to his characters. All the sardonic joy and seeming cruelty of natural forces at work are the outcome of his masterly courage in allowing Nature to speak always for herself, never impinging religious philosophy.

The violence of Nature in his early plays was ever-present. There was an eerie quality of shadow amid turbulent substance. Yet the characters had the distinctness of objects seen under the relentless light of mid-winter when the winds are whistling in the crags and there are no leaves upon the trees. For there is a type of intensity that comes from sources which are external to characterization, and Maeterlinck is a master of this artistic device. It is the mood that we find in almost all of these early plays. (p. 73)

He had written those early dramas ostensibly for marionettes, a form which fitted in with his theory of free will. Up until his secondary period, that of optimism, he held that man could not do very much of his own accord, that he was subject to the pulling of the strings, like marionettes. (p. 74)

[After *Monna Vanna*, however,] every play he was to write would be an expression of the inner struggle of the author's mind. Every play would be a struggle of the individual with himself. He was to show over and over again that there is no one logic, no one reason, but as many as there are individuals. If he offers religious balm to this age of dissenters, it is that which gives divine semblance to the rights and power of the individual. The Maeterlinckian heroines will choose even more complicated situations which will lead them to complete expression of their individuality. (p. 75)

Patrick Mahony, in his The Magic of Maeterlinck *(copyright 1951 by Patrick Mahony), House-Warven, 1951 (and reprinted by Kraus Reprint Co., 1969), 175 p.*

W. D. HALLS   (essay date 1960)

The phase [in Maeterlinck's career] of paramount literary importance is undoubtedly that which includes his Symbolist drama (1890-5). These plays are those which will survive to posterity, either as typical of the Symbolist theatre

—for example, the 'trilogy of death'—or for their own intrinsic worth, such as *Pelléas et Mélisande*. Yet this period is not that of the writer's greatest popularity, which was attained more by the plays . . . and by the essays that reflect the emergence of optimism. In this respect, the most outstanding theatrical work is *L'Oiseau bleu,* although its literary merit is little greater than that of *Monna Vanna*. Of the essays, *Sagesse et destinée* is more significant than *La Vie des abeilles:* Maeterlinck, at grips with his pessimism, is there striving to overcome it. Thus are made possible the plays of the 'second' [optimistic] theatre, which glorifies Love and diminishes the force of Destiny.

After the award of the Nobel Prize in 1911 there are no works that surpass or even reach the standard of earlier ones. Maeterlinck's powers of imagination, never very fully exercised—he probably leans more heavily for his inspiration on external sources than any of his contemporaries—seem to have shrivelled up within him. Perhaps his preoccupation with the great questions of life and death prevented him from giving his inventiveness full rein. Certainly all that follows is an unceasing revolving around the same stock of ideas, examined at every conceivable angle; yet in the end they lead the writer to no firm conclusions. The final deduction, if it may be so termed, is that all remains unknowable.

It requires little psychological knowledge to understand why his literary career followed this course. Beneath the taciturn exterior that Maeterlinck presented to the world in early manhood seethed an emotion that bubbled over in the lyrical outbursts of *Serres chaudes*. The dominant motif of the early plays is terror, most apparent when related to death, so vividly portrayed that it seems personal to the writer. It is succeeded by a calmer mood. . . . This he outgrew, like a child that ceases to depend on his mother. The preference that he then manifested for *Sélysette*—as against *Aglavaine*—personifying youth and innocence, signifies a reversion to the 'Pelléas type', infirm of purpose, lacking decision and willpower, and mistrusting the intelligence. The final pessimism was thus inevitable.

Pessimism at the end, as in the beginning. Thus the wheel of his thinking came full circle. In youth he had striven to shake off the shackles of nineteenth-century modes of thought. Positivism, a belief in progress, conventional religion . . . : such were the fetters that his spirit had to break asunder. On the material plane his revolt was against Philistinism and *idées reçues*. Once, however, he had rid himself of his chains, he found little solace elsewhere. Idealism was still a possible creed, but it was thwarted by the gross, practical side of his essentially Flemish disposition. Thus, in despair, he turned to the negative concept of agnosticism.

Yet, unfortunately, his belief in the impossibility of knowing was in continual conflict with his yearning for knowledge and certainty. He sought to resolve this fundamental opposition by turning his nature inwards upon itself. This accounts for the introspectiveness of *Le Trésor des humbles*, the constant 'quest' for the 'soul' within him. Such a mystical *voyage intérieur* led to disappointment. . . . By 1900, whilst denying the postulate of the supremacy of reason, he was closest to Stoicism and . . . had accepted the concept of progress. Yet the faint optimism he then reveals is always qualified.

Such a position, however, was difficult to sustain. The 'seekers' in his plays of the 'second manner'— and in this connexion the chronology of these dramas . . . is important —could not for ever end their quest unrequited. Thus, as this attitude becomes untenable, so does Maeterlinck relapse again into pessimism. His thoughts turn inward for the second time, to the realms of the subconscious, a process of withdrawal from the world that the catastrophe of 1914 accelerated. He began to examine the corpus of so-called occult knowledge whose tradition reaches back into the dim recesses of time. But in this vortex of esoteric thought he failed to distinguish the mumbo-jumbo of fraud from the genuine mass of scientifically unexplained phenomena. The true and false were accepted, for a time at least, with equal seriousness.

Finding in the occult no answer to his questions, he turned to science. Unfortunately, his scientific background was insufficient for him to evaluate the facts he considered and extract any coherent philosophy from them. His speculations became more and abstruse and incredible as he progressively abandoned the factual approach, blending the scientific with the occult.

The 'soul', Evolutionism, the occult, science: these were the laps of the race that he ran, the stages of a journey that was in essence the search for a faith. . . . [His] incapacity to examine dispassionately the validity of any 'revealed' religion is a kink in his psychological make-up.

Two ideas, however, although constantly changing in conception, remain always with him: Destiny and Death. In 1900, as his pessimism had waned, so had also the concept of a malevolent Fate. Yet the inexplicability of suffering and evil convinced him that, outside the sphere of the human, there existed a force that wittingly or unwittingly, with ill-will or with indifference, brought disaster upon the head of mankind. To the very end, even in his last plays, the figure of Destiny appears as a force to be reckoned with, one that is the ultimate arbiter of human action. Its ally in the early plays was Death, the word and concept that occurs unremittingly, unceasingly, and to satiety in all Maeterlinck's works, from first to last. . . . Around the problem of the end of this earthly existence and the speculations on what lay beyond, his mind was exercised without rest. In the end, the difficulties that these two extra-human factors presented were unresolved.

The most abiding impression one is left with after a study of his life and work is the sense of mystery. The mysterious may be clad in the forms of mysticism, or of the occult and the unknown, or of mere mystification. All these are present in Maeterlinck's work, sometimes simultaneously. . . . The unknown embraces the whole field of unexplained knowledge into which he ventured, from telepathy to ideas on the nature of God. . . . Maeterlinck may have advanced the boundaries of knowledge, but it was in reality the concept of the unknown that fascinated him more than the love of truth. This unknown he magnified, poeticized, and, on occasions, debased. (pp. 166-69)

If one characterizes Maeterlinck's work as being a *quest,* a seeking to explain life, one can only conclude that he failed. He failed to penetrate the mysteries of Destiny and Death, he did not discover the universal secret of wisdom and truth, nor capture the blue bird of happiness. In all the ways he trod he found no joy, but only ever greater ignorance. And in the end he could only make confession of his own failure. (p. 172)

W. D. Halls, "Conclusions," in his Maurice Maeterlinck: A Study of His Life and Thought (© Oxford University Press 1960; reprinted by permission of Oxford University Press), Oxford University Press, London, 1960, pp. 166-72.

CALVIN EVANS (essay date 1961)

If one does not agree with [Octave] Mirbeau that Maeterlinck is a greater dramatist than Shakespeare, it is difficult not to concede that Maeterlinck, more completely and more effectively than any predecessor, adapted to the stage the phenomenology of primitive man. The whole atmosphere takes on an oneiric quality. The spectator must sever himself from the intellect in order to establish any sort of empathy with the proceedings. He must allow himself to be mesmerized by the mystery of this dreamworld. His complete absorption therein would facilitate that same loss of identity experienced by the ancient Greeks when they viewed the cosmological history of the race through the medium of flesh-and-blood characters. (p. 56)

Few have seen in Maeterlinck's early drama an attempt to reproduce the phenomenology of the subconscious. Since the myth-making process, necessary to the development of tragedy and so natural to the primitive mind, remains vestigially in the dream life, one must therefore seek out the ritualistic raw material of tragedy at its natural source rather than in ethnic history. Maeterlinck, in his radical departure from conventional stage concepts, prepared the way for a genuine tragedy of the twentieth century. (pp. 56-7)

The Belgian dramatist is trying to bring us closer to the "ténébreuse et profonde unité" wherein psychic awareness had its genesis. His most successful attempt to accomplish this is in Act III, Scene II, of *Pelléas et Mélisande,* the "underground" scene: Golaud, who has just surprised Pelléas embracing the blond tresses of Mélisande, leads his younger brother into the subterranean passages beneath the castle. It is, or course, pitch dark therein and one must beware of abysses and dangerous escarpments. At one point the spectator senses the moral struggle within Golaud as he comes near to pushing Pelléas into a deep crevice. The atmosphere of the entire play is slung between the poles of light and shadow. . . . In the "underground" scene the unfathomable abyss of man's primitive phenomenology is made concrete by the murky gloom of the foundations under the castle. Here is projected dramatically into an exterior materialization the cavernous area of man's subconscious. If the castle is founded upon an unstable terrain full of stagnant pools . . . , so does the entire edifice of the intellect rest upon a dangerous fault that separates it precariously from the chaotic undersoil of the subconscious. In evaluating this scene phenomenologically one must constantly bear in mind that *Pelléas et Mélisande* represents one of the few dramatic expressions of the Symbolist movement, a movement which, above all, challenges the primacy of the intellect. With this play Maeterlinck himself descends from the tower of the castle into its "cave," i.e. he abandons intellect and penetrates the unconscious by making a clean break with the conventional perception of the naturalist stage. This scene is one of complete oneirism. Pelléas and Golaud are at once exploring the favorite haunts of their childhood. They are also restored to the psychic primitivity of the race. Darkness and the dank, fathomless

"grottes" suggest the crepuscular character of primitive perceptive processes. . . . Just as in Greek tragedy a barrier is erected against consciousness by the chorus, so does the decor of *Pelléas et Mélisande* draw the spectator into an insular area of self-communion. One sees bèfore him shadow figures which, in this state of hypnosis, are represented as projections of the subconscious psyche. Ideally, one descends with Pelléas and Golaud into the fetid underground. . . . One reverts momentarily to the phenomenology of the child who, when going down the cellar stairs, might imagine he sees all sorts of mysterious crawling creatures. . . . [We] are convinced that Maeterlinck achieves a materialization of [the subconscious] in his dramaturgy. If this be so, the Belgian dramatist deserves much greater consideration as regards his role in the providing of a fertile soil for the development of a genuine tragedy of the twentieth century. (p. 59)

Calvin Evans, "Maeterlinck and the Quest for a Mystic Tragedy of the Twentieth Century," in Modern Drama (copyright © 1961, University of Toronto, Graduate Centre for Study of Drama; with the permission of Modern Drama), Vol. 4, No. 1, May 1961, pp. 54-9.

JOAN PATAKY KOSOVE (essay date 1967)

[*Pelléas et Mélisande*] is neither about youth nor beauty, neither about love nor death. *Pelléas et Mélisande* deals with an intriguing and complex irony, the presentiment of disaster at the moment of happiness and calm. To the extent that the work succeeds, we experience not the presentiment but a modal effect appropriate to a realization about life that is part sad and part comic, part startling and part puzzling, but totally inevitable.

If the life stiuation that Maeterlinck deals with in this play is not inevitable, the play must fail, simply because it is the element of inevitability that justifies a static technique or a mystic philosophy. Characters in his work do not act; they await action, and if we are not convinced of the certainty of that action, we would be distracted by the resignation. The dramatic resolution must be shown to be the necessary part of the beginning situation or his audience will lose contact with the play trying to analyze the meaning of his technique. If given a chance, *Pelléas et Mélisande* will seduce the reader into weary acquiescence rather than prod him into critical analysis. (p. 781)

One might be tempted to categorize *Pelléas et Mélisande* as a tragedy. The play leaves us sad but somehow satisfied (catharsis?). This satisfaction grows out of our awareness that what was sad in the play is ultimately connected with what was happy. This play, however, is not a tragedy. Indeed one is tempted to call its outlook anti-tragic. For if one defines the tragic outlook as embracing a belief that our actions can control events, we have, in *Pelléas et Mélisande,* a play in which action is seen as futile. Further belief in the efficacy of action leads to an acceptance of responsibility just as a failure to believe in action negates responsibility. Compare the last words of Golaud, declaring that Mélisande's death was not his doing, with the terrible punishment Oedipus inflicts upon himself in Sophocles' *Œdipus Rex.* Such punishment and remorse on the part of Oedipus affirms his feeling of guilt which in turn demonstrates his belief that he could have avoided his patricide and incest. He was told his acts were predestined, but by his acceptance of guilt he denies such a belief. By Golaud's denial of guilt he affirms that Mélisande's death was predestined.

Indeed, if one must speak of Maeterlinck as an innovator, then he must be looked upon as the architect of an anti-tragic form where the characters in a play view their life as if it were a play in which all the lines and actions were already written by the unseen author, Fate. To the extent that such an outlook is dramatically represented by extreme techniques in speech and plot, Maeterlinck can be linked to the "Theater of the Absurd." To the extent that a preoccupation with determinism suggests the modern drama where man is seen more the victim rather than the shaper of forces, one may call Maeterlinck modern. (pp. 783-84)

The internal argument of Maeterlinck's work pleads no cause and makes no judgments. His art never becomes propaganda because he is concerned with fundamentals outside the reach of politics and psychiatry. His ultimate success as a playwright is to be seen in the subjective response his work evokes. We are not left with a desire to argue with him for he has pleaded no case; we are not anxious to examine his technique for his technique is interwoven with his substance. We are left only with a mood compounded of sadness and resignation; a mood that can only follow experience and discovery that somehow rest outside the limits of our intellect. (p. 784)

> *Joan Pataky Kosove, "Maeterlinck's 'Pelléas et Mélisande'," in* The French Review *(copyright 1967 by the American Association of Teachers of French), Vol. XL, No. 6, May, 1967, pp. 781-84.*

BETTINA KNAPP (essay date 1975)

Maeterlinck's theater has been variously labeled: a theater of silence, of stasis, of darkness, of the dream. His early dramas—(*The Intruder, The Blind, Pelléas and Mélisande*) —are all of these things. Yet, they go beyond such limited nomenclatures. In that they give primacy to ritual, myth, gesture, and the world of the occult, they may be looked upon as precursors to contemporary absurdist theater. In good Symbolist tradition—following the dictates of Baudelaire, Villiers de l'Isle Adam, and Mallarmé—symbols are the chief vehicles used in his dramas to arouse sensation, to breathe life into the ephemeral essences which people Maeterlinck's stage. (p. 9)

Maeterlinck's world is inhabited by mysterious and dreamy forces. Words and phrases, repeated at regular intervals during the performances, are designed to evoke sensations; the sets, stark in their simplicity, arouse man's fantasy world; the subdued light, cast in eerie hues, lends a tremulous and haunting note to the scene; sound effects, integrated into the body of the drama, are perceptible manifestations of an atemporal force—an unknown and terrifying destiny which hovered over each of the protagonists.

Maeterlinck frequently had recourse to the fairy tale structure in his plays. It best expressed his mystical ideations. Divested of cultural accouterments, the fairy tale is the profoundest and simplest expression of the collective unconscious. It brings forth a world of feeling, not the rational thinking function. Audiences, therefore, could respond viscerally, empathetically to a Maeterlinck play, be emotionally stimulated or pained as the case might be. (pp. 9-10)

With the passing of years, Maeterlinck altered his style.... His former ethereal, poetic, childlike heroines were now

transformed into *femmes fortes. Ariadne and Bluebeard* ... was the prototype of the feminist woman; *Monna Vanna,* the political heroine, yielded her body to the enemy for the collective good; *Mary Magdalene,* the religious martyr, accepted Christ's crucifixion rather than give herself to the Roman officer who desired her, convinced that her act was the highest and purest expression of divine love.

Maeterlinck's realistic-philosophical dramas were contrived. They lacked the intensity, the poetry and the authenticity of his early works. Of the twenty dramas he wrote after his Symbolist phase, only *The Blue Bird* is of superior quality. Here again he reverted to the fairy tale dimension, to the world of the child. (pp. 10-11)

[Like so many of Maeterlinck's works,] *The Intruder* is a play about death. A family, consisting of a blind Grandfather, an Uncle, a Father, and three girls, awaits the Mother's recovery after childbirth. A relative is expected. The Father and Uncle are convinced the Mother is out of danger. Only the blind Grandfather senses the hopelessness of the situation. The visitor finally arrives—in the form of Death. (p. 40)

The Intruder is constructed almost exclusively of the exteriorization of inner states. The actors, almost immobile throughout the performance, have pared their gestures down to the barest nuances of movement, underscoring by their very restraint the mounting terror of the situation. The dialogue is sparse. Words are enunciated with objectivity and yet with infinite tonal and rhythmic variations. They sometimes sound metallic; at other moments they take on the solemnity of a religious chant. (pp. 40-1)

Nor is the visual aspect of *The Intruder* neglected. The troubled characters grouped together on stage hide behind masks in the excruciating anxieties that corrode their lives.... Divested of personal elements, the characters in *The Intruder* are mythlike, mediumistic. They flay each other on stage in the subtlest of ways, compelled to do so, seemingly, by some invisible network of fatal forces.

Philosophically *The Intruder* is based on a series of vague or strange encounters, representing man's confrontation with occult forces over which he has no control. (p. 41)

Technically speaking, *The Intruder* is a modern piece, simple and poignant. The fact that *The Intruder* adheres to the French classical unities of time, place, and action is an indication of its conciseness and depth. There is no extraneous action, nothing superfluous. Everything on stage emerges directly from the body of the text. Action and playing time are the same: one and a half hours. The set does not change. It consists of a room with three doors and a window, the window opening onto a garden. The door to the left leads to the dying woman's room; the one to the right to the infant's room; the third, back center stage, leads to the outside world. The doors may be looked upon as three aspects of existence: death, life, and chance. Hovering over this ultrastationary and lugubrious atmosphere of doom are ... "enormous invisible and fatal powers."

The protagonists in *The Intruder* should not be looked upon as flesh-and-blood beings, rather as archetypes—primordial images arising from the profoundest layers of man's unconscious. (p. 43)

The Intruder is a play of cosmic dimension, a work that dramatizes a supreme interchange: the Mother, stage left, who is about to exit from life, and the infant, stage right, who is entering the earthly domain. It is a scenic depiction of life's cyclical orbit, what is termed in myths and religions a *rite de passage*. (p. 48)

For a number of years Maeterlinck had been drawn to the world of the marionette. . . .

[In the middle period] of his career, Maeterlinck felt that human actors, because they were restricted by their physical characteristics, were not appropriate vehicles to portray the archetypal figures with which he peopled his stage. Since wooden dolls were complex and ambiguous forces, they infused a super- or extrahuman dimension into the stage happenings. Inhabitants of two worlds, the real and the unreal, they could be transformed into anything at any time: god or man, saint or sinner. Like phantoms, they strutted about and stirred, terrified, and pained in a strangely inhuman way those who viewed them. Marionettes came to life only when the spectator projected his unconscious content onto them. (p. 77)

The Death of Tintagiles is [one] of Maeterlinck's dramas for marionettes. Here we are confronted with death in the form of a queen who dictates her inexorable blood wish and her maidservants who obey her will; thus showing once again man's impotence when dealing with destiny. (p. 84)

Death as expressed in *The Death of Tintagiles* is no longer a spiritual force that perpetually hovers over man as was the case in *The Intruder, The Blind, The Seven Princesses, Pelléas and Melisande,* and *Interior;* nor is death a senex figure who stealthily seeks out its victims. Death now has revealed itself, for the first time in Maeterlinck's dramas, in the form of a woman. . . .

Dual forces are at work in *The Death of Tintagiles.* The Terrible Mother figure on the one hand and the positive sisters (Ygraine and Ballangère) on the other. Both aspects of the female principle are present and do battle throughout. Although Tintagiles's sisters fail, they nevertheless fight valiantly.

The Death of Tintagiles may be looked upon as a *rite de passage* not only with regard to Tintagiles's life-and-death drama, but also in terms of Maeterlinck the playwright. Although still deeply entrenched in Schopenhauer's philosophy (man has no power over his fate; his life is constantly subject to outer-worldly forces), the fact that active forces emerge in *The Death of Tintagiles* and battle with fate indicates the end of Maeterlinck's passive acceptance of life's forces. (p. 85)

Maeterlinck's new dramatic style [as it developed after his period of marionette plays] (represented by *Aglavaine and Sélysette, Ariadne and Bluebeard, Sister Beatrice*) opted for a combined philosophical-thesis play in which problems were posed and answered and characters were of flesh and blood. Gone were the lyrical dramas replete with spiritualized essences and mysterious, hermetic, arcane ideations. No longer were spectators able to penetrate a world of feeling and experience fluid language—varied sonorities that flowed in and out of a dialogue resembling prolonged litanies, melopoeias, and aubades. . . . Maeterlinck's world now was, for the most part, existential. Whereas his protagonists had heretofore succumbed to an all-powerful heimarmene, and were powerless in dealing with the hidden forces fate had sent to destroy them, he now had them act overtly.

They participated in creating their future. Maeterlinck's earlier dramas had been spontaneous expressions of feelings, moods, and obsessions; his new brand of theatre would speak to the minds of spectators first—then, perhaps, to their feelings. (p. 107)

[Characteristic of the plays of this period is the strength of his women characters (les femmes fortes), such as Monna Vanna, who] is indeed a queenly figure. She uses her judging faculties, reasons out her situations, and acts with heart. . . . Once a forthright, open, loving wife, she has to be dishonest to become an authentic individual—to live life fully for the first time. Only [then] does her true identity emerge, giving her the strength to end a relationship that has grown sterile and destructive. (pp. 110-11)

Maeterlinck's plays are unique. The characters are not the flesh-and-blood human beings of conventional theater. They are, rather, presences, essences, will-less fantasy figures who move with an economy of gesture in an atmosphere of strange stillness amid subdued lights. They glide as if moved by some mysterious extraterrestrial force that compels them to fulfill their cosmic destiny. These haunting beings are essentially tragic. (p. 175)

To the extent that Maeterlinck's early plays are based on symbols, gestures, and the ritual, they may be considered as ancestors of absurdist theater. The conflict in dramas such as *The Intruder, The Blind, Interior, The Death of Tintagiles,* and *Pelléas and Mélisande* is experienced as an inward journey. The exteriorization of the protagonists' moods and feelings is effected by their physical demeanor and by the incantatory quality of their speech. Maeterlinck's language, punctuated with silences, relies heavily on repetition of sounds and phrases that frequently take on the power of a litany, a melopoeia, rediscovering in this form the original function of language, its supernatural and religious characteristics. Gone are the platitudes and banalities. Words no longer used in their habitual sense usher in a world of magic, arousing a multitude of associations and sensations that act and react viscerally upon the onlooker—not by brash or obvious means but rather by imposed restraints, nuances, and subtleties.

Everything within Maeterlinck's plays works toward a cohesive whole. The drama is tightly structured, adhering to the formulas of French classical theater; unity of time, place, and action. Language, decor, lighting, peripeteia, and gesture flow into one central image. Its impact, accompanied by powerful feeling tones, has a cumulative effect on the audience; nuances flay; feelings pain—until the weight of the experience becomes almost unbearable. (pp. 175-76)

Maeterlinck's early plays, like the fairy tale and the myth, are based on primordial experiences. They live on because they capture and materialize in the work of art the eternal part of man. (p. 176)

Bettina Knapp, in her Maurice Maeterlinck *(copyright © 1975 by G. K. Hall & Co.; reprinted with the permission of Twayne Publishers, A Division of G. K. Hall & Co., Boston), Twayne, 1975, 200 p.*

BIBLIOGRAPHY

Bailly, Auguste. *Maeterlinck.* New York: Haskell House Publishers, 1974, 156 p.

A survey of Maeterlinck's career concentrating upon the development of his mysticism.

Bithell, Jethro. *Life and Writings of Maurice Maeterlinck*. London: Walter Scott Publishing Co., 1913, 198 p.
    General study and biography.

Brachear, Robert. "Maurice Maeterlinck and his 'Musée Grévin'." *French Review* XL, No. 1 (October 1966): 347-51.
    Articulates Maeterlinck's theory that a drama's performance diminishes the effect of the written work.

de Soissons, S.C. "Maeterlinck as a Reformer of the Drama." *The Contemporary Review* 86, No. 467 (November 1904): 699-708.
    Analyzes Maeterlinck's theory of symbolic drama.

Hale, Edward Everett, Jr. "Maeterlinck." In his *Dramatists of To-Day*, pp. 174-217. New York: Henry Holt and Co., 1911.
    Survey of Maeterlinck's career which remarks upon the way his philosophical concerns were translated into drama.

Mahony, Patrick. "The Maeterlinck Centenary, 1862-1962." *Personalist* 43, No. 4 (Autumn 1962): 487-92.
    Appreciation and personal reminiscence of Maeterlinck.

Riffaterre, Michael. "Decadent Features in Maeterlinck's Poetry." *Language and Style* VII, No. 1 (Winter 1974): 3-19.
    Examines characteristically "decadent" themes and rhetoric in Maeterlinck's early poems and compares them with the work of other French authors connected with the decadent school.

Cesare Pavese

1908-1950

Italian novelist, poet, essayist, translator, and critic.

Pavese was one of the first modern Italian writers to break away from the academic tradition of literary Italian to create a vernacular style. His prose is lyric without rhetorical flourish and often approaches the expressive power of poetry.

A serious student of American literature, Pavese was well respected as a translator and literary critic. His familiarity with American literature had a profound effect on his own creative writing, with Whitman and Melville being important influences.

Pavese grew up in a rural village in the Piedmont hills. His fiction is dominated by a conflict between urban and rural, the cultured and the unsophisticated, the sense of present and past. He was a withdrawn man who formed few close relationships, but he sporadically involved himself in political causes. In 1935 he was arrested by the Fascist government for clandestine political activity and exiled for ten months in a Calabrian village. Afterwards, actual or symbolic confinement became an important image in his work. A similarly recurring motif is man's failure to communicate with others and his inability to make commitments. His narrators are typically outsiders, observers of action who are unwilling to consider themselves participants. Escapism is another constant theme, with the primitive countryside often viewed as a haven. These varied strands were drawn together in *La luna e i falò*, which many critics consider his best work.

Classified as a neo-realist, Pavese was not as concerned with the outside world as with how his protagonists came to terms with that world. For Pavese the present was understood by examining one's past, by creating a personal mythology based on experiences early in life, a philosophy which accounts for the sense his characters give of constantly living in the past. Pavese's work, as a whole, has also been viewed as a chronicle of the state of mind of Italy during and after the Second World War. His diary, with its clearsighted appraisal of his character, is considered a masterpiece of the literary journal.

In 1950 Pavese received the Strega Prize, Italy's most prestigious literary award. In the same year, at the height of his literary reputation, he committed suicide.

PRINCIPAL WORKS

Lavorare stanca (poetry) 1936

[*Hard Labor: Poems*, 1976]
Paesi tuoi (novel) 1941
[*The Harvesters*, 1961]
La spiaggia (novel) 1942; published in journal *Lettere D'oggi*
[*The Beach*, 1963]
Feria d'agosto (short stories, essays, and poetry) 1946
Il compagno (novel) 1947
[*The Comrade*, 1959]
Dialoghi con Leucò (prose dialogues) 1947
[*Dialogues with Leucò*, 1965]
La bella estate (novel) 1949; published with *Il diavolo sulle colline* and *Tra donne sole* as *La bella estate*
[*The Beautiful Summer*, published with *The Political Prisoner*, 1955]
Il carcere (novel) 1949; published with *La casa in collina* as *Prima che il gallo canti*
[*The Political Prisoner*, 1955]
La casa in collina (novel) 1949; published with *Il carcere* as *Prima che il gallo canti*
[*The House on the Hill*, 1956]
Il diavolo sulle colline (novel) 1949; published with *La bella estate* and *Tra donne sole* as *La bella estate*
[*The Devil in the Hills*, 1954]
Tra donne solo (novel) 1949; published with *La bella estate* and *Il diavolo sulle colline* as *La bella estate*
[*Among Women Only*, 1953]
La luna e i falò (novel) 1950
[*The Moon and the Bonfires*, 1952]
Il mestiere di vivere: Diario 1935-1950 (journals) 1952
[*The Burning Brand: Diaries 1935-1950*, 1961; published in England as *This Business of Living: Diary 1935-1950*, 1961]
Festival Night, and Other Stories (short stories) 1964
Summer Storm, and Other Stories (short stories) 1966

WILLIAM ARROWSMITH (essay date 1943)

Lavorare stanca is, unmistakably, an act of radical personal culture—the beautifully disciplined product of almost four years' obsessive, solitary labor in which the poet named himself and his world by bringing his personal demons firmly, though briefly, under the control of his art.

The poetry is also cultural in a larger sense. Apart from the section entitled "Green Wood," *Lavorare stanca* contains no political poetry, not a shred of ideology. Yet the book is clearly a political and a cultural act. Negatively, for instance, the Fascist experience of the twenties and thirties is perhaps remembered in the title . . . , but also in the tone, in the bleakness of some of the poems and the atmosphere of weary, suffering silence. Positively, it is present as the poet's radiant reaction to Fascist misery, in Pavese's laconic compassion and piercing sympathy. (p. xii)

Most Italian poets of the time, confronted with Fascism, chose conspicuous silence or withdrew into a sad "hermetic" inwardness (another, more literary, way of "saying nothing"). Pavese, instead, resisted; both his poetry and his translations of American authors were—and were understood to be—overt acts of literary rebellion against the regime. But his resistance was not merely negative defiance of official culture; it was an intense effort to rethink or create a valid Italian culture of his own. (p. xiii)

For this purpose realism was not enough, and certainly not the scrannel European variety. . . . To do this the poet had to stand open to the world and to others, to make his poetry *reveal* . . . the spiritual, mythical "presence" which things do not "express" but *are*. Hence the serious poet must reject the verbal and philosophical constraints of tradition, whether mandarin, Fascist, or simply *signorile*. The new poetry required a radically "new symbolism" (in Pavese's practice almost the opposite of conventional symbolism) and a new language: hard, colloquial, direct, but also austere and reticent, devoid of rhetoric, spurning all bookishness and decorative learning. The ultimate purpose of this new poetry was to replace Fascist (and traditional) culture with a new, noble (but unprivileged) indigenous culture. This new culture would reconcile (as Fascism had divided): nation and province; city and country, "language" (Tuscan) and "dialect" (Piedmontese); literate and illiterate; the concrete object and its numinous or spiritual "field." It was a wild, sublime, impossibly Whitmanian project. The poet's mission was literally to create his culture from scratch or to incarnate its noblest meaning in his striving; if he could not create culture, he could at least make poetry out of the intent (as Pavese thought Whitman had done). In Whitman, Pavese found not so much influence as affinity, a common taste for the sublime and unlimited aspiration. The point is crucial to an understanding of Pavese's life and work. Despite his low-keyed, self-effacing style and his temperamental shyness, nothing is more central to Pavese than his intense, vaulting ambition and his transcendental passion. The sublime, "the boundless dream," ran in his blood; he wanted to ennoble everything he touched. (pp. xiii-xiv)

Ultimately, I think, it will be recognized, even in Italy, that Pavese's poetry is strikingly original; that it is not an American "sport" but deeply (often perversely) Italian work; that the greatest Italian and classical writers are constant and pervasive presences. There is more Homer, for instance, in "South Seas" than Whitman or Melville. The project of creating a new culture, a new poetry, is at least as Vergilian and Dantesque as it is Whitmanian. Pavese's realism owes far more to Dante, Boccaccio, and Sacchetti than it does to Lewis or Dreiser. As for Dante, his influence is everywhere; positively, in Pavese's clawlike talent for seizing his object; negatively, in the principled refusal of figurative meaning. (pp. xix-xx)

Pavese never worked out a coherent statement of his aesthetics, and, apart from a group of late essays on myth and poetry, his views must be inferred from his criticism and practice. But, in one form or another, revelatory realism was the basic stance of all his work, both poetry and fiction (which for that reason differs *toto caelo* from Italian neorealism). But so far as the reader of *Lavorare stanca* is concerned, what matters is the recognition that very unusual demands are being made of him. Revelation, of course, is something we no longer expect, or perhaps even want, from poets, any more than we expect a character in a poem to reveal the universal traits of the species. Yet this is precisely what Pavese gives us. His characters, like the woman in "A Season" or the boy in "Atavism," are as much generic as individual portraits—incarnate "destinies," the universal looming in the individual. . . . To moderns [the] notion of character as expressive destiny is very strange, very Greek, indeed; even stranger is the idea, central to Pavese's work, that rhythm and meter are the temporal movement by which, *narrated,* this destiny is revealed. This, we like to think, is not the way poets (or anyone else) should talk, much less write. But Pavese's structure and techniques correspond to this revelatory purpose. Thus a Pavese poem (or novel) is not the familiar Empsonian object with its layered, ambiguous, and polysemous structure. It is instead a dynamic unfolding, along a single narrative level. Revelation takes place in two complementary ways: positively, by the staggered release of meaning by the poem's narration of its "imaginative links" . . . ; and negatively, by the gradual, crafted release of the meaning packed but suppressed in the poem's ellipses and silences. Pavese's reticence, in this respect, is structural technique, and the power of his poems to reveal is usually in direct proportion to what has been deliberately suppressed in its ellipses. The poem, in short, by verbal chiaroscuro, recreates the process by which the poet's darkness was first transformed into clarity and understanding; i.e., revelation. But this revelation is successful only insofar as it discloses the object or situation in its single entirety; quite consciously, I think, it sets out to frustrate the reader's expectation that the object be revealed as a sign or symbol of something else, that it show us, that is, a "deeper *level*" of meaning. Hence the reader conditioned to the pleasures of "layered" poetry is apt to find a Pavese poem flat, lacking in the polyvalent richness he has learned to demand. The problem, however, is not the poem but the reader's poetics, the routine critical insistence on polysemous structure and meaning. A Pavese poem asks just the opposite; it is the exact reverse of allegory (hence Pavese's quarrel with Dante). And its chief purpose is to make the object reveal the world it implies, to give back to the world the splendor of its own being, the richness of being *itself* and not some other thing. (pp. xxxvi-xxxvii)

William Arrowsmith, in his introduction to Hard Labor *by Cesare Pavese, translated by William Arrowsmith (English language translation copyright © William Arrowsmith, 1976; reprinted by permission of Viking Penguin Inc.; originally published as* Lavorare Stanca, *Giulio Einaudi, 1943), Grossman, 1976, pp. xi-xlii.*

LESLIE A. FIEDLER (essay date 1954)

To understand Pavese at all, we must learn to see in him as strangeness what strikes us as most familiar, his "Americanism." All his life, he pursued or retreated from a legendary America, a legendary American Novel, *the* American Novel. . . .

Pavese found in [American culture] a promise of freedom, cultural as well as political, a clue to a new kind of literary tradition, "a tradition of seeking tradition," to set against their own official culture, the legendary Mediterranean past which, under Fascist auspices, was being transformed from a museum to a prison. (p. 538)

The real unity which is discoverable in Pavese's work under its superficial shifts from realism to regionalism, from the political to the archetypal, is his preoccupation with the meanings of America; as essayist, poet, novelist, translator and critic, his chief effort was directed toward defining, discovering an America for his country and his time. (p. 539)

Pavese's impulse as an artist was toward a dimension he liked to call "mythic," a dimension he found in Melville and not in Flaubert. It is primarily through the author of *Moby Dick* that Pavese approaches American literature, and it is through him that he finds in our books an identity of word and thing that goes beyond mere anti-rhetorical immediacy to a special sort of symbolism: not the aristocratic *symbolisme* of the French, whose watchword is absolute transcendence and whose hero is the Dandy . . . but a democratic faith that a "colloquy with the masses" might be opened on the level of myth whose unity underlies the diversity of our acquired cultures.

Just as American literature had found a third way between the European poles of naturalism and *symbolisme,* so Pavese felt we had found an escape from the dilemma of classicizing traditionalism and romantic rebellion, between academicism and futurism. The American artist, Pavese believed, had discovered how to reject conformism without becoming "a rebel in short pants," how to be at once free and mature. The clue to this new kind of maturity Pavese found in the "intemperate autobiographism" of American books. (pp. 541-42)

In our classic books, Pavese found a method for making biography symbol, for transforming the most private impulses of the heart into myths of social utility; and for him the first of these myths was the image of America itself, a legend of a search for freedom, which Pavese used in order to transcend the limits of his own personality, to move his obsessions from the level of confession to that of communication. But there were other public legends to which he turned to redeem his private anguish, especially Communism and the myth of the Resistance, the Italian fable of themselves as their own sole deliverers. . . . Pavese, who embraced the new legend, America had to be transformed into the image of a false paradise, finally exposed as the land of universal lovelessness, alienation and discontent. (pp. 542-43)

His sense of the obligation of the artist to myth leads Pavese in one main line of his work to become more and more abstract, to abandon ever more the fable in favor of the ritual, until in *Feria d' Agosto* (*Summer Holiday*), a series of stories, essays and poems (the genre is indifferent) are worked into a musical confrontation as three hypostasized themes: the Sea, the City and the Vine; while in the *Dialogues with Leuko,* the book which Pavese considered his most significant work and which is surely his most beautiful, his most achieved effort, action has disappeared completely, and the characters have become "beautiful names, charged with a destiny but not a psychological character," who confront each other two by two to discuss certain classic myths in all their "problematic and anguished ambiguity."

As a matter of fact, Pavese himself insisted that all of his books were essentially as little realistic as the *Dialogues,* that in every one "the theme is the rhythm of what happens." But this contention taken alone is misleading; for, certainly, the line of books which reaches its climax in *The Moon and the Bonfires* has a tension between the temporal and the ritual lacking in the *Dialogues.* These novelistic books are by no means their mere metaphysics; but are full of jokes, local excitement, incest, murder, religion, politics, scenery, dialectics and poetry. It is true enough that *finally* every village fair becomes the Fair, every hill, the Hill—and even every life, Life, or as Pavese preferred to say, Destiny; and that therefore every book, even the most novelistic, is *at last* a dialogue between symbolic worlds, with their appropriate rhythms and images: the Hill and the Sea, the City and the Village, Virtue and Vice, the Child and the World, the Moon and the Bonfires. . . . But before the "finally," the "at last," there is room enough for all the accidents of grace, for the unpredictable collaboration of luck with art.

It is profitable in this light to compare Pavese's earliest work with his latest, to see what he did with certain characteristic themes before he really knew what they were trying to declare or had acquired the skill to control them. In *Paesi tuoi . . . ,* all his compulsive situations, the very ones he will be manipulating still in his last novel *The Moon and the Bonfires . . . ,* already exist but as mere obsessions and titillations, rendered in a tough, nervous style, self-consciously "American." The novel smacks of Erskine Caldwell in its gratuitous brutality, its pretended realism which is really an exoticism of the sordid. The story, seen through the eyes of a city-bred mechanic, deals with a peasant who ends by killing with a pitchfork the sister with whom he has been sleeping, when she tells him to use a dipper instead of drinking water directly out of a pail.

Implicit in the conception is a confrontation of City and Farm which is scarcely worked out, and the whole complicated fable of guilt and betrayal eventuates in detached images of violence which cry out to stand for something, but instead merely betray the writer's personal rage and frustration. The girl is obviously killed because her sexuality frightens Pavese, and must be at once penetrated and subdued, cancelled out in blood, while the craftiness and brutality of peasant life (a whole society turning on the question of who will *fregare* whom in all the senses of the word) is exploited only to reveal the author's sense of his own exclusion, his outsidedness. Under the hardboiled surfaces, it is the book of a terrified adolescent who can believe in society only as his private nightmare.

But when in *The Moon and the Bonfires,* Pavese returns for the last time to his familiar violated landscape, the same Piedmontese river and hill, to the compulsive themes of the beautiful girl slain in the full flush of her sexuality, and the almost pointless violence of peasant life, the blood under the fig tree—the valence of the images has changed. To begin with, Pavese has reached the peak of his mature style . . . , the control of prose rhythms which makes his language at once absolutely lucid and completely incantatory, weaving into the texture of the sentences the sense of remembering rather than inventing, of returning to something impossibly remote, yet knowing it for the first time.

But more than this, there is the feeling that Pavese is at last the master rather than the victim of his obsessions, that he has finally found a way to transform his realization of all that separates him from society and its typical experiences into a breakthrough to communication, a communion which must mean recognition and success. (pp. 548-50)

He had, at any rate, first politicized, then mythicized his themes: seeing the violence of the peasant now as a function of the *miseria* bred by the social system and upheld by the church; while the murdered enchantress became a symbol of the double agent, beauty as the whore of both sides in the struggle for social justice, and finally the accomplice of the Fascists. The death of all that is most desired becomes transformed into a brutal civic necessity, a crime which is also a deliverance, and toward which one must feel in unequal balance guilt and righteousness. But Pavese is not content to rest his case on social arguments, sensing that violence may merely call up counter-violence in an endless regress, and that crimes which depend upon a postulated future to justify them remain merely crimes when that future fails or is fumbled. It is on magical grounds that he finally stands, equating the death and burning of the beautiful daughter of a disappearing ruling class with the bonfires lighted to insure, not practically but ritually, the fertility of the earth.

For all the obliqueness of its reference, *The Moon and the Bonfires* is the most autobiographical of Pavese's fictions, almost cannibalistic in its effect; as if having been victimized by his life and having learned to control it, he wants now to consume it in a final fiction. . . . The protagonist is called "the American" for he is returning as the action begins, from a sojourn in America, as Pavese has returned to his own native earth from his imaginary expedition to the new world. There is irony in the plight of the returner, a bastard who does not know his parents, coming back to a home he has never had, to what is only a home by contrast with the lunar landscape of America, absolute homelessness made desert and mountains. (p. 551)

[But only] what eternally abides can be recaptured, and only this is truly new with the newness of the recurring seasons: the Hill, the River, the Grape Harvest, the Festivals with the young dancing until they fall in their places, and the musicians playing their way home through the sleeping countryside, the magic bonfires lit on the hills for the sake of the crops. To this alone can the bastard return, the archetypal earth: father and mother of the orphan, home of the homeless. If America is the land for which we can only set out, this is the anti-America, the land to which we can only come back. (p. 552)

Leslie A. Fiedler, "Introducing Cesare Pavese," in The Kenyon Review *(copyright 1960 by Leslie A. Fiedler), Vol. 16, No. 4, Autumn, 1954, pp. 536-53.*

NATALIA GINZBURG (essay date 1959)

[Pavese's] lines resound in our ears whenever we go back to [Turin] or think of it; and all that we know is they are beautiful lines, which are so much a part of us that they reflect the image of our youth for us, of those days now so far away when we listened to his lively voice for the first time; and discovered, with utter amazement, that even our grey, dull, prosaic city could be turned into poetry.

He lived in the city like a boy: and until the end he lived in this way. His days were very long, with plenty of time, like those of boys: he was able to find room both to study and write, to earn his living and to idle along the streets which he loved: and we who floundered, torn between laziness and industry, wasted the hours in uncertainty and making up our minds whether to be lazy or industrious. (pp. 22-3)

He was sometimes very sad: but we thought for a long time that he would be cured of that sadness as soon as he decided to grow up: because it seemed to us that his sadness was that of a boy, the voluptuous heedless melancholy of a boy who has still not come down to earth, and moves in the arid, solitary world of dreams. (p. 23)

He was not a leader for us, although he taught us many things: because we saw only too well the absurd and tortuous complications of thought in which he imprisoned his simple soul; and we in our turn wanted to teach him something, to teach him how to live in a more natural, relaxed way: but we never succeeded in teaching him anything, because whenever we tried to expound our ideas to him, he would lift a hand and say that he knew it all already.

In those last years, he had a furrowed, lined face, devastated by tormenting thoughts: but until the end his appearance kept its youthful gentleness. In those last years he became a famous writer, but this did not change his retiring habits in any way, or the modesty of his bearing, or his humility about his daily work, which was conscientious to the point of scruple. When we asked him if he liked being famous, he would reply with a superb grimace, that he had always expected it: at times he did have a superb shrewd frown, boyish and malevolent, which would light up and then disappear. But the fact that he had always expected it meant that when the thing was accomplished it no longer gave him any joy, because as soon as he had got anything, he was incapable of enjoying it and loving it. He said that he already knew his art so deeply that it could no longer offer him any more secrets: and if it offered him no more secrets, it no longer interested him. As for us, his friends, he told us that we had no more secrets for him either, and we wearied him infinitely; and we, terrified of wearying him, could not succeed in telling him that we saw only too well where he was going wrong: in not wanting to stoop to loving the mundane pattern of existence, which carries on regularly, and only seems to be without secrets. So it remained for him to conquer mundane reality: but this was forbidden and impregnable to him, who had both thirst and disgust for it; and thus he was only able to gaze at it as from distant spaces. (pp. 25-6)

Natalia Ginzburg, "Portrait of a Friend" (1959), in London Magazine *(© London Magazine 1968), Vol. 8, No. 2, May, 1968, pp. 21-7.*

LOUIS TENENBAUM (essay date 1961)

Almost invariably Pavese involves his narrators in a series of events, presented without dramatic tensions, which has deeply influenced their lives and from which they are groping to extract essential meanings. The narrative may move as sluggishly and forsake drama and passion as in *La spiaggia,* the unexciting account of a Ligurian coast vacation; or it can move from the monotonous torpor and heavily sensual atmosphere of the first half of *Paesi tuoi* to the explosive, incest-flavored murder which climaxes it. In neither case can the narrator escape the sense of participation, the feeling that he is involved with forces which transcend and will outlast him and which he cannot hope to control, in spite of the fact that he is a solitary figure who seeks to gain the inner strength needed to be independent of other men. Stefano in *Il carcere* is a good example of this central motif in Pavese's fiction, the conflict between the narrator's need for inner freedom or solitude and his awareness of his bonds with society and the world. First person point of view gives the storyteller the means to participate as well as to observe. The handling of this dual function is so skillful that the constant presence of the narrator (except in *Il carcere*) does not destroy the delicate balance by excessively obtruding itself into the story atmosphere. In this ideal scheme the narrator is not essentially interesting in himself, but becomes interesting through his relationships with the other characters he evokes. In the degree of intensity of these relationships much of Pavese's stylistic originality reveals itself. Recreated figures of the "hero's" past are endowed with a symbolism-tinged destiny, created and heightened by the evocation of leitmotival recurrences of characteristic attitudes, atmospheres, and events, achieving an almost rhythmic monotony, and a sense of invariability of movement.... [In the] Pavesian creation of the past the narrator recalls rhythmically, rather than chronologically, isolating from their original context and then joining, without reference to time disparities, units of experience which depend strictly on his very private myths. The dissimilarity with a stream-of-consciousness technique is obvious. Thus, in attempting to underline the individual's bond with a subjective as well as an objective reality, the novelist widens the scope of the narrative to include facts, impressions, observations, sentiments, and memories which other writers would probably exclude. In some of the novels this can lead to a sense of inconclusiveness, perhaps the strongest critical charge to be leveled at Pavese, as in *La spiaggia*, where significantly the narrator is most completely submerged in the accessory apparatus of the story. The delicate balance sought, what the writer called "the balance of the individual and the collective," he achieved with special success in *La luna e i falò*, where a Proustian remembrance of things past, skillfully divided between the "hero" Anguilla and his boyhood friend Nuto, emphasizes the sense of myth and destiny controlling life in the Piedmontese hills and valleys of Pavese's youth. (pp. 132-33)

Like Proust, Pavese viewed time as a destroyer of the unity life can offer us, and the process of memory functions in his novels to minimize the sense of time, enveloping his world in an aura of timelessness.... [Whereas] the nineteenth-century novel was concerned with the growth and development of the hero, the twentieth-century novelist prefers to stress his changelessness. *La luna e i falò* best illustrates this static relationship with time, in its concurrent unfolding on two time levels, that of reminiscence and memory, and that of an immediate past, mutually enriching and closely interwoven. (pp. 133-34)

The myth-seeking and the symbolistic quality of Pavese's fiction are closely allied and relate intrinsically to his concept of the function of character. Myth comports a certain amount of mystery, a residue of the inexplicable, an aura of the unknown. There is no attempt to paint a full portrait of the central character, who rigorously avoids self-analysis or explanation, while the secondary characters are seen even more fragmentarily. The symbolic function of the characters both relieves and justifies this sense of incompleteness, because as symbols they suggest more than they could possibly represent as finite individuals. Their participation in an atmosphere of myth and symbol reflects' a limitation of dimension, but not of realistically conceived significance. (p. 134)

The presence and influence of physical nature in the rhythmic pattern of Pavese's novels is as effective as the mythical qualities of his personages in contributing to the accessory role of character portrayal. The bond between man and nature is generally stronger than between men themselves; or it is in their awareness of their common bond with nature that men can find an essential kinship. The moral and ethical strength of the "hero" is usually closely bound to his feeling for nature. . . . The part played by the forces of nature, the seasonal rhythms, the effect of natural phenomena, the relation of man and environment enable Pavese to create a sense of destiny, of fateful development and direction in the people of his fiction. His minimization of character interaction, the static rather than active role one person plays in the drama of another, reflect his concern with the role of fate in human affairs, a concern colored by his Leopardian pessimism and sense of solitude. (p. 135)

> *Louis Tenenbaum, "Character Treatment in Pavese's Fiction," in* Symposium *(copyright © 1961 by Syracuse University Press), Vol. XV, No. 1, Summer, 1961, pp. 131-38.*

SUSAN SONTAG (essay date 1962)

Cesare Pavese began writing around 1930, and the novels which have been translated and published here—*The House on the Hill, The Moon and the Bonfires, Among Women Only,* and *The Devil in the Hills*—were all written in the years 1947-49, so that a reader confined to English translations can't generalize about his work as a whole. From these four novels alone, however, it appears that his main virtues as a novelist are delicacy, economy, and control. The style is flat, dry, unemotional. One remarks the coolness of Pavese's fiction, though the subject-matter is often violent. This is because the real subject is never the violent happening (e.g. the suicide in *Among Women Only;* the war in *The Devil in the Hills*) but, rather, the cautious subjectivity of the narrator. The typical effort of a Pavese hero is lucidity; the typical problem is that of lapsed communication. The novels are about crises of conscience, and the refusal to allow crises of conscience. A certain atrophy of the emotions, an enervation of sentiment and bodily vitality, is presupposed. The anguish of prematurely disillusioned, highly civilized people alternating between irony and melancholic experiments with their own emotions is indeed familiar. But unlike other explorations of this vein of modern sensibility—for example, much of French fiction and poetry of the last eighty years—Pavese's novels are unsensational and chaste. The main action always takes place off-stage, or in the past; and erotic scenes are curiously avoided.

As if to compensate for the detached relations which his characters have with each other, Pavese typically attributes to them a deep involvement with a place—usually either the cityscape of Turin . . . or the surrounding Piedmont countryside. . . . This sense of place, and the desire to find and recover the meaning of a place, does not, however, give Pavese's work any of the characteristics of regional fiction, and this may in part account for the failure of his novels to arouse much enthusiasm among an English-speaking audience, nothing like that aroused by the work of Silone or Moravia, though he is a much more gifted and original writer than either of these. Pavese's sense of place and of people is not what one expects of an Italian writer. But then Pavese was a Northern Italian; Northern Italy is not the Italy of the foreign dream, and Turin is a large industrial city lacking in the historical resonance and incarnate sensuality which attracts foreigners to Italy. (pp. 39-40)

[The] virtues of Pavese's fiction are not popular virtues. . . . Pavese's novels are refined, elliptical (though never obscure), quiet, anti-dramatic, self-contained. Pavese is not a major writer. . . . But he does deserve a good deal more attention in England and America than he has gotten thus far. (pp. 40-1)

> Susan Sontag, "The Artist As Exemplary Suffer-
> er" (1962), in her Against Interpretation (reprinted
> by permission of Farrar, Straus & Giroux, Inc.;
> copyright © 1961, 1962, 1963, 1964, 1965, 1966 by
> Susan Sontag), Farrar, Straus & Giroux, 1966,
> pp. 39-48.

GIOSE RIMANELLI (essay date 1964)

Pavese says of his poems that they were "an attempt to express a cluster of fantastic associations, of which one's own perception of reality consists, with a sufficient wholeness." . . .

A first exploration of Pavese's poems leads to an observation that is also a revelation, namely that they are "felt," *i.e.* they have rhythm. . . . They are suffused with an ineffable feeling that transcends reason. . . . The rhythm is constant and reflects the development of a situation that is always concrete, as are its particular elements themselves. But the relation between object and subject, between character and landscape is ungraspable because it is seamlessly fused together. . . . Pavese's concern was to suggest at first sight only an indistinct rhythm, an atmosphere which after all is naught else but a symbolic and primitive reality. (p. 20)

Even in the progression in the poems from the countryside to the city, from life as instinct to life as order, the poet's transcendent vision creates and recreates the associations and cadences of time as a dimension of absolute uniqueness. In the characters who have moved to the city there is always a sovereign need for release which remains ungratified. (p. 24)

The past is contemporaneous with the present in these confrontations that spring up spontaneously. A story unfolds as if the characters were confessing and laying bare their lives. Pavese's mythic time is not nostalgia, neither is it the Proustian "time of the mind," *i.e.* involuntary memory. . . . Nonetheless, for them, there is always an inner flux which brings those particular stratifications of the inner life to the surface in a vibrant and fresh form. But they are linked to the thrill of the unique feeling rather than to the remembrance of things past. For them, however, memory is a psychic kaleidoscope which is continually being reshaped within grooves that were staked-out in the consciousness in

a pre-rational age. Thus for Pavese the return of a "unique event" to the memory does not mean to isolate it in time and to contemplate it. Rather, it means to live it now, as if it were happening now for the first time. . . . The very rhythm of Pavese's poems, seemingly tranquil but unbroken, which immediately remind us of prose narratives, conceals a rhythm which confirms the artist's objectification with the material being dealt with. If story-telling means progression in time, Pavese understands this as a psychic progression, that is to say as a relation between consciousness and reality, an "inner relation between things." . . . This technique on occasion is reminiscent of a similarity with the "stream of consciousness." (pp. 25-6)

Thus for Pavese story-telling is tantamount to the invention of a landscape, which is the story itself. A hill, a landscape, a myth are fixed symbols. They exist indefinitely, in an absolute state. Myth is also the desire to endow the particular with an absolute value. This signifies making the profane sacred. Thus a hill becomes "all" hills, a sea "all" seas, etc. (pp. 26-7)

The dramatization of the myth, the establishment of relations between myth and temporal things and especially between myth and people are the constituitive elements of the epic. In the poems of *Lavorare stanca* the epic consists in reviving images of the past as over against the present. But this is not remembrance. Rather, it is a psychic process by means of which what occurred in the past invests the reality of the present. It is an evocation, not a re-evocation. (p. 27)

Lavorare stance is an epic, as has been said. Pavese defines the book as the "adventure of the adolescent who, proud of his countryside, imagines the city to be similar. Instead in the city he finds solitude and seeks a remedy for it in sex and passion which serve only to de-racinate him and hurl him far from both the countryside and the city into an even more tragic solitude which is the end of adolescence."

This is evident from the titles of the different sections of the book (Forefathers, After, City in the Countryside, Maternity, Green Wood, Paternity) in which the chronological progression remains implicit. There is no temporal development from poem to poem because Pavese is not "telling a story" about the physical evolution of a person in time. There are so many characters. What he registers is an attitude of the characters towards fixed symbols: hill, sea, city, countryside, etc. The interchangeable value which these symbols have for the boy, the adult and the old man constitute the unity of the book. (p. 28)

If there is a "meaning" in *Lavorare stanca*, it is that contained in the last lines of *Mari del sud* and in the poem *Mito*.

> But when I tell him
> that he is among the happy few who have seen the dawn
> on the most beautiful islands of the earth,
> he smiles at the memory and replies that the sun
> was rising but the day was old for them.

Life appears like an adventure to the boy. For the cousin life is experience, hard work. But in the poem *Mito* the "meaning" appears even more explicit. The protagonist notices that everything has changed since youth is over like summer. He no longer "feels" things as before. . . .

The youth is now alone. Even things are alien to him. He

has lost his innocence. He is cut off from his Eden. Life is no longer an emotive, sensual-spiritual apprehension of things. Experience is concept and category. And it is also time. He feels the weariness which is the day-to-day weariness of life. To work with weariness (*lavorare stanca*) means to live. It is only when the awareness that man is mortal sets in that there comes the realization that life is not a dream, when existence is accepted with all its burdens and sufferings, that maturity succeeds adolescence, and the young god becomes a man. (p. 30)

For the reason that the mythic vision is an intuition, a mystical participation in reality, these poems cannot be reduced to an idea and to a formulation. If this happens it is only because the poet has explained to himself the "meaning" of his intuition. He has tried, that is, to transform a sentiment, something unconscious, into something completely conscious. . . . Language is something completely objective. By way of language modern-day man does not feel but contemplates reality. Which is to say he is separated, alienated from it. The concept precedes the image. Man thinks in words which represent images. By way of the concept man can think of things which he has not even seen. . . . Concepts lend themselves to relations and implications. They are an inducement to expansion. They are system. Myth is coalition. It is something that happens in a time, in a place and in a peculiar way. What the poet feels is similarly unique, and essential. This is the lesson of *Lavorare stanca*. (p. 31)

Giose Rimanelli, "The Conception of Time and Language in the Poetry of Cesare Pavese," in Italian Quarterly, *Vol. 8, No. 30, Summer, 1964, pp. 14-34.*

A. E. MURCH (essay date 1966)

[In his early short stories, collected in *Summer Storm*, Cesare Pavese already shows himself] strongly affected by trends of thought that were to become characteristic of all his later work; his awareness of classical mythology, here hinted at in 'The Name', which he brought to full flower in his *Dialogues with Leuco;* his peasant-like, 'earthy' unquestioning acceptance of birth, mating, bloodshed and death, in 'First Love', and the theme of his novel *The Harvesters;* his deep conviction, expressed in 'Freewill' and again in 'The Family', that the whole of a man's future stems relentlessly from his childhood experiences; that a man's reaction to life's problems will always be the same; that, like a bridge, he can carry a certain, pre-determined load and no more.

Even in these early stories, Pavese clearly shows his distrust of women, whom he generally portrays as self-centred, 'treacherous and cruel as the sea'. Nora, in 'The Leather Jacket', Ernesta in 'The Family', and the prostitute, Mina, in 'The Idol', are typical of all Pavese's women characters. (pp. 8-9)

But Pavese's pity for the sufferings of men is deep and sincere; no one can doubt his quick perception of pain and his sympathetic portrayal of it in 'The Evil Eye', 'The Beggars', and 'The Leather Jacket'. It is the theme above all others that pervades his work and reveals his love for his fellow men, his realization of the mental anguish they often conceal beneath a mask of indifference. This is the outstanding quality in Pavese's work. In his diary for 28th January, 1938, when these early stories were being written, he

made a comment that could stand for all he ever wrote: 'Morality is not enough. The only creed worthy of respect is compassion, charity towards our fellow man. The teaching of Christ and Dostoievsky. All the rest is nonsense'. (p. 9)

A. E. Murch, in her introduction to Summer Storm *by Cesare Pavese, translated by A. E. Murch (translation © Alma Murch 1966), Peter Owen Limited, 1966, pp. 7-9.*

R. W. FLINT (essay date 1968)

A major literary figure by Italian standards, one whose immense popularity at home in recent years has surprised even his old friends and supporters, Cesare Pavese had the kind of essentially lyric and confessional genius that seems to spill over almost automatically into legend and scandal; he was, in a word, naïve. This word leads a curiously hectic life in literary discussions. No later critic has wanted to follow [Friedrich] Schiller in his use of the word as a virtual synonym for classic, in the famous essay on naïve and sentimental poetry; but every good critic is smitten with a restless sense of the word's value, even as he defers to common usage and sometimes takes it as a synonym for stupid. (p. 152)

[My purpose is to rescue Pavese] from the suspicion of having become popular for the wrong reasons and to justify the very high estimation in which he is held by a few intelligent and experienced people. Pavese's art—I use the word to include his *Dialoghi con Leuco,* his poetry, and his journal, *Il Mestiere di Vivere*—pleads for a revival of the word naïve for the most embracing technical, political, historical, social, and psychological reasons. Pavese lived his age with a high and deep generic typicality, as a result of which he became, throughout most of his short career . . . , as professionally misunderstood by his contemporaries as he was personally visible to the edge of caricature, the living spirit of middle-class literary Piedmont. (pp. 152-53)

Many native strains converge in his work—the volatility and musicality of Piedmont's "Celtic" inheritance from the northern invasions, the stubborn moral puritanism of a hill and mountain people, the musing, sometimes narcissistic reticence of the North-Italian bourgeoisie, Turin's natural eclecticism and fondness for the French, the ceaseless, unresolvable tension between a passion for technical renewal to match the new industrial age and an equal feeling for past literary glories, for formal subtlety and strength.

No matter how fresh and exact his observation may be, especially in [*La Casa in Collina*], or how cool, pungent, terse, elliptical and oblique his speech in the novels, his work only makes its full effect in its broadest lyric outlines, like Whitman's *Leaves of Grass*. . . . (p. 155)

Pavese was an obsessed, absorbed writer. The *simplex et unum* of neoclassical theory appealed to him naturally; he had a profoundly integrative mind. Consequently the whole *oeuvre* can be read as what in *La Casa* he calls "the history of a long delusion" and its conquest through art, the delusion that he was someone saved by his gifts from enduring the full misery of the age, excused from taking the militant politics of his city at their face value, an artist and therefore a privileged coward. The Pavese narrator is usually a difficult case, quite remote from the usual *simpatico* literary Italian. Hence the final impression of genial strength and power one takes from his writing has to rest on its widest lyric and panoramic frame. Often urbanely epic in tone, it is panoramic in technique and Arcadian at heart. But Arcadian in a surprising rebirth of this tired old tradition in Italian letters, Arcadian at the end of a long, agonized process of inner debate in which the rational man struggles mightily to keep his balance between the age's rational fanaticisms, between a Resistance that usually meant cultural reaction, and complicity with political reaction that often meant a degree of inner freedom. What emerges from these tempering fires is a faithful account of Italy's ordeal and a wonderfully affectionate, saturnine, loving portrait of his people and region that speaks to ordinary Europeans with a directness unmatched in Italy since the deaths of Verga and Svevo. (pp. 155-56)

[Pavese had] a sense of prose style honed razor-sharp on the novelists he had translated, especially Melville, Faulkner, Anderson, Stein, and Joyce. In addition to other things they had taught him the seeming looseness and carelessness with which he achieved his distinctively Piedmontese flavor; the knotty, emphatic, improvised syntax which brought down an absurd charge of "Americanism" from nice-minded readers.

Pavese's modernist eclecticism, however, was far from the whole story. He had what a critic well described as a "cordial austerity" that found echoes in the Greek dramatists and lyric poets, whom he knew in Greek, in Virgil, Dante, Manzoni, Leopardi and Foscolo, but most of all in Stendhal and Baudelaire. He was no mere provincial *bon élève*: the real issue, as he put it in the journal, was stylization rather than style. (p. 157)

Granted that Pavese actually succeeded in generating situations by the pure agency of style, how did this work in practice? What distinguishes him from, say, Silone, who uses the familiar loose narrative form he inherited from the historical novelists, or from Moravia, who writes an efficient prose, well suited to conveying ideas and large general images but too flat to challenge Pavese on his own ground. The first thing to remark is a basic turn of mind in which something is invoked, summoned to life, and then abruptly dismissed, often in one paragraph—a sort of *ave atque vale* trope. It lies at the bottom of a series of studied withdrawals and strategic leave-takings in his plots; it lies behind Pavese's clearly elegiac feeling for the very act of writing fiction. It suggests occasions for the highest, most moving pathos as well as the humbler "pathos of small circumstances" in Joyce's manner. (pp. 157-58)

R. W. Flint, "Translating Cesare Pavese," in Delos (copyright © 1968, by Delos), No. 1, 1968, pp. 152-64.

DONALD HEINEY   (essay date 1968)

[Pavese's] work is extremely diverse in style and genre, but certain consistent themes are evident in it from the beginning. The first of these is the contrast between the natural and the civilized, the rejection of *città* and the search for *paese*. In his own mind this took the form of a recovery of something lost, a search for his own origins comparable to Proust's search for lost time. (pp. 85-6)

America and American literature were mixed up with this idea of *paese* in a complicated way. . . . [Especially] in Melville and Anderson, he discovered another America,

"pensive and barbaric, blissful yet quarrelsome, dissolute, fecund; burdened with all the past of the world, yet youthful, innocent," an American that was *paese* not only for those who sprang from its soil but for all those who participated in the common experience of its literature. The American influence on Pavese's style, while important, has been overemphasized. But it is impossible to overemphasize the part this myth of America as primitive and elemental played in his inward development, his personal formation as an author. (p. 86)

Pavese's characters frequently—it can almost be said invariably—begin by evading a responsibility or running away from something, and then, after a certain period of exile, seeking a reconciliation which is sometimes successful and sometimes not. . . . [In his fiction and poetry the concept of escape is expressed in a number of recurring images. The first escape is to the city.] The sea too is escape; as elements of geographical symbolism the river and the Piedmontese hills are native, the sea foreign. The urban diversions—alcohol, easy sex, music, fashionable chatter, fast automobiles—are always connected in his fiction with evading genuine responsibilities. Work, including writing, is a form of commitment, but reading in the sense of "losing one's self in books" may be an escape, especially in wartime or in other times of crisis. The final evasion is suicide, the "absurd vice" that was Pavese's lifelong temptation and makes its way as a kind of subterranean motif through his work. Very few people die naturally in Pavese's fiction. For his characters death is less a result of disease or common human mortality than a conscious renegation, a failure to belong to life or find a place in it.

In spite of this constant search for the elemental and instinctive Pavese is a highly intellectual writer. Or, more precisely, he is that kind of a writer—like Lawrence and Rilke—who seeks out the elemental and primitive precisely because he is conscious of an over-intellectual tendency in his own personality. (pp. 87-8)

Pavese's effort to define himself as a writer can be expressed in a simple formula: from narrative poetry to poetic narrative. The early part of his career—roughly that to 1935—was devoted to the development of a poetry free from conventional metrics and expressed in a vernacular rhythm and diction: the poems of *Lavorare stanca*. . . . After the writing of his first novel in 1938-39 he returned to verse only sporadically, and always on occasion of involvements with women; Italo Calvino has pointed out that all the poems after the first volume in 1936 are *to* women. In Pavese's fiction, on the other hand, women are customarily regarded by the protagonist as enemies. (pp. 88-9)

[The early poems] relate in an important way to his fiction and are in fact the predecessors of the novels. Of these the most typical and probably the finest is the narrative poem "I mari del Sud" ["The South Seas"] which opens *Lavorare stanca*. All of Pavese is contained here in miniature: the theme is that of *paese* and wider world, the style anticipates the novels. . . . [It reflects the poetic he was in the process of constructing:] a precise and economic terseness with something of the quality of the native vernacular. This effort to combine vernacular and *lingua pura* continues throughout Pavese's work. . . . The essence of it is the effort to incorporate, not only the pattern and flow of common speech, but the mentality of the rural vernacular speaker—an intimacy with the earth, a sensitivity devoid of self-pity, a strain of sarcasm—into the framework of conventional Italian. (pp. 90-1)

From beginning to end his work is self-consistent and seems to be groping its way, book by book, toward the expression of a single rather complex statement. It is what used to be called an *oeuvre*, a career that in itself can be regarded as a single literary work visible through a long course of development. There are mistakes and wrong turnings in this development, but no actual dead ends. . . . Pavese's mistakes are in the main stream of his work, and they are never total mistakes; he always manages to salvage something and convert it to at least a partial success in a later novel. He did this with the somewhat contrived use of country mythology in *Paesi tuoi* and the treatment of rural aristocrats in stories like "Primo amore," for example; both were rewritten and improved later in *La luna e i falò*. There is only one narrator in the main body of Pavese's fiction, and he is essentially an autobiographical narrator. More precisely, since not all of Pavese's fiction is in the first person, this "narrator" is simply a consistent and identifiable consciousness through which the action of all of his fiction is seen. . . . In two curious cases (*La bella estate* and *Tra donne sole*) the autobiographical identity is switched in sex and becomes that of a woman. But it is still a consciousness that, transcending social class and even sex, remains fundamentally that of Pavese himself. It is a consciousness, for example, preoccupied with certain chronic problems: isolation vs commitment, work and the temptations that distract from work, the problem of transcending crude sex to arrive at some kind of genuine union of the spirit. It is even possible to trace a consistent imagery through Pavese's work: hills, crickets, sea, nudity, sun, moon, America, harvest, earth, perform the same symbolic or imagistic functions from his earliest published poems to his last novel. And yet in another sense he never repeated himself; each time he began a new work he struggled for a new framework, a new expression for his basic statement. . . . [The search for spontaneity] was a large part of his personal technical problem. The difficulty with his earlier fiction, particularly *Il carcere* and certain stories, is that on the one hand it follows the autobiographical experience too closely and on the other hand its thematics and symbolism are too contrived, too overtly literary. The difficult task of surmounting this synthetic method, of forgetting at least on the surface the sophistication he had gained as university student of letters, he accomplished fairly successfully before the end of his career. (pp. 92-3)

Il carcere is a novel with many technical faults or unresolved difficulties. The first of these is insufficient conversion of the autobiographical experience. (p. 96)

The recurring technical problem of Pavese's whole career, in fact, was that of combining a genuine personal commitment to his material with the objectivity of a finished work of art, and he was never successful at this except when he used one specific point of view: the first-person narrator who is basically a spectator but in another sense involved in or committed to the action. This is the method of *Paesi tuoi* and *La luna e i falò*, his two most successful novels, as well as some interesting half-successes like *Il compagno*. His attempts to experiment with other techniques always resulted in at least a partial failure of empathy. In *Il carcere* it is all "he" and "him" and it seems to be happening to somebody else, somebody neither the author nor the reader knows very well.

There are other difficulties: there are too many characters (again probably because Pavese was following his autobiographical experiences too closely) and they are not well enough defined, the necessary details of Stefano's previous life in Turin are lacking, the plot seems to be moving toward some resolution or statement and never gets there. (pp. 97-8)

[The key image of the novel is the word *carcere*, or prison. The family is a prison because] one is limited by it, is left unfulfilled and lonely in the midst of domesticity. Thus the family is only a microcosm of the world, and the world itself becomes a prison. This is the *carcere* of the title: not the cell of Regina Coeli, not the rented room by the railroad tracks, but the very immensity of a world in which the individual feels himself in some elusive and intangible way an exile, longing to establish contact with other men yet cut off from them by mysterious and invisible walls. And paradoxically it is this very sense of being cut off from others that leads Stefano to a realization of the kinship of all men, a kinship that subsists precisely in their common isolation. (pp. 99-100)

[*Paese tuoi; The Harvesters*] is different from anything in Pavese's earlier fiction. It is narrated in the first person, and yet the narrator is neither a directly autobiographical character nor a central figure in the events he relates. Instead he is that semi-involved spectator that Pavese had been working toward for some time, a spectator who is a projection of the author's consciousness and yet is a character apart from him. The empathy of the reader is broken into two parts. In one part of his mind he associates himself with the narrator, as the author does himself. But this narrator is empathetically involved with the central character whose story he is telling, sharing to a certain degree the emotions and inward reactions of this character. Thus that part of the reader's empathy not fixed on the narrator passes on to the central character, even though he is seen only at second hand through the consciousness of the narrator. The part played by this narrator is essentially the function performed by Marlow in *Heart of Darkness* and *Lord Jim*. . . . (p. 101)

[*La bella estate; The Beautiful Summer* and *Tra donne sole; Among Women Only* share a number of technical characteristics. The settings in both cases are urban.] The themes are similar, involving in some way the problems of self in relation to others, work vs love, producing and consuming. And, most important, both stories are told from the viewpoint of a female character. . . . Since a novel centering in a single consciousness can succeed only if the author identifies to a certain extent with his character, there is a certain inherent handicap in switching sexes in this way. . . . Women always remain objects rather than subjects for [Pavese]; he never succeeds in transcending his own sexuality to the point of understanding and regarding them as they understand and regard themselves.

Considering this, it is curious that he should have attempted these two novels related from the feminine viewpoint and concerned very largely with erotic relations. (pp. 109-10)

[The central character of *La Bella Estate* is Ginia. The root of the trouble in the novel] is not Ginia's weakness of character, although this is a factor. The real difficulty is that Ginia's weakness of character, her deficient culture, her sex, and a number of other qualities make her so different from the author that the result is a failure of commitment, of empathy between author and character, and the characterization is only partly convincing. To a degree the point of view is a technical tour de force, but the difficulty is that is remains only that. . . . In many ways it is smoother in its storytelling than either *Il carcere* or *Paese tuoi,* but never again was Pavese to confine himself to a narrative consciousness so limited and so different from his own. (p. 113)

Tra donne sole is narrated in the first person by a character with a good deal more sophistication and maturity [than Ginia], in short with a culture approaching Pavese's own. Yet the world of Turin *haute couture* is the same, a little more elegant and genuine perhaps, and seen a little more from the inside, and [the central character Clelia] . . . is really only Ginia in a later stage of development. The basic conflict [as in *La belle estate*] is still that of producing vs consuming, or useful work opposed to self-indulgence. (p. 114)

[But the fashionable society plot of *Tradonne sole* is much more complicated than the plot of *Paesi tuoi.*] Pavese portrays the aimless and decadent brilliance of the salon world with a certain skill, even though the reader is left the feeling that it is not quite his material. The technique is kaleidoscopic: the action shifts from character to character, place to place, with a kind of jerky impulsiveness. (pp. 116-17)

The difficulties of *Tra donne sole* are the complexity of the plot, which seems cluttered in so short a novel, and the characterization of Clelia. The device of the semi-involved spectator, relatively successful in *Paesi tuoi,* is somewhat less successful here. The difficulty is that the reader senses that Clelia's voice is actually Pavese's, that her personality is really only a kind of synthetic platform from which the author himself views his story. Her manner of reacting in the play of egos among persons is basically masculine. . . . Even if we concede that such personalities might have existed in the Turin salon world of 1949, or in other milieux where women are required to play a semimasculine role, the characterization stops short of verisimilitude; we cannot believe in, or at least cannot understand, the mental processes of such a person in such a time and place. She is really only the author clumsily disguised, and this leads to a kind of sex-switched *roman à clef* in which the protagonist is neither Pavese nor a real woman. The experiment was a particularly unfelicitous one for an author whose understanding of women was so subjective and so emotional. (p. 118)

[Taken] simply as an exercise in construction and technique [*La spiaggia; The Beach*] represents a considerable step beyond the three novels that preceded it. It is the first treatment of the theme of producing vs consuming that dominates *Tra donne sole,* and it forms an obvious bridge between his early "naturalism" and his later symbolistic style. Pavese was right in considering it his least characteristic novel in its ambience or narrative texture. But this is not the real source of its difficulties. Instead these are chiefly structural, the result of embarking into a far greater technical complexity than Pavese had attempted before. . . . The problem of point of view, one that preoccupied Pavese throughout his career, was fundamental to the nature of his work and his own relation to it. How can the novel be a personal expression and yet objective—simultaneously intimate and detached? [He solved this problem in *La spaggia* when he adopted the narrative framework he

was to use in all his subsequent works, that of male narrator who is partly involved in the plot and partly a detached spectator.] (p. 119)

[*La spiaggia* introduces the theme of responsibility to Pavese's work.] Once the emergence of the theme of responsibility has been noted in Pavese's work, it becomes apparent that the chief quality of the characters in *Il diavolo sulle colline* is their irresponsibility. The narrator and his friends Oreste and Pieretto are ostensibly university students but do very little studying; they spend most of their time roaming the Turin streets and the hills around the city at night. On one of these nocturnal expeditions they meet Poli, a wealthy and somewhat spoiled young man a little older than they are. At first they are a little sarcastic about his "advantages"—an expensive automobile, mistresses, liquor, drugs. But after a while they realize he is behaving about as they would if they had his money—what else, they ask themselves with a kind of sophomoric profundity, is there? For a good part of the novel they serve as somewhat ironic disciples of Poli's epicureanism. (pp. 124-25)

[The] ending is moving and succinct. The whole characterization of Poli—his sham philosophizing, his spasmodic generosity, his triste experiments in vice—is the best part of the novel. And yet the work in its totality is only partly successful, probably less successful than *La spiaggia* of which it was in a certain sense a rewriting. Part of the difficulty is that Pavese is not really comfortable in this milieu of the idle rich he attempted to deal with in both *La spiaggia* and *Il diavolo sulle colline.* (p. 127)

And a final difficulty with *Il diavolo sulle colline,* the reason why it seems even more fragmented and diffuse than *La spiaggia,* is that Pavese here tries to deal with three basic elements of conflict rather than two: the artificiality of city life, the "bestiality" of nature, and the refined vice represented by Poli. This complexity of conflict leads to a profusion of scenes, half-developed characters, images and suggestions that at first seem important and are then abandoned. . . . Pavese is not the kind of a writer who can juggle a great many characters, scenes, ideas, and settings at the same time. His best novels follow a single and graceful line that conceals, under the simplicity of its curve, an inner complexity. (p. 128)

[*La luna e i falò; The Moon and the Bonfires*] is the most finished and structurally symmetrical of his novels. A number of technical problems that had plagued him throughout his career were finally resolved. The first of these was point of view, or more precisely the psychological and linguistic relation of the narrator to the story he is telling. Like the earlier *Paesi tuoi, La luna e i falò* is told in vernacular language by a narrator who—at least on the surface—is only semi-involved in the story he relates. Because both narrators are of uncultured origin they speak naturally and simply, without literary affection. Thus Pavese in these two novels was able to achieve the vernacular or pseudo-regional language he had always sought for from the time of his earliest poetry, a style impossible in novels like *Il diavolo sulle colline* where the narrator is a person roughly of the writer's own cultural background. But *La luna e i falò* has an advantage in this respect over *Paesi tuoi.* The Berto of the earlier novel begins and ends as a Turin mechanic; his culture is insufficient to provide the proper language for the events he is relating, especially in their mythic or symbolic aspects, and Pavese himself was conscious of this difficulty. The unnamed narrator of *La luna e i falò* has grown up in a primitive Piedmontese village; his initial culture is even less adequate than Berto's. But he spends the middle part of his life wandering over the world, to Genoa and then to America, talking to many different people and working at many different jobs. With this relative sophistication he then comes back to the village and views it, in a sense, as a stranger, an American. (p. 136)

The most significant success of this novel, however, is the skill with which the symbolic or mythopoeic element is incorporated in an ostensibly realistic action. This was the most difficult of Pavese's problems, and the primary reason at least for the partial failure of both *Paesi tuoi* and *Il diavolo sulle colline*. And yet in its creation of a complex system of nature images *La luna e i falò* goes far beyond the earlier novels that had experimented tentatively with the technique. The images of crickets, moon, vines, bonfires, blood, hills, play a part in *Paesi tuoi* as they do in all of Pavese's fiction involving a country setting. The unlettered Berto of *Paesi tuoi* is aware of the power of these things, but the language he uses to express it is necessarily too subtle, too literary, to be wholly convincing. In certain other novels the problem is the opposite. The relatively sophisticated narrators of *La casa in collina*, *Il diavolo sulle colline*, and to a certain extent *La spiaggia* are capable of expressing the symbolism but not of believing in it in any mythic sense; the whole trend of their background and education inclines them to skepticism. In this regard the narrator of *La luna e i falò* is in a uniquely advantageous position. Within the framework of the novel it is necessary for both narrator and reader to accept certain premises: that the moon has an influence on crops, that bonfires "wake up the earth," that there is a mysterious connection between the body of woman and the body of the land. The narrator did believe in these things as a boy. . . . But under the influence of his friend Nuto, and under the very influence of the land, the moon, and the crops themselves, he comes to believe, or more precisely to return to his childhood belief; and in this gradual acceptance of belief the reader accompanies him. In this process Nuto, in his arguments with the narrator, serves not only as a kind of shaman but as a spokesman of rural folklore. . . . In the earlier novels, especially in *Paesi tuoi*, this whole structure of symbolism is simply imposed as a *fait accompli;* here Nuto as raisonneur introduces and justifies it step by step. The reader, if he accepts the apparatus of the novel at all, thus undergoes a process of conversion parallel to the conversion of the narrator. . . . It is obvious that this mechanism would be impossible without the complex point-of-view or psychological standpoint from which the narrator views the action. (pp. 138-39)

In his last novel Pavese finally achieved the simple and powerful narrative, the narrative unaffected and even naive in style and yet rich in unspoken implications, that he had worked toward for a lifetime. The final proof of this must, in the end, be a subjective one. The proof is that, as the reader loses himself in *La luna e i falò*, the sensations and reactions of this narrator who has no name and only a rudimentary education become his own sensations and reactions; that the reader, in short, forgets he is reading a novel

and directly shares the emotions of the storytelling voice. (p. 146)

Donald Heiney, "Cesare Pavese," in his Three Italian Novelists: Moravia, Pavese, Vittorini (copyright © by The University of Michigan 1968), University of Michigan Press, 1968, pp. 85-146.

BIBLIOGRAPHY

Biasin, Gian-Paolo. *The Smile of The Gods: A Thematic Study of Cesare Pavese's Works*. Translated by Yvonne Freccero. Ithaca, NY: Cornell University Press, 1968, 337 p.
   Identifies the inability to communicate as the central theme of Pavese's work and life.

Chase, Richard H. "Cesare Pavese and the American Novel." In *Studi Americani, Vol. 3*, edited by Agostino Lombardo, pp. 347-69. Rome: Edizioni di Storia e Letteratura, 1957.
   A detailed examination of the influence of American writers on Pavese, paying particular attention to his use of the techniques of Melville, Stein, and Anderson.

Flint, R. W. Introduction to *The Selected Works of Cesare Pavese*, by Cesare Pavese, translated by R. W. Flint, pp. v-xx. New York: Farrar, Straus, and Giroux, 1968.
   An introduction to Pavese's life and works.

Foster, David William. "The Poetic Vision of 'Le colline': An Introduction to Pavese's *Lavorare stanca*." *Italica* XLII, No. 1 (March 1965): 380-90.
   A discussion of Pavese's imagery and related poetic techniques.

Freccero, John. "Mythos and Logos: *The Moon and the Bonfires*." *Italian Quarterly* 4, No. 16 (Winter 1961): 3-16.
   A discussion of Pavese's concern with the cyclical nature of life in *The Moon and the Bonfires*.

Hood, Stuart. "A Protestant without God: On Cesare Pavese." *Encounter* XXVI, No. 5 (May 1966): 41-8.
   A discussion of the determinist nature of Pavese's vision of life.

Hutcheon, Linda. "Pavese's Intellectual Rhythm." *Italian Quarterly* 15-16, Nos. 60-1 (Spring-Summer 1972): 5-26.
   Sees Pavese as unconcerned with creating autonomous characters and instead creating mythic characters who draw their significance from their roles, not from any individual life they may possess.

King, Martha. "Silence, an Element of Style in Pavese." *MLN* 87, No. 1 (1972): 60-77.
   Pavese's use of silence in his narratives as an ironic expression of the incapability of language to relate experience.

Milano, Paolo. "Pavese's Experiments in the Novel." *The New Republic* 128, No. 18 (4 May 1953): 17, 23.
   A review of *The Moon and the Bonfires* which also includes a brief survey of Pavese's career.

Norton, Peter M. "Cesar Pavese and the American Nightmare." *MLN* 77, No. 1 (1964): 24-36.
   A study of the mythic elements of American culture as developed by Pavese in *The Moon and the Bonfires*.

Rimanelli, Giose. "Myth and De-mythification of Pavese's Art." *Italian Quarterly* 13, No. 49 (Summer 1969): 3-39.
   Explains why Pavese cannot be considered a neo-realist or an existentialist.

Dorothy (Miller) Richardson

1873-1957

English novelist, essayist, critic, translator, and short story writer.

Richardson was one of the principal authors of the twentieth century to conceive and practice the stream of consciousness technique. In fact, May Sinclair's 1915 review of Richardson's *Pointed Roofs* marked the first time that the philosophical concept of stream of consciousness was used to describe the style of a literary work.

Significant to Richardson's development as an author was the period that she lived in Bloomsbury and entered its artistic and intellectual society. Among her peers was H. G. Wells, with whom Richardson carried on one of the most important relationships of her life. Richardson used Wells as the model for the character Hypo G. Wilson in *Pilgrimage*.

In the twelve volumes of *Pilgrimage*, which she intended to be read as "chapters" of a single novel, Richardson explores the impressions of a single mind: that of her alter-ego, Miriam Henderson. Richardson's intention was to find, as she stated, "a feminine equivalent of the current masculine realism." Her method was to chart what she considered the transcendent insights and perceptions specific to a feminine consciousness. To achieve this she rejected earlier novelistic conventions and techniques for in her view they portrayed human experience in an artificial way. She attributed this artificiality to the analytical, exclusively masculine philosophical temper that she perceived in novelists of the past. These novelists, emphasizing plot causality, attempted to impose a structure upon life, while Richardson considered life a random series of events in continual flux.

Critics note that Richardson's concerns are clearly philosophical, her novels, for example, exhibiting her familiarity with Henri Bergson's ideas on the individual's perception of time.

Pilgrimage is significant as one of the earliest and most exhaustive demonstrations of stream of consciousness, a term Richardson herself said was "isolated by its perfect imbecility." Her work, however, has been overshadowed by that of her contemporaries Joyce, Woolf, and Proust, whose novels reveal similar techniques but offer greater stylistic and thematic interest. Current interest in Richardson focuses not on her technique, now commonplace in fiction, but on her illumination of feminine consciousness.

PRINCIPAL WORKS

The Quakers Past and Present (history) 1914
Pointed Roofs (novel) 1915
Backwater (novel) 1916
Honeycomb (novel) 1917
Interim (novel) 1919
The Tunnel (novel) 1919
Deadlock (novel) 1921
Revolving Lights (novel) 1923
The Trap (novel) 1925
Oberland (novel) 1927
Dawn's Left Hand (novel) 1931
Clear Horizon (novel) 1935
Pilgrimage (twelve-novel series, includes *Dimple Hill*) 1938
Pilgrimage (thirteen-novel series, includes unfinished novel *March Moonlight*) 1967

H. G. WELLS (essay date 1917)

[Miss Dorothy Richardson] has probably carried impressionism in fiction to its furthest limit. I do not know whether she will ever make large captures of the general reader, but she is certainly a very interesting figure for the critic and the amateur of fiction. In *Pointed Roofs* and *Honeycomb*, for example, her story is a series of dabs of intense superficial impression; her heroine is not a mentality, but a mirror. She goes about over her facts like those insects that run over water sustained by surface tension. Her percepts never become concepts. Writing as I do at the extremest distance possible from such work, I confess I find it altogether too much—or shall I say altogether too little?—for me. (p. xi)

> *H. G. Wells, in his introduction to* Nocturne *by Frank Swinnerton (copyright, 1917, by George H. Doran Company), George H. Doran, 1917, pp. vii-xiv.**

MAY SINCLAIR (essay date 1918)

By imposing very strict limitations on herself [Dorothy Richardson] has brought her art, her method, to a high pitch of perfection, so that her form seems to be newer than it perhaps is. She herself is unaware of the perfection of her method. She would probably deny that she has written with any deliberate method at all. She would say: "I only know there are certain things I mustn't do if I was to do what I wanted." Obviously, she must not interfere; she must not analyse or comment or explain. Rather less obviously, she must not tell a story, or handle a situation or set a scene; she must avoid drama as she avoids narration. And there are some things she must not be. She must not be the wise, all-knowing author. She must be Miriam Henderson: She must not know or divine anything that Miriam does not know or divine; she must not see anything that Miriam does not see. She has taken Miriam's nature upon her. She is not concerned, in the way that other novelists are concerned, with character. Of the persons who move through Miriam's world you know nothing but what Miriam knows. If Miriam is mistaken, well, she and not Miss Richardson is mistaken. Miriam is an acute observer, but she is very far from seeing the whole of these people. They are presented to us in the same vivid but fragmentary way in which they appeared to Miriam, the fragmentary way in which people appear to most of us. Miss Richardson has only imposed on herself the conditions that life imposes on all of us. (p. 5)

To me [*Pointed Roofs, Backwater,* and *Honeycomb*] show an art and method and form carried to punctilious perfection. Yet I have heard other novelists say that they have no art and no method and no form, and that it is this formlessness that annoys them. They say that they have no beginning and no middle and no end, and that to have form a novel must have an end and a beginning and a middle.... There is a certain plausibility in what they say, but it depends on what constitutes a beginning and a middle and an end. In this series there is no drama, no situation, no set scene. Nothing happens. It is just life going on and on. It is Miriam Henderson's stream of consciousness going on and on. And in neither is there any grossly discernible beginning or middle or end.

In identifying herself with this life which is Miriam's stream of consciousness Miss Richardson produces her effect of being the first, of getting closer to reality than any of our novelists who are trying so desperately to get close. No attitude or gesture of her own is allowed to come between her and her effect. Whatever her sources and her raw material, she is concerned and we ought to be concerned solely with the finished result, the work of art. It is to Miriam's almost painfully acute senses that we owe what in any other novelist would be called the "portraits" of [various characters].... The mere "word painting" is masterly. (pp. 5-6)

You look at the outer world through Miriam's senses and it is as if you had never seen it so vividly before. (p. 6)

It is as if no other writers had ever used their senses so purely and with so intense a joy in their use.

This intensity is the effect of an extreme concentration on the thing seen or felt. Miss Richardson disdains every stroke that does not tell. Her novels are novels of an extraordinary compression and of an extenuation more extraordinary still. The moments of Miriam's consciousness pass one by one, or overlapping, moments tense with vibration, moments drawn out fine, almost to snapping point. On one page Miss Richardson seems to be accounting for every minute of Miriam's time. On another she passes over events that might be considered decisive with the merest

slur of reference. She is not concerned with the strict order of events in time.... It is Miriam's consciousness that is going backwards and forwards in time. The time it goes in is unimportant. (pp. 7-8)

At the end of the third volume, *Honeycomb,* there is, apparently, a break with the design. Something does happen. Something tragic and terrible. We are not told what it is; we know as Miriam knows, only by inference. (p. 8)

Here Miss Richardson "gets" you as she gets you all the time—she never misses once—by her devout adhesion to her method, by the sheer depth of her plunge. For this and this alone is the way things happen. What we used to call the "objective" method is a method of after-thought, of spectacular reflection.... The firsthand, intimate and intense reality of the happening is in Miriam's mind, and by presenting it thus and not otherwise Miss Richardson seizes reality alive. The intense rapidity of the seizure defies you to distinguish between what is objective and what is subjective either in the reality presented or the art that presents.

Nothing happens. In Miriam Henderson's life there is, apparently, nothing to justify living. Everything she ever wanted was either withheld or taken from her. She is reduced to the barest minimum on which it is possible to support the life of the senses and the emotions at all. And yet Miriam is happy. Her inexhaustible passion for life is fed. Nothing happens, and yet everything that really matters is happening; you are held breathless with the anticipation of its happening. What really matters is a state of mind, the interest or the ecstasy with which we close with life. It can't be explained. (p. 9)

May Sinclair, "The Novels of Dorothy Richardson," in The Little Review *(copyright, 1918, by Margaret Anderson), Vol. IV, No. 12, April, 1918, pp. 3-11.*

RANDOLPH BOURNE (essay date 1918)

The sweetish-sour style and the strange, sensitive representations of a young English girl's impressions of her life are an acquired taste. "Pointed Roofs," with its flickering scenes of the German school where the girl goes as governess, was too insubstantial to stir the mind. "Backwater" might even have repelled you with its close sultry prison of the home to which she returns. But "Honeycomb" suddenly clarifies what the author is trying to do. Her idiom suddenly seems familiar, and the novel slant at which she looks on life captures your imagination as a genuine artistic creation, and not as that trick which it might have seemed.

The particular idiom and vision of [Dorothy Richardson] are the same as those of the makers of imagist-verse. Miriam, the girl, sees the world as a stream of sensed pictures, in hard clear outlines, where the form is more significant than the content.... People, house, and furnishings dissolve together and then flow back to her in intense forms and colors, exciting or depressing the reflections of her brain. The story is of her quick impressions and the racing stream of her inner thoughts, her puzzles and desires. Her contact with people, with social forms, with everything around her are contacts with something alive, hurting her, doing something to her. It is not the objective facts that make up her life, but these intensely felt pictures of what goes on around her, and her own wondering mind, jumping from idea to idea as, restless and rebellious, it tries to burrow its way out of its squirrel-cage into reality. Nothing could be more uncannily real than these quick chains of thought which run through Miriam's mind. Once you have acclimated yourself, you find in this flow between sensed outer picture and inner reflection the very quality of experience, caught with a precision that makes you marvel. (p. 451)

"Honeycomb" is not verse masquerading as a novel. It is an honest narrative, searching, living—fantastic only to those who cannot feel these very modern ways of looking at the world. The author has simply had the audacity to tell her story of this sensitive girl, neither child nor woman, from the attitude and with the values that those gifted young poets feel who have made us recognize in their naïve, cool vision of beauty, and in their sense of flowing life, new vistas of our own. And she has had the genius to make out of her few materials a book of beauty and truth. . . . This writer knows the cruelty of life as well as the high, clear, clean, fresh, fair things, for which her Miriam has so intense a love. I wonder if so completely feminine a novel as "Pilgrimage" has ever been written. (p. 452)

> Randolph Bourne, "The Imagist Novel," in The Dial (copyright, 1918, by The Dial Publishing Company, Inc.), Vol. LXIV, No. 766, May 9, 1918, pp. 451-52.

[VIRGINIA WOOLF] (essay date 1919)

[Miss Richardson's] is a method that demands attention, as a door whose handle we wrench ineffectively calls our attention to the fact that it is locked. There is no slipping smoothly down the accustomed channels. . . . If this were the result of perversity, we should think Miss Richardson more courageous than wise; but being, as we believe, not wilful but natural, it represents a genuine conviction of the discrepancy between what she has to say and the form provided by tradition for her to say it in. She is one of the rare novelists who believe that the novel is so much alive that it actually grows. . . . ["Him] and her" are cut out, and with them goes the old deliberate business: the chapters that lead up and the chapters that lead down; the characters who are always characteristic; the scenes that are passionate and the scenes that are humorous; the elaborate construction of reality; the conception that shapes and surrounds the whole. All these things are cast away, and there is left, denuded, unsheltered, unbegun and unfinished, the consciousness of Miriam Henderson, the small sensitive lump of matter, half transparent and half opaque, which endlessly reflects and distorts the variegated procession, and is, we are bidden to believe, the source beneath the surface, the very oyster within the shell. The critic is thus absolved from the necessity of picking out the themes of the story. The reader is not provided with a story; he is invited to embed himself in Miriam Henderson's consciousness. . . . The method, if triumphant, should make us feel ourselves seated at the centre of another mind, and, according to the artistic gift of the writer, we should perceive in the helter-skelter of flying fragments some unity, significance, or design. That Miss Richardson gets so far as to achieve a sense of reality far greater than that produced by the ordinary means is undoubted. But, then, which reality is it, the superficial or the profound? We have to consider the quality of Miriam Henderson's consciousness, and the extent to which Miss Richardson is able to reveal it. We

have to decide whether the flying helter-skelter resolves itself by degrees into a perceptible whole. When we are in a position to make up our minds we cannot deny a slight sense of disappointment. Having sacrificed not merely "hims and hers," but so many seductive graces of wit and style for the prospect of some new revelation or greater intensity, we still find ourselves distressingly near the surface. Things look much the same as ever. It is certainly a very vivid surface. . . . [Miriam's] senses of touch, sight and hearing are all excessively acute. But sensations, impressions, ideas and emotions glance off her, unrelated and unquestioned, without shedding quite as much light as we had hoped into the hidden depths. We find ourselves in the dentist's room, in the street, in the lodging-house bedroom frequently and convincingly; but never, or only for a tantalizing second, in the reality which underlies these appearances. In particular, the figures of other people on whom Miriam casts her capricious light are vivid enough, but their sayings and doings never reach that degree of significance which we, perhaps unreasonably, expect. The old method seems sometimes the more profound and economical of the two. But it must be admitted that we are exacting. We want to be rid of realism, to penetrate without its help into the regions beneath it, and further require that Miss Richardson shall fashion this new material into something which has the shapeliness of the old accepted forms. We are asking too much; but the extent of our asking proves that "The Tunnell" is better in its failure than most books in their success.

> [Virginia Woolf], "New Novels: 'The Tunnel'," in The Times Literary Supplement (© Times Newspapers Ltd. (London) 1919; reproduced from The Times Literary Supplement by permission), No. 891, February 13, 1919, p. 81.

[KATHERINE MANSFIELD] (essay date 1919)

Miss Richardson has a passion for registering every single thing that happens in the clear, shadowless country of her mind. One cannot imagine her appealing to the reader or planning out her novel; her concern is primarily, and perhaps ultimately, with herself. . . . Anything that goes into her mind she can summon forth again, and there it is, complete in every detail, with nothing taken away from it—and nothing added. This is a rare and interesting gift, but we should hesitate before saying it was a great one. (pp. 140-41)

["The Tunnel"] is composed of bits, fragments, flashing glimpses, half scenes and whole scenes, all of them quite distinct and separate, and all of them of equal importance. There is no plot, no beginning, middle or end. Things just "happen" one after another with incredible rapidity and at breakneck speed. There is Miss Richardson, holding out her mind, as it were, and there is Life hurling objects into it as fast as she can throw. And at the appointed time Miss Richardson dives into its recesses and reproduces a certain number of these treasures,—a pair of button boots, a night in Spring, some cycling knickers, some large, round biscuits—as many as she can pack into a book, in fact. But the pace kills.

There is one who could not live in so tempestuous an environment as her mind—and he is Memory. She has no memory. It is true that Life is sometimes very swift and breathless, but not always. If we are to be truly alive there are large pauses in which we creep away into our caves of contemplation. And then it is, in the silence, that Memory mounts his throne and judges all that is in our minds—appointing each his separate place, high or low, rejecting this, selecting that—putting this one to shine in the light and throwing that one into the darkness.

We do not mean to say that those large, round biscuits might not be in the light, or the night in Spring be in the darkness. Only we feel that until these things are judged and given each its appointed place in the whole scheme, they have no meaning in the world of art. (p. 141)

> [*Katherine Mansfield*], *"Three Women Novel-ists," in* The Athenaeum, *No. 4640, April 4, 1919, pp. 140-41.**

LAWRENCE HYDE   (essay date 1924)

[In *Pilgrimage*, Miriam Henderson] meets numbers of people, almost all of whom are of the most ordinary type, and no single one of whom is important enough to modify her life in any violent way, and during the whole time the interest of the record is steadily focussed on her stream of consciousness. The result is a curious production. As to the author everything which happens to her principal character is, for her present purpose of equal importance, the resulting work is a medley of heterogeneous impressions connected together by practically nothing more than the fact that they have all been received by one mind. The succession is that of the episodes in a cinematograph film with a tenuous plot. No preference is apparent for any particular type of experience; the author continues to turn the handle steadily, and everything, whether it be a sensuous impression, a casual conversation, or a complicated philosophical argument, is reproduced with equal fidelity. Not only is there no variety offered by the centre shifting for a time to another personality, there is not even escape possible in the dimension of time. While the thoughts which are in Miriam's head at the moment are set down whether they refer to past, present, or future events, everything which happens *to* her is described as she herself sees the experience at the time ... Nothing is interpreted unless Miriam happens to interpret it herself, perhaps two hundred pages later on.

Further, the reader is denied the satisfaction of contemplating such things as the logical development of a plot, the final harmonizing of initially postulated discords, the slow growth of a character. Naturally, Miriam develops in the course of the two or three years covered by *Pilgrimage,* but the reader's sense of this is obliterated by the emphasis laid by the writer on the impressions received rather than on the person who received them. Again, growth implies synthesis of experience, and throughout the work Miriam receives impressions far faster than she can deal with them. She serves principally as a delicate and efficient receiving instrument, a medium through whom we can look at life so surely and clearly that we forget that she is there between us and the pictures which are presented to us, forget even that the pictures are ostensibly only there because of the effect which they had on *her.* Thus, the real interest of the writer lies in the phenomena of life and not in the reaction to them of her heroine, who is only there to enable the author to envisage different aspects of it conveniently. The insubstantiality of Miriam is further enhanced by the fact that she scarcely ever acts, but only *re*acts. She criticizes, argues, explains as best she can, very occasionally flares

up, but practically never does anything more violent. She is, in fact, a pronounced "introvert." If she did anything more positive than look on, her *raison d'être* would disappear.

This last point may perhaps lead us towards an understanding of the genesis of this curious work. What is Dorothy Richardson trying to do? It should be clear by this time that she is not interested in telling a story, painting a portrait, writing a satire, constructing a drama, or doing any other of the things which she might be expected to in the course of two thousand odd pages. (pp. 510-12)

[For Dorothy Richardson] reality is a particularly evasive thing. To get down to it she must go farther along the path of unflinching description than anyone has done before. It is not enough to discard the "story"; or to content oneself with depicting smaller or larger "slices of life"; or to indulge in uncensored descriptions of people and their circumstances; or to pare away all sentiment and envisage one's characters as the products of the interplay of inescapable biological or economic laws. Life for her lies deeper. Life as she realizes it, in fact, seems to her hardly to have been described at all. It is going on all the time behind people's faces and words and gestures, but the real things are never set down.... (p. 513)

There was only one way to avoid this standardization, conventionalization, of experience, and that was to go back to consciousness and reproduce the flow of experience before the treacherous mind had begun to play upon it and distort it through the formation of these deadening, fixed conceptions. That way one certainly could not tell a story or indulge in architectonics, but at least honesty and immediacy would be preserved. It is a desperate device, this return to consciousness, and has been resorted to in different ways by such individual writers as James Joyce, T. S. Eliot, and Marcel Proust, the first with the resolve to hold nothing back at any cost (a step which the author of *Pilgrimage,* perhaps inconsistently, has abstained from taking; Miriam's reflection on the intimacies of sex, for instance, are completely unrecorded).... All of them have been driven steadily back from the orthodox positions until nothing remains for them but to set down as honestly as they can the activity of the mind with its endless associations, speculations, irrational side-jumps. Anything less immediate is exposed to the danger of becoming distorted, misrepresented, idealized.

But there are many objections to this method, even in the able hands of such a writer as Dorothy Richardson. For one thing, her Miriam is confronted with so many objects which serve to start her mind off on trains of thought which are never picked up again, that the reader, though delighted by the art with which these inner experiences are reproduced, ultimately becomes oppressed by the infinitude of loose ends out of which the whole is woven.... (pp. 513-14)

Miriam (whose attitude towards life one cannot help regarding as substantially representing that of her creator) is handicapped in her efforts to pierce to the significance of the life which surrounds her by a curious limitation, which always just serves to prevent her escape from the mental cell in which one feels her to be a prisoner—she is ... disappointingly negative; when the time comes for her to be positive she fails. Her sensitiveness and self-analysis lead her to the rejection of the fixed conceptions which dominate social life; she sees people all around her pretending in myriads of different ways; they go on doing one thing on the outside while inside they are doing something quite different; they have all sorts of natural movements in them towards freedom and beauty and liberty, but they stifle these back through fear or pride or confusion in their minds. It is amazing, but practically nothing is what it is represented to be; at times life seems simply a nightmare. The obvious deceptions, and a good many not at all obvious, she is able to lay bare, but there are multitudes of others, whose presence is revealed by a continuous succession of tiny signals—shades of expression on people's faces, sudden similarities which are sensed between things widely separated on the surface, unsuspected delicate identifications—which all speak to her for a moment and are then forgotten. (p. 516)

At present one has the impression that Miriam Henderson is somehow unworthy of the clairvoyance which has been bestowed on her. She is separated from life by a fatal coldness; she can love warmly, but her love is intimately bound up with her aesthetic appreciation—at the first touch of ugliness she turns away with a sort of nausea. There is absent in her that passionate driving force which compels the seer, even if his vision be but partial, to live out what he has seen at all costs. And so, instead of having taken the plunge into life, she remains on its periphery; the smells, the tastes, the delicate perceptions, the frenzied questionings continue, but there is never any laceration, any shattering of the outer form for the sake of embodying in life that which has been realized. Without this continual creation of something new through action there remains nothing but everlasting grey, negative criticism; life continues to unroll dark, inexplicable, and almost without hope. (p. 517)

> Lawrence Hyde, "The Work of Dorothy Richardson," in The Adelphi, Vol. II, No. 6, November, 1924, pp. 508-17.

CONRAD AIKEN (essay date 1928)

With *Oberland*, Miss Dorothy Richardson gives us the tenth volume of a serial novel, which is the closest parallel to Proust's masterpiece discoverable in the English language. This is not to say that Miss Richardson has the genius of Proust: nothing of the sort. But she shares many qualities with that great artist; she is as much a pioneer as he was; she has as much, or even more, influenced her own contemporaries, both in her own country and in America; and she is practically the first woman novelist to make an exhaustive serial study of a single female character, and with entire, or almost entire, detachment and honesty. This is a considerable claim to distinction. If one took a roll call of the novelists of the present day who owed a debt in technique and tone to Miss Richardson, it would include some impressive names. Among them would be Mr. Joyce, Mrs. Woolf, Miss Sinclair, Mr. Ford. She is in many respects the first careful or complete practitioner of the so-called stream-of-consciousness novel in English. And she is also still the only English novelist of the moment who has done this and nothing else.

This alone will secure for Miss Richardson, one would suppose, as precise and permanent a place in the history of literature as it is ever possible to predict for a living author. . . . [*Pilgrimage*] is Miriam Henderson's stream of consciousness going on and on . . . [There are readers] who

become bored with this minute recording, this almost seismographic charting, of sensations and moods and appetites and velleities; and again there are others who would be prepared to accept cheerfully enough this method as applied to the mind of a man, but who weary of it as applied to the mind of a woman.

Perhaps this distinction is invidious? Invidious or not, there is a little something to be said for it. For if one takes one's seat in the balcony, say, of such a mind as that of Stephen Dedalus, or even of Leopold Blum, it is obvious enough to any merely *male* reader that the variety of entertainment is going to be strikingly greater and richer and deeper. I am afraid Miss Richardson herself would be annoyed by this suggestion: for one of the curious features of her portrait of Miriam Henderson is her insistence on the superiority of her heroine's mind—on its (precisely) richness and power and depth, as compared (frequently) with the minds of the men whom she meets.

There is something a little pinched and sour and old-maidish in this. One begins pretty soon to resent this attitude of the heroine and to suspect that it is also the author's. It is, of course, a feminist attitude. . . . But it is also an attitude which, rightly or wrongly, the mere male feels to be the natural withering of the spinster. The air of challenge which marks the behavior of such a woman is dictated by a sense of inferiority; it colors her whole thought, her whole approach to the other sex; it urges her insensibly toward a kind of dry intellectual hypertrophy, an intellectualism which is curiously thin and bloodless.

This is a quality which is sometimes annoyingly characteristic of Miriam Henderson. If Miss Richardson has detachedly projected this, then one can only praise her skill in creation; but one feels a sneaking suspicion that the character lies pretty close to home; and all the more, therefore, one begins to resent this provincialism and smallness, just as one resents the rather ridiculous attitude toward America and Americans. And Miss Richardson is distressingly unaware, at times, of her complete failure to sound the real note of the masculine. . . . The whole dark, strange, horrible, fascinating, masculine mind remains an absolutely closed book to her.

This is the greatest single defect in Miss Richardson's series: a defect in the charm of her heroine. One has to forgive or overlook this. And then one is rewarded. For the skill and delicacy with which she evokes minor moods and despairs and happinesses, all the shoes and sealing-wax aspects of life, and the dissection of personal relationships, particularly those between one woman and another, are among the best things of the kind in this century. (pp. 329-31)

> Conrad Aiken, "Dorothy Richardson" (1928), in his Collected Criticism (copyright © 1935, 1939, 1940, 1942, 1951, 1958 by Conrad Aiken; reprinted by permission of Brandt & Brandt Literary Agents, Inc.), Oxford University Press, New York, 1968, pp. 329-31.

J. D. BERESFORD (essay date 1929)

[Miss Dorothy Richardson] is one of those inspired and yet deliberate experimenters who have founded a School. (p. 45)

[She] invented a new method. Many other novelists before

her had told their stories through the consciousness of one of their characters, but Miss Richardson's liaison with the consciousness of Miriam Henderson is so close that we see nothing, hear nothing, feel nothing except through Miriam's senses.

Now as a logical consequence of this—and Miss Richardson is essentially logical in the development of her method—there must be a different record of movement in space and time. The consciousness is not always attentive to its present circumstances. . . . [Often one's] thought may take a leap in space and time and I may for an instant or two be aware of myself in completely different surroundings and in another period of my life. To achieve that effect in a novel Miss Richardson had to invent a new method, and one of her aids to that end was the omission of the copula, whether a word, an explanatory sentence, or a movement in her story. In the series of books . . . dealing with the experiences of Miriam Henderson, the personality of Miss Richardson, the writer, is entirely absorbed into that of Miss Richardson the experiencer. She cannot, therefore, come out and join up her account of incidents or emotions as all other novelists do by a few words or lines of condensed explanation; for to do that would be momentarily to forsake the consciousness of Miriam Henderson. Thus whereas the orthodox novelist would explain that his heroine left the house, went out by the garden gate, walked across two or three fields and entered the wood; Miss Richardson either skips all account of the transition, or if some emotion experienced in the transit be necessary to her unfolding of Miriam, we suffer it subjectively. (pp. 45-6)

[Miss Richardson's technique in her novels is certainly a] most daring and far-reaching experiment. . . . We may find some precedent for it in the work of Marcel Proust . . . [and] another just recognizably similar experiment in James Joyce's *Ulysses*. But Miss Richardson's work is, nevertheless, unique in fiction . . . and has a metaphysical value that is absent in Proust or Joyce.

For neither of these writers is inspired by the mystical quality that is peculiar to Miss Richardson. Joyce and Proust are objective in their methods more often than not. We are constantly aware of the person of the recorder as opposed to that of the experiencer. Dorothy Richardson has assumed the existence of a soul to which the consciousness has much the same relation that the intelligence has to the consciousness. In *Pointed Roofs* . . . and in all the subsequent volumes, the ebb and flow of Miriam's consciousness, touched now and again to vivid response, at other times somewhat drearily aware of the limitations of physical experience, is the sole agent of the author's expression. (pp. 46-7)

The great moments of Miriam's experience are not found in moving adventure nor in moments of physical stress, but at those times when she is most keenly aware of herself in relation to the spirit that moves beneath and animates every phenomenon of the great phantasmagoria we know as life and matter. I am willing to maintain that the realistic method can go no farther than this, for reality is not a term that we can define, and the view of it differs with every individual. If, therefore, we wish to present an aspect of reality, we can do it consistently only by assuming its presentation through the consciousness of a single individual. (pp. 47-8)

> *J. D. Beresford, "Experiment in the Novel" (orig-*

inally a lecture delivered at City Literary Institute, London, 1929), in Tradition and Experiment in Present-Day Literature *(reprinted by permission of Oxford University Press), Oxford University Press, London, 1929, pp. 23-63.**

JOHN COWPER POWYS (essay date 1931)

In attempting to estimate [Dorothy Richardson's] work we must . . . ask what rivals does Miriam Henderson, the heroine of these nine books, find already existing in world literature? What has been already achieved by the human race along these lines? Miriam, simply considered as an interesting human soul, is quite the equal of the hero of Proust's work and a good deal superior to the hero of Rolland's *Jean Christophe*. To find her superiors in intellectual interest one is compelled to turn to such world-famous figures as Hamlet and Faust. But even Hamlet and Faust do not fill the spiritual gap, do not supply the sub-conscious material, claimed, as her right, by Miss Richardson's young woman. Why not? Because both of these are essentially projections of the *male* quest for the essence of human experience; and Miriam is a projection of the *female* quest for this essence. (pp. 5-6)

Dorothy Richardson is our first pioneer in a completely new direction. What she has done has never been done before. She has drawn her inspiration neither from man-imitating cleverness nor from narcissistic feminine charm but *from the abyss of the feminine subconscious*. (p. 8)

Without a hard, cold, clear, analytical core of the most ferocious masculine reason existing at the heart of her being, Dorothy Richardson herself would never have been able to articulate these things. All authentic human genius is, in some degree, bi-sexual; and it is only because she is the first *consciously to turn the two elements upon each other* in a reciprocal fury of psychological interpretation that her achievement is so startling, so important and so new. All the way through this extraordinary book the abysmal difference between the soul of a man and the soul of a woman is emphasized and enlarged upon. Upon this "tragic tension" . . . depends the whole method of Dorothy Richardson's art. (pp. 8-9)

But how far is this stupendous achievement of Dorothy Richardson's unique at the present hour?

It *is* almost unique. It *is* almost alone. And that is why it is so extremely difficult to do full justice to what she is about. . . . [In reading *Pilgrimage*, we] must cease to look for "charm and cleverness," and learn to look for something rich and strange, for something that has always been there and yet has never been given utterance.

But although Dorothy Richardson is alone in articulating the secret acceptance of life in this peculiarly feminine way-of-life as something that underlies both pain and pleasure, and returns upon the memory, when the pain is over, as sweet dregs to a bitter draught, one must remember that all the most interesting writers of fiction in our time, while aiming at some sort of rational synthesis, pick up on the shore of their effort much irrational flotsam. The difference is that, while the most significant discoveries of her contemporaries are made incidentally, hers are deliberate and premeditated. What she has achieved in this modern Pilgrim's Progress is a strange kind of "salvation" only to be attained by a certain peculiar awareness of an apparently purposeless life-flow. (pp. 9-10)

Dorothy Richardson is the only one who really continues—in her new, feminine way—the great egoist life-quest of Montaigne, Goethe, Wordsworth, Pater and Proust. And it is just because she has not deviated from this path that the rank-and-file find her so difficult an author. She *is* difficult. She is difficult in a way totally different from the way in which the objectively clever writers, the intellectual puzzle-mongers and riddle-makers are difficult. (p. 12)

[What] a triumph in portraiture Miriam is! It is hard to think of any woman in fiction more living, more real. One comes to know every cranny of her mind, every eccentricity of her feeling, every tangent of her thought. But the point I want to make is that this kind of portraiture differs completely from the outward, built-up reality which charms us so much in Jane Eyre, Becky Sharp, Beatrix in *Esmond,* Hardy's Tess. Such women are types. With Miriam it is not what she feels but rather the way she feels that makes her symbolic.

And the peculiar genius of these extraordinary volumes lies herein: that through Miriam's heightened awareness of them all the other characters in the book imbibe an intense life of their own, making them stand out in clear-cut relief against the ebb and flow of her feelings. (pp. 15-16)

[Three] rare qualities emerge as characteristic of Miriam's pilgrimage through modern life; in the first place the genius that has made of this young woman a symbol of universal human experience; in the second place the convincing reality of the various persons who compose the drama of the girl's practical and intellectual life; in the third place, and this the greatest of all, the secrets to which we are admitted in regard to Miriam's femininity. Yes; the first two of these attributes are but the rough-hewn scaffolding of the substantial edifice of Miss Richardson's art. . . . It is in the feminine substratum of this work that one grows aware of an entirely new element in fiction . . . something that we look for in vain in Jane Austen, in the Brontës, in George Eliot. These quiet and penetrating books represent, in fact, the only attempt that I am aware of to put into psychological fiction the real "philosophy," moral, aesthetic, spiritual, and that which underlies all these and escapes from all these and mocks at all these—of women where they differ most from men. (pp. 16-17)

Miss Richardson is a far more original writer, a far greater writer, than the clever philistine-culture of our age has the sensitivity to understand. She is an authentic philosopher, in the great "open-secret" tradition; the tradition that *excludes* Aristotle, Descartes, Kant, Russell, Whitehead, Watson, and *includes* Heraclitus, Pythagoras, Plato, Montaigne, Goethe, Emerson, Nietzsche, Spengler. The main point about this aspect of her work, however, is that she has carried this philosophy of the "a-logical, innocent eye" into a new dimension, the dimension of women's secret, instinctive sensitiveness to the mystery of life. She takes her place in the great rôle of thinkers who, like Heraclitus and Goethe and Nietzsche, are intent on Life Itself, in its mysteriously flowing stream, rather than any human hypothesis of its whence and whither. . . . [How] curious, how significant, that until Dorothy Richardson began to write her patient, convoluted, difficult books, not a single human thinker, whether in prose or poetry, has really made of the feminine attitude to life the vantage-ground for interpreting life! Did this distinguished writer know where she was going, and what she was doing, when she wrote

Pointed Roofs, her first book? For even there, her *method* is in full application. Where did she find this singular method? She can only have found it, like all mysterious discoveries in art-method, in some underlying fold or couch or secret volute of her own consciousness, unrolled there and brought to light for the first time. The literary student looks in vain for any earlier *fons et origo* of such daring innovation in fictional narrative. (pp. 17-19)

Dorothy Richardson is a Wordsworth of the city of London. . . . [She] is "after" precisely the same thing . . . something that is very old and very pagan and absolutely non-moral . . . what Wordsworth himself, indeed, calls quite simply, "the Pleasure which there is in Life itself." Most beautifully does Miriam Henderson in these books speak of her "profanity." This word "profanity" implies just exactly the non-moral, anti-social, lonely zest for the pure Life-Sensation, stripped of all surplusage, which Wordsworth, "suckled in a creed outworn," so indignantly advocates.

But Miriam's famous "profanity" implies much more than this. It implies far more important and serious change in our system of spiritual valuations than the literary critics of our time have had the wit to see. Miriam's "profanity" is indeed nothing more nor less than a very deep and original system of life based upon a mystical quietude; an intensity of entranced, receptive contemplation. . . . The obscurity of Miss Richardson is indeed, like the irony of Jane Austen, an integral part of her style and it is obscure, as I have already hinted, in the way wind-shadows on water are, or tree-creepers on trees, or caddis-worms on beautiful river-mud. It is in other words *organically,* not grammatically or philologically obscure. (pp. 19-21)

Dorothy Richardson's style has, like so many rare prose-styles, its distinct affinity with poetry, without in the least degree approximating to that bastard hybrid, "prose-poetry." Like poetry, what it desires to express is so evasive, so much a matter of what one feels, so to speak, through the pores of one's skin, that it has to be expressed in a gnomic, oracular, *idolatrous* way. To attempt to express it in plain, blunt prose would be to attempt to express logically, rationally, argumentatively, what is always killed and blown to bits by logic, reason, argument. You must remember that this pilgrimage of Miriam's is a sort of Quest of the Holy Graal. . . . What Dorothy Richardson's heroine is looking for is in fact the divine object of the ecstatic contemplative life, nothing less than the Beatific Vision; and not merely for this alone; for she is looking for this as it manifests itself, in diffused glory, throughout the whole inflowing and outflowing tide of phenomena.

And for the very reason that our author's protagonist is beating up such recondite game . . . it is clear that "style" in her work becomes like the holy language of a very complicated ritual, the only effective invocation of the shy *Numen* whose presence she is summoning. (pp. 22-3)

May it not be that the only possible purpose or unity or meaning in this story of Miriam is to be found in those words [she used when referring to something in herself that couldn't be touched or altered]—"perhaps it goes on getting stronger till you die"? It is here doubtless that Miss Richardson is the grand Heretic of Fiction. The very rudiments of the art of *the novel,* as distinct from the old story-telling of the famous "fabulators" of early times, are surely from the orthodox point of view that all "notes" should be gathered up in one crashing crescendo at the close. In the Miriam-story one begins to feel, as one reaches *Oberland,* that there has been no preparation at all, certainly no artful and elaborate preparation, for any kind of dramatic "finale." Miriam's life has been, and still is, an epitome, just as Faust's is an epitome of the spiritual growth of the human soul. (p. 38)

One deeply rooted trait in Miriam stems backwards, it is hard not to feel, directly to her author. I refer to her abnormal ear for musical euphonies and dissonances. Like Joyce, Miss Richardson is a born philologist; but, unlike Joyce, she uses her talent for word-coining not as an end in itself, full of metaphysical and scholastic revelations as to the cosmic constitution of things, but as a short-cut to the understanding and the exposition of human character. . . . She is indeed a most sardonic mimic; and these mimicries of deviations from "King's English" play a larger part in her method than they do in any other living writer that I know of. It is not only a matter of coining new words for subtle feelings. It is a matter of expressing—by the humour of clipping words and tumbling and towzling words —many shades of affectional and pathetical understandings and misunderstandings between intimate relations and friends. . . . [She also displays] contempt for the sort of human-too-human melodrama which has had such an appeal to writers of the Latin race. She gets rid of this human melodrama. . . . Where Latin writers—even the most cynical—display passionate seriousness she will ramble off, at any tangent, into all manner of whimsical, irresponsible *jeux d'esprit,* and where they—even the most sentimental— display levity she will display a profound, eager and disconcerting earnestness. Deeply English is her steady, persistent, undeviating preference for *the sensation of life* at all costs over the sentiment, or the passion, of the appropriate *gesture.* (pp. 41-3)

One grand advantage does the peculiar *proud-humbleness* of this writer give her above her sophisticated contemporaries—above Virginia Woolf, above the Sitwells, above Aldous Huxley. It enables her to retain her strong, fresh, exuberant, child-like zest for the old simple great things in philosophy and literature. She has not any need, as so many of us seem to have in these jaded days, to stir up her response to life by all manner of tricky "originalities." There is a certain obstinate, humorous, massive, deliberate *naiveté* about her approach to life that is not in the least degree ashamed of appearing pedantic. In this matter she is a true disciple of the wise Goethe. And it is just this refusal to play tricks with her natural intelligence that enables her authentic originality to sprout forth spontaneously, at its own sweet will, and that gives it, when it does so, that calm, magical, oracular quality that makes one think of those Pre-Socratic "logoi" of the old, great, natural philosophers, from whose vision of truth the direct, concrete, feminine insight has not been yet squeezed out by any dry, syllogistic, super-masculine Aristotle. (pp. 45-6)

John Cowper Powys, in his Dorothy M. Richardson *(reprinted by permission of the Estate of the late John Cowper Powys), Joiner and Steele, 1931, 48 p.*

HARVEY EAGLESON (essay date 1934)

To deny that Miss Richardson in *Pilgrimage* has accom-

plished her purpose is impossible, but to question whether that purpose was worth while is pertinent. No more careful, detailed and beautifully written psychological study of a woman has been made, but one wonders if *Pilgrimage* is not rather a case book than a novel, if it is not rather the materials of fiction rather than fiction itself. The book is a work of art in that it presents vividly, accurately, and convincingly a life, and through the medium of that life, all human life. But it is life that is static. It is a still photograph, not a moving picture. It is not that the still photograph is to be excluded from art. That is not the point. With Miss Richardson's work it is rather a question of prolongation. Except perhaps for the adding of meticulous detail Miss Richardson accomplishes her purpose in *Pointed Roofs,* the first volume of *Pilgrimage.* With that book the picture has been shown, and the observer has noted it. In the second volume one has a right to expect, if his interest is to be sustained, that there will be movement, progression, at least a new picture. But each successive volume of *Pilgrimage* merely adds detail to the first picture. This elaboration of the original, delicately and beautifully as it may be done, does not carry in itself sufficient cause for being. One feels rightly that it is elaboration to no end, because there is no end. Trite as the statement may be, it is no less true that a work of art must have a beginning, a middle, and an end. And it is there that the flaw in Miss Richardson's work is to be found. *Pilgrimage* is only a vast beginning. That Miss Richardson has something to say is patent, but that she says it repetitiously is equally evident. That she has elements of the highest greatness must be clear to any reader of discernment, but that she cannot arrive at greatness until those elements are focussed upon end rather than endlessness, must ever be a condition of her artistic status. *Pilgrimage* is the monumental pedestal for a statue of heroic size, but the statue is missing. (pp. 52-3)

Harvey Eagleson, "Pedestal for Statue," in The Sewanee Review *(reprinted by permission of the editor;* © *1934 by The University of the South), Vol. XLII, No. 1, Winter, 1934, pp. 42-53.*

FRANK SWINNERTON (essay date 1934)

[Dorothy Richardson] has invented a new kind of impressionism in literature. She does not dodge, as Virginia Woolf does, among the past and present moods and memories of her heroine, but with extremely dexterous selectiveness manages to tell a continuous life-story as if it were in progress under our eyes. . . . [She] makes every few weeks or months of [this story] fill three hundred pages and could seemingly go on for ever.

This is a feat. Still more of a feat is the fact that Dorothy Richardson manages to persuade the reader that she could not possibly be any more succinct. There is no haste in the ten volumes, but there is no padding either. They are all full to the brim of what seems much like actual history. That is just the doubt that assails my mind in contemplating *Pilgrimage:* I find it excellent as impressionism—tones, looks, turns of speech all as they might, as they *must,* have been. But if I am asked whether I consider such impressionism anything more than a marvellous feat of memory, of reproduction, I must answer that somewhere between volume one and volume ten there comes a moment in which one wishes that Miriam had died young, or that she had moved through life at a less even and ample pace. The whole question of "importance" in fiction seems to arise. (p. 386)

One is overwhelmed by the multitude of little things which Miriam notices in the course of her journey through life. They do not compose into a picture, but are like the collections of a lifetime, a boxful of scraps of old silk and stuff such as hoarding women gather and leave behind at death. That Miriam guesses a good deal at secrets half—or quarter—revealed by demeanour shows that she is not without inquisitiveness and even a rather harsh and ruthless judgment of other people, and so a picture of Miriam herself grows steadily, volume by volume. But how far deliberate is that portrait? Is it not there, inferentially, as it were, by the accident of accumulated indications? How far is the character *created*?

You see in Miriam what may be regarded as the first adumbration of Virginia Woolf's idea of character as no more than a series of reactions to milieu. She does not impose herself upon life, but suffers its impress and its humiliations. She does not act; she resents and records. She does this without apology or explanation from Dorothy Richardson, and so far is "presented" as she would be by an artist of importance. On the other hand, no attempt is made to extract significance from her experiences; and so the work is as little comprehensive as a tape-machine. At one time it was usual to call the method of Dorothy Richardson "the stream of life"; and I freely grant its interestingness as technical experiment. Its value in the art of fiction I find it less easy to admit. Curious, novel, for a time attractive, it seems to me in the end to be a little pointless. (p. 387)

Frank Swinnerton, "Post-Freud: May Sinclair, Dorothy Richardson, Rebecca West, E. M. Forster, D. H. Lawrence, James Joyce," in his The Georgian Scene: A Literary Panorama *(copyright 1934 © 1962 by Frank Swinnerton; reprinted by permission of Holt, Rinehart and Winston, Publishers), Farrar & Rinehart, 1934, pp. 379-420.**

GRAHAM GREENE　(essay date 1938)

In the monstrous subjectivity of [*Pilgrimage*] the author is absorbed into her character. There is no longer a Miss Richardson: only Miriam. . . . (p. 150)

There are passages of admirable description, characters do sometimes emerge clearly from the stream of consciousness. . . . There are passages, too, where Miriam's thought, in its Jacobean dress, takes on [the] wide impressionist poetry [of Henry James, Miss Richardson's master]. . . . (pp. 150-51)

But the final effect, I fear, is one of weariness (that may be a tribute to Miss Richardson's integrity), the weariness of the best years of life shared with an earnest, rather sentimental and complacent woman. For one of the drawbacks of Miss Richardson's unironic and undetached method is that the compliments paid so frequently to the wit or intellect of Miriam seem addressed to the author herself. . . . And as for the method—it must have seemed in 1915 a revivifying change from the tyranny of the 'plot'. But time has taken its revenge: after twenty years of subjectivity, we are turning back with relief to the old dictatorship, to the detached and objective treatment, while this novel, ignoring all signals, just ploughs on and on, [her] Saratoga trunk, labelled this time for Switzerland, for Austria, shaking on the rack, and Miriam still sensitively on the alert, reading far too much significance into a cup of coffee, a flower in a vase, a fog or a sunset. (pp. 151-52)

Graham Greene, "The Saratoga Trunk" (1938), in his Collected Essays *(copyright 1951, © 1966, 1968. 1969 by Graham Greene; reprinted by permission of Viking Penguin Inc.; in Canada by Laurence Pollinger Ltd. for The Bodley Head, Ltd.),* Viking Penguin, 1969, pp. 149-52.

ROBERT GLYNN KELLY　(essay date 1954)

In a time when Joyce, Proust, Virginia Woolf, and others labored to forge the fragments of experience into a new whole, Miss Richardson was affirming joyfully that the fragment was the whole, and that the new vision of life, for which these other writers had contrived their profound traps, was untrappable. . . .

Yet Miss Richardson is no mere curiosity. Her skill is so great and her devotion so relentless that her strange book is richer than many a more orthodox book. Like Woolf and Joyce, for example, she sharpens our vision for the world about us, showing us many things we looked at but did not see. Like them, she guides us into the surprising-familiar recesses of our own minds. . . .

But in her devotion to the stream of consciousness she is spectacularly unique. Other novelists have tended to use this technique simply as one technique among others, or as an exclusive technique for only one or two subjects. And usually they have attempted by various means to impose upon the stream of consciousness a structure more meaningful than its own. But not Miss Richardson. (p. 76)

She believes, first, that experience consists of a series of independent, equal fragments. Life for her, and for her heroine, Miriam Henderson, is a chain of "immortal moments"—sudden emotions, deep nostalgias; these alone are real. Therefore the stream-of-consciousness novel is the best approach to reality. . . . Miriam is not interested in the rational significance of things and events. Her world is full of meanings which cannot be reasoned out, which cannot be depended upon to be there when you methodically look for them, but which depend for their manifestation upon a sudden, transient concatenation of circumstances—and so "every moment things went by that could never be recovered." She does not try to analyze or organize her world, but rather in some mystical way to transcend it. (p. 77)

Miss Richardson believes, second, that literature which imposes upon life meaningful patterns is false. This she believes for two reasons. First, there are no such patterns in nature herself. Life, as we have seen, is but a series of equal fragments. . . . This belief, which is in part a reaction to the melodrama of romantic novels, leads Miss Richardson to flatten the hills and valleys of her narrative to a level as artificial as the exaggerated ups and downs she deplores. But the second and more important reason why one must not impose meaningful patterns upon life is that life has no meanings, there are no tragic or comic values. It is this idea, primarily, which governs Miss Richardson's thought, which leads her, for example, to see all traditional novel-forms as consisting merely of "excitement and suspense; uncertainty as to what, in the pages still to be turned, might befall the hero . . .". She finds man neither noble nor despicable, and without the capacity for being either. His behavior she does not even find interesting. And his mind is important only for its access to the divinity of Things. A plot, therefore, which dramatizes some theme—a plot which in a single *devised* action represents some principle of all action—is simply untrue. There was never an Oedipus.

This is the chief difference between Miss Richardson and James Joyce, for example, her chief stream-of-consciousness contemporary. For though Joyce shared many of her convictions (compare his epiphany to Miss Richardson's concept of the unique, fragmentary emotion), he by no means agreed that there were no patterns in life. (pp. 77-8)

But for Miss Richardson the larger patterns scarcely exist. Led by her simpler mysticism, she gives her novel no structure whatsoever. She follows the stream-of-consciousness technique stolidly to its uttermost implications, and arrives at simple chronological sequence. But even this she conceals from the reader so that he cannot bring it to bear upon the separate events. In *Pilgrimage* every fragment floats in a void. We are rarely sure where we are, or who is present, or what has happened. The slow years move by in imperceptible sequence, developing no action. (p. 78)

[In this narrative] there is not only no organization, there is ostensibly no selection. . . .

There are no categories in Miriam's world; one thing cannot represent another; every emotion is unique. And so the reader sits through lessons and lectures and goes on tiring walks, until when Miriam begins a new day he braces himself uneasily, as if for an actual physical effort. . . . (p. 79)

Yet with all this sacrifice to inclusiveness, Miriam's character is strangely incomplete, not only because the many details are not arranged in any clear pattern, or because their effect is diluted by so much irrelevance, but also because there are, after all, conspicuous omissions. For Miss Richardson, altogether unlike Mr. Joyce, is a prude. Though we plumb the depths of Miriam's mind, though we examine nearly every other trivial aspect of it, we never meet any of her sexual observations, nor even her most commonplace physical observations. The slightest physical detail is concealed in an awkward gap in the narrative, or simply lost in the mist of Miriam's astounding physical unawareness. Though we live with her, we discover none of her secrets. Eventually she creates in the reader an impression not only of a chaste mind, but even of an intangible body. And when after some thousand-odd pages one of Miriam's associates becomes so intimate as to clap his hands upon her knees, we are shocked not only at his being intimate, but at her having knees.

The third of Miss Richardson's beliefs—stated explicitly, with thundering conviction—is that man's greatest enemy is his reason. Miss Richardson's heroine, Miriam, is interested in nothing but her feelings. They alone will lead her to the truth of life—if only she can distract her attention, unfocus her mind, and let them run free. But always the rational mind is understanding things, obtruding surface meanings into her direct perception of subsurface reality. . . . Like Bergson, Miriam looks coldly upon the practical intellect and keeps it out of the way of her truth-perceiving intuition. (pp. 79-80)

This antirationalism is, moreover, strangely antimasculine. For Miriam, the difference between reason and intuition is largely the difference between male and female. The masculine mind is direct, rational, systematic, and practical—and misses the truth. The feminine mind is irrational, haphaz-

ard, sensitive, and intuitive—and finds the truth. . . . A strange heroine for a novel, one who is interested not in ideas or people, but primarily in things, Miriam aches always to be alone with a room or a bus or a bicycle. (p. 80)

Methodically, therefore, Miriam retires from the world as measured by reason, from the practical concerns of life—and from the moral. . . . Miriam's life will be a life of the mind, but not of thought. . . . She just sits in "silent, happy expansion." (pp. 81-2)

This is the culminating philosophy of *Pilgrimage*, which goes farther than any other novel in the strict employment of the stream-of-consciousness technique. This is the philosophy ideally suited to that technique, carried to its logical extreme. And that extreme is silence. (p. 82)

> *Robert Glynn Kelly, "The Strange Philosophy of Dorothy M. Richardson," in* The Pacific Spectator *(copyright © 1954 by The Pacific Coast Committee for the Humanities of the American Council of Learned Societies), Vol. 13, No. 1, Winter, 1954, pp. 76-82.*

LEON EDEL (essay date 1958)

Since [*Pilgrimage*] is written from the "inside" one either is able to move into the heroine's consciousness or is incapable of reading—or "experiencing"—the book. This would seem to be the long and the short of it. And since many of the book's critics seemed unaware of this, we find ourselves involved in large failures in empathy: gross failures to grasp the essence of Miss Richardson's quite extraordinary application of the Jamesian theory of the "point of view." (pp. 165-66)

Certainly there can be no question of placing her now on an equality of footing with Proust and Joyce. Miss Richardson was a journeyman beside the nimble-minded Irishman, nor did she have the Frenchman's capacity for discovering a universe in a perfume. She must be written down rather as one of the hardy and plodding experimenters of literature, the axe-swingers and stump-pullers, those who have a single moment of vision which suffices for a lifetime. There was a kind of Zola in Miss Richardson. . . . *Pilgrimage* is not a Rougon Macquart, but it is a long and detailed progress through the mind and emotions of an English girl who emerges from a Victorian adolescence and attains maturity and liberation in the early decades of our century. To reread Miss Richardson now . . . is to marvel at her unflagging zeal: the book is a victory of resolution, patience, and sensibility over limited artistic means. *Pilgrimage* for all its sprawling minuteness . . . contains distinct qualities of strength, insight and feeling, and above all vitality—the vitality of a purposeful individual who cannot be swerved from a creative task, who indeed converts the task into a self-education. (p. 166)

The true difficulty of *Pilgrimage* lies in its impenetrability. Readers of both sexes are asked to establish rapport with two thousand pages containing the flotsam and jetsam of consciousness, fragments of experience, emotions conveyed in emotion-limiting words. A reader can easily achieve a relation with a novel when he is on the outside, watching the story unfold; it is another matter to be "on the inside" looking out—and especially "on the inside" of an adolescent girl, in the first sections. This explains why the successful reading of the book seems to depend in a considerable measure on the reader's sex. Usually it is the women who speak of Miss Richardson's achievement as "uncanny" and filled with "intensities." Most men find it difficult to meet her requirement that they become the adolescent Miriam of *Pointed Roofs* and grow up with her in the succeeding volumes.

Few men—few critics of their sex—have been willing to climb into Miss Richardson's boat; the journey is long, the "stream of consciousness" difficult—raw unabstracted data, the absence of the omniscient author to serve as guide, the consequent need to become the author so as to bring some order into the great grab-bag of feminine experience offered us; and then the need, Orlando-like, to become the girl or woman, to become Miriam if we are to be her consciousness. Few writers have placed so double-weighted a burden upon their readers. And yet if the challenge is met and the empathy achieved, Dorothy Richardson offers us, on certain pages, a remarkable emotional luminescence—as well as, historically speaking, a record of the trying out of a new technique, the opportunity to examine a turning point in the modern English novel. (p. 168)

> *Leon Edel, "Notes and Discussion: Dorothy Richardson, 1882-1957," in* Modern Fiction Studies *(© copyright 1957 by Purdue Research Foundation, West Lafayette, Indiana), Vol. 4, No. 2, Summer, 1958, pp. 165-68.*

RACHEL TRICKETT (essay date 1959)

Dorothy Richardson is an unusual case of an experimenter who was not primarily interested in time nor in formal structure for its own sake. By her own confession, her experiments had a single aim: to discover the best way of expressing one particular kind of sensibility—a woman's. (p. 21)

It has often been noticed that [Virginia Woolf's] *To the Lighthouse* deals with many of the same themes as *Pilgrimage:* assumed masculine superiority, feminine 'being' as opposed to male 'becoming' (the terms are Dorothy Richardson's own), the perilous exclusiveness of love between two people, and the comprehensiveness of the solitary vision. But Virginia Woolf shows as much concern with the possibilities of her medium, and with the artist's peculiar realization of these themes, as with their actual truth. Dorothy Richardson, on the other hand, is a propagandist. She wants to convince us that these truths are neglected and important, and that without them any picture of life is incomplete. She is passionately concerned about them, with an emotion that spills over into all her characters, into Miriam who recognizes them, and into the others from whom she learns their meaning and significance. Perhaps because of this concern, Miriam Henderson, tiresome, priggish, intractable as she is, is more real than the half-symbolic Mrs Ramsay, while Hypo Wilson, Miriam's intellectual lover, and Michael Shotov, her Russian Jewish suitor, are more completely understood as characters than Mr Ramsay. Indeed there is nowhere in Virginia Woolf a character so lovingly realized as Shotov, or presented with such emotional truth and intimacy. . . . (p. 22)

[Dorothy Richardson] is, like most propagandists, a passionate sentimentalist. It is both her virtue and her vice, for while it prevents her from seeing her characters, and particularly her heroine, with any detachment, it compels her to love the feelings they arouse. Miriam, irritably searching after the inner integrity which she believes is truth, preserving her emotional virginity against all the onslaughts of experience and human relationships, yet has the paradoxical feminine quality of entertaining what she rejects, of accepting it intuitively in her heart and her imagination. Her precious isolation is always threatened by her sheer curiosity, her susceptibility to charm and ability to 'take' everything.

When they are discussing writers together, Hypo Wilson once suggests to Miriam that she should write novels like 'a feminine George Eliot'. It is not George Eliot who springs to mind when we read *Pilgrimage* though, but a less intellectual, a more prim and passionate interpreter of the woman's world—Charlotte Brontë. Dorothy Richardson for all her greater sophistication and poise has something of Charlotte Brontë's intenseness, her lack of humour, her fervour and integrity. She has the same intuitive love of people and places, and an obstinate desire to preach in the person of her heroine. But that best gift of feminine genius, the sense of the mundane poetry of common perception, is the finest quality they share. . . . Though she has rejected melodrama, Dorothy Richardson can convey, too, the same numb pain which comes from the pressure of the self that Charlotte Brontë shows in Lucy Snowe. But it is not, after all, surprising that, if she is like anyone, it should be Charlotte Brontë, the most feminine in her faults and her genius of the nineteenth century women writers.

Sensitivity is always counted the inevitable virtue of women's writing. But in spite of the delicacy of her impressions, Dorothy Richardson often seems almost insensitive, just as, in spite of reported witticisms and 'brilliant' conversations, she often seems humourless. Perhaps this is one of the penalties of the introspective method of narrative. . . . Sensitivity is a narrow word for her more common and instinctive quality, her power of realizing all the rich and various accumulation of raw material on which women's curiosity, their sentiments and sympathies are so lavishly expended. *Pilgrimage* reveals, with a paradoxically rich simplicity, that actual world of people and things which, in spite of ideals and aspirations that may defy it, women instinctively and tenaciously cherish. By the side of *Pilgrimage* Virginia Woolf's novels, with their beauty and formal skill, their far greater aesthetic power, seem scarcely feminine at all. In the last resort this is the measure of Virginia Woolf's superiority, but Dorothy Richardson's deliberate limitation, her fanatical devotion to the woman's outlook, is her unique claim on our attention, and, by its very completeness secures her a place among the writers whose work survives. (pp. 24-5)

> *Rachel Trickett, "The Living Dead: Dorothy Richardson," in* London Magazine *(© London Magazine 1959), Vol. 6, No. 6, June, 1959, pp. 20-5.*

CAESAR R. BLAKE (essay date 1960)

The twelve volumes of *Pilgrimage* compass the manifold experiences that show the *becoming* of Miriam and its reconciliation to the *being* that she must acknowledge in order to achieve a sense of the reality of identity and its consequent vision of the reality of life. The massive detail—some trivial and tiresome though functional; some profoundly suggestive of broad analysis and interpretation—is only secondarily important in itself: perhaps important in the sense of Dorothy Richardson's Miriam Henderson's "eye-view of the world," a "*Comédie Humaine* of English speaking Europe.'' It is indeed possible to read *Pilgrimage* with great profit as a vast critical commentary on humanity, society, art, religion, the English character. But the primary importance of the detail is its cumulative effect on the perceiving mind, as that mind seeks a perspective adequate to its demand for reality. Miriam is seventeen in *Pointed Roofs,* where she begins her life quest. In *Dimple Hill* she is over thirty. The years between, as selected for the novel, are crowded with great and minor experiences; some occur and pass quickly, flashing only m'mentarily a telling insight but residually important in future experiences; others occur and recur, modified by time and memory, and remain in the foreground of Miriam's consciousness as impetus to thought and action. Upon Miss Richardson's own advice, the reader can open the novel anywhere and find engrossment in the ''close texture,'' poetically rendered, of these experiences.

Beneath this quantity of complex detail, however, there are qualitative currents which define the developing consciousness successively in movements from youth and innocence to maturity and wisdom; from disillusioning conformity to enlightened individuality; from the opposition of feeling and thought to their reconciliation in belief; from dismay at life and the world to joy and wonder at life and the world transformed by the realized self. Miriam's stream of experience flows into larger currents persisting beneath the surface—at first separate, then conflicting, occasionally converging—themselves channelized finally in an achieved mystical vision.

In the first three chapters of *Pilgrimage*—*Pointed Roofs, Backwater, Honeycomb*—the reader meets Miriam Henderson, learns something of her essential character, and witnesses developments in her young adult life which motivate her extended pilgrimage and which provide the later conflictive movements of the novel. In *Pointed Roofs* the initial, circumstantial cause of Miriam's first independent journey into life is her father's financial collapse, a crisis serious enough to require radical readjustment of the Henderson family's life. (pp. 24-5)

In *Backwater,* the reader begins to formulate a conflict which fundamentally organizes the panoramic impressions of Miriam's Hanover and Banbury Park years. . . . [The] stimuli are various, but their effect is always an ideal condition of the self. It is a condition not always—not even often—possible of attainment in the individual's social existence. The ''solitary spring air'' is divorced from the realities of north London; this fundamental disparity between feeling and perception is the conflict formulated but unresolved in *Backwater.* (p. 30)

It is true that Miriam is adolescent in many of her attitudes and in much of her behavior: there is something distressingly familiar in her frequent flights to emotional finality and verbal superlatives in critical situations. . . . And it is true that Miriam is sometimes rather too ecstatic about soap, soft lights, or hot tea. Her redeeming quality is the unusual sensitivity which she frequently shows for the beauty of nature and music, for the nuances of human gesture and expression. The potential of this capacity prevents the reader from condemning her as entirely dull. He remembers that Miriam is seventeen, eighteen, nineteen and that Miss Richardson is concerned to document the girl's growth of personality. (pp. 33-4)

Miriam at Newlands is clearly more discerning and articulate than Miriam in Hanover; what, for instance, was a pouting distrust of men in *Pointed Roofs* has begun to emerge in *Honeycomb* as distaste for the characteristic habit of masculine minds—''propositional'' dogmatism. Similarly, for her ''illuminations,'' her distress about religion, her self-deprecation, or her impatience with social sham or pretense, Miriam at the end of *Honeycomb* has begun to focus her own experiences through the perspective of as yet embryonic attitudes about individuality and the integrity of the self, social duty, relations between the sexes, the relationship of God and man—in a word, about the reality of life. With these developing attitudes, she resumes her quest for the ''little coloured garden'' in the world of affairs; *The Tunnel* and *Interim* are the next course in its fulfillment. (p. 34)

The significance of *The Tunnel* and *Interim* is most apparent in a scene which allows Miriam to reflect on her several preoccupations, and in such a way as to indicate the advance she has made in her first London years. She attends a lecture on Dante, tolerating the lecture itself, but intently appreciating the reading of some of Dante's poetry. Listening to the ''voice of Dante,'' Miriam is impressed by a ''truth''—love as the fundamental moral imperative—which is true because it is self-evident to the individual. This value and its perception through intuition shows the impertinence and the falseness of values not consonant with love and not verifiable by vision. This is a promising perspective for Miriam, the furthest point of development she achieves in these chapters, but it is not a perspective which is totally meaningful to her. The insights occur in the context of Miriam's eager, half-critical pouncing on any and all ''truths,'' for in the Dante reverie she also concludes that post-office savings accounts, betting, gambling, and lotteries are wrong because they produce nothing. Hers is still a highly tentative mind, not yet poised in firmly grounded beliefs. (pp. 39-40)

Miriam has learned a great many things in *The Tunnel* and *Interim,* diffuse and unfocused as these things sometimes appear. Chiefly, she has learned the possibility of comprehending the world in relation to herself without lapsing impatiently into subjective finalities, as was her wont in the earlier chapters. She does not ignore or dismiss the social realities life inevitably presents to her; she makes some effort to understand and judge them through whatever resources of mind and spirit she has. This advance in her development can be seen in the greater number of illuminations she experiences in ''the world'' than before. (p. 41)

All in all, the gap between feeling and perception narrows. Perhaps the title *Interim* suggests a temporary, partial success to be challenged before a greater undertaking in the pilgrimage. (p. 42)

[The] successive volumes of *Pilgrimage* become increasingly complex. Miriam's consciousness is more and more filled with the cumulative effects of her experiences—intellectual, emotional, and physical. Their accessibility in memory and association is unusually facile, and thus her mind subjects even minor moods and perceptions to a kind of Proustian *approfondissement.* Passing an old woman on Shaftesbury Avenue can be as provocative for Miriam as remembering her first reading of Jevons. The consequent density of *Deadlock, Revolving Lights,* and *The Trap* is itself a measure of the ''different'' Miriam with whom we must deal.

In these chapters the first clear difference which the reader notices is a more self-assured Miriam. Between *Interim* and *Deadlock* several years pass; Miriam has apparently committed herself to an almost anarchic individualism. There is a contingent cynicism about "civilization" as it implies regulative institutions. (pp. 42-3)

[Miriam has] concluded firmly the supremacy of intuitive truth, and thus it is not surprising that she should find Emerson congenial to her present preoccupations. Not really possessing a temperament for sustained, rigorous metaphysics, Miriam finds in Emerson a similar temperament, and she exults in his poetized program for the divinely individual man. (p. 44)

[In *Revolving Lights*, the] choices between solitude and society, spiritual and physical satisfactions, different modes of conduct is not so simple as it seemed at Banbury Park or Newlands. Hence, the possible choices appear as lights, none entirely constant or direction-giving, but all revolving, beckoning her by turns, with Miriam figuratively unmoving as she contemplates their circular succession. Her defensive concern for "misunderstood" or unfairly treated womankind demands at times a program, but when the feminist organization is suggested to her, she rejects it by exclaiming: "Feminists are not only an insult to womanhood. They are a libel on the universe." . . . The chaos which men feel bound to overcome in the name of civilization and of which women are supposed to be a prime example is the principal masculine illusion, she argues. There never was that kind of chaos. Women exemplify the higher ordering of experience, of which masculine-minded men are incapable. The feminists want to prove women's equality by proving themselves masculine-minded. (p. 48)

There is a somber, brooding atmosphere [in *The Trap*] in sharp contrast to the intensities of *Deadlock* and *Revolving Lights*. (p. 53)

We cannot speak of the climax or climactic episode in *Pilgrimage;* its content is not conceived in terms of a dramatic development of successive actions. It is possible to speak only of a critical point or state of mind in the emergence of the consciousness defining Miriam Henderson. . . . From *Pointed Roofs* through *The Trap* the central disposition in Miriam's consciousness has been a transcendental individualism variously buffeted and variously justified, but ultimately contiguous to a [rigorously intellectual] philosophical idealism. . . . (pp. 56-7)

Miriam champions the higher order of intuitive perceptions, but the masculine part of her own intelligence seeks certainty in the systems she distrusts. The paradox suggests her lack of confidence in the sufficiency of the feminine consciousness, but it also suggests her dissatisfaction with the insufficiency of intellectual systems.

This dilemma is a major modification in her consciousness, which ultimately affects her partial commitment to philosophical idealism, for the conclusion of its logic is that there can be no substance or being superior to the finite individual except an absolute which . . . is virtually incomprehensible and thus approximates Nothing. (pp. 57-8)

Miriam's dissatisfaction with philosophical idealism is largely her uncertainty about the nature of being and the nature of God or an Absolute as such a system defines them. Because of this uncertainty, there frequently looms before Miriam an immensity called "life": the wholeness or unity behind disjunctive appearances or "living." The flux of experience needs the masculine genius to formulate external existence into manageable concepts and laws which make living orderly and predictable, but these provide no access to life. The feminine genius is to see behind the façade of the flux. (p. 58)

But there is not, at the end of *The Trap,* the characteristic effect of conversion or awakening; there have been "storm and stress, the vague cravings and oscillations," but the altered perspective of release into a "larger world of being" is missing. In the next chapter, *Oberland,* that effect, as Miss Richardson conceives it for Miriam's life, is accomplished.

Oberland is brief, joyous, lyrical. (p. 65)

The source of Miriam's Oberland joy is, in the mystic's language, "the revelation of an external splendour, the shining vision of the transcendent spiritual world." The joy itself is the mark of an accomplished awakening if there accompanies it its necessary complement: crystallization, participation, a "personal" and imperative concept that shows itself in changed behavior and attitudes. Miriam in *Oberland,* particularly her resolution to "live in its effect" in future, has experienced her awakening, her "release."

The title of the tenth chapter of *Pilgrimage—Dawn's Left Hand—*suggests its scope: the first, tentative emergence of the "new" Miriam. The effect of the Oberland experience is evident in Miriam's first renewals of her London life. (pp. 66-7)

The major part of *Dawn's Left Hand* is concerned with the remarkable travails of Miriam in love and sex. (p. 67)

The sex episodes are the central instance of Miriam's purification in *Dawn's Left Hand. . . .* (pp. 69-70)

It is not possible to mark a point at which one aspect or the other of purification begins or ends in *Dawn's Left Hand;* these chapters blend the two in a dense sequence of experiences that show Miriam negating or affirming their value depending on the extent to which they lend enhancement of the self she now cultivates. (p. 70)

In *Dimple Hill,* the last chapter of *Pilgrimage,* Miriam is taking a long, prescribed rest with a Quaker family in Sussex. The onset of [her] illuminative experience occurs early in the book. . . . (p. 73)

Though abrupt and amazing to Miriam, the "opening" [her illuminative experience] is the consequence of the psychological process she has undergone since her Oberland awakening. Intuitions are identified with, and confirmed by, God revealing Himself; feeling and perception are one in Miriam's admission to that certainty; the mode of her apprehension is both inner and outer, the heightened feeling within integrating with sensuous impression without. This has been the certainty Miriam sought, that her life might be unified in it. (p. 75)

Under the influence of Dimple Hill life, she begins writing a book, a long-cherished ambition only now possible of fulfillment. (p. 78)

Thus *Pilgrimage* ends, with no finality, but with a sense of the going-on, now differently, of a self realized in the mystic way. Miriam is not the fully developed religious mystic. She has achieved illumination, that of the religious mystic, and also that of the mystic-artist who seeks to communicate his vision of the transcendent reality to his fellows. (pp. 79-80)

Self-realization, achievement of personality, is harmonizing the two elements in the individual—what, Miss Richardson agrees, is meant by harmonizing Dr. Jung's division of the self into *persona* and *anima*, "the one turned towards objects, centrifugal, and the other towards inner experience, centripetal." For her, the more inclusive harmony is the *anima*-feminine. This is Miss Richardson's "feminism," which, inextricably connected with the psychological development of Miriam, is the thematic structure unifying *Pilgrimage*. (p. 81)

Pilgrimage exhibits in its entire sequence of chapters a broad contrasting alternation of moods that is a rhythmic movement of the novel; we would have to say specifically the rhythm of alternating qualities of feeling implicit in the mystic's quest. The general joyousness of *Pointed Roofs* is succeeded by the general gloom of *Backwater*. *Honeycomb* returns the arc to happiness; in its very last pages the mood is brought low again. Thence the arc rises again through *The Tunnel* and *Interim* to the uncertain tension of *Revolving Lights*. It falls again to dejection and gloom in *The Trap*. *Oberland* swings to an almost ecstatic happiness which is waveringly threatened in the smaller alternations of Miriam's "purgation" in *Dawn's Left Hand*. *Clear Horizon* is the final uncertainty before the full joy of Miriam's satisfied quest in *Dimple Hill*. (pp. 121-22)

[Dorothy Richardson] seems to speak for no major group, nor to be significantly close intellectually to other, better known writers in our time. And yet her early attempt to create an image of the age assures the historical importance of her work, even if we find her ultimate vision unsatisfying. And clearly her creative experiment in the techniques of fiction pioneered many of the achievements we associate with the modern novel. There is the added historical advantage that we may read *Pilgrimage* as a vast and specific reflection of the general upheaval which brought forth the best of Eliot or Joyce or Lawrence, an upheaval mirrored by a perceptive woman attempting in its midst a meaning and an aesthetic expression for its character. (pp. 190-91)

> *Caesar R. Blake, in his* Dorothy Richardson *(copyright © by The University of Michigan 1960), University of Michigan Press, 1960, 207 p.*

V. S. PRITCHETT (essay date 1967)

Miriam's ego is unflagging and I doubt if any reader has read the whole of *Pilgrimage* or can keep up with all the scenes in Miriam's endless intellectualisings and changes of mind. She asks too much. Her feminism is the driving engine; but her femininity really provides the best things. This quality was the making of the first volume, *Pointed Roofs*, which is a little masterpiece and which [Dorothy Richardson] never equalled. (Her single idea was ruined by being stretched for use in a chronicle). Here Miriam is a poor teacher at work in a girls' finishing school in Germany and there is nothing but originality and pleasure in her observation of the girls at the awkward age. Outside of Colette I can think of nothing like this book and, though Dorothy Richardson lacks the sensual and feline quality and is altogether too peering in her English way, she is able to catch the continuous ripples and whirls of feeling, the perpetual

posing, whispering and mood-play by which the girls live. One understands what she meant by the feminine sensibility to atmosphere. In this book she did not labour. There is no pretentiousness. It states simply Miriam's choice of that homelessness and loneliness as forms of adventure and happiness which runs almost lyrically through the whole of *Pilgrimage*. . . .

In spite of the 'stream of consciousness' . . . Dorothy Richardson's talent was for the page rather than for the chapter, the page done a good deal in the manner of the realists she was reacting against. . . . She appears to have written a good deal of *Pilgrimage* in the realist manner, but torn it up in the interests of the 'stream'. There are many times, when arriving in a state of intellectual exhaustion at some oasis of realism in this novel, that one is glad she did not tear up all. Miriam drifting on, Miriam tying herself into important looking knots, lasts less well than what Miriam saw. What this technician and experimenter was throwing away was, so often, art.

> *V. S. Pritchett, "Moral Gymnasium," in* New Statesman *(© 1967 The Statesman & Nation Publishing Co. Ltd.), Vol. 73, No. 1886, May 5, 1967, p. 619.*

WALTER ALLEN (essay date 1967)

What we have in *Pilgrimage* is the life story from moment to moment, almost one might say in close-up, of Miriam from girlhood to womanhood. It is the story of a woman's development at a specific time in history, roughly from 1890 to 1915. Miriam is very much of her time; indeed one feels she could have lived at no other era. This cannot be too strongly stressed, for it is in its portrayal of a woman of that time that a great part of the novel's value seems to me to reside. And seen in this light, some elements of the work that at the time of its first appearance were construed as blemishes appear rather differently. The most important of these is probably Miriam's aggressive feminism, her constant reaction, which a woman critic of our time has called fanatical, against what is felt to be the assumption of masculine superiority. (p. 6)

But the point is, Dorothy Richardson was a feminist in the full old-fashioned sense, and the writing of *Pilgrimage* was as much an assault, and conceived as such, on the citadels of masculine supremacy as any suffragette demonstration in Downing Street. (pp. 6-7)

[In] the end one comes back, considering *Pilgrimage*, to the world and the period which play upon, and are played upon by, Miriam's sensibility. It is largely the world of the ferment of ideas, of advanced thought, of which feminism was an important part, of the London from the nineties to 1914. *Pilgrimage* shows us, uniquely, what it felt like to be a young woman, ardent, aspiring, fiercely independent, determined to live her own life in the profoundest sense, at that time. It is not a small achievement; for the novels that continue to interest us are those, as *Pilgrimage* is, that are deeply rooted in a specific time and place. (p. 8)

> *Walter Allen, in his introduction to* Pilgrimage, *Vol. I by Dorothy M. Richardson (copyright © 1967 by Walter Allen; reprinted by permission of Alfred A. Knopf, Inc.), Knopf, 1967, pp. 3-8.*

SHIRLEY ROSE (essay date 1973)

Viewed as a whole, Dorothy Richardson's work expresses

a social commitment rare among the English literary avant-garde. She was remarkably strong emotionally and spiritually; she was convinced of her intellectual and aesthetic position. Though sharing the period's major literary preoccupation with the inner life of characters, she showed no interest in overtly depicting neurotic, nihilistic, alienated, frustrated, perverted, or pseudo-sophisticated tendencies examined by some of her prominent contemporaries. Above all, her outlook is affirmative, paradoxically linked to a qualified rejection of superficial social pressures. This outlook, based upon the traditional principles of individual worth and responsibility, is the result of a personal inner stability and illumination. The unusual qualities of abundant vitality and conviction in contrast to the twentieth-century artist's general preoccupation with moral and physical decay may be responsible in part for the critical neglect of her work.

Dorothy Richardson was not primarily an experimenter. What she sought to do in the novel was to develop a highly individual approach, to perfect a personally satisfying intellectual and aesthetic style and method. Although she was a pioneer of the new stream-of-consciousness technique, nearly a quarter of a century elapsed before twelve parts of *Pilgrimage* appeared. During this period, the technique, if not entirely abandoned by novelists, came to be adopted as a specific device rather than as an inclusive mode. (p. 93)

Criticism conditioned mainly by the aesthetic approach may fail to appreciate the variety of *Pilgrimage*. The dual nature of its concerns—that is, objective and subjective life, physical and mental activity, intellectual and emotional responses—is integral to both the novel's narrative and ideational structure. In applying herself to a consideration of varying modes of experience, technique is pushed to its farthest coherent limits. The world Dorothy Richardson creates has an objective reality to which she insists we attend. Yet her objective observation, for example, of time's continuity, and the subjective awareness of existence and experience removed from all concepts of time, are not conflicting ideas, but serve to affirm and confirm one another.

Dorothy Richardson's conception of subjective and objective reality in life and art shapes her social and aesthetic views. Concerned about the deterioration of the quality of life as a result of economic and class structure, she turned at first to socialism in the hope of remedy. Indeed, socialism plays an important role in the early years of Dorothy Richardson's writing career, and forms an important autobiographical element in the characterization of Miriam Henderson in *Pilgrimage*.... Ultimately, correlative ideas about the relationship of men and women, emphasizing the difference between the masculine and feminine consciousness, and feminism *per se,* become central to her work. (p. 94)

The "pilgrimage" increasingly comes to mean the journey of the artist not only to self-realization but, more practically, to the discovery of a unique creative form and expression. (p. 95)

> *Shirley Rose, "Dorothy Richardson: The First Hundred Years; A Retrospective View," in* The Dalhousie Review, *Vol. 53, No. 1, Spring, 1973, pp. 92-6.*

SYDNEY JANET KAPLAN   (essay date 1975)

[When] Dorothy Richardson created a consciousness for

Miriam, she did not merely demonstrate a feminine mode of thinking. Her radicalism is acted out through a definite assertion of the *superiority* of the feminine consciousness. Miriam begins her definition out of defiance at the evidence of masculine prerogatives that she sees everywhere around her. (p. 10)

Miriam's attempt to go beyond the prevalent belief in women's inferiority is complicated, however, by her own "masculine" attributes. She remarks about herself, "I am something between a man and a woman, looking both ways." ... Much of her hostility must be directed against that other side of herself. This makes it a double kind of hostility or opposition: against that other half of humanity who represent all the forces which suppress women, and also against that logical, classifying, intellectual part of herself which is so often at odds with her deeper, "intuitive" femininity.

Miriam's defensiveness is based partly on her own sense of inferiority and jealousy. (p. 11)

The basic component inherent to Dorothy Richardson's concept of the feminine consciousness as it is developed throughout *Pilgrimage* is Miriam's strong ambivalence toward her role as a woman. It is this ambivalence which charges with tension the attempted demarcation of feminine and masculine aspects of consciousness. It causes a separation between the verbalized, intellectual, and abstract statements Miriam makes about the feminine consciousness and her actual emotional reactions to situations in her life. This ambivalence is so important as a force behind any complete understanding of the concept that it is not going too far to say that it, more than anything else, is the primary ingredient in her development of a "feminine consciousness." (pp. 16-17)

Miriam's basic insecurity in her feminine role is closely related to her confused relationships with other women, which grow out of that early masculine self-identity as the "son" of her family. Since she is so aware that she is different from other women, she usually finds her relationships with them awkward and tense. Her feelings vacillate between a violent woman-hating (and here she blames women for their weakness, their acceptance of an inferior role, their insincerity, and their instability) and a romantic idolization of woman, complete with emotionality, self-abnegation, and desire. She must compete with women and yet too often finds herself shortchanged because she seems to lack "femininity." Thus she must either raise herself above the women she fears by despising them and casting doubt upon their values, or accept her latent masculinity and avoid competition with women by denying her inadequacies and taking on the male role, ... In fact, one might even say that her obsessions with women contain more desire, and more explicit direct expression of emotions, than her heavily intellectualized discussions of her relationships with men. It seems that here lie her most direct feelings. This is not to imply that Miriam should be viewed as a lesbian. Rather, one may see in her ambivalence over her role as a woman many elements of latent homosexual feelings. These complicate and cloud her division of consciousness into masculine and feminine components even further. (p. 28)

Miriam's conflict between masculine and feminine roles,

her desire for independence and feminine superiority, compete in various ways with her feelings for traditional values and behavior. As a result, she turns more and more to religious insights instead of rational observations as she matures. She begins to oppose the over-rationality of intellectuals, contrasting it with the intuitive awareness of people like the Quaker Roscorlas. She ties this growing sense of religious commitment to her view of the feminine consciousness. It is as if she accepts, at last, that part of herself which stems from her traditional background. But as much as she accepts it, she can never accept herself as totally a woman in the traditional sense. (p. 39)

Instead of developing the close human contact necessary for a complete sexual relationship, Miriam usually remains involved with her own self-development. Her moods of mystical absorption allow her to maintain individual identity. Her insistence upon "being" as opposed to "becoming" as the center of the feminine consciousness permits her to accept the self as a contained and basically unchanging center which is not affected by contacts with others. It is an abstract, isolated entity. Yet, in a sense, this whole concept of "being" runs counter to the purpose and plan of the novel and the telling of those innumerable experiences throughout those interminable pages. If "being" is a static thing, it might be revealed in a very short form. A single symbolic incident would probably be enough. Symbolism of a vague sort can be discovered in *Pilgrimage*, but it is not a distinguishing characteristic of it. Instead, the novel is discursive. . . . The whole process is described as a "pilgrimage," and so it does seem to be. (pp. 45-6)

This [process of] creation seems to be a form of "becoming"—changing, altering through the subtle pressures of external impressions and one's reflections upon them. Miriam learns and grows and changes, and seems to be in search of that "being" which she asserts exists without the searching. The completing irony of the whole process is that this "being" Miriam seeks, she believes to be a natural part of the feminine consciousness. But somehow it cannot be sought through accepting the sexual nature of femininity at all. Miriam insists upon its femininity yet refuses to put "femininity" into its natural, physical setting. This femininity is a femininity of mind, and Miriam does not seem to have it in herself with any great sense of surety. The "feminine consciousness" remains strangely abstract and separated from its normal connection with the body—which is the basic source of femininity—and its fullest revelation is to be a state of mystical awareness and communion with God. This is a lonely and asexual achievement of "being." (p. 46)

Sydney Janet Kaplan, "Dorothy M. Richardson,"
in her Feminine Consciousness in the Modern
British Novel *(© 1975 by The Board of Trustees*
of the University of Illinois; reprinted by permis-
sion of the author and the University of Illinois
Press), University of Illinois Press, 1975, pp. 8-46.

ELAINE SHOWALTER (essay date 1977)

The fiction of Dorothy Richardson, Katherine Mansfield, and Virginia Woolf created a deliberate female aesthetic, which transformed the feminine code of self-sacrifice into an annihilation of the narrative self, and applied the cultural analysis of the feminists to words, sentences, and structures of language in the novel. Their version of modernism was a determined response to the material culture of male

Edwardian novelists like Arnold Bennett and H. G. Wells, but, like D. H. Lawrence, the female aestheticists saw the world as mystically and totally polarized by sex. (p. 33)

The most consistent representative of female aestheticism was Dorothy M. Richardson, who might have been the Gertrude Stein of the English novel if she had been more self-promoting and more affluent. (p. 248)

Richardson's first literary efforts to define the female artistic identity took the form of a dialectic; eventually she wrote the anti-Wellsian novel. . . .

[Wells] was an Edwardian with Bennett and Galsworthy; [Richardson] was a Georgian with Forster and Woolf. Thus Richardson's repudiation of Wells was also a repudiation of the Edwardian novel of external realism and accumulated detail. It is also clear that to Richardson and Woolf the Edwardians represented a male literary culture. (p. 253)

Even though Richardson admired Wells and had been educated by him, she came to see him as an opponent, the quintessential male artist. Her name for him in *Pilgrimage* is "Hypo Wilson." . . . (p. 254)

Wells was concerned with the visionary and the Utopian; Richardson opted for the prosaic continual present. He chose a novel of ideas; she chose a novel of consciousness. He was politically engaged (and serially monogamous in his politics); she disdained any ideological or temporal division of the all-embracing female psyche. Wells constantly changed, shifted, developed, and exchanged old ideas for new; Richardson worked at *Pilgrimage* for thirty years without any significant modification of her style, approach, technique, or ideas. (pp. 254-55)

[Richardson] rationalized the problem of her "shapeless outpourings" by working out a theory that saw shapelessness as the natural expression of female empathy, and pattern as the sign of male one-sidedness. If a novel had symbolic form, that was because a man's truncated vision was responsible for it. . . . She was claiming that the entire tradition of the English novel had misrepresented feminine reality. (p. 256)

In pursuing a distinctively female consciousness, rather than attempting to explore female experience, Richardson was applying the ideas of the feminists, especially those of the social evolutionists and the spiritualists. She was fascinated by idealist theories of language and by the mystic's claims to being superior to the artist. (pp. 256-57)

Like Joyce, Richardson had philosophical objections to the inadequacy of language; unlike Joyce, she regarded language as a male construct. Richardson maintained that men and women used two different languages, or rather, the same language with different meanings. . . . Generally, she implies that women communicate on a higher level; in using the language—the "words," as she says—of men, they limit themselves the way an intergalactic race of telepathics would limit itself in using speech. (pp. 258-59)

The stream-of-consciousness technique (a term, incidentally, that Richardson deplored, and parodied as the "Shroud of Consciousness") was an effort to transcend the dilemma by presenting the multiplicity and variety of associations held simultaneously in the female mode of perception. . . .

[But] Richardson did not want to suggest intensity. As

many critics pointed out, her lack of punctuation, use of ellipsis, and fragmented sentences, worked against the structural potential of the sentence in terms of wit and climax, and main and subordinate ideas. Virginia Woolf was sufficiently impressed by this technique to call it "the psychological sentence of the feminine gender, a sentence of a more elastic fibre than the old, capable of stretching to the extreme, of suspending the frailest particles, of enveloping the vaguest shapes. . . . It is a woman's sentence, but only in the sense that it is used to describe a woman's mind by a writer who is neither proud nor afraid of anything she may discover in the psychology of her sex." (p. 260)

Richardson may indeed have fashioned the woman's sentence, or at least the chosen sentence of the female aesthetic. But Woolf is seriously mistaken in calling it unafraid. It is afraid of the unique, the intimate, the physical. By placing the center of reality in the subjective consciousness, and then making consciousness a prism that divides sensation into its equally meaningful single colors, Richardson avoids any discussion of sensation itself, especially as a unified and powerful force. Just as she would not commit herself to ideologies, she would not discriminate among her experiences.

Most of all, Richardson's art is afraid of an ending. Looked at from one point of view, her inability to finish is a statement in itself, a response to the apocalyptic vision of Wells and Lawrence. If men were so obsessed by their sense of an ending that they could not understand the present moment, women were outside of time and epoch, and within eternity. But as Richardson grew older, her relationship to *Pilgrimage* became more obviously possessive and anxious. The book was an extension of herself; to complete it was to die. (pp. 260-61)

> Elaine Showalter, "The Female Tradition" and "The Female Aesthetic," in her A Literature of Their Own: British Women Novelists from Brontë to Lessing (copyright © 1977 by Princeton University Press; Princeton Paperback, 1977; reprinted by permission of Princeton University Press), Princeton University Press, 1977, pp. 3-36, 240-62.*

BIBLIOGRAPHY

Beach, Joseph Warren. "Imagism: Dorothy Richardson." In his *The Twentieth Century Novel: Studies in Technique*, pp. 385-400. New York: Appleton-Century-Crofts, 1932.

Cites representative passages from *Pilgrimage* that warrant associating Richardson with the imagist movement in poetry. This essay also juxtaposes discussion of Emile Zola's and Knut Hamsun's literary techniques with discussion of similar techniques in Richardson's work.

Edel, Leon. "The Reader's Vision." In his *The Modern Psychological Novel*, pp. 65-74. New York: Grove Press, 1955.

An intriguing account of how the critic overcame his distaste for and learned to enjoy Richardson's work, which highlights the difficulties a male reader may find in responding to Richardson's achievement.

Fromm, Gloria G. *Dorothy Richardson: A Biography*. Urbana: University of Illinois Press, 1977, 451 p.

Most complete biography to date, though not designed to accommodate critical material.

Glikin, Gloria. "Dorothy Richardson: The Personal '*Pilgrimage*'." *PMLA* LXXVIII, No. 5 (December 1963): 586-600.

Excellent biographical essay.

Gregory, Horace. *Dorothy Richardson: An Adventure in Self-Discovery*. New York: Holt, Rinehart and Winston, 1967, 114 p.

Critical-biographical study that calls attention to the specific autobiographical elements in *Pilgrimage*, referring to the protagonist of the novels as Dorothy-Miriam.

Kaplan, Sydney. "'Featureless Freedom' Or Ironic Submission: Dorothy Richardson and May Sinclair." *College English* 32, No. 8 (May 1971): 914-17.*

Compares Richardson's and Sinclair's expression of feminine consciousness in their novels.

Rose, Shirley. "The Unmoving Center: Consciousness in Dorothy Richardson's *Pilgrimage*." *Contemporary Literature* 10, No. 3 (Winter 1969): 366-82.

Examines Richardson's critical view of the literary technique termed "stream of consciousness," and considers psychological and philosophical concepts of perception in her novels.

Rose, Shirley. "Dorothy Richardson's Theory of Literature: The Writer as Pilgrim." *Criticism* XII, No. 1 (Winter 1970): 20-37.

Insightful essay showing how Richardson's literary theories harmonize with her particular psychological and philosophical outlook.

Rose, Shirley. "Dorothy Richardson's Focus on Time." *English Literature in Transition* 17, No. 3 (1974): 163-72.

Examines Richardson's theories on the nature of consciousness and time as perceived by the individual.

Rosenberg, John. *Dorothy Richardson: The Genius They Forgot; A Critical Biography*. London: Duckworth, 1973, 212 p.

Far more biographical than critical.

Staley, Thomas F. *Dorothy Richardson*. Boston: Twayne Publishers, 1976, 145 p.

Critical study designed as a balanced evaluation of Richardson's achievement and literary importance.

Saki

1870-1916

(Pseudonym of H[ector] H[ugh] Munro) English short story writer, novelist, journalist, and historian.

Munro's commentators often credit him with literature's most vivid fictional preservation of the stock and staid figures of Edwardianism. His pseudonym, taken from Saki, the cup-bearer to the gods in the *Rubaiyat of Omar Khayyan*, came to be identified with a particular style of disdainful wit and with the Edwardian milieu that it satirized.

Munro's first published work was a history of Russia, a country for which he felt a lifelong fascination. He next published a series of political satires in the *Westminster Gazette*, these bringing him some measure of public notice. With the appearance of his first fiction, *Reginald*, Munro finally achieved the general renown that endured throughout his career.

The *Reginald* stories introduced readers to a type of protagonist who was to become well known for witty observations subversive to the values of the British upper classes. Reginald and his successor, Clovis, serve as Munro's satirical mouthpieces, voicing antagonism toward a wide range of stereotypical figures in elite society. Munro also wrote stories employing an understated savagery in place of clever satire, the result sometimes causing him to be labelled as a purveyor of immature brutality. This brutality is often attributed to his childhood under the guardianship of a pair of despotic aunts. One of Munro's best known tales, "Sredni Vashtar," narrates the horrible end of such an aunt to the delight of her persecuted nephew.

Critical attention has focused mainly on Munro's short stories, his two novels being generally held in lesser regard. The first, *The Unbearable Bassington*, was well received when published, but critics weren't prepared for the book's poignant misery which replaced the usual "Saki" flippancy. A second novel, *When William Came*, was intended as a timely and patriotic warning intended to draw attention to Britain's military vulnerability in the face of imminent war. With the onset of World War I, Munro lied about his age and enlisted in the army. Refusing a commission at least twice, he sought active duty and was killed in battle. Though he is commonly acknowledged as a writer of only minor achievement, Saki continues to draw a small yet loyal following.

PRINCIPAL WORKS

The Rise of the Russian Empire (history) 1900
The Westminster Alice (satirical essays) 1902
Reginald (short stories) 1904
Reginald in Russia, and Other Sketches (short stories) 1910
The Chronicles of Clovis (short stories) 1912
The Unbearable Bassington (novel) 1912
Beasts and Super-Beasts (short stories) 1914
When William Came: A Story of London under the Hohenzollerns (novel) 1914
The Toys of Peace, and Other Papers (short stories) 1919
The Square Egg, and Other Sketches, with Three Plays (short stories and dramas, includes *The Death Trap, Karl-Ludvig's Window, The Watched Pot*) 1924

(essay date 1900)

Mr. Hector H. Munro's account of "The Rise of the Russian Empire" . . . would be an excellent reference-book if it were supplied with a good index. The statement of the rise of the Rurikovitch dynasty, from the time of the first Russ-Varongian invaders in 862 to the extinction of the house in the sixteenth century, is given with a true appreciation of important events, and with a clear method. The history of this period has evidently been studied with thoroughness in such few sources as are available, and other authorities have been freely consulted. Thus the book becomes a valuable addition to a working library on history,—or, rather, it would be so were it not for the incompleteness of the aforementioned index. A masterpiece of historical writing the book is not, either in style, or in characterization of races and epochs. The style is not bad, it is merely mediocre, reminding one of the dry dust-and-bones writings of pedagogical historians, save only when the author has attempted to enliven his narrative by humorous comment,—and then the impression received is decidedly unfavorable, for such witticisms only rob the writing of its dignity without improving its general tone in the least. That luminous picture of peoples and of epochs, expected in these days from writers of general histories, is entirely lacking in Mr. Munro's book,—unless, indeed, an exception be made in favor of the portrayal of Russian political disorder and turmoil. This failure is, however, not the fault of the author, but of his subject; for surely it would be difficult for the most gifted historian to evolve any exact and clear-cut characterizations from the chaotic jumble of Russian politics, rulers, and races, in their earlier history. The author closes his account just when the Russian nation begins to assume a definite entity, and so denies himself the opportunity of showing his ability in dealing with a period where the subject people are better known, and the policy of rulers is more clearly defined. As a whole, the "Rise of the Russian Empire" is a serviceable book of reference, but it is not a great history.

> *"Briefs on New Books," in* The Dial *(copyright, 1900, by The Dial Publishing Company, Inc.), Vol. XXIX, No. 345, November 1, 1900, p. 310.*

(essay date 1914)

As a writer of grotesque social miniatures "Saki" stands in a class by himself. No one surpasses him in the art of condensation, or in creating the right atmosphere at the start. . . . Moreover, "Saki" has the complementary, but by no means invariably concomitant, quality of knowing how to leave off. . . . As a handbook of the gentle art of dealing faithfully with social nuisances—bores, cadgers, "thrusters," and "climbers"—*Beasts and Super-Beasts* is quite unique; but the enjoyment with which we read of their discomfiture is somewhat tempered by the fact that the executioners are not much better than their victims. To attempt to extract any moral lesson or edification from "Saki" would be as unprofitable a task as the effort to hatch a chicken from a hard-boiled egg. He is not an immoral, but for the most part a non-moral writer, with a freakish wit which leads him at times into inhumanity. He has no respect even for death, the references to which are frankly flippant, if we except the study of the old farm-servant called "The Cobweb." Death, in short, is treated either as a negligible or annoying incident in the social drama, or, as in the study of Laura's reincarnations, as a convenient jumping-off ground for incursions into uncanny levity. As an inventor of practical jokes to dislodge or disconcert tiresome people, "Saki" shows a mental resourcefulness bordering on the diabolical, but we like him best when he is least malicious. (pp. 60-1)

> *"Fiction: 'Beasts and Super-Beasts'," in* The Spectator *(© 1914 by The Spectator; reprinted by permission of* The Spectator*), Vol. 113, No. 4489, July 11, 1914, pp. 60-1.*

A. A. MILNE   (essay date 1926)

A strange, exotic creature, this Saki, to us many others who were trying to do it too. For we were so domestic, he so terrifyingly cosmopolitan. While we were being funny, as planned, with collar-studs and hot-water bottles, he was being much funnier with were-wolves and tigers. Our little dialogues were between John and Mary; his, and how much better, between Bertie van Tahn and the Baroness. Even the most casual intruder into one of his sketches, as it might be our Tomkins, had to be called Belturbet or de Ropp, and for his hero, weary man-of-the-world at seventeen, nothing less thrilling than Clovis Sangrail would do. In our envy we may have wondered sometimes if it were not much easier to be funny with tigers than with collar-studs; if Saki's care-

less cruelty, that strange boyish insensitiveness of his, did not give him an unfair start in the pursuit of laughter. It may have been so; but, fortunately, our efforts to be funny in the Saki manner have not survived to prove it.

What is Saki's manner, what his magic talisman? Like every other artist worth consideration he had no recipe. If his exotic choice of subject was often his strength, it was often his weakness; if his insensitiveness carried him through, at times, to victory, it brought him, at times, to defeat. I do not think that he has that 'mastery of the *conte*' which some have claimed for him. Such mastery infers a passion for tidiness which was not in the boyish Saki's equipment. He leaves loose ends everywhere. Nor in his dialogue, delightful as it often is, funny as it nearly always is, is he the supreme master; too much does it become monologue judiciously fed, one character giving and the other taking. But in comment, in reference, in description, in every development of his story, he has a choice of words, a 'way of putting things' which is as inevitably his own vintage as, once tasted, it becomes the private vintage of the connoisseur. (pp. 21-2)

> *A. A. Milne, in his introduction to* The Chronicles of Clovis *by H. H. Munro, in* The Works of "Saki" *(reprinted by permission of The Bodley Head), John Lane, 1926 (and reprinted as "Introducing Saki," in his* By Way of Introduction, *Methuen & Co. Ltd., 1929, pp. 19-23).*

MAURICE BARING   (essay date 1926)

[Saki's *The Unbearable Bassington* is] the most interesting, because the most serious and most deeply felt, just as from a literary point of view, it is likewise the most "important," because the most artistically executed of his books.

It is a tragic story; and it might have deserved as a work of art a still higher place, among the Tragedies of fiction, with Tourgene's *Father and Sons;* Meredith's *Feverel;* Maupassant's *Une Vie,* had there been in the book—for the *story* is as tragic as possible—a stronger dose of that without which a tragedy is not a tragedy: pity. But in the category of books that deal with the misfits, failures, misunderstandings and the minor victims of misunderstandings it is a masterpiece. . . . (pp. ix-x)

It is not that there is no pity in the book, the pity is there, but it is not strong enough to counter-balance and to mitigate the misery, nor to sweeten the bitterness of the misery.

In *The Unbearable Bassington* you see nearly all sides of Saki's peculiar talent; the only salient quality among those that distinguish and differentiate him as a writer from other writers, which is absent in this book, is his vein of macabre supernatural fantasy. There is a hint, but not more than a hint of this, in the farewell dinner party given to Comus.

He had the power of inspiring horror by a touch of the supernatural, but I doubt whether it was one of his most valuable gifts. It was perhaps in his hands too cruel.

The qualities of earlier stories are all to be met with in this book, and such limitations as were their inevitable complement. (p. x)

Saki could draw and create characters. The gift, in his case, is the result of a superfine sensibility and response to subtle and delicate shades of character and feeling. He could draw men, women, boys, children and even animals, and make

them live. He understood the English character, especially
the English female character, and best of all, the English of
the county families, the well-to-do prosperous men and
women who live in the Shires and hunt in the Midlands and
play Bridge in Belgravia.

His men especially, his prigs and his bores, are as sharply
drawn as his women. The characterization in both cases is
effected often by some little touch that reveals not only the
character, but throws light on a fundamental trait in human
nature. . . . (p. xii)

Next to his power of characterization, which is the most
important gift a novelist can possess, I should put his wisdom, his gift of light-hearted irresponsible nonsense, and
his wit; his barbed, sometimes bitter and sometimes cruel
satire; underneath and behind all these gifts there looms a
permanent sadness. His wisdom is revealed over and over
again in a broad gravity of outlook which foresees the inevitable consequences of folly, that effect can but follow a
cause; the rare gift of seeing that a moral "two and two"
make four. . . . (p. xiv)

Now for his wit. . . . Every page, or almost every page of
[*The Unbearable Bassington*] is starred either with epigrams, felicitous phrases, pointed comments or verbal py-
rotechnics.

At its worst, it is mere verbalism, an indulge in epigram
more for the sake of the sound than the sense, or for the fun
of twisting phrases or juggling with words and syllables and
antitheses; this is cheaper, it is the cardinal defect of his
quality; he is tempted in all his books to do it. But in this
book, *The Unbearable Bassington,* the level of Saki's wit
and the dexterity of his phrasing is high, and he might possibly, had he lived longer, have gradually discarded his
more facile verbalisms. . . . (pp. xv-xvi)

[*The Unbearable Bassington*] is a tragic story. The author
at the beginning tells us the story has no moral; he states an
evil and suggests no remedy—but . . . this book might have
been called "A Lesson to Mothers" or "Mother and Son."
There may not be one moral in it, there are very likely fifty
morals or more, for mothers, sons and every one else. It is
the story of a misunderstanding, of a mistake, and of a
wasted life: of a life which is wasted partly because of a
misunderstanding, and partly because of an ingrained egotism and lack of consideration which has for its inevitable
effect the retribution of an isolated death. (pp. xvi-xvii)

This is the tragedy of the book. The wall ["between mother
and son"] is nearly broken; it is nearly made to melt once
or twice, but never quite. The opportunities are misused.
The mother is tied to her possessions. (pp. xviii-xix)

A critical friend once said to me that the description of [the
mother's] last walk in St. James's Park seemed to him to be
the crown of miserable writing, unmitigated unhappiness. I
agree. . . . But the book as it is is an ironic tragedy on a
high level; and it is full of wit that has had time to turn to
tinsel, but has not been tarnished. (pp. xxi-xxii)

Maurice Baring, in his introduction to The Un-
bearable Bassington *by Saki, in* The Works of
"Saki" *(reprinted by permission of The Bodley
Head), John Lane, 1926 (and reprinted in* The
Unbearable Bassington *by Saki, The Viking Press,
1928, pp. ix-xxii).*

L. P. HARTLEY (essay date 1927)

[Munro] was a literary soldier, disciplined, not irregular,

who went the nearest way to his objective and generally
took it. One cannot, in thinking of him, get away from the
military metaphor. His style indeed was a more delicate
weapon than modern soldiers carry; it is a sister-blade to
Max Beerbohm's, stouter than his perhaps, and more prone
to frontal attacks, but not less piercing and leaving as clean
a wound. The conduct of his narratives, brief or long, resembles a campaign; the rough, rebellious surface of life is
mapped out; its defences are carefully enveloped, then
taken by surprise; finally with a grand assault its stronghold
is reduced, and the whole barren region is added to the orderly empire of art. How his stories sparkle, sometimes
with a distracting glitter! What traces do they not bear of
spit and polish, of superfluity discarded, of symmetry
achieved! Hardy, ascetic, mobile, what agonies of private
drilling must they have gone through, before they were allowed to appear in public, on parade, no paragraph incomplete, no comma missing, no sentence awry!

It is true that amid the rattle of rifles and light arms we
seldom detect the boom of a heavy gun. "Saki" carried few
heavy guns. What weight he had (and it was considerable)
was a personal quality and, like charity, it stayed at home,
forming the emplacement from which his machine-guns directed their devastating fire. Without this savage fundamental seriousness his shots would have gone astray; we
should have heard their impressive rattle, we should not
have seen the victims fall. We may tire of his exhibitions of
marksmanship; we may feel, in moments of satiety, that he
is only bringing down clay pigeons; but all the same there is
no disputing the deadliness of the shot or the accuracy of
the aim. Exactly from what dump Munro drew his ammuni-
tion it is hard to say, but it was inexhaustible. He hated,
and he believed. Perhaps it would be true to say that he
hated what he believed in, and believed in what he hated.
He believed that Nature was red in tooth and claw and that
Man was cruel, and he had some kind of respect for the
qualities in men which were consonant with such a view of
life. He believed in living dangerously, and he never mentions death, single or multitudinous, accidental or contrived, without a throb of delight. . . .

But for Munro cruelty was not so much the vehicle of humour as the source. It was not an escape from life but an
intensification of it. "Gentle dullness ever loves a joke,"
said Pope, but he would not have so described "Saki," who
was always willing to wound, and never afraid to strike. He
loves the spectacle of mankind brought to misfortune and
ridicule by its follies. He loves to see the unwary pedestrian
slipping on the orange-peel. He tolerates, he delights in
practical jokes; discomfiture and humiliation are as breath
to his nostrils, balm to his soul, and he always thinks them
funny. Time and again, as one of his characters is artlessly
preparing to sit down, does he (metaphorically) pull away
the chair and start the general laugh. He loathes meekness
and weakness; irony, the refuge of sensitive minds from the
world, is unknown to him; he is a satirist pure and simple.

Yet though he acquiesces in cruelty he does not spare the
cruel. Comus Bassington, the hero of his most considerable
book ["The Unbearable Bassington"], is within the limits
of his intelligence as odious a character as has ever been
drawn. The passage in which, when at school, he canes the
new boy who had been recommended to his protection, is a
masterpiece of venom. All the more hateful characteristics

of schoolboys, their herd-instinct, their desire and power to hurt, their ability to rise in their own esteem only upon the abasement of others, their fertility and resourcefulness in cruelty, all these traits are in a few brief pages exquisitely delineated. . . . But Munro has provided Comus with an Achilles heel. In the ways of the world he is fundamentally stupid—he doesn't know which side his bread is buttered; and so, as the moralist would say, he is shipped off to Nigeria to die of fever. His mother had doted on him, as far as her realisation that, if there were five plovers' eggs he would always take three, permitted her to dote. He and her one Old Master, cherished symbol of overt respectability and latent wealth, were the apples of her eye. On the same day, almost at the same moment, she finds she has lost both; Comus is dead and the picture is declared a copy.

"The Unbearable Bassington" would be a better book, as Mr. Baring has pointed out [see excerpt above], if it showed a sense of pity. It does, twice. Once when Lady Caroline hears of Comus's death; once when Elaine talks to the explorer and big-game hunter whose active life had been cut short by an accident. . . . [This] shows a side of Munro that he usually concealed. (pp. 215-16)

"Saki" then had a softer side, but it was the ferocious quality of his mind that gave life and impetus to his stories. This ferocity, let us hasten to add, is present in some, indeed in most, of his tales only as a rumour or a perfume, expressing itself in a thousand delicious shafts of malice, a hundred ingenious *dénouements*. Sometimes he thinks a story is funny in proportion as it is "tall"; sometimes his wit declines into facetiousness. But at its best it is admirable. True, the dialogue is artificial—people don't talk like that; but no doubt they would if they could. O! to be a Clovis, one thinks enviously, or a Reginald, who can subdue with a word the most insistent bore, encounter on equal terms the most brilliant Duchess. To have a life crammed with mirth-provoking incidents; to meet only two sorts of people; grindstones on which to sharpen the arrows of one's wit, plump defenceless bodies in which to plunge them. Though it is depressing to discover that not even Munro's silliest character, not even Merla Blathlington herself, can keep up her stupidity for long; she has to say something clever, or her creator would die of boredom. Munro will have a lasting reputation. His wit is not merely verbal, never merely a trick; it refreshes itself at a hundred sources and all his experience goes to feed it. His characters have a similarity, sometimes a sameness; his wit has an inexhaustible fertility and (a rare thing in this class of writing) it is reinforced by a sense of humour no less omnivorous. Dapper yet virile, cruel yet without personal animosity, the figure of "Saki" will be cherished by all who love first-rate craftsmanship in letters. (pp. 216-17)

> *L. P. Hartley, "Saki," in* The Bookman, *Vol. LXIV, No. 5, January, 1927, pp. 214-17.*

EDWARD DAVISON (essay date 1927)

"The Chronicles of Clovis" is, unfortunately, far from [Saki's] best book. . . . "The Chronicles" is an altogether delightful little collection of "pieces" (it is the best word) the full flavor of the author's work is not to be consistently tasted there. Once or twice he lapses badly into the mere humorist. Yet there is not a tale in his thirty (saving the two or three horror stories) without at least one touch of saving wit, while at least a dozen bubble champagne-like from beginning to end. . . .

Saki's tales are usually thinly disguised monologues and dialogues of which the dominating characteristic is a malicious cynicism mingling wit and nonsense. . . . Actual jokes are rare with him. He saves them for the situations on which his stories are grounded, stories like "The Unrest Cure" and "Mrs. Packletide's Tiger." . . .

But the best part of Saki is his dialogue. Here he matches the best in Oscar Wilde's comedies. He is at once urbane, ridiculous, cynical, spiteful, brilliantly superficial, epigrammatic, and sparkling. Like all such delicate growths it cannot be plucked for display in a review. A word must also be said of his variety. This volume includes two or three serious stories. For sheer grimness I can think of nothing in recent literature to approach "Sredni Vashtar." This very short story, which is a phenomenally fine piece of writing, bears the same relation to Saki's more characteristic work as "The Monkey's Paw" bears to the longshoreman yarns of Mr. W. W. Jacobs. "Filboid Studge" is sheer O. Henry anglicized; "The Music on the Hill" out-Machens Mr. Machen; but they are one and all Saki. He is a little classic.

> *Edward Davison, "An English Wit," in* The Saturday Review of Literature *(copyright © 1927 by Saturday Review), Vol. 4, No. 10, October 1, 1927, p. 147.*

CHRISTOPHER MORLEY (essay date 1930)

[For] the most part [Saki] preferred to sparkle and fume with incessant bubbles of wit; a wit for which such words as satire, cynicism, sophistry, are all too gassy. (p. v)

In recent revivals of his books distinguished enthusiasts have spoken handsomely of his urbane malice and charm. But in all those comments the friendliest critics have shown themselves instinctively puzzled how to proceed; all have fallen back upon quotation of Saki's own felicities. This is inevitable. The fact is there are few writers less profitable to write *about*. Saki exists only to be read. The exquisite lightness of his work offers no grasp for the solemnities of earnest criticism. He is of those brilliant and lucky volatiles who are to be enjoyed, not critic-handled. He will be instinctively recognized and relished by those capable. (pp. v-vi)

Both Saki and O. Henry are masters of the park-bench setting. Saki was less insistent on twisting the story's tail, but an equal master of surprise when he chose. Let the lover of O. Henry read Saki's *Dusk*, or *The Mouse*, or *The Reticence of Lady Anne*, or *The Open Window*, and see what I mean. The English flapper or Nut of pre-War days was anatomized by Saki as shrewdly as—and less sentimentally than—O. Henry's sheepherder or shopgirl. He could purge the decorous amenities of an English week-end party with blasts of cyclone farce. He could show the conversation of a few ladies at bridge as deadly and quick on the trigger of concealed weapons as a Western bar-room brawl. (p. vi)

Delicate, airy, lucid, precise, with the inconspicuous agility of perfect style, he can pass into the uncanny, the tragic, into mocking fairy-tales grimmer than Grimm. His phrases are always urbane and usually final. (pp. vi-vii)

Saki writes so lightly that you might hardly notice how beautifully also. And here and there, beneath so much enchanting play upon words, you will be startled and embarrassed by play upon hearts. (p. vii)

Christopher Morley, in his introduction to The Short Stories of Saki *by H. H. Munro (copyright 1930 by The Viking Press, Inc.; copyright renewed 1958 by The Viking Press, Inc.; reprinted by permission of the publishers), Viking Penguin, 1930, pp. v-vii.*

ELIZABETH DREW (essay date 1940)

Saki is the most impersonal of artists. His private emotions and enthusiasms, meditations or thoughts, have no place in the world of his art. Saki is not Hector Munro, any more than Elia is Charles Lamb. But the methods of the two writers are completely opposed. Lamb dowered Elia with all his own most lovable characteristics: his warm heart, his genius for friendship, his love of life. Hector Munro, though he was richly endowed with all these qualities, denied them to Saki. That artist, in all his short sketches and stories, is allowed but three strains in his nature: the high spirits and malicious impudence of a precocious child; the cynical wit of the light social satirist; and the Gaelic fantasy of the Highlander. We meet these three in turns: the irresponsible imp who invents unlimited extravagant practical jokes to mystify and enrage and outwit the heavy-minded adult world; the ironic mocker who speaks in the quips of Clovis and Reginald and the Duchess; and the Celt who sees the kettle refuse to boil when it has been bewitched by the Evil Eye, or hears Pan's laughter as he tramples to death the doubter of his powers. (p. 97)

There is an element of cruelty in a practical joke, and many readers of Saki find themselves repelled by a certain heartlessness in many of his tales. . . . It is the genial heartlessness of the normal child, whose fantasies take no account of adult standards of human behavior, and to whom the eating of a gypsy by a hyena is no more terrible than the eating of Red Ridinghood's grandmother by a wolf. The standards of these gruesome tales are those of the fairy tale; their grimness is the grimness of Grimm.

The other element in Saki's cruelty springs from a certain unsparing consistency of vision which will allow no sentiment to intrude. He speaks of one young man as 'one of those people who would be enormously improved by death,' and he never hesitates to supply that embellishment himself on suitable occasions. Stories such as 'The Easter Egg' and 'The Hounds of Fate' are tragedies entirely without pity, but their callousness is consistent with the hard cynical sanity which is behind even his lightest satire, and gives it its strength. His mockery is urbane but ruthless. His wit is in the tradition of Wilde and the lesser creations of E. F. Benson's *Dodo* and Anthony Hope's *Dolly Dialogues,* and in the modern world he has affinities with Noel Coward and the early Aldous Huxley. Like them, he creates an artificial world enclosed in an element outside of which it could no more exist than we could exist outside our envelope of ether. It is embalmed in the element of Wit. To talk about Saki's 'characterization' is absurd. His characters are constructed to form a front against which his light satiric artillery can most effectively be deployed. The forces against him are the common social vices of Vanity Fair: humbug and hypocrisy, greed and grab, envy and uncharitableness, sheer dullness and fatuity. (pp. 97-8)

But the situations and characters which, left to themselves, would develop into what Jane Austen called 'the elegant stupidity of a private party' develop instead into hilarious gayety and crackling brilliance, and it is Saki's wit and not

his satirical material, or any of his other literary material, which will make him live. (p. 98)

Elizabeth Drew, "Saki," in The Atlantic Monthly *(copyright © 1940 ℞ 1968, by The Atlantic Monthly Company, Boston, Mass.; reprinted with permission), Vol. 166, No. 1, July, 1940, pp. 96-8.*

GRAHAM GREENE (essay date 1950)

There are certain writers, as different as Dickens from Kipling, who never shake off the burden of their childhood. The abandonment to the blacking factory in Dickens's case and in Kipling's to the cruel Aunt Rosa living in the sandy suburban road were never forgotten. All later experience seems to have been related to those months or years of unhappiness. Life which turns its cruel side to most of us at an age when we have begun to learn the arts of self-protection took these two writers by surprise during the defencelessness of early childhood. How differently they reacted. Dickens learnt sympathy, Kipling cruelty. . . .

There are great similarities in the early life of Kipling and Saki, and Saki's reaction to misery was nearer Kipling's than Dickens's. (p. 127)

Unhappiness wonderfully aids the memory, and the best stories of Munro are all of childhood, its humour and its anarchy as well as its cruelty and unhappiness.

For Munro reacted to those years rather differently from Kipling. He, too, developed a style like a machine in self-protection, but what sparks this machine gave off. He did not protect himself like Kipling with manliness, knowingness, imaginary adventures of soldiers and Empire builders (though a certain nostalgia for such a life can be read into *The Unbearable Bassington*): he protected himself with epigrams. . . . Munro, like a chivalrous highwayman, only robs the rich: behind all these stories is an exacting sense of justice. In this they are to be distinguished from Kipling's stories in the same genre—*The Village That Voted The Earth Was Flat* and others where the joke is carried too far. With Kipling revenge rather than justice seems to be the motive. . . . (pp. 128-30)

Perhaps I have gone a little too far in emphasizing the cruelty of Munro's work, for there are times when it seems to remind us only of the sunniness of the Edwardian scene, young men in boaters, the box at the Opera, long lazy afternoons in the Park, tea out of the thinnest porcelain with cucumber sandwiches, the easy irresponsible prattle. (p. 130)

Graham Greene, "The Burden of Childhood" (originally published as the introduction to The Best of Saki *by H. H. Munroe, John Lane, 1950), in his* Collected Essays *(copyright 1951 © 1966, 1968, 1969 by Graham Greene; reprinted by permission of Viking Penguin Inc.; in Canada by Laurence Pollinger Ltd. for the Bodley Head, Ltd.), Viking Penguin, 1969, pp. 127-34.*

V. S. PRITCHETT (essay date 1957)

Saki was more than a wit. There was silence in him as well. In that silence one sees a freak of the travelling show of story-tellers, perhaps a gifted performing animal, and it is wild. God knows what terrors and cajoleries have gone on behind the scenes to produce this gifted lynx so contemptuously consenting to be half-human. But one sees the hankering after one last ferocious act in the cause of a nature abused. The peculiar character called Keriway who crops up unexplained in the middle of the Bassington novel tells the story of a "tame, crippled crane." "It was lame," Keriway says, "that is why it was tame." . . .

The Unbearable Bassington is a neat piece of taxidermy, a cheerful exposure of the glass case and contents of Edwardian society, a footnote to *The Spoils of Poynton*. In a way, Saki has been tamed by this society, too. Clovis likes the cork-pop of an easy epigram, the schoolboy hilarity of the practical joke and the fizz of instant success—"The art of public life consists to a great extent of knowing exactly where to stop and going a bit further" and so on—he is the slave of the teacup and dates with every new word. His is the pathos of the bubble. But Saki has strong resources: he is moved by the inescapable nature of the weariness and emptiness of the socialite life, though unable to catch, like Firbank, the minor poetry of fashion. Francesca is too shallow to know tragedy, but she will know the misery of not being able to forget what she did to her son, all her life. She is going to be quietly more humiliated every year. And then, Saki's other resource is to let the animals in with impudent cruelty. The leopard eats the goat in the Bishop's bathroom, the cat rips a house-party to pieces, the hounds find not a fox but a hyena and it comfortably eats a child; the two trapped enemies in the Carpathian forest make up their feud and prepare to astonish their rescuers with the godly news but the rescuers are wolves. Irony and polish are meant to lull us into amused, false comfort. Saki writes like an enemy. Society has bored him to the point of murder. Our laughter is only a note or two short of a scream of fear.

Saki belongs to the early period of the sadistic revival in English comic and satirical writing—the movement suggested by Stevenson, Wilde, Beerbohm, Firbank and Evelyn Waugh—the early period when the chief target was the cult of convention. Among these he is the teaser of hostesses, the shocker of dowagers, the mocker of female crises, the man in the incredible waistcoat who throws a spanner into the teacup; but irreverence and impudence ought not to be cultivated. They should occur. Otherwise writers are on the slippery slope of the light article. Saki is on it too often. There is the puzzling, half-redeeming touch of the amateur about him, that recalls Maurice Baring's remark that he made the mistake of thinking life more important than art. But the awkwardness, the jumpiness in some of these sketches, the disproportion between discursion and incident or clever idea has something to do with the journalism of the period—Mr. Evelyn Waugh's suggestion—and, I would add, some connection with the decadence of club culture. . . . But Saki's club prose changes when he is writing descriptions of nature [in which he is a minor master] when he describes animals and children or draws his sharp new portraits. His people are chiefly the stupid from the county, the natterers of the drawing-room and the classical English bores, and though they are done in cyanide, the deed is touched by a child's sympathy for the vulnerable areas of the large mammals. He collected especially the petty foibles and practical vanities of women (unperturbed by sexual disturbance on his part), and so presented them as persons, just as he presented cats as cats and dogs as dogs. . . .

I do not much care for Saki's supernatural stories, though I like the supernatural touch: the dog, for example, in *The Unbearable Bassington,* at the ghastly last dinner-party. His best things are always ingenious: the drama of incurring another's fate in *The Hounds of Fate,* the shattering absurdity of *Louis,* the artificial dog; and the hilarious tale of the tattooed Dutch commercial traveller who is confined to Italy because he is officially an unexportable work of art. The joke, for Saki, is in the kill. On the whole, it is the heart that is aimed at. He is always richly informed in the vanities of political life and does it in a manner that recalls Disraeli. (p. 18)

His next novel, *The Coming of William* . . . was good propaganda. He imagined an England annexed to Germany and it makes uncomfortable reading; for silly Society turns instantly to collaboration. There is a more serious discomfort here; a disagreeable anti-Semitism shows more plainly in this book and one detects, in this soldierly sado-masochist, a desire for the "discipline" of authoritarian punishment. He is festive and enjoyable as the wild scourge; but the danger obviously was that this performing lynx, in the demi-monde between journalism and a minor art, might have turned serious and started lecturing and reforming his trainer. In earlier and more spontaneous days, he would have eaten him. (p. 19)

V. S. Pritchett, "The Performing Lynx," in The New Statesman & Nation (© 1957 The Statesman & Nation Publishing Co. Ltd.), Vol. LIII, No. 1347, January 5, 1957, pp. 18-19.*

ROBERT DRAKE (essay date 1962)

[Exactly] what is Saki's world and what is his peculiar vision of it? On the one hand, it is the well-ordered country-house, tea-table world of the Edwardian aristocracy—often glittering in its elegance but usually replete with all sorts of "devitalizers": bores, prigs, hypocrites, and ordinary garden-variety fools. On the other, it is the wild, pagan (sometimes Oriental), supernatural world of a vengeful Terror which continually batters at the gates of respectability and decorum, showing no mercy in enlightening or destroying an aristocratic world which has mistaken means for ends and become complacently at ease in Zion. Perhaps here one might remark that there is, in many ways, little to choose between Saki's stories of laughter and his stories of terror; they differ more in degree than in kind. It is but a short step from Reginald and Clovis to Sredni Vashtar and the Hounds of Fate: they are all Terrors of a sort who bring enlightenment and sometimes destruction to the arrogant, the smug, and the willfully blind.

Saki's world is a loveless one. Hatred there is, and malice aplenty. Few writers in English have gloried more than he in the language of polished invective; one has to go back to the eighteenth century for his equal. But Saki was a "good" hater, and his "cruelty" is always directed toward the inflicters of cruelty. It is thus not really a morbid delight in the cruel act for its own sake but, rather, a meting out of cold justice. It is tempting here, of course, to see in Saki the boy who never grew up, avenging himself on his aunts and possibly his sisters; his justice is always channeled into an almost ritualistic form which its advocates will die to preserve. In this respect, Saki might even be compared with a writer so apparently different as Hemingway. They both, in a way, suggest that the world is a disordered, terrifying chaos; and they both suggest that about all one can do in the face of this disorder is to follow the code, to practice an aristocratic, lonely virtue. Saki's discipline is more rigorous and ascetic than Hemingway's, however; for his world is sterilized of that involving, and perhaps devouring, emotion, love. Kindness, *noblesse oblige,* indulgence he may show; but love, and certainly sex, is too big a risk. Family relationships, especially parent-child ones, are almost a blindspot with him: there are more often uncles, cousins, and, especially, aunts than mothers and fathers in his stories. Significantly, his principal attempt at a parent-child relationship, the mother and son in *The Unbearable Bassington,* is not really successful; the two antagonists are so devoid of real family feeling that they cannot properly collide, even tragically.

But in this terrible loveless world, Saki implies, you can stand up like a man and face the music. You may even go to die in the trenches, fighting against the very incarnation of deadening political and military Authority. Or you may face it more passively but resolutely like the Boy Scouts in that somewhat unsuccessful prophetic book, *When William Came.* But, at all costs, the image of the blind, devouring Authority (or anything else which makes for rigidity, inflexibility, and ultimately, perhaps, emasculation) must be shattered—either by such exotic Super-beasts as the Nuts and Flappers or the more ritualistic defenders of the organic, whole vitality which is Saki's ideal.

Saki cannot handle love; and he is not long on tenderness or compassion—whatever H. H. Munro was like in private life. Thus, he lacks the last, great gift of moving the heart. Sometimes, too, the journalistic vices intrude into his work: he writes too facilely, sometimes so pleased with the sound of his own voice that his wit declines into sheer verbalism. But at his best, in the stories, he exhibits a "rage for order" comparable to that of the Metaphysical Poets and a hatred as "regulated" as Jane Austen's. For the most part escaping the shoddy melodrama to which Wilde and his affinities were prone, Saki does not decline into the limp-wristed languor of Firbank, the brittle thinness of Noel Coward, or the bright prissiness of the early Evelyn Waugh. His genius may not be a great one, but it does burn with the hard and gem-like flame. (pp. 9-10)

> *Robert Drake, "Saki: Some Problems and a Bibliography," in* English Fiction in Transition *(copyright © 1962, Helmut E. Gerber and Helga S. Gerber), Vol. V, No. 1, 1962, pp. 6-26.*

ROBERT DRAKE (essay date 1963)

[There] are a substantial number of Saki's stories which, though they are by no means unrelated to the humorous stories, are decidedly nonhumorous in their effects. For want of a better term, one might classify them as stories of irony—an irony that ranges all the way from the mildly sardonic to the terrifyingly sinister. And though Saki's ironic stories have affinities with the works of other contemporary "ironists"—Ambrose Bierce, for example, they are nevertheless distinctively his own, both in their ironic perceptions and in the forms in which these perceptions are realized. These stories constitute, in many ways, no less important a part of Saki's work than his humorous stories. . . .

One of the most effective of the stories of this type is "The Music on the Hill." (p. 374)

It seems that in this story Saki is using a theme familiar in his humorous stories. He is once more constructing a situation in which a character—in this case, Sylvia—is brought by force to an awareness of some aspect of total reality to which he has been willfully blind. That this reality includes the existence of Pan and his dark mysteries and the necessity to do them reverence when within his domains and is contrary to what she believes "real" or perhaps "scientific" is possibly the bitterest irony of the story. But she, like many characters in the humorous stories, has been blind to the real situation as it exists. That is, she has refused to believe in Pan when she is at Yessney. Indeed, in a larger context, she has probably long ago "gone modern" and renounced any belief in the mysterious. But Mortimer sees the folly in not believing in him when he is in the country. Again, just as in the humorous stories, we have an incongruity in the implication that the sensible thing or norm lies really in someone or something that seemingly is not "sensible" or "normal." This paradox, of course, provides the fundamental humor of the Reginald, Clovis, and other "Nut" and "Flapper" stories. Here, though, the situation is significantly different. Cognizance of things as they exist *is* brought to Sylvia, but it comes *too late*. In her "initiation" she must die. There is no time for amelioration on her part. Perhaps this is the essential difference in the cognizance which is imposed on the self-deceived people of the humorous stories and that which is forced on the same sort of people in the nonhumorous stories, and thus the two types of stories may differ more in degree than in kind. (pp. 377-78)

The irony in ["The Hounds of Fate"] seems almost unbearable on the first reading. For a moment it seems that Stoner is victimized by some sort of blind fate which crushes him as relentlessly and remorselessly as one might step on a worm. Indeed, one is reminded of Gloucester's anguished cry in *King Lear:* "As flies to wanton boys are we to th' gods. / They kill us for their sport." But on closer examination there seems to be something besides this blind malignity in the conception of fate here. Stoner, in some respects, has been victimized by his own foolishness. He has been lulled by his lack of insight, the "natural slothfulness and improvidence" which probably explains his previous failures in life, into thinking he could "get away with something." He has, as it were, lived a lie. He is made to gain insight into the error of his ways; but again, as in the case of Sylvia Seltoun, it is too late. The means which brings this cognizance to him is Michael Ley, acting as the agent of a Fate which is not wholly blind but which, to some extent at least, rewards and punishes man on the basis of his own efforts. Stoner has erred in thinking of Fate as something which reaches out and stabs one in the back rather than something which man can help to make for himself. It is the Fate which he has manufactured *for himself* which finds him out in the "narrow lanes" and is "not to be denied." Thus Saki dramatizes the paradox of a blind Fate's not being so blind after all. Again, as in the case of Sylvia Seltoun, that which the protagonist does not believe in— Martin Stoner does not believe in a Fate which "sees"— brings about an awareness of it on his part but only when it is too late. (p. 380)

[The situation in "Sredni Vashtar"] is similar to the situations in the stories discussed previously. Conradin, a ten-year-old boy, has a degree of wisdom, a belief in the fanciful and imaginative that his guardian does not possess. He seems to get some of the full savor of life in his experience whereas Mrs. De Ropp is scornful, skeptical. She does not believe in the elusive, the mysterious, the exotic, represented by Sredni Vashtar [a polecat-ferret] and the cult which Conradin has built around him—the mysterious which is so essentially a part of the whole life. Instead, she is a dull, matter-of-fact person with no sympathy for Conradin, who believes most fervently in that which is not made with hands. Cognizance of the very thing she scoffs at is brought upon Mrs. De Ropp by the thing itself; but again it is too late. Again there is Saki's familiar incongruity of a child's superiority to adults in approaching a truly—and this may seem paradoxical—*mature* view of life. One can hardly take Conradin to task as even an indirect cause of Mrs. De Ropp's demise: she has brought it upon herself through her own refusal to acknowledge the existence of that which *seems* intangible. In this respect also she is like Sylvia Seltoun. They have both essentially denied the mystery inherent in life. (p. 385)

Saki's stories which are not humorous seem, if they have no other bond in common, to have a pervading irony—in some cases as bitter as that of "The Hounds of Fate" and in others only moderately saturnine as in "The Mappined Life." This irony usually consists in the principal character's bringing about his own downfall by scorning as "unreal" some aspect of total reality. In "The Music on the Hill" and "Sredni Vashtar" it is the mystical, imaginative side of human experience which is scorned. In "The Mappined Life" it is the polite fictions of civilization; in "The Hounds of Fate" it is the existence of a Fate which "sees"; and in "The Sheep" it is the existence of a universe which "plays for keeps," no matter how "sorry" the erring human player may be.

We acquire this knowledge of total reality, Saki seems to imply, *in extremis,* if not otherwise. . . . If we do not acquire it willingly, some day when we least expect it, we too are liable to find the hounds of Fate waiting in some narrow lane; we too may hear the music of Pan springing up at our feet and with it the echo of a boy's laughter. . . . (p. 388)

> Robert Drake, "Saki's Ironic Stories," in Texas Studies in Literature and Language (*copyright* © *1963 by the University of Texas Press*), Vol. V, No. 3, Autumn, 1963, pp. 374-88.

(essay date 1963)

The new worlds that were being explored by Edwardian writers like Wells and Bennett, the social problems investigated by Galsworthy, the scandalous social situations that provided subjects for Mr. Maugham, were either uninteresting or repulsive to [Saki].

Perhaps it is chiefly for this reason that there is little serious criticism of him, and that little is unsatisfactory. He has been compared with Max Beerbohm, O. Henry and John Oliver Hobbes, and Mr. Evelyn Waugh has said that he "stands in succession between Wilde and Firbank in the extinct line of literary dandies". Such comparisons seem not wrong but incomplete, because they ignore so much that can be found in his writing. It is true that some of his stories end with the snap of a tale by O. Henry. . . . But such tricks are the least part of Saki, and are found in comparatively few stories. He lacks the urbanity of Beerbohm, the good humour of Wilde and the irresponsible gaiety of Firbank. The chief characteristics of his writing are its casualness, flawed wit and cruelty. . . .

There is no indication that he ever talked about his own art, or about art at all, to his friends. Saki was a wit by nature, an artist by accident, and he was unlucky in the time at which his talent came to flower. Edwardian writers almost all show the touch of vulgarity that makes the whole world kin, and Saki is not immune from it. At its finest, his wit is the kind of verbal explosion that would sound even better on the stage than it looks in print. . . .

The Unbearable Bassington might easily have been an unbearably sentimental and whimsical book. In fact, it is a dazzling performance. Saki's wit is seen here to better advantage than in the short stories. It is more pointed, more elegant, and more relevant to the behaviour of the characters. The London settings against which refulgently witty dialogues are carried on, are done with marvellous careless skill. And the people themselves, not Comus alone but also his mother, the deeply egotistical Courtenay Youghal, and half a dozen minor figures, are examined with an intensity missing in Saki's other work. No doubt this is because here he at last approached the subjects about which he wanted to write.

> "A Crippled Crane," in The Times Literary Supplement (© *Times Newspapers Ltd. (London) 1963; reproduced from* The Times Literary Supplement *by permission*), No. 3221, November 21, 1963, p. 946.

J. W. LAMBERT   (essay date 1963)

There is no mystery about the continued popularity of Saki's stories. They make us laugh, they up-end respectability, they provide, in broad terms, unflagging entertainment. The deftness of their wit, the ingenuity of their anecdotes, are as effective as ever. The satire is still relevant, although its context was the luxurious, not to say bloated, world of upper-middle-class Edwardian England. . . .

[Behind] the artist's showing-up of blind materialism and dimness of spirit loom other, more disturbing qualities: ruthlessness tipping over into cruelty, a purely destructive rage, a remarkable limitation of sympathy, a preoccupation with revenge. . . .

[These attributes] give Saki a complexity which would not necessarily be of interest for its own sake; but which becomes so because its pressures made him, in advance of his time, into a one-man bridge between the Victorian world (of, for example, W. S. Gilbert) and the nervous vivacity of the post-war world (of, say, Noel Coward) which he did not live to see. (p. 7)

[In *Reginald in Russia*] all the notes in Saki's compass were struck: the purely frivolous, the frivolous-macabre, the rustic-horrific, the supernatural, the cynical, the deeply melancholy, and above all the calling-in of the brute creation to redress the inanity, or worse, of human beings. First, the stories made their mark, in both *Reginald* and *Reginald in Russia,* by their success in epigram and pinpoint flippancy. . . .

Saki's gifts in this direction being what they were, it is surprising that he did not—especially as he is known to have admired the plays of Wilde and Pinero—turn more wholeheartedly to the stage. (p. 39)

Like those of that far weightier decorator of trifle Henry James, Saki's prose narratives seemed to lean towards the theatre; like James, Saki was all the same unable to catch the dramatic note; and, again as with James, his tales have proved highly successful . . . when put into straight dramatic form by lesser but more theatrically expert hands.

With the publication of *The Chronicles of Clovis* . . . he signalized his arrival at a sort of maturity. His range was not enlarged, but these twenty-eight stories had an air of authority about them which was to be maintained in *Beasts and Super-Beasts* . . . , and in the best of the pieces in *The Toys of Peace.* . . . (pp. 40-1)

The Unbearable Bassington is open to adverse criticism on several counts. Its construction is clumsy, its emotion forced, several of its points made too hard and too explicitly. But then it is in fact a morality. Its villain is a grossly materialistic society, its victim a free spirit who, born and bred to the conventional world, can neither conform nor totally cut himself off. And at its best the novel reaches a fine level of tragi-comic intensity. Two farewell occasions, occurring before Comus leaves for Africa, wonderfully combine the dazzle of social comedy with an undertow of misery—a theatrical first night and a family dinner-party. Both focus the dissatisfaction which lay at the heart of Munro's temperament, if not his personality; and which was to express itself as strongly, though in a quite different form, in his next and only other full-length book, *When William Came.* Here the craft of fiction has given way almost entirely to a series of moralistic episodes. The tone is too often soggily emotional and the book is in no way a satisfactory work of art. Munro was trying, perhaps, to define a set of values, and to explore failures to live up to them. (p. 45)

When William Came is set in an England occupied by the Germans. But although it talks of the easy conquest of our unpreparedness (and earned the praise of Lord Roberts), it is not in fact another of those hortatory fictions . . . published in the twenty years or so before 1914. It is a picture of a society all too easily adapting itself to ignobility. The details of occupied London are presented with adequate imaginative vigour and a frequently savage wit; but the strength of the book lies in its contrast of temperaments. The spirit of resistance is embodied in a remote figure [Dowager Lady Greymarten] who does not play a large part, though her attitudes are clearly those to which Saki gives his allegiance. . . . And she stands for a fairy-tale England. . . . (pp. 45-7)

This is the England of George Eliot and Thomas Hardy turned over-ripe: the England of the fantasist, of Kenneth Grahame, of Evelyn Waugh (of P. G. Wodehouse, for that matter)—and still, I suspect, for most English people their private image of paradise, whether or not they also seek there standards of aristocratic verve, aplomb, responsibility, courtesy, and chivalry which centuries of high romantic dreaming have set up against the facts of life.

At the centre of *When William Came* stand not the Dowager Lady Greymarten but Murrey Yeovil and his wife Cecily. They are rich; and theirs is a loose-knit marriage. She, like Francesca Bassington, values most her comfortable home and the social London life of which it is the centre. Occupation, as such, by another nation, means little or nothing to her; if she can have her comfort, her attendant young men, her fair share of life in society she is content. When the book opens she is enjoying all these things in German-occupied London. Suddenly her husband returns

from a long spell of wandering in Russian central Asia. Unlike her, he is appalled by what has happened to his country. Here, again rather surprisingly, Saki brings off a striking picture of a man and a woman who, if love is too strong a word, deeply like and respect one another, and manage to preserve both liking and respect despite the abysmal difference which lies between them (but then, to do this, he must make the relationship—like all his relationships—entirely passionless). Yeovil, however (like the young Munro in Burma) has been fearfully ill in the course of his travels, and near to death. Back in England he bears a double cross. Much as he loathes, by instinct, the existing state of affairs, he finds the will to do anything but accept it ebbing away from him. And, taking himself off (again like the young Saki) for some recuperative hunting, finds himself slipping into friendly terms with the enemy, some of whom at least seem to have noticeably finer qualities than his own or his wife's friends. And Saki leaves him contented and ashamed.

Although *When William Came* ends with a moment of discomfiture for the German Emperor it is not in essence a merely patriotic book; it is rather a study in the decay of moral fibre—and of this, too, it seems likely, Saki accused himself. An attempt to define what values, precisely, this moral fibre should have been put to supporting must break down for want of evidence; but we are made to feel that they are very noble, and I see no particular indication that, as has been suggested, *When William Came* indicated any marked preference for authoritarian regimes; though it is true that this temperamental anarch clearly longed to identify himself with something, to find some sense in the pattern of society which he so relentlessly harried in his fiction. (pp. 48-9)

[Could] Saki ever have turned his satirical eye—. . . upon military disillusion as he had upon the Edwardian scene which so conspicuously failed to live up to his notion of what a civilized world should be like? An idle question, no doubt. Yet by way of answer the suspicion rises that Saki's work was done. Read as an Edwardian, he seems often strikingly modern in tone; imagined as an early post-war writer, he seems absurdly out of date.

The feral and pagan strain in him is one which has, at least for the moment, almost entirely vanished from literature. There is nothing unusual, even today, above preferring animals to human beings; but the lengths to which Saki carried the revenge of the animal kingdom or the use of the animal kingdom as agents of revenge is strange indeed. Tiger, elk, hyena, bull, ferret—his private ark resounds with the grunts and snarls of destructive, indeed murderous, brutes: and especially of wolves. These beasts recur in many stories, even the earliest and most frivolous. . . . (pp. 55-6)

Sometimes wolves, sometimes werewolves. Impossible not to sense, at times, the child who ran round the nursery crying 'I'm God, and I'm going to destroy the world' grown into the man whose pointed flippancy barely masked a deep desire to rend and tear the world which so betrayed his ideals. His supernatural stories—'Gabriel-Ernest,' 'The Hounds of Fate,' 'The Music on the Hill'—should not perhaps, after all, be regarded as merely exercises in a genre. He chose again and again, in the minority of stories set in the deep countryside, to highlight the ingrown brooding which he must have found easily enough in the North

Devon of his youth (and could find there today). And he broke the sullen hush with a panic scream which must have echoed something in himself.

Transplanted to London, trimmed into the conventions of the comedy of manners, the feral streak was not submerged. Saki was never a particularly striking satirist of immediate social issues; his occasional jabs at suffragettes, advertising, 'the Sherard Blaw school of discursive drama,' or the Jews . . . are no longer interesting. He worked best upon the perennial absurdities of human nature. He was a moralist who spoke sometimes through a brilliant image, sometimes through a well-turned epigram. . . . (p. 57)

Saki was no Pascal, no Chamfort; but on his level he reached out, from behind his mask and armour, and touched common human experience more widely and more perceptively than Wilde, though with less elegance and less intellectual verve.

Nursing a dream of chivalry, he could not suffer other people. . . . Society was for him a breeding-ground of inanity. When he turns from the attack he becomes a celebrant of loneliness. There is no close human relationship in any of his work, except the twisted skein which binds and cripples Francesca Bassington and her son. There is no physical passion: except in 'The Philanthropist and the Happy Cat' no hint of sex at all. Such marriages as he treats without scorn are companionate. . . . (p. 59)

Had he survived the war he might have matured; might, for example, have lived to write not a great war book but his own *Animal Farm* before George Orwell. . . . But his real contribution to a solemn world is his dazzling mischief. We can see now, in a time when black humour is almost a commonplace, the direction of his fantasy. Its comfortable setting and dexterous exposition make it acceptable to all. But it points, with hypnotic glee, towards the fragmentation of established, steady, solid society, the confusion of the bourgeoisie. . . . Saki sought in romantic patriotism the splendour he could not find in society, in anaesthetizing dreams of battles long ago the gallantry he missed in civilization. . . . He wrote too much, true. He remains a minor master, true. But, when pros and cons have been added up, influences dutifully noted; when a suitable docket for the literary card-index game has been prepared—there remains, beyond all his ingenuity as an anecdotalist, beyond his wit, far beyond his skirmishes with human nature, the buoyancy which irradiates all, which broke him out of his self-created prison, and leaves barely a hint of bitterness in our laughter as we watch this well-tailored Ariel at work on the Caliban in ourselves. (pp. 60-1)

> *J. W. Lambert, "Introduction" (© J. W. Lambert 1963; reprinted with permission of The Bodley Head), in* The Bodley Head Saki *by H. H. Munro, edited by J. W. Lambert, The Bodley Head, 1963, pp. 7-62.*

JANET OVERMYER (essay date 1964)

[Saki's] trademark is his wit, and to this may, in part perhaps, be attributed the absence of effusive and widespread acclaim. Our Puritan heritage still insists that no one who is funny can at the same time be profound. Saki's subject matter also seems remote; he is the satirical chronicler of the leisurely Edwardian era, which was characterized by week-long house parties, proper afternoon teas, servant difficulties, and the suffragette movement—a way of life that died with the First World War. The upper classes with which Saki was familiar and of which he wrote almost exclusively are no longer, even in England, as much looked up to as pace setters as they once were. (p. 171)

Also, fiction today dwells on the common man, the Willy Lomans and the Walter Mittys. It concerns itself with the inactive, the trapped, the frustrated; it is not receptive to Saki's protagonists, uncommon to say the least, who strike out boldly and outrageously, if sometimes foolishly and blunderingly, attempt grandly to solve their problems, and frequently succeed.

Not only Saki's content but his style also seems to be at war with contemporary fiction. Saki is a succinct, precise story teller; no character sketches or slice-of-life incidents for him. He is not particularly concerned with characterization at all, except as it emphasizes his ideas and sharpens his satire. This slight dehumanization of his people serves his purpose well. . . . (pp. 171-72)

Saki is a delightfully easy author to read. His aptness of expression is perfect; his stories move rapidly and frequently end with a twist; and he is wondrously witty. (p. 172)

But no matter how engaging, style is not, after all, its own excuse for being. It should not be laid on, like frosting, to hide unbaked content. But Saki's stylistic blend of wit and cruelty is not used to cover, but to expose. This combination is daubed on the tips of pointed barbs which are carefully aimed to puncture the weaknesses and affectations of those persons for whom Saki had an especial dislike, and who may all be included in the elastic category of fools. Saki did not suffer fools gladly; indeed, he did not suffer them at all. (pp. 172-73)

The ridiculous names and the absence of characterization in depth tend to so dehumanize them that the reader will not sympathize with them and the satire can then scathe more effectively. (p. 173)

But as Saki is capable of biting satire he is also capable of its opposite, heartfelt compassion. His tender solicitude shows as he relates the bittersweet concern for the church mice in "The Saint and the Goblin"; the description of the "elderly gentleman" in "Dusk" who "belonged unmistakably to that forlorn orchestra to whose piping no one dances"; and the heartbreaking doomed friendship of the little bird and the effigy of the Lost Soul in "The Image of the Lost Soul."

His compassion and cruelty come into careful balance when he writes of children. Saki loved and understood children as only a few adult writers are privileged to do, but his view of childhood is dark. He does not sketch the carefree, merry existence that adults like to think children lead. Instead, the children inhabit their own private, often grim world, one which is perfectly understandable to another child, but rarely to an adult. Children revel in the grimness since it is one way of alleviating the very cruelty of their actual existence. Children are cruel to one another because they openly and reasonably express their feelings of dislike. They are cruel to adults because the entire adult world is against them, and they are helpless to resist. They must therefore snatch their revenge whenever the opportunity arises. Saki chronicles children's cruelty with compassion; and this is not a paradox. He pities them, for they need pity; they must retaliate in kind because it is all they know.

Interwoven with Saki's attitude toward fools and children are four main themes, all of which fall under the general heading of man in relation to his environment. The themes are: supernatural beings and events, religion, hypocrisy, and death. The first two have in common their suggestion of tentative answers to man's questions about the unknown; the latter two have in common their inevitability. (pp. 173-74)

[It] is apparent that Saki took the supernatural seriously. Saki's characters have dreams which predict horse race winners, see signs which foretell death, put spells on one another, turn into ghosts or animals, and are startled by animals which have supra-animal powers. At no time is a rational explanation for these occurrences offered, and no character doubts their other-worldly source.

Saki's opinion of religion connects with his opinion of hypocrisy. Men endlessly pretend to one another, for both trivial and serious reasons. They glibly utter the "polite" white lie of thanking the giver for a useless Christmas gift, as in "Down Pens," and they just as readily dole out their friendship and pity openly to one of lower station only when it should be to their advantage, as in "The Wolves of Cernogratz."

Hypocrisy mars not only man's relation to man but man's relation to God. True Christians, actively practicing what they are supposed to believe, are almost impossible to find. Such stories as "A Touch of Realism" in which two Jews are marooned on a moor in a snowstorm as part of a Christmas game and "The Story of St. Vespaluus" in which a supposed Christian near-martyr is actually a pagan indicate that Saki distrusted genuine religious practices.

Polite tale-telling would thus seem to be necessary not only for a smooth-running society, but a smooth-running conscience. Man cannot face the truth about himself. Perhaps one reason why religion in Saki's stories is unworkable is that it will not permit man to lie to himself.

References to death recur repeatedly. It may be referred to flippantly, as in "The Lull," when a young girl describes the housemaid's identification of three bodies that have floated past the window during a supposed storm as her fiance. At times it is unavoidable doom, as in "The Hounds of Fate," when a young man is killed because of his resemblance to another; and at times it is a triumph of the human spirit as in "The Easter Egg" when a coward gives his life to save that of a prince. Saki's preoccupation with death would seem to say that an awareness of man's final end colors his every action. No matter how high he rises, death waits. But it need not be a total defeat; it may, in fact, be a victory. There is a correlation between this belief and the Christian philosophy, although the victory in Saki's stories refers to man's triumph over himself, not over death.

From a consideration of those persons Saki attacks and those themes that most interest him can be evolved an idea of his basic philosophy. All of his writing life Saki saw through a glass darkly. He attacks mercilessly because he sees life so clearly, both as it is and as he feels it should be. He cares so deeply about mankind that he cannot bear to see people dissipate their tastes and talents on the inconsequential. He so wants to incite them to productive action in order that they may achieve the great goals of which they are capable that he becomes cruel in pointing up their defects. And he finds it necessary to cover this bitter pill of cruelty with the jelly of wit. But the pill is still visible.

The jelly has two purposes. First, coating the bitterness makes the pill easier to swallow. For Saki attacks not *him*, but *me*, and no one enjoys having his own failings blatantly trumpeted. Saki's poker-faced satire exposes the faults of its reader as well as its victim, while it seems merely to be relating an amusing incident. While the reader is laughing, the rapier is slipping, almost unfelt, between his own shoulder blades. He must watch that he does not say, "How ridiculous he is," but "How ridiculous I am."

Wit is also a protection for Saki, as it is for Reginald-Clovis-Bertie—it wounds others before they can wound him. And it keeps the insensitive at a distance so they will not discover the sincere solicitude Saki felt for his fellows. For Saki, unlike Swift, can pity as hugely as he condemns because, as is evident from his many compassionate insights, he identifies himself with foolish, struggling, inept mankind.

But even while he is urging man on he says that, ironically, there is a barrier to complete success. Just as children can never win out against adults, so man can never win out against a force more powerful than he, which may be referred to as fate. Man may transcend himself for a moment and achieve a truly glorious triumph; but then he will be slapped back. And the final defeat is that of death. Nevertheless he must keep trying. The heroes are not those who win, for no one can win, but those who persist until they gain some small success before the greater power intervenes. It is the attempt that exalts. (pp. 174-75)

Janet Overmyer, "Turn Down an Empty Glass," in The Texas Quarterly (© 1964 by The University of Texas at Austin), Vol. VII, No. 3, Autumn, 1964, pp. 171-75.

PETER BILTON (essay date 1966)

Verbal wit is the ingredient for which Saki's stories are most admired, and the level at which criticism often stops, with some comment on the bright surface beneath which little can be found. But when Clovis says 'Waldo is one of those people who would be enormously improved by death', the wit works—as wit does—through the trick it plays on our conditioned expectations and responses, which were what Saki constantly tried to break down. At the same time, the remark has a disquieting chill about it, appropriate to Saki's views. When the twists of plot or sudden endings of the stories take us unawares, they are functioning in the same way as the wit: conventional expectations are upset, and life is shown as Saki thought it ought to be seen, as a source of constant surprise, shock—and interest. . . . The medium of wit, the setting amid society conventions, the plot aimed at the discomfiture of dulness: at all levels Saki made logically coherent choices. (That, surely, is structure.) (p. 440)

Perhaps Saki came to feel that the Universal Darkness—in his particular upper-class version—was triumphing nevertheless, or simply that with his stories he could lead his bores to laughter but could not make them think. Whatever the reason, one finds in a chronological reading of the stories a gradual decrease in the verbal wit, a more and more earnest or even bitter tone of voice, and a gradual increase in physical assault on his victims to accompany the mental. (Here let me express my wonder at the use of the word 'sadistic' in descriptions of the stories. Saki never goes into gory detail; when one of his animals takes life it happens quickly, cleanly, and above all naturally. Besides, the charge of sadism must refer to the writer's intention rather than to his subject matter. The verbal lashings and practical jokes in Saki's stories leave the air cleaner afterwards; even the deaths, though sometimes macabre, are never morbid.) (pp. 440-41)

[In] a few late stories, a passionate declaration of true values is allowed to reinforce the concerted attack on the false. The explicit statements in 'The Cupboard of the Yesterdays' or 'The Mappined Life' bring out what has been implied all along. To Saki the prospect that fatuous and self-satisfied Sheep should dwell in the land and possess it was far from soothing. He saw that passions were 'fast becoming atrophied for want of exercise', felt the 'charm of uncertainty and landslide', and pitied the 'legion of men who were once young and unfettered and now eat out their souls in dustbins'. He knew that 'there are heaps of ways of leading a real existence without committing sensational deeds of violence. It's the dreadful little everyday acts of pretended importance that give the Mappin stamp to our life.' Succinct anticipations of modern drama, and previews of modern life. Saki's crystal ball showed all to-day's triviality and mass-thinking. . . . (p. 441)

Peter Bilton, "Salute to an N.C.O.," in English Studies *(© 1966 by Swets & Zeitlinger B.V.), Vol. 47, No. 6, 1966, pp. 439-42.*

NOËL COWARD (essay date 1967)

Who could have dreamed fifty-two years ago when, at the age of fifteen, I first read [Saki's] "Beasts and Super-Beasts," that I should one day be in a position to reintroduce him to a reading public many of whom possibly have never heard of him. (p. xi)

On looking back I realise that the two most significant influences on my career as a writer were Saki and E. Nesbit. . . . (p. xii)

Many writers who raise youthful minds to a high pitch of enthusiasm are liable, when re-read in the cold remorseless light of middle age, to lose much of their original magic. The wit seems laboured and the language old-fashioned. Saki does not belong to this category. His stories and novels appear as delightful and, to use a much abused word, sophisticated, as they did when he first published them. They are dated only by the fact that they evoke an atmosphere and describe a society which vanished in the baleful summer of 1914. The Edwardian era, in spite of its political idiocies and a sinister sense of foreboding which, to intelligent observers, underlay the latter part of it, must have been, socially at least, very charming. It is this evanescent charm that Saki so effortlessly evoked. True, beneath the lightly satirical badinage of *When William Came* he sounds a prophetic note of warning which shows that he was by no means insensitive to the growing international tension. The idea of England being occupied by Germany . . . must have been fairly startling to the upper-middle-class complacency of 1912. It might have been more so if Saki had been more widely read, but alas he had only a limited public, possibly for the usual reason that he was ahead of his time. I don't feel, however, that this conclusion is really a valid one. At whatever time he had written, his talent, enchanting as it is to devotees like myself, lacks the necessary ingredients of a "best seller." It is too unsentimental and too superficially flippant. On the rare occasions,

such as the end of *The Unbearable Bassington,* when he attempts tragedy, the result is unconvincing and disconcertingly abrupt. His essays in the macabre are more successful. The sinister quality of "Sredni Vashtar" and "The Easter Egg" can be remembered with an authentic shudder. High comedy was undoubtedly his greatest gift. "The Schartz-Metterklume Method," "The Unrest-Cure" and "Tobermory" and "The Open Window" are masterpieces. I have often wondered, if he had survived World War I, how he would have reacted to the years immediately following it, that much maligned period now glibly referred to as "the Hectic Twenties" when upstart Michael Arlens and Noël Cowards flourished like green bay trees in the frenzied atmosphere of cocktail parties, treasure hunts, Hawes and Curtis dressing gowns, long cigarette holders and enthusiastically publicised decadence. He would undoubtedly have found many targets for his sardonic wit in that gay decade but I have an instinctive feeling that it wouldn't really have been his cup of tea. His satire was based primarily on the assumption of a fixed social status quo which, although at the time he was writing may have been wobbling a bit, outwardly at least, betrayed few signs of its imminent collapse. His articulate duchesses sipping China tea on their impeccable lawns, his witty, effete young heroes Reginald, Clovis Sangrail, Comus Bassington, with their gaily irreverent persiflage and their preoccupation with oysters, caviar and personal adornment, finally disappeared in the gunsmoke of 1914. . . . I am convinced that there will always be enough admirers of Saki to keep his memory fresh. I cannot feel that he would have wished for more. (pp. xiii-xiv)

Noël Coward, "Introduction" (1967), in The Complete Works of Saki *by H. H. Munro (copyright © 1976 by Doubleday & Company, Inc.; reprinted by permission of Doubleday & Company, Inc.), Doubleday, 1976, pp. xi-xiv.*

CHARLES H. GILLEN (essay date 1969)

[Munro's] first book, *The Rise of the Russian Empire,* was a rather heavy undertaking. (p. 28)

The principal fault of *The Rise of the Russian Empire* is the confusion it engenders in the general reader. The book's subject and its material are much too involved and full of incident to be compressed efficiently in the limits of a three-hundred-page book. . . .

At many points in the book Munro's style becomes lush and purple, a manner not at all typical of the later cool detachment of his fiction. Apparently, he was often carried away by the bloody, clashing pageantry of his subject. Indeed, the impression Munro leaves today is one of attempting to infuse life and color, by an art similar to the novelist's, into the hitherto dry and colorless writing of most history books. (p. 29)

The Rise of the Russian Empire presaged, however, many of Munro's writing characteristics. Munro as a writer had, for example, the ability to project his conceptions of people and places into the reader's imagination with extreme vividness. (pp. 29-30)

Many of the figures of speech in *The Rise of the Russian Empire* have the instantly recognizable Munrovian flavor and originality, with a predominant imagery of Russian princes, peasants, and invaders as wild birds and feral beasts. . . . (p. 30)

Munro, in his treatment of religion in the book, took a most patronizing and superior stand. He never bothered to conceal his contempt of all the religions, both formal and unsophisticated, with which he had to deal in the book. (p. 31)

Obvious also throughout the book is Munro's natural combativeness. He never wrote deprecatingly of the wastefulness of battles and wars, although he invariably wrote with contempt of the compromiser and the advocate of "peace at any price"—a revelation of Munro's own pugnacity. (p. 32)

The usual commentaries on *Reginald* have given these sketches a reputation for lightheartedly reporting the foibles of the stuffed shirts and overupholstered *grande dames* of London society while they are written with a giddy unconcern for the inequities of the social system which permitted such abuses. Munro in *Reginald* was occasionally critical of some of the sacred institutions of the upper world, but he criticized so lightly that his readers seldom felt his sting. . . .

Munro, through Reginald, was not always complacent when he wrote about the pomp and glittering surface of the great world. This "great world," as described in the *Reginald* sketches, was founded on exploitation, ignorance, and, above all, on widespread poverty. (p. 46)

Munro was not attempting to create a three-dimensional character in Reginald; no one could possibly have been so consistently artificial and flippant as Munro made him. When one gets past the irreverence and parasitism, there is very little else to uncover in the shallow Reginald character. . . . [In] creating Reginald, Munro pioneered in the exposition of a certain type of young man infesting the British upper classes, irresponsible and often scatterbrained. (p. 47)

One of Munro's writing distinctions is the manner in which he set out his truly unique fantasies. His straightfaced mendacity, for instance, was a frequent manifestation of this quality. Munro's readers knew, of course, that they were having their "legs pulled," but Munro did it with such appropriateness to his premises that the readers accepted it as slightly unfocused truth. (p. 72)

Munro's ability first to ideate his fantasies, then to develop them with all sorts of logical additions and reasonable comments, is another of his literary hallmarks. (p. 74)

Truly knowledgeable about the incidents and the backgrounds he was constantly observing in wealthy town houses and at weekend parties in the country, Munro wrote about these rarefied places and their habitués in a rather unflattering way. His was a sort of love-hate attitude; the milieu was Munro's own, the one into which he had been born, but he wrote about it in a dissociated and alienated way. (p. 75)

In a good many of his . . . stories, in the majority perhaps, Munro took as models the people of this upper world; but he never wrote of them with kindness or approbation. He criticized their habits, their beliefs, their characters; but he never once criticized the social system that permitted such beings to rest on the top of it. Because Munro believed in the rightness and inevitability of the class system, he was incapable of making any fundamental criticism of it. (pp. 76-7)

Munro's writing is archtypical of that halcyon prewar era of Edward VII and George V when, for the consumption of the wealthy and privileged, a caste of loving artisans labored in a small area of London's West End—the tailors, gunsmiths, bootmakers, vintners, hatters, tobacconists, jewelers, and haberdashers whose products play so large a part in Munro's fiction. No other writer has so fully bequeathed the feel and look of this vanished time of apparent solidity and order, when the happy few in Britain led their carefree lives in the country houses of "county" Society or in mansions in the sooty air of Town. (pp. 77-8)

Munro was the only writer of his day who consistently used the unhackneyed subject of the uncanny and supernatural. . . . [By] its nature the subject disqualified itself from use by the realists and social reformers, and probably could only be appreciated by a restricted and selective readership like Munro's. This subject might easily have degenerated into the merely silly, but Munro handled it with gravity and great writing skill, and he was helped in its development by something sympathetic in his nature. (p. 83)

[One] of Munro's traits is the effortless display of his cosmopolitanism. In "The Interlopers" he used the background of a forest in the Carpathians for two *mitteleuropa* characters most credibly drawn in this sketch of the old Austro-Hungarian Empire. The story "The Name-Day" also deals with the old Habsburg dominions; and, like "The Interlopers," it conveys the flavor of an exotic corner of the world. "The Wolves of Cernogratz" knowledgeably deals with the fulfillment of a legend in an east German castle, and in "Wratislaw" the badinage between a Gräfin and a Countess somehow imparts the gaiety of old Vienna. Munro casually injected Dieppe, Homburg, the Engadine, Novibazar, Paris, Pomerania, Burma, and other foreign places into his stories, always with the authenticity of having been to these places himself. Just as casually he introduced characters from the Russian nobility, the revolutionaries of the Balkans, the smug merchant class of the Far East, or the bohemian world of Paris; like the exotic backgrounds, these characters were authentic. (pp. 87-8)

The "Saki" short stories seem certain to endure; the latter-day reader finds something familiar and pertinent in Munro's cynicism and unflattering view of humanity. Munro's people are alive and contemporaneous: one still sees today the stuffed shirt, the persistent sponger, the social climber, the ambitious young politician, the black sheep, the self-satisfied incompetent, the wealthy idler, the silly, exploited woman, and, even occasionally, the wit. Munro's attractiveness for the modern reader is his surprising modernity. (pp. 89-90)

For the theme of [*The Unbearable Bassington*] Munro chose the sins of a young ne'er-do-well of the upper middle class, who—by rejecting opportunities of birth, position, and influence—alienated the people who tried to help him while he brought misery to those who loved him, as he obstinately traveled down his own road to perdition. (p. 91)

There is an obvious intent to convey an effect of impending, self-induced doom in the style and in the cumulative construction of [*The Unbearable Bassington*]; and, for all its digressions and its discursiveness, the novel does impart a feeling of portentousness and sinister inexorability that is a tribute to Munro's writing skill. He conveyed his motif of preordained misfortune, of impending disaster, in an ever-thickening atmosphere of nightmare inevitability. One way in which he did was to surround most of the characters in the book with an air of pessimism; they have a black outlook which is sensed even in their funniest observations. (p. 95)

Munro's attempt to make the fate of Comus Bassington into a "raw deal," something grossly unfair, a tragedy, does not stand up to the test of modern values. Many sons of the Establishment were "sent out" to earn a living in the unhealthier reaches of the British Empire; and many wild young men of this class, the black sheep and scapegraces like Comus Bassington, who were actually paid to stay from their respectable families in the home island, became "remittance men." It was not an unusual situation, and certainly Bassington's story was not tragedy.

There were sights, sounds, and events in London, right under Munro's nose, which were truly tragic: the unfortunates who had to spend their nights on the Embankment, the pavement artists, the cab touts, the tuberculars crowded into the warrens of the slums, the pageant of hunger, poverty, and ignorance that daily paraded through the city. Here was the stuff of real tragedy, tragedy of a scope and intensity never achieved in Munro's little book—a book whose characters, by contrast, underwent piffling misadventures. . . . (pp. 96-7)

Ingvar Andersson, Munro's Swedish critic, has suggested that a psychiatric examination of Munro's work by someone trained in both psychoanalysis and the creation of fiction would be very fruitful. It may be conceded without the psychoanalysis that Munro was a mass of complexes—he chose the Oedipal relationship as the main theme of *The Unbearable Bassington*—although that expression and other now familiar terms of Freudian jargon were then almost unknown—but never could he have brought himself to write baldly about sexuality, clever though he was at introducing its phenomena obliquely. Munro's theme of the mother-son relationship in *The Unbearable Bassington* is the mirrored obverse of his own personal history. . . . He seems to have chosen this Oedipus theme innocently for its relatively unhackneyed nature and with no premeditation of shocking his basically conventional readership by its unhealthy overtones.

There are many hints and rather open suggestions of sexual incidents throughout *The Unbearable Bassington* if the book is examined for them, but still it is apparent what [Evelyn] Waugh meant by his remark about "the complete exclusion of sex." Munro always wrote in a reticent manner about this most basic of topics, and though he was forced to deal with it, however gingerly, in *The Unbearable Bassington*, he almost invariably avoided it in his fiction. Was it natural reticence, distaste, or downright ignorance of the subject? Whatever the reason, the absence of this subject is another of the characteristics of Munro's writing, which is more the pity, because an occasional dollop of sexuality would have made his work all the more plausible and delectable. (pp. 101-02)

Munro, all through this book, introduced technical and sometimes clinical discussions of Parliamentary maneuvers and intrigues; it is almost as if his main theme of the scapegrace got away from him and the subject of politics became dominant. He himself had the common proprietary attitude toward politics, a trait which seems to have been characteristic of both the Liberal and Conservative paladins active in society. It mattered not too much to which party one belonged; the principal thing was to have the correct birth, background, schooling, and accent. And, because Munro was writing for this level, he had the honesty to write as a snob, snobbishly, and to portray the superiority in all respects of the wealthy, well-bred caste. He believed in this superiority with the deepest conviction; and, whenever he had occasion to introduce the lower orders into his plot, he mentioned them impersonally, like articles of furniture, as if they—the footmen, the maids, the crossing sweepers—were expected to be discreetly present whenever their services were needed. (p. 104)

The Unbearable Bassington is permeated with this unconsciously arrogant assumption of the superiority and deserved preferment of the wealthy and well-bred stratum. (p. 105)

And yet, for all Munro's mastery of his society milieu, there is a curious lack of verisimilitude in *The Unbearable Bassington,* an absence of realism in the presentation of how the Best People really spent their daily lives. . . . It is as if Munro had had a thesis to expound, as if he could not be bothered to make the characters who illustrated it into flesh-and-blood creations. (pp. 105-06)

In writing *When William Came* Munro had two purposes in mind: he wanted to make his own contribution to the cause of instituting universal military training in Great Britain, and he wanted to startle and shock the influential people of England out of their smugness and false sense of security by alerting them to the looming German menace. He undertook the job with all the seriousness and determination that underlay his superficial cynicism. . . . Even the chapter headings of *When William Came* are used as instruments of Munro's purpose; the chapters are not divided by chaste numerals, as in *The Unbearable Bassington,* but are satirical descriptions of the distasteful material each chapter treats of; and they become progressively more sardonic in their wording as one approaches the end of the book. (p. 112)

For one who had such a long and ramified military ancestry, and who himself was a militaristic, combative, hot-blooded man, Munro strangely enough skimped and even fudged the description of the Anglo-German war and the quick defeat of England in *When William Came*. Other contemporary writers, H. G. Wells for instance, would have made a description of such a war much more exciting and credible. It really is inexplicable that Munro did not make a greater effort at imagining and relating the details of so significant a war. Instead, Munro presents a perfunctory description of it in *When William Came*. . . . (p. 115)

The writing device most often used in *When William Came* is the illuminative-by-indirection dialogue, which Munro used throughout the book to emphasize the causes and consequences of a German victory over England. Murrey Yeovil has dialogues with a politically aware physician, a London policeman, a collaborating clubman, a Hungarian visitor to England, a combative young clergyman, and a *grande dame* of British politics. Cicely has inveigling conversations with her husband; a French naturalist converses with a British matron transplanted to India; and even a pair of German conquerors discuss the causes of English defeat and the possibility of German assimilation of the English. In all these dialogues Munro, without having to comment directly, was able to sidelight the horrible plight of defeated England and the folly of not being prepared militarily; it was an effective way of underscoring these two main issues. (pp. 116-17)

One thread which appears consistently in this book that is distasteful to the reader of the 1960's, who has been tragically educated by the world's more recent history, is Munro's anti-Semitism, the nearly universal anti-Semitism of his caste. His intense nationalism led him to impute in *When William Came* a tendency on the part of wealthy and influential British Jews to collaborate with the German conquerors and to take the places of those of the British aristocracy who had left England.... The emergence of Munro's anti-Semitism here, a typical Tory attitude of that day, has the appearance of his having seized an opportunity to air one of his prejudices. It certainly does nothing to amplify his theme of the necessity for military preparation in England. (p. 121)

The Death Trap and *Karl-Ludwig's Window* [are] of such brevity that their presentation even as curtain raisers would have been of debatable wisdom. They are little more than anecdotes, and much too stagy to be presented to a live audience, which might laugh in the wrong places. Munro seems to have written *The Death Trap* and *Karl-Ludwig's Window* in his late youth, before he attempted to become a professional writer, because they are certainly uncommercial, for their excess of gore and melodrama was outdated even at the turn of the century. These playlets illustrate, however, certain recurrent subjects in Munro's work in other media: his preoccupation with the blood lines and family trees of Continental royalty and nobility . . . ; his militarism; his admiration for the large gesture, the intransigence of youth; his deep sense of *noblesse oblige;* and a concern with death so pervasive that it can only be termed a death wish. (p. 124)

Although Munro made the protagonist of *Karl-Ludwig's Window* slightly older than the Prince of *The Death Trap* there is a similarity between these two militaristic playlets: finding a way out of an insoluble difficulty by committing a stiffly honorable suicide. Indeed, this Balkan setting, military background, and reverence for royalty would have been more suitable material for Munro's short stories, where they would not have seemed quite so ludicrous.

Both of these playlets may charitably be set down as mistakes of Munro's youth; apparently they were written as exercises, tentatively, before he determined to become a professional writer. Certainly their conception is very young, almost callow. About the only thing they indicate of the older Munro's writings is their mordant, rather nihilistic point of view. (p. 125)

The Watched Pot, for all its typical Munrovian attempts at originality in writing about the didoes of a group of young people, may very definitely be catalogued as a comedy of manners. It meets all of this medium's standards of lightness, flippancy, cynicism, and artificiality. The play acknowledges, without apology, the existence of a leisured class; and it dissects without apology their peccadilloes, affairs, and high-born attitudes. (p. 129)

Undoubtedly Munro broke new literary ground in his fiction; his quiet, disenchanted observations, inserted so suavely into his stories, on the human animal's foibles and follies, his mockery of human values, beliefs, institutions, his masterly use of the macabre, his great and constant wit, his genuine cosmopolitanism, and even his habitual use of surprise endings are some of the ingredients which were blended into the truly idiosyncratic works of "Saki." This work was fresh, if more than a little unsettling; and it was completely underived, owing nothing to any predecessor. (p. 158)

Munro's real accomplishment was to recognize the potential of the story material in the denizens and in the trappings of the upper classes. To him almost alone goes the credit of discovering and working this rich vein—the shallowness of the paladins who ordered his era and his world. Munro stands alone as *the* satirist of the grossnesses of Edwardian society; one cannot think of a better qualified Petronius in this narrow but fruitful field. This, then, is his contribution to English literature. (p. 159)

> *Charles H. Gillen, in his* H. H. Munro (Saki) *(copyright © 1969 by Twayne Publishers, Inc.; reprinted with the permission of Twayne Publishers, A Division of G. K. Hall & Co., Boston), Twayne, 1969, 178 p.*

BIBLIOGRAPHY

Chesterton, G. K. Introduction to *The Toys of Peace and Other Papers,* by H. H. Munro, pp. xi-xiv. London: John Lane, 1919.
Chesterton's ruminations on the title story of this collection.

Munro, E. M. "Biography of Saki." In *The Square Egg and Other Sketches, with Three Plays,* by H. H. Munro, pp. 3-103. New York: The Viking Press, 1929.
Anecdotal remembrances by Munro's sister, who is assumed to have destroyed many of Munro's papers and effects which would allow a more complete biography. This essay is particularly valuable for the letters by Munro that it reprints.

Nevinson, H. W. Introduction to *Beasts and Super-Beasts,* by Saki, pp. vii-xii. New York: The Viking Press, 1926.
Sees a "delightful and ingenious wickedness" in the stories of this collection.

Porterfield, Alexander. "Saki." *The London Mercury* XII, No. 70 (August 1925): 385-94.
Interesting survey of Saki's works which concludes that Saki will be remembered for his short stories rather than his novels which lacked the brightness and gaiety of his stories.

Pritchett, V. S. "Saki." *New Statesman* LXVI, No. 1703 (1 November 1963): 614-15.
Review of the Bodley Head edition of Munro's stories, along with a general appraisal.

Stevick, Philip. "Saki's Beasts." *English Literature in Transition* 9, No. 1 (1966): 33-37.
Freudian reading of Munro's *Beasts and Super-Beasts.*

Theroux, Paul. "Recalling Saki on His 100th Birthday." *Book World* IV, No. 51 (20 December 1970): 1, 3.
Brief biographical facts, with reflections on Saki's past commentators and his Edwardian milieu.

George Bernard Shaw

1856-1950

(Also wrote under pseudonym of Corno di Bassetto) Anglo-Irish dramatist, essayist, critic and novelist.

Shaw, an immensely popular playwright, is generally considered to be the best known English dramatist since Shakespeare. An outspoken public figure, he was famous worldwide for his concern with social reform and his iconoclastic wit.

Shaw was born into genteel poverty in Dublin. His father was an alcoholic; his mother, a lady of some refinement and culture, introduced her son to music and art at an early age. As a young man, Shaw left Dublin to join his mother in London, where she had established herself as a music teacher. For nine years Shaw was supported by his mother while he tended to his self-education. During this period he wrote five unsuccessful novels and through intensive reading in economics and politics gave himself the strong background that he would call upon all his life for his definite opinions on social subjects. Shaw established himself as a persuasive orator during this time, rising to prominence in the socialist Fabian Society. He was also prominent as a journalist, working as a book reviewer, an art critic, a music critic, and finally, in 1895, the drama critic for *The Saturday Review*. Shaw's criticism is witty, biting, and often brilliant.

Shaw has the unusual distinction of being a playwright whose work was successful in book form before it was successful on stage. His early career as a dramatist aroused the interest of a small enthusiastic audience, but several of his early plays were rejected for performance because they were believed to be unactable or risque. Nevertheless, six of these plays were collected in *Plays: Pleasant and Unpleasant,* accompanied by lengthy explanatory prefaces that many critics consider to be as significant as the plays. The success of this endeavor, along with his marriage in 1898 to Charlotte Payne-Townshend, a rich Fabian, proved a turning point in his fortunes. From that time on, Shaw was closely associated with the intellectual revival of the British theatre, two of his greatest critical successes being *Man and Superman* and *Saint Joan*. The comedy *Pygmalion* was his greatest commercial success, constantly revived, and was the basis for Lerner and Loewe's long-running musical, *My Fair Lady*.

The central criticism directed at Shaw as a dramatist is that his characters are intellectual rather than human creations. It is true that Shaw did not have the depth of Ibsen or Strindberg, nor did his characterization or dramatic technique grow richer or more complex over the years. But other critics find this to be Shaw's greatest strength. They regard Shaw's art as one in which intellectual conflicts are animated and enlivened. For this reason he is often considered to be a great dramatic teacher, with the theater as his classroom.

Shaw, an eccentric person, who was essentially shy, created the persona of "G.B.S.": showman, satirist, pundit, and intellectual jester, challenging established political and social beliefs. During his sixty years of literary activity, Shaw expressed his views on all subjects with great frankness and wit, producing a tremendous body of work. He declined the Order of Merit but was persuaded to accept the Nobel Prize in 1925.

PRINCIPAL WORKS

Cashel Byron's Profession: A Novel (novel) 1886
An Unsocial Socialist (novel) 1887
The Quintessence of Ibsenism (criticism) 1891
Widowers' Houses (drama) 1893
The Perfect Wagnerite: A Commentary on the 'Ring of the Niblungs' (essay) 1898
Plays: Pleasant and Unpleasant (dramas, includes *Widowers' Houses, The Philanderer, Mrs. Warren's Profession, Arms and the Man, Candida, The Man of Destiny, You Never Can Tell*) 1898
Love among the Artists (novel) 1900
Socialism for Millionaires (essay) 1901
Three Plays for Puritans (dramas, includes *The Devil's Disciple, Caesar and Cleopatra, Captain Brassbound's Conversion*) 1901
Man and Superman: A Comedy and a Philosophy (drama) 1903
The Irrational Knot (novel) 1905
On Going to Church: An Essay (essay) 1905
Dramatic Opinions and Essays, with an Apology (essays) 1906
John Bull's Other Island and Major Barbara (dramas, includes *John Bull's Other Island, How He Lied to Her Husband, Major Barbara*) 1907
The Admirable Bashville: or, Constancy Unrewarded; Being the Novel of Cashel Byron's Profession Done into a Stage Play in Three Acts and in Blank Verse (drama) 1909
The Shewing Up of Blanco Posnet: A Sermon in Crude Melodrama (drama) 1909
The Doctor's Dilemma, Getting Married, and The Shewing-

Up of Blanco Posnet (dramas) 1911

Androcles and the Lion: A Fable Play (drama) 1914

Misalliance, The Dark Lady of the Sonnets, and Fanny's First Play, with a Treatise on Parents and Children (dramas) 1914

Androcles and the Lion. Overruled. Pygmalion (dramas) 1916

Heartbreak House, The Great Catherine, and Playlets of the War (dramas, includes *Heartbreak House; The Great Catherine; Annajanska, the Bolshevik Empress*) 1919

Back to Methuselah: A Metabiological Pentateuch (drama) 1921

Saint Joan: A Chronicle Play in Six Scenes and an Epilogue (drama) 1924

The Intelligent Woman's Guide to Socialism and Capitalism (essay) 1928

The Apple Cart: A Political Extravaganza (drama) 1930

Immaturity (novel) 1930

The Adventures of the Black Girl in Her Search for God (short story) 1932

Music in London, 1890-94 (criticism) 1932

The Simpleton of the Unexpected Isles (drama) 1934

Too True to Be Good, Village Wooing, and On the Rocks (dramas) 1934

The Simpleton, The Six, and The Millionairess: Being Three More Plays (dramas) 1936; published in the United States as *The Simpleton of the Unexpected Isles, The Six of Calais, and The Millionairess*, 1936

London Music in 1888-89 as Heard by Corno di Bassetto (Later Known as Bernard Shaw) with Some Further Autobiographical Particulars (criticism) 1937

Geneva: A Fancied Page of History, in Three Acts (drama) 1939

Bernard Shaw's Rhyming Picture Guide to Ayot Saint Lawrence (poetry, with photographs by George Bernard Shaw) 1950

MAX BEERBOHM (essay date 1901)

I admit that [Mr. Shaw's youthful] serious plays were exceedingly good *pastiches* of Ibsen, and that in time he could have written serious plays to which one could have given higher praise than that. Nevertheless, he was not born to write serious plays. He has too irresponsible a sense of humour. This sense he never could have suppressed so utterly as to prevent it from marring his plays; and, as it is his greatest gift, one does not wish him to suppress it at all. Again, he is (though he may deny that he is) incapable of portraying satisfactorily those human passions which must form the basis of serious drama. In all his serious plays, he tried (and tried very cleverly) to reproduce Ibsen's women. These creatures are tolerable and admirable because they are warmly human, warmly alive. But Mr. Shaw never could get further than their surface-characteristics. And the result was that his heroines were quite appalling. They were just dowdy and ill-conditioned shrews—wasps without waists. I am glad to think that I have seen the last of them. Now that Mr. Shaw has got clean away from the Ibsen formula, and makes no attempt at dealing seriously with the great issues of human life, his heroines are quite delightful and (as far as they go) quite real. (p. 120)

I admit that the last play [of *Three Plays for Puritans*], "Captain Brassbound's Conversion," is not masterly. The admission is, indeed, wrung from me by the fact that I elaborately disparaged the play in these columns a few short weeks ago. Nevertheless, it marks a distinct advance from the serious plays: it is much more capable than were they of being treated with respect. Of the first play, "The Devil's Disciple," I have also written here, and, reading it, I have nothing to subtract from the praises I heaped on it after seeing it acted. The second play, "Caesar and Cleopatra," is quite new to me. It is, I think, far the best thing Mr. Shaw has yet done. Every scene in it is delicious. Most of the scenes are mere whimsical embroidery, a riotous sequence of broadly humorous incidents. But some of them, very cleverly woven in, are true psychological comedy. Both Caesar and Cleopatra are perfectly credible studies. Of course, if Mr. Shaw had tried to portray Caesar in some really serious love affair, or to give us Cleopatra in the Antonine phase, he would have failed utterly. But here, merely, is Caesar as an important public man who knows that a little chit of a girl-queen has taken a fancy to him, and is tickled by the knowledge, and behaves very kindly to her, and rather wishes he were young enough to love her. This kind of emotion Mr. Shaw can delineate sharply and truly. Nor could the kittenish admiration of Cleopatra for her hero have been more sympathetically shown to us. (p. 121)

I am not sure that Mr. Shaw's prefaces, notes, and stage-directions are not even more delightful than the plays themselves. In them, too. I find that Mr. Shaw has made real progress. He has always had a "style," in the sense that he has always been able to express accurately, in a live manner, the thoughts that are in him. But now he is evidently beginning to realise that a style may be beautiful, and ought to be beautiful, in itself. (pp. 121-22)

> *Max Beerbohm, "Mr. Shaw Crescent" (originally published in* The Saturday Review, *Vol. 91, No. 2361, January 26, 1901), in his* Around Theatres *(reprinted with permission of Granada Publishing Limited), revised edition, Rupert Hart-Davis, 1953, pp. 118-22.*

HENRY L. MENCKEN (essay date 1905)

In the dramas of George Bernard Shaw, which deal almost wholly with the current conflict between orthodoxy and heterodoxy, it is but natural that the characters should fall broadly into two general classes—the ordinary folks who represent the great majority, and the iconoclasts, or idol-smashers. . . . [When] Shaw chooses conspicuous fighters in this war as the chief characters of his plays, he is but demonstrating his comprehension of human nature as it is manifested to-day. In "Man and Superman," for instance, he makes John Tanner, the chief personage of the drama, a rabid adherent of certain very advanced theories in social philosophy, and to accentuate these theories and contrast them strongly with the more old-fashioned ideas of the majority of persons, he places Tanner among men and women who belong to this majority. The effect of this is that the old notions and the new—orthodoxy and heterodoxy—are brought sharply face to face, and there is much opportunity for what theater goers call "scenes"—*i.e.* clashes of purpose and will. (pp. xvi-xvii)

Dramatists of other days, before the world became engaged in its crusade against error and sham, depicted battles of other sorts. . . . Ibsen, except in his early poetical dramas, deals chiefly with the war between new schemes of human happiness and old rules of conduct. . . . Shaw is frankly a disciple of Ibsen, but he is far more than a mere imitator. In some things, indeed—such, for instance, as in fertility of wit and invention—he very greatly exceeds the Norwegian. (pp. xviii-xix)

Shaw is in no sense a preacher. His private opinions, very naturally, greatly color his plays, but his true purpose, like that of every dramatist worth while, is to give a more or less accurate and unbiased picture of some phase of human life, that persons observing it may be led to speculate and meditate upon it. (p. xxiii)

[Among] those who approach Shaw . . . honestly, there is little likelihood that he will ever grow more popular, in the current sense, than he is at present. In the first place, some of his plays are wellnigh impossible of performance in a paying manner without elaborate revision and expurgation. "Man and Superman," for instance, would require five hours if presented as it was written. . . . In the second place, Shaw's extraordinary dexterity as a wit, which got him his first hearing and keeps him before the public almost constantly to-day, is a handicap of crushing weight. As long as he exercises it, the great majority will continue to think of him as a sort of glorified and magnificent buffoon. As soon as he abandons it, he will cease to be Shaw.

The reason of this lies in the fact that the average man clings fondly to two ancient delusions: (*a*) that wisdom is always solemn, and (*b*) that he himself is never ridiculous. Shaw outrages both of these ideas, the first by placing his most searching and illuminating observations in the mouths of such persons as Frank Gardner and Sidney Trefusis, and the second by drawing characters such as Finch McComas and Roebuck Ramsden. The average spectator laughs at Frank's impertinences and at Trefusis' satire, and by gradual stages, comes to laugh at Frank and Trefusis. Beginning as comedians, they become butts. And so, conversely, McComas and Ramsden, as their opponents fall, rise themselves. In the first act of "Man and Superman," the battle seems to be all in favor of John Tanner and so the unthinking reader concludes that Tanner is Shaw's personal spokesman, and that the Tanner doctrines constitute the Shavian creed. Later on, when Tanner falls before the forces of inexorable law, this same reader is vastly puzzled and perplexed, and in the end he is left wondering what it is all about.

If he would but remember the . . . axiom that a dramatist's purpose is to present a picture of life as he sees it, without reference to any particular moral conclusions, he would better enjoy and appreciate the play as a work of art. Playwrights of Shaw's calibre do not think it necessary to plainly label every character or to reward their heroes and kill their villains in the last act. It is utterly immaterial whether Tanner is dragged into a marriage with Ann or escapes scot free. The important thing is that the battle between the two be depicted naturally and plausibly and that it afford some tangible material for reflection.

The average citizen's disinclination to see the ridiculous side of his own pet doctrines and characteristics has been noted by Shaw in his preface to Ibsen's plays. . . . One cannot expect a man, however keen his sense of humor, to laugh at the things he considers eminently proper and hon-

orable. Shaw's demand that he do so has greatly restricted the size of the Shaw audience. To appreciate "The Devil's Disciple," for instance, a religious man would have to lift himself bodily from his accustomed rut of thought and look down upon himself from the same distance that separates him in his meditations from the rest of humanity. This, it is obvious, is possible only to man given to constant self-analysis and introspection—the 999th man in the thousand.

Even when the average spectator does not find himself the counterpart of a definite type in a Shaw play, he is confused by the handling of some of his ideals and ideas. No doubt the men who essayed to stone the Magdalen were infinitely astounded when the Messiah called their attention to the fact that they themselves were not guiltless. But it is precisely this establishment of new view-points that makes Shaw as an author worth the time and toil of study. In "Mrs. Warren's Profession," the heroine's picturesque fall from grace is shown in literally a multitude of aspects. We have her own antipodal changes in self-valuation and self-depreciation, we have her daughter's varying point of view, and we have the more constant judgments of Frank Gardner, his father, Crofts, and the rest. It is kaleidoscopic and puzzling, but it is not sermonizing. You pay your money and you take your choice.

But even if Shaw's plays were not performed at all, he would be a world-figure in the modern drama, just as Ibsen is a world-figure and Maeterlinck another. Very frequently it happens, in literature as well as in other fields of metaphysical endeavor, that a master is unknown to the majority except through his disciples. (pp. xxiv-xxviii)

[Shaw] has shown variations sufficiently marked to bring him followers of his own. In all the history of the English stage, no man has exceeded him in technical resources nor in nimbleness of wit. Some of his scenes are fairly irresistible, and throughout his plays his avoidance of the old-fashioned machinery of the drama gives even his wildest extravagances an air of reality. (p. xxix)

Shaw's four published novels both suffer and gain by the widespread public interest in his plays; gain because this interest serves to keep them somewhat in the foreground, and suffer because, as the work of a very young man, they are ill-fitted to stand comparison with the literary offspring of his maturity. Of the four, "Love Among the Artists" is the best and "Cashel Byron's Profession" the most popular. "An Unsocial Socialist" is a wild extravaganza that has lived its day and done its task, and "The Irrational Knot" is forgotten. (p. 82)

The author was born with the dramatic instinct of a [Victorian] Sardou or a Hal Reid and throughout ["Cashel Byron's Profession"] there are scenes of tremendous excitement and clatter. Cashel fights fairly terrific battles—among others one with Miss Carew's footman, Bashville, who also loves her—and the general air of the book is distinctly warlike. Most of the minor characters are commonplace. (p. 84)

"An Unsocial Socialist" is a tract born of the nights that Shaw passed in pondering the philosophies. All of the ten articles in the manifesto of 1845 are preached in it, and in addition there is much that the Hon. "Tom" Watson, the Hon. Eugene Debs, and various other earnest gentlemen were destined to spout forth years later. . . . ["An Unsocial Socialist"] is the most riotous hodge-podge of cart-tail oratory and low comedy in the language. (pp. 84-5)

As in the case of "The Philanderer" a great many persons have wondered how Shaw could make such a ridiculous character of [Sidney Trefusis,] whose doctrines apparently coincide with his own. In truth, it is highly improbable that Shaw, or any other sane man, ever held to the ideas expressed by Trefusis. The latter's speech beside the corpse of his wife is without parallel in fiction. And some of his other utterances and acts—how royally and deliciously sacrilegious they are! Certainly an age that finds Schopenhaüer's essay on women a never-ending delight should be better acquainted with the ecstatic shocks of "An Unsocial Socialist." Trefusis, being utterly beyond the pale, is as productive of wicked little thrills to the orthodox and virtuous as McIntosh Jellaludin, David, Pantagruel, or the latest popular murderer.

"The Irrational Knot"—the theme of which is evident from the title—is now but a name. It was one of a vast multitude of similar books that saw the light at the time of its birth. Not one of the reviewers, eulogists or enemies of Shaw seems to think much of it. "Love Among the Artists," on the contrary, is a novel that deserves to rank with the really important fiction of the time. The theme is not startlingly original and in the 400-odd pages there are oceans of tiresome talk, but the work, as a whole, bears the stamp of distinction, and if only for the admirable searching portrait of the Polish *pianiste*, Aurélie Szczymplíça, it deserves some share of attention. (pp. 85-6)

Shaw was a newcomer in Bohemia . . . when he wrote this book and to this fact may be ascribed the freshness and virility of some of the characters—the Szczymplíça in particular, and Owen Jack, the eccentric composer. In the former the vagaries of the artistic mind are revealed with considerable originality and delicacy. If he was tempted to make a burlesque of the soulful little Aurélie, he kept a tight rein upon the impulse. Jack, on the contrary, is frankly a figure out of low comedy. Nothing more grotesque than his struggles with the Philistines is to be found in any of the Shaw plays. (p. 87)

Shaw's pair of critical pamphlets—"The Perfect Wagnerite" and "The Quintessence of Ibsenism"—will go down into history beside Robert Schumann's early reviews of the compositions of Chopin and Huxley's opening broadsides for Darwin. Each paved the way for better knowledge and better understanding. . . . [In "The Perfect Wagnerite"] Shaw undertook the vain task of proving the younger Siegfried a socialist—and succeeded in making his readers meditate upon Wagner. Thus he earned whatever money and fame he got from his pains.

"The Quintessence of Ibsenism" includes some wonderfully illuminative and searching passages, but on the whole it is rather out of date. Shaw makes the Norwegian a social-philosopher of most earnest purposes, and hangs upon the book an elaborate and ingenious theory of sham-smashing. As a matter of fact, we have Ibsen's own word for it that few of his plays contain much conscious preaching, and no doubt many of the alarming doctrines Shaw found in them were not there before he conjured them up. Nevertheless, the book remains the best estimate of Ibsen yet written in English. (pp. 87-8)

Henry L. Mencken, in his George Bernard Shaw: His Plays *(copyright, 1905, by John W. Luce & Company), Luce, 1905, 107 p.*

GILBERT K. CHESTERTON   (essay date 1905)

[The] sensation connected with Mr. Shaw in recent years has been his sudden development of the religion of the Superman. He who had to all appearance mocked at the faiths in the forgotten past discovered a new god in the unimaginable future. He who had laid all the blame on ideals set up the most impossible of all ideals, the ideal of a new creature. But the truth, nevertheless, is that any one who knows Mr. Shaw's mind adequately, and admires it properly, must have guessed all this long ago.

For the truth is that Mr. Shaw has never seen things as they really are. If he had he would have fallen on his knees before them. He has always had a secret ideal that has withered all the things of this world. He has all the time been silently comparing humanity with something that was not human, with a monster from Mars, with the Wise Man of the Stoics, with the Economic Man of the Fabians, with Julius Caesar, with Siegfried, with the Superman. Now, to have this inner and merciless standard may be a very good thing, or a very bad one, it may be excellent or unfortunate, but it is not seeing things as they are. It is not seeing things as they are to think first of a Briareus with a hundred hands, and then call every man a cripple for only having two. It is not seeing things as they are to start with a vision of Argus with his hundred eyes, and then jeer at every man with two eyes as if he had only one. And it is not seeing things as they are to imagine a demi-god of infinite mental clarity, who may or may not appear in the latter days of the earth, and then to see all men as idiots. And this is what Mr. Shaw has always in some degree done. When we really see men as they are, we do not criticise, but worship. . . . Mr. Shaw, on the practical side perhaps the most humane man alive, is in this sense inhumane. He has even been infected to some extent with the primary intellectual weakness of his new master, Nietzsche, the strange notion that the greater and stronger a man was the more he would despise other things. (pp. 62-4)

He is an almost solitary exception to the general and essential maxim, that little things please great minds. And from this absence of that most uproarious of all things, humility, comes incidentally the peculiar insistence on the Superman. After belabouring a great many people for a great many years for being unprogressive, Mr. Shaw has discovered, with characteristic sense, that it is very doubtful whether any existing human being with two legs can be progressive at all. Having come to doubt whether humanity can be combined with progress, most people, easily pleased, would have elected to abandon progress and remain with humanity. Mr. Shaw, not being easily pleased, decides to throw over humanity with all its limitations and go in for progress for its own sake. If man, as we know him, is incapable of the philosophy of progress, Mr. Shaw asks, not for a new kind of philosophy, but for a new kind of man. . . . Mr. Shaw cannot understand that the thing which is valuable and lovable in our eyes is man—the old beer-drinking, creed-making, fighting, failing, sensual, respectable man. And the things that have been founded on this creature immortally remain; the things that have been founded on the fancy of the Superman have died with the dying civilizations which alone have given them birth. (pp. 66-7)

Gilbert K. Chesterton, "Mr. Bernard Shaw," in his Heretics *(copyright, 1905, by Dodd Mead & Company), Dodd Mead, 1927, pp. 54-67.*

JAMES HUNEKER   (essay date 1905)

Whether we take him seriously or not, [Mr. Shaw] is a delightful, an entertaining writer. His facile use, with the aid of the various mouthpieces he assumes at will, of the ideas of Nietzsche, Wagner, Ibsen, and Strindberg, fairly dazzles. He despises wit at bottom, using its forms as a medium for the communication of his theories. Art for art's sake is a contradiction to this writer. (pp. 237-38)

[Mr. Shaw's] novels as a whole are disappointing. . . . Episodes of brilliancy, force, audacity, there are; but episodes only. The psychology of a musician is admirably set forth in *Love Among the Artists*, and the story, in addition, contains one of the most lifelike portraits of a Polish *pianiste* that has ever been painted. John Sargent could have done no better in laying bare a soul. Ugliness is rampant—ugliness and brutality. It is all as invigorating as a bath of salt water when the skin is peeled off—it burns; you howl; Shaw grins. He hates with all the vigour of his big brain and his big heart to hear of the infliction of physical pain. He does not always spare his readers. Three hundred years ago he would have roasted heretics, for there is much of the grand inquisitor, the John Calvin, the John Knox, in Shaw. (pp. 240-41)

Shaw despises weakness. He follows to the letter Nietzsche's injunction, Be hard! And there is something in him of Ibsen's pitiless attitude toward the majority, which is always in the wrong; yet is, all said and done, the majority. (pp. 241-42)

So he dips his subjects into a bath of muriatic acid and seems surprised at their wrigglings and their screams. "But I don't want to hear the truth!" yells the victim, who then limps back to his comfortable lies. And the one grievous error is that our gallant slayer of dragons, our Celtic Siegfried, does not believe in the illusions of art. Its veils, consoling and beautiful, he will not have, and thus it is that his dramas are amusing, witty, brilliant, scarefying, but never poetic, never beautiful, and seldom sound the deeper tones of humanity. With an artist's brain, he stifles the artist's soul in him—as Ibsen never did. (p. 242)

Velocity is one of Shaw's prime characteristics. Like a pianoforte *virtuoso* whose fingers work faster than his feelings, the Irishman is lost when he essays massive, sonorous *cantilena*. He is as emotional as his own typewriter, and this defect, which he parades as did the fox in the fable, has stood in the way of his writing a great play. He despises love, and therefore cannot appeal deeply to mankind. (p. 258)

> *James Huneker, "The Quintessence of Shaw," in his* Iconoclasts: A Book of Dramatists *(copyright © 1905 by Charles Scribner's Sons), Scribner's, 1905, pp. 233-68.*

JAMES JOYCE   (essay date 1909)

Shaw is a born preacher. His lively and talkative spirit cannot stand to be subjected to the noble and bare style appropriate to modern playwriting. Indulging himself in wandering prefaces and extravagant rules of drama, he creates a dramatic form which is much like a dialogue novel. He has a sense of situation, rather than of drama logically and ethically led to a conclusion. In [the case of "The Shewing-Up of Blanco Posnet"] he has dug up the central incident of his "Devil's Disciple" and transformed it into a

sermon. The transformation is too abrupt to be convincing as a sermon, and the art is too poor to make it convincing as drama. (p. 208)

> *James Joyce, "Bernard Shaw's Battle with the Censor: 'The Shewing-Up of Blanco Posnet'" (originally published in Italian in* Il piccolo della sera, *September 5, 1909), in* The Critical Writings of James Joyce, *edited by Ellsworth Mason and Richard Ellmann (copyright © 1959 by Harriet Weaver and F. Lionel Monro as Administrators of the Estate of James Joyce; reprinted by permission of Viking Penguin Inc.),* Viking Penguin, *1959, pp. 206-08.*

ASHLEY DUKES   (essay date 1911)

Bernard Shaw's outstanding position as dramatist is only comparative. His eminence is, as Renan said of Mill's, "largely due to the flatness of the surrounding country." (p. 122)

Shaw has made one attempt to write a tragedy in "The Doctor's Dilemma," and he has failed utterly. The dying artist Dubedat is not a tragic figure; there is no greatness in him. He is a more egregious poseur than Sergius in "Arms and the Man," or Napoleon in "The Man of Destiny." His death is a harlequinade. His final speech is a dialectical adventure, a proclamation of belief in "Michael Angelo . . . the majesty of colour and the might of design." Life must first be made real before death can be made tragic. And Dubedat is never real. There is no more life in him than in the ventriloquist's dummy. He sits upon his maker's knee, mouthing phrases as the strings are pulled, grinning pertly at the gods. . . .

I turn to the question of passion. Drama is a symphony of the passions. The melting mood is their sway of the hearer. Shaw's plays have one passion, and one only—that of indignation. Indignation against hypocrisy and lying, against prostitution and slavery, against poverty, dirt and disorder. (pp. 130-31)

[Take] Morell and Eugene Marchbanks in "Candida." A conflict of two wills, of two individualities? There is no point of contact. The person of Candida is only the apparent issue; actually she is always a spectator. The conflict is between two indignations. (p. 132)

[Shaw] makes the indignation palatable by his wit. The outburst creates a finely effective moment, and the Shavian drama is no more than a series of such moments. Persiflage links them together and weaves illusion. . . . This effect, however, cannot always be sustained. . . . The dramatist, like any other craftsman, is entitled to use all the existing devices and to invent others if he can. Intrinsically they are worth precisely their weight in illusion. But illusion without drama is impossible. Even the Shavian wit cannot make bricks without straw. (pp. 133-34)

Shaw's service to drama is first and foremost the revelation of a personality engaged in criticism of life. With one passion and much wit he has given this criticism dramatic force. Secondly, he has created more vivid individual types than any other living author. . . . Phases only, for they are types of reality intellectualised. There is no complete portrait that can be called great. . . . Shaw's comic spirit must be writ small; it has a narrow range. But [in the words of George Meredith] it "proposes the correcting of pretentiousness, of inflation, of dulness, and of the vestiges of rawness and grossness to be found among us." With that we must perforce be content. (pp. 134-35)

Ashley Dukes, "Bernard Shaw," in his Modern Dramatists, *Frank Palmer, 1911, pp. 120-35.*

ARCHIBALD HENDERSON (essay date 1913)

There are two fundamental ideas, consistently held and strenuously maintained by Shaw, which, rightly understood, effectually shatter the superficial theory that he is an artistic mountebank, exploiting the theatre as an instrumentality for shallow ends. Back of all surface manifestations lies the supreme conviction of Shaw that the theatre of today, properly utilized, is an instrumentality for the molding of character and the shaping of conduct no whit inferior to the Church and the School. (p. 341)

The theatre is a school of manners, of morals, both individual and social, exercising an influence that is none the less powerful in that it is indirect. Indeed, the subtle force of the comedies of Shaw is heightened through the enjoyment which they give. The bitter pill of the moralist is coated with the sugar of the artist. Shaw does actually continue the classic tradition of Molière who said that a comedy is nothing less than an ingenious poem which, in agreeable lessons, portrays human weaknesses. There is the deeper note in Shaw. He surpasses Molière as a moralist, because Molière was a censor of individual vices whilst Shaw is a censor of the sociological evils arising from the structural defects of modern society and modern civilization. (pp. 342-43)

The remarkable popular attention which Shaw won as a dramatic critic was due in great measure not only to his trenchant satire but also to the sincerity of his faith in the mission of the theatre. (pp. 343-44)

The prime fact which stamps Shaw's art into close correspondence with life is the fundamental note of *disillusionment* which is struck fearlessly and unfailingly throughout the entire range of his work. Just as all life is an evolutionary process, and all progress follows vision clarified through the falling of the scales from the eyes of the brain, so Shaw's drama is an ordered sequence of pictured incidents in which pitfalls are uncovered, illusions unmasked, and vital secrets displayed.... Shaw is so deeply impressed with the predominance of human activity which consists in the pursuits of illusions that he does not hesitate to denominate it the greatest force in the world.... It is not against the optimistic and progressive illusions, those indispensable modes of cloaking reality which possess the power to awake man's helpful interest and to inspire his best efforts, that Shaw directs his batteries of irony, of satire and of wit.... It is against those individual and social illusions, treacherous, ensnaring, destructive—prejudices, conventions, traditions, theological incrustations, social petrifactions—that Shaw brings to bear all the force of his trenchant and sagacious intellect.... Shaw's characters, whether involved in social labyrinths or confused by conventional dogmas, break through to the light by discovering their false allegiance to some stupid current fiction or some baseless fabric of cheap romance. (pp. 359-62)

If it be true that Shaw appears essentially simple and serious in mind and character, it is because ... he has succeeded in freeing his mind from all contemporary prejudice, has acquired the illimitable receptivity of the child, and has

effected the transition to that *second* state of innocence out of which proceed real art and simple truth. It is in this sense, indeed, that Shaw is a genuine *naïf*. Just as disillusionment is the defining quality of his art, *naïveté* is the defining quality of his temperament.... Someone has denominated Shaw a literary Peter Pan—a boy who has never grown up in literature. This is a peculiarly pertinent characterization of one who finds an "indescribable levity—something spritelike—about the final truth of the matter"; and who once said: "It is the half-truth which is congruous, heavy, serious, and suggestive of a middle-aged or elderly philosopher. The whole truth is often the first thing that comes into the head of a fool or a child; and when a wise man forces his way to it through the many strata of his sophistications, its wanton, perverse air reassures instead of frightening him." Shaw *is* a literary Peter Pan; and he takes the characterization as a very great compliment. "There was a time," Shaw once said, "when I was a grown-up man —more grown-up than anybody else. I was about eighteen at the time." But he added: "It was not until I became like Peter Pan that I was really worth anything." (pp. 363-65)

The apparent contrariety of ideas in Shaw's works is one of the elements that tend, not only to prevent comprehension of his purpose, but even to prompt suspicion of the seriousness of his purpose. The other element springs from the popular notion that wit and seriousness are two mutually contradictory entities. The really inspired man, in Shaw's opinion, is the man who brings you to see that there are certain delusions you must surrender; that there are certain steps forward that must be taken. Progress involves not only the sacrifice of certain obligations, but also the assumption of other obligations. But let the serious reformer dare to express his ideas in witty and paradoxical form, and he must answer the charge, not simply of being disagreeable, but also of being frivolous. (p. 366)

Bernard Shaw is the most versatile and cosmopolitan genius in the drama of ideas that Great Britain has yet produced. No juster or more significant characterization can be made of this man than that he is a penetrating and astute critic of contemporary civilization. He is typical of this disquieting century—with its intellectual brilliancy, its staggering naïveté, its ironic nonsense, its devouring scepticism, its profound social and religious unrest. The relentless thinking, the large perception of the comic which stamp this man, are interpenetrated with the ironic consciousness of the twentieth century. The note of his art is capitally moralistic; and he tempers the bitterness of the disillusioning dose with the effervescent appetizer of his brilliant wit. (pp. 367-68)

Archibald Henderson, "Bernard Shaw" (1913), in his European Dramatists (copyright © 1913, 1926, by D. Appleton & Co.; reprinted by permission of Prentice-Hall, Inc., Englewood Cliffs, New Jersey), Appleton, 1926, pp. 323-69.

DIXON SCOTT (essay date 1916)

Mr. Shaw became a dramatist—not as a result of predilection—but simply because he was propelled into the part by circumstances. Once one realizes that, one also sees the huge unlikelihood of him turning out the born dramatist he claimed to be; and, indeed, it could easily be shown that even his power "of conjuring up imaginary people in imaginary places and finding pretexts for theatrical scenes between them" (on which he plumes himself in the Preface to *Plays Pleasant*) is much more the novelist's dramatic knack than the playwright's, that his mere sense of the physically dramatic, taking that alone, is far from being the true sense of the theatre. But these initial, native deficiencies wouldn't have mattered so much if it hadn't been for [another] element; the grim fact that [given his early activities as a Fabian polemist,] the very circumstances which had made him dramatist had simultaneously robbed him of his best right to be one. Be one, that is to say, in his own high sense of it—a maker of works of art depicting the daily life of the world, phials filled with essence of actuality. A man of his wit and force couldn't, of course, fail to contrive stage-pieces with a good deal more pith and picturesqueness about them than the majority of plays turned out by the class of brains the stage deserves; but anything bigger, anything adequate to his own definition, he had already forfeited the faculty to produce. He was trebly disqualified. . . . Shaw really admitted his own incapacity for play-writing when he affirmed that the average audience was a set of soapy stupids, "part of them nine-tenths chapel-goers by temperament, and the remainder ten-tenths blackguards." For the stage at its best is only a mirror held up before the face of the watching house. The big play is composed of little players; it must comprehend them even when they don't comprehend it.

That, then, is the first of Mr. Shaw's three acquired deficiencies; his socialism has made him unsociable: his confirmed habit of wiping somebody out, which he formed among the Fabians because it was so effective there, becomes here a disastrous obliteration of his model. . . . And now . . . comes acquired defect number two. . . . All Shaw's early efforts as a writer were given . . . to the task of forming a medium of expression apt for physical utterance—a type of diction he could debate with and dictate with dogmatically, dealing it out from his hustings or stabbing it into his societies in successive sentences as pat and purposeful as neatly planted blows. Now, that meant good dialogue; and so, long before he had ever dreamt of turning dramatist, he had perfectly acquired the great trick which so many playwrights never do learn: the art of making all his words fit live lips and leap alertly off the tongue, as slick and natural as slang, fresh with the colours of actual intercourse. (pp. 39-41)

[But this] meant that the stage-door of his theatre had to be shut in the faces of a throng of very necessary characters; all the dim folk and foggy folk, the puzzled and perturbed, the groping, hoping, helpless, humble, unassertive humans, who act by instinct instead of by reason and whose deeds speak so much more clearly than their words—all these he was compelled to turn away. He couldn't employ them, for he couldn't equip them with a part. His sympathies, we have seen, were already limited—but even if he were filled with a positive affection for such characters he couldn't take them on—no, not even to take them off; for although he understood them they did not understand themselves; and for people who don't know their own minds and can't communicate the knowledge clearly, Shaw has no form of speech that will do. He can write none but definite dialogue; and definite dialogue entails definite minds; and the result is that all the members of his cast seem members of one exclusive caste. . . . Pass them in parade, from Vivie Warren to Andrew Undershaft, and you find they have all had to be endowed with this rare faculty—a power of quick, precise, and ruthless calculation and self-confidence, the

necessary adjunct to the way they'll have to speak. Each has a ready point of view, bright and finished as a rapier; and the drama has to resolve itself into the ring and rattle of these weapons, the multiplex duel we get when they all unsheathe their points and prettily proceed to cross opinions. What fun it is, how exciting it can be, we all, to our happiness, well know. But we have to admit that the mirror misses much. It is odd to reflect that his democracy is the cause of this exclusiveness.

Yet if these are serious handicaps I fear the third is even heavier. It was bad enough to be compelled to insist on his *dramatis personæ* all coming clearly provided with opinions; but what was worse was the fact that the exigencies of platform work had compelled him to add a pack of neat opinions to his own equipment, and that his haste and his innocence and the highly peculiar circle of his friends made the pack in many ways a faked one. . . . The pressure of those early days of gleeful mutiny, the need for being dogmatic, precipitated his young ideas in a premature philosophy, to which ever since he has clung; and at the same time the material out of which he had to get his ideas, the personal experiences he turned into opinions, were quite unfairly lopsided, incomplete, artificial. The idiosyncrasy of his troupe he might to some extent have counterbalanced by picking their points of view with care and then arranging these so that they partly reproduced the pattern and poise of reality; but such ingenuity availed nothing whatever against the bias of his own point of view. (pp. 42-4)

Mr. James has travelled tirelessly, shedding old shibboleths and learning the non-existence of horizons; whereas Shaw has always remained complacently satisfied that his early contact with life was remarkably complete. . . . He honestly believed that a brisk debate with Mr. Belfort Bax brought him very near to the simple heart of human nature. He felt that he understood the democracy because he knew so many democrats.

It was as a Fabian meeting multiplied, then, that Shaw first beheld the race of man; and his views of life were largely formed to fit this fascinating vision. (pp. 45-6)

[Once] the limitations of the plays are realized they cease to possess any; once you see that Shaw has done the best he could for us under the circumstances, then his effort is seen in relation to those circumstances and its errors instinctively allowed for. Recognize that a passion for purity, gentleness, truth, justice, and beauty is the force at the base of all his teaching, and you will find his message one of the most tonic of our time. Realize further how he has limited himself by the philosophy he has expounded, and you will escape all danger of being hurt by its deficiencies. And instead of the irritation, the bewilderment, or (what was worse) the priggish complacency with which you regarded them, you find yourself turning to them with sympathy, with comradeship and eager friendliness, able to use all their strong medicine without being embittered by the taste. It is only when you regard them, in short (and this is the summary of the whole irony), it is only when you regard them with the very sympathy they doggedly deride that you receive the help which they hunger to offer. (p. 47)

Dixon Scott, "The Innocence of Bernard Shaw" (originally published in a slightly different version in The Bookman, *Vol. XXXVIII, No. 1, September, 1913), in his* Men of Letters, *Hodder and Stoughton, 1916, pp. 2-47.*

JOHN FREEMAN (essay date 1916)

As a comic playwright [Mr. Shaw] has done all that a comic playwright who is not a poet can humanly achieve. Foolish critics in the haste of their pens and the hate of their hearts have condemned him because he will not be serious; more justly would they deplore the occasion when he is. He brings to comedy a broad natural portion of the comic spirit. (p. 7)

The whole of his characters move in a peculiarly rare atmosphere of inhumanity. They have movement, but they do not live:—rather should we say they are galvanically active. They are inhabitants of a country as essentially unreal as the country of Mr. Henry James's characters; they are citizens of a city where the unexpected always happens, and nothing is impossible but the normal. I do not think it would be true to say, as I was about to say, that they are unnatural, since unnatural persons are not uncommon: they are lifelike but unliving; they may be freakishly true portraits of certain actual persons, but they are not true within nature; they are cinematographic pictures of aberrations. And the reason of this is, I think, that his plays have not a "natural" origin: they are all illustrations of ideas. The folly of romance, the crime of criminal punishment, the economic oppression of woman, the cupidity of doctors, the prosaic reality of florid history—these are his theme. Some of his subjects he thinks unpleasant and calls the plays unpleasant; but it is the conduct of the play which is unpleasant, as, for example, in the excitement of sexual desire described in *Widowers' Houses* and glimpsed in *Mrs. Warren's Profession;* the unpleasantness, in short, is incidental and not inevitable. And so it becomes significantly easy, with some of the later plays, to describe them in a brief phrase. *Man and Superman,* for instance, is simply a comedy of inverted sex-pursuit; *John Bull,* a brisk political satire with a sweetening of sentimental passages; *The Doctor's Dilemma* a mere anti-medical philippic with remarks upon the immorality of genius; *Major Barbara* a mere anti-poverty philippic, with remarks upon the immorality of progress.

Nothing could have saved plays thus conceived but what has actually saved them—their author's high spirits. An intellectual buoyancy of remarkable pitch carries him through. With less of liveliness his plays would be detestable; with more of humanity they would be absurd. (pp. 8-9)

Since his plays do not arise from the development and opposition of character, but are mere illustrations of ideas, he cannot afford to let his characters speak for themselves. They have no proper speech of their own, for they must perforce play into each other's hands, exactly as, with Cinquevalli juggling, one ball is whipped from his palm in time for another to be received. So you find that one after another presents himself like an ignition strip, for the Shavian incarnation to rub the match of his wits upon. (p. 13)

He has mastered the trick of showing up one character vividly at the expense of another, but he has not mastered the trick of letting one character speak for itself and by itself, and without this visible foolish act of friction. His failure simply means that his characters never burn from within, but are artificially kindled from without; and the whole innocent conceit shows as clearly as has ever been shown the difference between vital and mechanical work, between the living creature and the galvanized puppet. (p. 16)

Mr. Shaw's mind is active yet inflexible, positive yet changeable, alert yet insensitive. That intemperance of language, that constant freedom of abuse, that reluctance to let words speak for themselves—what is behind it all but mere insensibility? (p. 44)

*John Freeman, "George Bernard Shaw," in his
The Moderns: Essays in Literary Criticism,
R. Scott, 1916 (and reprinted by Books for Libraries Press, Inc., 1967), pp. 1-51.*

WILLIAM LYON PHELPS (essay date 1920)

Shaw's pages bristle with ideas; and every living idea is a challenge. This is why his plays are so much more interesting than most plays. They answer no questions, but they ask many. For some in the audience the end of his play is the beginning of mental activity. Instead of giving us food, he gives us an appetite.

Bernard Shaw in one respect is the exact opposite of Shakespeare, and in this particular his dramas are the opposite of true drama. Shakespeare has presented every aspect of human life, and we do not know whether he was a Christian or an atheist, an aristocrat or a democrat, an optimist or a pessimist. His plays reach the goal of objective art—there is no alloy of the author in any of the characters, as there is in *The Ring and the Book.* Now Shaw is wholly subjective: even if he had not written the brilliant Prefaces, every play and every person represent the author. That he did write the Prefaces is a proof of his aim; so far from concealing himself, he uses every means to reveal himself.

He is a great Teacher; and if you ask me, What does he teach? I confess I do not know. The main business of the teacher is not to impart imformation, to transfer facts from his skull to the skulls of the pupils with as little friction as possible. The business of the Teacher is to raise a thirst. (pp. 82-4)

Although Bernard Shaw is an original writer, if there ever were one, he has learned much and been greatly influenced by his predecessors. That he has been profoundly affected by Schopenhauer, Nietzsche, and Ibsen would be perfectly clear even if he had not denied it; his debt to Samuel Butler he takes pleasure in acknowledging. (p. 85)

Although Rousseau and Shaw are about as different as two men could be, Rousseau's weapon being Sentiment and Shaw's Reason, still the latter shares the fate of all modern artists, thinkers, and writers in being influenced by Jean-Jacques, who was not only the greatest Force but the greatest Source in modern times. Nothing could indicate more clearly that the mass of men are swayed by emotion rather than by thought, than the absolutely universal influence of that eighteenth-century Frenchman. I had not supposed that it would be possible to point out any specific indebtedness, however, until I happened to see in *The Athenaeum* some years ago, the suggestion that Shaw took the hint for *Pygmalion* from Rousseau. (pp. 86-7)

Shaw's plays are cleanly, antiseptic, stimulating; his laughter clears the air. But plays that substitute the laughter of reason for the warm glow of romance lack something that is generally believed to be essential; instead of having an emotional interest, they have the keen play of dialectic. It is the same with his characters; even his greatest single character, *Candida,* has no charm; there is in all his plays only one figure that has any charm, and that is the Lion.

The beast is irresistible; everybody in the audience wants to stroke him. (p. 97)

William Lyon Phelps, "George Bernard Shaw" (1920), in his Essays on Modern Dramatists (© 1921 by Macmillan Publishing Co., Inc.), Macmillan, 1921, pp. 67-98.

J. C. SQUIRE (essay date 1922)

"Back to Methuselah" is one of the happiest conceptions [Mr. Shaw] has had; it catches one at once, and has the added advantage of meaning something. This, however, is what the reader does not understand immediately: there is, as usual, a preface interposed between the title-page and the play.

It is a long preface and not in every respect one of Mr. Shaw's best. The History of Evolutionary Thought is surveyed, with glances at the theatre, painting, politics, and theology. Mr. Shaw races along with fewer good witticisms than usual and fewer really provocative remarks. The sensation of speed is enjoyable at first. But after a while one tends to drowse; one ceases to notice the swift succession of passing objects, and is conscious only of the rhythmic rattle of the train. The upshot of it is that Creative Evolution is "the genuinely scientific religion for which all wise men are now anxiously looking." . . . The play that follows has a major and a minor theme. The major is Creative Evolution at work—mind conquering matter. The minor is a new instrument for accelerating the process. (pp. 122-23)

Mr. Shaw is as clever, as vigorous, as cunning, as high-spirited, as flippant, as curious as ever he was. There are conspicuous faults in this book. The preface, for all its merits, is rather inconsecutive, and gives one the feeling that although Mr. Shaw habitually thinks, he seldom stops to think. His characters are mostly sticks; his appeal is almost continuously to the intellect; the text is overloaded with topical references; a few passages are in bad taste and many pages are tiresome. Most of the middle of the play might have been taken for granted; we did not want that endless silly talk between Mr. Lloyd George, Mr. Asquith, and the rest, to help us form a conception of the present limitations of humanity; some scene much shorter could have furnished the necessary symbol. (pp. 124-25)

Mr. Shaw's qualities and faculties are precisely what they were; the faculty of being very boring was always amongst them, and he may cheer himself with the reflection that there is no fault here, large or small, which cannot be paralleled repeatedly from his earlier plays. I at least feel that in places Mr. Shaw is here surpassing his previous best, and notably in the first and last scenes. The whole play may be no more actable than the second part of "Faust" or yesterday's *Times*, but the first act and part of the last would be as effective in the theatre as anything that Mr. Shaw has ever done. The craftsmanship of the Eden scene deserves the much-abused epithet, "astonishing"; every sentence is revelatory, and moves the action forward; and the whole is a genuine re-creation of the legend. The illusion is perfectly imposed, and the temptation to cheap cleverness, which previous wits who have dealt with that story have not resisted, is avoided. Mr. Shaw's sympathy with the Serpent is scarcely veiled, but he does not obscure his intellectual conceptions with irrelevant jests as he has so often done, nor does he allow those conceptions, in their turn, to smother the dramatic progress of his story. In the last act

he comes nearer to poetry than he has ever come, and in the last pages nearer to awe. . . . There are elements in his composition which inhibit him from an even momentary abandonment to love or pity or aesthetic enjoyment, and he is incapable of fear. He is always "all there"; he possesses his subject and cannot be possessed by it; his sense of humour is never in complete abeyance; the strain of argument is always present; he is too interested in things in general to give his natural sympathy for individuals much play—being, like Nature, careful of the race, but careless of the single specimen; he despises the senses and, in so far as Art appeals to the senses, he despises Art. When he uses the mechanism of Strephon and Amaryllis, temple and bosky glade and pastoral dance, in the last act, our constant tendency to lapse into enjoyment of the idyllic element is checked by the pervasive sense of Mr. Shaw's irony; we know he thinks that all nonsense. Even at the close where, as I have said, he does actually come near awe, he does not quite achieve it: for in the imagined presence of the very spirit of Nature, to whom he has dedicated himself, Mr. Shaw's self-possession and detachment remain: it is as it were a theoretical awe struggling to carry conviction. Nevertheless, that scene, from the procession of primaeval ghosts to the last eloquent harangue of the symbolic Lilith, is conceived finely, and constructed with extraordinary skill. It leaves one with a sense of having had a glimpse of grandeur.

A cold and pagan grandeur; but there is Mr. Shaw's philosophy. (pp. 125-27)

J. C. Squire, "A Metabiological Pentateuch," in his Books Reviewed, George H. Doran Co., 1922 (and reprinted by Kennikat Press, 1968), pp. 122-28.

ST. JOHN G. ERVINE (essay date 1922)

["Heartbreak House" and "Back to Methusaleh"] are notable for a growth of religious conviction in their author which has brought him to a condition resembling, in the eyes of some, that of John the Baptist and, in the eyes of others (as I heard a clergyman of the Church of Ireland angrily assert) that of a religious fanatic. They are also notable for a weakening of technical skill as a dramatist. Mr. Shaw has set himself so ably to the task of rejecting drama from his plays, that unconsciously he ruins the effect of his lines by an excess of garrulity. (p. 211)

The difficulty a critic has in estimating Mr. Shaw's sense of the theatre is increased by the wilfulness with which he rejects technique: one is not always able to decide whether the lack of technique in the later plays is the result of intention or weakness. (p. 214)

Mr. Shaw, in his later pieces, leaves you with the sensation that he knows only too well what he means, but he will never admit that you are capable of understanding him. . . . I do not know of any writer who is so thrifty with his means as Mr. Shaw. Shakespeare, compared with him, is a prodigal and a spendthrift. . . . Any old plot, however disreputable it might be, would serve Shakespeare for drawing on to the stage a crowd of dissimilar persons and enriching their lives with his verse; and any old character, however remote from human semblance will serve Mr. Shaw as a vent for opinions. Shakespeare primarily was interested in people. Mr. Shaw primarily is interested in doctrine. The principal difference between a dramatist who is interested in people and a dramatist who is interested in doctrines, is that the former will delight in the creation of the greatest variety of characters whereas the latter will not trouble to create a new character if an old one will do. I doubt whether there are more than twelve distinct persons in the whole of Mr. Shaw's work. When he began his career as a dogmatist, he set himself to writing novels, but found after he had written five, of which only four have been published, that he could not use this instrument so effectively for his purpose as he could use the instrument of the play. And so he turned his attention to the stage. But he did not waste his novels: he dramatised them. He lifted passages from his books and put them into his plays. He took some of the novel-characters and, after he had tidied them and changed their names, forced them from between their covers on to the stage. There is little in the thirty-eight plays he has written which is not to be found, developed or suggested, in his four novels. He has preached one doctrine all his life, and has preached it with singular consistency. (pp. 215-18)

God, in Mr. Shaw's religion, is not just a God: he is a God determined to have His own way and entirely indifferent to the desires of His creatures. If man will not help God to fulfil His purpose, then God will destroy man and invent another and more submissive instrument whereby He may do so. Such is the Shavian gospel. In what respect does it differ from the most devastating and blasting form of Calvinism? When I was a child in Belfast, I was taught that if I persisted in being a wicked boy, I would be roasted for ever in a red-hot hell. Is there any real difference between the Calvinist who tells a child that he will be burned for all eternity and Mr. Shaw who tells it that it will be scrapped for all eternity? (p. 222)

Mr. Shaw's thirty-eight plays are not thirty-eight separate plays but one long, continuous piece, in which his twelve characters, in every conceivable disguise and situation, strive to elude the hand of God but are nabbed by Him in the end. Twist how you may, He'll get you in the end, unless, indeed, He wearies of trying to make use of you, when, inexorably, without a pang, He will cast you on to the scrap-heap where you will perish utterly as your little brothers, the mammoth beasts, perished long ago. (p. 224)

Mr. Shaw shows himself [like Shakespeare] indifferent to details when they no longer serve his purpose. He has been charged with spoofing his audience on occasion, notably in the first act of "Man and Superman" where he trumps up a case of impending maternity for shocking effects, and then, his purpose achieved, says no more about it for the remainder of the play! . . . I do not believe that Mr. Shaw had any intention of spoofing his audience when he invented [such] situations. He simply did not bother about the details. He had used the effect for his purpose, and since it was no longer servicable to him, he scrapped it without even troubling to clear away the debris—which, presumably, is what His God will do with us when He no longer needs us. . . . [A] propounder of doctrine pays little heeds to the laws of stagecraft or anything else. . . . Death and Tradition have no terrors for him. That is why, in face of the opposition of common sense and practical experience, he always does what he wants to do. (pp. 225-27)

["Heartbreak House"], in some respects the best that Mr. Shaw has written, is full of mad laughter, of bitter, self-mocking, torturing laughter . . . ; for "even in laughter the

heart is sorrowful, and the end of that mirth is heaviness." I feel about "Heartbreak House" . . . that here is a depth of feeling which cannot be fathomed. Like Job, Mr. Shaw cries out, "changes and war are against me," but, unlike Job, he finds no comfort in the end. "If men will not learn until their lessons are written in blood, why, blood they must have, their own for preference." As for him, he throws up the sponge. Our culture is but the plaything of fribbles; our democracy is merely government of fools by fools. "The question is," said Boswell to Dr. Johnson and Mr. Cambridge, "which is worst, one wild beast or many?" And the answer, in Mr. Shaw's terms, is "Both!" (pp. 231-32)

In "Back to Methusaleh," he seems to me to have suffered a spiritual set-back, and to be preoccupied by material considerations. We are no longer concerned with Man's Destiny and God's Purpose, but with matters of mere longevity. . . . Mr. Shaw tells us that if we *will* hard enough, we can achieve longevity, but, apart from the fact that longevity first happens in his play to people who have not willed it, but had it thrust upon them, I am puzzled to understand how Mr. Shaw expects mankind to will a state of existence which, portrayed by him, is extraordinarily repellent. (pp. 232-34)

His fearless, challenging spirit attracted all those who were in revolt against stagnant beliefs; and even now, when the multitude seems to have caught up with him and his views are less startling than they were a few years ago, he still stimulates the minds of the young and the eager and sends them bounding forward. "You should so live," he once said, "that when you die, God is in your debt!" He bids men and women strive to put more into the common pool than they take out, and he asserts with something like moral fury that any one who is taking more from the common pool than he puts in, is cheating both God and man. There are querulous persons who say that his work will not live. Their forefathers probably said that Shakespeare's work would not live, that Cervantes's work would not live, that Fielding's work would not live, that Dickens's work would not live; and no doubt they produced sound arguments to support their faith. (pp. 238-39)

St. John G. Ervine, "Bernard Shaw" (originally published in a slightly different version in North American Review, *Vol. CCXI, No. 774, May, 1920), in his* Some Impressions of My Elders *(reprinted by permission of The Society of Authors as the literary representative of the Estate of St. John Ervine;* © *1922 by St. John G. Ervine), The Macmillan Company, 1922, pp. 189-239.*

ST. JOHN ADCOCK (essay date 1928)

Shaw has been mistaken for an incorrigible jester because, instead of losing his temper and furiously denouncing the follies and hypocrisies of mankind, or going after the foolish with a whip (though he has done that on occasion), he is more inclined to laugh at them; he finds a subject for farce or comedy where the conventional reformer would find a text for a sermon. And, whatever can be said against them, it is some justification for his methods that while other sermons have emptied the churches, his have filled the theatres. (pp. 1-2)

[His] invincible common-sense told him he could do no effective preaching nor hope to sell even what was worth buying until he had secured an audience, and, laying himself open to the charge of being a quack and a charlatan, he deliberately adopted the practices of the mountebank to attract a crowd and to make it listen to him after it was collected. (p. 3)

[When] he disparaged Shakespeare and acclaimed himself as the greater dramatist, he was not actuated by vanity, but by a sound business instinct; since the world accepts a man at his valuation of himself, as a penniless author fighting for recognition and a livelihood, Shaw threw modesty to the dogs and instead of blushing unseen and wasting his sweetness on the desert air, accommodated himself to the world's stupidity. (p. 4)

You may see parsons, politicians, military men, business men, plebeians in the gallery and aristocrats in boxes and stalls listening to [his plays], . . . obviously enjoying the wit, the sly irony, the unorthodox teaching and humane, common-sense philosophy of them, even when these are levelled at their own beliefs and practises and satirise the opinions they hold and the lives they live. . . . [They] take their medicine gladly because the brilliance of his wit and the humour which clothes the sincerity of his hatred of wrong and cant and cruelty and humbug make it palatable. (p. 7)

I doubt whether any man has attacked more social evils and respectable shibboleths, or had a profounder, more far-reaching influence on his own time; yet . . . he has fewer enemies now than have most public men who, not having a tithe of his outspokenness, have never told any truths that were unpleasant to their own supporters. (p. 8)

> *St. John Adcock, "George Bernard Shaw," in his* The Glory That Was Grub Street: Impressions of Contemporary Authors, *Frederick A. Stokes Company, 1928, pp. 1-12.*

GEORGE JEAN NATHAN (essay date 1931)

Shaw's canon plainly betrays his dislike of sex and his evasion of it. In all his work from beginning to end I know of no instance where he has not deftly avoided self-commitment on the subject or has not indulged in equivoque of one sort or another in his treatment of it.

It is impossible, within the limits of the present chapter, to go fully into Shaw's writings and draw from them a comprehensive catalogue of illustrations. But one may suggest the color of his intrinsic and general attitude by skimming through them and extracting a few sufficiently pointed and revelatory examples. That, when he laid hold of the incalescent Cleopatra, he chose to contemplate her at the age of sixteen and, in spite of the fact that sixteen was maturity in that gala era, insisted upon comfortably regarding her as a species of pre-Mary Pickford flapper, that he presented the Caesar who had a baby by her as an historical Crocker Harrington, and that he once achieved the remarkable feat of writing sexlessly about the madam of a bordello, are phenomena familiar to everyone. (p. 170)

Let us glance haphazardly through Shaw's work. Having presented us with a virginal Cleopatra and a Caesar whose amatory exercises are confined to lifting her upon his knee and playing horsie, he presents us with the inflammable Great Catherine as one of the Four Marx Brothers, and not Harpo either. He gives us a Pygmalion who will have none of his perfected Galatea and who, to use Shaw's own

words, excuses his indifference to young women on the ground that they have an irresistible rival in his mother. (pp. 171-72)

Speaking of the marriage contract in one of his prefaces, Shaw alludes to sex stimulation as "the most violent, most insane, most delusive and most transient of passions," expresses his disbelief that married people as a rule really live together, and says that "a man as intimate with his own wife as a magistrate is with his clerk . . . is a man in ten thousand." . . . Lina, in "Misalliance," takes out her surplus energy on a flying trapeze and recommends the same diet to her adoring Tarleton. And in "Arms and the Man," we find the Shavian protagonist not too proud for sexual dalliance, but too tired.

The point is not that Shaw's imaginative writing is sexless —that is a fact too well known to call for repetition; the point is that the body of his work as a whole reveals a man to whom sex, in the sense that the word is commonly used, is at once unpleasant, deplorable and disgusting. There are times, true enough, when he seems to advance the opposite point of view, but it will be found that, when he does so, he does so only subsequently to refute and demolish it. Nor is his argument of the other point of view even momentarily persuasive; it hasn't the ring of sincerity; it is a dummy set up merely for tackling purposes. Among conspicuous modern English men of letters and English critics of life, he alone is indefatigable in waving the white banner of biological asceticism. One of the cleverest dialecticians of our time, he is sometimes successful in concealing his true attitude for a moment, in masking his ferocious personal convictions and in giving a bland performance in the rôle of a hell of a fellow, but it fools no one. Chesterton once observed that it is the weak man who always, when taking a walk, most vigorously thwacks the bushes along the roadside with his cane. A mistrust of his own philosophical attitude toward sex may similarly account for Shaw's disputatious thwacking of it. (pp. 173-75)

> *George Jean Nathan, "Chronicles," in his* Testament of a Critic *(copyright © 1931 by George Jean Nathan; reprinted by permission of Associated University Presses, Inc.), Alfred A. Knopf, Inc., 1931, pp. 97-178.**

ALEXANDER WOOLLCOTT (essay date 1933)

Taking a missionary Bible as her guidebook, [a] questing Black Girl visits all the authorities from the God of Noah to Mohammed and Voltaire [in *The Adventures of the Black Girl in Her Search for God*]. (p. 352)

When the story is finished, Mr. Shaw moves among the audience, distributing blueprints to explain his meaning. The English critics were irked by this medicine-man procedure, but that is only because they persist in thinking of Shaw as an artist when all his ancestral voices bid him strive to be not an artist at all but a teacher. And, though going on seventy-seven, he is, I think, the greatest of his time. When class is dismissed this time, I come away with a new notion about dear teacher. It suddenly occurs to me that his angers and emphases are more understandable to any reader who realizes that there is one scent which offends the Shavian nostrils beyond all others, one smell which, quite literally, maddens him. That is the odor of burning flesh. (p. 353)

Consider the Black Girl's encounter with the God of Noah.

She finds him a well-built, handsome, aristocratic man, wearing a beard as white as isinglass, a ruthlessly severe expression, and an absurdly decorous nightshirt. . . . [She] considers him a vain old bogy man of such bullying egotism as would be tolerated in an earthly father only if he were rich, aged, and of indisputable testamentary capacity. But this exigent Jehovah also demands that her relatives bring plenty of rams, goats, and sheep to roast before him lest he prove his greatness and majesty by smiting them with the most horrible plagues. And it is clear from the context that what Mr. Shaw most profoundly dislikes about the God of Noah is just this singular appetite for the "sweet savor" of sizzling carcasses. Indeed, you are driven to conclude, it seems to me, that not only Shaw's repudiation of that clumsily imagined god, but also his special anger at the martyrdom of Saint Joan and his horrified aversion to pork chops, are all, somehow, reflections of the same mysterious deep distaste for burning flesh. (pp. 353-54)

> Alexander Woollcott, "The Nostrils of G.B.S." (1933), in The Portable Woollcott, edited by Joseph Hennessey (copyright 1946 by The Viking Press, Inc.; copyright renewed © 1974 by The Viking Press, Inc.; reprinted by permission of the publishers), Viking Penguin, 1946, pp. 351-54.

FRANK SWINNERTON (essay date 1934)

Shaw has told the world that his ideas were derived from Wagner, Ibsen, Samuel Butler, and Nietzsche, and that his characters were stolen from Dickens. There is not a word of truth in all this. The cast of his mind, his mingling of kindness with an impatience of fools, his mingling of sense and nonsense, is altogether natural and peculiar. He has that intellectual simplicity to which all ideas are, as it were, foreknown. He had written in the manner of Ibsen before ever reading Ibsen; Wagner was a fellow-revolutionary; Nietzsche merely gave him the formula, the phrase, necessary for the expression of his own views; Samuel Butler had almost privately written down thoughts long familiar to Shaw. (pp. 51-2)

I think the real reason why he became a dramatist was that when as a young man he spent his evenings in debate he always found the opposition so weak that he longed to take both sides—all sides—himself, just to show how a case should be conducted. Most of his plays are dramatic debates, interspersed with farcical incidents. (p. 53)

[It] was not the themes of the plays that upset all who objected to Shaw. It was their verbal irreverence. Not what they said; but the nasty way they said it. To a people accustomed since the death of Dickens to a serious treatment of serious matters, a mocking attitude towards morals, parents, and respectability was abhorrent. (pp. 55-6)

[There] was nothing at all aesthetic in Shaw. Nor had these plays "dignity and memory and measure," in Henry James's sense. (p. 56)

Arms and the Man shows that Shaw had abandoned realism for ever. His sole connection with it henceforward was to be a persistent anti-romanticism. Where the realist coolly and fatalistically shows the inevitable sequence of events—Ibsen in his social plays is a realist,—Shaw leaps hither and thither among solemn follies and makes them ridiculous. He shows in this play, with a glee akin to that of Molière, the absurd impulse to lie and to pose which is dominant in men and women. And, instead of allowing the lie to persist, and

even to triumph, as a realist might justifiably have done, he makes every lie achieve the ignominy of ludicrous exposure. That is an unmistakable mark of comic genius, and in the field of farcical comedy *Arms and the Man* remains unequalled in Shaw's work. (p. 58)

> Frank Swinnerton, "Teachers: Shaw and Wells," in his The Georgian Scene: A Literary Panorama (copyright 1934 © 1962 by Frank Swinnerton; reprinted by permission of Holt, Rinehart and Winston, Publishers), Farrar & Rinehart, 1934, pp. 41-84.*

OSCAR CARGILL (essay date 1941)

Before the Intelligentsia discovered Nietzsche, they were very fortunate in having George Bernard Shaw for a back log and Bible, a thesaurus and jest book. Shaw, we hasten to add, seems to us to have some characteristics which set him apart from the Intelligentsia, but there is no denying that they have made most radical use of him, and that, until he can be weighed and sifted, bolted and bagged, we may count him their man. He has had for them an enormous appeal, for the very simple reason that they could turn to him for unconventional views on almost any topic—on prize fighting, art, church-going, diet, prostitution, home-rule, medicine, communism, feminine psychology, evolution,—just ask G.B.S., he has an iconoclastic opinion. (pp. 457-58)

Out of a variety of things which might be selected for the study of Shaw's development . . . , it is convenient to choose and to concentrate upon only three—those most influential in America: [the novel *An Unsocial Socialist*, the article "Socialism for Millionaires," in the *Contemporary Review;* and the play *Man and Superman: A Comedy and a Philosophy*]. . . . (p. 464)

An Unsocial Socialist is somewhat less revolutionary than a pan of biscuits which fail to rise, and less doctrinaire than a muffin. This is the more remarkable in that the novel was written when Shaw ostensibly was a simon-pure Marxist, just before he became a Fabian. As an afterthought, there is added to the book a letter from Sidney Trefusis to the author, in which Shaw's hero makes it clear that he is not a *revolutionary* Socialist (despite the fact that in the story he helps some men throw down a wall that an arrogant landlord has erected across a common path) but an *evolutionary* Socialist. The letter-writer is a converted Fabian, but from what is he converted? Not from his philandering, we hope, or he would have no charm or vitality whatever. Yet the idea that he has become an evolutionary voluptuary instead of a revolutionary one fills us with misgiving—we see in it the threat of the professional iconoclast which, apparently, it is possible even for an Irishman to become.

The enticing article "Socialism for Millionaires" was written when Mr. Shaw's dialectical powers presumably were at their best, ground, like a Sheffield knife, in the allegedly strenuous combats of the Fabian association and as an open-air speaker to dockhands. It does contain more than a suggestion of the gift of the capable extemporizer in getting a laugh out of nimble rhetoric. (pp. 464-65)

Shaw's next avatar is found in *Man and Superman* . . . [published] with an "Epistle Dedicatory" and a very important "Revolutionist's Handbook" attached. The play is an amusing adaptation of the old picaresque, Don Quixote-Joseph Andrews plot to the stage, in which a gentleman

Socialist, one John Tanner, is pursued down into Spain and there held captive by bandits long enough for his pursuer, a strong-willed young heiress, Ann Whitefield, to overtake and capture him. It tickles Shaw's fancy to treat Tanner as a modern Don Juan, reader of Schopenhauer and Nietzsche, student of Westermarck, concerned for the future of the race instead of being bent upon satiating his own appetites. This conceit permits the dramatist to introduce a graceful interlude on the stage as a dream of John Tanner, in which he as Don Juan engages the Devil in dialectics and ends by lecturing him. The Don attacks with astonishing venom (considering his past) the delusion that romantic love is the highest good of man. . . . With all the earnestness and vehemence of a Wesleyan preacher, the reformed libertine declares his conviction that a means will be found to avoid the present social consequences of passion. It will be found *because the Life Force wills it*. . . . It is thoroughly consistent, then, for Shaw in the appended "Revolutionist's Handbook" to renounce Fabianism and to declare himself for evolutionary socialism to be produced by the Life-Force. (pp. 466-67)

Yet so far as there is a true George Bernard Shaw, he may be said to be represented by the plays and pieces which we have surveyed. This is not the George Bernard Shaw, however, with whom Americans are acquainted or who has most influenced our thought. . . . American opinion of him has been formed in the main on other things, and because of this fact he does not appear to us either as a bewildered Socialist or baffled Irishman, but as an operatic Mephistopheles, the "tease" of the good and virtuous, the shocker of the moral and moderate, the cocksure diabolist. (pp. 469-70)

The consequences of Shaw's American reputation are that his one profoundly moving play, *Saint Joan* . . . , is prized most for its pseudo-cynical, apologetic epilogue, and that his popular *Candida* . . . , whose hold upon the public is really lodged in its Barryesque sentimentalism, is regarded as important for its satirical revelation of the weakness of the ministry. . . . A shelf of Shaw contains other recommendable treats, but it will take much new writing on the man to offset his deeply entrenched American reputation as an iconoclast and mere wit. He will probably remain the devil's disciple so far as America is concerned, the perfect exemplar of the especially privileged artist. (pp. 472-73)

> *Oscar Cargill, "The Intelligentsia," in his* Intellectual America: Ideas on the March *(reprinted with permission of Macmillan Publishing Co., Inc.; copyright 1941 by Macmillan Publishing Co., Inc.; renewed 1969 by Oscar Cargill), Macmillan, 1941, pp. 399-536.*

W. H. AUDEN (essay date 1942)

[Shaw] cannot, thank God, be serious for very long: the more logical his argument, the more certain he is to accompany it with a wink. Indeed his only insufferable characters are his good people (using "good" in the Shavian sense); like Candida who is a dreadful woman or Joan who talks like a lady novelist, and his most lovable characters are rogues like Candida's father.

For the same reason, perhaps, while no playwright has ever equalled Shaw in his insight into the effect of occupation upon character—he is the only writer who has read Karl Marx with real profit and most of his plays might be called

studies in occupational diseases—yet the occupational type which he cannot draw is his own, the artist: Marchbanks and Dubedat are the mustiest of theatrical props. His most first-hand, realistically unheroic observation is of the political hero, the stoic in a high position. . . .

His plays are a joy to watch, not because they purport to be concerned with serious problems, but because they are such wonderful displays of conspicuous waste, because the energy shown by any of his characters is so wildly in excess of what their situation practically requires that if it were to be devoted to anything "worthwhile," they would wreck the world in five minutes.

All his life Shaw has been devoted to music (he was probably the best music critic who ever lived) and, as he tells us, it was from Mozart's "Don Giovanni" that he learned "how to write seriously without being dull"; and this devotion is, perhaps, the clue to his work. For all his theater about propaganda, his writing has an effect nearer to that of music than the work of any of the so-called pure writers.

The Mozart of English Letters he is not—the music of the Marble Statue is beyond him—the Rossini, yes. He has all the brio, the humor, the tunes, the clarity, and the virtuosity of that great master of Opera Bouffe.

And this is a very great deal. If now we see errors in his doctrines, the credit must go to Hitler, not to our own acumen; and the present generation, if it is honest, will have to admit that in comparison with its own spokesmen, the "vulgar old buffer" not only had nicer manners, a kinder heart, and a more courageous will, but also wrote a lot better. (p. 13)

> *W. H. Auden, "The Fabian Figaro," in* Commonweal *(copyright © 1942 Commonweal Publishing Co., Inc.; reprinted by permission of Commonweal Publishing Co., Inc.), Vol. XXXVII, No. 1, October 23, 1942, pp. 12-13.*

RONALD PEACOCK (essay date 1946)

There is a certain quality of calculation in Shaw's approach to comedy. (p. 86)

Having turned to the theatre, it was undoubtedly a stroke of personal genius to choose comedy for his form in the conditions obtaining in the theatre and intellectual life generally at the turn of this century. Comedy carries didacticism with a better grace than other kinds of drama. . . . [It is] Shaw's own conviction, aggressively held, that art should always be parable. His work is the *best* effort of all the drama that was inspired by social criticism. It is even superior to Ibsen's, where Ibsen's implications are social. (p. 87)

Within the limits of the art of comedy he has displayed a striking originality in two principal directions; first in the point of view he adopts for his critical attack, and secondly in his adaptation of comedy to the naturalist technique.

Regarding the first point, Shaw conforms to tradition in the sense that you must have a fixed point from which to work, to launch your criticism. In Molière, for instance, the established position is generally interpreted as the rule of the golden mean of reason. Shaw is also devoted to reason. But whilst Molière takes his fixed point from the general experience of men as rational and social beings, Shaw takes his from a rational philosophy of his own. Hence he inverts the usual method. Instead of isolating the unreasonable character, he isolates the reasonable one. (pp. 88-9)

His main attack being on society, his transformation of traditional comic method is brilliant. Taking an unconventional character, a person with the gift of insight and freedom, he impinges it upon a group of conventional social animals, and the impact reveals at every turn stock notions and reactions, prejudices and dishonesties, in short the illusionary, the unreal, the irrational. Molière exposes one character in turn; Shaw the social herd, all together. And these characters of his are most certainly dramatic conceptions, because they create, by being what they are, startling situations. (p. 89)

Molière's Harpagon and Alceste, Jonson's Volpone and Sir Epicure Mammon, are imaginative creations. . . . Shaw's principals are not products of this kind of imaginative power. At the most it can be said that his series has a certain force and solidity because each member of it is a reflection of Shaw's own intelligence, and their effect is cumulative. The core of each one of them lies in their critical penetration, a quality of their creator. It is their only real vitality. They are without the vitality of instinct that makes a total living creature and on which the characters of Molière are based. . . . Shaw gives us but one image: of the critical mind acting as a solvent. There is a point outside the drama where the two authors meet, on the ground of philosophy and practical wisdom, or the effort towards it. It would be difficult to decide which is the greater intellect. But it is easy to judge Molière the greater artist, because he gives us forms, against which Shaw can only put a *perpetuum mobile* of critical comment. (p. 90)

His comedy flowing from his criticism of society, [Shaw] needs for his purposes the ordinary social milieu, with the sort of crisis that arises from typical bourgeois circumstances. In this milieu he lets his unconventional characters challenge the creatures of habit by word and action, and the rest follows. His material is that of all bourgeois drama since the middle of the nineteenth century, more particularly since Ibsen. One of the things he admired most in the latter was the way he made his audience feel that what they saw on the stage was what went on in their own homes. The direct attack is of the essence of Shaw's intention. His method in fact is to give us a comic version of Ibsen's principal theme, the rebel against society, the true man against the false. . . . In developing his work from this position Shaw achieves a remarkable feat. For in the first place comedy and wit introduce a compensating element of imagination into the lamentably prosaic waste of bourgeois realist drama; Shaw avoids the mistake of other imitators of Ibsen. And in the second place he liberates comedy from the cruder forms of its long-accustomed artificialities and tricks—the disguises, the eavesdroppings, the mistaken identities, the stock characters and so on. . . . Not that he foregoes altogether the prerogative of comedy in the matter of fantastic incident and improbable dénouement. In fact he gains here another advantage over the "serious" social problem dramatist, because he can treat more cavalierly the difficulty of contriving a probable end as well as a probable situation. He may use far-fetched incidents and dénouements, but they are not the part of his material that really counts. . . . [No] writer of stage comedy, not even Molière, can afford to neglect any source of amusement, and Shaw has the good sense to be as small on occasion as his greatest predecessor. But even so, the real Shavian comedy is independent of the bit of fantasy. . . . (pp. 91-2)

Our first impulse is to say: this is not comedy as it ought to be. Our second is to justify it as the proper mode for Shaw's idea. With our third impulse we look more closely at work that seems to owe no obligation except to its own law, its own subject-matter, and we discover that it does owe something to its genre, to its predecessors, to pre-existent authorities. It illustrates a continuity, not a break. Shaw adheres first to the principle that comedy must have a fixed vantage-point, though he transforms it to suit his own purpose. He retains, too, the prerogatives and tricks of comedy, without, however, the necessity of being chained to them. He also keeps to stock types for comic purposes, but his new social philosophy gives him a new set of types. Even in incidentals he can follow well-worn grooves of the art; the Straker-Tanner relationship in *Man and Superman* rests on the conventional master-valet set-up, given a completely new vitality from the new social background. And his second great obligation is to the dramatic developments that immediately preceded him and in which he was caught up. He uses the natural probable situation of bourgeois life, public or domestic, that focuses a problem of social behaviour. And he acknowledges the debt by originality of treatment; that is, he gives us what no one else gave and Ibsen had only hinted at, comedy. (pp. 92-3)

Ronald Peacock, "Shaw," in his The Poet in the Theatre *(reprinted by permission of Hill and Wang, a division of Farrar, Straus & Giroux, Inc.; copyright 1946, copyright © 1960 by Ronald Peacock), Harcourt Brace Jovanovich, Inc., 1946 (and reprinted by Hill and Wang, 1960), pp. 86-93.*

STARK YOUNG (essay date 1948)

Since Mr. Shaw himself goes to some length in the preface to invite more or less comparison of *Heartbreak House* with Chekhov's plays, we may sketch at least the beginning of such a comparison. Chekhov, he says, had produced four dramatic studies of *Heartbreak House*, of which three, *The Cherry Orchard, Uncle Vanya* and *The Sea Gull*, so far as England went, had got as far as a couple of performances by the Stage Society. The audiences had stared and said "How Russian!" To Mr. Shaw on the contrary it seemed that these intensely Russian plays fitted all the country houses in Europe in which . . . et cetera. Such a remark as that seems to me incredibly wilful and silly. The thesis of blind chaos and selfishness and of following the part of comfortable income and securities is a definite thesis. It may readily fit into the motif of a rotting Europe. But Chekhov would have been surprised to learn that his plays were a declaration in advance of all this. The Russian world of Chekhov can be only partially compared to the England that Mr. Shaw has diagrammed in *Heartbreak House.* A great difference arises from the fact that the expressiveness of the Russian temperament, with its gift and power of outpouring the far recesses of the heart, is a far more difficult matter for the English. This is not to say that either one or the other is better, but only that they are different. Where Tolstoy, Mr. Shaw says, was no pessimist and believed in the efficacy of violent measures, Chekhov, "more of a fatalist, had no faith in these charming people extricating themselves. They would, he thought, be sold up and set adrift by the bailiff; and he therefore had no scruple in exploiting and even flattering their charm."

What a patness and charm of persuasion this Mr. Shaw has! But the mere use of the words "flatter" and "charm" give away the British rubbish, or Teutonic conception, behind the idea. The references here are plainly to *The Cherry Orchard.* But no person in it wants to be flattered as to his special idiosyncrasy, nobody in this play is talking with that self-consciousness and varying degrees of egotism or no egotism so common to modest Englishmen. The charm of these people in *The Cherry Orchard,* and often of the Russians we meet is that nobody is thinking at all about being charming; nobody is self-conscious, nobody is affected. That sentence of Mr. Shaw's is a whole commentary on the difference between Chekhov's world and that British world which Mr. Shaw so pugnaciously caters to, rebukes so entertainingly, severely and sincerely, and makes a fortune out of.

The more you know of Chekhov's writing and of him and his life and friends, the more absurd Mr. Shaw becomes on the subject. It is all very well to use a man or a work of art to hit something or somebody over the head with; and certainly the sport is an old one. But nobody could be more astonished than Chekhov would have been to hear of his having no scruples about exploiting the people whose words and little ironic, tender or mad acts, and droll or dark life-patterns he put into plays and stories or left jotted down in his notebook. To "flatter" anything about them would not fit anything in him. What he did with his people was to turn them into theatre, just as Mr. Shaw in *Heartbreak House* turns Chekhov into a sort of literary Hyde Park soapbox dialectic for the theatre.

That such a man as Mr. Shaw could use the life that is presented in Chekhov's plays in Chekhov's way, and even some of Chekhov's ideas and attitudes, is obvious. In spite of the unsuccessful translations of the Chekhov plays into English, a great deal of him comes through; and I should think it possible enough that Mr. Shaw regards his own *Heartbreak House* as being technically related to the three Chekhov plays that he mentions, *The Cherry Orchard* especially. Whether he does so or not, the comparison is inevitable and the relationship plain. On that subject we should have to say that either he boldly exercised his usual independence in the way of doing things, or else he was blind as a bat to Chekhov's technique, stage-effects and spirit. We should be brow-beaten indeed to accept the idea that in *Heartbreak House* there is more than the merest hint or tiny reflection of Chekhov's true method, none of that pure, painstaking economy and drawing, none of that humility of vision, none of that shy certainty of intuition. And Mr. Shaw's play has none of the variety in emotional rhythm that Chekhov has, either in tone or in profound self-revelation among the characters.

Chekhov sees his people as rooted in something, which means that he begins with what they are, their quality, and from this he derives what they will express. Mr. Shaw, for all his prattle about their class, clichés, bogies, culture and complacent, urgent or ironic circumstance, sees his people in the light of their opinions. Such a course makes for certain effective dramatic patterns, for distinct *dramatis personae,* real or not real, and for straw men, to be set up or knocked over at will. But it is, I think, his greatest and his final weakness as a creative artist. And it provides the reason why no intelligent member of the traditional British ruling class has ever needed to fear Mr. Shaw very greatly. Nobody could ever take one of Mr. Shaw's magnates or autocratic ruling class characters as the real thing. They

may be arresting or provocative, but—for a while at least—it is their author, not themselves, that is so articulate. The portrayal, however, could be dangerous only when it came from the centre of the character himself. It is this quality of the centrifugal that makes Chekhov different from Mr. Shaw, though centrifugal seems a word too strong for that delicate, moving security and expressive freedom that Chekhov achieves for his people, and the matrix of gentle humor, like that of a wise doctor, within which he sees what they say or do, and for which he brings no compelling benefit or reform.

Taking a work of art as a kind of biological whole, which is the only way it makes any sense, I should say that nothing Mr. Shaw presents in *Heartbreak House* to prove his case could be a better evidence of the decay, if you like, of the English scene than this play itself is, with its lack of any organic unity or exciting technique, its fuzzy lack of power, its exhibitionistic self-assertion, its futile chatter in coquettish monotone about what the first bomb could obliterate or the first ism could make stale. (pp. 207-10)

Stark Young, "Heartbreak Houses," in his Immortal Shadows: A Book of Dramatic Criticism (abridged by permission of Charles Scribner's Sons; copyright 1948 by Charles Scribner's Sons), Scribner's, 1948, pp. 206-10.

EDMUND WILSON (essay date 1948)

Einstein has said that Shaw's plays remind him of Mozart's music: every word has its place in the development. And if we allow for some nineteenth-century prolixity, we can see in Shaw's dramatic work a logic and grace, a formal precision, like that of the eighteenth-century composers.

Take *The Apple Cart,* for example. The fact that Shaw is here working exclusively with economic and political materials has caused its art to be insufficiently appreciated. If it had been a sentimental comedy by Molnar, the critics would have applauded its deftness; yet Shaw is a finer artist than any of the Molnars or Schnitzlers. The first act of *The Apple Cart* is an exercise in the scoring for small orchestra at which Shaw is particularly skillful. After what he has himself called the overture before the curtain of the conversation between the two secretaries, in which the music of King Magnus is foreshadowed, the urbane and intelligent King and the 'bull-roarer Boanerges' play a duet against one another. Then the King plays a single instrument against the whole nine of the cabinet. The themes emerge: the King's disinterestedness and the labor government's sordid self-interest. The development is lively: the music is tossed from one instrument to another, with, to use the old cliché, a combination of inevitableness and surprise. Finally, the King's theme gets a full and splendid statement in the long speech in which he declares his principles: 'I stand for the great abstractions: for conscience and virtue; for the eternal against the expedient; for the evolutionary appetite against the day's gluttony,' etc. This silver voice of the King lifts the movement to a poignant climax; and now a dramatic reversal carries the climax further and rounds out and balances the harmony. Unexpectedly, one of the brasses of the ministry takes up the theme of the King and repeats it more passionately and loudly. . . . [She] launches into an extraordinary tirade in which the idea of political disinterestedness is taken out of the realm of elegant abstraction in which it has hitherto remained with the King and reiterated in terms of engineering: 'every little sewing machine in the Hebrides, every dentist's drill in Shetland, every carpet sweeper in Margate,' etc. This ends on crashing chords, but immediately the music of the cabinet snarlingly reasserts itself. The act ends on the light note of the secretaries.

This music is a music of ideas—or rather, perhaps, it is a music of moralities. . . . Shaw, like Plato, repudiates as a dangerous form of drunkenness the indulgence in literature for its own sake; but, like Plato, he then proceeds, not simply to expound a useful morality, but himself to indulge in an art in which moralities are used as the motifs. It is partly on this account, certainly, that Bernard Shaw has been underrated as an artist. Whether people admire or dislike him, whether they find his plays didactically boring or morally stimulating, they fail to take account of the fact that it is the enchantment of a highly accomplished art which has brought them to and kept them in the playhouse. . . . [Far] from being relentlessly didactic, Shaw's mind has reflected in all its complexity the intellectual life of his time; and his great achievement is to have reflected it with remarkable fidelity. He has *not* imposed a cogent system, but he has worked out a vivid picture. It is, to be sure, not a passive picture, like that of Santayana or Proust: it is a picture in which action plays a prominent part. But it does not play a consistent part: the dynamic principle in Shaw is made to animate a variety of forces. (pp. 182-84)

The principal pattern which recurs in Bernard Shaw—aside from the duel between male and female, which seems to me of much less importance—is the polar opposition between the type of the saint and the type of the successful practical man. (p. 185)

Certainly it is this theme . . . which has inspired those scenes of Shaw's plays which are most moving and most real on the stage—which are able to shock us for the moment, as even the 'Life Force' passages hardly do, out of the amiable and objective attention which has been induced by the bright play of the intelligence. It is the moment when Major Barbara, brought at last to the realization of the power of the capitalist's money and of her own weakness when she hasn't it to back her, is left alone on the stage with the unregenerate bums whose souls she has been trying to save; the moment when Androcles is sent into the arena with the lion; the moment in the emptied courtroom when Joan has been taken out to be burned and the Bishop and the Earl of Warwick are trying each to pin the responsibility on the other. It is the scene in *Heartbreak House* between Captain Shotover and Hector, when they give voice to their common antagonism toward the forces that seem to have them at their mercy. . . . It is the scene in *Back to Methuselah* when the Elderly Gentleman declares to the Oracle: 'They have gone back [the political delegation with whom he has come] to lie about your answer. I cannot go with them. I cannot live among people to whom nothing is real!'—and when she shows him her face and strikes him dead.

But now let us note—for the light they throw on Bernard Shaw in his various phases—the upshots of these several situations. In *Major Barbara,* the Christian saint, the man of learning, and the industrial superman form an alliance from which much is to be hoped. In *Androcles and the Lion,* written . . . in Shaw's amusing but least earnest middle period, just before the war, Androcles and the lion form an alliance, too, of which something is also to be

hoped, but go out arm in arm after a harlequinade on the level of a Christmas pantomime. In *Heartbreak House,* which was begun in 1913 and not finished till 1916, the declaration of war by the unworldlings takes place in the midst of confusion and does not lead to any action on their part.

In *Back to Methuselah,* of the postwar period, the Elderly Gentleman is blasted by the Oracle in a strange scene the implications of which we must stop to examine a moment. The fate of the Elderly Gentleman is evidently intended by Shaw to have some sort of application to himself: though a member of a backward community in which people have not yet achieved the Methuselah-span of life, he differs from his fellows at least in this: that he finds he cannot bear any longer to live among people to whom nothing is real. So the Oracle shrivels him up with her glance.

But what is this supposed to mean? What *is* this higher wisdom which the Elderly Gentleman cannot contemplate and live? So far as the reader is concerned, the revelation of the Oracle is a blank. The old system of Bernard Shaw, which was plausible enough to pass before the war, has just taken a terrible blow, and its grotesque and gruesome efforts to pull itself together and function give the effect of an umbrella, wrecked in a storm, which, when the owner tries to open it up, shows several long ribs of steel sticking out. The Life Force of the man and woman in *Man and Superman* no longer leads either to human procreation or to social-revolutionary activity. The Life Force has been finally detached from socialism altogether. In the *Intelligent Woman's Guide,* Shaw will reject the Marxist dialectic as a false religion of social salvation; but the Life Force is also a religious idea, which we have always supposed in the past to be directed toward social betterment, and now, in *Back to Methuselah,* we find that it has misfired with socialism. Socialism has come and gone; the planet has been laid waste by wars; the ordinary people have all perished, and there is nobody left on earth but a race of selected supermen. And now the race of superior human beings, which was invoked in *Man and Superman* as the prime indispensable condition for any kind of progress whatever but which was regarded by Shaw at that time as producible through eugenic breeding, has taken here a most unearthly turn. It has always been through the superman idea that Shaw has found it possible to escape from the implications of his socialism; and he now no longer even imagines that the superior being can be created by human idealism through human science. The superior beings of *Back to Methuselah* are people who live forever; but they have achieved this superiority through an unconscious act of the will. When they achieved it, what the Life Force turns out to have had in store for them is the mastery of abstruse branches of knowledge and the extra-uterine development of embryos. Beyond this, there is still to be attained the liberation of the spirit from the flesh, existence as a 'whirlpool in pure force.' (pp. 186-88)

Humanity, in *Back to Methuselah,* has dropped out for the moment altogether. The long-livers of the period of progress contemporary with the Elderly Gentleman are not the more 'complete' human beings, with lives richer and better rounded . . . : they are Shavian super-prigs who say the cutting and dampening things which the people have always said in Shaw's plays but who have been abstracted here from the well-observed social setting in which Shaw has always hitherto presented them. And the beings of the later epoch are young people playing in an Arcadia and ancients immersed in cogitations, alike—both cogitations and Arcadia—of the bleakest and most desolating description. There is in *Back to Methuselah* nothing burning or touching, and there is nothing genuinely thrilling except the cry of the Elderly Gentleman; and that, for all the pretense of revelation, is answered by a simple extinction.

In the *Tragedy of an Elderly Gentleman,* the Elderly Gentleman is frightened, but his tragedy is not a real tragedy. *Saint Joan . . .* is an even more frightened play, and, softened though it is by the historical perspective into which Shaw manages to throw it through his epilogue, it was the first genuine tragedy that Shaw had written. The horror of *Back to Methuselah* is a lunar horror; the horror of *Saint Joan* is human. The saint is suppressed by the practical man; and even when she comes back to earth, though all those who exploited or destroyed her are now obliged to acknowledge her holiness, none wants her to remain among them: each would do the same thing again. Only the soldier who had handed her the cross at the stake is willing to accept her now, but he is only a poor helpless clown condemned to the dungeon of the flesh. (pp. 188-89)

Heartbreak House has the same sort of setting and more or less the same form as such Shavian conversations as *Getting Married* and *Misalliance;* but it is really something new for Shaw. There is no diagram of social relations, no tying-up of threads at the end. . . . Heartbreak House, built like a ship, with its old drunken and half-crazy master, the retired adventurer Captain Shotover, is cultured and leisured England; but the characters are no longer pinned down and examined as social specimens: in an atmosphere heavily charged, through a progression of contacts and collisions, they give out thunder and lightning like storm-clouds. Brooding frustrations and disillusions, childlike hurts and furious resentments, which have dropped the old Shavian masks, rush suddenly into an utterance which for the moment has burst out of the old rationalistic wit. For once, where Bernard Shaw has so often reduced historical myths to the sharp focus of contemporary satire, he now raises contemporary figures to the heroic proportions of myth.—An air-raid brings down the final curtain: Heartbreak House has at last been split wide. The capitalist Mangan gets killed, and there is a suggestion that they may all be the better for it. (pp. 189-90)

Too True to Be Good [is] a curious 'political extravaganza,' in which he turns back upon and criticizes his own career. Here the theme of the bourgeois radical of the eighties, disillusioned with himself under stress of the disasters of the twentieth century, is treated in the same vein, with the same kind of idealist poetry, now grown frankly elegiac and despairing, which Shaw had opened in *Heartbreak House* and which had made the real beauty of *The Apple Cart.* (p. 191)

Shaw's most recent pieces are [weak]. *The Simpleton of the Unexpected Isles . . .* is the only play of the author's which has ever struck me as silly. In it, the Day of Judgment comes to the British Empire, and the privilege of surviving on earth is made to depend upon social utility. But, by setting up a purely theocratic tribunal, Shaw deprives this scene of social point: the principle of selection is so general that it might be applied by the fascists as readily as by the socialists, at the same time that the policy of wholesale extinction seems inspired by an admiration for the repressive

tactics of both. The play ends with a salute to the unknown future, which, like the vision of infinity of *Back to Methuselah,* seems perfectly directionless. *The Millionairess . . .* makes a farce out of the notion that a natural boss, deprived of adventitious authority, will inevitably gravitate again to a position where he can bully and control people, and sounds as if it had been suggested by the later phases of Stalin.

Here it cannot be denied that Bernard Shaw begins to show signs of old age. As the pace of his mind slackens and the texture of his work grows looser, the contradictory impulses and principles which have hitherto provided him with drama begin to show gaping rifts. In his *Preface on Bosses* to *The Millionairess,* he talks about 'beginning a Reformation well to the left of Russia,' but composes [a] panegyric on Mussolini, with . . . respectful compliments to Hitler. . . . (pp. 195-96)

Yet the openings—the prologue to *The Simpleton,* with its skit on the decay of the British Empire and the knockabout domestic agonies of the first act or two of *The Millionairess* —still explode their comic situations with something of the old energy and wit; and the one-acter, *The Six of Calais,* though it does not crackle quite with the old spark, is not so very far inferior to such an earlier trifle as *How He Lied to Her Husband.* It is interesting to note—what bears out the idea that Shaw is at his best as an artist—that the last thing he is to lose, apparently, is his gift for pure comic invention, which has survived, not much dimmed, though we may tire of it, since the days of *You Never Can Tell.* (p. 196)

Edmund Wilson, "Bernard Shaw at Eighty (1948)," in his The Triple Thinkers: Twelve Essays on Literary Subjects *(reprinted by permission of Farrar, Straus & Giroux, Inc.; copyright © 1938 by Edmund Wilson), revised edition, Oxford University Press, 1963 (and reprinted by Noonday, 1976), pp. 165-96.*

STEPHEN SPENDER (essay date 1949)

Perhaps Shaw is a two-dimensional giant moving in his own two-dimensional world. According to the rules of this two-dimensional existence, he never errs. . . . For him, in literature, the difference between poetry and prose is that poetry rhymes and has "number," prose doesn't. He found rhyming tedious; so he wrote his plays in prose. In private life, every problem should be solved by the kind of good sense which operates on the heart of the problem, reducing it to an abstraction dealt with by the intellectual will. . . .

In his plays Shaw develops artistically in the same two-dimensional way. Edmund Wilson has pointed out [see excerpt above]—what Shaw himself draws attention to— that there is musical art, borrowed largely from Mozart, in Shaw's plays. That is to say, he has learned from music the secret of external form and progression and sequence: movement of pattern within a mood which could be determined by a musical direction; the art of instrumentation by which dialogue is interwoven, like woodwind with strings. But while Shaw has learned the external tact of musicianship and applied it to drama, he has not learned the inwardness of Mozart. His art is the direction of dialogue from the outside, not the creating of character from within. When he tries (as in "Heartbreak House") to model a play on Chekhov's "inside" creation of character, he becomes, as when he tries (in "Saint Joan") to be poetic, self-conscious and almost embarrassing.

Thus Shaw's great achievement has been to stand outside and above the struggle with words, the struggle with the "blood and mire" of personal experience, which is the lot of other contemporary writers. He has conducted brilliant arguments with his generation in which his dialectical method has consisted in shifting the argument, constantly and with great skill, so that his opponent is left with the feeling that the ground, changed so often, has been cut from under his feet. . . .

[The] entertainer has immediate worth and therefore should be immediately accepted and rewarded. Shaw deserves to be a millionaire.

However, Shaw is more than entertainer, and this is where the difficulty for the critic arises. What is the central passion of his work? The answer is, I think, a kind of fanatical good sense, prepared to sacrifice feeling and enjoyment to good sense, and therefore sometimes fraying at the edges into vegetarian and anti-vivisectionist nonsense. (p. 504)

> Stephen Spender, "The Riddle of Shaw," in The Nation *(copyright 1949 by the Nation Associates, Inc.), Vol. CLXVIII, No. 18, April 30, 1949, pp. 503-05.*

WILLIAM IRVINE (essay date 1949)

Shaw wrote art criticism with indefatigable industry, brutal frankness, and elusive conscientiousness. He read the proper books, including those of Ruskin—whom he ultimately considered unreliable except where religion afforded a clue—but he thought it the critic's first duty to look at art. For years he was as inevitable as the pictures at an exhibition, and at the same time he refreshed himself regularly with the great masters at the National Gallery and at Hampton Court. . . . Shaw declares that in the development of his mind and art Michelangelo played a considerable part. "Michael Angelo, you see, taught me this—always to put people of genius into my works. I am always setting a genius over against a commonplace person."

Apparently Shaw did not begin his career in art criticism as an unqualified admirer of realism. (pp. 118-19)

[For one thing, the] puritan in him could take nothing but a regretful view of the nude. In 1901, with an optimism both Victorian and premature, he asserted as a chief advantage of photography over painting that it presented the nude in a manner too vivid to be endurable in art. (p. 119)

In discovering artistic good, he also discovered artistic evil. It was simply another form of universal evil, that is, of Victorian convention. Socialism had taught him that the Philistine kept his hand tightly in his pocket. Modern painting taught him that he kept his head in a cloud of sentimental illusion. And what was middle-class sentimentality but romanticism? Shaw had found a new antagonist. . . . His summing up of three figures in contemporary art rescues something of romanticism in the person of Watts: "Madox Brown was a man; Watts is at least an artist and poet; Leighton was only a gentleman." One is reminded of the damnation of Adrian Herbert in *Love among the Artists.* (pp. 119-20)

[Shaw] is a pragmatist. He wants not so much to discover truth as to increase it. He magnifies the crude veracity of

Madox Brown and decries the polished sentimentality of Leighton because thereby he hopes more effectually to teach the public to admire truth. Nevertheless, his early warfare against romanticism was not as ruthless as his later. Less venturesome than he was a few years afterward, he did not sacrifice undoubted genius to his cause. (pp. 120-21)

Shaw was artistically conscienceless only on high philosophical grounds. Otherwise, he was aggressively incorruptible. He was continually being fired from newspapers and journals because he refused to allow his criticisms to be padded with puffs. . . . At the cost of prodigious mental exertion, he was always improving his best, and by the time he was well embarked on music criticism, his best had become amazingly good. "Daily journalism," he declares, "is a superhuman profession." Good criticism, he decides, is rarer and more difficult than good creative writing. (p. 121)

Shaw was very sure both of his knowledge and his opinion and delighted in ramming both down the throat of the British reader. He understood not only the techniques of all sorts of instruments and voices but their physical basis in mechanical or physiological structure. With daring omniscience, he detects the slightest variation from legitimate scores, the slightest faults in voice technique, the slightest errors in Italian accent or English pronunciation, the quality and excellence of every instrument in a great orchestra. (pp. 125-26)

Though he was not above parading his knowledge, Shaw was thoroughly on guard against it. When it tended to minimize common sense and natural sensitivity, when it acted as a mechanical force obscuring imaginative insight, he disowned it. . . .

Shaw also brought to music criticism an extremely un-Shavian virtue: he had saved for music all the reverence of a highly irreverent nature. . . . The result is that in his musical criticism more than any other writing he shows genuine artistic conscience, a consuming puritanical passion for artistic perfection, the slightest infringement against which brings down whole thunderstorms of censorious wrath. He is the malignant personal enemy of every fallible musician. Usually he punishes quite impartially, but not always. Indeed he declares that justice is unattainable and truth is not a mean between extremes but "quite the most extreme thing I know of." His professed attitude is once more relativistic and pragmatic. He writes for immediate effect, in a gay and passionate effort to make audiences insist on better music and musicians and composers produce it. He coddles, bullies, lauds, insults, gadflying everybody to do his best. His criticism is propaganda for Wagner, for realistic costuming and staging, for precise and intelligent execution, for a dozen other causes and partial truths neglected at the moment. (p. 126)

The musical articles give a picture not only of the age but of Shaw himself. In fact, they reveal him in the very process of becoming himself. In the earlier numbers of *Corno di Bassetto* he does not differ widely from other men. He actually apologizes for bad manners and even expresses mild remorse for the literary murder of a fellow critic. (p. 128)

One is not surprised that music should have brought out in Shaw the wit and the dramatist or even the economist and the shrewd man of business; but one is a little surprised that it should reveal a man of deep and even romantic feeling or one so much concerned with mere immediate truth and justice. (p. 129)

William Irvine, in his The Universe of G.B.S. *(copyright, 1949, by William Irvine; copyright renewed, 1977, by Charlotte S. Irvine), Russell & Russell, 1949, (and reprinted by Russell & Russell, 1968), 439 p.*

ALLARDYCE NICOLL (essay date 1949)

[Precisely] as Shakespeare gives himself to his 'living' characters, so Shaw gives himself to his ideas. When Shakespeare throws himself into Claudius he still retains his comprehensive view of *Hamlet* and of Claudius' position in the story of that play: when Shaw throws himself into the embodiment of a particular thought he similarly remains at once true to the thought itself and to the general plan of which the thought forms merely one part.... Shaw being Shaw, what happens is that, as each idea presents itself, the playwright's gift of lucidity and sensitivity to dramatic effect make him devote all his strength and skill, for the moment, to the one object of producing conviction in the readers or in the audience. The idea steps out of the *corps de ballet* and executes a *pas seul* in mid-stage.

All Shaw's plays reveal this power, but none more clearly than *Androcles and the Lion* . . . , where the concepts of paganism, meek Christianity, and muscular Christianity are each put forward with such vigour, wit, and charm that while we listen to each sermon we are convinced that in it and in it alone must reside eternal truth. From this derives, ultimately, the interest of *Saint Joan.* . . . These are not living characters who inhabit here: they are all incorporations of spiritual things, the embodiments of faiths and beliefs, the human semblances of rationalizations. That extraordinarily powerful tent scene, wherein the Bishop of Beauvais confronts Warwick, gains its stageworthiness . . . from the skill through which Shaw makes two ideas assume the medieval garbs of layman and ecclesiastic, take on material form, and confront each other. The Bishop's arguments are so clearly and so trenchantly expressed that it seems they are irrefutable. . . . But we have only to listen for a moment to another speaker to hear a sermon equally true and equally sincere. In the final scene of the play the idea that is Joan and the idea that is the Inquisitor are both presented with absolute assurance. (pp. 747-48)

Because his characters are ideas, too, the atmosphere he invokes is of a kind absolutely distinct from anything the theatre has had in the past. *Saint Joan* ends with the burning of the heroine, but it is not a tragedy: our hearts are, again perfectly rightly, untouched, our withers unwrung. When Joan sits before the Inquisitor's court it is not a girl who is being tried: it is an idea that is being examined. (p. 749)

In *Saint Joan* Shaw reaches the peak of his art. Thereafter discursiveness, an increasing tendency towards the use of symbols, and a failure to bring his themes to any logical conclusion have been evident. . . .

The truth, of course, is that when a dramatist essays the bold and hazardous path of building his plays out of ideas rather than out of persons he denies himself the possibility of achieving anything between complete success and failure. . . . Where we have been moved even by a few scenes we are prepared to accept the play in its entirety and are content to view it with interest whenever it is presented before us. In the Shavian type of theatre we cannot do this. None of the characters in these last plays can make appeal

to us as human beings: even King Magnus, the most vital of them all, is cast in Shaw's familiar mould. The result is that, without human warmth to inspire us towards liking, structural weaknesses become more than commonly apparent, and these are made the more obvious in that, without realizing it consciously, we feel that the figures moving before us are rationalizations, and consequently that any logical failure in the conduct of the action is a betrayal of its very fabric. Logical errors may be condoned—indeed, freely accepted—in Shakespeare because the foundation of his work is emotional; in Shaw they must be condemned. (pp. 752-53)

Allardyce Nicoll, "Purposeful Laughter," in his World Drama: From Aeschulus to Anouilh *(reprinted by permission of George G. Harrap & Company Ltd.), Harrap, 1949 (reprinted by Harcourt Brace Jovanovich, Inc., 1950), pp. 741-62.*

HESKETH PEARSON (essay date 1950)

Shaw, like Ibsen and unlike Shakespeare, was intensely interested in the pressure of economic, political and religious institutions on his characters, finding it rich in dramatic situations and conflicts. His first play was denounced by the critics as a political pamphlet written by a Fabian crank utterly destitute of dramatic faculty. When this estimate became ridiculous, it was still contended passionately that his plays were "not plays," a position which he sardonically encouraged by calling them discussions, conversations, and the like. This was how he produced an overwhelming impression of novelty, audacity, and rupture of all the rules, whilst in his methods, far from advancing on the well-made play, he was deliberately going back to primitive dramaturgy. "Molière's technique and mine," he said, "is the technique of the circus, with its ring-master discussing all the topics of the day with the clown." (pp. 159-60)

Shaw's distinctive contribution to the theatre was first discernible in *Candida;* he was, and remains, the only playwright who has successfully dramatised the religious temperament, which, being the only temperament he completely sympathised with and therefore understood, was the source of all the emotion he was able to express on the stage. Shakespeare, one may add, completely understood every sort of character except the religious; and this is the real difference between the two as dramatists. (pp. 169-70)

Caesar and Cleopatra is the only play of Shaw's that has widely influenced the literature of his time, by initiating a natural and humorous treatment of historical subjects. In that respect it is his most notable achievement. . . . Shaw's is a fascinating and most endearing portrait; and if only the Caesars of this world had distantly resembled Shaw's comedian, the history of humanity would have been happier. But Shaw could not find the real Caesar in himself and so could not draw him. (p. 188)

Though Shaw could observe characteristics closely and reproduce them vividly, he could not penetrate to the emotions that lie at the root of character unless he shared them; he lacked Shakespeare's mediumistic faculty. Such knowledge as Shaw possessed of the man-of-action type came out, not in his full-length portrait of Caesar, but in his snapshot of Napoleon. . . . (p. 189)

Yet, though *Caesar and Cleopatra* is not as Shaw thought

it, "the first and only adequate dramatisation of the greatest man that ever lived," which he now repudiates as "a frightfully foolish remark if I ever made it," it is a unique and enchanting work, which contains incomparably the best of Shaw's self-portraits, some excellent scenes, many admirable strokes of character, and any number of fine phrases, such as Caesar's "He who has never hoped can never despair," and his "One year of Rome is like another, except that I grow older, whilst the crowd in the Appian Way is always the same age." The character of Caesar-Shaw is still the most satisfying male creation in English drama since Shakespeare, and Shaw was right when he asserted: "Cleopatra is not a difficult part: Caesar *is:* whoever can play the fourth act of it can play anything. Whoever can't, can play nothing." It goes without saying that Shaw's Caesar, like all his most vivid and deeply-felt creations, has a very un-Julian affinity with Jesus Christ. But then he strangely maintained that Jesus's strength lay not in his unlikeness to every one else, but in his likeness. (pp. 190-91)

Man and Superman was the first play Shaw wrote that had no reference whatever to the conventional theatrical requirements of his age; and it contains, in the long third act known as *Don Juan in Hell,* "a careful attempt to write a new Book of Genesis for the Bible of the Evolutionists." . . .

Briefly, Shaw's belief was in a God who achieves his purpose by Trial and Error. (p. 199)

[All Shaw's best characters] express religious emotion in one form or another; his other characters are self-conscious, or at least Shaw-conscious: that is, they say the sort of thing and strike the sort of attitude expected of them, conscious that it is funny, or profound, or stupid, or whatnot. Thus, apart from the religious, the only kind of character of which he can give a convincing portrayal is the purely self-conscious type, the polished, urbane, witty, intelligent, master-of-himself, Shavian aristocrat, such as the Emperor in *Androcles,* General Burgoyne in *The Devil's Disciple,* and Charles II, all of whom are the creatures of Shaw's intellect, just as his religious characters are the creatures of his soul. (pp. 257-58)

"Is there a conscious portrait of yourself in any of your plays?" I once asked him.

"No," he replied, "except the character of 'G.B.S.' in all of them."

Which explains why he never created a great character that was not an essential part of himself. But himself was that rarest of creations: a great character, whose humorous sanity irradiated an epoch which will probably be known to history as the Shavian Age. (p. 381)

Hesketh Pearson, in his G.B.S.: A Full Length Portrait and a Postscript *(copyright © 1950 by Hesketh Pearson; © 1976 by Michael Holroyd; reprinted by permission of Michael Holroyd), Harper & Brothers, Publishers, 1950, 381, 120 p.*

THOMAS MANN   (essay date 1951)

It was German music Shaw had in mind, and nothing else, when he spoke of German culture and his debt to it. He made that very plain and declared frankly that all the Western culture he had acquired was as nothing compared to his intuitive grasp of German music from its birth to its maturity. The son of a mother who was a singer and singing teacher, Shaw left a body of dramatic writing that is the epitome of intellectuality; yet the music of words is part and parcel of it, and he himself stressed that it was constructed on the model of thematic development in music. For all its sober brilliance, its alert and derisive critical judgment, it strives deliberately for musical effect. (p. 414)

In truth, Shaw, like every important dramatist before him, created his own idiom, a language of the theater at bottom as unrealistic as the chanted passion of the opera, exalted, exaggerated, terse, and striking, no less rhetorical than Corneille's verses or Schiller's iambic measures, and, strange as it may sound, no less pervaded with pathos, a term here not meant to imply unctuousness and bombast, but the ultimate in expression, an eccentricity of speech steeped for the most part in humor, full of *esprit,* challenge, effrontery—the ringing paradox. In his Preface to "Saint Joan," which is so good that it almost makes the play superfluous, he strips bare the scientific superstition of our times, insisting that the theories of our physicists and astronomers, and the credulity with which we accept them, would "have dissolved the Middle Ages in a roar of skeptical merriment." That sets the style. And not only does Shaw the essayist speak in this vein; he often—indeed, usually—has his characters speak in similar fashion, and it should be noted in passing that his figure of speech about dissolving an audience in a roar of skeptical merriment precisely describes his own effect on his spectators. (pp. 414-15)

He was no atheist, for he reverenced the vital force that is conducting so noble an experiment with man on earth, and was sincerely concerned lest God's experiment become a failure. Convinced that the esthetic element, creative joy, is the most effective instrument of enlightened teaching, he tirelessly wielded the shining sword of his word and wit against the most appalling power threatening the triumph of the experiment—stupidity. He did his best in redressing the fateful imbalance between truth and reality, in lifting mankind to a higher rung of social maturity. He often pointed a scornful finger at human frailty, but his jests were never at the expense of humanity. He was mankind's friend, and it is in this role that he will live in the hearts and memories of men. (p. 420)

Thomas Mann, "G.B.S.—Mankind's Friend" (copyright 1953 by S. Fischer Verlag GmbH, Frankfurt am Main), in The Yale Review, *Vol. XL, No. 3, Spring, 1951 (and compiled in German in his* Altes und Neues: Kleine Prosa aus Fünf Jahrzehnten, *S. Fischer Verlag, 1953), pp. 412-20.*

EDMUND WILSON   (essay date 1951)

Bernard Shaw, at the time of his death, left two books ready for the press. One of these—*Bernard Shaw's Rhyming Picture Guide to Ayot St. Lawrence*—is a thirty-one-page leaflet of photographs, taken by Shaw himself, of the village in Hertfordshire where he had his country place and where, for more than forty years, a good deal of his writing was done. The pictures are explained in a kind of verse which Shaw describes as Hudibrastic. . . . It is obvious . . . [that the pamphlet] was written in the expectation that Ayot St. Lawrence would become a shrine and that visitors would need a Baedeker. . . . Shaw was far from a master of verse, but the very badness of the rhyming and the raggedness of the meter make the whole thing rather touching and give it a certain charm. (p. 34)

Shaw's other new book is a volume of plays containing *Buoyant Billions, Farfetched Fables* and *Shakes Versus Shav*. The last of these little pieces is a blank-verse puppet play on the level of the *Rhyming Guide*. . . . [It] has one or two amusing moments, but it is rather as if Shaw's ghost were speaking, and it is not perhaps mere coincidence that the author, in his preface, discusses the "communications" that come to mediums through ouija boards. *Farfetched Fables*, though written even later—a product, Shaw says, of "the queer second wind that follows second childhood" —does have a certain eerie interest. It makes almost no attempt at drama but presents, in half a dozen brief scenes, a sort of postscript to *Back to Methuselah*. (p. 35)

There is a preface of some length, in which Shaw discusses, in his usual way, religion, politics and economics. Though he sustains his sharp phrasing, his vehement tone and his readiness with concrete examples, the whole effect is rather blurred. The overemphatic old talker sometimes loses his train of thought. And yet there is something impressive about this final volume of plays, turned out by Shaw in his nineties. It is interesting and satisfying to see evidence that so old a brain can go on thinking with animation almost to the last moments of consciousness. It lends a certain plausibility to Shaw's conception of the discarnate vortices; and it can almost make one believe that the intellect—this is a theme that runs through the whole volume—has, to some degree, mastered already the power of liberating itself from the flesh. (p. 36)

> *Edmund Wilson, "The Last Phase of Bernard Shaw" (originally published in* The New Yorker, *Vol. 27, No. 16, June 2, 1951), in his* The Bit Between My Teeth: A Literary Chronicle of 1950-1965 *(reprinted by permission of Farrar, Straus & Giroux, Inc.; copyright © 1951, 1959, 1960, 1961, 1962, 1963, 1965 by Edmund Wilson; copyright renewed © 1979 by Elena Wilson), Farrar, Straus & Giroux, 1965, pp. 34-40.*

JOSEPH WOOD KRUTCH (essay date 1953)

Next to his optimism and his energy, the most striking thing about Shaw was his furious eclecticism. He felt no necessity to choose between the various modern prophets. He would take something from them all, and moreover he would reconcile the most disparate. (p. 50)

One thing which made this possible was a sort of cheerful optimism enabling him to temper the more intransigent doctrines of his various masters and to fall back upon the formula "What this really means is . . ." Moreover, what it really meant was usually something less intransigent as well as frequently gentler and more kindly than the doctrine of his masters is generally assumed to be.

In the plays of the first decade especially, this cheerful determination to tame the wild men and to draw the fangs of revolution seems particularly striking. Nietzsche's doctrine of the superman—which might seem to others to foreshadow a blond beast, amoral and ruthless—tends to become no more than a rather extravagant method of recommending self-help and improvement. *The Revolutionist's Handbook*, supposed to have been written by the rebellious John Tanner, hero of *Man and Superman*, begins by breathing fire and then carefully explains that in democratic England there is all the revolution necessary every time the voters have recourse to the ballot box. In the same book a

shocking section ridiculing sexual morality and especially the sentimental word "purity" ends by demonstrating that, since the number of men and women in England is approximately equal, monogamy is the only sensible system. (pp. 50-1)

It is significant that [each] of Shaw's plots, even those of his most serious plays, is essentially farcical. That is another way of saying that it is at once perfectly logical and absolutely incredible. We do not for a moment believe that these events really happened. On the other hand, the reasons why they never could have happened are reasons which have to do not with logic, but with human psychology—and human psychology is something with which Shaw never bothers. He is never concerned with the way people do behave, but only with the way they would behave if they were characters in a Shaw play. (pp. 56-7)

Shaw does mean quite seriously and almost literally what *Back to Methuselah* whimsically presents: that only through a miracle—and a miracle not very likely to happen —can man be saved. (p. 63)

[Despite] his delightful, his irresistible comic gifts and despite what was originally a determined optimism born of a naturally sanguine temperament, Shaw's ultimate conclusions are in important respects considerably less different from those of other less outwardly cheerful "modern" dramatists than one would have expected. The longer he considers it, the wider and deeper the chasm between the past and the future appears to be and the greater is the difficulty of getting across it.

[Let us] consider the changes in his attitude as revealed in three successive plays written over a period of about a quarter of a century and spanning his most productive period. In the first, *Major Barbara*, we are told that we seem destined to reach peaceably, rather soon, and without any great effort on our part a happy society which is simply our own with all the difficulties and injustices removed. In *Heartbreak House* the difficulties and dangers have been greatly increased. The Marxian dialectic is no longer going to solve our problems for us. We shall have to learn the difficult art of navigation. Finally, when we get to *Back to Methuselah*, we discover an even greater difficulty. The necessary art of navigation is beyond our capacity to learn. Man as we know him is not smart enough to save himself. He will have to learn to live three or four hundred years or in some other way become much more intelligent and competent than he now is. Admittedly this is going to take many thousands of years at best. When and if it really does happen, neither man nor his society will be anything which we could possibly understand or have much interest in. Thus Shaw's "optimism" turns out to be more a matter of temperament than of philosophical conviction. The chief difference between him and the more usual despairing modern is simply this: Shaw takes his despair more cheerfully. He wears his rue with a difference. (pp. 63-4)

> *Joseph Wood Krutch, "Bernard Shaw and the Inadequate Man," in his* "Modernism" in Modern Drama: A Definition and an Estimate *(copyright © 1953 Joseph Wood Krutch; 1977 by the Trustees of Columbia University in the City of New York), Cornell University Press, 1953 (and reprinted by Russell & Russell, Inc., 1962), pp. 43-64.*

ANGUS WILSON (essay date 1956)

I think that one of Shaw's greatest contributions to the English theatre is his creation of characters who express themselves through ideas as well as emotions, who have heads as well as hearts. This view in itself runs counter to the opinion of many, particularly people in the theatre itself. They are never tired of reiterating that drama is a vehicle of emotion and passion not of ideas, that ideas are not 'theatrical'. . . . At his worst, Shaw tended to smother his very real thinking, feeling people beneath his own ideas, to drown the formal truth of his work beneath the Truth about Life shouted at the top of his own voice, to kill the wonderful vitality of his creation with his own pantomime of high spirits. In his best work—in most of the pre-1914 plays, in *Heartbreak House* and in part of *Saint Joan*—his own voice is only an accompaniment, powerful to contemporary audiences, but growing fainter and less important beside the total music of the plays as the years passed. (p. 55)

[Many of the modern critics of Shaw] cannot forget that he was one of the pioneers of the modern Welfare State and they read into his work all that they dislike in that society. It is peculiar because they . . . accompany their declaration that the plays are unreadable by great eulogy of his 'art', yet they do not seem to find that art powerful enough to overcome these immediate reactions. . . . If the attacks on brothels and slum landlordism savour too much of Socialism for these critics, then they should logically extend their dislike to Dickens and to Fielding. In fact, as many other critics have pointed out, Shaw was well aware that the remedying of material evils was only a preliminary, though an essential preliminary, to an ideal society; he was essentially religious. . . . For Shaw [evil and pain] always remained removables like poverty, to be divested of the sickly halo which Victorian sentimentalism and romanticism had placed around them and labelled petty crimes in good Erewhon fashion. But the reality of pain and evil have been foremost in the post-Hitler ordinary man's search for religion, and he is not likely to find satisfaction in a 'philosophy' that ignores it. The 'preaching' of Shaw, then, appears to be something of a bogy. In Shaw's best plays, it is largely irrelevant; in his later plays, after *Saint Joan,* which are his worst, it is unlikely to attract. Only *Man and Superman* is ruined by it.

In *Man and Superman,* however, Shaw's philosophy is shown from a different angle—the Life Force at work in the relations of the sexes. The conquest of Jack Tanner by Anne Whitefield, the natural selection of man by woman to fulfil her function, is a far more serious matter than the empty 'high thinking' of the ancients, for the theme runs through a great many of Shaw's good plays and makes some part even of the best almost intolerable, I think, to modern audiences. The treatment of the relations of the sexes is an even greater defect in Shaw's work than his treatment of art and the artist. Marchbanks and Dubedat talk foolish and embarrassing nonsense when they talk about art, but it is nothing to the embarrassment of the serious folly that almost any Shavian young man and woman talk to each other. The sexual qualities of most writers have both beneficial and maleficent effects on their work. It is possible that Shaw's energies, as he would have us believe, were the greater for other purposes by his dismissal of sex, though the Don Juan scene is as unconvincing as it is tedious. If Shaw had been able so summarily to dismiss sex as he wished, all might have been well, but it plays an es-

sential part in his neo-Darwinian scheme of things. It seems evident, whatever the number of affairs he is said to have had between his twenty-ninth year and his marriage, that Shaw had deep inhibitions about sex. He seems to have found the preliminaries deeply exciting and any physical expression distasteful. The chase was the thing, and the hunter in good Life Force manner—the woman. The result is a painful series of Benedict and Beatrice situations, arch, artificial—a kind of elderly male virgin's sex-teasing dream. Flirtatious sex-teasing women have clearly a place in comedy, but as the sole representatives of young women they strike an unpleasantly prurient note. . . : It is, I believe, this sexual aspect of Shaw's work—half naïveté, half prudish prurience, with which, of course, are bound to his total failure to appreciate the meaning of cruelty and his occasional straight childish vulgarities—that is most likely to prevent a modern audience from appreciating his plays. (pp. 56-7)

His inhuman detachment and his sexual naïveté combine to make him a writer who is seldom 'moving', in the sense that that word is usually employed now to mean 'moving to pity'. In *The Devil's Disciple* he achieves this effect, in the second act of *Major Barbara* and in parts of *Saint Joan,* but this is a less important defect than we may think, for Shaw is essentially a great comedian and above all, a man who understands the comic nature of language. . . .

[He] puts upon the stage characters who live on many planes and makes them speak in a language that is formally delightful without being artificial. He knew and really understood that people lived in their ideas and their words as much as in their emotions, that every character that an actor or actress has to play is himself acting a part that is quite as integral to him as his 'real self', that 'humours' and 'grotesques' and 'caricatures' are simply the social cloaks which men assume to protect their loneliness and that these cloaks 'are' them as much as the isolated creatures hidden beneath. His masters in this were Dickens and Ibsen. It would be absurd to compare the merits of the three, but Shaw at his best was the equal of his masters. Like them he had a superb eye for the 'new' types in society and his best plays are full of people who had never yet been brought on the stage. He had equally an eye for the type that was out of date and did not know it. Some of his most comic effects are achieved in this way. It is only in his later years when he had ceased to observe so brilliantly that his art lost its magic. It is from this modernity, this power of putting real people on the stage instead of worn out stereotypes that the dramatists of today can learn most from him; from that and his passion for language, his spoken prose which is far more theatrically powerful than any revival of verse drama can be. (p. 58)

Angus Wilson, "The Living Dead: Bernard Shaw," in London Magazine *(© London Magazine 1956), Vol. 3, No. 12, December, 1956, pp. 53-8.*

JACQUES BARZUN (essay date 1956)

[There] is such a thing as Shavian prose, which as a distinct creation assures its creator an immortality coterminous with the English tongue. . . . [The] Shavian sentence, by omitting connectives, becomes a sort of lash made up of fused ideas, written for ear and mind, and barbed to suit the occasion. . . . Like all good prose this is not identical with the spoken word—those who heard Shaw speak . . . will recall the difference—but it was learned on the soapbox and it gives the impression of speech; it is made for delivery, as Shaw's actors found out as soon as they opened their mouths instead of measuring the length of their sentences with the eye.

Sir Herbert Read truly says that in the undecorated English style, Shaw's prose ranks next to Swift's: it is limpid, passionate and tireless, never falling much below its own standard of perfection. The Shavian matter may be dry, the medium is invariably a polished work of art. Perhaps someday a detailed study of Shaw's diction will be made, which will include a guess at its lineal ancestors. It has affinities with Dickens at his best, exhibiting the same rapid variation of purpose and device, from colloquialism to a high abstraction which by some miracle makes itself concrete as it goes; and the same humor of words, which is something else than wit. The lashing effect owes something to Ruskin; and the shorter, simpler forms, which become more frequent in the last years, show cadences suggesting the Book of Common Prayer. But the pace and pointedness at all times are Shaw's own, like the motive which inspired it: "The more I learn about other men's methods, the more I perceive that nobody except myself ever dreams of taking the trouble to attain really exhaustive literary expression."

Fulfilling such an aim is quite enough to stamp a man as an artist, whether he uses his art to draft resolutions or write letters to his housekeeper. But Shaw, we must remember, made his reputation as a critic. Had he died at forty, we should know him today merely as one of the great judges of the theater with Hazlitt, Lamb, Lewes, and Agate, and as the only critic of music to put beside Berlioz. (pp. 253-55)

Shaw was an ethical critic. He could separate what he felt from what he ought to feel, what was actually given from what he might expect or like to be given. He was, moreover, indefatigable in acquiring information, knowing that to compare justly, the critic must know everything that has been said, composed, or painted since the beginning of time. . . . Shaw's music criticism, still instructive and enjoyable after sixty years, . . . is a measure not only of his critical genius, but of the difference between the art of criticism and the trade of reviewing. . . . (p. 255)

The part of genius in Shaw's critical work is his power to extract principles from the most unlikely materials, and to light up the confusions of intent and execution which affect particularly the arts of music and drama. He has, besides, a knack for touching off people, situations, sensations, merits, and faults; a readiness in illustration, a responsiveness to talents of all kinds—was he not the only London critic to praise Henry James's unlucky *Guy Domville* and to see that Wilde's plays were not pure *jeux d'esprit*?—above all, he has an incorruptible equity and courage, which taken together make him the critical intelligence personified. (pp. 255-56)

Assuming that drama is not mere physical motion, but psychological conflict which may occasionally turn into violence, we find Shaw lavish in both kinds: people slap each other, pull guns, raise pokers, hurl slippers, throw down vases in their rage, roll on the floor, besides doing the usual amount of direct name-calling. But what really counts for power, in action and comedy both, is that each speech shall genuinely grapple with the one before—by rebuke, ques-

tion, contradiction or misunderstanding—all this with a view to building up in a few minutes a recognizable human situation. Every step must be swift, unforced, and in itself worth hearing. Now at this sort of skill, Shaw has no rivals but Shakespeare and Molière. An excellent test is to open a Shaw play at random and feel the tenseness generated as you read. No need to remember the story or the background of the characters. Each person is fighting all the time, making drama as he goes: only recall the crowd under the rain at the opening of *Pygmalion* or the man buying apples in the grocery in Act II of *Village Wooing*. (p. 261)

[Shaw was] the first man in a hundred years to put on the stage characters capable of philosophizing. As such, too, they are able to take on the function of a chorus speaking for the author. Listening to Shaw thus calls for continual interpretation: his dialogue may branch out in three directions. This is equally true of Shakespeare or Molière, but the passage of time has made us think that whatever they do is perfectly natural. . . . (p. 262)

The objection remains that all this is brainwork. "Shaw is heartless and intellectualizes all hs sees." This is a natural illusion of the mentally indolent. One must reverse the proposition and say that Shaw is passionate and makes emotion out of all he conceives. What is vulgarly called "heart" is simply the accepted sentiments of the age. Mother love, demon rum, guilty passion, honest poverty, the equality of man, secret remorse—these things have been, still are, and will again be the objects of strong feeling for stage portrayal. But this does not mean that fears and hopes attached to other ideas do not also belong to the heart. Everyone understands Saint Joan's patriotism and her horror at the sentence passed upon her, but why suppose that in Sir Jafna's speech in *On the Rocks* we only hear Shaw lecturing? The outburst is in fact India's grievance against Britain and the white man; it is political passion personalized. What keeps us from recognizing this as legitimate emotion, and its dramatizer as a man with a heart fully as large as his mind, can only be the fact that Sir Jafna's motives are unfamiliar to us, too urgently contemporary and not decently hidden by official façade. In this and other Shavian scenes, we should prefer more pomp and a greater use of well-labeled attitudes—the prose of an editorial. We would then say "What a realist! How well he knows human beings!" for in stage dealing with history, ideas, or religion, we have come to want only the ritual hallowed by a thousand mediocre representations. We want sham Shakespeare or genuine Bulwer-Lytton. (p. 264)

He is in the great tradition, not in the little routine. Using everything in the theatrical shop, past and present, and holding in solution all that was stirring in the wide world of the author's mind, Shaw's plays form a dramatic legacy of the first magnitude. (p. 265)

Jacques Barzun, "From Shaw to Rousseau," in his The Energies of Art: Studies of Authors Classic and Modern *(copyright © 1956 by Jacques Barzun; reprinted by permission of Harper & Row, Publishers, Inc.), Harper & Brothers, 1956, pp. 245-80.*

SEAN O'CASEY   (essay date 1956)

What kind of a dramatist is Shaw? To what other dramatist does he correspond? None of the eminent, save perhaps Ibsen in his first polemical plays; with Ibsen, the poet, he has little to do. . . . He is nearer the Russian than he is to the German or the Frenchman, I think. By some cynical critics, Shaw has been called "a poet without the poetry," but that remark isn't at all fair, and true only within its own pontifical cleverness; for a lot of his plays are musical, and gleams of a poetical imagination stream out of them for all sensitive eyes to see. After some argumentative dispute with Shaw, [Yeats wrote to Lady Gregory] . . . saying, "Shaw seems to have no poetical sense. He is a logician, and a logician is a fool when life, which is a thing of emotion, is in question. It is as if a watch were to understand a bullock." Well, first, I'd say that Shaw understood more about a bullock than Yeats did. Emotion is part of life, but it isn't the whole of life; and logic comes well into life, too: the logic of growth, the infant, the child, the adolescent, the man; first the leaf, then the ear, then the corn in the ear. Christ was something of a logician, and something of a poet, too; and so was Shaw. Yeats was wrong, for it is poetical emotion to be sensitive to all the phases of life, its sorrow, its joy, success and failure, the wonder of children, the splendor of animated nature; all of which Shaw had in full, but Yeats only in part. . . . (pp. 202-03)

[By many] Shaw was thought to be "an irresponsible joker"; but his kind of joking is a characteristic of the Irish; and Shaw in his temperament is Irish of the Irish. . . . [We Irish are] often thought to be irresponsible, whereas, in point of fact, we are critical realists, while Englishmen often mistake sentimental mutterings for everlasting truths. This silvery thread of laughter runs through all of Shaw's plays, and most of his writing, weaving a delightful decoration into his keen thought and thrusting satire. This joking sage has been a godsend to England (and to Ireland, too), for his wisdom, his love of truth and freedom, his gay spirit and fearless conduct have been a banner before us, a banner and a bugle band leading the slow, the certain, the glorious ascent of man. (p. 204)

> Sean O'Casey, "A Whisper about Bernard Shaw," in his The Green Crow (reprinted with the permission of George Braziller, Inc., Publishers; copyright © 1956 by Sean O'Casey), Braziller, 1956, pp. 197-211.

BERTRAND RUSSELL   (essay date 1956)

Shaw, like many witty men, considered wit an adequate substitute for wisdom. He could defend any idea, however silly, so cleverly as to make those who did not accept it look like fools. I met him once at an "Erewhon Dinner" in honor of Samuel Butler and I learned with surprise that he accepted as gospel every word uttered by that sage, and even theories that were only intended as jokes, as, for example, that the *Odyssey* was written by a woman. Butler's influence on Shaw was much greater than most people realized. It was from him that Shaw acquired his antipathy to Darwin, which afterward made him an admirer of Bergson. It is a curious fact that the views which Butler adopted, in order to have an excuse for quarreling with Darwin, became part of officially enforced orthodoxy in the U.S.S.R.

Shaw's contempt for science was indefensible. Like Tolstoy, he couldn't believe in the importance of anything he didn't know. He was passionate against vivisection. I think the reason was, not any sympathy for animals, but a disbelief in the scientific knowledge which vivisection is held to provide. His vegetarianism also, I think, was not due to humanitarian motives, but rather to his ascetic impulses, to

which he gave full expression in the last act of *Methuselah*. (pp. 78-9)

In sum, one may say that he did much good and some harm. As an iconoclast he was admirable, but as an icon rather less so. (p. 80)

> Bertrand Russell, "George Bernard Shaw," in his Portraits from Memory and Other Essays (copyright © 1951, 1952, 1956 by Bertrand Russell; reprinted by permission of Simon & Schuster, a division of Gulf & Western Corporation; in Canada by George Allen & Unwin (Publishers) Ltd.), Simon & Schuster, 1956, pp. 75-80.

COLIN WILSON   (essay date 1957)

When Shaw is read in the light of the existentialist thinkers, a new philosophical position arises from his work as a whole, a position of which he himself was probably unconscious. It is this: that although the ultimate reality may be irrational, *yet man's relation to it is not.* Existentialism means the recognition that life is a tiny corner of casual order in a universe of chaos. All men are aware of that chaos; but some insulate themselves from it and refuse to face it. These are the Insiders, and they make up the overwhelming majority of the human race. The Outsider is the man who has faced chaos. If he is an abstract philosopher—like Hegel—he will try to demonstrate that chaos is not really chaos, but that underlying it is an order of which we are unaware. If he is an existentialist, he acknowledges that chaos *is* chaos, a denial of life—or rather, of the conditions under which life is possible. If there is nothing but life and chaos, then life is permanently helpless—as Sartre and Camus think it is. But if a rational relation can somehow exist between them, ultimate pessimism is avoided, as it must be avoided if the Outsider is to live at all. It is this contribution which makes Shaw the key figure of existentialist thought. (p. 289)

> Colin Wilson, "Bernard Shaw," in his Religion and the Rebel (copyright © 1957 by Colin Wilson), Houghton, 1957, pp. 242-89.

STANLEY WEINTRAUB   (essay date 1959)

Shaw, the playwright, could never divorce himself from Shaw, the novelist. His ideas for his plays often overflowed the form, necessitating long prefaces (sometimes—as with *Androcles*—longer than the play itself), notes and appendices (as in *Caesar and Cleopatra* and *Man and Superman*), and once a prose-fiction sequel, where we learn what happens to Eliza after the curtain drops on *Pygmalion*. In two of his novels (*Immaturity* and *Cashel Byron*) Shaw had previously used the epilogue, and a third—*An Unsocial Socialist*—overflows into an epilogue-apology in the form of a "Letter to the Author" from the fictional hero. (p. 330)

Much of Shavian drama is constructed around the inversion of a conventional theatrical situation. In *Widowers' Houses* the hero nobly refuses to live on his fiancée's tainted dowry, only to discover that his own income is equally tainted. Caesar turns out to be as far from a conventional conqueror-hero as Candida is from a conventional wife and mother. One of the most typical inversions is in *How He Lied to Her Husband* . . . , where the "deceived" husband is not outraged by his wife's extracurricular friendship with a youthful poet, but is outraged instead by the poet's feigned indifference to the charms of his wife. . . . *Arms and the Man* is typical of the group: the soldier-hero is really a coward in battle, and proud of it. Again conventional standards are held up to ridicule in this fashion, this time the theatrical view of war. (pp. 333-34)

[*Man and Superman*] seems foreshadowed in motif, especially in the Hell Scene, by a Shavian short story of the novel period, "Don Giovanni Explains" . . . , written as Shaw was embarking upon an abortive sixth novel. The play's more direct relationships to the novels lie elsewhere, however, one of them in the *raisonneur*-character of John Tanner, who, like others of his ilk, developed from a projection of Shaw—in the novels, often merely a wish-projection. (p. 340)

The Doctor's Dilemma—in the person of Dubedat, its hero —is . . . greatly concerned with man as artist. Though Shaw in the novels was generally unconcerned with a utilitarian function for art other than his own, he made through his plays several studies of the difference between the true artist (the genius) and the pseudo-artist (the pretender, the dilettante, the basely commercial or professional). Artists are significant characters in the novels—poets, artists, pseudo-artists, patrons, and patronesses appearing in *Immaturity* and in *The Irrational Knot*. By the third novel, *Love among the Artists,* the conflict of the true with the false in art becomes the thesis of the entire novel. In *Man and Superman,* . . . characters representing Shavian theories on art appear in a majority of Shaw's plays, and where none are present the prefaces often remedy the deficiency. (p. 344)

The interplay of mentor and disciple has always made for good drama, a fact which Shaw seemed to grasp instinctively when he began writing fiction. With a sure sense of paradox he portrayed his first such relationship in *Immaturity* as one between an immature tutor paralyzed with inhibition and a mature, self-assured pupil: Robert Smith and Harriet Russell. In *The Irrational Knot* Conolly attempts to re-educate his wife, and succeeds so well that she realizes their marriage was all a mistake. By his third novel, *Love among the Artists,* Shaw hit upon a formula which, transferred to the plays, created one of his greatest popular successes. In one of the parallel plots of the novel, Owen Jack, formerly "professor of music and elocution" at Alton College, trains Madge Brailsford in voice, elocution, and poise. She proves so adept a pupil that she eventually rises to star billing as an actress. After her success she seeks affection (and perhaps matrimony), having fallen in love with him in spite of his rudeness and abusiveness as a teacher and as a person. The tutor is too immersed in the interests of his own life, however, and rejects the notion of love or marriage.

If the names of mentor and pupil be changed to "Professor of Phonetics" Higgins and Eliza Doolittle, with Eliza's portrayal of a duchess considered her acting triumph, the scaffolding of the novel is seen as a striking anticipation of *Pygmalion.* It has not gone unnoticed. (pp. 348-49)

Stanley Weintraub, "The Embryo Playwright in Bernard Shaw's Early Novels," in Texas Studies in Literature and Language *(copyright © 1959 by the University of Texas Press), Vol. I, No. 3, Autumn, 1959, pp. 327-55.*

REED WHITTEMORE (essay date 1960)

The most cursory reading of [Shaw's] plays and prefaces reveals him as a "hard-facts" man. The word "facts" appears over and over again. . . . Fact vs. fiction. . . . [His] insistence upon a simple dualism is characteristic. Shaw's realities nearly always emerge as clearly and neatly set off from their intolerable opposites, illusion, fiction, myth, unreality. . . . Furthermore a persistent quality of the masters of reality (Caesar, St. Joan, Undershaft, etc.) is their commitment to the here and now, not to the past which they have been saddled with. . . . The realist, then, is the man who respects facts and lives with the facts of his own time. Therefore, if he is a writer, he is a journalist rather than a literary man. . . . Shaw makes all of this seem remarkably simple and clear. We go away amazed that anybody could be so foolish as to indulge in illusions, live in the past, or write with his eye on eternity rather than the present. But the simplicity and clarity of Shaw are, as many of his critics have noted, excessive; they are themselves not wholly respectful of hard facts. Hard facts are not clear and simple at all mostly, as any historian and almost any journalist except Shaw will tell us. In the first place we never *have* all the facts; in the second place we are frequently not sure that they *are* facts; and in the third place they are seldom "hard" in the sense of being understandable in only one, clear-cut way. And so Shaw, despite his protestations, has not gone down in the literary histories as a playwright of facts, or as a journalist, but as a playwright of ideas; he had many more and better ideas about facts than he had facts themselves, and he was in his element among ideas as he was not among facts, largely, I suppose, because ideas, unlike facts, are at their best clear and simple, and Shaw had a mind that respected the clear and simple, the orderly, the definable. Such a mind likes facts that will enable it to reject the whole of Western culture in a phrase, a whole religion in a sentence. The culture won't remain rejected, the religion won't stay scrapped—but at least the possibility will have been entertained pleasantly in the mind, which is where Shaw's reality is to be found.

In view of his odd detachment from the immediacies of the culture he was so fond of criticizing, we should not find it surprising that Shaw had a very lofty view of what a journalist is. I do not mean merely that it is odd for a journalist to take the drama as his chief medium, though it is. I mean also that Shaw seldom descended, either in his plays or out, to the affairs of the here and now, though he professed to. Instead he took a godlike view of daily affairs; he dealt with today in terms of yesterday and tomorrow, with the problems of English suffrage in terms of the general character of women in all ages and cultures, with Fabian methods for contemporary social reform in terms of Caesar, St. Joan, Don Juan, in short any suitable somebody *not* in the British swim in 1900-1910. And he refined his journalism further by having his mythical characters *act* like mythical characters: thus any businessman undertaking to emulate Undershaft could be expected to go bankrupt in a month. It is accordingly not surprising that when we look in the Shaw canon for instances of journalism in the most mundane sense— meaning the writing of a journal, the keeping of a regular daily account of public or private activity—we find very little. . . . I am not complaining about the omissions; I take them merely as a symptom of his remarkably abstract, impersonal view of the journalist's world. I am waiting for the psychological biography of Shaw which will explain all this. (pp. 132-35)

Reed Whittemore, "The Foundation of the

Abomination—Wells, Shaw, Ford, Conrad," in Browning *(copyright © 1960 by Richard Wilbur; reprinted by permission of Dell Publishing Co., Inc.), Dell, 1960 (and reprinted in his* The Fascination of the Abomination, *The Macmillan Company, 1963), pp. 129-66.**

RICHARD GILMAN (essay date 1962)

Saint Joan has its faults. Eric Bentley has commented on how stale the anti-English jokes are and on how the first part of the play, what Shaw called its "romance," is inferior to the later scenes. But there is a case to be made for its being, along with *Heartbreak House,* Shaw's greatest achievement, the nearest thing we have to a quintessence of Shavianism. For Shaw was fundamentally a dialectical thinker, a writer of dramas for the mind (something quite different from mental dramas), and in this play the clash of truths is on a heroic scale. (p. 65)

The usefulness [of *Saint Joan*] is that of all art to correct the imbalances and evasions of abstract intelligence. For the Catholic, if he is honest, there is a persistent difficulty with the double truth that the Church condemned Joan and then canonized her. Theology cannot really satisfy on the point, but art, Shaw's lucid, unafraid, *secularized* art is able to. Joan had to be condemned and had to be declared a saint: that is the truth of the play, and it is what lifts it above all those other approaches to Joan which see her as victim merely or as hold-out and exemplar, the free soul brought down by the enemies of freedom.

"A costly but noble tension." *Saint Joan* is concerned with that. Subdivided, the tension is of several kinds: between Church and State and between their institutional necessities and those of the individual; between change and tradition in its internal structure as a work of art, between tragedy and comedy. The two modes do not simply alternate but attain that creative fusion which is the mark of the best drama of our time, and we see it perhaps at its most intense point in the Epilogue, which so many misunderstanders of Shaw continue to disdain, the Epilogue whose dominant note is irony—a stance which participates as nearly equally in tragedy and comedy as any we can take. (pp. 65-6)

Richard Gilman, "The Special Quality of Joan" (1962), in his Common and Uncommon Masks: Writings on Theatre 1961-1970 *(copyright © 1971 by Richard Gilman; reprinted by permission of Random House, Inc.), Random House, 1971, pp. 64-7.*

MARVIN MUDRICK (essay date 1964)

Shaw is no more a dramatist than Voltaire. Intelligence having been banished from the English theater since 1700 (the sole anomaly is *The Importance of Being Earnest,* pastel fantasia on muffins and cucumber sandwiches), Shaw's mere rigid simulacra of intelligence on the stage dazed audiences into the hallucination that they were participating in a renaissance. The point is not that Shaw's plays are tracts, but that they are so much duller, clumsier, more banal than his undramatized tracts, prefaces, reminiscences, *feuilletons* on the arts, letters to newspapers and random correspondents. Any five consecutive pages of Shaw's four volumes of music criticism are superior in wit, humor, taste, discrimination, accuracy, robustness, exuberance, and human understanding to [the plays]. (pp. 108-09)

He was always ready to be excited by just about any topical and public issue, and had—perhaps still has—the power to convince many readers that his excitement is a portent and provocation of massive social changes; a politician's rather than a critic's power. It is characteristic of him that a collection of essays, prefaces, letters which the editor feels justified in titling *On Language,* and which Shaw took the trouble to turn out regularly over a period of fifty years, should be not on language but on the public symbols by which we make it out: on our inefficient alphabet. (p. 109)

Pygmalion is a pleasant and durable romantic comedy, flawed only by Shaw's preposterous insistence that his puppets not fall into each other's arms at the curtain. *The Devil's Disciple* has moments of blustery melodrama; the epilogue to *Saint Joan* almost achieves imagination. No doubt one could find salvageable phrases, perhaps speeches, in some of the other plays. *Heartbreak House,* which has been considered (by Shaw himself, among others) Shaw's "masterpiece," is Wilde without wit, Chekhov without pathos, Ibsen without iron—and Shaw without brains; Stark Young describes it as "garrulous, unfelt and tiresome" (epithets which will serve for almost any Shaw play). . . . *Man and Superman* has the style and present utility of a unicycle. (p. 115)

Shaw's prefaces *are* better than his plays. His journalism—especially on music—is best of all, the bright if somewhat metallic efflorescence of a mind that was most genial and active when it wasn't persuaded that it had a stage to conquer and immortal things to say. As the world grew less and less likely to accept the advice he so abundantly offered, Shaw—who had the asceticism of the painlessly self-deprived, and really didn't understand why people ate meat, drank alcoholic beverages, and fornicated at haphazard—grew more and more vindictively certain of its damnation. Shaw's latter years are disagreeable to contemplate not because like Swift he "expired a driveller and a show," or feared death like Voltaire, but because the spirit of Ruskin, William Morris, Sidney Webb—the spirit of Shaw's youthful awakening and his true faith—had turned out not to be capable of fulfilling itself; not in fact, after 1918, to be capable of working at all. It was the breath in the toy balloons of Shaw's plays; it was also the wind in the sails of Shaw's polemical writing. When it died, Shaw died with it, the millionaire socialist reduced to applauding the butcheries of a Stalin, the superannuated ghost making faces at itself in the mirror of history. (p. 116)

Marvin Mudrick, "Shaw" (1964), in his On Culture and Literature *(© 1970; reprinted by permission of the publisher, Horizon Press, New York), Horizon, 1970, pp. 108-16.*

BARBARA BELLOW WATSON (essay date 1964)

The woman who emerges at last from all Shaw's scolding, wooing, encouraging and instructive words is, like the society he envisions, a little beyond our reach. (p. 204)

Nothing in his long life's work has more moral elegance than Shaw's consideration of women. He began paradoxically by defending woman against her admirers, those woman-worshippers who demanded a paragon, chaste and selfless. Shaw pointed out that the exaggeration of differences between men and women, like the obsession with chastity, was an obsession with sex. He saw also that preserving the purity of women by keeping them out of business and politics, implied also a desire to preserve the impurity of business and politics and, by separating woman's innocence from man's drive for money and power, to avoid the pangs of confronting Christian and civilized ideals with the realities of *laissez-faire* capitalism. When Shaw speaks of woman as though she might save men's souls (or society, which is not so different a matter as it sounds), he intends quite a different process, one in which women plunge into practical matters and change reality instead of shunning it.

The Shavian woman, instead of being unselfish, is radically selfish. The selfishness Shaw recommends is extreme because only in its extreme form can it resist the insidious temptations of idealism, and also because selfishness, when finally freed from every petty concern, as it is in so many of the women in Shaw's plays, becomes a saintly assurance and strength. Certainly if evil and guilt be as extraneous to human life as they are to Shaw's consciousness, getting to the roots of the self may well be the only way to virtue. At any rate, Shaw's own tastes are so clearly superior to a vulgar, guzzling happiness, that the selfishness he recommends to woman can only mean honesty and self-respect.

The Shavian woman outrages the 'womanly' ideal further by being the aggressor in sex. That phrase has an unpleasant sound, but the Shavian huntress is by no means an unpleasant woman. Shaw considers courtship a game, not a war; therefore he endows his huntress with tact, wit, personal charm, and a strong sense of her own individuality, instead of making her the ferocious woman more timid authors imagine. Her outward pleasantness is matched by nobility of motive. In the woman who interests Shaw, the woman who is a vital genius, even unscrupulous or promiscuous behavior is interpreted as the working of the evolutionary appetite through the promptings of her unconscious self. Those who reject the mystical element in this process must account for Saint Joan's voices, which are no less voices from God for being just common sense or imagination. In the same way, a woman's pursuit of a lover need be no less the pursuit of an impersonal, evolutionary goal (a father for the Superman) simply because it is inspired by sexual attraction. In fact Shaw would claim that a conscious, dutiful choice of a genetically certified mate would be doomed to failure, since we cannot consciously know how to create something better than ourselves; therefore the voice of the unconscious is our only clue. (p. 207)

Shaw's opinions on the subject of marriage differ somewhat, depending on whether he is writing as a social critic, a husband, an evolutionist, or a playwright. As a playwright, he is in rebellion against the sentimental notion that marriage is a happy ending, and the convention that love interest is the one kind of interest essential to a play or novel. When Shaw does treat marriage as a happy ending, that is not with a view to personal happiness, but as a reminder of the supra-personal meaning with which he endows even the most fragile flirtation. Shaw's criticism of our marriage laws and customs is so radical and so well known, that it obscures the meaning of the many delightful marriages glimpsed in his plays. . . .

In *Getting Married* Shaw's indictment of marriage is consolidated, and the various ways in which marriage can become a slavery are both dramatized and described. Under capitalism, marriage means economic slavery for the dependent woman. The parallel between marriage and prostitution has a historical foundation in the venerable custom of buying wives and shows itself in our own times in the demand for virginity in brides and absolute fidelity in wives. Furthermore, as long as marriage remains an economic arrangement it cannot cease to be a spiritual slavery as well, for men and women alike. The more civilized and conscientious the man, the more he will feel compelled to sacrifice his inclinations and even his principles when they are in conflict with his obligations to his wife and children. (p. 208)

On the subject of that late-flowering luxury called love, for all his assurance, Shaw maintains his respect for the mysteries, subtleties and inconsistencies which remain even after the last reasonable word has been said, and therefore his attitude cannot be dismissed with the simple formulations that are customary. There is not a trace of bawdy in his writings; on the other hand, there is not a single character rendered unsympathetic by any breach of the sexual rules, not a single condemnation of any sexual act in itself. Shaw does employ a kind of euphemism which those born in the twentieth century find unnecessary; on the other hand, the euphemism of his language does not hide the realism of his thought, and he defends without reservation the writers who speak in the plainest terms about sexual experience, to the point of suggesting that budding girls be absolutely required to read *Lady Chatterley's Lover*. . . . He is scornful of people who allow sexual infatuation to rule their lives; on the other hand, he believes that the right to complete sexual experience is one which every political constitution should guarantee. Above all, he grants sexual freedom to women on absolutely equal terms, his feminine 'varietists' being, if anything, more at ease with themselves and more delightful to others than the philandering men. (p. 209)

It is never quite clear whether Shaw merely believes that the feminine view is needed to counterbalance the masculine, or whether he believes the feminine view is actually to be preferred. He does say flatly that if one had to choose between a parliament of women and a parliament of men, one should choose the women. After making the usual allowance for Shaw's playfulness and also his penchant for hitting a debating point as hard as possible, there are still two factors to consider. First, women have never had a chance to govern the world. A detached observer of the cruelty, waste and folly of our man-made society might well conclude that women could hardly have done worse, that almost anything done differently, in fact, must have been done better. This line of argument stands on emotion, not logic, but that does not prove it wrong. (p. 211)

The second factor is even less rational. There may have been, deep in Shaw's consciousness, a sense that it is the women who take care of us, in whom the final refuge and final comfort is to be found, and that whatever instinct it is that guides women in dealing with their sons and lovers, might guide them also in ruling the world. . . . If this idea has any validity, it may explain why no woman makes such extravagant claims for women as Shaw does.

None of his proposals, however, depends on this final reduction of the difference between the sexes to a mystical perception. Every one is made on solid, rational grounds. The flavor, however, the spirit in which the proposals are offered, not as grudging concessions, but as the gifts of a delighted giver, seems to result from the overflowing gratitude of love. Of course Shaw gives more reasoned arguments for his belief in the saving woman—chiefly the practical and life-conserving qualities of the mother-woman. Whatever his reasons, it is clear that all arguments are secondary to the presence of the saving woman in Shaw's plays. Candida, Major Barbara, Saint Joan—even the wild millionairess—and also the soothing wives and mistresses in the late plays, all indicate a sense that women have some resource that men have not. But whereas the traditional saving woman of literature saved by her innocence, these Shavian women do so by their unflinching realism. Male egomania falls in flimsy shreds when it encounters their clarity and decisiveness, the strength of which Shaw says (as others have said) comes of transcending the self. Yet again these women, so sensible, downright and unilluded, remain bewitchingly feminine. (pp. 211-12)

It is fair to say . . . that Shaw advocates all the equality between the sexes that nature will allow. He even goes so far as to favor a greater similarity between the sexes than has ever existed before. In the face of the irreducible differences which remain, however, he places the second sex first, but with a most important qualification. Woman may well be first in the sense that she has a closer connection with the evolutionary work of the Life Force; first in the sense that equal consideration will always dictate certain special privileges for her; first in the sense that her inspired practicality may be the salvation of a society that is heading for the rocks under masculine leadership. On the other hand, woman is never first for her own sake. Her evolutionary instinct, her reproductive labors and her place in the councils of state, all benefit her whole society. Shaw's inclusive spirit easily reconciles the good of society with the good of the individual woman, just as it reconciles a new appreciation of our common humanity with an unspoiled delight in sexual love. These are the fruits of an imagination which puts human qualities above all abstractions, and a spirit in which criticism and the joy of life are inseparable. (p. 214)

> *Barbara Bellow Watson, "Second Sex First," in her* A Shavian Guide to the Intelligent Woman *(reprinted by permission of W. W. Norton & Company, Inc.; copyright © 1972, 1964 by Barbara Bellow Watson), Norton, 1964, pp. 204-14.*

ROBERT BRUSTEIN (essay date 1964)

Shaw's "scientific religion" is actually a hodgepodge of ideas from the various nineteenth-century philosophers, artists, and scientists of whom Shaw approves, but primarily, it combines Bergson's "religion" of Creative Evolution with Lamarck's "science" of Functional Adaptation, both adapted to Shaw's visionary optimism. Familiar enough by now to be described briefly, the Shavian system holds that man has evolved, not through accident (as the Darwinists "mistakenly" assume), but through the exercise of a universal will—somewhat like Schopenhauer's *Wille* except that it is intelligent and benign rather than cruel and blind. Shaw, finding a rough English equivalent for Bergson's phase *élan vital,* calls this the Life Force. To Shaw, the Life Force is both immanent and transcendent—both in man and outside him—but its central purpose is the determination of man's evolutionary career. For just as the Life Force has made human beings superior to animals, so it will eventually create a being superior to humans. Following Nietzsche, who believed that "man is a bridge and not a goal," Shaw awaits the coming of the Superman. This crea-

ture represents to Shaw the last step in man's revolt against God. For with the advent of the Superman, Man will become God, and all social, moral, and metaphysical problems will be solved. (pp. 196-97)

[In] the doctrine of Shavianism, man becomes free only by ceasing to be man.

What this suggests is that behind Shaw's concern with the Super-human—the whole complex of messianic Shavianism—is a profound and bitter existential revolt. . . . For Shaw is not simply dissatisfied with certain human activities; he sometimes seems to be in rebellion against the very nature of human existence. . . . [Shaw] will neither explore his existential rebellion nor even acknowledge it. Nevertheless, it probably determines the shape of his Utopia in *Back to Methuselah;* and his outrage at human limitation undoubtedly determines the characteristics of his Superman. Thus, despite his pretense at destroying illusions, Shaw cannot accept the reality of his own feelings. And thus, he refuses to see what Arnold called "the object as in itself it really is."

He is, in fact, subject to the granddaddy of all illusions. . . . If Shaw is too much of a "realist" to don the mask of personal immortality, he is too much of an "idealist" to face the "dread" of the "Arch-Inexorable." And so he tries to propitiate, circumvent, and abolish death through a mask of his own invention—voluntary longevity. Philosophy, according to Montaigne, consists in learning how to die; but death has no place in Shaw's philosophy, since it calls an end to progress, and mocks all human aspiration. The ageless Ancient proceeds from the imagination of a man unable to look his "spectres in the face," lest he be forced back into existential despair. (p. 203)

Shaw's determination to keep his mask firmly fixed over his anguished features can be clearly observed in his remarks about *Too True to Be Good.* . . . In all other respects a pleasant light comedy, this work is intermittently suffused with the author's almost nihilistic bitterness on the subjects of the cruelty and madness of World War I, the futility of the Geneva negotiations, the aimlessness of the young, and the spiritual dislocation caused by Einstein's universe ("All is caprice; the calculable world has become incalculable"). And the last speech of the play, the concluding sermon of Shaw's protagonist, Aubrey, is a moving confession of messianic bankruptcy. . . . Shaw can look for a moment into the bottomless pit, but it is not long before he is whistling up his spirits again. His messianic rebellion is his last refuge, his Utopian idealism his last escape, from the tragic impasse of modern existence. (pp. 204-05)

The negative power of Shaw's rebellion in *Heartbreak House* brings the play closer to an authentic art of revolt than anything in the Shavian canon. Yeats has defined rhetoric as proceeding from the quarrel with others, poetry from the quarrel with ourselves—in this sense, *Heartbreak House* breaks out of rhetoric into genuine dramatic poetry, since there Shaw is disputing the entire philosophical basis of his work. There, too, it is possible to see that when Shaw drops the cheerful mask of the ethical reformer, the sorrow, bitterness, and strength of the existential rebel is deeply etched in his features. But he dropped his public mask too seldom; and if he is fading from us today, then this is because he stubbornly refused to examine, more than fitfully, those illusions he held in common with all men. Shavianism was that "mighty purpose" which kept Shaw writing when his heart said no; and though he continued to say no with wit and vigor, he could never quite sacrifice his delusionary yes. As a writer of high comedy, Shaw has no peers among modern dramatists; but his ambitions are larger; and he lacks, as a rebel artist, the stature of the men he admired and wished to join. If Strindberg thought he failed to be the man he longed to be, then Shaw's failure is the opposite: pursuing his ideal role, he failed to face the man he actually was. Yet, we measure this failure only by the highest standards, and it is because of his generous mind and talents that these standards continue to be applied to his art. (p. 227)

> Robert Brustein, "Bernard Shaw," in his The Theatre of Revolt: An Approach to the Modern Drama (copyright © 1962, 1963, 1964 by Robert Brustein; reprinted by permission of Little, Brown and Company in association with the Atlantic Monthly Press), Atlantic—Little, Brown, 1964, pp. 183-227.

JOHN F. MATTHEWS (essay date 1969)

It was Shaw's emphasis on "realism" which provides the answer to the otherwise rather inexplicable question (for the modern reader, anyhow) of what it was that he so greatly admired about Ibsen. . . . [For GBS Ibsen's plays] ranked with the greatest masterpieces of dramatic literature —mainly on the grounds that they found their inspiration in significant situations that could actually occur in real life, and then worked them out with implacable honesty in terms of what would actually *happen* in such circumstances. (p. 22)

Carried along by his determination to make the theatre a vehicle for truth, Shaw . . . began by accepting (apparently) the nowadays almost universal literary assumption that "truth" is identical with "unpleasantness," and that once the veil of socially acceptable appearances has been ripped away, the underlying reality consists entirely of things which are sordid, ugly, and cruel.

In this, rather than in its emphasis on contemporary settings and situation, lay the essential dynamic of Ibsenian and Strindbergian realism. . . . What is interesting so far as GBS is concerned is (*a*) that of all his plays, those first few in which he contentedly accepted this thesis now seem among the most dated, and (*b*) how quickly, thereafter, he moved off in a different direction, reinterpreting "realism" more broadly to fit his own tastes and experience.

It should be remembered, in this latter connection, that although Shaw was to spend most of his life attacking the society in which he lived, and the present form of nearly all its institutions, he never lost sight of the fact that in his own (and most people's) personal experience, there was a considerable amount of real good in the world. Any account of "reality" which did not take this into consideration was, from his point of view as a critic, liable to instant denunciation as a lot of pessimistic fiddle-faddle. . . . One of his personal aims as a dramatist, therefore, was to bring "good" characters to life as well as wicked ones.

[In *Arms and the Man*] Shaw not only found a way to do it but also concretized a new formula which was to serve him in a great variety of ways throughout the rest of his career as a dramatist. Here, as in most of the plays that follow, dramatic interest is aroused and sustained (à la Ibsen) by

revealing through action the contrast between appearance and reality. But what marks a departure from "orthodox" realism is that the *truth* uncovered is actually more interesting and attractive than the façade of trashy conventions which normally conceals it from our notice. (pp. 27-9)

What Shaw first utilizes, here, is the notion that when people are stripped down to where they "reveal" themselves, they often turn out to be, not worse, but *better* than expected. (p. 29)

In the long run, Shaw's tough-minded optimism enabled him to dispense almost entirely with conventional villains like Sir George Crofts [in *Mrs. Warren's Profession*], and to deal (somewhat in the mannter of Hegelian tragedy) with characters who are often partly *right* in what they do and think, but who come into conflict simply because they do not know enough about "reality." Which is not to say that his characters do not (in the more orthodox manner) sometimes turn out to be *worse* than expected. (pp. 31-2)

In the final analysis, Shaw had no faith in institutions (economic, political, *or* religious) but only in men. His experience of life was that of a resident alien: a clear-sighted, perceptive Irishman at large in a society which, however well he understood and analyzed it, always had less real meaning for him than the people he knew personally and felt affection for. What eternally delighted and fascinated him was not that various individuals agreed with him about anything, but rather that they possessed that mysterious inner force and consistency which transforms even the most "normal" of us, sometimes, into real *persons*. (p. 43)

> John F. Matthews, in his George Bernard Shaw (Columbia Essays on Modern Writers Pamphlet No. 45; copyright © 1969 Columbia University Press; reprinted by permission of the publisher), Columbia University Press, 1969, 48 p.

JOHN SIMON (essay date 1975)

Shaw has, after enormous success, proceeded neither to a peaceful place in the Pantheon of continued popularity and respect, nor fallen into the blatant eclipse that sometimes unjustly overtakes celebrity before father-killing is duly superseded by ancestor-worship. With Shaw, it is not just a case of his reputation having reached that uncertain age, too old to be loved, too young to be venerated; rather, the animus of some of his most brilliant contemporaries continues to hound him a quarter-century after his death, even as legions of solid citizens maintain his flame burning at medium-high. (p. 1)

Just as for his compatriot and colleague Oscar Wilde, the basic dramatic ingredient for Shaw was the paradox. But whereas Wilde kept it at the level of epigram, Shaw, both consciously and otherwise, let it permeate every aspect of his drama. For him, the most truly brave officer was to be the least heroic, even as his Saint Joan was to be chiefly a commonsensical peasant girl. . . .

[Shaw went] from wise child directly to pawky old man. . . . That skipping over central manhood is mirrored in the plays by two quintessential taboos: the fear of love, and the fear of death. For these, Shaw devised the twin remedies of the Life Force, the power of creative evolution that carries mankind willy nilly ahead, subsuming and neutralizing the chicanery of romantic love; and willed longevity, gradually leading toward immortality a mankind that has learned how to harness the Life Force. The traditional battle between Eros and Thanatos shifts in Shaw to Logos taking on the combined forces of Eros and Thanatos—but from such a largely dialectical contest it is hard to wrest tragedy.

Yet tragedy is indispensable to the vision of even a major comic dramatist; its lurking in the background contributes to the ultimate greatness of, say, "The Tempest," "Volpone," "The Misanthrope," and "Leonce and Lena." Shaw labeled two of his works as tragedies, but neither "The Doctor's Dilemma," good as it is, nor the fourth part of "Back to Methuselah," dreary (like the rest of the play) as it is, is tragic. But tragedy does skulk around "Heartbreak House" and "Saint Joan," two of his best plays, even if in the endings he cannot but fudge it over. Still, there is a way in which even the desperate evasion of the great poetic themes of love and death, by its very desperateness, creates a sociocomic intensity that rises to the heights of a poetry of the prosaic: of sense, rather than the senses, passionately embraced.

It is usually a poetry of pleading, of rational persuasion backed up with bounties of wit or dignified self-assertion—as in Caesar's nocturnal salute to the Sphinx, or Jennifer Dubedat's defense of her unworthy husband, to which the acquiescence of those who know better lends a beautifully absurd pathos. The only thing it never manages to be is a window on the absolute, on something beyond what can be apprehended by mere intelligence, however sensitized. . . .

[One] of the triumphs of Shaw's drama is that it reads as dramatically as its plays—just as it plays as intelligently as it reads. There is something irresistible about a dramatist who can write with equal ease, "That boy will make his way in this country. He has no sense of humor," and "this world . . . a place where men and women torture one another in the name of love." If Shakespeare had his infinite variety, Shaw, who mistakenly believed himself his superior, knew how to make his finitude look almost infinitely various. (p. 2)

John Simon, "The Definitive Bernard Shaw," in
The New York Times Book Review (© 1975 by
The New York Times Company; reprinted by permission), November 2, 1975, pp. 1-2.

ANDREW K. KENNEDY (essay date 1975)

Shaw only gradually recognized his distance from naturalism in his attitude to dramatic language. . . . Though Shaw may have been the first dramatist to exploit the comic potentialities of a phonograph on stage, he certainly had less use for that invention than any of the great prose realists. Not that the latter reproduce conversation, but they write from and against the felt pressure of 'men speaking to men'. . . . Instead, Shaw carried in his mind a prodigious gallery of known rhetorical models ready to be drawn on for 'power of expression'. It is a process of heightening from without, essentially different from Pirandello's definition of *spoken action:* 'immediate expressions inseparable from action . . . words, expressions, phrases impossible to invent but born when the author has identified himself with his creature to the point of seeing it only as he sees himself'.

This takes us to the essential distinction between 'spoken action' and 'verbal theatricality'. . . . The former goes with

authentic self-expression under the pressure of action; the latter with 'endowing' a character 'with conscious self-knowledge', or costume-speech. At its simplest this takes the form of comic-didactic bravura speech for a 'ventriloquist' like Doolittle, in *Pygmalion,* Act II. . . . Doolittle is told the 'floor is yours' [by Higgins and their] dialogue gives way to the dustman's tirades, including the well-known disquisition on middle class morality. . . . Here Shaw is exploiting, with the gay linguistic consciousness that fits in well with a comedy on the mechanics of speech, the simple comic tension in 'natural . . . rhetoric', vulgar eloquence. It does not wear well—it is too obvious—but it is certainly controlled. But in Shaw's more ambitious plays the pull of verbal theatricality against naturalism goes with a complex and often imperfectly controlled tension. (pp. 53-5)

[What] kind of dialogue does Shaw envisage in this 'return to nature' in dramatic art? The answer is the use of 'what has been used by preachers and orators ever since speech has been invented . . . rhetoric, irony, argument, paradox, epigram, parable'. And as if to underline how final this answer is, the chapter ends with a resounding restatement of what is to be substituted for the 'old stage tricks': 'a forensic technique of recrimination, disillusion, and penetration through ideals to the truth, with a free use of all the rhetorical and lyrical arts of the orator, the preacher, the pleader, and the rhapsodist'.

It is really the case that Shaw was, simultaneously, drawn to verisimilitude and driven to all the known forms of eloquence in dialogue by a contrary impulse. The linguistic gap that separates 'the natural that is mainly the everyday' and 'the free use of all the rhetorical and lyrical arts' fairly epitomises the duality found in all the plays. That is why one finds a hesitancy under the seemingly robust critical statements; and we are enabled, as if reading a code, to see how, whenever Shaw makes the attempt to come near to everyday speech, the dialogue is soon transposed into quite another key.

This is true even in those plays which are most nearly naturalistic in intention. Thus *Widowers' Houses,* the nearest thing in Shaw to the thesis-play, was, in Shaw's own words, 'distorted into a *grotesquely realistic* exposure of slum landlordism'. . . . [Theatricality] repeatedly triumphs over Shaw's intention to expose reality and move the audience to 'conviction of sin'. Sartorius, for example, . . . [explains his] view that his tenants are not fit to live in proper dwellings. . . . [His is a] 'Dickensian' voice in a supposedly 'Ibsenite' play; yet in the first Preface Shaw explains—has to explain—that Sartorius is no Pecksniff but a typical citizen; and elsewhere he argues that 'the Dickens-Thackeray spirit is that of a Punch-and-Judy showman . . . in contrast to Ibsen's power to move through every character'. (pp. 56-7)

The violent style-shifts from quasi-naturalism to hybrid modes of heightened expression can best be seen in *Major Barbara* and *Heartbreak House,* two central plays in Shaw's search for a theatre of parables. More extended study would show how the texture of either play is made up of continuous, and sudden, modulations from one key to another; the principle of selection is often arbitrary, for

Shaw is relying, above all, on what Francis Fergusson has called the 'perpetual-motion machine of the dialogue', and on his own expectation that the plays will be interpreted by actors displaying 'great virtuosity in sudden transitions of mood'. (p. 58)

[If in *Major Barbara*] Shaw still used melodrama as a ground bass for the 'Socratic dialogue' structure of the play, in *Heartbreak House* ... he is for the first time consciously aiming at a play—fusing leisurely discussion, 'fantasia' and parable—with a natural-sounding dialogue, dependent—in his own words—on 'nuances and subtleties'. Indeed, any good production of the play confirms that much of the dialogue has a spontaneity, a casual yet compelling rhythm, rare in earlier plays by Shaw. Yet in the presumably central scenes dealing with felt experience—the sequence of heartbreaks and the sense of being stripped naked—Shaw cannot decide whether to give such experience natural or posed expression. For example, Ellie, the *ingénue* turned Shavian heroine, is intended to speak with the voice of authentic experience, as in her long duologue with the Captain in Act II where she makes this inward discovery after a heartbreaking experience: 'I feel now as if there was nothing I could not do, because I want nothing.' Yet in the same Act we have Mangan's writhing and sobbing heartbreak in the midst of the trilling voices of the Captain's demon daughters (Hesione invoking the 'night in Tristan and Isolde'); and in Randall's shouting-foaming-weeping, Shaw falls back on an *opera buffa* heartbreak. The transitions from the expression of feeling to its parody are very precarious. And throughout the play the voices of personal experience are stylised in a manner barely distinct from the love-poses of the 'equestrian classes'—their galloping language predominates. (pp. 59-60)

After *Heartbreak House* Shaw's drama becomes, with a few exceptions, much more deliberately non-naturalistic. But the exception, *Village Wooing* ..., is worth brief consideration. For in this play Shaw does attempt to reproduce conversation; the playlet is a succession of three conversations. But what is striking is, firstly, that these duologues are between two cyphers: A, a literary gentleman who becomes a grocer, and Z, a bored young lady who becomes his 'slave' in the village shop; secondly, where the naturalistic dialogue has most vitality it anticipates Ionesco's later use of clichés in cross-talk as an assault on human reason.... Such a transition is almost an indulgence; an uneasy mixture between 'the thrilling voice' of the higher love in *Arms and the Man* and the earnest speculative rhetoric in *Methuselah*.

That Shaw had aspirations to naturalism is clear; it is equally clear that his attempts at naturalism were deflected by his emphatically different use of language. The early documentary plays turned into something else; melodrama when inverted—or used as the basis for a discussion play—left solid blocks of melodramatic dialogue in an otherwise changing form. And in his most memorable play on a contemporary theme, the rhythms of contemporary speech are like one thin voice in a many-voiced assembly. (pp. 61-2)

> Andrew K. Kennedy, "Shaw," in his Six Dramatists in Search of a Language: Studies in Dramatic Language (© *Cambridge University Press 1975*), *Cambridge University Press, 1975, pp. 38-86.*

BIBLIOGRAPHY

Allen, Walter. "Bernard Shaw: The Intoxication of Ideas." *The Times Literary Supplement*, No. 2839 (27 July 1956): 441-42.
  Examination of Shaw's beliefs and his works.

Bentley, Eric. "Bernard Shaw." In his *The Playwright as Thinker: A Study of Drama in Modern Times*, pp. 137-57. New York: Reynal & Hitchcock, 1946.
  Defense of Shaw's drama, and discussion of conflicting ideas within his plays.

Bentley, Eric. *Bernard Shaw.* New York: New Directions Publishing Corp., 1947, 242p.
  A seminal analysis of Shaw's dramas which was highly regarded by Shaw himself.

Bentley, Eric. "The Making of a Dramatist (Shaw: 1892-1903)." In *Theater in the Twentieth Century*, edited by Robert W. Corrigan, pp. 282-303. New York: Books for Libraries Press, 1970.
  Examination of the deceptive qualities that sometimes mask Shaw's dramatic brilliance.

Borges, Jorge Luis. "For Bernard Shaw." In his *Other Inquisitions: 1937-1952*, translated by Ruth L. C. Simms, pp. 163-66. Austin: University of Texas Press, 1916.
  Essay in which Shaw is praised for his ability to create characters superior to himself.

Brown, John Mason. "*Caesar and Cleopatra*." In *George Bernard Shaw: A Critical Survey*, edited by Louis Kronenberger, pp. 247-49. New York: The World Publishing Co., 1953.
  Critical applause for Shaw's dialogue and creation of characters in *Caesar and Cleopatra*.

Clarke, Arthur C. "Shaw and the Sound Barrier." *Virginia Quarterly Review* 36, No. 1 (Winter 1960): 72-7.
  An interesting sidelight on Shaw's interest in supersonic flight and space travel, including the contents of short letters sent by Shaw to Clarke.

Hale, Edward Everett, Jr. "Bernard Shaw." In his *Dramatists of To-day: Rostand, Hauptmann, Suderman, Pinero, Shaw, Phillips, Maeterlinck*, pp. 112-47. New York: Henry Holt and Co., 1911.
  Says that "Mr. Shaw is nowadays no mere dramatist: he is an Artist-Philosopher: he has a mission, a gospel, a message ...: he is an Interpreter of Life."

Hind, C. Lewis. "George Bernard Shaw." In his *Authors and I*, pp. 256-61. New York: John Lane, 1921.
  Tribute to Shaw's lively writing and lively character.

Masur, Gerhard. "The Confident Years." In his *Prophets of Yesterday: Studies in European Culture 1890-1914*, pp. 252-97. New York: The Macmillan Co., 1961.*
  Examination of Shaw's many beliefs.

Mencken, H. L. "The Ulster Polonius." In his *Prejudices: First Series*, pp. 181-90. New York: Alfred A. Knopf, 1924.
  Critical praise for Shaw's originality in dramatically presenting commonplace ideas and situations.

Murry, J. Middleton. "On Dependable Writers." In his *Pencillings*, pp. 90-8. New York: Thomas Seltzer, 1925.
  Laudatory appraisal of Shaw's literary criticism.

Pritchard, William H. "England Seen Through." In his *Seeing Through Everything: English Writers 1918-1940*, pp. 23-50. New York: Oxford University Press, 1977.*
  Examination of *Heartbreak House* and brief critique of *Saint Joan*.

Stewart, J.I.M. "Shaw." In *Eight Modern Writers*, edited by F. P. Wilson and Bonamy Dobree, pp. 122-83. Clarendon: Oxford University Press, 1963.
  Critical overview of Shaw's work.

Symonds, John. "The Unclouded Eye." *London Magazine* 18, No. 2 (May 1978): 59-72.*

  Sketch of the state of the theater in the 1890s, and criticism of Shaw's entry into the world of drama as an attention-starved, naive playwright.

Vidal, Gore. "Bernard Shaw's *Heartbreak House*." In his *Homage to Daniel Shays: Collected Essays, 1952-1972,* pp. 58-66. New York: Vintage Books, 1973.

  Critical attack on content and form of *Heartbreak House,* and on Shaw also.

Ward, A. C. *Bernard Shaw*. Harlow, England: British Council, 1970, 60 p.

  Biography of Shaw, tracing his career and illuminating his philosophies.

Yeats, W. B. "Unity of Being: Unity of Culture." In *Major British Writers, Vol. II,* edited by G. B. Harrison, pp. 652-53. New York: Harcourt Brace and Co., 1954.*

  Impressions of the first performances of *Arms and the Man,* noting the play's rousing reception by its audiences.

Robert E(mmet) Sherwood

1896-1955

(Also wrote under pseudonym of Brighton Perry) American playwright, biographer, novelist, essayist, and screenwriter.

Sherwood was a popular playwright whose work was consistently informed by his opposition to the tyranny of power or ideas. However, critics find that his desire to entertain his audience often obscured the serious themes of his plays. His thematic intentions, as stated in his prefaces, are often left undeveloped in the midst of slick showmanship. His prefaces, in fact, are generally more weighty than the plays themselves.

The evolution of Sherwood's thought is typical of the changing attitude of the generation that came of age with the First World War. Like so many other writers of his generation, Sherwood served in the war and was thoroughly disillusioned by the senselessness and horror of his experience. War is a constant presence in his work and his attitude toward war evolved in three stages: an early group of plays that ridiculed traditional concepts of honor and glory, as in *The Road to Rome;* a group of plays, typified by *The Petrified Forest,* which are peopled with frustrated idealists who passively sacrifice themselves for others; and his ultimate position, exemplified in *The Rugged Path,* that fighting, however personally abhorrent, is sometimes necessary to insure basic freedoms. All of his work reflects his concern with the power of the individual to shape or alter events.

Sherwood received Pulitzer Prizes for three of his plays: *Idiot's Delight, Abe Lincoln in Illinois,* and *There Shall Be No Night.* In 1940 he became a speechwriter and advisor to President Franklin D. Roosevelt and this experience led to his historical work, *Roosevelt and Hopkins,* for which he received his fourth Pulitzer Prize. Sherwood also won an Academy Award for his screenplay *The Best Years of Our Lives.* He was a pioneer in his early work as a movie reviewer, which treated motion pictures as a serious art form.

Although Sherwood's works are infrequently staged today, they are valuable as a mirror of his generation's changing attitudes toward war.

PRINCIPAL WORKS

The Love Nest   (unpublished drama, first performed in 1927)
The Road to Rome   (drama)   1927
The Queen's Husband   (drama)   1928
Waterloo Bridge: A Play in Two Acts   (drama)   1930

This is New York: A Play in Three Acts   (drama)   1931
The Virtuous Knight   (novel)   1931
Reunion in Vienna: A Play in Three Acts   (drama)   1932
Acropolis   (unpublished drama, first performed in 1933)
The Petrified Forest   (drama)   1935
Idiot's Delight   (drama)   1936
Abe Lincoln in Illinois: A Play in Twelve Scenes   (drama) 1939
There Shall Be No Night   (drama)   1940
The Rugged Path   (drama)   1946, published in *Best Plays of 1945-46*
Roosevelt and Hopkins, an Intimate History   (history) 1948
Small War on Murray Hill: A Comedy in Two Acts   (drama)   1957

ROBERT EMMET SHERWOOD   (essay date 1928)

The American writer is desperately afraid of glamorous romance. . . . He knows, because the critics have told him so, that Romance is Hokum, Fantasy is Hokum, and Sentiment is the lowliest Hokum of all. Poetry may also be hokum unless it is salted with references to "muscles," "guts," "blood" and "sweat." (p. xv)

It may be as well to eliminate hokum from the novel . . . ; but the elimination of hokum and buncombe from the theatre would result in the elimination of the theatre itself. Hokum, as the term is applied in these disillusioned states, is the life-blood of the theatre, its animating force, the cause of and the reason for its existence. The theatre is and always has been a nursery of the arts, a romping-ground for man's more childish emotions. (p. xvi)

The theatre is no place for consciously superior persons. It is a place for those incurable sophomores who have not been blessed by God with the power to rise above their emotions. The theatre is and forever will be the theatre of Rose Trelawney and Fanny Cavendish and the Crummels family. (p. xviii)

[It] is my firm and unshakable belief that a playwright should be just a great, big, overgrown boy, reaching for the moon.

The moon is not unattainable. Playwrights have reached it in the past; they have even brought it down to earth, and pasted it on a back-drop. The moon is never more beautiful than when it is seen shining down on an insecure balcony, in a canvas Verona. (p. xix)

> Robert Emmet Sherwood, in his preface to his The Queen's Husband (*abridged by permission of Charles Scribner's Sons; copyright © 1928 Charles Scribner's Sons), Scribner's, 1928, pp. vii-xix.*

STARK YOUNG (essay date 1930)

["Waterloo Bridge"] was evidently written in haste, the lines contain no meat of any kind and no dramatic diction, no dialogue with point, no speech that has any reality of any kind or any sort of edge; and yet, by virtue of its resting on a story that is safe stage platitude, and through the staking out of the curtains and main points in the story, a considerable effect of drama arises. It is all very dull but it stalks its way more or less evenly through all the stages till we reach the end.

In spite of the dullness and platitude, this new piece of Mr. Sherwood's is in one sense the best play he has done, which means that it is less uneven and less insecure than "The Road to Rome," for example, though "The Road to Rome" was worth fifty of it in any other sense. Such is the theater.

By cooking up a sufficient bouquet of situations and motives and mishaps for them, and letting the actors occupy the stage often enough, you can get a surprising return on a very small outlay of dramatic writing and idea. And though "Waterloo Bridge" remains rubbish, it is the well-scrutinized rubbish of an intelligent man, and so, at least, it does not block the actors' steps. (p. 251)

> Stark Young, "Mostly the Actors," in The New Republic (© *1930 The New Republic, Inc.), Vol. 61, No. 790, January 22, 1930, pp. 250-51.**

JOHN HOWARD LAWSON (essay date 1936)

Sherwood's approach to his material [in *The Petrified Forest*] is as static as the point of view of his hero. The conception underlying the play is as follows: men are drifting toward a doom over which they have no control; if we are to be saved at all, we must be saved by the instinctive rightness of our feeling (exemplified in the love story between Gabby and Squier); but in this world of chaos, the only men who are able to act with instinctive decision and purpose are men who are desperate and evil (as typified in the gangster). Thus Sherwood's thought follows the time-worn circle: the philosophy of blood and nerves leads to pessimism; the denial of reason leads to the acceptance of violence.

The only definite action in *The Petrified Forest* is the killing which takes place at the end of the play. The gangster and the intellectual have an intuitive bond between them, an understanding which has no rational basis. In the final scene, the gangster, as he is escaping, turns and empties his machine gun into Squier as a *favor to him,* because he instinctively realizes that this is what the other man genuinely desires. This violent whim justifies the gangster; it is accepted as what Hedda Gabler called "a deed of spontaneous beauty."

From a structural point of view, the deed is neither climactic nor spontaneous, because it is a *repetition-situation.* Every element of this climax has been presented in the early part of the first act, and has been repeated throughout the play. The first act conversation between Gabby and Squier reveals the sense of futility, the girl's artistic aspirations, the dawning love between them—and the fact that death offers the only solution. (pp. 143-44)

The plot-structure centers around Squier and Gabby. Their relationship undergoes no change. They feel drawn to each other from the moment they meet; but this has no effect on them or their environment. Gabby wants to study art and Squier wants to die; these conscious wishes form the thread which integrates the action; but blind fate contrives the solution without the exercise of will on the part of either of the characters.

The play is not a study of an intellectual's mind and will, facing a problem which he must solve, or die. The play is based on the preconception that struggle is useless. Social causation is disregarded, and absolute necessity governs Squier's puzzled mind and the gangster's brutal whim. (p. 144)

[This] conception is socially conditioned; it involves the acceptance of man's fate on any terms which Nature (blind necessity, operating in us and around us, causing events in which we take part but over which we have no control) may dictate. Cruelty and violence seem to play a necessary part in Nature's scheme. Since emotion is absolute, it includes both good and evil; the life-force operates through love and violence, sentiment and cruelty, sacrifice and sadism. We find this dualism in the final scenes of *The Petrified Forest.* Squier finds love: "I think I've found the thing I was looking for, I've found it here, in the Valley of the Shadow." As he dies, Gabby says to him, "I know you died happy. . . . Didn't you, Alan? *Didn't* you?" Love has no positive value; it gives Squier no wish to live, and no strength for further conflict; it is a mystic escape, which gives him the *immediate* sense of union with a power higher than himself. It also sanctifies the needless act of violence which causes his death. (pp. 144-45)

> John Howard Lawson, "The Technique of the Modern Play," in his Theory and Technique of Playwriting (*reprinted by permission of Brandt & Brandt Literary Agents, Inc.; copyright © 1936, 1949, 1960 by John Howard Lawson), Hill & Wang, 1936, pp. 142-62.**

ELEANOR FLEXNER (essay date 1938)

Robert E. Sherwood tends to repetition in the matter of plots. A man—wise, cynical, and charming—finds the answer to his quest for a meaning in life, in a woman; suddenly he falls in love, no less suddenly his life is wrenched violently from its old pattern, and in three cases out of four he goes gallantly to his death in consequence. The exception is *The Road to Rome;* the other three instances are *Waterloo Bridge, The Petrified Forest,* and *Idiot's Delight.*

Another item common to all these plays is a background of war or violence which endangers the lives of the characters. This is Sherwood's device for sustaining tension, a device forced upon him by his inability to construct a play in which suspense will arise from the actions of the characters themselves. The reason for this is, particularly in his more recent plays, because the central character is completely passive, a symbol of futility. And since . . . such immobility makes for a poor brand of theatre, Sherwood falls back on air raids and gangsters to bolster up his plots.

The same cause eventually leads him to the dramatic formula which is becoming so common among our writers of comedy: a room full of contrasting types (the Bar-B-Q in the Arizona desert in *The Petrified Forest,* the hotel lounge in *Idiot's Delight*) who exchange reflections, and comment on Life with a capital L. Such a reiteration of formula and of types can only reflect the mind of the dramatist himself. (pp. 272-73)

Among Sherwood's intellectual comedies with their macabre backgrounds the best is the deftly ironical *Road to Rome,* incidentally his first play. . . . The only scene in the play which holds the interest not by the flamboyance of its dialogue ("I wonder what it feels like to be violated?"), but by dramatic contrast and tension, is that in which Amytis gradually breaks down Hannibal's only aim in life, and reveals him to himself. . . . Having asserted her hold on him by all the weapons at her disposal, she eventually convinces him of the futility of his life. . . . It is characteristic of Sherwood that the resolution of the play should consist in the dissipation of action before words: Hannibal, the man of force and action, is stripped, emasculated, becomes the victim of abstract ideas. (pp. 273-74)

Reunion in Vienna itself is one of the most brilliantly witty of our comedies in recent years, in which the philosopher and dramatist in Sherwood are briefly fused. The comedy is two-edged, for the writer is mocking, not only the faded glamour of Viennese imperial glory, but the cocksureness of the new psychology, which presumes to weigh human emotion with chemical accuracy, and admits of no incalculabilities. (pp. 274-75)

In *The Petrified Forest* Sherwood celebrated the death pangs of the age of individualism. Alan Squier regards himself as "a survival of the in-between age," and [equates himself with T. S. Eliot's "The Hollow Men."] . . . Although there is an element of truth in Sherwood's observations on a decaying class as represented by Squier, he is grossly sentimentalized. Squier is the attractive, "appealing" victim of fate. We deprecate far more than we despise him. (pp. 276-77)

To admit the theatricality of Sherwood's conception, the tension which hangs over the temporary inmates of the Bar-B-Q, the comedy of some of the lines, is only to underline the meretriciousness of *The Petrified Forest.* For thus slicked up for popular consumption, Mr. Sherwood has served up one of the most amoral hodgepodges of philosophy that ever rejoiced the hearts of our dramatic critics and fashionable audiences. (p. 278)

[In *Idiot's Delight*] we find the author discussing the problem of war through the mouths of a group of cosmopolitans isolated in a mountain resort in the Italian Alps at the moment of outbreak of the next and presumably last-because-all-destructive slaughter. With the same mixture of "just so far" realism, Sherwood lashes out at the forces which breed wars—jingoism, the accumulated injustice of the Versailles Treaty, and the international munitions racket. . . . (p. 279)

Dramatically, interest depends on a skillful alternation between wisecracks, and the tension induced by air-raid sirens, off-stage executions, and the imminence of general destruction. Action, in terms of conscious choice, of character determining events, of mind shaping life, is not only absent, but is implicitly denied. (p. 280)

What it does convey, of course, is a picture of Mr. Sherwood's own mind. . . . It also furnishes additional proof that the line between tragedy and comedy on our stage is growing steadily less palpable. Mr. Sherwood is not the only alleged writer of comedy who more and more approximates the perplexity and gravity of our avowedly serious dramatists. (p. 281)

> *Eleanor Flexner, "Robert Sherwood," in her American Playwrights: 1918-1938 (copyright © 1938, 1966, 1969 by, Eleanor Flexner; reprinted by permission of Simon and Schuster, a Division of Gulf & Western Corporation), Simon & Schuster, 1938 (and reprinted by Books for Libraries Press, Inc.), pp. 272-82.*

EDITH J. R. ISAACS   (essay date 1939)

[The] outstanding fact about Sherwood's work is that while most of the other creative writers of his age and inclination have forgotten the war, by preference or because they could not live and write if they remembered it too steadily and too acutely, Sherwood seems never to have been able consciously or subconsciously to forget it. The terror and stupidity, the brutality and waste of those days and the disillusion that followed them remain constantly with him, in one way or another showing through everything of importance that he has written.

Sherwood's concentration on the idea that peace is better than war did not add to his craftsmanship. It seems for a considerable time to have interfered with it, to have gotten in the way of his plots and his characters, to have cramped a style that was neither sure enough nor sizeable enough to give his ideas range and form. Judging from the early plays, you would say that although the author admired the theatre as an effective medium, he did not respect it any too highly, and often took the theatre's easiest way, rather than its best way, to a given end. He learned very early how simple it was to get laughter and applause by certain theatrical tricks. He seemed to know instinctively how to pick a dramatic situation and the characters to enliven it. But he could not complete a plot or develop a character. So, to make his action progress he would often—unconsciously perhaps—shift his own ground, play up his guns and bombs and drums, and make puppets of his people.

Probably no dramatist who has had a success on the level of Sherwood's has ever written prefaces about the materials and the themes of his plays which show so clearly how far the plays themselves—all of the early ones down to *Reunion in Vienna*—are from his idea of what they were to be. (p. 32)

[In his preface to *The Road to Rome* he reveals what he intended to create in Hannibal's character.] But read the play, and there is little of [his intention] in it, except the event of Hannibal's leaving, with a cause which translates its reason into a woman's whim. Neither Hannibal nor Amytis, the Greek wife of the Roman dictator Fabius Maximus, who undertakes to conquer Hannibal by her feminine wiles, has any reality of character. Sherwood tried, in his use of historic material, to give the play the flavor of modernity by the use of colloquial language. But his people, though dressed in historic costume, were only clichés out of the modern theatre, speaking the language of Broadway. *The Road to Rome* is actable comedy, as its long and successful career shows, but it is essentially a false, rather than a theatrical, play. . . .

The preface to *Waterloo Bridge* is one of the best essays Sherwood has written. It is a picture of the war as reflected in London. . . . (p. 33)

[There] is no complaint when Sherwood chooses to show what the war was like—at the moment when Gotha bombers were hovering over London—through the fortunes of two Americans, a little chorus girl . . . , and a young soldier from Syracuse. . . . The only complaint with *Waterloo Bridge* is that even within the small theatrical strip he has chosen, Sherwood again fails to make use of the theatre's power of characterization and of illusion. The play has sentiment, a certain wistful sympathy, a picturesque realism in the early scenes, but little vitality. (p. 34)

A turn in fortune came with *Reunion in Vienna*, the first play in which Sherwood showed an aptitude for developing a good theatre situation after he had created it. From this point on, you begin to see clearly in your mind's eye the people of whom he wrote, and although you do not always see them as people walking beside you in the world, they remain with you in the shape of the actors who took part in his plays. If they are not yet people of the real world, they are real people of the theatre world, and for certain kinds of plays, such as *Reunion in Vienna*, that is quite enough. . . . The comedy has brisk action throughout, dialogue that is constantly lively and crisp, and enough undercurrent of mischief—suspected but unproved—to keep the interest challenged all the way. (pp. 34, 37)

Several years elapsed between *Reunion in Vienna* [and *The Petrified Forest*]. . . . Critical opinion of Mr. Sherwood's work had settled down comfortably in the meantime with the decision that here was a writer of comedy, learning his craft a step at a time but steadily, sure to go on providing bright entertainment for his audiences. (p. 37)

Then, to disturb the critics' placidity, came *The Petrified Forest*, with one of the best first acts Sherwood has ever written . . . , and with a second act that rides full tilt into the most specious hokum with which the playwright has ever made a compromise. It is sincerely to be hoped that Mr. Sherwood regrets writing *The Petrified Forest* after *Reunion in Vienna*. It is all well enough to say that he intended to set the portrait of the man of action, the gangster-murderer Duke Mantee, against that of the intellectual man of inaction, Alan Squier, to show their equal futility. But conceding the dramatist's right to his choice of material and purpose, you must still ask, Did he do it?—to which the answer in this case is, No; and, Was it worth doing?—to which the answer is, Decidedly, no. (pp. 37-8)

Abe Lincoln in Illinois says what all Sherwood's other serious plays and serious prefaces have tried to say. . . . Much of *Abe Lincoln* is in Lincoln's own words—his homely phrases, his anecdotes, his famous speeches; but the play is none the less Sherwood's creation. He has so immersed himself in Lincoln's style of simple, direct, rugged speech that you pass from Sherwood's words to Lincoln's with no sense of change. Every speech is in character as Sherwood has recreated Lincoln, and within that character a great man, a national hero with all of a nation's

legend behind him, lives and moves as a man among men. (pp. 39-40)

Edith J. R. Isaacs, "Robert Sherwood: Man of the Hour," in Theatre Arts *(© 1939 by Theatre Publications, Inc.), Vol. XXIII, No. 1, January, 1939, pp. 31-40.*

CARL SANDBURG　(essay date 1939)

"Abe Lincoln in Illinois" by Robert E. Sherwood is the first full-statured drama [about Lincoln] that has come around the legend.

Also it is the first shaped by a playwright who went to the main studies derived from basic source materials—and delved extensively himself in the actual sources.

The extent to which he realized his responsibility—in availing himself of a dramatist's license to depart from the facts—is soberly told in his supplementary notes. (p. xi)

Having seen Sherwood's play, and having noticed how the audience itself participated, I believe it carries some shine of the American dream, that it delivers great themes of human wit, behavior and freedom, with Lincoln as mouthpiece and instrument.

Also there are moments when the lines of Sherwood . . . achieve an involved, baffling Hamlet of democracy. Or again there are twilights of motive as curious as a Chekhov short story. And one goes away from seeing the play haunted by some reality persuasive of Lincoln's presence, of his sobriety and wit, of his somber broodings over the Family of Man on the earth and the strange prices of devotion and discipline paid for the getting and keeping of freedom. (p. xii)

Carl Sandburg, in his forward to Abe Lincoln in Illinois *by Robert Emmet Sherwood (abridged by permission of Charles Scribner's Sons; copyright © 1937, 1939 Robert Emmet Sherwood), Scribner's, 1939, pp. xi-xiii.*

JOSEPH WOOD KRUTCH　(essay date 1939)

[Mr. Sherwood] proved that he could invent for himself a form as thoroughly American as it was novel, and he produced with great success two plays [*The Petrified Forest* and *Idiot's Delight*] of which the second at least, may perhaps best be described as a didactic vaudeville—a melodramatic farce-with-a-moral in which the author manages to discuss a current problem while maintaining all the superficial excitement, all the bustle and all the raffish humor, of *Broadway*. (p. 217)

Of the two plays, the one which it is most easy to take with complete seriousness is *The Petrified Forest*. . . . Mr. Sherwood had something to say and he was obviously in earnest. He was also, however, too accomplished a craftsman to ask indulgence from any Broadway audience, since he knows the tricks of his trade and has a witty fluency quite sufficient to make something out of nothing. . . . *The Petrified Forest* could succeed upon its superficial merits alone, and one has some difficulty in deciding whether or not one has been charmed into granting it virtues deeper than any it really has.

To begin with, the play is quite capable of standing on its feet as a simple comedy melodrama of a familiar type. The lonely filling station on the edge of the desert has been used before, and so has the band of fleeing desperadoes which descends upon it to take charge temporarily of the assorted persons who happen to find themselves there. In itself all this is merely sure-fire theatrical material, and so is the fresh and innocent rebelliousness of the budding young girl, who happens in this case to be the proprietor's daughter. Add, for love interest, a penniless young man who has made a failure at writing, and there is still little to distinguish the play from very ordinary stage fare. Imagine further that the dialogue is bright and the characterization crisply realistic. You have now a play admirably calculated to please anyone intelligent enough to prefer that even the routine should be well performed. What is more, this routine play can easily be detached from all the meanings which Mr. Sherwood has given it. It is complete in itself and it is, as I remarked before, quite capable of standing alone.

Yet for all this, it is plain enough that the play is double and that the familiar situations may be taken, not at their face value, but as symbols. Solidly realistic as the filling station is, it is obviously intended also as a place out of space and time where certain men can meet and realize that they are not only individuals but phenomena as well. Though there is no obvious patterning, no hint of plain allegory even for an instant, the characters represent the protagonists in what the author conceives to be the Armageddon of society. The young man is that civilized and sophisticated intelligence which has come to the end of its tether; the young girl is aspiration toward that very sensitivity and that very kind of experience which he has not ceased to admire but which have left him bankrupt at last. About them are the forces with which they realize they cannot grapple: raucous bluster in the commander of the American Legion, dead wealth in the touring banker, primitive anarchy resurgent in the killer and his gang. By whatever grotesque name the filling station may call itself, . . . the desert tavern is also Heartbreak House, a disintegrating microcosm from which the macrocosm may be deduced. And the moral—or at least the only one which the only fully articulate person in the play can deduce—is a gloomy one. What Mr. Sherwood calls Nature, and what a poet once called Old Chaos, is coming again. (pp. 217-20)

I have, to be sure, a lingering feeling that there are dangers inherent in the effort to write on two levels at once, and some scruples about accepting as symbols things as familiar in their literal use as some which *The Petrified Forest* employs. There is an unresolvable ambiguity at times, not only concerning the meaning but also concerning the emotional tone, and the melodrama as such sometimes gets in the way of the intellectual significance. But such objections are purely intellectual. Mr. Sherwood achieved the almost impossible feat of writing a play which is first-rate theatrical entertainment and as much more than that as one cares to make it. (p. 221)

[*Idiot's Delight*] takes the simple theme of the horrors of war and treats it in a play remarkable for the extent to which certain tendencies observable in *The Petrified Forest* are exaggerated until the manner becomes, at least in the light of all the conventions to which we are accustomed, monstrously incongruous with the subject matter. Here again Mr. Sherwood is discoursing upon one of the grimmest of topics—namely, the social and spiritual bankruptcy of modern life. . . . But even in *The Petrified Forest* it was

somewhat disconcerting to find the author delivering his message with all the disarming facility of the parlor entertainer. He was not merely skillful; he was positively slick; and in *Idiot's Delight* he is the same, only more so. (pp. 221-22)

At the same time the theme is, if anything, even more grim. . . . Whatever else *Idiot's Delight* may or may not be, it is the result of the most accomplished showmanship exhibited in New York since *Broadway* and, indeed, there is much in both the pace and the methods by which the pace is maintained to suggest those of that phenomenal melodrama. (p. 222)

The scene is a resort hotel high in the Italian Alps. The chief characters are the leader of a group of night-club entertainers . . . , an international munitions magnate, and his mistress. . . . (p. 223)

None of the gaudy situations obviously possible from this set-up is missed, and much of the time the action is kept going by means of a series of "gags," both verbal and practical, some of which are clever and original, some of which . . . are adaptations of material very decidely in the public realm. The fact remains nevertheless that the effect is irresistibly lively and—what is more important as well as more puzzling—that despite all the gags Mr. Sherwood manages frequently to treat his serious theme with no little effectiveness. . . . [If] the author's main contention—namely, that men are too emotional and too childish to carry to a successful issue any plan for abolishing war—is not especially encouraging, it is at least tenable enough as well as grim enough. When all has been said and done, there is no doubt about the fact that despite all the comic interludes the sense of the folly and the horror of war has been conveyed almost as effectively as it has ever been conveyed upon the stage. (pp. 223-24)

Joseph Wood Krutch, "Comedy" (1939), in his The American Drama Since 1918: An Informal History *(reprinted by permission of George Braziller, Inc., Publishers; copyright © 1939, 1957 by Joseph Wood Krutch), revised edition, Braziller, 1957, pp. 134-225.**

FRANCIS FERGUSSON (essay date 1940)

[In *Abe Lincoln in Illinois*] Mr. Sherwood claims the dramatist's license to distort the facts for artistic reasons, but adds that in dealing with Lincoln, "a strict regard for the plain truth is more than obligatory, it is obviously desirable. His life as he lived it was a work of art." There is both in Mr. Sherwood's thinking and in his play some confusion between Lincoln as the symbol of American democracy, the external facts of whose life may have some emotional effect in the theater; and a Lincoln who must be invented, like Brutus or Antony, if he is to be the central figure in a drama. . . . But Mr. Sherwood is trying to write a drama, he tells us that this is to be "a play about the solidification of Lincoln himself." And accordingly we see Lincoln learning grammar, chivalrously threatening to "outrassle" the local bully, and stumbling over his feet in Mary Todd's parlor. But here Mr. Sherwood relies on the "plain facts" too much and uses the dramatic imagination far too little. Mary Todd, Speed, and the rest owe their existence to the books, they have no life of their own. They are perfunctory, like Martha Washington in the school pageant. . . . The series of scenes becomes simply a series of references to the stories, and though Lincoln explains himself at each stage, nothing ever happens to him. We never get the immediate sense of actuality which good drama gives and which comes from the vitality and dramatic necessity of each character and the imaginative consistency of the whole. If Mr. Sherwood wanted to write a drama he should have used that poetic license far more than he did; the facts won't serve—they may be history, they may be souvenirs, but they are not drama. (pp. 560-61)

Mr. Sherwood has not written a good play, but he has demonstrated once more his natural grip on a certain influential audience. (p. 561)

> *Francis Fergusson, "Notes on the Theatre" (copyright, 1940, by Francis Fergusson), in* The Southern Review, *Vol. 5, No. 3, Winter, 1940, pp. 560-62.**

S. N. BEHRMAN (essay date 1940)

Sherwood feels that his career began with *The Petrified Forest*. But though he may believe that the integration between what he is and his work, which was to find completion in *Abe Lincoln in Illinois* and *There Shall Be No Night*, began with *The Petrified Forest*, that integration really began with *Acropolis*, which was produced unsuccessfully in London in 1933. He wrote this play immediately after reading *Mein Kampf* and it was intended to illustrate the incursion of totalitarianism (Sparta) on an intellectually free city state (Athens). Between these five plays—*Acropolis, The Petrified Forest, Idiot's Delight, Abe Lincoln in Illinois,* and *There Shall Be No Night*—there may be traced a creative blood transfusion. Lines and ideas which Sherwood dropped out of one he used in another, and some of the speeches that were not uttered by Pericles in *Acropolis* appeared in the last letter written by the Finnish Dr. Valkonen to his wife in *There Shall Be No Night*. (p. 142)

> *S. N. Behrman, "Old Monotonous" (originally published in* The New Yorker, *Vol. XVI, Nos. 16 and 17, June 1 and 8, 1940), in his* The Suspended Drawing Room *(copyright © 1939, 1940, 1944, 1945, 1946, 1947, 1965, by S. N. Behrman; reprinted with permission of Stein and Day Publishers), Stein and Day, 1965, pp. 137-63.*

WINIFRED L. DUSENBURY (essay date 1960)

[Modern critics] question whether or not the Aristotelian concept of the tragic hero as a great man should be revised. Even in the case of *Abe Lincoln in Illinois* it is of course a nobility of spirit rather than an inherited aristocracy which can be claimed for the hero. In spite of other differences as well, there are many similarities in the dramatization of the ancient and modern hero, to both of whom the adjective "lonely" applies.

Abe Lincoln in Robert Sherwood's play is driven by an inexorable fate as surely as is Oedipus. The gods will not be placated until Abe has fulfilled the function in life provided for him. . . . [After] the self-recognition scene, in which the hero comes to an understanding of his true destiny, Abe appeals to Mary to be his wife with . . . stoical avowal. . . . As the curtain falls upon Mary's protestations of love, Abe, holding her in a loose embrace, stares down at the carpet. The American predilection for the happy love affair has never altered the view that Abe's relationship with Mary was not a happy one for him personally. As Oedipus de-

stroys himself to save his country, so Abe Lincoln renounces personal happiness to become the savior and uniter of his country. (p. 181)

Mary is in the anomalous position in the play, as in the myth, of being honored by a grateful country for prodding, Abe into the presidency while being disliked for her lack of understanding and inability to inspire him with love. . . . Mary Todd thus becomes not so much a character in her own right as the *deus ex machina* of the drama. (p. 182)

Robert Sherwood has subtitled his story of Abe Lincoln, "A Play in Twelve Scenes," apparently wishing to indicate that, in spite of the divisions into three acts, the continuity of the hero's life flows unbroken by dramatic technique. (p. 183)

Lincoln's life follows most closely of all, perhaps, that of Christ, with its humble beginning, unpretentious rise, and martyr's death. Sherwood's drama covers only the middle span of Lincoln's life, but the audience's knowledge of his beginning and tragic conclusion adds weight to the significance of the action portrayed. (p. 184)

As a contrast to his treatment of America's hero, in *The Petrified Forest*, written three years earlier, Robert Sherwood does some satirizing of American hero worship within an exciting melodramatic plot. No less lonely than Lincoln, Alan Squier is the opposite to the President-hero in that he has no ideals to live by, no thought of service to his fellow man, and nothing but disillusionment about life in general. . . . Had Sherwood's play about Abe Lincoln been as dramatically effective as this semisatirical portrayal of the lonely hero, it might well be the mainstay of little theaters through the years; episodic and constricted perhaps by the use of excerpts from Lincoln's own speeches, it does not attain dramatic heights. (p. 185)

> *Winifred L. Dusenbury, "The Lonely Hero," in her* The Theme of Loneliness in Modern American Drama *(© 1960 by the Board of Commissioners of State Institutions of Florida), University Presses of Florida, 1960, pp. 179-96.**

R. BAIRD SHUMAN (essay date 1964)

Although *The Road to Rome* has some severe technical flaws, the popularity of the play is undeniable. The characterization is superb, the plot construction is generally well planned, much of the humor is appealingly sophisticated—the dependence upon modern colloquialism notwithstanding—the element of irony is very well handled, and the dialogue, though occasionally overburdened with philosophizing, is usually sprightly and spirited. The major flaw—aside from the jarring use of slang . . .—is that the basic theme of the play is obscured by the heavy emphasis which Sherwood places upon the theme of pacifism in the second and third acts.

Actually, pacifism should be a secondary theme in the play rather than the main one. As the action is developed, the main theme, and the real point of the play, is presented through Amytis who asks Hannibal of his four years of conquest, "Why have you done it?". . . . [Hannibal has no real answer and from this point forth he comes increasingly to acknowledge by deed, and finally consciously by word, ". . . that there's a thing called human equation."] Amytis personifies this theme; her every act reinforces it. . . . However, as the dialogue is increasingly diluted with speeches about the futility of war, the main theme is driven into the background and ultimately is subordinated to the pacifist monologues. The whole broad idea of the potency of words and of human reasoning . . . is made distinctly secondary to the narrower, more specific theme of pacifism. (pp. 38-9)

The characterization in *The Road to Rome* is well handled and is generally convincing. The play belongs primarily to Amytis and secondarily to Hannibal; however, the supporting characters are well drawn and give strength and dimension to the production. (p. 39)

In a sense the whole question of personal morality versus public morality is at the heart of this play. The play's great irony is that personal morality on the part of Amytis wins the day for Rome; but public morality, of which her husband and mother-in-law are the prime exemplars, receives the credit. (p. 45)

The plot of *Waterloo Bridge* is as old as literature itself. An unregenerate streetwalker meets an innocent youth who falls in love with her, and she is purified through his love. (p. 77)

The most serious weakness of *Waterloo Bridge* is the plot. The writing is generally polished and the characterization is handled expertly. . . . [Handicapped] by the banality of the plot, Sherwood proceeded unhesitatingly to display all of the stock elements which the situation suggested; and the result is that the positive features of his work were obscured almost totally by its negative features.

In defense of the play, it must certainly be admitted that the first scene has a pace unusual for the first act of a Sherwood play. The writing here, while not the work of a consummate artist, is surely the work of a practiced, skillful craftsman. (pp. 77-8)

If Robert Sherwood were to be remembered for any one of his plays, it is likely that the play which would fix his name in the galaxy of the immortals is *Abe Lincoln in Illinois*. The Lincoln play is not his best drama, but more people have probably seen it and been affected by it than by any of his other productions. (p. 83)

It is a mirror held up to a universal type of situation which must be dealt with by a man who is essentially simple and peace-loving. He tries to follow a moderate course, but the circumstances of the situation make such a course impossible.

No other Sherwood play is so completely an individual portrait as this one. In his earlier plays, the author had been mastering the technique of using his minor characters to reinforce his characterization of major characters. In *Abe Lincoln in Illinois* the technique has been thoroughly mastered and is skillfully used. No character in the play is seen except in relation to Lincoln; no character other than Lincoln is developed unless such development becomes a significant part of the growth of the protagonist. This technique accounts for the completely one-sided development, for instance, of Mary Todd Lincoln and of Ninian Edwards, both of whom are more fully developed than the other supporting characters in the play. (pp. 83-4)

[Sherwood] wanted the play to be more than biography; he wanted it to represent his stand on a major and current social and political issue—how to deal with the spread of Fascism. Lincoln was his perfect protagonist for the accomplishment of this wish, for Lincoln was a common man faced with a huge problem involving thousands of human lives. (p. 85)

Lincoln was also the symbol of the common man caught in the dilemma of having events antithetical to the aims of human liberty close in upon him. . . . The allegory here is subtle. The play can be taken at face value as a biographical drama. But few people seeing it in 1938 and 1939 could fail to draw conclusions regarding the similarity between Lincoln's plight in 1861 and that facing the free world just prior to World War II. *Abe Lincoln in Illinois* was Sherwood's first obvious step in rejecting total pacifism. (p. 86)

The Lincoln play is the first production which Sherwood really approached with a feeling of awesome respect and virtual reverence. The result is that many of the devices of his earlier plays, which the critics labeled "hokum," are not present. (p. 92)

That Robert Sherwood was not effective as a novelist is clearly evident to one who has read *The Virtuous Knight*. . . .

In any consideration of Sherwood's literary and philosophical development, *The Virtuous Knight* cannot be ignored. In this book one finds Sherwood experimenting rather fully with themes which are later to emerge in his plays, or which, in some cases, have already been used in his earlier plays. He is also experimenting with techniques of characterization, and much that is later to appear full-blown in *Abe Lincoln in Illinois* is found in the novel, usually in a rudimentary stage of development.

If one can pinpoint a single major flaw in *The Virtuous Knight*, it is its lack of solid form. The plot is allowed to meander, and the result is that much of the emphasis is wrongly placed. . . . (p. 112)

The conflict in *The Virtuous Knight* is largely one between Martin, who is unbelievably good most of the time, and society, which is quite believably bad—or at least immoral—all of the time. (p. 113)

[Sherwood's] plot is so contrived and so tired that one cannot read it with any enthusiasm. Its every turn is predictable. Further, each turn is achieved not through any notable structural development, but through the author's omniscient relating of events. It is further apparent that Sherwood grew very tired of what he was doing long before he had finished his novel. . . .

It must be said of Martin's virtue that the extreme depiction of goodness is consistent with much medieval chivalric writing, and Sherwood was undoubtedly trying to achieve this effect in *The Virtuous Knight*. However, he undermines this effort most severely by superimposing upon the story his own observations regarding war. (p. 116)

From the time that he wrote *The Road to Rome* . . . until he wrote *Reunion in Vienna* . . . , Robert Sherwood was groping for a satisfactory means of saying what was in his mind. . . .

The failure of Sherwood's works which fell between *The Road to Rome* and *Reunion in Vienna* is due largely to his attempts to be essentially philosophical and serious most of the time, relieving the seriousness only occasionally with often untimely bursts of broad humor. But in *Reunion in*

Vienna the philosophical level is underplayed, and the broad humor is replaced with sophisticated wit. Philosophically, the play carries less weight than *The Road to Rome*. However, in terms of urban humor, *Reunion in Vienna* surpasses anything that Sherwood has written. (p. 121)

Essentially it can be said that *Reunion in Vienna* is a non-philosophical play with an extremely philosophical preface. The gloom of the preface is totally in opposition to the light frivolity of the play itself, and is led into by Sherwood's admission that the play is an escape from reality on his part. He then launches into a presentation of reality as he sees it. . . . But none of the gloom of this preface is transmitted to *Reunion in Vienna,* and the drama does not consider in detail the more profound and serious questions of life. (p. 133)

It cannot be honestly said that *Reunion in Vienna* has a very original theme or that its development is very original. [The play is concerned with the retreats that men make into the past in order to blind themselves to the rapid changes their society foists upon them.] But the undeniable charm of the play places it many levels above most plays which have dealt with similar topics in a comic way. And in Sherwood's comedy there is a sadness at the passing of something about which people can feel the sort of sentiment which Sherwood saw in the Viennese. (p. 141)

In a period of some four decades, [Sherwood] established his name among the notables in the American theater as a playwright and as a moving force behind the Playwrights' Producing Company and the American National Theatre and Academy. . . . However, despite the eminence which Sherwood gained, there are few critics who would call him a truly great figure in American theater; the statures of Eugene O'Neill, Tennessee Williams, Arthur Miller, and William Inge overshadow that of Robert Sherwood. But Sherwood was an engaging and urbane playwright. More than half of his plays were excellent theater and were received warmly by audiences. Even his less successful early plays had about them a suggestion that the author was gaining mastery over his technique, and such imperfect works as *The Queen's Husband* and *Waterloo Bridge* were relatively well received. (pp. 142-43)

Sherwood's most apparent and significant idea is the continuing and developing theme of pacifism which pervades all of his writing in one way or another. *The Road to Rome* is a statement of absolute pacifism under any circumstances, and this attitude is to be noted in all of Sherwood's works up to and including *Idiot's Delight.* However, with *Abe Lincoln in Illinois* Sherwood's pacifism becomes more moderate than it had been; and *Abe Lincoln in Illinois* leads directly into *There Shall Be No Night* in which the theory of peace at any cost is replaced by the one that freedom must be preserved even if its preservation necessarily involves its defenders in war. By the time Sherwood came to write *The Rugged Path,* he was willing to justify the idealist's going to war and dying for the cause of freedom. Unfortunately, Sherwood's loftier message in *The Rugged Path* is vitiated and obscured by the fact that Morey Vinion is escaping into war; he leaves behind him an intolerable situation and war gives him the opportunity to regain the individuality that a bourgeois society has seriously threatened to deprive him of. Sherwood permits his protagonist in this play to lose sight of the ideal which initially motivates him.

Sherwood was accused of doing an about face when he wrote *There Shall Be No Night.* Some pacifists for whom he had once been an eloquent spokesman now considered him a warmonger who had utterly deserted his former ideals. However, it must be remembered that Sherwood's pacifism was always moral rather than political and that his whole reaction to the rise of the Axis powers was predicated more on basic morality than on political considerations. (pp. 143-44)

This brings us to another point which must be made in any chapter containing conclusions about Sherwood: as an author, Sherwood was never really ahead of his time. He sensed the sentiments of the liberal, intelligent segment of American society and his plays were generally in complete accord with these sentiments at a given time. Sherwood did not purposely set out to mirror the philosophy and reactions of his society; however, his thinking was never revolutionary. It gave American intellectuals reassurance; it corroborated their deepest sentiments. Sherwood's plays gave utterance to what his audiences had been thinking, but they did not generally cause audiences to think in a new dimension. Audiences would nod in assent to the philosophy of Sherwood's plays, but they would not be led to action by it. (p. 144)

His plays, for the most part works which demonstrate a high degree of competence, reflect his warm humanity and his genuine concern for mankind. (p. 146)

> *R. Baird Shuman, in his* Robert E. Sherwood *(copyright © 1964 by Twayne Publishers, Inc.; reprinted with the permission of Twayne Publishers, A Division of G. K. Hall & Co., Boston), Twayne, 1964, 180 p.*

JOHN MASON BROWN   (essay date 1965)

For Sherwood *The Road to Rome* was . . . a successful entrance to a new career [as a playwright]. Audiences flocked to it, relishing its performances, delighted by the flippancy with which it dealt with history, smirking at its audacities, and roaring at its togaed versions of contemporary speech. (p. 219)

Many playgoers preferred to overlook the comedy's deeper reachings, or at best put up with them. Their search was for laughter and romance, with both of which it provided them bounteously. At its core there was more to *The Road to Rome* than that. This became manifest after the first act when, regardless of the questions he left unanswered, Sherwood changed his manner. Possessed by the largeness of his concerns, he began to write with the smooth-flowing, simple clarity which was later to distinguish his best dialogue and endow it with a cadence, style, and eloquence very much his own.

[*The Road to Rome*] was Sherwood's first sustained public antiwar statement, written from the deepening disillusionment which the peace had brought him. Although his subject seemed to be an enthralled leader, a lightheaded charmer, and brazen coquetry or sacrificial adultery, his title could have been *What Price Glory?* as [Alexander] Woollcott noted. (pp. 219-20)

To most theatre-goers his comedy was a spoof on Rome; to Sherwood it was an oblique attack on America. He, like many another, saw a "deadly and disturbing" parallel between the materialism of ancient Rome and Coolidge's

America. His fear was that the Roman faults rather than the Roman virtues were in the ascendant in this country, his hope that audiences would recognize the similarities between our go-getters and his antique Romans, and come to question their efforts and their values. (p. 220)

He deplored what he saw going on in [the realistic theatre of the twenties]. The theatre seemed to him to be turning its back on itself. Romance, sentiment, and enchantment were being driven from it by the tough journalistic tradition which had come to dominate our literature. (p. 238)

He blamed the critics who had told the American writer that romance is hokum, that fantasy is hokum, and that sentiment is the lowest of all. Because of this instruction the American writer had come to know that he must be literal. He must be an iconoclast, a misanthrope, and a fearless exposer of the mediocrity and hypocrisy of life. (pp. 238-39)

Sherwood was tired of the ex-newspapermen who, as essayists, novelists, and dramatists, were forever giving the lowdown on religion, the lowdown on love and marriage, on patriotism or motherhood, the lowdown on anything and everything. His conviction was that hokum was "the life blood of the theatre, its animating force, the cause and reason for its existence." . . . [See excerpt above.] (pp. 239-40)

To him life was one thing, the theatre another, and neither reporting nor debunking was the theatre. He wanted the theatre to be theatre. He did not want it to reject its special possibilities as a medium. He wanted it to rejoice in them, unashamed of sentiment, unafraid of glamour, unintimidated by romance, a release for the emotions, a dispenser of wonder. He was growing up when he was young enough to swear allegiance to a painted moon, and growing up in many ways, but he was never to outgrow completely the boy within him. (p. 240)

> John Mason Brown, in his The Worlds of Robert
> E. Sherwood: Mirror to His Times 1896-1939
> (copyright © 1962, 1965 by John Mason Brown;
> reprinted by permission of Harper & Row, Pub-
> lishers, Inc.), Harper, 1965, 409 p.

WALTER J. MESERVE (essay date 1970)

[Sherwood] thought in terms of rather sweeping ideas; generally he regarded concepts and characters from an idealized position; and he accepted uncomplicated, frequently romantic solutions in his plays. Yet he was a man deeply concerned with the human condition and interested in making meaningful comments on that condition. . . . He was thoughtful, but he was not profound. It would almost seem that his demand for wit and humor, from both himself and others, veiled a fear of the strictly intellectual approach to life. Simplicity, indeed, is a key. Philosophically, he leaped great spans of thought without concern for chasms of conflicting ideas or history which might slow down or overwhelm a less determined reformer. Idealistic oversimplification, then, became his weakness as well as his strength—a strength because he made his points extremely well during a period (1937-1940) when these ideas were needed, a weakness because his plays reveal him as incapable of dealing effectively with man's essential problems. With an artistically effective theatrical flourish he managed only to ripple the surface of the "human equation" that he wanted to probe in depth. (pp. 14-15)

[Sherwood began his career as a movie reviewer.] In most respects Sherwood's reviews are similar to those of present-day movie critics. He was perceptive; he wrote well; he took seriously a relatively new form of art. His main distinction, however, is that he was one of the first writers to view movies as a critic. . . .

There is no doubt that Sherwood received supreme satisfaction in expressing his views, while the kind of comments he made revealed his interest at this time. For example, he rarely mentioned the thought in a movie, or the effect of the movie either emotionally or intellectually upon a sensitive viewer. (p. 30)

Sherwood had no regular format for a review, but he spent a considerable portion of each column commenting on actors and directors. Rudolph Valentino was a newcomer to the screen in *The Four Horsemen,* and Sherwood accurately saw him as a potential star. (p. 31)

At a time when little that was meaningful about movies appeared in print, Sherwood's generally thoughtful comments earned him a significant place among American movie reviewers. Of much greater importance, however, was the value of the experience for Sherwood as a future scenarist and playwright. His scenario for *The Adventures of Marco Polo,* for example, was considered an exemplum for many writers. Although it is probably impossible to assess the effect of Sherwood's movie-going on his plays, one can see in most of his work some of the same standards he asked of the movies. (p. 33)

Robert Sherwood was one of a select number of ambitious dramatists whose plays during the late twenties and throughout the thirties provided a distinction in American theatre which propelled it toward a place in world drama. He was not an experimenter in form or structure, it is true. Neither was he a dramatist of searching ideas or deep insight, although he had a compassionate understanding of man and definite views concerning social, political, and moral behavior. He simply knew how to write a play; he was a sincere craftsman with a skill in dramaturgy which made it possible for him to produce frequently excellent entertainment. He was, therefore, that substantial and necessary element in a developing theatre—a dramatist who could please an audience while suggesting ideas concerning man and his society. (p. 36)

It is difficult to take *The Road to Rome* seriously because Sherwood refused to take himself or his play seriously. And yet there are some provocative ideas in the play. Sherwood had something to say, but he seemingly felt obliged to undercut his ideas with a humor that dramatizes his uncertainty about himself. . . . Sherwood noted much later . . . that his message was simply his opposition to war. In accomplishing his purpose, however, he used, as he once said, "every style of dramaturgy." In turn he was a poet, a wisecracker, a propagandist, a farceur, a satirist, a writer of historical burlesque, and a serious commentator on American life. There are ideas in the play which should be taken seriously, but they are obscured by numerous *double entendres,* some hilarious one-line jokes, scenes constructed only for humor, and a general approach which systematically undercuts a serious purpose. (pp. 42-3)

The message of the play, the comments on the uselessness and wastefulness of war, were not emphasized by early critics who saw the play as comedy mixed with farce—

which is what it is! Before an audience it is an extremely humorous play; the reader gets the antiwar message more clearly. (pp. 43-4)

While the relation of sex to an antiwar theme is peripheral, it is clear that Sherwood provides climaxes and solutions that are too easy. Consequently, Amytis' words mean relatively little: her concept of "truth," the "human equation," the "glory of submission" seem empty words and phrases in a sex-motivated plot. This is unfortunate because Sherwood is clearly serious in his ideas, and these ideas are not without power. In this instance, however, he did not have adequate faith in his ideas and felt impelled to resort to the techniques which made him a success with the [Harvard] Hasty Pudding productions. It would be a long time before he could strike a balance between his comic propensities and his desire to say something serious. Not until he wrote *Abe Lincoln in Illinois* did he put hokum aside, while his earlier serious play of ideas, *Acropolis,* he could never finish. (pp. 45-6)

Like his other plays, [*Reunion in Vienna*] was sentimental and frivolous. Critics were aware of his skill and his wit, but they missed the more serious undertone that they expected and which Sherwood felt he had written. (p. 78)

Dr. Krug is science; and for his wife, his students, and the whole world he is a god who controls himself and solves all problems. . . . Here in a single individual were all of the formalized characteristics that made Sherwood . . . despair of science and all of those who believed in it as the "ultimate ant-hill." . . . In a meaningful if obscure way Sherwood has Dr. Krug ridiculed, cuckolded, and defeated. Humanity, not science, becomes the victor. No critic, however, seems to have sensed Sherwood's serious idea in this play, and that is perhaps understandable. It was not clearly dramatized, and Sherwood never tried to explain himself. (p. 80)

[With *The Petrified Forest* it] would seem that Sherwood was becoming more in tune with the problems of the times as well as with the demands of Broadway. He had always been a dramatist in sympathy with man at the same time that he seemed occasionally overwhelmed by man's hopelessness. . . . [Until the mid-thirties,] however, he had been swept along by a superficial romanticism in such plays as *The Love Nest, The Queen's Husband, Waterloo Bridge,* and *Reunion in Vienna.* A kind of romantic idealism, of course, always remained a part of Robert Sherwood, but his criticism of man and society was becoming a more definite aspect of his dramaturgy and of his philosophy of life.

For Sherwood the essence of *The Petrified Forest* was in Alan Squier's statement: "I belong to a vanishing race. I'm one of the intellectuals." Perhaps Sherwood expressed some personal vanity or sense of persecution in this idea. If so, he was reflecting the disillusionment of his age as well as the personal disillusionment he fought throughout his life. . . . There is no doubt that at the time, and in his particular frame of mind, Sherwood wanted to write a play with a serious point. Where does man go? To the petrified forest, as "Homo Semi-Americanus—a specimen of the in-between age"! That was part of Sherwood's thought. The rest was romantic idealism involving illusion and escape. Accomplished craftsman that he was, Sherwood worked all of this into his play and hoped, as always, that people would understand.

As theatre, *The Petrified Forest* was a brilliant and instantaneous success. . . . (p. 103)

In close scrutiny the ideas in *The Petrified Forest* are certainly garbled, and neither Alan Squier nor Gabby has a sufficiently substantive character development to dramatize the ideas that Sherwood had in mind. It is, in fact, Sherwood's hasty perusal of these ideas that makes the play ineffective as thesis drama. He seems to be concerned with the intellectual in modern society, a theory of man and Nature, traditional values, rugged individualism, freedom, truth, and the necessity for illusions. But his concern as well as his effect is scattered. He lacks a penetrating and unified approach and, as he obliquely admitted, had to resort to a hokey and romantic conclusion. All of which simply says that he was not a philosopher. He was, however, a good playwright, and he offered palatable food for thought even if it was somewhat garbled. (p. 105)

There Shall Be No Night is a play of seven scenes divided into three acts. Structurally, it is an episodic play filled with "editorialized" speeches and little cause and effect action. War is the topic, and the characters respond to this force and make the choices which decide their fate. Like *Abe Lincoln in Illinois,* the play has no hokum and few lines that show Sherwood's light touch. Instead, he is deadly serious watching people face death. The main thesis dramatizes the decision of Dr. Kaarlo Valkonen, medical doctor and winner of the Nobel Prize, to forego his life of helping man and instead shoulder a gun and be killed in the front lines. . . . His goal as a human being, a scientist, and a Christian remains the same, but he has to try a different means of achieving it, one thrust upon him. This was Sherwood's message, and with letters, song, and poetry, as well as the trustworthy elements of sentimental melodrama, he made his point. It was a powerful message for a particular people and a particular time, but neither then nor now have critics called it good drama. (pp. 148-49)

[Anyone] reading the play from a reasonable perspective of time realizes that it really is not much of a play. In terms of plot there is only a series of episodes held together by Sherwood's message. There is no character development, although Sherwood clearly wanted Valkonen's decision to be dramatic and compelling. Unfortunately, he showed Valkonen's true thoughts in Scene 1 and then brought about the doctor's major decision offstage in a period of a few hours. (p. 152)

If, then, there is little plot action, no real character development, and no effective conflict among or within the characters, the play must get its power from some other source. And it does—from Sherwood's occasionally eloquent and emotional message supported by his well-established theatrical craft. . . . In general the characters are . . . worn but, in this instance, effective devices: morose and sensitive musician sees hope, ineffective woman becomes a potent force, young aspiring poet is killed, scientist gives life for beliefs.

Dramatically, *There Shall Be No Night* offers little for the student of well-structured drama, but for the student of theatre as a propaganda force Sherwood shows why F.D.R. did well to select him as a speechwriter. He had a full bag of tricks, and he used each one successfully. (pp. 152-53)

There is no doubt that *The Rugged Path* [the first play Sherwood wrote after his years as a White House speechwriter] was a meaningful play for Sherwood, as it dramatized his personal revelation and also seemed to be a defense or an explanation of his actions. But the play shows the disservice which F.D.R.'s invitation did to Sherwood's art. It would seem that Sherwood's four years of writing propaganda had seriously impaired his ability to see shadings in life or complexities in issues. Dealing as he had in the war years with emotional phrases, simple black and white meanings, and short slogan-type sentences, he now had difficulty developing characters and dramatizing conflicts. Although in both *Abe Lincoln in Illinois* and *There Shall Be No Night* he had used speeches so long they suggested a debater's point of view or an editorial comment, in *The Rugged Path* the journalistic effect seemed blatant, nothing less. There was only one character who interested Sherwood, and that one, Morey Vinion, carried his message like a banner. All subtleties were abandoned. There was a single issue, a simple idea [the need for a man and country to die for their beliefs], and Sherwood beat it out like a Ten-Twenty-Thirty melodrama without complications. Attempting to dramatize his own discovery and preach that gospel as the only road to the salvation of the world, he showed mainly a point of view that suggests strong but surface passion rather than thought-provoking ideas. Why, as a fine student of human nature during the war, he did not realize that in 1945 people would be anxious to forget the war is another question. But, of course, he did not want people to forget the war or the reasons for which it was fought. (pp. 188-89)

By the time *The Rugged Path* left the Broadway stage Sherwood was already at work on another large project—a history of the war years as reflected in his knowledge of Roosevelt and Hopkins. . . . It was Hopkins who had planned to write of his war years with Roosevelt, and it was Hopkins who had collected much of the necessary information. With his death, however, Sherwood was a logical person to write his book. . . . In his research and perhaps in his writing Sherwood had excellent help, and the book shows a careful attitude toward research which had seldom been a strong point in Sherwood's writing. Probably Sidney Hyman deserves more plaudits for his assistance than Sherwood was willing to allow him. (pp. 190-91)

The publication of *Roosevelt and Hopkins* . . . brought Sherwood back into the world of humanities with a distinction. Immediately recognized as the best book on World War II by an American, the history provided a very readable view of an important period in American Life. For those interested in some more or less intimate views of the White House . . . Sherwood supplied a fine touch. He also provided a sensible exposition of many of Roosevelt's problems which he documented with considerable skill. . . . The informed and balanced view throughout the volume makes Sherwood sound like a sensible, accurate recorder of events, even like a political expert. And indeed he was, whatever assistance he may have had. But he was also the same Sherwood who enjoyed theatre, and much of the flavor of the book comes from Sherwood's enthusiasm for his own experiences. . . . Sherwood knew that he was involved in history, and he was both excited and sometimes awed by his own experiences. (pp. 191-92)

His years away from the theatre and with Roosevelt obviously had their effect upon his dramatic talents. . . . Once past that high point in his career, he created on a dimin-

ished scale. This was the more painful because, being aware of his problems in writing plays, he tried other theatre avenues, such as the musical and television, and could satisfy neither himself nor others. (p. 192)

Sherwood had noted that the theatre had two diametrically opposed but equally essential functions: to entertain and to bring stern realities to the audiences. For Sherwood these two functions became two horns of a dilemma from which he never quite freed himself. (p. 215)

It is easy enough to describe the part that Sherwood did not play. He was not an experimenter nor an innovator, nor was he an influential dramatist in the developing American theatre. He was not a theorist; in fact, one of his friends and directors stated that he did not have a theory of drama, although for a time Sherwood waved a banner emblazoned with *hokum* as a basis for his work. Stated bluntly, he was not a cerebral dramatist. Some critics have described him as a superb craftsman, but that position is sometimes difficult to defend, perhaps depending upon a definition of the term. Careful analysis of his plays certainly brings to light serious flaws and problems with his play structure, characters, motivations, and climaxes. One of his contemporary dramatists has noted that Sherwood was not a fine craftsman although he worked hard at his craft. (p. 221)

He was, of course, a dramatist who naturally and frankly dealt with the emotions that America wanted to feel, who knew how to express them in good theatre. As well as any of his contemporaries and better than most, he knew the theatrical tricks which would bring laughter and applause. People want to be entertained, and he gave them the hokum that he loved and the spectacle that he did so well, at the same time providing simple messages that were effective in the theatre. In an exciting manner, he protested certain aspects of life when it was astute to protest. Never a great playwright, he spoke intensely and with wit and integrity during a period in history when such plays as his were needed. He provided excellent plays for the moment, out of the moment, just as he later fitted neatly into F.D.R.'s administrative machine. This was his greatness, and he was well paid by a grateful generation. (p. 222)

Walter J. Meserve, in his Robert E. Sherwood: Reluctant Moralist *(© 1970; reprinted by permission of the publisher, The Bobbs-Merrill Company, Inc.), Bobbs-Merrill—Pegasus, 1970, 360 p.*

BIBLIOGRAPHY

Anderson, Maxwell. "Robert E. Sherwood." *Theatre Arts Monthly* XL, No. 2 (February 1956): 26-7, 87.
 A brief appreciation by a fellow dramatist and friend.

Broussard, Louis. "Everyman at Mid-Century: Robert E. Sherwood." In his *American Drama: Contemporary Allegory from Eugene O'Neill to Tennessee Williams*, pp. 104-10. Norman: University of Oklahoma Press, 1962.
 Examines *The Petrified Forest* as an allegorical treatment of the decline of Western institutions and a celebration of man's capacity for sacrifice and courage.

Brown, John Mason. "America Speaks: Allegory and Mr. Sherwood." In his *Two on the Aisle: Ten Years of the American Theater in Performance*, pp. 163-68. New York: Norton, 1938.
 A contemporary review of *The Petrified Forest* and *Idiot's Delight*. Brown applauds the former as an amusing melodrama

and profound allegory of the human spirit. He hints at the allegorical nature of the latter but primarily applauds its showmanship.

Brown, John Mason. *The Ordeal of a Playwright: Robert E. Sherwood and the Challenge of War*. Edited by Norman Cousins. New York: Harper & Row, 1970, 320 p.
A biographical study concerned primarily with Sherwood's political beliefs and his service as a speechwriter and propagandist for the Roosevelt administration. The book includes the play *There Shall Be No Night* and Sherwood's preface to that play.

Commager, Henry Steele. "Franklin Roosevelt's Alter Ego." *The New York Times Book Review* (24 October 1948): 1, 38-40.
A review of *Roosevelt and Hopkins* that applauds Sherwood's control of a massive amount of detail and his revelations about American policy during World War II.

Dusenbury, Winifred L. "Myth in American Drama between the Wars." *Modern Drama* 6, No. 3 (December 1963): 294-308.
A short examination of Sherwood's plays which contends that his satirical tone and rational approach nullify the mythic element of his heroes.

Gould, Jean. "Robert Sherwood." In her *Modern American Playwrights*, pp. 99-117. New York: Dodd, Mead & Co., 1966.
A serviceable short biography.

Lausch, Anne N. "Robert Sherwood's 'Heartbreak Houses'." *The Shaw Review* VI, No. 2 (May 1963): 42-50.

Comparison between Shaw's *Heartbreak House* and Sherwood's *The Petrified Forest* and *Idiots' Delight*. Lausch notes that both Shaw and Sherwood confront the problem of evil, Shaw seeing evil on a more universal scale than Sherwood. Sherwood's plays, she finds, have too narrow a perspective of evil and thus have not survived.

Miller, Evelyn E. "A Trilogy of Irony." *English Journal* 59, No. 1 (January 1970): 59-62.
A study of Sherwood's use of irony in *Idiot's Delight*, written for a high school audience.

Schlesinger, Arthur, Jr. "Portrait of Hopkins." *The Nation* CLXVII, No. 23 (4 December 1948): 638-40.
A review of *Roosevelt and Hopkins* which praises its documentation and the personal insight it offers.

Sherwood, Robert E. "Footnote to a Preface." *The Saturday Review of Literature* XXXII, No. 32 (6 August 1949): 130, 132, 134-35.
A brief synopsis by Sherwood of his career and the important dramatic talents of his time. He bemoans the scarcity of new and creative dramatic writing in America.

Thorp, Willard. "Dramatic Interlude, 1915-1940." In his *American Writing in the Twentieth Century*, pp. 63-109. Cambridge: Harvard University Press, 1960.
Interesting synopsis of Sherwood's plays tracing the development of his thought from intellectual activism, to disillusion, to political activism.

Henryk (Adam Aleksander Pius) Sienkiewicz

1846-1916

(Also wrote under pseudonym of Litwos) Polish novelist, short story writer, and journalist.

Though in his homeland Sienkiewicz is a major literary figure, readers worldwide primarily remember him as the man who wrote *Quo Vadis*. He was considered a patriot of stature and indeed Sienkiewicz's expressed purpose in writing his *Trilogy* was to fortify the moral awareness and national pride of his people. He achieved this through the recreation of the dramatic and traumatic episodes of seventeenth century Poland. Critics have challenged the historical accuracy of some of the events and characterizations in the *Trilogy*, but Sienkiewicz was an informed researcher of the past. Thus the dispute is not over his knowledge but over the way he adapted this material for use in his fiction. He was aware of the artistic pitfalls facing the historical novelist and commented on them in his essay "On the Historical Novel."

Throughout his career Sienkiewicz alternated between portraying life of the past, such as first century Rome in *Quo Vadis*, and that of the present, as in *Without Dogma* and *Children of the Soil*. His first stories were realistic tales modelled partly on the sociological doctrines of positivism, which he later abandoned as alien to his nature. In 1876, Sienkiewicz came to America as a correspondent for the *Gazeta polska*, relaying a series of travel letters homeward. While in California he helped found an experimental, though unsuccessful, utopian community of Poles. It was following his return to Poland that Sienkiewicz began the major artistic phase that produced the *Trilogy*, a work which had all the characteristics of vigor and panoramic scope that were to form his identity as an author.

Though his most famous works are renowned for their realistic and vivid depictions of war, Sienkiewicz himself was the first man for five generations of his family not to choose a career in the military. Sienkiewicz was awarded the Nobel Prize for Literature in 1905. He died in Switzerland while working for the Polish Red Cross during World War I.

PRINCIPAL WORKS

Na marne (novel) 1872
 [*In Vain*, 1899]
Hania (short stories) 1876
 [*Hania*, 1897]
Listy z podróży do Ameryki (letters) 1876-78; published serially in newspaper *Gazeta polska*
 [*Portrait of America: Letters*, 1959]
Ogniem i mieczem (novel) 1884
 [*With Fire and Sword*, 1890]
Potop (novel) 1886
 [*The Deluge*, 1891]
Pan Wołodyjowski (novel) 1887-88
 [*Pan Michael* 1893]
Bez dogmatu (novel) 1891
 [*Without Dogma*, 1893]
Listy z Afryki (letters) 1892
Rodzina Połanieckich (novel) 1895
 [*Children of the Soil*, 1895; also published as *The Irony of Life: The Polanetzki Family*, 1900]
Quo Vadis (novel) 1896
 [*Quo Vadis*, 1896]
Krzyżacy (novel) 1897-1900
 [*Knights of the Cross*, 1897-1900; published in England as *The Teutonic Knights*, 1943]
Sielanka: A Forest Picture and Other Stories (short stories) 1898
Na polu chwały (novel) 1906
 [*On the Field of Glory*, 1906]
Wiry (novel) 1910
 [*Whirlpools: A Novel of Modern Poland*, 1910]
W pustyni i puszczy (novel) 1911
 [*In the Desert and Wilderness*, 1912; also published as *Through the Desert*, 1912]

*These are multi-volumed works.

EDMUND GOSSE (essay date 1897)

[Before] beginning the great historical epos which has made him famous, Sienkiewicz collected his shorter stories and sketches into three volumes under the general title of "Pisma." ... [Sienkiewicz's early short stories and sketches] are mainly village-idylls, *dorfgeschichten*, which suggest the influence of Jeremias Gotthelf and Auerbach. They are, however, more incisive and photographic, and in their mixture of realistic description and idealistic sentiment they come, sometimes, very close to the early manner of Björnson. ... [This] minute and romantic observation of episodes in the life of peasants, which was already so familiar to German, Swiss, and Scandinavian readers, had the charm of novelty for Poles; but the general European critic will not see much positive originality in these agreeable early tales of Sienkiewicz. (p. 519)

Sienkiewicz is certainly slow in warming to his work. The openings of his novels are hard reading. Doubtless, the cause of this is the fact that he paints on a very large scale, and that the panoramic style excludes the possibility of finishing up corners and edges. But, unquestionably, the great historical trilogy ["With Fire and Sword," "The Deluge," and "Pan Michael"] cannot be approached with a light heart. (p. 520)

[The] plan of Sienkiewicz [is] to create a vast, uni-colored background, tempestuous or sullen, and here and there, against it, to paint in vivid, even brilliant hues, the humors of exceptional figures. So that the plan has an artificiality, a remoteness from actual experience, very unlike the conscientious art of Tolstoi in "Peace and War," yet highly impressive in its broad way. A single page of Sienkiewicz conveys nothing to the imagination, a single chapter produces a faint effect, but long before we are half through a volume the epic grandeur of the treatment, its fierce, heroic vitality, have seized our attention. Hence, the interest and even the merit of the book seem regularly to advance, simply because, as the canvas the writer has to cover grows larger, his swift and sweeping brush produces an impression of greater *bravura*. (pp. 521-22)

As is inseparable from the panoramic manner, there is a tendency [in "With Fire and Sword"] to make . . . persons carry a sort of ticket of identity, so that Zagloba cannot be introduced for a moment without . . . expatiating on food and drink; Pan Longin's desire to cut off three Cossacks' heads at one blow . . . is mentioned on every occasion; and we can never look at Pan Michael but his moustaches rise in tufts. Were the author not to do this, however, in a work planned on such a prodigious scale, we might fail to recognize promptly enough the recurrent personages. The way in which these three ceaselessly tease and chaff one another, in a very happy reconstruction of the pedantic humor of the seventeenth century, singularly lightens the gloom of the story, and the more so because of the continuous development of melancholy in the grave figure of Pan Yan [the hero] himself.

That Sienkiewicz shines in his episodes has already been suggested; he is even methodically episodical. It is doubtless the only way in which vitality can be given to such a theme as his. . . . And if to be novel and to be spirited is to succeed in the historical episode, Sienkiewicz succeeds, whoever fails. (pp. 522-23)

On the whole, the impression which the talent of Sienkiewicz produces is one of breadth and vigor rather than of subtlety. . . .

It is certainly the great constellation of romances of seventeenth-century history which lifts Sienkiewicz out of the category of ordinary writers of meritorious fiction. It is these fierce vast panoramas of war which give him for the present his claim on our attention. They are in the highest degree remarkable, and it is much to be desired that he should return from spheres where others hold more authority than he to this one province where he reigns supreme. His three romances form a cycle of genuine grandeur. In them he has contrived to create a huge army of

hurrying, desperate men, driven over the monotonous world by storms of vague, homicidal frenzy. It is not finely and minutely painted. It is not Tolstoi or Meissonier; it is rather the work of a gigantic scene-painter filled with enthusiasm for his work and standing on a ladder twelve feet high to paint a hero in a cloud of blood. It is all grandiose and magnificent, yet preserved, by an undertone of poignant melancholy, and by a constantly supported distinction of sentiment, from the merely melodramatic and tawdry. (p. 527)

Edmund Gosse, "Henryk Sienkiewicz," in The Living Age *(copyright 1897, by the Living Age Co.), Vol. XIV, No. 2759, May 22, 1897, pp. 517-27.*

WILLIAM LYON PHELPS (essay date 1910)

The three great Polish romances [Sienkiewicz's historical Trilogy] were all written in the eighties; and at about the same time the author was also engaged in the composition of purely realistic work, which displays his powers in a quite different form of art, and constitutes the most original —though not the most popular—part of his literary production. The *Children of the Soil,* which some of the elect in Poland consider his masterpiece, is a novel, constructed and executed in the strictest style of realism; *Without Dogma* is still farther removed from the Romantic manner, for it is a story of psychological analytical introspection. Sienkiewicz himself regards *Children of the Soil* as his favourite, although he is "not prepared to say just why." And *Without Dogma* he thinks to be "in many respects my strongest work." It is evident that he does not consider himself primarily a maker of stirring historical romance. But in the nineties he returned to this form of fiction, producing his Roman panorama called *Quo Vadis,* which, although it has made the biggest noise of all his books, is perhaps the least valuable. Like *Ben Hur,* it was warmed over into a tremendously successful melodrama, and received the final compliment of parody. Toward the close of the century, Sienkiewicz completed another massive historical romance, *The Knights of the Cross,* which, in its abundant action, striking characterisation, and charming humour, recalled the Trilogy; this was followed by *On the Field of Glory,* and we may confidently expect more, though never too much; he simply could not be dull if he tried. (pp. 117-18)

Is the *romanticist* Sienkiewicz an original writer? In the narrow and strict sense of the word, I think not. He is eclectic rather than original. He is a skilful fuser of material, like Shakespeare. At any rate, his most conspicuous virtue is not originality. He has enormous force, a glorious imagination, astonishing facility, and a remarkable power of making pictures, both in panorama and in miniature; but his work shows constantly the inspiration not only of his historical authorities, but of previous poets and novelists. . . . The influence of Homer is seen in the constant similes, the epithets like "incomparable bowman," and the stress laid on the deeds of individual heroes; a thing quite natural in Homeric warfare, but rather disquieting in the days of villainous saltpetre. The three swordsmen in *With Fire and Sword*—Pan Yan, Pan Podbienta, and Pan Michael—infallibly remind us of [Alexandre] Dumas's three guardsmen; and the great duel scenes in the same story, and in the *Knights of the Cross,* are quite in the manner of the Frenchman. . . . In the high colouring, in the management of historical events, and in patriotic enthusiasm, we cannot help thinking of [Walter] Scott. (pp. 121-22)

With reference to the much-discussed character of Zagloba, I confess I cannot join in the common verdict that pronounces him a "new creation in literature." . . . Zagloba is a Polish Falstaff, an astonishingly clever imitation of the real thing. . . . The real triumph of Sienkiewicz in the portrayal of the jester is in the fact that he could imitate Falstaff without spoiling him, for no other living writer could have done it. A copy that can safely be placed alongside the original implies art of a very high class. (pp. 122-23)

In power of description on a large scale, Sienkiewicz seems to take a place among the world's great masters of fiction. The bigger the canvas, the more impressive he becomes. His pictures of the boundless steppes by day and night, and in the varying seasons of the year, leave permanent images in the mind. Especially in huge battle scenes is his genius resplendent. It is as if we viewed the whole drama of blood from a convenient mountain peak. The awful tumult gathers and breaks like some hideous storm. So far as I know no writer has ever excelled this Verestchagin of the pen except Tolstoi—and Tolstoi's power lies more in the subjective side of the horrors of war. . . . Sienkiewicz becomes at times merely sensational. There is no excuse for his frequent descent into loathsome and horrible detail. The employment of human entrails as a necklace may be historically accurate, but it is out of place in a work of art. . . . The love of the physically horrible is an unfortunate characteristic of our Polish novelist, for it appears in *Quo Vadis* as well as in the Trilogy. The greatest works appeal to the mind rather than the senses. *Pan Michael* is a great book, not because it reeks with blood and abounds in hell's ingenuity of pain, but because it presents the character of a hero made perfect through suffering; every sword-stroke develops his spirit as well as his arm. Superfluous events, so frequent in the other works, are here omitted; the story progresses steadily; it is the most condensed and the most human book in the Trilogy. Again, in *The Deluge*, the author's highest skill is shown not in the portrayal of moving accidents by flood and field, but in the regeneration of Kmita. He passes through a long period of slow moral gestation, which ultimately brings him from darkness to light. (pp. 123-25)

Sienkiewicz is undoubtedly one of the greatest living masters of the realistic novel. In [*Children of the Soil* and *Without Dogma*], the most minute trivialities in human intercourse are set forth in a style that never becomes trivial. He is as good at external description as he is at psychological analysis. He takes all human nature for his province. He belongs not only to the "feel" school of novelists, with Zola, but to the "thought" school, with Turgenev. The workings of the human mind, as impelled by all sorts of motives, ambitions, and passions, make the subject for his examination. In the Trilogy, he took an enormous canvas, and splashed on myriads of figures; in *Without Dogma,* he puts the soul of one man under the microscope. . . . Every futile impulse, every vain longing, every idle day-dream, is clearly reflected. It is a melancholy spectacle, but fascinating and highly instructive. For it is not merely an individual, but the national Slavonic character that is revealed.

Sienkiewicz is not only a Romanticist and a Realist—he is also a Moralist. The foundations of his art are set deep in the bed-rock of moral ideas. As Tolstoi would say, he has the right attitude toward his characters. He believes that the Novel should strengthen life, not undermine it; ennoble, not defile it; for it is good tidings, not evil. . . . The fact is, that at heart Sienkiewicz is as stout a moralist as Tolstoi, and with equal ardour recognises Christianity as the world's best standard and greatest need. (pp. 126-28)

Sienkiewicz seems to have much the same Christian conception of Love as that shown in so many ways by Browning. Love is the *summum bonum,* and every manifestation of it has something divine. Love in all its forms appears in these Polish novels . . . from the basest sensual desire to the purest self-sacrifice. There is indeed a streak of animalism in Sienkiewicz, which shows in all his works; but, if we may believe him, it is merely one representation of the great passion, which so largely controls life and conduct. (pp. 130-31)

Sienkiewicz is indeed a mighty man—someone has ironically called him a literary blacksmith. (p. 131)

> *William Lyon Phelps, ''Henryk Sienkiewicz,'' in his* Essays on Modern Novelists *(reprinted with permission of Macmillan Publishing Co., Inc.; ©️ copyright 1910 by Macmillan Publishing Co., Inc.; renewed 1938 by William Lyon Phelps), Macmillan, 1910, pp. 115-31.*

LACY LOCKERT (essay date 1919)

We live in an age of literary tabloids, and Sienkiewicz created leviathans. . . . His huge canvases are covered with figures whose strange Polish names are discouraging if not repellent to us. . . . Moreover, Sienkiewicz's novels of Polish history are not likely to invite one who is a stranger to those complex annals; while in them and in his modern stories alike one is ill at ease amid the unfamiliar customs of a foreign people and the sometimes mystifying idioms of that people. . . . (pp. 257-58)

Throughout his historical fiction Sienkiewicz is supreme as a descriptive artist. His pictures of the boundless steppes and his great battle scenes are alike unrivaled; in all the myriad of combats he never repeats himself. The narrative is sustained with a graphic power and breathless intensity that sweeps the reader with it like a flood. . . .

The last half of *With Fire and Sword* is unsurpassed anywhere in the work of its author; the earlier portion of the book drags at times, especially the second fifth, and contains too much rather confused fighting, too many unimportant battles. (p. 263)

In the second section of the series, however—*The Deluge* . . .—Sienkiewicz masters his material. That stupendous novel, the hugest of his books, is the greatest, not only of the Trilogy, but of all the novelist's productions—perhaps of all the productions of all novelists. Only once in its thirteen hundred odd pages, and then for less than one hundred, does the story flag. Throughout the broad-flung welter of battle and siege and sally and ambuscade and duel and daring exploit, of plot and counterplot, of love and intrigue, of public war and private feud—runs one binding thread: the regeneration and development of a man's soul. The character of the hero, Kmita, is the subtlest, though not the most spectacular, of his creator's psychological studies, and the story of how from a ruffian and an outlaw he becomes ten times over the savior of his King and country is worked out with masterful power and art. (pp. 263-64)

[The last of the series, *Pan Michael,*] is the most human of the three—both shorter and more like the general run of novels. Its plot is closer knit—less episodic—than those of the others; but it represents a falling off in power and, though a supreme achievement by any lesser standard, really cannot compare with the preceding two.

In considering the Trilogy as a whole, the word "epic" comes constantly to the mind and to the lips. Sienkiewicz has himself mentioned his indebtness to Homer in the management of great masses of men and mighty conflicts. But beyond this and the Iliad-like accounts of the prowess of individual champions, there is a world of minutiae that hails straight from the Greek epos. The epithets and indeed the figures of speech, especially the similes, are Homeric. . . . [The] historical novels of Sienkiewicz have an epic objectivity that is absolutely unique in fiction of this type. For that reason they are at once less popular and greater than other war novels. The average reader likes to know how war would look to him or feel to him. Zola, in *La Débâcle,* gives us realism. He photographs the incoherent chaos, the unvarnished horrors of war—not as the combatants see it, but as he, Zola sees it—and from the *outside.* Tolstoy, in *War and Peace,* represents the other pole. He is the great emotional exponent of war. He describes, not war itself, but what men feel who are engaged in it. . . . [Sienkiewicz] alone among novelists shows us that age, not as a picture spread before us that we can see, or through the magic lens of his own eyes—but through the eyes of the people who lived and acted them—not a panorama unfurled, but a cyclorama amid which we stand: confused, terrible, magnificent—faithfully reproduced both in its glory and in its frightfulness; and it is just for that reason that he is incomparably the greatest of all historical novelists. (pp. 264-65)

In general, historical novelists might be divisible into the school of Scott and the school of Dumas. Scott's productions are costume pieces. . . . Those of Dumas, on the other hand, are primarily tales of adventure, recounted with gusto and careless irresponsibility. . . . But Sienkiewicz takes a lesson from both his great predecessors; he seizes the outer aspect of an age with all the broad grasp of Scott, and peoples it with characters as vivid, virile, keen-witted, and heroic as those of Dumas, involved in an action narrated with scarcely less compelling sweep than is found in the works of the French wizard of plot—and, like neither of those predecessors, strikes below the surface events which concern his heroes and heroines to deeper issues, more solemnly momentous than the lives of men and women. Throughout the Trilogy there is no one, not even Pan Michael, who is the real centre of interest, the protagonist: it is Poland. *Her* peril, her salvation, her suffering, her glory, are all-important, the matters that enthrall our care. No sacrifice is so great, no personage so beloved, that we, in reading, deem the price too hard. And in the individuals themselves the mere question of safety or death, of happiness or disaster, is felt to be, after all, a thing of minor importance; everywhere we encounter a deep psychological interest, the working out of an inner problem, the struggle in noble minds between selfishness and duty. (pp. 266-67)

[Though] they would be classed together as historical fiction, the Trilogy and *Quo Vadis* are totally unlike in both field and method. The ephemeral fame, built on false values, which the new work enjoyed has tended to obscure its

real merit. Its plot, despite the usual comprehensive sweep, is more closely knit than is customary in the loose-woven fabrics of Sienkiewicz—is dramatic rather than epic—and the old descriptive power loses nothing in the depiction of imperial revels, the burning of Rome, or the scenes of the arena. The delicate task of presenting the figures of Peter and Paul is not unsatisfactorily discharged; whereas the opposed portrait of Nero, while a perversion of historical fact and a slander upon the otherwise sufficiently dubious fame of that emperor, is self-consistent, plausible, and luridly powerful. It is, indeed, in characterization that *Quo Vadis* is most notable. Nero and Chilo would suffice to dignify any work, but in Petronius *Arbiter* Sienkiewicz has, I believe, painted his absolute masterpiece. (pp. 273-74)

[*Knights of the Cross*] is a complete return to the epic type of historical novel. . . . Of all the works of Sienkiewicz, it gives the greatest impression of vastness; it lacks, however, the striking characterization of the Trilogy. . . . Everything considered, *The Knights of the Cross* should probably rank third in order of excellence among Sienkiewicz's novels, yielding precedence to *The Deluge* and *With Fire and Sword.* (p. 274)

[*Whirlpools*] is the least impressive product of his pen after he reached maturity. The author has elsewhere expressed his entire lack of sympathy with didactic fiction, declaring the novel should be above all things a work of art. In *Whirlpools* the purpose obtrudes upon the story; yet Sienkiewicz was by nature unfitted for his task, his mind preferably illuminating a subject by glancing though often subtle flashes, rather than with the inexorable, steady light of syllogistic proof. (p. 275)

[*Through Desert and Wilderness*] is less a novel than a boy's book of adventure, raised to the nth power—a sort of glorified *Swiss Family Robinson.* . . . It is rather a tremendous *tour-de-force* than a work to add to the reputation of its author. Yet in two ways it is characteristic and fitting as his farewell creation: it offers one more testimonial to his infinite variety, and in the figure of its boy-hero, whose pluck and ingenuity surmount every difficulty, there is, as it were, a symbol of Sienkiewicz's faith in the Polish people—in their capacity of rising to any occasion, of being equal to any task—and a final bugle-call to the pride and self-reliance of his land. (pp. 275-76)

Sienkiewicz's literary theory was that love, as the universal emotion, should be the basis of all fiction. In each of his novels, however wide a circle may be fetched around it, a love-story is the integrating principle of the narrative. . . . Sienkiewicz is preëminently the novelist of love, but the climax of *The Deluge,* his most enthralling love-story, is when the hero, Kmita, at the call of his country's need, abandons the search which apparently is necessary to deliver his sweetheart from death or worse. That clear, strong, unfailing perception of relative values is like the salt sea-breeze blowing amid the rose vapors of sentimental emotionalism. (pp. 279-80)

Sienkiewicz's portrait gallery of heroines has not always received due appreciation at the hands of even his admirers. Those of his works which have been most widely read—*Quo Vadis, With Fire and Sword,* and *The Deluge*—have no female figures of real distinction, save the somewhat statuesque heroine of the last-named novel. But if all his books be taken into account, a collection of lovely women may be culled, who bear a curious resemblance to the heroines of Shakespeare—not in their individual characters, but in the manner of their drawing: in outline, with bold, simple strokes, and a tendency to delicate idealization in contrast to the realism with which the men of both authors are treated. . . . [One] may, for the most part, divide them into groups: Olenka, Marynia Plavitski, and Miss Anney—strong yet gentle, quietly brave; Anusia, Zosia, Aniela, Danusia, and the Marynia of *Whirlpools*—innocent, simple, child-like, clinging natures; Helena, Krysia, and Lygia, reserved, timid, and somewhat languidly lovely; and finally, best of all, the Amazons—the little hoyden, Basia, of *Pan Michael,* and the radiant Yagenka of *The Knights of the Cross.*

What place shall we assign Sienkiewicz among the world's great novelists? (p. 282)

In consideration of [his] vast, complex, and glorious achievement, only one novelist can contest Sienkiewicz's claim to preëminence: the colossal Balzac. . . . If, therefore, we feel inclined to dub Balzac "the Shakespeare of the Novel," we should hail Henryk Sienkiewicz as its "Homer." (p. 283)

> Lacy Lockert, "Henryk Sienkiewicz," in The Sewanee Review (reprinted by permission of the editor; © 1919 by The University of the South), Vol. XXVII, No. 3, Summer, 1919, pp. 257-83.

ROMAN DYBOSKI (essay date 1924)

Sienkiewicz, in his great later novel from contemporary life, *The Połaniecki Family* [also known as *Children of the Soil*], definitely adopted a consistent and thorough-going Conservatism. His mastery is here shown . . . in a gallery of life-like types drawn from modern Polish society; but the limited outlook of the commonplace hero, a narrow-minded, business-like Pole of the kind produced after the last insurrection by the stress of economic forces, is emphasized with irritating persistence; the equally irritating passiveness of his devoted wife is idealized over-much; and at the end the policy of 'back to the land' is advocated too unreservedly for the judgement of the more thoughtful spectator of the industrial and commercial development of society. The author went even further in this direction [in *Whirlpools*] when he used his waning powers to reveal his want of sympathy with the impatient and misguided outburst of those young Poles who, during the revolutionary ferment in Russia about 1905, thought the moment come for a corresponding rebellion in their own country. The very title of Sienkiewicz's work, *Whirlpools*, is significant of his opinions, but in the eyes of the critic it also indicates with involuntary irony a failing clearness of vision. (p. 36)

Quo Vadis is certainly the most successful presentation by a modern writer of the conflict between decaying Roman civilization and the rising moral power of Christianity. The grandeur of the historical vision, its wealth and vivid colour of detail, the creative force which gives life to a crowd of Roman and Christian characters, the fullness of antique culture as embodied in Petronius, have been justly admired by readers of many nations. Blemishes have become apparent as the work has been more widely read: the central figures of the lovers are somewhat bloodless, the great Christian leaders somewhat abstract in their perfection, the Roman revels and the tortures of the Christians occasionally somewhat too crude in their laboured realism. But it may be said

that these are errors such as a Michelangelo might have fallen into in dealing with so vast a theme; its greatness tends to impair the writer's sense of proportion; under its moral inspiration he over-intensifies in his picture the lights and shadows of reality. (pp. 36-7)

Sienkiewicz is now receding into the secure distance of history, across the dividing gulf of the war. In historical perspective he will undoubtedly for ever stand out as the greatest Polish writer of his age. (p. 39)

> Roman Dyboski, "From Realism to New Romance," in his Modern Polish Literature: A Course of Lectures (reprinted by permission of Oxford University Press), Oxford University Press, London, 1924, pp. 31-9.

MONICA M. GARDNER (essay date 1926)

Sienkiewicz was among the first of Polish novelists to consecrate his pen to peasant themes, which have since played so great a part in Polish literature. He is not out to idealise, still less to make poetry out of prose. What he saw in the peasants he describes: their hardships, their struggles with the red tape of official petty tyranny, their restricted intelligence, their roughness, their rugged fidelity, their deep piety.

Sienkiewicz called the earliest of his peasant tales *Sketches in Charcoal.* (p. 4)

In this story the sarcasm of the author is more frank than it is elsewhere, and more youthful: it has, in fact, a touch of crudeness. The overpiling of the agony with, as its result, a certain distortion of the truth are faults from which Sienkiewicz did not entirely free himself till later. (p. 6)

Sketches in Charcoal was followed by the best of his short stories. *Janko the Musician, For Bread, The Lighthouse Keeper* and *Bartek the Conqueror* are all peasant tales. Each of these, but most noticeably *Janko* and *The Lighthouse Keeper,* is tinged with the peculiarly Slavonic atmosphere, ghostly and unearthly, that is so marked in the first and third parts of the Trilogy. (p. 7)

In *For Bread* and *The Lighthouse Keeper* Sienkiewicz gives us his peasant no longer in the Polish village, but in exile, in America. Here he portrays with tender pathos the Polish peasants at their best. (p. 11)

When Sienkiewicz's subject is a peasant he becomes a peasant himself, with the addition of the sympathetic insight of genius. He relates a peasant story from within, not from without. The very narrative of what the peasant thinks and sees is generally couched in peasant idiom. This explains the intense humanity of Sienkiewicz's peasants. They are flesh and blood, not figures on paper. (p. 16)

The beauty and pathos of [*The Lighthouse Keeper*], built on the slenderest of frameworks, its delicacy of touch and artistic handling, place it with the masterpieces of Polish literature. . . . The atmosphere of *The Lighthouse Keeper* is integral to the story, and that atmosphere is the sea. (p. 17)

All [the earliest and best of Sienkiewicz's short stories] are sad, albeit the humour in *Bartek* only yields to tragedy at the end of his story: but with the exception of *Bartek* and *The Lighthouse Keeper* their melancholy tends to pessimism. This is comprehensible enough when we recall the terrible national circumstances under which Sienkiewicz wrote them. The fact remains that the great novelist who became as a tower of strength to his country began his life's work by a strong inclination to pessimism, to a morbid one-sidedness, as in *Janko* and *Sketches in Charcoal,* that becomes exaggeration, to a certain softness that might easily have degenerated into sentimentality. His peasants, as he tells their stories, find not a soul to help them in their distress. His aristocrats are callous, frivolous, unpleasant. . . . Again, if we look closely, all the actors of these stories are more or less in the same psychological position: they are all at grips with some inimical force: it is only the treatment that varies. So masterly is, however, this treatment that superficially the short tales are not alike, and have each their own distinct character.

These are merely the flaws in creations that are masterpieces: and with what must have seemed to his readers dramatic swiftness, Sienkiewicz shook himself free of this inclination to morbidity and consequent exaggeration that would not only have marred his work as an artist but wrecked his work as a patriot. The last of his stories [*Tartar Captivity*], before he turned to the historical novels that took his nation's heart by storm, contains in germ much of what was to develop into the moral force whence the author's compatriots drew fortitude and comfort. (pp. 43-4)

In more than one sense this tale is the prelude to the Trilogy, set as it is in the Ukrainian steppes of *With Fire and Sword;* the steppes where the Cossack border soldiery of Poland patrolled her eastern frontiers. (p. 46)

It is interesting to note that Sienkiewicz never plunged into the exacting form of a long novel without first testing his powers by some shorter attempt in the particular line which that novel was to take. *Tartar Captivity* paved the way for the Trilogy. *Let us follow Him,* a sketch of two young pagans won to Christ by witnessing His passion, was Sienkiewicz's preparation for his great romance of the first ages of Christianity, *Quo Vadis.* So *Hania,* though it lacks the power and penetration of the later novels, and is not written as they were for a moral purpose, foreshadows *Without Dogma* and *The Polaniecki Family.* (pp. 165-66)

Hania was one of the earliest things that Sienkiewicz wrote, and together with *The Old Servant* at once took the public fancy. The plot . . . is too threadbare and conventional to account for the fascination of *Hania.* The charm of the story lies in the freshness of its style, the vividness of its types, and—to the foreign reader at all events—in the attractive pictures it presents of the old Polish manor house of Sienkiewicz's youth. . . . (p. 166)

Both *Without Dogma* and *The Polaniecki Family,* written in the maturity of Sienkiewicz's genius, have behind them a very decided intention on the part of the author of straightening false ideas and pointing to a moral. But as we have already observed, in no case is Sienkiewicz's moral aim ever allowed to interfere with the claims of art or the truth of his representation of life. Sienkiewicz is a great moral force: but he is as great an artist. (pp. 170-71)

The two social novels, published in the nineties of the nineteenth century, are, on the contrary, in close touch with the psychological analysis of the modern novel. This is especially true of *Without Dogma.* (p. 171)

The plot of the book is ordinary enough, and its working out, related in the shape of a diary, might have proved wearisome in the extreme. The book is not ordinary, and it is not wearisome. The pitiless analysis of Ploszowski's character is so masterly that it carries the reader through a narrative where events are slight and personages few. The idea underlying the story is more concisely worked out than is usual with Sienkiewicz; the mortal struggle between the man and woman one of his finest psychological studies. (pp. 175-76)

The evolution of Ploszowski's love for Anielka . . . is worked out with extraordinary skill. The man who, at the moment in which he begins his diary, is mentally too inert to feel much emotion over any subject, becomes a possessed soul who sees nothing, hears nothing, except Anielka's face, Anielka's voice. Healthy work of any sort is unknown to him. At the time when passionate love of an oppressed country was almost a religion in the heart of every Pole, Ploszowski cares nothing for his country. He is an absentee, only choosing to return to his native land when driven thereto by circumstances. He owns he has no aim in life to which he might dedicate his life: a confession, says Dr. Kallenbach, terrible upon Polish lips. (p. 179)

The protagonist of *Without Dogma* presents the extreme consequence of moral and spiritual stagnation, and was Sienkiewicz's warning to his young compatriots.

The Polaniecki Family . . . has already left that side of life behind. There is no room here for the futility of a Ploszowski. The second social novel is more filled with life and action than *Without Dogma,* and its heroine, Marynia, if too much in the nature of a patient Grizel to be wholly pleasing to a modern audience, holds her high place in Sienkiewicz's portrait-gallery of beautiful women. But the book has not the brilliance and the incisive penetration of Ploszowski's diary: it is on far more commonplace lines, and at first sight does not show the cohesion of one idea that gives *Without Dogma* its singular power. In fact, at the outset, we cannot follow the thread that binds these apparently loosely-assorted groups of human beings together, or fathom what the author has in his mind regarding them. But, leaving aside for the moment certain outstanding psychological factors that will presently be visible in the histories of all these people, we shall follow their story better if we bear in mind that *The Polaniecki Family* is a human comedy. We must read it as such: and the men and women who are the actors in its scenes are so extraordinarily alive that the book commands our unflagging interest. (pp. 187-88)

By the time . . . the book ends, we have grasped our main ideas. Above all, the sanctity of marriage; in a lesser degree, the sanctity of work and the sanctity of the soil: in these things Sienkiewicz finds the salvation of society and therefore of a nation. (p. 189)

The Knights of the Cross is the last of Sienkiewicz's great works. The book is not on a level with the Trilogy, nor equal to *Quo Vadis.* It yet remains a masterpiece. Here Sienkiewicz leaves his beloved eastern frontiers with their wild border wars, their ghosts, their steppes, and turns to the marsh and forest lands of West Poland. The book has in consequence a more familiar ring than the Trilogy, and is more akin to the historical fiction of other countries. Its epoch is mediaeval, and it proceeds on the clear-cut, simple lines of the mentality of the Middle Ages. There is the atmosphere of chivalry and tournament, the rough and tumble of mediaeval life, its lack of subtlety, its primitive conceptions. The characters are the least interesting in all Sienkiewicz's greater books. . . . And yet *The Knights of the Cross* attracts the reader only little less than the other historical novels. If as regards its power and artistic treatment it is their inferior, its interest is undoubted, while it steers clear of the long-windedness of *The Deluge*. There are, moreover, chapters in this work when the historical element almost ceases to be, and it becomes a delicious story of long days in the forest spent by the boy and girl in hunting bear and beaver. (pp. 238-39)

In the romance that he entitled *On the Field of Glory . . .*, [Sienkiewicz] returns to his favourite figure of Sobieski, and amplifies the episode of the relief of Vienna by the Polish army upon which he had touched in the epilogue of *The Little Knight*. But it was inevitable that the hand which had painted the gorgeous colours of the Trilogy was nearing its exhaustion, and could not again grapple successfully with the same theme. The book has its fine passages: but it is unfinished, and will be forgotten, while the Trilogy, *Quo Vadis* and *The Knights of the Cross* live. (p. 266)

> *Monica M. Gardner, in her* The Patriot Novelist of Poland: Henryk Sienkiewicz, *J M Dent & Sons Limited, 1926, 281 p.*

WACLAW LEDNICKI (essay date 1948)

In his first writings—short stories and sketches—Sienkiewicz followed the main ideas of positivism—he fought against romantic sentimentality and devoted his main attention to the fate of the peasant. . . . However, even in these stories some traits of the art of Sienkiewicz are distinctly revealed. He is first of all a painter, his gift is plasticity, the evocation of revealing physical detail; his interest is preeminently in the man, in his hero. . . . The interest in the man, the type, the human personality was much stronger in him than interest in social, political, or intellectual currents. . . . It will become his greatest power, especially in his historical novels. Tarnowski rightly asserted that the heroes of the *Trilogy* became for the whole of Poland true living people. But between that escape from positivism and his long expedition into the field of the historical novel there took place an extremely important event in the life of Sienkiewicz—his travels in America. (pp. 14-15)

Letters From America [gives] an extremely colorful, picturesque, and lively picture of America sometimes serious and perspicacious, sometimes funny and amusing. The attentive and friendly, from time to time even enthusiastic traveler, often clever in his irony and jokes, still young but already mature, did not fail to see and reproduce the most varied aspects of American life. In his later career, Sienkiewicz traveled extensively and he wrote his famous *Letters from Africa* and his excellent book for children, *In the Desert and in the Jungle*. The foretaste of these appears in his excellent descriptions of California, of his travels through the whole American continent, of the exuberant American nature, of its fauna, wonderfully rich at that time. All animals, all birds, fish, reptiles, insects, trees, herbs, flowers, appear in crowds and swarms in that magnificent panorama. (p. 16)

If one seeks to reduce Sienkiewicz's technique of the historical novel to its main elements, one may easily be tempted to regard the *Trilogy* as a renewal of Walter Scott and [Alexandre] Dumas. We have in the *Trilogy* a combination of purely historical motifs with motifs of a love story, which is the essential trait of the novels of Walter Scott and Dumas. The similarities between the *Trilogy* and *The Three Musketeers* are easy to discover, beginning with the fact that both Dumas and Sienkiewicz presented four and not three "musketeers." But this is not important—what is important is that Sienkiewicz's heroes are marvellously true to the essential traits of the Polish national character. Sienkiewicz has been criticized for having amplified his fictional heroes to such a degree that they eclipsed the figures of historically known persons. Another accusation has been that he reduced his picture of Poland of the seventeenth century to only war and love, splitting his heroes between these two spheres of life. . . . But this accusation is not realistic; even in the war through which we have just passed our soldiers were split between the same two spheres of life. Brückner has justly observed in his *History of Polish Literature* that one must be thankful to Sienkiewicz for raising his novels from the sand of the small petty details of everyday life in which the romances of our disciples of Walter Scott were plunged. Besides, it is not true at all that Sienkiewicz is guilty of such a reduction. To be sure, his chief heroes might be considered symbolic figures representing the mass of the nation, but he surrounded them with an innumerable crowd of secondary types and presented various scenes of the life of the community in towns and country.

The structure of his novels is uniform; the characters are generally divided into two contrasting parts, just as in Tolstoy's *War and Peace:* Poles and enemies. But Sienkiewicz is fair to the political enemies of the Poles, and his novel is not at all a novel of xenophobia. This method of contrasting juxtapositions is in general characteristic for Sienkiewicz. This trait appeared in his earliest stories, such as *Janko the Musician*, where the poetic soul of a peasant child is opposed to the selfish Philistinism of the "cultivated" landlords. We have the same in the story of *Bartek the Conqueror*. This method will prevail in Sienkiewicz's later works. (p. 19)

Each novel in the *Trilogy* has a siege as a center; in *With Fire and Sword*—Zbaraz, in *The Deluge*—Częstochowa, in *Pan Michael*—Kamieniec. His "private" heroes are deeply involved in historical events, and they surround the historical figures of the period; these latter appear only from time to time and always in a special light, on a special level. Therefore the accusation that historical figures are eclipsed by the private heroes is entirely unfounded: the physical laws ruling this world prevent it. There are three chief historical figures: in the first novel—Prince Jeremi Wiśniowiecki, in the second—the priest Kordecki, in the third—King Jan Sobieski. Together with the three sieges they represent historical, geographical, and moral centers.

Sienkiewicz's novelistic mastery is manifest in three achievements. First, in his language, with its really epic descriptions of nature and events; its amazing richness of historical, political, and military vocabulary; wonderful command of dialogue; excellent reproduction of the everyday speech of the seventeenth century (which he could find in the memoirs of that time). His historical stylization never becomes pedantic—the author found a mysterious principle for his marriage of the modern with the old. And sometimes, in especially pathetic episodes, his speech becomes truly moving.

Second, in the organization of his plot—here his imaginative resources are really inexhaustible, in spite of the fact that his novel, being a novel of incident, automatically uses all kinds of technical clichés such as separation of the lovers, fights for the bride, abductions, kidnaping, sudden attacks, escapes, battles, flights and pursuits, and duels. Therefore, Sienkiewicz of course repeats himself very often, but each time the situation and the tension which he creates fascinate the reader, and the reception of impressions is never automatic, the mystery of surprise still remains efficient.

Third, Sienkiewicz has an incomparable power of plastic evocation. In this field I think a comparison with Tolstoy might be justified. His descriptions of battles, of landscapes, of collective scenes and, of course, of individuals are always clear, precise, and genuine. (p. 20)

In his *Trilogy,* Sienkiewicz reveals himself as a wonderful painter, and as such he has created a historical fresco unique in its suggestivity, with epically great figures whose psychology is reduced to the most fundamental human feelings, attitudes, and actions. One must not forget that the *Trilogy* is a novel of incident and not a psychological novel. However, the typically Polish quality of his characters is amazing. One especially, Zagłoba, the Polish Falstaff, is the best example of his technique. Sienkiewicz . . . knew excellently the Polish writers of the sixteenth and seventeenth centuries. This knowledge armed his language; hence, Zagłoba speaks indeed as one taken from the marvelous memoirs of Pasek. On the other hand, we know—and this from the memoirs of Helena Modjeska—that Sienkiewicz met in California the real prototype of Zagłoba, in San Francisco, among the Polish émigrés he saw on his trip in 1876. Sienkiewicz knew how to form a living man in his historical costume. Besides, the *Trilogy,* especially in its first and third parts, gives us a truly poetic sense of the special atmosphere of Ukraina and the steppes—one feels as if having been transported into the regions of Malczewski and Słowacki. The picturesque and colorful quality of the oriental world (of the Tartars and Turks) deserves mention; particularly since some beautiful short stories are interwoven with the novel. Finally—the brilliancy of some episodes in *The Deluge* and the masterfully done characteristics of different figures, such as the Radziwills, for instance, and scenes of domestic life in camp in *Pan Michael.* (pp. 20-1)

The chief traits of his talent and of his aesthetic methods manifested themselves in [*Without Dogma* and *The Połaniecki Family*] with the same clarity as in the *Trilogy.* However, some new traits appeared also. First of all, Sienkiewicz here again deals with individuals much more than with society as a whole, much more with the concrete story of a human life than with any abstract social, philosophical problems. True enough, both books, and especially when taken together present a social program. But at the present moment this social program has scarcely any interest although some of Sienkiewicz's views, especially his presentiment of the approaching catastrophe of European civilization, are very striking in the light of our days. The method of contrast prevails—it prevails within these two novels taken separately, and it also prevails in another sense—*The Połaniecki Family* and its chief hero are a kind of corrective to *Without Dogma* and to Płoszowski. But even if one takes *Without Dogma* itself, one sees that juxtaposition is still Sienkiewicz's hobby. The novel is a triangle, and in this triangle the main juxtaposition is between the tragic lover and the woman. . . .

[From] the point of view of realism Sienkiewicz achieved

one characteristic artifice: the author ignores entirely the fact of the presence of Russia, Prussia and Austria in his Poland. It is as if he had by a kind of enchantment created a free Poland at the end of the nineteenth century. It is quite true that this absence of any political detail in the book might be connected with the main character of the novel—for people like Płoszowski life was reduced to all the pleasures and enjoyments which birth and money secure—women, Havana cigars, good wine, travels, *belles lettres,* fine arts, and music. (p. 25)

Sienkiewicz's novel contains, besides that dogmatic didacticism, various subtle and delicate yet really daring insights into man's psychology. It is not only the story of *la peur d'aimer* which ends with a tragic love. It is more than the story of a *déraciné* (uprooted)—it is more than the picture of sickness of will, of lack of vitality, of the split personality of a man who is an actor and a spectator at the same time, a story of the tragedy of inconsistency and irrational caprice which captivate and strike Sienkiewicz's readers. It is more than the story of a modern Hamlet. Sienkiewicz sometimes dares to draw back the curtains of the elegant scenery of the life he represents and show some Freudian complexes in man's soul. (p. 26)

Finally, the last word about this novel—its end is remarkable. After a detailed, somnolent, dreamy diary written with quietly selected words, at the moment when the catastrophe is at hand and death is approaching Anielka, the reader witnesses a sudden, violent change in the rhythm and mood of Płoszowski's diary: under the blow, Płoszowski writes in short, abrupt sentences; one feels as if fate indeed were insistently knocking at the door of the defeated man. (p. 28)

Without Dogma is the story of a generation perishing because of lack of guiding ideas. The hero commits suicide. [In *The Połaniecki Family*] the writer provides ideas and principles. Strangely enough, in this novel Sienkiewicz, after his romantic and even decadent excursions, seems to return to the harbor of positivism. From a certain point of view it is indeed so. He tries to put the Polish society on a real ground, and he launches three main salutary ideas: the sanctity of marriage (already in *Without Dogma* the same tendency has been revealed), the sanctity of work, and the sanctity of soil. This is probably why the English translator called *The Połaniecki Family, Children of the Soil.* Tolstoy . . . praised very highly this novel (and *Without Dogma* also) and affirmed that he found in it the picture of an attractive society. I share Tolstoy's opinion about the novel, but I should not agree that the society presented by Sienkiewicz in this novel is attractive. Sienkiewicz appears here as a psychologist of shallow, mediocre characters with only a few exceptions, among them some of his feminine types. It is indeed as if a development of the first act of Krasiński's *Undivine Comedy.* It is a "human comedy" in which trivialities make up human life. The same method of contrasting juxtapositions prevails here once more. In the middle of a gallery of excellently drawn types belonging mostly to the bourgeois stratum . . . appears the charming figure of Marynia Pławicka-Połaniecka around whom Sienkiewicz has created a special atmosphere of captivating kindness. She corrects silently the life of her mediocre husband, she corrects it not by words, not even by actions, but simply by her presence in that life, by a kind of mysterious emanation of her moral prestige. . . . There are daring but never repulsive insights into the region of human sensuality and passion. Sienkiewicz's revelation of the irrational, destructive, and irresistible power of desire is the more striking because it appears in a story full of solid, firm bourgeois virtues. This combination of lucid observation of human trivialities and mediocrity with a deep knowledge of the inexhaustible tenderness of the human heart is perhaps the most attractive trait of this novel of double vision of human life. This is probably why Tolstoy liked so much *The Połaniecki Family,* and [William Lyon] Phelps justly stated that "Sienkiewicz is undoubtedly one of the greatest living masters of the realistic novel." . . . This novel was also guided by the Catholic idea of suffering and purification through suffering—it ends with a strangely touching presentation of the mystery of pardoning: Sienkiewicz knows indeed how to be tender. (pp. 28-9)

From the purely literary and technical point of view [*The Teutonic Knights*] was perhaps Sienkiewicz's greatest achievement. For his *Trilogy* Sienkiewicz had plenty of sources and Polish texts at his disposal—literary as well as historical. He was in just as favorable a situation with *Quo Vadis?.* But his problem became completely different at the moment when he had to deal with the end of the fourteenth and the beginning of the fifteenth century in Poland. All Polish documents and works of that period were written in Latin. The rigid Latin of the Polish historian, Długosz, covered with a classic toga the life and speech of the growing Polish nation. How could Sienkiewicz achieve the miracle of his language? Aleksander Brückner has justly said that the strong conservatism of the Polish language helped Sienkiewicz. The preservation of the old language in the speech of the peasants—this is what helped Sienkiewicz. And again, as in his *Trilogy,* but this time through the speech of the peasants, he created a highly convincing evocation of the Polish middle ages. The chief charm of the novel is hidden in the wonderful poetical feeling that Sienkiewicz himself had and conveys to his reader of the historical, elemental, powerful mobilization of the whole nation for fight, of a nation which was at that time building her great country. . . .

This was his last great work. Whatever he wrote or started to write after *The Teutonic Knights* showed that the writer had become tired. But he was indeed the father of the modern historical novel. (p. 31)

> *Waclaw Lednicki, in his* Henryk Sienkiewicz: 1846-1946 *(copyright 1948 by the Polish Institute of Arts and Sciences in America, Inc.), Polish Institute of Arts and Sciences in America, 1948, 38 p.*

MANFRED KRIDL (essay date 1956)

In the author's own words, *The Trilogy* is a 'war novel'; this designation indeed describes its character better than the usual term 'historical novel.' . . . The first two novels deal almost exclusively with war, the third devotes much space to other problems. The accounts of these wars are presented in such a way as to set the victories, heroism, and glory of the Polish forces very much in the foreground and to conceal the failures and defeats in the background. That is why the humiliating flight of the army from the camp at Pilawce is only mentioned in an indirect report, while the crushing Polish victories in small or large battles with the Cossacks and Tatars are described in detail and with great pathos. In *With Fire and Sword* the heroic de-

fense of Zbaraż becomes a kind of symbolic central motif. A similar focal point in *The Deluge* is the defense of Częstochowa (an old shrine city) and, in *Mr. Wolodyjowski,* the defense of Kamieniec Podolski. Such inglorious facts as the treason of some Polish magnates and their going over to the Swedish side are confined to a single, though powerful, scene in the castle of Prince Radziwill. The reader finds out only indirectly and fragmentarily about the seizure of Kraków and Warsaw by the Swedes. Naturally, a writer has full right to choose for his novels whatever motifs he likes, but this very choice describes the author's personality and the character of his work. . . . (p. 382)

The war-like character of the novel is emphasized even more forcefully by the almost complete absence of cultural and social life, while the national mores are indicated only where they influence the ways of war. . . . [It] is useless to complain, as did both older and more recent critics, that *The Trilogy* gives a one-sided and even distorted picture of the past. This is true if we compare *The Trilogy* with historical documents. But to compare history with a fictional work of creative imagination is always dangerous, for it confuses two completely distinct domains. Much was written about the fact that Prince Jeremi Wiśniowiecki, known in history as a brawler and cruel oppressor of the Ukrainian peasants, is presented in *The Trilogy* as a shining hero and the savior of the Republic. The point is, however, that the fictitious Wiśniowiecki must not be treated as a 'falsified' historical figure but in his own right as the hero of a novel, a fictional hero, who is quite different from his historical namesake. (pp. 382-83)

[*The Trilogy*'s] concentration on action naturally affects the portrayal of the characters, which is simple and without any indication of the more subtle issues of personality or psychology. The characters give the impression of being carved in one solid block: we have a great leader, an excellent soldier, a noble knight, a bragging coward, and a meek giant of athletic strength (Podbipięta). It is easy to understand them, for they present no enigmas, they do not perplex the reader who likes them for their simplicity. (p. 384)

Another trait of the structure of *The Trilogy* is the alternation of historical and fictional motifs, as well as of scenes full of horror and dramatic suspense, with happy and even humorous scenes. The latter device is particularly valuable in avoiding monotony. Sienkiewicz also makes frequent use of the familiar device whereby a hero is placed in a desperate situation only to be rescued in the most unusual manner; or he has him overcome an enemy whose invincible strength has been much touted. (pp. 384-85)

[*Quo Vadis*] deals by its very nature with other subjects than war; more space is given the social and historical background, the characters are more carefully and substantially drawn and differentiated as human beings, not simply as social types. . . . But the action is nevertheless the dominant element, built on a complex of historical and fictional plots. . . . As in *The Trilogy,* historical scenes are interwoven with fictional ones, the grim episodes with happy ones. The pagan world is more impressive and colorful than the Christian, which is somewhat stiff and pale, overpowered by the magnificent scenes of the raging Rome of the Caesars. The juxtaposition of these two worlds is artistically to the advantage of the pagan, a result which was even used as a reproach against the author. The reason for this inequality may result from the fact that Sienkiewicz's sensuous imagination reacted more forcefully to the world of external, physical phenomena than to the purely spiritual ones which necessarily predominated in the life of the Christians. If they also had their dramas and conflicts, these were of an entirely different kind from those of the pagan world. We do not even see them in the novel. We find, on the other hand, scenes of Christian martyrdom which showed Sienkiewicz's talent at its greatest. (p. 385)

[Neither] psychology nor contemporaneity were fields well suited to Sienkiewicz's talent. In [*Without Dogma*] he paid tribute to the fashion set up by Bourget; [*The Polaniecki Family*] is a rather accidental and transitional literary experiment, after which he returned to his proper genre, the historical novel. This field lay closer to the natural bent of his imagination and his finest accomplishments are all in this genre. (p. 386)

> Manfred Kridl, "Positivism and Realism," in his A Survey of Polish Literature and Culture, *translated by Olga Scherer-Virski (copyright 1956 by Mouton & Co., Publishers), revised edition, Mouton Publishers, The Hague, 1956, pp. 347-402.**

MIECZYSLAW GIERGIELEWICZ   (essay date 1968)

In Sienkiewicz's hands, the short story became an instrument of definite action; its purpose was to stir public opinion and to provoke repercussions. Later, this tendency did not disappear completely, but practical aims were replaced by more general motifs. (p. 74)

Structurally a number of the stories were ambitious undertakings containing a résumé of the protagonist's life with one striking episode standing out as the main component. Those in this category are "The Lighthouse Keeper of Aspinwall," the portrait of a political refugee; "Lux in Tenebris Lucet," a sketch of an unsuccessful artist; "The Organist from Ponikla," a biography of a country musician; "From the Memoirs of a Poznan Tutor," an account not only of a pupil, but also of a tutor who realized that he was ill with consumption and that his days were numbered. They were not just casual sketches but studied portraits. The intense emotional coloring was tied in with Sienkiewicz's main characters. They were often helpless, born to be victims and provoking compassion.

Sharp contrast was one of the favorite structural devices which the author used in order to enhance the emotional impact of his stories. A satirical attitude was often juxtaposed with that of pathos. Irony was another means which the author introduced with considerable skill.

For a long time, the writer's pessimism weighed heavily on his heroes. Most of the stories ended with the demise of the main characters. The author patiently traced a path of disaster in which human lives were threatened with grief, lunacy, and extinction.

Some incidents kept cropping up in the author's works. In both "Jamiol" and "The Organist from Ponikla," the victims could not walk through deep snow, became tired and sat down, only to meet their deaths. Another episode the author tended to repeat was the description of prolonged dying, which occurred in "Lillian Morris," "Yanko the Musician," "From the Memoirs of a Poznan Tutor," "Lux in Tenebris Lucet," and "Let Us Follow Him." It was fascinating to observe how the identical motifs acquired a different emotional tone.

The effectiveness of some tales depended on their language. In stories dealing with life in the country, the author confronted the peasant dialect with the vulgar jargon of officials and the elaborate elegance of the speech of the gentry. In "Charcoal Sketches" he inserted a parody of typical church sermons, which were so abstract and sublime as to be totally incomprehensible to the parishioners. The *pointe* in "The Lighthouse Keeper of Aspinwall" was dependent upon the poetic charm of *Pan Tadeusz*. "The Tartar Captivity" and "Memories of Mariposa" indicated the writer's fascination with the language of the seventeenth century, which was so important in the *Trilogy*. Among other works the brief "Sabala Fairy Tale" was written in the dialect of the Polish highlanders.

The best stories were probably those in which Sienkiewicz's satirical vein found its expression, e.g., "Bartek the Conqueror", and those with a highly coherent structure and artistic economy, e.g., "The Lighthouse Keeper of Aspinwall." (pp. 74-5)

The texture of the *Trilogy* belonged to history, but some recent incidents also left their mark. During the long work on the cycle many events occurred to which the writer could not remain indifferent. When he started to write *With Fire and Sword*, there were reports of anti-Semitic disturbances taking place in some Ukrainian cities. These might have inspired the wild mob scenes included in the novel. (p. 84)

Such links with then current problems enriched the texture of the *Trilogy* and added to its emotional vigor. It could be taken by the readers not only as a historical narrative but as a camouflaged struggle with timely, burning issues as well. This made the *Trilogy* more meaningful to Sienkiewicz's countrymen; but its initial success among foreign admirers resulted only from its narrative value and qualities of craftsmanship. (p. 88)

Recently [Zygmunt] Szweykowski produced a . . . theory, suggesting that Sienkiewicz intended to write a legend of the national past rather than a truly epic work. If this interpretation were to be accepted, it would scamp the writer's careful and systematic study of historical sources and his defense of the historical novel as a legitimate literary genre. Moreover, his contemporaries received the *Trilogy* as a truly historical narrative, and it would hardly be reasonable to assume that the author's estimate of his own book differed so drastically from that of his readers. For succeeding generations of Poles, the historical material contained in the work became less significant and was overshadowed by the fictional components. Naturally enough, they began to attribute to the work a legendary flavoring. However, this was due rather to the changed attitude of the readers than to the intricate qualities of the *Trilogy*. (p. 91)

The structure of the *Trilogy* is better appreciated when it is remembered that each novel appeared initially in periodical installments. . . . Some drawbacks of serialization were noticed by French critics who found it perilous to literary craftsmanship and protested against its abuses. One of the most obvious difficulties was the writer's inability to see the work as a whole and to add the necessary final touches. (pp. 96-7)

From the very start, Sienkiewicz introduced in *With Fire and Sword* a device aimed at maintaining cohesion in the story. He anticipated prospective events by referring to the widespread custom of predicting the future by observing nature.... (p. 98)

Another means of strengthening the unity was the use of flashbacks. They were especially helpful when they were repetitive and showed the same episode from different angles. (pp. 100-01)

Flashbacks mixed occasionally with predictions, especially if the unity of the work stood a more prolonged test. (p. 101)

Coordinated anticipation and retrospective flashes acted as an additional means of enhancing suspense. They kept interest alive despite the fact that serialization extended reading for many months and, even when occasional links were overlooked, they produced an illusion of continuity.

Naturally, such repetitive passages also performed other esthetic functions.... Such artful detours twist a straightforward narrative into a whimsical, multistoried edifice. The depicted object is shown on different levels which inevitably delays the climax and serves as a "brake of action."

In serialized novels some authors introduced spectacular collective scenes in which a large number of characters were involved. They clarified the mutual relations among the co-actors and helped to coordinate the elements of the narrative; they provided an opportunity to solve the major problems of the novel in such a way that the solution directly affected the whole party; the effect was comparable to a dress rehearsal. (p. 102)

Sienkiewicz used these collective scenes with moderation. Complicated adventures of his heroes made their simultaneous meetings difficult and rather awkward. Yet he did not disregard this device.... In all three novels, the author arranged a large collective scene at the finale.

Mastery in creating suspense was one of the striking features of the whole *Trilogy*. Despite the considerable length of the separate novels, each produced tension lasting to the very final episode. Incidents of the plot were coordinated in such a way that curiosity never subsided.... If a temporary lull took place, it usually anticipated new dramatic complications and harder trials. Whenever the mood of the narrative brightened, the author staged some theatrical surprise. (pp. 102-03)

There were cases when Sienkiewicz's technical vigilance apparently slackened. This occurred mainly in the chapters in which the romantic element prevailed. The obvious reason for this was the need of a more relaxed mood, either in view of the content or in order to settle the preliminaries for some major events. (pp. 105-06)

Sienkiewicz did not create a new means of narrative expression, sought no new devices of narrative technique, but he became a master craftsman with the tools already available. Whatever can be said of the historical background of the *Trilogy*, its treatment was colorful, infectious, and impressive. If it is ignored as history, it acquires a refreshed meaning as a legendary vision. The cycle does not reveal any new psychological or social aspects of the era, but it introduces a great number of believable characters and persuasive episodes.

The Polish controversy provoked by the *Trilogy* resulted mainly from its message. The opponents reproached the writer for a tendentious presentation of history and for complacency in undermining national vigilance and soundness of judgment. Some critics disapproved of its esthetic qualities. It has often been defined as Sienkiewicz's best achievement and the mainstay of his fame. (p. 108)

Sienkiewicz believed that there was an analogy between the dissolution and moral chaos of his own epoch, and the Rome of the pre-Christian era. He wanted to show that the same expedient which had revived the ancient world contained hope and promise for his generation. (p. 134)

Some incidents of the novel are reminiscent of the *Trilogy*. Yet in *Quo Vadis?* there is less artistic justification for adventurous components. They are loosely blended with the main conflict between Christianity and paganism, and occasionally they appear too flimsy. What in the *Trilogy* seems a natural emanation of the chivalrous era, in *Quo Vadis?* looks like a stereotyped set of tricks. It is possibly this inconsistency which discouraged some sophisticated readers. (p. 139)

Notwithstanding the meticulous planning of the plot, Sienkiewicz increased cohesion by using his well-tested devices of anticipation and flashbacks. Predictions appeared almost from the outset. (p. 140)

The composition of the novel owes its monumental outline to the distinct prominence of a few collective scenes devised on a grandiose scale. There are only four of them, distributed in the narrative with majestic symmetry: Caesar's banquet, the gathering of the Christians in the catacombs, the holocaust in Rome, and the triple martyrdom of Christians. Around these basic components, the author arranged the other episodes. (p. 143)

Sienkiewicz' place in the history of Polish literature is well determined. His international standing, though subject to obvious limitations, can hardly be ignored. He found the way to millions without debasing his literary craft or vocation. He did not discover any new vehicles of expression, but he combined skillfully the inherited ones and raised them to the level of virtuosity. He did not pave the way to the future but was a gifted exponent of the tendencies of his own period, which he reflected with dignity and dedication. (p. 165)

> *Mieczyslaw Giergielewicz, in his* Henryk Sienkiewicz *(copyright © 1968 by Twayne Publishers, Inc.; reprinted with the permission of Twayne Publishers, A Division of G. K. Hall & Co., Boston), Twayne, 1968, 192 p.*

BIBLIOGRAPHY

Birkenmajer, Jozef. "Henryk Sienkiewicz." *Thought* XIV, No. 55 (December 1939): 579-93.
> Biographical background to Sienkiewicz's literary career, from earliest ambitions to final writings, with brief, general discussion of individual works.

Curtin, Jeremiah. "The Author of *Quo Vadis?*: My Aquaintance with Sienkiewicz." *The Century Magazine* LVI, No. 3 (July 1898): 428-32.
> Anecdotal essay by Sienkiewicz's first English translator recalling visits with the author. Little is revealed here concerning Curtin's actual process of translation.

Gardner, Monica M. Introduction to *Tales from Henryk Sienkiewicz*, by Henryk Sienkiewicz, pp. vii-xi. London: J M Dent & Sons, 1931.

General appraisal of Sienkiewicz's novels and short stories and the relationship between them.

Lednicki, Waclaw. *Henryk Sienkiewicz: A Retrospective Synthesis*. The Hague: Mouton, 1960, 81 p.

Expanded version of *Henryk Sienkiewicz (1846-1946)*, with additional and updated information on Sienkiewicz and his work, along with a brief biography, bibliography, and photographs.

Segel, H. B. "Sienkiewicz's First Translator, Jeremiah Curtin." *Slavic Review* XXIV, No. 2 (July 1965): 189-214.

Describes personal and professional relationship of Sienkiewicz and his English translator, with a critical evaluation of Curtin's translations.

May Sinclair

1865?-1946

(Born Mary Amelia St. Clair Sinclair; also wrote under pseudonym of Julian Sinclair) English novelist, short story writer, essayist, biographer, and poet.

Sinclair broke new ground regarding acceptable subject matter about which women could write. Some of her novels, for example, represent a revolt against religious hypocrisy, and against Victorian sexual and social values, particularly the value of self-sacrifice, which Sinclair viewed as a destructive influence on people.

Sinclair was influenced by the works of James Joyce and Dorothy Richardson, and was the first to apply William James's term "stream of consciousness" to a literary style. As a friend of Ezra Pound and other members of the imagist group, and a student of the theories of Freud and Jung, Sinclair was conversant with contemporary ideas in literature, philosophy, and psychology. She utilized the theories of Freud in *The Three Sisters* and *Mary Olivier*, the latter considered by many to be her greatest work. Her unassuming, solitary lifestyle, reflected in the subject matter of some of her novels led Joseph Wood Krutch to say that Sinclair 'watched life rather than lived it.'

Initially Sinclair's works were poorly received in England by readers and critics alike. Only after the success of *The Divine Fire* in the United States did she receive attention in her own land.

Before World War I Sinclair was a suffragette, and during that conflict she served in an ambulance unit on the Belgian front. Her experiences at the front provided material for several books, including *The Romantic* and *The Tree of Heaven*. Sinclair also maintained an interest in psychic phenomena and spirituality, writing several short stories on those subjects. Although Sinclair was recognized in her own time as an important writer and thinker, her reputation has not endured.

PRINCIPAL WORKS

Audrey Craven (novel) 1897
Mr. and Mrs. Nevill Tyson (novel) 1898; published in the United States as *The Tysons (Mr. and Mrs. Nevill Tyson)*, 1906
Two Sides of a Question (novellas, includes *Superseded* and *The Cosmopolitan*) 1901
The Divine Fire (novel) 1904
The Helpmate (novel) 1907
The Judgement of Eve (short story) 1907
The Immortal Moment: The Story of Kitty Tailleur (novel) 1908; published in England as *Kitty Tailleur*
The Creators: A Comedy (novel) 1910
The Flaw in the Crystal (novel) 1912
The Combined Maze (novel) 1913
The Judgement of Eve, and Other Stories (short stories) 1914
The Three Sisters (novel) 1914
The Belfry (novel) 1916; published in England as *Tasker Jevons: The Real Story*
A Defence of Idealism: Some Questions and Conclusions (essay) 1917
The Tree of Heaven (novel) 1917
Mary Olivier: A Life (novel) 1919
The Romantic (novel) 1920
Mr. Waddington of Wyck (novel) 1921
Anne Severn and the Fieldings (novel) 1922
Life and Death of Harriet Frean (novel) 1922
The New Idealism (essay) 1922
Uncanny Stories (short stories) 1923
Arnold Waterlow: A Life (novel) 1924
A Cure of Souls: A Novel (novel) 1924
The Dark Night (poetry) 1924
The Rector of Wyck (novel) 1925
Far End: A Novel (novel) 1926
The Allinghams (novel) 1927
History of Anthony Waring (novel) 1927
Tales Told by Simpson (short stories) 1930
The Intercessor and Other Stories (short stories) 1931

WILLIAM LYON PHELPS (essay date 1916)

May Sinclair is to-day the foremost living writer among English-speaking women. She has a hectic, feverish, high-tension manner that is not really unhealthy; it is more the overflowing of pent-up passion. For none of her books is made by the scraping together of what lies in the dusty corners of the mind; and no one of her books is made to order; they are more like escaping steam, that cannot be repressed another instant. They are the outcome, in other words, of fiercely held convictions. If she could not write, she would burst.

This white-hot intensity is just as characteristic of *The Helpmate, The Judgment of Eve, The Three Sisters, The Belfry,* as it is of *The Divine Fire. The Helpmate* and *The Judgment of Eve* represent exactly opposite points of view, for which, however, these two books afford excellent illustrations. (pp. 226-27)

Miss Sinclair is a looker-on at the game of marriage, which gives her the vantage-ground for observing the mistakes of both players. *The Helpmate* castigates the woman, and *The Judgment of Eve* lashes the man. The whip in each case descends on the guilty party, although women are sure to believe *The Helpmate* most needed, while men will own to the necessity of *The Judgment of Eve.* (p. 227)

In *The Three Sisters,* Miss Sinclair approaches perihelion. This is the best book she has written, wrought with an art that has become thoroughly mature. The influence of the three Brontë sisters is more real than apparent; the spirit of the book shows the same unsatisfied thirst for life, the same frustration of passion, that one feels in *Jane Eyre* and in *Wuthering Heights.* Woman's inhumanity to woman is the basis of the plot; and although the scene is laid in a country parsonage, although the rector and his three daughters are all technically virtuous, the divine fire has become sulphurous; it is really the flame of hell. . . . (p. 228)

No *man* by any possibility could ever have drawn that oldest sister; she is a "designing creature," presented with subtle art. This is a real novel, an important novel; it has a real story, startlingly real characters, has no thesis, and means nothing except as a significant representation of life. (pp. 228-29)

Miss Sinclair has made astonishing progress in literary art since the composition of *The Divine Fire;* there is no comparison at all between that book and *The Belfry.* No two of her books are alike; she is more than versatile: she has something of the range of humanity itself. What an extraordinary power of contrast is shown in the clergyman of *The Three Sisters* if you compare him with the Canterbury cleric in *The Belfry!* The two men, however, are no more unlike than the two books they adorn. As Miss Sinclair grows older, her eyes become more and more achromatic: in *The Divine Fire,* she saw life through all kinds of fantastic colours; now she sees the world as it really is. (pp. 229-30)

William Lyon Phelps, "Conrad, Galsworthy and Others," in his The Advance of the English Novel *(copyright, 1915 by Dodd, Mead and Company; copyright, 1916 by Dodd, Mead and Company, Inc.; reprinted by Dodd, Mead and Company, 1929), Dodd, Mead, 1916, pp. 192-231.**

GERTRUDE ATHERTON (essay date 1919)

"Mary Olivier" is not a novel or a romance but a biography, and in covering the life of a woman from the age of two until forty-seven Miss Sinclair has adopted the happiest possible method. The suave and flowing style would consume far too much space. The book consists of a long series of vignettes, brief and sharply cut. The style is telegraphic, short sentences often without subject or predicate. Some critics of English object bitterly to this departure from the good old rules, but for my part I cannot see that anything but results matter, and Miss Sinclair certainly gets results. Her carefully considered brief sentences are winged, and fly into your brain like so many sharp little arrows. There must be thirty of forty characters in the book, and each is

as distinct and memorable as if as much time had been given to their delineation as to the cool and deliberate calculation involved in their conception. They are likeable or detestable, according to the reader's point of view—once more the futility of criticism—but I cherish a private belief that Miss Sinclair has been at pains to specialize in the detestable. It certainly gives enormous scope to her talent.

Mary Olivier's life as sketched in a rapid series of episodes, progressive and cumulative, leaves you with the impression of having watched her for forty-five years through the wrong end of an opera glass: in which you have seen her remotely but with a good measure of distinctness. She never comes anywhere near as close as the minor characters, but you know her nevertheless. Whether you like her or not again depends upon your personal bias. Certainly you are forced to sympathize with her, whether she is writhing in the sharp pangs of adolescence, or in the claws of a spiteful fate; and you close the book with a feeling of satisfaction that the climacteric is evidently deferred, and that, as she is still young, like many other intelligent and active women of today at the age of 47, she may yet meet a man who will really compel her to fall in love with him. (p. 445)

[Miss Sinclair] has given us a new gallery of portraits which we may not like but always remember. Her bounders, in which she has specialized, for instance, are inimitable. You never for a moment question the truth of her portraits. While you sense remorselessness you do not accuse her of personal prejudice against the sex in general. She has merely chosen a different line, and if she has "put it over," as we say, so much the more honor to her talents.

She had one moment of weakness in "Mary Olivier." Jimmy Ponsonby promised to be the very flower and perfection of England's manhood. The reader fell as pleasurably in love with him as the little girl did. But Miss Sinclair promptly extinguished her sinful lapse and our hopes. She accused him of some unmentionable crime and packed him off to Australia. He survived only in the memory of the heroine, and was, we suspect, the secret but inexorable rival of the men to whom she was tenuously drawn thereafter. . . .

Nothing could be more striking than the contrast between our earlier New England stories of stranded old maids, whose martyrdom consisted in banishing lovers and all their other rights in life for the sake of an invalid and selfish mother, and the excessively modern treatment of the same theme in "Mary Olivier." True, Mary did not take to suffrage, or even to authorship, until late in life, but she had an incurable optimism and a buoyant philosophy founded on the somewhat vague pantheism of her early girlhood, and cemented by her conversion to the didactic Germans. She lived for the most part in the intellectual ether and finally achieved a high measure of self-hypnotism, during which she banished importunate desires and regrets.

I fancy this last phase of her development will appeal to many women. . . . Miss Sinclair's method—I shall not give it away—is . . . picturesque, and while beyond the reach of the average woman—Mary Olivier was a poet—is highly to be recommended to the imaginative. (p. 446)

Gertrude Atherton, "May Sinclair's Biographical Novel," in The New York Times Book Review *(© 1919 by The New York Times Company; re-*

printed by permission), September 7, 1919, pp. 445-46.

R. BRIMLEY JOHNSON (essay date 1920)

[Miss Sinclair's] genius for moving with the times is evidenced . . . by her appreciation of Miss [Dorothy] Richardson (the most advanced of all our novelists). . . . But it is equally obvious in her own work. "The Tree of Heaven," for instance, reflects the war atmosphere most poignantly from the point of view of those who were young then. (p. 34)

[No] national or race psychology is here attempted. The world-tragedy is used, by a great artist, as local colour for private tragedies. Nowhere else, however, can we discover so striking a proof of Miss Sinclair's unconquered vitality. Suffering everywhere is—inevitably—supreme. The noblest of parents are left bereft: youths of promise are cut off in their prime: their sister loses the lover she had just realised: the torture of a sincere conscientious objector is laid bare. Yet the impression remaining is one of beauty and happiness, faith and love. What we remember most vividly, what we recognise as the permanent gift from the whole story, is a fine picture of the splendid possibilities within humanity. Men and women are shown mighty in tribulation; as they had been glorious in joy. In part, no doubt, this effect is produced by the rare understanding between two generations, the comradeship of both Father and Mother with children, the fine sanctity of marriage. But, though we have doubts and difficulties—without which life cannot be—the best pervades all. Because there is patience in misunderstanding, and trust under the clouds, none of the characters prove ultimately false to themselves. Faith is justified of her children. (pp. 40-1)

Once more, again, Miss Sinclair proves her vitality, her adaptability, and her continued youth, in "Mary Olivier," where all these conditions are reversed. This is a profound tragedy, the poignant record of a wasted life. But, on the other hand, it is a successful experiment in the manner of Miss Richardson. Of course, Miss Sinclair is too great an artist to imitate. Superficially, she does not recall the model. But she has here entered right into the last stronghold of the new movement; adopting a scheme and manner that is absolutely the same. Which is to say that this whole, fascinating story is a record (*not* a composed picture) of one life, the experience of daily emotion given to one charming girl. All the characters, all the events, each stage of Mary's development, are drawn from within; as they rise gradually above the horizon of her consciousness. We have, not only her words and deeds; but her thoughts, her emotion, her instincts—even the sub-conscious self. The actual story, indeed, has more form than any of Miss Richardson's—something not altogether unlike a beginning and an end; the persons and the happenings are more closely linked and dramatically arranged; but it is written with the same "final" realism, the same inward atmosphere, the same devotion to reality. Even the terrible shadow of inherited insanity, from which none of the family is quite exempt, comes to us only as its hold tightens round Mary herself. It is not implanted from without by the onlooking novelist: he who knows what the victim only suspects. It is not, perhaps, over-fanciful to find in it some justification (or explanation) of the *composed* narrative. Lives so tortured do often move in a vicious circle: and being largely cut off from humanity at large, *are* rounded off and completed after a fashion

more nearly akin to fiction than to the experience of ordinary, more fortunate, individuals. (pp. 41-2)

[We regard "Mary Olivier" as] the one deliberate variation (from an experienced novelist) of Miss Richardson's new methods: an indication, perhaps, of the permanent influence they may be destined to effect upon English literature.

It is not necessary to enlarge upon the art of Miss Sinclair in general terms. Its essential qualities are capability, catholic sympathy, and generous optimism. But here, and for us, its value depends on the fact that, through maintaining her youth, seeing and welcoming the best in all new movements and tendencies, she has moved with the times; so that, although she has been writing for over twenty years, she is yet absolutely one with the art of to-day, a leader among war-novelists as advanced as the most original. (pp. 42-3)

R. Brimley Johnson, "May Sinclair," in his Some Contemporary Novelists (Women), *Leonard Parsons, 1920, pp. 33-43.*

ROBERT MORSS LOVETT (essay date 1921)

Miss Sinclair's work has approached such dimensions that it is appropriate and convenient to speak of it by periods. *The Divine Fire* has the characteristics of an early novel of extraordinary promise. *The Three Sisters* is the work of a mature and practiced hand, a genuine fulfilment, a classic in its balance and symmetry, its understanding and authority. In this novel, as in *The Tree of Heaven*, the author works in the frame of family life, and develops a pattern of considerable breadth and variety through the interaction of her characters. In *Mary Olivier* the tendency is perceptible to limit her theme to the interests of a single personality, to replace width of application by depth of implication, and to seek compensation for the narrower outlook by more intense penetration. This tendency becomes more marked in her last novels, *The Romantic* and *Mr Waddington of Wyck*, but instead of pursuing an autobiographic method of self-analysis, Miss Sinclair presents her heroes objectively, as seen by other characters and tested by them. (p. 699)

In *The Romantic* Miss Sinclair works through tragedy; in *Mr. Waddington of Wyck* through comedy. The former remains a masculine, the latter a feminine book. It satisfies George Meredith's definition of comedy, and presents a world which, for all the titular distinction of man, is really dominated by shrewd, witty, clear-eyed women. Miss Sinclair succeeds better with comedy than with tragedy. There is over-emphasis in *The Romantic*, an insistence on the detail of every occurrence, as well as a certain apparent striving for unity and strain to preserve the point of view by having everything seen by Charlotte. The fact that she loves John Conway and that she pays with her love for every episode in his revelation makes the story quiver with pain. *Mr Waddington of Wyck* is exact in design and perfect in texture without a moment of self-consciousness on the part of the author. It has an atmosphere of good-nature about it. . . . Among the minor artifices of the story the skilful use of properties with their Freudian connotation should not be forgotten. Mr Waddington's canary yellow waistcoat, and his pyjamas flaming in orange, are like Malvolio's cross-gartered stockings, the symbol of the self-love with which he is sick. (p. 703)

Robert Morss Lovett, "Miss Sinclair's Later Work," in The Dial (*copyright, 1921, by The Dial*

Publishing Company, Inc.), Vol. LXXI, December, 1921, pp. 699-703.

BERTRAND RUSSELL   (essay date 1922)

[Miss Sinclair belongs to] the tradition of Descartes, Spinoza, Locke, Berkeley, and Hume—of those who pursue philosophy in the time they can spare from their regular avocations. Such writers have a certain quality of freshness and lively interest which is difficult to preserve when teaching and examinations fill a large part of the working day. This quality exists in Miss Sinclair's philosophical writing, and gives it a value not dependent upon its claim as an actual contribution to the corpus of philosophy.

"The New Idealism" is concerned to defend the primacy of mind, and its essential contribution to the objects of knowledge, against the attacks of the so-called "new realists," especially [Samuel] Alexander, [Alfred North] Whitehead, and [Charlie Dunbar] Broad. The defence is somewhat marred by the fact that the various writers who may be roughly called "realists" are treated too much as if they were all one. They differ widely *inter se*, and their merits are diverse. Some are good on one point, some another; by criticizing each where he is weakest, a case may be made out which would fail if each were taken as contributing only his best to a whole which is not yet complete. Not that Miss Sinclair shows any unfair spirit; on the contrary, she does the fullest justice to the authors whom she examines. But she seems not to realize what is the distinctive characteristic of the school, in so far as there can be said to be a school. The distinctive characteristic is not any metaphysical tenet, such as realism; a man might quite well be an idealist in metaphysics and yet belong to the school and be in vital disagreement with Miss Sinclair. What is distinctive of the school is a method—a method which its adherents regard as simply that of science, applied to material which has hitherto been treated in quite a different way. . . .

The philosophers with whom Miss Sinclair is disagreeing hold that all the ordinary stock notions of traditional philosophy—cause, matter, mind, space, time, knowledge, will, &c.—are hopelessly vague, and must be replaced by quite different notions before it is possible to say anything either true or false in any precise sense.

[Unfortunately, the technique of the "new realists"—the technique of analysis followed by mathematical logic—] requires familiarity with mathematical symbols, which is not possessed by most philosophers. Consequently, philosophical writers do not understand what has been done, and do not know that they do not understand it. Miss Sinclair, for example, maintains that space-time must be continuous, and that the difficulties of continuity have not been solved by Cantor and Dedekind. No person having the necessary knowledge would agree with either of these statements. . . . Much of what Miss Sinclair says about Dr. Whitehead rests upon sheer misunderstanding; but for this she is hardly to be blamed, as his books are exceedingly difficult. Moreover, she prudently confesses that this is very likely to be the case. (p. 625)

Apart from criticisms of the "new realists," Miss Sinclair's positive doctrine rests upon a distinction between what she calls primary and secondary consciousness. Primary consciousness consists of all that does not imply reflection, while secondary consciousness consists of the reflective or self-conscious parts of the mind. . . .

But we are not told what is meant by "the mind," or by being "within" the mind, so that we are left in doubt as to what is meant by saying that mind is necessary to its objects. Certain passages suggest that the difference between Miss Sinclair and some of the realists might turn out to be partly verbal, and to depend upon a difference as to the definition of the word "mind." Her emphasis upon will as the creative force in the world is, however, something which few realists could accept.

Although the above review is mainly critical, the present reviewer considers that the book is one of the best defences of idealism that have appeared in recent years. It shows admirable patience in mastering books with which the author does not agree, and does complete justice to their merits. Particularly, the well-deserved tribute to Professor Alexander shows a generous appreciation which is not as common in philosophy as it ought to be. (p. 626)

Bertrand Russell, "Philosophic Idealism at Bay," in The Nation and The Athenaeum, *Vol. XXXI, No. 19, August 5, 1922, pp. 625-26.*

REBECCA WEST   (essay date 1922)

[Miss Sinclair] is too rebellious to see quite straight as an artist. *Anne Severn and the Fieldings* is, in any case, not one of Miss Sinclair's best books because, although it contains the essential truth about all its characters, it is not true enough to the appearances of the world. The myth she has designed to express her discovery hardly holds together. There is reality in the theme of Jerrold, the man who is everything that is noble and fine, but who is evasive and turns his back on unpleasantness. . . . But the circumstances of the book are so casually imagined that the mind is sceptical. . . . [More] damaging to the effect of *Anne Severn and the Fieldings* than . . . mechanical defects is Miss Sinclair's reaction against the fluffy feminine ideal, which is the [joy of some of today's authors]. . . . Anne Severn is her author's declaration that a woman can be passionate and sexual and yet a cool and dignified human being. She is rather more that than she is a person. She has something of the almost priggish open-airiness and self-reliance that the early pioneers of the higher education of women strove to inculcate in their pupils. She interrupts the story to say "Yea" to a "Nay" that was uttered in a controversy outside it. When she intervenes in the processes of the tractor ("she stooped, did something mysterious and efficient with a lever; the wheels dipped, raising the shares to their right level, and the tractor set off again") there is a surface on the description of her action, a glossy surface such as one sees on those big advertisements that hang in railway stations, which proceeds from Miss Sinclair's consciousness that many people have alleged from time to time that the things that women do with levers may be mysterious but are not efficient. It is this slight disingenuousness in the conception of the principal character that makes the book distinctly less impressive than Miss Sinclair's novels usually are. For it is primarily a novel about passion; and when one is shown Anne consumed by passion, the very power of her creator makes us shocked and incredulous. This is the real thing; but how startling it is that Anne should have felt it. One feels as a headmistress might if she discovered that the head prefect was engaged in an ardent love affair. This is not to say that Miss Sinclair is not a gifted and delightful artist. She has shown herself that in other volumes; she shows herself that here, in the description of the happy peace of Wyck on the Cotswolds, and in the characterisation of the Fieldings. But perhaps just because here is a romantic theme, that might well involve its writer in adherence to the romantic conception of women, she has forfeited one tiny part of her artistry. (pp. 270, 272)

Rebecca West, "Notes on Novels: 'Ann Severn and the Fieldings'," in New Statesman (© 1922 *The Statesman Publishing Co. Ltd.), Vol. XX, No. 503, December 2, 1922, pp. 270, 272.*

JEAN DE BOSSCHERE (essay date 1924)

["Mary Olivier"] is undoubtedly the toughest, the most compact of Miss Sinclair's works. It is built of even, well-laid bricks, bound together by a mortar which is consistently good in quality. The whole is a harmonious composition. "The Three Sisters" is Miss Sinclair's masterpiece, but "Mary Olivier," equally among her works and among the best literary productions of the last few years, holds a special position. It is the model of modern romance, and is as far removed from the old convention as are the novels of Dorothy Richardson and James Joyce, except where it shows too great a respect for certain dead institutions or laughable professions of faith. But this defect is its sole weakness, and is weakness, moreover, only to the philosopher or anarchist. In avoiding cynicism, the author is sometimes betrayed into the use of ancient currencies. In any case, she is the least conventional of women writers.

The form of "Mary Olivier" is new; it is an experiment—a sudden intellectual gesture of the author. This experiment is a complete success. Besides being solid and compact, the book contains a quick succession of pictures. One gets the impression of an album of highly finished engravings, filled with useful details, well-grouped, and not interfering one with another. Moreover—and this is most remarkable considering the complete revolution in Miss Sinclair's style—these pictures have her old perfection of finish. They are harmonious. Through many pages I detect more than the ordinary cadence of prose. There are two rhythms—now appearing in the thought, now in the structure. When the rhythm is closely allied to thought, it echoes in the cadence of phrases, their punctuation, their length; when the rhythm merges into structure, the prose leads up to a culmination and finishes abruptly with some curious climax, which invariably haunts the memory. (pp. 82-3)

Miss Sinclair's pitifulness has made her the champion of [the] hidden tragedies of the misunderstood. With infinite subtlety and justice she reveals the useless sacrifices and fruitless devotion of humble and obscure souls, who are groping towards each other in a fog of misunderstanding, ignorant of each other's psychology and tendencies. One of her books, "The Life and Death of Harriet Frean," deals with a similar theme. But here is no such secret bond as enables the ignorant to understand the enlightened; the humble, the conceited; the simple, the complex. And at the end, after her mother's death, the daughter, who is the central figure of this novel, discovers her mistakes, and is horrified at the futility of her sacrifice, of sacrifices which in her mother were equally mistaken. The author's insight, or her charity, creates from this theme a short, simple tale—a study in fine parallels, as well as in correct and studied angles. (pp. 83-4)

[Miss Sinclair] manages, by virtue of the wholeness and confidence of her gift, to see the world without a veil, with directness, as if it were the first time it had been looked upon. (p. 85)

When Miss Sinclair depicts a mediocrity such as Ranny Ransome in "The Combined Maze," or a determined constructor like Jevons in "Tasker Jevons," our desire for direct communication with another human being is aroused. . . . If Ranny Ransome were to tell us the story of his life, there would be nothing in it but relative truths, truths relative to things and to institutions in which we may not believe. But when Miss Sinclair tells us the story of this mediocrity, we are brought face to face with a personality who is a type, the representative of a struggle, obscure and sombre in its anonymity. He is enhanced by every-day misfortunes which are diabolical in their paltriness. We see in him the history of Everyman. Ranny is one of Shakespeare's puppets. He does not know he is a puppet, a phantom like everyone else. May Sinclair knows it; what is more, she loves him. And from her knowledge of this universal misery and her love, is born her greatness as a writer.

If she had not first given herself to them completely, Miss Sinclair would not have been able to understand the infinitely small creatures she has often shown as struggling on the world's stage. She knows that vast charity is the key to the secrets of the heart. (pp. 86-7)

The multitude of the characters appearing in Miss Sinclair's work is proof enough that she has penetrated into all kinds of people. But she specially inclines towards the humble, on the one hand, and the creators, on the other, poets or writers, living on the proceeds of their art.

She must from the first have had some presentiment of her own strength. Her early figures—as in "Two Sides of a Question" and "Mr. and Mrs. Nevill Tyson"—are good outline sketches of those which appear later on, like Waddington, Charlotte Redhead, and the characters in "Mary Olivier"; and if these early figures are wanting in force and emphasis, it is due to the author's lack of practice in writing. A writer does not master his medium all at once. But in "The Divine Fire" Miss Sinclair has acquired the master's certainty of touch. The personality of the hero is indicated in a few strokes. One does not desire the smallest elaboration or re-touching. And when, after reading Miss Sinclair's later volumes, one re-reads "The Divine Fire," one sees it in a new light. The characters are renewed, and one feels that if the author was less practised at the outset; she was not less inspired or less immersed than she is today. Her grasp of her characters is always so powerful as to give at first the impression that it is purely intuitive. But this impression does not linger. It is swept away by recurrent evidence of close analysis—a meticulous examination of the atoms forming the whole, with no sign of effort or fatigue in the examination. One feels, particularly in the later novels, that she has not fastened upon her atoms as one does upon a calculation that will furnish the solution of a problem. They were, from the first conception, part of her vision of the whole. I do not think that her characters grow in her mind; they appear to her at once, complete. She meets them suddenly, just as Hambleby appeared in Hyde Park, splendid and definite, to a novelist she has drawn for us in "The Creators." (pp. 87-8)

There is no distinctive stylism in May Sinclair's writing; but harmony and precision of form are born naturally of the sentiments and the ideas that she expresses. In this way, without artifice, her talent has become prodigious. It is not a congeries of theories and mannerisms somehow contrived together. It is simple in a way that may not be called facile. The unity of her style defies even the closest analysis, for its elements are poured into a clear fine mould. To have a just idea of the inner beauty and force of her writing, one must consult her later books: the first pages of "Tasker Jevons," for example, the whole of "Mary Olivier," long parts of "Harriet Frean," or certain passages, perhaps the most enchanting of all, in "The Three Sisters." The ardent, serious play of "The Three Sisters" could not be sustained without the quality which I have mentioned. It is there, sensibly, throughout. In "Tasker Jevons" the fabric of the book is inspiration from end to end, so that it seems as if there were no construction. It is life, laid bare with an unfailing and even violent clarity. This constancy, this infallibility of touch, itself produces harmony.

Books like "The Three Sisters" and "Tasker Jevons" are a proof that the abundance, the apparent confusion, of "The Divine Fire" and "The Creators" is the result of the tireless domination of the clear spirit of the author. There is no real confusion in "The Divine Fire" and "The Creators," but a mind which absorbs everything, treating with equal power both the diversity of detail and the salient figures. In Miss Sinclair's fear of omission, this burning desire to say and to express everything, I can see a fine honesty, a prodigious fecundity, and, above all, a beautiful candor. It is evident that the author, in the fever of writing, forgets her readers and forgets their demand for simple reading, for reading that shall not be too tiring. Far from bowing to her public, she has extended her material, writing three novels at once, or rather one in which three are found interlaced. Five or six books written round a common centre—forming together an incomparable work—each tells the story of a single life. But in this extension of material nothing of the author's characteristic depth, nothing of the lucid ardor of the investigation has been sacrificed. (pp. 89-90)

> *Jean de Bosschere, "Charity in the Work of May Sinclair," in* The Yale Review *(© 1924 by Yale University; reprinted by permission of the editors), Vol. XIV, No. 1, October, 1924, pp. 82-94.*

J. W. KRUTCH   (essay date 1924)

No English novelist has more calm, keen intelligence than Miss Sinclair, and she has never had a subject better suited to her talent than that of "A Cure of Souls." To me she seemed in her last book before this to be quite lost when she ventured into dim emotional regions and attempted effects which intelligence alone cannot reach, but here she returns to her own field and, seizing upon a perfectly definite character, she reveals its every turn and traces out its effects with a skill and finality which are completely satisfying to the mind. . . .

["A Cure for Souls"] is the story of one man [Canon Chamberlain] and one trait [his lust for a life of ease]. Yet so skilful is Miss Sinclair's analysis that, though we know from the beginning what the result will be, the interest never falters and each incident has in its perfect fitness the charm of surprise. . . .

If success in achieving the end proposed were, as it is sometimes said to be, the sole test of literary greatness, then "A Cure of Souls" would be superlatively great. But it

is hardly that, for it comes too largely from the mind and is addressed too nearly exclusively to it. When Miss Sinclair decided long ago to watch life rather than to live she imposed upon herself certain limitations not of intellectual but of emotional understanding. Ignorance is the last thing that one would accuse her of. Indeed, because of her aloofness she probably knows more about life than most who have been more passionately concerned with some part of it, but she understands more than she feels, and her triumphs are triumphs of penetration rather than of participation. The great passions of humanity do not sweep through her books, but seem to come to her as things heard of and then thought about, analyzed, and evaluated rather than as resistless and compelling to herself. Even the [story's] old maid, a genuinely tragic figure, is dissected with cruel detachment. Miss Sinclair seems perched above the tumult on Lucretius's Mountain top and here there is a kind of greatness which she does not achieve. When one has finished a great novel of another tradition, "Crime and Punishment" or "Tess of the D'Urbervilles," the tumult within will not die down when the book is closed, and one is driven into the streets or fields to recover peace of soul. But no one will be compelled to walk off "A Cure of Souls." When he has finished the book his feelings will be not disturbed but calmly content, and he will be more in the mood to think quietly, to take all human life as an interesting story than to live intensely. (p. 535)

> *J. W. Krutch, "From Wisdom's Mountain Height," in* The Nation *(copyright 1924 by the Nation Associates, Inc.), Vol. CXVIII, No. 3070, May 7, 1924, pp. 535-36.*

GERALD GOULD   (essay date 1925)

The very name, "The Three Sisters," is ominous; it suggests weirds and how to dree them. The witches in "Macbeth" were three sisters, and so were the Gorgons, and so were the Fates. But then so, on the other hand, were the Graces. In Mary, Gwendolen, and Alice Cartaret there is something at once of the Witch, the Gorgon, and the Grace; there is something at once terrible, bodeful, and beautiful in them; their setting of straggling northern village and wild northern moor is singularly appropriate to their unhappy story—unhappy with an unhappiness that paradoxically seems half wanton and half inevitable: very subtly and artistically are the discriminations among their characters set off against the over-brooding family likeness. I have called their story "unhappy," though two out of the three "heroines" find certain satisfactions and adequacies in life to outweigh in the long run the sufferings and frustrations. (pp. 33-4)

[There is] the suggestion of sexuality; and, indeed, but for the free poise and speed, the touch of Artemis, in Gwendolen, and the chilly element in the calculations of Mary, the whole story might be called a study in the sexual. . . . [Sex] broods and glooms like a monstrous evil spirit over the whole. If I understand Miss Sinclair aright (and her treatment is all that there is of the most delicate and allusive), the vicar, the father of the three girls, is over-sexed to the verge of insanity. . . . This peculiarity is repeated in his youngest daughter, for whom the doctor quite frankly says that marriage and madness are the alternatives. Now, I am not protesting against this theme. . . . [But it] seems to me that the whole thing is kept at an unnatural pitch and strain. I find Miss Sinclair's pages too oppressive; even her humour gives small relief. She never allows one to breathe the common air; her very language is breathless. (pp. 34-5)

Miss Sinclair's "The Tree of Heaven" [is] . . . not the best of the novels of war-time, but the most clearly symptomatic of war-time's effect upon the novel. (pp. 64-5)

Miss Sinclair's tree grows in the garden of the Harrisons' house, a house which, as she puts it with characteristic wit, has "the air of all the old houses of Hampstead, the wonderful air of not acknowledging the existence of Bank Holidays." Anthony Harrison is a successful business man—successful not merely by grace, but by nature. . . . [Beyond his] family looms The Family. There [are] Anthony's . . . wife's mother, "Grannie," and Grannie's three unmarried daughters—Auntie Louie, Auntie Emmy, and Auntie Edie. These three aunties are—as is proved by the very fact of their usually being thought and spoken of as aunties—only subsidiary adjuncts of the main story: they are, however, the most effective and memorable part of the book. They are all starved, warped, defeated. Miss Sinclair's method of dealing with them is entirely objective and pitiless. Every detail of their physical unattractiveness, every variation of their jealousies and disappointments, is emphasized with that uncanny insight and thoroughness of which she is past master. It is a hard picture: it is not correlated with the larger solaces and redemptions of the spiritual life. But, for what it is, it is wholly successful. It reminds us that peace hath her miseries no less profound than war. . . . I am inclined to think that the book loses somewhat in artistic proportion through the extraordinary power and finish of the subsidiary part devoted to the "aunties." Attention is distracted from the far larger but slightly less successful story of the Harrison children themselves. The story is *their* story, even though it is primarily their mother's, for their mother lives in them: and it is their story because it is designed to show the effect of war upon them. The fact that Miss Sinclair succeeds with the "aunties," who are within her compass, and fails with the war, which necessarily is not, is a summary criticism of all this type of literature. (pp. 66-8)

> Gerald Gould, "Psychological: The Influence at Work" and "Sociological: War-Time," in his The English Novel of To-day, *The Dial Press, 1925, pp. 27-40, 59-68.**

ABEL CHEVALLEY (essay date 1925)

When one reads Miss May Sinclair's books successively, what strikes one at first is the predominance in the principal characters (almost all feminine) of what is most elementary in nature: the physical instinct of love. They are all haunted by it. It is an obsession: The Divine Fire is also the human fire, which consumes while it purifies.

There is no shadow of brutality or sensuality, still less, be it understood, is there any obscenity or conscious or unhealthy excitation in these sometimes burning pages. But the eternal voice of sex sounds through them all without respite. A long, slow clamour emanates from them, telling of the human being's blind aspiration toward love, his catastrophes, his punishments, his illusions and his disillusions. Since Jane Eyre, no woman has more completely expressed the instinct of woman.

If there is one woman novelist of our day who is seemingly dedicated to interpret anew the Brontë sisters, it is as-

suredly Miss May Sinclair. In a considerable portion of her work, she combines and blends the principal traits of the characters of Charlotte and Emily. She continues the inspiration of their work; with the freedom of a freer day, in the light of a more advanced knowledge of the soul and body, she completes it and refines upon its execution. She knows, in particular, the gamut of hysteria, and one is sure, only by reading certain of her books, that she is acquainted with modern psychiatry and thoroughly familiar with nervous disorders.

It is not imitation, but the spontaneous meeting of two kinds of temperament, that links her to the Brontë sisters. In the novel which I consider her masterpiece, *The Three Sisters,* it happens that the external circumstances recall the parish of Haworth. There is here only a pure coincidence, that has no connexion with the drama, but it adds to the interest of this remarkable book. (pp. 198-200)

The minister Carteret has killed his first wife by a succession of incautious childbirths. His second wife has left him because she was suffocating in the atmosphere of pious egotism that he breathes. . . . Carteret, with his three girls, has left his important parish in the south and abandoned his hopes of quick advancement. He has taken refuge in an obscure northern parish. . . . It is there that the three sisters are to meet their fate.

They are equally the victims of instinct, of the physical need of loving. Miss May Sinclair is not among those English women novelists who conceal the existence of such a thing. Mary, placid, waits. Alice, impulsive, is subject to disquieting disturbances of mental and physical health. [Gwendolen's] temperament is no less vigorous, but it is allied to an imagination, an artist's intelligence, and a true woman's heart. She is a natural masterpiece set between two works of nature.

The three sisters, one mature, another a child, seem condemned to celibacy, when a young doctor comes to establish himself in the neighbourhood. He is the one possible husband, and they are three. . . . (pp. 200-01)

[The] predominance of carnal love [is discernible throughout the novel]. . . . There are a thousand other things in *Three Sisters:* realism of depiction, idealism of intention, influence of heredity and of temperament; bitter criticism of the conventions which, had they been respected, would have led to the degradation of Alice; apology for the instinct and logic of life which saves two human beings by their very sins; and, finally, the irreducible opposition of generations. One feels that Samuel Butler has passed this way. In contemporary fiction there is no longer a self-respecting novel in which the father is not detestable and abhorred.

The true subject of the drama is not only the battle for the husband; it is the calm ferocity of instinct in Mary, its beauty in [Gwendolen], and its violent weakness in Alice. In this familiar setting, what a tragedy is this merciless competition for love and marriage! Here again Samuel Butler and Bernard Shaw have passed: it is the woman who is the aggressor.

There are long stretches in this novel, there are digressions, and sometimes rhetoric. But it is none the less admirable for its unity. The unique motivating power of all these human beings is the very one which assures the continuity of the race. (p. 203)

[Miss Sinclair's] latest books witness a sensible change [from her earlier sexual preoccupation]. She has discovered other fields and other types in which the instinct of action, the desire for production, supersedes that of reproduction. The style of these books is renovated, rejuvenated. Her first novels were written in a quasi-prophetic language, and there still remained something ecstatic in those that followed. The latest are infinitely more direct. (p. 204)

Despite her deplorable abundance, she is, it seems, the most representative woman novelist of contemporary England. If new evidence of this were required, it could be found in *Mary Olivier* . . . which is not far from equalling *The Three Sisters* in power and interest. It is again the physio-psychological story of one of those "normally tainted" families that Miss May Sinclair has persistently unveiled for us in healthy England.

As a matter of fact, one doubts that the mental and moral health of the middle classes among our neighbours is either better or worse than elsewhere. But no one, in the British novel, has done the work of dissection that Flaubert, Zola, Maupassant and their disciples accomplished in France towards the close of the last century. With more real knowledge and less brutality, Miss May Sinclair, bending tenderly over the body and heart of the modern woman, knows how to reveal the weakness of her sex without killing our respect for it, knows how to reveal the powerful human force without doing violence to a single feminine charm. (pp. 205-06)

> *Abel Chevalley, "Miss May Sinclair," in his* The Modern English Novel, *translated by Ben Ray Redman (copyright © 1925 by Alfred A. Knopf, Inc.; reprinted by permission of Oxford University Press, Oxford), Alfred A. Knopf, Inc., 1925, pp. 198-207.*

ROBERT MORSS LOVETT and HELEN SARD HUGHES (essay date 1932)

Miss Mary Sinclair's career deserves special notice because it spans the entire period from the publication of *Jude the Obscure* to the present, and reflects in a long series of novels the changing social attitudes and technical resources of the new century. She is an eclectic novelist. In various aspects her novels recall Meredith, Hardy, Butler, and suggest parallels to, if not the influence of, Shaw, Lawrence, and Dorothy Richardson. Her early work culminated in *The Divine Fire* . . . , a Meredithian novel in which the soaring spirit of Keith Rickman, poet, is contrasted with that of the earth-bound critic, Horace Jewdwine, with pointed satire of the London intelligentsia, dominated by organs of official criticism and rival publishing houses. *The Helpmate* . . . and *The Judgment of Eve* . . . are concerned with Shavian themes of the subjection of women to the family, in the bearing and rearing of children; and *The Combined Maze* . . . deals with the tragedy of youth seeking its true mating in a society ridden by marriage conventions. *The Three Sisters* . . . suggests the social criticism of Butler and the psychoanalysis of Lawrence. (pp. 427-28)

Miss Sinclair, like D. H. Lawrence, uses the method of psychoanalysis, approaching the normal through the abnormal. Her situations are built on complexes, unfulfilled desires, compensations, frustrations, wish-fulfillments, and dreams. Like Lawrence, she leans heavily on the unconscious and meets the difficulty that this region can be sug-

gested only through the conscious. It is clear also that she regards society as suffering from neuroses similar to those of its members, and reacting miserably upon the individual. The conventions, spiritual and social, of the Victorians, she views as sources of tragedy for the normal individual, especially for women. . . . (pp. 429-30)

As a whole, Miss Sinclair's novels represent the revolt against the Victorian conception of the family, against the egoism of fatherhood and motherhood, against the religious sanctions and ideals of renunciation which destroy the individual. How far this revolt has gone, how intense social criticism has become, may be estimated by comparing her treatment of maternal selfishness in Mrs. Olivier, Mrs. Fielding, or Mrs. Waterlow with Jane Austen's unforgettable picture of the same quality in Mrs. Bennet. Like George Eliot, Miss Sinclair works steadily from a theme (and like her predecessor she sometimes forces her story to its exemplification); but if her problems are similar, her solutions are obviously different. (pp. 431-32)

> *Robert Morss Lovett and Helen Sard Hughes, "The Georgians" in their* The History of the Novel in England *(copyright © 1932 by Robert Morss Lovett and Helen Sard Hughes; reprinted by permission of Houghton Mifflin Company), Houghton, 1932, pp. 413-64.*

THEOPHILUS E. M. BOLL   (essay date 1973)

[May Sinclair] belongs in that channel of the English novel that flows from the confluence of the more romantic and compassionate current of the Brontës, Mrs. Gaskell, and George Eliot, and the more realistic, more ironic, more intellect-displaying current of George Meredith, George Gissing, Walter Pater, George Moore, and Samuel Butler. (p. 314)

My complete sympathy with all three writers would place May Sinclair on a level with Virginia Woolf and the Arnold Bennett of all but his four greatest novels. My more moderate sympathy with D. H. Lawrence as a novelist moves me to rank her body of novels above his.

The core of meaning running through May Sinclair's novels is a person's progress toward becoming an individuated self, against forces outside the person, such as family, class, and convention, and inside the person, such as racial, hereditary, and singular forces. . . .

Her study of metaphysics focused her attention on the idea of reality, and her innate concern for the subjective level of life led her to make the search for the experience of reality an important theme for psychological narrative. She developed the subjective phase of what had been from the time of George Gascoigne's novel an almost objective, certainly a dramatic theme: a person's achieving the perception of reality in the form of insights into others, into himself, and into human values. (p. 315)

I offer some qualities of hers to test May Sinclair's right to a place of honor among the novelists of her time, and therefore of all time: an unseduceable integrity as an artist; substantial fresh discoveries of human behavior, of women and of men; an increasingly perfected dynamics of causation leading to an inevitable ending and a clear spire of meaning; characters who are entered to their conscious and unconscious depths, and so thoroughly comprehended as to become irrefutably real; careful, credible dramatic preparation, and the bold use of episodes as symbols to establish the drift; ingenious ligaturing of chapters; a style recognizable as hers alone, free from all clichés, rare in its slips into analytic cant, delighting with fresh images, inspired figures, and varied rhythms, and not allowing a word or a phrase to evade a supremely sensitive critical scanning; care in each novel to balance moods or modulations of a mood; freshness from book to book; an increasingly disciplined, selfless economy of means; dramatic dialogue at its best; many flashes of wit and the adequate relief of tension through comedy or irony; the recurrence of a theme (like the study of a life, or of lives, in a family setting) managed so as to surprise the reader with the variations that it has undergone; a unique honesty and fairness in reexploring earlier insights with a fresh development and a fresh conclusion to offer a balance of possibilities; and not least, the frequent excitement and even exaltation that we can identify as the lift of poetry. . . .

I have confidently placed her among the major English novelists from Samuel Butler to Storm Jameson. . . . (p. 316)

> *Theophilus E. M. Boll, "Her Place and Her Meaning," in his* Miss May Sinclair: Novelist; A Biographical and Critical Introduction *(© 1973 by Associated University Presses, Inc.), Fairleigh Dickinson University Press, 1973, pp. 312-16.*

HRISEY DIMITRAKIS ZEGGER (essay date 1976)

May Sinclair's statement that "James has influenced me considerably" is borne out by *The Cosmopolitan* and to a lesser extent by *The Divine Fire*. Both novels center on the development of the protagonists, and this development follows the same pattern F. W. Dupee found in all of Henry James's chief protagonists: "a process of coming into one's own, attaining a sense of identity, through moments of awareness and acts of renunciation." Another Jamesian characteristic found in Sinclair's two novels is a fastidiousness of tone, a preoccupation with what is noble, and a subtly developed moral sense. The protagonists themselves are scrupulous in their conscience and subtle in their analysis of the meaning and effects of their own and other characters' actions. Like many of James's characters, Frida [of *The Cosmopolitan*] wants to plunge into experience and at the same time has the impulse to renounce it.

The influence of James is most apparent in Sinclair's use of a central intelligence in *The Cosmopolitan;* indeed, the painter Durant, from whose point of view the story unfolds and the characters are portrayed, is like the Jamesian central observer—intelligent, sensitive, sympathetic, and curious. Sinclair referred to Durant in a letter as being "very Henry Jamesy." Frida is revealed through his eyes only gradually by hints and glimpses; and, as he tries to "make Frida out," he engages in considerable speculation about her motives and feelings as well as about those of the characters surrounding her.

Henry James's influence on May Sinclair's early novels was not altogether a fortunate one, since she responded to and emulated one of James's lesser aspects—what one critic has described as James's "bleak world of Higher Perceptions, Noble Ideals, Tender Restraints and Unsung Heroisms." Moreover, James tended to be somewhat veiled and restrained when touching upon such abstract and elevated matters; but Sinclair was unabashedly definite and

even allegorical. For example, in *The Wings of the Dove* James surrounded Milly Theale with a veil of tender sentiment; but Sinclair became irksomely allegorical when she described Frida in her death as having "stretched out her hands to the . . . incomprehensible, finite, infinite whole." . . . This penchant for the noble and the ideal that May Sinclair shared with Henry James became more a liability in her case because she expressed herself in philosophical and abstract terms. Whereas James emphasized "solidity of specification" and keeping close to reality, in these early novels Sinclair drew characters and actions to illustrate a predetermined set of ideas. (pp. 32-3)

Between 1908 and 1914, Sinclair's interest was beginning to shift to "things insubstantial, intricate, and ill-defined"; and she found James's later methods more suitable for this subject matter than the realism of social conditions she used in *The Combined Maze*. These Jamesian short stories have a more intricate subject matter and are concerned with vagaries of human feelings and with what is going on in the hinterland of the human psyche. These short stories show Sinclair's growing interest in psychology, anticipate her psychological novels, and mirror some Jamesian subjects and techniques.

"The Gift" . . . is indicative of Sinclair's new emphasis on her characters' inner life, on complex relationships between people, and on the theme of emotional waste; and these interests were to occupy her in all her psychological novels. Some of the themes of this story are Jamesian; and so also is the technique of the story: it is structured in a series of scenes made up of dialogue and narrative that contain the inner thoughts of the two main characters. (p. 61)

In 1911, May Sinclair wrote two short stories that show not only her familiarity with psychoanalysis but also her indebtedness to James. "The Intercessor" is a ghost story in which a young man named Garvin takes a room with an uncommunicative, apparently troubled family, the Falshaws, and begins to hear cries of a young child in the house. Before long, the ghost of a little girl is haunting his room; and he eventually realizes that the ghost is Mrs. Falshaw's dead daughter who was rejected and mistreated by her mother. Mrs. Falshaw is now tortured by her guilt and by her fear of the ghost. Garvin feels pity for both Mrs. Falshaw and the ghost; and, because of his pity and his understanding, he acts as the intercessor between the two. Through him, Mrs. Falshaw loses her fear and guilt and can accept the memory of her dead child; and the child-ghost can now rest in the knowledge of its mother's acceptance.

In contrast to Sinclair's earlier fiction, in which the supernatural is used to convey metaphysical truths, she uses the supernatural in this story to reveal emotions of fear and guilt and the darker side of human nature. Like James, Sinclair uses ghosts as representations of states of mind; and, through them, she explores human relationships. The ghost is a personification of the mother's guilt; and the intercessor, Garvin, is essentially doing the work of the psychoanalyst. The first half of the story is strangely affecting, largely because she so vividly created an atmosphere of unknown terror and oppressiveness that surrounds the house and family. The last part of the story, when the intercessor begins to exercise his influence over the mother and child, is somewhat too neat and diagrammatic and is in this respect different from James's use of the occult. In *Mary Oliver*, Sinclair's chief psychological novel, the relationship be-

tween the protagonist and her mother follows the same pattern of longing for acceptance and rejection as in "The Intercessor." (pp. 62-3)

Although May Sinclair in her reviews of other writers' works was often enthusiastic, wholehearted, and confident, she showed a certain diffidence about her own work. While this timidity about her own capabilities enabled her to learn from the criticisms of others, it also had the unfortunate effect of making her rely too much upon other writers for models: H. G. Wells for *The Combined Maze*, the Brontës for *The Three Sisters*, and [Dorothy] Richardson for *Mary Olivier*. (p. 144)

Yet May Sinclair made some contributions to the English novel and to English literature. She was one of the first English novelists to absorb the theories of psychoanalysis and to make creative use of them in *The Three Sisters*, and his novel adumbrates the lifelong themes of D. H. Lawrence. By her awareness and expression of her characters' unconscious—the sexual drives of the Cartaret sisters, the dreams of Mary Olivier, and the final unconscious musings of Harriett Frean—Sinclair brought into her novels a level of reality deeper than that which existed in the realistic novels of the previous decade. (p. 145)

Sinclair's originality in connection with the stream-of-consciousness novel was in her critical appreciation of its aims and methods, which she revealed in her critical article about [Dorothy Richardson's] *Pilgrimage*. In this article, she gave adequate definition, sympathetic understanding, and enthusiastic support to the stream-of-consciousness novel which most critics at that time misunderstood and which, as a result, they regarded unsympathetically and critically. All later criticism of the stream-of-consciousness novel, including Virginia Woolf's essay "Modern Fiction," is strongly indebted to Sinclair's article. In Sinclair's own use of the stream of consciousness in *Mary Olivier* and *Harriett Frean*, she made a number of modifications which made the style more readable and also assimilated it to other more traditional methods of structuring novels.

Not the least of Sinclair's contributions to the English novel was in helping to bury Mrs. Grundy's standards in literature by writing about sex in greater detail and with more honesty than critics of her time desired or approved. Sinclair was also a discriminating critic of modern poetry and played a part in fostering some of the best poets of her day, most of whom at the time were still unrecognized.

If one looks for the continuation of the tradition of Sinclair's novels among present day novelists, the writers who come to mind are Doris Lessing, Ivy Compton-Burnett, and L. P. Hartley. (pp. 145-46)

Finally, many of Sinclair's works can be read with pleasure for their own sake. Through the corpus of her work from *Superseded* in 1902 to *A Cure of Souls* in 1924 she presented a comprehensive view of English society of the time and provided the reader with the pleasure of seeing an intelligent, courageous, and honest mind dealing with the problems and recreating the ambience of the time. She was a distinguished and careful stylist who wrote with wit, grace, and subtlety. In her novels, Sinclair showed an imaginative sympathy for and an ability to create a wide range of characters from many classes and social milieus, from the lower middle-class Rannie Ransom in *The Combined Maze*, the farmer Jim Greatorex and the servant Essy and her mother

in *The Three Sisters*, to the squire and rector in her comic novels. Between these two classes, and most often, she wrote about English middle-class family life: the effete gentility of the London Freans; the harsh puritanism of the Vicar Cartaret in a Yorkshire village; and the sacrifice of individual thought, feeling, and aspiration to the tyranny of good manners and conformity of the suburban Ilford Oliviers.

She was at her best in recreating the world of the middle-class, dependent women in late Victorian times. Beginning with Juliana Quincey in *Superseded* and going on to the vicar's daughters in *Three Sisters*, the three maiden aunts in *Tree of Heaven*, Mary Olivier and her two maiden aunts, and Harriett Frean, Sinclair recreated the social and psychological life of these women with a completeness, sensitivity, and honesty that one seldom finds in her contemporaries. . . . Much of the continued viability of Sinclair's novels stems from her recreation of the lives of these women. Sinclair will survive as a novelist with her own particular vision because of her portraits of the dependent and often repressed women of her era in *Superseded, The Three Sisters, Mary Olivier,* and *Life and Death of Harriett Frean.* (pp. 146-47)

> *Hrisey Dimitrakis Zegger, in his* May Sinclair *(copyright © 1976 by G. K. Hall & Co.; reprinted with the permission of Twayne Publishers, A Division of G. K. Hall & Co., Boston), Twayne, 1976, 176 p.*

BIBLIOGRAPHY

Atherton, Gertrude. "The Changing Genius of May Sinclair." *Literary Digest International Book Review* I, No. 1 (December 1922): 11-12, 69.
    A review of *Anne Severn and the Fieldings* and discussion of the weaknesses of Sinclair's changing technique.

Braybrooke, Patrick. "May Sinclair." In his *Philosophies in Modern Fiction*, pp. 53-7. New York: Books for Libraries Press, 1965.
    An essay criticizing Sinclair as a pessimist, who "writes of a world of shadows, and sees it to be a world of shallow people who are merely interested in their own ambitions and comforts."

Brewster, Dorothy, and Burrell, Angus. "Post-Freudian Apron-Strings: *Mary Olivier* and *Sons and Lovers*." In their *Dead Reckonings in Fiction*, pp. 215-23. New York: Longmans, Green and Co., 1924.*
    A psychological rendering of *Mary Olivier* and *Sons and Lovers,* and comparison of the two novels.

Cooper, Frederic Taber. "May Sinclair." In his *Some English Story Tellers: A Book of the Younger Novelists*, pp. 252-79. New York: Holt, Rinehart and Winston, 1912.
    Cooper believes *Divine Fire* to be Sinclair's only completely fulfilled novel and points out several ways in which her other novels fail.

Gorsky, Susan. "The Gentle Doubters: Images of Women in Englishwomen's Novels, 1850-1920." In *Images of Women in Fiction: Feminist Perspectives*, rev. ed., edited by Susan Koppelman Cornillon, pp. 28-54. Bowling Green: Bowling Green University Popular Press, 1973.*
    A short study of several of Sinclair's works from a feminist perspective.

Kaplan, Sydney. "'Featureless Freedom' or Ironic Submission:

Dorothy Richardson and May Sinclair." *College English* 32, No. 8 (May 1971): 914-17.*
An examination of the lives of Sinclair's Mary Olivier and Richardson's Miriam Henderson, and of their self-fulfillment through developing intellectually and sexually at the expense of an otherwise suppressed lifestyle.

Mansfield, Katherine. "The New Infancy." In *Novels and Novelists*, edited by J. Middleton Murry, pp. 43-5. New York: Alfred A. Knopf, 1930.
A review of *Mary Olivier.*

Myers, Walter L. "General Aspects of Recent Characterization: The Incongruous." In his *The Later Realism: A Study of Characterization in the British Novel*, pp. 58-77. Chicago: The University of Chicago Press, 1927.*
An overview of Sinclair's grafting of elements of the unconscious sex drive into her stories, and of how this method mars her stories.

Steell Willis. "May Sinclair Tells Why She Isn't a Poet." *Literary Digest International Book Review* II, No. 7 (June 1924): 513, 559.
A brief interview with Sinclair, in which she discusses her books, her publishers, and her domestic life.

Swinnerton, Frank. "Post-Freud: May Sinclair, Dorothy Richardson, Rebecca West, E. M. Forster, D. H. Lawrence, James Joyce." In his *The Georgian Literary Scene: 1910-1935*, pp. 295-327. London: Hutchinson, 1969.*
A comment on the groundbreaking effect of Sinclair's work along with other writers of her day.

Tynan, Katharine. "Life's Many-Coloured Twist." *The Bookman* XLIV, No. 259 (April 1913): 30-1.
A review of *The Combined Maze*, described by the critic as "the height of [Sinclair's] achievement."

Wellington, Amy. "An Artist of the Supernormal." *The Dial* LXIII, No. 00 (13 September 1917): 195-98.
Analysis of two supernormal stories "The Flaw in the Crystal" and "The Intercessor" acknowledging Sinclair as an important contributor to this type during this era.

Wallace Stevens

1879-1955

American poet and essayist.

Stevens's poetic achievement is one of the most conspicuously important of the twentieth century. In his poetry Stevens blended a self-consciously elegant style with the thematic concerns of a philosopher, producing a unique and distinguished literary voice. He insisted he was essentially a romantic poet, though critics have noted more obvious artistic sympathies with the French symbolist and later imagist movements. These influences are particularly apparent in the early poetry.

For much of his life Stevens worked as an executive for an insurance firm, eventually becoming a vice-president and remaining in this position until his death. This identity as a professional businessman has puzzled Stevens's biographical and critical commentators, though perhaps no more so than were his fellow executives when they learned of his avocation as a poet. His first poems and verse plays were published in *Poetry* magazine as early as 1914, but Stevens was in his forties before *Harmonium*, his first collection, appeared.

Critics have observed that Stevens's work exhibits a greater degree of artistic wholeness than other authors whose writing is more easily divisible into discrete periods and styles. The characteristics of comic irony, a learnedly obscure vocabulary, and a somewhat mannered eloquence were already evident in *Harmonium* and endured into later work. Also noticeable in this volume is what was to be Stevens's lifelong attitude of religious agnosticism, which is clearly dealt with in the poem "Sunday Morning."

A theme crucial to an understanding of Stevens's work is the predicament of the agnostic poet in his attempt to find and fix some kind of philosophical truth. For Stevens this truth was to be attained largely by viewing existence through what he termed the "Supreme Fiction" of poetry. Some critics have found this relief from metaphysical uncertainty a bit rarefied and impersonal, and a frequent criticism of Stevens is that his poetry is overly abstract and does not portray recognizably human characters and situations.

Stevens's literary concern was primarily with subjects other than the human social order: the "order" in his book *Ideas of Order* is pre-eminently that of the mind and aesthetic sensibility. The resultant abstract quality of the poetry is acknowledged in *Notes toward a Supreme Fiction,* in which one of the three sections is titled "It Must Be Abstract." The title of another major poem, "The Man with the Blue Guitar," is

derived from the painting by Picasso and points out Stevens's aesthetic affinities with highly theoretical modernist movements in the visual arts.

Throughout Stevens's work there is evident the ambition to reach conclusions about reality through what he considered the only authentic method available—the creative use of the imagination. The poetry that grew out of this ambition represents one of the major accomplishments in modern literature. Stevens won the National Book Award in 1950 and the Pulitzer Prize in 1955.

PRINCIPAL WORKS

Harmonium   (poetry)   1923
Ideas of Order   (poetry)   1935
Owl's Clover   (poetry)   1936
The Man with the Blue Guitar and Other Poems   (poetry)   1937
Notes toward a Supreme Fiction   (poetry)   1942
Parts of a World   (poetry)   1942
Esthétique du mal   (poetry)   1945
Transport to Summer   (poetry)   1947
The Auroras of Autumn   (poetry)   1950
The Necessary Angel: Essays on Reality and the Imagination   (essays)   1951
Collected Poems   (poetry)   1954
Opus Posthumous   (poetry, dramas, and essays)   1957
Letters   (letters)   1966

EDMUND WILSON   (essay date 1924)

The poems of Mr. Wallace Stevens have now been collected in a volume, with the title *Harmonium*. Mr. Stevens is the master of a style: that is the most remarkable thing about him. His gift for combining words is baffling and fantastic but sure: even when you do not know what he is saying, you know that he is saying it well. (p. 49)

He is ironic a little in Mr. Eliot's manner; but not poignantly, not tragically ironic. Emotion seems to emerge only furtively in the cryptic images of his poetry, as if it had been driven, as he seems to hint, into the remotest crannies of sleep or disposed of by being dexterously converted into exquisite amusing words. Nothing could be more perfect in its tone and nothing by itself could be more satisfactory than such a thing as *Last Looks at the Lilacs*. But when we have gone all through Mr. Stevens, we find ourselves putting to him the same question that he himself, in the last poem of his book, puts *To a Roaring Wind*:

> What syllable are you seeking,
> Vocallissimus,
> In the distances of sleep?
> Speak it.
>
> (p. 50)

Edmund Wilson, "Wallace Stevens and E. E. Cummings" (1924), in his The Shores of Light: A Literary Chronicle of the Twenties and Thirties *(reprinted by permission of Farrar, Straus & Giroux, Inc.; copyright 1924 by Edmund Wilson), Farrar, Straus & Giroux, 1952, pp. 49-56.* *

GORHAM B. MUNSON   (essay date 1928)

Until the advent of Wallace Stevens American literature had lacked the dandy. Of swaggering and nonchalant maca-ronis there had been a-plenty, but . . . these artists are not impeccable, and impeccability is the sine qua non of the true dandy.

The impeccability of the dandy, when reflected upon, resolves into two elements: correctness and elegance. (p. 78)

Certainly as a poetic craftsman, Wallace Stevens is eminently correct—notwithstanding the probable testimony of professorial versifiers to the contrary. For they confuse the pale correctness of the copyist who adds nothing, with the fresh correctness of the creating poet who extends the range of the existing poetic order or refines upon it. But Stevens' knowledge of verbal music is profound: he has presumably absorbed the teachings of the academy: at any rate he can trust himself to make departures and yet obey the underlying laws. (pp. 78-9)

Wallace Stevens takes all the musical risks of poetry (alliteration, free irregular rhyming, irregular stanzaic forms, and vers libre) and can be counted on to overcome them because for one thing he is so cognizant of dangers. Nor is his musical range limited. It touches at one extreme the light measures of *The Apostrophe to Vincentine* and at the other the deep organ-tones of *To the One of Fictive Music* with most of the intervening tonalities perfectly under control. (p. 80)

Wallace Stevens gains elegance in large measure by his fastidiously chosen vocabulary and by the surprising aplomb and blandness of his images. . . . The whole tendency of his vocabulary is, in fact, toward the lightness and coolness and transparency of French, into which tongue he sometimes glides with cultivated ease. As for his images, they are frequently surprising in themselves, yet they always produce the effect of naturalness by virtue of their consistency with the design and the flowing motion that Stevens imparts to them. (p. 81)

The safeguards that Stevens employs to keep "the torments of confusion" from rumpling his attitude are three: wit, speculation and reticence. . . . [By] wit and mockery one maintains one's perfect poise. (pp. 82-3)

[Stevens' discipline] is the discipline of the connoisseur of the senses and the emotions. His imagination comes to rest upon them, it is at their service, it veils them in splendor. It is clearly not in the service of the mind which is philosophical and constructed for the plumbing of life in the large, and consequently in the final analysis Wallace Stevens is a temperate romanticist. The integration he achieves is exclusively one of feeling.

But Stevens has a quality that is very rarely associated with romanticism, a quality that his illustrious predecessor, Baudelaire, lacked, . . . [for] tranquillity enfolds and inheres in all of Stevens' production. (p. 85)

Because of this tranquillity, this well-fed and well-booted dandyism of contentment, Stevens has been called Chinese. Undeniably, he has been influenced by Chinese verse as he has been by French verse, but one must not force the comparison too strongly. For Chinese poetry as a whole rests upon great humanistic and religious traditions: its quiet strength and peace are often simply by-products of a profound understanding, and its epicureanism is less of an end and more of a function in a wider pattern of living than Stevens expresses. To this critic, at least, Stevens' tranquillity is decidedly American. (pp. 86-7)

Growing more reckless, we might say that if Dr. Jung is correct in asserting that in American psychology there is a unique alliance of wildness and restraint, then Stevens would seem to have another general tie with his country. I do not discover in him the ferocity that some critics have remarked upon, but there is at least a flair for bright savagery, for "that tuft of jungle feathers, that animal eye, that savage fire": he has at least an appreciative eye for "raspberry tanagers in palms, high up in orange air." With some romanticists such symbols would betray insatiable longings, the desire for a nature that never existed. But in the case of Stevens they are purely spectacular. He has achieved the restraint of a spectator, but he prefers to view the wildness of the tropical. The Old World romantic, restless amid the stratifications of his culture, yearns for the untamed: the New World romantic, a participant in the unsettled, prefers to assume the easy posture of an audience. (pp. 87-8)

No American poet excels him in the sensory delights that a spick-and-span craft can stimulate: none is more skillful in arranging his music, his figures and his design. None else, monocled and gloved, can cut so faultless a figure standing in his box at the circus of life.

There are, as A. R. Orage once observed, masters of art and art-masters. The virtue of the former is wisdom, and the virtue of the latter is impeccable form. Nowhere has Wallace Stevens been more canny and more definite than in distinguishing between major and minor, than in observing to the letter the restrictions of the art-master. (pp. 88-9)

Gorham B. Munson, "The Dandyism of Wallace Stevens," in his Destinations: A Canvass of American Literature Since 1900 *(copyright, 1928, by J. H. Sears & Co., Incorporated), Sears, 1928, pp. 75-89.*

R. P. BLACKMUR   (essay date 1931)

The most striking if not the most important thing about Mr. Stevens' verse is its vocabulary—the collection of words, many of them uncommon in English poetry, which on a superficial reading seems characteristic of the poems. An air of preciousness bathes the mind of the casual reader when he finds such words as fubbed, girandoles, curlicues, [etc.]. . . . Hence Mr. Stevens has a bad reputation among those who dislike the finicky, and a high one, unfortunately, among those who value the ornamental sounds of words but who see no purpose in developing sound from sense.

Both classes of reader are wrong. Not a word listed above is used preciously; not one was chosen as an elegant substitute for a plain term; each, in its context, was a word definitely meant. The important thing about Mr. Stevens' vocabulary is not the apparent oddity of certain words, but the uses to which he puts those words with others. It is the way that Mr. Stevens combines kinds of words, unusual in a single context, to reveal the substance he had in mind, which is of real interest to the reader. (p. 68)

If Mr. Stevens stretches his words slightly, as a live poet should and must, it is in such a way as to make them seem more precisely themselves than ever. The context is so delicately illuminated, or adumbrated, that the word must be looked up, or at least thought carefully about, before the precision can be seen. This is the precision of the expert pun, and every word, to a degree, carries with it in any given sense the puns of all its senses. (p. 72)

Mr. Stevens' tropes, in his best work and where he is most characteristic, are neither visual like Pound nor dramatic like Eliot. The scope and reach of his verse are no less but are different. His visual images never condense the matter of his poems; they either accent or elaborate it. His dramatic statements, likewise, tend rather to give another, perhaps more final, form to what has already been put in different language. . . .

His kind of condensation, too, is very different in character and degree from Eliot and Pound. Little details are left in the verse to show what it is he has condensed. And occasionally, in order to make the details fit into the poem, what has once been condensed is again elaborated. It is this habit of slight re-elaboration which gives the firm textural quality to the verse. (p. 89)

[Eliot and Stevens] work in contrary modes. Eliot places a number of things side by side. The relation is seldom syntactical or logical, but is usually internal and sometimes, so far as the reader is concerned, fatal and accidental. He works in violent contrasts and produces as much by prestidigitation as possible. (p. 88)

That is the method of a dramatic poet, who moulds wholes out of parts themselves autonomous. Mr. Stevens, not a dramatic poet, seizes his wholes only in imagination; in his poems the parts are already connected. Eliot usually moves from point to point or between two termini. Mr. Stevens as a rule ends where he began; only when he is through, his beginning has become a chosen end. The differences may be exaggerated but in their essence is a true contrast. (p. 89)

Two poems occur where the rhetoric is the vital trope—"A High-Toned Old Christian Woman" . . . , and "Bantams in Pine-Woods". . . . The first and last distichs [of "Bantams"] are gauds of rhetoric; nevertheless they give not only the tone but the substance to the poem. If the reader is deceived by the rhetoric and believes the poem is no more than a verbal plaything, he ought not to read poetry except as a plaything. With a different object, Mr. Stevens' rhetoric is as ferociously comic as the rhetoric in Marlowe's *Jew of Malta,* and as serious. The ability to handle rhetoric so as to reach the same sort of intense condensation that is secured in bare, non-rhetorical language is very rare, and since what rhetoric can condense is very valuable it ought to receive the same degree of attention as any other use of language. Mr. Stevens' successful attempts in this direction are what make him technically most interesting. Simple language, dealing obviously with surds, draws emotion out of feelings; rhetorical language, dealing rather, or apparently, with inflections, employed with the same seriousness, creates a surface *equivalent* to an emotion by its approximately complete escape from the purely communicative function of language. (pp. 92-3)

His great labour has been to allow the reality of what he felt personally to pass into the superior impersonal reality of words. Such a transformation amounts to an access of knowledge, as it raises to a condition where it may be rehearsed and understood in permanent form that body of emotional and sensational experience which in its natural condition makes life a torment and confusion. (p. 93)

Mr. Stevens is a genuine poet in that he attempts constantly to transform what is felt with the senses and what is thought in the mind—if we can still distinguish the two—into that realm of being, which we call poetry, where what is thought is felt and what is felt has the strict point of thought. And I call his mode of achieving that transformation rhetorical because it is not lyric or dramatic or epic, because it does not transcend its substance, but is a reflection upon a hard surface, a shining mirror of rhetoric. (p. 100)

> R. P. Blackmur, "Examples of Wallace Stevens" (1931), in his The Double Agent: Essays in Craft and Elucidation (copyright, 1935, by Richard P. Blackmur), Arrow Editions, 1935 (and reprinted by Peter Smith, 1962), pp. 68-102.

MARIANNE MOORE (essay date 1937)

For some of us, Wallace Stevens is America's chief conjuror—as bold a virtuoso and one with as cunning a rhetoric as we have produced. He has, naturally, in some quarters been rebuked for his skill; writers cannot excel at their work without being, like the dogs in *Coriolanus*, "as often beat for barking As therefore kept to do so." . . . His repercussive harmonics, set off by the small compass of the poem, "prove" mathematically to admiration, and suggest a linguist creating several languages within a single language. . . . The playfulness, that is to say humor, of such rhymings as *egress* and *negress, Scaramouche* and *barouche,* is just right, and by no means a joke; one's sense of humor being a clue to the most serious part of one's nature. But best of all, the bravura. Upon the general marine volume of statement is set a parachute-spinnaker of verbiage which looms out like half a cantaloupe and gives the body of the theme the air of a fabled argosy advancing.

A harmonist need not be proud of dominating us illusorily, by causing a flower in bloom to appear where a moment before there was none; and not infrequently Wallace Stevens' "noble accents and lucid, inescapable rhythms" point to the universal parent, Shakespeare. A novice of verse, required in an examination to attribute to author or century the line, "These choirs of welcome choir for me farewell," might pay Wallace Stevens a high compliment.

> Remember how the crickets came
> Out of their mother grass, like little kin,

has perfectly Shakespeare's miniature effect of innocent sadness, and the consciously pertinaciously following of a word through several lines, as where we see the leaves

> Turning in the wind,
> Turning as the flames
> Turned in the fire,

are cousin to the pun of Elizabethan drama. We feel, in the tentatively detached method of implication, the influence of Plato; and an awareness of if not the influence of T. S. Eliot. (pp. 401-02)

Again, and moreover, to manner and harmonics is added a fine and exultant grasp of beauty—a veritable refuge of "blessed mornings, meet for the eye of the young alligator"; an equivalence for jungle beauty, arctic beauty, marine beauty, meridian, hothouse, consciously urban or unconsciously natural beauty—which might be alarming were it not for the persistent foil of dissatisfaction with matter. (pp. 402-03)

Unanimity of word and rhythm has been attained, and we have the seldom exhilaration of knowing that America has in Wallace Stevens at least one artist whom professionalism will never demolish. (p. 403)

> *Marianne Moore, "Unanimity and Fortitude," in* Poetry *(© 1937 by The Modern Poetry Association; reprinted by permission of the Editor of* Poetry*; excerpted by permission of The Estate of Marianne C. Moore), Vol. XLIV, No. V, February, 1937 (and reprinted as "The Poetry of Wallace Stevens," in* Literary Opinion in America, *Vol. II, edited by Morton Darwen Zabel, revised edition, Harper and Brothers, 1951, pp. 401-03).*

YVOR WINTERS (essay date 1943)

[Stevens'] fundamental ideas are stated in *Sunday Morning,* an early poem, and in some ways his greatest. . . .

The first stanza sets the stage and identifies the protagonist. We are given a woman, at home on a Sunday morning, meditating on the meaning of death. The second stanza asks the question which provides the subject of the poem; it asks what divinity this woman may be thought to possess as a recompense for her ultimate surrender to death; and having asked the question, it replies that her divinity, which must live within herself, consists wholly in her emotions—not in her understanding of the emotions, but in the emotions as a good in themselves. This answer is not quite the orthodox romantic answer, which would offer us in the emotions either a true guide to virtue or a more or less mystical experience leading to some kind of union with some kind of deity. Any philosophy which offers the cultivation of the emotions as an end in itself, I suppose, is a kind of hedonism. In any event, that is the kind of philosophy which we find here. (p. 431)

Whatever the defects of the hedonistic theme, and with the possible but by no means certain exception of a few short poems by Stevens and of two or three poems by E. A. Robinson, *Sunday Morning* is probably the greatest American poem of the twentieth century and is certainly one of the greatest contemplative poems in English: in a blank verse which differs, in its firmness of structure and incalculable sensitivity of detail, from all other blank verse of our time save that of a few poems by Hart Crane which were in some measure modeled upon it, it renders the acute uncertainty of what we are inclined to consider the modern mind, but it does so with no uncertainty of method or of statement; it renders an acute consciousness of the imminence of death, of the sensory and emotional richness of life on this bewildering planet, and of the heroic magnificence of the religious myths which are lost to the poet and to many of the rest of us, except as memories of things long past. (p. 433)

[In] the sixth stanza of *Sunday Morning,* the stanza in which Stevens projects into the eternity of paradise the highest good which he can imagine, there appears a weary dissatisfaction with the experience, a hint of the dissatisfaction which might imaginably appear in our present life if the experience were too long protracted. This dissatisfaction is familiar to students of romantic literature under the name of ennui; it is the boredom which eventually overtakes the man who seeks for excitement instead of understanding. In the poem entitled *The Man Whose Pharynx Was Bad* we find a statement of this boredom which is both extreme and explicit. (p. 437)

The poet has progressed in this poem to the point at which the intensity of emotion possible in actual human life has become insipid, and he conceives the possibility of ultimate satisfaction only in some impossible emotional finality of no matter what kind. (p. 438)

Unless one change one's entire philosophy, having arrived at this impasse, there can remain open to one only two modes of action: one may renounce one's art and subside into a kind of stoical silence; or one may pursue, not greater intensity of experience, for human language and the human organism alike set a certain limit to progress in that direction, but experience increasingly elusive and incomprehensible. Stevens has considered both of these possibilities, but since he has chosen the latter, we may fairly examine first the mode of action which he has considered and discarded. It so happens, incidentally, that his meditation upon the possibility of renunciation has resulted in his longest single work [*The Comedian as the Letter C*]. (p. 439)

[The quality of the rhetoric employed in *The Comedian as the Letter C* at the point at which the renunciation takes place, about half-way through the fifth section: "Was he to bray . . . Because he turned to salad beds again?"] helps us profoundly to understand Stevens himself. . . . What I wish the reader to note is this: that the passage describes Crispin's taking leave of his art, and describes also his refusal to use his art in the process of leave-taking, because the art is, after all, futile and contemptible. Yet for Stevens himself the entire poem is a kind of tentative leave-taking; he has not the courage to act as his hero acts and be done with it, so he practices the art which he cannot justify and describes it in terms of contempt. Furthermore, the chief instrument of irony in this passage, and throughout the poem, and indeed throughout much of the rest of Stevens, is a curious variant on the self-ridicule, the romantic irony, with which we are familiar from Byron through Laforgue and his modern disciples; the instrument is self-parody, a parody occasionally subtle, often clumsy, of the refined and immutable style of Stevens at his best. (pp. 443-44)

Since the poet, having arrived at the predicament to which we have traced him, however, is not to abandon his art, there remains only the possibility that he seek variety of experience in the increasingly perverse and strange; that he seek it, moreover, with no feeling of respect toward the art which serves as his only instrument and medium. In the poem entitled *The Revolutionists Stop for Orangeade,* we are given the theory of this type of poetry. . . . And from this point onward there remains little but the sly look and a perverse ingenuity in confusing the statement of essentially simple themes. *The Man with the Blue Guitar,* for example, which is one of his most recent performances, is merely a jingling restatement of the old theme of the severance between the rational understanding and the poetic imagination. But the statement is never quite clear; and since the theme, though unsound, is far from difficult to understand, one is inclined to suspect that the lack of clarity is the result of a deliberate choice, a choice motivated, perhaps, by the hope that some note more moving than the poet has a right to expect may be struck from the obscurity. And if one does not always encounter such wilful semiobscurity in the later poems, one much too commonly encounters the kind of laborious foolishness to be found in . . . *The Mechanical Optimist. . . .* (pp. 444-45)

The generating mood [of *The Mechanical Optimist*] is one of ennui; the style represents an effort, half-bored and half desperate, to achieve originality; the victim of the irony is very small game, and scarcely worthy of the artillery of the author of *Sunday Morning;* the point of view is adolescent. The author of *Sunday Morning* and of *Le Monocle de Mon Oncle,* the heir of Milton and of Jonson, is endeavoring, in his old age, to épater les bourgeois. The poem is the work of a man who twenty or twenty-five years earlier was one of the great poets of the English language. (p. 446)

> *Yvor Winters, "Wallace Stevens or the Hedonist's Progress" (1943), in his* In Defense of Reason: Primitivism and Decadence *(© 1937, 1947 by Yvor Winters; reprinted by permission of Ohio University Press, Athens), The Swallow Press & W. Morrow and Company, 1947 (and reprinted by University of Denver Press, 1959), pp. 431-59.*

ROBERT LOWELL   (essay date 1947)

The subject throughout Stevens's poems is the imagination, and its search for forms, myths, or metaphors that will make the real and the experienced coherent without distortion or simplification. . . . In his later poems Stevens often uses an elaborate machinery of abstractions, but what he is saying has changed very little. His world is an impartial, hedonistic, speculative world—he is closer to Plato than to Socrates, and closer to the philosophy and temperament of George Santayana than to Plato. Directly or indirectly much of his thought is derived from the dialectical idealism of Hegel. (p. 400)

His places are places visited on a vacation, his people are essences, and his passions are impressions. Many of his poems are written in a manner that is excessively playful, suave, careless, and monotonous. And their rhetoric, with its Tennysonian sound effects, its harmonious alliteration, and its exotic vocabulary, is sometimes no more than an enchanting inflection of the voice.

The [poems in "Transport to Summer"] are more philosophical, and consider many things in this world of dark-

ness ("Lenin on a bench beside a lake disturbed / The swans. He was not the man for swans") which the Stevens of "Harmonium" would have excluded as unpoetic. His language is simpler and more mature. But structural differences makes all that has been gained precarious. Nothing like the dense, large-scale organization of his "Sunday Morning," or even the small perfection of his "Peter Quince at the Clavier," is attempted. The philosophy is not exhaustive and marshaled as in Lucretius; and it is seldom human and dramatic as in Donne. When one first reads this poetry that juggles its terminology with such lightness and subtlety, one is delighted; but as one rereads, it too often appears muddled, thin, and repetitious. How willingly one would exchange much of it for the concrete, gaudy wit of "Harmonium."

The points that I have been making are probably overstated, and they are necessarily simplified. But few poets of Stevens's stature have tossed off so many half-unfinished improvisations. Underneath their intellectual obscurity and whimsey, their loose structures, their rhetorical and imagistic mannerisms, and their tenuous subject matter, there seems to be something in the poet that protects itself by asserting that it is not making too great an effort.

The best poems in "Transport to Summer" are as good as anyone is writing in English. . . . In spite of a few beautiful sections—particularly *Begin, ephebe, by perceiving; The first idea was not our own; Not to be realized; It feels good as it is; The great statue;* and *A lasting visage*—and many fine moments, the whole [of "Notes Toward a Supreme Fiction"] seems to me to be unsuccessful. Its structure is sloppy, idiosyncratic, and repetitious. It rambles and rambles without gathering volume, and many of the sections are padded to fill out their twenty-one lines. Much of the rhetoric is extremely mannered. Certain details, such as Canon Asperin, and Nanzia Nunzio Confronting Ozymandias, seem written for Stevens's private amusement. Of the shorter poems, I think the best is "No Possum, No Sop, No Taters." It is objective and subtle in its rhythms and perceptions, and is certainly one of Stevens's most magical and perfect slighter pieces. Other small poems in "Transport to Summer" approach it in excellence but are imperfect, or have much less to them. "Dutch Graves in Bucks County" is much grander and more ambitious. The past and the present are opposed thematically. . . . It is written with tremendous feeling, pathos, and power. I think that no living poet would be able to match the magnificence of its rhetoric and resonance. A few lines are slightly mannered, and there is something a little long, formless, and vague about its development. But it is a very large undertaking wonderfully executed. (pp. 400-01)

["Esthétique du Mal"] is about as good and important a poem as T. S. Eliot's "Four Quartets" or "Ash Wednesday." Its subject is: How shall the imagination act when confronted with pain and evil? The structure is not very tight, two or three sections are not particularly good, and several others have a great number of bad or overwritten lines. The good parts can be detached, but they lose some of their momentum. But "Esthétique du Mal" is more in the grand manner than any poetry since Yeats's; and it reminds one of parts of "Cymbeline" and "The Winter's Tale"—slow and rapid, joining the gorgeous with the very simple, wise, elaborate, open, tolerant without apathy, understanding with the understanding of having lived long. (p. 402)

Robert Lowell, "Imagination and Reality," in The Nation (copyright 1947 The Nation Associates, Inc.), Vol. CLXIV, No. 14, April 5, 1947, pp. 400-02.

DONALD DAVIE (essay date 1953)

Stevens deserves nearly everything that his admirers have claimed for him. He is indeed a poet to be mentioned in the same breath as Eliot and Yeats and Pound. That is his place, and that is the company he must keep. We are called upon now not to assign a status but to define an excellence. (p. 455)

Le Monocle de Mon Oncle, for all its precious title and a few jazzy superficialities ('connaissance'), is a strikingly old-fashioned poem. This is as true of the movement of thought, as of the versification. . . . The poet thinks in Keatsian terms throughout, and the movement of thought is Keatsian too. . . . Stevens's poem, like an ode by Keats, is . . . *discursive;* it moves from point to point, always forward from first to last. Lose the thread, and you may go back and look for it. In *The Waste Land,* by contrast, it is only when the poem is grasped as a whole that each part of it falls into place.

The difference between *Sunday Morning* and *Le Monocle* on the one hand, *The Waste Land* and *Mauberley* on the other, can be put in another way. Except at certain key-points, like the image at the very end of *Le Monocle* ('That fluttering things have so distinct a shade'), the poetry and the meaning do not coincide. To get at the meaning, you have to go *behind* the poetry, whereas if you go behind Eliot's poetry you have gone behind the meaning too. Understanding *Le Monocle* is a matter of groping through a dazzle, or stripping off the caparisons, until you come, behind the rhetorical magnificence, at a structure of plain sense that is quite lean and skeletal. (pp. 456-57)

Stevens has insisted repeatedly that he is a 'Romantic' poet. This, together with what we find in the verse of *Le Monocle de Mon Oncle,* for instance, advises us of one way in which 'Romantic' may be understood. Stevens is a Romantic in the sense that Keats was a Romantic—his is to be a poetry of excess, among other things of rhetoric in excess of meaning, rhetoric for its own sake, for its 'essential gaudiness'. (p. 457)

Perhaps the most striking thing about the poetry of Stevens is its metrical conservatism. 'To break the pentameter,' said Pound, 'that was the first heave.' Stevens has never made the break; the greater part of his poetry is written in quite regular iambic pentameters. One can read critic after critic without finding this really striking feature even acknowledged. Yet there can be no adequate account of Stevens that does not take note of one of his most striking eccentricities—his extreme metrical conservatism in an age of revolutionary metrical experiment. If I am right in thinking that a Keatsian allegiance is the clue to Stevens, then his metres are accounted for—his conservatism in this department is part and parcel with his conservatism in structure and in rhetoric. (p. 458)

For Stevens, 'style', whether in life or literature, is only 'affectation' or 'mannerism' that succeeds. Admittedly the splendid hat of *The Pastor Caballero* is examined from the point of view of the beholder, not the wearer. But observe that *Infanta Marina* makes gestures of thought not *with* the motions of her wrist, but *of* those motions. The movement of the wrist does not express the motions of the mind; it invokes them and creates them. She behaves grandly not because she thinks grandly, but in order to do so. So, in *Le Monocle de Mon Oncle,* the poet's solution for the drabness and sterility that comes upon him, is 'bravura', 'the music and manner of the paladins'. If a man can no longer think and feel grandiosely, then he acts grandiosely or he makes a grandiose speech, and this renovates and exalts his thinking and his feeling. The cure for sterility is to act and speak as if it did not exist; by so doing, one destroys it.

Stevens is always mannered and affected. The affectation of his poorer poems reflects back out of the poetry upon Stevens the private individual; in his better pieces the affectation succeeds and becomes style because it stays in the poetry and builds up the public and representative figure of the poet. Where the affectation is a way of dealing with experience, with the theme of the poem, it justifies itself as poetic style; where it is a way of dealing with society, represented by the reader, it may be justified in terms of social behaviour, but not in terms of poetry. (pp. 461-62)

I am nothing if not profoundly grateful for the significant beauty that Stevens so generously provides. Only if that point is taken, can I go on to admit that, for my own part, I think the very greatest poetry is more chaste, less florid than this. . . . Yet it is Stevens's achievement that whenever we pick up his poems, he makes such reservations seem graceless and niggling. He is a great poet indeed. (p. 462)

Donald Davie, "'Essential Gaudiness': The Poems of Wallace Stevens," in The Twentieth Century (© The Twentieth Century, 1953), Vol. 153, No. 916, June, 1953, pp. 455-62.

RANDALL JARRELL (essay date 1955)

The *Collected Poems* of such a poet as Stevens—hundreds and thousands of things truly observed or rightly imagined, profoundly meditated upon—is not anything one can easily become familiar with. Setting out on Stevens for the first time would be like setting out to be an explorer of Earth. (p. 56)

Collected Poems is full of extraordinary things, and the most extraordinary of all is the section of twenty-eight new —truly new—poems called "The Rock." . . . These are poems from the other side of existence, the poems of someone who sees things in steady accustomedness, as we do not, and who sees their accustomedness, and them, as about to perish. In some of the poems the reader feels over everything the sobering and quieting, the largening presence of death. The poems are the poems of a very old man, "a citizen of heaven though still of Rome"; many of their qualities come naturally from age, so that the poems are appropriately and legitimately different from other people's poems, from Stevens's own younger poems. These poems are magnanimous, compassionate, but calmly exact, grandly plain. . . . (pp. 57-8)

[As we read "To an Old Philosopher in Rome" it] seems to us that we are feeling, as it is not often possible for us to feel, what it is to be human; the poem's composed, equable sorrow is a kind of celebration of our being, and is deeper-sounding, satisfies more in us, than joy; we feel our own natures realized. . . . (p. 59)

This is a great poem of a new kind. The completeness and requiredness of the poem's working-out, the held-back yet magically sure, fully extended slowness with which these parallel worlds near each other and meet remind one of the slow movements of some of Beethoven's later quartets and sonatas. But poems like these, in their plainness and human rightness, remind me most of a work of art superficially very different, Verdi's *Falstaff*. Both are the products of men at once very old and beyond the dominion of age; such men seem to have entered into (or are able to create for us) a new existence, a world in which everything is enlarged and yet no more than itself, transfigured and yet beyond the need of transfiguration. (pp. 59-60)

Stevens has always looked steadily at the object, but has looked, often, shortly and with a certain indifference, the indifference of the artist who—as Goethe says—"stands above art and the object; he stands above art because he utilizes it for his purpose; he stands above the object because he deals with it in his own manner." But now that the unwanted, inescapable indifference of age has taken the place of this conscious indifference, Stevens is willing to be possessed by "the plain sense of things," and his serious undeviating meditation about them seems as much in their manner as in his. His poetry has had "the power to transform itself, or else / And what meant more, to be transformed." The movement of his poetry has changed; the reader feels in it a different presence, and is touched by all that is no longer there. Stevens's late-nineteenth-century orchestration has been replaced, most of the time, by plain chords from a few instruments—the stir and dazzle of the parts is lost in the sense of the whole. The best of these late poems have a calm, serious certainty, an easiness of rightness, like well-being. (pp. 61-2)

When the reader comes to aberrant poems like "Page of a Tale" and "A Rabbit as King of the Ghosts," he realizes how little there is in Stevens, ordinarily, of the narrative, dramatic, immediately active side of life, of harried actors compelled, impelled, in ignorant hope. But how much there is of the man who looks, feels, meditates, in the freedom of removedness, of disinterested imagining, of thoughtful love! As we read the poems we are so continually aware of Stevens observing, meditating, creating, that we feel like saying that the process of creating the poem is the poem. Surprisingly often the motion of qualification, of concession, of logical conclusion—a dialectical motion in the older sense of *dialectical*—is the movement that organizes the poem; and in Stevens the unlikely tenderness of this movement—the one, the not-quite-that, the other, the not-exactly-the-other, the real one, the real other—is like the tenderness of the sculptor or draftsman, whose hand makes but looks as if it caressed. (pp. 63-4)

At the bottom of Stevens's poetry there is wonder and delight, the child's or animal's or savage's—man's—joy in his own existence, and thankfulness for it. He is the poet of well-being. (p. 67)

He has spoken, always, with the authority of someone who thinks of himself as a source of interest, of many interests. He has never felt it necessary to appeal to us, make a hit with us, nor does he try to sweep us away, to overawe us; he has written as if poems were certain to find, or make, their true readers. Throughout half this century of the common man, this age in which each is like his sibling, Stevens has celebrated the hero, the capacious, magnanimous,

excelling man; has believed, with obstinacy and good humor, in all the heights which draw us toward them, make us like them, simply by existing. (p. 71)

Stevens has spoken with dignity and elegance and intelligence—with eloquence—of everything from pure sensation to pure reflection to pure imagination. . . . (p. 73)

> Randall Jarrell, "The Collected Poems of Wallace Stevens" (originally published in The Yale Review, Vol. XLIV, No. 3, Spring, 1955), in his The Third Book of Criticism (reprinted by permission of Farrar, Straus & Giroux, Inc.; copyright © 1955 by Mrs. Randall Jarrell), Farrar, Straus & Giroux, 1969, pp. 55-73.

MARIUS BEWLEY (essay date 1955)

I think it is possible to gain a fresh insight into Stevens' poetry by considering him as an American Transcendentalist poet. There are some serious difficulties in the way, but there are also some rewards. Viewed in this way, he is no longer a sport in the American tradition, a rather dandified anomaly, but an explicable phenomenon.

Traditional American Transcendentalism is hard to define, but if it stood for anything as a movement, it was for the capacity to apotheosize the soiled pragmatic world, to justify the grubby fact in a higher realm of intuition. Such a transcending process is essentially a motion, a becoming. But it is not necessarily a flight from material reality. It can be an intenser apprehension of life—a kind of spiritual metabolism by which the boundaries of the physical are canceled, its substance becoming a part of some ultimate, central vision that is the highest life. For Stevens the exercise of the creative vision was the means towards achieving this intenser state of being. He never submitted this state to dogmatic definition, but he celebrated it in a great many poems. (p. 272)

Stevens [has said] that the poet's imagination "may be part of a larger, much more potent imagination, which it is his affair to get at." The imagination when spoken of in these terms is not only unmistakably the Romantic imagination as it developed during the last years of the eighteenth century and the first quarter of the nineteenth—it also has strong affinities with Emerson's Over-Soul. It is clear I think that Stevens has not, except now and then, gone along with the implications of his statement which I just quoted. And indeed the Over-Soul may not impress many people today; but something of its kind (failing some species of religious orthodoxy) is still a necessary support for the kind of inner illumination both Emerson and Stevens wished to achieve.

Although this one difference is crucial enough to warrant our looking for an essential difference in the character of their respective goals, if we reread "Prologues to What Is Possible" and compare it with Emerson's talents of the soul, both poets seem to be talking about the same thing. Here is Emerson on the soul, which for thinkers like these two may also be called the imagination: "The soul circumscribes all things. As I have said, it contradicts all experience. The influence of the senses has in most men overpowered the mind to that degree that the walls of time and space have come to look real and insurmountable; and to speak with levity of these limits is, in the world, the sign of insanity. Yet time and space are but the inverse measures of the force of the soul."

In Emerson's thinking the soul has this creative and destroying power, in some considerable degree, from the outside. It is able to transcend its usual limitations because it has superior assistance; but Stevens usually sheers away from this conclusion, although it is really implicit in his poetry, as the "mystical" overtones of so much of the imagery, especially in his late verse, indicate. (pp. 278-79)

I doubt if Stevens would have welcomed the comparison with Emerson I have made here, but despite differences in outlook, the affinities I have pointed to (as well as the differences) seem to me to reveal a great deal about Stevens' poetry. Poetry is not metaphysics, but there is such a thing as a philosophical poet, and both Stevens and Emerson deserve this title for reasons that are very similar. (p. 280)

> *Marius Bewley, "Wallace Stevens and Emerson" (originally published in* Commonweal, *September 23, 1955), in his* Masks & Mirrors: Essays in Criticism *(reprinted by permission of Atheneum Publishers; copyright © 1970 by Marius Bewley), Atheneum, 1970, pp. 271-80.**

G. S. FRASER (essay date 1955)

The whole tone of polite irony, of urbane mystification that pervades Mr. Stevens' work stems, I think, from [the] central predicament of the reflective aesthete who, philosophically, is a kind of pragmatic solipsist. The world, for Mr. Stevens, that the poet lives in is the world that he chooses to shape by the arbitrary emphases of a detached attention —an attention not itself shaped by the compulsions, for instance, of hunger or love. We feel continually, in reading Mr. Stevens, that his actual *gifts* are comparable with those of the very greatest poets. . . . Probably no modern poet has a more supple, rich, commanding, and evocative vocabulary; within certain limits—Mr. Stevens would be incapable of achieving the changes of pace, and the suddenings, slackenings and concentrations, of *The Waste Land* or *Ash Wednesday*—few modern poets are more notable masters of rhythm; very few contemporary poets, again, combine as Mr. Stevens does the three apparently disparate gifts of evoking impressions with Imagistic vividness, shaping long poems with musical care, and pursuing through a long poem a single, very abstruse, metaphysical argument. Yet in one's heart one does not quite think he is a "great" poet in the sense that, say, Yeats and Eliot are "great" poets. What is it that one misses? Partly, or perhaps mainly, the whole area of life that lies between detached aesthetic perception and philosophical reflection on it; and, as a chief corollary to that, the urgency of ordinary human passion, the sense of commitment and the moment of final concentration. In one crude human sense, Mr. Stevens' enormous talents are being exploited a little frivolously; in all one's continuing pleasure and admiration, while reading him, there is the sense all the time of a lack of the highest tension. (p. 356)

> *G. S. Fraser, "E. E. Cummings and Wallace Stevens" (1955), in* Literature in America, *edited by Philip Rahv (© 1957 by The World Publishing Company), World Publishing Co., 1957, pp. 350-57.**

DELMORE SCHWARTZ (essay date 1955)

The very charm and beauty of Stevens' language misleads the reader often: delighted with the tick and tock, the heigh ho of Hoon and Jocundus, "jubilating," "in the presto of the morning," the reader often missed the basic substance, the joy that for the moment at least the poet has grasped "the veritable *ding an sich* at last": for Stevens was essentially a philosophical poet, the rarest of all kinds, seeking always "in a good light for those who know the ultimate Plato," to see and possess "the nothing that is not there, and the nothing that is." It is natural enough not to recognize that a poem called *Le Monocle de Mon Oncle* is a serious discourse on the nature of love; a poem named *The Comedian As the Letter C* may be a serious analysis of the perennial attitudes toward experience, but it is much longer than most poems that most readers of poetry read; and the title of *Thirteen Ways of Looking At a Blackbird* hardly makes clear the fact that its subject is everything involved in looking, loving, and living. (p. 195)

> *Delmore Schwartz, "Wallace Stevens: An Appreciation" (1955), in* Selected Essays of Delmore Schwartz, *edited by Donald A. Dike and David H. Zucker (reprinted by permission of The University of Chicago Press; © 1970 by The University of Chicago),* University of Chicago Press, 1970, pp. 192-96.

WILLIAM CARLOS WILLIAMS (essay date 1956)

The satiric spirit of Stevens' first poems went out of them as time advanced; he became contemplative, more thoughtful, as happens to us all unless we die young. At first it was not so.

An inquiry from Santayana, the philosopher, who had seen his early poem, *Thirteen Ways of Looking at a Blackbird*, may have taken its toll.

This was the phase of the French influence on his style or the influence he conceived to be French, though it was no more French than that of Robert Louis Stevenson. Baudelaire would have found nothing French about it. That was during his alliterative period. . . . (p. 234)

Stevens' thought was like that of a New Englander, but he was not from New England.

That made for a cryptic quality to his verses that was never resolved, a ritualistic quality as though he were following a secret litany that he revealed to no man. Over and over again, as he reached his later years and suddenly began to be recognized for what he was, a thoroughly equipped poet, even in such a late book as *The Auroras of Autumn*, he could be detected to the surprise of the world, in this secret devotion. He was in the midst of a life crowded with business affairs a veritable monk.

At first when he took his annual sojourns to Florida, where orange trees were blooming, his poems were filled with their flowers. The hibiscus was his true nature. There is an opulence that shows itself in an imagery that was florid and full as he permitted himself to make it. That to me was Stevens at his best. (p. 235)

He was a man who would never acquire the stigma of a popular appeal. He never stepped down to that. Therefore he earned an undeserved reputation for coldness if not sterility. Time alone will have to rescue him from the implied obloquy.

Technically Stevens was not, as were many of his contemporaries, an experimentalist. He did not write staid classroom lines that can be regularly scanned, but they lie, for all that, in regular units of 2s and 3s and 4s quite according to custom. There is an intrinsic order which they follow with a satisfying fidelity which makes them indefinably musical, often strongly stressed by Stevens, his signature.

His is not strictly speaking a colloquial diction, but there are especially in his later works no inversions of phrase, "for poetic effect," no deformities of the normal syntax. He liked to use unusual, often foreign words for the sheer tactile qualities, such a word as "Badroulbadour," a decoration which many poets before him have affected. Perhaps he was more concerned with these effects that he should have been but it has its uses. Even so it diminishes the force of the epithet. Stevens seldom comes down on a statement of fact. It is always, "thirteen ways of looking at a blackbird," which cannot but weaken any attack. (pp. 235-36)

From the first his poems invoke only one mood, restraint. He was at times whimsical even gay. He loved words as if they were as they must be to the poet, precious things. What he did with them was fascinating to the ear. He loved alliteration and used it copiously. (p. 236)

There was a quality in Stevens' work that while academic, in no way experimental, makes it definitely of the New World: much as he wanted to cling to the old. He's an American even if it hurts, even when he speaks of the "Puella Parvula" or says, in a title "Cy Est Pourtraicte, Madame Ste Ursule, et Les Unze Mille Vierges." These examples show him most nostalgic toward a gone beauty much as was Yeats or Ezra Pound but we forget it as we turn toward, *Dutch Graves in Bucks County*. The technique is not, alas, altered.

Or if it does show pressures from the world about us it is, for me, in Stevens' relaxed stanzaic formations, regular but not, at the same time, slavishly so. You can hear above the words the new accent, difficult to isolate and capture in a phrase. He is writing English but no Englishman writes like that.

He abounds in felicitous titles, *Last Look at the Lilacs; Peter Quince at the Clavier*. He was a formalist as much as Rimbaud or Baudelaire or Remy de Gourmont were so. The poems of Walt Whitman meant nothing to him, the entire "free verse" movement left him cold—which marks in the beginning (because he never went astray) the modern return to accepted verse forms of the present day and yet there are Americanisms all through his writing—an overall quality which is plainly evident. It is the best part of him. (pp. 237-38)

William Carlos Williams, "Wallace Stevens," in Poetry (© 1956 by The Modern Poetry Association; reprinted by permission of the Editor of Poetry *and New Directions, agents for the Estate of Florence H. Williams), Vol. LXXXVII, No. 4, January, 1956, pp. 234-39.*

NORTHROP FRYE (essay date 1957)

Wallace Stevens was a poet for whom the theory and the practice of poetry were inseparable. His poetic vision is informed by a metaphysic; his metaphysic is informed by a theory of knowledge; his theory of knowledge is informed by a poetic vision. He says of one of his long meditative poems that it displays the theory of poetry as the life of poetry . . . , and in the introduction to his critical essays

that by the theory of poetry he means "poetry itself, the naked poem". . . . He thus stands in contrast to the dualistic approach of Eliot, who so often speaks of poetry as though it were an emotional and sensational soul looking for a "correlative" skeleton of thought to be provided by a philosopher, a Cartesian ghost trying to find a machine that will fit. No poet of any status—certainly not Eliot himself—has ever "taken over" someone else's structure of thought, and the dualistic fallacy can only beget more fallacies. Stevens is of particular interest and value to the critical theorist because he sees so clearly that the only ideas the poet can deal with are those directly involved with, and implied by, his own writing: that, in short, "Poetry is the subject of the poem". . . . (p. 353)

[What Stevens considers "central poetry" is] based on the concrete and particular act of mental experience. . . .

This central view of poetry is for Stevens based on the straight Aristotelian principle that if art is not quite nature, at least it grows naturally out of nature. He dislikes the term "imitation," but only because he thinks it means the naive copying of an external world: in its proper Aristotelian sense of creating a form of which nature is the content, Stevens' poetry is as imitative as Pope's. Art then is not so much nature methodized as nature realized, a unity of being and knowing, existence and consciousness, achieved out of the flow of time and the fixity of space. (p. 356)

A world of total simile, where everything was like everything else, would be a world of total monotony; a world of total metaphor, where everything is identified as itself and with everything else, would be a world where subject and object, reality and mental organization of reality, are one. Such a world of total metaphor is the formal cause of poetry. Stevens makes it clear that the poet seeks the particular and discrete image: many of the poems in *Parts of a World*, such as "On the Road Home" . . . , express what the title of the book expresses, the uniqueness of every act of vision. Yet it is through the particular and discrete that we reach the unity of the imagination, which respects individuality, in contrast to the logical unity of the generalizing reason, which destroys it. (pp. 364-65)

The theoretical postulate of Stevens' poetry is a world of total metaphor, where the poet's vision may be identified with anything it visualizes. For such poetry the most accurate word is apocalyptic, a poetry of "revelation" . . . in which all objects and experiences are united with a total mind. (p. 367)

Just as the "poetic" is derived mainly from the reverberations of tradition, so it is clear that the anti-"poetic" quality in Stevens is the result of his determination to make it new, in Pound's phrase, to achieve in each poem a unique expression and force his reader to make a correspondingly unique act of apprehension. This is a part of what he means by "abstract" as a quality of the "supreme fiction." It was Whitman who urged American writers to lay less emphasis on tradition, thereby starting another tradition of his own, and it is significant that Whitman is one of the very few traditional poets Stevens refers to, though he has little in common with him technically. It is partly his sense of a poem as belonging to experiment rather than tradition, separated from the stream of time with its conventional echoes, that gives Stevens' poetry its marked affinity with pictures, an affinity shown also in the curiously formalized symmetry of the longer poems. "Notes Towards a Supreme Fiction," for instance, has three parts of ten sections each, each section with seven tercets, and similarly rectangular distributions of material are found in other poems.

When we meet a poet who has so much rhetorical skill, and yet lays so much emphasis on novelty and freshness of approach, the skill acquires a quality of courage: a courage that is without compromise in a world full of cheap rhetoric, yet uses none of the ready-made mixes of rhetoric in a world full of compromise. Stevens was one of the most courageous poets of our time, and his conception of the poem as "the heroic effort to live expressed As victory" . . . was unyielding from the beginning. Courage implies persistence, and persistence in a distinctive strain often develops its complementary opposite as well, as with Blake's fool who by persisting in his folly became wise. It was persistence that transformed the tropical lushness of *Harmonium* into the austere clairvoyance of *The Rock*, the luxurious demon into the necessary angel, and so rounded out a vision of major scope and intensity. As a result Stevens became, unlike many others who may have started off with equal abilities, not one of our expendable rhetoricians, but one of our small handful of essential poets. (p. 370)

Northrop Frye, "The Realistic Oriole: A Study of Wallace Stevens," in The Hudson Review *(copyright © 1957 by The Hudson Review, Inc.; reprinted by permission), Vol. X, No. 3, Autumn, 1957 (and reprinted in his* Fables of Identity: Studies in Poetic Mythology, *Harcourt, Brace & World, Inc., 1963, pp. 352-70).*

HOWARD NEMEROV (essay date 1957)

Stevens is most difficult at precisely the moments of greatest simplicity, where the world, so far as meaning is concerned, is summed up and destroyed in a phrase usually balanced upon the point of the verb "to be". . . .

This principle of composition, which revokes at once all other principles and makes something uniquely recognizable of Stevens' figures, is given us more or less diagrammatically at the beginning of a poem called "Connoisseur of Chaos". . . . (p. 77)

[This may be] said about the figurative center of Stevens' poetry: that every object, in the poet's mind, becomes the idea of itself, and thereby produces the final illumination which in the Platonic philosophy would have been produced by the view of the archetypes themselves; save that this illumination, final as it is, is meaningless, repetitious as prayer, yet "responsive as a mirror with a voice"—the epiphany not of what is real, but of the self poetizing. This is our reality, that "we believe without belief, beyond belief," that "Life consists / Of propositions about life," and that "The poem must resist the intelligence / Almost successfully." (p. 80)

What follows from the principle of poetics which I have attributed to Wallace Stevens is this, that the poet's art constitutes the world. This contention is also, I think, the chief subject of his poems, which meditate the ambiguity, old as Genesis, whether this poetic act is a creation *ex nihilo* or the ordering and making perceptible in language the immense possibilities of chaos, the establishment of what Joyce called "the ineluctable modality of the visible." The dominance of this subject, which makes the freedom and

particular strangeness of Stevens' poetry—since all objects may be exalted into poems, the act of looking at them being what is at issue—also sets their limits and is responsible for their repetitive and sometimes bemused character—since the meditation is endless, or ends only with death (an end but no solution). . . . (p. 81)

The principle of composition, whereby—to put it very roughly—all particulars may "represent" all general statements, makes for an immense variety of apparently individual subjects and images; yet I have been able to make out some strains of iterative and thematic imagery whereby the central tension is composed many times, and I will indicate briefly the most important of these.

The chaos of the actual is represented . . . in sea, storm, wind, darkness; also in the figure of the jungle: Venezuela, Africa, Brazil, Yucatan, "Florida, Venereal Soil," the Everglades, and (epitomizing its qualities) "that alien, point-blank, green and actual Guatemala," whose antithesis, in a sadly satiric poem, is the Waldorf,

> Where the wild poem is a substitute
> For the woman one loves or ought to love,
> One wild rhapsody a fake for another.

Most often, though, the jungle of immediate experience is placed over against the image of the statue, which may appear in very various forms: the snow man, the Founder of the State, allegorical emblems of Fides, Justitia, Patientia, Fortitudo, "those sovereigns of the soul / And savings banks," Belshazzar, Stalin, Xenophon, etc. (p. 83)

The statue, like the jar in Tennessee or the valley candle, orders the wilderness (usually a park) in which it is set, providing a center and focus for all that green; but beyond that it alludes to all that is dominating and heroic, all that is too big for man, until, in its remotest ranges, it becomes indistinguishable, with Platonic piety, from the One, and is identified with soldier, giant, hero, captain—"outer captain, inner saint," "a large-sculptured, platonic person, free from time," "the soldier of time grown deathless in great size."

It is between these extremes of the jungle and the monumental hero that the poet produces—with a wistful, hankering eye on the One—his transformations, "As of a general being or human universe," whereby the most random experiences are to be reflected mythically in "the central man," "the impossible possible philosophers' man,"

> our oldest parent, peer
> Of the populace of the heart, the reddest lord,
> Who has gone before us in experience,

with the foredoomed, ruefully Platonic object of "The essential poem at the centre of things."

It is part of this poetical bargain with the world, of course, that one does not bring forth the essential poem at the center of things. The poet, as musician and clown, as Crispin, Peter Quince, Man with the Blue Guitar, must daily renew the contest with chaos which he cannot win; the tenacity with which Stevens held himself at this frontier between the actual and the mind characterizes both the successes and the failures of his genius. (pp. 83-4)

Howard Nemerov, "The Poetry of Wallace Stevens," in The Sewanee Review *(reprinted by permission of the editor; © 1957 by The University of*

the South), Vol. LXV, No. 1, Winter, 1957 (and
reprinted in his Poetry and Fiction: Essays, Rutgers University Press, 1963, pp. 75-85).

J. V. CUNNINGHAM (essay date 1958)

Most of what is interesting in Stevens issues from [a]
problem. It can be put in various terms. It is the problem of
traditional religion and modern life, of imagination and reality, but it can be best put for Stevens in the terms in which
it is explicitly put in *The Comedian*. The problem is the relationship of a man and his environment, and the reconciliation of these two in poetry and thus in life. The two terms
of this relationship are really Wordsworth's two terms: the
one, what the eye and ear half create; the other, what they
perceive. The reconciliation in Wordsworth is in a religious
type of experience. . . . The reconciliation in Stevens is
sought in poetry. . . . For poetry is the supreme fiction of
which religion is a manifestation. . . . What Crispin is
seeking is such a reconciliation, a oneness between himself
and his environment. He began in the illusion that he was
the intelligence of his soil, but the experience of reality
overwhelmed him, and he came to believe that his soil was
his intelligence. At this extreme he wrote poems in which a
person is described by his surroundings. But he perceived
that this too was sentimental, and so he settled for the ordinary reality of daily life, married, had four daughters, and
prospered. However, he did not give up poetry entirely; he
recorded his adventures in the poem, and hoped that the
reader would take it as he willed. . . . (pp. 234-35)

The central concern of Stevens' poetry, the concern that
underlay Crispin's voyage and the poet's meditative argument with the woman in *Sunday Morning,* as well as most
of the more or less curious divergencies of his career, is a
concern to be at peace with his surroundings, with this
world, and with himself. He requires for this an experience
of the togetherness of himself and Nature, an interpenetration of himself and his environment, along with some
intuition of permanence in the experience of absoluteness,
though this be illusory and transitory, something to satisfy
the deeply engrained longings of his religious feeling. (pp.
240-41)

Stevens attempted to will it into being. He constructed a
series of secular myths, like the one in *Sunday Morning,*
that affirm the traditional religious feeling of the nobility
and unity of experience, but the myths remain unconvincing and arbitrary, and conclude in grotesqueries that
betray the poet's own lack of belief in his invention, as in *A
Primitive Like an Orb*. . . . (p. 241)

He has attempted to contrive it by a doctrine of metaphor
and resemblances, which is precisely Wordsworth's doctrine of affinities. He has sought to present in a poem any
set of objects and to affirm a resemblance and togetherness
between them, but all the reader can see is the objects and
the affirmation, as in *Three Academic Pieces*. . . .

But there is a poem in *Transport to Summer,* one of the
perfect poems, as far as my judgment goes, in his later
work, that achieves and communicates this experience. It is
a short poem in couplets entitled *The House Was Quiet and
the World Was Calm.* There is no fiddle-dee-dee here. The
setting is ordinary, not exotic. It is about a man reading
alone, late at night. The phrasing is exact and almost unno-
ticeable. The style is bare, less rich than *Sunday Morning,*
but with this advantage over that poem, that none of its ef-

fect is drawn from forbidden sources, from what is rejected.
The meter is a loosened iambic pentameter, but loosened
firmly and as a matter of course, almost as if it were speech
becoming meter rather than meter violated. It has in fact
the stability of a new metrical form attained out of the inveterate violation of the old. It is both modern and traditional. . . . (p. 242)

*J. V. Cunningham, "Tradition and Modernity:
Wallace Stevens," (originally published in*
Modern Literary Criticism: An Anthology, *edited
by Irving Howe, Beacon Press, 1958), in his* The
Collected Essays of J. V. Cunningham (© *1976 by
J. V. Cunningham; reprinted by permission of
Ohio University Press, Athens and the author),*
The Swallow Press Inc., *1976, pp. 225-43.*

A. ALVAREZ (essay date 1958)

Stevens worked his talent to its full. He might very easily
have been a worse poet. It is hard to see that he could have
been any better. His standard is that of accomplishment.
And it is very high. (pp. 124-25)

If Stevens owes anything to a modern poet, it is to Eliot.
He is one of the few important poets whose language was
influenced by Eliot's own practice instead of by the earlier
authors Eliot made fashionable. . . . Stevens's world is one
of luminous and distinct images which earn their place not
as they approximate to something he has gone through but
as they justify ideas. The tension and pressure of Stevens's
verse is all in the ideas.

He is, in fact, at a level of considerable subtlety, something
of a philosophical poet; his poetry comes to rest in the
clarity of abstractions rather than of experience. (pp. 125-
26)

In a way, Stevens was the only poet ever to take Imagism
seriously. That is, he took it to its conclusion. The bulk of
Imagist poetry was a more or less high-minded game played
out in the consciously pregnant silences around the images.
It needed an audience to be shocked into exclaiming: "How
can you say so little?" and a poet who, with some satisfaction, could turn the question back on the asker: "How can
you *see* so little?" But Stevens, not content with the occasionally wise passiveness the pure Imagist might, with luck,
attain, made his poetry out of the problems with which
those silences teemed. (pp. 128-29)

[His theme] is almost a denial of Imagism, as though by
practising the style Stevens had arrived at its contradiction.
It is a poetry of irritation. He seems to be continually baffled by the impossibility of describing anything at all with
finality. A motion of the wrist, the slightest variation in
light or in the mood of the observer, and the object is utterly different. The impossible endlessness of observation,
then, is Stevens's creative premiss. (p. 129)

Stevens at his best . . . is not merely acting on poetic principle, on something that will give him the best practical results; he is involved in a tense logical process which takes
him from the purity of the description to the idea of the
thing described. He has come out on the far side of Imagism into its opposite, the Platonic world of Ideas.

Of course, there is no clear-cut ontology in Stevens's poetry, no world of meaning that has its separate existence
aside from the poetry, like the "meaning" of Spenser's
allegory—whatever that is. Stevens's style is too rooted in

images for generalizations ever to get away in it on their own. But his preoccupations take him off into a realm where his poetry must get along on a rarified diet. It is a question of what the poet feels strongly about. And Stevens has great feeling for two things: for the truth that lurks below the changing surface of appearances, and for the mode by which this is perceived, the imagination. Certainly, the truth Stevens's imagination seizes upon is kept supple and varied by its dealings with images; but its method of dealing with them is more questionable. (pp. 130-31)

[Not] only are his poems again and again about themselves, about the imagination, about the validity of metaphor, and so on; underneath all his work is an abiding *belief* in abstraction. His poetic method is controlled by an abstracting principle. Unless you are willing to treat his imagery only as a set of toy bricks, carefully made and elegantly arranged, you find yourself forced away continually into a spare, abstract world. (pp. 131-32)

There is a point with Stevens, and he reaches it often, at which profundity becomes blurred with rhetoric.

His rhetoric is at times a distraction from what he is saying, at others it is the whole tale. Stevens's fatal Cleopatra was undoubtedly the turn of phrase. I find it difficult to know quite how to take his encrusted style.... And yet his extraordinary rhythmical control, that sense of perfect balance and strictness without ever using, or needing, rhymes, is an assurance at least that the hesitation is not in the craftsmanship. It is a matter, I think, of the medium itself. Throughout his work, and particularly in *Harmonium*, Stevens seems to me to be writing in a language that does not quite belong to him. (pp. 134-35)

Stevens's style, of course, is in no way imitative; but it is something contrived. Often there is a disparity between his elaborate furnishings and the rather stringent bareness of the ideas. And even in those poems where meaning and style go most together he still moves, and is moved, by indirections.... For all the incisive delicacy and wit [of "The Bird with the Coppery, Keen Claws"], there is some sort of deliberate redundance in the writing. He proceeds like a fashionable hostess at someone else's party; at each step he pauses for an elaborate gesture: "Aloe of ivory, pear of rusty rind", "Of his gold ether, golden alguazil". No doubt part of the wit lies in the exotic style; here the grandiose exaggeration is very much to the point. But often the gestures claim all of your attention—the over-rated "Bantams in Pine-Woods", for example—and then the poems hardly exist below the level of style.

The poems that have received too little attention are a number of far quieter ones, in which the style is subdued into clarity, and the lack of surface commotion leaves the metrical perfection to speak for itself.... And yet the absence in these poems both of the dominant themes and the hard surface of stylistic device makes me feel that Stevens did not set very much store by them. They seem to have happened a little to one side of his main creative effort. Yet the qualities he set most by—sustained precision of movement and sustained richness of style—which at other times puff his poetry up, as though with ambition, in these poems relax into a slighter and more personal perfection. (pp. 136-37)

Perhaps the word "ambition" is the key to all the hesita-

tions I have about Stevens's poetry. He is content to let these smaller poems go with personal statements. But his bigger themes are entangled with his theory of abstraction and a purity of perception which has only disdainful truck with the personal world. (p. 138)

Stevens was too intelligent and too gifted to be content with small subjects. His grand purpose was serious, lucid and difficult. Twice he achieved it, in "Sunday Morning" and "Notes Toward a Supreme Fiction", and these are great poems; a number of times he got very near it, in, for example, "Le Monocle de Mon Oncle", "Peter Quince at the Clavier", "The Idea of Order at Key West"; he also wrote a number of excellent and much slighter poems. But in his ambitious failures—"An Ordinary Evening in New Haven", for example, or "The Comedian as the Letter C"—he leaves you only with the precision and elaboration of method and ideas. Personally, I don't share his enthusiasm for these. And so I find the poems dull. It may be a little late to begin to quibble with words, but there is one hair that needs to be split: at some time while Stevens was discovering what he had to say about the world, he became muddled in the distinction between poetic *intellect* and poetic *intelligence*. The first he always has—hence the rigour and tight-lipped skill of his verse. The other, like most other poets, he can only fully achieve from time to time. (pp. 138-39)

A. Alvarez, "Wallace Stevens: Platonic Poetry," in his Stewards of Excellence: Studies in Modern English and American Poets *(abridged by permission of the author; in Canada by Chatto & Windus Ltd; copyright © 1958 A. Alvarez), Scribner's, 1958 (and published in Britain as* The Shaping Spirit, *Chatto & Windus Ltd, 1958), pp. 124-39.*

ROBERT PACK (essay date 1958)

There is no contradiction between imagination and reality in the poetry of Wallace Stevens; he is concerned with an antinomy. As he regards the flourishing and mystery of human consciousness, he is neither academic nor aesthetic —but comic.

Comic imagination always fixes itself first on common things, it is concerned with the ordinary rather than the exotic, society rather than the solitary spirit in its romantic loneliness or isolation. The comic spirit is concerned with practical things, with the everyday world, and the voice of its conscience speaks of making ends meet, of getting along, and when inspired, of finding the amusement and delight in daily life, of finding the extraordinary hidden within the ordinary. This for Wallace Stevens is the task and challenge the human imagination must meet. (p. 3)

It is perhaps Stevens' most central and appealing belief that Man cannot conceive of a paradise superior in bliss to that we experience in our own world, our ordinary lives....

The drama of ["Sunday Morning"] is in the testing of the idea of earth as paradise. Stevens does this by conjecturing about the meanings of their separation and about the literal and metaphorical possibilities of their coming together. (p. 25)

"Esthétique du Mal" can profitably be read as a sequel to "Sunday Morning," for not only is it like "Sunday Morning" in form and style but it picks up the question of whether earth can be a paradise where the "ambiguous undulations'' of ''Sunday Morning'' and the ''fluttering things'' of ''Le Monocle de Mon Oncle'' leave off. Having accepted, rather embraced, death and mutability in the earlier poem, Stevens goes on in ''Esthétique du Mal'' . . . to consider the place of evil and pain in his paradise on earth. As the title suggests, evil becomes a question of aesthetics, and ultimately serves an aesthetic end. (p. 34)

Wallace Stevens is a philosopher as well as a connoisseur of physical sensations and perceptions. . . . But Stevens never merely philosophizes, using the form of verse as a temptation; he presents the drama of the mind as it manipulates the details of perception; he shows us how the mind receives and resists the world, and teaches us that thought has its own emotions. What is it like to have an idea? What is it like to perceive things and to know that one is perceiving them, and to be aware that this knowing becomes part of the perceiving? To these questions Wallace Stevens brings the wisdom of his imagination. And the theory that is a product of this inquiry is at the heart of Stevens' poetry. (pp. 53-4)

An object loses its independence as it becomes involved in the particular history of the perceiving mind, and we must begin to speak of the apprehension of this object, for it is seen within a particular psychological and aesthetic reference. From this point on, the higher consciousness comes into play in the further ordering of the apperception. The relationship between the newly perceived object and other remembered objects forms a correspondence, and thus is evolved a complex organization, a conception. It is the discovery and succeeding organization of resemblances and correspondences that for Stevens is the work of poetry, and in this activity lies his most profound pleasure which is also the pleasure of improvisation, of ''merely circulating.''

In the continual ordering of the ambient flow of images, all life tends to become literature. There are three types of relationships which this ordering produces, and in each case we observe the process of perception becoming apperception and culminating in conception. *Resemblance* is the discovered relationship between external objects. (p. 56)

The more complex resemblance is the ''metaphor,'' which is a description of something in terms of something else that in immediate perception it does not resemble. The metaphor seeks out a hidden similarity, it reveals the quality of things. . . . (p. 58)

The relationship of the internal and the external, of inner feeling and outer fact, is a ''correspondence.'' As resemblances are similarities between externals, correspondences are similarities between states of mind and material phenomena. (p. 59)

Wallace Stevens' search for correspondences is . . . an exploration for the possible as part of the real. Intuition is the discovery of such possibility, and expression therefore is not merely the mirror of reality but also its extension. Sensation alone records only an aspect of what it responds to, while the imagination, according to the principle by which it lives, knows that every finite thing has an infinite existence. (p. 61)

The apparent dichotomy between things as they are known to the perceptual eye and things as they are known by human feeling and imagination is Stevens' greatest concern. Infinite reality does not prefer one or the other, but rather includes both. And if a satisfactory resolution is to be achieved, then these antinomies must be seen as aspects of one thing: for Stevens this thing is *change*. In a world without change it is possible to be completely rational. Devoid of happiness and unhappiness, the only feeling one could have is to know, and though this might be bliss for angels, it would not be bliss for men whose irrationality is often the source of their deepest feelings. In the cycle of abandonment and return to strict, perceptible reality the imagination, in its flight, has added itself to ''things as they are.'' (p. 76)

In ''Notes toward a Supreme Fiction,'' Stevens presents to us the abstraction—a supreme fiction—which would totally disabuse us of our disillusionment and would fill reality with the ultimate fullness of imagination. Such a ''fiction'' can, of course, only be approached, not reached, and so Stevens' ''Notes'' move ''toward'' it. (p. 94)

In *The Necessary Angel* Stevens tells us that the imagination has no material existence but is an essence that is vividly present and is analogous only to light. Therefore, space, air, the depths of the sky, symbolize, for Stevens, the infinity of reality's possibilities into which the imagination can begin to see, and the sky is then like a mirror which reflects an image of the abstraction of collective man. (pp. 108-09)

''Nothingness'' in Stevens' vocabulary represents the reality one would see with the perfect perceptual eye devoid of all imagination. It is the reality of the world stripped of all its ''seeming.'' It is the poverty suggested by winter when everything is reduced to its minimum, when the tree stands before us in its nakedness merely as fact, and we have forgotten the leaves it once bore and will flourish again in the summer winds. To understand the abstraction of ''nothingness'' is to have the earliest vision of reality, for ''nothingness,'' like winter, is a beginning.

It is this beginning that will lead to the summer imagination by which reality will be known in its fullness. And it is this movement from winter to summer that postulates as its culmination the ''supreme fiction,'' which is the ultimate description of reality. ''Nothingness'' and the ''supreme fiction'' are polarities that are never reached, but within which we move through a cyclical change, like the cycle of the seasons. These abstractions are themselves conceptions of the mind and, as such, are part of the total reality that includes the imaginary as well as the material. . . . The abstraction of a ''supreme fiction,'' then, describes reality as the relationship of facts and our correspondence to them; while the abstraction of ''nothingness'' describes reality as isolated fact, fact unchanged by our perception of it. This explains why Stevens says the ''opposite of 'fiction' is not 'truth' but 'fact' ''. . . . (pp. 121-22)

In the cycle of the imagination moving from its latest attempt to achieve the ''supreme fiction'' back to ''nothingness,'' reality's source, there is the possibility of infinite change. The process of change is a dialectic of fictions in contention as descriptions of reality. At the moment when one idea, one fiction, has been rejected, and before a new fiction, a new idea, has been conceived, we are in what Stevens calls ''chaos.'' Chaos is part of the principle of change. (pp. 127-28)

To be in chaos is to know a particular without knowing its relation to the universal. . . . (p. 131)

Stevens' hero is not a man among us, but a man beyond us. He does not exist in our world except as abstraction. But, conscious of the idea of the hero, men labor to achieve nobility in the quotidian world, and it is the poet's work to make this idea vivid. . . . (p. 147)

The hero exists in our fictions, and Stevens says that the myth for our time in which the hero lives must be an ideal which becomes "blooded" as our belief in it grows and as we act according to its wisdom. The myth that enfolds the hero is made out of the appearances of things, which Stevens gives the elaborate dress of rhetoric and dazzling vocabulary. (pp. 147-48)

As "nothingness" is an expression for the infinite possibility of reality, so the hero is an expression for the infinite possibility of man. The hero, then, will be the poet who composes the central poem, and he will also be its subject. (p. 148)

Poetry is the finite embodiment of the infinite idea of the hero, for he exists beyond, always in the end untouchable. . . . (p. 153)

"To know" is to recognize the world as a structure of relationships, of resemblances and correspondences, and to feel that one belongs to this structure. And "to love," in Stevens' meaning, is to feel the intensity of this belonging in that it relates, each in his unique way, man to man, man to woman, and man to his work and his world, and to feel that this belonging is sufficient—the source of final peace and acceptance. (p. 179)

Robert Pack, in his Wallace Stevens: An Approach to His Poetry and Thought *(copyright © 1958 by Rutgers, The State University; reprinted by permission of Rutgers University Press), Rutgers, 1958, 203 p.*

MICHEL BENAMOU (essay date 1959)

[In] a paper entitled "The Relations Between Poetry and Painting," which Stevens read at the Museum of Modern Art in 1951, . . . he defined four main areas of influence: sensibility, subject matter, technique, and aesthetics. He did not cite his own work as illustration, but he was so careful to keep to the craftsman's viewpoint, discarding any mysterious *Zeitgeist,* that his words bear the sigil of self-analysis. He said, in effect, that a poet can learn his trade by reading what painters reveal about theirs, and by looking at their pictures. It is not irrelevant that Stevens was a great reader of exhibition catalogues. He called them "the natural habitat for prose poems". . . . (pp. 3-4)

One feels in the poetic universe of Wallace Stevens a sort of pulse that alternately dilates and narrows the field of vision. At its widest it resembles the world of an open-air landscapist; at the other extreme, it has the limits of a painter's studio. One pole corresponds to the broad landscapes of the Impressionists, its opposite to the still lifes and the compositions of decorative Cubism.

The more lasting influence on Stevens' vision was perhaps that of Impressionism, which he called "the only great thing in modern art." He regarded it as "poetic." By this, it seems to me that he meant an element of sensibility, a sensitiveness to the flux and change of nature. Both Monet and Stevens express the poetry of a fluent universe, a vast stage for the wind, rain, sun, and moonlight, a poem of skies and waters in which the key word is weather. Their

insistence on weather, season of year, and time of day stems from an acute sense of visible changes caused by the condition of lighting. The great Impressionists, Monet, Sisley, and Pissarro, carried this concern to the extreme that they no longer painted objects so much as the light on them and the air round them. Stevens, who dubbed himself "pundit of the weather," wrote "Evening Without Angels" as a hymn to "the great interests of man: air and light." (pp. 4-5)

A constant preoccupation of the Impressionist, whether painter or poet, is to restore the innocence of the eye. (p. 6)

The freshness of Stevens' poetry is largely due to what Delmore Schwartz called "a vision instructed in the museums," rather than to the glass-pane purity of naked sight. Was not the very transparence which he praised in impressionistic landscapes a product of artifice? (p. 7)

Parts of a World and later collections, too, seem cluttered with the paraphernalia of Cubism, the guitars and mandolins, the still lifes arranged on tables, the plaster heads, the bits and odds that painters hoard for their collages, parts of a world rescued from the dump. To the reader looking for Stevens' subject, it may appear that the use of art as a source of inspiration entails a narrowing of the poetic range, limited as it is to studio objects. . . .

But the real subject of Stevens' poetry and the real subject of Cubist painting is not immediately perceptible: it is poetic imagination. The merit of the poem or picture arises from the degree of concentration with which the imagination refracts the object. The meanest and most derelict thing can thus be made significant, beautiful. "A Post-Card from the Volcano" typifies this procedure. . . . (p. 8)

Thus the poetry of Wallace Stevens incorporates conflicting elements from Impressionism and Cubism: naturalness and artificiality, delight in appearances and metamorphosis of appearances. A baffling sum of relations—for where in these extreme ranges is the identity of a poet's sensibility?

The identity is in Stevens' concern with change. Impressionism shows the *passive* principle of change. The eye must be as candid as possible and merely relay the variations of light and colors. But in Cubism, "more than changes of light" are involved. Imagination is the *active* principle which transforms and extends the object by multiplying resemblances. The metaphors of poetry and the metamorphoses of painting tap the same reservoir of analogies. (pp. 10-11)

Michel Benamou, "Wallace Stevens: Some Relations Between Poetry and Painting," *in* Comparative Literature *(© copyright 1959 by University of Oregon), Vol. XI, No. 1, Winter, 1959 (and reprinted as "Poetry and Painting," in his* Wallace Stevens and the Symbolist Imagination), *Princeton University Press, 1972, pp. 3-24.*

GRAHAM HOUGH (essay date 1960)

[One] reproach aimed at Stevens is unjustified. It is often said that he held the proper subject of poetry to be poetry, that he endlessly wrote poems about the process of writing poems, and that he remains enclosed within this sterile infinite regress. But for him poetry was simply the embodied imagination; and the imagination is the primary source of value in human life. It is clear then that he is not in intention confining himself to the artist's dilemma; he is discussing something central to all living human experience. It is true that intentions in literature count for little; what is actually achieved is all; and it is true too that the imagination as Stevens conceives it does not even attempt to exercise its transforming power on some of the most important areas of human experience. But his central problem has nothing to do with the intricacies of a craft; it does not exist in hermetic isolation; it is one of the problems of man as man:

Another deduction is that the claims made for the imagination, though highly pitched, are not really very great. Poetry may be the necessary angel, but the conception of it is a minimal one. . . .

The world remains the pragmatical preposterous pig that it has always been, quite irremoveable. It is hard to be sure, but it seems that Stevens' conception of 'reality' was that of a naive positivism. The world is irreducible brute fact; the way to make something of it is by abstraction; to contemplate not the thing, but the patterns that, in collaboration with the human imagination, the thing is capable of making. (p. 213)

It seems that Stevens uses principally two kinds of verse, and that these correspond, broadly speaking, to two poetic manners. The first is blank verse—meditative, undramatic blank verse, of a perfectly orthodox and unexperimental kind. . . . He contrives in most of the blank verse poems to make it something extremely distinguished and distinctive, by the use of a heightened vocabulary, a rather lofty, sometimes ironical, literary tone that yet, by perceptible prayer and fasting, always avoids an obvious poeticism. This manner is a considerable feat of craftsmanship, sometimes a positive *tour de force;* and it gives the pleasure that such achievements have the right to give. Some of his finest poems are written in this style. But there is another manner, becoming more frequent later on, and another kind of verse. I suppose we must call it free verse, useless as that term is to describe anything. It is at any rate mostly rhymeless; it avoids the iambic rhythm of most English verse and relies on the looser, flatter rhythms of common speech. But the lines are usually of similar length, and they are grouped in symmetrical stanzas, so that the effect is not one of informality. And the language is bare, stripped, reduced to the range of common speech. In trying to summarise the argument of poems like this I have found that there are no words plainer or more economical than those of the poem itself. After the leaves have fallen we return to a plain sense of things; and in spite of the greater celebrity of his bravura manner I believe that it is in the bare, extremely individual expressiveness of this second style that his greatest triumphs are to be found. Perhaps there is another manner too, mostly in a few later poems, where a lyrical tenderness of movement is combined with a pure, translucent vocabulary. (p. 217)

[Once] we have come to know his work, especially in its quieter and less frequented reaches, he is a poet we cannot do without, a necessary angel. His intricacies and felicities of language are a delight, but an expendable delight. What makes his poetry an indispensable possession is that it gives us something else, not the highest gift of which poetry is capable, but still the satisfaction of a continual need. It is an illustration of how to make something of this preposterous pragmatical pig of a world, by accepting daily experience in all its uncompromising banality, without fibs or

metaphysics, and then re-forming it in the light of the imagination. (p. 218)

Graham Hough, "The Poetry of Wallace Stevens," in Critical Quarterly, *Vol. 2, No. 3, Autumn, 1960, pp. 201-18.*

FRANK KERMODE (essay date 1960)

It is a fundamental principle for Stevens that there exists no difference between poetry and the *materia poetica;* a poem is reality discovered or revealed in the experience of the artist. "Poetry means not the language of poetry but the thing itself, wherever it may be found." Consequently the poetry of Stevens is a finding of reality in his own experience; his life is a discovering of poetry. (p. 3)

[Although] it is clear that Stevens was affected by the Imagists, by French poetry, by Whitman—and that later he felt the influence of Eliot and many others—the strong tang of a highly individual consciousness penetrates even the earlier work, to the degree that we can tell a Stevens failure as we detect the rottenness of a particular fruit: it is bad in its own peculiar way, a corruption of the good, an evil parody of banana.

That he was much affected by French poetry is certain and not at all unexpected. . . . Mallarmé, Verlaine, and Laforgue were assimilated by Stevens and powerfully affected *Harmonium.* The influence of Valéry, who was almost Stevens' contemporary, became more powerful later. (pp. 10-11)

Harmonium is on the whole very much more concerned than the later poetry with establishing the contours, the colours, the fortuity of Stevens' world—with reality "arranging itself into poems" of the "gaudiness" necessary to the fictive presentation of its own texture, its own strangeness. This is its theme, and it is a theme of delight. *Harmonium* has little—but not quite nothing—to say of what Stevens later came to call "poverty"—meaning the absence of a fruitful union between imagination and reality. Almost its only poverty is that of age and death, when the glitter dims and disappears, and the unexpected less often or never arranges itself into poems. That is a real impoverishment; and, like Coleridge his direct ancestor, Stevens is always conscious that the creative power may withdraw, that the time may come when one may see, without feeling, how beautiful the world is. But the main object of *Harmonium* is to be accurate. . . . [*Harmonium*] is a volume of poems which live or die as physical objects radiating the freshness and pleasure of transformed reality. (p. 25)

[It is true] that many of the short poems in *Harmonium* owe something to the ideals of Imagism, the catching of the exact curve of a thing, the rendering of what Hulme called the "intensive manifold," in rhythms untrammelled by conventional metre: brief insights into the physique of the world. (p. 26)

[But just] as Imagism is to Stevens a discipline interesting but not requiring submission, so the examples of Verlaine, of Mallarmé, of Laforgue, of the early Eliot, are studied and assimilated. (p. 29)

Reality, in *Harmonium* as throughout Stevens, is that which the imagination, in different ways at different times and in different places, must contend with, compound with. (p. 38)

Bergson and Santayana provide strong philosophical links with the Romantic-Symbolist tradition in which Stevens as a poet inevitably found himself, and they provided him with ways of thinking about the world as transformed by the mind. The poems, though philosophical, are never philosophy; they aspire to that condition of philosophical poetry which Coleridge thought to be within the power of Wordsworth, whose theme was also the interdependence of imagination and reality. Such poetry differs from philosophy in that it is "part of the *res* itself and not about it." The poem is not a comment but a fact never before realised, a contribution to reality. Compared with philosophy it is disorderly, because it depends on *trouvailles*, and because it has an indispensable element of unreason. The *fonction fabulatrice* is irrational; so is metaphor (resemblance pleases in so far as it is not identity). Finally, the reality of poetry is a reality "flicked by feeling." "The irrational element in poetry is the transaction between reality and the sensibility of the poet from which poetry springs." (p. 83)

One is left, after a reading of the prose, with the sense that one has assisted at the process of thinking rather than that one has heard doctrine preached. Nevertheless Stevens on the imagination, on religion, on style, on the kind of image that is the basis of more explicitly poetic meditation elsewhere, has in the end perhaps more clarity because the presiding personality is that of a poet and not of a temporary aesthetician. At all events the prose makes clearer a difference between him and his great contemporaries which all their agreements (and they are many) cannot obscure. Yeats, for example, could not have borne this labour to deprive the world of gods, to give it the brilliance of every paradise; he sought no victory over the incredible; not, anyway, the kind of victory Stevens could approve. In an age of poetic myth making Stevens is almost alone in his respect for those facts which seem "in disconnexion, dead and spiritless." (p. 92)

> *Frank Kermode, in his* Wallace Stevens (© 1960 *by J. F. Kermode*), Oliver and Boyd Ltd., 1960, *134 p.*

KENNETH REXROTH   (essay date 1961)

The terrible truth to tell, Stevens wrote precisely like an insurance executive. (p. 216)

His line was insurance. He stood quietly on the sidelines and took bets from the Power Elite on the chances of their meeting with disaster or the consequences of their folly. That is what his poetry says. Never believe for an instant that it has anything to do with the seven types of ambiguity and the pure, aesthetic, self-contained systems of his Higher Critic expositors. . . . Always, in every poem, Wallace Stevens struggled to catch and hold and keep and be true to the simplest animal wisdom and hence the most human and humane—the profound skepticism of the organism that acts in perfect confidence. (p. 217)

Certainly Stevens never, in a long and very distinguished career, came up to the high point from which he started in his first book, *Harmonium*. That little book sold only a few copies, but it hit my generation with an unforgettable impact. *The Waste Land* may have made more noise, but when it was over, it left only a pose. *Harmonium* left wisdom—its own rather privileged kind of wisdom, but real nonetheless. I suppose the wisdom is riper in the late poems in this book [*Opus Posthumous*]; it is certainly very

ripe, but the poetic excitement is a good deal less and sometimes is lacking altogether. . . . Many of the later poems are deeply moving, but they are, by and large, put together with what is called quiet mastery, one of art's less exciting characteristics. Once in a great while [as with "A Child Asleep in Its Own Life"] this quiet assurance envelops you in its own very special mystery, the mystery of animalism and skeptic faith. . . . (pp. 218-19)

> *Kenneth Rexroth, "Wallace Stevens," in his* Assays (© 1961 *by Kenneth Rexroth; all rights reserved; reprinted by permission of the author*), New Directions, 1961, pp. 216-19.

ELIZABETH JENNINGS   (essay date 1961)

Wallace Stevens is a poet without faith in the religious sense, nor does he affirm in the familiar humanist sense. He would have agreed only with the second half of Keats' dictum about 'the holiness of the heart's affections and the truth of imagination.' But he pursued truth *through* imagination with as much rigour and passion as mystics seek God or philosophers seek meaning. Every poem he wrote is fundamentally about the same thing—the search for reality by means of imagination. His poetry enacts his philosophy; one cannot extract the thought, the content, the meaning, without emptying out, as it were, the whole poem. Yet there is nothing purely abstract in his work. Indeed, a superficial reading might persuade the reader that Stevens is a hedonist, a self-indulgent pleasure-seeker. His poems abound in scents, sounds and tangible objects. Often his images arise from paintings or *objets d'art*. Anything which appeals to the senses may, in fact, be the springboard to his inquiries. But these things are present for their significances not merely for their sensuousness. (p. 201)

In a poem called *Of Modern Poetry* [Stevens] speaks of 'the poem of the act of the mind'. This is metaphysics in the strictly philosophical sense, but with Stevens it is also something more. The poem which is 'the act of the mind' is created by the imagination working on the findings of the senses, and working on them not to elaborate them but to elucidate them. If Stevens's attitude is agnostic, if his answers are often negative, his poems are, nevertheless, a repudiation of chaos, a gesture against disorder. And where the mystics make contact with God through their wills and their intellects, Stevens makes contact with reality through his own poetic imagination. All poets do this, of course, but not all poets make this very search the prevailing subject-matter of their verse. In this sense, Stevens is a poet in the pure state, constantly reiterating and calling in question what most poets take for granted. And this search has its own torments since so much intrudes between the poet and his vision. (p. 202)

It would be easy, too easy, to lay great stress on Stevens's use . . . of religious or ritual terms such as 'sacrament'. In fact, he appropriates such terminology for purely secular and utilitarian purposes. His tone, his personal voice, is created by an extraordinarily rich vocabulary. He draws his language from art, philosophy, poetry, nature and many other things. But he impresses these words not so much with his own personality (he is, in most ways, a remarkably impersonal poet) as with the colour and light of his own vision of the world. The vision is, as it were, trapped in this highly idiosyncratic yet extremely decorous language.

Sunday Morning is a poem about a world without faith yet

it is neither a negative poem nor a despairing one. As with his language, so with his imagery—Stevens draws upon every resource of language to express his ideas. In this poem he uses the articles of Christian faith (the doctrine of the Resurrection in particular) to lend colour to his verse, to intensify his vision. . . . (pp. 203-04)

Stevens's final rejection of God is a melancholy one and yet, because he must have order, he makes the measure of his verse impose order even upon what he feels is without design or meaning. . . . (p. 204)

Stevens's view of the universe is not entirely unlike Rilke's. Both poets seek for reality by means of the imagination but where Rilke, at the end of the *Duino Elegies,* is prepared to admit a transcendent vision, Stevens remains content simply with the relation between the mind and the objective world. He needs no mediator but his own imagination and this limitation perhaps accounts for the repetitiveness (even though it is an exquisite and compelling repetitiveness) of his poems. His mind never rests but must always be teasing at his one great theme. He knows nothing of 'negative capability' or serene receptiveness. In a sense, Stevens is to his poetry what the God he himself cannot believe in is to the world of the Christian visionary. Yet Stevens's vision is quite without pride or megalomania; he celebrates only what he can affirm. The tension in his verse, that tension which is the life of all important poetry, resides in the struggle for something which he feels his intellect cannot accept. So he transfers the idea of divinity to the realm of art. . . . (p. 205)

The poet, by means of his poetry, makes contact with reality and tries to maintain that contact. It is in this attempt at adherence, at unity, that Stevens's conception of the poet approximates to the Christian idea of the mystic. At the beginning of *Notes Towards a Supreme Fiction,* he makes poetry the embodiment of reality, the apex of truth. It is a lofty vision and also a supreme act of faith by a man who in all other ways would have regarded himself as an agnostic. Indeed, it may very well be that there is something at the heart of poetry which forbids the total gesture of agnosticism. Simply to write is, after all, some kind of affirmation, but to lay upon poetry, as Stevens does, all those things which other men have assigned to religion and philosophy, is a kind of enthronement of credence itself. (p. 207)

Stevens's world is, on the whole, an impersonal world. The people in it tend to be merely figures in a landscape or images to which the poet can attach his own meanings. They are, in short, his raw material and no more and no less august or important than the *objets d'art* or natural phenomena which he also incorporates into his verse. It is the *being* of his men and women, their mere existence, that Stevens is concerned with, not their emotions or conflicts—still less, his own. Paradoxically, Stevens's fastidious care for particulars is, in fact, only an exquisite mask over a passion for generalities. His work is highly sophisticated, yes, but it lacks the supreme sophistication of the great humanist poets (Chaucer, Shakespeare, Yeats) who are concerned not so much with meaning as with feeling. If there is tragedy in Stevens's work it is a tragedy not of individual emotions and sufferings but of a vision of the world as a place which can only be illuminated by the fitful insights of the individual imagination. Thus a poem entitled *God is Good. It is a Beautiful Night,* turns out not to be the

celebration of a moment of human awe and reverence, but simply one more examination of order. . . . (pp. 208-09)

[Stevens] is a poet of *being* yet his doctrine of existence is closer to Plato's timeless essences than to modern existentialism. His infinite caution in proposing absolutes sometimes conceals not only a concern for but also an unawakened belief in absolutes. In other words, his poems sometimes go further than his severe beliefs would lead us to expect. It may be indeed, as I have suggested already, that poetry is of its nature antagonistic to complete incredulity or negation; a 'willing suspension of disbelief' is, perhaps, at the heart of poetry as well as at the heart of the perfect reading of poetry. Certainly, with Stevens, his poems appear sometimes to catch him off guard and amaze him with an affirmation. . . . For Stevens, the imaginative faculty is august and autonomous and also, as Coleridge has said, 'the living power and prime agent of all human perception'. The senses supply it with material from which it shapes images and then gropes towards order.

Crowded with *objets d'art,* fastidiously selective, uncompromisingly honest, quick to detect error—Stevens's art is all these things. On the surface it appears, in his own words, 'less and less human', but this is only because he takes things at their source; he is concerned with perception, feeling, desire in their pure state, before they have become involved in passion or personal conflict. Yet his verse takes its tension from a battle between disinterestedness and self-expression, since all poems are made with feelings as well as with thought. Stevens's passion is a controlled passion but it is a passion nonetheless. (pp. 211-12)

Elizabeth Jennings, "Vision without Belief: A Note on the Poetry of Wallace Stevens," in her Every Changing Shape *(copyright © 1961 by Elizabeth Jennings), Andre Deutsch, 1961, pp. 201-12.*

WILLIAM YORK TINDALL (essay date 1961)

[Wallace Stevens] poems are of two kinds: the one strange and imagistic, the other lean and discursive. Both are odd and both persist from start to end of his career. There is little real development in theme or method. Analogy and interaction remain his principles.

From start to finish there are manners, each from a persona or mask, at once expressive and defensive. Sometimes the mask is that of the dandy, sometimes of the magnifico, sometimes of the rabbi. These masks are absurd, but so is he who speaks through them, so those who listen, and so the nature of things. Behind each mask is the poet-insurance man, obsessed by ideas that excited him, and what excited him produced his poems. These poems unite mask, man, and idea in forms that consist of rhythm, sound, tone —of words, in short—and their interaction. To single one element out is a mistake, and the commonest mistake to take Stevens as a philosopher. . . .

His themes are limited. Despite an insistence on personality, Stevens is rarely personal. However lyrical, he seldom deals with love. Over and over again, excited by those few ideas, he deals with imagination and fact or subject, object, and the nature of reality. . . .

What strikes one on looking into *Harmonium* is an air of florid elegance. Plainly, Stevens has his mask of dandy on. In the later volumes, instead of gallant artifice, fastidious gaudiness, and "quirks of imagery," we commonly find the elegance of severity. The "final elegance," he says, is "plainly to propound." (p. 12)

Not only a mask, dandyism is a dress and a style. The poem is its style, says Stevens, the style is the poet, and a change of style is a change of subject. Adjusting ruffle and cravat in vacant lot or, better, on the dump, Stevens displays Stevens and dump and Stevens on dump. *(Chacun à son égout.)* Whatever his style, he was always a realist and never more than when most elegant. (p. 13)

At a time when poets were commonly descending to common speech the speech of Stevens was uncommon, "besprent" with archaisms, foreign intrusions, neologisms, and insolent hoo-hoos. Rejecting the logical positivists, lamenting those who, prejudiced against perfection, demand plain English for all occasions, Stevens announced that poems may require a "hierophantic phrase." For the poet there is no common speech. Consisting of the right words in the right places, poems sometimes call for the "gibberish of the vulgate," sometimes for a "lingua franca et jocundissima." Whatever the words, Anglo-Saxon or Latin, they must be exact. (p. 15)

The interaction of [opposites] is one of Stevens' constant means. . . . (p. 19)

Perhaps the most splendid example of harmony and contrast is "Peter Quince at the Clavier." This imitation of symphonic form has four movements, each related to the others by theme and motif, each different from the others in rhythm and key. The first movement, quiet and meditative, is a thought process, logical in frame, yet consisting of two analogies to be elaborated: that of music and that of Susanna and her red-eyed elders. Odd rhymes and "pizzicati," interrupting sobriety at the end, promise another development. The second movement, an andante, reveals Susanna bathing in green water. A dramatic intrusion of cymbal and horn introduces the third movement, a scherzo. Elegant couplets and absurd rhymes suit tambourines and "simpering Byzantines." The last movement, returning to the meditative mode of the first, renders "on the clear viol of her memory" the composer's ruminations about body, death, and beauty. His composition is at once musical, logical, and brightly imagistic. Rhythm, curious diction and rhyme, the interaction of contrasting movements, and, above all, those two elaborated analogies produce the strange radiance.

Suggestive of music, maybe, the poem is not music. An approximation in shape and rhythm, it is as close to music as one whose genius was pictorial and meditative could get. . . . Stevens, who thought himself *"chef d'orchestre,"* lacked the high musical abilities of Milton or T. S. Eliot. Music for Stevens was another analogy; and a harmonium, after all, is a little organ. (pp. 20-1)

Ascetic poems on emptiness, interacting with their bizarre companions, occur even in *Harmonium,* where one kind sets the other off. The bizarre, creating feelings in which ideas play a part, are florid; the ascetic, devoted to expressing ideas in which feelings play a part, are bare. In the later volumes austere poems outnumber the florid. . . . Yet, however much the two kinds differ—the one concrete, the other more or less abstract, the one imagistic, the other more or less discursive—there is less difference than there seems. Each kind offers immediate experience, and each is elegant. The first has the elegance of abundance, the second the elegance of severity. (p. 22)

Stevens wrote three long poems on aesthetics and several short ones, all longer, however, than his "Anecdote," the first great statement of the theme. Of the long poems "The Comedian as the Letter C" is the earliest and the least successful. Yet, fascinating as document, it is a comprehensive display of the things that teased him.

Crispin, the hero of "The Comedian," is a philosopher, poet, and clown—or so he is labeled—and, as his name implies, he is also valet and saint. Overtly, the poem is about his journey from Bordeaux to Carolina. Less like that of Candide than of Bunyan's Christian, this voyage is an allegorical "pilgrimage." Places and people are insistently significant. At journey's end, for example, Crispin, an abstraction, cultivates a garden and raises four allegorical daughters. Like any allegory, this "anecdote" is a "disguised pronunciamento . . . invented for its pith"—"not doctrinal in form but in design." The end of Bunyan's Christian is a place in heaven. By no means transcendental, that of Stevens' Crispin is a place on earth. His quest is for an "aesthetic." Christian's pilgrimage is up moral hills and down moral valleys. Crispin's is an "up and down between two elements," imagination and fact or intelligence and soil, until he finds their point of balance. The poles between which he oscillates bear allegorical tags: moon and sun, north and south, blue and green. Their conflict and synthesis are dialectical. Controlling theme, Stevens' principle of interaction controls manner and method, too. (p. 25)

Failing to follow the transformation of Crispin from traditional European to bare American, the style remains more "poetic" than prosaic. . . . In a contest between the elegance of abundance and the elegance of severity, abundance wins. This, after all, is early Stevens. But maybe—and we are left with buts and maybes—pomposity is the narrator's comment on himself. Far from representing imagination in conflict with sense, the style represents fancy alone. (p. 27)

In "The Man with the Blue Guitar," his second long poem on aesthetics, he reviews the themes of the first, but with more assurance and greater success. A product of what we call the creative imagination, "The Blue Guitar" is poetry, we say. This composition is a suite of thirty-three short parts in four-beat couplets, sometimes rhymed, commonly unrhymed. These parts are variations on a theme.

Bright, clear images strike one first, and after this an air of tidiness and the gaiety that Stevens prized. The last of these effects comes from imagery in part, an imagery both familiar and strange, and in part from quick rhythms, neat structure, and a diction that successfully combines exactness with ambiguity. Order plays a part and so does drama. Each of the parts is a little drama with its conflict, climax, and appeasement, a drama not only of ideas but of structure, rhythm, and tone. In the conflict between clarity and obscurity that serves as underplot, clarity, after many trials, triumphs; for the play is a comedy. Among the personae, suitably masked, are a marionette and a clown. Though sedentary, the man with the guitar is more of an actor than either. (p. 28)

The matter he chose to shape into a work of art is the work of art—or it seems so on first reading. Choice of subject reveals the poet's personality, said Stevens, and what is poetry but a transaction between a person and something else? The poet writes about what he must. The subject Stevens had to choose for his ["Notes Toward a Supreme Fiction"] is not so remote from our general interests as it seems. If the work of art is an arrangement of reality, he is writing about ways of accosting reality. The ostensible subject, however, is not the real one. Not the formulation of an aesthetic but the experience of trying to formulate it is the subject here: how it feels to think things out. "Not to impose," he says, but "to discover." When he wanted to announce his aesthetic he wrote an essay or made a speech. This poem is an essay only in the sense of being an attempt to fix the feeling and quality of an experience. Less rational than it seems, this poem is not philosophy; for nothing here approaches systematic thought. Rather, it is a meditation and a drama of thought in progress with all its hesitations, failures, and triumphs. (p. 32)

> William York Tindall, in his Wallace Stevens (American Writers Pamphlet No. 11; © 1961, University of Minnesota), University of Minnesota Press, Minneapolis, 1961, 47 p.

DANIEL FUCHS (essay date 1963)

[Stevens'] insight into the gains and losses of the imaginative man in our society, his sustained attempt at the promulgation of a new fiction in the face of the breakdown of belief, his awareness of the personal disorder of our time testify to the ultimacy of [his] seriousness. An astonishing stylist, he is yet so much more than a fine writer. (p. 16)

A common criticism of Stevens' poetry is that there are no people in it. It is more accurate, if less grammatical, to say that Stevens is all the people in his poetry. His masks provide a sense of drama which other poets—Whitman, Frost, Eliot—achieve, in part, by a novelistic gift. This self-dramatization of his comic sense makes Stevens both wit and butt. Like the comic style of Laforgue and the early Eliot, Stevens' comic style is full of travesty and self-irony, full of integrations of the frivolous and serious. It is both a parody of a stately, grand style and a burlesque of the poet who cannot possess one. For Stevens is at once a leading modern exponent of an elevated style and one of its archenemies. The poet who wrote "Sunday Morning" and "Esthétique du Mal" also wrote "The Emperor of Ice-Cream" and "The Man on the Dump." There is a constant tension in his poetry between the promulgation of a new seriousness and the deflation of a grandeur which he can see only as ridiculous. With dandiacal superiority, elegance, and detachment, he can wryly caricature the conventionally sacred. . . . (pp. 24-5)

Those who say that he is a sentimentalist of the imagination, that he shows, for example, none of the Yeatsian doubt of the imagination, do not take into account the great self-irony which is central in his work. They do not take into account the comic projection of the poet's plight in a work like "Sailing after Lunch," and the poems like it in tone. The best expression of this self-irony is Stevens' great comic poem "The Man on the Dump." It is the best expression of Stevens' indecorous treatment of the merely sentimental imagination. Obsolete purple poetry, abstruse philosophy, the idea of absolute truth—all come in for a satiric once-over. For these are contrary to our contemporary experience, signified by a garbage heap. The man on the dump is the poet, who, in his effort to salvage something clean and true, must encounter not only the sordid miscellany of contemporary life but the obsolete romantic rhetoric

which it conceals itself behind. The poem is consequently parody as well as satire. It is a poem which is a travesty on what we are meant to consider the traditional matter of poetry. In this sense, it is an anti-poetic poem. (pp. 112-13)

It takes the uncommon intelligence, the inner violence, the intense imagination—or what Stevens likes to call the romantic—to see what is merely sentimental and archaic in the romantic. The man on the dump is, despite his surroundings, a romantic. Despite the muck about him, his perception is unsullied. Among the dung, his imagination remains pure. . . . The romantic poet, in Stevens' view, is one who treads the uneasy line between the integrity of the imagination and the test of that integrity, the insistence upon coming to terms with reality. Whether directly on top of the dump or somewhat higher above it, the poet knows that it composes a good part of the ineluctable landscape. It is his ivory tower, his unviolated imagination, that makes the dump livable, even interesting. This ivory tower is not an escape, but a necessity; the necessary vantage point from which the dump may be seen in its true perspective. (pp. 117-18)

[At the heart of Stevens] is the joy of finding a new aesthetic, an aesthetic which is humble when compared to the grandiose myths of the past. When Stevens called "The Comedian" an "anti-mythological poem" he might have been speaking for all of his poetry, which is anti-mythological in the sense of its being aloof from any of the myths which make claims for man's heroic nature, or the identity of moral perfectibility in the universe and in man. It is indifferent to Platonic perfection, to Verrocchio nobility, to Puritan intimidation. Stevens, of course, has a myth of his own to make, a plain myth of human existence, an anti-mythological myth. Rejecting essense in the sense of ontological priority, he always prefers the human, secular predicament to a grand faith. For him, as for Sartre, the human condition—the necessity to exist in the world and to act there—is essence. As one of the apostles of existence he must make arrogant assertions for humility. He finds infinite possibilities in man's admission of his finite capabilities. He sees imaginative riches in the recognition of man's essential poverty. (pp. 155-56)

Stevens makes an aesthetic of evil because he sees human disorder in the life about him.

Human existence, in all its poverty, is the starting point of this aesthetic. Just as Stevens' poetry is an instance of a typically modern task, the labor of denudation, it is also typically modern in its relentless quest for reality, in its attempt at reconstructing a sense of order, of direction, to human effort. Stevens' tone in this effort at reconstruction is, as we have said, humble. It is the humility of someone starting anew. He writes only "Notes" toward a supreme fiction—not necessarily exhaustive notes at that. His aesthetic is admittedly "du Mal." . . . He so often has in mind an opposition between his way and what he considers generically as the traditional. His way is more tentative, but it is never ridiculous. The very title of his brilliant first volume of verse, Harmonium, implies this opposition; he is announcing himself as a voice to be heard, sonorous, melodious—but different from the authoritative old organ voice. Stevens is never grandiose; despite the stateliness of much of his verse he makes clear at the outset that he is a small, sometimes playful, kind of organ voice. Whatever his stateliness, whatever his gaiety, it all stems from the modern attempt at making a modest appraisal of human life. Engaged in a labor of reconstruction he starts from scratch, making no *a priori* assumptions about the order of the universe. This is one advantage of a secular metaphysics. Stevens has the further advantage, an historical one, of living in a time when it requires no great effort of the imagination to have a vision of the poverty of human life. The poet indeed lives in the world of Darwin, not Plato. (pp. 157-58)

Yvor Winters, who perceives neither the seriousness of Stevens' intentions nor the motivation behind his various masks, rebukes Stevens—rigidly—for not having had the "courage" of Crispin and taken leave of "the art which he cannot justify" [see excerpt above]. Winters sees Stevens as a victim of what he calls hedonism, a poet of "emotion divorced from understanding" who can find a subject for poetry "only in new degrees of intensity and strangeness"; "and as each new degree achieved becomes familiar it is submerged in the monotone of that which is no longer new, so that the search is equally devoid of hope and significance." This judgment is a misinterpretation of one of the first-rate reflective poets of our time, a poet whose meditations give rise to the most intense sort of emotion. How wrong-headed is Winters' assertion that Stevens is the victim of a philosophy "which offers the cultivation of the emotions as an end in itself," in the light not only of Stevens' poetry but of his commentary on poetry. Winters says this of a poet who indulges in a "neverending meditation" on the possible new insights into reality, a poet for whom "there is no wing like meaning" (*Adagia*). Far from being an end in itself, the most intense emotion in Stevens accompanies integrations of imagination and reality. Yet Winters, in a dubious coupling, classifies Stevens with Poe as one who "sought only emotional stimulation in the arts" and therefore "considered novelty, and novelty of a fairly crude kind, to be an essential of good art." True, Stevens is an apostle of the new, but for very different reasons. Winters sees him cultivating the new out of some decadent necessity. Emotion-seeking, after all, leads to the dead end of trying to recapture the desired emotions in new ways, trying to preserve the intensity of the experience by cultivating its strangeness. However, Stevens creates the new as an act of faith, as an act of meaning. Reality is to be perceived anew or not at all. Surely this is what Stevens means when he says, in *Adagia,* "Poetry is a renovation of experience." In confusing the new with novelty, Winters does Stevens a great injustice. Although Stevens would consider, say, surrealism, mere novelty, he has great praise for the new (having, no doubt, his own poetry in mind): "Newness [not novelty] may be the highest individual value in poetry. Even in the meretricious sense of newness a new poetry has value" (*Adagia*). For Stevens, then, novelty is the reverse of the emotional decadence which Winters accuses him of. It is for nothing less than a very much needed grasp of modern reality and modern beauty that Stevens is an apostle of the new.

Stevens' irony comes of the awareness of the limitation of his position. How can we see beauty in things which are in some sense not beautiful—imperfections, limitations, pains, and wrongs? Of course, it would be wrong to say that Stevens, who started writing poetry with some of the mannerisms and tastes of the dandy, thinks of beauty only in terms of the wry. There is the incipient lotus-eater in him. . . . [He] is a poet with a magnificent sense of natural beauty, beautiful beauty. A poem like "Meditation Celestial and

Terrestrial" in which the vaunted mind of winter dissolves because of the inebriating influence of summer is not the exception, nor is it a contradiction of the *esthétique du mal,* but another aspect of a poet who seeks the true and complex grounds of pleasure. (pp. 164-65)

[It] is clear that a poem like "The Revolutionists Stop for Orangeade" is, despite its apparent frivolousness, a serious attempt at arriving at aesthetic truth. Winters sees this poem with his characteristic humorlessness. "Since the poet, having arrived at the predicament to which we have traced him [Winters is still equating Stevens with Crispin], however, is not to abandon his art, there remains only the possibility that he seek variety of experience in the increasingly perverse or strange; that he seek it, moreover, with no feeling of respect toward the art which serves as his only instrument and medium. . . ." We are led to the conclusion that Stevens is literally an old sailor drunk in his boots, catching tigers in red weather.

The thing Winters misses, above all, is Stevens' irony. His moral absolutist position forces him into misleading statements about Stevens' irony and irony in general. He sees Stevens as one of a group of poets—Byron, Laforgue, Corbière, Eliot, Pound are the others—which he calls romantic ironist. . . . Romantic irony is, to be sure, an irony often directed at the ironist, stemming from a sense of traditional values lost. But if it is a wry comment on the difficulties of the modern man of feeling or the modern poet, it is often a criticism of the cultural origins of these difficulties. It is an irony directed not only at the ironist but at the reader. It is not only a torment but a weapon; it not only controls the ironist but is controlled by him. It may not occur to Winters that his position is an object of this irony; Winters should lament, not the self-destructive quality of this irony, but its effectiveness in destroying the values which he does not like to see disturbed. In reality, it is not "careless feeling," much less "careless writing," which irritates Winters, but the jarring moral and aesthetic dissonance created by bold and original minds who dare disturb the universe. . . . Stevens' irony is most effective [contrary to Winters' accusation of no control] precisely because of his control, his double-edged control. It is like the irony of the modern sculptor, who, in his impoverished aesthetic, uses wire, bolts, and rope instead of marble, in an effort to bring us to life's essential prose, to the world that surrounds us. It is an irony of a disillusioned and sly awareness, directed mainly against a stale past, a dull bowl of clichéd carnations, empty rhetoric. It is an irony which introduces a tough aesthetic—tough-minded and tough to swallow, as we have said—the way Stevens handles it. . . . Stevens wants to make poetry an integral part of our lives once more. He wants it to vex us into a true sense of self-awareness. The pretty is not enough. The heroic is too much. (pp. 165-67)

Stevens has come a long way from his inability to see much point in the life of the ordinary man. It was one of the fashionable poses of the twenties, carried somewhat over into the thirties, to be indifferent to politics and the plight of the ordinary man. . . . A long depression and a second World War had led Stevens to the realization that to speak of man is to speak of all men. (p. 168)

It may strike the reader that too often in Stevens a person is a personification. Instead of "The major man" we may want a major man or a minor one; instead of "the figure of youth" we may wish to know a particular youth living in a particular house with a particular problem; instead of "the imagination," various imaginations; instead of "it," you; in addition to more light, more heat. Yet if Stevens lacks the most intense sort of personal emotion he finds corresponding advantages. "Poetry is not personal," he spunkily asserts in *Adagia*. With his distinct rabbinical preference for thoughtful solitude to personal surrender, Stevens establishes in his large, flaunty way a relationship of self to world, a connection between his predicament and the historical moment. What poet of our century has told us more about the condition of the well-above-average sensual man? Who has studied his imaginative life more intricately or celebrated it more eloquently? Who has so happily adjusted the possibilities of life to an increasingly diminished concept of the self? (p. 192)

> *Daniel Fuchs, in his* The Comic Spirit of Wallace Stevens *(reprinted by permission of the Publisher; copyright 1963 by Duke University Press, Durham, North Carolina), Duke University Press, 1963, 201 p.*

IRVING HOWE (essay date 1963)

At the base of Stevens' work, as a force barely acknowledged yet always felt, lies a pressing awareness of human disorder in our time—but an awareness radically different from that of most writers. Only rarely does it emerge in his poems as a dramatized instance or fiction; Stevens seldom tries and almost never manages to evoke the modern disorder through representations of moral conduct or social conflict. When in *Owl's Clover* he did write a poem with a relatively explicit politics, the result, as he later acknowledged, was unfortunate: rhetoric overruning thought, an assault upon a subject which as a poet Stevens was not prepared to confront.

Lacking that "novelistic" gift for portraiture-in-depth which is so valuable to a good many modern poets, Stevens does not examine society closely or even notice it directly for any length of time; he simply absorbs "the idea" of it. A trained connoisseur in chaos, he sees no need to linger before the evidence: there is enough already. And that is why it seems neither a paradox nor a conceit to say that in Stevens' poetry the social world is but dimly apprehended while a perspective upon history is brilliantly maintained: history as it filters through his consciousness of living and writing at a given time. The disorder that occupies the foreground of so much modern literature is calmly accepted by Stevens, appearing in his work not as a dominant subject but as a pressure upon all subjects.

In a somewhat similar way Stevens, though sharply responsive to the crisis of belief which has troubled so many sensitive persons in the twentieth century, is not himself directly or deeply involved in it. He knows and feels it, but has begun to move beyond it. (p. 160)

Accepting the condition of uncertainty and solitariness as unavoidable once man has freed himself from the gods, Stevens poses as his ultimate question not, what shall we do about the crisis of belief, but rather, how shall we live with and perhaps beyond it? And one reason for thinking of Stevens as a comic poet is that he makes this choice of questions.

How shall we live with and then perhaps beyond the crisis of belief?—it is to confront this question that Stevens keeps returning to the theme of reality and imagination. Not merely because he is interested in epistemological forays as such—though he is; nor because he is fascinated with the creative process—though that too; but because his main concern is with discovering and, through his poetry, *enacting* the possibilities for human self-renewal in an impersonal and recalcitrant age. (p. 163)

The elaborate conceptual maneuvers of Stevens' longer poems have as their objective not any conclusion in the realm of thought but a revelation in the realm of experience. They are written to rediscover, and help us rediscover, the human gift for self-creation; they try to enlarge our margin of autonomy; they are incitements to intensifying our sense of what remains possible even today. Each nuance of perspective noted in a Stevens poem matters not merely in its own right, but as a comic prod to animation, a nudge to the man whose eye is almost dead. And in Stevens' poetry the eye is the central organ of consciousness.

When Stevens writes about the writing of poetry, he needs to be read not only on the level of explicit statement, but also as if the idea of poetry were a synecdoche for every potential of consciousness, as if poetry were that which can help liberate us from the tyranny of mechanical life and slow dying. Stevens is a revolutionist of the imagination, neither exhorting nor needing to exhort but demonstrating through poetry the possibilities of consciousness. And he can do this, among other reasons, because in the background of his work loom the defeats and losses of the century.

Time and again Stevens turns to the clause, "It is as if . . . ," for that clause charts a characteristic turning or soaring of his mind, which then is followed by another opening of perception. And these, in turn, are openings to the drama of the mind as it reaches out toward new modes of awareness and thereby "makes" its own life from moment to moment. There may be thirteen or three hundred and thirteen ways of looking at a blackbird, but what matters is that the eye, and the mind behind the eye, should encompass the life of these possible ways and the excitement of their variety. What also matters is that the mind behind the eye should remember that the blackbird, no matter how it may be seen, is always there in its mysterious tangibility.

Putting it this way I may seem to be making Stevens into a moralist of sorts: which readers awed by his urbanity of style might well take to be implausible. But in his relaxed and unhurried way Stevens is, I think, a moralist—a moralist of seeing. (pp. 164-65)

> *Irving Howe, "Wallace Stevens: Another Way of Looking at the Blackbird," in his* A World More Attractive: A View of Modern Literature and Politics *(© 1963, reprinted by permission of the publisher, Horizon Press, New York), Horizon, 1963, pp. 158-67.*

WILLIAM VAN O'CONNOR (essay date 1964)

To read Stevens with enjoyment and understanding it is necessary to perceive that each subject, however commonplace or esoteric, becomes a variation upon the all-controlling theme: the role of the human imagination. In writing of the "death of Satan," Lenin, a city getting ready for bed, a bowl of peaches, a lion roaring, modern poetry, a sea voyage, love, war, or whatever, the basic theme is always the same. Consequently in the body of Stevens' poetry one lives in a world of related ideas, with infinite variations and subtleties. (pp. 29-30)

In reading Stevens it is helpful to know in advance that he is employing a complex, ever enlarging symbolism, and a dramatis personae. The abstractness of the later poetry is in part in the mind of the reader who fails to perceive the complexity and to feel the weight of meaning borne by the symbols and characters that live in his mythology. (p. 31)

The primary emphasis, the *sine qua non,* of Stevens' [two plays, *Three Travellers Watch a Sunrise* and *Carlos among the Candles,*] is theme. They may be characterized, providing the term is not used as a pejorative, as closet dramas. It may well be that the writing of these plays convinced Stevens that his talent is philosophical, expository, and narrative rather than dramatic. If there is a characteristic persistent throughout Stevens' work, it is his impersonality. . . . It is also true that there are no *people,* there are merely generally symbolic figures, in his poems or in his plays. There are only ideas about people and aspects of people. There is, on the other hand, a constant process of abstraction that serves his theory of poetry. As one looks back over the range of his work it becomes evident that Stevens' interests have always been in the direction of theory. His advice to William Carlos Williams in 1917 was that the poet needs a focus and a central point of reference. Instead of shifting and changing points of view the poet holding to a single focus would enlarge and qualify his understanding of his subject. Stevens in holding over the years to his subject has enlarged his understanding of the nature of poetry and the implications of its enormous role. (pp. 39-40)

Two figures in the mythology of Stevens' poetry which seem to be closely associated and his own personal creations are Chocorua and Hoon. Chocorua, a mountain in Vermont, has a place in New England legends. The story is that a white hunter pursued an Indian chief, who leapt from a precipice and was killed. But this story, which may have suggested the symbol to Stevens, is not necessary to an understanding of the meaning of Chocorua in his poems. In them, it has become the mountain of the self, huge and shadowy because of the power of the imagination to magnify and to soar in an immense heaven of its own creation, but it also is of this earth, the "flesh, the bone, the dirt, the stone." Hoon functions somewhat similarly. It suggests solitariness, detachment, indifference to human imaginings. Ironically, it is also a part of the self.

The most persistent symbol of the unthinking sources of life in Stevens' poetry is the sun. (p. 81)

Stevens is aware, much more keenly than most of his contemporaries, that *reality* in our time is used honorifically, associated with such ideals as practicality, objectivity and rationality; he is aware, that is, of the old dichotomy between objectivity and subjectivity, between reality and appearance. Stevens knows, as anyone should who stops to consider the matter, that in our minds the two are never separate. We feel about an object according to our beliefs, our likes and dislikes. Whether the image of it in our mind is to be labeled *true* or *illusory* will depend to a considerable extent on the beliefs, likes and dislikes in the mind of the one doing the labeling. Is there really a separation between imagination and things-as-they-are? (p. 91)

That Stevens was never taken in by the twentieth-century

cult of "reality" is demonstrated readily by his acceptance of the reality of the imagination, its workings and its products. (p. 96)

Stevens is concerned with style both as a poet and as a student of the imagination. His reputation for many years was as a stylist alone, as though he were concerned with words or with style *per se*. Edmund Wilson, for example, once called him "a charming decorative artist." He has been accused of mere verbal legerdemain, as though a style worthy of acclaim could be created that expressed an insubstantial or, almost, a nonexistent subject matter. During that early period of his career, of course, writers were striving to be simple and direct: the naïve ideal was to get beneath style to the essential subject. Content was real. Style, thought of as rhetoric, was artificial. A style that hinted at the grand manner, even though checked by self-mockery, was suspect. With these attitudes toward style Stevens has been strongly in disagreement. (p. 97)

Stevens has from the beginning used color both descriptively and in support of his theme or subject. . . . To know the world is to know it in its color. (p. 98)

Reality has been an honorific term, but *imagination* a pejorative. Stevens realizes the terrible irony of decrying imagination, the agent for the creation of values, in a time so desperately in need of it. And in his creation of an interrelated body of images and symbols, collectively giving evidence of "solid reality," he has demonstrated both our need for an imagined reality and the absurdity of pretending that reality has significant relationships only with rationality. (p. 104)

For Stevens the imagination is the agency that creates values. It does not follow that he believes it can create a rigorously explicit set of values. . . . A way of life evolves slowly, by trial. The values a people live with are affected by the conventions of their past, their surroundings, and their currently influential notions and attitudes. . . . In our time because of a few simple-minded emphases, such as the distrust of imagination, together with certain forces largely outside our control, such as the almost incessant bombardment of stimuli that disturbs our peace of mind and ease of contemplation, we seem unable to conceive and maintain images of the nobler aspects of man. (p. 105)

The doctrine of "correspondences," a term with many meanings and covering a broad range of experiences, finds a place in Stevens' poetry. It would seem that this doctrine arose from a sense of the need to express relationships between the world of matter and spirit. It gave rise to the attempt to translate one sense impression into another. For Stevens the doctrine of correspondences is included in his concern with the realm of resemblances, with the ability of the imagination to see resemblances between things. (p. 123)

Stevens is deeply concerned with the ideal, but for him it is to be found in the individual's imagination, not in some transcendental or Platonic realm of Ideas. The poet can create a unity, draw seemingly divergent things together, but he is working from within his own mind. (p. 124)

Stevens' symbolist esthetic includes the translating of one sense impression into another. Poetry is identified with "sound," "music," or painting, an idea merges with a color, a thought with an odor or perfume. Presumably he believes that synesthesia is a fact of the mind which should be recognized and given its place in the language of poetry. Taken together, all the arts suggest a common concern, a reaching toward the ideal that each individually expresses in a fragmentary way. Perhaps the most notable examples of "correspondences" in Stevens' poetry are in "Peter Quince at the Clavier". . . . (p. 125)

Stevens' usual, or at least very frequent, method in writing a poem is to make a general initial statement. . . . Usually, too, the statement is elaborated, qualified, enlarged, and probed. And all the while, there is being evoked, as well, by means of metaphor, variant phrases, and the employment of deftly appropriate rhythms, a conviction or strong sense of the experience generalized about in the introductory abstraction. (p. 129)

Stevens' tone is necessarily ironic. In his view of the world and man's role there is no blinking at the difficulties or harsh realities. . . . Irony is a kind of guaranty against excesses, against exaggerated rhetoric, sentimentality or empty assertions. Stevens' irony is a mode of analysis, facile, perceptive and witty. There is a good deal of self-mockery evident in the titles of his poems, as though he were guarding against taking his own assertions too seriously. . . . [His] irony helps hold him close to the natural. There is an easy casualness even in his elegance. (pp. 138-40)

Stevens has the sense for the precise word or phrase as well as the sensibility and imagination necessary to creating the radiant atmosphere in which the commonplace and the real can be seen freshly and newly. "The morality of the poet's radiant and productive atmosphere," he has said, "is the morality of the right sensation." Stevens himself has in great abundance, to the point of genius, the powers he ascribes to the poet of creating "a truth that cannot be arrived at by the reason alone, a truth that the poet recognizes by sensation." (p. 140)

> William Van O'Connor, in his The Shaping Spirit: A Study of Wallace Stevens (copyright, 1950, Henry Regnery Company; copyright renewed, 1978, by Mary O'Connor), Russell & Russell, 1950 (and reprinted by Russell & Russell, 1964), 146 p.

JOSEPH N. RIDDEL (essay date 1965)

Stevens' achievement must be measured in the continuity and development of his work, as it expresses a life lived in the mind, a life not only recorded but realized in poetry. In this corpus of poetry he fulfills his own need; but more than that, he realizes his belief that poetry is the provenance of man's being as well as the highest form of articulating that being. In an age angrily secular, romantically antiromantic, and resignedly naturalistic, this was a credence nowise popular or well-founded and hardly conducive to the ordinary life of poetry. For it demanded that the poet justify his poetry even as he wrote it, to prove the poem by way of proving himself. Such was Stevens' task as he inherited it from his romantic predecessors and shared it with his peers. (p. 4)

With good enough reason, many critics have considered Stevens a poet notable for a handful of exquisite poems and a canon full of indifferent ones, a poet who above all failed to develop. . . . The question of Stevens' development is indeed crucial. To deny him that, it seems to me, is to deny his greatness: not only because it assumes that in his first

volume, Harmonium . . . , Stevens reached the pinnacle of style and idea, but because it implies that Harmonium's strengths (the alternating gaiety and world-weariness, the musical range, the brio and wit, the impeccable craftsmanship) are the measures, not to say forerunners, of his failure to mature. Yet it seems equally questionable to praise him as a philosopher; for his thought, if consistent, is hardly systematic. (pp. 4-5)

I am prepared to accept Stevens' own suggestions of how his poetry developed: that it did develop and mature rather than simply change, and that the evidence of this development lies in neither his ideas as such nor in basic stylistic changes as such, but in the inner life of a changing and aging sensibility. . . . It is no proof of Stevens' maturing that he abstracted the tissue of ideas (his aesthetic) repeatedly stated in his late poems from the vivid experiences of his earlier ones, or that his late abstractions are simply enlargements and proliferations of his earlier images. There is every indication that his ideas in the abstract were fully formed (if not clearly refined) in the early poems, and fully in-form them. Stevens did more as he developed, however, than peel away the rich texture and expose the core of abstractions. His development is manifest in an evolution of style, and thus of the self it expresses, in a continuum of poems that become a body of poetry, a total structure. Moreover, the single poem, as distinguished from poetry, constitutes but a moment of reality, an achieved form in the ever-flowing life of imagination, as Stevens conceives the incessant conjunctioning between mind and world. The poem is a form, life come to order in a vidid abstraction (in metaphor, the sound of words), and thus to reality. Life is a rhythm, a grammar, of forms. The poet's total achievement, his "book," is a life manifest in forms, and hence the fullest realization of the life of the imagination which Stevens insisted is the life we live everyday.

Now this romantic notion is repugnant to the traditional conceptions of poetry, inverting as it does the ratio of poetry to life. There is no apologizing for it on the grounds that it is one man's faith, no more than on the grounds that the romantic metaphysics or epistemology on which it builds is ipso facto true. For now it is enough to insist on Stevens' premise. This is the burden he placed on poetry, its centrality in his life, which allowed him to shift with ease between the masks of amateur and professional poet. (pp. 5-6)

Stevens was a poet who knew very well how man aspired toward final forms, to know the absolute, to complete the circle. And he knew just as well how this aspiration reached beyond life, willing a negation to it and its poems.

Stevens implies, nevertheless, that his poems as individual pieces take on a new import in the continuous life of the whole. . . . Indeed, his willingness to let his poems stand for what they (and he) were at the time of their composition, with a minimum of revising, would suggest his satisfaction that poetry must be the "cry of its occasion, / Part of the res itself and not about it" [Collected Poems]. This is the very opposite of James updating his sensibility, or Yeats remaking his earlier self, or Auden his ideology. The minor exercises, the casual asides, along with the stately, elaborating, enlarging meditations—this collage of perceptions and thoughts, images and metaphors—finally compose their separate occasions into the continuous and developing life of the mind. (pp. 7-8)

[The] later poetry as it grows out of the earlier becomes the normative activity of any imaginative mind, not the special perceptions of a private sensibility, and hence a metaphor for the possibilities of the human mind creating the forms of the world in which it lives. If it echoes the earlier themes, if it parades many of the familiar images in but slightly different dress, the later style issues in a different poetry: its images are refined and memorable, not immediately felt; they are no longer the tenor of perception but the vehicle of meditation. The poem becomes an action rather than a perception, a process rather than a form. Whether one calls it a poetry of meditation, or of process (a poetry constantly becoming), it cannot, I think, be wholly measured by the traditional forms, largely romantic meditations, which it so readily suggests. It is a poetry which not only extends and completes the essentially traditional style of *Harmonium,* but provides the standard by which the early poetry must be understood. *Harmonium,* in other words, must be seen in the light of the whole rather than the whole in the light of *Harmonium.* (pp. 9-10)

The critic of Stevens is confronted with a number of basic contradictions. He is and is not an intellectual poet, is and is not a "pure" poet. He is a romantic, but disconcertingly impersonal; a traditional poet, yet experimental; an imagist, but also a symbolist of sorts; a lyrical and meditative poet who wears equally well the masks of clown and pedagogue. The fact is, he can be at any one time any and all of these, which should, I think, give pause to those who would either praise his poetics or censure his obsession with one limited and vague idea. Stevens resolves the contradictions in a poetry which is neither pure lyric nor intellectual argument, but which at any one time may pose as either. Accused, especially in his early poetry, of being a hedonist pure and simple, Stevens was no less a reflective poet from first to last. The experience of his poetry, even at its most militantly antirational, is within the mind rather than at the tip of the senses. (p. 11)

Compared with [William Carlos] Williams or Marianne Moore, contemporaries whom he most nearly resembled, Stevens was never an objectivist or descriptive poet. "Not all objects are equal," he once wrote *en passant.* "The vice of imagism was that it did not recognize this" [*Opus Posthumous*]. This attitude defines his style from the beginning and separates him fundamentally from Williams. Indeed, his lifelong quarrel with Williams was on this point of how far the imagination could or should remake the world: that is, evolve a qualitative reality of mind from the quantitative reality of pure perception, yet still savor the essential life of things as they are. (p. 12)

[The] traditional forms and even the language of early Stevens become in the later simply a framework which is the essential form of all acts of mind, while within the framework, like the bed of a river, there flows the ever-changing, ever-various process of reality. The structure of a poem, for Stevens, becomes the action of metaphors. The landscape of his poems, whether it be "Sea Surface Full of Clouds" or "Credences of Summer," is in the mind. His subject is the activity of this mind, the act of creation, to which the reader is witness and in which he is involved. It was Stevens' faith that by being true to himself, by exercising his own imagination upon the world (whether external or internal), he could manifest the possibilities of every mind, and hence create for his time the idiom of man. (p. 15)

This ambition bespeaks Stevens' limitations. We know them well enough: abstractness, impersonality, a poetry without people and drama, a world without passion in which suffering is academic and tragedy nonexistent, a solipsistic poetry.... The movement from the personal voice of *Harmonium* to the impersonal, vatic "I" of the later poems evidences Stevens' attempt to hypostatize his humanity, not transcend it—a development from what Emerson called "mean egotism" to a human state of "Man Thinking," or to what Thoreau described as his cabin on the frontiers of thought. One has but to give himself up to the activity as well as the idea of Stevens' last poems to discover the intense passion there, a passion seeking form.... It was the necessary result of his desire to write the great poem of Man or earth, now that the great poems of Heaven and Hell had been written, and Heaven and Hell had proved to be of man's making. (pp. 15-16)

Accepting the challenge to prove the being of man in a secular age, stripped of his divinity and left an impoverished animal, Stevens pursued the human with an energy and intrepidity unequalled in our time. Whether or not he asked too much of poetry, history will judge. (p. 16)

Looking at *Harmonium* retrospectively, we can see that it is a poetry more traditional than modern. We can see it, too, as a *vade mecum* for the later work. There are, for example, poems almost exclusively of the imagination, and oppositely, poems exalting the sensuous world (a geo-poetical America, a virgin land of imagination) which in its vitality (and vulgarity) overwhelms the imagination or defies it. On the other hand, the major poems are reflective, meditations upon the meaning of the self's isolation in reality, upon time and transience. Or they are dramatic, presenting the intercourse between mind and world in all its comic variety. In the largest sense, these are poems about poetry, about the poet in search of how far he can go in re-creating the world in feelings and words, and how much he is held by reality to the world as it is. They are poems of a sensitive, alienated self, the poet as outsider seeking to be an insider, trying heroically to find his way through the world rather than beyond it. (p. 57)

Harmonium, pretty clearly, was present knowledge, and in the course of Stevens' growth and development there came the greater knowing. Not transcendental, this "distant away" was, on the contrary, a knowledge of what the self can know, what it can create, and hence what it is. (p. 269)

The elegance of *Harmonium* ... is a strategy of the sensibility, trying on clothes of definition, changing its costume as the needs of the self change. But the volume has more drift than direction, and it exists almost exclusively on the level of "present knowledge." It is a period poetry, even if in the long run it has proved to be more. Yet this is the volume by which Stevens is mainly known. There is no denying that as individual poems his earliest ones, along with a few of his very last, are the most easily accessible. But any ultimate placement of Stevens will need to account for the continuity of his development of self, and the style of that self. And this involves an understanding of his poetics, which if implied in *Harmonium* are refined and even essentially altered by the changing and aging poet, the poet who unlike any of the masks of *Harmonium* aspired to achieve a "theory of poetry" that would be a "theory of life." (p. 270)

Joseph N. Riddel, in his The Clairvoyant Eye:

The Poetry and Poetics of Wallace Stevens *(copy-right* © *1965 Louisiana State University Press),* Louisiana State University Press, 1965, 308 p.

J. HILLIS MILLER (essay date 1965)

[The] vanishing of the gods, leaving a barren man in a barren land, is the basis of all Stevens' thought and poetry. His version of the death of the gods coincides with a radical transformation in the way man sees the world. What had been a warm home takes on a look of hardness and empti-ness, like the walls, floors, and banisters of a vacant house. Instead of being intimately possessed by man, things appear to close themselves within themselves. They become mute, static presences. (p. 219)

There are only two entities left now that the gods are dead: man and nature, subject and object. Nature is the physical world, visible, audible, tangible, present to all the senses, and man is consciousness, the nothing which receives na-ture and transforms it into something unreal—"description without place".... In conceiving the world in this way Stevens inherits the tradition of dualism coming down from Descartes and the seventeenth century. Like that tradition generally, he is an unfaithful disciple of Descartes. The Cartesian God disappears from his world, and only mind and matter remain, mind confronting a matter which it makes into a mirror of itself. This bifurcation of reality is the universal human condition, from the creation until now.... (pp. 221-22)

"Sunday Morning" is Stevens' most eloquent description of the moment when the gods dissolve. Bereft of the super-natural, man does not lie down paralyzed in despair. He sings the creative hymns of a new culture, the culture of those who are "wholly human" and know themselves.... (p. 222)

The dialogue between subject and object is Stevens' central theme, and it seems that this interchange can become a "mystic marriage," like that of the great captain and the maiden Bawda in "Notes toward a Supreme Fiction".... Imagination and reality can merge to produce a third thing which escapes from the limitations of either, and we can triumphantly "mate [our] life with life".... (p. 224)

From one end of his work to the other he reiterates a single idea, and all his work is an attempt to explore the endlessly variable perspectives from which reality can be viewed by the imagination. He is resolutely carrying out Nietzsche's injunction that man the survivor of God should experiment tirelessly with new truths, new representations, new life forms.

And yet—Stevens' poems are rarely celebrations of the triumphant ease with which man "imposes orders as he thinks of them".... They describe instead a universal fluc-tuation. This motif is especially evident in *Harmonium*, but it is a constant theme throughout. (pp. 225-26)

[The] absence of any transcendent reality to which images might refer is related to Stevens' assumption that things are what they appear to be: colored forms in motion. Poetry need concern itself solely with "the surface of things" ..., for "the aspects of earth of interest to a poet are the casual ones, as light or color, images" ..., and "art, broadly, is the form of life or the sound or color of life".... This no-tion leads Stevens to write what might be called expres-sionist poems, poems which attempt to create, as does

much modern painting, a surface of colored forms without depth. These force the spectator to remain close to a primi-tive level of sensation where the hue, shape, texture, or sound of a thing is more important than the fact that it is an identifiable object. (p. 228)

This universalizing of particulars is evident in Stevens' con-stant use of the four primitive elements—bare earth; wind blowing beard and pine tree alike; water, which transforms all things it touches, as Crispin is washed away by magni-tude; and fire, absorbing everything in its flaming metamor-phosis, leaves, peacocks' tails, and planets. A restricted image like blue and white larkspur becomes an expression of totality by blending with one of these elements. Each cosmic constituent means the same thing. Even bare earth must yield to time and the round of the seasons. Every-where in Stevens the reader confronts another proof that the sovereign law of reality is change. (p. 231)

This motion is the combined oscillation of mind and things, as the mind wanders here and there seeking to capture a reality which is itself eternally changing. Imagination and reality are like two charged poles which repel one another as they approach and can never touch, though the relation between them creates a vibrant field of forces. Existence is neither imagination alone nor reality alone, but always and everywhere the endlessly frustrated attempt of the two to cross the gap which separates them. (p. 233)

Stevens' poetry defines a realm in which everything "is not what it is".... His poetry is not dialectical, if that means a series of stages which build on one another, each tran-scending the last and moving on to a higher one in some version of the Hegelian sequence of thesis, antithesis, syn-thesis. It is impossible to organize the stages of Stevens' thought in this way. A new stage merely contradicts the first, and the first remains just as valid in its own way. In fact there is no first stage. They are all equally prior and equally final. There is no progress, only an alternation be-tween contradictory possibilities. (p. 259)

The elaboration of such a mode of poetry is Stevens' chief contribution to literature, and in the meditative poems of his later years he takes possession of a new domain....

"The Man with the Blue Guitar" has a special place in Ste-vens' work. It marks his turning to the new style. The reader has the feeling that the poem has been going on for some time when he hears the first words, and the last verses are not really an ending. The twanging of the strings continues interminably. (p. 260)

Life as it is is a sequence of states of consciousness with neither start nor finish. If a poem is to be true to life it must be a constant flowing of images which come as they come and are not distorted by the logical mind in its eagerness for order. (p. 261)

The structure of a book of poems by Stevens is on a larger scale like the structure of "The Man with the Blue Guitar." Every poem is a movement toward the perfect poem which never quite gets written. (p. 262)

Stevens' poetry contains in its inner development an im-plicit rejection of technological civilization and its meta-physics. That civilization has been built both theoretically and literally on the idea that it is possible to understand and control reality by doing something to it, whether this takes the form of trying to possess things by turning them into images, perspectives, metaphors, "world views," or whether it is the literal making of machines out of the earth. Stevens, like Gerard Manley Hopkins, sees modern civilization as an obscuring of reality which leaves man in possession of a two-dimensional façade. (p. 267)

The later Stevens is beyond metaphysical dualism, and beyond representational thinking. It is no longer a question of some reality which exists already in the world, and of which the poet then makes an image. The image is inextricably part of the thing, and the most extreme imaginative distortion is still based on reality. There is only one mode of existence: consciousness of some reality. Imagination never exists separately. Reality never exists separately. All that ever exists, anywhere, for man, is imagination-reality, an imaginary reality, or a real imagination. (pp. 274-75)

"It is a world of words to the end of it" . . .—this is apparently Stevens' ultimate position: the reconciliation of imagination and reality in a theory of the identity of poetry and life, and the development of a poetry which will sustain this identity. There is one more aspect of his thought, however, and this the most difficult to see or to say.

It begins with a movement toward nothingness in his later poetry. Along with the development of a poetry of the swarming moment there is something different. As its tensions are resolved, Stevens' poetry gets more and more disembodied, more and more a matter of the spirit's alchemicana and less and less a matter of the solid and tangible, the pears on their dish, the round peaches with their fuzz and juice. His verse becomes more and more insubstantial as the oscillations between imagination and reality get more and more rapid, until, at the limit, the poem seems about to evaporate altogether. At the extreme of speed all solidity disappears. The mobility which allows beginning and ending to merge releases something else: a glimpse of the nothingness which underlies existence. (pp. 276-77)

Stevens seemed to be approaching a full possession of plenitude of things, but as the tension between imagination and reality dimishes there is an emptying out of both, until at the moment they touch, in the brevity of a poem which includes beginning and ending in a breath, the poet finds himself face to face with a universal nothing.

This apparent defeat is the supreme victory, for the nothing is not nothing. It is. It is being. Being is a pervasive power, visible nowhere in itself and yet present and visible in all things. It is what things share through the fact that they are. Being is not a thing like other things and therefore can only appear to man as nothing, but it is what all things must participate in if they are to exist at all. Stevens' later poetry has as its goal the releasing of that evanescent glimpse of being which is as close as man can come to a possession of the ground of things. The paradoxical appearance of being in the form of nothing causes the ambiguity of his poetry. (pp. 278-79)

> *J. Hillis Miller, "Wallace Stevens," in his* Poets of Reality: Six Twentieth-Century Writers *(copyright © 1965 by the President and Fellows of Harvard College; excerpted by permission of the author and publishers), Cambridge, Mass.: Harvard University Press, 1965, pp. 217-84.*

FRANK DOGGETT (essay date 1966)

The concepts that emerge from long reading of the poetry of Stevens are so slight and so basic that any elementary course in philosophy or even a few years of interested reading could yield all of them; yet, these concepts taken together are not mere miscellaneous samplings, for there is an accordance among them. The accordance is probably a result of Stevens' preference for naturalistic thought and for ideas that lean on the imagery of organism. . . . Still, there is no dialectic to support them, and they never cohere into an organized body of thought. In general, throughout Stevens' poetry, the only continuous strand of thought is a fundamental naturalism that is immediately apparent in the poems of *Harmonium*. This naturalism is as much a sentiment, as much an expression of an allegiance—a piety and an affection—as it is an expression of thought. The allegiance is to earth, and the sentiment is expressed in many celebrations of the reality that is the substance and support of his existence.

The concepts that are submerged in Stevens' poetry are usually some variation of the idea of the subject-object relationship—what Stevens so often refers to as "the interrelation between reality and the imagination" that he says is "the basis of the character of literature." . . . For the critic of Stevens, it is of paramount importance to notice that the poet sees an idea as the fundamental implication of one of his own poems. (pp. ix-x)

[Stevens] hoped his poems bore "some feature, some richness, even if only half-perceived," of the reality of earth, "of the planet of which they were a part." It was the wish of a poet who found the central concern of his poetry in the estrangement of the self from a world external to it. (p. 1)

One necessity of individual being . . . is mortality, and another is subjectivity, for the mind is a specific of time as well as a specific of existence or point of identity from which all the world radiates. These two aspects of being— mortality and the interdependence of mind and world—engross most of the discourse of this poetry.

The unique, conceiving, reflecting self of Stevens' poetry is both container and contained. The world exists only within the mind, and yet the mind exists only within the world. (p. 4)

Stevens' ardent longing for the physical reality of burgeoning life is a central thesis of his work, and throughout his many years in poetry, from his early days as dweller in the dark cabin crying hail on the watermelon pavilion to the gold-feathered bird singing in the palm at the end of the mind, he celebrates simple vitality. (p. 8)

Male and female principles in the poetry of Stevens are often representations of consciousness as male lover and of reality as anonymous woman—unknown because reality can never be realized objectively. (p. 24)

The poet in his nostalgia for the real had conceived of reality as woman and found (just as Jung did) one that is both the beloved object of desire and the eternal mother of all. (p. 39)

The innocence of the archetypal woman is that of the course of nature that proceeds without any untoward purpose. (p. 41)

Only rarely is Stevens' archetypal woman touched by the literary mythology that he eschews. She is never individualized, is usually naked and nameless, and sometimes appears only in the hint given by the use of a personal pronoun. Her symbolic function is provisional, and if interpretation be pressed, she is best understood as an embodiment of an attitude toward the content of objective experience. The attitude is often that of a longing suddenly realized by a vivid image of woman, as in "Debris of Life and Mind". (p. 45)

The inamorata or nameless beloved of Stevens' poetry is myth in its incipient form because she is a spontaneous and natural embodiment of feeling and a surrogate for an unknown. The image gives identity to the random events, the disparate objects encountered in a fortuitous existence. When reality is configured by myth, the miscellany of things on every side becomes one world conjoined by a latent centrality of being; its shifting appearances are held together by a figure of reality or nature. The woman as mother or as inamorata reflects this sense of person felt within the reality of the world, derived perhaps from a projection of self but always known to be something apart —intimate but elusive, continually desired and never truly attained. (p. 46)

"An Ordinary Evening in New Haven" ends with a phrase that expresses Stevens' sense of the flux of things: "A force that traverses a shade" affirms the domination of time and process over a world continually passing away. Stevens' poetry is permeated by the idea of time, and a great deal of the poetry can be known only in terms of his concept of process and the relevance of many of his images to this concept. (p. 55)

[Stevens] conceives of the self as a center of change and animation, sometimes in terms of the idea of the inner flow of experience, at other times of an interior person or creature, or again with no more than a suggestion of the secret activity of life "in the central of our being." Stevens uses *humming* to suggest that animation is a continuous inner commotion and implies by this image that he shares Bergson's idea of the flux as the coursing of the interior life, of "duration," as Bergson terms the interior flux of experience. (p. 57)

It is because of incessant passage in the present moment that the world is seen only the moment after, and this lightning passage occurs within the life of experience in such a way that whatever is entering that life is simultaneously departing. . . .

The poetry alternates between a consideration of the coming and of the going. (p. 59)

No matter how slight, how unobserved, one minute shifting of relations, one added light "creates a fresh universe by adding itself." The universe that he imagines as an objective and vast quietude is inherently active with power and potential for all changes. The newness, the freshness of each moment and its fresh universe is what he calls "time's given perfections." This freshness is the element by which men exist—an element that fulfills the need of each generation and its culture to be actual and as it is. (pp. 60-1)

One could not know oneself from moment to moment if there were no persistent elements in one's world, if it did not always seem the same place. In Stevens' sense of the flux, there is a mingling of repetition and alteration. Out of the alteration comes the eternal novelty of experience, and out of the repetitions of one's world, the continuance of one's identity. (p. 62)

Stevens' symbolic and anecdotal representations show that he feels the self to be capable of infinite variations, of division into multiple selves, a chameleon of weather and feeling—one moment bright and single, the next "the evilly compounded, vital I." He seems to regard the interior life as fluid and formless and composing a specific character only out of integrations of animal feeling. (p. 87)

If Stevens ever has a moral, it is the one that he indicates [in "Notes toward a Supreme Fiction": the poet's occupation of song is "A thing final in itself and, therefore, good"] and that he repeats in many versions throughout his productive life in poetry. He emphasizes his moral with his singing hidden rhymes and illustrates it with his symbolic picture of wine coming to men in a wood who enjoy the good that comes to them just as they do the contemplation of the simple activity of that which exists, of the leaf spinning, paradigm of the spinning world. To put his moral in paraphrase: experience is a good in itself. (p. 118)

The supplemental opposites, physical life and cognition, represent two ways of knowing the world, and a number of Stevens' poems express the theme that the world is truly realized in the life of the body and that abstract thought is itself a separation, a removal from the reality it considers. (pp. 143-44)

The notion that to know is merely to regard one's own idea, that knowledge about is a poor substitute for an experience of, that an idea is always and inherently fictive permeates all of the poetry of Stevens. (pp. 148-49)

Stevens' skeptical view of reason is reinforced by his naturalism. Right or wrong, to speculate is the nature of the conscious self. . . . Perception of anything, of "A Dish of Peaches in Russia," is an engagement of the body with the world. And the body is also one with the self and all its history of affections, its identity spilled out in its individuality of memory merged with the present personal consciousness. (p. 149)

The body as an irrational animal is an archetype. "Poetry Is a Destructive Force" uses this image to show the whole man composed of a body and its dormant emotions bearing the wakeful consciousness that is the rational man. These dormant emotions are sleeping beasts, and the reason lives within this animality. (p. 150)

[The] animal nature of man, Stevens indicates [in "An Ordinary Evening in New Haven"], has an inherent need for the illusions that enable him to increase the range and variety of conceptual life, the fictions by which he may live, awake or conscious. (p. 161)

By the evidence of many poems, it is obvious that Stevens assumed that there is a naturalistic basis for the life of the imagination and that poetry itself is a flowering of the natural world. Just as consciousness is a temporary waking from the sleep of the unconscious natural world, just as reason is the illusion of self-command of the irrational natural creature, just as the attempt to know reality and all the subtlety of thought is only the self-regard of nature, with reality looking into that mirror, the mind: "a glass / The sun steps into, regards and finds itself"—just as all these things are aspects of the natural world, so also the voice of poetry is only a sound like all the other real noises of things and voices. Poetry is a form of ordered meaning abstracted from the sound that words make. All intentional meaningful utterance is ultimately no more than sound, like the spontaneous cries of all the creatures of the world or like the accidental noises of things shaken or in motion: sound of wind, water, things in friction or impact. (pp. 162-63)

In a great many of Stevens' poems, his ideas, like the slight action usual in most lyrics, provide a surface for immediate attention and give the poem a guise or a role to perform. This guise for Stevens is that of an intuition of reality; thus, idea carries on for him a function for the whole poem that resembles the function of an action in a poem with a dominant dramatic character. His poetic ideas engage us in a semblance of an experience that is specific in character and expresses a certain individual sense of the world.... We are accustomed to poems in which a fiction, an invented situation or a particular mode of action, becomes a representation of an abstraction by standing as symbolic of an idea, or as part and instance of a universal. Thus, the specified thing or event, transformed by implication, is turned into a general concept. Stevens' poems are often made of this traditional experience-into-cognition arrangement; but just as often he reverses it with an arrangement of idea into experience. (pp. 207-08)

Stevens himself insists on the value of his ideas, but he also insists that this truth value exist only in the particular sense of existence given in one of his poems; for the kind of truth value that an idea in a poem by Stevens normally has is intuitive and revelatory rather than practical and applicable beyond the context. His realizations or "secretions of insight," as Stevens calls them, embody experience as though the idea created special circumstances in which the world could be known but only in a certain way and according to the terms of the idea itself. The idea of "On the Road Home" has such a function. Its contrast of the old philosophic pair, the one and the many, is no more than a simple rejection of one and vindication of the other in terms of a new realization of living, a result of his awareness of the vividness and particularity of immediate experience. (p. 209)

It was in "On the Road Home" that Stevens says that he became aware that anything real is individual and exists only in a particular experience of it. Thus it is that pluralism gives the real things within the flux, and man standing in that flux stands alone. (p. 210)

[Stevens] finds *the* truth falsely enshrined; and finding reality in the idea of pluralism, like a poet but unlike a philosopher, he turns it into a way of regarding the world, and the idea is dissolved in an experience. (p. 211)

[Stevens' ideas] have other purposes than philosophic ones and are really only half ideas after all. Stevens in his poetic wisdom never made them more.

The secret of the effect of these ideas is their lack of elaboration. Stevens' usual plan for cognition in a poem is to use an abstraction as an over-all expository scheme and then within that scheme to move from one idea to another, these contained ideas being almost discrete and used to support the emotional implications of the major ideas rather than to express abstract import. In other words, his subsidiary ideas do not elaborate the over-all idea; they elaborate its emotional implications. Stevens is too knowing a poet to subject his poems to an overwhelming cognitive content. What appears to be an elaboration of an idea may only be the repetition of its slight meaning. (p. 213)

Frank Doggett, in his Stevens' Poetry of Thought *(copyright © 1966 by the Johns Hopkins Press), The Johns Hopkins University Press, 1966, 223 p.*

JAMES BAIRD (essay date 1968)

The adventure in the total structure and the ritual of its making—in the view of Wallace Stevens these are the acts of the poet. As the supreme motions of the mind in its encounter with a world in motion, they justify the will of the artist. In a comment on the critic Paul Rosenfeld, Stevens wrote: "... [he] was a shaper, that is to say, a *Schöpfer,* who lived for the sake of *Schöpfung....* This constant shaping, as distinguished from constancy of shape, is characteristic of the poet." *Schöpfung.* The English equivalent will not serve. Stevens returns to his European heritage. He must be satisfied in his naming of creative restlessness. (p. 1)

The nature of architecture is the nature of the process celebrated as *Schöpfung....* [The] concept behind architecture as an art of shaping was mandatory for Stevens.... Beneath the crafted object is the living and moving idea of the object. The Platonic metaphor of the golden form is merely another name for the fact of organicism. (pp. 2-3)

The one architectural form in the poetry of Coleridge that may have engaged Stevens' attention is, of course, the pleasure-dome of "Kubla Khan." But as a fanciful structure it is dream alone, wholly unrelated to things of a "stone" reality-made-ideas. The dome of Stevens rests upon the rigid, indifferent base; it preserves a total poetic process, steel above stone. Coleridge's dome of Xanadu is scarcely attributable to the hand of an adjacent architect, any more than the peculiar power of Alph, the sacred river, is measurable, as it flows through caverns to a sunless sea. The pleasure-dome has "caves of ice"; its shadow floats "midway on the waves." Remarkable as this poem is in hallucinatory power, it is a water-borne mirage. The imagination dictates images in a state of riot unchallenged by poetic will. Such antecedence is of no value in a study of Stevens. One may as well attempt to urge a prefiguring eminence for the white radiance beyond Shelley's "dome of many-coloured glass" in "Adonais".... These domes are imposed, rather than integral, structures. (p. 39)

For Stevens the lesson of Laforgue has the ... significant consequence of imaginative play upon the idea made of the object from an implacable reality. The "Dimanche" poems of Laforgue's *Des Fleurs de Bonne Volonté*—a title exactly compelling for Stevens, flowers, flourishings from a will (imposed upon the commonplace)—seem to me to be of real consequence in a later American expression. "Dimanche" is the symbol of the banal, the quotidian. The eleventh poem of the *Fleurs* opens with "O forbidden Sundays of the infinite ..." and continues, "Sunday citizens, entirely quotidian...." Sunday becomes the symbol of the banality of bourgeois commonplaceness, the quotidian of the "old can-can" (the *only* bourgeois dance), of sordidness, of rain, of "damp tobacco" in an endless succession. Sunday-made-idea is rendered again and again by the imagination. Each time it reappears, it is cast in a different mode. The subject remains the same. This method of imaginative play upon mediocrity, the quality of the quotidian—in other words, the flat and senseless endurance of a commonplace reality untransformed by imagination—is the method of Stevens. The symbol of Sunday perseveres in him: it is first exploited in "Ploughing on Sunday"; it is asserted again in "Sunday Morning"; it is recast in the fourth section of "Owl's Clover"; it reappears in a distant poem of the last meditations, "The Old Lutheran Bells at Home." It has its own architectural significance in the continuity of the poetry. When one adds to this evidence Stevens' speculation upon the quotidian in "The Comedian as the Letter C," this sapping power, this insidious weight that gives nothing in return save an "unkeyed" music . . . , it seems clear that Laforgue had been regarded intently and closely remembered. (pp. 50-1)

With Emerson, nature moves as an outward display of inner reality; with Stevens it moves in a pattern willed by the observer's self alone, and it displays nothing save the reality made by the imagination. Emerson should be regarded as on the American way to Stevens.

But one notes immediately that the province of central man is the paradigm common to both poets. Within this native America area, the self is wholly the tyrant of the field of vision. Emerson is the first theorist, the archdisputant. (p. 67)

Emerson is again a threshold for Stevens in his American decree of the poet as "the namer." We understand this master author to be the poet-self, the originator of the essential name. (p. 68)

An examination of Stevens as architect must encompass [the] feeling of structure as process. To see the act of the artist in terms of geometric forms and relationships is to recognize the compulsion of the draftsman. (p. 80)

[The] one abstraction of Stevens [is] major man, the imagination. We understand that any art devoted to a thoroughly mathematical conception of the world was for him insupportable. The imposition of free movement by an imagination playing upon physical nature is . . . denied. Surrender to the "clanking mechanism" amounts to an endless winter of the artist. . . .

It was Cézanne's insistence upon the structure of physical reality, the authority of natural form beneath imaginative rendering, which finally marked his separation from pure impressionism. The same insistence is obvious in Stevens, even when one considers his judgment of impressionism as "the only really great thing in modern art." It is certainly of some significance that Cézanne is mentioned far more frequently in the critical prose of Stevens than is any other modern painter. This preoccupation would seem to come of an awareness of Cézanne's postimpressionist advance into problems of structure. (p. 84)

A geometric precision remained the prize above the imperfect. He continued to order the points of his reference. The arrows described their arcs. They fell at the points that he plotted. It is perhaps not generally recognized that the arrangement of the last four lyrics in the *Collected Poems* is the final evidence of precision. I take these strictly in the order presented: "St. Armorer's Church from the Outside," the survey of the design completed, however imperfect to the poet, however rare to us; "The Planet on the Table," the farewell to the imagination; "The River of Rivers in Connecticut," the farewell to American earth and American being; "Not Ideas about the Thing but the Thing Itself," the salutation to the new poet to follow, the next voice in the endless succession of central man. (p. 90)

The metaphor of the arc is related to every mathematical projection of Stevens in the act of design. Invariably it represents the thrust into the future. . . .

At any point on any arc the act of the poet predicts his own future in imagination. . . . To the very end of Stevens' poetry the requirement of *materia poetica* from reality of place endures. Yet the dome in air, made by a free imagination, is an aggregate description without place. Finally, when there is no longer a future, the woman-genius of the poet takes refuge in the enclosure of summer, as though it were a *last* summer, "Like a shelter not in an arc . . ." ("Celle Qui Fût Héaulmiette," . . .). She is *helmeted* there; and . . . this helmet is the completed dome. (p. 96)

Stevens is not a maker of a new sun-myth; nor is he an anthropological historian of an old one. As the imagination, endlessly preserved in major man, is the inner center of the individual's life, so is the sun, endlessly primary in the phenomena of earth, the outer center of the individual's sight. From these centers stream two courses of vitality, man-exerted and sun-exerted. Stevens names these *bars*. (p. 107)

[The] sun remains the source of man's existential courage. . . . Once Adam woke in morning light, endowed with his first human power to make a metaphor of the world, "While all the leaves leaked gold". . . . His was the first human experience with the sun. But it was he who malformed the metaphor. The world malformed became paradise malformed. We may assume that with the myth of Adam's fall Judaeo-Christian man was forever to be denied the freedom of a self-wrought metaphor. The objective of human life became, in this tradition, bondage to an imagined state of existence *beyond life*. Now, far into history, we say that "the solar chariot is junk". . . . This saying, Stevens reminds us, is not a variation upon sun-myth, but an end of myth. (And we acknowledge, in this sense, that the myth now dead was itself foreign to the Judaeo-Christian theocentrism that began with Adam.) But the possibility of man in a world-as-metaphor remains. He has a power of shaping his world when he continues "to stick to the contents of the mind / And the desire to believe in a metaphor . . .". . . . The sun inspires him; the self derives from the sun a strength to believe in its metaphor of the world, a metaphor of the untrue, and yet a defiance of the reality of self-nothingness in the universe. (pp. 111-12)

[It] is Stevens as a modern man who writes the tale of ultimate sun-disaster. In the total range of American expression in this century there is perhaps no poem approximating his "Page from a Tale". . . . If modern man has no kinship with Delos or any other sun-altar, his thought of the sun is no less awesome: he possesses modern physics. This late poem of Stevens' is compelled by twentieth-century science. It is strange that its apocalyptic vision has been so little noticed. Here is an imagery which blazes with awesome force. (p. 113)

The longest of Stevens' sequences under an encompassing title is "Notes Toward a Supreme Fiction." I take this as the supreme statement, the crown of the dome. In this work all the arcs will be found to cross. I think of it as the point of intersection. (p. 114)

James Baird, in his The Dome and the Rock: Structure in the Poetry of Wallace Stevens *(copyright © 1968 by the Johns Hopkins Press), The Johns Hopkins University Press, 1968, 334 p.*

DENIS DONOGHUE (essay date 1968)

Stevens was not a philosopher, a systematic thinker. Stevens did not play with philosophic ideas: he was too scrupulous to frivol with the gravity of other men. Moment by moment, poem by poem, he committed himself to the 'mental state' of the occasion, doing his best to make it lucid if nothing else. If it occurred to him that these local commitments were contradictory, he was not distressed, because he trusted that the work would conform to the nature of the worker, and no other conformity was required. (p. 225)

[We] might call him a metaphysical poet, for the sufficient reason that his themes are often metaphysical; Appearance and Reality; the One and the Many; Being (as, specifically, in 'Metaphor as Degeneration'); Knowledge; Image and Idea; Metamorphosis. But this would mean going against Stevens's wish. . . .

Trying again: it would be possible and decent to think of Stevens as a mythological poet, on the particular authority of that passage in 'The Comedian as the Letter C' in which he says

> What counted was mythology of self,
> Blotched out beyond unblotching. . . .

or that late poem in which he says that, 'A mythology reflects its region.' And this, at the least, would be preferable to the poverty of calling Stevens a symbolist poet; especially after 'This Solitude of Cataracts'; in which the poet repudiates the language of wild ducks or mountains that are not mountains. But then we remark, with some embarrassment, that Stevens also wrote 'The Poem that Took the Place of a Mountain'; so we are advised to take another tack. (p. 227)

My predicate runs somewhat on these lines. Stevens wrote his poems for a hundred reasons, including this one: to pass the time, to get through the evening. He wrote while waiting: for what? For the maximum disclosure of his own poetic powers. And because this is eight words he often reduced it to one, calling it God: or sometimes to three, calling it the human imagination. Hence and meanwhile there was something to be done. Good or bad, it would be better than its alternative—nothing, the grand zero. He had his own powers: and he had the language, in its dazzling resource. (p. 228)

Stevens, like Santayana, is an inquisitor of structures, and he will test them as severely as he can. He knows as well as any other modern poet that one can be self-indulgent in words even more easily than in action or evasion. And he knows . . . that words are a great defence of the mind against being possessed by thought; a defence and an ease of mind. Words alone are certain good, Yeats said, and only half-believed: the other half of the belief was taken up by Stevens, for whom the world had to issue in the word or declare itself redundant. (p. 234)

The basic motive of *Notes Toward a Supreme Fiction* is to offer man a substitute for God; to show him how he may transfer to himself the attributes and reverberations of the divine. This involves the replacement of certain fundamental terms in accordance with the idea that 'God and the imagination are one'. If they are one, the former may be replaced by the latter. So the idea of God is replaced by the idea of the imagination. Theology becomes Poetry, Meta-

physics becomes Aesthetics. Faith is now addressed to the relation between the imagination and the structures of its own invention. The priest is replaced by the poet. Hence the Supreme Fiction is the Theme, of which only a few variations are known; the theme itself is not known, since it is beyond all the variations. The purpose of the *Notes* is to find the most persuasive variations; hence to imply the Theme by urging the imagination to reach it. The relation between theme and variations is like the relation between the body's beauty, which never dies, and the body, which always dies; or the relation between perfection and 'the imperfect', which is meanwhile 'our paradise'; or the relation, in 'The Comedian as the Letter C', between the text and its glosses; or the relation, in 'The Emperor of Ice Cream', between the 'be' which is the finale and the 'seemings' which lead up to it.

Meanwhile Stevens offers to translate the old terms. If God is the human imagination, Life is what the human mind has come to know: time is the continuum in which the mind acts: the self is the locus of the imagination. Fact is the instrumental matter through which the mind declares itself. . . . Value is the glow surrounding the acts of the mind. Notes toward a Supreme Fiction: supreme, meaning 'fully answerable to man's needs and desires', leaving no ache behind; fiction, meaning a structure of man's invention, corresponding not to an impersonal, objective reality but to the nature of the inventor; great because he is great. 'The image must be of the nature of its creator.' . . . The fiction is in man's image as the theologians say that man is created in God's image. (pp. 267-68)

[We] are tempted to read Stevens's *Notes* as a humanist answer to the *Four Quartets*. Think of the poems together, the unwilling light they cast upon each other. Both are didactic, large statements, couched in grand terms with the support of many earlier experiments in the resource of language. . . . When Eliot points to the Negative Way, the way of purgation, Stevens translates the admonition into humanist terms; each of us must become 'an ignorant man' again, until we can see the sun clearly 'in the idea of it', the dazzle of perception. (pp. 268-69)

Stevens's object is to see how much of human life is in the power of the imagination. If the answer is: All; then man is indeed God. (p. 269)

[The] Supreme Fiction, which must be abstract and must change, must also give pleasure. One of the most compelling patterns in Stevens takes this line: why do we do such-and-such?; because we like doing it. And why do we like doing it? Because doing it satisfies something in our nature. But why does it satisfy? We do not know—to proceed beyond this is to 'say more than human things with human voice,' and, 'That cannot be.' (pp. 281-82)

[The] last phrase of the Epilogue stays in mind; 'the bread of faithful speech'. If we are ironists we reflect that man may in some sense live on this bread, but only after his requirements in the more prosaic kind of bread are satisfied. This is one of the dissatisfactions which persist; the feeling that to Stevens bread is something to which we listen rather than something we eat. Things become metaphorical and figurative before they have long established themselves as things. Yeats said that *Marius the Epicurean* taught him and his fellow-poets 'to walk upon a rope tightly stretched through serene air', and they were left to keep their feet upon 'a swaying rope in a storm'. Stevens is a virtuoso in this manoeuvre. What Pater called 'the gypsy phrase' is an essential part of his poetry: finding little nourishment in the gibberish of the vulgate, he had to rely upon his own. He cared little for the dialect of the tribe: he did not feel called upon to purify it.

There are other sources of dissatisfaction. Stevens never quite persuades us that consciousness is the centre of all human circles. While reading him we are persuaded that the only relevant human act is consciousness, but when we put down the book and read something else or nothing at all, we cease to believe him. Other things assert their importance; spontaneous, daily things, hardly conscious at all. Sometimes in Stevens the imaginative act seems too easy, the resistance not great enough. Reality seems to be merely an instrument for the disclosure of the human mind: the world is merely adjectival to the noun, the imagination. . . . But the real difficulty in Stevens is that the individual John Smith tends to be dissolved in the idea of John Smith and finally in the idea of Man. The reason is clear. If John Smith lives and moves without my *fiat*, his life and motion are an affront to my imagination. Stevens does not always think so, as we have seen, but the thought came easily when it came at all. He would sometimes allow that 'the plum survives its poems', but this allowance came hard. This is why he would have asked to live in essence rather than in substance or existence. He found it a little too easy to abstract himself. (pp. 286-88)

[The] satisfactions in reading Stevens are so great that to qualify our pleasure seems the work of a churl. But vagabond doubts persist. I think it a limitation in the *Notes* that they seek a Supreme Fiction rather than a viable Truth. In the *Adagia* Stevens says, 'In the long run the truth does not matter,' and we respect his meaning. But if you opt out of a search for truth your traversing acquires the gaiety of freedom at the cost of being arbitrary. You can assert that there is a relation between the proffered image and the nature of its creator, but you can merely assert it; there is no proof. This is why the reader remembers, in Stevens, the labials of certain exquisite moments, moments of a consciousness almost Decadent, making us revel in Decadence against our sharper judgement; and then we put down the book and move back into the world of gutturals, half in relief. Fiction is such a relief from fact, until fact becomes a relief from fiction. (p. 288)

In Stevens's greatest poetry the purity of the fiction is wonderfully thwarted by his sense of the palpable world, the sundry of things, and especially in his later poems he gave the world its due. I have argued elsewhere [in *Connoisseurs of Chaos*] that in *The Rock* the poetry is sustained by a vigorous tension between principle and particle; between 'intelligence' and 'soil', to use the terms of 'The Comedian as the Letter C'. Where the tension fails, the poetry is slack; and slackness is Stevens's characteristic fault. He is not a dramatic poet: his bearings are aesthetic at some cost to all the other considerations, moral, social, and political. He tends to place his qualified spectator at a suitable vantage-point, looking at the world with his own imaginative eyes: hence the poetry of meditation and survey. But the tension between thesis and instinct on these occasions often results in Stevens's greatest poetry. . . . (pp. 288-89)

Denis Donoghue, "Nuances of a Theme by Stevens" and "On 'Notes Toward a Supreme Fiction'," in his The Ordinary Universe: Soundings in Modern Literature *(reprinted with permission of Macmillan Publishing Co., Inc.; copyright © 1968 by Denis Donoghue), Macmillan, 1968, pp. 221-40, 267-90.*

JAN PINKERTON   (essay date 1971)

Many refinements of epistemological thinking that have been attributed to Stevens are simply statements of a worried man's response to a world he sees as giving in to such evils as high taxes and socialism. These so often are the "pressures of reality" which critics have leaped to define in ways that would have pleased Stevens, a man of philosophical pretensions, but which he clearly had not originally intended. Stevens' prose has been elaborated on by critics seeking to prove his profundity, but a more realistic appraisal of it indicates a man with some philosophical but very little historical understanding, whose imprecise phrasing conceals the voice of a businessman who finds the world going downhill, away from the Protestant virtues on which he was raised and away even from the recognition of aristocratic tastes that justify an elite in a world of vulgarity.

Stevens' gradually escalating defense of the poet, in other words—starting, say, with "The Man with the Blue Guitar" —is most accurately seen as a defensive withdrawal from a declining world of increasing vulgarity, a world which he realized was not susceptible to his poetic legislation. The qualities of his mind, moreover, cannot be understood until he is rescued from the hyperboles of his critics. He was a man who tried to understand modern society, but whose limitations of background, personality, and intellect kept him from such an understanding and made many of his pronouncements both fatuous and naïve. Being a skillful poet does not make one a purveyor of wisdom; it is time to reassess all such claims that have been made on Stevens' behalf. . . . (p. 576)

Despite avowals that the poet has no social obligation, despite insistence that his poetry is "pure," Stevens was obsessed with a world gone wrong, and the reality that he came to speak of was basically a new and confusing political and economic reality. Yet he was naïve and totally lacking in historical understanding, and his pronouncements tended to be both muddled and inaccurate. He did not have a tough mind, nor did he have the kind of mind capable of the reconstruction of the world that his critics have claimed for him. What he ultimately did offer in his prose statements was a belief, never clearly explained, that poetry could offer some sort of psychic salvation to men of understanding and sensibility living in a world of disquieting and threatening social upheaval. Indeed, such an existence, made bearable by poetry, was man's heroism. (p. 601)

Jan Pinkerton, "Political Realities and Poetic Release: Prose Statements by Wallace Stevens," in The New England Quarterly *(copyright 1971 by The New England Quarterly), Vol. XLIV, No. 4, December, 1971, pp. 575-601.*

HUGH KENNER   (essay date 1975)

[The great novelty of "Sunday Morning"] is the way the poem opens not into a world, still tenuously Aristotle's, of place and person, but into a becalmed world of visual arrangement: Painting. (p. 77)

If you imagine a painted woman having thoughts, you are passing (it is hard to say how far) beyond any intent of the painter. The eye is caressed by appearance, arranged appearance, appearance arranged within art's silent world. "The Man with the Blue Guitar" in the same way takes off from the Picasso of the blue landscapes and emaciated harlequins, and offers the unplayed music, silent speech, unstatable statement which, obligated by the pressure of Picasso's vision, might be expected to issue from a guitar in a painted universe.

This may be Stevens' chief technical insight. Very early in his career he appears to have sensed that in the time since Wordsworth's enterprise foundered it has been the painter who has developed the only feasible relationship of the sole man to the mute universe. The painter's works cling to its dimension, the visual, and share its muteness. Pictures do with the visible universe what poetry once did with the universe the visible universe superseded, the universe of speech, which traced everything to the *logos* and heard everything informed with divine and human voices (for Bryant the voice of Nature is a convention, vestigial). So Stevens allows the painter to precede him, performing the first selection, the first arrangement, the first concretion of images. The strange dimension in which his language operates, employing in recognizable sentence patterns words you can look up if you don't happen to recognize them, always seeming to be saying in an orderly way something really simple which we find we cannot quite follow, is accounted for and perhaps obliged by the metaphor of the painting: familiar language transmuted into a self-contained system by exactly the same means Picasso has employed in transmuting familiar visual facts into a self-contained system: language caught up into the world of the painted guitar.

Which is why, in Stevens' world, there are no actions and no speeches, merely ways of looking at things. The long tradition of mimesis uses words to imitate actions and speeches; but confronted by a world of matter and motion, from which actions and speeches have departed, mimesis can only imitate (1) old poems, or (2) the movements of the mind transposing and reconstituting what is seen. Old poems Stevens frequently imitates, their way, their air, their rituals. The movements of the transposing, reconstituting mind, these he imitates habitually, and it is frequently the movements of the painter's mind that he elects as model. And so we have a poem called "Thirteen Ways of Looking at a Blackbird."

Stevens might have invented the Blackbird. It performs no Aristotelian actions: in ways accessible to poetry, it neither does nor suffers. You could not write a tragedy about it. It is presumably sentient, yet alien; yet not more alien, in the cosmos of Newton, than any other sentient thing: than Mrs. Pappadopoulos, say, or the Friends from Pascagoula. And the blackbird is alien from the kingdom of traditional poetry, where he obtains a visa only as part of the company baked in a pie; and alien also from that sphere of feeling which Wordsworth denominated "Nature." No sense sublime of something far more deeply interfused has its dwelling, so far as we intuit, in him. He will serve very nicely as the projection into art's cosmos of the Solitary (archetype of Wordsworth's Leech Gatherer): instantly visible, the inevitable focus of attention in any picture or poem in which he appears, a black shape, a hoarse cry. (pp. 77-9)

The thirteenth way, its turns out, is simply to look. . . . If we are not conscious of any difficulty in doing this, that is because of our experience with the coincidences of the visible universe, where dark snowy afternoons and blackbirds often engage in mutual coexistence. This sequence of words no more holds up the mirror to Nature than did any of the preceding ones. But for once a correspondence of two *Gestalts,* this of words, that of natural things, can persuade us that dissonances have been dissolved. Language, it would seem, can mime the wordless world only by a kind of coincidence, as when a stain on the wallpaper resembles a face. The sequence coheres by postulating a maximal separation between what is said and what is experienced, so that it can produce a climactic flat recognition by making their contours momentarily coincide. This assumption is the polar opposite of Williams' assumption that words share thinghood with things, and that language is a social fact needing no explanations. A Williams poem becomes as unintelligible, if we make a puzzle of how words relate to reality, as a Stevens poem does if we do not.

Each of the thirteen ways of looking at a blackbird is a way of playing with the *word* blackbird, setting it in a miniature context, bounded by the shape of a stanza or the rules of a sentence, exactly as a painter might play with the *shape* blackbird, placing it somewhere within his rectangle among a gamut of accessories: trees, houses, glass coaches. (pp. 80-1)

Wallace Stevens was the Last Romantic, the last poet of a long era that believed in "poetry," something special to be intuited before the words had been found, something of which one's intuition guided the precious words. (p. 185)

Hugh Kenner, in his A Homemade World: The American Modernist Writers *(copyright © 1975 by Hugh Kenner; reprinted by permission of Alfred A. Knopf, Inc.), Knopf, 1975, 221 p.**

RICHARD EBERHART (essay date 1976)

It is rather dangerous for me to read Wallace Stevens in 1976; it would have been better in 1956. I felt him to be the large general mentor of the times, whom I looked up to as commanding the scene. I took comfort in this. I knew my man and believed in the excellence and durability of his stance. To me it was a high artistic position comporting with an acceptance of an America it represented. Having suffered T. S. Eliot and living in the surround of Eliot for decades, as had those of my generation, it was a distinct refreshment of taste to transfer to Stevens one's beliefs and wishes. He was above the battle, while happily engrossed daily in the business of business. There was this secure moment, a moment of a few years, when Stevens satisfied the capacity to live with belief within a sophisticated poetry. It seemed to have everything: the serious, the grand, the concise, temperamental extravaganzas, periods made memorable by fantastic grammar, a love of this world seen through a repetitious philosophy, a sinister darkness still with the power to charm, a colorful grotesquerie with the skill not to abate interest. His poetry succumbed to endless resources to overcome itself. He overwhelms sensory predicaments by tactile arrangements of style without overwhelming the substratum of sheer and embroidered intelligence. He could write problem poems like "The Emperor of Ice Cream" and the "Anecdote of the Jar," but he was not limited to anthology exercises and could walk and ramble through miles of Stevens territory in his long poems which never dragged foot. He was my specialist of the exquisite, the refined, and he was my expert in the grand, the noble, the generous, a poet of large statements and design. He was as readable as his handwriting was unreadable. One wanted to go on reading and reading, making the Stevens voyage into infinities of metaphors and tropes, a great health of the spirit. I thought he represented America at its best.

Now we have to look at Stevens in another way. (pp. 214-15)

In 1976 Stevens represents a part of the American poetry scene of the past quarter-century or more, but maybe what we yearn for is less nobility, less imaginative detachment from society; maybe we want a man as big as the continent we live on, a Walt Whitman or his like, a poet of universal, nor particular, consciousness. But Stevens was universal in his way, too. (p. 215)

> *Richard Eberhart, "Reflections on Wallace Stevens in 1976" (copyright, 1976, by Richard Eberhart), in* The Southern Review, *Vol. 12, No. 3, July, 1976 (and reprinted in his* Of Poetry and Poets, *University of Illinois Press, 1979, pp. 214-15).*

HAROLD BLOOM (essay date 1976)

[Wallace Stevens has written] the poems of our climate more definitively than any American since Whitman and Dickinson. What justifies an estimate that sets him higher than Frost, Pound, Eliot and Williams? If he is, as so many readers now believe, a great poet, at least the equal of such contemporaries as Hardy, Yeats, Rilke and Valéry, what are the qualities that make for greatness in him? How and why does he move us, enlighten us, enlarge our existences, and help us to live our lives? (p. 103)

The reader who loves Stevens learns a passion for Yes, and learns also that such a passion, like the imagination, needs to be indulged. "It must give pleasure," Stevens says, following a supreme tradition, and his poems do give pleasure. This pleasure, though naturalistic, essentially helps to satisfy the never-satisfied mind. . . . (p. 104)

Several critics have regarded Stevens as essentially a comic poet. I think this characterization is not adequate to even his more sardonic aspect, but at least it reminds us of how humorous he could be. One of my favorite poems in *Harmonium,* which I rarely persuade anyone else to like, is called "Two Figures in Dense Violet Light." I take it as being a superbly American kind of defeated eroticism, the complaint of a would-be lover who is ruefully content to be discontent, because he rather doubts that high romance can be domesticated anyway in a world still so ruggedly New. One might think of this poem's speaker as being a decadent Huckleberry Finn dressed up to play the part of Romeo. . . . (pp. 104-05)

Though more than usually mocking and self-mocking, this is surely another of Stevens' hymns to the Interior Paramour, another invocation of his Muse, his version of Whitman's Fancy. But Whitman's Fancy, though she rarely emanated very far out from him, did have a touch or two of an exterior existence. Stevens' Paramour, poor girl, is the most firmly Interior being in Romantic tradition. Compared to her, the epipsyches of Nerval, Poe, Shelley and the

young Yeats are buxom, open-air, Renoir-like ladies. Stevens knows this, and the violet light of his poem is so dense that the two figures might as well be one. "What a love affair!" we cannot help exclaiming, as the Grand Solipsist murmurs to his Paramour: "Speak, even, as if I did not hear you speaking, / But spoke for you perfectly in my thoughts." This is a delicious Dialogue of One, all right, and we find its true father in some of Emerson's slyly bland observations on the Self-Reliance of Spheral Man. Recalling one Boscovich, an Italian Newtonian who had formulated a more-than-usually crazy version of the molecular theory of matter, Emerson mused: "Was it Boscovich who found that our bodies never come in contact? Well, souls never touch their objects. An innavigable sea washes with silent waves between us and the things we aim at and converse with."

In Stevens, this "innavigable sea" is called "the dumbfoundering abyss / Between us and the object," and no poet has been more honestly ruthless about the actual dualism of our everyday perceptions and imperceptions. Except for a peculiar roster of fabulistic caricatures, there aren't any *people* in Stevens' poems, and this exclusion is comprehensive enough to include Stevens himself as whole man or as person. But the "whole man" or "person" in a poem is generally only another formalizing device or dramatizing convention anyway, a means of self-presentation that Stevens did not care to employ. (pp. 106-07)

For all his antimythological bias, the old Stevens turned to Ulysses, "symbol of the seeker," to present his own final quest for a transcendental self. Unlike the Ulysses of Tennyson, at once somewhat Homeric, Dantesque, Shakespearean and Miltonic, the Ulysses of Stevens is not seeking to meet anything even partly external to himself. What other Ulysses would start out by saying: "As I know, I am and have / The right to be"? For Stevens, "the right to know / And the right to be are one." . . . (p. 107)

For the absolutely transcendental self, the man-god, we read Whitman only, but I am astonished always how much of it abides in Stevens, despite nearly all his critics, and despite the Idiot Questioner in Stevens himself. His evasive glory is hardly distinguishable from his imperfect solipsism, or from ours. And there I verge upon what I take as the clue to his greatness; in the curiously esoteric but centrally American tradition of Emerson, Whitman, Thoreau and Dickinson, Stevens is uniquely the twentieth century poet of that solitary and inward glory we can none of us share with others. His value is that he describes and even celebrates (occasionally) our selfhood-communings as no one else can or does. He knows that "the sublime comes down / To the spirit and space," and though he keeps acknowledging the spirit's emptiness and space's vacancy, he keeps demonstrating a violent abundance of spirit and a florabundance of the consolations of space. He is the poet we always needed, who would speak for the solitude at our center, who would do for us what his own "Large Red Man Reading" did for those ghosts that returned to earth to hear his phrases, "and spoke the feeling for them, which was what they had lacked." (pp. 108-09)

Stevens celebrates an apprehension that has no social aspect whatsoever and that indeed appears resistant to any psychological reductions we might apply. As no one is going to be tempted to call Stevens a mystical poet, or in any way religious, we rightly confront a considerable problem in description whenever Stevens is most himself. His True Subject appears to be his own sense of glory, and his true value for his readers appears to be that he reminds us of our own moments of solipsistic bliss, or at least of our aspirations for such moments.

The Stevens I begin to sketch has little in common with the poet of "decreation" most of his better critics have described for us. There is indeed a Stevens as seen by Hillis Miller, a poet of the almost-Paterian flux of sensations, of a cyclic near-nihilism returning always upon itself. There is also truly a Stevens as seen by Helen Vendler: Stevens the venerable ironist, apostle of "the total leaflessness." I do not assert that these are merely peripheral aspects of the poet, but they seem to me aspects only, darker saliences that surround the central man, shadows flickering beyond that crucial light cast by the single candle of Stevens' self-joying imagination. . . . (pp. 109-10)

Stevens is a priest, not of the invisible, but of that visible he labors to make a little hard to see. He serves that visible, not for its own sake, but because he wants to make his own sublimity more visible to himself. Endlessly qualifying his sense of his own greatness, he still endlessly returns to rest upon such a sense. Yet he knows that he needs us, his possible readers, to do for him "what he cannot do for himself, that is to say, receive his poetry." As he proudly tells us, he addresses us as an elite, being in this one respect, at least, more honest than a far more esoteric and difficult poet, Whitman. (p. 113)

The principal difference between Stevens and Whitman appears to be that Stevens admits his mind is alone with its own figurations, while Whitman keeps inaccurately but movingly insisting he wants "contact" with other selves. . . . "Poem With Rhythms," like so much of Stevens, has a hidden origin in Whitman's "The Sleepers," particularly in a great passage apparently describing a woman's disappointment in love. . . . (p. 116)

This juxtaposition of major Whitman to relatively minor Stevens is not altogether fair, but then I don't think I hurt Stevens by granting that Whitman, upon his heights, is likely to make his descendant seem only a dwarf of disintegration. Whitman-as-Woman invokes the darkness of birth, and blends himself into the mingled Sublimity of death and the Native Strain. Stevens-as-Interior-Paramour invokes only his mind's own figurations, but he sees himself cleansed in the vitalizing mirror of will as he could never hope to see himself in the mere outwardness of air. Whitman oddly but beautifully persuades us of a dramatic poignance that his actual solipsism does not earn, while Stevens rather less beautifully knows only the nondramatic truth of his own fine desperation. (p. 117)

Stevens, I suggest, is the Lucretius of our modern poetry, and like Lucretius seeks his truth in mere appearances, seeks his spirit in things of the weather. Both poets are beyond illusions, yet both invest their knowing of the way things are with a certain grim ecstasy. But an American Lucretius, coming after the double alienation of European Romanticism and domestic Transcendentalism, will have lost all sense of the communal in his ecstasy. Stevens fulfilled the unique enterprise of a specifically American poetry by exposing the essential solipsism of our Native Strain. No American feels free when he is not alone, and every American's passion for Yes affirms a hidden belief

that his soul's substance is no part of the creation. We are mortal gods, the central strain in our poetry keeps saying, and our aboriginal selves are forbidden to find companionship in one another. Our ecstasy comes only from self-recognition, yet cannot be complete if we reduce wholly to "the evilly compounded, vital I . . . made . . . fresh in a world of white." We need "The Poems of Our Climate" because we are, happily, imperfect solipsists, unhappy in a happily imperfect and still external world—which is to say, we need Stevens. . . . (pp. 118-19)

Harold Bloom, "Wallace Stevens: The Poems of Our Climate," in his Figures of Capable Imagination *(copyright © 1976 Harold Bloom; used by permission of The Continuum Publishing Corporation), The Seabury Press, 1976, pp. 103-19.*

SAMUEL FRENCH MORSE (essay date 1979)

More than half a century after its publication, *Harmonium* still seems full of extraordinary sounds and words; it was, as [Stevens] put it in a later note, a demonstration that "poetry is a recitative in the midst of a hubbub," in which one hears both the recitative and the hubbub, and also "a recreation of [his] sense of the world"; it was a collection of pieces illustrating various forms associated as often with oral as with written tradition. . . . (p. 923)

The poems of *Ideas of Order* were anything but the "iridescent notes" he had hoped for, although some of them must be ranked among the great ones: "The Idea of Order at Key West," "Evening without Angels," and "A Postcard from the Volcano." The ambitious series he thought of calling "Aphorisms on Society," but published as *Owl's Clover,* was an attempt "to dip aspects of the contemporaneous in the poetic," but the result was what he said one critic seemed to think of it: "a lot of Easter eggs." "The Man with the Blue Guitar" was more successful, although the confrontation between poet and audience with which it began tailed off into meditations on what he called "the incessant conjunctions between things as they are and things imagined." (p. 928)

[*Notes toward a Supreme Fiction* was] the culmination of his preoccupation with "the indefinite, the impersonal, atmospheres and oceans, and, above all, the principle of order," which were, he said, "precisely what I love," and which provided both the "true subject" (or "Canonica") and the "poetry of the subject" (or "Illustrations of the Poetic as a Sense") of *Parts of a World.* . . . Some of these "theoretic poems" have become classics of Stevens' "middle style". . . . Throughout the book, "the presence of the determining personality . . . that reality" without which "no amount of other things matters much," was everywhere apparent.

What Stevens meant by that "presence" was very different from the identifying voice and manner a reader comes to expect of a poet, often seeing in a change of style a failure of the maker's powers rather than any lack of adaptability on his own part. For Stevens, the maker's view was paramount. . . . (p. 930)

After 1937, the long poems often seemed to become "part of the never-ending meditation" that could also be "practicing in order to make perfect" or even "practicing in order to get at his subject," whether the subject was "a supreme fiction" or "An Ordinary Evening in New Haven," "two pears" or "the common life," "Variations on a

Summer Day" or "A Primitive like an Orb," "Not Ideas about the Thing but the Thing Itself." The shorter poems were sometimes "favors" dropped from his "prolonged attention" to longer pieces; but sometimes his "prolonged attention" was itself an attempt to get at his subject, "faintly" or "obscurely" delineated, as in "Extracts from Addresses to the Academy of Fine Ideas" or "Esthétique du Mal," and the short poems that followed were those that brought "his subject into that degree of focus at which he [was] able to represent it in exact definition."

A poetic career that may have begun in the tentative statement of a single theme, the variations of which provided a ground for his serenade and an unmistakable identity, concluded in "the complicate, the amassing harmony" of "The Whole of Harmonium," which is the proper context, finally, for an appreciation of both the short and the long poems and any examination of the relations between them. Such a context adds depth and meaning to his statement that "it is the explanations of things that we make to ourselves that disclose our character: The subjects of one's poems are the symbols of one's self or of one of one's selves." To some of his more high-minded critics, such a statement may suggest an inconstancy little short of betrayal; but it provides, in fact, a place in the canon for those "secretions of insight" that give pleasure like those "prismatic formations that occur about us in nature in the case of reflections and refractions," those "effects of analogy" that allow the poet the freedom to indulge his sense of humor and his skepticism as well as his belief in "the greatness of poetry." It does not diminish the great poems in which "the theory of poetry" is "displayed" as "the life of poetry," to say that some of the short poems of *The Rock* and the few last poems may prove to be those in which the words "surrender, reveal, that in itself" which their maker loved as much as he loved "supreme fiction," that "living name" and place made visible and "confess[ing] openly all the bitter secretions of experience." These, rather than the grander *Notes* or "The Auroras of Autumn," may move us most deeply. We should not have the later long poems, in any case, without the short ones, nor the short ones without the long ones. Which is simply to assert that the theory and the practice were inseparable, as the maker intended them to be. . . . (pp. 931-32)

> *Samuel French Morse, "Wallace Stevens: Instances, Illustrations, Ideas" (copyright, 1979, by Samuel French Morse), in* The Southern Review, *Vol. 15, No. 4, October, 1979, pp. 921-32.*

BIBLIOGRAPHY

Bates, Milton J. "Major Man and Overman: Wallace Stevens' Use of Nietzsche." *The Southern Review* 15, No. 4 (October 1979): 811-39.
    Examines Stevens's familiarity with Nietzsche's ideas and their influence on the poetry Stevens wrote between 1936 and 1947.

Bevis, William. "Metaphor in Wallace Stevens." *Shenandoah* XV, No. 2 (Winter 1964): 35-48.
    Analyzes Stevens's use of metaphor as a means of apprehending and understanding experience.

Bloom, Harold. *Wallace Stevens: The Poems of Our Climate.* Ithaca: Cornell University Press, 1976, 413 p.
    Thorough study of Stevens's work that uses a particular crit-

ical schema described as the "'antithetical' mode of poetic interpretation."

Buchsbaum, Betty. "Wallace Stevens: The Wisdom of the Body in Old Age." *The Southern Review* 15, No. 4 (October 1979): 953-67.
    Discusses Stevens's ultimate philosophical positions as found in the late poems.

Buttel, Robert. *Wallace Stevens: The Making of "Harmonium."* Princeton: Princeton University Press, 1967, 269 p.
    Follows Stevens's early development as a poet, closely examining the poetry written at Harvard through the composition of the poems in *Harmonium*.

Caldwell, Price. "'Sunday Morning': Stevens' Makeshift Romantic Lyric." *The Southern Review* 15, No. 4 (October 1979): 933-52.
    Looks at "Sunday Morning" in light of the norms of Romanticism and analyzes the poem's structure.

Carpenter, Lynette. "The Evolution of 'The Latest Freed Man' in Three Poems by Stevens." *The Southern Review* 15, No. 4 (October 1979): 968-84.
    Sees three poems from *Parts of a World* as being thematically related, with a central character who is to some extent autobiographical.

Doggett, Frank. "The Transition from *Harmonium*: Factors in the Development of Stevens' Later Poetry." *PMLA* 88, No. 1 (January 1973): 122-31.
    Sees Stevens's work after *Harmonium* as becoming progressively more concerned with ideas as opposed to a former aesthetic of "pure poetry" without a predominance of intellectual content.

Doggett, Frank. "Stevens on the Genesis of a Poem." *Contemporary Literature* 16, No. 4 (Autumn 1975): 463-77.
    Discusses Stevens's ideas on the creative process, how a poem is conceived and composed, and Stevens's theory of his own artistic methods.

Eberhart, Richard. "Emerson and Wallace Stevens." *The Literary Review* 7, No. 1 (Autumn 1963): 51-71.*
    General evaluation of Stevens as "the aristocrat of emotional and intellectual fascination."

Ellman, Richard. "Wallace Stevens' 'Ice-Cream'." In *Aspects of American Poetry,* edited by Richard M. Ludwig, pp. 203-22. Columbus: Ohio State University Press, 1962.
    Treats the theme of death in Stevens's poetry.

Enck, John J. *Wallace Stevens: Images and Judgements.* Carbondale: Southern Illinois University Press, 1964, 258 p.
    Accessible critical study forming a good introduction to the themes and structure of Stevens's poetry.

Gollin, Richard M. "Wallace Stevens: The Poet in Society." *Colorado Quarterly* IX, No. 1 (Summer 1960): 47-58.
    Examines the relationship between Stevens's art and life, especially his career as an insurance executive.

Hughson, Lois. "Stevens and the Sufficiency of Reality." In her *Thresholds of Reality: George Santayana and Modernist Poetics,* pp. 158-75. Port Washington, N.Y.: Kennikat Press, 1977.
    Discusses Stevens's use of the imagination as a faculty for perceiving and transforming reality.

Kessler, Jascha. "Wallace Stevens: Entropical Poet." *The Wallace Stevens Journal* 1, No. 2 (Summer 1977): 82-6.
    Contends that Stevens's last poems represent the reversal of a former nihilism.

Lensing, George S. "From Pieces of Paper: *A Wallace Stevens Notebook*." *The Southern Review* 15, No. 4 (October 1979): 877-920.
    Reprints a fourteen-page notebook of phrases and scraps of poetry, many of which Stevens later used in poems. There is an analysis of Stevens's method of composition following the notebook.

Lentricchia, Frank. "Wallace Stevens: The Ironic Eye." *The Yale Review* LVI, No. 3 (Spring 1967): 336-53.

Discusses the ironic tension in Stevens's poetry between an objective reality and the artist's subjective perception of it.

Middlebrook, Diane Wood. *Walt Whitman and Wallace Stevens.* Ithaca: Cornell University Press, 1974, 238 p.*

Three chapters concerning Stevens, the first of which discusses his theories of artistic creativity and the nature of poetry. The other chapters are devoted to establishing "the relevance of Whitman as a model and symbol in Stevens' work."

Morris, Adalaide Kirby. *Wallace Stevens: Imagination and Faith.* Princeton: Princeton University Press, 1974, 205 p.

Considers Stevens's poetry as a transformation of art into religion, corresponding specifically with Christianity. The critic claims that "as the Supreme Fiction overthrew the Supreme Being, it assumed many of the accoutrements of traditional religion."

Olson, Elder. "The Poetry of Wallace Stevens." *College English* 16, No. 7 (April 1955): 395-402.

Discusses Stevens's intensely conscious use of imagery and poetic imagination.

Regueiro, Helen. "Stevens." In her *The Limits of Imagination: Wordsworth, Yeats, and Stevens,* pp. 147-218. Ithaca: Cornell University Press, 1976.

Analysis of Stevens's concern with the imagination as a medium through which the poet apprehends reality.

Sheehan, Donald. "Wallace Stevens' Theory of Metaphor." *Papers on Language and Literature* 2, No. 1 (Winter 1966): 57-66.

Attempts to resolve conflicting theories of metaphor in Stevens's work.

Stevens, Holly. *Souvenirs and Prophecies: The Young Wallace Stevens.* New York: Alfred A. Knopf, 1977, 288 p.

Biographical commentary on Stevens's early years interwoven with excerpts from his journal.

Symons, Julian. "A Short View of Wallace Stevens." *Life and Letters Today* 26, No. 37 (September 1940): 215-24.

Regards "The Man with the Blue Guitar" as one of the most notable poetic achievements of the past two decades.

Vendler, Helen Hennessy. *On Extended Wings: Wallace Stevens' Longer Poems.* Cambridge: Harvard University Press, 1969, 334 p.

Contends that Stevens's "experimentation toward his own voice" in the longer poems was "directed toward a proper mode for his austere temperament."

(Sir) Rabindranath Tagore

1861-1941

(Pseudonym of Sir Ravīndranāth Thākura; also transliterated as Ravīndranátha, Rabindra Nath) Indian poet, playwright, novelist, short story writer, essayist, and philosopher.

Tagore, renowned as one of India's greatest lyric poets, also pioneered a new direction in Bengali literature with his prose. Tagore created a prose form that used conversational idioms instead of the formal literary style of the time.

Tagore was raised on the family estate of Joransanko in Calcutta and the beauty and impact of these natural surroundings figure in his poetry. He began publishing at fifteen, and the next fifteen years of his career consisted mainly of his writing for his brother's journal, *Bharati*. The bulk of his literary work shows the influence of three revolutions in India with which Tagore had sympathy: the religious movement of Raja Ramohan Roy; the literary movement of Bankim Chandra Chatterjee and other Bengali writers like him; and the political movement against the cultural and political oppression of the West. It was Tagore's belief that the East and West had much to share, a view he expressed in *The Hope and Despair of Bengalis*.

Many critics consider Tagore's mature work to date from the death in 1884 of the sister-in-law who was his close friend. Death is the central theme of his poetry of this period. Years later, he returned to melancholy themes when he published *Katha* and *Smaran*, which were written for his son and his wife respectively. Following his wife's death in 1902, Tagore retreated to the Himalayas; the subsequent deaths of his son and daughter resulted in his retirement from public life in 1907.

During travel suggested by his doctors after a serious illness, Tagore translated some of his work into English. It was Yeats who, after reading the translation of *Gitanjali*, introduced Tagore to the English-speaking world and saw to the publication of this collection in 1912. The following year, Tagore was awarded the Nobel Prize in Literature, mainly for this work. Further distinction came in 1915 when Tagore was knighted, a title he relinquished four years later as a protest against the violence of the British suppression of the Punjab rioting. He was later to use the title again in some of his published work.

Tagore composed about 2000 songs and wrote, staged, and acted in numerous plays at Santiniketan, the school which he established in 1901 to promote the freedom of the individual in education. Santiniketan later developed into an international university called Visva-Bharati.

Often imbued with a tragic quality, Tagore's work is a tribute to nature and to the dignity of the individual. He conveys throughout an attitude of optimism, humility, and respect which he both taught and lived.

PRINCIPAL WORKS*

Sandhyā Sangīt (poetry) 1882
Prakritir Pratiśodh (drama) 1884
   [*Sanyasi; or, The Ascetic* published in *Sacrifice, and Other Plays*, 1917]
Rājā-o-Rānī (drama) 1889
   [*The King and the Queen* published in *Sacrifice, and Other Plays*, 1917]
Mānasī (poetry) 1890
Vāsarjan (drama) 1890
   [*Sacrifice* published in *Sacrifice, and Other Plays*, 1917]
Chitrangadā (drama) 1892
   [*Chitra*, 1913]
Sonār Tarī (poetry) 1894
Mālinī (drama) 1896; published in *Kāvya Granthāvalī*
   [*Malini* published in *Sacrifice, and Other Plays*, 1917]
Gāndharir Āvedan (drama) 1900; published in *Kahīnī*
   [*The Mother's Prayer* published in *The Fugitive*, 1921]
Karna-Kunti Samvad (drama) 1900; published in *Kahīnī*
   [*Karna and Kunti* published in *The Fugitive*, 1921]
Satī (drama) 1900; published in *Kahīnī*
   [*Ama and Vinayaka* published in *The Fugitive*, 1921]
Naivedya (poetry) 1901
Gītāñjali (poetry) 1910
Gorā (novel) 1910
   [*Gora*, 1924]
Rājā (drama) 1910
   [*The King of the Dark Chamber*, 1914]
Achalāyatan (drama) 1912
Dākghar (drama) 1912
   [*The Post Office*, 1914]
Balākā (poetry) 1916
Ghare-bāire (novel) 1916
   [*The Home and the World*, 1919]
Lipikā (prose poems, allegories, and stories) 1922
   [*Lipika*, 1969]
Muktadhārā (drama) 1922; published in journal *Pravasi*
   [*The Waterfall* published in journal *The Modern Review*, 1922; also published as *Mukta-dhara* in *Three Plays: Mukta-dhara, Natir puja, Chandalika*, 1950]

Raktakarabī (drama) 1924; published in journal *Pravasi*
[*Red Oleanders: A Drama in One Act*, 1925]
Natīr pujā (drama) 1926
[*The Dancing Girl's Worship* published in journal *The Visva-Bharati Quarterly*, 1927; also published as *Natir puja* in *Three Plays: Mukta-dhara, Natir puja, Chandalika*, 1950]
Śesher Kavitā (novel) 1929
[*Farewell, My Friend*, 1949]
Yogāyog (novel) 1929
Punaścha (prose poems) 1932
Chār Adhyāy (novel) 1934
[*Four Chapters*, 1950]
Prāntik (poetry) 1938
Señjuti (poetry) 1938
Ākāś pradīp (poetry) 1939
Navajātak (poetry) 1940
Rogaśayyāẏa (poetry) 1940
Sānāi (poetry) 1940
Ārogya (poetry) 1941
Janmadine (poetry) 1941
Śesh Lekhā (poetry) 1941
[*Tagore's Last Poems*, 1972]

Principal English-language translations not previously listed:

Gitanjali (Song Offerings) (prose poems) 1912
The Gardener (prose poems) 1913
Glimpses of Bengal Life, Being Short Stories from the Bengali of Rabindranath Tagore (short stories) 1913
Fruit-Gathering (poetry) 1916
The Hungry Stones, and Other Stories (short stories) 1916
Stray Birds (poetry) 1916
Lover's Gift and Crossing (poetry) 1918
Mashi, and Other Stories (short stories) 1918
The Fugitive (poetry, sketches, and drama) 1921
Poems from Tagore (poetry) 1922
Broken Ties, and Other Stories (short stories) 1925
Rabindranath Tagore (poetry) 1925
Fifteen Poems of Rabindranath Tagore (poetry) 1928
Sheaves, Poems and Songs by Rabindranath Tagore (poetry) 1929
The Golden Boat (poetry, prose poems, allegories, and short stories) 1932
Collected Poems and Plays of Rabindranath Tagore (poetry and drama) 1936
Poems (poetry) 1942
The Parrot's Training, and Other Stories (satire and short stories) 1944
A Flight of Swans: Poems from Balākā (poetry) 1955
A Glimpse of Tagore's Poems (poetry) 1956
The Runaway, and Other Stories (short stories) 1959
Poems from Puravi (poetry) 1960
Wings of Death: The Last Poems of Rabindranath Tagore (poetry) 1960
A Tagore Reader (letters, short stories, autobiographical writings, drama, essays, and poetry) 1961
One Hundred and One: Poems (poetry) 1966
Fifteen Longer Poems of Rabindranath Tagore (poetry) 1969
Collected Stories, from Rabindranath Tagore (short stories) 1970
Later Poems (poetry) 1974

*Many of Tagore's works were not translated as a whole. Rather

selections from his works were translated in various volumes, thus the separate listing of many English titles.

W. B. YEATS   (essay date 1912)

[These] prose translations from Rabindranath Tagore [*Gitanjali* and *Fruit Gathering*] have stirred my blood as nothing has for years. . . . (p. vii)

I have carried the manuscript of these translations about with me for days, reading it in railway trains, on the tops of omnibuses and in restaurants, and I have often had to close it lest some stranger would see how much it moved me. These lyrics—which are in the original, my Indians tell me, full of subtlety of rhythm, of untranslatable delicacies of colour, of metrical invention—display in their thought a world I have dreamed of all my life long. The work of a supreme culture, they yet appear as much the growth of the common soil as the grass and the rushes. (pp. xiii-xiv)

Rabindranath Tagore, like Chaucer's forerunners, writes music for his words, and one understands at every moment that he is so abundant, so spontaneous, so daring in his passion, so full of surprise, because he is doing something which has never seemed strange, unnatural, or in need of defence. These verses will not lie in little well-printed books upon ladies' tables, who turn the pages with indolent hands that they may sigh over a life without meaning, which is yet all they can know of life, or be carried about by students at the university to be laid aside when the work of life begins, but as the generations pass, travellers will hum them on the highway and men rowing upon rivers. Lovers, while they await one another, shall find, in murmuring them, this love of God a magic gulf wherein their own more bitter passion may bathe and renew its youth. At every moment the heart of this poet flows outward to these without derogation or condescension, for it has known that they will understand; and it has filled itself with the circumstance of their lives. . . . A whole people, a whole civilization, immeasurably strange to us, seems to have been taken up into this imagination; and yet we are not moved because of its strangeness, but because we have met our own image. . . . (pp. xiv-xvii)

An innocence, a simplicity that one does not find elsewhere in literature makes the birds and the leaves seem as near to him as they are near to children, and the changes of the seasons great events as before our thoughts had arisen between them and us. (p. xxi)

> *W. B. Yeats, "Introduction" (1912), in* Gitanjali *and* Fruit-Gathering *by Sir Rabindranath Tagore (reprinted with permission of Macmillan Publishing Co., Inc.; © 1916, 1918, by Macmillan Publishing Co., Inc.; in Canada by A. P. Watt Ltd., agents for the estate of W. B. Yeats), Macmillan, 1916 (and reprinted by Macmillan Inc., 1918, pp. vii-xxii).*

EZRA POUND   (essay date 1913)

The appearance of "The Poems of Rabindranath Tagore" is, to my mind, very important. (p. 571)

The movement of his prose may escape you if you read it only from print, but read it aloud, a little tentatively, and the delicacy of its rhythm is at once apparent.

I think this good fortune is unconscious. I do not think it is an accident. It is the sort of prose rhythm a man would use after years of word arranging. He would shun kakophony almost unwittingly.

The next easiest things to note are the occasional brilliant phrases, now like some pure Hellenic, in "Morning with the golden basket in her right hand," now like the last sophistication of De Gourmont or Baudelaire.

But beneath and about it all is this spirit of curious quiet. We have found our new Greece, suddenly. As the sense of balance came back upon Europe in the days before the Renaissance, so it seems to me does this sense of a saner stillness come now to us in the midst of our clangour of mechanisms. (p. 573)

There is in [Mr. Tagore] the stillness of nature. The poems do not seem to have been produced by storm or by ignition, but seem to show the normal habit of his mind. He is at one with nature, and finds no contradictions. And this is in sharp contrast with the Western mode, where man must be shown attempting to master nature if we are to have "great drama." It is in contrast to the Hellenic representation of man the sport of the gods, and both in the grip of destiny. (p. 574)

If we take these poems as an expression of Bhuddistic thought, it is quite certain that they will change the prevailing conception of Bhuddism among us. For we usually consider it a sort of ultimate negation, while these poems are full of light, they are full of positive statement. They are far closer in temperament to what we are usually led to call Taoism. (p. 575)

Briefly, I find in these poems a sort of ultimate common sense, a reminder of one thing and of forty things of which we are over likely to lose sight in the confusion of our Western life, in the racket of our cities, in the jabber of manufactured literature, in the vortex of advertisement.

There is the same sort of common sense in the first part of the New Testament, the same happiness in some of the psalms, but these are so apt to be spoiled for us by association; there are so many fools engaged in mispreaching them. . . . (pp. 575-76)

If these poems have a flaw—I do not admit that they have —but if they have a quality that will put them at a disadvantage with the "general reader," it is that they are too pious.

Yet I have nothing but pity for the reader who is unable to see that their piety is the poetic piety of Dante, and that it is very beautiful. . . .

I do not think I have ever undertaken so difficult a problem of criticism, for one can praise most poetry in a series of antitheses. In the work of Mr. Tagore the source of the charm is in the subtle underflow. It is nothing else than his "sense of life." (p. 576)

[Rabindranath Tagore] has given us a beauty that is distinctly Oriental, and yet it is almost severe, it is free from that lusciousness, that overprofusion which, in so much South-Oriental work, repels us. His work is, above all things, quiet. It is sunny, *Apricus,* "fed with sun," "delighting in sunlight."

One has in reading it a sense of even air, where many Orientals only make us aware of abundant vegetation. (p. 579)

Ezra Pound, "Rabindranath Tagore," in The Fortnightly Review, *Vol. 99, No. DLX, March, 1913, pp. 571-79.*

JOYCE KILMER   (essay date 1915)

There is a poet and essayist whom Mr. Yeats ranks with Saint Francis and Thomas à Kempis and William Blake. It is a wierd combination, but it is Mr. Yeats's own. And the name of this paragon is Rabindranath Tagore.

No one will deny that Mr. Tagore is an able literary craftsman. He is not, as he has been called, the greatest living poet, but he is the most versatile writer living; he is almost as versatile as the late Andrew Lang. He writes in English as skilfully as in his native Bengali; his love-songs are graceful; his poems about children are whimsical and dainty; his one-act plays, although not strikingly original, are imaginative and dexterously put together; and his philosophical essays are thoughtful.

But Blake and Saint Francis and Thomas à Kempis! What have they to do with this talented Hindu? . . .

If Mr. Tagore had been born in Brooklyn, he would never be a fashionable poet. There is a quaint exotic aroma about his poems, like sandal-wood or stale cigarettes or the back room of a Chinese laundry. He writes about temple-bells and water-jars and the desert: it is all so nice and Oriental! And then he teaches such a comfortable philosophy: just have a good time and love everybody and your soul will migrate and migrate and migrate until finally it pops off into the Infinite! The pearl slips into the lotos; *om mani padmi oum* and all that sort of thing.

Well, that is all right in its way unless you happen to be a Christian. "Go to the dogs and be drunken," says Mr. Tagore. "Be drunken and go to the dogs." M. Baudelaire gave the same advice, in a poem which this well-read poet may possibly have seen. But M. Baudelaire was merely praised with faint damns for writing it. Mr. Tagore is almost worshipped; he is hailed as a genius, a philosopher, a benefactor of the world, a religious leader, and—of course—a mystic.

Mr. Bassanta Koomar Roy has every right in the world to celebrate his compatriot and co-religionist. But the Americans and Englishmen who are humbly kneeling before the clever Oriental journalist who bids them "leave this chanting and singing and telling of beads," who would substitute fatalism for hope, Nirvana for heaven and a blue-faced lecher named Krishna for Jesus Christ; what in the name of common sense are they thinking about? Isn't there heathenism enough in this country already without importing a supply from India? Are we really so jaded and worn that we take a perverted pleasure in throwing away all our standards of conduct, all our traditions, all our faith? . . .

Some other novelty will come along, a Greek dancer or a Turkish fiddler, and Mr. Tagore's works will go up into the garret with the Ouija board and the ping-pong rackets.

But meanwhile I wish that Mr. Yeats would stop calling Mr. Tagore a mystic. It is so silly! Mystics don't commune with the Infinite and then sell their communings to a magazine. Mystics don't have their photographs taken for frontispieces of their biographies. Mystics don't get fifteen per cent royalty on their meditations. If Mr. Yeats only would read a mystical work some day—he could buy a "De Imitatione Christi" for a shilling—he'd see how ridiculous it is to call Mr. Tagore a mystic. He might as well call him a Neo-Celt.

If people would stop calling Mr. Tagore a mystic, I wouldn't so much mind them calling him "the East Indian Whitman." That is not a true characterization, but it has an element of truth in it. Mr. Tagore's verses are like Whitman's in that they are exclamatory and unrhymed and unrhythmical.

> *Joyce Kilmer, "Rabindranath Tagore," in* America (© America Press, 1915), Vol. XIII, No. 14, July 17, 1915, p. 355.

ERNEST RHYS (essay date 1915)

[As we read Rabindrinath's short stories] we feel at once the touch of the born tale-teller. . . . [We] find that it is not the traditional tale-teller, reappearing with a modern difference, who offers us his wares. For while the traditional has undoubtedly helped him in his interpretation of Bengal life, there is a rarer savour in it altogether, a savour peculiar to the writer himself. (pp. 47-8)

[As] Rabindranath has proved himself in other ways a close student of foreign literatures, so here he has known how to develop for his own use a sympathetic and thoroughly congenial form of short story. In it he combines, not hard and fast realism, but the human realities with his romance, and truth to nature attends his wildest apparent improvisations. He is able thus to gain effects which a Nathaniel Hawthorne or a Turgenief might envy him. Dr. Seal . . . has pointed out that his stories resemble most closely (if they are to be held like anything in European literature) the shorter tales of Flaubert. The finer art of the tale began in Bengal with the "Vaishnavas," who gave the Indian tale, or *Katha,* a more finished form; from them Rabindranath took it over, and made of it a pliable or adaptable instrument. (p. 49)

The scenes of Indian country life which they contain . . . grow as intimate and real in his telling as those familiar in our everyday English fiction.

It is remarkable too how often the story is directed to showing the devotion and the heroism of the Hindu wife or woman. In one which he calls "The Ghât" he makes the river-stair itself turn narrator; and its reminiscences culminate in the fate of the girl Kusum. The opening discovers the instinctive sense of place and the affectionate regard for his neighbourhood that inspire the narrator. No western writer, not even Turgenief in his *Note-Book of a Sportsman,* or George Sand in *La Mare au Diable,* is better able to call up the illusion and the aroma of a scene in the printed page. . . . Of the two, Flaubert is more sure and artistically exact; Tagore more imaginative, more suggestive of the moods and hidden spirits of the creatures and places he evokes with the tale-writer's talisman. (pp. 50-1)

In ["The Ghât"] Rabindranath Tagore reveals the heart of Kusum by the slight interrogatory touches which he often uses to give reality to his spiritual portraits of women. He is one of the very few tale-writers who can interpret women by intuitive art. The devotion and the heroism of the Hindu wife he paints are of a kind to explain to us that though the mortal rite of Suttee is ended, the spirit that led to it is not at all extinct. It lives re-embodied in a thousand acts of sacrifice, and in many a delivering up of the creature-self, and its pride of life and womanly desire.

Such a tale of the slow Suttee is told by Rabindranath in "The Expiation," in which the little Bengali wife of a splendid drone and do-nothing takes on her own head his guilt, when he turns thief in order to get money to go to England. While he lives there and casually picks up an English wife she pawns and sells her jewels to support him. What the wife Bindhya does in this apologue is only the sacrifice and self-annihilation of the funeral pyre in another form. In [, "Auspicious Look,"] the tale of another more attractive kind of parasite—Rasik, the fond brother—Bansi shows the same extraordinary devotion and Souravi, who loves Rasik, is a companion portrait worthy to set by Bindhya's.

There you have only one motive out of many dealt with in these tales of Bengal. Among the creators of the fantasy of place there are few who can call up as he does by direct and indirect touches the illusion of a scene. He is particularly skilful in working the charm by means of an agent of romance, youth or maid, man or woman, who is at odds with ordinary good fortune, yet at one with the given environment.

In the story of the "Auspicious Look"—that is the look given by a bridegroom to his bride at the customary wedding-rite—there is a savour of childish mystery about the girl who is the signal figure. She is very beautiful, and, like the figure of Kusum in the story of the Ghât, her charm is used to evoke the spirit of a riverside scene. She comes to the water with two ducklings pressed to her bosom with both her hands; she wishes to let them go in the water, and yet she is afraid they will stray out of her reach, and as she stoops, with the river-side grass glistening bright at her feet and the morning light playing upon her form, the dramatic moment arrives when Kanti, the hero of the tale, catches sight of her. (pp. 54-6)

In the story of another child of nature, "Sweet Tongue"— so called before she is discovered to be dumb—we have for setting another waterside village. . . . Nature seemed to wish to lend the silent girl a voice, the lapping of the water, the trilling of birds, the rustling of leaves, join themselves to the voices of the crowd and the boatmen's songs, and all mingle together with the constant movements and agitation of Nature, and break, as it seems, like the surf on the sea-beach, in her ever-silent breast. In such tales Rabindranath confesses, as he does in his songs, his belief in the identity of nature and man, of nature and supernature.

So far the tales described have been virtually of everyday life in Bengal. But one remains . . . , "The Hungry Stones," which shows a truly uncanny power in romance. In it the place-interest centres in a dead and deserted palace of white marble, very stately in its Persian courts and galleries, standing above a Ghât or river-stair in Hyderabad. (pp. 58-9)

Rabindranath Tagore indeed is a place-charmer in his tales. For him, houses have souls, old ruins may be powerful as witches in their sorcery, a river-stair can count the footfalls of ages, and a door can remember its dead.

This is only part of his tale-teller's equipment; for he is very tender to his human folk, especially to his women of sorrow and children, and, what is perhaps his favourite among them all, the child of nature—what the Bengali calls sometimes a "mad Chandi," a possessed one, with a certain tenderness as for a creature held by a spirit beyond the common. His page often tells of the unconscious creature that is very near the sources of nature, drinking her clear dew and becoming one with her in her play of life and death.

His stories, finally, . . . are written in a style of their own, here and there reminding one a little of Hawthorne in his most elusive vein, or Turgenief in his romantic tales. It is as if a folk-tale method were elaborated with literary art, inclining to the imaginative side of everyday life, yet dwelling fondly on the human folk it portrayed. (pp. 62-4)

> *Ernest Rhys, in his* Rabindranath Tagore: A Biographical Study *(reprinted with permission of Macmillan Publishing Co., Inc.; in Canada by Macmillan, London and Basingstoke; © 1915 by Macmillan Publishing Co., Inc.), Macmillan, 1915, 157 p.*

E. M. FORSTER (essay date 1919)

When a writer of Tagore's genius produces such a sentence as "Passion is beautiful and pure—pure as the lily that comes out of the slimy soil; it rises superior to its defilement and needs no Pears' soap to wash it clean"—he raises some interesting questions. The sentence is not attractive—in fact, it is a Babu sentence—and what does Tagore, generally so attractive, intend by it? Is he being dramatic, and providing a Babu of his creation with appropriate English, or is he being satirical, or was there some rococo charm that has vanished in the translation, or is it an experiment that has not quite come off? Probably an experiment, for throughout [*The Home and the World*] one is puzzled by bad tastes that verge upon bad taste. . . . [When] the theme is developed, one receives inappropriate emotions, and feels that the contrast is not so much between the Home and the World as between the well-bred and the ill-bred. The Home is not really a home, but a retreat for seemly meditation upon infinity. And the World—it proves to be a sphere not for "numberless tasks," but for a boarding-house flirtation that masks itself in mystic or patriotic talk. . . . The tragedy is skilfully told, but it all seems to be about nothing, and this is because the contrast does not work out as the writer intends. He meant the wife to be seduced by the World, which is, with all its sins, a tremendous lover; she is actually seduced by a West Kensingtonian Babu, who addresses her as "Queen Bee," and in warmer moments as "Bee." In spite of the beautiful writing and the subtle metaphor and the noble outlook that are inseparable from Tagore's work, this strain of vulgarity persists. It is external, not essential, but it is there; the writer has been experimenting with matter whose properties he does not quite understand.

Why should he care to experiment? Here is a more profitable but more difficult question. Having triumphed in *Chitra* or *Gitanjali,* why should he indite a "roman à trois" with all the hackneyed situations from which novelists are trying to emancipate themselves in the West? These Bengalis—they are an extraordinary people. Probably this is the answer. They are more modern and mentally more adventurous than any of the other races in the Indian peninsula. They like trying, and failures do not discompose them, because they have interest in the constitution of the world. (pp. 330-31)

> *E. M. Forster, "'The Home and the World'" (1919), in his* Abinger Harvest *(© 1936, 1964 by E. M. Forster; reprinted by permission of Harcourt Brace Jovanovich, Inc.; in Canada by Edward Arnold Ltd. in connection with King's College, Cambridge and The Society of Authors as the literary representatives of E. M. Forster's Estate), Harcourt, 1936, pp. 330-31.*

EDWARD J. THOMPSON (essay date 1921)

[Though] Rabindranath has never ceased to learn, and is as great a thief as any in all literature, it is in the pre-*Mānasi* period that we must look for influences. First, of course, are the Bengali Vaisnava lyrists. The poet's own authority compels this statement, for did he not in the *Bhānu Singha* songs carefully catch their very notes? And he has never ceased to praise them, has translated them, and always refers to them as his masters. Be it so, then; one must suppose that they are. Yet I have always been rebellious under the importance he ascribes to them, and I believe he does them too much honour. I will say frankly that I am sure they have not influenced him to anything like the extent he has persuaded himself. He is grateful to them because they put him in the way of finding his gift of pure song, and therefore he is more filial than he need be, mistaking for parents those who are only among his chief teachers. . . . Rabindranath's real master has been Kalidāsā. He never misses a chance of paying Kalidāsā homage, either by explicit panegyric or by the subtler way of paraphrasing or quoting. . . . Frequently, when the strain is ostensibly a Vaisnava one, and the theme is Krishna and Rādhā, the real mood is not Vaisnava at all, but, as obviously as possible, is Kalidāsā's. The two poets [Kalidāsā and Rabindranath], the greatest India has ever produced, differ as strikingly as they resemble each other. The one is the poet of mountains, rejoicing in their strength and vastness. The other is the poet of rivers and of quiet places. But the two between them so completely represent Indian landscapes, that any third poet hereafter must seek some other way to fame. Both are passionate lovers of the rains, and have given us picture after picture of them which is perfect in faithfulness and charm. Both, again, love the gentler beauties of Nature and character; and both are at home in symbolism and mingle with easy grace in the affairs of Gods and Immortals.

A very important strain in Rabindranath's work is the influence of folk-tale and folk-poetry other than Vaisnava. This is responsible for many charming moments, and also for occasional moments of dulness, when it contributes to that cult of the trivial which is the defect of his great quality of interest in the smallest things. The great epics, too, have given him thoughts and incidents that have touched him to fine issues. . . . He was called, while in his teens, the Bengali Shelley, and he has translated Shelley, and has acknowledged him as an influence. The *Hymn to Intellectual Beauty,* he says, was like a transcript of his mind in his youth. 'I felt as if I could have written it.' . . . Shelley's mythopoea, his compound adjectives, his personifications, his unhappiness, especially his vague, poetical unhappiness,—these things fill *Evening Songs.* (pp. 52-4)

From Keats's *Odes* he learnt, if my guess is right, to build up magnificent stanza-forms in his own tongue, by which he enriched it immensely. His stanzas are very many, and carried Bengali poetry far beyond the metres introduced by Hemchandra Banerji. . . .

But a stronger influence than Keats was Browning. This influence came as he entered upon maturity. It is very marked in the new psychological interest of many poems in *Mānasi*, it is present in that first group of non-symbolical plays, it is present most strongly and nobly of all in the short dramatic dialogues of the later nineties, *Gāndhāri's Prayer* [*Gandharir Avedan*], and *Karna and Kunti*. In his novel, *The Home and the World*, he has made a striking adaptation of the scheme of *The Ring and the Book*, telling the one story through different minds.

But, in the case of a wide and desultory reader like Rabindranath, it is not possible to say where he found the suggestion for this or that idea or phrase. It is enough, that he has 'taken his own where he found it,' and has laid under contribution German, and French, and Russian literature, as well as Sanskrit and English. (p. 55)

It must be admitted that he has written a great deal too much, and that the chief stumbling-block in the way of accepting him among great poets is the inequality of his work. . . . There is a recurrence of a certain vocabulary, of flowers, south wind, spring, autumn, tears, laughter, separation, tunes, bees, and the rest, which sometimes is positively maddening. This sort of thing is most apparent when he is least inspired, but it is by no means absent from his best work. . . . Even in much of the noblest work of his later years, his incorrigible playfulness, the way in which, often when most serious, he will fondle and toss with fancies, spoils some splendid things. . . . From all this comes sometimes a sense of monotony, which hides from the reader the richness and versatility of his work. This is the great weakness of his earlier work, that which finishes with *Chaitāli*. One is often surprised, on analysis, to find how much of even his most exquisite work is built upon themes well-worn with him. . . . *Moon, Spring, sigh, eternal separation, night and full moon, laughter, flute, unrest, tears, weeping, Hope,*—these are the old performers. . . . There is many a passage in Rabindranath when you might call the roll, and, if one of these were present, all the rest would click their heels and answer. Here, in the supreme inspiration of *Urbasi*, they are transfigured into unsurpassable loveliness, which no criticism can touch. Yet, as the flawless Idea which lives in God's presence suffers loss with the judgment of us mortals for the faulty embodiments of that perfection which we see and have made, so even on the best of the poems of his early period some shadow falls from memory of the many passages which have their accidents without their essential of inspiration.

Yet this fault really witnesses to a great strength, his wonderful abundance of imagery. . . . Here we get very close to the heart of his genius, and can confidently claim for him the title of great poet. No poet that ever lived (I shall use this phrase again) has had a more constant and intimate touch with natural beauty. He can use, at his best, the same images and pictures, the oldest ones in the world, a score of times in as many lines, and each time with freshness and charm. His wealth here is inexhaustible, and it is manifest in prose as in verse, and today, after his swift advance in mastery of the tongue, is almost as manifest in English as in Bengali. (pp. 55-7)

[Too] many suppose that Rabindranath is a poet of softer beauty, evading the sterner. But this was never the case, even in his early work; at any rate, was never the case after *Evening Songs*. In *Mānasi*, for example, is one of the grandest and most terrible sea-storms in the world's literature—written, not by an Englishman, but by a Bengali. (p. 57)

He has a thousand pictures, all distinct from each other, and all perfect, of every Indian season. Autumn is a favourite of his, as she deserves to be; and he personifies her as Lakshmi, the gracious goddess. Noon in the summer heats is another favourite; and he can make the page quiver with its tense, blinding quietness. (p. 60)

Again, no poet that ever lived has shown such a power of merging not only himself but his human figures with their landscape. Here he is absolutely great, and absolutely original. Sometimes, the mingling is a matter of subtle and exquisite perception of the intimate inter-relation between mind and matter. . . .

This rich, individual gift of his nowhere finds more satisfying expression than in his short stories. . . . [There are] outstanding qualities of the best stories . . . which put him among the world's greatest short story writers. First among them is their range and variety. This writer or that has surpassed Rabindranath in some quality or other. But where are we to find a writer of stories so different and so good as *Hungry Stones, Living or Dead, Subhā, Cloud and Sun, The Kingdom of Cards, The Trust Property, The Riddle Solved,* and *The Elder Sister*? Four of these eight are of the deepest tragedy, a very unusual feature in an Indian writer; two are of tragedy of a less mixed and absolute kind, but sufficiently poignant, with irony salting the bitterness and with tender laughter softening the pathos; one deals with a realm of sheer phantasy, two are ghostly; several are masterly psychological studies. It is strange that his stories have received so little fame in the West; they are the most under-rated of all his work. (pp. 61-2)

Edward J. Thompson, in his Rabindranath Tagore: His Life and Work, *edited by Kalidas Nag (reprinted by permission of Oxford University Press, New Delhi), Y.M.C.A. Publishing House, 1921, 112 p.*

P. GUHA-THAKURTA (essay date 1930)

Wherein lies the secret of [his] power? It certainly does not lie in the action of the plays or even in the psychological analysis of the characters. For, Rabindra Nāth does not aim at constructing a story consisting in merely objective action, nor does he occupy himself exclusively with the tracing of the innermost workings of the minds of his characters. His power seems to lie in his amazing vitality of imagination and his remarkable ability to create an atmosphere which grows upon the mind, not by the repetition of any central idea, but by magic, as it were. He weaves his words into a most delicate pattern of poetic prose. He can hold up the action with talk that makes action superfluous and the merely objective relation between one character and another seem unnecessary. His plots are nothing but little suggestive sketches meant to induce and express only an attitude of mind. Having set us laughing at a folly or weeping over the futility of human passions, he suddenly turns our laughter and tears alike into an emotion which is more exalted than either of them, to which he gives a lyrical expression of unearthly and romantic beauty. . . . The extremely rhetorical and sometimes paradoxical way in which all his characters speak makes it impossible for him to make them live before us in a convincing way. He uses much wit but little humour, much mockery but little irony, much keenness of intellect but little precision and straightforwardness. So his plays become merely plays of ideas, the reality of which is hidden behind a persistent and determined illusion. Even a most startlingly realistic plot becomes a cloak for symbolism. Everyone in his plays is his puppet. His characters are all as poetic as himself and one can never escape from the feeling that they are actors staging an idea, symbols, not human beings. His drama like his music, therefore, is just a rhythmic ebb and flow of many tunes, all alike apparently unsuited for harmonic orchestration. It is indeed capable of poetic heights, because the artist is intensely subjective and sensitive, but it is very apt to lose its simple and strange beauty in the endless maze of a useless reiteration of words and phrases. And in any case, the truth which he seeks to paint is never merely an objective or material thing but an abstract truth, a spiritual idea. . . . The fact is that the drama or the theatre is for Rabīndra Nāth just a device and an excuse for self-expression. (pp. 215-17)

[Rabīndra Nāth] only chooses to analyse exceptional characters in exceptional circumstances, and always aims at the expression of the ultimate, final essence of subjective life and consciousness. If his characters had more triviality they might have been more true to real life; but they all live in a world which can only be understood by rising above the plane of matter. In this respect and also in his attempt to systematize his ideas and principles of symbolist art, Rabīndra Nāth has many striking points of resemblance with Maurice Maeterlinck. (p. 219)

Rabīndra Nāth, like all true romanticists, has set up primitivism or the natural goodness of man as a philosophy or even as a religion. He redeems the cruelty of civilization and decorum by that touch of wildness, that pleasant air of irresponsible discursiveness, that flavour of the open air and the free man. He invents a type of literary vagabond, with a gipsy strain in the blood, with an ingrained distaste for the routine of everyday life and conventionality. His Bāul or Blind Bard in *Phālgunī;* his Biśu Pāgal in *Rakta Karabī,* his Thakurdādā in *Sāradotsab,* his Dādā Thākur in *Achalayātan* are the varying types of such a vagabond and care-free soul. He either tramps along the open road or butts in into the action of the play with his mystical talk of the problems of life and the universe and transcendental beauty. He is splendid in his garulity and ecstatic in his musical moods. He is something more than a mere lover of Nature; he is a worshipper of Nature with all the passionate ardour of his soul. (pp. 221-22)

[Rabīndra Nath's] individuals *are* extraordinary men and women, such as can best serve his self-expression. Thus he continually sacrifices the probable for the picturesque. He breaks up the smooth and tiresome surface of ordinary normal life by the pursuit of surprise and strangeness. For, reality to his mind can not be locked up in any set of formulae. So he gives to his work a gusto, a zest and a thrill impossible to an ordinary realist. He denies the very conditions which determine the special technique of realistic stage-craft. He becomes a "mighty prophet" and "a seer blest." It is, indeed, much easier to be an original genius than to be an artist on the terms imposed by the realities of the ordinary common-place things of life. Yet, if one looks back at his early lyrical and musical sketches and over the lengthening life of his dramatic dialogues and symbolical plays, one feels that from the first to the last they are all linked up and related to each other by a charm of personality that gives strength and beauty to them all. (p. 223)

> *P. Guha-Thakurta, "His Dramatic Art," in his* The Bengali Drama: Its Origin and Development *(a revision of a thesis given at London University in 1926; reprinted by permission of Routledge & Kegan Paul Ltd), Kegan Paul, Trench, Trubner & Co., Ltd., 1930, pp. 215-24.*

SISIRKUMAR GHOSE (essay date 1947)

[While] revealing new tendencies [the period covering the last ten years of Tagore's life] contains, at the same time, a summary of all, or nearly all, his earlier styles and attitudes. . . . [Along] with, and even more than a recapitulation of the past, it is also an anticipation of the future. . . . [It] is characterised by experiences and experiments that are unusual even for Tagore. The prose poems, for instance. . . . [Also], the period coincides with an excited outburst in painting. The same creative energy overflows in poetry, though not quite in the same manner. Images are a poet's colour, the symbols of his meaning, and the imagery of the later poems is something new in Tagore. A study of the imagery of Tagore still awaits investigation. And not only the imagery but also the syntax. (pp. 17-18)

[This last period of Tagore's writing] opens with a new experiment—prose poems. (p. 29)

[The] simplicity of the prose poems is deceptive. It can be said definitely that the common man and the common reader—both risky abstractions—prefer the earlier Tagore to the later. The appeal of the sophisticated writer of prose poems is confined to an ever-shrinking coterie. Social stratification, the absence of generally shared cultural values or "public themes," contribute to this failure. It is not enough to blame the poet and it is not his honesty that we question, but the adequacy of the measure adopted. It must be put down to Tagore's extraordinary awareness that he acknowledges this failure more than once, sometimes coming close to the real reason that had been hidden from him so far. The prose poems may not have achieved the great things he had expected from them, but that, at their best, they have their own excellence and their own justification will not be denied. . . .

Tagore himself liked to think that this change in form was due to a change in his point of view, what is called in art-history a change in "the form of beholding." He also felt that, in the process, he might come closer to the spirit of the age and the people. It was, in this sense, an attempt at greater intimacy and exploration of areas of self and society which had so far escaped his notice, a reaching towards the source, a closer contact between life and poetry. There is an obvious increase in the references to neglected aspects of life, of the voiceless millions, "the tragedy of the pariah dog." (p. 32)

Conscious, as never before, that his art did not belong to the people, Tagore now wishes to voice their still, sad, music. In this he thinks—that way error lies—that prose will be the way out. Tagore's use of colloquialism is amazing, but it is colloquialism supported by long years of culture. Its sensitive sophistication is beyond the reach of the poor folk whose mouthpiece, for the nonce, he wanted to be. He has drawn freely from indigenous traditions, such as those of the *bāuls,* for instance, but always from the top, as it were. In the phraseology of the Left, he has not "de-classed" himself. Try as he would, he could not be common, much less a revolutionary or a proletarian poet. (p. 37)

Nothing is, apparently, more common in the later poems than the first person singular. Personal details are included in a manner as if he were writing a kind of private diary, or for circulation among friends and acquaintances. (p. 53)

And yet his poetry is not altogether an autobiographical exercise nor can he be accused of being unduly self-centred. To feel, if not to lose himself in the All, has been, at all times, one of his basic urges. A wider relation or reference is a necessity of his nature. In this respect some of the finest poems of the period are those written on or round his birthday. In these the facts of his life easily merge into, or are set against, a wider background, often a cosmic background, of pain, delight and, above all, mystery. Where this does not happen the poem fails. Also, it should be noted, that this wider reference, relation or symbolism is not something deliberate—the result of an effort. On the contrary, the transition is almost casual and hence more convincing. It shows how naturally our poet is drawn to the heights of sublimated poetic intelligence.

Metaphysically, Tagore is on the side of the concrete and the diverse; socially, he stands, or wishes to stand, for experience that belong to men of all times, what Tagore calls *chiramānab.* . . . The poet of personality, he wants to be free from the inferior promptings of the separative ego. He does not wish to live apart, in and for himself. (pp. 53-4)

Like the Vedic poets he too prays that the Golden Lid covering the face of Truth may be removed and reveal the Purusha within. Of course the manner of writing here is more ethical than poetical, and depends more on statement than on experience, but it shows the way his mind moves in these matters. (p. 56)

Those who like to think of the prose poems, if not the entire later poetry, as nothing but the product of a period of tiredness, and consequently an attempt at philosophizing, will meet with many surprises. (p. 67)

The verses of *Prantik* are some of the strongest, as they are among the most significant, that Tagore ever wrote, . . . because they are creatures of [his] churning. It is perhaps the most considerable as well as the most compact of all his later works. It is poetry throughout and contains more poetry than any other single volume under consideration.

From the point of technique its grave sonnet-like form is an immense advance on the lolling prose poems. The diffuseness is gone at a stroke, instead we are faced with a tension that almost never slackens. Concentrated in effect and detail, *Prantik*'s close interwoven texture reveals—because it is the result of—a difficult and delicate adjustment between disparate impulses and attitudes. Each poem is marked by a passionate internal order, indeed, the entire book is of a piece and may be treated as one continuous poem. The unity and passion are due to its central experience. What is this experience or what are these experiences?

The very first lines of the first poem strike an austere note, bringing us straight to the heart of the mystery—the nearness of death and, along with it, the familiar idea of rebirth through suffering, a dying into life. (pp. 80-1)

Heavily conditioned by illness and a sense of crisis, the poems of *Prantik* reveal a tension that is ever at the bursting point. Rich in subtle psychological analysis of a soul caught in the throes of a further advance, it is equally impressive as poetry.

The triumph of *Prantik* lies, I think, rather in the intensity and the contraries that it evokes so powerfully, with such agonizing immediacy, than in the conciliation that it achieves. In other words, the peace does not come from the plane from which the disturbance arises, at least it is the states of disturbance that are really more impressive. Tagore is not a native of the regions that now engulf or open out before him, a vast inner kingdom of penultimate chaos and confusion, of doubt and debate, pulls and pressures of different kinds. He is not happy about these "unknown modes of the being" which sweep over him fitfully and leave him utterly exhausted. Unexpected onslaughts—all the more hard to bear because they come on the crest of extreme physical pain and suffering. But he faces their revelations bravely, he can be heroic even in distress. It is true that in some part of his mind there still lurks a resistance, or unresolved conflict. This, while it makes the poems so unusually dramatic, also turns them into something of a stormy vision. *Prantik* is as near to the poetry of *Angst* as Tagore ever wrote. (pp. 81-2)

Prantik is a proof of his unimpaired energy, novelty and sincerity. It brings a magnificence to the short poem that it had not known before. (The poems of the last two years will show an even greater advance along the line.) In *Prantik* he has taken a new direction, added a new dimension to his poetry. (p. 84)

The background [of *Senjuti (Evening Lamp)* and *Akashpradip (Skylight)*] is one of the "deepening gloom of twilight." As a rule, the poems of *Senjuti* have fewer details than those of *Akashpradip*. They are barer and more reflective, here are thoughts of an old man, while the dusk descends. Lightly philosophical, he accepts the mystery of existence, but the mood is one of obvious tiredness. . . . The tone of it makes one feel that this is far from that total awareness for which he prays elsewhere in his stronger moments. Against the flux of events and the uncertainty of the future, he sets up lyric joy as a defence. (pp. 103-04)

The symbolism is clearly autobiographical. It is a gentle comment on his own creative leanness, very different from the note of self-defence of the prose poems. In its own way *Senjuti* shows an awareness of the coming dark, though . . . without the tension and agony of *Prantik*. (p. 105)

Senjuti is important for another reason—the concept of time which some of these poems suggest or develop. The subdued tone of these poems brings many facts of life into a new focus. As is natural, he begins with the fact of change, time's surest seal and handiwork. This he first works out through a series of shifting pictures, but he soon passes on to the change of attitude that these imply or reinforce. That is, we have both facts and interpretation. This is a somewhat new, at least a growing, note and may be connected with the "historical consciousness" that critics have noticed in his work of the period. (p. 107)

Akashpradip continues and completes *Senjuti*. There is an increasing self-consciousness, and old memories return, especially memories of early childhood. . . . The landscape he has known is now no more, or faded. Naturally, he notices the change in terms of his own life. (p. 109)

"The Peacock's Vision," the last poem in the volume, is written in an apparently autobiographical vein. The peacock strutting about the garden does not seem to care for the love's labour of our poet. As a result he becomes a bit uneasy. In his present mood this becomes a symbol of Nature's indifference to all human and creative activity....

In such a chastened and somewhat depressed mood he looks at the poem he has been writing. It seems to him like a host of insects waiting for Time's holocaust. He feels that if he were to tear these pages that will only advance their certain burial tomorrow. But how can he end on a note like this? Soon recompense returns, in the shape of an admiring grand-daughter.... A brief conversation follows, in course of which all losses are restored. (p. 120)

Nabajatak's [also transliterated as *Navajatak*] undertones are made up of many motives, some of them pressing motives. They force to the front the social outlook of the poet (his idealism no less than his uncertainty), we are struck by his fluent denunciation as well as the faith in a spiritual solution. He can no longer keep his eyes shut to what is taking place in the world outside. This and the very title of the book ["nabajatak" means "newly-born"] has drawn attention. And yet *Nabajatak* is perhaps not as novel and important as the title or its Preface would seem to suggest. It is more an assortment of tendencies than any steady or whole view that we have here. The sense of fullness or direction is yet to come. (p. 122)

Nabajatak contains poems of social, political and historical import. But very often the poet's emotional unease prevents a clear or complete statement. In other words, the poems are not always unified and the poet has not completely mastered his material. Extraordinary isolated passages, or single phrases, are no doubt to be found everywhere, but rarely a poem that can be accepted in its entirety. Between prayer and self-defence poetic intensity is apt to be lost. The result is either pathos or rhetoric, or both—but rarely poetry that will remain when the immediate provocation is forgotten. There is a sense of bitterness, excitement and even helpless rage about some of these poems. This may be due to an unpreparedness to meet situations that are now being forced upon his attention and from which there is now no escape. (p. 123)

Nabajatak presents us with ... adjustments and modifications, other ... than those raised or made available by science and history. Some of these centre round ancient, obstinate questionings. At this period they are never far from the poet's mind. Indeed, they acquire a new intensity, what one might call a note of high scepticism. Tagore has often been troubled by a spirit of negation and pessimism; more than is suspected. He is not alien to the sense of tear in human things, the sense of waste, of meaninglessness that weighs so heavily on the inquiring mind. The surface of his poetry is not all sunlit, or perhaps it is only the surface that is. Underneath there are darker zones, dubious promptings, goblin voices. For instance, [the poems] "Why" and "Question." (p. 131)

Tagore's last four books form a moving human document, centring round "the phantasmal light of the sick bed." Of the critical consciousness generated by illness and convalescence there are few records more complete or revealing. But he has made it look so natural that it has escaped notice. (p. 144)

In these poems Tagore speaks from the inmost depths of his being, depths which had not been touched in like manner before. He is now *most* himself, bereft of all superficial appeal. The poems are often brief and bare, but the range of emotion and the range of the instrument are now greater than the later poems have so far revealed.... Their subtle strength is fed from obscure and opposing sources, of thrill and terror, submission and defiance, energy and weariness. But their newness reinforces, not rejects, his earlier work. (pp. 144-45)

Death and darkness draw him to their opposites: life and light. They lead him to reaffirm the values he has held dear, but with a new poignancy, values tested in the flame of suffering. (p. 146)

[The] ambivalence of his later poems adds a new note to Tagore's works, remarkable as they have been—creates a new richness. But since the poems are so subtilised that one may as well call it a new barrenness. It is the nudity of the heights. Whatever phrase we may choose to describe it, there can be little doubt that through it all he was tending towards a greater maturity and inclusiveness. (p. 151)

The poems in *Arogya* are, as a rule, tired and soft, without the vividness of *Rogsajyae* [also transliterated as *Rogasayyaya*]. *Arogya* has a pervasive pathos about it, in which the love of the earth and every common sight blends with premonitions of the beyond. (p. 154)

In a mystical phrase we might say that the poet is "recollecting," only there is nothing deliberate or disciplinary about it. Whatever discipline there is, is one of art and often there is not enough of that. The whole thing is almost casual, something like the "stream of consciousness" method or "automatic writing" of which we have heard and read so much. Such recollections, which occur in any life that claims to be mature, are not an escape from present reality and are to be distinguished from the day-dreaming of poets and the worship of the past. They are a process in self-integration and self-knowledge and form one of the distinctions and attractions of the later poetry.... He now prays for the total vision, the vision that escapes and allures him. The Bard must know the past, present and future, he has to unite being with becoming. That is his ideal role as seer and prophet and this ideal Tagore does not renounce. (p. 156)

We cannot hope to understand the innermost Tagore if we eliminate the imaginative ideal in terms of which he was moving, or in terms of which he wanted to complete his vision; the overtures he made, and for what.... [A] just view of the poetry of the last phase must recognise that he was hinting at new levels of inclusiveness and awareness, and that it is a development towards a higher degree of knowledge and finer modes of perception. (pp. 156-57)

Janmadinay [also transliterated as *Janmadine*], the penultimate volume—and the last to be published in his lifetime—continues the notes of *Rogsajyae* and *Arogya*. But it is fuller and has more variations. A sense of death, or distance, overhangs the whole of it, and it is this which provides the overtone for most of these poems of parting. Its grave beauty is touched by a near sense of the Unknown, we feel as though we were witnessing the ritual of man's entry into other modes of being. In this there can be no question of self-indulgence or delusion. His bare majesty, and the essential reality of these his last acts outtop all attitudinising. (pp. 158-59)

On his own admission the relation between the finite and the Infinite has been the major theme of his poetry. Now there is a slight change in emphasis, it is the relation between the manifest and the unmanifest that interests him more. Of course he feels it less as a philosopher and more as a poet, mixing emotion with speculation. The awareness of these wider and, as some think, somewhat remote experiences has become quite natural for him and we find it not only in the death poems, but also in the birthday poems. (p. 161)

[At] the end of his long life the individualist and idealist poet can no longer hide from himself the limitations of his temperament and tradition, the limitations of the *milieu* from which he rose. He senses a failure, the failure to treat of the common man, his hopes and fears, his role in the making of history. . . . The closing years of Tagore's life were marred by continued illness, but perhaps even more than this was the embitterment of his mood and mind, the rude shocks to his earlier untroubled faith (p. 164)

As it is, the strange fact remains that out of his failures he can make beautiful poems, that is, even his negations are creative. (pp. 167-68)

Some of the poems seem to be wanting in actuality, so subjective is the temperament, so tenuous, "free from the taint of the actual," as he himself had noted in a different context. Tagore remains true to his genius and does not bow before fashions in literature, though he is quick to catch the slightest change in the world around him. . . . For him the world's troubles are almost an occasion for emotional outburst or a detached picture. It is rarely that his whole personality is involved in the process. . . . Also, the crisis as Tagore sees it is mainly moral, calling for conversion or penance. . . . In [the] matter of political poems, or poems with a political theme, his reaction sways between prayer and petulance, condemnation and a search for refuge. This is not to deny their energy, and the subtlety of some of them at least, but they all point to a certain unresolved conflict in his being. But whether he is cursing like a prophet betrayed and unheeded, or simply confessing his own limitations compared to the trash of most political verse, these few poems of his, in their sadness and their beauty, the honest portrayal of his inner difficulties and his warning against facile sentiments, are a touching testament. (pp. 171-72)

The movement of Tagore's sensibility is a delicate balancing of opposites, and it is not easy to say to which side he leaned more, the here or the hereafter, to man or to the Absolute. There is in many of the closing poems the sense of something novel, the pressure for a change—not necessarily physical death—which can no longer be postponed. This change which he desires and towards which his being tends is also one that he often dreads and refuses to face fully. . . . But it is a crisis mostly in undertones, the poetry largely depending on the pathos of indecision. This is the difficulty of all genuine unifiers, those who wish to build a bridge between, what the Chinese call, "This" and "That." Tagore's yoga has been in the main unconscious, and now that he is faced with a decision, the hour of leave-taking becomes all the more tender. It is a farewell to all that he has loved and held dear, and the poetry of renunciation is another name for tender apology. (p. 175)

Sesh Lekha, No. 15, [was] the last poem to be dictated by the poet on his death-bed. Rarely has the drama of creation, its dichotomous design, the mystery of its half-light, pain and misery, evil and disharmony littered along the human journey found such mature and concentrated expression either in his works or in those of other poets. Language never fails him and the lyric takes on an epical or tragic dignity. The burden of this "impersonal verse" forces us to look at Tagore's poetic career in a new light. It is the winning of the sorrow-minted faith that is the sign of its maturity—no lilting muse here—his unquestionable integrity, and the integrity of his poetry. The crisis itself, however, suggests that a solution cannot be far off. He has been shaken and scorched to the roots, the purifying fire has touched and made him whole, burnt away all dross and debility. Now, and not before, has he won the "unwasting right to peace." (p. 180)

Without claiming much for the scheme it may be said that [Tagore's later] poems fall into a rough pattern, of alternate rhythms, of valley and peak. . . . The prose poems, often expository, are deliberately "low," but are shot with such exceptions as *Patraput,* No. 3, and "Sishutirtha." . . . *Prantik* stands out in relative aloofness, opens up a world of swift and searching inner exploration. It is a world full of dark splendour. . . . *Senjuti, Akashpradip, Nabajatak* and *Sanai* form another group. The first two, as the titles indicate, are soft and tired, mainly works of recollection. *Nabajatak,* however, is a germinal volume and hints at a number of possibilities, of these historical consciousness is one of the most significant. *Sanai* is in many ways a throwback to the early Tagore. Then comes the last quartet—*Rogsajyae, Arogya, Janmadinay* and *Sesh Lekha.* The scene shifts further inwards. The first two centre round the sick bed without, however, being clinical. A few are frankly personal but there are others that are not only impersonal, but cosmic. *Janmadinay,* No. 5, gives an exalted summary of individual existence in terms of the emergent Purpose. The book also contains the famous tribute to the toilers and a confession of failure (already hinted at in *Arogya* and even earlier). *Sesh Lekha* is valued not for its soft poems—on the *chorui pakhi* or the fifth wedding anniversary of the grand-daughter—but the austere poems, especially the last two, with which Tagore's poetic career closes. In them the conflict of *Prantik* finds an even more dramatic and piercing exposition. The end is near indeed—the first poem in *Sesh Lekha* is a funerary piece. Some of these raise the note of agony and mystery to a pitch beyond which poetry can hardly hope to go, without turning into something else. (pp. 185-86)

The duality, of within and without, the earth and the Beyond, the individual and the transcendent, of illusion and reality, runs throughout the poetry of Tagore. The later poems are no exception. But in the end he, even he, cannot relate the World and the Self and we are faced with a final merger in Space or Silence. Do what the poet will, the gap remains, widens, till "surrounded by precipices, for ever on the verge of the unknown," it swallows up both poet and poetry. (p. 200)

Till society accepts the supra-social religion of the poet, and it will be a long time before it does, Tagore is bound to remain largely isolated, if not inexplicable. (p. 204)

Sisirkumar Ghose, in his The Later Poems of Tagore (© *Sisirkumar Ghose 1961; originally written in 1947), Asia Publishing House, 1961, 304 p.*

EDWARD THOMPSON (essay date 1948)

When *The Broken Heart* was written, Rabindranath was well launched upon those stormy seas which begin a poet's career, the period of his introspective sorrows; of his journeyings, not home to his habitual self, but to a false self, full of mournings, sensitive and solitary. . . . [*Evening Songs*] represents a big stride forward, in style and mastery of material, from *The Broken Heart* and *The Genius of Vālmīki*. But in its lyrics everything draws its hues from the poet's mind. The atmosphere is sombre to monotony; thought is choked by vague emotion, or shines dimly through the mists of imaginary feeling. (p. 35)

Yet the poems, in the expressive simplicity of their diction, were in advance of anything then being written. The whole book points to his later achievement, and has an importance out of proportion to its merits. He is feeling his way, and has no sureness of touch in metre, no firm control of cadence. But already there is no mistaking the master of language, the magician who can call up cloud after cloud of rich imagery. (pp. 35-6)

[If] we take *Evening Songs* at their best, how beautiful in their languorous fashion these poems are! One of the finest songs is *Evening*—prophetic title and theme. Already there is his power of making an atmosphere. The poem has all the shortcomings of *Evening Songs*, yet it transcends them triumphantly. There is no depth of feeling—feeling has not begun. It is all abstractions; and the poet is obsessed by the image of a mother and child. But out of this tenuous stuff he makes a lullaby. The metres, winding their cunning monotonous coils, suggest the weaving of spells. . . . (p. 40)

Morning Songs shows the rising of his healthier intellectual self above the mists—the miasma, almost—of self obsession, the vague miseries of adolescence. The book has its own faults of over-emphasis, of dwelling on his new-found freedom with a convert's earnestness, till the aggressive assertions of mental robustness and of catholic sympathy take on a monotony of their own. Their zest, however, makes them endurable when the languors of *Evening Songs* pall; and the poems witness to a remarkably quick escape from that slough of despond which seems to engulf almost all poets early in their race. In this fact lies the importance of *Morning Songs*—the poems face his future and resolutely forsake his past. Their metre, also, is firm and sure, after *Evening Songs*. Repetitions are fewer, and his mannerisms are temporarily in some abeyance; while almost every strain to be found in his poetical range in later days has its preluding note struck in some poem. (pp. 42-3)

Pictures and Songs broke into [Rabindranath's] first dramatic period. The name is fitting, almost all the pieces being sketches, often carefully detailed, or lyrics. The book is the record of his sensitiveness to sights and impressions, the notebook of his spirit. . . .

The pieces mark a further advance in command over form. Unhappily, his mannerisms are again intensified. He fills up whole stanzas with repetition and parallelism, and *tears, laughter, flowers, light,* and the rest—for they act as if under foremen, the mention of one serving as evocation of the whole troupe—are as tiresome as *beauty* and *April* and *blood* in some English 'Georgian' verse. There are far too many flutes, the cowherd fraternity apparently existing to make distant music at eventide; and far too many lost forest-wanderers. Nevertheless, the series represents a

wider range of theme and experiment than anything he had done before. (p. 52)

There can be no question that *Sharps and Flats* is a richer and better book than any before it. Its variety is the more welcome, because his previous books seemed to say that, whatever other merits this poet might have, he would not have this one. Sonnets take up a large part of the book, some of them of the ordinary Elizabethan form, others variations of the Italian one, with every conceivable arrangement of rhyme and differing length of line.

One group of sonnets at once made the book a storm-centre. This group was defiantly erotic; sonnets on his mistress's kiss, her arms, feet, body, smile, the wind of her skirt, the sky of her heart, two on her breast, one on her nakedness. One sonnet, *Bodily Union,* is as frank as D. H. Lawrence. *Her Arms,* like so much of his work, omits nothing that occurs to him, and is distressing to read. (pp. 55-6)

He is trying to prove that he is a realist, a catholic lover of beauty, to whom nothing is common or unclean. His preoccupation with the body is literary rather than genuine; to me, at least, these sonnets read very insincerely. (p. 56)

The prevailing note of [*Mānasi*] is quiet certainty; it marks his definite attainment of maturity. He was never to cease from experiment, in the attempt to enlarge his own range and that of his tongue. But after *Mānasi* he was master of a sure style. The metres owe much to English stanza-forms; and he is master of the ode, as it had been written by Keats, with consummate interweaving of line and rhyme. (pp. 65-6)

Chaitāli closed [the] first lap of his poetic race. Hitherto, his achievement had been predominantly lyrical: even the dramas have a lyrical ground, especially *Chitrāngadā* and *Mālini.* They have dramatic qualities . . . but that is not their highest excellence; this is rather in the lyrical cry, the note which is heard in the Sannyasi's fierce soliloquies, in the ecstasies and despairs of Chitrangada, in the eddying passions round Malini's dim goddess-form. This quality appears pure in the songs and the best poems of *Chitrā, The Golden Boat,* and *Mānasi.* His reflective and descriptive power finds expression in *Chaitāli* and *Pictures and Songs:* and the two gifts, the lyrical and the descriptive, mix throughout. In his later work, he hardly surpassed his expression of these, but he kept his gift of song, he learnt to draw with deeper sympathy the sorrows of humble lives, and he added a power of mystic interpretation of religious experience which the whole world recognized as exceptional. Also, in at least two books, *Kathā* and *Palātakā,* he showed a fine gift of verse narrative. (pp. 138-39)

Kshanikā by its title—'What is Momentary'—suggests a lighter mood and manner and choice of themes, the poet's tentative entry on his later work. The book was revolutionary in style. No man, as Ajit Chakravarti observes, can jest in Sanskrit; the poet in the muses' name boldly seized the colloquial tongue. For the first time, he used extensively the *hasanta,* or truncation of a word by omission of a vowel last syllable. . . . [By] reducing the super-abundance of vowel-sounds which make Bengali a soft rather than a powerful tongue, it gave Rabindranath's verse a ruggedness and craggy strength. . . . Rabindranath, in *Kshanika,* by a stroke of perception of philological genius, placed himself in such a position as Chaucer had, when he could revive or slur over at will those light final e's which were about to fall off from the language like withered leaves. This meant an extraordinary access of resource to him as a lyrist. He could make the verse soft and musical, by a full use of all its vowel-strength; or by the use of *hasanta* he could give it a sharp break, as of a rock outjutting amid musical waves, and provide the voice and rhythm with something to ripple against. 'Obstructed by the pebbles of *hasanta,* the tune dances.' This became his usual style, and the book was a watershed. . . . Rabindranath's new style completely conquered in the end, and became dominant. (pp. 173-74)

In *Naivedya,* there is not the abundance of the *Chitrā* period; but neither are there the old faults. In the best pieces . . . his qualities shine in purity and simplicity. His interest in the most trivial things can give us such a generalization as 'Thy centuries follow each other, perfecting a small wild flower'. He has found that poise and calm of spirit which are perhaps his chief gift to the world, judged as teacher rather than as poet. *Naivedya* has power to heal and help, from its richness of personal experience. (p. 181)

Gitānjali brings the poet into closer and more familiar contact with the natural world than any previous book. This is not to say that its natural effects are truer or brighter or lovelier than many that have been attained by him before. It is a matter of atmosphere, of being steeped in sound and sight and colour. The book's mood is grey, its key is almost always minor, its pictures mournful, or, at best, untouched by exhilaration. Probably the impression of monotony comes from this oneness of mood, an impression as of a wind wailing through rainy woods, and from the fact that the book gets its effects out of the merest handful of illustrations. Rarely was fine poetry, one thinks, made out of less variety; rain and cloud, wind and rising river, boatmen, lamps, temples and gongs, flutes and *vinās,* birds flying home at dusk, travellers tired or with provisions exhausted, flowers opening and falling. It is astonishing what range the poet gets out of these few things—they are far too naturally and purely used here to be called properties, as they justifiably might be in much of his work. (pp. 216-17)

[The] metrical achievement of *Gitānjali* is impeccable. The poems were written to be sung; but they sing themselves. (p. 219)

[*Gitmālya—Song Garland—*] is perhaps his greatest book of songs. The criticisms I have passed on the others apply to this also, but in smaller measure. The book is one of his most joyful, full of songs of service, of trust in God, of thankfulness for the beauty of the world. (p. 223)

[*Gitāli—Songs—*] is a much less valuable assemblage. It contains 108 pieces, the number of beads on a Vaishnava rosary; and the artificial character suggested by this exact number is borne out by the details of the collection. . . . Most of the pieces are made of the old stuff which he kept so plentifully on hand. Long before the rosary is counted, we weary most utterly of storms and boats, helmsmen and travellers, flowers and flutes and lamps. He has no book which has so large a proportion of pieces worthless as poetry, and his technical skill is wasted. (p. 227)

[*Balākā* is] his greatest book of lyrics. . . . Its title, *A Flight of Cranes,* is symbolical, for migratory birds have always stood for the soul in its passage through these phenomenal skies to eternity. The title has a special fitness, for these lyrics are pilgrim-songs, eagerly looking beyond this plane

of time and sense to other lives, whether reincarnate here or placed beyond our sun and stars. . . . His favourite imagery is of a river. In this there is nothing new; but the river is now not always, or even usually, one which flows through these lands of his sojourn. Often it is an aerial river, the magnificent streaming of that space-flood on whose eddies the stars are floating lilies. In these lyrics his intellectual greatness is revealed. His mind is like a spring from whose depths thoughts and similes bubble incessantly. The effervescence of ideas is never checked for a moment, and especially notable is the flow of abstract ideas. The life of grass and blossom is as dear as ever, and even more delightfully handled; but the poet is not the slave of his fancy, a sterner or, at any rate, a stronger mood being in possession of his fleeting moments. . . . In *Balākā,* not only has the more abstract side of his mind found expression at last, but in diction he has struck a balance, after his experiments, between the colloquial tongue and the rich Sanskrit vocabulary. This balance is as perfect as can be, a marriage of poise and dignity, of lissom ease and power. (pp. 230-31)

The form of *Balākā* is extraordinarily free. He can do what he likes with metre and rhythm, and he no longer cares for any rules except those that justify themselves by resultant beauty or force. Sometimes his metres stream and scatter over the page, like fountains making their way down a Himalayan height. There is practically nothing second-rate. The least important group of lyrics are altogether joy-bringing. (pp. 231-32)

[*The Home and the World*] is essentially a psychological and introspective novel, for it is not to be supposed that ordinary folk would understand and portray themselves as accurately as they do here. The scheme of *The Ring and the Book* is adapted; English literature served him well again, in setting his mind working to such result. Following on such a songtide and on *Phālguni,* the book is a great proof of the vigour of his inspiration. Nikhil and his master are excellently conceived characters. In Amulya, that 'piece of childhood thrown away', we see what sacrifices were demanded by the cruel deity of racial hatred. Bimala, the superficially attractive, yet deeply commonplace woman, is less clearly drawn. Yet she is human; neither for her, nor even for the base self-worshipping Sandip, do we lose all sympathy. The novel would always keep a niche, if only for its historical interest, as the best picture of Bengal's time of political awakening. (p. 246)

Palātakā—'The Runaway'—consists of fifteen pieces . . . which show his narrative gift at its very best. Very few are prolix; most are direct straightforward story-telling, with just sufficient admixture of brooding moralization and reflection. The style is simple and extremely colloquial, almost slangy. The verse, though loose, never quite oversteps art's domain, into the realm of formlessness. 'I wanted to write in that broken verse.' Ornament is austerely used. The poetry is in the texture of the stories themselves, or flashes out in a pregnant sentence or two. (p. 250)

Palātakā could not have been written by any but a great poet. The ease and freedom are extraordinary, slang losing its slanginess and sliding into poetry. (pp. 255-56)

This same untiring interest in form showed itself in . . . [*Lipikā.*] One or two of these are almost a naturalizing in Bengali of *vers-libre;* others are descriptive prose-poetry; others are allegories and apologues. They are a mixture of subtle thought and extraordinarily close observation and of conceits, sometimes very thin. They show him more and more an observer, detached and intellectual. Old griefs find calm but touching remembrance; 'what was sorrow once has become peace'. The poems were rapturously received by his admirers, who felt that they added new modes of imaginative expression to their tongue. The unfaltering beauty of phrase and rhythm deserve gratitude and the book is much more than a fine example of his technical skill. (pp. 270-71)

Tagore's dramas fall into three main groups: (1) the earliest, non-symbolic, of which [*Visarjan*] *Sacrifice* is the best as drama, and *Chitrāngadā* [*Chitra*] and *Malini* the loveliest as poetry. All of these, except *Mālini*, are in blank verse; they are of the Shakespearian type, with five acts. (2) The group of short dramas based on Sanskrit (or, in the case of *Sati* [*The Faithful Wife;* also translated as *Ama and Vinayaka*], later) heroic story. These are in rhymed couplets and are short. (3) The later dramas, all in prose, which are symbolical. Whatever fire of human interest was present in the earlier plays is fading out; ideas gain the mastery, almost the monopoly, of the poet's stage.

Taking the longer dramas, whether blank verse or prose—that is, groups (1) and (3)—it is to be noted that they do not master form. *Mālini* is almost an exception; and *Chitrāngadā,* as presented in English (but not in Bengali), is quite an exception. The blank verse plays take over the Elizabethan model, especially as we find it in the lesser plays. Hence the multiplicity of scenes, many of them representing no real break or division in the action, the subplots, the welter of declamation. The talk distracts attention and sympathy from the characters. From the Elizabethan drama, at first necessarily the only European drama known to him at first-hand, Rabindranath got his rags of convention, rags long gone out of fashion. This makes these earlier dramas seem curiously obsolete, as they did when translated into English.

The prose dramas, though equally weak in construction, except [*Maktadhara*] *The Free Current* [also translated as *The Waterfall*], have escaped from both Elizabethan and Sanskrit models. It is unfair and unsatisfactory to consider them simply as literature, for they were very much in line with that contemporary movement which strove to make the drama a synthesis of all the arts—pageant and scenery, dancing and costume and music, being as essential as the words. Just as many of Rabindranath's later songs seem nothing on the printed page, but when winged with their own haunting tunes carry the mind far out of itself and float it along rainy dark skies or place it beneath a blazing heaven, on a cracked parched earth that is famishing and craving showers, so many of these pageant-plays, which read more or less thinly, when seen are a delight which never falters from the first word to the last. Both in the case of his songs and these plays, the poet is entitled to every bit of credit for his many-sided success, for the tune and the song, the play and the pageant, were twin-born, and neither element is more essential than the other. This development of his drama brought his prose plays into line with the most modern drama of the world. It had been an independent development, in the main; but he was well aware of what was happening outside India, and to his mind a hint was more than a full exposition is to most poets. (pp. 292-94)

Taking simply the printed page, then, it is to be noted that

in these latest dramas the dramatic fire is dying after its flashing intensity in *Sati* and [*Karna-Kunti Samvad*] *Karna and Kunti,* plays which we have still to consider. Also, he mixed his lasting stuff with whims and fads of his own, streaking everything with a thread of caprice. He did not like this or that class of men—the fact appears repeatedly. He used one theme, one person or set of persons, again and again. I sometimes feel as if he had written only one play since *Karna and Kunti,* as if each successive play were just a redaction of the previous one. This, of course, is by no means the case; but he only once broke ground that was really new, in *The Free Current.* (pp. 294-95)

Rabindranath's people . . . have a great gift of folk-drama, of ready racy extemporization, of dialogue which comes straight from the road or the bazaar. This gift, a very living one, was his, and came to him directly from his motherland, out of whose soil it seems to spring spontaneously. (p. 295)

But this side of his genius reached its highest expression in *The Free Current.* He never gave his dramatic gift development or even a fair chance, and it is in this late drama that control of form is most masterly and the allegory kept in place, as contributory but not ruling and obtrusive, and—best of all—it is the one in which the very breath of his land has found dramatic expression, in the voice of her different classes mingling on the highway.

Both these groups, the earliest plays and the latest, have a great deal of achievement. The earlier group abound in poetry, and in their sub-group, the 'literary' plays—*Chitrāngadā,* [*Viday-Abhisap*] *The Curse at Farewell,* and *Mālini*—are noble literature. (p. 296)

But it is in the short plays of group (2) that Rabindranath showed his highest powers as a dramatist. These swift studies recapture more than verisimilitude, they recapture life itself; and their variety is remarkable. All that can be said against them is that their stage and cast are restricted and meagre, and their presentation of life fragmentary and detached. (pp. 296-97)

There is yet another gravest fault of all. With all [Rabindranath's] busyness, all the glancing curiosity of his mind, there went a certain mental laziness, except when deep feeling roused him. If we refuse to allow ourselves to be satisfied with the rich and often wonderful beauty of his work, declining to sink back on pillows of such variegated softness, asking instead what is its value for the mind and spirit of man, we often feel there is a slackness somewhere, probably at the very springs of thought and conception. His poems rarely fail in beauty of style; but they often fail in grip. This is the special failure of *Chitrā,* so fine lyrically. Many of its poems trail, spreading the central conception loosely. He often does not keep control of his mental processes, but lets the thought slide whither it will, prolixly. We have seen how he stops short of dramatic success, when it was within his grasp, in *Mālini* and elsewhere—stops short because of some lack of power or willingness to concentrate and to stake all on the last throw. He plays too much with externals, with ornamentation. The worst flaw of his later work is this lack of serious intellectual effort. His mastery of expression had long been consummate and his metrical accomplishment impeccable. But, more and more, he embroidered the margins of truth, treating it as a missal to be illuminated. Yet *Balākā, Palātakā, Lipikā,*

Puravi, and *Mahuyā*, all books of his last twenty-five years, showed how amazingly varied, as well as superbly easy, was his workmanship, nor was it inadequately sustained by imagination and thought.

Leaving empty and false pieces aside—their number is not great comparatively, it is their existence at all in the work of maturity that is significant—there is an enormous body of beautiful work by Rabindranath, probably a larger body of really beautiful work than any other poet can show. It will never cease to delight, and it will keep his name honoured. Nevertheless, I find it hard to persuade myself that work which so rests in secondary details, and is so occupied with beauty of ornament, rises into the extremely small class of first-rate poetry, except rarely. If it does so at all, Rabindranath's claim to the title of great poet is secure; if it does not do it often, that means only that he is not a Shakespeare or a Sophocles or a Dante. He may well be a Hugo or a Wordsworth, or greater than either. (pp. 302-03)

Buddhadeb Bose claims that [Rabindranath] is the world's greatest lyric poet; and, though on his translations I know it sounds absurd to agree with this, yet, when I remember his unrivalled variety of lyric measures, his unfailing certainty of touch, the gaiety and liveliness as well as gravity which were at his command, his power of noble thought and emotion, joined to this luxuriance of imagery which varies despite its sameness—as the natural world also varies amid repetition—I am disposed to believe it.

His countrymen find his greatest gifts to be this interpretation of nature and his interpretation of sorrow. It is the former that is to be the more unhesitatingly accepted. I believe it to be his greatest quality, and the quality in which no other poet surpasses him. It goes very much deeper than the fresh open-air quality of which I have been speaking, his gift of landscape. He has put his heart so close to the world about him, that his sympathy seems to pass into its body, returning thence charged with a knowledge and subtle understanding that make his language haunted. Looking into Nature's face, he remembers; once the dust that is now his limbs was dust that grew her rice and banyans, or was rocked in the sway and toss of her surges. (pp. 307-08)

He has been both of his nation, and not of it; his genius has been born of Indian thought, not of poets and philosophers alone but of the common people, yet it has been fostered by Western thought and by English literature; he has been the mightiest of national voices, yet has stood aside from his own folk in more than one angry controversy. His poetry presents the most varied in the history of Indian achievement. (pp. 309-11)

> *Edward Thompson, in his* Rabindranath Tagore: Poet and Dramatist *(reprinted by permission of Oxford University Press, New Delhi), revised edition, Oxford University Press, London, 1948, 330 p.*

HERMANN HESSE   (essay date 1957)

Tagore's reputation [is in partial eclipse] in the West today. . . .

I see no cause for bitterness or complaint. He owes part of his reputation to the rich heritage of ancient Indian philosophy, for which he reclaimed a place of honour in the West, at least for a time. In some minds and hearts the effects

have lived on and borne fruit, and this continuing influence —impersonal, silent and in no way dependent on fame or fashion—may in the final analysis be more appropriate to an Indian sage than fame or personality cults. . . .

I would be happy if I lived to see his triumphant re-emergence after the testing period of temporary oblivion.

> *Hermann Hesse, "Hermann Hesse on Tagore" (1957), in* Later Poems of Rabindranath Tagore, *translated by Aurobindo Bose (© 1974 Peter Owen Ltd; translation © 1974 Aurobindo Bose), Peter Owen, 1974, p. 7.*

EDWARD C. DIMOCK, JR.   (essay date 1959)

Rabindranath as a poet and as a thinker lies well within the tradition of a long line of Indian poet-saints, and . . . his roots are far more deeply buried in medieval Bengal than they are in the West. This is not to say that Rabindranath was uninfluenced by Western thought and literature. Indeed, I should find that very difficult to argue, particularly on the literary level. I do feel that he lives today in Bengal as he did fifty years ago because he is first and foremost a Bengali poet and speaks out of a tradition of Bengali poets. He is great because he had profound insight and rare lyric genius. These are the exclusive property of no language or tradition. He is great to non-Indians perhaps because the tradition out of which he comes is not the highly complex Sanskrit classical tradition which speaks primarily to the educated and sophisticated people of India, but the simple, personal, emotional tradition of the poet-saints who wrote for the people. But for most non-Indians, he is no longer living. He is an isolated figure. For us, he is not part of a living tradition.

That Rabindranath had a profound interest in such non-Bengali medieval poets as Kabīr and Dādū, as well as in the Vaisnava poets of medieval Bengal and the Bengali Bāuls, is quite clear. . . . But the Bāuls held his attention the most. He is known as the "discoverer" of the Bāul songs, who by his discovery "added greatly to the wealth of Bengali literature." (p. 34)

Who then are the Bāuls? The word itself means "mad." When Bengalis use the term, they usually mean to indicate a type of mendicant religious singer who, dressed in tattered clothes deliberately made up of the garments of both Hindus and Muslims, wanders from village to village celebrating God in ecstatic songs, existing on whatever his listeners choose to give him. . . . In his songs one can find traces of Sūfī Islam, of Sahajiyā or Tantric Buddhism, of Caitanyite Vaisnavism, and perhaps other religious strands not as easily isolable. . . . The Bāul recognizes no divisions among men either social or religious; he holds that all men are but travellers on the same road toward God. . . . (pp. 36-7)

Finally, all those who go by the name of Bāul seem somehow to come as strangers to the world. They accept no tradition or custom of society. An overwhelming feeling of the presence of God drives them to search for him. They feel that man is deluded by his senses, trapped by the snare of the body. The flesh, the attraction of the senses to the world, is strong. . . . Like other men, the Bāul has followed many paths, wandering near and far in search of the source of the flute of God which echoes always in his ears. The true Bāul finally realizes that the sound of the flute which has driven him mad comes from within his own heart. Then his madness becomes the madness of joy, the madness of the realization that he contains the seeds of bliss within himself. (pp. 38-9)

In a certain doctrinal and literary sense, . . . Rabindranath was profoundly influenced by this Bāul mysticism. In a social and perhaps an intellectual sense, he was a long way from being a Bāul. He was, in the first place, the son of a very rich and aristocratic family. As much as he tried, he never quite reached the common man. He was not a common man. . . . Many things are left unsaid by the Bāuls, things which are reflected in their attitudes but not in their thought. Such things are often explicitly stated by Rabindranath. (p. 39)

Rabindranath is frequently characterized as a poet of joy. Assuming that "joy" means not "happiness," but implies a realization of the transcendant, this characterization is certainly not false. . . . [There] is [also] a deep awareness of the tragic, a sense of melancholy and longing underlying the joy. In Rabindranath, longing for fulfillment and joy in fulfillment seem somehow to be one: each potentially contains the other. The loneliness of Rabindranath, and the loneliness of the Bāuls, is the loneliness of man's soul separated from God. (pp. 39-40)

The Bāul songs rest heavily upon the longing of man's soul for God, upon the despair and pain of separation, upon the lower self, the senses, as hinderances to realization. This element of monism can be found in Rabindranath. But there is in his thought another element, a dualistic conception that worship is the true end of man. Worship is impossible if the human and the divine are the same. (p. 50)

Rabindranath then finds more delight, more worshipfulness, more pure beauty in the world than do the Bāuls. The significant thing for him is the unity of man and nature. In one sense, he is like the Bāuls, feeling that the earthy nature of man keeps him from knowledge of his true nature. In another sense, the body is good; the body is that through which one knows the world, a place of transcendant joy. . . .

Other such differences between the doctrines of Rabindranath and those of the Bāuls could be noted, as indeed could many other such inconsistencies within the poetry of Rabindranath itself. But if Rabindranath's views seem sometimes inconsistent, it must be remembered that a poet need not be a logician. A poet interprets the world as he feels it, and Rabindranath felt it in many different ways at different times. . . . His interests, his language, his imagery were constantly changing. It is therefore far from my purpose to imply that all his writings can be interpreted in terms of the Bāuls. . . .

[These] few songs indicate that at least some of the sources both doctrinal and stylistic of Rabindranath's poetry lie neither in Sanskrit nor in European literature, but in the oral literary tradition of Bengal itself. (p. 51)

Edward C. Dimock, Jr., "Rabindranath Tagore—'The Greatest of the Bāuls of Bengall'," in Journal of Asian Studies *(copyright 1959 by the Association for Asian Studies), Vol. XIX, No. 1, November, 1959, pp. 33-51.*

BHABANI BHATTACHARYA (essay date 1961)

Rabindranath Tagore, one of the greatest poets of all time, wrote several novels. . . . (p. 96)

All, or nearly all, of them are novels of ideas. That is, the dramatization is devised to express an idea, a philosophic motif, in terms of life and action. Each novel grows in its own individual mould, different from what has preceded it or comes afterward. Some are more or less traditional in manner, others a total departure. *Gora* may be classed in the former category in the sense that it picks up the thread of a tradition and ties it to a new unwinding thread-reel of its own.

This is a voluminous work, much longer than all the other novels. A good part of it is filled with polemics, more than the craft of fiction would normally permit, since even the novel of ideas must dramatize what the essayist has simply to state. But the polemics in *Gora* seems inevitable in view of the time of its composition. The Partition of Bengal in 1905 was a historical event in more than one sense. While it stirred the national consciousness of the country and gave rise to the first great political movement in India on a mass scale, it brought about an intellectual ferment as an inevitable corollary—a great awakening of the spirit cannot but touch and transform every aspect of life. (p. 97)

However, it is as creative writing that *Gora* has its assured place in literature. Its real interest lies not in the pages of brilliant dialectic, but in the projection of ideas in the form of living images. *Gora* is contemporary and yet timeless; it is set in a certain social class, a vivid rendering of their life and mind, and yet it reaches out towards the universal. . . . In his portrayal of the characters Tagore exposes whatever was ridiculous or false not only in the old religious system but also in the orthodoxy of the new, the 'enlightened'. Everywhere in the world, in different spheres, there is constant recurrence of the same phenomenon—a new tyranny substituted for the old—and in that context the stern satire in *Gora* is of perennial interest. (pp. 97-8)

The political motif of *Gora* repeats itself in a different way in *Ghare-baire (The Home and the World)*. The Partition of Bengal, the blaze of national awakening that it meant, makes the background. Some of the unfortunate aspects of the national movement—the angry intolerance, the racial hatred leading to terrorism, the uncritical acceptance of a rigid line of action—draw Tagore's condemnation, which, it may be noted, he has also expressed on later occasions, heedless of the wrath it must arouse. However, it is the human interest in *The Home and the World* that mainly counts. The characters are no pawns in the hand of history, even if they are good symbols. The story is a total departure from the traditional form. It is built through the awareness of each of the three main characters by the introspective use of the first person singular. There is Nikhil, calm and perfectly balanced, watching the current events with eyes that look beneath the surface; there is his teacher, the impassioned political worker Sandip, egocentric and devoid of scruples; and between the two stands Nikhil's young wife, Bimala, bespelled by the false patriot, a helpless moth drawn despite herself towards the many-tongued flame. (pp. 98-9)

This work has an added interest as a memorable milestone: here the poet in Tagore who, in *Gora* a decade earlier, had surrendered his claims to the novelist, recovers every inch of the lost ground. He not only dominates over the novelist but, once in a while, hustles his rival out of the scene. The reader may at first have a fretful feeling that, with the superb rhetoric, the glittering ornamentation of the language, the 'poet' has been slowing the pace of the story and dimming the characters under his own shadow. But in a while the sheer beauty of language has an overwhelming effect. Dissatisfaction goes; the critical voice is shamed. And at the end of it one hates to think that the book could have been other than what it is, a poet's novel.

The poet, having asserted his domination over the novelist, does not fumble ever again. With *Sesher Kavita* he achieves further consolidation of his might. Here the theme from beginning to end is love. As a matter of fact love is the all-powerful theme in every Tagore novel, and even *Gora* is far from an exception.

It must be understood that love in Tagore is free from every trace of sentimentality. That is one reason why no Tagore novel has attained the wide popular appeal of the work of the other top-ranking novelist of Bengal, Saratchandra Chatterji, whose strong point is sentimentality itself. But then, the breath-taking tenderness that Tagore calls forth with an amazing economy of words is a literary miracle. The evocation of youthful love until its intensity is an agony too hard for the spirit to bear—that is a recurrent theme in several Tagore stories; and at that level love's fulfilment is in tragedy alone. Tragedy cannot but have the last word. Here is an idea that challenges language. The words needed for the nuances of feeling in terms that carry communication are, indeed, a severe test for any language, and passing through the test language recreates itself.

Love's asceticism and utmost dedication attains its last word in *Sesher Kavita* (translated by Krishna Kripalani under the title, *Farewell, my Friend*). Its young heroine (if one must use the word), Labanya, is middle-class, studious, rich with a serenity of temperament. The hero, Amit Ray, is sophisticated with his intellectual brilliance and great flights of poetic fancy, and if he is a rebel from high-society he belongs to it essentially. The philanderer is suddenly caught in the meshes of love amid the sylvan splendour of Shillong, and the great wonder of love has overtaken Labanya equally. But in a while Labanya realizes that it is, after all, her idealized image that has fascinated Amit. She has no heart to play up to that image, she has to be just herself, just a woman of common clay. Heartbreak at this stage would be easier to bear, she decides achingly, than heartbreak after marriage, and she strips her finger of the engagement ring and gives it back to her lover.

Perhaps it is unfair to state *Sesher Kavita* in such bald terms. Its beauty of feeling is as indescribable as its beauty of language—every passage is a unique and startling prose poem—and the astounding fact is that such freshness, such youthfulness, could come from a writer in his seventieth year. Somewhere in him Tagore was reborn, as it were, over and again so that the rich exuberance of the young in spirit along with the depth of understanding of the true seer made a perfect amalgam for his creative genius.

Four years later he wrote his last novel, *Char Adhyay (Four Chapters)* which bears a certain semblance to *Sesher Kavita,* though the story and setting are altogether apart. Ela is in a way related in spirit to Labanya, even if she is less serene, more passionate, more 'woman' in the earthly sense. And Atindra is far more mature than Amit Ray. The Terrorist movement gives the story its framework. Ela has pledged herself to that movement and into it she draws Atindra with whom she is in love. (pp. 99-100)

The four chapters in which the story is set are virtually four acts in a play. It is all dialogue, so vibrant with passion that the prose has to stand the hardest strains. Perhaps nowhere has the expressive power of Bengali prose been so well vindicated as in *Char Adhyay*.

In chronological order *Jogajog* [also transliterated as *Yogayog*], the other peak achievement of Tagore, comes a full decade before *Char Adhyay;* it belongs to the same period as *Sesher Kavita,* but the two have no points of contact. In technique it is closer to *Gora* in the sense that the poet and novelist are not in conflict on its pages, they have agreed to share the materials in hand equitably.

Jogajog, like *Gora,* has a clear-cut story line in which structure carries as much value as mood or thought, but all such means, all inventiveness, is tied to the focal point of characterization. Madhusudan is one of Tagore's most flesh-and-blood creations. Proud, all ego, vulgar in tastes and requirements, the self-made millionaire marries a young girl from the aristocratic house with which his ancestors had been in bitter feud—that house has nothing left to it except its great heritage of culture. All might have been well if Kumudini were tempted by her golden cage, but she has no use whatsoever for wealth, for attractive tinsel. Her heart has been brimful with worship for her husband; but where is the deity to whom she can make her offering? Her mind-picture of him shrivels before the reality. Madhusudan, utterly insensitive, alien to all refinements, hurts her with his baseness and revolts her with his crudities from the very first moment of their life together—there is no chance for her to adjust her dreams and make compromises. The great gift which could have been her husband's must go to waste. (pp. 100-01)

The great power of *Jogajog* is in its clear portrayal of psychological subtleties. It is, from one point of view, the most satisfying of all the novels Tagore has written. . . .

To sum up: Had Rabindranath Tagore written nothing but novels . . . he would still be the most predominant figure in the literary history of Bengal. (p. 101)

> *Bhabani Bhattacharya, "Tagore As a Novelist,"
> in* A Centenary Volume: Rabindranath Tagore,
> 1861-1961, *Sahitya Akademi, 1961, pp. 96-101.*

BUDDHADEVA BOSE (essay date 1961)

The prose of Rabindranath Tagore is as much a poet's work as his verse; at their best the two have the same quality and affect us in a similar fashion. If for a minute it were possible to imagine that the whole body of his verse had disappeared, leaving in our possession nothing but his essays, plays and novels, the palpable presence of a great poet would still shine through those proliferating pages of fiction, drama and essayistic prose.

It's literally true: his essays would give away the secret no less than his short stories or symbolical plays. And by the essay I mean not only forms like the memoir or travel-diary whose natural pliancy is favourable to poetic treatment, but also his discourses on set themes, his polemics, and his critical writings on history, religion, prosody and literature. There is a brilliance, a vibration, a certain inflexion of voice which means a little more than the topic or the content of the essay; and this vibration, which haunts and remains with us even when the theme has ceased to be exciting, we finally learn to identify with the unique personality of Tagore.

It has often been said or implied that poetry and discursive writing are incompatibles and Tagore's prose is defective because it is not logical enough. This view I can quite understand and have even been tempted to corroborate. Tagore's repetitions are far from few, his tangential passages are numerous; he uses imagery rather than reasons, and metaphors rather than facts; he starts with the professed intention of proving a thesis and ends by sharpening our perceptions; where an intellectual debate is expected he makes the illicit move of producing enchantment. Despite these defects, however, it is possible to extricate the message from metaphors when he is discussing matters like politics, education or social reform, but when literature—his dearest concern—is the theme, he becomes elusive to the point of apparently refusing to yield a tangible or workable hypothesis. At any rate he lays down no law, nor offers clean definitions; an extreme reluctance to arrive at a definite conclusion makes him contradict his own statements— may be within a minute of having made them. No one can deny that Tagore is not even a critic, in the sense that Aristotle or Anandavardhan is one. (p. 102)

Just as his prose piece *Basantayapan* (Passing the Spring) is really a poem in the essayistic form, so are poems like *Ebar Phirao More* (Make me Return) or *Basundhara* (The World) didactic or descriptive essays in verse. We could blame him for using verse and prose for the same or similar purposes. We could even say that in certain cases, where he writes prose in the poetic manner and uses prose matter in hundreds of lines of verse, he has done justice to neither; but can we, for these reasons, ever leave him aside? . . .

A Tagore free from his faults would not be Tagore at all; therefore, even while quarrelling with much of his doings, we accept him just as he is, and accept him whole. . . . We, who were nurtured on him and to whom the world was revealed through his words, are now in a position to give a pitiless account of his failings, and to say in the same breath that, although we have travelled much and treasure the memory of many shrines, Tagore is the house-god whom we perpetually need. (p. 103)

In Bengal and the whole of India Tagore has been elevated, or shall we say *reduced,* to an institution: he is an idol, a symbol of pan-Indian glory, a perennial prop for our national self-respect, and as such he is automatically accessible to whoever is born on the Indian soil. But it is not this formalized and devitalized Tagore that I should wish to stress, for public utility is very different from private enjoyment, and however easy it may be to invoke his authority in the beginning of all our ceremonies and in support of whatever creed we happen to hold, no reader can approach him, or any other poet, without a readiness to exert himself. However celebrated the name, a reader is always on his own; he can take nothing on hearsay; his job is not to join in the cheers of the multitude but to form a personal relationship with the book or author in question. And it is as an individual reader, and not merely as a member of a nation, that we must discover wherein the permanence of Tagore lies.

The great obstacle to a proper appreciation of Tagore is that he is both voluminous and unequal; the profusion and diversity of his works, comparable only to Goethe's, becomes bewildering when we reflect that, unlike Goethe, he has left no supreme single achievement by which we could justifiably judge him. . . . Indeed, there could be no better image of his career than the one he himself used for this purpose—I am referring to *Nirjharer Svapnabhanga* (The Awakening of the Waterfall), that prophetic poem of his youth in which for the first time he discovers and describes his possibilities: all Tagore's diversities may be likened to the turns and twists of a waterfall which flows the more excitedly for being impeded by boulders. . . . Poetry is the elemental stuff in Tagore, and his prose is one of its manifestations. Not that the flame does not flag now and then, and that is as true of his verse as prose; but no one who was not a poet to his very bones could have produced a critical essay like Tagore's on Bengali nursery rhymes, or his works on prosody and linguistics, or the sequences of *Sahaj Path,* that shining little masterpiece of an alphabet book combining pedagogic excellence with an astonishing beauty of diction. (pp. 104-05)

Tagore uses what is known as the general style; his arrangement of sentences and paragraphs are not apparently different from others'; and it is not until the nineteen-twenties that we catch him consciously trying to elevate prose to the level of verse. Moreover, he was capable of writing on depressingly mundane subjects, such as current politics or even co-operative banking. That his prose has dull moments is therefore not surprising; the marvel rather is that so much of it, irrespective of subject-matter, is haunting and resonant, capable of taking possession of our memories and delighting us by its very presence. (p. 105)

What Tagore did was to repeat in verse what he had said in prose, and *vice versa;* in him the two forms not only complement each other but are sometimes almost interchangeable. Lest the acolytes of modernism should regard this as heretical, I hasten to adduce the example of Charles Baudelaire—the prime source of modern poetry—who enriched his prose by borrowing phrases, imagery and at times whole stanzas from his verse, composed variations of the same poem in verse and prose, and whose poetry and art criticism occasionally sprang from the same material. And this is part of Tagore's practice, but where it differs from Baudelaire's is also important. Instances are not lacking where, using the same substance, Tagore is terse in prose and prolix in verse, while the prose of Baudelaire's essays is playful and even diffuse and his verse intensely concentrated.

A case in point is Tagore's *Balakà,* a volume of odes regarded by many Bengalis as an achievement, where the best piece, commemorating a long-lost beloved in page after page of breathless verse, is an expansion and elucidation of what he had said in two quiet prose paragraphs in the 'Bereavement' episode of his autobiography. . . . Tagore . . . lets his poems run away with him, with the result that sometimes his verse is distinguishable from his prose only by the use of metre or a visually different arrangement of the lines. Not a few of his poems have what we might call prose matter; the message in these could be delivered as well or more effectively in prose; and this can be seen in much of the prose he wrote during the last two decades of his life. . . . Of the art of versification Tagore was so much a master that he suffered from this very mastery, as when, during his last phase, he built poems round chance phrases or fleeting thoughts he had hit upon while sending off some letter or other—poems which add little to the prose form in which the thought was first captured. Tagore's verse and prose did not develop on parallel lines—we realize this the moment we view them in their entirety; for his verse style did not undergo any fundamental change after the turn of the century, whereas his prose went through a series of metamorphoses right through the nineteen-thirties. In verse he was an emperor crowned by Nature herself; and a safe assumption for his countrymen and almost for himself, was that any lines of verse would be poetry or at least well worth reading, simply because they bore his signature. But in prose he was much more of a conscious artist and aware of models and competitors in his own language, subject to unrest and the need for revisions, and incessantly striving to surpass himself.

Thus has this incredible thing happened to our literature that the greatest poet in the Bengali language is also supreme in prose. I say Bengali, but, once we except the creator of that eternity known as the *Mahabharata,* he being one who makes all comparisons absurd, Tagore as a poet has absolutely no equal in the whole history of Indian culture. And it is he who created Bengali prose. . . . Tagore did more to Bengali prose than any other writer before or after him; starting modestly in the footsteps of Bankimchandra [Chatterji] he ended by changing his style so radically that the gap between Bankimchandra's early works and Tagore's later ones may appear to be not of one but several centuries. In the pages of Tagore is recorded the whole evolution of our prose from the point where Bankimchandra left off, for he assimilated all viable innovations attempted by his successors and contemporaries, reflected all phases and transitions, and through a series of daring experimentations, perfected what is now understood to be modern Bengali. The productions of the six decades of his working life constitute the microcosm of Bengali prose, and, judging by volume and variety, its macrocosm as well. All moods and shades are there: the ponderous and the light, the simple and the ornate, ceremonial Sanskritisms and colloquial vigour, wit, fervour and gaiety, restraint and opulence, outspoken directness and the subtlest obliquity. Judging by the cool, measured and impeccably lucid periods of *My Reminiscences,* we can say that Tagore 'wrote like a gentleman'—in the eighteenth century English sense of the word; yet in the novel, *The Home and the World,* published only three years later, the style is almost suffocatingly rich, as loaded with rhetorical devices as a poem of Kalidasa's. Again in *Lipika,* a volume of prose-poems and a very close successor to *The Home and the World,* we behold yet another act of this magician: here the artifice employed is the apparent rejection of all artifice; the sentences are short, the adjectives few, and the words chosen from the homely diction of men and women—I daresay of women in particular. What Tagore seems to be doing here is to take the speech of Bengali womenfolk, to whom are attributed many of our immortal fairy-tales, purge it of its 'folkishness' and vulgarisms, and extract the whole of its lovely and loving simplicity. Here, as in the earlier work, *The Post Office,* Tagore achieves miraculous effects by purifying and elevating the merely natural. So great is the range of his prose style, and so frequent his alternations between rhetorical weight and sheer simplicity, that by studying him alone one can get to know all the modes of Bengali prose, all the styles that were and are living, and also those which contain the germs of the future. And there is no other Bengali writer of whom we can say this. Others have excellence of one kind or another, but in the single figure of Tagore is contained the essence of all that has

happened to our language in modern times. With all respect to his forbears and successors, it is impossible not to recognize that he, our master-singer, is also the perfect mirror of Bengali prose. (pp. 106-08)

[When Tagore was about fifty, he joined hands] with Pramatha Chaudhuri in effecting what we call a revolution in Bengali prose; sundering himself from Bankim and his line, he creates what is literally a *new* prose and the voice of a new century. . . .

It was a change-over from literary formalism to an approximation of living speech. . . . The struggle between *sadhubhasha* and *chalitbhasha*—or the 'noble' or 'elegant' and the 'common' or 'current' language, as we call them in Bengali —dragged on for years before the latter won the day, thanks to the polemics of Pramatha Chaudhuri and the prodigious inventiveness of Tagore. (p. 109)

Tagore, however, was ambidexterous in his prose writings. I mean he was happy either way; the books he wrote specifically for publication—again with the exception of plays— were all in *sadhubhasha,* but his letters and travel-diaries, starting from the earliest ones, were written in a conversational style which lacked neither grace nor power nor confidence. Thus the prose that Tagore wrote from youth to middle age falls into two distinct groups—the public and the private, or the 'official' and the 'homely'; and although I do not mean the former term in a pejorative sense, I must say that some of his correspondence of this period, written in vivid colloquial Bengali, make better use of the resources of our spoken language than any other work of the time. (p. 110)

I hope I am not understood as saying that books in *chalitbhasha* are necessarily better than those in the old style. That would verge on absurdity. The best of our nineteenth century prose is very good indeed; and much of Tagore's best is in *sadhubhasha.* What should be noted, though, is that once having adopted the new style—for public as well as private purposes—Tagore never went back to the old; and as time passed, more and more writers of the younger generations were won over by his example. By the time he died in 1941 there hardly remained an area which *chalitbhasha* had not taken over and to-day the once-lauded 'elegant style' is stepping downhill toward oblivion by way of school-texts and newspapers.

Another thing that Tagore did to Bengali prose was to impart movement. In saying this I am not counting the distinction between *sadhu-* and *chalitbhasha,* for in his case both have the same kind of movement, though not to the same degree. I am rather trying to define the difference, in terms somewhat more precise, between his prose and let us say Bankimchandra's. Not that Bankimchandra did not have movement—it is impossible to write either prose or verse without movement of some sort—but Tagore made the language *flow,* giving it a flexibility we do not find in his elders. (p. 111)

It seems to me that Bankimchandra built up his prose in a succession of single sentences, but in Tagore the unit is the paragraph, and the link between the paragraphs and the sentences of which they are composed, is provided not merely by grammar or logical coherence, but by another element, less easy to define, which remains off stage as it were and yet animates the whole. It is something like the pulse-beat in the body of a living animal, and this we can finally recognize as the very rhythm of the language. This rhythm—of which Mallarmé spoke—is what was lacking in Bengali prose before Tagore and which he brought to it. Tagore's sentences do not merely follow a logical sequence, but remain sensuously in touch with one another; they are like a troupe of ballet dancers who have plastic limbs and sinuous movement and who can produce the most overwhelming effects by doing not what is expected but what is barely felt to be possible. Perhaps it would be nearer the truth to say that they satisfy our immortal longing for harmony, and by harmony I mean an organization which can combine a very great variety of movement, including dissonance and violation of symmetry. In Tagore's prose long and short sentences jostle one another; meandering complexities lead to an abrupt decision couched in a statement of two words; no two consecutive sentences begin or end in the same way, and closed and open sounds caressingly alternate. And Tagore does all this intuitively, with an apparent ease which baffles us all, and he does this in a language whose resources, when he came to it, were certainly small compared to English or French.... [It] was Tagore who showed how much Bengali can gain in speed, strength and richness by adopting parentheses, inversions and several other devices which are common in English and all other languages which have developed a prose literature.... Perfected by Tagore, this new syntax is the style of modern Bengali; it is absurd to say that any such thing as a 'pure Bengali syntax' is any longer possible, or that our prose has corrupted itself by deviating from the norm of medieval verse-couplets, which trudged as best they could on the stilts of their single and double stops. The truth is that the style of Tagore makes full use of the natural rhythm of spoken Bengali; neither stuffily Sanskritic nor loosely colloquial, it is rather an idealized form of the living speech of his countrymen. The very inflexions of our voice, ranging from assertion to the whispered word, from dejection and doubt to passionate belief—all this is heard in the prose of Tagore. In other words, it is rhythmic in the way of prose, and removed as far as possible from metrical beats; it moves in the same way as the *alap* or overture of Indian music, which follows tempo, but rejects melodic measure.... Tagore, *the* poet, writing prose as only a poet can, never admits in it the faintest echo of metrical effects, not even in the prose-poems of his later years. And this, I think, is his great achievement as a prose writer. (pp. 112-13)

> Buddhadeva Bose, "Rabindranath Tagore and Bengali Prose," in A Centenary Volume: Rabindranath Tagore, 1861-1961, *Sahitya Akademi, 1961, pp. 102-13.*

MARY M. LAGO (essay date 1967)

With a unanimity rare among literary critics, four contemporary Bengali scholars [Srikumar Banerjee, Sukumar Sen, Bhudev Chaudhuri, and Buddhadeva Bose] agree that with the work of Rabindranath Tagore the short story "came of age" in Bengali literature. (p. 24)

In Bengal, as in the countries of the West, [the 1890's were] a time of economic and social ferment, of cultural revival and personal readjustment.... In such a situation a thoughtful person could scarcely avoid questioning both himself and others. We are primarily concerned here with the placement and the mode of Tagore's questioning in two of his early "modern" stories: "Punishment" (*"shasti"*)

..., and "A Lapse of Judgment" (*"durbuddhi"*).... The action in "Punishment" arises from a crime and its retribution, in "A Lapse of Judgment" from a dilemma involving moral choice, but in both stories something important occurs in the background. This something important is a process of implied questioning that forces the reader to recognize change and the need for change. In "Punishment" the changes relate to the social scene, and in "A Lapse of Judgment" they arise from an inner moral scene. (p. 25)

Tagore's commitment to the lyric poem has a fundamental relationship with his affinity for the short story as a literary form. Both lyric and short story provide the reader with little more than an outline map for the imagination's explorations.... From beginning to end, this process of imaginative exploration is a mode of self-questioning. It leads the reader, if he pushes it to its logical conclusion, to the making of value judgments about society and about himself.

A type of Bengali lyric that profoundly influenced the tone of Tagore's work was the *pada,* the principal devotional expression of the Vaishnavas [who were followers of Khrishna]. (p. 27)

The continuing theme of these [Vaishnava] lyrics is the endless mutual search of God and the human soul for each other. In Vaishnava thought, God needs Man as much as Man needs God, and neither can be complete or contented without the other. This theme is allegorized in the love story of the divine Krishna and Rādhā as Krishna's mortal reflection. Every episode of their meeting, separation, search, and reunion is lyrically dramatized.... *Biraha,* separation, and *milan,* reunion, are cyclical; and the mood is one of sustained and thoughtful—but not fatalistic—waiting. (pp. 27-8)

In the best of Tagore's short stories, also, we find the present-yet-absent detachment of the Vaishnava lyricist. Such a posture is admirably suited to objective examination of the status quo, and we shall find in the two stories that I discuss here that the meeting of the pragmatic and the lyrical, somewhere in the background of the primary action, is the reader's cue to raise an important question.

In "Punishment," a young village wife goes to the gallows for a murder she has not committed and thereby punishes the husband who forces her to plead guilty in order to spare his brother, who is the real murderer. The moral questions raised by the story reach to the darkest corners of human behavior, but at the same time the background is marked out with Tagore's double-edged questions about certain flaws in the social structure and about the rôle of material property in the life of the individual. (p. 28)

[The wife's] tragedy is the tragedy of *biraha,* separation, without hope of *milan,* reunion. She is a paradigm for Rādhā without Krishna, for Man without God. She is cut off through no fault of her own, and the world offers her no escape and no explanation.... Tagore was indignant at the economic state of Bengal, but his greater grief was for the *ryot*'s [the peasant's] inarticulate submission.

"A Lapse of Judgment" deals with an ethical dilemma and a moral choice. Again lyricist and pragmatist meet in the background of the primary action. Nature, in its most literal sense of natural setting, is their meeting-place. Again Tagore uses (whether consciously or unconsciously is irrelevant here) a concept from the heart of Vaishnava thought.

In the Vaishnava lyrics, natural setting has both functional and symbolic uses. Rādhā is described leaving the warmth and security of home and family to go out into the stormy night in search of Krishna. . . . She is buffeted by wind and drenched with rain, and it is truly a dark night of the soul for Nature here is a mirror of mankind, who is God's other half. (p. 32)

The protagonist in "A Lapse of Judgment" is a Bengali doctor in government service. He is a widower, the father of an only daughter, and a friend of the local police inspector, a back-country bureaucrat who has made it financially worthwhile for the doctor to manipulate medical certificates. The doctor has drifted for some time with this questionable current, fanned by the breezes of expediency. (p. 33)

The death of Harināth's daughter [and the doctor's subsequent betrayal of his friend Harināth] does not touch the doctor's conscience until his own Shashi falls ill and dies. Even then he shows no resistance, either active or passive, to the police inspector's domination. It is [a] nameless peasant's wordless submission that finally makes the doctor speak out. (p. 35)

The tensions accumulated during [the doctor's] own wordless complicity with the inspector are released along with the rains which, because they symbolize the reunion of lovers and the renewal of life, make absence or alienation doubly painful. Tagore used this motif, repeated over the centuries in uncounted numbers of Bengali lyric poems, as catalyst for the resolution of a moral predicament that finds more than enough analogies in our own lives and times. In both "Punishment" and "A Lapse of Judgment," the lyric motif is a device for emphasizing a fundamental irony and a practical lesson: Man is separated from God whenever he ignores factual truth, or manipulates it for selfish ends.

Tagore, whom critics were to call to account all his life for apparent self-contradictions, was already using realism and romanticism to temper each other. The technique of balancing them was sometimes far from perfect in his stories; he, like writers in Europe and the Americas at that time, was still learning his craft. But it is worthwhile to note that at a time when recognized fictionists were still plagued by the "dear reader" authorial syndrome, Tagore was successfully using devices that are hallmarks of good fiction today: a consistent point of view, a detached narrative stance, titles whose double-edged connotations make them functional parts of the story, and open-ended conclusions that make the reader a participant in the action.

The techniques he used in these stories show that he knew how to make apparently contradictory approaches complement each other. By pointing the way to questions that cry out for answers, Tagore the lyric poet puts his own imagination at the service of the inarticulate, and Tagore the pragmatist indicates those situations that call for social or moral action. Finally, he pays his readers the compliment of assuming that they are mature enough to spell out their responsibilities by reading between his lines. (pp. 35-6)

> Mary M. Lago, "Modes of Questioning in Tagore's Short Stories," in Studies in Short Fiction (copyright 1967 by Newberry College), Fall, 1967, pp. 24-36.

MARY M. LAGO (essay date 1976)

Even if Tagore's novels, in their turn, strike the reader somewhat as period pieces, some of the characterizations are unforgettable. As in the short stories, one is struck by the vividness and the strength of Tagore's women characters. This is especially true of *Cokher Bali* [*Eyesore*], whose heroine, Binodini, is a young widow who comes into a middle-class home and refuses to accept the restrictions upon what she feels is every woman's right to love and domestic happiness. Her situation is like that of Charulata, in [*Nashtanir*] *The Broken Nest,* insofar as Binodini knows that she possesses talents and great intelligence; her resentment and restlessness are fed by the realization that those talents will never be used, and her passionate revolt finally tears the family to pieces. "Half a century ago, when *Cokher Bali* was first published, in the eyes of Hindu society, Binodini's image was appalling," Buddhadeva Bose has commented. "Then, one had to be really reckless to write this book." Yet even Tagore, for all his recklessness, was intimidated by public opinion, for even the fiery Binodini capitulates at the end, to the great detriment of the novel. She tells the man who really loves her and wants to marry her that marriage is impossible: "'The very thought of it is shameful,' said Binodini. 'I am a widow and, besides, a woman in disgrace. I can never allow you to lose caste on my account. Please, don't ever again utter such words.'"

Similar motifs and evidences of social restrictions appear in [*Ghare-Baire* (At Home-Outside), translated as *The Home and the World; Nouka-Dubi* (Sunken Boat), translated as *The Wreck;* and *Gora*], and their timing was not auspicious. The war was over, and English liberals clamored for belated reforms, among them women's suffrage, liberalized divorce, and property inheritance laws. Imperialists of an evangelical bent could easily interpret such episodes in Indian novels as proof that English rule had not yet delivered India from a benighted state, and therefore the Englishman must not lay down that burden just yet. Readers who held such views would have been quick to notice that the plot of *The Home and the World* was centered upon an episode typical of abuses within the Swadeshi movement, which was even then causing the Government of India no end of trouble, and upon an unscrupulous organizer for that movement. They would not have known—for the copyright page of the translation gives no hint of it—that *The Wreck,* written in 1906, was well on its way to becoming a period piece, but they would be quick to note that it dealt with a young woman victimized by a restrictive society. And *Gora* was a study of the relation between Hindu orthodoxy and Indian nationalism. This is by no means to suggest that the novels should not have been translated and published, but one must say that novels like these bore a very heavy responsibility, coming at such a time from a writer of such prominence. (pp. 121-22)

If Bengali novelists were somewhat behind Western novelists in refinement of literary techniques, Indian readers would find [*The Home and the World*] decidedly up to date: the anti-British sentiment of which Swadeshi was the expression—however it might be conveyed in novels—*was* a product of Indian nationalism. *The Home and the World,* whatever its faults as fiction, demonstrated the consistency of Tagore's view that positive ends never justify negative means. (p. 125)

> Mary M. Lago, "The Other Tagore: Dramas, Novels, Personal Writings," in her Rabindranath

BIBLIOGRAPHY

Bose, Abinash Chandra. "Rabindranath Tagore." In his *Three Mystic Poets: A Study of W. B. Yeats, A.E., and Rabindranath Tagore*, pp. 103-53. Darby, PA: The Folcroft Press, 1970.
   Chronological overview of Tagore's poetry, with an emphasis on its religious and mystic elements.

Chakravarty, Amiya. Introduction to *The Housewarming and Other Selected Writings*, by Rabindranath Tagore, translated by Mary Lago, Tarun Gupta, and Amiya Chakravary, pp. vii-xii. Westport: Greenwood Press, 1965.
   Biographical and cultural background to Tagore's work.

Chakravorty, B. C. *Rabindranath Tagore, His Mind and Art: Tagore's Contribution to English Literature*. New Delhi: Young India Publications, 1971, 304 p.
   A thorough survey of Tagore's career stressing the development of his philosophical humanism.

Henderson, Alice Corbin. "Rabindranath Tagore." *The Drama IV*, No. 14 (May 1914): 161-76.
   Biographical sketch, with a survey of Tagore's early plays in English.

Lago, Mary M. Introduction to *The Broken Nest (Nashtanir)*, by Rabindranath Tagore, translated by Mary M. Lago and Supriya Sen, pp. 1-18. Columbia: University of Missouri Press, 1971.
   Discusses social and political background to *The Broken Nest*, tracing the emergence of Bengali as a literary language.

Mackenzie, Kathleen Cuffe. "Rabindranath Tagore." *The Dalhousie Review* 25, No. 1 (April 1945): 68-78.
   Biographical sketch.

Roy, Basanta Koomar. *Rabindranath Tagore: The Man and His Poetry*. New York: Dodd, Mead & Co., 1916, 223 p.
   Romantic narrative biography, with intermittent criticism.

Sanyal, Hirankumar. "Tagore's Place in World Drama." *Natya, Special Issue:* Rabindranath Tagore (1961): 68-76.
   An excellent survey of Tagore's drama which focuses upon the innovations he made in the Indian and world theaters.

Shridharani, Krishnalal. "Rabindranath Tagore, 1861-1941." *Saturday Review of Literature* XXIV, No. 17 (16 August 1941): 3-4, 14-15.
   A look at Tagore's influence and reception in western countries.

Katharine Tynan (Hinkson)

1861-1931

Irish poet, novelist, and journalist.

Although she was the author of more than one hundred novels, Tynan is remembered principally as an early member of the Celtic Revival and as a minor poet of nature and devotional lyrics. Among her friends in the Young Ireland circle were figures such as W. B. Yeats, A.E., and Alice Meynell. Tynan's work, however, does not significantly share the characteristics of Celtic spirituality and pagan myth prominent in the writing of her contemporaries. Her literary themes more often derive from Christian legendry, and she maintained an orthodox Catholicism throughout her life. Religion and family were both important foundations of Tynan's world. The experience of motherhood served as inspiration for the kind of sentimental and deeply personal poetry on which her reputation flourished.

It was in a second phase of her literary career that Tynan became the author of popular novels of romance and adventure. These books, written primarily to support herself and her children, were also sincere reflections of her own moral, spiritual, and social values.

Today Tynan's work is probably of most interest and importance to students of the Irish Literary Renaissance.

PRINCIPAL WORKS

Louise de la Vallière, and Other Poems (poetry) 1885
Shamrocks (poetry) 1887
Ballads and Lyrics (poetry) 1890
Cuckoo Songs (poetry) 1894
Miracle Plays: Our Lord's Coming and Childhood (poetry) 1895
The Way of a Maid (novel) 1895
Lover's Breast Knot (poetry) 1896
Poems (poetry) 1901
Innocencies: A Book of Verse (poetry) 1905
Twenty-Five Years: Reminiscences (autobiography) 1913
Irish Poems (poetry) 1914
The Holy War (poetry) 1916
Lord Edward: A Study in Romance (novel) 1916
Herb O'Grace: Poems in War-Time (poetry) 1918
Love of Brothers (novel) 1919
The Years of the Shadow (autobiography) 1919
Denys the Dreamer (novel) 1920

Memories (autobiography) 1924
A Fine Gentleman (novel) 1929
The Admirable Simmons (novel) 1930
Collected Poems (poetry) 1930

W. B. YEATS (essay date 1892)

[In reading Miss Tynan's *Ballads and Lyrics*] I feel constantly how greatly she has benefited by study both of the old Irish ballads and of the modern [Irish] writers. . . . Her first book, *Louise de la Valliere,* was too full of English influences to be quite Irish, and too laden with garish colour to be quite true to the austere Celtic spirit. *Shamrocks* was better, and now *Ballads and Lyrics* is well nigh in all things a thoroughly Irish book, springing straight from the Celtic mind and pouring itself out in soft Celtic music. Though perfectly original, I can yet feel in it the influence of more than one master of Celtic speech, and in thus gaining nationality of style, Miss Tynan has found herself and found the world about her. The landscapes are no more taken from the tapestry-like scenery of Rossetti and his imitators, but from her own Clondalkin fields, and from the grey Dublin hills. She apologises for the charming provincialism in an "Apologia" as exquisite as Allingham at his best, but with an added richness. . . .

In Miss Tynan's earlier books colour was too often sought for its own sake, as if an artist were to rest satisfied with the strange and striking combinations of the colours spread upon his palettes, instead of using them to make manifest the beautiful things about him. In this book, however, is many a fine landscape and much fine portraiture of noble woods. How well-suggested is the gloomy landscape in "The Children of Lir" and how subtly expressed are their wistful human souls wrapped around with birds' bodies.

How rare a thing is good religious poetry is known to all reviewers, and yet some of the most successful poems in this book are on the most hackneyed symbols of Christianity. Miss Tynan charms from them even some new and quaint beauty. Some of her religious poems have the *naïveté* of mediaeval song; nor is their simplicity any the less genuine for being conscious—for being a product quite as much of art as of impulse. (pp. 181-82)

Here and there is a poem that leaves me cold, a song that

does not seem to me to sing, a ballad where art has become artificial and [has] stifled impulse instead of guiding it; but what need is there to single them out, when there is so much beauty, so many verses that may well be dear to the heart of our people, when I who write and you who read are under the green grass or "where the thistles grow." (p. 183)

W. B. Yeats, "Notes: Poems by Miss Tynan" (originally published in a different version in the Evening Herald, January 2, 1892), in his Letters to Katharine Tynan, edited by Roger McHugh (copyright 1953 by Clonmore & Reynolds, Ltd.; reprinted by permission of A. P. Watt Ltd.), Clonmore and Reynolds, 1953, pp. 181-83.

KATHERINE BREGY (essay date 1913)

In the garden of Mrs. Hinkson's poetry it is quite possible to sort and sift the flowers—even to trace by their sequence the progress of her own seasons. . . . *Louise de la Vallière* [was] as like as possible to the pale sweet crocus of earliest springtime. . . . Like most youthful songs they were shy, romantic, idealistic; tenderly but not fastidiously wrought, and preoccupied with the minor music of life. The title poem was a monologue of much grace and pathos. . . . *Joan of Arc* again takes the monologue form, and the book holds a charming tale of King Cophetua's Beggar-Queen. A poem upon Thoreau gave prophecy of the Franciscan sympathies which have dominated so much of Katharine Tynan's later work: and there was already, in more than one poem, touches of that sweet and altogether reconciling comprehension of *death* which has given largeness and serenity to her pages. (pp. 208-09)

[In *Shamrocks*] there was the forward leap. In its *Angel of the Annunciation* one discerns the golden germ later to develop into the First Book of *Miracle Plays;* just as *The Heart of a Mother* anticipates that whole group of poems which one shall find clustering about the thought of the little dead child. (p. 209)

[*Ballads and Lyrics*] gave us the first of those delicious verse *apologias* which Mrs. Hinkson's readers have learned to expect by way of introduction—as also that little trick of the refrain which she has used so repeatedly and so refreshingly. Nowhere is it more refreshing nor more persistent than in the now familiar *April* lyric. . . . In that we come upon the strain which Mrs. Hinkson's friends will like to label the essential Katharinian! (pp. 209-10)

Of very different tenor was the *Countess Cathleen*. . . . To handle with any sort of *vraisemblance* this tale . . . would seem a work of peculiar difficulty. It is a far more mystical version of the Monna Vanna problem—something of Faust to boot. But there is no doubt that it has proved immensely stimulating to the poets. When Katharine Tynan pictured her Cathleen going forth from the palace . . . she achieved one of her most beautiful passages. (pp. 210-11)

[In *Cuckoo Songs*] there was a noticeable deepening of the personal note. To Katharine Tynan (or as she had now become, Mrs. Henry Albert Hinkson) there had come a new power of self-expression and of soul-expression.

In the main, and all along, this has been most successful in concrete forms. *God's Bird* is both noble and tender; but most readers will recognize in *House and Home* a rather unique combination of "the dream and the business," and

withal a very convincing piece of feminine (if not "feminist") psychology. . . . (p. 211)

[*Miracle Plays*] was a most lovesome recasting of the mediaeval strain, a series of little poetic plays upon our Lord's Birth and Childhood, very devout, very naïve, very artistic; and full (as the best mediaeval ones were also full) of a vital and simple humanism. Although cast in dialogue form, their strength is mainly lyrical; and at the beginning and end of all six parts there are lyrics of extremely quotable beauty. (p. 212)

The dramatic sense is nowise deficient, for all this lyricism: one meets it in the characterization of the three kings, in the exquisite little scene with Simeon at the Presentation, in the song of Dimas' Mother. St. Joseph was to take on personality later, in that poem of glorified domesticity, *The Man of the House*, and was but slightly defined in the *Miracle Plays*. But the Virgin moves like a pearl across the pages. . . . It is a mystical, childlike Mary in the early scenes, bowered among her blossoms and her birds; a very woman in the hours of stress; a very mother in her sweetly fearful dominance of the final episodes.

Love and motherhood and then death had laid their seal upon Katharine Tynan's life—perhaps, indeed, they must needs have laid their seal, every one of them—before she could conceivably have given us her *Lover's Breast Knot*. She herself has named the flowers it brought into the garden—heartsease and love-lies-bleeding: heartsease for the "marriage of true minds," a *woman's* love songs, infinitely tender, scarcely passionate; and love-lies-bleeding to rest, like a sprig of rosemary, on the grave of the little lost son, Godfrey. Here, in truth, was passion enough; no passion of ineffectual tears, but the agony of motherhood made barren, the surpassing wistfulness of eyes which must look all the way into eternity before the heart's delight be found. . . . It is a note less of tragedy than of consummate, quintessential pathos, and without it Mrs. Hinkson's poetry could never have attained its most piercing loveliness. (pp. 212-13)

Katharine Tynan's experiences are all innocencies: praises to God for the beauty of earth, for the serviceable senses, for sweet memories and sad, for friends and gardens and the quiet of meadowpaths, for sunlight and shadow, and all the comfortable and common things of life. (p. 214)

It would be very easy to over-accentuate this note of serenity in Mrs. Hinkson's work. It is always easy to overstress the obvious, and to hear only the loudest music. But there are many distinct "motives" in these songs of the seasons, and it is not alone in the most joyous that she has proved a true poet. . . . No one has sung more enchantingly of the birds: very few more sympathetically of the beasts. But Francis himself was scarcely joyous when he looked upon the burdens of Brother Ox or Brother Ass. In Katharine Tynan's *Shamrocks* there was a version of that old sweet legend of Christ and the "pitiful dead dog" lying in the streets of Jerusalem: and soon, in the volume not yet published, her readers will come upon a lyric, *The Ass Speaks*, in her best manner and of tear-compelling potency. (pp. 215-16)

Something of this tender, colloquial note goes into all of Katharine Tynan's devotional poetry. It was the charm of the *Miracle Plays* and the *Man of the House*, and it gave sincerity to the more ornate pre-Raphaelite pieces. By temperament, Mrs. Hinkson would seem less mystical than Crashaw or Francis Thompson or even Dante Rossetti; but in the best of her religious pieces she becomes mystical, precisely because of the definite intimacy with which she handles Uranian themes. There is a beautiful youthfulness in the sharp sweet music of her *Garden;* a lyric breath, it might be, from the unspoiled hills of Oberammergau. . . . (p. 217)

It was not in the nature of Mrs. Hinkson's poetry to fall into the snare of didacticism; if she teaches, we do not know it; and she is wise enough to seem ignorant of it herself. Yet we cannot ignore the peculiar nobility with which, from almost every angle, she has treated the subject of death. It is not merely in the religious pieces; nor in that spirited and singing bit of symbolism, *Planting Bulbs;* it is the pervading message of her song. From that early recognition of Azrael . . . in the very youth of her work, our poet has simply dismissed the traditional fear of death. . . . She has found a stronger thing—Love which casts out fear; and she carries it unhesitatingly into every human relationship. Hence we find the constantly recurring motive of the return of the dead: the motive of the dead child . . . remembering and comforting the mother still "under sentence of life." More insistent still is the theme of the dead mother, who returns to watch over her little ones upon earth. *Shamrocks* gave us the first of these valiant, piteous women: then came *The Widowed House* of *Cuckoo Songs,* a brief piece of haunting power and pathos. . . . (p. 218)

There is nothing in all the love poems of Katharine Tynan to equal the passion of *Maternity.* Yet, although romantic love has scarcely been a favorite theme with her, and although it has been a theme treated with reticence, she has given us authentic love songs none the less. In the early poems there was often a note of wistfulness; but in all the mature work it is calm and sweet fruition, a deep but scarcely ruffled music. Once again domesticity dominates; as in *House and Home* and the *Country Lover* the sea surges toward harbor lights. For sundered lovers, staggering separately the long Via Crucis till paths converge at last—for lovers who must needs do battle in the dust and heat and darkness—for lovers bruised and broken by the pitiless waves of life—our poet has no word. But the *True Marriage* of hidden grace and manifest love, the union grown purer by long use and daily sacrifice, she has interpreted with delicate and exquisite fervor. (p. 220)

Katharine Tynan's garden has, in all truth, been rich: in sympathy, in variety, in those rarer virtues of sincerity and idealized realism. Her poetry is highly emotional, but not, for the most part, stirred by the profundities of passion or conviction. It knows little of conflict. It is gentle, gracious, intensely personal. When it reaches out to experiences as old and as large as humanity, it does so by the simple right of having lived and felt one life sensitively. There is no effort of the poet to "project" her soul—to speak oracularly or vicariously. Indeed, she is no lover of abstractions in divine or human things. There is little in her work of what we are fond of calling Celtic other-worldliness: a thing beloved of poet and dreamer, not unknown, perhaps, to peasant or beggar; but no whit more real, and not one-tenth as general as Celtic domesticity. There is no more home-making race on earth than the Irish, and the Irishman as lover (not in any precise sense mystical!) has become a fable to the nations. In this engaging sense Mrs. Hinkson's poetry is Celtic enough! (p. 221)

Katherine Bregy, "The Poetry of Katharine Tynan Hinkson," in Catholic World *(copyright 1913 by The Missionary Society of St. Paul the Apostle in the State of New York), Vol. XCVII, No. 578, May, 1913, pp. 208-21.*

ERNEST A. BOYD (essay date 1916)

It is not easy to understand why what [Katharine Tynan] herself describes as a "very-much derived little volume" [*Louise de la Vallière*] should have had a fate so different from that of the first work of so many young poets. *The Dead Spring, Joan of Arc, King Cophetua's Queen* and many of the other poems, are obviously inspired by the Pre-Raphaelite movement, and cannot be said to reveal anything of the poet's personality. On the other hand, two sonnets on *Fra Angelico at Fiesole,* though perhaps derived from the same source, are more characteristic of Katharine Tynan's later manner. They have something of the innocent tenderness, the devotional sensitiveness to external beauty which are associated with her best work. These elements are more clearly present in such a poem as *An Answer,* which, in its absence of word-painting after Rossetti, foreshadows more precisely the style of much of her subsequent poetry. The promise of this volume would have been imperfect, however, had the note of nationality been absent. Beautiful as are some of the poems already mentioned, they could not have warranted the general recognition of Katharine Tynan as the singer of a distinctively Irish song. The Pre-Raphaelite tinge of *Louise de la Vallière* made the book one which might have been written by a young disciple of Rossetti, were it not for the five poems—the most stirring of all—whose theme was patriotic or national. The best of all these is *Waiting.* . . . The element of mystery is here combined with a living patriotism which give to this poem a thrill of reality contrasting with the rather imitative echoes of the verses of more commonplace inspiration. The lines on the death of A. M. Sullivan, entitled *The Dead Patriot* and *The Flight of the Wild Geese,* though less remote in their subjects, are not more intensely felt than this poem of legend. They, too, are infused with the emotion which is necessary to the creation of genuine poetry. (pp. 103-04)

[In *Shamrocks*] we find Katharine Tynan occupied more frequently with Celtic themes. The first and longest poem, *The Pursuit of Diarmuid and Grainne,* was one of the earliest attempts to make use of the Ossianic material in Anglo-Irish poetry. Though it is spoiled by rather conventional diction, there are many charming pictures which give to it an interest other than that necessarily attaching to the early poetry derived from legendary and historical sources. *The Story of Aibhric* and *The Fate of King Feargus* also witness to the poet's increased attention to Gaelic subjects. . . . The religious feeling so noticeable in Katharine Tynan's work comes out very definitely in this volume. *St. Francis to the Birds* is one of her best and most characteristic impressions of that simple piety which imbues so much of her verse, and has again and again drawn her to the gentle figure of Assisi. *Ballads and Lyrics* . . . contained several poems relating to St. Francis, but none of these is superior to the first. This book, however, represents more adequately all the phases of the poet's talent, and shows a great advance upon its predecessors. There is a more pronounced individuality in this work than heretofore, and many of her previous themes are here rehandled with a surer touch. The opening verses, *The Children of Lir,* are far superior to the preliminary treatment of the same subject in *The Story of Aibhric,* already mentioned. Christian and pagan folk-lore are the basis of most of this volume, *Our Lady's Exile, The Hiding-Away of Blessed Angus, The Fairy Foster-Mother* and *The Witch* are typical poems of a kind Katharine Tynan has familiarised in many later books. They combine those two striking traits of Irish peasant character: an unlimited faith in the possibilities of witchcraft together with a profound belief in the more picturesque legends of Catholicism.

Ballads and Lyric is Katharine Tynan's most representative, and probably her best volume, as it is certainly that which bears most distinctly the Celtic imprint. *Cuckoo Songs* . . . suffers, by comparison, owing to a certain monotony due to the predominance of the devotional element, nor did the author recover the variety of *Ballads and Lyrics* in the four years' interval that preceded the publication of *The Wind in the Trees.* Here, the sub-title, "A Book of Country Verse," announced a certain limitation of scope. The entire volume is devoted to a series of intimate impressions of external nature, of the beauties of leaf and flower, all conceived in the vein of simple, loving admiration which has made her the sympathetic interpreter of mediaeval Catholicism. In spite of the charm of such pictures as *Leaves, The Grey Mornings,* the volume can hardly be said to mark any progress, unless it be in a more careful technique. This halt in the development of Katharine Tynan's talent may be due to the fact that she has been too prolific for one whose gift is manifestly of slender proportions. Had she written but three volumes, they would easily have held the best of her inspiration. Using the word in its best sense, we may describe her as an essentially minor poet, though a minor poet of the first rank. Narrative verse was not her forte and she abandoned it early for lighter forms. Her themes have constantly been those of minor poetry, the birds and flowers of the countryside, the green fields and in general the simpler emotions derived from nature. She has treated these subjects with frequent delicacy and skill, and to them she owes her greatest successes. Nevertheless, she has continued to publish regularly books of this unsophisticated verse, each resembling its predecessor, alike in form and content. This inability to understand how rapidly such a vein becomes exhausted has resulted in the swamping of much good work by such volumes as *New Poems* . . . , where there is hardly a line that could not have been written by the average young lady and gentleman with a facility for rhyme. (pp. 104-07)

If her poetry has suffered by being subjected to the same exploitation as her prose, Katharine Tynan is none the less an interesting figure in contemporary literature. She is almost unique in that she is the only writer of any importance whose Catholicism has found literary expression. (p. 107)

Katharine Tynan, though also associated, to some extent, with the group of poets [that included A. E. and W. B. Yeats], remained uninfluenced by the revolt which led them to the very sources of Celtic spirituality. She remained undisturbed in her acceptation of the simple teaching of the Catholic Church, and it is just in so far as she approximates to the attitude of the country people that she is a Catholic poet. One does not find her expressing the profounder aspects of Catholicism, the exaltation and rapture of belief, for these belong to a more emotional and intellectual religion than that of the Irish Catholic. . . . Katharine Tynan's

verse, therefore, voices that naïve faith, that complete surrender to the simpler emotions of wonder and pity, which characterise the religious experiences of the plain man.

Her delight in St. Francis is typical of her general manner. She never touches the speculative depths of such Catholics as Pascal, the doubts and ecstasies of the great believers are not hers. She sees nature with the eyes of devout reverence, and in her tender descriptions of all the small creatures of God, her love for the old or the helpless, she excels in conveying a sense of child-like admiration for and confidence in the works of an Almighty Power. Her *Rhymed Life of St. Patrick* accurately reproduces the popular view of the saint, widely different as that is from the facts. . . . [In *Miracle Plays*] there is a rather too careful simplicity, giving an air of artificiality not usual, for spontaneity is a noticeable feature of her devotional outpourings. But it must be said that here also she has failed to exercise any restraint. (pp. 110-11)

Interesting though she may be as the only important Catholic poet in Ireland, Katharine Tynan will hardly rank with the best writers of the Literary Revival. (p. 112)

> *Ernest A. Boyd, "The Revival, Poems and Ballads of Young Ireland: Katharine Tynan," in his* Ireland's Literary Renaissance *(copyright 1916 by John Lane Company), John Lane, 1916, pp. 103-12.*

HAROLD WILLIAMS (essay date 1925)

[*Louise de Vallière, Shamrocks,* and *Ballads and Lyrics*] are disfigured by many lapses in taste and style. The rhymes—"sweeter, glitter, palace, trellis, sward, herd"— are often inexcusable; and [Mrs. Hinkson] is sometimes guilty of cacophonies in music and rhythm which go far to ruin a whole poem. 'Rosa Spinosa,' for example, both in content and form rises above the standard of her earlier work, but she damages it irretrievably with the jangle of the closing couplet. . . . Many of her poems are songs of childhood and children, pretty and graceful, but not rising above the commonplace in thought or descriptive power. The *Cuckoo Songs* . . . showed, however, a distinct advance upon the work of the earlier volumes. Especially beautiful in this volume is 'The Sad Mother,' which rises above Mrs. Hinkson's graceful sentimentality to a note of tragic pathos which is true and deep. And in some of the dialect poems, notably in 'The Train that Goes to Ireland,' in *New Poems* . . . , she reaches a higher level than her ordinary manner. But there is little, in general, to distinguish from each other the many volumes of verse she has published. The garden in spring and winter, the birds chirruping, the love of children, pieties and religious observances, these form the staple of Katharine Tynan's verse. There is seldom any strong emotion in thought or originality in phrase, nor, again, is she the possessor of any personality in style. (p. 210)

> *Harold Williams, "Irish Poetesses: Katharine Tynan," in his* Modern English Writers: Being a Study of Imaginative Literature 1890-1914, *revised edition, Sidgwick & Jackson, Limited, 1925, pp. 210-11.*

HERBERT S. GORMAN (essay date 1927)

Katharine Tynan's . . . "Twilight Songs" is, unfortunately for her, a thin book. She has done better work before this, work in which the spirit of her native Ireland has manifested itself delicately. The reader has always been aware (and he will still be aware of it in the lesser verses of "Twilight Songs") that a substance of being essentially Celtic albeit not profoundly deep, urges Mrs. Hinkson into poetic expression. She is one of the lesser figures of the Irish Renaissance, a thin, cool voice like the far-away whistle of a blackbird. Immersed in a Catholic tradition it is but natural to find her poetry colored by a religious ardency that approaches the mystic at times. In "Twilight Songs" such pieces as "Ireland Long Ago," "The Tramping Woman," "The Exile" and "A Song of St. Anne" are not without a fastidious merit. The pulse beats feebly, however. (p. 17)

> *Herbert S. Gorman, "Countee Cullen Is a Poet First and a Negro Afterward," in* The New York Times Book Review *(© 1927 by The New York Times Company; reprinted by permission), August 21, 1927, pp. 5, 17.**

A.E.   (essay date 1930)

Katharine Tynan was the earliest singer in that awakening of our imagination which has been spoken of as the Irish Renaissance.... Irishmen of letters, Yeats, Synge, O'-Grady, Stephens, Dunsany, Joyce, O'Casey, O'Flaherty, and most of their contemporaries have [the] tendency to turn from the hearth and to roam in uncharted regions of the psyche. Katharine Tynan has her own spirituality, but she has kept closer to the normal than any except Padraic Colum. She had something which is rather rarer among poets than most people imagine, a natural gift for song.... The first perfect saying of verse I ever heard was when she read me the just-written *Children of Lir,* and I listened to a voice which gave its perfect resonance and rhythm and emotional quality to every line. I may be mistaken: but I think it has been easier for her to work in the craft of poetry than it has been with any of the poets I have known. But because it was easy and she has written many books of verse, it would do her wrong to think that what was written with a natural ease was not memorable. There was a mould in the psyche into which thought and emotion were poured, and the lyric record was almost always shapely.... What is common to Katharine Tynan's lyrics out of whatever mood she writes is a shapeliness in their architecture. This can be seen to perfection in *Sheep and Lambs,* in *Larks,* and in *Lux in Tenebris.* (pp. vii-ix)

I like her poetry best when she draws some shy beauty out of its recesses as in [the] little lyric which she named *Drought....* (p. x)

It was the same brooding love which enabled her to interpret *Summer Airs,* to pass beyond odour of heather or ocean, beyond memories of lakes and islands, to discover that some wind out of Paradise is mixed with the air we breathe. (p. xi)

I like Katharine Tynan's poetry best where I find her nature harmonious with my own. Others may take much more pleasure in poems whose art I admire but which are born out of emotions I have not shared, or use a symbolism with which my childhood was not familiar, so that I could not make it a stepping-stone to the reality it stands for. But to the majority of my countrymen the symbols she uses are keys to a sanctuary they often enter. (pp. xii-xiii)

> *A.E., in his foreword to* Collected Poems *by Katharine Tynan (reprinted by permission of Colin*

> *Smythe Ltd), Macmillan and Co., Limited, 1930, pp. vii-xiii.*

PATRICK BRAYBROOKE   (essay date 1931)

Mrs. Tynan is not in any sense a great novelist. She has no place in the same rank as Sheila Kaye-Smith, she has not a masterly touch of creation, but she can give us a very good story. I do not want to be misunderstood if I say that Mrs. Tynan is more than anything else the type of novelist who gets a rather obvious but good plot. Sometimes we are in danger of forgetting exactly what a plot is.... But in the stories of Mrs. Tynan we are introduced not only to a good plot but to an exciting tale and a tale which is always perfectly clean.... Mrs. Tynan is clever without being in the least subtle. She is smart without letting her fiction become merely shallow smartness. (p. 209)

[Mrs. Tynan] is an independent novelist who still believes that the kind of novel which has a melodramatic background can find acceptance in this age which is sceptical of anything it can easily understand. We have the old-fashioned attributes of the old-fashioned novel in her stories. (p. 210)

In ["Denys the Dreamer"] we discover Mrs. Tynan venturing rather near a psychological study. But all the time she keeps a good story going. Denys is a dreamer, and like many dreamers he gets things done. He is brought into line as it were by the mildly contemptuous attitude which is adopted towards him. It does not make him sullen, but it gives him an obstinacy which refuses to be beaten.... So we see a picture of Denys getting the impetus, and all the time we feel that Mrs. Tynan is plunging along quickly and certainly with her story. (pp. 210-11)

Sometimes in true novelist fashion, Mrs. Tynan exaggerates. She creates in a somewhat superficial manner a philanthropic moneylender and possibly her creation is absurd. (p. 212)

Mrs. Tynan brings out very clearly that the chief fault of Denys is really quite a good fault. He is full of impetuosity, he takes matters into his own hands and very nearly annoys his employer. All the way through we are quite conscious that Mrs. Tynan is dealing with a reaction. From being a great dreamer Denys becomes a great man of action. The transition carries with it a certain hardness and want of heart in the character of Denys. He jumps to conclusions and does not consider the preliminary steps. Mrs. Tynan without, as I say, concentrating on a psychological study to the exclusion of a story, allows Denys to develop himself quite logically. (p. 214)

Mrs. Tynan is always a thoroughly sympathetic writer. She is broad-minded without acquiescing in every kind of conduct. Quite gently now and then she disagrees with her characters.

Like all novelists who can write a really good story, by which I mean a story that has both imagination and invention, Mrs. Tynan has considerable powers of description. Perhaps her type of description can best be called "straightforward" description.... She uses an economy of words, but is never mean. (pp. 216-17)

[In] "A Fine Gentleman," we discover that she is equally skilful in dealing with a young man of a completely different type from Denys. Mrs. Tynan is not in any way class conscious in that she is awkward with any particular class of person. In the novel . . . we have to deal with a young officer. No kind of individual offers less scope to the novelist. . . . Without being unmoral they do not usually stand out against the accepted code, which I am bound to say is not particularly stringent. And yet without in any way encroaching on the bounds of probability Mrs. Katharine Tynan manages to give us a story about an officer who is neither a prig nor a prude and will not budge one inch from the high standard he has set himself. (pp. 218-19)

Mrs. Tynan has a great power of never holding up the tale. . . . That is a very pronounced characteristic of much modern fiction. This extraordinary fashion of dalliance, this remarkable habit of holding up the story for a kind of psychological digression, almost a kind of investigation, not by a novelist but by a brain specialist. Now Mrs. Tynan does not do this. She gets along through her story quickly and yet without any suggestion of rushing. (pp. 223-24)

In "The Face in the Picture" Mrs. Tynan relies on one of the simplest of themes. . . . In this kind of story she is not in any sense whatever a pioneer. She does not wish to try the novel in a new form, but is content to rely on an old kind of "stock" tale. And it is both courageous and sensible to do so. We have evolved from the type of tales that Mrs. Tynan writes, but I am inclined to think that we shall revolve back to them. We are quite often in grave danger of having thrust upon us a kind of fiction which is nothing more or less than pen portraits of neurotic or erotic people. Catholic novelists have a very great chance in keeping this kind of hothouse fiction in the background. Novelists like Mrs. Tynan do no little to help. It can be said all the way through that her work invariably infers Catholicism. . . . [It] is not necessary to read between the lines to know that Mrs. Tynan stands rigidly for all that Catholics hold dear. She shows us that clean, healthy fiction, not by any means great fiction, can still hold and interest us. She proves to us . . . that love is a clean and glorious romance, and not something fleshly and sensual. (pp. 227-28)

> Patrick Braybrooke, "Katharine Tynan and Her Stories," in his *Some Catholic Novelists: Their Art and Outlook*, Burns Oates & Washbourne Ltd., 1931, pp. 209-30.

MARILYN GADDIS ROSE (essay date 1974)

Katharine Tynan . . . is a woman writer who sees herself and expresses herself in terms of women's roles. As to what a woman's role is or has to be, she begrudgingly accommodates herself to the functional definitions established by male consensus. In her poetry, her most rigorously controlled genre by any set of standards, her low expectations of every man outside her own family are not completely sublimated, but they are so conventionally disguised that they would neither offend a male reader nor alarm a female reader. In her fiction, her least controlled genre, her plots and characterizations are woven with implicit criticism of men's inevitable inadequacies, with which women's resourcefulness must forever cope. In her journalism, she is quite explicit that a man's world is not the best of all possible worlds for a woman. (p. 16)

Thus, she writes to women, about women, and on behalf of women, and when she writes directly about herself, it is only as a slightly exceptional, somewhat encouraging example of a type.

She eschews self-analysis altogether. On the one hand, this is commendable, for it means that she does not indulge in self-pity or waste time with personal problems that cannot be solved. On the other hand, she may have hampered the development of her own genius, for at times in her memoirs she seems to lack self-awareness. As a writer, she does not seem to have been capable of self-criticism. In her work there are frequent slips that show an uncritical acceptance of class prejudices. When she avoids plumbing her own depths, she may well prevent herself from knowing anyone else in depth. (p. 17)

All her poems in [*Louise de la Vallière and Other Poems*] give evidence of an impressive facility with language. They would conform admirably to lay preconceptions of poetry. The diction is chaste, in tone that of English poetry since William Collins. It rarely exceeds the rhyming license allowed to popular ballad. Yet the diction is not that of any level of speech, colloquial or formal. This is somewhat surprising when the poems are either monologues of an adopted *persona* or of herself as a *persona*. No one, not even she herself, speaks in character. Her poetic voice speaks the way a "poet" is supposed to. (p. 35)

"The Children of Lir" . . . represents a poetic *persona* that is feminine: motherly, affectionate, and by virtue of these, condescending. (p. 43)

[*A Lover's Breast-Knot*] was better than her preceding books in craft and sincerity. It is clearly a touching example of self-therapy. She is making a desperate, determined appeal to her religion to sustain her amidst these examples of cosmic injustice. "Love Comfortless" is a simple ballad about her buried child. She cannot bear to think of him as a cold lorn corpse, so she must fantasize for herself a Nursery in Heaven. (p. 51)

Nowhere does her acceptance of the values of her class emerge more strongly than in her extremely popular volumes of poetry, [*The Holy War* and *Herb O'Grace*]. . . .

Her diction is simple and natural. Mother of two sons in action, she can only be sincere. Our perspective on World War I and wars in general has changed so drastically that these books seem curiously dated and strange to us. The only poem that we can accept is "Haymaking, In Connaught, 1915," spoken by the farmer whose son is buried in France: "But the heart o' me's cryin' this minit, / For the boy that'll never come home." (p. 55)

[*Love of Brothers*] gives an authentic picture of upper-class ruthlessness and the gamut of skulduggery and decency found among the lower classes. The plot, intricate as it is, is actually a simple one by comparison with most of her novels, for she came to exploit more and more her ability to tell a tale and consequently had to slight characterization. Because of her goodwill and perhaps also because of her Catholic belief in repentance, she usually lets the villain redeem himself by the end of the novel, even if such a reprieve seems totally inconsistent. Thus it is good strategy on Mrs. Tynan Hinkson's part to have us too preoccupied by the movements of the plot to notice that the characters are acting out of character. (pp. 57-8)

[In her nature poem "August Heat"] Mrs. Tynan Hinkson makes no pretensions to saying anything beyond the words themselves. A newly married woman soon to be fruitful, she sees the August harvest as something that nature arranges by its own tranquilizing processes. She is unquestioning, contented to be a part of the scene that she describes.

To write even one such good nature poem is a feat. It is not a feat, however, that distinguished her work from that of other poets, for English and Anglo-Irish poetry is rich in nature poems.

Her distinctive poems are those on the eros of motherhood. A well-bred woman of her class cannot speak too openly of love, even conjugal love. If Mrs. Tynan Hinkson had for her husband feelings comparable to Elizabeth Barrett's for Robert Browning, she was too inhibited to write them down. But she did not feel inhibited about speaking openly on the ecstasy of motherhood. On this subject she can let herself go without offending her readers. These poems are honestly, innocently sensual. (pp. 61-2)

[The poems of *Innocencies*] have very simple meters and use language that she could have used in conversation. They bear the stamp of sincerity, and there is every reason to believe that they reflect her most intimate and deeply felt erotic experiences.

There may be no more sensual poetess of motherhood. The purely feminine cast of her writer's personality may have been a deficiency when she was writing a third-person novel; it was an experiental drawback certainly when she is commenting upon the Easter Rising or poeticizing the glories of wartime combat. But for poems on motherhood she could only be authentic. (p. 64)

Mrs. Tynan Hinkson has a penchant for sensational plots couched in nonshocking language. An Irish setting, and a plot tied in with one of her projects for human betterment ensure her authenticity. (p. 72)

In showing the terror and abuse caused by drunken men, the disease-breeding conditions of Dublin slums, the toll wreaked upon the poor slum mothers, who are the ineffectual martyrs of the environment, Mrs. Tynan Hinkson is fearlessly graphic. She does not analyze the causes of degradation. Her stated antipathy to labor leader James Larkin, whom she considered a demagogue, might lead us to deduce that she could not have believed that unrestrained capitalism or British colonial mercantilism was in any way responsible for the demoralizing conditions of the Dublin disadvantaged. But as to the effects of the system, whatever it is, on children and women, she is alert, responsive, and aggressive.

These remarks hold generally for all her committed writing, whether reported as fact or dramatized as fiction. She does not concern herself with the probable roots; her only cure is a hope that people who are advantaged will be unselfish. She considers it her role to move in quickly with maternal solicitude, using her pen to bestir the consciences and open the pocketbooks of her more fortunate readers.

She saw life, in short, as possessing the potentiality for happiness; earth, as possessing the potentiality for paradise. Whereas her feature writing and fiction showed what needed to be changed, her poems showed what should be kept. In this respect, she had nothing new to say. (pp. 75-6)

[Mrs. Tynan Hinkson's] corpus contains no quintessential piece, no major work. It is consensus that poetry is her best genre. . . . She bombarded the market with novels. All are

of a piece. We could be missing vast amounts of her fiction and still have an accurate estimation of what she had to say and how she would say it. . . . Much of her writing, as she herself admitted, had to be potboiling. As it happens, she wrote very few entirely satisfactory works. So, if we can talk about commendable characteristics of her work as a whole, we can find few thoroughly commendable works. She was too closely tied to her class to transcend it. (pp. 79-80)

Although she could be quite explicit when describing substandard living conditions, she is careful not to shock the conventional reader. She avoids the sexual and the vulgar. (p. 80)

This does not mean, however, that she did not take up threatening behavior or work out fantasies that must have been veritable nightmares. She spun plots that could exceed any grisly feature story in sheer extent of horror and brutality. Her plots typically follow a pattern of delayed achievements: protagonist X, after overcoming innumerable formidable obstacles, succeeds in performing task Y and in winning reward Z. Any of these algebraically indicated elements may be multiple. There may be more than one hero or heroine working together or on parallel tracks. All will receive rewards, and, typically, if at all possible, their antagonists will have a change of heart that will allow them to share in the reward. There are few unmixed villains, and Mrs. Tynan Hinkson is ever alert to extenuating circumstances to provoke our pity and understanding. The pattern that I have just described could be applied to many novelists: Hawthorne's novels fit the pattern perfectly; so do most works by Thackeray, Meredith, and George Eliot, to restrict the example to works that Mrs. Tynan Hinkson would know. Where her plots differ from theirs is in the accumulation of obstacles to be overcome and the *faits divers* incredibility of them. (pp. 81-2)

Some of the typical givens in her fiction show how well she manipulated—unconsciously, I am convinced—the threats and fears of a middle-class woman's imaginary life. The chief of these is the threatening female. Although we have seen in "The Comfort" in *Herb O'Grace* that Mrs. Tynan Hinkson is capable of telling a mother that having her son die in battle spares her the misery of having to share him with a wife, generally she takes the side of the younger woman against the man's mother or mother surrogate. . . . She has a more curious, perhaps even unique, female villain who stands in for the shameless Jocasta: a vampire nurse. This terrifying victimizer stalks through novels set after World War I and keeps her veteran victim bound to her through exploitation of his illness, which, by the time the younger woman comes along to rescue him, is largely a psychological dependency. The older woman relies on medicine, magic, and more experience, and will accept morbid dependency when erotically colored filial love is no longer forthcoming. The younger woman represents normal activities and confidence-inspiring innocence. (p. 82)

The second threat in a woman's life is the disappointing male. . . . At best, the disappointing male, as Mrs. Tynan Hinkson portrays him, is the husband not sufficiently resourceful to earn a steady income. In novels set after World War I, such a man is not condemned, because he has been debilitated or bestialized by his battle experiences. Or he can be a well-meaning drunkard or blackguard. (Men, she implies, are such weak creatures.) Mrs. Tynan Hinkson democratically finds drunkards and blackguards in all social classes. It is not an oversimplification to say that her expectations for men are lower than her expectations for women. When a man is weak, a woman must compensate for his weaknesses with a smile and a prayer; when a woman is weak, another woman must be called in to help the man concerned. A man is threatening in the long run simply because he is biologically stronger; a woman can usually outwit him, and only a woman can rout the female villain. (p. 83)

Kate Tynan's poetic *persona* is indeed her most endearing, whether the mask is her kind Irish face or a congenial one borrowed from history. The self that wrote her poetry distilled what was the best in her. The class prejudices that mar her fiction, the self-promotion and self-justification that make her memoirs unwittingly ironic, these rarely intrude in her poetry. (p. 89)

[Mrs. Tynan Hinkson] set out to be a minor writer. AE linked her name favorably with Christina Rossetti's. Miss Rossetti's religious orientation was attractive to Kate Tynan. I have compared her in passing with Elizabeth Barrett Browning, who could write from marital experience. Yet, both as Katharine Tynan and Mrs. Tynan Hinkson, she set too close a goal for herself for her ever to equal their achievements. She never developed the former's vir-

tuosity in form and inventiveness and in poetic substance; she diverted her own inventiveness into fiction when with patience she quite probably could have written excellent long narrative poems. She never allowed herself to express the latter's intensity or passion. . . . (p. 91)

In the end, she excels only other Irish poetesses, not poets, of her own generation. Susan Mitchell, Dora Sigerson, and Eleanor Hull do not equal her in skill or substance. This is a very modest field of excellence.

But these remarks, while denying her a place as an exemplary writer, do not keep her from being an exemplary woman. (p. 92)

> *Marilyn Gaddis Rose, in her* Katharine Tynan (© *1974 by Associated University Presses, Inc.), Bucknell University Press, 1974, 97 p.*

BIBLIOGRAPHY

"Katharine Tynan." In *Catholic Authors: Contemporary Biographical Sketches, 1930-1947,* edited by Matthew Hoehn, pp. 743-44. Newark: St. Mary's Abbey, 1948.
> Includes background on some of Tynan's works, with a chronological listing of major novels and poetry collections.

Sigrid Undset

1882-1949

Norwegian novelist, short story writer, essayist, critic, biographer, poet, and dramatist.

Undset is a dominant figure among Scandinavian novelists and one of the foremost literary proponents of Christian ethics and philosophy. Her major works, *Kristin Lavransdatter* and *The Master of Hestviken*, are skillfully rendered portrayals of medieval Norwegian life and have been praised as exemplary models of historical fiction, evidencing a detailed knowledge and keen sympathy with their subject. On the strength of these works she was awarded the Nobel Prize in literature for 1928.

Before her medieval masterpieces, however, Undset produced several works of contemporary realism which reflect her experience as a young working woman of the middle class. Her father was a prominent archaeologist, and Undset too was expected by her family to follow a scientific career. After her father's death she instead enrolled in business school and eventually made a living as an office clerk, during which time she produced a number of books that were only modestly successful. With the success of *Jenny* she was able to devote herself to writing as a livelihood.

In 1924 Undset became a convert to the Roman Catholic Church, whose philosophy and ideals were already evident in the saga of Kristin Lavransdatter. Choosing the Middle Ages as a background to her novels enabled Undset to develop her characters within the specifically Christian context natural to the period. Throughout her subsequent works Undset promoted the orthodox tenets of Catholicism, stating in one of her essays that the future of European culture depends on the continued prevalence of Christian theological and moral concepts. She deprecated the values of liberalism and humanism as spiritually destructive falsehoods and rejected the model of human life provided by science and psychology. The vision of life found in Undset's novels is often described as brooding and painfully realistic, her portrayal of human relationships as unsentimental, and her character studies as profound.

Most of Undset's later fiction returns to contemporary subjects, but the themes of religious quest that subtly pervade the medieval novels became obtrusive when transplanted to the modern era. In *The Wild Orchid, The Burning Bush*, and *The Faithful Wife*, for example, Undset overtly confronts the conflicts between the modern world and the dogmatic traditions of Christianity. Unlike her earlier works, which masterfully combined realism and symbolism, these later works are often regarded as increasingly dogmatic.

During World War II Undset was forced to flee Norway, where the Nazis were destroying her books, and emigrate to America for the duration of the war. After her return to Norway she was honored by King Haakon VII with the Grand Cross of the Order of Saint Olav, the first woman after Crown Princess Märtha, and only commoner, ever to receive that award.

PRINCIPAL WORKS

Fru Marta Oulie (novel) 1907
Den lykkelige alder (short stories) 1908
Fortaellingen om Viga-Ljot og Vigdis (novel) 1909
 [*Gunnar's Daughter*, 1936]
Jenny: Roman (novel) 1911
 [*Jenny: A Novel*, 1920]
Fattige skjaebner (short stories) 1912
Vaaren (novel) 1914
Splinten av troldspeilet (novellas, includes *Fru Waage*
 and *Fru Hjelde*) 1917
 [*Images in a Mirror*, translation of *Fru Hjelde*, 1938]
De kloge jomfruer (short stories) 1918
Kristin Lavransdatter: Kransen (novel) 1920
 *[Published in England as *The Garland*, 1922; published
 in the United States as *The Bridal Wreath*, 1923]
Kristin Lavransdatter: Husfrue (novel) 1922
 *[*The Mistress of Husaby*, 1925]
Kristin Lavransdatter: Korset (novel) 1922
 *[*The Cross*, 1927]
Olav Audunssøn i Hestviken (novel) 1925
 **[Published in two sequential volumes: *The Axe*, 1928;
 The Snake Pit, 1929]
Olav Audunssøn og hans børn (novel) 1927
 **[Published in two sequential volumes: *In the
 Wilderness*, 1929; *The Son Avenger*, 1930]
Gymnadenia (novel) 1929
 [*The Wild Orchid*, 1931]
Den braendende busk (novel) 1930
 [*The Burning Bush*, 1932]
Ida Elisabeth (novel) 1932
 [*Ida Elisabeth*, 1933]
Etapper: Ny raekke (essays) 1933
 [*Stages on the Road*, 1934]
Elleve aar (autobiography) 1934
 [*The Longest Years*, 1935]
Den trofaste hustru: Roman (novel) 1936

[The Faithful Wife, 1937]
Madame Dorthea: Roman (novel) 1939
   [Madame Dorthea, 1940]
Tilbake til fremtiden (autobiography) 1943
   [Return to the Future, 1942]

*These novels were collected as *Kristin Lavransdatter* in 1929.
**These novels were collected as *The Master of Hestviken* in 1932.

SIGNE TOKSVIG (essay date 1921)

Jenny has been labelled immoral by some reviewers, probably because an illegitimate child appears in it, and Jenny Winge, the heroine, is loved by her fiance's father. But the sad fact about Jenny Winge is that, in spite of undeniable appearances, she is stiffly and terrifyingly moral, if morality means having high ideals and going as far as death because they can't be lived up to. (p. 165)

Jenny is not one of Sigrid Undset's best books. It is too rigid, too full of fine-spun agonies. If humor is defined as a lack of the sense of proportion, then it fails by being humorless. It seems to justify ever so little those who speak about Norwegian gloom. And yet there is in it so much ability to ensnare visual beauty and so many wise and delicate perceptions that one must hope for translations of Sigrid Undset's maturer works. (p. 166)

> Signe Toksvig, "Review of Books: 'Jenny'," in
> The New Republic (© 1921 The New Republic,
> Inc.), Vol. 28, No. 357, October 5, 1921, pp. 165-
> 66.

EDWIN BJORKMAN (essay date 1923)

What seems to be the trouble with most [historical novels] and what tends to make me, for one, rather indifferent toward their *genre*, is that, as a rule, they present the life of past ages from the outside, so to speak. . . .

It is the glorious characteristic of Sigrid Undset, and the chief reason of her rapidly spreading reputation, that what has just been set down does not apply to her wonderfully vivid and convincing re-creations of bygone days and bygone generations. She is now regarded as the foremost Scandinavian woman writer with the sole exception of Selma Lagerlöf, while in her own Norway they hold her the peer, if not superior, of all writers, male or female, but Hamsun. And though she has written some very telling fiction in contemporary settings, it is by her historical works that she has won the position she holds to-day.

The trilogy of which "The Bridal Wreath" forms the first part is beyond all doubt her most pretentious effort, and also her most successful one. She has undertaken two things in this monumental work: first to give us pictures of the early fourteenth century in Norway so intimate that they make us feel as if we were reading about this morning's happenings in our own particular back alley; and, secondly, to trace the life thread of a strikingly unusual woman from the cradle to the grave. Both these purposes of hers have been achieved to my thinking.

Kristin Lavransdatter is one of those figures which, although woven out of a poet's fancy, yet tend to take on more reality than the men and women with whom we touch elbows on the streets. . . .

Of sentimentality the whole book has not one trace, and if it had Fru Undset would not be the artist she is. We meet with Kristin as she really is . . . a frail yet firm and fundamentally righteous human being who has the courage to follow her instincts in the face of the whole little world surrounding her. Out of this pertinacity issues no fairy tale happiness, but a fulfilment of her own nature that carries her through sorrows and trials of tragic height to a haven that loses none of its promised satisfaction because she has reached it through shame and humiliation.

Fru Undset is frank, but not needlessly so. She tells the truth without fear, but also without defiance, and of offensive details there are none. Much of what to our own day will seem questionable is nothing but veracious echoes of a life that had still to struggle through centuries to reach such restraints and refinements as, normally at least, must be reckoned ours. As we get that life in Fru Undset's pages, it comes to us with a strange sense of inevitableness. We become part of it and feel that thus would we have acted, thus would we have looked upon things, had we lived in that same period. Beneath the color that may be called local or periodical we see all the time a broad human basis that has shifted but little since the days when poor Kristin loved and suffered and triumphed.

Around the central figure of Kirstin there is grouped a whole gallery of men and women no less lifelike and convincing than herself. Her parents in particular bid fair to root themselves in the reader's consciousness no less firmly than will their daughter. Even minor figures, like that of the wandering monk, Brother Edwin, are drawn with as much care and love as those more in the foreground. Taking it all in all, Fru Undset's book must be held one of the biggest that have come over to us from those northern countries in a long while.

> Edwin Bjorkman, "Making the Past Live," in Literary Review, Vol. 3, No. 33, April, 1923, p. 624.

(essay date 1927)

[Sigrid Undset's] robust romanticism, with its winning but not obtrusive mystical strain, the vehement, easeful authority with which she controls her ample canvas, her living background, and, above all, her tolerant, all-embracing humanism are colored with an epic intensity which gain for her the reader's eager assent. The three novels, "The Bridal Wreath," "The Mistress of Husaby" and now "The Cross," give a striking picture of Norway in the fourteenth century, yet they are by no means exclusively historical. . . .

A part of the secret of the conviction that the story of Kristin Lavransdatter carries is ascribable to Sigrid Undset's choice of a period. . . . It is not alone in this tacit comparative philosophy, an unearned, or at least unlabored, increment of the narrative, that Sigrid Undset's magic power resides. Her supreme achievement is in the appealing humanity and fallibility of her characters. "The Bridal Wreath" gives the troubled, passionate girlhood of Kristin Lavransdatter and her pursuit of Erlend Nikulausson, for whose gay and heedless sage she broke her promised word. "The Mistress of Husaby" shows Kristin in the midst of the brave and ceremonious "kurtesie" which was the lot of the wife of a great feudal noble. "The Cross" works out Kristin's ambitions, and develops further the drama between her steadfast and unbending integrity and the compliant, willful, impulsive Erlend, especially as it is reflected in the unfolding lives of her seven sons. (p. 8)

"'*Jennifer*' and Other Recent Works of Fiction," in The New York Times Book Review (© 1927 by The New York Times Company; reprinted by permission), February 20, 1927, pp. 8-9.*

CHARLES WHARTON STORK   (essay date 1928)

"The Axe" presents Norway in the Middle Ages with an intimacy of psychological and physical detail that reminds one of Balzac. It may at least be said that no one to whom Balzac's method is repugnant will enjoy a book in which the salient events are few, and the minutiæ abundant and predominantly disagreeable.

It is on the courage of truth, not on the seduction of beauty, that Sigrid Undset bases her appeal. She has realized her people, major and minor, with an energy that leaves us unable to doubt them and, furthermore, she has realized them as individuals. In this respect we are reminded less of Balzac than of George Eliot and Sheila Kaye-Smith. The result in connection with her antique background is both disturbing and stimulating. The Middle Ages so inevitably connotes romance to us that the frequent mention of dead fish and manure heaps demands a considerable readjustment of approach. . . .

As the ugliness of fact is nowhere avoided in the setting, so the unheroically human traits of the characters are faithfully developed. Many readers will find the treatment of the heroine in the second half of the book too pathological. The tone is in fact not so much fatalistic, like that of Hardy . . . as scientific, almost medical. . . . "The Axe" is not so much a novel as an experience understandingly analyzed. Not that the style is cold, it is only unflinchingly strict. . . .

[Despite] its sordidness, there is a bracing quality in the novel as a whole. . . . The landscape backgrounds are done with fine sympathy and reserve. The picture of medieval Norwegian life and customs is most interesting, particularly in the complicated legal questions that arise as to blood-money, marriage tithes, etc. These are skilfully woven into the main story. In fact, so complete is the representation that on laying down the book one has to rub one's eyes in order to be sure that one is in modern America, not on the estate of an ancient Norwegian baron.

Charles Wharton Stork, "In Medieval Norway," in The Saturday Review of Literature (copyright © 1928 by Saturday Review), Vol. 4, No. 45, June 2, 1928, p. 930.

HANNA ASTRUP LARSEN   (essay date 1929)

There is a distinct line from [Sigrid Undset's] first book to her last; and while it is customary to divide her works into two groups, the modern and the medieval, they all, however different in subject matter, are filled with the same underlying motive. She is and has always been a thinker along conservative lines, supremely interested in the relation of the individual to the race through marriage and parenthood. She is and has always been a moralist, a champion of those "banal and shopworn truths" which human beings have tested by centuries of experience. In her earliest works she simply sees and describes with pitiless realism the disaster that overtakes an individual who attempts to break away from the ties that bind the race together; later

she formulates her vision as a definite theory of life; and, finally, she comes to base her ethical convictions on a deep and passionate religious faith.

It is proof of her greatness as a creative artist that she knows how to project her ideals through living characters. They are never the puppets of her theories; she never condescends to them or preaches at them. She lives with her people and makes us experience with them the struggles through which their view of life changes and develops. The message of the book is never a foregone conclusion; it is born in travail.

To her own countrymen Sigrid Undset's novels of contemporary life brought a flash of recognition. She had chosen to describe a group that is both large and important in Norway, the educated but impecunious middle class. It is a class that has been little exploited in fiction, perhaps because its modest ambitions, small drab joys, and petty economies do not lend themselves to picturesque treatment. (pp. 344-45)

Sigrid Undset derives perhaps more from Jonas Lie than from any other of the older [Norwegian] writers. She resembles him in the ability to reveal personality by the casual words and tiny actions of everyday life, as also in the almost uncanny gift of reproducing local color by catching some little daily experience or current slang or even the very intonation of a word that reveals the milieu. It is true, her heavier and more somber nature completely lacks Jonas Lie's blithe geniality. She has fewer illusions than the older author, but she is fully his equal in her sympathy for even the most commonplace and obscure of the characters that make up her world. The men who plod in their profession with no hope beyond meeting the family bills; the wives who try to salvage some remnant of graciousness while they toil in kitchen and nursery; the lonely old maids upon whose door romance has never knocked,— all become endowed with a living humanity. Though she is pitiless in revealing their frailties, she never allows us to lose our fellow-feeling for them. Like Jonas Lie again, she is never present in her stories. We see the events through the eyes of her characters, and sometimes she will even relate the happenings of years by letting them pass in retrospect through the mind of one of her characters. In this way we gain a wonderful knowledge of her people from within; and though she sometimes puts in their mouths great thoughts which we know they could not have uttered so trenchantly, she thereby manages to keep her solid objectivity and to avoid the didactic. (p. 345)

[*Fru Martha Oulie*] is the story of a woman who has been unfaithful to her husband. . . . Martha Oulie has married a man somewhat beneath her in taste and intellect. . . . [When] her passion has cooled, her husband bores her. . . . Then she meets again an old friend, a cousin of congenial tastes. . . . He makes love to her, and she yields to him; but when her husband is suddenly stricken with a deadly malady, she feels that her lover is nothing to her, and it is only her life with husband and children that really matters. . . . Some critics have held that there is another story concealed beneath the obvious one, and that Martha Oulie is deceived by her own remorse into thinking she cares more for her husband than she actually does, while it is the cousin she really loves. This seems somewhat beside the point. The author's meaning is perfectly clear: no matter which of the two men she ought to have married, the fact that she did marry one of them makes bonds that she cannot break. Their natures have become entwined one with the other. This is the theme that recurs again and again in Sigrid Undset's books and is never more nobly set forth than in . . . the great tetralogy of Olav Audunssön.

Fru Martha Oulie was followed by several stories dealing with the lives of self-supporting young girls. . . . The author's heroines from that period are all of the same type, but so varied and vividly conceived that each stands out as a complete personality. They are girls of good family, proud, self-contained, knowing the makeshifts of poverty and suffering keenly from them. They are often stiff and unable to play, but underneath an apparent coldness they have a passionate conviction that somewhere there exists a warm and throbbing life which they long to become a part of. Their jobs do not interest them, and the society they can get in cheap boarding-houses or studios holds no satisfaction for them. When the sense of loneliness and chill has become unendurable, they easily compromise with their ideals. (pp. 346-47)

Jenny [in *Jenny*] is, so far as I remember now, the only one of Sigrid Undset's characters who runs away from life. Usually her people have a dogged strength that makes them endure to the end, carrying whatever burdens fate lays upon them. We are told that she failed because of her very delicacy and purity, that she was like a lily or some other flower on one slender stalk which, once bruised, never holds up its head again. I have never felt that her sordid tragedy was in keeping with her nature as the author makes us see it. But be that as it may, the book was an outstanding achievement. The lure of the artist's life, the colorful background of Rome, the dramatic conflicts, and the daring treatment of a woman's erotic life all combined to make it something of a sensation. . . . In its intensity of emotion and daring frankness of treatment it foreshadowed her medieval books. (p. 348)

In *Spring* (Vaaren . . .) Sigrid Undset essayed to show that compromising with one's own feeling could be as dangerous in marriage as in a more irregular union. . . .

The book is a conscientious study of the struggles which two fine and sensitive individuals have to go through before their natures blend, but the conflict seems somewhat too finespun for the great breadth of detail. Among the minor characters the study of Rose's mother is most interesting. . . . (p. 349)

Much more clearly drawn and incisive than *Spring* is *Fru Hjelde* in which I believe most readers will agree with me Sigrid Undset has reached the highest point in her interpretation of modern life. . . . In picturing the tortures of genteel poverty Sigrid Undset can compete with Strindberg himself. (p. 350)

[*Fru Waage*] is more tragic, but far less appealing [than *Fru Hjelde*]. None of the chief persons in it rouse our sympathy or even our pity. Harriet Waage has been married off, while still very young, and almost without her own volition, to a wealthy cousin, a kindly and decent fellow, but a thorough Philistine and slightly ridiculous. The author, however, is far from making these circumstances an excuse for the wife's faithlessness. Involuntarily one remembers how in *Ghosts* Fru Alving throws the blame for her misery on her mother and aunts who had married her off to Captain Alving. Harriet Waage's marriage had come to pass in very

much the same manner, but Sigrid Undset does not for a moment allow her to take shelter behind that fact. With her the convenient scapegoat "Society" which bore the sins of an earlier generation in Norwegian literature—we need only remember Nora [protagonist of Ibsen's *A Doll's House*]—is never pressed into service. Her people have to bear the consequences of their own acts. In *Fru Waage* she is pitiless in her dissection of the idle self-indulgent woman who ruins two homes and must perforce marry her lover after she has come to a realization that the new union will not bring her any more happiness than the old. (pp. 351-52)

. . . . .

Even if she had written only her stories of modern life, Sigrid Undset's position as an author of rank would have been well established, and yet it was not before she began to choose her subjects from the Middle ages that she came into the full possession of her powers. . . . In medieval life she found greater heights and darker depths, more color and glamor, bolder passions and more profound remorse.

The new milieu not only released her latent powers as an artist, but it appealed in a peculiar way to her taste and sympathies. She has always been by temperament and conviction opposed to many of the tendencies current in her own age. She has never had any respect for the kind of liberality that would efface the sharp distinction between right and wrong. (p. 406)

Much has been written about Sigrid Undset's method of dealing with medieval life. Scholars have acclaimed the solidity of her knowledge, and literary experts have pointed to her manner of approach as something absolutely new in historical fiction. The fact is, she has assimilated her scholarship so perfectly that she is able to write about people in the fourteenth century with the same wealth of realistic detail that she lavishes on her modern books. In this way she achieves a marvellously vivid background, but she never falls into the temptation of using her people as lay figures to drape in garments of historical fashion. On the contrary, she uses external details to deepen and heighten and intensify the expressions of inner life. (p. 407)

The heroine of *Kristin Lavransdatter* is very much of the same type as the author's modern heroines . . . but the life-force in her is stronger; everything about her, more spacious. Her emotions are deeper, her repentance is more agonizing—as it must be when wrong was not merely a mistake but a sin against God; but her love, too, has a deeper intensity, dearly as she must pay for the joy it brings.

Transported to a more masculine age, Sigrid Undset, who never before created a masculine type of as distinct individuality as her women, succeeds in drawing the figures of two men as unforgettable as Kristin herself. Lavrans Björgulfsson, Kristin's father, stands out in bold, clear outline, a noble, stately figure, with all the best qualities of the old Norsemen softened by Christianity. . . . Erlend Nikolaussön is the exact opposite. . . . Lavrans has about him something of the universal father. Erlend is the eternal lover, who charms and baffles, fascinates and disappoints. His generosity can be like a white leaping flame; he is incapable of a mean impulse, but in his thoughtlessness he does things that entail worse consequences than other people's wickedness. His love for Kristin never wavers, but the woman who loves him is predestined to suffer. At last she has to take the ordering of their common life into her own hands, but she knows, even when she opposes him, that she would not have had the strength to do it but for the fire which this man had once for all kindled in her blood. As Lavrans and Erlend are in their way types, though fully individualized, so there is about Kristin a kind of universality, and her experience as daughter, mistress, wife, and mother is the common lot of woman deepened and intensified. (pp. 408-09)

Kristin Lavransdatter is full of stirring and colorful scenes.... Almost intolerably poignant is the description of Kristin's penitential walk to Trondhjem to lay upon the altar of God the maiden's garland of gold which she had worn unrighteously on her wedding day. And yet, with all the severity that belongs to the age, there is a freshness about it too: the walk in the morning through the dewy forest; the vigorous young woman whose joy in her own body and happiness in the child on her back cannot be dashed even by bare feet and penitential garb; the first sight of the beautiful city by the fjord as she ascends the pilgrims' "Hill of Joy"; and the overpowering emotion that lifts her out of herself when she hears mass in the great cathedral.... These are intensities to which modern life offers no parallel. They might well tempt an author with Sigrid Undset's power of describing human emotions. (pp. 409-10)

The trilogy is such an absorbing study of human relations that we hardly realize to what an extent it is also the study of a human soul in its relations with God....

The tetralogy *Olav Audunssön* is also the story of a human being from childhood to the grave, but it is far more somber than *Kristin Lavransdatter*. There is less of color and pageantry, and little of the softness and grace that captivate us in the description of Kristin's childhood home. Olav's life holds little of the raptures that vibrate in the story of Kristin's and Erlend's love, and the entire work wears a bleaker aspect.... [But] its dissection of one human soul gains impressiveness from its intense concentration. (p. 410)

The entire conception of Olav's spiritual history is Christian through and through, and even though Protestants may balk at the apparatus of the Confessional and the large space it occupies, they cannot, and will not want to, deny that Sigrid Undset has given flesh and blood to the very essence and inmost heart of Christianity. (p. 413)

If *Olav Audunssön* has less of medieval pomp and splendor than *Kristin Lavransdatter,* it seems to penetrate even more deeply into the medieval spirit. The author is becoming more and more familiar with the age she describes and moves in it with an ever surer touch, giving us more and more intimate glimpses of the people. Here, as in her modern works, she is supremely interested in the life of the family. (pp. 413-14)

While in the main she confines herself to descriptions of family life, she suggests how far the Norsemen of the day roamed for purposes of trade or adventure.... Sigrid Undset has re-created such a trip so convincingly that we almost see medieval London with the eyes of Olav Audunssön—a farmer from a simpler land—and almost experience with him the squalor and magnificence, the barbarism and holiness that made a strange medley in the great city. Though the chapters recounting Olav's adventures there have but little significance to the story, we could ill

spare them from the book. They belong to a complete picture of Norwegian life in the fourteenth century.

Sigrid Undset's medieval works have made us feel our common humanity with the people of a bygone age, and have enriched our minds by letting us see how the people of our own flesh and blood lived and worked and suffered and rejoiced in that distant time. (p. 414)

> Hanna Astrup Larsen, "Sigrid Undset: Modern Works" and "Sigrid Undset: Medieval Works," in The American-Scandanavian Review (copyright 1929 by The American-Scandinavian Foundation), Vol. XVII, Nos. 6 & 7, June and July, 1929, pp. 344-52, 406-14.

VICTOR VINDE (essay date 1930)

[Undset's] work is essentially personal. Her heroes are always, even in little things, alike; they have the same faults and the same virtues—yes, they even have practically the same experience of life and love. Moreover, their experience stops short at the point of the novelist's own limitations, and increases proportionally as these are extended. The truth is that fiction plays an insignificant part in the work of Sigrid Undset: observation and experience are everything.

Although Sigrid Undset is subjective to the point of being partial and unjust, it must not be thought that she is lacking in the ability to observe. Indeed, she has extremely clear vision regarding human beings and objects.... She is unable, however, to depict her heroes completely in a short space; her method is to build them up by brief touches here and there, with the result that although the process resembles a picture-puzzle, the completed picture is marvelously adequate. A mannerism of speech, a hesitancy, or a laugh, gives us a clue to the character sketch which the author is so carefully working out, and leads us to imagine the complementary action or trait which is to follow.

Her view, meanwhile, errs through a congenital weakness: she chooses always one and the same point of observation —her inner self. She finds it impossible to depict her heroes from an external point of view; it is always from within, and with personal feeling. Thus the perspective is falsified. And her portraits fail to be realistically exact also because she reproduces only portions of reality: light and shade, greyness, but never bright and happy colors. Happiness itself never is presented except as a forerunner of disaster and grief. According to Sigrid Undset the storm alone must claim the attention of the artist, and it alone is a faithful image of reality. In short, her conception of reality is a subjective and particular one; not a 'slice of life' but a state of soul. (pp. 16-17)

[Undset's temperament] is extremely idealistic and extremely sensual. She possesses inexhaustible resources of moral and physical energy, and an integrity of character which nothing could divert from its path, but her mind is pedantic, rigid and without nuances, as though carved from a block of stone. At times she seems to us rather inhuman, with her too highly elevated ideals and her morals for supermen. One wishes that she might speak to us sometimes of other virtues than grand passions—of little vices and little virtues belonging to all those persons who are neither particularly vicious nor particularly virtuous.

In her modern novels, Sigrid Undset has never attempted to

be modern—that is, to reflect the color of the age—except in the ideas with which she endows her characters, and these are of the late nineteenth century. There is in her novels no trace whatsoever of the great political and social events which took place at the beginning of the century, nor is there any allusion to the moral and religious ideas which stirred the epoch during which her characters lived. These are contemporary only in the sense that they have inherited the morality and the spiritual world of the novelist herself, who acquired them in turn from the masters of the late nineteenth century. She is a psychologist, and is interested only in conflicts of the soul and of the heart.

That is why, when Sigrid Undset turned to the Middle Ages, she made no effort at all to be 'historical.' She wished to portray the emotional world of a fifteenth-century individual, without regard to anecdote or historical fact. Thus [in *Kristin Lavransdatter* and *The Master of Hestviken*] she has not written an 'historical novel,' but a novel in which men of the Middle Ages live. It is their thoughts and their reactions which interest us—in short, their inner lives. (pp. 24-5)

The drama which unfolds in these great epic poems of Sigrid Undset is developed on two planes: physical love and spiritual love. The one conditions the other. Physical passion is the generator of sin, for it violates both human and divine law. (p. 28)

The story of Erlend and Kristin, and that of Olav and Ingunn, is the classic and tragic story of Adam and Eve. Human beings love, win each other, repulse each other, and wound each other in a merciless combat which, because of its definitely physical character, is especially bitter —a combat in which the only possible armistice is that imposed by physical desire, and which ceases only with death.

The struggle for their souls which God grants to Kristin and Olav is touching because it is so unfair. As yet imperfectly instructed in Christian morality, they are easily led into sin, and it seems, indeed, as though God makes use of his advantage by laying snares for them in order that he may punish them. Is it not the passion with which nature has endowed them that incites them to sin against chastity, to taste love before the divine benediction has been pronounced—and is it not this sin which engenders all other sins? If it is not mere chance that sows their path with temptations, then who but God can be responsible? Satan, perhaps? In any case God and Satan combine forces to break the pride of these human beings, to crush them beneath calamities, and finally to bring them, repentant but stubborn sinners, before the altar, where they kneel in conscious shame. (pp. 29-30)

If in her contemporary novels, the technique seems crudely realistic, it is because the material is dominant. The style is certainly lax and incoherent, the construction of the story often lacking balance. One gets the impression that the author has employed words haphazard, as they come to mind, without exercising choice.

It would be easy to discover in her stories and novels written before *Kristin Lavransdatter,* a number of tedious superfluities, as well as repetitions, improbabilities, and undeveloped or obscure passages. Setting herself to a study of laborers and *petits bourgeois,* she has her characters speak colloquially, as is proper; but as the author rarely

interrupts the narrative with comments of her own—allowing her characters to resort to monologue whenever dialogue is impractical—she is forced to employ from beginning to end the same familiar language, which finally tires even the most indulgent reader. Her style is intended to reflect life, and to be as much a reality as herself; thus it acquires great power of suggestion, but at the same time it loses all literary quality.

In her historical novels Undset uses a completely different method. Discarding all biographical elements—that is, her own past—which had formed the basis of her earlier work, she frankly essays fiction. Her problem is no longer to render experience and observation, to reproduce a reality which she has observed near at hand, but to re-create from certain documents a vanished world whose re-creation is dependent upon her imagination. Her great epics are obviously *built up,* and they rest upon carefully laid foundations. Even her style is a masterpiece of construction; the archaic language is enriched with wise borrowings from the old Norwegian, and the syntax recalls that of the Icelandic sagas. By a *tour de force* she succeeds in creating a new style, a style which is supple and living and yet clearly archaic.

But if from a technical point of view, her manner is changed, her method of psychological investigation remains the same. With these mediaeval characters she proceeds in the same way as with modern characters. Instead of explaining them or commenting on them, she lets them explain themselves. She actually relives the life of each of her characters, and thus brings them to life. They think and act without any intervention on the part of the author.

To the same degree that this method proved tiresome when applied to human beings without exciting inner lives, as in some of the modern stories, it becomes a marvelously effective device in the revivifying of mediaeval persons, who are moved by open and violent passions.

A decidedly feminine sensibility, a strong sensuality, an extraordinary psychological sense, and a keen faculty of observation combined to enable Undset to write novels that are at once beautiful and moving, and to contribute to literature human documents of the first order of importance, yet all her realistic production was but preparation—a long and painful schooling during which she learned to reconcile life and art. It is thanks to this apprenticeship that she was able eventually to create her masterpieces, *Kristin Lavransdatter* and *The Master of Hestviken.* . . . (pp. 32-5)

Meanwhile, the world of Sigrid Undset, a world of desire and sin, of fire and blood, of heroism and abnegation, is a horribly limited world, cramped and airless. Undset reduces the enigma of life to a simple sexual problem, and the human being to a level essentially animal. Apart from the desire for physical possession there is no creative element. All life is sex. The sensual instinct inspires our actions and guides our steps, pushes us down the slope of sin and carries us to the pinnacle of sublime sacrifice. Prisoners of their bodies, the characters of Sigrid Undset can free themselves from bondage only by accepting a new bondage fully as heavy: the bondage of God. There is no date set for deliverance: to be slave to the body or slave to God—there is no alternative and no escape.

That which seems to Sigrid Undset to nullify the gifts or the potentialities of life is the fact that life begins under the curse of the original sin committed by our ancestors, Adam and Eve. All her heroes and heroines taste of the forbidden fruit, and for this sin God punishes them by sowing between man and woman discord and hate. This existence becomes a purgatory where man is necessarily brought, by his very nature, to commit new sins engendered by the first error, until that day when, vanquished by the trials forced upon him by God, and war-weary, he answers the call of instinct and gives himself to God.

The moral betterment which Christianity has wrought, though which humanity would probably have acquired anyway, does not exist in the world of Sigrid Undset. Man is not a being capable of self-amelioration; he is but a toy of a superior and supernatural force. The story of humanity, that succession of magnificent victories of the human mind over matter, and of genius over nature, is for her only a tragic Calvary of the conflicts of love. We are not, according to Sigrid Undset, cave-men who through joy and suffering have achieved noble conquests over ourselves and the forces of nature; we are only sinners driven from Paradise.

Hers is a world where the human spirit is solidly surrounded by physical desires; a world where the spiritual never prevails over the temporal except by the negation of life itself. . . . (pp. 36-7)

> *Victor Vinde, in* Sigrid Undset: A Nordic Moralist, *translated by Babette Hughes and Glenn Hughes (copyright, 1930, by Glenn Hughes), University of Washington Book Store, 1930, 37 p.*

HARRY SLOCHOWER (essay date 1937)

Kristin Lavransdatter presents in a human and historic setting two forces at war: Pagan passion and Christian piety, embodied in the clash between Norse tradition and feudal Catholicism. In a wider sense, the story pictures the dissolution of medieval collectivism and the entry of Protestant individualism. Behind these historic currents, lie fundamental conflicts between the call of the sea and attachment to the soil, between waywardness and stability. These are fought out by Kristin Lavransdatter, in her choice between surrender to a knightly, adventurous lover and marriage to a staid, conservative Northerner. It is a battle between her pagan blood and Gothic milieu. (pp. 26-7)

Kristin Lavransdatter is a profound rendering of basic human emotions. Although the novel is set in a definite period, it is not a historical novel, in the sense that the works of Scott and Tolstoy are. Undset has chosen a time when little of historic significance took place. . . . This choice of a period, in which historic happenings are unimportant, suggests the irrelevancy of the temporal factor, tends to indicate that the theme has universal and eternal import, that the issues presented are perennial.

The story of Kristin Lavransdatter is, in a sense, quite unexceptional. Joy and pain are caused by no untoward occurrences, but issue from the normal and necessary phenomena of life. The instability and hazard which operate in the life of this family, simply "happen" everywhere and always. So effective is Undset's underscoring of the inescapable difficulty of the human way, that the total impression created is of man placed in a great, wide expanse, in which unknown and treacherous winds blow, where tragic chance threatens, where nothing is certain except death,

and individual frustration. The characters of this drama put up a kind of resistance; in the end, they turn, like frightened children, to run home and hide under the great white apron of their mother—the Catholic Church.

But Undset does not escape time. This is shown first by the conception of the position and the rôle of woman in *Kristin Lavransdatter*. Kristin becomes a strong woman; but she remains first and foremost a wife and a mother. Kristin's final insight that the highest self-development is impossible apart from acquiescence to one's social and religious tradition can be understood only in view of her particular milieu. Moreover, the central tragedy in the novel emerges from the transitional character of the period. The old paternal agrarianism is being challenged by a feudalism of absentee ownership and by a new economic aristocracy, the commercial bourgeoisie which arose toward the end of the thirteenth century. This new individualism of incipient Protestantism and commercialism, symbolized by Jofrid and her people, meets the old individualism of Nordic knighthood, represented by Erlend. Erlend dies, but Jofrid and Gaute go on. The existing order is shaken, the institution of the family tradition is no longer firm. Adultery and disobedience are widespread and frequent. Even Simon yielded somewhat to the new spirit when he allowed his betrothal to Kristin to be broken, and then he did something "unheard of in his kindred," wooed a widow independently of his father's consent. Lavrans' household itself disintegrates.

Kristin Lavransdatter expresses the religious yearning for salvation through surrender. In a time when the pillars of society are crumbling, religion provides man with a feeling that he is not altogether helpless and alone. By portraying the futility of revolt, religion also helps for the "stabilization" of existing institutions. Individual revolt against social conventions is shown to result in dreadful consequences. "Disobedience," Kristin confesses at the end, "was the chief of my sins."

Undset's *Kristin Lavransdatter* is, despite its apparent medievalism, a characteristic modern expression. This appears both by implication and directly. Even though Undset argues for humility and resignation, her *art* reveals her attraction for the sinners. The presentation of young Kristin is more living than that of the older woman. Her drawing of Erlend excels that of Simon. Furthermore, while the novel purports to glorify religious piety, conformity to the godly way does *not* bring happiness to the characters. Lavrans and Simon suffer greatly, suffer more than the bohemian Erlend. Kristin's unhappiness actually *begins* with the assertion of her religious background and, what is even more significant, her very religious mood leads her to be *unjust* to Erlend. The religious attitude, instead of bringing peace and love, makes for turmoil and bitterness.

The novel pays tribute to the traditional family idea. But its overemphasis may mean that children will be ill prepared to cope with problems outside the home. In this sense, the Ragnfrids and the Lavranses as well as the Kristins are poor parents, precisely to the extent that they severely adhere to the family ideal. This absence of broader social interests also accounts for the total emptiness that enters, once the family group is broken up. After the death of Lavrans and of Erlend, their wives, Ragnfrid and Kristin, find nothing to live for. Thus, the very values championed in Undset's novel lead to frustration. It shows the irreligious consequences of religion, the disintegration of the individual members of a group through the narrowing circle of the family, the self-extinction that results from the quest for the Absolute. Kristin's last act is to "save" a dead body and the story of Kristin Lavransdatter "ends" in the Black Death.

There is another and direct aspect from which Undset's Catholic plea is modern. Protestantism was more akin to early capitalism, while Catholicism is nearer to the collectivism of developed capitalism. And divested of dogma and tie-up with business, Catholicism is close to the ideal communal spirit of socialism. As practiced by Lavrans and Kristin in her old age, Catholicism spells a sense of social responsibility for the downtrodden. . . . It should be further noted that socialist doctrine exposed only the bourgeois family as the bulwark of private property, which in turn became instrumental in the disintegration of home and family life. . . . Undset's conception of the family may be viewed as a symbolic representation of its break-up due to the modern chaos of capitalism, and her plea as compatible with and supporting the socialist conception. To be sure, in her novel, Undset presents an unreal dilemma in offering a choice between an extreme irresponsible, unconscionable individualism (Erlend) and a self-effacing collectivism (Kristin), between living for one's body and living to save dead bodies. (pp. 44-8)

[Reactionary] practices are not inherent, but extrinsic to the anti-commercial ethic of Undset's Catholicism. *Kristin Lavransdatter* ends with two men whose Christian names are almost identical, with Eilif, the priest and Ulf, the faithful servant. Both have been friends to men and servants of God. These two alone remain alive at the end, a symbolic union of matter and spirit, earthliness and godliness. Both are dear to the author. (pp. 48-9)

> Harry Slochower, "Feudal Socialism: Sigrid Undset's 'Kristin Lavransdatter'," in his Three Ways of Modern Man (copyright, 1937 International Publishers Co., Inc.), International, 1937, pp. 25-49.

ALRIK GUSTAFSON   (essay date 1940)

Sigrid Undset is a moralist, first of all, though she is certainly not by temperament an ascetic. She has a profound, brooding awareness of the domination of the flesh in the average human life, the central place of passion in the average human destiny. To Sigrid Undset the immediate, as well as the ultimate, truth about purely human life is the central reality of sex; and in the recognition of this truth she is one with not a few of her contemporaries. Still she does not—as do some modern authors—accept the actual dominance of sex in human life as essentially a blessing, for which man must be grateful, or as a primarily constructive fact of human existence, upon which an adequate positive philosophy of life may be built. Though sex is to her of central importance, the free, natural functioning of sex is not looked upon by her as an unmixed blessing. It is, rather, simply a fundamental condition of human existence which has in it much of evil, simultaneously with some good—and man never attains the complete, the *good life* by means of it alone. Hers is, in the last analysis, a severe, a high morality: between the flesh and the spirit there exists a constant, intensive strife—and the spirit must eventually triumph over the flesh if man is to be good. This is the dominant theme of Sigrid Undset's two greatest works, the his-

torical novels *Kristin Lavransdatter* . . . and *The Master of Hestviken* . . . , as well as her novels dealing with contemporary life which have appeared after *The Master of Hestviken;* and the theme is more or less explicit in the long series of early stories which came from her pen before the composition of *Kristin Lavransdatter.*

It is perhaps largely in consequence of such a rigid, uncompromising morality that the picture of the world which we come upon in the pages of Sigrid Undset is so heavy, so unyieldingly realistic, so essentially tragic in most of its immediate implications. (pp. 286-87)

We find in [her] early work much that is characteristic of Sigrid Undset at her greatest: a drab, severe, uncompromising realism, quite unafraid in its intensely honest depiction of those narrowly limited milieus in which her characters must live and move and have their being; a sombre, probing preoccupation with human character, for whom she reveals deep sympathies, and yet upon whom she does not hesitate to pass severe judgments; and a thoroughly unsentimental moral idealism, transforming itself by degrees—especially in the novels and short stories which come after *Jenny* . . .—into a morality increasingly affected by a profound religious instinct. All of this . . . moves again in *Kristin Lavransdatter* and *The Master of Hestviken.* In these two great historical novels, however, all of this is given a more magnificent perspective: it moves more freely, more easily, more naturally, yet without any loss of solidity, of mass, of honest, forthright realism; and it is conceived with a moral grandeur which is the mark of only the highest tragedy. But these are differences largely in degree, not in kind. (p. 299)

The bare outline of the story and the theme of *Fru Marta Oulie* [Sigrid Undset's first work] seems to suggest a very ordinary tale of modern married life enforcing a very trite and commonplace "moral." . . . [It] is not, however, quite as naïve in tone or ordinary in its manner of development as . . . its contents might suggest. . . . [In] one regard—its steady, sober realism, its honest analysis of human passion, never led astray into hysterical sentimentalities or melodramatic poses—this little novel about domestic life has its own genuine fictional distinction. It is to be emphasized, moreover, that Sigrid Undset's "moralizing" in this novel is motivated neither by the repression complex of mere Puritanism nor by a timidly feminine escape psychology.

Neither in *Fru Marta Oulie* nor anywhere else in her work does Sigrid Undset seek to deny the central validity of love —even passionate love—in human life. In this respect, at least, she is sufficiently "modern." . . . Passion—Sigrid Undset insists already in her first novel—must not be denied; rather must it be subordinated to certain higher laws of being. These higher laws of being—so runs the reasoning in *Fru Marta Oulie*—have found expression in certain human institutions, particularly in the institution of the home. Later in Sigrid Undset's work we shall find her conservative moral instincts finding other than merely human authority for her conception of the sacred inviolability of the home. For the present she is satisfied with an idealism founded upon purely natural and human grounds. (pp. 302-03)

Den lykkelige Alder ("The Happy Age") [is] a volume taken up almost entirely by two short stories ["A Stranger" and "The Happy Age"] which are even more characteristic of Sigrid Undset's early years as an author than is *Fru Marta Oulie*. In a sense these stories remind one of her earlier novel; but on the whole they represent a distinct advance in narrative technique, being more vivid, more alive, and carrying their moral more naturally, less obtrusively. Both of these short stories deal with young women. . . . (p. 303)

The first of these two tales has a rather artificial plot, and it reflects at times a form of idealism that seems high-flown and forced; but the tale is saved from being a failure because of the intimately realistic study in milieu which it contains. The second—the tale which is concerned with Charlotte Hedel and Uni Hirsch—bears the stamp of living reality throughout; it remains to the present day one of Sigrid Undset's most consistently living fictional performances despite its short, concentrated *novella* form. Into the two young women's characters Sigrid Undset has poured a great deal of herself: she has not only *observed* such young women—in a sense she has *lived their lives*. She pours all of her sound, healthy natural instincts into Uni Hirsch, whose early dreams are not realized but who finally comes to find in her life certain solid human values of which her late adolescent world of romantic yearnings had never dreamed. Charlotte Hedel, on the other hand, is conceived largely in contrast to Uni Hirsch, especially toward the end of the story. She too has her dreams; but when they cannot be realized in the form which they had originally taken in her dreams she becomes a tragic victim of the eternal conflict between dream and reality. (pp. 303-04)

I cannot say that I share the almost unreserved admiration which Norwegian critics and literary historians have showered upon [*Jenny*], though it is doubtless to be ranked as the most *considerable* work of Sigrid Undset's before the publication of *Kristin Lavransdatter*. The novel employs somewhat improbable situations in order to prepare the reader for its final tragic action; it is not without episodes in a highly theatrical, even melodramatic manner; and its composition seems at times more wooden, more self-conscious than is usual even in Sigrid Undset's early work. . . . Despite these faults, however, the novel does somehow affect one: we do become intensely concerned about the destiny of Jenny—perhaps so much so that we are to an extent revolted (and *not* sentimentally) by the severe judgment which Sigrid Undset comes finally to pass upon her heroine. (pp. 305-06)

It is characteristic of Sigrid Undset that seventy pages . . . are devoted to a minute, circumstantial depiction of the horrors of the lonely, terror-filled period of [Jenny's] advanced pregnancy and childbirth and the violently tragic aftermath [of her suicide] in Rome. The novel reminds one of Guy de Maupassant's *Une Vie* in its brutal *lingering* over the sad details of the tragic dénouement. A normally precipitate tragic action is not permitted here. The reader must concentrate, with whatever patience he may have, upon a slow, steady *accumulation* of tragic detail: he must linger, all but sadistically, over the gradual stages in Jenny's final decay; he must finally come to see, always directly, never by subtle narrative implication, the "inevitability" of Jenny's tragic fate in the light of the severe ethical idealism of her earlier years. . . .

Sigrid Undset's heroines after Jenny, however, are almost without exception not tragic characters in this sense. Most of them ultimately learn to adjust themselves to life, though only after a more or less severe struggle. This is true of Rose Wegner in *Vaaren* ("Springtime" . . .), Sigrid Undset's most important work in the decade between *Jenny* and the publication of *Kristin Lavransdatter*. This is true also of most of the women characters in the two collections of short stories *Splinten av Troldspeilet* ("The Splinter of the Troll Mirror" . . .), and *De kloge Jomfruer* ("The Wise Virgins" . . .). And this is preeminently true of Kristin in *Kristin Lavransdatter*. . . . (p. 309)

It is to be noted that the moral emphasis in the stories which succeed *Jenny* becomes more pronounced with each new volume; and we find more and more that the prevailing moral emphasis in these stories becomes gradually invested with an increasingly significant religious element. In *The Wise Virgins* (the title itself is fraught with strong religious associations) the relation between religious faith and morality is clearly implied. The recurrent theme of this collection of stories is the necessity of a profound spiritual experience as the foundation for any sound, lasting love. (pp. 309-10)

Kristin Lavransdatter is certainly to be counted among the greatest historical novels of all time, and my feeling is that it ranks first among novels dealing with the Middle Ages. (p. 311)

[The] first thing that impresses us in *Kristin Lavransdatter* is the apparent *effortlessness* of the artistic performance, the seeming lack of any conscious narrative devices or tricks, the complete absence of *style* in the narrow literary sense of that word. It has been maintained by some critics, indeed, that Sigrid Undset is not an artist; and insofar as this means merely that she disdains the formal tricks of the conscious literary artist the judgment is true. She never resorts to artistic artifice; she does not pause to form her sentences with sedulous care, nor does she see any virtue in carefully turning her phrases, in searching intently for *le mot juste*. . . . Sigrid Undset's art—such as it is—simply *grows,* naturally, intensely, sometimes with strangely awkward pregnancy of utterance, out of the plentiful resources of a deeply sensitive, a profoundly serious genius. In consequence it has its faults: there are passages which might profit by greater concentration of phrasing; there are episodes which might move more swiftly, more decisively; there are details which at times might better be omitted. But by these we are only momentarily disturbed, if at all; for there is so much else in Sigrid Undset's pages to impress the reader—so much more to make him intensely conscious of the existence in *Kristin Lavransdatter* of a kind of truth in art that is more than art alone.

She has no "style," it is true—she merely *writes,* seemingly without especial care, without any particular form, yet under the marvelously sensitive intuitive guidance of an artistic spirit which has been gripped so deeply in her problem that she somehow finds the word that is appropriate, the image that is inevitable, the stylistic tempo and the narrative tone that fits the peculiar burden of her story. The secret of her art in *Kristin Lavransdatter* is to be found in the remarkable intensity, the brooding tenaciousness with which she comes to grips with her subject. (pp. 315-16)

The note is already struck in the forthright directness of the opening paragraphs in the novel; it accounts for much of the medieval idiom . . . which gives a natural color to the dialogue; it is characteristic of the incidental manner in which both historical background and natural background are employed throughout the novel; it is the secret of the leisurely tempo maintained in the novel's general narrative movement, and explains the apparently sudden intensification of this movement which we come upon in certain crucial scenes; and finally, it is present in Sigrid Undset's deliberately minute analysis of Kristin's character, and in the author's brooding awareness of the ethical values involved in Kristin's struggle with immediate circumstances and with her God. Some critics have insisted that there is nothing really natural in Sigrid Undset's almost morbid preoccupation with the general problem of evil; but this would be to insist upon a very limited conception of what constitutes "the natural." The most superficial analyses of Sigrid Undset's genius must admit that *to her,* at least, *the sombre is the natural*—to brood intently is to live deeply, strongly, completely. Though such a brooding preoccupation with the problem of evil might tend to lead other novelists to a spirit of complete disillusionment, to a sense of unrelieved, futile tragedy, even to a state of morbidity which would seem to be the opposite of the natural, it leads Sigrid Undset, in fact, to a grandeur of tragic moral conception which we have become accustomed to identify with great tragedy, with the tragic *katharsis* of the Aristotelian aesthetics. (pp. 316-17)

Sigrid Undset was guided by a marvelous artistic intuition when she placed the action of *Kristin Lavransdatter* in what one Norwegian critic has aptly called "an historical vacuum" . . . ; for our very lack of precise, detailed historical information on the period from 1320 to 1350 permits the imagination of the novelist to range freely, unobstructed by any of the rigidities of actual historical events. . . . The details of dress; foods and drink, and their preparation; household customs of all kinds; characteristic turns of speech; the manner of thinking and feeling in a still half-primitive Norwegian society;—these are the "historical materials" that are woven into the marvelously detailed and complex pattern of *Kristin Lavransdatter*. It is in this sense, primarily, that the novel is to be considered "historical." The reader is at no time particularly conscious of the actual historical precision with which Sigrid Undset handles her materials; for they are so subtly subordinated to the absorbing central motive of the novel—the story of Kristin—that they never call attention to themselves.

Natural background plays just as important a part in the novel as does historical background; but Sigrid Undset no more permits natural scene to dominate than she does the pageantry and intrigues incidental to historical episode or the numerous paraphernalia of medieval dress and custom and idiom. We are always subtly aware of the magnificent Norwegian landscape. . . . Yet natural background, impressive as it is . . . , is never described for its own sake; always it is introduced as an integral, and merely supporting, adjunct of the central action in the novel. (pp. 318-19)

She knew the Norwegian landscape with which she deals here into its minutest details. . . . Not only does she *see* these details; she *feels* their surfaces, their varied textures, with an acutely delicate and sensitive touch; she *hears* their faintest traces of sound with an ear that is marvelously alert; and, above all, she *smells* every pungent, acrid odor as well as every gentle fragrance given off by nature in her manifold sensory manifestations. And despite the careful,

minutely realistic intimacy with which the reader becomes acquainted with the innumerable details of this natural background, Sigrid Undset can on occasion introduce a superb sweep, a magnificently broad perspective to her natural scene. (p. 320)

In its purely narrative movement the novel is slow, leisurely, unhurried, proceeding with a quietly deliberate solemnity, never impatient of detail, ever subtly alert to all those minute forms and phases of outward phenomena which register their impressions upon human character and human destiny. And yet this steady stateliness of general narrative movement gathers itself together at times, leaps into a blazing intensity of feeling or of action in certain individual episodes, only to recede again into its unhurried way —as unhurried as the ceaseless processes of nature and eternity and God. Suffusing it all there is a note of unutterable majesty, even of sublimity—the poignant sublimity with which a story of human fate can become invested when a profoundly unhurried artistry touches it and brings it into the delicately penetrating focus of an intensely serious creative imagination. In Sigrid Undset's work the majesty of nature combines subtly, as at times in life, with the majesty of a severely elevated moral consciousness; and her unhurried narrative movement is but the inevitable technical accompaniment of her sombre moral theme. Any other narrative tempo would be inconceivable in a story such as *Kristin Lavransdatter*.

Unhurried as the general narrative movement is, however, the story is never flat or insipid or tedious. . . . And Sigrid Undset shows herself master of a wide range of human emotions in her creation of the crucial episodes in her novel: they vary in their central motifs as well as in their use of detail, in their tempo as well as in their moods. (p. 324)

[In *Kristin Lavransdatter*] Ragnfrid's morbidly violent brooding over her secret sin—a brooding which amounted to a kind of self-immolation of the spirit—is typical of the central feminine characters almost everywhere in Sigrid Undset's novels. But in *Kristin Lavransdatter* this type of woman is developed with a relentlessly probing minuteness of psychological analysis nowhere else attained in these novels. Kristin herself is Sigrid Undset's greatest creation in this type of woman, though Kristin has her fictional prototypes in both Jenny Winge and Vigdis Gunnarsdatter. . . . Each of these women is violently intense in her inner idealisms, never capable of compromise, ever severe in judgement both upon herself and upon others. In *Jenny* this severity of judgment takes its toll primarily upon the heroine herself. In *Gunnar's Daughter* the heroine takes a fierce, thoroughly pagan vengeance upon the man who had wronged her, this despite the fact that she loved him. And in *Kristin Lavransdatter* both Kristin and Erlend must suffer because of Kristin's constant, brooding consciousness of a past sin, and her tendency, in weak moments, to hold Erlend responsible for all that had befallen her. In each case it is the heroine's inability to forget a wrong which accounts for her brooding, and for her distracted efforts to right in some way or other the wrong that had been done.

In *Kristin Lavransdatter* the type is much more convincing than in either of the earlier novels, perhaps largely because of Sigrid Undset's profoundly understanding ability to conceive of her central character over against a magnificently appropriate background—the complicated, restlessly paradoxical milieu of a relatively primitive society undergoing civilizing processes which as yet have only partially conquered the passionate brutality of an age which had but recently passed. (pp. 328-29)

Some critics have hailed the character of Kristin as Sigrid Undset's great triumph in the creation of the universal woman—a woman who, in her relation to her parents, her husband, and her children, as well as to the whole general world of moral and religious values, gives a profoundly moving expression to the noble urge supposed to exist in some form in all women of all times toward an ideal moral and religious order. In a sense, possibly, such a judgment is sound; and yet it is not the primary truth about Sigrid Undset's creation of Kristin—for Kristin Lavransdatter is, first of all, *a woman of medieval Norway.* Her unique temper, that which most immediately and most consistently attracts the discerning reader, is that she represents in her person a strong-willed, essentially pagan spirit being slowly broken —in a sense, perhaps, transformed—by the severe moral dogma of the medieval Church. In her we come to find perhaps the most profound delineation in world literature of the struggle between a Christian ethics and a pagan world.

It must be emphasized, then, that Sigrid Undset's analysis of Kristin's character is a triumph first of all in *historical* portraiture; only secondarily, if at all, is she to be considered representative of the purely hypothetical "universal woman" of which some critics have made so much. It is only if we look upon Kristin as a woman of medieval Norway that we can explain the fierce intensities of her moral brooding, the massively sombre coloring of her tragic earthly experience. (pp. 332-33)

[*The Master of Hestviken*] is even more heavy and sombre in tone and movement than is *Kristin Lavransdatter*. . . . [It] is definitely more unrelieved and dreary in its coloring, more stark in its general narrative outlines, and more relentlessly bleak in its portrayal of the inner moral struggle of its central character. (p. 346)

Only in the opening chapters is the reader given a glimpse of something fresh, buoyant, hopeful—this in the innocent youthful love of Olav and Ingunn. Brutally tragic forces lurk on every hand, however, and the charming young love idyll of Olav and Ingunn soon becomes a pathetic sacrifice to the darkling forces of violence and hatred which surround them. Before the end of *The Axe* . . . Olav has committed the sin of the flesh with Ingunn and has killed two men by violence; and yet he is a mere youth in these years, and by nature he is one who loves peace rather than violence. It is clear that the world of *The Master of Hestviken* is primarily a man's world, a world in which the moral struggle is bound to be very harsh in its outlines and in its inner complications—bleak and grim and starkly bare as a far northern landscape. (pp. 346-47)

That *Kristin Lavransdatter* is in the last analysis a greater novel than *The Master of Hestviken* must certainly be granted; but its relative greatness is hardly to be found in the fact that it is less gloomy, less essentially tragic in its final moral implications than is *The Master of Hestviken.* The latter novel is inferior to *Kristin Lavransdatter* for another reason.

The chief difficulty with *The Master of Hestviken* is that the religious dogma which determines its moralizing is entirely

too obtrusive—never sufficiently subordinated to the narrative pattern of the novel. It must be admitted that *Kristin Lavransdatter* is almost equally full of long moralizing passages, which upon even cursory analysis are seen to contain formal Catholic dogma; but in *Kristin Lavransdatter* such dogma is far more capably worked into the normal narrative processes, and so we find ourselves little disturbed by the dogmatic implications of the novel. In *The Master of Hestviken,* on the other hand, the free flow of narration is too often interrupted by the long moral homily, by a forced and definitely obtrusive religious dogma. In fact, Sigrid Undset is so intently concerned with purely dogmatic questions in this novel that she at times apparently introduces episodes merely for the purpose of providing a background or an occasion for the expression of a given dogma. (pp. 348-49)

In most respects, however, the story which is unfolded for us in *The Master of Hestviken* is quite convincing. The historical background, everywhere founded upon a minute knowledge of the times, is subordinated to the main narrative pattern with a rare intuitive power; the characters of Olav and Ingunn are revealed with that intimacy and penetration which one might expect from the author of *Kristin Lavransdatter;* the natural scene is marvelously alive and thoroughly congruous with the sombre moral theme; and the moral itself, though obtruding too obviously in certain episodes, is managed on the whole with a naturalness and power only exceeded by *Kristin Lavransdatter.* It might be added, in passing, that *The Master of Hestviken* has in it touches of humor too frequently lacking in *Kristin Lavransdatter,* though the latter novel is not entirely devoid of humor. The humor of *The Master of Hestviken* is distinctly broad, sometimes harsh and grim; but it serves admirably the twofold purpose of providing occasional bits of not unwelcome comic relief and of adding to our sense of historical illusion. (pp. 349-50)

Upon the completion of *The Master of Hestviken* Sigrid Undset returns again to the contemporary scene in a group of four novels. . . .

[*The Wild Orchid, The Burning Bush, Ida Elisabeth,* and *The Faithful Wife*] lack that sense of an immediate, pulsing physical life characteristic of her earlier, less ambitious tales dealing with contemporary life; and they fall far short of *Kristin Lavransdatter* and *The Master of Hestviken* in rich, intimate intensities of character portrayal. They deal, however, with their immediate contemporary problems in the spirit of straightforward, wholly unsentimental honesty that one has come with the years to associate with Sigrid Undset; and with all of their shortcomings as compared with Sigrid Undset's great historical novels, they are among the most important novels that have come out of Norway in the last ten years.

The chief fault of at least the first two of Sigrid Undset's late group of novels dealing with contemporary life is that they are too patently motivated by a particular religious dogma, that of the Roman Catholic Church. In the historical novels the central inclusion of religious dogma seems, on the whole, natural enough, these novels dealing with historical periods when "the Church" was coming increasingly to dominate human thought and human conduct in the North; though, as we have seen, a too intent preoccupation with dogmatic questions in *The Master of Hestviken* leads Sigrid Undset at times into serious artistic difficulties. In the later novels dealing with contemporary life, however, there seems to be far less necessity for a particular kind of religious emphasis; and it is obvious that Sigrid Undset's inclusion in these late novels of the materials of something just short of religious propaganda has resulted in a distinct falling off in the quality of these novels.

It must be said to Sigrid Undset's credit, however, that her propaganda is effective. . . . (pp. 354-55)

[Her charges] are in the last analysis to be considered only as particular phases of an aggressive frontal attack upon the whole structure of post-war materialism, whose characteristic doctrines, she insists, must be replaced by those of a dogmatic authoritarian Church if society is to survive. This becomes apparent in her late contemporary novels to anyone who reads with but ordinary discernment; and it becomes the central thesis of a series of critical essays [*Etapper: Ny raekke* ("Stages on the Road")] which she has published in the two decades which followed upon the fearful cataclysm of the World War.

These essays [are] often penetrating analyses of post-war psychology and post-war politics. . . . They represent, as the titles hint, certain "stages"—or better, perhaps, "halting-places"—in Sigrid Undset's religious and intellectual development; and as such they are of first importance in any careful study of her general development as a thinker and as an artist. (pp. 356-57)

In these essays Sigrid Undset seems to have managed to shake off, at least for the moment, the narrower aspects of a purely Catholic dogma in the interests of a more inclusive, universal Christian view. In fact, she goes even farther at times, championing a kind of general religious view of life in broad opposition to certain tendencies in contemporary European national politics. (p. 357)

In her novels and essays are to be traced fairly clearly the successive steps in Sigrid Undset's religious growth. At first she developed a kind of moral idealism, which later became identified with a sort of ethical Christianity independent of church institutions or church dogma, and only finally, in the 1920's, took on a positive, specifically Catholic, form. (p. 359)

Sigrid Undset stands among the great novelists of all time. Among living novelists one is prone to rank her next to Thomas Mann. Among Scandinavian novelists she has no peer. Among women novelists she probably stands alone. (p. 360)

> *Alrik Gustafson, "Christian Ethics in a Pagan World: Sigrid Undset," in his* Six Scandinavian Novelists *(copyright © 1940 by the American-Scandinavian Foundation), Princeton University Press, 1940 (and reprinted by The University of Minnesota Press, 1967), pp. 286-361.*

N. ELIZABETH MONROE   (essay date 1941)

Mrs. Undset's work helps to correct three destructive tendencies of the modern novel: the movement away from life, which has devitalized the novel, the loss of a spiritual conception of personality, and the loss of a sense of community, which has resulted from disintegration in society and in the novel. (pp. 41-2)

The passion of Mrs. Undset's mind has saved her from any temptation to play with life or art. Her early writing was crude but not unreal. She uses the novel as a means, not an end, and explores the complex problems of modern life and the eternal themes of faith and suffering with care and penetration. Her modern novels examine marriage and divorce with fearless realism. The myth of romantic love, invented as much by the realistic as by the romantic novelist, suffers a severe blow from these novels. She has always been interested in the problem of order and charity and justice in an industrial and materialistic society. (p. 42)

Mrs. Undset's work has also done much to restore personality to the novel. . . . By the very nature of her faith Mrs. Undset is bound to describe man completely. No novelist without faith can invent situations that are as dramatic and binding as those which entangle Kristin and Olav. Their plight is dramatic to begin with and is intensified by the obligations that surround them. Ties such as these make man significant, however humble his lot may be. It is noteworthy that all the characters of her historical novels are obscure people. They do not depend on their position or involvement in great and stirring events for their importance. Yet these characters seem larger than life, moulded in greatness, because their temptations and their sufferings are great. They are interesting because of the psychological subtlety of the analysis. Mrs. Undset drops a plumb-line deep into man's consciousness and lets the character unfold naturally from within. She uses mood and revery and the direct examination of conscience, but never as ends in themselves. They do not interrupt the action but supply its motivation or, through their dramatic context, give the impression of action or carry the action on in another sphere. (pp. 42-3)

Whatever Mrs. Undset's concern—the social problems of our day or the conflict between a pagan and Christian order—she has brought to her work the force of a great personality. Though not dependent on subjective experience, her work carries a personal stamp much as Dostoievsky's novels are marked by his profound and tortured nature. This is not a question of being autobiographical or even subjective. Tolstoy's novels are all parts of his search for truth; they are directly personal experience. But the works of Dostoievski and Mrs. Undset have arisen from deep and vital personalities; their writings do not carry their individual experiences, but take the mold of their thought and feeling. (pp. 46-7)

Mrs. Undset avoids two dangers of the modern novel, the failure to go beyond the concrete and particular, and the failure through over-abstraction to breathe life into a story. . . . Mrs. Undset is helped in this regard by her profound religious experience. Her stories always move on two levels. The reader can enjoy these narratives without regard to their representative level, or without believing in the supernatural destinies the characters are working out in their lives, but the literary effectiveness of having natural motives reinforced by supernatural motives cannot be denied. Although intensely interested in ideas, she never lets ideas take the place of story. She knows how to set characters into action and to involve them in tense situations. Their ideas are enthralling because they lead to action, or deflect the course of action, or call forth deep resources of spiritual energy to motivate the rest of life. They never turn ideas over in their minds as a mere form of intellectual exercise or become the mouthpieces of propaganda; their ideas are given only when they help to determine their lives. (pp. 47-8)

Though [*Jenny*] is morbid, it shows the direction of Mrs. Undset's genius. She creates scenes and relationships with unflinching realism, but has not yet learned to build character in the round. The book is a daring exploration of the erotic impulse in woman. Mrs. Undset is trying to get at its very basis. A woman's sound instincts may protect her from free love but not always from the need of self fulfillment and the desire to love and be loved. Jenny is an appealing character—young, clear-sighted, generous, independent. (p. 52)

The fact that parts of the book sound like a reconstruction of Mrs. Undset's own experience has limited its appeal. The exploration of woman's emotions is convincing, but the characters, especially the men, are shadowy. Even at this early period she knew how to create relationships. The tensions of the Gram household convince the reader only too well. . . . The other concerns of this book are to appear again in later novels—the basis of leadership in modern society, socialism, and the introduction of an authentic culture in Norway, which has turned all its energies to providing food and the latest comforts and a veneer of culture. (p. 53)

In *The Faithful Wife*, Mrs. Undset shows how narrow and egotistical people become, who have nothing but themselves to believe in. They take up the new morality of enlightened self-interest, only to find it a mushroom growth, or try to fulfill all of life in purely human relationships, only to find them barren and insecure without something greater than themselves as a measure. In this book, as in her mediaeval works, she sees that the individual is not significant, except in his own esteem, unless he is the child of God. Then he has a destiny toward which all his powers should lead. (pp. 59-60)

These two mediaeval novels, *Kristin Lavransdatter* and *The Master of Hestviken,* stand among the great stories of all time. This is in part because they employ great themes and explore them with unparalleled depth and penetration, and in part because Mrs. Undset has the art of telling a story so that what happens next becomes of supreme importance at every turn in the way. This is a remarkable achievement for stories with a slow, leisurely pace and great density of material. Perhaps the first thing the reader notices about the narrative is its apparent effortlessness. Everything springs naturally from the central situation, and the separate incidents are closely connected, but the author has used no conscious devices to hold them together or to emphasize the drama. On the whole this is a mark of greatness, but there are occasions when foreshortening would have helped the proportions of the story, and the tendency of a naturally dramatic art to become melodramatic could have been reduced by subjecting the narrative to rigid control. The incidents are so rich and well-rounded and so much a part of the story that they almost never call attention to themselves. (pp. 64-5)

Mrs. Undset gives the impression of the very movement of life: time passes . . . ; the seasons come and go; man is thrown into actions he has not intended; he grows old and dies. At the same time the pattern of causality is everywhere present: Olav's past life follows him relentlessly, calling for resolution; his sorest trial, Eirick, becomes the husbandman of his goods; Kristin's disobedience runs like a scarlet thread through all the pattern of her life, until she offers the whole fabric to God. (p. 65)

Sigrid Undset has gone right to the center of things from the start. It is because she writes against a background of ultimate ideas and because her characters are answerable to two orders that her stories are poignantly dramatic. The purely aesthetic effects of a dramatic situation are sharpened immeasurably by the moral conflicts involved. This is not to say that Mrs. Undset is a propagandist, except in the very broad sense in which all great art persuades us to belief. This is simply her way of apprehending life. Her aim is not to convince the reader that the ideas held by her characters are true but to reconstruct a world in which men believed them to be true. In this world the outlines of character are not blurred or obliterated and the tragedy of every conflict is deepened by its spiritual consequences, and man is still a resident of two spheres. (p. 71)

[In *Ida Elizabeth, The Faithful Wife,* and *Madame Dorothea,*] Mrs. Undset discusses ideas without any reference to religion. Here she is trying to get at the fact that morals are older than religion, that a moral conception of life is simply the rational way of looking at things. *Madame Dorothea* . . . is not altogether successful. For the first time in her career Mrs. Undset makes the erotic impulse too vivid; at least she explores it more intensively than is necessary to establish its reality. But she has an intelligent purpose here. Madame Dorothea realizes that there would be much less confusion in a woman's sex life if she managed to work out a harmony between instinct and reason, instead of assuming that instinct must be thwarted in a good life. (p. 72)

Mrs. Undset's contribution to culture is memorable. She is one of the greatest historical novelists of all times. She has succeeded in describing the Middle Ages honestly, without romanticizing the past or concentrating on what is merely picturesque. Even when her stories are not altogether successful as novels, they have the quality of greatness because they enthrall the mind through the moving drama of human life. Everything about them seems important and dramatic. This is because Mrs. Undset's mind fastens on her theme with great intensity and allows nothing to interfere with its real and dramatic expression. Mrs. Undset's use of the interior dialogue and impassioned mood and memory is far more remarkable than Mrs. Woolf's experiment with the stream of consciousness, because it motivates action or takes the place of action. (pp. 86-7)

To be able to use the materials of her craft so that finite and infinite, sense and super-sense, are visible together, has formed for her a great and rare triumph. (p. 87)

> *N. Elizabeth Monroe, "Art and Ideas in Sigrid Undset," in her* The Novel and Society: A Critical Study of the Modern Novel *(copyright, 1941, by the University of North Carolina Press), University of North Carolina Press, 1941, pp. 39-87.*

A. H. WINSNES (essay date 1949)

[Sigrid Undset] does not experiment with new forms of literary expression, with a technique better fitted to grasp concrete realities, in the manner of a Virginia Woolf or a James Joyce. In this respect at least, she is old-fashioned. She carries on the tradition of the great realistic writers of the nineteenth century, Balzac, Dickens, Tolstoy, the style which began in Norway with Camilla Collett and achieved its triumph in Kristian Elster the elder, Alexander Kielland, Jonas Lie and Amalie Skram.

But she is bolder in her description of reality than were

most of her great predecessors. The picture she gives of humanity, the passions, hate and love, betrayal and loyalty, the idyllic and the tragic, of the whole of life from the movement of the embryo in the womb to the withering of the body and death, from the smell of blood which a human child draws in as it comes into the world up to the highest forms of conscious existence—all this is presented by her without a trace of romantic idealisation or artificiality. Few writers have seen deeper into the unpleasantness of life, into mankind's destitution and wretchedness. (pp. 2-3)

Mrs Marta Oulie [(*Fru Marta Oulie*)] is written in the form of a diary, but it cannot be said to have a confessional character. An individual stamp is given to this remarkable first work . . . by the detached presentation, the cool objectivity, which nevertheless grips the reader. In the retrospective entries in this journal, almost in the same way as in the dialogue of a play by Ibsen, the curtains are drawn back to reveal the past and to enable us to follow step by step the belated self-realisation of the unfaithful wife. (p. 38)

The Happy Age [(*Den lykkelige alder*)] is the most sensitive piece of writing about girlhood that has ever appeared in Norwegian,—at the same time it is nearest to reality. These young women have a certain coolness and reserve, but these lie only on the surface, and are no more than the shield which covers the warmth imprisoned within. Casual love-affairs are not much heeded in the milieu of lodging-houses and rented rooms in which they live. But these girls are so constituted that they cannot regard them so lightly, whether their attitude is natural in them or depends on the inheritance they have brought with them from their homes. As Sigrid Undset writes of one of them, there is something in them which makes any stain show up clearly not only to others but, above all, to themselves. They are not prudish, but they live with the dream of something worthy of complete surrender, something which will demand their faith utterly and absolutely. (p. 43)

Jenny, like *Mrs Marta Oulie*, is also a kind of *roman expérimental*. Its tone is quite different, however, since in *Jenny* the author experiments with the possibilities lying within herself, and in making them actual she identifies herself with their extension into reality. In consequence, the novel has the character of a confession. Jenny belongs with the young women in *The Happy Age*, related not so much to Edele Hammer and Uni, both of whom succeed at last in making a compromise between their dreams and reality, as to Charlotte Hedels, who could find no object for her consuming longing and took her own life.

It is Charlotte's story which is told in new and profounder form in *Jenny*,—a love-story, sordid and unpleasant, but with a brilliance lent to it by Italy, Rome and the Campagna, by the life which blossoms in it, by the writer's joy in art and nature, and by the dream which comes true. (pp. 52-3)

There is not only the sheen of Italy over *Jenny*; one also finds occasionally a supernatural element. This is due to Jenny herself, for the foundation on which her character is built is her inherent religious nature. She is in fact intensely religious, longing to serve someone she sets higher than herself. But she does not believe in God. If she has faith in anything, it is in herself and her own strength. How far will that carry her?—that is the theme of the book. (p. 53)

Jenny is one of the most distinctive women characters in

Norwegian literature. It would not seem out of the way to compare her to Ibsen's Nora and Gunnar Heiberg's Karen. . . . Jenny is no less exacting in her demands than Nora and Karen, but it is always on herself in the first place that those demands are made. It is not simply that she is more intelligent than they—there is in her a spiritual ferment, a more highly developed consciousness, with which Nora and Karen are unacquainted. (pp. 55-6)

The new elements in Sigrid Undset's writing in the years immediately following *Jenny* do not make themselves evident in any obvious or demonstrative fashion. The material in [*Poor Fortunes (Fattige skjaebner)*, *Spring (Vaaren)*, *The Splinter of the Magic Mirror (Splinten av troldspeilet)*, and *The Wise Virgins (De kloge jomfruer)*] is on the whole the same as before—the reality of everyday life, with characters drawn chiefly from the middle-classes in Oslo. But to some extent, the attitude towards the material is different. The tone of personal confession, which often breaks through in her earliest writing, is now rarely heard, and when heard is damped down and restrained. The presentation of a story may now take on a retrospective character. On the whole, her material now seems to have been set at a greater distance. The intensity may be less, but not the fervour of her mind, not the sympathy and clearsightedness. There may be keen and clever satire, as in the descriptions of poor souls like Selma Brøtter and Miss Smith Tellefsen, but there is satire too of the tenderest kind, where it trembles on the verge between tears and laughter, as in the masterly short story *Simonsen*, where the dissonances of life are resolved in a humour closely related to that of Dickens.

A love-story forms the theme of her great novel, *Spring*, as it does in other of her books. But the history of the child-love of Torkild Christiansen and Rose Wegener, their engagement and marriage, the collapse of that marriage and its resurrection, is related from a clearly conscious social point of view. *Spring* is essentially a social novel, and the story of Torkild and Rose and the people around them is used to throw light on a concrete social phenomenon—the home. All the characters are seen in relation to the homes from which they come, and they are explained, tried and judged, according to their ability to shoulder the responsibilities which the home, as the protocell of the life of society and of all higher culture, thrusts upon them. (pp. 67-8)

Closely related to *Spring* is *The Splinter of the Magic Mirror*. . . . It consists of two stories, one called *Mrs Hjelde*, the other *Harriet Waage*, though it is not by accident that the two are set side by side in the same volume. . . . The essential fact is that the two women, each in her own way and in quite sharp contrast to the other, are illustrations of the same case. Each of them has a splinter of the magic mirror in her eye—the mirror which, according to Hans Andersen, made people see everything crooked and distorted. (pp. 70-1)

The three stories in *The Wise Virgins* deal with characters from a more ordinary background. Here, as elsewhere, it is the common stuff of humanity that Sigrid Undset wishes to grasp, the instincts, needs and desires which may appear differently under different circumstances, but which remain essentially the same. The lives of the servant-girl, Helene Johansen, the dressmaker Fanny Erdahl, Klara in the factory and Emma in the milk-shop, are different in their externals from the lives of Mrs Hjelde and Mrs Waage. Nevertheless, where something primary like the sexual life is concerned, they belong to the same human family. Some women feel their sex as an impulse to live for someone else; others feel it as something which gives them the right to live on someone else. But splinters of the magic mirror have not perhaps reached so many of those who live in the milieu described in *The Wise Virgins*. All three stories are variations on the same theme of mother and child. The development of the theme in *Tjodolf* is masterly. The story of Helene Johansen's love for a little child she has taken to herself but must give up again, is one of Sigrid Undset's loveliest pieces on the theme of mother-love. It is built up with an eye to the effect of contrast, but there is nothing schematic or artificial about it. The opposition between the frivolous Fanny Erdahl, the real mother of the child, and the steadfast Helene, has the same solid basis in living reality as the opposition between Harriet Waage and Uni Hjelde in *The Splinter of the Magic Mirror,* or between the homes of Torkild Kristiansen and Rose Wegener in *Spring*. *Tjodolf* is more than a deeply moving and pathetic story: it bears the stamp of greatness, because in a flash it gives us insight into a mother's love, the love which in the psychic organism of this one human being is the very thread of life.

Some critics spoke scornfully of the moral messages in *Spring, The Splinter of the Magic Mirror* and *The Wise Virgins*. But this is not moralising literature—a better name for it would be literature about moral values and moral heroism. (pp. 73-4)

Sigrid Undset is in a special position. In none of the other writers of the period do we find such a fundamental revolt against the materialist interpretation of life, with a criticism of contemporary culture so firmly based in point of principle and inspired by so clear a religious ideal. This applies both to her controversial and historical writing between the wars and to the novels of contemporary life which she also wrote in this period, particularly *The Wild Orchid (Gymnadenia)* and *The Burning Bush (Den broendende busk)*. (p. 155)

She is no less a realist than before, and no less a realist than other contemporary Christian novelists, like François Mauriac and Georges Bernanos in France and Graham Greene and Evelyn Waugh in England. But, once again, she must be placed in a separate category. The psychological penetration of a writer like François Mauriac, for example, fastens above all on the evil in man and his wretchedness without grace. In this series of her modern novels, Sigrid Undset is chiefly occupied with man's inherent tendency towards truth and virtue. Sin and the sense of guilt, remorse and penitence, which were vital elements in the medieval novels, continue to play an important part, but another aspect also claims attention. In the medieval novels we meet the Augustinian type of Christianity. In the story of the conversion of Paul Selmer, in *The Wild Orchid (Gymnadenia)* and *The Burning Bush (Den broendende busk)*, we find another type, which the French philosopher, Etienne Gilson, calls Thomist. (pp. 175-76)

These books contain some biting satire. It tends to be somewhat stylised when it is aimed at the Protestant clergy, especially the liberal theologians; but it is mercilessly accurate when it touches such things as the boom-mentality, baseness and superficiality, which prevaled amongst large social groups in Norway during the first World War. Equally sure and unsparing is her exposure of the self-satisfaction and fatuity of the un-Christian middle-class, or, as

in *Ida Elisabeth,* her exposure of idealistic self-deception and the "nature-idyll".

The satire remains of minor significance, and here, as elsewhere, her greatness lies in her powers of self-identification with ordinary people. She had possessed that faculty from the beginning, but her ability to share in the life of others has perhaps never extended so far as in her portrayal of such "anonymous" characters as Lucy Sippen in *The Wild Orchid,* Ida Elisabeth in the novel which bears her name, and Nathalie in *The Faithful Wife (Den trofaste hustru)*. This activity of her imagination has gained new strength from the Christian attitude, which conditioned the creation of these novels. (p. 176)

The novels, [*Ida Elisabeth* and *The Faithful Wife*] . . . , mark a new departure in Sigrid Undset's realistic treatment of modern life. In none of her other books is the everyday quality of both material and method so intimately connected with the whole idea of the novel and its artistic unity. Nevertheless,—or perhaps for this very reason— women characters like Ida Elisabeth or Nathalie in *The Faithful Wife* are endowed with monumental greatness. . . . Their greatness is revealed in their relationship to the common round of life. They neither flee from it nor are they swallowed up by it. They are loyal souls, and extract gold from the dross of everyday life. In a chaotic world, they stand for something stable; while the world totters on its supports, we find in them that which, in the final count, holds everything together. The art which portrays Ida Elisabeth and Nathalie is as far removed as can be from the art which idealises and embellishes, but in these characters we are given a glimpse of the eternally feminine, the prototype of womankind, in the Christian sense. (pp. 194-95)

Although the religious idea is the essential impulse in both these novels, it does not appear with such clarity and directness as in *The Wild Orchid* and *The Burning Bush*. Their construction depends on the opposition between those fundamentally different adjustments which a person can make to life—the natural on the one hand, the supernatural on the other—the antithesis, that is, between man's ineradicable need of the transcendental and that other view of life, which sees human beings as citizens only of this world. (p. 195)

In form *Ida Elisabeth* and *The Faithful Wife* are ordinary realistic novels of married life. The method is basically the same as in the experimental novel of the Zola school. But the Christian experimental novel certainly comes to very different conclusions from those of the naturalistic type. The Christian outlook counts on man's freedom. It is perhaps for that reason that the poetry does not fade away, and one feels it throughout as an undercurrent, a vital source, or as an effluence permeating the whole. Latent in these two novels is a hymn in praise of the ideals of virginity and Christian marriage and in honour of the traditional Christian institution of the family. (p. 204)

In Norwegian literature, *Eleven Years* [(*Elleve aar*)] is a unique volume of memoirs, recollections of past life which have their origin in a mental process of the kind described by Henri Bergson in *Matière et mémoire*. He calls it *mémoire pure*—memories which can well up when some chance sensation sets in motion a mental life which has, as it were, lain dormant. (p. 205)

With all its concrete objectivity and despite the absence of "the intoxicant of recollection", *Eleven Years* is none the less a work of the creative poetic imagination, and it is this which makes it such a remarkable study of child-psychology. An academic psychologist can observe and describe the same facts about a child, but only a writer has the power to fit them into a real and concrete whole, the complete context of which they form part, and then interpret them in relation to this totality. We see the child's world come into being: the intense egotism, contact with an outside world, dawning awareness of things and people and of an external will which interferes and against which revolt is made. We see the reactions, negative and positive, towards parents and towards reprimand and punishment; the world of religious ideas which is built up; the first acquaintance with sex; and the child's instinctive reaction against being prematurely snatched out of its feeling of security by adults. We see all the small events, in themselves insignificant, which can make a child intensely happy or intensely unhappy, the wounds which may never heal in a whole lifetime. And finally we see the home as a living organism, an integrating unit, where almost imperceptibly the child learns to understand what it is that gives substance to life. (p. 207)

[Sigrid Undset] sees isolated man's need for fellowship and his desperate attempts to find the communal solidarity, without which he cannot live. As no other contemporary writer, she has laid bare, in all its crying nakedness, the pseudo-liberalism of the nineteenth century and every form of irresponsible individualism. But she has been equally caustic and merciless in unmasking and branding the collective movements into which rootless modern man has flung himself in order to escape from his isolation. For this very reason, she is in a position to present the fellowship which does not engulf the individual but liberates him—Christian universalism. (p. 248)

In an age which was moving generally towards an anthropocentric philosophy of life, an age in which men were adopting the cult of self-worship, she declared the eternal message of religion—*Soli Deo Gloria*—and created one of the great monuments of our literature to stand high over the spiritual pilgrim-path of man. (p. 250)

> *A. H. Winsnes, in his* Sigrid Undset: A Study in Christian Realism, *translated by P. G. Foote (copyright 1953 Sheed and Ward, Inc.; reprinted with permission from Andrews and McMeel, Inc.; originally published as* Sigrid Undset: En studie i Kristen realisme, *Aschehoug, 1949), Sheed and Ward, Inc., 1953, 258 p.*

JAMES WALTER McFARLANE (essay date 1960)

It is the endless and seemingly effortless stream of realistic detail that is the first conspicuous quality of [Sigrid Undset's] work. At bottom, it is the realism of a diagnostic report, drafted in great elaboration with the earnest purpose of assisting the individual to a greater awareness of himself, the whole then powerfully enriched by the concentrate of years of minute observation and dedicated historical study.... Indeed the term 'realism', in its application to Sigrid Undset, is one of rich contradiction: the observed detail of her contemporary world, the grey and sombre setting for those characters whose longings are frustrated by routine work and financial cares, seems to possess all the poetic precision of an imaginative reconstruction; whilst the studied detail of the medieval works is shot through with all the vividness one might expect from an observer's report.

But all the apparently inexhaustible detail of 'landscape', of setting, of milieu, however integral it is to the purpose and direction of the novels, remains subsidiary to their moral purpose. It provides a background, it sets up a backcloth, it marks out an arena, against which and within which are performed a series of moralities. Each individual novel is disposed about a moral and religious axis in a fashion reminiscent of the way in which the whole corpus of Sigrid Undset's work is arranged about her year of decision—1924, the year of her conversion to the Roman Catholic faith. It is not merely that her decision was taken at very nearly the mid-point of her adult life; rather it is the astonishing way in which the one half of her work presents what is very nearly a mirror image of the other, with the fact of her conversion standing to the design of her life as a kind of axis of symmetry. Immediately to either side of it come the two first-magnitude, historical works, *Kristin Lavransdatter* ... and *The Master of Hestviken*.... Flanking these are the two groups of 'contemporary' narrative works: the three novels and four volumes of short stories she published between 1907 and 1918; and the four, rather more confessionally inspired, modern novels that belong preponderantly to the 'thirties. And ultimately, providing yet further reinforcement for the idea of symmetry, one remarks the two other historical 'outriders', stationed thirty years apart and equidistant from her conversion, [*Gunnar's Daughter (Fortællingen om Viga-Ljot og Vigdis)* and *Madame Dorthea*].... (pp. 158-59)

The change [in Undset's work] from 'contemporary' to 'historical' [novels], the displacement of the action from the twentieth to the fourteenth century that came with *Kristin Lavransdatter* was essentially a technical change, on a par with the change in scale; ... the characters in it, like those in her 'modern' works, are embodiments of a humanity and a human frailty that is timeless. The basic texture is the same; and if there seems at times a greater colourfulness in contrast to the earlier greyness, it is rather the lighting that has changed, and not the weave—like sackcloth illumined by stained glass. Some moments hint at the sagas, some of the linguistic elements of her style have a medievalism that is occasionally just a little indiscreet. But the realism is that of an author quite evidently much more at home in the chronicle than in, say, the *Novelle*. Her realism exploits the arrangement of mass detail rather than the economical selection of significant, and regards elaborateness itself as something inherent in life which, if subject to too severe a selective process, inevitably suffers distortion. (p. 162)

The emphasis in the design of [*Kristin Lavransdatter*] rests on the relations between individuals rather than on the qualities of the individuals themselves; and there is built up a network of relationships in which Kristin herself is the central and co-ordinating element. In one respect the trilogy serves as a disquisition on woman's loyalties: on the one hand, those which her menfolk importunately claim, her father, her husband and her sons; and on the other, those absolute loyalties she owes to God. It traces the consequences which this multi-dimensional conflict of claims has upon her life, upon her standards of conduct, her sense of integrity and self-respect; it considers how these claims often merge with other factors, the calls of instinct and impulse and desire, the dictates of will and conscience. It examines the nature of the accessory phenomena of sin and guilt and remorse, making a boldly patterned design, in which the pieces belong together with all the digressionary consistency of an individual life. The progression of the narrative through childhood and early maturity to adulthood, parenthood and age has the rhythm of organic growth, in which each moment has a significance and each stage a meaningfulness quite apart from its relevance to the ultimate design of things. Sigrid Undset is not concerned merely to complete her narrative pattern, but is intent on examining her theme at each stage in its development, and on demonstrating the consequential changes that occur in the total design with the advent of each new motif. (pp. 164-65)

Sigrid Undset, like her heroines, betrays an interest in stability that is almost obsessive. (p. 165)

[The] defining characteristic of her early heroines was an unstable equilibrium as they crossed and re-crossed the frontiers of respectability and disrepute, living between self-discipline and self-indulgence, between the observance of traditional decencies and the wilful pursuit of pleasure. Furthermore, it was the tampering with this situation that seems to make the later batch of 'contemporary' novels less of an artistic than a devotional expression. Sigrid Undset's conversion marked the completion of a process whereby her earlier scepticism of 'received' views found solace in the acceptance of dogma.... The artistic consequences were what D. H. Lawrence would not have hesitated to call 'immoral': 'Morality in the novel is the trembling instability of the balance. When the novelist puts his thumb in the scale, to pull down the balance to his own predilection, that is immorality.' (p. 168)

James Walter McFarlane, "Sigrid Undset," in his Ibsen and the Temper of Norwegian Literature *(© Oxford University Press 1960; reprinted by permission of Oxford University Press), Oxford University Press, London, 1960, pp. 158-68.*

CARL F. BAYERSCHMIDT   (essay date 1970)

[In *Fortellingen om Viga-Ljot og Vigdis (Gunnar's Daughter)*] Sigrid Undset has made an attempt to imitate the style and spirit of the Old Icelandic saga. The tale reflects all the stark violence consistent with the spirit of this early Christian period. In the silent fortitude with which she faces adversity, Vigdis is a woman of heroic grandeur, but she displays a relentless fury in the manner in which she carries out her vengeance to the grave. Despite the slightly conciliatory tone of the conclusion, Christianity had made no impression upon the minds of the principal characters of this tale. The world of dark violence is relieved but little by the humanity and understanding which Sigrid Undset shows in her later works.

In imitating the style of the saga Sigrid Undset has been only moderately successful. The Icelandic saga writers present the external facts in a clear and lucid style and let the reader draw his own conclusions from the circumstances as described. Character is revealed through the

subtle technique of understatement and through terse utterances and cutting rejoinders rather than through psychological analysis. In this way the author does not intrude upon the scene of action nor does he permit himself to make any moral judgments. Sigrid Undset attempts to observe a certain epic objectivity, but it is difficult for her with her great love for detail to adapt herself to the rigid limitations of such a style. As a woman of strong imagination and feeling she looks into the hearts of her characters. Behind the facts she sees human relationships where others see only drab details. *Gunnar's Daughter* is a tale written from a woman's point of view, and many of its passages, charged with emotion, are conceived in a style completely foreign to the saga. This genre did not allow Sigrid Undset the proper freedom which she needed in order to make full use of all her knowledge of the Middle Ages and to unfold a tapestry which depicts so brilliantly the atmosphere and color of bygone times. It was in her medieval novels that she was to find the proper vehicle for her narrative and expository talents. (pp. 66-7)

Carl F. Bayerschmidt, "Early Works," in his Sigrid Undset *(copyright © 1970 by Twayne Publishers, Inc.; reprinted with the permission of Twayne Publishers, A Division of G. K. Hall & Co., Boston), Twayne, 1970, pp. 55-67.*

BIBLIOGRAPHY

Beach, Joseph Warren. "Variations: Sigrid Undset." In his *The Twentieth Century Novel: Studies in Technique*, pp. 263-72. New York: Appleton-Century-Crofts, 1932.
  Analyzes the narrative devices that structure the chapters in Undset's novels.

Beck, Richard. "Sigrid Undset and Her Novels on Medieval Life." *Books Abroad* 24, No. 1 (Winter 1950): 5-10.
  Biographical sketch and introductory survey of the major novels.

Brady, Charles A. "An Appendix to the Sigridssaga." *Thought* XL, No. 156 (Spring 1965): 73-130.
  A discussion of Sigrid Undset's literary sources in the Nordic sagas, with an annotation and commentary by the novelist.

Dunn, Margaret Mary. "*The Master of Hestviken*: A New Reading: I and II." *Scandinavian Studies* 38, No. 4 (November 1966): 281-94; 40, No. 3 (August 1968): 210-24.
  Argues that Professor Alrik Gustafson's interpretation of *The Master of Hestviken* (see excerpt above) is a misreading that ignores the essentially "triumphant" vision of the work when seen as a whole. This is a two part article which examines *The Axe* and *The Snake Pit* in part one and *In the Wilderness* and *The Son Avenger* in part two.

McCarthy, Colman. "Sigrid Undset." *The Critic* XXXII, No. 3 (January-February 1974): 59-64.
  Biographical sketch and overview of the major novels, with plot outlines.

César (Abraham) Vallejo

1892-1938

Peruvian poet, journalist, playwright, and novelist.

Vallejo has been ranked with Pablo Neruda as one of the greatest South American poets of the century. His earthy, boldly-stated imagery and irrational personal logic, developments of the techniques of Apollinaire, set Vallejo's work apart from that of the more literary poets writing in Spanish during the twenties and thirties.

Death is a recurrent theme in Vallejo's poetry, and absurdity his consistent stance. In reaction to a God that he believed to be indifferent to human suffering, Vallejo pleaded for neighborly compassion in order to ease the pain of life. As a young man he became involved in leftist political activities in response to the social injustices, particularly the abuse of Indians, that he observed about him. Vallejo was jailed in 1920, by most reports unjustly, for his political activities. His bitterness over his imprisonment was reflected in *Trilce*, a collection of poems characterized by their pessimism and concern with death.

Vallejo left Peru in 1923 and settled in Paris. He never returned to his homeland. The revenue brought in by the leftist books and articles he wrote during the years in exile barely supported him, and he lived in illness and poverty to the end of his life. He briefly visited the Soviet Union several times, and eventually joined the Communist Party. Vallejo was expelled from France for political reasons in 1930. While visiting Spain he met several writers and thinkers of the Generation of 1927, including Rafael Alberti and Federico Garcia Lorca. He returned to Spain during the Civil War as a supporter of the Loyalists. His experiences in that land inspired Vallejo to write the poems collected in *España, aparta de mí este cáliz*. These poems and *Poemas humanos* were completed under the strain of mortal illness. It is believed that most of Vallejo's works remain unpublished in the possession of his widow.

PRINCIPAL WORKS

Los heraldos negros: Poemas (poetry) 1918
Trilce (poetry) 1922
Rusia en 1931: Reflexiones al pie del Kremlin (essays) 1931
Poemas humanos (1923-1938) (poetry) 1939
  [*Poemas humanos: Human Poems*, 1968]

España, aparta de mí este cáliz (poetry) 1940
  [*Spain, Let This Cup Pass from Me*, 1972]

XAVIER ABRIL (essay date 1958)

Many of the pages of *Human Poems* have an indefinable Chaplinesque tint, especially those that are charged with the feeling of desolate misfortune or stark abandonment, in which misery is like an X-ray of hunger and horror. Not merely in the characters, orphaned and abandoned in the world, who live like phantoms of pain, but, even more deeply, in the compassionate thought of some of the poems there is a cry of the age as well as the lament of time.

The accent of Vallejo that recalls Chaplin is by no means an echo of the great clown, the creator of the dramatic, subconscious victim, but lies rather in the coincidence of human emotion and human suffering. Long before Chaplin had developed his gesture of the laughing buffoon towards the tragic chill of *The Circus* and *The Gold Rush*, Vallejo had, in certain poems of *The Black Heralds* [*Los heraldos negros*] and *Trilce*, already sounded the note of hunger, pain, solitude, and death within the abstractions and shifts of time. (pp. 172-73)

Hunger, transcended, dreamlike, is what links Vallejo to Chaplin within the trend of a new aesthetic humanism. . . .

In the "Epistle to Passers-By," whose title somehow suggests Whitman and Chaplin at the same time, Vallejo alternates a satiric tone with images of pain and suffering. . . .

[Within the poem the] relationship to Chaplin is suggested . . . by the humorous contrast of two concepts, the two words, *rabbit* and *elephant;* the idea of work, suggested by the contrast of *day* and *night*, provides the impulse toward comedy. (p. 174)

[The last line "suffering as I suffer from the lion's direct speech] is one of Vallejo's most surprising, whose mysterious dual origin, spirit and animality, seems to spring powerfully from the metaphysical source of language itself. It is an expression which reaches out and touches an anthropomorphical god. The poet officiates with his own essence, suffers from the unknown malady of speech, whose symptoms are the symbolic, the sacred. (p. 175)

[In another stanza, the imagery of a dirty] shoe (a touch of Van Gogh?) is just like a portrait of Chaplin, the sharpest expression of his inner being, the classic attribute of the tramp. The nomad's shoe becomes a symbol which is inseparable from the nomad himself.

This poem is Vallejo's great farewell. In other poems one finds isolated allusions to a sense of approaching old age, allusions that together define his mortal vocation; but none are like those in "Paris, October 1936." Here the poet confines himself to his particular case in such an organic way that he reconciles subjective self-analysis with objective confrontation of reality. With his peculiar and characteristic sense of synthesis, dazzled by fatality, he has achieved what might be called a sum of the senses, a sum of the most apt and exact concepts of physical and spiritual crisis. Intuition and experience have influenced and determined the achievement of this chilling poem which seems to have written itself at the very limits of awareness and horror.

After a study of Vallejo's autobiographical poem, which to my mind so marvelously corresponds to the dramatic vision Chaplin hints at in the dimensions of the visual and the plastic, there remain other metaphors of the poet which show how the process has been more or less synchronized. (pp. 176-77)

["Stumble Between Two Stars" is] one of the most extraordinarily human poems that Vallejo ever wrote. . . . [It contains] the most vehement expressions of the poet's shattered and defenseless sensibility. Each line has an absolute value, and its unity is of a higher order and greater than the sum of its structure and its form. The variety and richness of the images run the whole gamut of adversity as well as of irony, elementality, pathos, despair, misery, pity, lyricism, and love, always love, for the saddest and most incredible things.

These very images most vividly bring to mind, both in actuality and in imagination, the being and the possibility of being which, to us, are "Chaplin."

Human Poems and *Spain, Let This Cup Pass* are something more than two books. They are a quarry and a fountain of inexhaustible prophecy. They are the glorious work of a poet filled with all the experiences of life, with the highest as well as the meanest records of consciousness, neither cancelling out the other as so often happens in unperceptive "surrealist" art. As the subconscious registers both light and darkness, chaos and order, so Vallejo has confronted and squarely faced the dregs of his soul and of the world. (pp. 178-79)

Vallejo's work cannot be compared to any other seemingly similar work. The dialectical Vallejo surpasses in imagination and in realism all the alchemists of verse, the strategists of rhetoric, the useless shipwrecked victims of language: greedy victims, fat with the sweet bloat of the baroque. (pp. 179-80)

In Vallejo's poetry man exists with all his vicissitudes, hopes, and despairs, as he does in Chaplin's art. . . . In *Black Heralds* there are some allusions to labor, to peasants, to field workers, and teamsters, but the word "worker," the reference to the proletariat, appears for the first time in *Trilce,* and is to be repeated later, soberly, in *Human Poems* and in *Spain, Let This Cup Pass.* (pp. 187-88)

[Within his poetry], the word "worker" is not excessively used and it is for this very reason that the theme of the worker achieves a much greater intensity in Vallejo than it does in whole books dedicated exclusively and demagogically to slogans and propaganda. Here lies the difference in attitudes between the propagandist and the true poet. Vallejo does not idealize the worker as such, because he is interested in the human condition above all contingencies and classifications. There is no hidden motive in his work that could displace his legitimate defense. In Chaplin, the same specific and free vocation also prevails, over and above the fleetingly tendentious. (p. 188)

The relationship between Chaplin and Vallejo dates back to *Black Heralds* and *Trilce,* but it reaches its deepest intensity in *Human Poems* and *Spain, Let This Cup Pass.* (p. 189)

Chaplin comes across to me from the sensitive medium of the film as mocked and fallen. He was, like Vallejo, the chosen victim of crows and watchdogs. Descendants of Don Quixote, they are brothers in their fate, now in the cause of liberty, now in its sequel, prison. (p. 190)

> *Xavier Abril, "Chaplin and Vallejo" (1958), translated by Tina de Aragon, in* Odyssey Review *(copyright © 1962 by the Latin American and European Literary Society, Incorporated), Vol. 2, No. 1, March, 1962, pp. 172-90.*

CLAYTON ESHLEMAN   (essay date 1968-69)

[For Vallejo, Spain's *agon* of revolution] became his own in the *España* sheaf, . . . although in *Poemas Humanos* this struggle is interiorized & then projected to all man, in Vallejo's own person, as contradiction & violence therein. Only one of *Poemas Humanos* is overtly political, "Angelic Greeting," written in the early thirties at the height of his Marxist Conversion. Even then he was not much off his own center: he believes and doesn't believe; revolution, he says, thru its violent means of betrayal is and is not a solution; perhaps it is the best non-solution. For in Vallejo there is no solution other than death, as "solution" dissolving all. . . . All solutions as such fade, in *Poemas Humanos,* before all-powerful death; it is as if man never dies but lives eternally at the edge of death; Vallejo is the great poet of the End and in this respect he reminds one of Baudelaire—he is filled with it, an anguish, a Black Midas. (pp. 73-4)

> *Clayton Eshleman, "Translating César Vallejo: An Evolution," in* TriQuarterly *(© 1968 by TriQuarterly), No. 13/14, Fall-Winter, 1968-69, pp. 55-82.*

GEORGE GORDON WING   (essay date 1969)

While recognizing the incalculable value of [Eduardo] Neale-Silva's pioneering work [see excerpt below] . . . , nevertheless I should like to propose in this essay a variant of his reading of *Trilce I.* . . . [From] among the many possible approaches to this key poem which might have shed light on the essential qualities of Vallejo's achievement, it seems to me that he has elected the one that is perhaps least fruitful—he reads it as an allegory. In the case of *Trilce I* this approach is fatal, for it involves the arbitrary superposition of a rational *a priori* scheme—the allegorical framework—on the poem from without, an initial step for which the poem itself provides no real justification or evidence to support what Neale-Silva considers its central meaning. . . .

In short, it seems fairly obvious that Neale-Silva's allegorical framework was derived largely from a knowledge (real or mythical) of Vallejo's life rather than from the context of the poem itself. (p. 269)

Trilce I is a poem in which the separate elements are loosely organized around a central theme, never stated explicitly, but which is, as we shall see, a variation on one of the most familiar in all of Vallejo's poetry—orphanhood. Moreover, as in so many of the poems of *Trilce*, the dramatization of the poetic process itself, the poet's struggle against the inadequacy of traditional form and conventional language, must be considered an integral part of the theme. Of course, it may be possible for the reader to appreciate the poem without consciously recognizing the ubiquity of the main theme, for Vallejo has hidden it away like a deeper figure in the carpet which the surface imagery both reveals and conceals. Nevertheless, the total effect of the poem depends ultimately on Vallejo's technique of indirection—the sporadic, gradual, and perhaps deliberately incomplete revelation of the theme, which becomes the most important unifying factor in a poem marked by external formlessness and apparent internal disorder, hallmarks of *Trilce* as well as of so much of the new poetry of the period in which it was written. (p. 270)

One of the most damaging omissions of Vallejo's critics . . . has been their failure to recognize the central role of the comic in *Trilce*. It is literally impossible, for example, to appreciate *Trilce I*, unless we are prepared to see it as a marvelous *jeu d'esprit*, an extended joke of Rabelaisian proportions in which Vallejo, adopting a tone of ironic self-mockery, resorts to punning, burlesque, and in general to the humor of the absurd. Moreover, the mockery is double-edged, aimed also at those unimaginative readers and hyper-genteel critics whose responses to the basic situation of the poem, obtuseness and timorous prudery, doubtlessly foreseen by Vallejo, make of them a kind of unconscious and greatly exaggerated caricature of the "dramatic I" or *persona* of the poem who is faced with the same situation.

The basic comic effect of the poem derives, of course, from the disproportion that most adult readers would feel to exist between the banality and coarseness of the "dramatic situation" (a man's privacy threatened as he defecates) and the high seriousness of the theme (man's essential solitude and orphanhood). Indeed Vallejo exploits the ludicrous sentimentality inherent in this disproportion, not by denying the emotions which most of us (including no doubt the poet himself) would consider excessive or unwarranted by the situation, but rather by employing reticence and indirection, concealment and ambiguity in the imagery with which he evokes the situation itself. The exaggerated use of reticence throughout the poem is, of course, a kind of parody of the "normal" human reaction on discovering that one's emotions have been triggered by an apparently unworthy and perhaps unmentionable stimulus. It is this choice of reticence, furthermore, which dictates the basically comic strategy of the poem and accounts for a great deal of its complexity—the imagery designed to conceal as well as reveal the "dramatic" situation of the poem is also the source of its wry humor and irony because of the extravagance of the puns, metaphors, and implied comparisons. On the other hand, the complexity of the poem and its total impact is greatly increased by the fact that the same imagery must point beyond this situation in itself and evoke the anguished feelings of homelessness and orphanhood arising naturally from it. In short, although Vallejo's general tone and attitude are essentially comic, the total effect of the poem is deliberately ambiguous and its impact depends on the tension generated by the confrontation of unresolved opposites. In a sense, then, the real subject of *Trilce I* is the self-dramatization of the poetic "I" in a manner that points up the fundamental division of the mind. This dramatization is at once a comment on the human condition in general and the expression of the moral and psychological terrors that haunt a concrete modern man. (pp. 271-72)

[Vallejo] is by temperament essentially a romantic. Indeed, most of the poems of *Trilce* are clearly intended to be self-expressive of a poetic "I" that is probably meant to differ in no significant respect from César Vallejo himself. The subject matter of the poems is invariably the private experience and emotions of the poet, and if we tend to think of *Trilce* as a completely revolutionary book, we should do well to keep in mind that it also represents the culmination of the romanticism of a poet for whom Wordsworth's dictum that "all good poetry is the spontaneous overflow of powerful feeling" would surely strike a responsive chord.

It is this concept of the poem as spontaneous self-expression (implicit in *Trilce*) that distinguishes Vallejo from Mallarmé and the literary symbolists. The idea of the poem as a skillfully constructed artifact for producing purely aesthetic effects, or of the poet as an impersonal craftsman working with abstract, algebraic language is completely alien to Vallejo. Therefore, when I have spoken of the dramatization of the poetic process itself as a kind of theme in *Trilce*, this is not to say that the reader must look for a classical ordering of the various linguistic counters in an aesthetic object intended to be autonomous and completely self-reflexive. Dramatization of the poetic process in a poem by Vallejo must be understood as a function of the problematic relation of the poetic "I" to the external world, a dramatization of the refractory nature of language as a mediator between the poet and his human environment. It is a dramatization of an indomitable will to communicate specifically human experiences and feelings in a language that is shown to be agonizingly inadeqate. Finally, the importance given by Vallejo to the comic and the absurd is also a clear indication that temperamentally and artistically he stands at the opposite pole from the symbolists whose unrelieved gravity and solemn humility befitted the priesthood of a movement that had deified art at the expense of the artist.

In retrospect, it should be apparent that Vallejo's *Trilce* is a product of the general literary and artistic climate of the pre-surrealistic stage of the French and Spanish avant-garde movements of this century. Huidobro and the Ultraists, for example, with whose works Vallejo was certainly acquainted, were part of a general movement that was based on the negation of what Roger Shattuck has called the earlier arts of *transition* (including the essential classicism of Mallarmé) in favor of a radical art of *juxtaposition*. (pp. 282-83)

George Gordon Wing, "Trilce I: A Second Look," in Revista Hispánica Moderna: Columbia University Hispanic Studies, *Vol. XXXV, No. 3, January-April, 1969, pp. 268-84.*

M. L. ROSENTHAL   (essay date 1969)

Slightly more than half the manuscripts of "Poemas Humanos" were dated by the poet; they appear to have been written, or at any rate to have reached final form, over a three months' period at the end of 1937. . . .

[The] 52 dated poems are indeed a unique constellation. These are poems of cruel suffering, physical and mental, which yet have a kind of joy of realization in their singular music, harshness, humor and pain. They are clear as brook-water; you can see through them to the specific awareness and feeling, the sharply exuberant self, green and alive, growing at the bottom, while at the same time they are elusive and changing.

Motifs flow together, and an imagery of bitter, impotent male love moves through transferences of direction into wider implications, perhaps political, perhaps philosophical, and constantly elegiac; often some witty reversal of image will suddenly and unsentimentally turn the tone into one of affirmation as if in spite of itself. Even when Vallejo seems to *want* to be sentimental (as in the untitled poem beginning "There comes over me days a feeling so abundant, political"), his phrasing crackles so brilliantly with its own life that it carries him into an original statement of the predicament of a would-be generous, truthful spirit.

The technical range of these poems, as well as of many of the undated ones, is striking in its variety and its functional virtuosity. They are sometimes tightly formal structures and sometimes quite improvisational ones, and they move easily between colloquial directness and the most exquisitely pure and imaginative language reaching toward complex and concentrated effects. A poem like "Yokes" is a triumph at once of structural simplicity and of emotional projection through sheer mastery of syntax. And although Vallejo, described by Pierre Lagarde as having "invented Surrealism before the Surrealists," could proliferate metaphors like meteors, he shows by his endings that he was not just "letting go"—fascinating as that can be—but was able to recognize and control the design of image-motifs despite the tremendous speed with which they emerged in his poems.

Vallejo is like Keats in his enhanced sense, related to his illness and concerned anguish, of life-on-the-edge-of-death. He adds certain dimensions of a later sensibility—of the literal, the violent, the seedy, the hard-pressed. He is the essential poet of the modern city, the infinitely charitable man himself in need of charity who can summon up Dante and Chaplin as alternative selves in the same line.

> M. L. Rosenthal, "Poems of Singular Music, Harshness, Humor and Pain," in The New York Times Book Review (© 1969 by The New York Times Company; reprinted by permission), March 23, 1969, p. 8.

EDUARDO NEALE-SILVA   (essay date 1970)

[For] many students of literature, *Trilce* . . . is César Vallejo's most important and most challenging work from the standpoint of both form and content. . . .

We believe that it is precisely in the totality of each poem where the meaning of much of Vallejo's poetry is to be found. A good example is *Trilce I*. . . . (p. 2)

A cursory examination of this poem brings to the minds of most Spanish-speaking readers a confusing mixture of ideas that do not fall into a clear pattern. The language and struc-ture seem to contribute to the poem's obscurity. . . . The poem also contains ambiguities, solecisms and double meanings. (p. 4)

It may be quite possible that a poet—and we know this was Vallejo's case—may purposely seek to convey a plurality of meanings. (p. 5)

Trilce I can be read on two semantic levels. The primary level weaves into a surrealistic pattern the various components of a Peruvian seascape: guano islands, pelicans, squawks, shrieks and Nature's balance. The poem, however, cannot be reduced to such simple terms. It contains many connotations that clearly point to a secondary semantic level: "to give testimony" (*testar*), "insular heart" (*insular corazón*), "unafraid" (*impertérrita*), etc. All these quotations suggest a human content and some kind of interaction allegorically related to the seascape.

It is difficult to believe that as discerning and conscientious a writer as Vallejo would have been satisfied with a simple scene of bird defecation or, for that matter, with the concept of universal elimination for the opening selection of his new book. . . . Vallejo most likely felt that his forthcoming volume also required some sort of preliminary statement, especially in view of the radical departure from Hispanic models implicit in his Trilcean verses. To be sure, he could anticipate a negative reaction in most readers and critics. (p. 8)

When *Trilce* finally appeared . . . even some perceptive students of literature were puzzled. What could the poet expect from others, from ordinary readers, from pedestrian critics?

Vallejo must have felt like a solitary island surrounded by a sea of incomprehension. The image of the sea so often present in his poetry as an ominous expanse of water must have come to his mind time and again. "I withdraw from the sea," he states in *Trilce XLV;* "how awful, how atrocious you look," he adds in *Trilce LXIX.* The sea remained in his mind as the symbol of a "philosophy of black wings." The association of the ocean with the guano islands was the next step. These islands are the habitat of millions of sea birds whose droppings are sold as fertilizer. Vallejo must have meditated on his poetic self in connection with these islands, which he specifically mentions again in *Trilce XXV:* ". . . from the guano islands / to the guano islands." In *Trilce XLVII* he even identifies himself with a plankton-covered rock (*ciliado arrecife*).

Right here is the key to the secondary level of meaning: Vallejo was anticipating the unceremonious reception he would have and wished to affirm his decision to weather the shower from the pelicans of criticism. (pp. 9-10)

Trilce I is a reaffirmation of the artist's faith in himself. What Vallejo said of the "pelicans" is exactly what Darío had stated in the introduction to *Prosas profanas* (Profane Proses) concerning the "geese" of criticism: "The hissing of three hundred geese will not prevent you, oh, Silvano, from playing your magic flute." In a larger sense, Vallejo's protest is the same one any man would voice when he has been maltreated by untutored, self-appointed judges. (pp. 15-16)

Vallejo is a poet of subtleties, one who demands a special mental attitude of empathy and collaboration and also a willingness to let imagination project and construct. (p. 16)

Eduardo Neale-Silva, "The Introductory Poem in Vallejo's 'Trilce'," in Hispanic Review, *Vol. 38, No. 1, January, 1970, pp. 2-16.*

ANDREW P. DEBICKI (essay date 1970)

César Vallejo's poetry reveals a profound sense of the tragedy of life. The irrational, unjustified sufferings burdening Man are first stressed in *Heraldos negros,* pervade the later *Trilce,* and culminate in the emotionally charged *Poemas humanos.* As Vallejo's poetry develops, it comes to stress brotherhood among men as a means of overcoming such unjustified sufferings.

This theme of human suffering could easily have led Vallejo's poetry into sentimentalism, into an expression of feelings which we as readers would not share. The tragic nature of life is hardly news, and a declaration concerning it could easily become commonplace. A defense of solidarity as a solution for Man seems like a narrow message, not a full poetic experience. Yet Vallejo, working with a theme and a view very difficult to embody in poetry, somehow manages to avoid both sentimentality and narrowness of scope. His best poems transcend commonplace romantic laments and limited messages concerning solidarity.

They do so, to my mind, by means of several poetic techniques. One of the most important, which appears in all of Vallejo's books of poetry, is the use of a particular point of view. A poem is uttered by a specific down-to-earth speaker, who focuses on physical details of reality. This speaker brings a tragic outlook on life down to a very concrete level. At the same time, by finding wider meanings in the common objects around him, he draws a significant vision out of ordinary settings. At times, especially in the later poems, he shifts tones and comments ironically about himself. In all cases, he turns Vallejo's theme into an experience which is on the one hand tangible and complex, and on the other essential and far-reaching. In this fashion, he keeps the poem from being either simplistic or commonplace.

Some of this is apparent in "La de a mil," from *Heraldos negros.* . . . In linking God with a lottery ticket seller, the poem obviously suggests the arbitrary and meaningless nature of divine fate in the world described. . . . Everything [in the poem] echoes the pessimistic vision of our world's order which pervades all of *Heraldos negros.* (pp. 247-49)

[We] notice that the same physical details which give immediacy to the poem point, at the same time, to its wider vision. . . . The lottery ticket salesman so vividly observed by the speaker becomes a metaphor for an impotent divinity: his cries offer a meaningless fate, his tickets are unreachable rewards. Vallejo is making the speaker of his poem simultaneously underline the tangible aspects of the scene, and find within these aspects indications of a wider vision. In this fashion he brings together, and fuses, a particular experience and a significant outlook. His poem becomes a "concrete universal," free of unreal abstractions and equally free of inconsequential trivia.

"La de a mil" does not contain any obvious irony, such as we will see in some later poems of Vallejo. But the perspective of its speaker does create a tension in the reader. The latter is obviously surprised at the joining of two such disproportionate elements as the theme of a meaningless fate and the story of a lottery seller. He may also find surprising

the simultaneous emphasis placed on the tangible reality and on a wider theme. Such juxtapositions help the poem; they dispel the danger of its seeming commonplace or cliché. They lead, in addition, to a yet more important effect. (pp. 249-50)

Having initially shocked us by a comparison between a trivial character selling tickets and a divinity tragically misleading Man, the speaker gradually works out a series of relationships between the two. He makes us see that a connection can be made. In the process, he dramatizes again the finding of a wider theme in a common, tangible reality. In this way too he merges the descriptive and the philosophic levels of the work, helping create an experience both particular and absolute, a good poem. (p. 250)

Vallejo's *Trilce,* on first impression, differs greatly from *Heraldos negros.* The lack of a logical structure in many poems, and the presence of seemingly disconnected and enigmatic images and of word-play, make the book resemble some of the "dehumanized" vanguard poems of its era. Yet, as Luis Monguió has noted, an emotive vision akin to that of *Heraldos negros* underlies the book. The images and other elements of many poems of *Trilce* may not connect rationally, but they do embody very effectively the state of mind of an anguished speaker, and in that way convey Vallejo's vision. The non-logical links and the syntheses of various realities make us aware that the episodes of the poem are seen and transformed by this anguished speaker's perspective. In that fashion, they stress the tragedy of a specific being, crystalized in a given state of emotion at a particular setting. They keep the poem from falling into a generalized sentimental message.

This is evident in Poem II of *Trilce.* . . . In it the protagonist finds in a country scene details which he connects with his feelings about the monotony and the suffering brought on by time. . . .

Everyday scenes linked to a speaker's tragic awareness abound in *Trilce.* In Poem LXIII, a rainy morning evokes melancholy and nostalgia; in Poem XXI, December represents collapse and misfortune; in Poem XXVIII, a lunch among strangers recalls the speaker's loneliness; in Poem VI, dirty clothes stand for injustice. Throughout the book, bits and pieces of ordinary experiences are recalled to embody an attitude of meaninglessness and anxiety. These elements are therefore signs, sometimes even symbols, of wider concerns. Very much like the everyday details in "La de a mil," they embody more elusive meanings in ordinary and tangible objects. Yet they are always seen through the eyes of a particular speaker, and acquire further meanings in his view. Therefore their suggestive or symbolic nature does not make the work abstract or excessively philosophic. It serves, rather, as one more way of tying wider issues to immediate experience.

Occasionally we find in *Trilce* ironic statements directed at himself by the speaker. . . . (p. 253)

In other poems, Vallejo obtains similar results without . . . evident irony; he does so by shifting from an elevated to a pedestrian tone. . . . Such shifts in tone avoid cliché and sentimentalism by surprising us, as well as by undercutting the protagonist's previous declarations. They too illustrate how Vallejo keeps using tone and point of view to situate the pessimistic vision of *Trilce* in concrete experience, and to avoid excess rhetoric, abstraction, and sentimentalism.

A particular speaker who finds wider meanings in the details of ordinary reality, and whose tone affects our reaction to these meanings, is even more apparent in Vallejo's *Poemas humanos.* In "Los nueve monstruos," such a speaker presents the sufferings of modern man and the need to alleviate them. . . . (p. 254)

A violent declaration of human suffering is here modified by the objects mentioned [in the poem]. A random list of modern items sets the scene in our common world, brings the subject close to the reality we know. . . . In addition, by addressing itself to the minister of health instead of a traditional muse or divinity, the poem becomes an ordinary modern plea to the authorities.

More importantly, the random list of objects, or chaotic enumeration, calls attention to the speaker. In themselves, the items named do not relate to each other; nor do they objectively reflect human suffering. By mixing them together and by finding suffering in all of them the poem adopts the perspective of a particular anguished person, who desperately picks out objects at random and reads his vision into all of them. . . . The very difference between the items named stresses that the protagonist can manage to find suffering in anything, and on any plane. This technique, therefore, makes us very aware that the poem is spoken by a particular emotive being, and not by a generalized poetic voice. The poem becomes the embodiment of this particular being's plight, not a generalized lament and sermon by Vallejo, which we might have dismissed. (p. 255)

Normally, a shift from an elevated to a pedestrian tone would seem comic; it has been used for comic effect by prose writers as different as Ricardo Palma and Camilo José Cela. Yet here it makes us, instead, understand and sympathize with the speaker's plight. This confirms, in my opinion, the view that the irony is here a poetic technique which protects the work from sentimentality. It balances what would have been excessive complaining on the part of the speaker with an awareness of his own limitations. Thus it makes his (and the poem's) outlook a complex, yet at the same time cohesive rendering of Man's tragedy—and not a mere contrast to make us laugh.

An ironic tone is [also] noticeable in "Traspié entre dos estrellas." . . . The poem presents an important theme of *Poemas humanos,* the desire of overcoming suffering by means of love and solidarity among men. The protagonist's plea for humanity, which could so easily have seemed sentimental, avoids that danger. His use of trivial details and comic vignettes, especially when linked with parallelistic phrases which create a litany-like tone, suggest the same self-awareness which we noted in "Los nueve monstruos." Allusions to petty and comic human figures indicate that the speaker makes his plea not in romantic ignorance of human weaknesses, but in spite of a full awareness of these weaknesses. This makes his plea not the facile ravings of a sentimentalist, but the insightful search for ideals on the part of someone who realizes all too well the limitations of his world, and of himself.

In all three of César Vallejo's major books of poetry a specific speaker, focusing on concrete details, gives immediacy to wider themes, and protects them from seeming commonplace and sentimental. As Vallejo's poetry develops and as its vision of life's tragedy intensifies, this speaker's role becomes more and more evident. In the process, ironic comments and tone shifts become more frequent and important, and the concrete details used point more directly to the speaker. Throughout all of the poems studied, however, the techniques of point of view, tone, and description which we have observed convert an emotive theme and outlook into full and acceptable experiences for the reader—into good poems. (pp. 257-58)

Andrew P. Debicki, "César Vallejo's Speaker and the Poetic Transformation of Commonplace Themes," in Kentucky Romance Quarterly (© University Press of Kentucky; reprinted by permission of Kentucky Romance Quarterly), Vol. XVII, No. 3, 1970, pp. 247-58.

JAMES HIGGINS (essay date 1970)

[*Los heraldos negros*] contains sixty-nine poems grouped rather arbitrarily in six sections. Only two of these sections —*Nostalgias imperiales* and *Canciones de hogar*—have any real unity and character of their own. *Nostalgias imperiales* initiates a current of nativism and localism in Peruvian poetry. These are poems about the Peruvian countryside, its people, their labours, their diversions, their way of life. The *canciones de hogar* are among the best poems in the collection. Vallejo identified happiness with the integrated and protected world of the home and the family. *Los pasos lejanos* and *A mi hermano Miguel* . . . mark the beginning of the break-up of that world. The latter poem is addressed to the poet's elder brother Miguel, the playmate of his childhood years, who died on 22 August 1915. The effectiveness of the poem proceeds from the opposition of past and present and the alternate superimposition of the one on the other. (p. 7)

[*Enereida*] presents a vision of the paternal home in Santiago. The poet is absent and the other children have also left home, so that the parents are alone. The poem is concentrated on the figures of the father, characterized by his noble and generous heart, and the mother, the image of maternal love. The poem stresses the silence and emptiness of the house: now that the children have grown up and left, the parents feel old and lonely. The son, by his absence, introduces bitterness into the harmony of the family circle. He experiences a sense of guilt and a melancholy tenderness. Separated from his parents in space, he returns to them through his love. . . .

A large proportion of the poems deal with love themes. *Setiembre* and *Heces* refer to a relationship with Zoila Rosa Cuadra in Trujillo in 1917. (p. 8)

The best poems in the volume are those dealing with existential themes. *Los heraldos negros* is a poetry of suffering: of anguish in face of existence. *Espergesia* . . . introduces us to a theme that is to recur in Vallejo's later poetry, that of the outsider, the man whose vision of life is different from that of other people, who has perceived the meaninglessness of life and can no longer feel himself at home in the universe as others do. (p. 9)

In Vallejo's world some dark, menacing force of evil pursues man and strikes down blows of misfortune upon him. The poem *Los heraldos negros* . . . opens with an affirmation of the existence of such blows. The poet feels himself to be in the presence of something hostile but is unable to understand or explain or even describe these blows. The most he can do is to advance a series of approximations: it is as if God, with all his omnipotence, had directed all his hatred against man; it is as if all the suffering of the past had erupted in the present, so that a lifetime's suffering is experienced in a single moment. In the following stanzas the poet describes physically the effect of these blows and enumerates a series of images in a renewed attempt to describe and explain them. Towards the end of the poem, however, he abandons this attempt and offers us an image of man: a prey to terror, he looks over his shoulder waiting for the next blow to fall. In the course of the poem there is no progression. The poem ends, as it began, with affirmation of the existence of these blows and the poet's inability to understand them, and suffering appears as a vicious circle with no way out. It is significant that this poem should open the book and give it its title: Vallejo clearly intended that it should set the tone for the whole collection. The dark forces of evil hang menacingly over the whole volume. (pp. 10-11)

Los heraldos negros is essentially a book of transition: in it we see Vallejo gradually free himself from literary influences and move towards a poetry that is a genuine expression of his own personal experience and emotions. The influence of Romanticism is to be noted in poems such as *Los dados eternos* and *La de a mil* which tend to be cerebral and unspontaneous in their conception and in their treatment of existential situations, while there is also a tendency to strike attitudes, as in *Espergesia*. Several poems are purely literary, dealing with themes that are part of the baggage of Modernism. Thus, *Nochebuena,* with its *fête galante* atmosphere, recalls [Ruben] Darío's *Era un aire suave*. The poem is set in moonlit gardens where music and perfume fill the air and shadowy female figures flit past in the darkness. In this refined setting the woman appears as a divine being whose love, like Jesus, offers redemption. There are also reminiscences of Darío in the poet's obsession with the flesh and his subsequent moments of repentance as in *La copa negra* and *Amor prohibido*. The influence of Modernism is also evident in the expression, in a tendency to poeticize reality, dressing it up in pretentious literary language and imagery.

At the same time there is a process of purification as Vallejo gradually breaks loose from these influences. The poems become more authentic, more personal and spontaneous in their inspiration and the poetic emotion is expressed simply and directly. (pp. 14-15)

Trilce is a collection of seventy-seven poems, each of which is designated by a Roman numeral. The principal theme of the volume is perhaps the destruction of the happiness of the past. In poem *XXXIII* . . . Vallejo states that he cannot free himself from the misery of his present situation. It is not what life holds in store for him that causes him anguish, but what has been taken away from him and never recovered. Happiness is identified with the past and with people who have gone out of his life—his mother, now dead, and Otilia, now separated from him—and consequently it is irredeemably lost.

A series of poems follow on from the *canciones de hogar* of *Los heraldos negros,* which, as we have seen, signal the beginnings of the break-up of the integrated world of the home and the family. In *Trilce* the death of the poet's mother has completed the destruction of that world. Poem *LXI* . . . is a vision of the poet's return to Santiago on the eve of the feast of St. James. He arrives home late at night and calls at the door, but the house is in darkness, the door is closed and no one answers. The home that once rang with the playful laughter of children is now silent. Instead of the loving family circle he expected he finds only an empty house. For Vallejo the home and the family represent the supreme value and this abandoned house is the symbol of the emptiness and desolation of his adult life. (pp. 17-18)

The volume also contains a number of love poems, most of which seem to refer to Vallejo's affair with Otilia. Some are characterized by their eroticism. Thus poem *LXXI* . . . describes a moment of unity and fulfilment achieved through the sexual act. Knowing only too well that such moments are short-lived, the poet tries to shut out of his mind thoughts of future unhappiness. In his state of orphanhood he must snatch at happiness wherever he can find it.

In general, however, the stress is less on the sexual aspect of love than on woman's maternal nature. Vallejo seems to seek in Otilia a substitute mother figure. (p. 20)

A series of poems refer to Vallejo's persecution and imprisonment. In poem *XXII* . . . the poet, in hiding, feels that he is being persecuted by the inhuman representatives of bourgeois society because of his ideals of equality and justice which are feared as a threat to the established order. Outside the sun is shining but it is raining, so that the sun appears as a broken-down lamp and seems to be begging from itself the light it has lost. The sun is the image of the poet's own condition and in a sense his fate is linked to it. The light of his liberty has been darkened and he longs for it to be restored. But the sun is also a symbol of hope, for if he can look forward to the prospect of a full sun which will light up the dark corners of his room, he can equally look forward to the prospect of liberty. He promises that when he is free he will work towards his ideal of a just world in which all men will be united in brotherly love. Thus, despite his persecution, his morale and his ideals remain intact. (p. 22)

One of the most important themes of the volume is the attempt to transcend the misery and limitations of the human condition and to attain a meaningful and satisfying existence. (p. 25)

Trilce, then, is a poetry of existential anguish. For Vallejo the happiness of the past has been destroyed and he is trapped in the misery of the present. He desperately strives to break out of the vicious circle of his suffering in two directions. He struggles to find an individual solution to his own personal dilemma, and he moves towards his fellow men. These two aspects come together in his later poetry as he realizes that his own situation is linked to that of others and that redemption can be thought of only in collective terms. (p. 31)

[In] *Trilce* most of the poems lie between two extremes. On the one hand, there are poems in which the language is relatively simple and straightforward and the imagery clear. Such poems generally refer to concrete experiences—childhood, imprisonment, a love affair—and the poet's response to them tends to be emotional. On the other, there are poems in which the language is complex and contorted and the imagery hermetic. These generally refer to the anguish of the poet's condition and are intellectual and abstract in character. In a number of poems both expressions exist side by side. Most poems contain obscurities. Occasionally a poem is completely incomprehensible. . . .

In common with other avant-garde poets Vallejo tends to reduce poetry to essentials, eliminating the anecdotic and descriptive, cutting out adjectives whose function is purely decorative, and suppressing intermediate phrases and connectives. Consequently, his poetry is remarkably elliptic and concentrated. (p. 33)

Vallejo stands apart from other modern poets in that the basis of his poetry is not imagery but language, and his originality springs from his original use of language. It has been said that Vallejo writes as if he were unaware of the existence of language and syntax and creates his own. (p. 36)

Vallejo's final works move between two poles, the absurd world of the present and an ideal world of the future. On the one hand, most of *Poemas humanos* expresses the poet's anguish, the misery of the human condition, the absurdity of existence; on the other, [*España, aparta de mí este cáliz*] and a number of compositions from *Poemas humanos* prophesy a future in which man will dominate nature and control his destiny. (p. 44)

In an absurd world the poet, aspiring to unity, finds himself surrounded by chaos, disorder, division. To translate this disorder and chaos Vallejo employs two basic techniques. One is to break with the norms of logic, reversing the order we normally assume to be present in the universe. In *Los nueve monstruos* . . . he explains that experience of suffering opens our eyes to the chaos around us. Then we see things in reverse: water flows vertically, eyes are seen instead of seeing, ears emit noises instead of hearing them. The second technique is much more common: the juxtaposition of opposites. Vallejo was obsessed by the contradictions inherent in life, with the fact that day cannot exist without night, heat without cold, good without bad, life without death, etc. This obsession manifests itself in the form of verbal oppositions. Thus ¿ *Qué me da* . . . ? . . . is made up of couplets in which the last term of the second line opposes the last term of the first. Those stanzas which do not conform exactly to this pattern contain some element of opposition within them. In this way the poem opposes eternity and time, life and death, body and soul, the individual and his fellow men, aspiration and reality, sorrow and joy. In the last line the poet states that he is neither alive nor dead. More exactly, he is alive in so far as he is breathing, but he is dead in that he does not live fully. He indicates, too, that these contradictions have ceased to matter to him: in an absurd world nothing matters, nothing has any importance. (p. 45)

Vallejo's preoccupation with death is nowhere more clearly expressed than in *Sermón sobre la muerte* . . . where death is seen as an advancing army sweeping before it all the things of life. The poem is based on a series of rhetorical questions revolving around three basic points which particularly torment the poet. Firstly, if man must die, what need does he have of food and sermons? What does it avail him to sustain body and soul if he is to die anyway? All provisions to sustain life are superfluous since they are useless. Secondly, if man must die, why must he die little by little? Why must each moment of life be a death, why must life be a constant and progressive dying? Thirdly, what meaning do human activities and values have in face of death? What lasting significance do the achievements of human civilizations have? Death seems to make life pointless. None the less, the poet expresses his determination to resist death with all the resources he can call forth. He will continue to

struggle against the absurd, praying with his whole being for a better world and striving to achieve peace and repose. He will multiply himself so that he is in all places ready to ward off an attack from whatever side it may come. He takes pride in his struggle against the absurd and its ultimate manifestation, death, for it is in this struggle that human dignity resides. (pp. 53-4)

A feature of *Poemas humanos* is the absence of references to God. In Vallejo's universe God does not manifest himself: man is abandoned to his own resources and can expect no aid from a divine source. (p. 56)

[The idea that the way out of the impasse of the absurd is through human solidarity] is expressed in *Hasta el día en que vuelva*. . . . Here life is seen as a journey which ends at its starting-point: the poet must live his life knowing that he must return to the void from which he has come, symbolized by the stone. He goes through life a cripple, incomplete and incapable of attaining his goals, embittered by one disappointment after another, yet holding his head erect. The poet affirms that the absurdity of existence does not give man the right to comport himself in a cynical and egoistic fashion: he has a responsibility towards his fellow men. He sees death as a day of final judgement but significantly speaks not of a judge but of judges: he will be judged not by God but by his fellow men and the criterion of a good life is his comportment towards others. The poem ends with an apotheosis of man: in spite of the fact that he must disappear into the void, in spite of the absurdity of life and his own insignificance, man can achieve a certain grandeur. The context of the poem seems to imply that he will do so by facing up' to the misery of life with dignity and by recognizing and fulfilling his responsibility towards his fellows. (pp. 65-6)

The poems of *España* . . . refer to the Spanish Civil War and celebrate the heroes of the Republic. But for Vallejo this is not simply a struggle of the workers against Fascism: it is an episode of man's struggle to create the new universal society and the Republic is the symbol of that society. Thus in the *Himno a los voluntarios de la República* . . . Vallejo prophesies the reign of peace, harmony and justice that will come into being as a result of the sacrifice of the Republican militiamen. (p. 67)

Despite the messianic nature of his later poetry Vallejo realizes that theories and doctrines in themselves are insufficient to change the world. He realizes that men must have recourse to practical action, that they must take up arms and fight. Thus in the *Himno* . . . he calls on the *voluntarios* to kill in order to create a new and better life. . . . [Vallejo] believes in the necessity of armed revolution, but it is to be emphasized once again that for him the Revolution is not simply a struggle of the workers against capitalism: it is a struggle of humanity to create a world of peace and love. (pp. 69-70)

Though obscurities still exist, *Poemas humanos* is less difficult, less incoherent, more immediately communicative than *Trilce*. In a sense it represents a break with *Trilce,* a reaction away from the avant-garde mentality towards a poetry more easily accessible to the ordinary reader. It is also an evolution. In *Trilce* the desire to innovate tended to carry the poet to extremes of incoherence and hermeticism. Now he has mastered the new techniques and they no longer obtrude but exist alongside more traditional techniques. In a sense *Poemas humanos* might be said to be more "classical". (pp. 77-8)

James Higgins, in his introduction to César Vallejo: An Anthology of His Poetry *by César Vallejo (copyright © 1970 Pergamon Press Ltd.), Pergamon Press, 1970, pp. 1-82.*

CANDACE SLATER (essay date 1976)

Vallejo's *Spain, Take This Cup From Me* . . . presents us with a passionate spokesman for an impassioned age. . . . [The] collection includes fifteen poems written around the time of the Spanish Civil War, which first exploded in 1936. In *Spain, Take This Cup From Me*, the translators have made every effort to create English poems whose author remains, nevertheless, Vallejo. (p. 96)

Written in direct response to the Spanish experience, the poems comprising the collection reflect Vallejo's personal struggle to force language to convey his overriding sense of universal human suffering ending in death and succeeded by violent redemption possible only through a unanimous love. While these poems, in their pain and beautiful, difficult deformations, could only have been written by Vallejo, they also mirror a good deal of a more general aura surrounding the Spanish Civil War. . . . In reading *Spain, Take This Cup From Me*, we are struck above all by its enormous sense of potential. To Vallejo, nothing appears easy yet all seems possible. . . . Although Vallejo cannot be considered a surrealist. . . . he does share the iconoclasm of the European Vanguard of that time. Spain for Vallejo, as for Neruda, Hemingway, Eluard, Aragon, Malraux, Auden, Macniece and countless others, should be seen as the testing ground for what so many envisaged as a new world. (pp. 96-7)

What makes the Peruvian poet particularly interesting is that while many other writers achieved universal significance through their commitment to national causes, Vallejo found an almost perfect metaphor for his already existing universal preoccupations in Spain. The great paradox of these poems lies in the fact that while they could have been written about no country other than Spain, Spain herself finally becomes first and foremost a metaphor. . . .

Spain, for Vallejo, is the androgynous parent, "mother Spain" who is "right this moment distributing / her energy among the animal kingdom / little flowers, comets & men," but also the masculine Spain of blood, iron and dust. (p. 97)

Even the most cursory reading of *Spain, Take This Cup From Me* will reveal a number of symbols traditionally associated with the Spanish landscape. The dust, the olive trees, the wolves, the pebbles, the rivers, are to be found not only in Vallejo but in Lorca or Hemingway or Aragon, as well as writers who had taken Spain for their subject centuries before. Vallejo's use of these objects makes his poetry at once concrete and particular. . . .

Having established that Spain is, indeed, a particular country, we must go on to point out that it is also a symbol, and an excellent one for Vallejo's wholehearted celebration of the Common Man. Spanish poverty is viewed by the poet as a source not only of suffering but of redemption at a time in which W. H. Auden was asserting, "We must love one another or die." (p. 98)

The title, *Spain, Take This Cup From Me*, lets us know

from the outset that Vallejo's political positions reflect a sort of religious intensity. He is not a propagandist, but a believer with a fervent faith in redemption through human means. The savior to whom he looks is thus not Christ, but the silent defenders of Guernica, "the barber next door— maybe he cut me, / but a good man & besides, unfortunate; / the beggar who yesterday was singing across the street, / the nurse who today passed by crying, / the priest burdened with the stubborn highness of his knees. . . ." He is both spokesman for, and champion of the lowly. . . . (p. 99)

The really extraordinary thing about Vallejo is his fever-pitch belief, never drummed up for the occasion but totally true. *Spain, Take This Cup From Me* is a remarkable witness' account of an experience which he both lived and observed. Although unfailingly on the side of the fallen peasant, of the bound word and rented sky, he is never shrill nor doctrinaire, and his hatred of the oppressor is virtually nonexistent when compared with his love for the oppressed. . . . Looking forward into days when the blind will see, the deaf will hear and the ignorant will be wise, a future in which death will die as all men work, beget and understand, Vallejo's verse is charged throughout with "the direction of water that runs to see its limit before burning," which cannot and yet which will explode. (pp. 99-100)

Candace Slater, "The Water That Runs to Its Burning," in Review *(copyright © 1976 by the Center for Inter-American Relations, Inc.), No. 17, Spring, 1976, pp. 96-100.*

JEAN FRANCO (essay date 1976)

The title of Vallejo's first collection, *Los heraldos negros*, belongs to the vocabulary of Romantic alienation, with the poet as dark voice of destruction and negation instead of the herald of light and order. (pp. 30-1)

The motive of the [title] poem arises out of the gratuitous nature of evil, and the conclusion that suffering without apparent cause can only come from the hatred of God. Yet even to suppose a hating God destroys the notion of a creator and hence removes any prospect of salvation. What distinguishes Vallejo's poem from dozens of similar statements of despair and death is the manner in which he builds the uncertainty-principle into language itself, and makes the poetic voice the voice of ignorance and negation. The Orphic role of the poet has been destroyed by those blows, so that he can no longer claim to be a secular priest with a vision of unity unperceived by ordinary men. The poet's [repetitive] 'I do not know' casts him into the common pit, a victim of destruction, as impotent as any other person to make a whole out of the fragment. Instead of channelling the goodness and the grace of creation, the waters of human suffering have stagnated in the soul without possibility of issue. The sense of stagnation is important, for it eventually threw Vallejo back on to the domain of the given; and even in this comparatively early poem, the verb 'to open' refers not to escape or transcendence but to the furrows made by suffering on man's own body, on which Vallejo will eventually rewrite the Holy Scriptures. In *Los heraldos negros* man's attempt to get beyond the divided self is thwarted, and his gaze turns backward as if to try and identify the source of his alienation rather than looking forward into a future in which his state might be changed. (pp. 31-2)

It is above all the disparity between the promise of the sacred book and the insignificance of modern man that bursts through traditional systems of analogies in Vallejo's poems. The Romantics had already contributed to the instability of language by extending notions such as 'God' or 'love' greatly beyond a Christian significance; and Vallejo now pushes the consequences of this over-extension to the limits of absurdity. There is hardly an act of daily life—travelling, eating, sleeping, hardly a common object—water, bread, rivers, mountains, cities, which has not been used to suggest the supernatural and the infinite. Vallejo is concerned with the loss of the spiritual power that formerly attached to these, and the loss too of that divine magic he had felt in childhood and which contrasted so brutally with the trivialization of language in the modern world. In the absence of Logos, man is left with words, with a language which can no longer refer to the infinite. The immediate consequence is that the Passion of Christ is no longer a single unique event which bestows meaning on the multiplicity of passions upon earth. Once pluralized, the notion of Christ loses all meaning. To refer, as Vallejo does, to 'Los Cristos del alma' (the soul's Christs), to 'Marías que se van' (Marias who go away) devirtualizes Christian myth and, by association, all other metaphors related to the Passion. 'The red crown of Jesus' becomes a term of comparison for the moon, though the very notion of Christ's sacrifice is inconsistent with the planetary circle. The poems speak of '*one Palm Sunday*', '*a host in red blood*', '*a sinning Christ*', '*a Baptist*' instead of John the Baptist, '*one eternal morning*' instead of eternity, '*a Good Friday*', instead of Good Friday, '*this bohemian god*' instead of God. When, in a love poem, Vallejo declares that '*the child Jesus of your love was born*', the trivialization is complete. The profane world has taken over. But though Christ and the Passion are rendered insignificant, other nouns—*Vida* (Life), *Luz* (Light), *Sombra* (Shadow), *Razón* (Reason), *Muerte* (Death), *Verano* (Summer) are capitalized, a typographical device which puts them into the same category of substantives as God or Christ. And this is not simply a device but represents a re-evaluation of categories and shows how universal categories are created out of human experience. (pp. 35-6)

'Nostalgias imperiales' are the only poems which are written in the tradition of poems of provincial or rustic life which were much in vogue at the turn of the century. But even these poems which are strongly marked by the influence of the Uruguayan Modernist, Julio Herrera y Reissig centre on the spiritual loss of the indigenous peoples. By choosing to evoke the 'imperial nostalgias' of the Peruvian Indians, Vallejo relates the universal loss of faith to the specific peoples whose degradation he had witnessed both in the northern areas of Peru and during his brief stay in the Sierra de Pasco, where the sad plight of the modern Indian was even more evident. Thus the first four sonnets of 'Nostalgias imperiales' are structured around images of desacralization and emptiness. There is a closed chapel, a desecrated altar with the bell tolling in the distance, the snow-white eyes of an old woman coloured by a 'blind sun without light', a lake (of stillness or stagnation) in which the Inca Emperor and Sun-God Manco-Capac weeps as he drowns. Cut off from any possibility of future, the figures and landscapes are bathed in the fading light of what has gone. (p. 54)

Trilce is an extreme book, revolutionary in its exploration of an authentic language, yet curiously at odds with the fact that between 1918 and 1922 the poet still seemed to be living within the structures of Romanticism, still paying homage to the rhetoric of José Santos Chocano and practising the 'bohemianism' that had come to seem the indispensable mode of existence for the poet. It seems as if, while exploring the pains and delusions of the individuation principle that was the heritage of Romanticism, Vallejo also glimpsed [a] terrifying vision of utter emptiness and chaos.... The crisis that produced *Trilce* was probably precipitated, as much as anything, by the profound contradictions Vallejo discovered between the Romantic exaltation of the self and the displacement of man from the central role in creation which had followed from evolutionist theory. (p. 79)

[This was] the terrifying void which Vallejo glimpsed in *Trilce*. Later on, Vallejo would relate language closely to the ideology of individualism, and in one of his articles he talks of the 'blind and unchecked supremacy of Archimedes's law and the crudely positivist enthusiasm which has been responsible for bomber planes and war', relating this to the crisis in civilization from which the only salvation could be a new Logos: 'the supremacy of the Word which discovers, which unites and which takes us beyond transient self-interest and egoism'. By this, he did not of course mean some avant-garde revolution of the word, nor did he believe that by spelling 'destierra' 'DestieRRa', he would change man or society. It is rather that consciousness and language are one, and there can no more be a new consciousness without a new language than there can be a new language without a new consciousness. But in *Trilce* he is faced with a demystifying task—that of showing the inoperability of traditional images and metaphors, the speciousness of 'harmony' in the Modernist sense. That is why the poems lurch forward in a series of shocks, discontinuities, verbal games, outrageous puns. That is why *Trilce* rejects homogeneity of mood, refuses comfort and solace. That is why the poems are anti-divine, anti-prophetic, anti-heroic, satiric. (p. 83)

The *Poemas humanos* are shot through with the sadness of the 1930s, when disasters were large and the human individual seemed of little account. Massed at Fascist rallies, standing in dole queues, shipped off to concentration camps, people were dispensable parts of a powerful system. Chaplin's little tramp, struggling to hold on to the shreds of dignity, had become the epitome of the lonely individual's tragi-comedy in a dehumanized world. It was war—and first of all the Spanish Civil War—that paradoxically restored something of a sense of purpose, or at least gave individuals an intenser glow. For this reason Vallejo's 'Spain' poems are not only complementary to *Poemas humanos* but represent, so to speak, the apocalyptic backdrop against which man's obsession with the trivial is heightened to grotesque proportions, somewhat like Orwell's condemned man avoiding a puddle of water on the way to his execution.

The *Poemas humanos* and the 'Spain' poems are more than the schizoid halves in the poetic production of a Vallejo who had a public and a private personality. Rather they confirm that it was not possible for him to separate man from the society he had made and whose values he has internalized. Even Death and Birth are not grasped in terms of archetypal myth but rather in their specific manifestations, with man's allotted span reduced to a 'stumbling between two stars', a mere parenthesis between two moments of nonbeing, a losing battle in which he appropriates the objects of his environment only to find that they are in no sense really *his*. In the poem, 'Esto / sucedió entre dos párpados' (It / happened between two eyelids) . . . the dying man holds tight to a solitary shoe which has been *produced* by human hand; something which the individual regards as *his* is no longer so. There can be no more exact image of reification nor of man's alienation from others, trapped as he is in his lonely linear cage.

If death assumes supreme importance in these poems, it is because (to use a cliché) it is a moment of truth; though in capitalist society the lonely Passion of the cross is a less appropriate symbol than the conveyor belt to the grave. To diminish the importance of death is to lessen the importance of life; so that in a world of reified objects, man has no mirror in which to find a reflection of his dignity and worth. This 'fall' translates itself into this collection of poems, whose central devices are synecdoche and anti-climax, a poetry in which the subject is constantly forced to accept humble and tautological propositions about the self like 'I'm here because I'm here.' In many of the poems, he is reduced to affirming his existence by touching himself. . . . (pp. 192-93)

What immediately strikes a reader of the *Poemas humanos* is the setting of the trivial within the perspective of death, which recalls the poetry of the Golden Age. The traces are there in the use of rhetorical figures, in the binary patterns of imagery, whose opposing tensions are brought together in the *summa* at the end of the poem, in the recurrence of certain conventional metaphors like 'gold', 'snow', 'light'. Above all, paradox becomes of central importance, though it is not identical with seventeenth-century paradox which referred to an apparently untrue, outrageous or irrational statement which, in the light of Christian belief (or commonly accepted practice), could be seen to be true. The rich man, according to Christian doctrine, is really poor, for it is hard for him to enter the kingdom of Heaven. The poor man is spiritually rich. What at first reading seems to be a similar paradox in Vallejo's poems turns out to be very different, for there is no totalizing system to turn the paradox into common-sense. . . . (p. 194)

The bleakness of many of the *Poemas humanos* is unquestionable, a bleakness, however, that is solemnized by a language whose appropriateness conditions derive from death. While, on the one hand, the colloquial demeans existence, confirming the automatic nature of our responses, heightened language makes life portentous. Where portentousness is inappropriate, poetry turns into hollow sound or parody. . . . [Vallejo's poems] function on a knife-edge between life and death and between tragedy and farce, for though he behaves as if every moment might be his last, he cannot, for all that, entirely rescue his life from triviality. (pp. 195-96)

The passion recorded in *España, aparta de mí este cáliz* is that of an entire people; the collection combines the messianic spirit of the Old Testament with the message of the New Testament that humanity can be saved from death. The fifteen poems include a hymn, a response, a prayer, a litany and a prophecy; in them, the Christian symbols which in *Trilce* and *Poemas humanos* had become empty vestiges now recover referential value. Bread once more refers to the bread of life and water to the water of grace though both life and grace are produced by the material world. When we recall how difficult the simple act of speaking and writing had been in some of the *Poemas humanos*, the tone of *España, aparta de mí este cáliz* is even more astonishing. Words like 'grandeza', 'llamar', 'grito', can now be used without irony for man finally lives up to the grandeur of language. The poet, meanwhile, does not assume the role of prophet but is simply a witness who bears the marks of a past which has been superseded by the events he describes. . . . (p. 233)

Many poems in this collection deal with the accidental victims of war—the peasants of Extremadura, the people of Guernica, Madrid and Bilbao who faced bomber-raids, the victims of the fall of Gijón and those who made the horrifying retreat from Málaga. Apart from the Italian campaign in Abyssinia, it was the first large-scale modern war to involve the civilian population, and newspapers of the time were full of horrified eye-witness accounts. (p. 245)

Images of fire and water recur throughout the poems of this collection, signifying salvation and purification, grace through destruction. Now fire tempers even the ruminants, turning the peaceful into fighters. Yet [in 'Invierno en la batalla de Teruel'] when the poet calls out, 'Who goes there?', it is life itself which is found beneath the snow, 'wagging its tail, with its second rope'. This grotesque image is followed by two lines in which the alliterated *d* [of the verb 'dar'—'to give'] mimes the sound of war guns. . . . The suggestion is that war is 'man-like', that there is something horribly human about it. This reading is supported by the final verses in which the poet addresses a comrade who 'treads on his own arm distractedly among the corpses'. The very fact of mortality makes both the killing and the risk of death paradoxically human. Yet it is hard for Vallejo to humanize technological warfare or to persuade us that one side may bring 'grace' rather than simply destruction. And this is all the more difficult when the poet himself is horrified by his own mortality, at his own shrinking from death, as he reveals in the final 'Down with my body' of the last line of the poem. *España, aparta de mí este cáliz* creates a rhetoric of commitment though at a price. The poet can no longer afford irony or doubt though it is difficult for him to celebrate the war in full consciousness of death and destruction. Based on a socialist realist aesthetic, the poems celebrate exemplary heroes, collective bravery or disaster in a manner that recalls other Communist writing of the time. If Vallejo was willing to accept a socialist poetics, it was because he considered that the collective spirit of the Spanish militiamen represented a qualitative leap beyond individualism. That is why, even when he foresaw the defeat of the Republican side, he could not really countenance it in his poetry. To do so would have been to cross the limits into the realm of the unthinkable. (pp. 248-49)

Jean Franco, in his César Vallejo: The Dialectics of Poetry and Silence (© *Cambridge University Press 1976), Cambridge University Press, 1976, 296 p.*

BIBLIOGRAPHY

Bly, Robert. "What If After So Many Wings of Birds." In *Neruda and Vallejo: Selected Poems,* edited by Robert Bly, translated by Robert Bly, John Knoepfle, and James Wright, pp. 169-74. Madison, MN: Sixties Press, 1962.

Calls *Los heraldos negros* "the greatest single collection of poems I have ever read."

Eshleman, Clayton. "César against Vallejo." *Parnassus* 1, No. 2 (Spring-Summer 1973): 38-41.
   A short essay on Vallejo's life, and on *España, aparta de mí este cáliz.*

Higgins, James. "The Conflict of Personality in César Vallejo's *Poemas Humanos.*" *Bulletin of Hispanic Studies* XLIII, No. 1 (1966): 47-55.
   A discussion of Vallejo's poems that deal with man's dual nature: the struggle between lofty spiritual aspirations and physical limitations.

Knoepfle, John. "Thoughts on César Vallejo." *Twenty Poems,* by César Vallejo, edited and translated by John Knoepfle, James Wright, and Robert Bly, pp. 7-8. Madison, MN.: Sixties Press, 1962.
   A short essay on Vallejo's bold use of startling metaphors in his poetry.

Obarrio, Felipe. "Life, Death, and César Vallejo." *Américas* 20, Nos. 11-12 (November-December 1968): 46-8.
   An essay on the recurring theme of death in Vallejo's work.

Squirru, Rafael. "Vallejo in Translation." *Américas* 20, Nos. 11-12 (November-December 1968): 48-9.
   A review of Eshleman's translation of *Poemas humanos.*

Terry, Arthur. "Surrendering to the Species." *The Times Literary Supplement,* No. 3934 (5 August 1977): 964.
   A review of Jean Franco's *César Vallejo: The Dialectics of Poetry and Silence,* and examination of Vallejo's style and beliefs.

"Visions of Solidarity." *The Times Literary Supplement,* No. 3526 (25 September 1969): 1098
   An overview and comparison of *Los heraldos negros, Trilce,* and *Poemas humanos.*

Wright, James. "A Note on César Vallejo." In *Twenty Poems,* by César Vallejo, edited and translated by John Knoepfle, James Wright, and Robert Bly, pp. 9-11. Madison, MN: Sixties Press, 1962.
   Terms Vallejo "one of the greatest modern poets," commends especially his poems about his family.

Giovanni Verga
1840-1922

Italian novelist, dramatist, and short story writer.

Verga is a major figure both in Italian literature and in the evolution of modern western literature. During the era of his mature genius he was the leading voice of the *verismo* school, an Italian movement of literary realism roughly corresponding to the French naturalism of Emile Zola. Verga's innovations on the realistic technique created a style that described a fictional environment from within; the form, diction, and tone of a story mirroring the attitudes and consciousness of its characters, both individually and collectively. This method was particularly effective in Verga's depictions of Sicilian peasant life, enabling an acute and subtle articulation of a fundamentally inarticulate stratum of society. One of Verga's most successful examinations of this peasant world was *Cavalleria Rusticana*, which the author wrote as both a short story and a drama, and which was adapted as the libretto for Mascagni's well known opera of the same title.

Verga was born in Sicily into an upper-class family, and for a time he studied law at the University of Catania. His interests, however, were resolutely literary, and after publishing some undistinguished early novels he decided to leave Sicily and pursue his career in the more exciting and diverse centers of Florence and Milan. The novels he produced in this period were fashionable romances dealing with the passions of the rich, and they did not yet display his ultimate style. It was while living in northern Italy that Verga's artistic concerns altered dramatically. "Nedda," which Verga subtitled "a Sicilian sketch," is one of the earliest stories to exhibit the cultural and stylistic focus of his later genius. The culture was no longer high society but the rural life that surrounded him when he was growing up; the style was a realism that sought to efface the author's identity and allow the fictional subject to dictate the form of the work. In his later short stories and novels Verga let the dialects and idioms of his characters permeate every level of his narrative, a technique he intended to use to represent faithfully all levels of society.

I Malavoglia and *Mastro-don Gesualdo* are the only completed works of a five-novel project which Verga titled *I Vinti* (*The Defeated*). Each successive novel was to portray a more sophisticated social world, from one of poverty to one of prosperity and finally political dominance. The two novels, however, along with his short stories, are sufficient to place Verga among the artistic forerunners of such modernist devices as interior monologue and stream of consciousness. Although he produced the body of his work in the nineteenth century, it is perhaps in the light of twentieth-century literature that Verga is best understood.

PRINCIPAL WORKS

Una peccatrice   (novel)   1866
Storia di una capinera   (novel)   1871
Eva   (novel)   1873
Tigre reale   (novel)   1873
Eros   (novel)   1875
Vita dei campi   (short stories)   1880
   [*Cavalleria Rusticana, and Other Tales of Sicilian
      Peasant Life*, 1893]
I Malavoglia: Romanzo   (novel)   1881
   [*The House by the Medlar-Tree*, 1890]
Il marito di Elena: Romanzo   (novel)   1882
Novelle rusticane   (short stories)   1883
   [*Little Novels of Sicily*, 1925]
Per le vie   (short stories)   1883
Cavalleria Rusticana   (drama)   1884
Vagabondaggio   (short stories)   1887
Mastro-don Gesualdo: Romanzo   (novel)   1889
   [*Master Don Gesualdo*, 1893]
Don Candeloro e c'   (short stories)   1894
   [*Don Candeloro and Co.*, 1958]
La lupa. In portinaio. Cavalleria Rusticana. Drammi
   (dramas)   1896
La caccia al lupo. La caccia alla volpe. Bozzetti scenici
   (dramas)   1902

W. D. HOWELLS   (essay date 1890)

I can praise [*The House by the Medlar-Tree*] without reserve as one of the most perfect pieces of literature that I know.

When we talk of the great modern movement towards reality we speak without the documents if we leave this book out of the count, for I can think of no other novel in which the facts have been more faithfully reproduced, or with a profounder regard for the poetry that resides in facts and resides nowhere else. . . . [Signor Verga] offers us a masterpiece of the finest realism. (pp. iii-iv)

Few tales, I think, are more moving, more full of heart-break than this, for few are so honest. By this I mean that the effect in it is precisely that which the author aimed at. He meant to let us see just what manner of men and women went to make up the life of a little Italian town of the present day, and he meant to let the people show themselves with the least possible explanation or comment from him. The transaction of the story is in the highest degree dramatic; but events follow one another with the even sequence of hours on the clock. You are not prepared to value them beforehand; they are not advertised to tempt your curiosity like feats promised at the circus, in the fashion of the feebler novels; often it is in the retrospect that you recognize their importance and perceive their full significance. In this most subtly artistic management of his material the author is most a master, and almost more than any other he has the rare gift of trusting the intelligence of his reader. He seems to have no more sense of authority or supremacy concerning the personages than any one of them would have in telling the story, and he has as completely freed himself from literosity as the most unlettered among them. (pp. v-vi)

> *W. D. Howells, in his introduction to* The House by the Medlar-Tree *by Giovanni Verga, translated by Mary A. Craig (copyright © by Harper & Brothers), Harper, 1890, pp. iii-vii.*

D. H. LAWRENCE (essay date 1928)

[It] was only in middle life that the drama of peasant passion really made an impression on Giovanni Verga. His earlier imagination, naturally, went out into the great world. (p. 7)

A true provincial, he had to try to enter the *beau monde*. (p. 8)

He did so: and apparently, with a certain success. And for nearly twenty years he lived in Milan, in Florence, in Naples, writing, and imagining he was fulfilling his thirst for glory by having love-affairs with elegant ladies: most elegant ladies, as he assures us.

To this period belong the curiously unequal novels of the city world: *Eva, Tigre Reale, Eros*. They are interesting, alive, bitter, somewhat unhealthy, smelling of the 'seventies and of the Paris of the Goncourts, and, in some curious way, abortive. The man had not found himself. He was in his wrong element, fooling himself and being fooled by show, in a true Italian fashion.

Then, towards the age of forty, came the recoil, and the *Cavalleria Rusticana* volume is the first book of the recoil. It was a recoil away from the *beau monde* and the "Continent," back to Sicily, to Catania, to the peasants. (p. 9)

[In *Cavalleria Rusticana* Verga] recoils savagely away from the sophistications of the city life of elegant little ladies, to the peasants in their most crude and simple, almost brute-like aspect. (p. 13)

Verga's people are always people in the purest sense of the word. They are not intellectual, but then neither was Hector nor Ulysses intellectual. Verga, in his recoil, mistrusted everything that smelled of sophistication. He had a passion for the most naïve, the most unsophisticated manifestation of human nature. (p. 15)

Verga turned to the peasants to find, *in individuals*, the vivid spontaneity of sensitive passionate life, non-normal and non-didactic. He found it always *defeated*. He found the vulgar and the greedy always destroying the sensitive and the passionate. The vulgar and the greedy are themselves usually peasants: Verga was far too sane to put an aureole round the whole class. (p. 24)

Cavalleria Rusticana and *La Lupa* have always been hailed as masterpieces of brevity and gems of literary form. Masterpieces they are, but one is now a little sceptical of their form. After the enormous diffusiveness of Victor Hugo, it was perhaps necessary to make the artist more self-critical and self-effacing. But any wholesale creed in art is dangerous. (p. 26)

But Verga was caught up by the grand idea of self-effacement in art. Anything more confused, more silly, really, than the pages prefacing the excellent story *Gramigna's Lover* would be hard to find, from the pen of a great writer. The moment Verga starts talking theories, our interest wilts immediately. The theories were none of his own: just borrowed from the literary smarties of Paris. . . . And when he starts putting his theories into practice, and effacing himself, one is far more aware of his interference than when he just goes ahead. Naturally! Because self-effacement is, of course, self-conscious, and any form of emotional self-consciousness hinders a first-rate artist. . . . (pp. 27-8)

Therefore in *Cavalleria Rusticana* and in *La Lupa* we are just a bit too much aware of the author and his scissors. He has clipped too much away. The transitions are too abrupt. All is over in a gasp: whereas a story like *La Lupa* covers at least several years of time.

As a matter of fact, we need more looseness. We need an apparent formlessness, definite form is mechanical. We need more easy transition from mood to mood and from deed to deed. A great deal of the meaning of life and of art lies in the apparently dull spaces, the pauses, the unimportant passages. They are truly passages, the places of passing over.

So that Verga's deliberate missing-out of transition passages is, it seems to me, often a defect. And for this reason a story like *La Lupa* loses a great deal of its life. It may be a masterpiece of concision, but it is hardly a masterpiece of narration. It is so short, our acquaintance with Nanni and Maricchia is so fleeting, we forget them almost at once. *Jeli* makes a far more profound impression, so does *Rosso Malpelo*. These seem to me the finest stories in the book, and among the finest stories ever written. *Rosso Malpelo* is an extreme of the human consciousness, subtle and appalling as anything done by the Russians, and at the same time substantial, not introspective vapours. You will never forget him.

And it needed a deeper genius to write *Rosso Malpelo* than to write *Cavalleria Rusticana* or *La Lupa*. (pp. 28-9)

This business of missing out transition passages is quite deliberate on Verga's part. It is perhaps most evident in [*Cavellaria Rusticana and Other Stories*], because it is here that Verga practises it for the first time. It was a new dodge, and he handled it badly. The sliding-over of the change from Jeli's boyhood to his young manhood is surely too deliberately confusing!

But Verga had a double motive. First was the Frenchy idea of self-effacement, which, however, didn't go very deep, as

Verga was too much of a true Southerner to know quite what it meant. But the second motive was more dynamic. It was connected with Verga's whole recoil from the sophisticated world, and it effected a revolution in his style. Instinctively he had come to hate the tyranny of a persistently logical sequence, or even a persistently chronological sequence. Time and the syllogism both seemed to represent the sophisticated falsehood and a sort of bullying, to him. (pp. 29-30)

Verga tried to convey [illogical thought patterns of the emotional mind] in his style. It gives at first the sense of jumble and incoherence. The beginning of the story *Brothpot* is a good example of this breathless muddle of the peasant mind. When one is used to it, it is amusing, and a new movement in deliberate consciousness: though the humorists have used the form before. But at first it may be annoying. Once he starts definitely narrating, however, Verga drops the "muddled" method, and seeks only to be concise, often too concise, too abrupt in the transition. And in the matter of punctuation he is, perhaps deliberately, a puzzle, aiming at the same muddled swift effect of the emotional mind in its movements. He is doing, as a great artist, what men like James Joyce do only out of contrariness and desire for a sensation. The emotional mind, however apparently muddled, has its own rhythm, its own commas and colons and full-stops. They are not always as we should expect them, but they are there, indicating that other rhythm. (pp. 32-3)

> *D. H. Lawrence, in his preface to* Cavalleria Rusticana and Other Stories *by Giovanni Verga, translated by D. H. Lawrence (copyright © renewed 1955 by Frieda Lawrence; reprinted by permission of The Dial Press), Dial, 1928 (and reprinted by Greenwood Press, Publishers, 1975), pp. 7-33.*

THOMAS GODDARD BERGIN (essay date 1931)

[Verga's early works] are all cut from the same cloth; there is a similarity in plot, characterization, style, and general tone which makes it possible almost to reduce these tales to a formula. . . . Consider the Hero.

Pietro Brusio, the protagonist of *Una peccatrice,* is described in enthusiastic detail by the author. A young man of about twenty-five, he is, of course, handsome in a rather exotic way . . . , he dresses carelessly and affects indifference to the opinions of others. Perhaps too *"nobile"* for the unworthy society of the present day, he has a generous though sometimes impetuous character. He has an almost superstitious belief in his star, and because he has achieved some slight literary success he looks forward with impatient confidence—with rare alternations of profound despair—to a brilliant future.

Need one insist upon the obvious resemblances to the author? . . . The device is certainly not a new one; it was ever so with the young romantics: the author and the Hero are one. (pp. 15-16)

With the later novels comes an interesting development. The protagonist becomes slightly idealized: Giovanni Verga no longer sees himself quite as he is, nor perhaps even as he would really wish to be, but on the background of Brusio he embroiders new refinements that he observes in the gay bucks of the north. The melodramatic pose of his first heroes fades gradually into a rather more sophisticated cynicism. . . . (pp. 16-17)

[Our] author drew his materials not from literature but from life. For lack of better models he depicted himself. As his horizon widened he was enabled to find a series of new characters to graft on to the old. But there is this general consistency. Throughout these youthful romances he described only what he actually saw. If he is in Sicily, so is his hero. If he is in Milan, the hero is either Milanese or living in Milan. The protagonists, too, grow progressively older as the author does. (p. 17)

Brusio is meant not only to be another Verga but also to typify the Sicilian character. The question of Sicilian jealousy comes up in his case and again in Lanti's [in *Eva*] as an integral part of the plot. The almost superstitious cult of the home, moreover, . . . is found in all the tales that have a Sicilian protaonist, and always as a powerful emotional stimulus to the character concerned.

In the stories where the protagonists are northern aristocrats rather than poor Sicilian artists Verga tries to bring out in their characters what he felt were the dominant elements in the fashionable society about him. They are cynical young men, devoid of all illusion and belief. (p. 20)

In these later tales, too, the study of Sicilian character is replaced by a somewhat more objective consideration of the *mores* of the north, just as the passionate young artist is replaced by the *poseur.* This world of *salotti* and cynical love affairs, in which the actors seem never to lose a certain self-consciousness, is presented before us in some detail. The weary love-making that seems to have been the principal occupation of that society forms also the principal subject of Verga's work, receiving most extensive treatment, of course, in the well-named *Eros.* (p. 21)

It seems quite legitimate . . . to say that the purpose of these early romances is to depict contemporary upper class society. The inspiration is originally autobiographic and the local color and sociological studies in the early novels are based either upon experience or first-hand observation by the author. (pp. 23-4)

[Despite the realism of the most fantastic plots of Verga's early period, he] frequently built a rather baroque edifice on the staid foundations of his own observation. Except for *La storia di una capinera,* the plots of these youthful romances, quite conveniently for us, and perhaps inevitably for the young Verga, all follow the same general outlines. Here is the formula: a young man, usually an artist of good family and social position, meets, under circumstances which differ in detail but are alike in their melodramatic setting, a strange woman, usually older than himself and possessed of a mysterious and overpowering charm. After struggles of varying intensity he yields to this charm and the two become lovers. Follows a period of intense passion succeeded—refreshingly enough—by a reaction. One of the two lovers tires; the deserted one usually dies, thus conveniently ending the novel. (pp. 25-6)

It may be safely said that the heroine of these tales represents the fantastic, the exaggerated and the unreal, just as the hero represents the true and the realistic. The heroines are, one and all, rare, seductive creatures whose principal charm is an unhealthy and overwhelming sensual attraction. (p. 27)

[Their charm] is purely sensual. But one must insist upon the exotic nature of this sensuality. They are incomprehensible creatures, sometimes foreigners, always out of the circle to which the hero belongs. *Tigre Reale* is the ideal example, a combination, formidable indeed, of the cossack, the parisian, and the bohemian. (pp. 27-8)

The sensual element—since we are tracking it down—creeps out also in occasional details. There is a description of Brusio's study in *Una peccatrice:* soft lights, deep carpets. . . . (p. 28)

Those twins of melodrama, sensualism and sentimentalism, are seldom found alone. Certainly not in these tales. Just as there is in all these novels a *"donna corruttrice,"* so there is also an innocent victim, sometimes more than one, of the *grande passion* created by the siren. Sometimes our pity is asked—openly or tacitly—for one of the two lovers. This is the case, of course, in the *Storia di una capinera.* In *Eva* we are supposed to pity Lanti. . . . Narcisa takes poison and dies quite pathetically, with one eye, as it were, on the audience, and so, somewhat more artistically, does Nata. Alberti after numerous stimulating flights on the wings of Eros finally becomes a very dutiful husband, so that when his wife dies he shoots himself, thus atoning for his early viciousness. This type of sentimental treatment is often necessary to compensate for the excesses of sensualism that we have observed. . . . (p. 29)

There is, however, another basis, and perhaps a more legitimate one, for sentimentalizing. Our magnificent lovers practically always enjoy their guilty passion at the expense of someone else's happiness. And the victim is—it was inevitable—the Home. Lanti's tragic death causes unutterable grief in his home in Sicily and there are numerous moving passages where Verga indicates how he had not hesitated to spend on Eva the remittances that his proud and hopeful parents had sent him. (pp. 29-30)

From the presence of these two elements, sensualism and sentimentalism, there arises logically a tendency to moralize. Verga tries to keep it impersonal from the very beginning, but he sometimes slips and steps, unconsciously as it were, into the well-adorned tale to point a moral. (p. 30)

Paradoxically enough, for all the broken hearts and homes and commandments, the author attempts to blame none of his characters. There are weak and immoral characters in these tales but there are no villains. It is all fate. . . . It will be seen that this theory which puts humanity at the mercy of a destiny over which it has no control makes it conveniently possible for the author to adopt an attitude of sympathy toward his characters at the same time that he disapproves of their actions. (p. 31)

The plot [in *Nedda*], as almost invariably with Verga, is extremely simple. . . . The background is no longer the theater, club, or *salotto* of the great northern cities but the bleak Sicilian countryside. With the loss of this background goes of necessity the loss of tone of the other romances for the details added to give realism are essentially gross where formerly they were elegant. Perhaps even more important is the disappearance of the sensual element. There is no glorification of the flesh in *Nedda.* Indeed far from being beautiful is the heroine for the author informs the reader that, as a result of hard work and privations, she has almost ceased to look like a human being. There is, furthermore, no moralizing. Paradoxically enough, with *Nedda* the real moral force of Verga's cycle begins, but it lies in the story, perhaps even in the reader. Certainly neither author nor characters do any moralizing.

So much for what is lost in the formula. Are there any new elements to replace these losses? Doubtless even Verga himself must have been conscious of the fact that artistically *Nedda* was his first success. It possesses a concentration and a unity that his other works had lacked. This concentration might almost be called impact, so striking it is in its effect. . . . [For] the effeminate artist there has been substituted the less complex but undoubtedly more robust figure of the peasant. The people are coming into their own. (pp. 38-40)

Another novelty, introduced perforce with the character of the peasant, is the rôle of nature. Nature ceases to be a casual background and begins to take a very definite part in the story. Not only is it a hot summer day which causes Nedda to yield to Janu, but far more deeply than that natural forces shape the destiny of the characters. The *contadini* depend for their very existence on the whims of the weather. When it rains Nedda is unable to work in the fields, hence her mother gets no money for medical attention. If the *annata* is good, all is well; if not, then those on the margin of society pay the price. It is no one's fault, as Nedda herself says; it is starkly inevitable. This sense of an irresistible destiny created by elemental forces differs somewhat from the rather vague, romantic fatalism that, as we have seen, frequently creeps out in the early novels; but it represents the same attempt of the author, much more logically supported, to assume an impersonal attitude. There arises from this latter fatalism a curious, perhaps unconscious, anti-Christian feeling which is to grow stronger during the later period of Verga's work. God is as remote and impersonal as nature. He may do us good but he is more likely to do us harm. His Church turns away from the sinner; Nedda, carrying her illegitimate child, is not allowed to enter the church on Easter Day. And the irony seems to become almost bitter at one point. When Janu leaves Nedda she bids him take care of himself, as he is all she has in the world. "God will take care of me," he replies, and in a few weeks he is dead. (pp. 40-1)

[It] may well be believed that the young Verga was not without the love of fine phrases common to most young authors and encouraged probably by the poets, artists, and wits that he came to know during this period. This false elegance may be said to have the following traits . . . : (1) numerous inversions, (2) frequent use of foreign words and phrases, (3) occasional similes somewhat too daring for good taste. (p. 102)

[With *Nedda,* however,] he introduced to his readers not only a new character and a new atmostphere, but a new and startling style. This he later perfected in *I Malavoglia* and *Vita dei campi,* and it remained characteristically his style, save on the occasions when he returned to the northern background for his stories. The single word that can best describe this new style—and it is a word which makes the contrast between the new and the old style very startling—is "conversational." He tried to write as the Sicilians talked; he tried to put into his novel exactly the ways of speech, the vocabulary and syntax of the peasant or fisherman. And because he knew these people well he succeeded well in his task, and his accomplishment is among the major glories of modern Italian prose.

The artistic triumph of this prose is, however, a little difficult for a foreigner to understand. I have said he reproduced the speech he heard about him. So he did, but if he merely reproduced exactly he would be writing Sicilian and not Italian. Some enthusiastic regionalists thought he would have done better if he had used the dialect. But it was Verga's idea to reproduce the sense of the dialect, to give the impression of dialect and at the same time to write his tales in good standard Italian. It will be seen that it was a very delicate task; much more so than simply telling the story in dialect or using a few words of *argot* for local color. His method is to arrange good Tuscan words in Sicilian word order and to make the reader aware of the rhythm of dialect under the Italian sentence. (pp. 106-07)

[His style] is artfully simple and has a vividness that is unsurpassed in modern prose. . . . It is, indeed, safe to say of Verga's style exactly what we have said of his work as a whole: when it is based on first-hand observation it is strong and trenchant; it is likely to be unconvincing only when, as in the youthful attempts at Tuscanism, it is built on literary models or linguistic conventions. (p. 110)

[Only] a pagan can have the peculiar, deep sympathy for humanity that is characteristic of Verga. For him no man is guilty of sin: we are what we are because destiny has so willed it. And this sentiment is predominant in all Verga's work. (p. 117)

Not unlike Thomas Hardy. Yet there is a difference, and a difference that goes far, I think, toward explaining the relative unpopularity of Verga's novels. Hardy makes his fatalism a personal issue; his Fate or his God seems at times rather a malevolent sort of creature and the author puts a good deal of personal emotion into depicting the sad lot of his characters. Not so Verga. It is here that he is most truly impersonal. The universe is as it is; no one is to blame. Things are what they are; they are unquestionably very sad but they *may* be for the best. He will not commit himself. Is it because after all his Catholic training exercises some restraint on his pessimism? More likely, it seems to me, it is the character of Giovanni Verga. (pp. 117-18)

> *Thomas Goddard Bergin, in his* Giovanni Verga *(copyright, 1931, by Yale University Press), Yale University Press, 1931, 135 p.*

LUIGI PIRANDELLO (essay date 1931)

[Verga's] early works are the expression of his romantic and sensual sentimentality: a world created from the outside and—what may seem paradoxical—without any direct feeling on his part. Not because at the time he did not actually have those feelings, but because he had too many and they were too close to him. Consequently, he was unable to clothe reality from within, unable to see it and place it objectively in a character, in the very character that as a story-teller he aspired to create. In other words, Verga's ambition was to live these novels while writing them; and only artifice could be the result. His aspirations remained muddy and confused, and never became purified in the filter of art.

But it was an experience necessary to his passionate nature which was trying to incarnate itself in art, trying to find its novel, and which began by forming it artificially, lodged within models that came to him from France. All this romantic dross had to burn so that the gold could flow more pure. Verga had first to reach that conclusion which we read in his youthful work *Eros:* "All knowledge of life lies in simplifying human passions and reducing them to their

natural proportions." That is to say, it lies in the small area that must be dug in depth, so that the oak's roots may reach as far down as its branches grow in height and firmness into the sun. It does not lie in the vast field to be tilled on the surface only, so that the plants of one season may sprout in it merely to be beaten down by the first blast of wind. In brief, the fire of art, having burned the dross, had to sweep over him to the very marrow of living matter.

But when this happened, when Verga was through with living his adventure and began the toil and labor of creation, the work that was born no longer had any resonance. It was mute. (pp. 109-10)

Verga is dialectal. Dialectal, but in a manner suited to a nation that lives the varied life and therefore uses the varied languages of its many regions. "The "dialecticism" of Verga is truly a formal creation, which cannot be considered part of "the question of the language," in the usual manner, noting its often strictly Sicilian syntactical structure and its idioms.

In the case of Verga, "idiomatic" means "right." The life of a region in the reality that Verga gave it, as he saw it, as it took form and movement in him, that is to say, as it created itself in Verga, could not be expressed differently: that language is the very creation of that region. (pp. 111-12)

Those who think that the work of Verga's maturity was intentionally patterned on an artistic method suggested by others and imported from outside Italy, without having developed within him as his own living subject matter, are mistaken. That method was Verga's, not because it came to him from the French naturalist school, but because it was his, the intimate law of his being as a writer, the free and spontaneous expression of his own personal image of life that being free and spontaneous could take no other form than the form it took. So much so that now, after so much time has elapsed, Verga's work survives whole and perfect, with all its unique elements marvelously interrelated and cooperating with one another to form a living body. And there is no reason to think that the form of any of these elements is what it is because of the artist's desire to conform to any of the canons of the French naturalist school, canons that we do not even remember. (pp. 115-16)

Verga—as he developed within the history of his own time, in his particular way of being, conditioned by his time and changing with it—had no active faith, no norm and direction in his life; nor did he seek one, for he thought that none existed. Actually he did have one but it was hidden, obscure as are all things that reside in feeling and not in intellect. Verga's faith had to do with his affections, his immediate affections: his family, his land, the customs of his people, their interests and their passions. And, indeed, it was only in this area that he was able to set "a reality" for himself. Thus he did not create a world ideologically; he was not able to construct it to correspond to an abstract idea, from the outside, within a reality going beyond it, that is, beyond himself. He accepted the world within that obscure reality which his feelings dictated, from within himself, piecemeal; and he said that reality was as it was because that is how it was. Naturally, since his feelings took this form by chance and without the aid of the intelligence, they became progressively sadder, drying up bit by bit, like a mechanism governed by some anguished destiny. He pictured the almost fatal existence of those feelings in realities that can only be exactly as they are, because those feelings are what they are and cannot be otherwise—so sad, so implacably sad!

And so we have *Vita dei campi,* and the *Novelle rusticane,* and *Per le vie,* and *Vagabondaggio,* and *I Malavoglia,* and *Mastro don Gesualdo.* And yet Verga thought that the restlessness of his vagabond imagination could find peace quietly "in the serenity of sweet, simple feelings, succeeding one another calmly and regularly from generation to generation." He thought that he could find peace by considering worthy of the deepest respect the tenacious attachment of a poor people to the rock on which fate had decreed that they be born, their resignation to a life of hardship, the religion of the family casting its sober light on their work and home, on the stones that surround that home. But instead of finding peace in all this, he perceived something like a fatal necessity in the tenacious affections of the weak, in the instinct of the humble to band together in order to protect themselves against the storms of life; and he tried to decipher the modest and nameless drama that defeats the plebeian actors of his masterpiece, *I Malavoglia.* The essence of this drama he himself described: "When one of those humble ones tries to leave the group, either because he is attracted by the unknown, or because he desires to improve his lot, or because he is curious about the rest of the world, the world, hungry fish that it is, swallows him and those closest to him as well."

This is the idea that lights up his feelings. But what a sad light it is! And the feelings—his love for those humble ones, for those weak ones, for those poor beings—become passion in that light, and the passion becomes torment. Quite the contrary of sweet peacefulness! Quite the contrary of serene peace! Quite the contrary of gentle, simple feelings, of a calm succession of events, unchanged from generation to generation! This is a world, a poor world of fundamental necessities, of basic affections, intimate, primitive, naked, a world of naked things, of elemental simplicity, abandoned to some fatal necessity. He is the first to suffer because of it, but the light of the intellect immediately convinces him that it can only be thus, that there is no escaping into any other reality—a reality that would be different if one were to look at it from another angle, if the feelings of the characters were to mirror themselves even just fleetingly in the reflection of someone standing on the outside, as so often happens in [Alessandro] Manzoni. No, Verga looks at this reality steadily, always from within, with the eyes of his characters, continually identifying with them. And reality is only that reality, as the feelings of his characters create it, implacably, inexorably, always that reality. Not that it is not sometimes comic, or that it may not turn an ironic glance upon itself, in the comments of the other actors on the scene, or in the contrasts—often cruel and awkward—of life in the provinces or life in the country. But here too that necessity is always present, turning even irony into melancholy and awkwardness into sadness, as is the case in "Malaria," and in "Il Reverendo," and in "Cos'è il Re," or in "Licciu Papa," and a bit everywhere in the short stories, and in *I Malavoglia* and *Mastro don Gesualdo.* One must come to terms with this impending fate, and woe to him who doesn't do so, or doesn't want to do so; he will have the damage and the scorn. This is the nature of Verga's resignation and it is so bitter. Not "rationality" then, which gives the idea of a mechanical rigidity, but resignation to a fatal necessity that vanquishes all and allows no one to rebel. (pp. 120-22)

[For] Verga the domestic hearth is sacred. . . . In almost all of Verga's work there is not other sacred pivot than this. Verga always looks at it through the eyes of his characters with veneration, nostalgia, and tenderness. He is filled with pity for those who have no hearth, for those condemned to leave it or to lose it, because of want and poverty. "To each bird its nest is beautiful." Oh the proverbs of Padron 'Ntoni Malavoglia, for whom men are made like the fingers of a hand! Oh unforgettable house of the Medlar Tree! And all the hardships to win it back only to end up dying far away, in the poorhouse in the city, with eyes glued to the door to see if no one is coming to take one back to where one can no longer live but one could at least die! And what is saddest for Mastro don Gesualdo is to have to die like a dog in his daughter's palace, he who in his eagerness "to amass things" had never allowed himself a moment's rest.

But don Gesualdo Motta is inferior to Padron 'Ntoni Malavoglia. Not because don Gesualdo's figure doesn't stand out powerfully in full relief, nor because his deeds, his feelings, his every smallest act, and those of the others about him, aren't portrayed even more skilfully than in the first novel. But don Gesualdo's story is already constructed with elements that obviously go beyond him, without the compact and sincere naturalness of the other novel, so much more admirable and almost miraculous. For we do not know how all the life of that fishing village can be so tightly knit around the house of the Medlar, and how this novel, whose plot is non-existent and whose events occur almost by chance, can be so full of passion.

One cannot claim that all this was not intentional, for it was part of Verga's aspiration, as he revealed it in dedicating the short story "L'amante di Gramigna" to Salvatore Farina. In that dedication he wrote that the triumph of the novel would occur "when the affinity and the cohesion of its every part will be so complete that the process of creation remains a mystery, like the development of human passions; when the harmony of its forms will be so perfect, the sincerity of its reality so evident, its mode and reason for being so necessary that the hand of the artist will remain absolutely invisible. Then the novel will have the stamp of a real happening, and the work of art will seem to *have produced itself,* to have matured and grown spontaneously like a fact of nature without maintaining any point of contact with its author. . . ." (pp. 123-24)

This aspiration became a reality with *I Malavoglia.* (p. 124)

The work is admirable, but the commitment from which it springs is even more admirable. Its new and inevitable style keeps it alive forever as a work of art, more alive today than ever before, as a model of action and faith, and even aside from any literary considerations, as an act of life. (p. 125)

Luigi Pirandello, "Pirandello on Verga" (1931), in Verga's Milanese Tales *by Olga Ragusa (copyright, 1964 by S. F. Vanni), S. F. Vanni, 1964, pp. 106-26.*

D. H. LAWRENCE (essay date 1936)

Verga is one of the greatest masters of the short story. In the volume *Novelle Rusticane* and in the volume entitled *Cavalleria Rusticana* are some of the best short stories ever written. They are sometimes as short and as poignant as Tchekhov. (p. 271)

[*Storia di Una Capinera*] is rather sentimental, maybe. But it is no more sentimental than [Hardy's *Tess of the D'-Urbervilles*]. And the sentimentality seems to me to belong to the Sicilian characters in the book, it is true to type, quite as much so as the sentimentality of a book like Dickens's *Christmas Carol,* or George Eliot's *Silas Marner,* both of which works are "ridiculous", if you like, without thereby being wiped out of existence.

The trouble with Verga, as with all Italians, is that he never seems quite to know where he is. . . . [He] seems to have a borrowed outlook on life: . . . borrowed from the French. . . .

This is the trouble with Verga. But on the other hand, everything he does has a weird quality of Verga in it, quite distinct and like nothing else. And yet, perhaps the gross vision of the man is not quite his own. All his movements are his own. But his main motive is borrowed. (p. 272)

[*I Malavoglia*] is a great book. But it is *parti pris*. It is one-sided. And therefore it dates. There is too much, too much of the tragic fate of the poor, in it. There is a sort of wallowing in tragedy: the tragedy of the humble. It belongs to a date when the "humble" were almost the most fashionable thing. And the Malavoglia family are most humbly humble. Sicilians of the sea-coast, fishers, small traders—their humble tragedy is so piled on, it becomes almost disastrous. . . . It is a great book, a great picture of poor life in Sicily, on the coast just north of Catania. But it is rather overdone on the pitiful side. . . . Nevertheless, it is essentially a true picture, and different from anything else in literature. . . .

The trouble with realism—and Verga was a realist—is that the writer, when he is a truly exceptional man like Flaubert or like Verga, tries to read his own sense of tragedy into people much smaller than himself. (p. 273)

Not all the noble sympathy of Flaubert or Verga for Bovarys and Malavoglias can prevent the said Bovarys and Malavoglias from being commonplace persons. They were deliberately chosen because they *were* commonplace, and not heroic. The authors insisted on the treasure of the humble. But they had to lend the humble by far the best part of their own treasure, before the said humble could show any treasure at all. . . .

Mastro-don Gesualdo, however, is not nearly so much treasure-of-the-humble as *I Malavoglia*. Here, Verga is not dealing with the disaster of poverty, and calling it tragedy. On the contrary, he is a little bored by poverty. He must have a hero who wins out, and makes his pile, and then succumbs under the pile. (p. 274)

Gesualdo is attractive, and, in a sense, heroic. But still he is not allowed to emerge in the old heroic sense, with swagger and nobility and head-and-shoulders taller than anything else. He is allowed to have exceptional qualities, and above all, exceptional force. But these things do not make a hero of a man. A hero must be a hero by grace of God, and must have an inkling of the same. . . .

Gesualdo is just an ordinary man with extraordinary energy. That, of course, is the intention. But he is a Sicilian. And here lies the difficulty. Because the realistic-democratic age has dodged the dilemma of having no heroes by having every man his own hero. (p. 275)

Gesualdo seems so potent, so full of potency. Yet nothing emerges, and he never says anything. . . .

And you have a wretched, realistic kind of tragedy for the end. And you feel, perhaps the book was all about nothing, and Gesualdo wasn't worth the labour of Verga.

But that is because we are spiritual snobs, and think, because a man can fume with "To be or not to be", therefore he is a person to be taken account of. Poor Gesualdo had never heard of: To be or not to be, and he wouldn't have taken any notice if he had. He lived blindly, with the impetuosity of blood and muscles, sagacity and will, and he never woke up to himself. Whether he would have been any the better for waking up to himself, who knows! (p. 279)

> *D. H. Lawrence, "'Mastro-don Gesualdo'," in* Phoenix: The Posthumous Papers of D. H. Lawrence, *edited by Edward D. McDonald (copyright 1936 by Frieda Lawrence; renewed copyright © 1964 by the Estate of the late Frieda Lawrence Ravagli; reprinted by permission of Viking Penguin Inc.), The Viking Press, 1936 (and reprinted in* Selected Literary Criticism, *edited by Anthony Beal, William Heinemann Ltd., 1955, Viking Press, 1956, pp. 207-72).*

RAYMOND ROSENTHAL (essay date 1964)

The House by the Medlar Tree is the artistic expression of precisely this theme: the sacredness of the indefinably, primitively human, and the childish cry of pain which all injustice, whether the product of aimless fate or callous men, wrings from the human heart. Its unity of artistic means and thematic ends is so exquisite and perfect that one can only compare it to the art works of more forthright, instinctive ages than ours—the paintings of Masaccio, say, or the music of Pergolesi. It is perhaps the last great Christian novel in modern times, and, ironically enough, it was written by a firm unbeliever and anticlerical. (p. vii)

Verga's choral method permits him an emotional ductility and ambiguity, a gay irony that, throughout all the episodes, is counterpointed against the grave ground bass of the novel's dominant tone. From the very first the author vanishes and his characters take the center of the stage, and the charm of their bustling, eruptive, vociferous existence lies in the fact that they are at once predictable and unpredictable, since what they have to say is always being qualified, or distorted, or turned completely around, by its relation to the vicissitudes of the central story. Verga is a master of vivid transitions, constantly catching us off balance, constantly forcing us to see his characters in another light, and this gives his novel the quick, blurred, spontaneous, glancing effect that life itself has upon us. (p. ix)

[Verga] invented a language in which to tell the story of *The House by the Medlar Tree* that, although outwardly observing the forms of correct Italian, was wholly based on the inner rhythms and cadences, the locutions, of Sicilian dialect. But his linguistic submission to the world of poor fishermen was only the outward sign of his willingness to submit to something much profounder and more meaningful that he found there; and his entire novel is, in the truest sense, the expression, in Simone Weil's pregnant words, of "the supernatural virtue of humility in the domain of thought." (pp. xi-xii)

> *Raymond Rosenthal, in his foreword to* The

House by the Medlar Tree *by Giovanni Verga, translated by Raymond Rosenthal (copyright © 1964 by Raymond Rosenthal), The New American Library, 1964, pp. v-xii.*

V.S. PRITCHETT (essay date 1964)

Cavalleria Rusticana is an admirable, naked story, ruthlessly economical and as plain a piece of surgery on the passions as you could ask for. It is more than surgery; the more terrible Sicilian knife is at work. *La Lupa* . . . is another of the same kind. There is something superb, an excess which amounts to the poetry of pride, about these acts of transcendent psychological justice among people who are blinded by the rage of honor, amid starvation, crippling toil and rags. (p. 322)

In [*Mastro-Don Gesualdo*] we find what it is that lies behind the Sicilian violence. The answer, according to Verga, is more violence. Violence of tongue, violence of will, greed, push, scramble, gossip, the awful ruthless, comic, bitter, incorrigible barnyard belligerence of family life; fights for money, fights for food, fights for possession. Misery is the basis of it, the misery of poor land, the misery of the isolated towns where the nail scratches of scandal and contempt are scrawled over everyone's life. The beautiful are the humble and submissive who refuse to join the fight; worse luck for them, they are kicked out and trodden on and their poor-spiritedness is a byword. So we should describe the people in Verga's novel and yet they do not distress us. Only the suburban townsman idealizes the countryman and is shocked by the malignance of country life and its poisoned solitudes. Only the suburban townsman conveniently forgets that the countryman must fight for money and property like the rest of the world. Far from distressing us, Verga's people gradually take possession of our minds, seize us with their grasping hands, harangue us about their case until we are forced to see the point of it, and to see that here, in this ludicrous family screeching about pride, money, marriages, and ownership, something elemental is taking place. His people are able to convince us of this not merely because it is true but because Verga is a very considerable novelist. He has a rich range of mood, a pungency of metaphor; something in him is equal to the clamor of the heart; he has a comprehensive grasp of scene; and without being naturalistic he seems to be able to pull up people by the roots straight out of nature and put them, rife as they are, upon the page. They come out with such vocal, physical emphasis that at first one is stunned and deafened. Verga depends on the crackle of his dialogue and on an allusive atmosphere which each sentence creates. You have to watch that and keep your senses keen or you will miss his transitions. (pp. 323-24)

You notice that Verga is not a regional novelist in the provincial sense of the word. *Mastro-Don Gesualdo* is no more regional in this rather derogatory meaning, than Turgenev was in *Lear of the Steppes*. No, Verga is European and modern. His visual power, which is heightened by his constant use of peasant metaphor and his identification with the peasant mind, is very modern. . . . Verga, no doubt like Cézanne, supposed he was being scientific. Now the visual, oral style becomes monotonous, unless the human heat of the book grows until it becomes convulsive and momentous. And Verga's story does grow. (p. 324)

The intensity of Verga is achieved by dense detail. He is totally without rhetoric. . . . But thinking about this in-

tensity has led me to forget Verga's comic gift. Verga saw the fantastic comedy of the family struggle. He saw the sardonic farce of Sicilian politics, and how much they depended upon local personality. (p. 325)

Verga is one of the great in this novel, a Balzacian. He sees a society and that society working in men and women. Perhaps, like the Sicilian sun, he hammers his words too pitilessly on our heads and batters us with the theme of self-interest; but he has the space of the masters. (p. 327)

V. S. Pritchett, "'Cavalleria Rusticana'," in his The Living Novel and Later Appreciations *(copyright 1947 © 1964; renewed 1975 by V. S. Pritchett; reprinted by permission of Random House, Inc.; in Canada by Literistic, Ltd.), revised edition, Random House, 1964, pp. 320-27.*

SERGIO PACIFICI (essay date 1967)

The world of Verga's primitives is distinguished by its simple feelings, its modest aspirations. . . . (p. 11)

Few stories could actually be simpler than the one told with consummate skill by Verga in *The House by the Medlar Tree*. It is a tale revolving around the many vicissitudes that strike a family of fishermen, the Malavoglia. In the course of the story, the heroes discover the meaning of death, defeat, moral degradation, fear, misery, and love. (p. 16)

Verga's technique is one based on direct and indirect discourse; we either hear the characters speak or we are told, by one of the characters, the essence of what has taken place. Indeed, what the characters say is often reported indirectly in a way that mirrors the spoken rather than written speech. The so-called minor characters often act as a chorus, whose function, much like a Greek tragedy, is to comment upon the dramatic events of the story.

Nowhere does Verga attempt to make a direct comment on, or judgment of, the action he describes, and much less does he try to influence the opinion of the reader. The method he selects is that of a novelist whose function must be deceptively limited to providing the information in as vivid and complete a manner as possible so the reader may see and judge for himself. In addition, in the novel seeing is combined with hearing. What we *hear* a character say, or what is said about him, enables us to recognize him by his personal idiosyncrasies, by his speech and action. Our insights into their quality as human beings are extended by frequent opinions and gossip offered by friends and relatives, whose conversations reveal an intimate, but never offensive, concern for life in the community. (p. 19)

The relatively few descriptive passages of *The House by the Medlar Tree* . . . are written as though they were in fact spoken by an unidentified villager whose manner of speech follows a pattern familiar to us since we have encountered it many times in the unfolding of the tale.

The novel's setting is kept purposely narrow: practically the entire story takes place in the town of Aci Trezza. Conversely, the cast of characters . . . is comparatively large. . . . Everything in the novel helps create the illusion that we are in a small town: the small talk we hear, the provincial attitude of the peasants, the petty jealousies and nagging grievances, the unobtrusive manner in which some of the extraordinary or important happenings that take place in the mainland reach the town as faint echoes. . . . We are truly cut off not only from the continent but from history itself. We live a drama with many self-repeating acts, a drama whose heroes change their names but not their roles for they are all equally involved in the endless struggle for survival and furtherance of their own selfish interests. We are thrust into a world where misery is rampant and greed is frequently out of proportion with what is at stake; a world of hard work and sorrow accepted with resignation as the lot of man. In such a world there is little awareness of the tragic fact that, sooner or later, everyone will be overcome by the vicissitudes of life. (pp. 19-20)

Verga relies exclusively on a few bold strokes and details to give his heroes a quality and dimension we are not likely to forget. It is his economy of means coupled with the adroit device of allowing his characters to define themselves through their acts and utterances, complemented by the comments made by the other personages of the book, that constitutes one of the fresh and vital aspects of the work. (p. 22)

The novel's events are sparse and modest almost to the point of seeming trivial. It is one of the many achievements of the book, however, to show us that what it presents is no inconsequential struggle, but a dramatic battle that takes place, in a larger scale and on a vastly more complicated stage, in life as we know it. Only by viewing the book from a distance are we able to study its architecture and begin to discover the perfection of its design. There is both progress and continuity in the story. Whatever happens to its heroes manages to keep us in a continual state of suspense, even though we expect that our feelings will not be betrayed. . . .

Tragic and comic touches alternate in the novel, for this is no bleak account of the numerous disasters that have hit the family and have destroyed its confidence in life itself, but a tale of the irony and humor of life. (p. 26)

Verga offers no answers to the eternal riddle of existence, no program of action, no staunch commitment to a religious faith. In some ways, Verga has something in common with Albert Camus in indirectly asserting that only a genuine solidarity with other human beings is ultimately capable of alleviating, and rendering more bearable, the suffering and tragedy that mankind has to endure. (p. 28)

> Sergio Pacifici, "The Tragic World of Verga's Primitives," in The Modern Italian Novel from Manzoni to Svevo (copyright © 1967 by Southern Illinois University Press; reprinted by permission of Southern Illinois University Press), Southern Illinois University Press, 1967 (and reprinted in From Verismo to Experimentalism: Essays on the Modern Italian Novel, edited by Sergio Pacifici, Indiana University Press, 1969, pp. 3-34).

D. WOOLF (essay date 1975)

By the time Verga came to write the *Novelle rusticane* his conception of realism had undergone a radical change, probably under the influence of his work on *I Malavoglia*. The essence of the change is this, that whereas formerly Verga's realism consisted in giving an undistorted portrayal of individual destinies, it now lies in the accurate revelation of the common experience of life. *Vita dei campi* tells of such things as Jeli's crime, Rosso's philosophy, gnà Pina's passion. The *Novelle rusticane* are about law and society, attitudes to authority, class structure and so on. In short, the themes of *Vita dei campi* are personal and individual while those of the later collection are social and general. (pp. 257-58)

One of the judgements most commonly made of the *Novelle rusticane* is that they bear witness to a deepening of the author's pessimism. This judgement is based upon the following points: that "la roba," by which is understood the passion for material gain, is the leit-motif of the entire collection; that the author is concerned to show the spiritual degradation caused by this passion that warps sentimental and moral values alike; and that his preoccupation with these ideas shows a darkening of his own spirit and a disillusioned view of life in general. This judgement appears, however, to be untenable on several counts. The passion for material gain is not a general theme among the stories. It is the basis of one story (*La roba*) and plays an incidental part in some others (e.g., *L'asino di San Giuseppe*, *Il Reverendo*) but it does not appear at all in stories such as *I Galantuomini*, *Il Mistero*, *Malaria* and *Cos'è il Re*. Similarly, the adulteration of sentiment which is the theme of *Gli orfani* plays a minor role in some of the other stories but by no means in all of them. But, more importantly, the view that the *Novelle rusticane* reflect the author's personal pessimism fails to take into account the nature of the stories themselves. It is legitimate to speak of pessimism in a story like *Pane nero* where the destiny of the characters is manipulated to express a certain interpretation of a certain situation but the other tales in the collection do not follow this pattern. They do not express the author's feelings and opinions but are, as we have seen, illustrations of significant aspects of a particular society, designed to make that society comprehensible. Where life in a particular society is thus illustrated and that life is harsh and the harshness is shown, one cannot charge the author with pessimism save in his choice of subject, for the sombre color of his work is not then pessimistic but realistic. (pp. 259-60)

> D. Woolf, "Three Stories from the 'Novelle rusticane'," in Italica, Vol. 52, No. 2, Summer, 1975, pp. 235-61.

GIOVANNI CECCHETTI (essay date 1978)

[In "Nedda,"] Verga turns his attention to the lowest social levels in Sicily and to characters who are passionate and honest, but who also have great difficulty in winning their battle for survival. The theme of the story will not, then, spring from his personal involvement in, and direct observation of, high society, but from the memories of his own childhood and adolescence. . . . (p. 32)

[The uncomplicated plot of "Nedda"] contains all the ingredients of the works of Verga's maturity. The characters, hopelessly trapped in extreme poverty, are destroyed by events, without being able to do anything to change their destiny. Their psychology has repeatedly been called the psychology of the doomed, which consists not so much in an inevitable defeat as in an innate resignation to the blows of life and in the unshakable belief that things have always been so and will never change. Verga places a great emphasis on the background and social environment of his protagonist. Poverty is viewed not only as a deterministic element, but as the most decisive of forces. Even Nedda's physical appearance has been shaped by poverty. Her destiny is the same as that of all the other poor, and no one can conquer it. The man she loves tries to earn some extra money, but as a result he dies, and in turn her little girl dies too. Love and the possibility of having a family are indeed luxuries the poor cannot afford. The power of the economic factor, which was already present in *Una peccatrice* and in *Eva,* is now explored anew, and far more convincingly. The writer has transplanted it into its own natural ground.

Verga's attitude throughout the story is one of unwavering compassion for the creature "crouched on the lowest step of the human ladder." ... He manages to bring out her feelings more successfully than he had done with any other character, but he also allows his personal compassion to lead him into frequent moralizing. He constantly calls Nedda "poor girl" and constantly attacks the people around her for being inhuman. Such direct intrusions and comments constitute one of the shortcomings of the story. The true artist does not judge; he represents. The judgment may spontaneously emerge from the page, but it is never expressed directly. Verga is not as yet capable of portraying the world of the poor in its stark inevitability by letting the facts speak in their own voice. This inability is reflected also in his style, which continues to be marred by frequent lapses. (pp. 34-5)

"Nedda" cannot be considered either Verga's first mature work or a sample of what he would do in the years ahead. It carries the seeds of a great story, but great it is not. While it affords us a glimpse into his future achievements, it also bears witness to Verga's groping past. It is the somewhat clumsy product of a man who has finally discovered a compatible world, but does not yet understand it fully. That the dialogues are often so natural and spontaneous is partly due to the novelty of that world. Verga cannot escape a style and a language that are more sober, more concrete, more fitting to the innate reticence of his Sicilian peasants, and, therefore, free of sophistication and falsification. But when he presents his characters and their background directly, and speaks and describes on his own, his prose reveals the same old blemishes. (pp. 36-7)

With "L'amante di Gramigna" ["Gramigna's Mistress"] Verga began to strive for the greatest economy of words and for maximum condensation. Not only did he refrain from any direct intrusion into his text, but eliminated everything that could be suggested between the lines. Above all, he avoided traditional descriptive passages. The very fact that he was narrating with the words of his people forced him to be unceasingly intent upon their individual reactions. As a result, he could mention external elements only when those people mentioned them—that is to say, when they found them relevant to their everyday lives. Thus description per se was automatically eliminated. (p. 51)

In a story of only a few pages Verga manages to create a highly poetic character. His stylistic compression, rather than preventing, helps him to evoke some profound human associations. A few words, or the repetition of a key phrase, are enough to bring to the surface even what lies hidden in the subconscious. With "L'amante di Gramigna" Verga has definitely opted for certain characters and has conquered a prose born of their inner world. Although they are the poor and the oppressed, these characters are full of existential intensity, and although they cannot rebel against a social structure that has from time immemorial assigned them to their present condition, they do indeed live by their desires and aspirations, and above all by their dignity and sense of morality. Verga has them express the ordinary/extraordinary events in their lives with a vehemently personal language, through which they stand out and tower. Thus he turns the poor and the oppressed into the heroes of his time. (pp. 52-3)

Strikingly different from "La lupa" and "Cavalleria rusticana," ["Jeli il pastore" ("Ieli")] is a novelette in which Verga explores the possibiltiy of a new narrative rhythm and the relationship between chronological and psychological time. He closely watches the development of a peasant boy who is left entirely to himself, for whom life is an unending series of discoveries, and who grows up to be a man with the same feelings and the same sense of justice as those who have been guided and indoctrinated by a social group. (p. 59)

[Verga] intended, among other things, to examine the past of a man who, having grown up in a friendly, primitive environment, is naïvely optimistic and, consequently, is slow in understanding the everpresent treachery of life. Thus the fabric of "Jeli il pastore" comes to rest on the dialectical conflict between such naïve optimism and the realities of the human condition. We may even venture to state that in it Verga is tacitly arguing against one of the most popular among the late Romantic views of life. The happiness of childhood, he seems to say, can neither last nor can it be recaptured; in fact, it should not be. Man must grow up to be alert, well-prepared and well-armed to defend himself from both circumstances and the ruthless selfishness of the adult world, or he will be destroyed. (pp. 59-60)

[In] "Jeli il pastore" Verga pursues also a narrative exploration of the interrelationship between chronological and psychological time, and opts for the latter. He almost totally disregards the actual sequence of time periods and dwells exclusively on events with a lasting emotional impact. There is no way to tell, for example, how many years elapse between the beginning and the center of the story. Ieli was a happy child, and suddenly he is an adult facing the difficulties of life. The transition is merely hinted at by the incidental phrase: "so much water had passed and passed under the little bridge" .... as if all that had left an indelible mark on the child had already been told and the rest represented nothing more than the repetition of obvious thoughts and of obvious gestures. Interestingly, we do not feel we miss any details. If anything, we are even under the impression that the narrative pace is slower, more leisurely and more diffuse, than in the other stories. And in spite of the chronological gaps, we know that the three parts constitute an indivisible unity, all imbued with the same, deep-flowing lyricism.

Through memory man instinctively selects from his past a related event and fully relives it in a special dimension—as belonging exclusively to the present. At that moment, time in a chronological sense does not exist. We may object that in life there is always a sequence, a before and an after; however, the perception of this sequence is the product of our rational faculties, which compel us to see events in a so-called logical order, or, rather, to translate the subconscious into the conscious. When by association we relive past experiences, we actually make them contemporary. Then only psychological time does really exist, and it is unidimensional: present. In "Jeli il pastore" Verga has to reconcile the protagonist's continual withdrawal into this dimension of past-present with the possibility of his becoming fully aware of what is happening around him. To do so, he has decided to tell the story on two different but synchronously amalgamated planes, without ever losing sight of either one of them. (pp. 61-2)

If in "Jeli il pastore" Verga had eliminated many transitions, the reader could still perceive some sort of chronological sequence. [In "Rosso Malpelo"] even this barely perceptible sequence seems to have been abolished, so that we are left with the impression that many events take place simultaneously. Reading "Rosso Malpelo" is like watching a canvas being slowly uncovered, piece by piece, until we can finally see it in its entirety. (p. 63)

Not very much seems to happen in the story, and yet we feel it overflow with momentous events, due to the fact that Verga does not narrate directly but through his protagonist's remarks. The flashback on Malpelo's father's death appears to function as the mover of the entire story. Not only all of Malpelo's observations on life and man, but even his final decision to go underground, spring from that same remote source. . . . It is the theme of the relationship between Malpelo and his dead father that makes it possible for Verga to remain on a purely psychological level, while leaving actual chronology almost completely aside. Malpelo's stark and ruthless philosophy (similar to that of a primitive Machiavelli planted in a hostile world) also grows out of such a theme. By meditating on his father's death, he discovers the substance of the struggle for survival and can synthesize it into a personal concept of human existence.

The story as a whole is a magnificent piece of prose. It gives the full measure of Verga's narrative skills and orginality of style. Here many of the features that we have discovered in the previous stories stand out with an even greater degree of maturity. (pp. 64-5)

[*I Malavoglia* is] the story of the house by the medlar tree —the very symbol of the family roots and of its unity—and of how it was lost. Together with the house there is the fishing boat, the *other* house, the home away from home, which makes survival possible. The grandfather, Master 'Ntoni, in full possession of the wisdom of the centuries, is the skipper. When he speaks, he utters proverbial maxims, because "the sayings of the ancients never lied." . . . He is firmly planted in tradition. He knows that whatever is being done now has been done an infinite number of times in the past; that life consists in the perennial repetition of the same gestures for the same perennial purpose of surviving; that in our voyage we can travel only the path that has been found and marked from time immemorial; and whoever decides to change cannot reap anything but sorrow, and perhaps death. These fundamental truths can be expressed only with the words that have always contained them. . . . Master 'Ntoni's proverbs insist on the inevitability of social organization, with a man in charge who gives the orders. As is peculiar to primitive, natural wisdom, he derives his basic metaphor from the human body, from how it is structured, with each organ and each limb having a well-defined function, and being at the same time related to, or dependent upon, the functions of the others. (pp. 75-6)

[Verga] had insisted that the novel should develop with the same natural spontaneity as human passions—a principle that, if applied to psychological analysis, would produce a work mirroring the most elusive ripplings of the psyche without the intrusion of the author's hand. In *Il marito di Elena* [*Helen's Husband*], however, Verga does not succeed in bringing this ideal of impersonality to fruition. In fact, he is often present with expressions of either approval or disapproval, which ring as his own even when stylistically they may appear to be spoken by the invisible observer. (p. 99)

Imprecision is one of the weaknesses of the novel. It is rooted in the author's inability to view his characters and their vicissitudes from a certain distance, with the result that the characters themselves are described rather than presented. Verga intends to analyze their psychology, and yet he is unable to go beyond a somewhat reflective, at times vacuously emphatic and exclamatory, commentary from the outside. In the last pages of the novel, he proceeds through a string of exclamations on the assumption that they reflect Cesare's psychological condition in that tragic moment. Instead they sound almost like the transcription of the reactions of a superficial observer, of one who is not present but is told about the event in a moment of inebriated elation. Thus what could have been an intense drama is translated into light melodrama—and a rather poor one at that. (p. 100)

[There is] a great deal of humor in [*Novelle rusticane*], but it is a dark and bitter humor—the result of a pessimistic outlook on life by a writer who has grown both fatalistic and unable to find any redeeming traits in his own people's actions. He seems to insist that the hand of fate weighs heavily on each of us, and there is nothing we can do to lift it. Yet the main theme of the book is economic: property and money on one side, and poverty and near starvation on the other; those who have and those who have not, with the latter being subjected to the former, and with all of them pursued by a relentless destiny. The style, enriched with all the discoveries of the previous "Sicilian" books, is supple and complex, and the people's lives are perfectly fused with the heavy atmosphere of the desolate countryside; they are created and accompanied by the rhythm of the words, and by the slow, intriguing music of sentences that are often imbued with such continuity as to reach symphonic proportions. (pp. 104-05)

Mastro-don Gesualdo is the epic of the economic compulsion relentlessly driving a man toward the acquisition of greater and greater wealth and toward the power that such wealth generates. Throughout his previous works Verga had regularly stressed the significance of financial well-being and of how its presence, or its absence, conditions all other aspects of human life. Now he pulls together all those considerations and observations to fuse them into a new and vigorous unity. Greed for riches obsesses nearly everyone of the numerous characters in the novel—yet only the protagonist, Gesualdo, rises above the pettiness and the abjection of the others. He wants wealth; yet he does not conceive of it as an end unto itself, but rather as a means to power: the power to realize many other aspirations—such as that of reaching the top of the social ladder and dominating an entire town. The philosophy standing as a motivating force behind the novel may be found summarized in two familiar-sounding aphorisms: "The world belongs to those who have money" . . . and "Everyone works in his own interest." . . . But even though Gesualdo's plans and actions are in harmony with these principles, he never appears narrow-minded or narrowly self-centered. "His own interest" often may signify also the interest of many other people; yet the philosophy that brings him success carries within itself the seeds of his destruction. . . . Gesualdo is not satisfied with money and land: he wants respectability, which he believes he can attain by marrying into the town aristocracy. It will be precisely this vanity—a new and different kind of greed—that will cause him to lose everything to the equally greedy, aristocratic son-in-law, and to die alone. Yet, throughout the novel both the town and every one of its inhabitants exist only as a function of Gesualdo. But when he himself is vanquished, his defeat is born of the power he exerts on his environment and not of anyone's actions.

The ironic double epithet—*mastro-don*—refers to the standing of Gesualdo Motta—the name of a commoner—in the society of Vizzini (the Sicilian town where most of the action takes place). *Mastro* defines an independent workman, a skilled laborer, or—as is our case—a mason; a *Don*, on the other hand, is a member of the land-owning gentry. Mastro-don, therefore, gives us at once the past and the present of the protagonist, his roots in the working class as well as his claims to the aristocratic level. But, more importantly, it points out the attitude of the townsfolk.... We must add that it also stresses the power of Gesualdo's personality over all those who delude themselves in belittling him. (pp. 128-29)

With *Mastro-don Gesualdo*, Verga concluded a decade of so intense a literary production as to establish himself as the greatest and the most innovative Italian writer of the second half of the nineteenth century. (p. 141)

> Giovanni Cecchetti, in his *Giovanni Verga* (copyright © 1978 by G. K. Hall & Co.; reprinted with the permission of Twayne Publishers, A Division of G. K. Hall & Co., Boston), Twayne, 1978, 172 p.

BIBLIOGRAPHY

Alexander, Alfred. *Giovanni Verga: A Great Writer and His World.* London: Grant & Cutler, 1972, 252 p.
 A life of Verga that deals almost entirely with the social background of the author, with little critical commentary.

Bates, Ralph. "Verga Reconsidered." *New Republic* 113, No. 17 (22 October 1945): 525-26.
 Discussion of what the critic considers Verga's artistic failures and how they exemplify the inadequacy of pure realism as literary dogma.

Biasin, Gian-Paolo. "Narcisa's Poison." In his *Literary Diseases: Theme and Metaphor in the Italian Novel*, pp. 36-62. Austin: University of Texas Press, 1975.
 Examines *Una peccatrice* in connection with morbid aspects of romanticism.

Cambon, Glauco. "Verga's Mature Style." *Comparative Literature* XIV, No. 2 (Spring 1962): 143-52.
 Analysis of Verga's literary technique: his use of dialect, unobtrusive narrative tone, and the way he allows style to reflect a character's consciousness.

Cecchetti, Giovanni. "The Last Stories of Giovanni Verga." *Italian Quarterly* 1, No. 2 (Summer 1957): 8-14.
 Examines *Don Candeloro e Compagni*, Verga's last collection of short stories. There is also a general discussion of Verga's "free indirect style."

Cecchetti, Giovanni. Introduction to *The She Wolf and Other Stories*, by Giovanni Verga, pp. v-xx. Berkeley: University of California, 1973.
 Overview of Verga's life and works, with a particular emphasis on the stories in this collection.

Chandler, S. B. "The Movement of Life in Verga." *Italica* XXXV, No. 1 (March 1958): 91-100.
 Analyzes the vision of human existence implicit in Verga's work.

Chandler, S. B. "The Primitive World of Giovanni Verga." *Mosaic* 5, No. 3 (Spring 1972): 117-28.
 Discusses Verga's rejection of urban society in favor of the traditions and stability of rural society.

De Vito, Anthony J. "The Struggle for Existence in the Work of Giovanni Verga." *Italica* XVIII, No. 4 (December 1941): 179-85.
 Discusses how Verga's realistic fiction depicts the hardships of its Sicilian characters.

De Vito, Anthony J. "Disasters and Disease in the Work of Giovanni Verga." *Italica* 46, No. 1 (Spring 1969): 279-91.
 Considers the role of natural calamity in Verga's fiction and how this illuminates the author's view of existence.

Erickson, John D. "A Milanese Tale by Giovanni Verga." *Symposium* XX, No. 1 (Spring 1966): 7-13.
 Examines Verga's objective technique and the way it harmonizes with subject matter in "L'ultima giornata."

Goldberg, Issac. "Giovanni Verga." In his *The Drama of Transition*, pp. 141-45. Cincinnati: Stewart Kidd Co., 1922.
 Sketch of Verga's work and style, with a brief discussion of his dramas.

Jones, James F. "Narrative Technique in Verga's 'Le storie del castello di Trezza'." *Italica* 52, No. 2 (Summer 1975): 221-34.
 Analysis of Verga's literary experimentalism in this story.

Patruno, Nicholas. "An Interpretation of Verga's *Eva*." *Romance Notes* 17, No. 1 (Fall 1976): 57-65.
 Appraisal of this work of Verga's as exhibiting greater artistic maturity than previous critics had attributed to it.

Pritchett, V. S. "Verga." In his *Books in General*, pp. 19-24. London: Chatto & Windus, 1953.
 Focuses on Verga's style and realistic technique.

Schorer, Mark. "The Novels of Giovanni Verga." *New Republic* 130, No. 1 (11 January 1954): 17-19.
 Introductory overview of Verga's fiction and some of its commentators.

Edith (Newbold Jones) Wharton

1862-1937

American novelist, short story writer, critic, autobiographer, and poet.

Wharton is best known for satirically illuminating the manners and cruel excesses of aristocratic society. Her subject matter, tone, and style have often been compared with those of Henry James, her friend and mentor.

A member of New York's upper class society, Wharton was educated at home and in Europe by governesses and tutors. During her youth, the established gentry of New York were slowly usurped by the new business tycoons, and it was against these culturally pretending philistines that Wharton later directed her literary firepower.

In her early years, unsatisfied with society life and ill-matched in marriage, Wharton turned to writing for a measure of fulfillment. From the start of her professional writing activities and through many years Wharton was advised and encouraged by her cousin and friend, Walter Berry. Romantic allusions about them are made by various biographers, while a character similar to Berry has figured in her works. With the breakup of her marriage, Wharton took up permanent residence in France. It was there that she wrote one of her most famous works, *Ethan Frome*.

Wharton threw herself into France's service during World War I, organizing relief and caring for Belgian orphans, work that earned her the French Legion of Honor. Her war novels *The Marne* and *A Son at the Front* are, however, undistinguished. In 1921 she won the Pulitzer Prize for *The Age of Innocence*, which along with *The House of Mirth* and *Ethan Frome* is considered one of her three masterpieces. In *The Age of Innocence* Wharton masterfully chronicled the old New York of her childhood.

During her later years, Wharton's novels were strained with bitterness toward an increasingly harsh-mannered world, and they are, with few exceptions, considered inferior to her prewar works. She died in St. Brice-sous-Forêt, with her final effort, *The Buccaneers*, lying unfinished.

Wharton's fiction is not widely-read today, although, as Margaret McDowell has stated, she provided an important "link between the morally and psychologically oriented works of Hawthorne and James, who preceded her, and the later realists like Sinclair Lewis or F. Scott Fitzgerald with their tendency toward the sardonic and iconoclastic."

(See also *Dictionary of Literary Biography*, Vol. 4)

PRINCIPAL WORKS

The Decoration of Houses [with Ogden Codman, Jr.] (nonfiction) 1897

The Greater Inclination (short stories) 1899

The Touchstone: A Story (novella) 1900; published in England as *A Gift from the Grave: A Tale*

Crucial Instances (short stories) 1901

The Valley of Decision: A Novel (novel) 1902

Sanctuary (novella) 1903

The Descent of Man (short stories) 1904

Italian Villas and Their Gardens (essays) 1904

The House of Mirth (novel) 1905

Italian Backgrounds (memoirs) 1905

The Fruit of the Tree (novel) 1907

Madame de Treymes (novella) 1907

The Hermit and the Wild Woman, and Other Stories (short stories) 1908

Tales of Ghosts and Men (short stories) 1910

Ethan Frome (novella) 1911

The Reef: A Novel (novel) 1912

The Custom of the Country (novel) 1913

Xingu, and Other Stories (short stories and novella) 1916

Summer: A Novel (novel) 1917

The Marne (novella) 1918

French Ways and Their Meanings (essays) 1919

The Age of Innocence (novel) 1920

The Glimpses of the Moon (novel) 1922

A Son at the Front (novel) 1923

Old New York (novellas, includes *False Dawn: The 'Forties, The Old Maid: The 'Fifties, The Spark: The 'Sixties,* and *New Year's Day: The 'Seventies*) 1924

The Mother's Recompense (novel) 1925

The Writing of Fiction (criticism) 1925

Here and Beyond (short stories) 1926

Twilight Sleep (novel) 1927

The Children (novel) 1928

Hudson River Bracketed (novel) 1929

Certain People (short stories) 1930

The Gods Arrive (novel) 1932

A Backward Glance (autobiography) 1934

The World Over, (short stories) 1936

Ghosts (short stories) 1937

The Buccaneers (unfinished novel) 1938

HARRY THURSTON PECK (essay date 1899)

We could count upon the fingers of one hand the books of the past year that any one would ever think of reading a second time or of referring to hereafter, and one of these rare exceptions to the general rule of mediocrity and dulness we have found in a volume of eight short stories [*The Greater Inclination*] by Mrs. Edith Wharton. . . . [The] whole eight, with one exception, deserve in their collected form the most respectful consideration.

At the very outset it is necessary to set forth the undoubted fact that Mrs. Wharton, both in her choice of themes and in her treatment of them, has been influenced by the example of Mr. Henry James. At times one comes upon resemblances that are positively startling. Yet this is said in a purely scientific spirit and with no intention whatsoever of regarding Mrs. Wharton as an imitator. (p. 344)

[We] cannot say that she has imitated him, because to our mind her stories, with the exception already noted, are superior in many ways to those of Mr. James's. She has caught his later manner, but she has improved upon his later workmanship, and, therefore, she deserves a wholly independent criticism.

Of the stories in this book, three have to do exclusively with the sex-relation, and these are the strongest of the eight. One of the others, entitled "A Journey," is a study in nervous tension. Another, called "A Cup of Cold Water," is a powerful bit of emotional psychology. The last one in the book, "The Portrait," is slight in its workmanship, but ingenious in its theme. The fifth story. . . . "A Coward," is the one failure to be noted, since it lacks in some inexplicable way the sort of constructive coherence that ought to bind together the parts of even the very slightest work of fiction; for while a reader as a rule finds pleasure in the unexpected, the unexpected when once revealed ought to be quite in consonnance with what has led up to it; and in "The Coward" this is not the case.

Mrs. Wharton's most amusing piece of work, as it is the one most strongly suggestive of Mr. James's lighter manner, is that which is called "The Pelican." It is a perfectly delicious study of the typical "lady lecturer," and is full of pure delight from the beginning to the end. (pp. 344-45)

In the way of fiction we have seen nothing this year that has impressed us so much as Mrs. Wharton's book. There is a finish, an assurance, and a tenacity of grasp about her work that show her to be already an accomplished literary artist; while, as we have said before, Mr. James himself has nothing to teach her in those half-elusive but exquisitely effective strokes that reveal in an instant a whole mental attitude or the hidden meaning of a profound emotion. (p. 346)

Harry Thurston Peck, "A New Writer Who Counts," in The Bookman, *Vol. IX, June, 1899, pp. 344-46.*

WILLIAM MORTON PAYNE (essay date 1906)

"The House of Mirth" appears to be the novel of the season in the sense that it is the novel that has occasioned the most discussion of a serious sort. It is a work which has enlisted the matured powers of a writer whose performance is always distinguished, and whose coupling of psychological insight with the gift of expression is probably not sur-passed by any other woman novelist of our time. It is a story elaborated in every detail to a high degree of refinement, and evidently a product of the artistic conscience. Having paid this deserved tribute to its finer characteristics, we are bound to add that it is deficient in interest. The reason is not far to seek. There is no section of American society—or of society anywhere, for that matter—so absolutely devoid of appeal to the sympathies of normally-constituted intelligences as the vain and vulgar element that disports itself in our larger cities as the only society worth considering, this pretension being based upon wealth alone, with its natural accompaniment of self-seeking display and frivolity. A novelist of archangelical powers could not make interesting so sorry a phase of humanity as this, and because Mrs. Wharton has described for us this type and this alone, we turn her pages impatiently, and look in vain for relief from their emptiness. What she can do with real material she has evidenced in "The Valley of Decision," a book that we admire heartily enough to permit us the severity with which we are appraising the content, as distinguished from the form, of the present work. What justification may be offered for the book as a portrayal of any sort of human life is found in the plea of its satiric intent—of its character as an American "Vanity Fair,"—but this will not take us very far. The pungent wickedness of Becky Sharp gives her a reasonable excuse for being, but we cannot find in Lily Bart the positive qualities for either good or evil that make it worth while to follow her fortunes through five hundred and more pages of print. . . . We are much inclined to doubt that it was worth while—for a writer of Mrs. Wharton's exceptional gifts. (pp. 15-16)

William Morton Payne, "Recent Fiction: 'The House of Mirth'," in The Dial *(copyright, 1906, by The Dial Publishing Company, Inc.), Vol. XL, No. 469, January 1, 1906, pp. 15-16.*

HENRY DWIGHT SEDGWICK (essay date 1906)

When Mrs. Wharton's stories first appeared, in that early period which, as we have now learned, was merely a period of apprenticeship, everybody said, "How clever!" "How wonderfully clever!" and the criticism—to adopt a generic term for indiscriminate adjectives—was apt, for the most conspicuous trait in the stories was cleverness. They were astonishingly clever; and their cleverness, as an ostensible quality will, caught and held the attention. And yet, though undoubtedly correct, the term owes its correctness, in part at least, to its ready-to-wear quality, to its negative merit of vague amplitude, behind which the most diverse gifts and capacities may lie concealed. No readers of Mrs. Wharton, after the first shock of bewildered admiration, rest content with it, but grope about to lift the cloaking surtout of cleverness and to see as best they may how and by what methods her preternaturally nimble wits are playing their game,—for it is a game that Mrs. Wharton plays, pitting herself against a situation to see how much she can score.

To most people the point she plays most brilliantly is the episode, which in the novel is merely one of the links in the concatenation of the plot, but in the short story is the form and substance, the very thing itself; and so to be mistress of the art of the episode almost seems to leave any other species of mastery irrelevant and superfluous. In Mrs. Wharton this aptitude is not single, but a combination. It includes the sense of proportion, and markedly that elementary proportion of allotting the proper space for the introduction of the story,—so much to bring the *dramatis personæ* into the ring, so much for the preliminary bouts, so much for the climax, and, finally, the proper length for the recessional. It includes the subordination of one character to another, of one picture to another, the arrangement of details in proper hierarchy to produce the desired effect. (p. 217)

Some readers deem the dialogue the strongest point of Mrs. Wharton's game, it is so pithy and witty. Others, again, among the various excellences, prefer the author's own observations and comments. Still others like best the epigrams or the dramatic interest of the incident itself.

If the reader, after he has gone over these various points in the game, attempts to sum up his impressions, to his astonishment and dismay he finds himself again face to face with his old adjective *clever*. At first he surmises that this is a trick of his own indolence, which, lazily yielding to habit, offers him this serviceable word; but upon reflection he perceives that the adjective has a positive merit. It is a word of limitation; it fences in its own domain, and excludes other regions beyond. Mrs. Wharton's stories are not original like Miss Wilkins's, not poetic like George Eliot's, not romantic like Bret Harte's, not rippling with muscular energy like Kipling's, nor smooth with the dogmatic determinism of Maupassant. To none of those story-tellers would one apply the word clever; and though Mrs. Wharton cannot very well monopolize the adjective, by her high level of skill, by her ready command over her own resources, by her tact, by her courage,—no situation daunts her,—and especially by her limitations, she wholly justifies the public in crying out, "Oh, clever Mrs. Wharton!" (pp. 217-18)

When [*The Valley of Decision*] was first published, the fashion was to disentangle and distinguish,—as one ruminates and speculates over the flavors of a salad,—to separate the several ingredients culled from many books, and to crow over the discovery or attribution; in blindness to the fact that the somewhat royal levy of tribute was the object of the book, open, obvious, proclaimed, and carefully planned. The story, of purpose, is subordinated to its setting. The actors are necessarily a little frigid, the hero, unwillingly perhaps, a *poseur,* the heroine willingly a *poseuse;* but the scenery in which they carry about their rarefied and cool personalities is very attractive. (pp. 221-22)

All life is but a transmutation of materials, and novelists may use whatever they can find in books, in history, in life, in imagination; the point is to create life again. One would hardly go so far in praise of *The Valley of Decision* as to think of it as creating life out of its literary materials. It did not do that; it made a very entertaining, interesting, and agreeable book. (p. 222)

[The] volumes on *Italian Villas and Their Gardens* and on *Italian Backgrounds* came [out] with some interval between them. The name *Italian Villas and Their Gardens* carried with it a special aroma, and gave a fillip to expectation. At last we were to get at the meaning of Italian gardens, which to our ignorance appeared so inferior to the English in all usual horticultural appointments ... Whether Mrs. Wharton's hand had not complete control, or whether she was impatient of a prescribed task, or whether the translation of the inner delicacies of an Italian garden into American notions was a task unsuited to her talents, or whatever the

reason, the book had a cold, perfunctory, mechanical ring. (pp. 222-23)

In *Italian Backgrounds* she is on surer footing. She is familiar with Italy, and she has a very wide knowledge of the best that has been thought and said of Italy. She is hand and glove with the critics of art. She never enters a town in Italy, no matter how small, but she has in her handbag Crowe and Cavaleaselle, Kugler, Burckhardt, Morelli, Berenson, and a half dozen more. She looks at every picture, every fresco, every bit of sculpture and carving, like a constitutional queen, and they are her responsible advisers; she judges cherubim, madonnas, portraits, choir-stalls, proportions of height and breadth, contrasts of light and shade, relations of Gothic to Romanesque, of the *quattrocento* to the *cinquecento,* of masters to pupils, all according to the laws and rules adopted by her learned advisers, to which she gives full assent and approval. Certainly she does this well. There are no errors to be subsequently corrected, no rash ventures to be regretted; but ill-regulated readers sometimes long to fling authority to the winds. Give us not what Morelli thought or Burckhardt, but what you think, Mrs. Wharton; pitch your portable library out of your *vettura,* send Berenson to Jericho, make mistakes on every page, and let's hear how beautiful Italy impresses you. It is your personal intimacy with Italy that interests us. (p. 223)

On reading *The House of Mirth,* the first sensation of everybody ... was one of exultation, of "I told you so," as they recognized all Mrs. Wharton's talents, but better and brighter. Her mastery of the episode is as dashing as ever, and more delicate. The chapters are a succession of tableaux, all admirably posed. And yet this mastery, by its very excess, has marred the work of its necessary companion art, the hymeneal art of uniting episodes; it will not suffer any episode to remain in a state other than that of celibate self-sufficiency. But in a novel no episode can be self-sufficient; it must proceed from the episode before and merge into the episode that follows. In this part of her craft Mrs. Wharton has always shown a certain lack of dexterity; and the general effect of *The House of Mirth* is to throw this difficulty in high relief. There are places where the junction of two episodes appears no more than as the scar of an old inadequacy; and then again there are others where the episodes seem animated by a desire to break away from the trammels of the plot and pose by themselves. They remind one of the succession of prints that constitute *The Rake's Progress.* Like the rake, Lily Bart proceeds downward from print to print, from Trenor circle to Gormer circle, from the Gormers to Norma Hatch, from Norma to millinery; and so on, from morn to noon she falls, from noon to dewy eve, down to her catastrophe; each stage is a distinct episode, a scene which Hogarth—with Sir Joshua Reynolds to paint Lily's picture—might have portrayed.

The epigrams are as luminous as ever, but they are no longer firecrackers; they are brightened and softened to electric lights ensconced in Venetian glass, where they shed both illumination and color. They maintain their old electric vivacity,—Mrs. Bart sits at her husband's bedside "with the provisional air of a traveler who waits for a belated train to start,"—but now they serve a purpose, they explain, they emphasize, and in no readily forgettable manner. (pp. 224-25)

The less artistic traits, which revealed themselves at times in the stories, show a great gain in self-effacement. Mrs.

Wharton's nervous American energy has become far less tense, less fitful, far more even and self-controlled. Her luxuriant artistic and literary information is never put obviously forward; nevertheless, unjustly perhaps, one cannot shake off a somewhat uncomfortable suspicion that a great deal of the book is rather the product of culture than of real human knowledge; that it has been approached by the circuitous way of the authorities,—Stendhal, Bourget, Henry James,—rather then by grubbing in life itself. . . .

Mrs. Wharton, in her early period, acquired a habit of using men and women as butts for satire, masks for a dialogue, candelabra for epigrams,—as something other than human beings living in and for themselves; and that habit is a hindrance in her present task of studying them humanly. With her talents, with her growth in artistic feeling,—a growth that is conspicuous throughout *The House of Mirth,* —Mrs. Wharton will, no doubt, free herself from these trammels. (p. 225)

Mrs. Wharton, it would appear, has been limited to one somewhat narrow species of men and women, a species in which, perhaps, human nature does not find its freest expression. For the purpose of portraiture any species serves as well as another,—our interest in an artist's perception of our fellow beings is inexhaustible,—but to enable an artist to acquire a knowledge of humanity one species is too narrow a field of study. As soon as Mrs. Wharton leaves the Trenor set (supposing that that set is taken from life), she is forced to draw, and always more and more, upon the stores of her imagination and of her general literary information. The Gormers, though they, to be sure, are but temporary wheels to roll the plot forward, evince a disinclination to become solid and substantial. Even Simon Rosedale, with all the advantages of individuality conferred by his race, offers a by no means irrefutable argument for his verisimilitude. Mrs. Norma Hatch flutters beyond the frontier of Mrs. Wharton's experience, and the charwoman, who as a *dea ex machina* shoves the plot onward, does so very unhandily.

A statement of the fact that Mrs. Wharton does not give to her characters the illusion of reality is no explanation of her motive in not doing so. One vaguely surmises that she feels she cannot attain the flashes of revelation of the great masters, and disdains the counterfeit procured by elaborate descriptions of petty details, and therefore rests content with her own individual, if arbitrary, representation of human life. But one has also a subsidiary feeling that it is safer to suspend judgment until one has approached this matter from another point.

This failure to observe the primary tenets of realism is not the only instance of Mrs. Wharton's disregard of ordinary rules; she does not adhere to the rule of inevitability. There is no inevitable connection between the last chapter of *The House of Mirth* and the first; the bottle of chloral may be the last link of a chain of which the visit to Seldon's apartment is the first, but it does not fasten upon us a sense of necessary connection. The reader is in doubt as to the intervening links; he snuffs, as it were, traces of indecision as to the termination of Lily's career. (pp. 226-27)

The reason for Mrs. Wharton's indecision must perhaps be sought in the episodical character of her vision; possibly in the difficulty of discovering the inevitable thread. A better solution, justified by the fact that it also explains her neg-

lect of the commandment of realism, is that, as an artist, she finds neither rule of advantage to her, and therefore brushes them aside with the elegant ease of an American woman passing the customs. Certainly *The House of Mirth* shows a marked advance in acceptance of responsibility to art, a far larger sense of the value of composition, and a great increase of power in putting that sense to use. It is her feeling for composition that causes her to disregard both literary determinism and realism; these she deliberately sacrifices for the sake of obtaining the desired emphasis upon the figure of central interest. All the minor characters in the novel are adjuncts and accessories, illustration and decoration, to display the commanding figure of Lily Bart; she stands conspicuous, and all the others derive their importance from their relations to her. What they do, say, and think, is done, said, and thought in order to explain and give a high relief to Lily Bart. This mastery of composition is the great artistic achievement of the book, and justifies its immense success.

Otherwise, . . . Mrs. Wharton in *The House of Mirth* displays no new aptitude, no new sensitiveness, no new accomplishment. The plot, wholly apart from any question of determinism, is uninteresting,—if one may say this when so many episodes are extremely interesting. There is a monotony, due to the iteration of motive, like that in the dimly remembered figures of the Lancers at dancing-school,— "forward and back," ladies' chain, pirouetting, and so on, over and over, in interminable sequence. Lily's behavior is mechanical; she whirls round and round, fresh and glittering, like waters in the upper basin of a fountain; then tumbles into the basin beneath, whirls and eddies with breaking bubbles, and tumbles again, and so down and down, until at last her continual falls from set to set sound painfully like a neglected faucet. One might suppose that this would produce what in current criticism is called the "note of inevitableness;" but it does not; the reader is continually expecting Mrs. Wharton to get up and turn it off.

Her failure in the construction of the plot in this respect, so far as it is due neither to the episodical character of her vision nor to the imperious demands of composition, is because she lacks the talents of a story-teller; for Mrs. Wharton cannot, at least, she certainly does not, put forward any claim to be a raconteur. In the short stories this lack was concealed by her mastery of the episode, but in *The House of Mirth* it is betrayed by the mechanical monotony that, even in all the brilliancy and glamour of episodes, of epigrams, of Lily herself, oppresses us with drowsy remembrances as of a too familiar tune. (p. 227)

Henry Dwight Sedgwick, "The Novels of Mrs. Wharton," in The Atlantic Monthly *(copyright © 1906 by The Atlantic Monthly Company, Boston, Mass.; reprinted with permission), Vol. XCVIII, No. 2, August, 1906, pp. 217-28.*

CALVIN WINTER [Frederic Taber Cooper] (essay date 1911)

[The] first thing that must strike a discriminating critic, whether he makes [Mrs. Wharton's] acquaintance through the medium of [an early short story, such as] "The Muse's Tragedy" or [a later story, such as] "The Letters" is that he has to do with an author of rare mental subtlety and unusual breath of culture; a worldly wise person with rather wide cosmopolite sympathies, yet rather rigid prejudices of social caste. One would guess, with no further help than the light shed by her own writings, that here was a mind that might be likened to a chamber of art treasures—not over-crowded, but sufficiently rich to offer a pleasing harmony of colour and form. Such, at all events, is the impression that one gathers from her stage setting. She lingers over each interior, its portières and wall-papers, its etchings and mezzotints, its choice old furniture and fragile porcelain with the grudging reluctance of a bibliophile relinquishing a first edition or a priceless binding. So far as the atmosphere of her stories goes, there is everywhere a pervading sense of art and literature and culture; a sense, as it were, of sunlight softly filtering through richly stained glass, of life seen relentlessly within the limits of a definite angle. Mrs. Wharton's literary activity has resulted, up to the present day, in somewhat more than fifty short stories and novelettes, and three novels; and of these the great majority deal frankly with the literary and artistic circle. One has only to run over in memory the separate stories to realise the truth of this. There are, for instance, no less than a dozen in which the hero is by profession an author; . . . and next to authors her favourite heroes are artists. . . . Yes, her angle of outlook upon the world is rather narrow, but, like the proverbial still waters, it runs rather deep.

Yet if Mrs. Wharton shows a predilection for artistic and academic society, she nevertheless has a far-reaching—I was tempted to say, an exaggerated—instinct of social values. In all the various settings of her stories, whether in the self-satisfied provincialism of a New England college town, or the full floodtide of New York life to-day, or of Lombardy a century ago, she never for an instant allows you to lose sight of the fact that there exists a local social code more potent than any laws of Medes and Persians; a fine, stratified caste system, too attenuated for any but the native born to grasp in all its details, yet inflexible in matters of cause and effect. Her subtle sense of the far-reaching significance of some quite trivial, perhaps unconscious infringement of these unwritten rules of conduct, gives us the real key to a number of her strongest situations. Her understanding of human nature, her relentless pursuit of a motive down to its ultimate analysis, her deliberate stripping off of the very last veils of pretense and showing us the sordidness and cowardice of human souls in all their nudity, are unsurpassed by any other woman novelist now living. She has a trick not merely of describing even her secondary characters so clearly that you feel you can see them both inside and out, but she often flings out some single line of description which ever afterwards sticks to that particular character like a burr and is probably the first thing we think of each time that character reappears. For instance, in "Souls Belated," "Mrs. Tillotson, senior, dreaded ideas as much as a draught in her back"; in "A Coward," "Mrs. Carstyle was one of the women who make refinement vulgar." . . . (pp. 302-03)

But this is merely a superficial aspect of Mrs. Wharton's treatment of character and of life. And to some extent the surface sparkle of her style is at times a blemish; we find ourselves straying away from the central interest of the story in order to relish for a moment the sheer verbal cleverness of some casual epigram, such as "Genius is of small use to a woman who does not know how to do her hair." . . . Her whole attitude toward the personages of her stories is a direct application of La Rochefoucauld's maxim that in the sorrows and misfortunes of our friends we find something that is not altogether displeasing. And her stories allow her abundant opportunity to do this. From first to last

they deal with the victims of fate—men and women who are caught in the meshes of circumstance and struggle with as hopeless impotence as so many fish in a drag-net. Mrs. Wharton may not be conscious of it, but there is a great deal of predestination in the philosophy of her stories. Nearly all her heroes and heroines seem foreordained to failure. Of struggle, in the sense in which drama is defined as a struggle, a conflict of wills, her books contain little or nothing. Her tragedies belong to one or the other of two classes, or to a combination of the two: on the one hand, to the complications arising from not understanding, from the impossibility of ever wholly getting inside another person's mind; and on the other, from the realisation that one cannot escape from one's environment, that one's whole family and race have for generations been relentlessly weaving a network of custom and precedent too strong for the individual to break.

As for the first of these tragic keynotes, that of *misunderstanding,* it is only necessary to glance through a few of the separate stories chosen almost at random to see how the word recurs over and over, with or without variations, like a *leitmotiv.* Thus, in "In Trust," Halidon sums up the crucial point with the words, "I can't make her see that I'm differently situated"; in "The Last Asset," Garnett lays his finger on the difficulty, "Ah, you don't know your daughter!" (pp. 303-05)

The other tragic motive, that of the inexorable demands of social traditions, the unwritten law of *noblesse oblige,* we find forming the very warp and woof of all Mrs. Wharton's bigger and more serious efforts. In *The House of Mirth,* Lily Bart is tossed as helplessly as a cork in the whirls and eddies of the social stream—tossed and buffeted and finally dragged under with her eyes wide open to her own helplessness. In *The Valley of Decision,* Odo Valsecca and Fulvia Vivaldi sacrifice their happiness to the obligations of rank, a prince's duty to his people; and they do this not in the spirit of generous sacrifice, but rather because they recognise the impossibility of doing anything else. And so again in *Madame de Treymes,* even an American finds that all the vaunted freedom and independence of our republic avails nothing when confronted by the impalpable yet unyielding wall of French family tradition and prejudice.

So much for the general character of Mrs. Wharton's situations and problems. Before turning to take a more specific glance at some of the separate stories, it is well to get the following points clearly in mind regarding her technique of construction. Mrs. Wharton is one of those exceptional writers who do not greatly concern themselves with conventional rules of length and breadth. Economy of means is a principle which never binds her against her will. Her short stories frequently lengthen out into the structure and dimensions of a novelette; her novelettes might so easily have been expanded into full-length novels. She writes apparently to suit herself, in whatever way the narrative comes most naturally to her. A Maupassant with a different ideal of story structure, a more relentless self-discipline, would have used a vigorous pruning knife on almost any of her stories and gained, it might be, sharper effects, but at the sacrifice of much delightful cleverness and some rare and subtle half-tones. We must accept Mrs. Wharton as she is, recognising frankly that she is one of those writers who must do the thing their own way if they are to do it at all—but do not let us fall into the widespread error of assuming that because her stories are so remarkably good she necessarily has a flawless technique.

It would be impracticable as well as bewildering to attempt a detailed survey of all or even a majority of Mrs. Wharton's stories. We must necessarily make a slender choice, touching only the higher places. The first volume, however, *The Greater Inclination,* needs closer attention for the purpose of pointing out some structural weaknesses. The opening story, "The Muse's Tragedy," deals with a young critic's interest in an older woman who in earlier years was the source of inspiration of a now deceased poet.... Now the central idea of this story is clear as crystal, the tragedy of an unloved woman as seen through the eyes of another man. Two men and one woman, and a single point of view. That, I think, is the way Mrs. Wharton would have written the story ten years later; she would have done it more in the manner of "The Dilettante," and by so doing she would have gained in power.

"A Journey," Mrs. Wharton's second story, offers one of the strongest situations she ever used: a woman, bringing her invalid husband home to New York, discovers in the morning, shortly after leaving Buffalo, that he is lying dead in his berth. To avoid being put off the train she all day long keeps up the pretence that he is too ill to be disturbed, and breaks down under the strain only at the moment when the train slides into the Grand Central Station. Now the greatness of a short story very largely depends upon the trick of choosing all details of structure with the idea of making each in turn add its share to the poignancy of the situation. In the present case it seems axiomatic that the ultimate tragedy of the situation would depend upon the degree of affection that the woman felt for the dead man. Mrs. Wharton has chosen to tell us without reserve that the wife had ceased to care for him at all. She is a frail woman, physically unstrung, a little frightened at her isolation and helplessness; but that ultimate turn of the screw which comes of a great personal bereavement is missing.

And thirdly, we come to that much-praised story, "The Pelican"; the history of a woman who, finding herself a widow with a small child and no property, undertakes to support herself by lecturing in hotel parlours and before women's clubs.... Thirty years later she is still making the rounds of clubs and parlours for the purpose of raising money to educate that same boy. Now the crucial moment of the story comes when that boy, a bearded man of thirty, runs across her at a hotel, discovers her subterfuge and demands an explanation. All this is natural enough, but the story is told in the first person by an old friend of the mother; the son drags this old friend, a stranger to him, into his mother's presence, and before him denounces her in terms that make one wince. His whole manner is in bad taste—perhaps Mrs. Wharton meant him to be precisely that kind of a man, but one doubts it. At all events, if she were writing that story to-day she would not have made him a man of quite that kind; at least she would have smoothed over his raw edges a little more carefully.

In this way we might take up those early stories one by one and show how they miss that finer perfection which Mrs. Wharton began to show in *Crucial Instances,* and which she shows so triumphantly in *The Descent of Man.* It is hard in speaking of this third volume to discriminate in favour of any particular stories—they are all so extremely good. (pp. 305-06)

But unquestionably, if we must discriminate, we shall do so in favour of "The Other Two," the story of a woman twice divorced and a third time married. When Waythorn married Alice Varick, who had earlier been Alice Haskett and who brought with her Haskett's little daughter, "he had fancied that a woman can shed her past like a man." But in this he was to learn slowly that he was mistaken. Both of his predecessors are still alive; both of them, by a series of quite natural coincidences, come into contact with himself and Alice.... He rebels at first fiercely, but impotently; then little by little accepts the inevitable; and the curtain falls at last on the group of all three husbands, past and present, assembled in Waythorn's sitting-room with Alice placidly pouring tea for them. There is not a single brush stroke, a single touch of colour in the whole picture that one could afford to alter. It is a little masterpiece of its kind, a deliciously ironical apotheosis of conventionalism. (p. 307)

Calvin Winter [pseudonym of Frederic Taber Cooper], "Representative American Story Tellers: Edith Wharton," in The Bookman, *Vol. XXXIII, No. 3, May, 1911, pp. 302-09.*

HENRY JAMES (essay date 1912)

There are fifty things I should like to say to you about [*The Reef*], and I shall have said most of them in the long run; but there are some that eagerly rise to my lips even now and for which I want the benefit of my "first flush" of appreciation. The whole of the finest part is, I think, quite the finest thing you have done; both *more* done than even the best of your other doing, and more worth it through intrinsic value, interest and beauty. (p. 282)

To attempt in [my present state of illness] to rise to any worthy reference to *The Reef* seems to me a vain thing; yet there remains with me so strongly the impression of its quality and of the unspeakably *fouillée* nature of the situation between the two principals (more gone into and with more undeviating truth than anything you have done) that I can't but babble of it a little to you even with these weak lips. It all shows, partly, what strength of subject is, and how it carries and inspires, inasmuch as I think your subject in its essence [is] very fine and takes in no end of beautiful things to do. Each of these two figures is admirable for truth and *justesse;* the woman an exquisite thing, and with her characteristic finest, scarce differentiated notes (that is some of them) sounded with a wonder of delicacy. I'm not sure her oscillations are not beyond our notation; yet they are so held in your hand, so felt and known and shown, and everything seems so to come of itself. I suffer or worry a little from the fact that in the Prologue, as it were, we are admitted so much into the consciousness of the man, and that after the introduction of Anna (Anna so perfectly named) we see him almost only as she sees him—which gives our attention a different sort of work to do; yet this is really, I think, but a triumph of your method, for he remains of an absolute consistent verity, showing himself in that way better perhaps than in any other, and without a false note imputable, not a shadow of one, to his manner of so projecting himself. The beauty of it is that it is, for all it is worth, a Drama, and almost, as it seems to me, of the psychologic Racinian unity, intensity and gracility. Anna is really of Racine and one presently begins to feel her throughout as an Eriphyle or a Bérénice: which, by the way, helps to account a little for something *qui me chiffonne* throughout: which is why the whole thing, unrelated and unreferred save in the most superficial way to its *milieu* and background, and to any determining or qualifying *entourage,* takes place *comme cela,* and in a specified, localised way, in France—these non-French people "electing," as it were, to have their story out there. This particularly makes all sorts of unanswered questions come up about Owen; and the notorious wickedness of Paris isn't at all required to bring about the conditions of the Prologue. Oh, if you knew how plentifully we could supply them in London and, I should suppose, in New York or in Boston. But the point was, as I see it, that you couldn't really give us the sense of a Boston Eriphyle or Boston Givré, and than an exquisite instinct, "back of" your Racinian inspiration and settling the whole thing for you, whether consciously or not, absolutely prescribed a vague and elegant French colonnade or gallery, with a French river dimly gleaming through, as the harmonious *fond* you required. In the key of this, with all your reality, you have yet kept the whole thing: and, to deepen the harmony and accentuate the literary pitch, have never surpassed yourself for certain exquisite *moments,* certain images, analogies, metaphors, certain silver correspondences in your *façon de dire....* There used to be little notes in you that were like fine benevolent finger-marks of the good George Eliot—the echo of much reading of that excellent woman, here and there, that is, sounding through. But now you are like a lost and recovered "ancient" whom *she* might have got a reading of (especially were he a Greek) and of whom in *her* texture some weaker reflection were to show. For, dearest Edith, you are stronger and firmer and finer than all of them put together; you go further and you say *mieux,* and your only drawback is not having the homeliness and the inevitability and the happy limitation and the affluent poverty, of a Country of your Own (*comme moi, par exemple!*) It makes you, this does, as you exquisitely say of somebody or something at some moment, elegiac (what penetration, what delicacy in your use there of the term!)—makes you so, that is, for the Racinian-*sérieux*—but leaves you more in the desert (for everything else) that surrounds Apex City. But you will say that you're content with your lot; that the desert surrounding Apex City is quite enough of a dense crush for you, and that with the *colonnade* and the gallery and the dim river you will always otherwise pull through. To which I can only assent—after such an example of pulling through as *The Reef.* Clearly you have only to pull, and everything will come. (pp. 283-85)

Henry James, in his letter to Edith Wharton on December 4, 1912, in The Letters of Henry James, Vol. II, *edited by Percy Lubbock, (abridged by permission of Charles Scribner's Sons; copyright 1920 by Charles Scribner's Sons; renewal copyright 1948 by William James, Margaret James Porter), Scribner's, 1920, pp. 281-86.*

EDWIN BJÖRKMAN (essay date 1913)

The thread of events used by Mrs. Wharton for her purpose [in "Ethan Frame"] is of the slimmest and simplest. (p. 291)

Few features of this remarkable book stand out more strikingly than its general design, by which the author has managed to satisfy at once our craving for surprise and our dislike of too much surprise. From the very start the shadow of that final "smash-up" lies over the pages of the book. (p. 294)

[Ethan lives] his spoiled life between those two spectres of his lost hopes: the woman he needed [Zeena] and the woman he loved [Matt]. All other tragedies that I can think of seem mild and bearable beside this one. What is death, or sorrowing for the dead, in comparison with a life chained to the dead remains of what might have been love? (p. 295)

[One] redeeming factor asserts itself subtly throughout the book, though Mrs. Wharton never refers to it in plain words. It is this: that, after all, the tragedy unveiled to us is social rather than personal. It is so overwhelming that the modern mind rebels against it as a typical specimen of human experience. (p. 296)

"Ethan Frome" is to me above all else a judgment on that system which fails to redeem such villages as Mrs. Wharton's Starkfield. (p. 297)

Those who dwell in our thousand and one Starkfields are [as] wrecked mariners, fallen into their hapless positions by no fault of their own. And though helpless now, they need by no means prove useless under different conditions. Vessels should be sent to take them off their barren hillsides— or social effort should by employed in making those hillsides fruitful once more. (p. 298)

[Mrs. Wharton] has done—and all she was called on to do —was to reveal the presence of Starkfield and its population of Fromes within a social body that should contain nothing but living and growing tissue. In doing this, and doing it with her usual exquisiteness of word and phrase and portraiture, Mrs. Wharton has passed from individual to social art; from the art that excites to that which incites.

Glancing over the all too brief volume in retrospect, I can find only one point where it suggests a certain degree of failure, of growth still unachieved. With the building of the tale as it now stands I can have no fault to find. It is against a certain lack of outlook, a certain onesidedness of conception, that I direct my adverse criticism. And to what I say along this line, the author may, of course, reply that what I am wishing for did not fall within the scope of her plan. And yet I wish it had! (pp. 299-300)

As I read the book now, I come away with an impression that, in the author's mind at least, the one thing needed to change Ethan's life from a hell to a heaven would have been the full and free expression of his love for Matt. (p. 300)

Romantic love, as idealized for us by our sentimental-minded forefathers, has long ago gone into bankruptcy. (p. 301)

Had Zeena died and Matt married Ethan—well, it is my private belief that inside of a few years life on that farm would have been practically what it was before Matt arrived, with Matt playing the part of a Zeena II—different, of course, and yet the same. For the life in our Starkfields is cursed or saved not by this or that single incident, not by the presence or absence of this or that individual.... The curse lies in staying there, in breathing the crushing, choking atmostphere of Starkfieldian sterility. (p. 303)

Edwin Björkman, "The Greater Edith Wharton," in his Voices of To-morrow: Critical Studies of the New Spirit in Literature *(copyright 1913 by Mitchell Kennerley), Kennerley, 1913, pp. 290-304.*

obviousness and slickness. She has always been the Sargent of American fiction and as time goes on seems to become more and more willing to deal facilely with her subjects.

Perhaps it is Mrs. Wharton's long residence abroad which makes her novels run a little thin nowadays. . . . *The Age of Innocence,* surely one of the best of her novels, succeeds through the intensity of the emotion it conveys rather than through the sort of vividness she once commanded; its settings and characters, admirable as they are, have some of the vagueness of memories. And the realities of *Old New York* are vaguer and more remote still. Nonetheless, as details in Mrs. Wharton's extraordinary history of the New York civilization these stories are, of course, not negligible. The inferior boundary of that history is now marked by the first story in the collection, *False Dawn;* the superior boundary, I suppose, by *A Son at the Front*—though she leaves the New York scene itself with the elaborate and violent *Custom of the Country,* in which the city is already becoming too complicated and chaotic for the author of *The Age of Innocence* much to enjoy grappling with it any longer. Too chaotic and vulgar today; yesterday too correct and narrow. Mrs. Wharton has written the tragedy of the New York soul caught between the millstones of these two eras. She is probably the only absolutely first-rate literary artist, occupying himself predominantly with New York, that New York has ever produced. Henry James was born here and understood the city well, yet never treated it intensively. But the brick fronts of Washington Square, the brown monuments of Park Avenue, the glittering apartments of the upper westside—Madison Square, the Grand Central Station, the Weehawken Ferry and the downtown office-buildings seem still to burn with a sort of incandescence from having become the prisons of Mrs. Wharton's passion and the symbols of her indignation.

> *Edmund Wilson, "Review of Books: 'Old New York'" (reprinted by permission of Farrar, Straus & Giroux, Inc.), in* The New Republic, *Vol. 39, No. 497, June 11, 1924, p. 77.*

ROBERT MORSS LOVETT (essay date 1925)

No one will question the fact that Mrs. Wharton's impression of life is usually direct and personal. She does not see the world as a vast field of phenomena, an infinite spectacle of the human comedy. She has marked her separation from the great masters of the panorama of life in her own literature, Fielding, [Tobias George] Smollett, Dickens, Thackeray. She belongs to the group looking back to [Samuel] Richardson, who make a virtue of their limitation of experience, and who seek in a restricted field to present the pattern of life rather than its monstrous confusion. The three principles which determine her pattern, morality, culture, and class, are the three which Richardson asserted. Her world, like his, is one of subtleties of conscience, and niceties of deportment, of respect for education and cultivation, of recognition of superiority embodied in an aristocracy. For her, it is true, morality has ceased to be the assertion of external authority, and is a matter of fine perception of the responsibilities of men and women toward each other in their mutual bonds and contacts: she is not concerned with didactic methods or the teaching of etiquette to the middle classes, but rather with what George Meredith says the English race has never spiritually comprehended, "the signification of living in society," and the enhancement of life

by the finer social processes and a sense of the inheritance of beauty and order from the past. She has abandoned the crude romantic motive, common in English fiction, of promotion from the lower to the upper class as a reward of virtue. For her the intellectual class is a fact of high importance because there, through the operation of consciousness, the social experiment is carried on under most favorable conditions, and the discovery of what makes life worth living is most hopefully sought. "Cultivated men and women," says George Meredith, "who do not skim the cream of life and are attached to its duties, yet escape the harsher blows, make acute and balanced observers. Molière is their poet." Meredith himself and Henry James are their novelists in England, and Edith Wharton in America. (pp. 78-80)

It is true, as Fielding long ago remarked, that the upper classes make thin soil for the novel. And it is to be noted further that the American upper class is not deeply rooted in the soil by the long feudal process, but grows rapidly, rankly, in the forcing house of wealth, lacking power to seed itself, propagating by graft. . . . The nearest approach to a genuine upper class with ancestral and traditional qualifications is to be found about the sites of the three earliest settlements, among the descendants of the planters of Virginia, the patroons of New York, the traders of Massachusetts Bay. One of these groups Mrs. Wharton possessed by inheritance and in it she found her best material; but it is here where she is strongest that her inferiority to Jane Austen is apparent. The comparison has often been made between the two writers, both dealing with a limited society, both possessing similar powers of observation and penetration, of detachment and irony. The difference is that Miss Austen's people are real in spite of and because of their conventions and prejudices, which have the force of inherited characteristics. They are part of an institution, stable, self-perpetuating, permanent. They are in true relation to their environment, and racy of the soil. By contrast Mrs. Wharton's society is transitory, imitative, sterile. Miss Austen is provincial; Mrs. Wharton is colonial. (pp. 80-2)

English and American contemporaries alike find themselves novelists of social change, but the former have to record the slow crumbling of a tough and resisting order which in its dissolution leaves the solemn regret that "that which once was great has passed away." Mrs. Wharton's class denies her this consolation of tragedy in her art except as it is felt, by herself perhaps most keenly, as the tragedy of failure.

Mrs. Wharton's effort to supplement the resources of social class by those of culture and art is doomed for the same reason. Here again the limitation imposed by her material is apparent. As she is unfamiliar with the America of pioneering and industry, so she is equally indifferent to the attempts, often painful and crude, to find a form which shall be expressive of the spirit of America in its travail, the symbol of its bringing forth. The art of which she thinks is imitative and derivative. As one reads the catalogue of mythical authors, painters, books, and pictures in her fiction, one is impressed by their ghastly unreality. They are only as real as their conditions would permit them to be—as real as the acres of Americana on the walls of our galleries and art institutes, or the forgotten books of ten or twenty years ago. It is fair to say that Mrs. Wharton uses these things chiefly as counters in her game, the object of which is a symmetrical pattern of life, or the Q.E.D. of a moral theorem. It is significant, however, that in the most humanly real of her accounts of the artistic conscience, *The Recovery,* Keniston abandons the colonial experiments of his first, second, third, and fourth periods for the Louvre.

It is to be said, however, that Mrs. Wharton never makes expatriation an end in itself. That problem of the colonial novelist, to which Henry James returned again and again, appears only incidentally in her stories; and in them she shows no sympathy with the feeling that the good life is to be found only in Europe. . . . In spite of her long residence abroad she has remained in matter and point of view an American. Unlike Henry James she is a part of American literature. (pp. 82-4)

To compensate for the softness of the material upon which she sought to stamp her impression of life, and to enhance the vividness of that impression, Mrs. Wharton brings certain unimpeachable literary gifts and attainments. Her style is a clear, luminous medium in which things are seen in precise and striking outline. If the figures are pale in coloring they have definiteness of line. She never fell victim to the self-conscious mannerisms of Meredith and James. Her early addiction to epigram became more and more restrained, and the marks of imitation and erudition vanished as her style became more and more her own. (p. 85)

[Humor] remains one of her steadfast qualities. It shows itself broadly as caricature of the Philistines of Apex City, or more subtly as satire of those within the pale. Even in the great emotional crisis of the war she could see the absurd pretensions of her country-women of both sexes, expending themselves in activities which merely enriched their self-importance. In her irony, she realizes George Meredith's definition of comedy as "the humour of the mind." . . . (p. 86)

Mrs. Wharton can stand outside of her world to criticize—not to create. She lacks the power of imagination to follow the leadings of her experience and the phenomena of her environment into other fields, to transpose the themes of her chamber music into larger harmonies and discords of the full orchestra. And the age upon which Mrs. Wharton has been cast has become increasingly impatient of art in its refinements as a criticism of life, or for any purpose except large representation and bold decoration. After the brief interlude of civilization in the nineteenth century the world has reverted toward barbarism. . . . The substitution of the theme to live well for the theme to live seemed to the last century a natural development in its art, but the unleashing of the cruder forces in the racial and industrial conflict has thrown the world back into a more primitive phase of the evolutionary struggle. All this has come to pass since Edith Wharton made her appearance in literature nearly thirty years ago. She cannot claim to have been born out of her due time, but it is among the happy consequences of her persistence in her original well-doing that she remains for us among the voices whispering the last enchantments of the Victorian age. (pp. 86-7)

> *Robert Morss Lovett, in his* Edith Wharton *(copyright, 1925, by Robert M. McBride & Co.), McBride, 1925, 91 p.*

FRED LEWIS PATTEE (essay date 1930)

In technique and finish all [Mrs. Wharton] has touched is distinctive. Edged with satire, pointed with wit, [her works]

are French rather than American or English. To compare them to the work of Henry James is conventional, but it is also unavoidable. The tap-roots of the art of both pierce through the Anglo-Saxon into Gallic strata. Only in her materials is she American. She can make a volume on "The Writing of Fiction," noting all forces and all writers that have contributed to the evolution of the novel, and allude to only three Americans: Poe, Hawthorne and Henry James, in the section treating the short story, noting only that their work was really not of short-story texture. Both James and Mrs. Wharton must be classed as virtuosi trained in the school of Stendhal, Balzac, Flaubert, and Turgeniev. Both must be classed as intellectuals, concerned fundamentally with form, with manners, with art.

One does not read long in a volume like "The House of Mirth" without being impressed with its atmosphere of artificiality. In technique it is near perfection, but one cannot breathe. It is the artificiality of the city as contrasted with the naturalness of the country. Its author is dealing with metropolitan society, with vast wealth, monstrous personalities, vain, empty of all save selfishness. All her women are parasites, cruel as leeches and as soulless. To be good in this Vanity Fair, this sleek den of leopards, is impossible. Lily Bart, the best character in her novels, elaborated with all the detail of a Becky Sharp, attempted morality in its polluted circle and failed. The ball-and-chain of her inheritance dragged her down to its level.

Her novels are not muck-rake work though they came, the earliest of them, in "the shame of the cities" era, and though they lay bare social evils with the unction of an Upton Sinclair. Never is she furnishing propaganda, with a vision of reform. Her function is diagnosis of the diseases incident to the artificiality of modern civilization, diagnosis clear and positive. Not for her the surgery.

Of her major novels after her first venture the best is "The Age of Innocence," New York society as she knew it in the seventies, New York with the Indian summer light upon it of remembered childhood. After it in value come "The House of Mirth" and "The Custom of the Country." "Ethan Frome" in its brevity seems more perfect, but the novel is a structure with complexities; its difficulties are architectonic—the difference between a villa and a cathedral. It centers in the portrayal of character, whereas the short story centers about a situation. In a novel we live long with the characters and learn to know them intimately, so intimately indeed that, if the work be well done, we close the book with a sigh and awake as from an experience that has taken us from the actuality of our own living. But the short story is a flash, a glimpse, a humor, a situation not lived with. It is a moment of feeling, like a lyric.

Like Henry James, Mrs. Wharton has carried parallel with her major pieces of fiction numbers of [her] shorter-length works—more than fifty in all. They have been praised more than her novels have, and they deserve praise. Nowhere can one find in English better models for study, better illustrations of all the devices of the modern and complicated art of short-story creation. Yet, as we have seen, they must not be rated above her major novels, which are architecturally as perfect. Artistry reveals itself more readily always in the small-wrought area than in the large. Her success with a small canvas like "Ethan Frome" we can account for. The *conte,* the modern short story, is an art form: technique is its life-blood, and Mrs. Wharton first of all is a craftsman.

And here again we must note that her art is fundamentally intellectual, just as Mrs. Atherton's is emotional. It is at this point that she fails of reaching the heights where the great masters stand. Her works are mere *works*. Great art must have in it more than faultless technique: it must have something that lifts it into the realm of the spiritual, it must have *soul*—that which one may feel but no man define. This final touch she has seldom been able to give. Even in so perfect a bit of artistry as "Ethan Frome" it has all but escaped her. (pp. 251-53)

Despite her artistry . . . Mrs. Wharton has failed, as the eighteenth century failed, by her insistence upon definitions of life in terms of the artificial, in terms of civilization rather than in the fundamentals of Nature. Of the great quivering, suffering, laboring human mass she knows little. . . . Nature unadorned she views with all the horror of an Addison or a Pope. She is at home only in landscaped grounds with topiary-bordered walks and green lawns, with mansion houses and servants, where perfectly dressed drones take tea. (pp. 253-54)

> Fred Lewis Pattee, "The Feminine Novel," in his
> The New American Literature: 1890-1930 (copy-
> right, 1930, by The Century Co.), Century, 1930,
> pp. 245-69.*

FRANCES THERESA RUSSELL   (essay date 1932)

[Melodramatic] signs and tokens abound in Edith Wharton's work, and they manifest themselves in her plots, characters, backgrounds, emotions, ideas, and the style that depicts them all. She says herself that "The art of rendering life in fiction can never be anything but the disengaging of crucial moments from the welter of existence." . . . Her process is carefully selective, as she illustrates in one of her first titles, "Crucial Instances", and the selection is aided by an imagination with a strong preference for the extraordinary and marvelous.

Mrs. Wharton's fictitious world is one in which total strangers sit aimlessly chatting on hotel verandahs just in time to overhear a remark that reveals their mutual interest in the woman under discussion, and betrays the subterfuge that sacrificing "Pelican" had been carrying on for years. . . . It is a world in which a middle-aged divorcée achieves her first real romance with a younger man who afterwards is discovered to be her own daughter's fiance; a Henry Esmond situation with ramifications that would make simple Thackeray cock a startled eye. . . . And when the plot does not quite coagulate into a coincidence it thickens to a good stiff consistency with complication and linked intrigue long drawn out. (pp. 427-28)

Better still as a guaranteed thriller is the summoning of the supernatural to the human conclave. In the nine or ten short stories of this type, in which Edith Wharton is perhaps most directly influenced by Henry James, she invokes her ghosts with an extra gusto, as if herself fascinated by the gruesomely eloquent eyes, the avenging hounds, the uncanny bell, the phantom factotum who strangles disobedient housekeepers, and all such apparitions. To present these inhabitants of an immaterial sphere as though taken seriously may imply a belief in the esoteric that amounts to a philosophy, or may be simply an exercise of efficient artistry. To infer either intent or attitude would be dogmatic, but the fact that Mrs. Wharton's spectral phenomena are not explained away as hallucinations or tricks or any kind

of abnormal psychology, but are accredited by the flesh and blood they haunt if not by the author of them all, is cited for whatever significance it may have. (p. 428)

[In] the case of an intellectual such as Mrs. Wharton [we are] likely to find mind functioning more spontaneously than heart. Exposition and analysis gush forth over her pages at the slightest turn of the faucet, whereas feelings enter with more effort. Perhaps it is that the opinions are her own while the feelings mostly belong to other people that her depicted emotions have often the coolness of mental processes and the ideas have the warmth of sentiment. In any event, her beliefs frequently have the emphatic insistence of melodrama. No comment could be wider of the mark than that "As a cosmic thinker she renounces all standards and viewpoints." On the contrary, while there is nothing cosmic in her thinking, she is as full of standards and viewpoints as she can stick.

When these are disapproving they are vented with the pungent aid of satire, a condiment that permeates her entire work with, caustic tang. (p. 432)

She meditates a good deal over this and that: the evils of divorce, the aftermaths of deception, the individual versus society, the need and the danger of joy, the gulf between ambition and ability; and she hatches a whole brood of concrete problems to serve for her themes and theses. But they turn out rather inconclusive. Her run-away wives, for instance, either come timidly back or accept a bribe to keep themselves scarce. Not one of them gets the five-pound look. *The Children* exhibits the muddled families that come from many marriages but the charm of the story lies in the glomerate hilarity of the Step, Half, and Whole Wheaters. Kate Clephane in *The Mother's Recompense* was a poor excuse of a mother and she had no recompense, except the satisfaction of a futile renunciation and a gratuitous martyrdom. She might have justified her hitherto useless and expensive existence by marrying staunch Fred Landers and salvaging something for the two of them, but she preferred to plume herself on the vague virtue of expiation. This tale is Mrs. Wharton's most sentimental, and *The Custom of the Country* the most sensational. The strange case of Miss Undine Spragg with her tractor career is as riotous melodrama as the doings of Deadwood Dick but it sounds the thus-far-and-no-farther warning to pampered and greedy American women.

Of romantic comedy this voluminous writer furnishes only one instance, in *Glimpses of the Moon*, and of complete tragedy none at all. One title, *The Tragic Muse*, brings in the phrase but not the whelming catastrophe. It is *Ethan Frome* that has the reputation of being the most perfect tragedy in our literature, but even that poignant story of frustration and cruel defeat lacks the gallant hopeless struggle and the total irrevocable loss that lift the tragic above the acquiescent level of pathos. Yet the Wharton characters are not wholly puppets of a capricious destiny, not being fashioned by an avowed ironist or determinist. The moral failures are offset reasonably enough by the successes. The American volunteers, Troy Belknap and George Campion, are sincere in their idealism; the Mornways place honor above reputation; Ned Halidon and Ned Stanwell, Delia Ralston and Lizzie Hazeldean, are capable of the hardest kind of sacrifice—that which by its very concealment puts one under the cloud of misinterpretation; Newland Archer shows that when one makes the best of a bad bargain instead of sulking or storming, the best may turn out to be pretty good.

Nor is it an artistic flaw to stop short of an ultimate coherent Weltanschauung while pushing details to extremes, since novelists need not be philosophers, but it does indicate an interest in the sensational for its own sake. And if Edith Wharton's specific sagacities are not welded into profound wisdom, any such deficiency is no more than the natural limitations that define a strong personality. A specialist is bound to be restricted. It is merely that the restricted areas of this writer are more conspicuous by belonging to a less generally familiar realm. Fewer writers as well as fewer readers know the upper crust of life better than the lower. And since our conclusions are of necessity conditioned by experience, none of us can escape our allotted boundaries. (pp. 433-34)

Mrs. Wharton's manner, of course, harmonizes beautifully with her matter. It is as objective and detached yet as acutely conscious of its calculated and cunningly wrought effects. Whether the story is told in the third person or in the first of an invented speaker, it has firm structure and high polish,—qualities that are at least a relief after a good dose of the grotesque sprawlings and sloppy irrelevancies of the modern mode. . . .

The novelist's glitter comes largely from her epigrams, aphorisms and metaphors, a garniture profusely laid on with both comic and serious effects. Many of these have only ordinary gleam and luster but ever and anon they strike with dazzling force. (p. 435)

Dynamic as she is in style, however, Mrs. Wharton is static in substance. In nearly four decades of production the only evidence of change is in externals. Her earlier characters rang for cabs and turned lights up and down instead of on and off. Her later actors ride in taxis and press buttons, though even in the *Hudson River Bracketed* . . . ladies wear tea-gowns of an afternoon and start the alcohol burner under the tea-kettle. This last novel of hers spins nearly six hundred pages about the most egregious ass that ever kept out of the Home for Feeble Minded, yet she seems to think he is something of a genius. Her very latest volume, like her first, is a collection of short stories, and its menu offers very much the same succession of courses,—a subtle futility, a dismal crime, a pathetic illusion, a chivalric romance, a mistaken-identity farce, and a baleful ghost. They confirm the impression that she will continue to write with a pearl-handled gold pen to the end of her days. (p. 436)

> *Frances Theresa Russell, "Melodramatic Mrs. Wharton," in* The Sewanee Review *(reprinted by permission of the editor; © 1932 by The University of the South), Vol. XL, No. 4, Autumn, 1932, pp. 425-37.*

JOSEPH WARREN BEACH (essay date 1932)

["The House of Mirth" has a subject] suggestive of James —the shifts and compromises of a young woman brought up to the luxury of society life but without a sufficient income. Lily Bart, by her intelligence and charm as well as by her situation, reminds us of Charlotte Stant, Kate Croy, and Fleda Vetch. It is inevitable that her story should be told largely from her point of view. But Mrs. Wharton has not conceived this as an artistic principle to which sacrifices must be made, and she finds it more convenient to present many passages of the story from the point of view of Sel-

den, and even of such insignificant characters as Mrs. Peniston, Mrs. Stepney, Gerty Farish, and Trenor. Mrs. Wharton sometimes leaves the point of view of her heroine to tell us how she looked, or passes lightly from her thoughts and feelings to those of her companion. (pp. 291-92)

[While] Mrs. Wharton has a distinct tendency to make much of the impressions of her important characters, she had not at this date the intention of rendering her story exclusively through these, but followed naturally the traditional method of objective narrative.

This is even more iking in novels like ["The Fruit of the Tree" and "The stom of the Country"] . . . , in which the interest is di   ted over a larger number of principal characters, who succeed one another alternately as the center of the picture, and give way often to quite secondary characters where the exposition requires it. Very frequently, in "The Custom of the Country," the author begins her chapter . . . in a purely objective manner, setting the stage and marshaling the characters for half a dozen pages before any one of the persons emerges and begins to interpret the action in terms of his own impressions.

And there is a particular reason why, in this book, Mrs. Wharton cannot maintain the James technique of restricted point of view. The central person, Undine Spragg, a common young woman from the back country, who uses her beauty as a means of making successively more brilliant marriages, and so raising herself in the social scale, is a noble forerunner of Lorelei in "Gentlemen Prefer Blondes". . . . But Mrs. Wharton does not tell her story, like Anita Loos, in the diary manner. And the irony with which her career is chronicled does not admit of our losing ourselves in her point of view. Her vulgar smartness is a very different thing from the sensitive intelligence of Fleda Vetch or Lily Bart, and cannot be expected to render more than the gross and superficial aspects of the world she views. So that with the best of intentions, with the modern disposition to let the character speak for herself, the author cannot very whole-heartedly identify herself with Undine Spragg, and we are forever conscious of her critical gaze upon the motives and behavior of her shoddy heroine.

But any reader coming to "The Custom of the Country" directly from, say, "Vanity Fair" will be struck by the enormously greater use made in the later novel of the impressions of the characters themselves—even Undine's—as the means of rendering the action. This tendency toward intensifying the point of view is perhaps what should be emphasized in a discussion of any of these earlier novels of Edith Wharton rather than their departure from the limited point of view.

Meantime, in several very short novels or novelettes she had been experimenting with the absolutely limited point of view. In "Madame de Treymes" . . . , strongly reminiscent of "The American," of "Madame de Mauves," and of other stories of James, long and short, the point of view is, without exception, that of John Durham, the counterpart of Christopher Newman and Longmore, Americans similarly caught and bewildered in the mazes of French aristocratic society. In "Ethan Frome" . . . , inside the framework provided by the imaginary narrator, the point of view is exclusively that of Ethan Frome. Thus Edith Wharton followed exactly the evolution of James in this matter, even to the first application of the restricted point of view in stories long enough to be published each in a single volume, though not long enough to be classified securely as novels.

In "Summer" ... the same technique is extended to a novel of almost average length; and after "The Age of Innocence" this technique is the rule rather than the exception. In "A Son at the Front" ... and "The Children" ... the story is given altogether from the point of view of the central character. In "Hudson River Bracketed" ... it is given alternately from the standpoints of the two principals. But none of these novels of Edith Wharton after "The Age of Innocence" is on a level of interest with "The House of Mirth" or "The Custom of the Country." Taken together they are symptomatic of the overwhelming trend in her toward the restricted point of view. But of all her books, it is "The Age of Innocence" that stands out as the best example of the well-made novel in its various implications. (pp. 292-94)

If Edith Wharton shows her expertness more in one thing than another, it is in her dialogue. But it is the dramatic continuity of issue that gives its point to the dialogue and determines that it shall have structural, functional value as well as interest for itself alone. In "The Age of Innocence," certainly, she does not indulge herself with talk which is merely entertaining, which is devised for setting forth certain pet opinions of the author or for displaying the humors and eccentricities of the characters. Some aspects of New York society tone are amusingly hit off in certain passages of dialogue, but she manages to subordinate this interest strictly to that of her theme and make it serve the major issue. Her dialogue has some of the point of Thackeray's, but it is more dramatically knit together.

It is in general pointed and crisp from pruning and selection and from concentration on an issue. She is very deft in the springing of new items of information, carefully prepared, the timing of curtains, the isolation of significant bits. There are no long fat speeches of explanation, as so often in Hugh Walpole, for example; it is all broken up into half-utterances, challenges, questions, meanings developed through the give-and-take of dialogue. The chapters are short, and the chapter-divisions serve to set in provocative relief the culminating lines, like Sillerton Jackson's remark at the end of the first chapter, "I didn't think the Mingotts would have tried it on." (pp. 298-99)

The dialogue of Edith Wharton is so much slighter, brighter, smarter, wittier than that of James. The issues are so much more obvious; the story moves forward so much more swift and sparkling. One does not have in her the feeling of threading a long and arduous labyrinth. The development of situation in James is carried out with all the fullness and relentlessness of Ibsen. In Wharton one thinks rather of something in French comedy. (p. 301)

[In Edith Wharton] we have a follower of James as different from him as she is like him. Even in her handling of the point of view—perhaps most of all in her handling of this very problem—we find the difference. In "The Age of Innocence" and many other stories she is as strict as James in the observance of the limited point of view, but the effect is not the same. Everything is rendered through the consciousness of Newland Archer, but nothing is made of his consciousness.

Newland Archer is one of the palest and least individual-

ized characters ever offered to the public by a distinguished writer of fiction. He is hardly more than a device for projecting a situation and characters much more real than himself. We do not dwell with him in the narrow prison of his predicament. ... The limited point of view is here a compositional device of great value; it serves to focus the attention upon the simple issues. It gives sharpness and precision. But it does not serve as in James for enrichment and deepening of the effect. It is not a means of steeping us imaginatively in the special and rare solution which is the essence of a unique personality.

For this very reason Mrs. Wharton is a more popular writer than her master. There is so much less weight of the "subjective" to make the story drag. And if she has adopted the "dramatic" device of the limited point of view, she has avoided that over-emphasis on the conscious process which makes it bad "theater." (pp. 302-03)

> *Joseph Warren Beach, "The Well-Made Novel: Sedgwick, Wharton," in his* The Twentieth Century Novel: Studies in Technique *(© 1960; reprinted by permission of Prentice-Hall, Inc., Englewood Cliffs, New Jersey), Appleton-Century-Crofts, Inc., 1932, pp. 287-303.**

JOHN CROWE RANSOM (essay date 1936)

[It] came to pass that Edith Wharton, tutored by no less a technician than Henry James, expert in her rendering of the smart scene and the better sort nearest to her, must spend a time in the Massachusetts back country which was quite long enough to make her sensible of a new scene and set of characters, and to acquaint her with a local tragedy that clamoured to be told. How should she tell it? We must judge from the odd structural pattern of *Ethan Frome,* as well as from its unsatisfactory detail, that the problem gave her trouble. We are told as much in the Preface. It is an honest Preface, and only slightly disingenuous.

To the natives of Starkfield Mrs. Wharton must have been something of a foreign wonder; classifiable, being a "New York lady", yet a strange and outland personage. She evidently struck herself, too, as alien to the mind of the Starkfielders, in fact to a degree that threatened to inhibit her representation of Ethan, who was a particularly grim and taciturn one of them. Who should tell Ethan's story? For there must be means to bring his story, "in a way at once natural and picture-making, to the knowledge of its narrator", and through the narrator to the knowledge of the readers. If Ethan should tell it himself, it would not be identifiable with the main body of Mrs. Wharton's fiction. But if she should tell it, it would very likely be the story of a rather metamorphosed Ethan. (pp. 271-72)

Of what use in a case like this was her trained and sophisticated sensibility? It was that which would have falsified the whole.

Mrs. Wharton compromised; or rather, since she did not thoroughly reform her usual practice, she temporized. She invented a special reporter for Ethan in the person of a young man of sensibility and education very like her own. In theory it gained her this, that the reporter became a man; and this, that not being herself he need not render quite the complete spiritual history of events associated with her name as an author. In effect, it gained her very little. Spiritually, this gentleman is cousin to the gentlemen who relate stories for Joseph Conrad and Willa Cather, and he could probably trace descent from one ghost writer to another who had been in Henry James's own employ. She makes for him a temporary residence in Starkfield and acquaints him with Ethan, at a time just twenty-four years after the event that is the heart of Ethan's story. How can he participate in it? He gets nothing out of Ethan, and only scraps of information out of the villagers, but manages finally to find himself snow-bound for the night at Ethan's house. Now Ethan's story is of a man, a wife, and an extra woman, and in Ethan's kitchen the reporter actually finds these three characters, still surviving, dumb and wretched, in the most enduring triangle that fiction has recorded. The scene is illuminating. But we catch only a glimpse of it. The reporter finds the illumination much before we do, and begins at once to spin the story, starting the twenty-four years back. To put together "this version of the story"; the phrase being followed by three rows of points or ellipses, and Chapter One. The story which we have heard of, and despaired of, has begun. It goes on. After nine chapters it is complete, externally with respect to events, and internally with respect to Ethan's mind. It sees Ethan just past the tragic smash. The last word is followed, in my edition, by four rows of ellipses and the resumption of the sketchy account of how the reporter later ferreted out the outlines of the story he has already told.

This is fairly remarkable, though not unique, since we have stories from Conrad which play similar tricks. We are allowed to anticipate the reporter who is gathering the story, and then we go back and see him make slight detective motions at gathering it; but we are forced to conclude that he did not gather it really; that, mostly, he made it up. Why a special reporter at all? And why such a peculiar chronological method? These are features which picture to me, if it is not impertinent, the perturbation of an author wrestling with an unaccustomed undertaking, uneasy of conscience, and resorting to measures.

Forgetting the Preface, and the exterior or enveloping story, we attend strictly to Ethan's story, and discover that the fictitious reporter has had the goodness to enter Ethan's own mind and present events under the form of a focussed and continuous inner experience. That is, we are made to identify our own existence with Ethan's and to live his story with him. Or we are expected to, but to the best of my knowledge we cannot quite do it, we cannot become naturalized in Ethan's world. The tone is not always Ethan's, I think, imagining I know him better than Mrs. Wharton does. . . . [There] is the feeling that, identified with Ethan, we are not having quite as much sheer experience as the events would entitle us to have; and reflecting upon this, we first recall, and then reject, Mrs. Wharton's intimation (the prefatory one) that Ethan did not have any complicated experience to record. The suspicion arises that, rather than this, Mrs. Wharton is merely not familiar with Ethan's variety of complications. The book is half long enough, or less; it is a "study", a well-proportioned first-draft or outline for the real circumstantial thing that was to come, that would have been fiction.

In view of Mrs. Wharton's successes with her own sort of material it will not be invidious to point to this relative failure, a case illustrating a difficulty that besets the conscientious author. Henry James himself would have failed in this particular undertaking; or if not, it is because his sense of tactics would not have permitted him to try it. (pp. 272-75)

John Crowe Ransom, "Characters and Character," in The American Review, *Vol. VI, No. 3, January, 1936, pp. 271-88.**

Q. D. LEAVIS   (essay date 1938)

[Let us] compare Edith Wharton with George Eliot. George Eliot was a simple-minded woman except where great sensitiveness of feeling gave her a subtle insight—even her learning was deployed with solemn simplicity. Undeniably Mrs. Wharton had a more flexible mind, she was both socially and morally more experienced than George Eliot and therefore better able to enter into uncongenial states of feeling and to depict as an artist instead of a preacher distasteful kinds of behavior. Her Undine Spragg is better sustained and handled than the other's Rosamund Vincy. Undine's sphere of action is dazzling and she always has a fresh surprise for us up her sleeve in the way of moral obtuseness; it was cleverer to make Undine end up at the top of the tree with her only disappointment that her last husband couldn't get made Ambassador (on account of having a divorced wife) than to involve herself in disasters like Rosamund: the manifold irony of worldly success is more profitable than any simple moral lesson and artistically how much richer! Mrs. Wharton writes better than George Eliot, who besides lacking grace rarely achieves the economy of language that Mrs. Wharton commands habitually. Her technique is absolutely right and from the works I have instanced it would be difficult to alter or omit without harm, for like Henry James she was the type of conscious artist writing to satisfy only her own inflexible literary conscience. Now George Eliot in general moves like a cart-horse and too often takes the longest way round. But again it is George Eliot who is the great novelist.

I think it eventually becomes a question of what the novelist has to offer us, either directly or by implication, in the way of positives. In *Bunner Sisters, Summer,* and some other places Mrs. Wharton rests upon the simple goodness of the decent poor, as indeed George Eliot and Wordsworth both do in part, that is, the most wide-spread common factor of moral worth. But beyond that Mrs. Wharton has only negatives, her values emerging I suppose as something other than what she exposes as worthless. This is not very nourishing, and it is on similar grounds that Flaubert, so long admired as the ideal artist of the novel, has begun to lose esteem. It seems to be the fault of the disintegrating and spiritually impoverished society she analyses. Her value is that she does analyse and is not content to reflect. We may contrast Jane Austen, who does not even analyse, but, having the good fortune to have been born into a flourishing culture, can take for granted its foundations and accept its standards, working within them on a basis of internal relations entirely. The common code of her society is a valuable one and she benefits from it as an artist. Mr. Knightley's speech to Emma, reproving her for snubbing Miss Bates, is a useful instance: manners there are seen to be based on moral values. Mrs. Wharton's worthy people are all primitives or archaic survivals. This inability to find any significance in the society that she spent her prime in, or to find 'significance only through what its frivolity destroys,' explains the absence of poetry in her disposition and of many kinds of valuable experience in her books. She has none of that natural piety, that richness of feeling and sense of a moral order, of experience as a process of growth, in which George Eliot's local criticisms are embedded and which give the latter her large stature. Between her conviction that the new society she grew up into was vicious and insecurely based on an ill-used working class and her conviction that her inherited mode of living represented a dead-end, she could find no foundation to build on. (pp. 274-75)

Mrs. Wharton, if unfortunate in her environment, had a strength of character that made her superior to it. She was a remarkable novelist if not a large-sized one, and while there are few great novelists there are not even so many remarkable ones that we can afford to let her be overlooked. (p. 276)

> *Q. D. Leavis, "Henry James's Heiress: The Importance of Edith Wharton," in* Scrutiny, *Vol. VII, No. 3, December, 1938, pp. 261-76.*

ALFRED KAZIN (essay date 1941)

It is easy to say now that Edith Wharton's great subject should have been the biography of her own class, for her education and training had given her alone in her literary generation the best access to it. But the very significance of that education was her inability to transcend and use it. Since she could do no other, she chose instead to write, in various forms and with unequal success, the one story she knew best, the story that constituted her basic experience—her own. Her great theme, like that of her friend Henry James, became the plight of the young and innocent in a world of greater intricacy than they were accustomed to. But where James was obsessed by the moral complexity of that theme and devoted his career to the evaluation and dramatization of opposing cultures, Edith Wharton specialized in tales of victimization. To James the emotional problems of his characters were the superficial expression of that larger world of speech, manners, and instinct—whose significance was psychological and universal. He saw his work as a body of problems that tested the novelist's capacity for difficulty and responsibility. To Edith Wharton, whose very career as a novelist was the tenuous product of so many personal maladjustments, the novel became an involuted expression of self. She was too cultivated, too much the patrician all her days to vulgarize or even to simplify the obvious relations between her life and her work; she was too fastidious an artist even in her constricted sphere to yield to that obvious romanticism which fulfills itself in explicit confession. But fundamentally she had to fall back upon herself, since she was never, as she well knew, to rise above the personal difficulties that attended her career. She escaped the tedium and mediocrity to which her class had condemned her, but the very motivation of that escape was to become a great artist, to attain by the extension of her powers the liberation she needed as a woman; and a great artist, even a completely devoted artist, she never became. James, who gave her friendship, could encourage but not instruct her. Actually, it was not to become such a writer as he, but to become a writer, that she struggled; and what he had to give her—precision of motive, cultivation of taste, the sense of style—she possessed by disposition and training. James's need of art was urgent, but its urgency was of the life of the spirit; Edith Wharton's was desperate, and by a curious irony she escaped that excessive refinement and almost abstract mathematical passion for art that encumbered James. She could speak out plainly with a force he could never muster; and her own alienation and loneliness gave her a sympathy for erratic

spirits and illicit emotions that was unique in its time. It has been forgotten how much Edith Wharton contributed to the plain-speaking traditions of American realism. (pp. 105-06)

The greater consequence of Edith Wharton's failure to fulfill herself in art was its deepening of her innate disposition to tragedy. She was conscious of that failure even when she was most successful, and in the gap between her resolution and her achievement she took recourse to a classical myth, the pursuing Eumenides who will not let Lily Bart—or Edith Wharton—rest. She was almost the only one in her generation to attain the sense of tragedy, even the sense of the world as pure evil, that found expression in the biting edge of her novels and the utter fatalism of their drama. "Life is the saddest thing," she wrote once, "next to death," and the very simplicity and purity of that knowledge set her off in a literary generation to whom morality signified the fervor of the muckrakers and for whom death as a philosophical issue had no meaning. Spiritually, indeed, Edith Wharton was possessed of resources so much finer than any contemporary writers could muster that even the few superior novelists of her time can seem gross by comparison. It was a service, even though, like so many artistic services, it was an unconscious one, to talk the language of the soul at a time when the best energies in American prose were devoted to the complex new world of industrial capitalism. (pp. 105-07)

Edith Wharton knew well enough that one dynasty had succeeded another in American life; the consequences of that succession became the great subject of her best novels. But she was not so much interested in the accession of the new class as she was in the destruction of her own, in the eclipse of its finest spirits. Like Lily Bart, Ellen Olenska, Ralph Marvell, she too was one of its fine spirits; and she translated effortlessly and pointedly the difficulties of her own career into the difficulties of young aristocrats amidst a hostile and alien culture. It is the aristocrat yielding, the aristocrat suffering, who bestrides her best novels: the sensitive cultivated castaways who are either destroyed by their own class or tied by marriage or need to the vulgar *nouveaux riches*. Henry James could write of revolutionaries and nobility, painters and politicians, though all talked the Jamesian language at the same polysyllabic pitch; Edith Wharton's imagination was dominated always by the fellow spirits of her youth. Though she had been hurt by her class and had made her career by escaping its fundamental obligations, she could not, despite all her fertile powers of invention, conceive of any character who was not either descended from that class or placed in some obvious and dramatic relation to it. At bottom she could love only those who, like herself, had undergone a profound alienation but were inextricably bound to native loyalties and taste. Indeed, their very weakness endeared them to her: to rise in the industrial-capitalist order was to succumb to its degradations. "Why do we call our generous ideas illusions, and the mean one truths?" cries Lawrence Selden in "The House of Mirth." It was Edith Wharton's stricken cry. She had accepted all the conditions of servitude to the vulgar new order save the obligation to respect it values. But it was in the very nature of things that she should rebel not by adopting a new set of values or interesting herself in a new society, but by resigning herself to soundless heroism. Thus she could read in the defeat of her characters the last proud affirmation of the caste quality. If failure was the destiny of superior men and women in the modern world, failure was the mark of spiritual victory. For that is what Edith Wharton's sense of tragedy came to in the end: she could conceive of no society but her own, she could not live with what she had. Doom waited for the pure in heart; and it was better so.

Is not that the theme of "Ethan Frome" as well as of "The House of Mirth?" Ethan, like Lily Bart or Ralph Marvell, fails because he is spiritually superior and materially useless; he has been loyal to one set of values, one conception of happiness, but powerless before the obligations of his society. It was not a New England story that Edith Wharton wrote in "Ethan Frome." She knew little of the New England common world, and perhaps cared even less; the story was begun as an exercise in French while she was living in Lenox, Massachusetts, and she wanted a simple frame and "simple" characters. The world of the Frome tragedy is spaceless. She never knew how the poor lived in Paris or London; she knew even less of how they lived in the New England villages where she spent an occasional summer. There is indeed nothing in any of her work, not even in the one notable story she wrote of people who work for a living, "The Bunner Sisters," to indicate that she had any conception of the tensions and responsibilities of even the most genteel middle class poverty. Sympathy she possessed by the very impulse of her imagination, but it was a curious sympathy which assumed that if life in her own class was often dreary, the world "below" must be even more so. Whenever she wrote of that world, darkness and revulsion entered her work mechanically; she thought of the poor not as a class but as a condition, and the qualities she automatically ascribed to the poor—drabness, meanness, anguish—became another manifestation of the futility of human effort.

Edith Wharton was not confined to the lachrymose; she could hate, and hate hard, but the object of her hatred was the emerging new class of brokers and industrialists, the makers and promoters of the industrial era who were beginning to expropriate and supplant her own class. She disliked them no less fiercely than did the rebellious novelists of the Progressive era—the Robert Herricks, the David Graham Phillipses, the Upton Sinclairs; but where these novelists saw in the brokers and industrialists a new and supreme condition in American society, Edith Warton was merely offended. It is the *grande dame,* not the objective novelist, who speaks out in her caricatures of Rosedale and Undine Spragg. To the women of the new class she gave names like Looty Arlington and Indiana Frusk; to their native habitats, names like Pruneville, Neb., and Hallelujah, Mo. She had no conception of America as a unified and dynamic economy, or even as a single culture. There was old New York, the great house in Lenox (from which she gazed down upon Ethan Frome), and the sprawling wilderness that called itself in the Middle West, a land of graceless manners, hoary jests, business men, and ridiculous provincial speech. It was condescension that evoked in her that crackling irony that lunges through her best novels like a live wire; it was the biting old dowager of American letters who snapped at her lower-class characters and insulted them so roundly that her very disgust was comic. As the world about her changed beyond all recognition, she ignored the parvenu altogether and sought refuge in nostalgia. Her social views, never too liberal or expansive, now solidified themselves into the traditional views of reaction. After 1920, when she had fulfilled her debt to the past with "The

Age of Innocence," she lost even that interest in the craft of fiction which had singled her out over the years; and with mechanical energy poured out a series of cheap novels which, with their tired and forlorn courtesy, their smooth rendering of the smooth problems of women's magazine fiction, suggest that Edith Wharton exhausted herself periodically, and then finally, because she had so quickly exhausted the need that drove her to literature.

If it is curious to remember that she always suggested more distinction than she possessed, it is even more curious to see how the interests of the American novel have since passed her by. James has the recurrent power to excite the literary mind; Edith Wharton, who believed so passionately in the life of art that she staked her life upon it, remains not a great artist but an unusual American, one who brought the weight of her personal experience to bear upon a modern American literature to which she was spiritually alien. (pp. 108-11)

> Alfred Kazin, "The Lady and the Tiger: Edith Wharton and Theodore Dreiser," in Virginia Quarterly Review *(copyright, 1941, by the* Virginia Quarterly Review, *The University of Virginia), Vol. 17, No. 1 (Winter, 1941), pp. 101-19.*

BLAKE NEVIUS (essay date 1953)

Early and late, from the publication of *The Greater Inclination* to the obituaries of its author nearly forty years afterward, it was customary to remark that [Edith Wharton] was a disciple of [Henry James] and to let it go at that. Until all of the evidence is in (I am thinking particularly of the James letters to Mrs. Wharton which are part of the collection at Yale), it would be fairer to both writers to modify the usual view of their relationship by reminding ourselves that, roughly speaking, they started from the same position, proceeded by the same path, and that somewhere around 1900 they separated—with James taking a high road where the atmosphere, for Edith Wharton, proved too rare. It was in 1904 that she wrote to W. C. Brownell: " . . . The continued cry that I am an echo of Mr. James (whose books of the last ten years I can't read, much as I delight in the man) . . . makes me feel rather hopeless." Certainly the usual view is complicated by the fact that the two novelists' origins, background, and class outlook, as well as their literary ancestry, were almost identical. The most we can say for sure is that James led the way and that up to a certain point Edith Wharton found it easy to follow, and that rarely has there been so striking an affinity between two writers.

With certain departures, *The Writing of Fiction* is a highly simplified restatement of James's basic theory of fiction, but precisely for that reason—because of its orthodoxy and its determinedly impersonal quality—it is, for the student of Edith Wharton's own novels, an exasperating document. Mrs. Wharton had a mind of her own, but it expressed itself less in the form than in the tone and content of her fiction. If her literary intelligence was less patient and subtle than James's, it was usually more direct. Moreover, her strongest work is not her most Jamesian, so that any attempt to perpetuate a simple cause-and-effect view of their relationship is bound to be as misleading as the attempt to minimize Edith Wharton's debt to James in order to enhance her independent stature.

Although the general agreement in outlook and method between the two novelists cannot be deduced solely from

TWENTIETH-CENTURY LITERARY CRITICISM, Vol. 3   WHARTON

Mrs. Wharton's early short stories, a certain area of it is already apparent. For James, his friend recalled, "every great novel must first of all be based on a profound sense of moral values ('importance of subject'), and then constructed with a classical unity and economy of means." Leaving aside for the moment the question of form, we may protest, however mildly, that this is an oversimplification of James's doctrine as formulated first in "The Art of Fiction" and later in his preface to *The Portrait of a Lady*. James was always more cautious than Edith Wharton in isolating and defining the various functions of a work of art. No statement so flatly confident, so open to a multitude of questions, as her paraphrase of his supposed doctrine would have been possible from him.... Nevertheless, in her early stories Edith Wharton tacitly recognized James's dictum by carefully assigning the point of view to the "finest" consciousness available, and in an unpublished critical fragment she acknowledged the dependence of the moral sense of a work of art on "the amount of felt life concerned in producing it" in her statement that "the immoral (or at least the harmful) novelist is he who handles a sombre or a complex subject without sufficient power to vivify its raw material." Allowing for Mrs. Wharton's occasional oversimplifications, she and James are in perfect agreement. "The ultimate value of every work of art," she insisted, "lies, not in its subject, but in the way in which that subject is seen, felt, and interpreted." Consequently, in her essay on Marcel Proust she took that writer gently to task for his failures of moral sensibility. Her position is worth emphasizing because ... first in *The Reef* ... , but particularly in the novels she wrote following *The Age of Innocence* ... , her own moral sensibility is progressively inadequate to the demands made upon it by her subjects, with the result that her comments on Proust must strike the reader of *A Son at the Front* and *The Mother's Recompense* with an unexpected effect of irony.

What Edith Wharton said of George Eliot, that she "vibrated to *nuances* of conduct as an artist vibrates to subtleties of line and colour," could be said of both her and James at [the outset of their writing careers]. Unlike Miss Talcott, the heroine of her short story "A Cup of Cold Water," who is unable to "distinguish the intermediate tints of the moral spectrum," Edith Wharton sometimes allowed the intermediate tints to usurp the function of primary colors with the result that the dramatic texture of some of her early stories is perilously thin. Nevertheless, her problem was the same as James's: how to express the nuances. And it is in this connection that her most reliable and Jamesian cluster of metaphors comes into play. Her characters, in the early short stories and in *The Reef* particularly, are intensely aware of one another; they respond to the slightest changes in the atmosphere of thought and sensation conveyed by another presence; and they are equally alive to impressions generated by their physical environment. The general image by which this empathy is expressed occurs in the reference to George Eliot just quoted: the individual becomes an instrument capable of transmitting and receiving the most delicate vibrations. When Edith Wharton is most conscious of James's example, she falls most easily into his manner. *The Reef* alone supplies countless variations of this central metaphor: " ... Darrow, on meeting her again, had immediately felt how much finer and surer an instrument of expression she had become" ... ; "He recalled with a faint smile of retrospective pleasure the

girl's enjoyment of her evening, and the innumerable fine feelers of sensation she had thrown out to its impressions." ... Another metaphor, by no means uncommon in fiction, but which is especially active in both James and Mrs. Wharton, is that of the moral or emotional abyss which is constantly opening at the characters' feet, dividing them from each other or from their own better natures. One recalls particularly those situations in James, frequently duplicated in Mrs. Wharton, where his heroes, confronted by a sudden demand on their feelings (usually made by a woman who has some claims on them), make a bridge of evasive words to carry them safely across this frightening abyss. It is apparent, in short, that the sensibility embodied in the point of view employed by both novelists is almost identical and therefore expresses itself in much the same terms.

In the early stories and novels the dialogue, too, is frequently Jamesian in its hesitations, seeming *non sequiturs,* and unfinished statements.... But James's conversations are carried on in a denser and more highly charged atmosphere. Questions hang in the air unanswered, and the silences are oppressive. The air surrounding Edith Wharton's characters is of a thinner texture; remarks have a greater tendency to evaporate in it. Her dialogue is ordinarily brisker than James's and more emphatic.

Such parallels as I have suggested are confined to the realm of technique.... It would be easy, of course, to point up the resemblances in situation between *The Age of Innocence* and *The Europeans,* between *The Buccaneers* and *The Portrait of a Lady,* between *Madame de Treymes* and both *Madame de Mauves* and *The American;* but it could be argued that they are the natural result of two writers, related in background and temperament, working on the same general subject. It should be clear by now, however, that the reader who knows his James is at least half prepared to understand Edith Wharton on first acquaintance. (pp. 30-6)

Blake Nevius, "Reconnoiterings," in his Edith Wharton: A Study of Her Fiction *(copyright © 1953 by The Regents of the University of California; reprinted by permission of the University of California Press), University of California Press, 1953, pp. 12-36.*

LOUIS O. COXE (essay date 1955)

Times and readers change [, but *The Age of Innocence*], written at the height of Edith Wharton's powers, retains a power the gradual release of which one becomes aware of with time, with acquaintance, with a more delicate attuning of the ear and the sensibility to the things Edith Wharton was writing about. And it seems to me one of the graces and delights of *The Age of Innocence* lies exactly in the multifariousness of its thematic material, in its refusal to tie itself down to "meaning," the while that it glitters with a density, a hardness of surface that only a truly novelistic eye could have seen and an informing mind recreate. (pp. 155-56)

I know of no other American novelist with Edith Wharton's power (in this book, at any rate) of simple vision, of showing us who was there and in what grouping, what juxtapositions.... Nowhere does Edith Wharton's grip relax; her hold on actuality is everywhere firm. She has been there—she knows. From the smallest flower in the Beaufort

567

conservatory to the styling of dresses by Worth in the Seventies—she knows it all and she knows how to put it before us in all its appeal of the rare, the far-off, the perhaps absurd. And in so doing, she does not partronize either her readers or her characters and their world. . . . (p. 156)

The scenes strike us so vividly throughout the novel are of different sorts, and not one seems there for its own sake. . . . [They illustrate] a lively sense of surface and attitude, without which no deeper probing is possible. And the probing is possible. And the probing takes us deep enough for comfort, down to the quick of a society, a world, a whole history of the American sensibility.

That indeed seems to emerge as the finest quality of Edith Wharton's theme in *The Age of Innocence,* the whole question of the old and the new, of passion and duty, of the life of the feelings and that of the senses. For us, reading the book some decades after its publication, the complexities of meaning alone make the novel seem far richer than many another more highly touted. And again, here is no apparatus composed by symbols, near-allegory and didacticism, but a tissue of objects, places, attitudes, and desires.

If one can plump for a single "meaning" that the book may hold for us today, it may well be that of the lost life of feeling, the kind of life, the kinds of feeling, that Newland Archer's son seems utterly incapable of understanding or knowing. At the very end, when Newland Archer, for the last time, retreats from Ellen Olenska and from the sort of experience his son Dallas is only too glad to meet, we feel the fullness of the irony. Archer, with his insecurity, his sensitivity, and his passion has obeyed the moral imperatives of his class and time and has given up Ellen and love for the furtherance of the shallow-seeming aims, all amorphous as they are, of his world. He has stuck to May and to his New York, giving up another world. (pp. 156-57)

Can Dallas or anyone like him begin to understand the meaning of the kind of feelings Archer has known? Have they the time? the imagination? the passion? What can the notion of a buried life mean to one who can conceive only of surface? As Archer himself puts it to himself, "the thing one's so certain of in advance: can it ever make one's heart beat wildly?"

Newland Archer does not say this to his son. Times have changed and the steady cultivation of the affections, of nuances of feeling which only an ordered society allows seems to the new generation "a deaf and dumb asylum." (p. 158)

Edith Wharton seems to be saying that only if America can evolve a society which feels deeply and can say what it feels can it do more than shift from generation to generation, without a sense of the past, without depth, without blessing. (p. 159)

Edith Wharton is very clear about all of this: she opposes Archer, the near-rebel, with May, the total conformist. Here a lesser novelist would have been content to rest, in the mere showing of the processes by which an American with separatist tendencies is broken to harness and curb. That she does not leave it at this adds dimension to the book and to the novelist's vision. The emphasis here rests finally upon the ways in which an individual, in more or less settled times, can come to identify his illusions with

those of his world. The rightness or wrongness of such identification we may determine if we can, though for my part I would say that the triumph of Edith Wharton's realism strikes one as most sweeping in just her very refusal to draw any such line: she seems merely to say, that is the way things were for these people. Had you done differently, it would have been a different time, place and cast.

If this novel is not quite a retelling of *Bérénice* there is in it some, at least, of Racine's sense of fatality and of the course of duty as a form of fate to be defied at one's peril. As Archer quite clearly sees, to follow one's simple duty means that one must in some sense lose one's life. Yet this in not really the tragedy for Archer; it comes at last . . . to his final inability to see that if he cannot—must not—have Ellen and the rich life of "Europe," he still has May. But having once had a vision of Ellen Olenska and her passion, May, the white and conventional counterpart of Ellen, must figure to him as the embodiment of the society that denies the vision's fulfillment. It is not so, of course. With his careful, lifelong cultivation of the sensibilties and the passions, Newland Archer has unfitted himself for passionate, devoted action. . . . [That] very capacity to feel and to suffer serves as a cousinly and female bond between May and Ellen. Archer, the object of two such loves, has never been able to take the risk of either. (p. 160)

Louis O. Coxe, "What Edith Wharton Saw in Innocence" (copyright © 1955 by Louis O. Coxe; reprinted by permission of the author), in The New Republic, Vol. 132, No. 26, June 27, 1955 (and reprinted in Edith Wharton: A Collection of Critical Essays, edited by Irving Howe, Prentice-Hall, Inc., 1962, pp. 155-61).

JOSEPH X. BRENNAN (essay date 1961-62)

In spite of the critical interest it has continually aroused . . . and the popularity it has from the first enjoyed, *Ethan Frome* has yet to receive the kind of detailed textual analysis many lesser works have long since enjoyed. To be sure, it has evoked a variety of commentary, respecting its theme and narrative framework especially, but due attention has yet to be directed to its elaborate metaphorical patterns and the intricate relationship of those patterns to the narrator's sensibility. Only in a close study of these aspects of the novel, which determine its very tone and structure, can one begin to comprehend the reasons for its strange power and durability.

In her brief but illuminating introduction to *Ethan Frome* Mrs. Wharton directed the greater part of her attention to the narrator framework of the novel, which she presumably regarded as her chief problem and special achievement. Whatever her real convictions many have been concerning her solution, John Crowe Ransom is certainly right in regarding the results as less than satisfactory [see excerpt above]. For the close reader readily discerns that the engineer-narrator did not really gather his story "bit by bit, from various people," but having been inspired by a few bare hints and scraps of information, created his "vision" of what *might* have been almost entirely out of the stuff of his vivid imagination. In short, the narrator who presents himself as an engineer in the realistic framework of the novel is actually a writer in disguise with the technical skill of a professional novelist and the sensibility of a poet; and his imaginative reconstruction of Ethan Frome's story, in view of what little he had to go by, is really no more than a brilliant fiction. Once one recognizes this fact, however, that we have to deal here with an overt fiction within a fiction, it is expedient, if not indeed necessary, to accept this arrangement as the very form of the novel and to analyze it as such. Hence the need for a close examination of the "vision" within the novel in relationship to its narrator as well as on its own terms.

From the many descriptions of the setting which one encounters in both the narrative framework and the "vision" of the novel, it is clear that the engineer-narrator is not only intensely responsive to the beauty of the natural scene and the seasons, but has a distinct predilection also for rendering his response in imagistic or poetic language. . . . The narrator's acute sensitivity to the beauty of nature, in fact, accounts for much that is profoundly moving and memorable in *Ethan Frome,* so thoroughly does it permeate the whole novel, framework and vision alike.

It is not surprising, therefore, that in projecting the character of Ethan the narrator has liberally endowed him with much the same sensitivity he himself possesses. Though there is not the slightest indication from any source of evidence to which the engineer has access that either Ethan or Mattie was especially sensitive to the beauties of nature, the narrator has so thoroughly indued the two of them with this susceptibility that it both motivates and dominates their relationship. . . . (pp. 348-49)

This special sensitivity, shared equally by the narrator and his imagined characters, accounts, moreover, for the many skeins of imagery which pattern the envisioned story. It accounts, first of all, for the chief pattern of contrast which runs throughout this story, that between indoors and outdoors, between the house as the symbolic stronghold of moral convention and conformity, and the open countryside as symbolic of natural freedom and passional abandon. And it accounts also for the elaborate system of metaphorical characterization developed in direct relationship to this basic symbolic pattern.

Of the many natural objects and locations which constitute the pattern of outdoor imagery, the two black Norway spruces are surely the most important, since they provide the setting for the lovers' uttermost passion and final fatal resolve. In their symbolical dark shadows, indeed, the story of Ethan and Mattie's secret passion virtually begins and ends. When for the first time in Chapter II they stand together in this darkness, their deep mutual passion is no less intense, and all the more painful, for being unexpressed and forbidden. . . . In Chapter IX, when they again stand together under these spruces, they give passionate avowal to that love, of which, but three nights earlier, there had been only mute intimations. And it is in this darkness, finally, a darkness now of utter hopelessness, that they resolve to die together. Thus the spruces both shelter their forbidden love and foreshadow its tragic ending, forming a kind of dark parentheses to the brief interlude of their passion. (p. 350)

Insofar as the narrator has imagined and set these scenes, this symbolic use of the Norway spruces directly reflects his informing sensibility. The characterization of Mattie and Zeena, however, though ultimately derived from the narator's sensibility also, nevertheless becomes the immediate responsibility of Ethan in the envisioned story, for it is through his sensibility and from his point of view that this vision is projected. The distinction, of course, is a logical

rather than real one, since the two sensibilities are really only one.

The imagistic light in which both Mattie and Zeena are consistently regarded by Ethan, in any event, is directly related to this larger pattern of contrast. In Ethan's mind, it is interesting to note, Mattie is constantly associated with the most lovely and delicate objects in nature. Her face "always looked like a window that has caught the sunset"; "it was part of the sun's red and of the pure glitter of the snow"; "it was part of the sun's and it "changed with each turn of their talk, like a wheat-field under a summer breeze." Noteworthy also are the descriptions of Mattie's hair. Seen from behind, as she carried a lamp before her, it looked to Ethan "like a drift of mist on the moon"; and while she washed the dishes, the steam tightened "her rough hair into little brown rings like the tendrils of the traveller's joy." (p. 351)

Especially important, and even symbolic, is the frequent association of Mattie with birds: for Ethan, "the motions of her mind were as incalculable as the flit of a bird in the branches"; and "her hands went up and down above the strip of stuff, just as he had seen a pair of birds make short perpendicular flights over a nest they were building." To him, also, her voice was a "sweet treble," and "the call of a bird in a mountain ash was so like her laughter that his heart tightened and then grew large." Of particular interest, therefore, is the manner in which, after the smash-up, Mattie's whimpering is confused in Ethan's mind with the sound of both a bird and a field-mouse. . . .

Since Zeena, as we shall see below, is consistently associated with and even identified by her cat, this shift from the image of the small bird, the eternal but more elusive quarry of cats, to that of the field mouse, their more defenseless prey, is obviously symbolic of Zeena's final victory over Mattie. (pp. 351-52)

Into the characterization of Mattie, furthermore, the narrator has quite deliberately woven a streak of symbolic red; she is so frequently connected with this color, in fact, that by the end of the story her personality is vividly imbued with the passion, vibrancy, and daring nonconformity which red traditionally connotes. . . . Of particular import in [one] scene . . . is the "dish of gay red glass" which Mattie had taken down from the forbidden shelf of Zeena's special possessions. As an object of beauty and gaiety, which Zeena, significantly, had never used once since her wedding, this gay red dish suggests symbolically the pleasure and passion that Ethan had sought and Zeena had thwarted in their marriage. As Zeena's property by marriage and by right, it represents also, respecting Ethan and Mattie, a forbidden pleasure and illicit passion. The shattering of the red dish, moreover, clearly prefigures the final shattering of their limbs and ill-starred love.

In direct contrast to this rendering of Mattie in terms of nature and vibrant reds, are the descriptions of Zeena suggesting the artifical, angular, and unhealthy. . . . In contrast to Mattie's vivid coloring and beauty, Zeena's face was "drawn and bloodless," "grayish," and "sallow," with "fretful" "querulous lines"; her hair was "thin," her lips "straight," her eyes "lashless," and her looks "queer." (pp. 352-53)

Countering the metaphorical association of Mattie and birds, moreover, is the more literal and obvious relationship between Zenobia and her cat. In the long anticipated evening of Zeena's absence, in fact, the cat directly becomes her watchful surrogate: "The cat jumped into Zeena's chair . . . and lay watching them with narrowed eyes." Earlier in the evening the cat had disrupted [the lovers'] happiness even more violently by breaking the red pickle-dish, the symbol of their forbidden passion. In its cunning, cruelty, and languid domesticity the cat indeed is the perfect representative of its mistress. It seems, too, that the stuffed owl in the parlor was introduced to further suggest Zeena's affinity for the artificial and predaceous. In any event nothing natural and beautiful seems to thrive in her domain of drugs and patent medicines; even the kitchen geraniums fade and "pine away." From the characterization of Zeena in both the narrative framework and the story proper, moreover, one is evidently intended to infer that she gathers a certain morbid strength from the weakness and illness of others: vulture-like she diligently attends the dying.

In close connection with this pattern of contrasts in the characterizations of Zeena and Mattie, there appears another set of contrasts in which Ethan himself figures. At the beginning of the novel, when the narrator first beholds Ethan, twenty-four years after his smash-up, the things which most impress him are his deep taciturnity and moral isolation. . . . It is interesting to note, therefore, that as the narrator envisions Ethan's relationship with Mattie, twenty-four years earlier, "she, the quicker, finer, more expressive, instead of crushing him by the contrast, had given him something of her own ease and freedom." And since she is most frequently associated with summer imagery, it is not surprising that as they make their way home the first evening, Ethan's growing conviction of their mutual love is paralleled by an imagistic progression from spring thaw to summer warmth and flow. . . . The joyful anticipation of spending the evening alone with Mattie further unlocks Ethan from his wintry taciturnity: "he, who was usually so silent, whistled and sang aloud as he drove through the snowy fields. There was in him a slumbering spark of sociablility which the long Starkfield winters had not yet extinguished." . . . In their most passionate embrace two nights later under the Varnum spruces, this progression from wintry cold to summer heat reaches its culmination: "once he found her mouth again, and they seemed to be by the pond together in the burning August sun." (pp. 353-55)

In opposition to the imagistic warmth and ease characterizing his relationship with Mattie is the chill, numbness, and paralysis which typifies his relationships with his wife. Ironically it was Ethan's very dread of loneliness, silence, and isolation—all symbolically related to winter—that had induced him to marry Zeena in the first place. Before long, however, he became increasingly aware of Zeena's real nature, of her hypochondria, her "narrow-mindedness and ignorance." "Then she too fell silent"; and recalling his mother's growing taciturnity, Ethan began to wonder if Zeena were also turning "queer." "At times, looking at Zeena's shut face, he felt the chill of such forebodings." By the time of Mattie's arrival, nevertheless, the estrangement of the couple was so complete that even with his love for Mattie suffusing his whole being, the mere mention of her name was sufficient to seal him in silence: "Ethan, a moment earlier, had felt himself on the brink of eloquence; but the mention of Zeena had paralyzed him."

Just as the house stands in symbolic opposition to the out-of-doors, so too the bedroom of Zeena and Ethan is the direct symbolic counterpart of the shadows of the Norway spruces. For at the end of Chapter II and the beginning of Chapter III, it is evident that the bedroom represents for Ethan his suffocating marital commitment to Zeena and his frustrating separation from Mattie. The bedroom, moreover, is the scene of the first incident "of open anger between the couple in their sad seven years together"; in this scene, the obvious antithesis to that of the lovers under the spruces, "their thoughts seemed to dart at each other like serpents shooting venom." Thus Ethan's desertion of his bed that same night and his retirement to the study below foreshadow his subsequent resolution to desert Zeena and run away with Mattie.

Ethan's hope of an escape from his bondage to Zeena, however, soon withers in the harsh light of day and reality: "The inexorable facts closed in on him like prison-warders handcuffing a convict. There was no way out—none. He was a prisoner for life. . . ." Returning now to the narrative framework, one notes that this image of the shackles reappears in the description of Ethan's lameness "checking each step like the jerk of a chain." His very attempt to escape through suicide, in fact, had only doubled the bonds of his captivity; for his crippled body only objectifies the warped state of his soul, now chained to the ruins of a tragic marriage and even more tragic love. It is no wonder, then, that Ethan appears to the engineer to be already "dead" and "in hell." Here there is no hope or meaningfulness at all—only the endurance of despair.

In retrospect it may be seen more clearly how intricately *Ethan Frome* is structured. In spite of the obvious formal distinction between the framework and the narrator's "vision," the two parts are nevertheless complexly interrelated; the account of Ethan's tragic love, in fact, is so thoroughly informed by the sensibility and imagination of its narrator that the story can be adequately analyzed only in terms of that relationship. Since the narrator has had to imagine almost the whole of Ethan's history and the most important traits of his character as well, in many respects, inevitably, the sensibilities of the two are indistinguishable.

It seems to me, therefore, that it would be much more reasonable to judge the novel in terms of the special character of the narrator's mind—his predilection for poetic, symbolic design and an abstract ideal of human nature—rather than in terms of psychological realism. For even within the formal structure and statement of the work, Ethan and Mattie and Zeena are much more imagined than real characters. One may take issue, perhaps, with the rightness of the narrator's vision but certainly not with his right—or the right of the author—to imagine it as his peculiar sensibility dictates. (pp. 355-56)

Joseph X. Brennan, "Ethan Frome: Structure and Metaphor," in Modern Fiction Studies (© copyright 1961 by Purdue Research Foundation, West Lafayette, Indiana), Vol. 7, No. 4, Winter, 1961-62, pp. 347-56.

LOUIS AUCHINCLOSS (essay date 1961)

The tales in *The Greater Inclination* . . . and in its successor, *Crucial Instances* . . . , have some of the flavor of James's stories of artists and writers of the same period. They are apt to be set against European backgrounds and to deal with such themes as the temptation to the serious artist of commercial success or the bewildering influence upon him of the art of an older, richer civilization. They are clever and readable, if a trifle thin, and in three of them, "The Pelican," "The Rembrandt," and "The Angel at the Grave," Mrs. Wharton shows herself already in full command of the style that was to make her prose as lucid and polished as any in American fiction. It is a firm, crisp, smooth, direct, easily flowing style, the perfect instrument of a clear, undazzled eye, an analytic mind, and a sense of humor alert to the least pretentiousness. We may later wonder if her style was adapted to all the uses to which she put it. . . . The defect in Edith Wharton's poetry, of which she published three volumes, is that this same style, consciously ennobled and stripped of laughter, becomes as dull and over-ornamented as the privately printed verse of any number of aspiring ladies who sought refuge from the distraction of social life. But poetry is subjective, and Mrs. Wharton, like many persons of wide reading and disciplined exterior, was inclined to be mawkish in subjective mood.

Her first novel, *The Valley of Decision,* . . . is laid in Italy, that charnel house of English and American historical fiction. It is Edith Wharton's *Romola,* except that it is a better book than George Eliot's, for the fruits of her research are strewn attractively through the pages and not spooned into the reader like medicine. But although she captures remarkably the spirit and color of the eighteenth century, nothing can save the novel from its pale and lifeless characters. It is like a play with perfect settings in which the actors stand stiffly in the middle of the stage, their eyes fixed on the prompter. (pp. 9-10)

The Descent of Man . . . is another volume of short stories, similar in tone to the earlier ones except for "The Dilettante," which marks an advance in the development of a male character who is to pervade all of Mrs. Wharton's fiction, the cold, cultivated, aristocratic egoist who feeds on the life and enthusiasm of simpler souls. (p. 11)

The House of Mirth . . . marks her coming of age as a novelist. At last, and simultaneously, she had discovered both her medium and her subject matter. The first was the novel of manners and the latter the assault upon the old Knickerbocker society in which she had grown up of the new millionaires, the "invaders" as she called them, who had been so fabulously enriched by the business growth following the Civil War. . . . Mrs. Wharton saw clearly enough that the invaders and defenders were bound ultimately to bury their hatchet in a noisy, stamping dance, but she saw also the rich possibilities for satire in the contrasts afforded by the battle line in its last stages and the pathos of the individuals who were fated to be trampled under the feet of those boisterous truce makers. (pp. 11-12)

The different levels of society in *The House of Mirth* are explored with a precision comparable to that of Proust whom Mrs. Wharton was later so greatly to admire. . . . Lily learns that money is the common denominator of all these worlds and that the differences between them consist only in the degrees of scent with which its odor is from time to time concealed. (p. 13)

I do not suppose that Mrs. Wharton intended Lawrence Selden to constitute the last and greatest of Lily's trials, but so he strikes me. He is a well-born, leisurely bachelor lawyer, with means just adequate for a life of elegant solitude, who spends his evenings, when not leafing through the pages of his first editions, dining out in a society that he loves to ridicule. . . . Mrs. Wharton's attitude toward Selden's type of man is enigmatic. He may be a villain in "The Dilettante," or he may at least pose as a hero in *The House of Mirth.* . . . I incline to the theory that Mrs. Wharton really intended us to accept this plaster-cast figure for a hero, but that she had a low opinion of heroes in general. When Lily suddenly retorts to Selden that he spends a great deal of his time in a society that he professes to despise, it is as if the author had suddenly slipped into the book to express a contempt that the reader is not meant to share. (p. 14)

The Fruit of the Tree is an experiment in a totally new field, the novel of reform. Mrs. Wharton began her task of research conscientiously enough with a tour of a factory near her country home in Lenox, Massachusetts, but she soon lost interest in her theme and succumbed to an unworthy compromise. In order to be able to draw her factory manager and trained nurse from models in her own world, she endowed them both with old and distinguished families which had only recently lost their money, thus giving to these parts of her book a curious air of social masquerade. Even so, the reader's interest is caught when Amherst, the priggish manager, marries the widow owner of the factory, having misconstrued her passion for himself as a zeal for the cause of the workers, and settles down in blithe ignorance to what he imagines will be their shared task of reform. But at this point Mrs. Wharton changes her theme altogether. Bessie Amherst, bored with the workers and interpreting, perhaps correctly (again the enigma of the Wharton hero), her husband's interest in reform as indifference to herself, goes galloping over icy roads until she falls from her horse and receives an incurable back injury, which condemns her to a long period of hideous and futile agony. The novel now turns abruptly into a problem novel about euthanasia in the manner of Bourget, for Bessie's sufferings are abbreviated by the needle of the trained nurse with the social background. Mrs. Wharton handles both themes competently, but the book simply collapses between them. (pp. 17-18)

[*Tales of Men and Ghosts*] contains some superb chillers. A tricky ending to a serious short story will sometimes detract from the total effect and make it seem superficial or sentimental, or both, but in a ghost story it has a valid, even an indispensable, function. The egotism of Mrs. Wharton's constantly recurring bachelors is brought out more effectively in "The Eyes" than in any of her other short stories or novels. (pp. 18-19)

Mrs. Wharton's other ghost stories may be considered out of chronology because their style and effectiveness does not vary, except to improve, with the years. This kind of tale requires a skill that never left her, the skill of telling a story reduced to its bare bones, without the aid of social problems or manners or mores or even of human nature, except in its most elemental sense. She always believed that the storytelling faculty was basic and indispensable in any writer. She was like a representational artist who looks askance at an abstract painting and wants to know if the man who executed it can really draw. At times she would try her hand, almost as one might try a puzzle, at a story that was nothing but technique, like "Roman Fever," where the interest and excitement is concentrated in the last line that gives the whole meaning to what has gone before. Her technique in ghost stories is to keep the supernatural to the minimum that will still irradiate the tale with horror. Character can be important as in "The Eyes," but it is by no means essential. As long as there is one plain human being, as in "All Souls," to register terror for the reader, there is an adequate cast.

Time . . . brought to Mrs. Wharton an attitude of disapproval toward the changing social scene which was to sour her later work, but the ghost stories, by their very nature, escaped this, and her grasp of the secret of chilling her reader continued to improve to the end. (pp. 19-20)

When I think of [*Ethan Frome*], I visualize a small painting, perfectly executed to the last detail, of three silent figures in a small dark cottage kitchen, with snow glimpsed through a window, the terrible Zeena in the center, white and pasty and gaunt, and, scattered on the table, the pieces of a broken dish. But I could never put the story as fiction in the same class with *The House of Mirth* on the very ground that to me it is a picture and, as such, one dimensional. Lily Bart and the society in which she lives are turned around and around and studied from different angles. It is not fair, of course, to compare a long novel with a novelette, but the tremendous reputation of *Etham Frome* evokes such a defense.

There has been some disposition in critics to view with distrust Mrs. Wharton's excursions into life among the needy, as evidenced by *Ethan Frome*, "The Bunner Sisters," and *Summer,* to see her as the great lady from "The Mount" in Lenox, peering at Ethan and his womenfolk from the back seat of her big motor. I doubt if these comments would have been made had the stories been published under another name, for the keeness of Mrs. Wharton's observation was not affected by the social status of her models. Only, in later years, when she attempted to describe persons and places that she had never seen did she fail in her job. I am totally persuaded of the reality of that notions shop kept by Ann Eliza Bunner and her sister and by the dank public library where Charity Royall dreams away her listless days. The reason why *Summer* and "The Bunner Sisters" are less convincing than *Ethan Frome* does not lie in any failure of observation or imagination on the part of the author, but in the fact that one feels her presence, which in *Ethan Frome* the device of a narrator has successfully eliminated. (pp. 21-2)

[*The Reef*] was greeted with a burst of congratulation from all the Jamesian circle. "Racinian" was the adjective used by the master, and indeed a Racinian unity of mood is achieved by centering the action in an old, high-roofed chateau of brick and yellowish stone, bathed in the pale light of October afternoons. The rooms in which the characters tensely talk are like a series of paintings by Walter Gay. It is a quiet, controlled, beautiful novel, but its theme has always struck me as faintly ridiculous. Mrs. Leath, a widow, is at last about to marry George Darrow, her old bachelor admirer, and her stepson, Owen, is entertaining a similar plan with respect to the beautiful young family governess, Sophy Viner, when the discovery that Darrow and Sophy have once been lovers reduces all the characters to a state of quiet desperation. Even conceding that in 1912 such an affair might have disqualified Sophy as a bride for Owen, would Mrs. Leath, a woman who had lived all her adult life in France, consider that her own happiness had to be sacrificed as well? Of course, Mrs. Wharton's answer would be

that Mrs. Leath is a woman of the finest sensitivities and that the affair occurred at a time when she had every reason to believe Darrow attentive to herself, but I still cannot get away from the suspicion that at least part of the horror of the situation lies in the fact that Sophy is a governess. The final chapter, so jarringly out of tune with the rest of the book, tends to confirm this suspicion. When Mrs. Leath goes to Sophy's sister's hotel to tell Sophy that she has given Darrow up, she is received by the sister in a dim, untidy, scented room, complete with lover and masseur. (pp. 22-3)

[*The Custom of the Country*] is a return to the rich, sure ground of New York and the novel of manners, only this time the central character in the conflict of social groups is not a victim but an invader. Undine Spragg is a creature of alloy, as sentimental in her judgments of herself as she is ruthless in her judgments of others. A father is only a checkbook, a husband a means of social advancement, a baby a threat to the figure. . . . She never knows the toll in human misery of her advance to the social heights, for it never occurs to her to look back. The story of how she hews her way through the old New York ranks . . . is vivid and fascinating. Undine gets into as many dangerous corners as Lily Bart, but by miscalculation rather than by inertia, and the same shrewd, restless cerebration that gets her in can be counted on to get her out. In *The House of Mirth* our compassion goes out to Lily; in *The Custom of the Country* it goes out to the society which Undine is trying to crash.

The flaw in the novel that keeps it from ranking equally with its predecessor is that Mrs. Wharton hates Undine too much. She sees in her incarnate the devil of the modern world, that world where all fineness of soul and graciousness of living have been submerged in a great tide of insipid and meretricious uniformity whose origin seems to lie vaguely in the American Middle West. . . . What Mrs. Wharton fails to prove is that Chelles would have married Undine at all. For she is really too awful to be quite so successful with quite so many men. Her vulgarity destroys the allure that such a woman would have been bound to have and that her creator was not to understand until her last, unfinished novel. (pp. 23-5)

[Mrs. Wharton] regarded the war from a simple but consistent point of view: France, virtually singlehanded, was fighting the battle of civilization against the powers of darkness. It was the spirit that made men fight and die, but it has never, unfortunately, been the spirit of fiction. Reading *The Marne* . . . and *A Son at the Front* . . . today gives one the feeling of taking an old enlistment poster out of an attic trunk. It may be a significant comment on the very nature of Armageddon that the only literature that survives it is literature of disillusionment and despair. Mrs. Wharton knew that the war was terrible; she had visited hospitals and even the front itself. But the exhilaration of the noncombatant, no matter how dedicated and useful her services, has a shrill sound to postwar ears. (p. 27)

The title, *The Age of Innocence,* refers to the New York of the 1870's . . . and gives to the book the flavor of a historical novel, as is often pointed out by critics. The fact not always recognized by critics is that it was a habit of Victorian novelists to set their stories in the era of their childhood. The novelist of manners has since shown a tendency to revert to a usually recent past where social distinctions, which make up so much of his subject matter, were more sharply defined, or at least where he thinks they were. *The Age of Innocence* . . . is written in a Proustian mood of remembered things that evokes the airless atmosphere of an old, ordered, small-town New York as vividly as a conversation piece by Eastman Johnson. Here the dilettante bachelor, Newland Archer, as usual a lawyer, is at last placed in a story adapted to bring out the best and the worst in him. For he must have enough passion and imagination to aspire to break through the barriers of convention that surround him and yet be weak enough so that he cannot finally escape the steely embrace of an aroused tribe. Newland knows that he never really has a chance from the beginning; that is his pathos. (p. 29)

We see him more completely than any other of Mrs. Wharton's heroes. . . . (p. 30)

The Age of Innocence is the first of Mrs. Wharton's novels to have all the action seen through the eyes of one character. The interest is thus centered in Newland Archer. . . . Unlike James, however, she refused to be limited in her own comments to her central characters point of view. Archer's conventional way of looking at life, at least in the first half of the book, is too dull a lens for the reader, and his creator never hesitates to peer over his shoulder and point out all kinds of interesting things on the New York scene that we would otherwise miss. James would have objected to this. He would have argued that the spiritual growth of Archer, like that of Lambert Strether in *The Ambassadors,* would have a richer significance if viewed entirely through Archer's mind. It was one of their principal points of division. Mrs. Wharton refused to subordinate to any rule of design the "irregular and irrelevant movements of life" that to her made up the background of her stories.

It is interesting that her name should be so constantly linked with James's, considering how different were their approaches to their art. His influence is visible, superficially, in her early work, and, of course, they were both interested in Americans in Europe, but there the resemblance ceases. James was subtle, speculative, and indirect; Edith Wharton was always clear and to the point. . . . She dealt with definite psychological and social problems and handled them in her own definite way. Her sentences never have to be read and reread, like James's, for richer and deeper disclosures. (pp. 30-1)

[*The Glimpses of the Moon*] was first serialized in the *Pictorial Review,* which may give the clue to its author's remarkable lapse of style and taste. The jacket of the book depicts an Italian villa on Lake Como by moonlight to evoke the mawkish, gushing mood of an opening chapter which makes the reader rub his eyes and look again to be sure that he is dealing with Edith Wharton. Nick and Susy Lansing, two bright young penniless hangers-on of the international set, have married on the understanding that their bond may be dissolved at the option of the first to find a richer spouse. Nick is again the dilettante hero, writing a novel about Alexander the Great in Asia because it takes less research than an essay, but now, for the first time, reader and author see him from radically different points of view. To the reader he is, quite simply, an unmitigated cad, perfectly content to live in the borrowed houses of rich friends so long as his wife agrees not to steal the cigars or to take any overt part in the blindfolding of their hostesses' deceived husbands. On these two commandments hang all

his law and his prophets, and when Susy has violated both (in each case, for his sake), he abruptly abandons her to pursue an heiress. It is impossible to imagine how Mrs. Wharton could have picked such a man as the hero of a romance unless she seriously believed that he represented what a gentleman had sunk to in the seventeen years which had elapsed since the publication of *The House of Mirth....* Mrs. Wharton's preoccupation with vulgarity had for the moment vulgarized her perceptions. (pp. 32-3)

Fortunately the novels that followed *The Glimpses of the Moon* are not all quite so slick. If they are not good novels, neither are they potboilers. But it seems a pity that Mrs. Wharton should have chosen to lay all the blame for the shapelessness of the postwar world on her native land. In book after book her complaints grow shriller and shriller until at last everything [on the American side of] the Atlantic is tainted with the same grotesque absurdity. She gives to her American towns such names as Delos, Aeschylus, Lohengrin, and Halleluja, and to their inhabitants, in their brief hours away from money-making, a total gullibility in dealing with religious and medical charlatans. Their fuzzy zeal for good causes envelops their hideous skyscrapers in a stifling cloud of euphoria. (pp. 34-5)

So far Mrs. Wharton had only skirmished with America. . . . But she was preparing herself for a closer study of what had happened to America, and she had now spotted a type that she considered a representative victim of the disease of modern vulgarity, if, indeed, it was not the virus itself. Pauline Manford in *Twilight Sleep* . . . is the daughter of an invader from "Exploit" who has first been married to a son of the age of innocence, Arthur Wyant. But time has profoundly altered both types. The invader's daughter is no longer prehensile or even crude; she has become bland and colorless and pointlessly efficient, building a life of public speeches and dinner parties around causes that she does not even try to understand, while Wyant, no longer the cool, well-dressed New York gentleman with a collector's eye for painting and porcelain, has degenerated to a foolish gossiping creature whom his wife has understandably divorced for a sneaky affair with his mother's old-maid companion. That is what has come of the merger of the old and new societies; it has cost each its true character. Pauline Manford, with invader's blood, has survived better than has Wyant, but hers is a lonely and precarious survival in a rosy cloud floating on an ether of fatuity from which she views with frightened eyes the moral collapse of her family. The invaders and their daughters have in common the faculty of immense pre-occupation, the former with their businesses, the latter with their causes. But both are blinded to all that is beautiful or significant in the world around them by the dust stirred up by their febrile activities. (pp. 36-7)

[The] most ambitious experiment of her literary career [was] the fictional biography of a young middle western American writer, Vance Weston, told in two novels: [*Hudson River Bracketed* and *The Gods Arrive*]. . . . She opens his story in a town which is, typically enough, called "Euphoria" and plunges fearlessly into details of middle western life, as if Sinclair Lewis by dedicating *Babbitt* to her had given her some special insight into an area of America that she had never even seen. The result is as bad as might be expected, but Vance Weston soon leaves his home town and comes to New York and an old house on the Hudson where his creator is on more familiar ground. . . . (p. 39)

It is easy to ridicule this long saga with its distorted picture of the New York publishing world, its uncouth young writers and artists . . . , its irritatingly efficient heroine who can change travel accommodations and rent villas as easily as she can spout Goethe, its insensitive hero whose obsessive egotism becomes ultimately tedious, its ponderous satires of popular novelists and literary hostesses, but it nonetheless contains a strong picture of a young genius who educates himself and fights his way to literary success with a ruthlessness of which he is too preoccupied to be more than dimly aware. We sympathize when he is stifled in the ignorant, carping atmosphere of his invalid first wife's home and with his artist's need to rip away even at the most basic family ties. Here at last in Edith Wharton's fiction is a picture of a man. It may have all kinds of personal significance that he is neither a New Yorker nor a gentleman. As he develops cultivation in Europe, however, he develops some of the hardness of the older Wharton heroes, and when he leaves Halo at last for a round of parties in London, there is not much to choose between him and Martin Boyne. But that is in the second volume which, like so many sequels, should never have been written. Both reader and author have become bored with Vance. (p. 40)

[Wharton's] ultimate reputation in American letters will rest upon only a fraction of [her work]. *Ethan Frome,* I have no doubt, will always be read, but it is out of the main stream of her work. I believe that she will be remembered primarily for her two great novels of manners: *The House of Mirth,* and *The Age of Innocence.* In these she succeeded in re-creating an unadventurous and ceremonious society, appropriately sheltered behind New York brownstone, looking always to the east rather than to the west, and the impact upon it of the winds that blew from both directions. There were plenty of minor writers who attempted to delineate this society, but among those of the first rank Mrs. Wharton, at least in the first decade of our century, had it to herself. It is true, of course, that some of James's characters come from the same milieu, but they are rarely considered in relation to their native land or cities. The reason Mrs. Wharton succeeded where so many others have failed is that in addition to her gifts as an artist she had a firm grasp of what "society," in the smaller sense of the word, was actually made up of. She understood that it was arbitrary, capricious, and inconsistent; she was aware that it did not hesitate to abolish its standards while most loudly proclaiming them. She knew when money could open doors and when it couldn't, when lineage would serve and when it would be merely sneered at. She knew that compromises could be counted on, but that they were rarely made while still considered compromises. She knew her men and women of property, recently or anciently acquired, how they decorated their houses and where they spent their summers. She realized that the social game was without rules, and this realization made her one of the few novelists before Proust who could describe it with any profundity. In American fiction her nearest counterpart is Ellen Glasgow. (p. 423)

Louis Auchincloss, in his Edith Wharton *(American Writers Pamphlet No. 12;* © *1961, University of Minnesota), University of Minnesota Press, Minneapolis, 1961 (and reprinted by the University of Minnesota, 1966), 46 p.*

IRVING HOWE (essay date 1962)

Mrs. Wharton's best novels portray the life of "old New York" during the latter third of the nineteenth century. (p. 48)

"[Old] New York" was a world that had entered its decline. . . .

She loved "old New York" with that mixture of grieving affection and protective impatience Faulkner would later feel toward Mississippi and Saul Bellow toward the Jewish neighbourhoods of Chicago. Yet it also left her dissatisfied, on edge, unfulfilled. . . . [She] yearned for a way of life that might bring greater intellectual risks and yield greater emotional rewards than her family and friends could imagine, and only after a time did she find it in her dedication to writing. Just as Faulkner's attitudes toward his home country have kept shifting from one ambiguity to another, so Mrs. Wharton combined toward her home city feelings of both harsh rejection and haughty defence. There are moments, especially in *The House of Mirth,* when she is utterly without mercy toward "old New York": she sees it as a place of betrayal, failure, and impotence. In her old age, when she came to write her autobiography, she was mellower—though perhaps the word should really be, harder—in spirit. (p. 49)

While a final critical estimate of her novels can hardly rest on such considerations alone, one reason for continuing to read *The House of Mirth, The Custom of the Country,* and *The Age of Innocence* is the shrewdness with which Mrs. Wharton, through an expert scrutiny of manners, is able to discriminate among the gradations of power and status in the world of the rich. To read these books is to discover how the novel of manners can register both the surface of social life and the inner vibrations of spirit that surface reveals, suppresses, and distorts. (pp. 49-50)

[In] books like *The House of Mirth* and *The Age of Innocence* she could work on the assumption, so valuable to a writer who prizes economy of structure, that moral values can be tested in a novel by dramatising the relationships between fixed social groups and mobile characters. In the fiction thus engendered, moral values come to be seen not as abstract categories imposed upon human experience but as problems, elements in the effort of men to cope with conflicting desires and obligations. . . . Because Mrs. Wharton is so completely in control of her material, the meanings of the book emerge through a series of contrasts between a fixed scale of social place and an evolving measure of moral value.

But as she herself knew quite well, there was little in Mrs. Wharton's world that could provide her with a subject large in social scope and visibly tragic in its implications. Had "old New York" gone down in blind and bitter resistance to the *nouveaux riches,* that might have been a subject appropriate to moral or social tragedy; but since there was far less conflict than fusion between the old money and the new, she had little alternative to the varieties of comedy that dominate her books. Only once in her novels did she achieve a tragic resonance, and that was in *The House of Mirth* where Lily Bart is shown as the victim of a world that had made possible her loveliness and inevitable her limitations. Even here we must reduce the traditional notion of the tragic to the pathetic on one side and the bleak on the other, if the term is to be used with approximate relevance. . . . Her later novels are shoddy and sometimes mean-spirited in the hauteur with which she dismisses younger generations beyond the reach of her understanding or sympathy. These novels bristle with her impatience before the mysteries of a world she could not enter, the world of 20th-century America, and are notable for a truculence of temper, a hardening of the moral arteries. I would offer the speculation that Mrs. Wharton, whose intelligence should never be underestimated, was aware that the ground on which she took her moral stand was dissolving beneath her. . . . She turned, at times with open savagery and at other times with a feeling as close to wistfulness as she could tolerate, to the world of her birth, hoping to find there some token of security by which to satisfy the needs of her imagination. In the inevitable disappointment that followed. Mrs. Wharton, though extremely conservative in her opinions, proved to be the American novelist least merciful in her treatment of the rich. She kept harassing them, nagging at them in a language they could not, with the best will in the world, understand; and then she would become glacial in her contempt, almost too willing to slash away at their mediocrity because she did not know anyone else to turn toward or against. (p. 50)

The texture of Mrs. Wharton's novels is dark. Like so many writers whose education occurred during the latter decades of the 19th century, she felt that the universe—which for her is virtually to say, organised society—was profoundly inhospitable to human need and desire. The malaise which troubled so many intelligent people during her lifetime, the feeling that they were living in an age when energies had run down, meanings collapsed, and the flow of organic life had been replaced by the sterile and mechanical, is quite as acute in her novels as in those of Hardy and Gissing. Like them, she felt that somehow the world had hardened and turned cold, and she could find no vantage point from which to establish a protective distance from it. . . .

In Mrs. Wharton's vision of things—and we can only speculate on the extent to which her personal unhappiness contributed to it—human beings seem always to prove inadequate, always to fail each other, always to be the victims of an innate disharmony between love and response, need and capacity. Men especially have a hard time of it in Mrs. Wharton's novels. In their notorious vanity and faithlessness, they seldom "come through"; they fail Mrs. Wharton's heroines less from bad faith than weak imagination, a laziness of spirit that keeps them from a true grasp of suffering; and in a number of her novels one finds a suppressed feminine bitterness, a profound impatience with the claims of the ruling sex. This feminist resentment seems, in turn, only an instance of what Mrs. Wharton felt to be a more radical and galling inequity at the heart of the human scheme. The inability of human beings to achieve self-sufficiency drives them to seek relationships with other people, and these relationships necessarily compromise their freedom by subjecting them to the pain of a desire either too great or too small. Things, in Mrs. Wharton's world, do not work out. (p. 51)

A good many of Mrs. Wharton's critics have assumed that she was simply a defender of harsh social conventions against all those who, from romantic energy or mere hunger for meaning in life, rebel against the fixed patterns of their world. But this is not quite true for many of her books, and in regard to some of them not true at all. What is true is that

most of her plots focus upon a clash between a stable society and a sensitive person who half belongs to and half rebels against it. At the end he must surrender to the social taboos he had momentarily challenged or wished to challenge, for he either has not been able to summon the resources of courage through which to act out his rebellion, or he has discovered that the punitive power of society is greater than he had supposed, or he has learned that the conventions he had assumed to be lifeless still retain a certain wisdom. Yet much of Mrs. Wharton's work contains a somewhat chill and detached sympathy for those very rebels in whose crushing she seems to connive. Her sense of the world is hardly such as to persuade her of its goodness; it is merely such as to persuade her of its force. (pp. 51-2)

In a final reckoning, of course, Mrs. Wharton's vision of life has its severe limitations. She knew only too well how experience can grind men into hopelessness, how it can leave them persuaded that the need for choice contains within itself the seeds of tragedy and the impossibility of choice the sources of pain. Everything that reveals the power of the conditioned, everything that shreds our aspirations, she brought to full novelistic life. Where she failed was in giving imaginative embodiment to the human will seeking to resist defeat or move beyond it. She lacked James's ultimate serenity. She lacked his gift for summoning in images of conduct the purity of children and the selflessness of girls. She lacked the vocabulary of happiness.

But whatever Mrs. Wharton could see, she looked at with absolute courage. She believed that what the heart desires brings with it a price and often an exorbitant price. (p. 52)

Irving Howe, "The Achievement of Edith Wharton," in Encounter *(© 1962 by Encounter Ltd.), Vol. 19, No. 1, July, 1962, pp. 45-52.*

R.W.B. LEWIS (essay date 1962)

Lily Bart [in *The House of Mirth*] is one of the authentic creations of American fiction. She is by turns admirable, touching, exasperating, forlorn, sturdy, woefully self-deceptive, imprudent, finely proud, intuitive—and, for one reader at least, not much less than humanly adorable. She is not a tragic heroine. She does not have a truly fatal flaw, only a dangerous weakness: an inability to resist a certain kind of temptation. The temptation is not erotic; Lily Bart is not vulnerable (as are some of her associates) on the sexual side. She can imply a promise of exquisite intimacy; the gesture by which she leans forward to light her cigarette from the tip of Selden's has more real suggestiveness (and I do not mean symbolism) than a dozen pages of anatomical espionage from popular fiction. But Lily Bart is a creature, not of sexual passion but of a physical passion of a different order. She is, let us say, a nymphomaniac of material comfort; *that* is what she is helpless to resist. Her entire being in this respect is characterized by her attitude toward the notion of marrying Rosedale—that "plump rosy man of the blond Jewish type," whose "smart London clothes fit[ted] him like upholstery," and who somewhat surprisingly is permitted by Edith Wharton to manifest qualities ("a certain gross kindliness," "a rather helpless fidelity of sentiment") that distinguish him favorably from his gentile social superiors. Lily cannot quite bring herself to like him, or anyhow to like him enough; and as she contemplates married life with him . . . , "she did not indeed let her imagination range beyond the day of plighting; after that everything faded into a haze of material well-being, in which the personality of her benefactor remained mercifully vague." Into that same haze of material well-being, Lily's sexual reactions regularly tend to fade.

The career of Lily Bart (the action of *The House of Mirth*) is . . . determined by the interplay of the character outlined above and the social scene in which she is required to make her moves. But the game is really lost in advance. For the only society in which Lily might have found the combination she sought—the older New York society, where decency did blend with an adequate material ease—was not observable on her horizon. It had been superseded by the house of mirth; and what was left of it had retreated into "the republic of the spirit." Entrance into the house of mirth had to be paid for by marriage to someone like the intolerable Percy Gryce; and, although Lily attributes her failure to establish a footing there to her own "unsteadiness of purpose" . . . , it was due in fact to a habit of discrimination that all her self-delusion cannot overcome. Edith Wharton's private feeling of belonging and not belonging to the social order that flourished in the 1870s and '80s was greatly exacerbated in Lily Bart's contradictory attitude—her urge toward and repugnance to—the Trenor society of a generation later. At every turn she undercut or slid away from her material opportunities, always regarding her refusal to make the final compromise as a failure of nerve. But the only alternative she is ever made conscious of (apart from the curiously compassionate proposals of Rosedale) is Lawrence Selden and his spiritual republic.

Lily Bart's journey is punctuated by the shifts in her relation to Selden. Each of the two books begins as Selden and Miss Bart are drawing toward one another, and each ends in separation. Through the house party at Bellomont and the New Year's gathering at the Brys in Book I, their intimacy and understanding grow to the point where Selden is about to ask Lily to marry him. Lily, while assuring herself that she will not of course accept him, is half-ready to hear him out—until the affair is blasted by the dreadful contretemps with Gus Trenor. In Book II, Selden is again caught up in Lily Bart's troubles and again rises to that point of animation where he is determined to propose to her. But while he is on his way to her shabby room, Lily takes an excessive dose of sleeping drops, and just before he arrives, she sinks through unconsciousness to death—a manipulation of timing and incident by Mrs. Wharton that would seem tediously contrived and melodramatic were not the mode of Lily's death the almost inevitable culmination of her sagging career. The relation between Selden and Lily Bart thus gives the novel that "he loves me, he loves me not" pattern in terms of which *The Age of Innocence* is so much more smoothly constructed, and which, in the latter novel, is announced in the very opening scene by the song from *Faust* (*"M'ama, non mi ama"*) the main characters gather to hear in the old Opera House.

What Lawrence Selden has to offer but never quite nerves himself to offer is companionship in "the republic of the spirit." . . . [It] is not only because Mrs. Wharton's view of the male sex, and her usual narrative strategy as well, led her time and again to depict her masculine figures as all too unmasculine, as intelligent but ineffectual (Selden, George Darrow in *The Reef,* Ralph Marvell, Newland Archer). It is

also, and I think more importantly though relatedly, because Mrs. Wharton knew something else, an insight she shared with Henry James (who dramatized it, for example in *The Spoils of Poynton*), but one that readers of both novelists have often failed to understand.

Edith Wharton knew that in the fatal modern dislocation between manners and morals, between actual conduct and ethical principle, as the former become crude, the latter become bloodless. This is not a matter of allegory; it is a matter of fact. Selden is dimmer, dryer, harder to discern than, say, Rosedale, with his vigorous vulgarity, because that kind of psychological fade-out is (Mrs. Wharton saw) what is likely to happen to a man who achieves the freedom arrived at by Selden—freedom not only from material anxiety, but almost freedom from the material world itself, from the flesh and blood of the actual. In *The Age of Innocence,* the unfortunate split in question would be explicitly named, as a division between "the actual" and "the real." But while we have long been accustomed to accounts of the terrible effect upon the actual of its divorce from the real (or ideal), we hear less often about the opposite—how the real goes dry and sterile when dissociated from the actual. There is a portion of anxiety, or shall we say of moral alertness, that goes with the condition of being human; and to break free of that is to break away from humanity itself. The point about the republic of the spirit is not (or not only) that Lily Bart is too impurely devoted to material things to get into it, but that it is too airless for anyone with blood in his veins to survive in it.

This great divorce is the "malice of fortune" which Lily Bart vaguely invokes, along with her own infirmity of purpose, as the cause of her failures. It is a historical malice, a calamity brought about by historical developments within the social and moral order; and Lily's infirmity is in good part due to her bemused awareness that neither alternative that the times can offer will satisfy. She wilfully spoils her chances for marrying into the house of mirth; but she distrusts the republic of the spirit. She has no place to go. (pp. 144-47)

> *R.W.B. Lewis, "Introduction" (1962), in* The House of Mirth *by Edith Wharton (reprinted by permission of New York University Press; copyright © 1963 by R.W.B. Lewis), Houghton Mifflin Company, 1963 (and reprinted as "Edith Wharton and 'The House of Mirth',*" *in his* Trials of the Word: Essays in American Literature and the Humanistic Tradition, *Yale University Press, 1965, pp. 129-47).*

MARGARET B. McDOWELL (essay date 1970)

Edith Wharton's ghost stories represent, in general, the work of a mature and sophisticated artist. These works form a well-defined group in subject and technique, and they provide a convenient focus for an inquiry into Mrs. Wharton's methods and achievements in short fiction. Like the best of her other efforts in this genre, the short stories of the macabre and the supernatural, more often than not, manifest in concentrated fashion the careful technique, the evocative style, and the concern for aesthetic order that she revealed in her best novels. (p. 133)

All things considered, her ghost stories illustrate meticulous craftsmanship and imaginative power as they drive toward what she called "the thermometrical quality" of successful ghost tales, the sending of "a cold shiver down one's spine." Still, her finest efforts in this mode are notable precisely because they are more than adroit evocations of the otherworldly.

Edith Wharton maintains in the preface to *Ghosts* that the "moral issue" question is irrelevant in estimating the aesthetic excellence of a supernatural tale. Her immediate aim, which she implied was enough in itself, was to generate an atmosphere conducive to such psychic states in the reader as fear, dread, terror, and horror. In *The Writing of Fiction* she had asserted that for most ghost-story writers it is enough to invoke "simple shivering animal fear." But, like *The Turn of the Screw* which she praised so highly, her own stories go beyond her initial aim and reveal her extraordinary psychological and moral insight.

In fact, these stories achieve ultimate distinction, I think, to the degree that she explores in them, often symbolically, human situations of considerable complexity. . . . Superficially it seems that fantasy, involving spectres and other extraordinary phenomena, would have little bearing upon the realms of social experience and philosophical value. In Edith Wharton's best tales of the supernatural, however, fantasy provides, by an unusual angle of penetration, a new perspective from which to review the mundane and the perhaps unfamiliar problems of human beings. (pp. 133-34)

[In] the preface to *Ghosts* Edith Wharton was to stress the artist's sense of continuity with human traditions if he were to create a compelling supernatural tale, and a corresponding sense of continuity in the reader if he were to respond fully to it. She felt, moreover, that all readers retain atavistically a preoccupation with, or fear of, the supernatural and reveal "states of mind inherited from an earlier phase of race-culture"; that they recognize instinctively the appearance and effects of ghostly phenomena; and that they are ready to accept the illusion of probability to account for the most improbable circumstances. Whether we believe in ghosts or not, we are likely to be fascinated by them and to fear them. The dread we feel thus derives, she asserts, not only from the writer's technical skill, but from our stimulated imaginations as we become gradually involved in preternatural evil and horror.

[Like] Hawthorne and James, Edith Wharton recognized the ambiguities in inner experience, in human behavior, and in all ethical and metaphysical formulations. Sensitive as she was to the complications inherent in human motives and values, she tended in her work, as James did in his, to illuminate rather than resolve the complex issues and situations that she subjected to her scrutiny.

Mrs. Wharton reveals such strength and subtlety of insight in one of her best tales, "The Eyes," an acute analysis of the blindness of the aesthetic temperament. She is concerned in this tale with the ramifications of Andrew Culwin's moral deficiencies as they have undermined his own life and the lives of others. A gracious, wealthy, cultured man, Culwin surrounds himself with disciples and does help them to mature intellectually and to define their own ideas; and yet his interest in these young men is that of the amused spectator, not that of the deeply-concerned friend and mentor. Passively, he is also able to satisfy the homosexual bent of his emotional nature which he never frankly acknowledges.

Twice at times of self-satisfaction when he has judged that he has acted in a kindly and disinterested way, he has had a vision of leering red eyes at night in his bedroom. Whether they are the result of his own faulty vision, whether they are a hallucination, or whether they are "a projection of my inner consciousness," we are free to decide. We do not have to rule out entirely the first two explanations to accept more readily than for years Culwin does the fact that these eyes are indeed a symbol of his own corruption.

A master at self-deception, Culwin cannot see, until the final moment in the story, that the eyes are a symbol of his own hidden weaknesses. Mrs. Wharton often made use of such a single obsessive and obtrusive image to organize a given tale. (pp. 135-37)

"Miss Mary Pask," an extraordinary *tour de force*, again exposes moral weakness. . . . The story is . . . a triumph in tone and atmosphere. And indeed, it is Mrs. Wharton's ability to assimilate the very landscape into her art, to make of natural setting as it were an active agent in the unfolding psychic drama that distinguishes her work in this realm from James's and brings it, in this respect as in some others, closer to Hawthorne's. The fog-enshrouded loneliness of Mary Pask's Brittany residence, the absence there of all sound except the sea, and the narrator's nocturnal encounter with her spectral figure, dimly illumined by candlelight, intensify for us her unwilled isolation and the pathos informing her situation. The psychological insight and the intensity of mood present in the story compensate for the elements of contrivance: the narrator's forgetting, almost inexplicably, the news of Miss Mary Pask's death when he plans his visit, and the reversal at the end when the narrator learns that she is alive by virtue of a cataleptic trance that had been at first interpreted as death. (p. 138)

"Pomegranate Seed" is in part effective because the tangible acts of its spectral figure, Elsie Ashby, impinge so decisively on the personal and moral lives of her widowed husband, Kenneth, and his new wife, Charlotte, although Charlotte never actually confronts her ghostly rival. Elsie's authority is expressed through the actuality of the letters she sends to her living husband and through their disintegrative effects upon him and his new wife. The observable disasters attributable to these letters argue, in short, for the reality of their sender, who is otherwise almost excessively wraithlike even for a ghost. Suffice to say, Elsie resents her husband's happy second marriage and connives to possess him beyond the grave. Outward suspense and inner psychic tension parallel each other in "Pomegranate Seed," with the result that the tale is finally imposing for its moral and psychological significance, not simply for its convincing supernatural aspect. (p. 139)

"The Triumph of Night" derives its power from the way in which the protagonist develops also an awareness of perfidy and evil when he visits a remote estate inadvertently. Mrs. Wharton in this tale powerfully evokes the New England mansion and rural scene in winter. She thus centers her moral and psychic drama in an American setting. . . . When Faxon's new employer fails to meet him, he accepts the invitation of a young stranger, Rainer, to spend the night at the nearby estate of his uncle. During the evening Faxon learns that John Lavington (the uncle), despite his wealth, his taste in painting, his love of flowers, his graciousness as a host, and his effusive concern for his nephew's welfare, is self-centered and vicious. Faxon, as the experiencing consciousness in the tale, is enlightened by a malevolent ghost, which only he sees as it stands behind Lavington. . . . The repulsive apparition in Mrs. Wharton's story is, in fact, an exact double for the "kindly" uncle and a symbolic projection of the actual evil in his soul, which Faxon only gradually perceives. The uncle, so solicitous about his nephew's health, really wishes his death in order to control his money.

Mrs. Wharton's virtuosity in this story is masterly. The isolation of the uncle's house, the omnipresent cold, the compression of the action into a few hours and the contrast between the uncle's gracious hospitality and the sinister threats emanating from his double—all intensify the inevitability of Rainer's doom. Mrs. Wharton establishes the reality of the ghostly-double, all the more forcibly perhaps, by implying that the apparition might have been a hallucination of Faxon's. . . . But we choose to believe that the sinister alter-ego did stand behind Faxon's host and that Rainer's fate might have been avoided had Faxon acted decisively after he saw the leering apparition. We accept these conclusions because we identify strongly with Faxon and his interest in Rainer. The pathos of the tale is increased by Rainer's being an archetype of the beautiful, gifted youth who will be cut down in his prime. His coughing of blood and his withered hands are symptomatic of his mortality and his doom, a symbolic intimation that the good and beautiful are aliens in our imperfect world. He is the innocent creature trapped in the web spun out by his insidious, hypocritical relative.

The chilling effect of the tale also derives from Faxon's gradual recognition of the fact that he might have saved Rainer. Faxon has been reluctant to face the evil that, as a responsible moral agent, he ought to have combatted strenuously, once he was apprized of it. Instead, his one action—fleeing through the snow-covered landscape—becomes the immediate cause of Rainer's death when the consumptive youth pursues him. (pp. 141-43)

Witchcraft . . . dominates "Bewitched," a powerful tale of the effects of isolation in remote New England and one of Edith Wharton's most artistically accomplished narratives. The rural New Englanders in the story are narrow and provincial in outlook; but they are intense and reveal for us the psychic conflicts inevitable among people who have lived a withdrawn existence for too long. (p. 145)

In the tale Mrs. Wharton traces the disintegrating effects upon several characters of a supposed supernatural visitation. Here we have the same situation explored as in Henry James's "Maud-Evelyn"—the psychic disablement of a living individual by the spirit of a dead one—but texture in Mrs. Wharton's story is less finely spun and the characters exert a crude and vulgar power unknown to James's decorous personages. (p. 146)

The effectiveness of "Bewitched" mostly derives from the iron force exerted by Mrs. Rutledge and from the imaginative intensity with which Mrs. Wharton envisioned her. She is the person whose monolithic beliefs and prejudices generate the action and the conflicts among the characters, and she may have, in fact, "bewitched" her husband into a conviction that he is being haunted by a spectral presence or else driven him into the sexual embraces of another being, demon or living woman as the case may be. (p. 147)

The effectiveness of "Bewitched" also depends on Mrs. Wharton's understanding of the difficulties to be endured in New England rural life, an understanding likewise evinced in *Ethan Frome* and *Summer*. The hardships of ordinary living give rise to rigid beliefs in an implacable God and to a grim, cheerless view of man and his destiny in this life. From the opening of the story, isolation and the ingrown life lead to a destructive sickness of the spirit. (p. 149)

It is no accident that the tale . . . takes place in the depth of winter when the physical landscape can reinforce the psychic tensions oppressing the people in the community. Snow becomes an animated force, as if it is bound to exact from the human pygmies in the tale the greatest amount of physical pain and mental anguish. Mrs. Wharton is especially adept in relating exterior nature to the psychic states of Orrin Bosworth. As the snow and cold dominate the exterior landscape, so do they enshroud the inner state of Bosworth's consciousness. An "icy chill" goes down his spine when Mrs. Rutledge names the ghost who has bewitched her husband; at the pond the cold penetrates "his very marrow" and before the funeral "an icy sweat" covers him when he saws wood, despite the coldness of the day. Continually in this tale exterior nature is assimilated into interior states of consciousness. When Bosworth declares that "miles ain't the only distance," he underscores one of Mrs. Wharton's chief preoccupations in "Bewitched," the charting of the vast stretches of interior distance within the psyche and the corresponding distances that may obtain in a remote region among individuals who live in the closest proximity. So the natural slips by degrees into the supernatural, and the sharp line between psychic dislocation and the spirit world dissolves. (p. 151)

First-class achievements such as these predominate in *Ghosts;* but there are other stories wherein the supernatural is evoked to little purpose, wherein technique obtrudes at the expense of mental conflict, moral complexity, and psychological penetration. In such stories as "Mr. Jones," "Afterward," "The Lady's Maid's Bell," and "A Bottle of Perrier" the reader no doubt experiences "the cold shiver" that Edith Wharton wished him to; but they exert less imaginative pressure upon him than the stories we have already discussed. These lesser tales register more as contrived exercises in a literary mode than as moments of significant experience given permanent form and perennial fascination as viable works of art.

Margaret B. McDowell, "Edith Wharton's Ghost Stories" (revised by the author for this publication), in Criticism *(reprinted by permission of the Wayne State University Press; copyright, 1970, Wayne State University Press), Vol. XII, No. 2 (Spring, 1970), pp. 133-52.*

RICHARD H. LAWSON (essay date 1977)

Despite Wharton's professions of happiness in *A Backward Glance,* she was an unhappy human being. One even feels she was unhappy as a woman. Her society subjected women to special disadvantages; in this connection we think of the plight of Lily Bart. This society subjected a brilliant woman, like Wharton, to additional humiliation by simply not recognizing her brilliance or her literary accomplishment—those were things one did not talk about. Wharton was a feminist, however, only in a limited way. Social class was more important to her than sexual equality. She deplored the double standard as it applied to Lily Bart or Ellen Olenska; she defended it as it applied to Sophy Viner. Moreover, Wharton preferred to speak in fiction with a man's voice, to work from a fictional perspective which was male. That is, whenever she employed the device of the fictive narrator, that narrator was a male. And her narrators were in every way valid and convincing in their male perspectives.

On the whole Wharton did not deal kindly with the members of her own sex as they appeared in her fiction. Her special gifts as a writer of fiction were in the areas of plotting and style. She was not an innovator of novelistic form, but she did develop the possibilities of the traditional nineteenth-century novel as far as her virtuosity could take her, which in the cases of *The House of Mirth, Ethan Frome, The Custom of the Country,* and *The Age of Innocence* was very far indeed.

It has been frequently said that Wharton's novels consist of the trivial doings of trivial people. That is largely true. But her fictional people, with whom she was for the most part on remarkably close terms of acquaintance, were part of, acted in, and typified a society in crisis, about which there were things to be said. Wharton said them, and what she did not say she ironically implied.

There is a surge of interest in Wharton today, reflected in frequent reprinting of her works as well as in the publication of biography, interpretation, and criticism. It is a more substantial surge than that which often attends the rediscovery of a first-rate writer several decades after his or her death. The reason may lie in Wharton's particular appeal to a torn society, reflecting at once deep cynicism and muted, if occasionally effective, idealism.

It is not, however, as simple as our society being a mere copy, writ large, of Wharton's society. But we and Edith Wharton share the experience of living through a relatively rapid and perceptible social upheaval. Then, for example, materialism with its social reflections was coming in, and despite her very material comfort, she was materialism's sworn enemy. Now materialism is on the defensive; and we savor the accuracy, the bite, of Wharton's attack, perhaps admiring along the way, or perhaps not entirely grasping, her erudition. Then, there was social and sexual discrimination. There still is. Wharton supported the first, decried the second, as long as it did not impinge on the first. But she did decry, and that was something, then quite likely a lonelier role than now. Wharton had courage. We find that admirable. And if it was expressed, or implied, pointedly and with wit, we find it even more admirable. (pp. 97-9)

> *Richard H. Lawson, "Conclusion," in his* Edith Wharton *(copyright © 1977 by Frederick Ungar Publishing Co., Inc.), Ungar, 1977, pp. 95-9.*

EDMUND WILSON (essay date 1978)

[The] catastrophe in Edith Wharton's novels is almost invariably the upshot of a conflict between the individual and the social group. Her tragic heroines and heroes are the victims of the group pressure of convention; they are passionate or imaginative spirits, hungry for emotional and intellectual experience, who find themselves locked into a small closed system and either destroy themselves by beating their heads against their prison or suffer a living death in resigning themselves to it. Out of these themes she got a sharp pathos all her own. The language and some of the machinery of *The House of Mirth* seem old-fashioned and rather melodramatic today; but the book had some

originality and power, with its chronicle of a social parasite on the fringes of the very rich, dragging out a stupefying routine of week-ends, yachting trips and dinners, and finding a window open only twice, at the beginning and at the end of the book, on a world where all the values are not money values.

The Fruit of the Tree, which followed it . . . , although its characters are concerned with larger issues, is less successful than *The House of Mirth,* because it is confused between two different kinds of themes. There is a more or less trumped-up moral problem *à la* Bourget about a 'mercy killing' by a high-minded trained nurse, who happened to have an 'affinity,' as they used to say at that period, with the husband of the patient. But there is also the story of an industrial reformer, which is on the whole quite ably handled—especially in the opening scenes, in which the hero, assistant manager of a textile mill, is aroused by an industrial accident to try to remove the conditions which have caused it and finds himself up against one of those tight family groups that often dominate factory towns. . . . (pp. 161-62)

Edith Wharton had come to have a great hand with all kinds of American furnishings and with their concomitant landscape-gardening. Her first book had been a work on interior decorating; and now in her novels she adopts the practice of inventorying the contents of her characters' homes. Only Clyde Fitch . . . in those early nineteen-hundreds made play to the same degree with the miscellaneous material objects with which Americans were surrounding themselves, articles which had just been manufactured and which people were being induced to buy. . . . [In] the case of Edith Wharton, the *décors* become the agents of tragedy. The characters of Clyde Fitch are embarrassed or tripped up by these articles; but the people of Edith Wharton are pursued by them as by spirits of doom and ultimately crushed by their accumulation. These pieces have not been always made newly: sometimes they are *objets d'art,* which have been expensively imported from Europe. But the effect is very much the same: they are something extraneous to the people and, no matter how old they may be, they seem to glitter and clank with the coin that has gone to buy them. A great many of Mrs. Wharton's descriptions are, of course, satiric or caustic; but when she wants to produce an impression of real magnificence, and even when she is writing about Europe, the thing still seems rather inorganic. She was not only one of the great pioneers, but also the poet, of interior decoration.

In *The Custom of the Country* . . . , Mrs. Wharton's next novel about the rich—*The Reef* is a relapse into 'psychological problems'—she piles up the new luxury of the era to an altitude of ironic grandeur, like the glass mountain in the *Arabian Nights,* which the current of her imagination manages to make incandescent. . . . In the last pages—it is an admirable passage—Undine Spragg's little boy is seen wandering alone amid the splendors of the Paris *hôtel* which has crowned his mother's progress from the Stentorian: 'the white fur rugs and brocade chairs' which 'seemed maliciously on the watch for smears and ink-spots,' 'his mother's wonderful lacy bedroom, all pale silks and velvets, artful mirrors and veiled lamps, and the boudoir as big as a drawing-room, with pictures he would have liked to know about, and tables and cabinets holding things he was afraid to touch,' the library, with its 'rows and rows of books, bound in dim browns and golds, and old faded reds as rich as velvet: they all looked as if they might have had stories in them as splendid as their bindings. But the bookcases were closed with gilt trellising, and when Paul reached up to open one, a servant told him that Mr. Moffatt's secretary kept them locked because the books were too valuable to be taken down.' (pp. 162-64)

The other side of this world of wealth, which annihilates every impulse toward excellence, is a poverty which also annihilates. The writer of one of the recent notices on Mrs. Wharton's death was mistaken in assuming that *Ethan Frome* was a single uncharacteristic excursion outside the top social strata. It is true that she knew the top strata better than she knew anything else; but both in *The House of Mirth* and *The Fruit of the Tree*, she is always aware of the pit of misery which is implied by the wastefulness of the plutocracy, and the horror or the fear of this pit is one of the forces that determine the action. There is a Puritan in Edith Wharton, and this Puritan is always insisting that we must face the unpleasant and the ugly. Not to do so is one of the worst sins in her morality; sybarites like Mr. Langhope in *The Fruit of the Tree*, amusing himself with a dilettante archeology on his income from a badly managed factory, like the fatuous mother of *Twilight Sleep*, who feels so safe with her facial massage and her Yogi, while her family goes to pieces under her nose, are among the characters whom she treats with most scorn. And the three novels I have touched on above were paralleled by another series —*Ethan Frome, Bunner Sisters* and *Summer*—which dealt with *milieux* of a different kind.

Ethan Frome is still much read and well known; but *Bunner Sisters* has been undeservedly neglected. It is the last piece in the volume called *Xingu* . . . , a short novel about the length of *Ethan Frome*. This story of two small shopkeepers on Stuyvesant Square and a drug-addict clockmaker from Hoboken, involved in a relationship like a triple noose which will gradually choke them all, is one of the most terrible things that Edith Wharton ever wrote; and the last page, in which the surviving sister, her life-long companion gone and her poor little business lost, sets out to look for a job, seems to mark the grimmest moment of Edith Wharton's darkest years. . . . (pp. 165-66)

Summer . . . , however, returns to the Massachusetts of *Ethan Frome*, and, though neither so harrowing nor so vivid, is by no means an inferior work. . . . [The] heroine of *Summer* recoils from the nethermost American social stratum, the degenerate 'mountain people.' Let down by the refined young man who works in the public library and wants to become an architect, . . . she finds that she cannot go back to her own people and allows herself to be made an honest woman by the rather admirable old failure of a lawyer who had brought her down from the mountain in her childhood. It is the first sign on Mrs. Wharton's part of a relenting in the cruelty of her endings. (pp. 166-67)

[*The Age of Innocence*] is really Edith Wharton's valedictory. The theme is closely related to those of *The House of Mirth* and *Ethan Frome*: the frustration of a potential pair of lovers by social or domestic obstructions. But setting it back in the generation of her parents, she is able to contemplate it now without quite the same rancor, to soften it with a poetic mist of distance. And yet even here the old impulse of protest still makes itself felt as the main motive. If we compare *The Age of Innocence* to Henry James's *Europe-*

ans, whose central situation it reproduces, the pupil's divergence from the master is seen in the most striking way. In both cases, a Europeanized American woman—Baroness Münster, Countess Olenska—returns to the United States to intrude upon and to disturb the existence of a conservative provincial society; in both cases, she attracts and almost captivates an intelligent man of the community who turns out, in the long run, to be unable to muster the courage to take her, and who allows her to go back to Europe. . . . [One] still feels an active resentment against the pusillanimity of the provincial group and also, as in other of her books, a special complaint against the timid American male who has let the lady down.

Up through *The Age of Innocence,* and recurring at all points of her range from *The House of Mirth* to *Ethan Frome,* the typical masculine figure in Edith Wharton's fiction is a man set apart from his neighbors by education, intellect and feeling, but lacking the force or the courage either to impose himself or to get away. . . . [These] men are usually captured and dominated by women of conventional morals and middle-class ideals; when an exceptional woman comes along who is thirsting for something different and better, the man is unable to give it to her. This special situation Mrs. Wharton, with some conscious historical criticism but chiefly impelled by a feminine animus, has dramatized with much vividness and intelligence. But there are no first-rate men in these novels.

The Age of Innocence is already rather faded. But now a surprising lapse occurs. (It is true that she was now nearly sixty.) (pp. 167-69)

With her emergence from her life in the United States, her settling down in the congenial society of Paris, she seems at last to become comfortably adjusted; and with her adjustment, the real intellectual force which she has exerted through a decade and a half evaporates almost completely. She no longer maims or massacres her characters. Her grimness melts rapidly into benignity. She takes an interest in young people's problems, in the solicitude of parents for children; she smooths over the misunderstandings of lovers; she sees how things may work out well enough. She even loses the style she has mastered. Beginning with a language rather ponderous and stiff, the worst features of the style of Henry James and a stream of clichés from old plays and novels, she finally—about the time of *Ethan Frome*—worked out a prose of flexible steel, bright as electric light and striking out sparks of wit and color, which has the quality and pace of New York and is one of its distinctive artistic products. But now not merely does she cease to be brilliant, she becomes almost commonplace.

The Glimpses of the Moon, which followed *The Age of Innocence,* is, as someone has said, scarcely distinguishable from the ordinary serial in a women's magazine. . . . *A Son at the Front* is a little better, because it had been begun in 1918 and had her war experience in it, with some of her characteristic cutting satire at the expense of the belligerents behind the lines. It is not bad as a picture of the emotions of a middle-aged civilian during the War—though not so good as Arnold Bennett's *The Pretty Lady*.

Old New York was a much feebler second boiling from the tea-leaves of *The Age of Innocence*. . . . *Twilight Sleep,* is not so bad as her worst, but suffers seriously as a picture of New York during the middle nineteen-twenties from the author's long absence abroad. Mrs. Wharton is no longer up on her American interior-decorating—though there are some characteristic passages of landscape-gardening. . . . (pp. 169-70)

[*A Backward Glance*] I found rather disappointing. The backward glance is an exceedingly fleeting one which dwells very little on anything except the figure of Henry James, of whom Mrs. Wharton has left a portrait entertaining but slightly catty and curiously superficial. . . . [Her] later works show a dismay and a shrinking before what seemed to her the social and moral chaos of an age which was battering down the old edifice that she herself had once depicted as a prison. Perhaps, after all, the old mismated couples who had remained married in deference to the decencies were better than the new divorced who were no longer aware of any duties at all.

The only thing that does survive in *A Backward Glance* is some trace of the tremendous blue-stocking that Mrs. Wharton was in her prime. The deep reverence for the heroes of art and thought—though she always believed that Paul Bourget was one of them—of the woman who in earlier days had written a long blank-verse poem about Vesalius, still makes itself felt in these memoirs. (pp. 171-72)

> *Edmund Wilson, "Justice to Edith Wharton" (originally published in a different version in* The New Republic, *Vol. 95, No. 1230, June 29, 1938), in his* The Wound and the Bow: Seven Studies in Literature *(reprinted by permission of Farrar, Straus & Giroux, Inc.; copyright © 1938 by Edmund Wilson; copyright renewed © 1966 by Edmund Wilson), Farrar, Straus & Giroux, 1978, pp. 159-73.*

BIBLIOGRAPHY

Anderson, Hilton. "Edith Wharton as Fictional Heroine." *South Atlantic Quarterly* 69, No. 1 (Winter 1970): 118-23.
　　Interesting look at the parallels between Wharton's heroines and her own life.

Andrews, Wayne. "The World of Edith Wharton: Fragment of a Biography in Progress." In *The Best Short Stories of Edith Wharton,* by Edith Wharton, edited by Wayne Andrews, pp. vii-xxvii. New York: Charles Scribner's Sons, 1958.
　　Short biography of Wharton, including excerpts from her journal concerning her love for Walter Berry.

Auchincloss, Louis. "Edith Wharton and Her New Yorks." *Partisan Review* XVIII, No. 4 (July-August 1951): 411-19.
　　Overview of Wharton's novels illustrating Wharton's love-hate relationship with American values.

Bell, Millicent. "The Eagle and the Worm." *London Magazine* 6, No. 4 (July 1966): 5-46.
　　An account of the friendship between Henry James, Edward and Edith Wharton, and Walter Berry, told largely through excerpts from James's letters.

Clough, David. "Edith Wharton's War Novels: A Reappraisal." *Twentieth Century Literature* 19, No. 1 (January 1973): 1-14.
　　Examines *The Marne* and *A Son at the Front,* illuminating American attitudes of World War I and the significance the war held for Wharton.

Coolidge, Olivia. *Edith Wharton, 1862-1937.* New York: Charles Scribner's Sons, 1964, 221 p.
　　Biography of Wharton.

Coxe, Louis O. "What Edith Wharton Saw in Innocence." *The New Republic* 132, No. 26 (27 June 1955): 16-18.
　　Examination of *The Age of Innocence,* in which the critic attempts to reintroduce "one of the fine novels of our century" to the contemporary reader.

Hackett, Francis. "Mrs. Wharton's Art." *The New Republic* X, No. CXIX (10 February 1917): 50-2.
　　Review of *Xingu and Other Stories* commenting on Wharton's deficiency in comedy and her excellences in portraying human relations in the upper classes.

Hopkins, Viola. "The Ordering Style of *The Age of Innocence.*" *American Literature* XXX, No. 3 (November 1958): 345-57.
　　Examination of the stylistic elements within *The Age of Innocence.*

Jessup, Josephine Lurie. "Edith Wharton: Drawing-Room Devotee." In her *The Faith of Our Feminists,* pp. 14-33. New York: Richard R. Smith, 1950.
　　Study of the male-female conflicts in Wharton's fiction. The critic sees women portrayed as preeminent beings, with their men "trailing at heel."

Kronenberger, Louis. "Mrs. Wharton's Literary Museum." *The Atlantic Monthly* 222, No. 3 (September 1968): 98-100, 102.
　　Critical overview of many of Wharton's short stories and novels.

Lewis, R.W.B. "Edith Wharton: The Beckoning Quarry." *American Heritage* XXVI, No. 6, (October 1975): 53-73.
　　Interesting overview of little-known, recently discovered biographical information about Wharton and her lovers and friends.

Lubbock, Percy. *Portrait of Edith Wharton.* London: Jonathan Cape, 1947, 222 p.
　　Genteel biography of Wharton, consisting of reminiscences of her friends and excerpts from letters.

McDowell, Margaret B. "Viewing the Custom of Her Country: Edith Wharton's Feminism." *Contemporary Literature* XV, No. 4 (Autumn 1974): 521-38.
　　Thoughtful study of Wharton's implicit feminist concerns and her changing attitudes toward women throughout her life.

McDowell, Margaret B. *Edith Wharton.* Boston: Twayne Publishers, 1976, 158 p.
　　Insightful biography, and analysis of Wharton's canon.

McManis, Jo Agnew. "Edith Wharton's Hymns to Respectability." *The Southern Review* 7, No. 4 (October 1971): 986-93.
　　Study of the theme of self-sacrifice in Wharton's characters and the motives behind their sacrifice.

Plante, Patricia R. "Edith Wharton as Short Story Writer." *The Midwest Quarterly* IV, No. 4 (July 1963): 363-79.
　　Careful study of the various collections of Wharton's short stories and critical reactions to them.

Thorp, Willard. "*The Age of Innocence.*" In his *American Writing in the Twentieth Century,* pp. 1-24. Cambridge: Harvard University Press, 1960.
　　Critical look at Wharton's works, and assessment of her strengths as a writer.

Trilling, Diana. "*The House of Mirth* Revisited." *Harper's Bazaar* LXXXI, No. 12 (December 1947): 126-27, 181-86.
　　Examination of *The House of Mirth,* and biographical sketch of Wharton the aristocrat.

Trilling, Lionel. "The Morality of Inertia (Edith Wharton: *Ethan Frome*)." In *Great Moral Dilemmas in Literature, Past and Present,* edited by R. M. MacIver, pp. 37-46. New York: Cooper Square Publishers, 1964.
　　Discussion of *Ethan Frome* and the "morality of inertia" presented within: morality imposed by social demand, circumstances, habit, and biology.

Wegelin, Christof. "Edith Wharton and the Twilight of the International Novel." *The Southern Review* 5, No. 2 (Spring 1969): 398-418.

    Discussion of Wharton's international novels, and of the European-American cultural clashes presented within them.

Wolff, Cynthia Griffin. *A Feast of Words: The Triumph of Edith Wharton*. New York: Oxford University Press, 1977, 453 p.

    Biography of Wharton, and examination of the author's major works as reflections of her psychological development.

Appendix

THE EXCERPTS IN TCLC-3 WERE REPRINTED FROM THE FOLLOWING PERIODICALS:

Accent
The Adelphi
America
American Literary Realism
American Literature
The American Review
The American-Scandinavian Review
The American Scholar
Anglo-Welsh Review
The Antioch Review
The Argosy
The Athenaeum
The Atlantic Monthly
AUMLA
The Bookman
Books Abroad
Catholic World
Chinese Literature
CLA Journal
College English
Commonweal
Contemporary Review
Critical Quarterly
Criticism
Critique
Current Literature
The Dalhousie Review
Delos
The Dial
The Drama
Drama Survey
Encounter
English
English Fiction in Transition
English Studies
L'Esprit Créateur
Evening Herald
The Fortnightly Review

The French Review
Genre
The German Quarterly
Harper's
The Harvard Journal of Asiatic Studies
Hispania
Hispanic Review
Horizon
The Hudson Review
The Huntington Library Quarterly
Il piccolo della sera
Italian Quarterly
Italica
James Joyce Quarterly
Journal of Asian Studies
Kentucky Romance Quarterly
The Kenyon Review
The Literary Review
The Little Review
The Living Age
London Magazine
The Markham Review
Modern Drama
Modern Fiction Studies
Modern Language Notes
The Nation
The Nation and The Athenaeum
Negro American Literature Forum
The New England Quarterly
The New Republic
New Statesman
The New Statesman & Nation
The New Yorker
The New York Review of Books
The New York Times Book Review
The North American Review
Odyssey Review
Orbis Litterarum

The Pacific Spectator
Partisan Review
Philological Quarterly
PHYLON
Poet Lore
Poetry
Polemic
Quadrant
The Quarterly Review
Religion in Life
Renascence
Review
Revista Hispánica Moderna
Romance Notes
Saturday Review
Scrutiny
The Sewanee Review
South Atlantic Quarterly
The Southern Review
The Spectator
Studies in Scottish Literature
Studies in Short Fiction
Symposium
The Texas Quarterly
Texas Studies in Literature and Language
Theatre Arts
The Times Literary Suppement
Topic
TriQuarterly
The Twentieth Century
The Victorian Newsletter
Virginia Quarterly Review
Western American Literature
Western Humanities Review
Yale French Studies
The Yale Review

THE EXCERPTS IN TCLC-3 WERE REPRINTED FROM THE FOLLOWING BOOKS:

Adams, Marion, Gottfried Benn's Critique of Substance, *Van Gorcum, 1969.*

Adcock, A. St. John, The Glory that Was Grub Street: Impressions of Contemporary Authors, *Stokes, 1928.*

Aiken, Conrad, Collected Criticism, *Oxford University Press, 1968.*

Alvarez, A., Stewards of Excellence: Studies in Modern English and American Poets, *Scribner's, 1958 (published in Great Britain as* The Shaping Spirit, *Chatto & Windus, 1958).*

Archer, William, English Dramatists of To-day, *Sampson Low, Marston, Searle, & Rivington, 1882.*

Auchincloss, Louis, Edith Wharton, *University of Minnesota Press, 1961.*

Baird, James, The Dome and the Rock: Structure in the Poetry of Wallace Stevens, *Johns Hopkins University Press, 1968.*

Bannister, Winifred, James Bridie and His Theatre, *Rockliff, 1955.*

Baring, Maurice, Landmarks in Russian Literature, *Methuen, 1910.*

Barzun, Jacques, The Energies of Art: Studies of Authors Classic and Modern, *Harper, 1956.*

Bates, Scott, Guillaume Apollinaire, *Twayne, 1967.*

Bayerschmidt, Carl F., Sigrid Undset, *Twayne, 1970.*

Beach, Joseph Warren, The Twentieth Century Novel: Studies in Technique, *Appleton-Century-Crofts, 1932.*

Beckett, Samuel, et.al., Our Exagmination Round His Factification for Incamination of Work in Progress, *New Direction, 1972.*

Beerbohm, Max, Around Theatres, *rev. ed., Rupert Hart-Davis, 1953.*

Behrman, S. N., The Suspended Drawing Room, *Stein and Day, 1965.*

Benamou, Michel, Wallace Stevens and the Symbolist Imagination, *Princeton University Press, 1972.*

Bentley, Eric, In Search of Theater, *Knopf, 1953, Vintage, 1957.*

Beresford, J. D., Tradition and Experiment in Present-Day Literature, *Oxford University Press, 1929.*

Bergin, Thomas Goddard, Giovanni Verga, *Yale University Press, 1931.*

Bermel, Albert, Artaud's Theatre of Cruelty, *Taplinger, 1977.*

Bewley, Marius, Masks & Mirrors: Essays in Criticism, *Atheneum, 1970.*

Bjorkman, Edwin, Voices of To-morrow: Critical Studies of the New Spirit in Literature, *Mitchell Kennerley, 1913.*

Blackmur, R. P., The Double Agent: Essays in Craft and Elucidation, *Arrow Editions, 1935.*

Blake, Caesar R., Dorothy Richardson, *University of Michigan Press, 1960.*

Bloom, Harold, Figures of Capable Imagination, *Seabury, 1976.*

Bogan, Louise, Selected Criticism: Poetry and Prose, *Noonday, 1955.*

Boll, Theophilus E. M., Miss May Sinclair: Novelist; A Biographical and Critical Introduction, *Fairleigh Dickinson University Press, 1973.*

Bone, Robert A., The Negro Novel in America, *Yale University Press, 1958.*

Bonheim, Helmut, Joyce's Benefictions, *University of California Press, 1964.*

Bowra, C. M., The Creative Experiment, *Macmillan, 1949.*

Boyd, Ernest A., Ireland's Literary Renaissance, *John Lane, 1916.*

Braybrooke, Patrick, Some Catholic Novelists: Their Art and Outlook, *Burns Oates & Washbourne, 1931.*

Brée, Germaine, and Guiton, Margaret, An Age of Fiction: The French Novel from Gide to Camus, *Rutgers, 1957.*

Breunig, Leroy C., Guillaume Apollinaire, *Columbia University Press, 1969.*

Brown, John Mason, The Worlds of Robert E. Sherwood: Mirror to His Times 1896-1939, *Harper, 1965.*

Brown, Sterling, The Negro in American Fiction, *Associates in Negro Folk Education, 1937.*

Brown, Sterling, Negro Poetry and Drama and The Negro in American Fiction, *Atheneum, 1972.*

Brustein, Robert, The Theatre of Revolt: An Approach to the Modern Drama, *Atlantic-Little, Brown, 1964.*

Burgess, Anthony, ReJoyce, *Norton, 1965.*

Bush, William, Georges Bernanos, *Twayne, 1969.*

Butor, Michel, Inventory: Essays by Michel Butor, *ed. by Richard Howard, Simon & Schuster, 1968.*

Campbell, Joseph, and Robinson, Henry Morton, A Skeleton Key to "Finnegans Wake," *Harcourt, 1944.*

Cargill, Oscar, Intellectual America: Ideas on the March, *Macmillan, 1941.*

Cecchetti, Giovanni, Giovanni Verga, *Twayne, 1978.*

Chesterton, Gilbert K., Heretics, *Dodd Mead, 1927.*

Chevalley, Abel, The Modern English Novel, *trans. by Ben Ray Redman, Knopf, 1925.*

Cobb, Carl W., Antonio Machado, *Twayne, 1971.*

Connelly, Thomas E., ed., Joyce's Portrait: Criticisms and Critiques, *Appleton-Century-Crofts, 1962.*

Connolly, Cyril, Previous Convictions, *Hamish Hamilton, 1963.*

Costich, Julia F., Antonin Artaud, *Twayne, 1978.*

Coustillas, Pierre, and Partridge, Colin, eds., Gissing: The Critical Heritage, *Routledge & Kegan Paul, 1972.*

Cruse, Harold, The Crisis of the Negro Intellectual, *William Morrow, 1967.*

Cunningham, J. V., The Collected Essays of J. V. Cunningham, *Swallow, 1976.*

Currey, R. N., Poets of the 1939-1945 War, *rev. ed., Longmans, Green, 1967.*

Daiches, David, New Literary Values: Studies in Modern Literature, *Oliver & Boyd, 1936.*

Davies, Ruth, The Great Books of Russia, *University of Oklahoma Press, 1968.*

Doggett, Frank, Stevens' Poetry of Thought, *Johns Hopkins University Press, 1966.*

Donnelly, Mabel Collins, George Gissing: Grave Comedian, *Harvard University Press, 1954.*

Donoghue, Denis, The Ordinary Universe: Soundings in Modern Literature, *Macmillan, 1968.*

Drew, Elizabeth, The Novel: A Modern Guide to Fifteen English Masterpieces, *Dell, 1963.*

Dukes, Ashley, Modern Dramatists, *Frank Palmer, 1911.*

Dusenbury, Winifred L., The Theme of Loneliness in Modern American Drama, *University Presses of Florida, 1967.*

Dyboski, Roman, Modern Polish Literature: A Course of Lectures, *Oxford University Press, 1924.*

Eglinton, John, Irish Literary Portraits, *Macmillan, 1935.*

Eliot, T. S., The Three Voices of Poetry, *Cambridge University Press, 1953.*

Ervine, St. John G., Some Impressions of My Elders, *Macmillan, 1922.*

Esslin, Martin, Antonin Artaud, *Penguin Books, 1977.*

Fergusson, Francis, The Idea of a Theater: A Study of Ten Plays; The Art of Drama in Changing Perspective, *Princeton University Press, 1949.*

Flexner, Eleanor, American Playwrights: 1918-1938, *Simon & Schuster, 1938.*

Folsom, James K., The American Western Novel, *College & University Press, 1966.*

Forster, E. M., Abinger Harvest, *Harcourt, 1936.*

Fowlie, Wallace, Age of Surrealism, *Indiana University Press, 1960.*

Franco, Jean, César Vallejo: The Dialectics of Poetry and Silence, *Cambridge University Press, 1976.*

Freeman, John, The Moderns: Essays in Literary Criticism, *R. Scott, 1916.*

Fuchs, Daniel, The Comic Spirit of Wallace Stevens, *Duke University Press, 1963.*

Fuller, Edmund, Man in Modern Fiction: Some Minority Opinions on Contemporary American Writing, *Random House, 1958.*

Gardner, Monica M., The Patriot Novelist of Poland: Henryk Sienkiewicz, *J. M. Dent, 1926.*

Garnett, Edward, Friday Nights: Literary Criticisms and Appreciations, *Knopf, 1922.*

Gapp, Samuel Vogt, George Gissing: Classicist, *University of Pennsylvania Press, 1936.*

Gerhardi, William, Anton Chehov: A Critical Study, *Duffield, 1923.*

Ghose, Sisirkumar, The Later Poems of Tagore, *Asia Publishing House, 1961.*

Giergielewicz, Mieczyslaw, Henryk Sienkiewicz, *Twayne, 1968.*

Gilbert, Stuart, James Joyce's 'Ulysses': A Study, *rev. ed., Knopf, 1952.*

Gillen, Charles H., H. H. Munro (Saki), *Twayne, 1969.*

Gilman, Richard, Common and Uncommon Masks: Writings on Theatre 1961-1970, *Random House, 1971.*

Gilman, Richard, The Making of Modern Drama: A Study of Büchner, Ibsen, Strindberg, Chekhov, Pirandello, Brecht, Beckett, Handke, *Farrar, Straus & Giroux, 1974.*

Givens, Seon, ed., James Joyce: Two Decades of Criticism, *Vanguard, 1963.*

Gloster, Hugh M., Negro Voices in American Fiction, *University of North Carolina Press, 1948.*

Godwin, A. H., Gilbert & Sullivan: A Critical Appreciation of the "Savoy Operas," *J. M. Dent, 1927.*

Goldberg, Isaac, The Drama of Transition: Native and Exotic Playcraft, *Stewart Kidd, 1922.*

Gorky, Maxim, Reminiscences of Anton Chekhov, *trans. by S. S. Koteliansky and Leonard Woolf, B. W. Huebsch, 1921.*

Gorky, Maxim, Reminiscences of Leonid Andreev, *trans. by Katherine Mansfield and S. S. Koteliansky, C. Gaige, 1928.*

Gorky, Maxim, Reminiscences of Tolstoy, Chekhov, and Andreev, *trans. by Katherine Mansfield, S. S. Koteliansky, and Leonard Woolf, Hogarth, 1948.*

Gorman, Herbert S., The Procession of Masks, *Brimmer, 1923.*

Gould, Gerald, The English Novel of To-day, *Dial, 1925.*

Greene, Graham, Collected Essays, *Viking Penguin, 1969.*

Greene, Naomi, Antonin Artaud: Poet without Words, *Simon & Schuster, 1970.*

Guha-Thakurta, P., The Bengali Drama: Its Origin and Development, *Kegan Paul, Trench, Trubner, 1930.*

Gustafson, Alrik, Six Scandinavian Novelist, *Princeton University Press, 1940.*

Halls, W. D., Maurice Maeterlinck: A Study of His Life and Thought, *Oxford University Press, 1960.*

Hambuger, Michael, Reason and Energy, *Grove, 1957.*

Hebblethwaite, Peter, S. J., Bernanos: An Introduction, *Hillary House, 1965.*

Heiney, Donald, Three Italian Novelists: Moravia, Pavese, Vittorini, *University of Michigan Press, 1968.*

Henderson, Archibald, European Dramatists, *Appleton, 1926.*

Hicks, Granville, Figures of Transition: A Study of British Literature at the End of the Nineteenth Century, *Macmillan, 1939.*

Highet, Gilbert, The Classical Tradition: Greek and Roman Influences on Western Literature, *Oxford University Press, 1949.*

Hingley, Ronald, Chekhov: A Biographical and Critical Study, *rev. ed., Allen & Unwin, 1966.*

Hoffman, Frederick F., Freudianism and the Literary Mind, *Louisiana State University Press, 1945.*

Howarth, Herbert, The Irish Writers 1880-1940: Literature under Parnell's Star, *Rockliff, 1958.*

Howe, Irving, A World More Attractive: A View of Modern Literature and Politics, *Horizon, 1963.*

Howe, Irving, ed., Edith Wharton: A Collection of Critical Essays, *Prentice-Hall, 1962.*

Howe, Irving, ed., Modern Literary Criticism: An Anthology, *Beacon Press, 1958.*

Huneker, James, Iconoclasts: A Book of Dramatists, *Scribner's, 1905.*

Hutman, Norma Louise, Machado: A Dialogue with Time; Nature as an Expression of Temporality in the Poetry of Antonio Machado, *University of New Mexico Press, 1969.*

Irvine, William, The Universe of G.B.S., *Russell & Russell, 1949.*

Jackson, Holbrook, Romance and Reality: Essays and Studies, *Grant Richards, 1911.*

Jackson, Robert Louis, ed., Chekhov: A Collection of Critical Essays, *Prentice-Hall, 1967.*

James, Henry, The Letters of Henry James, Vol. II, *ed. by Percy Lubbock, Scribner's, 1920.*

James, Henry, Notes on Novelists, with Some Other Notes, *Scribner's, 1914.*

Jameson, Storm, Modern Drama in Europe, *W. Collins Sons, 1920.*

Jarrell, Randall, The Third Book of Criticism, *Farrar, Straus & Giroux, 1969.*

Jennings, Elizabeth, Every Changing Shape, *Andre Deutsch, 1961.*

John, Alun, Alun Lewis, *University of Wales Press, 1970.*

Johnson, R. Brimley, Some Contemporary Novelists (Women), *Leonard Parsons, 1920.*

Joyce, James, The Critical Writings of James Joyce, *ed. by Ellsworth Mason and Richard Ellmann, Viking Penguin, 1959.*

Kahn, Lothar, Insight and Action: The Life and Work of Lion Feuchtwanger, *Fairleigh Dickinson University Press, 1975.*

Kahn, Lothar, Mirrors of the Jewish Mind: A Gallery of Portraits of European Jewish Writers of Our Time, *Thomas Yoseloff, 1968.*

Kaplan, Sydney Janet, Feminine Consciousness in the Modern British Novel, *University of Illinois Press, 1975.*

Kaun, Alexander, Leonid Andreyev: A Critical Study, *B. W. Huebsch, 1924.*

Kazin, Alfred, The Inmost Leaf: A Selection of Essays, *Harcourt, 1955.*

Kazin, Alfred, On Native Grounds: An Interpretation of Modern American Prose Literature, *Reynal & Hitchcock, 1942.*

Kennedy, Andrew K., Six Dramatists in Search of a Language: Studies in Dramatic Language, *Cambridge University Press, 1975.*

Kenner, Hugh, Dublin's Joyce, *Indiana University Press, 1956.*

Kenner, Hugh, A Homemade World: The American Modernist Writers, *Knopf, 1975.*

Kermode, Frank, Wallace Stevens, *Oliver & Boyd, 1960.*

Kindilien, Carlin T., American Poetry in the Eighteen Nineties: A Study of American Verse, 1890-1899, *Brown University Press, 1956.*

Knapp, Bettina L., Antonin Artaud: Man of Vision, *David Lewis, 1969.*

Knapp, Betinna L., Maurice Maeterlinck, *Twayne, 1975.*

Korg, Jacob, George Gissing: A Critical Biography, *University of Washington Press, 1963.*

Kridl, Manfred, A Survey of Polish Literature and Culture, *trans. by Olga Scherer-Virski, rev. ed., Mouton, 1956.*

Kronenberger, Louis, ed., Novelists on Novelists, *Doubleday, 1962.*

Krutch, Joseph Wood, The American Drama since 1918: An Informal History, *rev. ed., Braziller, 1957.*

Krutch, Joseph Wood, "Modernism" in Modern Drama: A Definition and an Estimate, *Cornell University Press, 1953.*

Lago, Mary M., Rabindranath Tagore, *Twayne, 1976.*

Lavrin, Janko, Russian Writers: Their Lives and Literature, *D. Van Nostrand, 1954.*

Lawrence, D. H., Phoenix: The Posthumous Papers of D. H. Lawrence, *ed. by Edward D. McDonald, Viking, 1936.*

Lawrence, D. H., Selected Literary Criticism, *ed. by Anthony Beal, William Heinemann, 1955, Viking, 1956.*

Lawson, John Howard, Theory and Technique of Playwriting, *Hill & Wang, 1936.*

Lawson, Richard H., Edith Wharton, *Ungar, 1977.*

Leal, Luis, Mariano Azuela, *Twayne, 1971.*

Lednicki, Waclaw, Henryk Sienkiewicz: 1846-1946, *Polish Institute of Arts and Sciences in America, 1948.*

Lehmann, John, The Open Night, *Longmans, Green, 1952.*

Levin, Harry, James Joyce: A Critical Introduction, *rev. ed., New Directions, 1960.*

Lewis, Sinclair, The Man from Main Street: Selected Essays and Other Writings, 1904-1950, *ed. by Harry E. Maule and Melville H. Cane, Random House, 1953.*

Lewis, Wyndham, Time and Western Man, *Harcourt, 1928.*

Lin, Yutang, ed., The Wisdom of China and India, *Random House, 1942.*

Linklater, Eric, The Art of Adventure, *Macmillan, 1947.*

Little, Roger, Guillaume Apollinaire, *Athlone Press, 1976.*

Loftus, Richard J., Nationalism in Modern Anglo-Irish Poetry, *University of Wisconsin Press, 1964.*

Lovett, Robert Morss, Edith Wharton, *McBride, 1925.*

Lovett, Robert Morss, and Hughes, Helen Sard, The History of the Novel in England, *Houghton, 1932.*

Lukács, Georg, The Historical Novel, *trans. by Hannah Mitchell and Stanley Mitchell, Merlin Press, 1962.*

Lumley, Frederick, Trends in 20th Century Drama: A Survey since Ibsen and Shaw, *Rockliff, 1956.*

Luyben, Helen L., James Bridie: Clown and Philosopher, *University of Pennsylvania Press, 1965.*

Lyell, William A., Jr., Lu Hsün's Vision of Reality, *University of California Press, 1976.*

McFarlane, James Walter, Ibsen and the Temper of Norwegian Literature, *Oxford University Press, 1960.*

Magalaner, Marvin, ed., A James Joyce Miscellany, *Southern Illinois University Press, 1959.*

Magarshack, David, Chekhov the Dramatist, *Hill & Wang, 1960.*

Mann, Thomas, Last Essays, *trans. by Richard and Clara Winston and Tania and James Stern, Knopf, 1959.*

Marker, Lise-Lone, David Belasco: Naturalism in the American Theatre, *Princeton University Press, 1975.*

Martin, Jay, Harvests of Change: American Literature, 1865-1914, *Prentice-Hall, 1967.*

Matthews, John F., George Bernard Shaw, *Columbia University Press, 1969.*

Mencken, H. L., A Mencken Chrestomathy, *Knopf, 1949.*

Menchen, H. L., Prejudices: First Series, *Knopf, 1919.*

Meserve, Walter J., Robert E. Sherwood: Reluctant Moralist, *Bobbs-Merrill-Pegasus, 1970.*

Miller, Henry, The Henry Miller Reader, *ed. by Lawrence Durrell, New Directions, 1959.*

Miller, J. Hillis, Poets of Reality: Six Twentieth-Century Writers, *Harvard University Press, 1965.*

Mirsky, D. S., A History of Russian Literature, ed. by Francis J. Whitefield, *rev. ed., Knopf, 1955.*

Mirsky, D. S., Modern Russian Literature, *Oxford University Press, 1925.*

Monroe, N. Elizabeth, The Novel and Society: A Critical Study of the Modern Novel, *University of North Carolina Press, 1941.*

Morgan, H. Wayne, American Writers in Rebellion: From Mark Twain to Dreiser, *Hill and Wang, 1965.*

Moses, Montrose J., the American Dramatist, *rev. ed., Little Brown, 1917.*

Mudrick, Marvin, On Culture and Literature, *Horizon, 1970.*

Munson, Gorham B., Destinations: A Canvass of American Literature since 1900, *Sears, 1928.*

Murry, J. Middleton, Katherine Mansfield and Other Literary Studies, *Constable, 1959.*

Natan, Alex, ed., German Men of Letters, Vol. III, *Oswald Wolff, 1964.*

Nathan, George Jean, Testament of a Critic, *Knopf, 1931.*

Nathan, George Jean, The Theatre Book of the Year 1950-1951: Record and an Interpretation, *Knopf, 1951.*

Nathan, George Jean, The Theatre, the Drama, the Girls, *Knopf, 1921.*

Nemerov, Howard, Poetry and Fiction: Essays, *Rutgers University Press, 1963.*

Newcombe, Josephine M., Leonid Andreyev, *Ungar, 1973.*

Nevius, Blake, Edith Wharton: A Study of Her Fiction, *University of California Press, 1953.*

Nicoll, Allardyce, World Drama: From Aeschylus to Anouilh, *Harrap, 1949.*

Norris, Margot, The Decentered Universe of "Finnegans Wake": A Structural Analysis, *Johns Hopkins University Press, 1976.*

O'Casey, Sean, The Green Crow, *Braziller, 1956.*

O'Connor, William Van, The Shaping Spirit: A Study of Wallace Stevens, *Russell & Russell, 1950.*

Pacifici, Sergio, ed., From Verismo to Experimentalism: Essays on the Modern Italian Novel, *Indiana University Press, 1969.*

Pacifici, Sergio, The Modern Italian Novel from Manzoni to Svevo, *Southern Illinois University Press, 1967.*

Pack, Robert, Wallace Stevens: An Approach to His Poetry and Thought, *Rutgers, 1958.*

Parrington, Vernon Louis, Main Currents in American Thought: The Beginnings of Critical Realism in America, 1860-1920, *Harcourt, 1930.*

Pattee, Fred Lewis, The New American Literature: 1890-1930, *Century, 1930.*

Peacock, Ronald, The Poet in the Theatre, *Harcourt, 1946.*

Pearson, Hesketh, G.B.S.: A Full Length Portrait and a Postscript, *Harper, 1950.*

Persky, Serge, Contemporary Russian Novelists, *trans. by Frederick Eisemann, J. W. Luce, 1913.*

Phelps, William Lyon, The Advance of the English Novel, *Dodd, Mead, 1916.*

Phelps, William Lyon, Essays on Modern Dramatists, *Macmillan, 1921.*

Phelps, William Lyon, Essays on Modern Novelists, *Macmillan, 1910.*

Phelps, William Lyon, Essays on Russian Novelists, *Macmillan, 1911.*

Pitcher, Harvey, The Chekhov Play: A New Interpretation, *Chatto & Windus, 1973.*

Powys, John Cowper, Dorothy M. Richardson, *Joiner and Steele, 1931.*

Pritchett, V. S., Books in General, *Chatto & Windus, 1953.*

Pritchett, V. S., The Living Novel and Later Appreciations, *rev. ed., Random House, 1964.*

Ragusa, Olga, Verga's Milanese Tales, *S. F. Vanni, 1964.*

Rahv, Philip, ed., Literature in America, *World, 1957.*

Redding, J. Saunders, To Make a Poet Black, *University of North Carolina Press, 1939.*

Rexroth, Kenneth, Assays, *New Directions, 1961.*

Rhys, Ernest, Rabindranath Tagore: A Biographical Study, *Macmillan, 1915.*

Riddel, Joseph N., The Clairvoyant Eye: The Poetry and Poetics of Wallace Stevens, *Louisiana State University Press, 1965.*

Ritchie, J. M., Gottfried Benn: The Unreconstructed Expressionist, *Oswald Wolff, 1972.*

Roback, A. A., The Story of Yiddish Literature, *Yiddish Scientific Institute, 1940.*

Rose, Marilyn Gaddis, Katharine Tynan, *Bucknell University Press, 1974.*

Russell, Bertrand, Portraits from Memory and Other Essays, *Simon & Schuster, 1956.*

Sahitya Akademi, A Centenary Volume: Rabindranath Tagore, 1861-1961, *Sahitya Akademi, 1961.*

Schorer, Mark, ed., Society and Self in the Novel, *Columbia University Press, 1956.*

Schwartz, Delmore, Selected Essays of Delmore Schwartz, *ed. by Donald A. Dike and David H. Zucker, University of Chicago Press, 1970.*

Scott, Dixon, Men of Letters, *Hodder and Stoughton, 1916.*

Segel, Harold B., Twentieth-Century Russian Drama: From Gorky to the Present, *Columbia University Press, 1979.*

Shaw, George Bernard, Shaw's Dramatic Criticism, *ed., by John F. Matthews, Hill & Wang, 1959.*

Shestov, Lev, Anton Tchekhov and Other Essays, *trans. by S. Koteliansky and J. M. Murry, Maunsel, 1916.*

Showalter, Elaine, A Literature of Their Own: British Women Novelists from Bronte to Lessing, *Princeton University Press, 1977.*

Shuman, R. Baird, Robert E. Sherwood, *Twayne, 1964.*

Slochower, Harry, No Voice Is Wholly Lost...: Writers and Thinkers in War and Peace, *Creative Age Press, 1945.*

Slochower, Harry, Three Ways of Modern Man, *International, 1937.*

Sokel, Walter H., The Writer in Extremis: Expressionism in Twentieth-Century German Literature, *Stanford University Press, 1959.*

Sontag, Susan, Against Interpretation, *Farrar, Straus & Girous, 1966.*

Spalek, John M., ed., Lion Feuchtwanger: The Man, His Ideas, His Work—A Collection of Critical Essays, *Hennessey & Ingalls, 1972.*

Speaight, Robert, Georges Bernanos: A Study of the Man and the Writer, *Liveright, 1974.*

Spector, Ivar, The Golden Age of Russian Literature, *rev. ed., Caxton, 1943.*

Spell, Jefferson Rea, Contemporary Spanish-American Fiction, *University of North Carolina Press, 1944.*

Spender, Stephen, The Struggle of the Modern, *University of California Press, 1963.*

Squire, J. C., Books Reviewed, *George H. Doran, 1922.*

Starkie, Walter, Jacinto Benavente, *Oxford University Press, 1924.*

Stewart, J.I.M., Eight Modern Writers, *Oxford University Press, 1963.*

Stroup, Thomas B., and Stoudemire, Sterling A., eds., South Atlantic Studies for Sturgis E. Leavitt, *Scarecrow Press, 1953.*

Sutton, Max Keith, W. S. Gilbert, *Twayne, 1975.*

Swinnerton, Frank, George Gissing: A Critical Study, *George H. Doran, 1923.*

Swinnerton, Frank, The Georgian Scene: A Literary Panorama, *Farrar & Rinehart, 1934.*

Symons, Arthur, The Symbolist Movement in Literature, *rev. ed., Dutton, 1919.*

Taylor, Una, Maurice Maeterlinck: A Critical Study, *M. Secker, 1914.*

Thompson, Edward J., Rabindranath Tagore: His Life and Work, *ed. by Kalidas Nag, Y.M.C.A. Publishing House, 1921.*

Thompson, Edward J., Rabindranath Tagore: Poet and Dramatist, *rev. ed., 1948.*

Thompson, William Irwin, The Imagination of an Insurrection, Dublin, Easter, 1916: A Study of an Ideological Movement, *Oxford University Press, 1967.*

Tillyard, E.M.W., The Epic Strain in the English Novel, *Chatto & Windus, 1958.*

Timberlake, Craig, The Bishop of Broadway: The Life & Work of David Belasco, *Library Publishers, 1954.*

Tindall, Gillian, The Born Exile: George Gissing, *Temple Smith, 1974.*

Tindall, William York, Wallace Stevens, *University of Minnesota Press, 1961.*

Tolstoy, Leo, Tolstoy's Letters: 1880-1910, Vol. II, *ed. and trans. by R. F. Christian, Scribner's, 1978.*

Toumanova, Nina Andronikova, Anton Chekhov: The Voice of Twilight Russia, *Columbia University Press, 1937.*

Trend, J. B., Antonio Machado, *Dolphin, 1953.*

Valency, Maurice, The Breaking String: The Plays of Anton Chekhov, *Oxford University Press, 1966.*

Van Doren, Carl, Contemporary American Novelists: 1900-1920, *Macmillan, 1922.*

Vinde, Victor, Sigrid Undset: A Nordic Moralist, *trans. by Babette Hughes and Glenn Hughes, University of Washington Book Store, 1930.*

Wagner, Jean, Black Poets of the United States: From Paul Laurence Dunbar to Langston Hughes, *trans. by Kenneth Douglas, University of Illinois Press, 1973.*

Walcutt, Charles Child, American Literary Naturalism, a Divided Stream, *University of Minnesota Press, 1956.*

Ward, A. C., Gissing, *British Council, 1959.*

Warren, L. A., Modern Spanish Literature: A Comprehensive Survey of the Novelists, Poets, Dramatists and Essayists from the Eighteenth Century to the Present Day, Vol. II, *Brentano's, 1929.*

Watson, Barbara Bellow, A Shavian Guide to the Intelligent Woman, *Norton, 1964.*

Weales, Gerald, Religion in Modern English Drama, *University of Pennsylvania Press, 1961.*

Weinstein, Arnold L., Vision and Response in Modern Fiction, *Cornell University Press, 1974.*

Whittemore, Reed, Browning, *Dell, 1960.*

Whittemore, Reed, The Fascination of the Abomination, *Macmillan, 1963.*

Williams, Harold, Modern English Writers: Being a Study of Imaginative Literature 1890-1914, *rev. ed., Sidgwick & Jackson, 1925.*

Williamson, Audrey, Theatre of Two Decades, *Rockliff, 1951.*

Wilson, Colin, Religion and the Rebel, *Houghton, 1957.*

Wilson, Edmund, Axel's Castle: A Study in the Imaginative Literature of 1870-1930, *Scribner's, 1931.*

Wilson, Edmund, The Bit Between My Teeth: A Literary Chronicle of 1950-1965, *Farrar, Straus & Giroux, 1965.*

Wilson, Edmund, The Shores of Light: A Literary Chronicle of the Twenties and Thirties, *Farrar, Straus & Giroux, 1952.*

Wilson, Edmund, The Triple Thinkers: Twelve Essays on Literary Subjects, *rev. ed., Oxford University Press, 1963.*

Wilson, Edmund, A Window on Russia, *Farrar, Straus & Giroux, 1978.*

Wilson, Edmund, The Wound and the Bow: Seven Studies in Literature, *Houghton Mifflin, 1941, Farrar, Straus & Giroux, 1978.*

Winsnes, A. H., Sigrid Undset: A Study in Christian Realism, *trans. by P. G. Foote, Sheed and Ward, 1953.*

Winter, William, The Life of David Belasco, Vols. I-II, *Moffat, Yard, 1918.*

Winters, Yvor, In Defense of Reason: Primitivism and Decadence, *Swallow & W. Morrow, 1947.*

Woodward, James B., Leonid Andreyev: A Study, *Oxford University Press, 1969.*

Woolf, Virginia, The Second Common Reader, *Harcourt, 1932 (published in Great Britain as* The Common Reader, second series, *Hogarth, 1932).*

Woollcott, Alexander, The Portable Woollcott, *ed. by Joseph Hennessey, Viking Penguin, 1946.*

Yates, May, George Gissing: An Appreciation, *Manchester University Press, 1922.*

Yeats, W. B., Autobiographies, *Macmillan, 1955.*

Yeats, W. B., Letters to Katharine Tynan, *ed. by Roger McHugh, Clonmore and Reynolds, 1953.*

Young, Howard T., The Victorious Expression: A Study of Four Contemporary Spanish Poets, *University of Wisconsin Press, 1964.*

Young, Stark, Immortal Shadows: A Book of Dramatic Criticism, *Scribner's, 1948.*

Zabel, Morton Dauwen, ed., Literary Opinion in America, Vol. II, *rev. ed., Harper, 1951.*

Zegger, Hrisey Dimitrakis, May Sinclair, *Twayne, 1976.*

Ziff, Larzer, The American 1890s: Life and Times of a Lost Generation, *Viking Penguin, 1966.*

Cumulative Index to Authors

AUTHOR INDEX

Cumulative Index to Critics

CRITIC INDEX

CRITIC INDEX

CRITIC INDEX

CRITIC INDEX

CRITIC INDEX

CRITIC INDEX